PENGUIN REFERENCE

The Penguin Guide to th*...Ireland*

Steve Roud is Local Studies Librarian for the London Borough of Croydon and served as Honorary Librarian of the Folklore Society for over fifteen years.

He has been researching British folklore for over thirty years and is the joint author of the *Oxford Dictionary of English Folklore*, plus other books on traditional drama and folk song. He also compiles the *Folk Song Index* and the *Broadside Index*, two internationally known computer databases of traditional folk and popular song.

Steve Roud lives in Sussex.

The Penguin Guide to the

Superstitions
of Britain and Ireland

Steve Roud

General Editor: Jennifer Westwood

PENGUIN BOOKS

For Kate and Mark and the new little one

PENGUIN BOOKS

Published by the Penguin Group
Penguin Books Ltd, 80 Strand, London WC2R 0RL, England
Penguin Group (USA) Inc., 375 Hudson Street, New York, New York 10014, USA
Penguin Group (Canada), 90 Eglinton Avenue East, Suite 700, Toronto, Ontario, Canada M4P 2Y3
(a division of Pearson Penguin Canada Inc.)
Penguin Ireland, 25 St Stephen's Green, Dublin 2, Ireland
(a division of Penguin Books Ltd)
Penguin Group (Australia), 250 Camberwell Road, Camberwell,
Victoria 3124, Australia (a division of Pearson Australia Group Pty Ltd)
Penguin Books India Pvt Ltd, 11 Community Centre,
Panchsheel Park, New Delhi – 110 017, India
Penguin Group (NZ), cnr Airborne and Rosedale Roads, Albany,
Auckland 1310, New Zealand (a division of Pearson New Zealand Ltd)
Penguin Books (South Africa) (Pty) Ltd, 24 Sturdee Avenue,
Rosebank, Johannesburg 2196, South Africa

Penguin Books Ltd, Registered Offices: 80 Strand, London WC2R 0RL, England

www.penguin.com

First published 2003
Published in paperback 2006
1

Typeset in Minion by Palimpsest Book Production Limited, Polmont, Stirlingshire
Printed in England by Clays Ltd, St Ives plc

ISBN-13: 978–0–140–51512–1
ISBN-10: 0–140–51512–7

Contents

List of Illustrations

Introduction

It is the hardest thing in the world to shake off superstitious prejudices: they are sucked in as it were with our mother's milk; and growing up with us at a time when they take the fastest hold and make the most lasting impressions, become so interwoven into our very constitutions, that the strongest good sense is required to disengage ourselves from them. No wonder therefore that the lower people retain them their whole lives through, since their minds are not invigorated by a liberal education, and therefore not enabled to make any efforts adequate to the occasion.   Gilbert White (1788) 184

More than 200 years after Gilbert White made this observation, many would agree with his assessment that family tradition and childhood impression are important ways in which superstitions are disseminated, but few would be so confident that a liberal education is all that is needed to shift them. Indeed, after a century of compulsory schooling and far-reaching scientific advancement, superstition is still a commonplace of modern society. Many people still avoid walking under a ladder or refuse to open an umbrella indoors, and, whether we believe them or not, superstitions still have the power to fascinate us. Much has been written on the subject since White's time, and since the foundation of folklore studies in late Victorian times a general consensus that superstitions are survivals from ancient times has been reached. As will be seen later, one of the main purposes of this book is to refute that consensus and to bring a new historically based method to the subject.

'Superstition' is not an easy word to deal with. It has been used in numerous contexts, with roughly the same meaning, since at least Chaucer's time, but it is always the context in which the word appears which matters. By its very nature the concept of superstition is highly subjective, and this is seen most clearly in the use of the word as an adjective. Any person or group can call another 'superstitious', but this tells us

The superstitious nature of rural workers was frequently mocked, as in this illustration by George Cruikshank, c.1840.

nothing about the beliefs of those thus described, while it does reveal something of the relationship between the parties involved. The only certainty is that the person using the word disapproves of, or wishes to belittle, the belief or custom which s/he is so labelling. In general, dominant elements in a society dismiss the beliefs of less powerful elements as superstitious. In the relationships between religions, classes, nations, regions, ethnic groups, and so on, the label 'superstitious' is always available to put someone else down, but no one labels their own beliefs as superstitious. It is because of this cultural baggage that modern folklorists tend to eschew the word 'superstition' and prefer to use other terms such as 'alternative belief'.

Unfortunately, such attempts to alter perception by changing language are rarely successful. Outside the strictly scientific spheres, meaning is not under the control of the specialist, and in everyday language any new term is likely to already have its own baggage. If 'alternative belief' is useful at all, it is a broader concept than 'superstition' and, indeed, includes it, and we therefore lose clarity and precision by its adoption. Despite the grossly subjective nature of the adjectival form, in modern Britain there is a general consensus about what constitutes a 'superstition'. People may not be able to define a 'superstition' but they can certainly name some and describe their basic characteristics. On the other hand, most people will understand the term 'alternative belief' to mean something like aromatherapy, acupuncture, or Scientology.

Definitions

In most traditional dictionary definitions of superstition, the central point is *irrationality*:

Irrational belief usually founded on ignorance or fear and characterized by obsessive reverence for omens, charms, etc.   Collins English Dictionary (1986)

In the modern world, however, we are often uncomfortable with the assumption that there is only one valid form of 'rationality'. The *Encyclopaedia Britannica* is clearly uneasy on this point:

Belief, half belief, or practice of which there appears to be no rational substance. Those who use the term imply that they have certain knowledge or superior evidence for their own scientific, philosophic, or religious convictions. An ambiguous word, it probably cannot be used except subjectively.   Encyclopaedia Britannica (15th edn, 1974) 401.

Nevertheless, we must have a working description, even if we cannot achieve a strict definition. For the purposes of this book, a superstition includes one or more of the following elements:

1. Luck
Belief in luck as a real and not simply a metaphorical force in human life, and that future luck can be manipulated or influenced by present behaviour.

2. Omens/Signs
Belief that the future can be foretold or predicted by physically unconnected events such as the presence or behaviour of birds or animals or accidental occurrences in everyday life.

3. Beginnings
(a) Belief that situational elements which pertain at the beginning of a project, journey, period of time, etc., predict how it will continue or determine its outcome.
(b) Belief that situational elements which pertain at the beginning of a person's life predict or determine future character, prosperity, etc.
(c) Belief that coincidences have deeper meaning and significance than random accident.

4. Occult powers
(a) Belief in divination.
(b) Belief in magic.
(c) Belief in 'witchcraft' or powers by which one person can physically harm another by casting spells, saying words, or making gestures.
(d) Belief in the power of words to affect physical change, to cure, or to protect from harm.
(e) Belief in the power of amulets or other items worn to cure or protect the wearer from harm.
(f) Belief that items once physically connected retain a sympathetic connection even when apart.

These descriptions beg the further question of what is 'belief'. Do people really believe, pay lip service to, or simply know of the superstitions without following them? In very many of the examples discussed in this book, we have insufficient information about 'belief' as such, but can merely register that a superstition was *recorded* at a particular time and place. While we can be sure that Samuel Pepys believed in the efficacy of his hare's foot, because he says so in his diary, we do not know whether William Shakespeare believed that cobwebs were good for stopping bleeding when he referred to the notion in *A Midsummer Night's Dream* with the line 'I shall desire you of more acquaintance, good Master Cobweb; if I cut my finger I shall make bold with you.'

In the human mind, 'belief' is far from constant and can vary over time according to situation. Despite Gilbert White's pessimism, many of the beliefs we hold as children are discarded as we get older. But we can still happily 'half believe' something, we can even believe and not believe at the same time if we want to. We may notice omens on the way to an important interview but not on other days, and our belief can result in action at some times and not at others. We are told by folklorist Edward Lovett, for example, that the carrying of mascots and lucky charms increased dramatically during the First World War. Presumably, many individuals who started carrying them at that time knew of mascots before, but did not bother about them until a particular need arose. This seems to confirm that a key factor is the feeling of vulnerability, and that superstition thrives in an atmosphere of fear, uncertainty, or perceived lack of control over one's fate. It is no surprise therefore that superstitious feeling appears to proliferate during such periods of particular stress as war, or in occupations which face daily danger (fishing, mining), or where success appears to depend largely on 'luck' (acting, sports). But this does not explain why some people are superstitious all the time, and others not.

Echoing Gilbert White's emphasis on education, the modern hard-line rationalist has no problem with this last question: s/he argues that superstitious thinking is simply ignorance which the human race will gradually grow out of. Superstition represents a failure to apply intelligence and proper inductive reasoning or to distinguish between appearance and reality, and the phrase *Post hoc ergo propter hoc* ('after that, therefore because of that') is often quoted to explain how erroneous connections are sometimes made by less than rigorous thinking. Certainly, the principles involved in most superstitions do not normally bear rational scrutiny, but people often manage to believe in the teeth of all evidence to the contrary.

Even within the world of superstition, thought processes are not clear. Omens, by definition, are warnings of things to come, but they were often treated as if they were *causes* rather than simply signs. Certainly, when the key omen is man-made – such as a grave being left open over Sunday, which predicted another death in the parish – it is impossible to say that this action, or inaction, was not the cause. Similarly, why should an unusual occurrence be deemed ominous?

[c.1914] *At long last our Dad has it calved, a terrible freak of a creature with two heads and eight legs. Farmers feared freaks, for they were always considered to be bad omens. And indeed there were plenty of folk about to verify about freaks a-being born and the owners dying unnatural deaths soon after.*   Stewart (1971) 90

It is clear that tradition plays a strong part, but other than that the problem is circular. Why do people believe strange things? Because they are superstitious. Why are they superstitious? Because they believe strange things.

Deconstructing superstitions

One of the regrettable by-products of the assumption that superstitions have ancient origins is that it has prevented any genuine analysis of how superstition is structured and how it functions. Commentators have usually assumed that knowing that superstitions are ancient survivals is all we need to know, and have been more concerned with inventing origins than with analysing the beliefs themselves. The alternative approach adopted in the present work is one which comes most naturally to a folklorist. It is clear from even a casual glance that beliefs are not random and unconnected but share basic principles and include recurrent formulas or motifs in the same way as other folkloric forms, such as folk-tales. The identification and analysis of these motifs is highly rewarding, and tells us far more about the workings of belief than any supposed origin. Principles such as 'do not tempt fate', 'begin well to continue well', 'the natural world following the prevailing religion', 'avoid acts of finality', 'anything unusual is likely to be threatening', 'like cures like', and so on are found in the vast majority of beliefs and are thus reflected in the majority of entries in this book.

The vast majority of superstitions are concerned with bad luck rather than good, and the superstitious view of the world is indeed a bleak one. Death and injury lurk around every corner; pride, achievement, and good fortune will be punished by a vengeful fate or by our neighbours who are so jealous of any potential success that they may cast an evil eye on us at any time.

Other folkloric processes are also involved. Superstitions expand into narratives, becoming embedded into local stories which simultaneously help to disseminate the core belief and legitimize it with local and personal details. Other beliefs are similarly supported by simple stories about Jesus or the Virgin Mary, and thus appear to have the backing of the Church. Some superstitions become so widespread that they achieve the status of well-known sayings in themselves. In Victorian times, 'a letter in the candle' or the 'stranger on the bar' were as instantly recognizable as 'I'll cross my fingers for you' or 'touch wood' are in modern times.

A word must also be said about the relationship between superstition and religion. For many commentators in Britain, superstitions were clearly the inventions of the Devil:

The observation of omens, such as the falling of salt, a hare crossing the way, of the dead-watch, of crickets, &c. are sinful and diabolical: they are the inventions of the Devil, to draw men from a true trust in God, and make them his own vassals. For by observations as these, they are slaves of superstition and sin, and have all the while no true dependence upon God, no trust in his providence.   Henry Bourne, *Antiquitates Vulgares* (1725)

Alternatively, they were seen as remnants of discredited faiths, which should be rooted out. For Protestants, the Roman Catholic Church was the arch progenitor of superstition. On the other hand, some could quite happily incorporate superstitions into their religious faith:

[Death omens] *Many pious people also improved the circumstance, pointing out that these omens were evidence of God's great mercy, inasmuch as He vouchsafed to give a timely warning in order that the dying persons might prepare for death, and make their peace with the great Judge.*   Napier (1879) 56–7

The relationship between religion and superstition exists on several levels, but cannot be ignored. It has already been indicated that many regard other people's religious beliefs as superstitions, and, indeed, to the atheist, they all are. Christianity, in its various forms, has been by far the strongest and most constant influence on the daily lives of people all over Britain for over a thousand years, and many superstitions are clearly based on its teachings in one form or another. Some were simply survivals of previous rites and customs now superseded in the official church, others were misunderstandings or misappropriations. The common people, for example, have regularly appropriated passages from the Bible into their charms and divinations, as, indeed, they had to do, for no one would have tolerated overtly non-Christian material in such contexts. All the major Christian festivals and occasions, such as christenings, weddings, and funerals acquired unofficial superstitious overtones and practices. However much the church authorities have tried to distance themselves from belief in witchcraft and magic, it has been a constant uphill struggle, hampered by the fact that their own holy book includes stories of magicians and witches. The niceties of theological doctrine have often passed the common folk by, but the Bible speaks directly to us.

Another category of material is also represented by some entries in the present work – what were previously termed 'vulgar errors'. These are erroneous 'scientific' facts which were widely believed and slow to be exploded. Most people in the early nineteenth century, for example, were firmly convinced that horse hairs placed in water turned into eels. It seems ridiculous now, but there are plenty of equally unfounded beliefs still in circulation, and probably always will be. Many people believe that your hair can turn white instantly through shock or fear. Others believe that it is illegal to place a stamp upside down on an envelope, as the disrespect to the Queen counts as treason, or that a tooth placed in Coca-Cola will dissolve overnight. These beliefs are the stuff of contemporary legend and, in general, are excluded here, but a few of the more interesting ones of the past have crept in (see also the entry under 'legal errors').

A historical approach

As already indicated, it is the central premise of this book that the popular idea that superstitions are very old, and that they reflect the thought processes, fears, and preoccupations of our remote ancestors, is mistaken. The roots of this notion lie in the development of folklore studies in Victorian times and have a complex history, but suffice it to say here that the whole notion of folklore being necessarily very old is groundless and flies in the face of most of the evidence which has been amassed over the past century or so. Many of our well-known modern superstitions cannot be found before the late nineteenth or even early twentieth centuries. It follows that all the thinking based on assumed antiquity needs to be re-evaluated. Even if 'superstitious ways of thinking' are endemic to the human brain, which is still debatable, there is no evidence that individual superstitions are immutable cultural constants which reveal deep hidden truths about the national psyche. Indeed, like all other traditional forms, they are subject to change and adaptation. They are invented, and go in and out of fashion. It follows that the penchant for inventing origins by extrapolating backwards from modern beliefs, shown in virtually all popular writing on the subject, is pointless and leads to a completely erroneous picture of the material and what it means.

This dismissal of the 'ancient origins' theory is not the only departure represented by this present book. With one honourable exception, modern books on superstition are of little use to the historian, the scholar, or even the general reader who seeks a genuine understanding of the subject. There is no shortage of popular dictionaries of superstition, nor of articles in newspapers and magazines, but they are composed entirely of unsupported assertions and material recycled without regard to provenance or context. The honourable exception to this blanket condemnation is the *Dictionary of Superstitions* compiled by Iona Opie and Moira Tatem, and published by Oxford University Press in 1989. This truly seminal work represents the only serious attempt to present superstitions in a historical context, and it must be the starting point for any future research for a long time to come. Without it, this present Guide would have taken years more to compile and would have been much poorer.

The present Guide shares with Opie and Tatem the attempt to set superstitions into a genuine historical and geographical framework, without which we are completely in the dark. They built their dictionary on 'historical principles', providing dated examples of usage, including the first known occurrence of each belief. They thus provide the opportunity to work from evidence rather than supposition, but their format precludes any commentary and occasionally obscures a geographical perspective.

The approach taken in the present work allows more room for commentary and analysis, and attempts to present the evidence in as full a form as possible within the confines of a single volume. The references which follow each entry may not be needed by the casual reader, but they are an essential component of the book's *raison d'être*, and they serve several purposes. As with all references, they provide readers with the scholarly equivalent of an audit-trail, allowing them to check my assertions and quotations against the originals. But they also have value in themselves, in providing as detailed an overview as is practical of the geographical and chronological spread of the known material and thereby some measure of the relative popularity or rarity of the belief in question. Although no entry can include every single known reference, the majority of known examples are always given, and the number of references thus provides a rough guide to relative popularity. In addition, anyone interested in a particular period, or more likely a particular region, can use these references to isolate material of interest to them.

The book is therefore fiercely historical – bound by historical dates and chronologies in a way that some readers may find too rigid. The main principle adopted is that if the first known reference to a superstition occurs in 1850, then we need other evidence to make us believe it to be any older. Obviously, it is quite feasible that it *is* older, and that either it did not leave any evidence or we have simply failed to find the references which do exist. If the former is the case, there is little we can do about it, but for the latter situation we at least have the consolation that as further serious investigations are undertaken, our coverage of the literature will gradually improve in both depth and breadth. As each study is published, we can be more confident that we have not missed something.

Clearly, any statement of 'earliest date' must therefore be handled with caution. In some cases, indeed, I have allowed myself a modest degree of speculation beyond the first known publication date. Where, for example, several references occur in rapid succession from different parts of the country, we can draw on our knowledge of the basic workings of traditional materials to suggest that as cultural items take a while to spread geographically, any widely spread item is likely to have been around for a while. Obviously, the complicating factor here is fashion. An item can be widely reported simply because it is in fashion at the time, and fashions are usually for *new* rather than *old* things.

One further aspect of historical dating needs discussion, to caution the unwary not to jump to conclusions. Some of the beliefs reported in Britain in recent centuries have close analogues in the writings of classical authors from around the time of Christ and even long before. Where these analogues have been found, they have been noted in the appropriate entry. It must never be assumed in these cases, however, that the belief has survived intact in Britain for all that time – that is so unlikely as to be almost beyond the bounds of belief. Given the changes in race, culture, language, and religion which have taken place in the British Isles in the intervening millennia, and the fact that there is no single case where it can definitely be shown to have occurred, it is another of the nineteenth-century notions which must be discarded.

What must be taken into account, however, is the tremendous popularity of classical writings with the educated elites of all European countries, including Britain, from the late Middle Ages onwards. It is only a slight exaggeration to say that the thoughts and practices of writers such as Pliny were more familiar to many educated British people than the contemporary customs and beliefs of their own lower classes. Classical material had immense status for the educated minority, especially when supported by Continental authorities.

Being in the country in the vacation time not many years since, at Lindly in Leicestershire, my father's house, I first observed this amulet of a spider in a nut-shell lapped in silk, etc. so applied for an ague by my mother: whom although I knew to have excellent skill in chirurgery, sore eyes, aches, etc. and such experimental medicines, as all the country where she dwelt can witness, to have done many famous and good cures upon divers poor folks, that were otherwise destitute of help – yet, among all other experiments, this, methought, was most absurd and ridiculous: I could see no warrant for it. Quid arraneæ cum febre? [Why a spider for a fever?] For what antipathy? Till at length, rambling amongst authors (as I often do) I found this very medicine in Dioscorides, approved by Matthiolus, repeated

by Aldrovandus . . ., I began to have a better opinion of it, and to give more credit to
amulets, when I saw it in some parties answer to experience.

Robert Burton, *Anatomy of Melancholy* (1621) Pt 2, Sec. 5, Mem. 1, Subs. 5

This is particularly true in the realm of medicine, as reflected in the influential herbals
published from the fifteenth century onwards. In all the surviving Anglo-Saxon medical
manuscripts of the tenth and eleventh centuries, the majority of the material was copied
from written classical sources.

The evidence is pretty clear. Those ideas and practices which closely follow classical
models have not survived on the ground for all the intervening time but have been introduced to Britain via a literary tradition in the modern period, and have therefore quite
literally skipped a thousand years or so.

One of the severe limitations of the present approach, however, is its narrow geographical focus on the British Isles. Again, this is partly a reaction against earlier methods, in
the tradition of Frazer's *Golden Bough*, which allowed the pulling of examples from around
the world regardless of context, chronology, or possible connection, but it is mainly
because meaningful comparative work can only be done if one has confidence in the material being used. The further one moves from one's own culture the more difficult it is
to know who to trust. Imagine a foreign writer using any of the recent popular books on
British superstition as evidence, and the problem becomes clear. Only if we have an Opie
and Tatem for each country can we proceed with confidence.

Nevertheless, the nettle must be grasped soon. Even with the present narrow focus, there
are tantalizing glimpses of where further investigation could take us. It seems, for example,
that Friday 13th suddenly became known in Britain, America, and Germany at the same
time, and the Tooth Fairy, which we in Britain presume to have been imported from the
USA in the 1960s, was also brand new there at the same time. It is interesting to compare
the lists of superstitions given in Thorpe's *Northern Mythology* (1851) with what we know
of British beliefs of the period. For example, of the eighty-two beliefs from 'Netherlandish
popular tradition' first published in 1843, well over thirty have almost exact analogues in
nineteenth-century British traditions – 'For thirteen to sit at table is ill-boding', 'The
howling of a dog forebodes the death of a person in the neighbourhood', 'To overthrow
a saltcellar is not good, strife will follow', and so on. Many others work on recognizable
principles – 'If a bride tears her bridal dress, it is not good; she will undergo much trouble.'
Others, however, seem completely foreign – 'Those who do not like cats will not get handsome wives.' In previous times it would be assumed that such similarities exist because
the beliefs go back to our common ancestors, many centuries ago. But as we have rejected
that theory, we are left with two possibilities, which may not be mutually exclusive. One
is that similar superstitions arose spontaneously and independently in more than one
place – it may be argued, for example, that an itching hand meaning money coming or
going is sufficiently obvious to occur in more than one culture. The other possibility is
international dissemination – one society learnt it from the other – and the scale and
scope of this transnational borrowing would be fascinating to unravel.

Another deliberate narrowing of focus relates to the basic subject-matter of the book.
Folklore genres are not clearly defined, mutually exclusive territories, and there is much
overlap between them. Superstition shades off into a number of neighbouring areas,
including *narrative* (legends, by definition, include an element of belief), and *calendar*

customs (some customs take on superstitious elements, while some superstitions are carried out on certain days of the year). *Weather-lore* is excluded, on the grounds that it is usually based on the observation and interpretation of physical signs and thus might, perhaps, have a scientific basis. Other major omissions are *supernatural beings*, such as fairies, elves, and ghosts, as they are too large a subject to do justice to here; similarly, astrology and witchcraft are not as fully covered as I would wish.

It is one of the joys of research in folklore that evidence can be found in almost any imaginable place. Certainly, any published source is grist to the mill – newspapers, magazines, plays, poems, novels, scientific treatises, Acts of Parliament, memoirs, letters, diaries, children's books, dictionaries, political cartoons, advertisements, and so on can all include valuable information, and have all been used in the present work. We also possess a great number of specialist publications which include material collected by folklorists, both amateur and professional. The wonderful *Notes and Queries* (N&Q), launched in 1849, is mentioned on nearly every page, and the journals of the Folklore Society, *Folk-Lore Record* (1878–82), *Folk-Lore Journal* (1883–9), *Folk-Lore* (1890–1957), and *Folklore* (1958 to date) also include a wealth of superstition material, collected in villages and towns all over the country, as well as articles of commentary and analysis. County and regional collections of folklore appeared regularly from Victorian and Edwardian times onwards, and local periodicals such as *Transactions of the Devonshire Association* preserved numerous beliefs for posterity. Indeed, there is no shortage of material. One type of source which I have not been able to use as fully as it deserves is the wealth of manuscript materials in folklore repositories in Ireland, Scotland, and Wales. These need to be consulted, and the current imbalance towards England redressed.

The references at the foot of each entry are organized primarily in geographical rather than chronological order, although places are not normally given at lower than county level. Each listing starts with **England**, progressing from south to north, followed by **Wales**, **Scotland**, **Ireland**, **Channel Isles**, and **Isle of Man**. Sources which are clearly reporting a tradition in a particular place, without making it clear where, are listed as **Unlocated**, followed by **General** descriptions, and **Literary** treatments. If a particularly important source exists, it is included in **Major studies**, and lastly any **Foreign** or **Classical** references are listed.

It was surprisingly difficult to pinpoint the geographical location of many sources, and the result is only accurate to a fairly broad level. One anomaly should be mentioned: S. O. Addy's important book *Household Tales* or *Folk Tales and Superstitions* (1895) covers Yorkshire, Lincolnshire, Derbyshire, and Nottinghamshire, and as I could not think of an adequate name for this area, it is given as **England**, but appears alongside Derbyshire in the list.

Early and literary sources are mostly given in full in the references, but the majority of the rest are given in abbreviated form, e.g. Smith (1980), which can be further identified in the Bibliography.

Are we more or less superstitious than we used to be?

The difficulty of identifying levels of belief has already been discussed, and it is thus extremely difficult to compare degrees of superstition across time or space. Nevertheless, the question is often asked whether we are more or less superstitious today than we used to be. Any answer also has to be qualified by the lack of a clear-cut time-frame boundary. We live in the twenty-first century, but anyone over the age of three was born in the twentieth, and there are still many people around who were born in the first quarter of that century. Beliefs learnt in the period of the First World War are still in the heads of many old people in Britain today.

It is common in popular works on superstition to claim that we are still very superstitious; depending on your definition, this may be true, and anyway it makes good copy. Undoubtedly, there are still people who would be described as 'very superstitious', and it would be a very bold person who claimed to have no superstitious beliefs at all. Nevertheless, from the evidence presented in this book and in Opie and Tatem, it is clear that, as a society, we are immeasurably less superstitious than we used to be. This is true on all levels – we do not know so many superstitions, we do not believe so deeply, we do not act upon them so much, and the ones we still possess have generally been sanitized to mean 'bad luck' instead of 'someone will die soon'. Indeed, it is no exaggeration to say, in comparison to a hundred years ago, that we *play* at being superstitious. Try a small exercise. Answer the following questions:

1) You are the manager of a shop. An employee fails to turn up for work on several occasions because he returns home every time he sees a single magpie. Do you accept this as a valid excuse?

2) You have applied for a job for which you are well qualified. You are turned down because you have red hair. Do you think that is fair?

3) Your daughter cuts herself and is bleeding heavily. Your neighbour says, 'Don't worry – I know a charm that will stop that.' Do you (a) Believe him and wait for the charm to work, or (b) Take your daughter to the hospital immediately.

4) Your eighteen-year-old niece is having a church wedding, the banns are called for three weeks in advance, and she is in church to hear them read. Do you tell her that because of this her first baby will be born deaf and dumb? Even if you believed it, would you *say* it?

5) Your sister lives in a fishing village and does the family washing on New Year's Day. Her husband is unfortunately lost at sea. Do you point out to her that she is guilty of 'washing him away'?

6) You wish to help find a cure for cancer. Do you give money to scientific research or to the faith healer in the next village?

7) Things seem to be going wrong in your life. You are having a run of bad luck. Do you think that someone has bewitched you? If so, do you find the nearest old woman and scratch her face to make it bleed, to break the spell?

These are not obscure beliefs but were all very widespread only a few years before our current oldest inhabitants were born, and the examples could be multiplied many times over. Compare these to the colourless present-day beliefs that it is unlucky to walk under a ladder or to open an umbrella indoors. It is only now that superstition plays such a minimal role in medicine and everyday life that we can afford to be nostalgic about it and say we regret its passing.

Top ten superstitions 1998

In 1998 Jacqueline Simpson and I undertook a brief survey of superstitions in England, with the assistance of the Folklore Society. The survey was a single sheet which was circulated to Society members with a request that they pass it on to others (i.e. not Society members). The sheet asked people to list ten superstitions, or more if they knew more. We deliberately offered no definition of superstition, nor did we ask if people believed them or not. We wished to test two basic hypotheses: firstly, that people would readily understand the word 'superstition', and secondly, that the range of superstitions known today is severely limited, and that the same few beliefs would be reported over and over again.

The survey was not a scientifically valid project, but we believed that it would provide at least an indication of the current situation. We received 215 completed sheets. The responses came from various parts of the country and from a range of ages (but no children). The vast majority of beliefs listed were already familiar to us. The superstitions included by most respondents, together with the percentage of respondents who mentioned them, are as follows:

1   Unlucky to walk under a ladder 83%
2   Lucky/Unlucky to meet a black cat 67%
3   Unlucky to break a mirror 54%
4   Unlucky/Lucky to see magpies 47%
5   Unlucky to spill salt 44%
6   Unlucky to open an umbrella indoors 39%
7   Thirteen/Friday 13th unlucky 36%
8   Unlucky to put shoes on a table 35%
9   Unlucky to pass someone on the stairs 21%
10 Lucky to touch wood 16%

Within the limited terms of reference, both our hypotheses were confirmed. Apart from a few items of weather-lore, such as 'Red sky at night', . . . all the items listed were recognizable superstitions, and there was remarkable conformity across the board. Some respondents gave many more than ten, some could not manage ten, but as will be seen from the list above, the top three were cited by over half the respondents, and the top eight by over a third. Informal research since that time has consistently confirmed these findings.

Some commentary on these results is necessary. Although 67 per cent listed the black cat superstition, they were about evenly split in regarding it as lucky or unlucky, and some wrote that they could not remember which it was. Few people gave the whole magpie rhyme, but all agreed that seeing *one* was bad. Friday and Friday 13th are given a combined total here because they seemed to be linked in many people's responses, but it is arguable that they should be treated separately (see their main entries).

The only real surprise was that 'touch wood' scored so badly. We believe that this is evidence that it is passing out of the arena of superstition and becoming simply a saying which we utter in certain social situations, for example when we seem to boast or be too confident.

Further analysis of the list sheds interesting historical light. These are not, by any means, ancient superstitions. Only two, for example, (black cat and spilt salt) are included in John Melton's 1620 list (see pages 447–8). Comparing the list with the relevant entries in this present work, and in Opie and Tatem's *Dictionary of Superstitions*, shows that only one (Friday) can be dated possibly to the fourteenth century; one (salt) possibly to the sixteenth century; one (black cat) to the seventeenth century; three (ladder, mirror, magpies) to the eighteenth; and four (umbrella, shoes, stairs, touch wood) to the nineteenth.

Acknowledgements

My most immediate debt of gratitude is to Iona Opie and Moira Tatem. The influence of their *Dictionary of Superstitions* will be found on every page of this book. Of the many published folklore collections, Roy Vickery's *Dictionary of Plant Lore* was particularly useful. Thanks, also, to numerous folklore colleagues, past and present; in particular, for this project, Jacqueline Simpson, Jennifer Chandler, and Caroline Oates, all of the Folklore Society.

Much of the best material on folklore topics in recent decades has been written by historians, and I would like to acknowledge in particular the work of Owen Davies, Ronald Hutton, and Keith Thomas, whose books are informative, stimulating, and, above all, sensible.

Thanks to the staff of that wonderful institution, the London Library, for their unfailing courtesy and assistance, and similarly to the staff of the inter-library loans department at Croydon Libraries (David Wood, Jayne Raper, Frances King, and Louise Adrados) for finding obscure material. A special vote of thanks also to my colleagues in Croydon's Local Studies Library and Archives (Chris Corner, Margaret Mumford, Grace Woutersz, and Chris Bennett) for their unfailing friendship, support and forbearance.

Writing a reference book like this is really an exercise in plundering other people's work, but I hope that I have given credit to previous workers in the field where it is due. I hope also that my book is deemed worthy of plunder in its turn.

The Guide

abracadabra

Long before the word 'abracadabra' became the stereotypical phrase of the stage magician, it was believed to be a powerful CHARM against ague, toothache, and various other ailments. Written repeatedly on a piece of parchment as an inverted triangle, with each line omitting some letters, and hung round the neck, it acted as an AMULET:

To cure an ague – Write this following spell in parchment, and wear it about your neck. It was be writ triangularly. With this spell, one of Wells, hath cured above a hundred of the ague.

Unlocated Aubrey, *Miscellanies* (1696)

Aubrey's is the first known example of the word in English, but he claims that it was already in use. Within a year it was also published by John Durant, and there is little doubt that it was introduced to British tradition directly by some such translator of classical works, probably only a short time before Aubrey.

A cigarette card from 1923 showing 'abracadabra' in an inverted pyramid shape – the usual form in which it appears when used as an amulet.

The word is first found in a Latin poem by Q. Severus Sammonicus, physician to the Emperor Carcalla in the second century AD, where it was already recommended to be hung round the neck as a protective charm. The inverted triangle, it has been suggested, symbolized – or physically forced – the disease to diminish as the letters do in the charm.

The origin of the word is unknown, but this has not prevented numerous guesses that it is a secret word for a god, or the name of a demon. Astrologers and would-be sorcerers in Britain and abroad, from early modern times to the present day, have been fascinated by words which can be written in geometric shapes, especially if they can be read in various directions, believing that such words must have special powers.

In essentially the same form, the amulet was still being reported in the twentieth century.

Devon Hewett (1900) 73. **Herefordshire** [1804] Leather (1912) 74–5. **Wales** Davies (1911) 283–4; Jones (1930) 143. **Unlocated** Aubrey, *Miscellanies* (1696/1857) 134–5; John Durant, *Art and Nature Joyn Hand in Hand* (1697), quoted *Folk-Lore* 23 (1912) 236; Grose (1787) 57. **General** *Jewishencyclopedia.com.*

acorns

Acorns only feature in scattered folk medicine references. They are one of the many items which could be carried about the person, or placed in the bed, as a cure for CRAMP or RHEUMATISM. They could also be taken internally, either chewed, or heated and powdered, for stomachache, diarrhoea, and the AGUE. In addition, an apparently unique LOVE DIVINATION procedure was reported from the Channel Islands:

A spell which requires to be performed in society is as follows. On any of the solemn nights about Christmastide, when spells are supposed to be efficaciously used, a number of girls meet together and make a chaplet in perfect silence, by stringing grains of allspice and berries of holly alternately, placing, at intervals of twelve, an acorn, of which there must be as many as there are persons in the company. This chaplet is twined round a log of wood, which is then placed on the blazing hearth, and, as the last acorn is being consumed, each of the young women sees the form of her future husband pass between her and the fire.   Guernsey MacCulloch MS (1864)

A more mundane way of trying your future prospects was to name two acorns, one for yourself and your sweetheart, and drop them into a basin of water. Marriage was predicted if they floated close together.

See also OAKS.

Devon [c.1912] Lakeham (1982) 48. Essex [c.1939] *Folk-Lore* 62 (1951) 263. Bedfordshire Marsom (1950) 183. Worcestershire/Shropshire *Gent. Mag.* (1855) 384–6. Suffolk Pigot, *Gent. Mag.* (1867) 728–41; Vickery (1995) 264. Lincolnshire Sutton (1992) 148. Guernsey MacCulloch MS (1864) 410. Unlocated Radford (1971) 254.

actors

see THEATRE.

adders

see SNAKES.

adder-stones

see SNAKESTONES.

Agnes

Lincolnshire dialect expert Edward Peacock twice reported the strange belief that 'Persons called Agnes always go mad'. He gave no reason for this astonishing assertion, nor has any other corroborative reference so far come to light.

Lincolnshire N&Q 1S:8 (1853) 382; Peacock (1877) 3.

ague

An older name for malaria, or any fever, 'the ague' was formerly widespread, and a bewildering variety of cures for it were current well into the twentieth century. In addition to numerous herbal cures, the ague was thought susceptible to magical approaches by CHARMS:

When Jesus saw the cross whereon he was to be crucified he trembled and shook and the Jews asked him, 'art thou afraid or hast thou the ague?' Jesus answered and said, 'I am not afraid neither have I the evil ague, whoever wears this about them shall not be afraid nor have that evil ague'.
Herefordshire [1804] Leather

As with most charms, this could be recited over the sufferer, or written down and worn or carried about the person. It is also a regular characteristic of the genre that many are little more than a story about Jesus or his disciples. Other charms were also widely used, including the word ABRACADABRA, first recorded by John Aubrey in 1696.

Another common cure which lasted from at least the seventeenth century to within living memory was to imprison a SPIDER or other small creature in a bag and wear it around the neck, or swallow it alive. Elias Ashmole recorded in his diary for 11 June 1681: 'I took early in the morning a good dose of elixir, and hung three spiders about my neck, and they drove my ague away – Deo gratias' (Ashmole, 1927). The principle here seems to be LIKE CURE LIKE, in that a shivery creature cures a shivery disease. Less easily explained is the idea that a piece of wood taken from a GALLOWS or gibbet and worn round the neck would cure the fever. Some writers commented on the particularly unpleasant nature of ague cures:

Chief among the ailments of Marshland in olden days was ague, and some of the many remedies prescribed were so horribly filthy that I am inclined to think most people must have preferred the ague, or the race could hardly have survived. It will, perhaps, be enough to say that the chief ingredient in one such decoction consisted of nine worms taken at midnight from a churchyard sod and chopped up small!   Lincolnshire Heanley (1902)

Some beliefs held that the ague could also be caused by careless behaviour or magical methods. It was said that you caught it by burning green ELDER wood, while others maintained that you could deliberately cause ague by utilizing procedures similar to offensive counter-witchcraft (*see* WITCH BOTTLES).

It is said in Devonshire that you may give [the ague] *to your neighbour by burying under his threshold a bag containing the parings of a dead man's nails, and some of the hairs of his head; your neighbour will be afflicted with ague till the bag is removed.*   Devon Henderson (1866)

Charms: Kent N&Q 3S:2 (1862) 343. Sussex [c.1710] *Sussex N&Q* 2 (1929) 27. Cornwall Couch (1871) 148;

Folk-Lore Jnl 5 (1887) 202. **Herefordshire** [1804] Leather (1912) 73. **Worcestershire** N&Q 2S:10 (1860) 184. **Lincolnshire** [*c.*1858] Gutch & Peacock (1908) 125; N&Q 4S:7 (1871) 443; Heanley (1902) 18. **Shropshire** [*c.*1810] *Folk-Lore* 6 (1895) 202–4. **Wales** Jones (1930) 143. **Co. Leitrim** *Folk-Lore* 5 (1894) 198. **Unlocated** Aubrey, *Miscellanies* (1696/1857) 134–5; Grose (1787) 57; Halliwell (1849) 208; N&Q 1S:5 (1852) 413; Henderson (1866) 137; N&Q 4S:7 (1871) 483.

Spiders or cobwebs: **Sussex** *Sussex Life* (Jan. 1973) 34. **Somerset** N&Q 1S:2 (1850) 130; Henderson (1866) 118; Poole (1877) 52; N&Q 10S:1 (1904) 273–4. **Devon** [1781] N&Q 10S:1 (1904) 205. **Oxfordshire** *Oxf. FL Soc. Ann. Record* (1956) 11. **East Anglia** Varden (1885) 102. **Suffolk** *East Anglian Mag.* 14 (1954/5) 349. **Lincolnshire** N&Q 10S:1 (1904) 273–4; Gutch & Peacock (1908) 116. **Yorkshire** [1871] N&Q 10S:1 (1904) 317–18. **Lancashire** Harland & Wilkinson (1882) 75. **Western Scotland** Napier (1879) 95. **Southern Ireland** N&Q 1S:2 (1850) 259. **Unlocated** (1743) Chambers 1 (1878) 732. **General** John Wesley, *Primitive Physic* (13th edn, 1768).

Gallows: **Co. Durham** Brockett (1829) 291. **General** Browne, *Pseudodoxia Epidemica* (1650/6th edn., 1672) Bk 5, Ch. 23; Grose (1787) 57. *Gent. Mag.* (1796) 636; Brand (1810) 107.

Other cures: **Sussex** Latham (1878) 39. **Hampshire** *Athenaeum* (1849) 814; N&Q 6S:10 (1884) 18. **Devon** Henderson (1866) 118. **Hertfordshire** N&Q 1S:6 (1852) 5. **Buckinghamshire/Middlesex** N&Q 3S:5 (1864) 237. **Gloucestershire** N&Q 4S:4 (1873) 500; *Glos. N&Q* 1 (1881) 43; Hartland (1895) 51. **Bedfordshire** *Bedfordshire Mag.* 2 (1950) 163. **Cambridgeshire** N&Q 4S:8 (1871) 133; N&Q 5S:1 (1874) 204. **Suffolk** *Gent. Mag.* (1867) 728–741; Gurdon (1893) 29; *Folk-Lore* 10 (1899) 365. **Norfolk** N&Q 1S:4 (1851) 53; Varden (1885) 102; *Folk-Lore* 40 (1929) 115; Haggard (1935) 21; Chadwick (1960) 86. **Lincolnshire** N&Q 2S:1 (1856) 386; Henderson (1866) 118–19; Peacock (1877) 134; Heanley (1902) 18; Gutch & Peacock (1908) 124–5; Sutton (1992) 146. **Staffordshire** Hackwood (1924) 150. **Wales** Trevelyan (1909) 316–17. **West Wales** Davies (1911) 283. **Co. Cavan** Maloney (1972) 71. **Unlocated** Melton (1620); N&Q 2S:12 (1861) 492; N&Q 4S:12 (1873) 469; Chambers 1 (1878) 732.

air cures

The idea that the air we breathe is important to our general health hardly counts as superstition, and a 'change of air' has been prescribed for many medical problems for generations. Among the staple folk-cures of WHOOPING COUGH and other respiratory diseases, however, are many that recommended the inhaling of certain pungent fumes and special atmospheres. Often quoted in this context are the by-products of industrial processes such as gas-making and lime-burning, charcoal-burning, and the manufacture or use of tar:

In Dublin there was a cure which must have been used on hundreds of thousands of Dublin children: nearly every Dublin person from whom I enquired knew all about it and many of them had

been treated with it. The child was taken to some place where tar was being used and kept there sniffing the hot tar. The usual place was where some convenient road was being tarred, but if this was not possible, the child might be taken to any factory where tar was being used and made to smell it . . . Usually one treatment at the tar was not enough and treatment had to be continued for a number of days. Dublin Logan (1981)

In contrast, the fresh air of particular moors, mountains, and at the seaside was also regularly prescribed, as were the breezes found on BRIDGES, and even in canal or railway tunnels:

I was once travelling from Whitchurch to Tutbury along the North Staffordshire line, when at the Harecastle Tunnel I pulled up the window (third-class); on which a respectable woman opposite to me, with a child in her arms, pulled it down again hastily, and lifted the child to the open window. When we got out of the tunnel she explained that she had been advised that the air of the tunnel was good for whooping-cough.
Shropshire Burne (1883)

Other regular cures in rural areas included inhaling the smell of newly turned earth, the breath of a donkey or piebald horse, being carried through a flock of sheep, or, simply:

[When I was a child] delicate children were sent to stay on the farms because 'the smell of the manure' gave them strength.
Shropshire *Folk-Lore* (1938)

See also GASWORKS; LIME-KILNS; TIDE; WHOOPING COUGH

Devon [1945] *Devonshire Assoc.* 91 (1959) 199. **Surrey** [1920s] Surrey Fed. W. I.s (1992) 123. **London** *Cornhill Mag.* (Apr. 1917) 469. **Oxfordshire** *Folk-Lore* 68 (1957) 415–16. **Essex** [*c.*1939] *Folk-Lore* 62 (1951) 259–60. **Herefordshire** Leather (1912) 82. **West Midlands** W. Midlands Fed. W. I.s (1996) 73. **Suffolk** *Gent. Mag.* (1867) 728–41. **Shropshire** Burne (1883) 190; *Folk-Lore* 49 (1938) 228. **Staffordshire** Poole (1875) 81–2. **England** Addy (1895) 90. **Westmorland/Lancashire** [1939] *Folk-Lore* 62 (1951) 259–60. **Banffshire** Gregor (1874) 270. **Dublin** Logan (1981) 44.

alabaster

Alabaster, a form of gypsum, much used for statues, was long held to have medicinal qualities when finely powdered and administered in an ointment or poultice for sore legs, breasts, and other ailments, or even for internal use:

Leave Cardigan, take the road to Llanfernach

Bridell Church. Meet a man who carries a stone about the country, which he calls Llysfaen. Scrapes it into powder with a knife, and sells it at about five shillings an ounce as an infallible remedy for the canine madness. He says this stone is only to be found on the mountains after a thunderstorm, and that every eye cannot see it. He showed me the stone, and when I assured him and a little crowd that had gathered about him, that the stone was only a piece of Glamorgan alabaster, the poor fellow was confounded and seemed very angry; but I was surprised to hear many positively assert that they had actually seen the hydrophobia cured in dogs, and man, with this powder given in milk, and used as the only liquid to be taken for nine days, and the only food also.   Cardiganshire Extract from the *Diary* of Iolo Morganweg, 1802, quoted in N&Q (1912)

Alabaster taken from statues inside or on the outside of churches was regarded as particularly efficacious, and Exeter Cathedral is one of those buildings which long bore the evidence of the parishioners' habit of chipping bits of the fabric over the years. In some cases, particular figures acquired a curative reputation:

About a century ago the effigy of a knight in armour in Royston Church suffered considerable injury from scraping, the resultant powder being utilised for some medicinal purpose.
Hertfordshire N&Q (1912)

The medicinal use of alabaster has a long history. Its virtues are quoted, for example, in Salmon's *Pharmacopoeia Londinensis* (first published 1678) and in the *Medicinale Anglicum* (c.AD 950) *see* N&Q 11S:6 (1912) 175). As such, it must have had a general reputation, but folkloric references to it are almost entirely from western England and Wales, where its use lasted well into the twentieth century.

See also LEAD: CHURCH ROOF.

Devon Henderson (1866) 124; N&Q 11S:6 (1912) 175; *Devonshire Assoc.* 67 (1935) 133. *Devonshire Assoc.* 83 (1951) 74; *Devonshire Assoc.* 86 (1954) 299. New Forest Wise (1867) 176. Hertfordshire N&Q 11S:6 (1912) 129. Cardiganshire [1802] N&Q 11S:6 (1912) 234–5. N. Wales N&Q 4S:12 (1873) 385.

albatross

The belief that it is extremely unlucky to kill an albatross is entirely due to its inclusion in Samuel Taylor Coleridge's popular poem *The Rime of the Ancient Mariner* (written in 1797 and first published the following year). The albatross

motif was suggested by Coleridge's fellow-poet William Wordsworth, who came across the idea in Capt. George Shelvocke's *A Voyage Round the World by Way of the Great South Sea . . . 1719–1722* (published 1726). There is no evidence that the albatross superstition existed in Britain before the publication of Coleridge's poem, and, indeed, it was its very air of exotic mystery which suited the poem, in a way that a prosaic local belief would not have done. Such was the poem's popularity that the belief rapidly entered popular consciousness and, as in the nature of these things, was presumed to be ancient. Although almost everybody is aware of this superstition, not many authenticated examples have been reported. Whether it was believed or not is largely academic, as few inhabitants of the British Isles would come across an albatross anyway.

The albatross motif does provide an example of how one superstition can be brought in to explain another:

Question: Why is it considered bad luck to carry a box of Swan Vestas aboard a boat or ship? Answer: The earlier answer saying it's not considered bad luck may apply on Merchant Navy ships but is certainly wrong for fishing boats. I was given a dressing-down for carrying Swan Vestas while at sea and was told the swan on the box is held to represent the unfortunate albatross from Coleridge's epic poem The Rime of the Ancient Mariner. *In some cases the skipper will throw the matches over the side, circle them three times and return to port.*
Northumberland *Daily Mail* (21 Apr. 1994) 58

almanacs

Almanacs were annual publications, produced in large quantities for mass sale, and cheap enough for almost everyone to afford. They contained a wealth of practical information, including a calendar, TIDE tables, lists of markets and fairs, historical chronology, and medical advice, but also weather predictions, the phases of the MOON, simplified astrology, and predictions for the coming year. In times of major unrest, as in the second half of the seventeenth century, they also participated in the great political and religious controversies of the day, but for most of their existence they filled a more humble role.

The faith which some of our country folk place in almanacular prognostications is quite implicit. These annual publications are held in great esteem. There is nothing like a good comet year for the sale of them. On such occasions alarmist predictions are wont to swell the pages of these productions. And not a few of the more nervous portion of the community well-nigh tremble and quake with fear.   Yorkshire Morris (1911)

At a time when the printed word was still a mystery to much of the population, almanacs were sold in huge quantities. By the 1660s, combined almanac sales were about 400,000 a year. Probably one in three of families in England owned one. The leading titles became household names – *Raphael's, Zadkiel's, Old Moore's* – and in the late nineteenth century *Old Moore's* alone could sell a million copies.

In Gloucestershire, Zadkiel's is the orthodox almanac among the farmers, who, for the most part, firmly believe in his prediction of weather and political events. Moore's mystical guides them as to minor operations of tail-lopping, and the like, on lambs and foals, etc., which are never undertaken unless 'Sol' is in Aries, Taurus, or the right sign of the zodiac.   Gloucestershire N&Q (1873)

The almanac provided much support for local beliefs and superstitions. They were the main way in which simplified astrology was disseminated among the labouring classes, and provided information which was necessary for everyday life:

About the close of the last century, a medical practitioner of great eminence in Suffolk sent a purge to a patient, and desired him to take it immediately. On the following day he called at his home, and inquired how it had operated. The patient (a substantial farmer) said he had not taken it; and upon the doctor's remonstrating against his disobedience, the sick man gravely answered, 'That he had looked into his almanack, and seeing the sign lay in "bowels", he thought that, and the physic together, would be too much for him.'   Suffolk Forby (1830)

Gloucestershire N&Q 4S:11 (1873) 500; *Folk-Lore* 16 (1905) 169–70. Yorkshire Morris (1911) 160. Suffolk Forby (1830) 403–4. General Thomas (1971) esp. 347–56; James (1976); Capp (1979); Curry (1989); Perkins (1996); Davies (1999 a & b) 153–7.

ambulances

A superstition, apparently confined to children, dictated that on sight of an ambulance one must hold one's collar for a specified time, often until one sees a four-legged animal, and usually accompanied by a short rhyme:

[Chelsea in 1920s] *If we saw an ambulance or even heard its distant bell ring, we clawed dramatically at our throats, licked our fingers and touched the ground, gabbling 'touch collar, never swaller, never get the fever'. Fever meant diphtheria.*   London Gamble (1979)

First recorded in North London *c.*1906, the belief was widespread across Britain until the 1950s, and lingered until at least the 1980s. The rhyme varied considerably, but the 'Collar Swallow' couplet was the most common element:

Touch collar
Never swallow
Never get the fever
Touch your nose
Touch your toes
Never go in one of those.

Newcastle Opie (1959)

Other variant elements included SPITTING, CROSSING FINGERS, and TOUCHING WOOD.

There is little doubt that the belief started with the introduction of special conveyances for transporting people with contagious diseases and was later extended to include all ambulances. It would be useful if we could identify a connection between the children's response to meeting an ambulance and that of meeting a funeral, but the only noticeable similarity is that in some later instances of the latter, the trigger for ceasing the protective action was the same: 'If you see a funeral cross your fingers till you see a four-legged animal' (Opie & Tatem, 171). On the theoretical level, the underlying premise of meeting sickness and death may be the same, but in the case of the 'fever van' the notion of 'contagion' is more physical than magical. Nevertheless, at least one version voiced a more altruistic feeling: 'If you don't do this the person in the ambulance will die' (Opie (1959) 211).

Compare FUNERALS; FLOWERS.

London [*c.*1906] Rolph (1980) 55; [1920s] Gamble (1979) 89–90. Glasgow [Late 1940s] MacLeay (1990) 48. Various places [1930, 1953, 1954, 1983] Opie (1959) 210–11 Various places & dates Opie & Tatem, 2.

amputations

It was widely thought that at the day of judgement we would be expected to account for any missing body parts. Some took this quite literally and carefully kept any TEETH which were extracted in their lifetime, instructing their next of kin to place them in the coffin for burial. Those unfortunate enough to lose limbs or other body parts took steps to get them buried, if possible somewhere near where their body would eventually lie:

Andrew Bohan, living in Glenmacnass, County Wicklow, received an injury to his leg which resulted in subsequent amputation at the knee. The doctors who performed the operation were desirous of sending the leg to the medical school at Trinity College, Dublin, but Bohan's friends, hearing of their intention, broke into the house of Dr. Garland at Laragh, County Wicklow, and carried away the leg, burying it at once in the churchyard at Glendalough.   Co. Wicklow *Folk-Lore* (1907)

Devon *Folk-Lore* 20 (1909) 226; *Devonshire Assoc.* 59 (1927) 158. Oxfordshire *Folk-Lore* 19 (1908) 234. Norfolk *Folk-Lore* 21 (1910) 105. Shropshire [1799] *Folk-Lore* 21 (1910) 387. Cumberland Gibson (1858) 107–8. Northumberland *Folk-Lore* 20 (1909) 226. Co. Kerry *Folk-Lore* 18 (1907) 216. Co. Wicklow *Folk-Lore* 18 (1907) 82–3.

angels

There are few significant folk beliefs regarding angels. Babies who smile in their sleep are occasionally said to be seeing them, which was already regarded as an 'old saying' in a 1660 diary entry:

. . . and being in a slumber in my arms on my knee, he would sweetly lift up his eyes to heaven and smile, as if the old saying was true in this sweet infant, that he saw angels in heaven.
          Yorkshire Thornton (1875)

and was still current over two hundred years later. Another version, however, features fairies rather than angels:

When babies laughed or smiled in their sleep, the Welsh nurses in the long ago said the fairies were kissing them.   Wales Trevelyan (1909)

A more widespread tradition holds that a sudden lull in a conversation, usually taking place around twenty past or twenty to the hour, is occasioned by an angel passing by or over the house, although others say it is a spirit, or even 'the parson'. Thus, in a humorous piece detailing superstitions held by old people:

[after a silence] a spare, wrinkled lady . . . interposed to inquire whether or not we believed that an angel's wing had touched Mr. B.'s shoulder when he broke that pause in the conversation to which we have alluded.
          Unlocated *Illustrated London News* (27 Dec. 1851)

and:

'A host of angels must be passing by', said Mr O'Brien, 'what a silence there is!'
          Wales Thomas (1940)

In a story which prefigures the famous 'Angel of Mons' legend of the First World War (*see* Simpson & Roud (2000, 5–6), the nature writer Richard Jefferies reported an angel in the sky:

Now and then the western clouds after the sunset assume a shape resembling that of a vast extended wing, as of a gigantic bird in full flight – the extreme tip nearly reaching the zenith, the body of the bird just below the horizon. The resemblance is sometimes so perfect that the layers of feathers are traceable by an imaginative eye. This, the old folk say, is the wing of the Archangel Michael, and it bodes no good to the evil ones among the nations, for he is on his way to execute a dread command.
          Southern England Jefferies (1879)

See also TALKING.

Southern England Jefferies (1879) 113. Kent [1923] Opie & Tatem, 95. Somerset [1952] Opie & Tatem, 95. Herefordshire Leather (1912), 88. Lincolnshire Peacock (1877), 6. Yorkshire Thornton (1875), 124. Wales Trevelyan (1909) 267. Thomas (1940) 243. Unlocated *Illustrated London News* (27 Dec. (1851). *Sunday Express* (23 Sept. 1973) 13.

animal infestation

It has been widely believed that reptiles, insects, and other creatures can enter the human body, live, grow, and sometimes breed there. This is a topic which highlights the fuzzy nature of arbitrary theoretical distinctions between folklore genres, by straddling the boundary between superstition and CONTEMPORARY LEGEND. Of all the narrative sub-genres, contemporary legends rely most heavily on 'belief', and most of the examples listed below are in the form of stories told 'as true'.

The most common traditional examples in Britain involve amphibians who supposedly live in people's stomachs, but the genre also includes earwigs which have long been believed to eat their way into the brain after entering through the ear, insects believed to live in the lacquered bee-hive hairdos of young women in the 1960s, and baby spiders which issue from 'boils' contracted abroad by modern holidaymakers. The motif is also exploited regularly by makers of horror and science fiction films.

Frogs, newts, or snakes are the most common animals reported to be found in stomachs, but sometimes more exotic species such as octopi or wolves are reported to have been found. The stories warn against drinking pond water, eating unwashed watercress or over-ripe fruit, and so on, or simply sleeping in the fields. In some stories, the animal is enticed out by placing a bowl of milk near the person's mouth, or stupifying it with fumes, but in many cases the person dies and the full horror is then exposed:

She knew herself a young woman who was ill in bed, and had a glass of milk left on the floor at night by the bedside. She drank it and must have drunk some beetles with it, for, 'when she died, the doctors opened her and found her full of holes and blackbeetles'.   London *Folk-Lore* (1926)

In Irish tradition, it is the NEWT which is particularly feared in this context:

The man-creeper is elsewhere called 'man-keeper', 'man-lepper', 'dark-looker', 'alpluachra', and other names. The belief that it will enter the mouth of a sleeping person, and live inside him till he dies, seems to be universal in Ireland, and is well illustrated by a story in Douglas Hyde's Beside the Fire. *I have been told in Co. Louth that a decoction of nettles is beneficial in such a case, and that the man-creeper dies if laid on a bunch of nettles.*
     Ireland *Folk-Lore* (1908)

It is no coincidence that these stories of animal infestation are similar in both broad scope and detail to many descriptions of possession by the Devil and other evil spirits which emerged in witchcraft trials of the sixteenth and seventeenth centuries. These spirits were often described as having taken physical form and residence either in the witch's or her victims' bodies. What still needs to be clarified, however, is whether, as seems likely, the witch confessions took the form they did because they were part of an existing infestation tradition.

Sussex [1790] *Folk-Lore* 41 (1930) 105–6; Latham (1878) 48–9. Surrey *Folk-Lore* 37 (1926) 79–80. London *Folk-Lore* 37 (1926) 78–9. Oxfordshire [1890s] Thompson (1939) 116. Gloucestershire *Folk-Lore* 28 (1917) 313. Birmingham N&Q 1S:6 (1852) 466. Suffolk *Gent. Mag.* (1867) 728–41. Norfolk *Folk-Lore* 40 (1929) 120. Shropshire *Folk-Lore* 49 (1938) 230. Cheshire N&Q 1S:6 (1852) 338. Yorkshire N&Q 1S:6 (1852) 221–2; [1878] Addy (1895) 69. Lancashire [1920s] Naughton (1988) 141–2. Ireland *Folk-Lore* 19 (1908) 317. Co. Meath/Co. Tipperary *Folk-Lore* 15 (1904) 460. Co. Laoighis *Béaloideas* 9 (1939) 33. Co. Leitrim Logan (1981) 63. Guernsey [1589] *Channel Islands Ann. Anth.* (1972–3) 19. Unlocated Lupton (1631) Bk 5, para. 95.
For many more folkloric examples, *see* the bibliography of contemporary legend material by Bennett & Smith (1993). For spirit possessions, *see* Oldridge (2000) Ch. 6.

animals kneeling

A widespread belief holds that at midnight on Christmas Eve, all the cattle and other farmyard animals kneel in their stalls or in the fields in honour of the birth of Christ:

Christmas Eve – The country people have a notion that on this evening oxen kneel in their stalls and moan. In boyhood I was induced more than once to attend on the occasion; but whether for want of faith, or neglect of the instructions given me, I know not – they would not do their duty.   Northern England Brockett (1829)

Some writers report that their informants claimed to have successfully witnessed these events on a regular basis, but in other traditions it was regarded as sacrilegious to attempt to do so:

At midnight on Christmas Eve cattle are supposed to kneel in their stalls in adoration of the Saviour. It is said that anyone who enters the stable to test this, will be struck dead.   Jersey L'Amy (1927)

As with other seasonal beliefs, the reform of the CALENDAR in 1752 caused confusion for the faithful, who were forced to choose between the new official calendar and 'old style' dates eleven days later. Many chose to stick with tradition:

My grandmother believed that on Old Christmas Day (January 6th) all oxen knelt down at a certain hour to do homage to the Saviour, and that a flower bloomed for a short time.
     Yorkshire *Folk-Lore* (1910)

Variations on the same theme exist in less common beliefs that at Christmas BEES in hives hum the One Hundredth Psalm, animals in the field turn to the east and bow, and DONKEYS kneel at Easter. Occasionally, the same things are reported at HALLOWE'EN, and even ST MARK'S EVE.

These beliefs are a clear example of the standard motif that nature observes the Christian calendar, which provides both a charming vignette to be told to children, and a proof and legitimization of the religion for the faithful. Belief in the Holy THORN and the sun dancing at EASTER have the same basis. The first clear documentation of cattle kneeling is by Brand in 1790, and it is widely reported through the nineteenth and early twentieth centuries, although on present evidence, it seems that Scottish animals were less devout than others in the British Isles. Brand suggests that the belief originated in a popular print of the stable scene, in which the oxen are shown kneeling down, and this certainly seems likely provided that the picture can be shown to predate the superstition.

Cornwall Couch (1871) 163. Devon/Cornwall [1790] Brand (1849) 1, 473–4. Sussex *Folk-Lore* 25 (1914) 368. Kent Igglesden (c.1932) 105. Berkshire *Folk-Lore* 5

apples

The main area of superstition in which apples feature is LOVE DIVINATION, of which there are several distinct strands in the following entries. For some reason, apples seem to have been connected in the popular mind with love and sex, an echo perhaps of the belief that the fruit which Eve gave Adam to eat was an apple. Two other widespread beliefs are given separate treatment: the simultaneous appearance of blossom and fruit on the same tree as a death omen, and the use of apples in curing WARTS.

A few of the many other miscellaneous beliefs concerning apples are as follows:

To eat an apple without rubbing it first is to challenge the Evil One.   Surrey Igglesden (*c*.1932)

If it is a good season for gooseberries, it will be a bad season for apples.
      Devon *Devonshire Assoc.* (1892)

If the sun shines at 12 o'clock on Christmas Day it will be a good year for the apples.
      Lincolnshire Rudkin (1936)

If you have sore eyes, poultice them with decayed apples.   England Addy (1895)

Eat an apple going to bed
Knock the doctor on the head.
      Somerset Tongue (1965)

When it is a good apple year, it is a great year for twins.   Unlocated N&Q (1862)

The latter belief can be compared with a similar saying about NUTS.

Devon *Devonshire Assoc.* 24 (1892) 51. Somerset Tongue (1965) 220. Surrey Igglesden (*c*.1932) 221. Lincolnshire Rudkin (1936) 14. England Addy (1895) 91. Unlocated N&Q 3S:1 (1862) 482.

(1894) 337. Oxfordshire *Folk-Lore* 24 (1913) 89. Herefordshire *Folk-Lore* 51 (1940) 297. Northamptonshire Sternberg (1851) 186. Norfolk *Norfolk Archaeology* 2 (1849) 296. Shropshire *Folk-Lore* 49 (1938) 233. Lincolnshire Peacock (1877) 57; N&Q 7S:8 (1889) 388; Rudkin (1936) 40. Northern England Brockett (1829) 68. Yorkshire *Folk-Lore* 21 (1910) 225; Morris (1911) 218. Lancashire N&Q 2S:8 (1859) 242. Northumberland Bigge (1860–62) 92. Ireland Wilde (1888) 207. Guernsey De Garis (1975) 124–5. Jersey L'Amy (1927) 99.
Bees: Worcestershire *Folk-Lore* 26 (1915) 97. Lancashire N&Q 2S:8 (1859) 242.
Donkeys at Easter: N. Ireland Foster (1951) 130–1.

apples: blossom

The simultaneous appearance of blossom and fruit on a tree was widely held to be ominous, usually predicting an imminent death in the owner's family:

Last year I was walking in the garden of a neighbouring farmer, aged seventy-one. We came up to an apple tree, heavily laden with nearly ripe fruit; and perceived a sprig of very late bloom, a kind of second edition. He told me, rather gravely, that in his boyhood this occurrence was invariably held to herald a death in the family within two or three months. On my joking him about Welsh credulity, he pretended not to believe the idle lore, but evidently was glad to pass from the subject. His brother, aged sixty-eight, in perfect health then, who resided in the same house, was dead within six weeks. A few weeks afterwards, walking in our own orchard, I discovered a still later blossom on a Ripstone Pippin tree; and called a man-servant,

aged sixty-three, to look at it. He at once told me, with some concern, that it always foretold death in the family; he had known many instances. Singularly enough, he himself was dead within a very few weeks!   Wales? N&Q (1854)

There seems to be no rational explanation for such belief, beyond the fact that the superstitious mind abhors anomalies in nature such as albino animals, crowing hens, and birds trying to come indoors. Late blossom on fruit trees is not that rare an occurrence, but it was widely feared. The earliest reference only dates from the mid nineteenth century, and it was still being quoted well into the late twentieth.

Dorset N&Q 4S:10 (1872) 408. Hampshire [1962] Opie & Tatem, 32, Somerset [1912] Tongue (1965) 137. Devon *Western Antiquary* 9 (1889–90) 34, 64; *Devonshire Assoc.* 61 (1929) 125. Berkshire *Folk-Lore* 5 (1894) 337; Salmon (1902) 423. London [1978] Vickery (1985) 30–1. Buckinghamshire *Folk-Lore* 43 (1932) 107. Gloucestershire N&Q 4S:10 (1872) 183. Herefordshire Leather (1912) 20. Worcestershire/Shropshire *Gent. Mag.* (1855) 385. Northamptonshire Sternberg (1851) 161–2; [1982] Vickery (1985) 30–1. East Anglia Varden (1885) 117. Suffolk N&Q 6S:10 (1884) 187. Norfolk Fulcher Collection (*c*.1895). Rutland N&Q 4S:8 (1871) 322. Lincolnshire N&Q 6S:10 (1884) 158; *Folk-Lore* 19 (1908) 467. Yorkshire Nicholson (1890) 121. Wales? N&Q 1S:10 (1854) 461.

apples: mirror divination

MIRRORS are uncanny things, and feature in a number of superstitions which are based on the fear of seeing unwanted reflections of the dead, the Devil, and so on. In this entry, however, the conjuring of a lover's reflection is the purpose of the ceremony. The apple is again linked with LOVE DIVINATION:

'I'll eat the apple at the glass' – Take a candle, and go alone to a looking-glass; eat an apple before it, and some traditions say you should comb your hair all the time; the face of your conjugal companion, to be, will be seen in the glass, as if peeping over your shoulder.

Scotland Robert Burns, 'Halloween' (1786)

Only a few examples have been recorded, but as they cover a spread of over 150 years, this form of divination is likely to have been more popular than these few references would suggest.

Compare LOVE DIVINATION: MIRRORS .

England Addy (1895) 84, Cumberland *Folk-Lore* 40 (1929) 285. Wales Davies (1911) 10. Scotland Robert Burns, fn to 'Halloween' (1786). Co. Longford *Béaloideas* 6 (1936) 269. Unlocated [*c.*1870s] Wright (1913) 261.

apples: peel divination

A relatively well-known simple LOVE DIVINA-TION ceremony in which the questioner must peel an apple, taking care that the peel remains in one long piece, and then throw the peel over his/her shoulder. The shape it takes will resemble the initial of the future lover's name:

*This mellow pippin which I pare around
My shepherd's name shall flourish on the ground
I fling the unbroken paring over my head
Upon the grass a perfect L is read.*

John Gay, *The Shepherd's Week* (1714)

Gay's description provides the earliest reference, and it is reported in similar fashion right into the twentieth century. Most sources stipulate no special date on which the act should take place, but some give HALLOWE'EN which, given its regular connection with apples, is unsurprising. Two authorities, Halliwell and Hewett, stipulate 28 October, the day dedicated to Saints Simon and Jude, and accompany the action with the following rhyme:

*St. Simon and Jude, on you I intrude
By this paring I hold to discover
Without any delay, to tell me this day
The first letter of my own true lover.*

Unlocated Halliwell (1849)

One further variation is reported from Lancashire:

Popular opinion directs that if a lady desires to infer the name of her future husband she must peel an apple without breaking the rind, and hang the shred on a nail behind the door – the initials of the name of the first gentleman who enters the house after this has been done will be the same as those of the person she will marry.

Lancashire Harland & Wilkinson (1873)

Occasionally, it is a turnip which is specified rather than an apple.

Devon Hewett (1900) 70; *Devonshire Assoc.* 70 (1938) 116. Essex [1953] Opie & Tatem, 3. Wiltshire *Wilts. N&Q* 1 (1893–5) 151. Norfolk [1875] Hope-Nicholson (1966) 134–5. Lincolnshire [1837] Peacock (1877) 189. Derbyshire [1890s] Uttley (1946) 124. Nottinghamshire Addy (1895) 82–3. Yorkshire Nicholson (1890) 122. Lancashire Harland & Wilkinson (1873) 230. Cumberland Gibson (1858) 105. Carmarthenshire Davies (1911) 78. Pembrokeshire *Folk-Lore* 39 (1928) 173. Western Scotland Napier (1879) 123. Dumfriesshire Corrie (1890/91) 39–40. Unlocated Halliwell (1849) pp. 216–17; N&Q 176 (1939) 333. General *The Everlasting Fortune Teller* (1839) 11–12, quoted Opie & Tatem, p. 3. Literary John Gay, *The Shepherd's Week* (1714); *Connoisseur* 56 (1755) 335; D.H. Lawrence, *The White Peacock* (1911) Pt 1, Ch. 8.

apples: pin divination

Sticking PINS into objects is not confined to malevolent purposes, it is also used in LOVE DIVINATION procedures. A Guernsey example includes the instruction: 'Into a golden pippin stick eighteen new pins, nine in the eye and nine in the stem, tie round it the left garter and place it under the pillow', and then get into bed backwards, accompanied by a rhyme in French (N&Q (1850)). A Jersey variant gives further details:

*Good St. Thomas do me right
And bring my love to me this night
That I may view him face to face
And in my arms may him embrace.*

Jersey *Folk-Lore* (1914)

This procedure does not appear to have been particularly widespread, but was reported several times from the Channel Islands. By far the earliest description appeared in 1685 in the CHAP-BOOK entitled *Mother Bunch's Closet Newly Broke Open.*

Guernsey N&Q 1S:2 (1850), 509–10; MacCulloch MS (1864), 408–9. Jersey *Folk-Lore* 25 (1914), 247. General *Mother Bunch's Closet Newly Broke Open* (1685) 8–9.

apples: pip divination

Apple-pips feature in several LOVE DIVINA-
TIONS, in which the mode of handling varies
considerably. The simplest, and apparently the
oldest, is to press a number of pips to your face
and see which falls off last.

*I am sure Mr. Blossom loves me, because I stuck
two of the kernels [apple pips] upon my forehead,
while I thought upon him and the lubberly squire
my pappa wants me to have: Mr. Blossom's kernel
stuck on, but the other dropt off directly.*

Connoisseur 56 (1755)

Only two sources describe versions of this procedure. Both are from the eighteenth century, with
John Gay's (*Shepherd's Week* (1714)) the earliest.
   More commonly reported, but considerably
later in time, is a procedure whereby the pips are
placed in the fire, usually on a shovel or other
metal implement, and, as in a similar exercise
with NUTS, the prediction is taken from the
behaviour of the pips:

*Burning apple pippins is a very common test, and
is practised in almost every cottage. In this case we
are directed to place two pippins on the mouth of
a pair of tongs, so as to touch each other. The lady
who is performing the experiment now gives her
own name to the left-hand pippin, and that on the
right must bear the name of the person whose
intentions are being tested. The tongs must now be
placed in a hollow portion of the fire, where the
heat is most intense, and if both pippins fly off on
the same side, the parties will be married; if on
opposite sides, there will be no union; and if both
burn together without flying off, the gentleman will
never propose to the lady who is placed beside him.*

Lancashire Harland & Wilkinson (1873)

The third method involves squeezing the pips
between the fingers to make them fly out, throwing them in the air, or shaking them between two
cupped hands. The direction in which the pips
move, or point, indicates the quarter from which
the desired lover will come:

*Take an apple-pip between the forefinger and the
thumb, flip it into the air, saying: 'North, south,
east, west, tell me where my love doth rest' and
watch the direction in which it falls.*

Cornwall *Folk-Lore Jnl* (1887)

Face: Literary John Gay, *The Shepherd's Week* (1714);
Connoisseur 56 (1755) 335.
Fire: Suffolk N&Q 1S:2 (1850) 4; *Bye-Gones* (1 June
1887) 317. **Lincolnshire** Peacock (1877) 161–2.
Lancashire Harland & Wilkinson (1873) 230–1. **Co.
Durham** Brockie (1886) 209–10. **Denbighshire** *Bye-Gones*
(19 Jan. 1887) 227. **Unlocated** Halliwell (1849) 224.
Fingers or Hands: Cornwall *Folk-Lore Jnl* 5 (1887) 215.
Lancashire N&Q 4S:6 (1870) 340; *Lancashire Lore* (1971)
50. **Wales** Trevelyan (1909), pp. 237–8. **Western Scotland**
Napier (1879), p. 123.

apples: wart cures

One sub-category of WART cures is to rub them
with some particular plant matter which is then
buried or thrown away. In a few cases, an apple
is specified:

*Or they cut an apple in two, rub the warts with
each half, tie the halves together again, and bury
them in the ground. In the latter case, as the apple
decays, the warts will disappear.*

Co. Durham Brockie (1886)

Shropshire Burne (1883) 200; **Co. Durham** Brockie
(1886) 223; **England** Addy (1895) 89.

aprons

see CLOTHES: APRONS; MOON: TURN YOUR
APRON.

Ascension Day: lightning

The oldest tradition of Ascension Day holds that
eggs laid on the day protect a house from lightning, or other calamity. This was known in the
sixteenth century:

Ascension Day (Holy Thursday)

In the Christian church, Ascension Day is the day
on which Christ ascended into Heaven, forty days
after Easter Sunday. Its exact date therefore varies
from year to year. A small number of beliefs
pertained to Ascension Day; however, most of
these also occurred at other times of the year, and,

except for the ones concerning water, their connection with this particular day seems relatively weak.
Compare EASTER; GOOD FRIDAY.

For Ascension Day customs, *see* Simpson & Roud
(2000) 10; Wright & Lones 1 (1936) 129–48.

*To hang an egg laid on Ascension day in the roof
of the house, preserveth the same from all hurts.*
                                                Scot (1584)

and was also reported from the mid nineteenth
century:

*Another protection against fire and other calami-
ties is believed, in Nottinghamshire, to be an egg
laid on Ascension Day and placed in the roof of
a house.*   Nottinghamshire [1852] Wright & Lones

while in Staffordshire it was a piece of hawthorn:

*At Eccleshall . . . a piece of hawthorn gathered on
Ascension Day is the proper thing* [to preserve
houses from lightning], *as I have heard more than
once. A yeoman farmer's wife there tells me that
it must be brought to you, not gathered on your
own ground. She has a piece brought to her every
year, and hangs it with her own hands among the
rafters in the 'cock-loft', which is now nearly full
of these charms.*   Staffordshire *Folk-Lore* (1896)

Staffordshire *Folk-Lore* 7 (1896) 381. **Nottinghamshire**
[1852] Wright & Lones 1 (1936) 147. **General** Scot (1584)
Bk 12, Ch. 18.

Ascension Day: washing

Ascension Day shares with Good Friday, and
New Year's Day, the stipulation that no WASH-
ING should be done:

*If you wash sheets on Holy Thursday you will be
laid out in those sheets as a corpse before the next
Holy Thursday comes.*   Yorkshire *Folk-Lore* (1909)

Oxfordshire *Midland Garner* 2 (1884) 19.
Worcestershire *Folk-Lore* 20 (1909) 345. **Lincolnshire**
The Times (8 May 1934) 12. Yorkshire Addy (1895) 116;
Folk-Lore 20 (1909) 349.

Ascension Day: water

The strongest association of the day is with water.
Ascension Day appears regularly as the key time
to visit healing or holy wells, and many English
well-dressing customs take place on the day.

*North Molton – Holy well – On Thursday last,
Ascension-day, this celebrated well was as usual
visited early in the morning by suffering mortals
with various diseases. Like many advertised
medicines, the water is, by the simple, believed to
be a cure for 'all the ills that flesh is heir to'. One
lady came from Tiverton to bathe, and some from
neighbouring parishes, while a few natives
availed themselves the cheap universal remedy.*
                    Devon *Devonshire Assoc.* (1884)

More widely reported is the notion that rain
which falls on Ascension Day has healing powers,
keeps fresh for a long time, and is particularly
effective for sore eyes:

*Rain which falls on Ascension Day is a favourite
remedy for bad eyes, and, like Good Friday bread,
is supposed to keep good for years. 'Of course, it
must be corked up in a clean bottle', explained
Mr. Munby's Shropshire servant. Old Mary Gale
of Edgmond bathed her eyes in 1874 with
Ascension Day rain-water which she had caught
and bottled three years before.*
                        Shropshire Burne (1883)

Several informants stressed the need for a clean
bottle, while others stipulated that the rain had to
fall directly into the bottle or, in one variant, was

*caught in the hollow formed by the leaves of a
species of dock by brook sides.*
                    Worcestershire Salisbury (1893)

The idea that Ascension Day rain 'keeps sweet'
and is medicinal is an echo of the much more
widely spread beliefs about GOOD FRIDAY bread.
The available references do not imply any great
antiquity for these beliefs. The earliest known
connection between water, eyes, and Ascension
Day is from Wales in 1804, and that refers to a
local well. The first to mention rain is from
Oxfordshire in 1848, and if it were not for two
or three from outside the area, all the references
would be from the Midlands.

It would not be surprising if further research
labelled this a recent and relatively localized
belief.

Devon *Devonshire Assoc.* 16 (1884) 122–3. **Surrey** N&Q
6S:6 (1882) 45. Oxfordshire *Athenaeum* (1848) 142.
Gloucestershire [1900] *Trans. Bristol & Glos. Arch. Soc.* 53
(1931) 264. *Folk-Lore* 20 (1909) 489. **Worcestershire**
Salisbury (1893) 70; N&Q 10S:4 (1905) 497; *Folk-Lore* 20
(1909) 491; Berkeley & Jenkins (1932) 33. **Worcestershire/
Buckinghamshire** N&Q 6S:6 (1882) 155. **Warwickshire**
Guardian (19 May 1869). **Northamptonshire** N&Q 1S:9
(1854) 542. **Cambridgeshire** N&Q 10S:4 (1905) 447.
Shropshire N&Q 5S:3 (1875) 465; Burne (1883) 191. **Wales**
Hoare, *Itinerary Through Wales* 1 (1804) 133, quoted Opie
& Tatem, 5.

Ascension Day: working on

A handful of reports indicate a reluctance to work
on Ascension Day, particularly in Welsh quarries:

*The whole of Lord Penrhyn's slate quarrymen
took a holiday on Ascension Day, because of the
universally prevalent superstition that a fatal
accident will inevitably cut off those who work*

during that day. This strange superstition is common among the thousands of quarrymen engaged in North Wales. **Wales** N&Q (1886)

A similar avoidance of work seems to affect some birds, particularly rooks, who were reputed to refuse to build their nests on the day.

Birds: Norfolk [1920s] Wigby (1976) 69. **Shropshire** Burne (1883) 217–18. **Yorkshire** Addy (1895) 116. **Humans: Yorkshire** Addy (1895) 116. **Wales** *Daily News* (8 May 1880) 6; N&Q 7S:2 (1886) 166; *The Times* (11 May 1888) 5.

---

ash leaf divination

A form of LOVE DIVINATION which involved finding an ash leaf with an even number of leaflets. In the simplest versions it was enough to find such a leaf to be lucky, but there were more complex versions:

The following Midsummer Eve superstition has been given me: Pluck an even ash leaf, and, putting it into the hand, say:

The even ash leaf in my hand
The first I meet shall be my man
Then, putting it into the glove, say:
The even ash-leaf in my glove
The first I meet shall be my love
And, lastly, into the bosom, say:
The even ash-leaf in my bosom
The first I meet shall be my husband
Soon after which the future husband will make his appearance.

                                        Unlocated N&Q (1865)

The belief was so well known that the phrase 'even ash' was almost as proverbial as 'four leaf clover' is today. It can also be noted that both beliefs run counter to the general superstitious principle that odd NUMBERS are inherently more lucky than even ones.

See also CLOVER.

Somerset [1923] Opie & Tatem, 6; Tongue (1965) 221. **Dorset** Hone *Year Book* (1832) 588; Udal (1922) 254; *Folk-Lore* 89 (1978) 155–6; Vickery (1995) 15. **Devon** Hewett (1900) 25; [1910] *Folk-Lore* 28 (1917) 313; Crossing (1911) 147. **Cornwall** Hunt (1865) 225; Couch (1871) 155. **Wiltshire** *Athenaeum* (1846) 1068, 1142. **Oxfordshire** Thompson (1943) 323–4. **Worcestershire** *Folk-Lore* 20 (1909) 343. **Cambridgeshire** N&Q 165 (1933) 371. **Northamptonshire** Sternberg (1851) 163. **Northern England** *Denham Tracts* 2 (1895) 70–1. **Yorkshire** *Athenaeum* (1846) 1142; Addy (1895) 88. Co. **Durham** Leighton (1910) 54. **Wales** Brand 1 (1813) 302; Howells (1831) 67. **Flint** [c.1815] Lucy (1983) 23. Co.

Antrim Patterson (1880) 35. **Unlocated** Halliwell (1849) 222–3; N&Q 1S:2 (1850) 259; N&Q 3S:8 (1865) 494; N&Q 165 (1933) 371.

---

ash-riddling

A divination custom carried out at NEW YEAR or on ST MARK'S EVE, designed to indicate if any one in the household was destined to die in the following year:

The last thing done on the last day of the year was to 'rist' the fire, that is, cover up the live coals with the ashes. The whole was made as smooth and neat as possible. The first thing on New Year's morning was to examine if there was in the ashes any mark like the shape of human foot with the toes pointing towards the door. If there was such a mark, one was to be removed from the family before the year was run.

                Northeast Scotland Gregor (1881)

A common detail, missing in this description, is that the ashes were sieved, or riddled – hence the usual name of the custom – ash-riddling.

A variant on the same theme was sometimes reported. The search for the footprint was the same, but the ash was found in a different way:

When the corpse is lifted, the bed-straw, on which the deceased lay, is carried out and burnt in a place where no beast can come near it, and they pretend to find next morning, in the ashes, the print of the foot of that person in the family who shall die first.   **Morayshire** Shaw (1775)

All the examples found are from Scotland, Isle of Man, and northern England.

See also CHAFF-RIDDLING for a similar procedure.

Northern England Brockett (1829), 11; Henderson (1866) 34. **Yorkshire** N&Q 5S:6 (1876) 323; Robinson (1876) 6. **Northeast Scotland** Gregor (1881) 160. **Morayshire** Shaw (1775) 249. **Shetland** Tudor (1883) 174. **Isle of Man** Train (1845) 115–16. **Unlocated** Brand 1 (1849) 193; Chambers (1878) 550.

---

ash trees

A classic example of sympathetic magic in a cure. A child suffering from rupture was passed through a split made in a young tree, and the split was then bound up to ensure that the wood grew together. As the tree healed, so would the child:

An old woman in this parish, J.W., who works at the vicarage, told me that her son, now a guard on the Great Western Railway, and a little over thirty, was born ruptured. When the child was nearly a year old her husband went into the wood on the road between Calne and Chippenham, and split a 'maiden ash' tree – a tree which had never been pruned – about as thick as a broom stick, and tied it up with a withy. The next day, May 1st, the child was passed at sunrise, with its head towards the sun, through the tree, which was tied up again. The tree grew well afterwards, and the child was cured of its rupture. She mentioned several other children with whom this had been done. It seems that if the tree does not thrive, the child is not cured.   Wiltshire Eddrup (1885)

Various other details are given, some of which appear in the above extract. The child must be passed through a set number of times (three is common, sometimes nine), facing a certain way (towards the sun), and the child must be naked. Sometimes set words or a prayer were recited. At Broxwood, Herefordshire, this was simply, 'The Lord giveth', and 'The Lord receiveth', said in turn by two men as they passed the child from one to the other (Leather (1912)).

Some reports do not specify the type of tree, but the ash is by far the most commonly cited. In many instances the locals believed that the tree and the health of the child would continue to be linked throughout life, and were concerned to keep the tree unharmed.

The symbolism of the rupture and the repaired split tree is obvious, but the same procedure was also recommended for other complaints, such as RICKETS, EPILEPSY, WHOOPING COUGH, and 'weakness in children', where the connection is less clear. It would seem likely therefore that the process was originally for rupture, and later extended as a general cure. A correlation between this cure and that of creeping, or being passed through, a holed stone is usually presumed in the literature, but this may not be a useful analogy. The hole in the tree is bound up, grows, and is 'cured': this sets it apart from the stone, which must obviously remain, in these terms, uncured. While the surface details are similar, the principles involved are therefore very different. Furthermore, in the absence of any obvious meaning, many earlier writers assumed that the symbolism of passing through a stone symbolized the patient's rebirth, and they assumed that this would be the same for the split tree. This notion remains speculative at best, and is unlikely to be of relevance here. It is more useful to view the passing-through as setting up the connection between patient and tree, while the binding up and re-growth effect the cure. It must be admitted, however, that this

argument is occasionally challenged by a handful of examples where a convenient naturally holed tree has been used (see, for example, the willow tree reported by Leather (1912)).

There is no direct evidence that this is an ancient cure, although it is usually assumed to be such. The first references come thick and fast in the late eighteenth century – Gilbert White in Hampshire in 1776, J. Cullum in Suffolk in 1784, and Grose in 1787 – which argues for a custom already widespread and well known, but until further examples are brought to light its early development will remain a mystery. It was certainly widely reported in the nineteenth and early twentieth centuries.

See also SNAKES: ASH TREES.

Sussex Latham (1878) 40–1. *Sussex County Mag.* 5 (1931) 122. **Somerset** [1938] Tongue (1965) 221. **Devon** *Devonshire Assoc.* 8 (1876) 54; *Devonshire Assoc.* 9 (1877) 94–6; *Devonshire Assoc.* 17 (1885) 119; Hewett (1892) 27; Wright (1913) 236. **Cornwall** N&Q 1S:12 (1855) 37; Hunt (1865) 224; Couch (1871) 166; *Jnl Royal Inst. Cornwall* 20 (1915) 128. **Wiltshire** Smith (1874) 323–4; Eddrup (1885) 331; E.P.E. (1889) 344–5. **New Forest** Wise (1867) 177. **Hampshire** [1776] White (1788) 184–5; *Devonshire Assoc.* 17 (1885) ... Herefordshire Leather (1912) 80–1. **Worcestershire** Berkeley & Jenkins (1932) 36. **Warwickshire** *Gent. Mag.* (1804) 512, 909; Langford (1875) 20. **East Anglia** Varden (1885) 103. **Suffolk** Cullum (1784) 234; *Gent. Mag.* (1867) 728–71; Gurdon (1893) 28; *Folk-Lore* 56 (1945) 270. **Norfolk** [c.1870s] Haggard (1935) 15. **Shropshire** Burne (1883) 196–7. **Monmouthshire** *Folk-Lore* 16 (1905) 65. **Western Scotland** Napier (1879) 95–6. **Co. Donegal** [1890] *Béaloideas* 3 (1931) 332. **Jersey** *Folk-Lore* 25 (1914) 248. **Unlocated** Grose (1787) 58; Chambers 1 (1878) 732.

Aurora Borealis (Northern Lights)

Spectacular celestial phenomena such as ECLIPSES, COMETS, and major STORMS were regularly taken as portents or the result of great things afoot. The grander the show the more elevated the people or events that were involved. The Aurora Borealis have excited awe and interest in all cultures that can see them, and Britain is no exception:

The Northern Lights are supposed to be a sign of war and conflagration. The winter of 1870 was remarkable for the splendid displays of crimson and orange streamers, which were looked upon as the reflection of the immense destruction caused by the Franco-German war.
   Yorkshire Nicholson (1890)

They also provided poets with ready-made atmospheric detail, such as William Aytoun's description of the Edinburgh sky after the battle of Flodden field: 'Fearful lights, that never beckon, Save when kings or heroes die' (Aytoun (1849)). Where they are not normally seen, the sudden appearance of the lights could cause unease. The vicar of East Dereham, for example, recorded their effect in his diary:

[9 Mar. 1861] *A beautiful Aurora Borealis, which so alarmed the servants that they all came into the dining-room to know what it could mean.*

Norfolk Armstrong (1949)

Things had hardly changed sixty years later:

Natural phenomena were always regarded with awe and apprehension. The Northern Lights were seen with great foreboding – some thought a national disaster was imminent, others that the end of the world was nigh.

Essex [*c.*1920] Ketteridge & Mays

Essex [*c.*1920] Ketteridge & Mays (1972) 143. **Norfolk** Armstrong (1949) 78. **Yorkshire** Nicholson (1890) 45. **Shetland** Thomas Pennant, *Arctic Zoology* 1 (1784). Ch. 28. **General** N&Q 175 (1938) 113–14. **Literary** Aytoun (1849) 'Edinburgh after Flodden', Pt 1; John Clare, *Shepherd's Calendar* (1827) 111.

babies: carried up

A neat piece of symbolism equates 'going up in the world' in the literal and metaphoric senses, and results in a very widespread custom to ensure that a newborn baby does both:

When a child was taken from its mother and carried outside the bedroom for the first time after its birth, it was lucky to take it up stairs, and unlucky to take it down stairs. If there were no stairs in the house, the person who carried it generally ascended three steps of a ladder or temporary erection, and this, it was supposed, would bring prosperity to the child. Western Scotland Napier (1879)

In the absence of a step-ladder, the resourceful nurse would step on to a box or a chair. Some authorities developed the notion further, saying that failure to carry the baby upwards would result in its early death and the ultimate trip down into the grave.

This superstition is probably behind the comment in Congreve's play *Love for Love*, in a scene which includes references to many other omens and beliefs:

and I came upstairs into the world, for I was born in a cellar. William Congreve, *Love for Love* (1695)

but the first indisputable example is much later:

a letter to 'My dear, dearest Molly' begging her, when she left her room, whatever she did, to go upstairs before going down.

Mrs Gaskell, *Cranford* (1853)

The notion lasted well into the twentieth century.

Devon N&Q 5S:10 (1878) 255–6; *Devonshire Assoc.* 67 (1935) 139; *Devonshire Assoc.* 79 (1947) 48. **Wiltshire** *Wilts. N&Q* 1 (1893–5) 102. **Berkshire** *Folk-Lore* 5 (1894) 337. **Oxfordshire** *Folk-Lore* 34 (1923) 326. **Gloucestershire** N&Q 5S:10 (1878) 255–6. **Warwickshire** Langford (1875) 14. Bloom (*c.*1930) 18. **East Anglia** Varden (1885) 107. **Suffolk** Chambers 2 (1878) 39. **Norfolk** Dew (1898) 77–81; *East Anglian Mag.* (Aug. 1935) 93. **Shropshire** Burne (1883) 285; *Folk-Lore* 49 (1938) 224. **Derbyshire** [1890s] Uttley (1946) 125. **Yorkshire** Henderson (1866) 10; N&Q 5S:10 (1878) 205. **Co. Durham** Brockie (1886) 182; Leighton (1910) 47. **Co. Durham/Northumberland** N&Q 5S:10 (1878) 205. **Western Scotland** Napier (1879) 31. **Highland Scotland** Polson (1926) 5. **Dumfriesshire** Corrie (1890/91) 37. **Glasgow** N&Q 5S:10 (1878) 255–6. **Jersey/Guernsey** *Folk-Lore* 38 (1927) 179. **Unlocated** *Spectator* (18 Jan. 1902) 82. **Literary** William Congreve, *Love for Love* (1695) 2:1; Mrs Gaskell, *Cranford* (1853), Ch. 5.

babies' clothes

A belief concerning the way a baby is dressed has been reported a few times since the 1860s, but on present evidence cannot be said to be widespread:

When an infant is first dressed, its clothes should never be put on over its head (which is very unlucky) but drawn over its feet.

Co. Durham N&Q (1867)

Most informants stated that this policy must be continued until the baby is christened, but no reason is quoted as to why this should be. Another warning about clothes, from about the same time, has been recorded even less frequently:

If a mother gives away all the baby's clothes she has . . . she will be sure to have another baby, though she may have thought herself above such vanities. Suffolk [1864] Chambers

This idea fits so well with the basic principle of tempting fate that it would be surprising if this notion was not in the mind of many a mother since, when handing clothes on to others. A number of other miscellaneous beliefs are included in the references below.

See also GOOD FRIDAY: WEANING BABIES.

Somerset [1920] Tongue (1965) 143. **Suffolk** [1864] Chambers 2 (1878) 322. **Wiltshire** *Wilts. N&Q* 1 (1893–5) 102. **West London** [1987] Opie & Tatem 12. **East Anglia** Varden (1885) 107. **Lincolnshire** Swaby

(1891) 88–9. **Co. Durham** N&Q 3S:12 (1867) 185; Leighton (1910) 47; [1953] Opie & Tatem, 12. **Northumberland** Bosanquet (1929) 33. **Wales** Trevelyan (1909) 268.

babies' fingernails

see FINGERNAILS: BABIES'.

babies: first food

A number of traditions existed as to the first food given to a newborn baby, but butter and sugar was a particular favourite:

In this part of Yorkshire, new-born infants receive as their first food a teaspoonful of butter and sugar. This custom no doubt dates from the time when honey was used instead of sugar, and is a literal carrying out of the prophesy 'butter and honey shall be eat', with an expectation that it will produce the remainder of the promise 'that he may know to refuse evil and do the good' [Isaiah 7:15].   Yorkshire N&Q (1886)

A different tradition is indicated in a Scottish reference:

Immediately after birth, the newly-born child was bathed in salted water, and made to taste of it three times. This, by some, was considered a specific against the influence of the evil eye; but doctors differ, and so among other people and in some localities, different specifics were employed.   Western Scotland Napier (1879)

Herefordshire Leather (1912) 112. **Warwickshire** Bloom (*c.*1930) 18. **Shropshire** Burne (1883) 284. **Yorkshire** N&Q 7S:2 (1886) 145. **Western Scotland** Napier (1879) 30. **Co. Longford** *Béaloideas* 6 (1936) 258.

babies: first teeth

see TEETH: BABIES' FIRST.

babies: first visit

The principles of BEGINNINGS and HAND-SELLING are strongly evident in traditions regulating what to do the first time a new baby is brought to visit you, or the first time you meet it elsewhere. In most cases in the past, the mother would not bring the baby to visit until she had been CHURCHED and the baby CHRISTENED. Highly symbolic items were then given, usually including an egg, salt, bread, and money (often

specifically silver), and sometimes matches, but this varies a little:

On the occasion of a baby's first visit to a house, it should receive an egg, suet, and a silver coin ('the child's alms'). It will never want if it thus receives food and money.
    Northumberland *Folk-Lore* (1925)

Egg, salt, and bread are the three items recommended in the two eighteenth-century references (Hutchinson and Grose) and in most of the early nineteenth-century sources, but by the later twentieth century only money was given. The need to follow tradition still remained very strong:

The giving of gifts to a new-born child is usual . . . in rural Ulster . . . the gift tends to take the form of money. I was very surprised, although I should have known better when an old lady who had been in the habit of calling at my mother's house for a weekly alms, presented my baby daughter with a shilling to 'hansel her'. ('Hansel' means to protect from evil or to bring luck). The money is never handed to the parent; it is always placed in the child's hand.   N. Ireland Foster (1951)

After a birth in our family, in 1946, an old farm-labourer, reputed to be 'a bit wanting', knocked at the door, and handed me sixpence, saying, 'A tanner for the babby'. I gave him a slice of christening cake, which he spat on before putting in his pocket. The wife of a Black Country (north Worcestershire) vicar told me that a box or bowl was always left in a conspicuous place after a birth, for the reception of silver coins, and no one would visit the house without contributing to it.
    Worcestershire *Folk-Lore* (1957)

If the coin was placed in its hand, the baby's future character could be gauged by whether it grasped the money or not (*see* BABIES' HANDS).

The custom is widely recorded from the 1770s onwards, and was clearly common all over the British Isles, although Wales is strangely absent from the references listed below. Giving a new baby a gift is, of course, still the norm, and although the symbolic items have largely disappeared, the feeling that a coin is appropriate 'for luck' is still very strong.

Somerset [1923] Opie & Tatem, 11; Tongue (1965) 135. **Devon** N&Q 10S:12 (1909) 66; *Devonshire Assoc.* 96 (1964) 98; *Devonshire Assoc.* 103 (1971) 268; *Devonshire Assoc.* 104 (1972) 267. **Oxfordshire** *Folk-Lore* 68 (1957) 413–14. **Worcestershire** *Folk-Lore* 68 (1957) 502. **Northamptonshire** N&Q 1S:2 (1850) 164. **Bedfordshire** *Folk-Lore* 37 (1926) 77. **Lincolnshire** *Gent. Mag.* (Dec. 1832) 492; N&Q 5S:10 (1878) 216; Watkins (1886), 12. **Leicestershire** N&Q 1S:7 (1853) 128. **England** Addy (1895)

95. **Derbyshire** [1890s] Uttley (1946) 125; Addy (1895)
128–9. **Northern England** Brockett (1846) 90; *Denham Tracts* 2 (1895) 25, 48. **Yorkshire** Young (1817) 883; N&Q
1S:1 (1850) 349; N&Q 5S:9 (1878) 138, 299, 477; Addy
(1888) xxv; *Folk-Lore* 5 (1894) 341; *Folk-Lore* 21 (1910)
225–6; *Observer Supp.* (24 Nov. 1968) 10. **Lancashire**
Harland & Wilkinson (1882) 262. **Cumberland** *Folk-Lore*
40 (1929) 279. **Co. Durham** Brockie (1886) 183; Leighton
(1910) 47; [1984] Opie & Tatem, 11. **Northumberland**
Hutchinson 2 (1778) 4; N&Q 5S:10 (1878) 37; *Folk-Lore* 36
(1925) 256. Bosanquet (1929) 33–5; [1985] Opie & Tatem,
11. **Scotland** N&Q 2S:4 (1857) 25. **Western Scotland**
Napier (1879) 33. **Highland Scotland** Polson (1926) 5–6.
Ayrshire [1962] Opie & Tatem, 11. **Aberdeenshire** *Folk-Lore* 6 (1895) 394. **Glasgow** [c.1820] Napier (1864) 397.
Orkney N&Q 1S:6 (1852) 311–12. **N. Ireland** Foster (1951)
10. **Connemara** *Folk-Lore Jnl* 2 (1884) 257. **Co. Antrim**
[1905] McDowell (1972) 129. **Guernsey** De Garis (1975) 7.
Jersey L'Amy (1927) 97. **Unlocated** Grose (1787) 64.

babies' hands

In the symbolism of superstition, hands have an
integral part to play in luck, and they are usually
connected with money (see, for example, HANDS:
ITCHING). This is the context for the widespread
idea that one should not wash a baby's hand, for
fear of washing away its luck, or future riches:

*I have often and very recently seen the creases in
the palms of children's hands filled with dirt; to
clean them before they were a year old would take
away riches – they would live and die poor.*
                              Cornwall *Folk-Lore Jnl* (1887)

In some versions it is only the right hand which
matters, and some keep it unwashed only until
the christening. Although reported widely, this
belief has not been found earlier than the second
half of the nineteenth century, whereas a
different prognostication on babies' hands is
demonstrably older.

*It was observed how infants held their hands for
some time after birth. If they kept them closed it
was a sure sign they would hold fast the money
that came in their way, and the remark about
such a child would have been heard, 'He (she) 'll
be a grippie, that ane', or 'he'll be a gey grippie
lad'. If, on the contrary, the hands were kept open,
the money would go as fast as it came. It was a
common custom to make a present of a coin to
an infant the first time a friend went to see the
mother, and to put it into the infant's hand. If the
child closed the hand over the coin, then the
money gained during life would be well looked
after, but if the coin was allowed to drop from the
hand, then the earnings would go as fast as they
came.*   Aberdeenshire *Folk-Lore* (1895)

In essentially the same form, this idea was
included in John Bulwer's treatise on hands,
Chirologia (1644), and was still being noted in
the later twentieth century. It is still common for
adults, when meeting a baby for the first time,
to give it a coin 'for luck' (see BABY: FIRST
VISIT), and the humorous comments which are
often made if the baby immediately grasps the
coin tightly, show that the idea of the prediction
of future character is far from dead.

Unwashed hand: **Western England** Henderson (1866) 9.
Somerset [1923] Opie & Tatem, 13. **Devon** *Devonshire
Assoc.* 9 (1877) 90. **Cornwall** *Folk-Lore Jnl* 5 (1887) 207–8;
Old Cornwall 1:9 (1929) 41; *Old Cornwall* 2 (1931–6) 39.
Herefordshire Leather (1912) 113. **Worcestershire**
Berkeley & Jenkins (1932) 36. **Lincolnshire** Swaby (1891)
88–9. **Staffordshire** Poole (1875) 85. **Northern England**
Henderson (1866) 9. **Co. Durham** N&Q 3S:12 (1867) 185;
Brockie (1886) 183; Leighton (1910) 47. **Orkney** *Farmers
Weekly* (9 Jan. 1970) 75.
Open hand: **Lincolnshire** *Gent. Mag.* (1832) 492.
Aberdeenshire *Folk-Lore* 6 (1895) 394. **Orkney** *Farmers
Weekly* (9 Jan. 1970) 75. **General** John Bulwer,
Chirologia (1644) 62.

babies: measuring

see MEASURING BABIES.

babies: mirrors

see MIRRORS: BABY SEEING ITSELF.

babies: 'Monday's child'

See also BABIES: WHEN BORN.

An extremely well-known rhyme, even in the
present day, which purports to predict a child's
character or fate from the day on which it was
born. Despite being reported from a wide range
of places, over more than 160 years, the wording
has remained remarkably stable. Compare the
earliest known version, published in 1838, with
one noted from a 56-year-old woman in Surrey
in 2001, who learnt it from her mother:

*Monday's child is fair in face
Tuesday's child is full of grace
Wednesday's child is full of woe
Thursday's child has far to go
Friday's child is loving and giving
Saturday's child works hard for its living
And a child that's born on Christmas day
Is fair and wise, good and gay.*
                              Devon Bray (1838)

Monday's child is fair of face
Tuesday's child is full of grace
Wednesday's child is full of woe
Thursday's child has far to go
Friday's child is loving and giving
Saturday's child works hard for a living
But the child that is born on the Sabbath day
Is bonny and blithe and good and gay.

Surrey [2001] Steve Roud Collection

It is not clear how seriously this was taken as a superstition, and those who print it do so without comment. It must be said that it has a 'bookish' air to it, as if it started life in some 'improving' children's book, but if such a publication were sufficiently popular to launch such a well-known rhyme, it is strange that it has not been identified. Certainly, if such a rhyme had been well-known in previous centuries, it is strange that, for example, the prolific seventeenth-century playwrights do not refer to it, as it seems tailor-made for them. Similarly, the distribution is puzzling. Whatever the situation nowadays, the historical record shows a heavy preponderance of English versions – only two from Scotland, one from Ireland, and none from Wales – but further research would be necessary before anything can be read into this distribution.

A small number of versions start on Sunday, and the character attributes therefore fall on different days but are in the same order, and a handful (as in the earliest version) have Christmas instead of Sunday. But of the 28 versions noted below, virtually all have the fair face/grace couplet for Monday and Tuesday (or Sunday/Monday).

The idea that the day of birth might be significant is not confined to this rhyme. Opie and Tatem, for example, quote Thomas Nashe's *Terrors of the Night* (1594) – 'I have heard aged mumping beldams . . . tell what luck everie one should have by the day of the weeke he was borne on', and the whole basis of astrology links birth and time in determining character. But the rhyme does not fit with other beliefs about DAYS of the week, most notably the almost universal notion that FRIDAY was the most unlucky day, particularly for starting anything important. Of the 28 citations, only two have a negative meaning for Friday's child. An alternative, non-rhyming view of birthdays shows that the rhyme is not necessarily the last word on the subject:

If a man-child was born on a Sunday it was believed that he would live without anxiety and be handsome. If born on a Monday he was certain to be killed. Those born on a Tuesday

grew up sinful and perverse, while those born on a Wednesday were waspish in temper. A child born on Thursday, however, was sure to be of a peaceful and easy disposition, though averse to women. Friday was supposed to be the most unlucky day of all, it being prophesied that a child born on this day would grow up to be silly, crafty, a thief, and a coward, and that he would not live longer than mid-age. If born on a Saturday, his deeds would be renowned; he would live to be an alderman, many things would happen to him, and he would live long.

Northumberland/Co. Durham Neasham (1893)

Dorset Udal (1922) 178. **Somerset** [1923] Opie & Tatem, 27. **Devon** Bray (1838) 287–8; N&Q 1S:4 (1851) 98; Hewett (1892) 26; Crossing (1911) 134. **Cornwall** Hunt (1865) 237; Couch (1871) 164. **Surrey** [2001] Steve Roud Collection. **Warwickshire** Bloom (c.1930) 21. **Norfolk** Fulcher Collection (c.1895); Dew (1898) 77–81. **Lincolnshire** Rudkin (1936) 18–19. **Shropshire** *Bye-Gones* (21 July 1886) 94. **England** Addy (1895) 119. **Northern England** *Denham Tracts* 2 (1895) 102. **Yorkshire** [1987] Opie & Tatem, 2. **Co. Durham** Brockie (1886) 182; Leighton (1910) 46. **Northumberland** Bosanquet (1929) 33, 75. **Northumberland/Co. Durham** Neasham (1893) 251. **Highland Scotland** Polson (1926) 4. **Aberdeenshire** *Folk-Lore* 6 (1895) 394. **Co. Antrim** [c.1905] McDowell (1972) 130. **Unlocated** Halliwell (1849) 228; N&Q 1S:2 (1850) 515; N&Q 3S:2 (1862) 342; N&Q 5S:7 (1877) 424.

babies: nuts

A direct link was presumed by many to exist between human fertility and aspects of the natural world, and clues could be gleaned from various signs. The most regularly reported was that 'a good year for nuts was a good year for babies':

In 1950 a vicar's wife of my acquaintance remarked to her charwoman that the number of births in the parish had been unusually large that year. The woman replied that this was only to be expected because there had been a very fine crop of nuts in the previous Autumn. When questioned further, she could not explain the connection; she only knew that it was an accepted local sign and, in her experience, a true one.

Unlocated *Folk-Lore* (1957)

Over a century before, William Cobbett quoted what he called an old saying, 'A great nut year and a great bastard year' (*Rural Rides*), which perhaps explains the charwoman's reticence in producing an explanation for the vicar's wife. 'Going NUTTING' has long been a euphemism for rural sexual encounters:

It is probable that many a poor country labour-
ing man may be horrified this month, when their
wives go into the wood, picking of nuts, for oppor-
tunity has been the occasion of making many a
man a cuckold.   Poor Robin's Almanack (1668)

This notion obviously means that the good year
for babies is the one *after* the good year for nuts,
but the direct sexual overtones are lost in many
of the later versions. It was still being quoted at
the end of the twentieth century.

The sexual implication does not explain other,
less common, ideas of a connection between
nature and humans, such as 'When it is a good
apple year, it is a great year for twins' (Unlocated
N&Q (1862)) and:

In the East Riding they say that if animals are
fortunate in bearing young, for example, if sheep
yield good 'crops' of lambs in the spring, the same
spring will be lucky for women and babies. It is
said that 1874 'was a terrible year for farmers and
husbands, for so many sheep and wives died'.
                                     England Addy (1895)

See also LIONS; BEARS.

Hampshire [1968] Opie & Tatem, 290. Dorset Vickery
(1995) 172. London Folk-Lore 37 (1926) 365. Herefordshire
[1856] Leather (1912) 256. Shropshire N&Q 5S:3 (1875)
465. Shropshire/Worcestershire Gent. Mag. (1855) 385.
England Addy (1895) 96. Mid-Wales Davies (1911) 221.
Neath Phillips (1925) 592. Denbighshire [1984] Opie &
Tatem, 290. Unlocated Folk-Lore 68 (1957), 411; N&Q 3S:1
(1862), 482. General Poor Robin's Almanack (1668);
William Cobbett, Rural Rides (30 Aug 1823).

babies: sneezing

see SNEEZING: BABIES.

babies: teething

see TEETHING.

babies: tempering

A neat pun on the word 'temper', as verb and
noun, led to a charming idea that the first person
to kiss a baby was particularly important:

A good-tempered person should be selected as the
first to kiss the baby, as the good influence will
persist through life. A lady told me that her old
nurse was much disturbed because the wrong
person had kissed and so 'tempered' the baby.
                              Norfolk Folk-Lore (1929)

The handful of examples all come from East
Anglia, but the belief is unlikely to be quite so
regionally restricted.

Suffolk Folk-Lore 35 (1924), 349. Norfolk Dew (1898)
77–81; Folk-Lore 40 (1929) 122–3.

babies: tickling

A handful of references report that if you tickle
a baby's feet it will grow up with a stammer.

Somerset [1905–58] Tongue (1965) 138. Devon Devonshire
Assoc. 104 (1972) 267. Guernsey De Garis (1975) 8.

babies: weaning

see GOOD FRIDAY: WEANING BABIES.

babies: when born

In addition to the widespread 'Monday's Child'
rhyme which assigns different character traits to
those born on each day of the week (*see* BABIES:
'MONDAY'S CHILD', a number of other beliefs
were concerned with when a baby was born.
Taken together, they do not constitute anything
approaching a unified scheme, and indeed are
sometimes contradictory:

Those born on a Sunday are free from evil
spirits.   Somerset Tongue (1965)

A child born on a Sunday will be fortunate.
                              Wales Trevelyan (1909)

Born on a Sunday and you're a tyrant all your
life.   Norfolk Fulcher Collection (c.1895)

A Sussex child born on Sunday can neither be
hanged nor drowned.   Sussex Lucas (1904)

Sunday is the day most often singled out, but
other circumstances of birth are also commented
upon in traditional belief:

To be born at night made one open to see visions,
ghosts, and phantom funerals . . . A child born
during a storm would lead a troublesome life . . .
To be born when the moon is on the increase is a
good omen.   Wales Jones (1930)

Children born in hot weather are not supposed
to live long.   Co. Durham Folk-Lore (1909)

Children born at certain phases of the MOON,
on Christmas day, NEW YEAR'S DAY, and other
special days, were also declared to have certain
characteristics. In Ireland, a particular horror

was reserved for those born at WHITSUN, as they were said to later either kill or be killed. The remedy was to give the baby a mock burial, or to crush an insect in its hand:

On a Whit Sunday (1821) a child was born to Pat Mitchell, a labourer. It is said that the child born on that day is fated to kill or be killed. To avert this doom, a little grave was made, and the infant laid therein, with clay lightly sprinkled on it, sod supported by twigs, covering the whole. Thus was the child buried, and at its resurrection deemed to be freed from the malediction.

Unlocated [1821] N&Q

See also MAY: BABIES BORN IN; MOON: BIRTHS AND DEATHS; WHITSUN.

Sussex Latham (1878) 9; Lucas (1904) 76. **Somerset** Tongue (1965). **Dorset** Udal (1922) 178. **Cornwall** *Folk-Lore Jnl* 5 (1887) 208. **Gloucestershire** *Folk-Lore* 68 (1957) 413. **Warwickshire** Langford (1875) 13–14. **Norfolk** Fulcher Collection (c.1895). **Lincolnshire** N&Q 1S:8 (1853) 382. **Co. Durham** *Folk-Lore* 20 (1909) 74. **Northumberland/Co.** Neasham (1893). **Wales** Trevelyan (1909) 265, 267, 270; Jones (1930) 196–7. **Aberdeenshire** *Folk-Lore* 25 (1914) 349. **Ireland** Wilde (1888) 140–1, 204. **Co. Longford** *Béaloideas* 6 (1936) 259. **Guernsey** De Garis (1975) 6. **Isle of Man** Moore (1891) 157. **Unlocated** [1821] N&Q 5S:6 (1876) 463. *Folk-Lore* 68 (1957) 413.

babies: wrapped in old clothes

Some traditional nurses and midwives indulged in a custom of wrapping babies first in old clothes:

A new-born child should be wrapped in something old, preferably an old flannel petticoat. An old-fashioned nurse told me she never liked to dress babies in new clothes for the first time, if she could avoid it. She always took an old flannel petticoat with her, to be the first garment worn by each baby she nursed.

Herefordshire Leather (1912)

The reasons for this appear to vary considerably. It may have been to avoid tempting fate by avowing pride in the new life, but sometimes the father's clothes were chosen as a protection, or for intrinsic value:

The baby should be wrapped in an old shirt of its father's, to ensure it being strong.

Norfolk *Folk-Lore* (1929)

In some reports, the clothes are specifically those of the opposite sex to the baby. This may have been to confuse the fairies or other ill-wishers, but it was also believed that this would make the child attractive to the opposite sex in later life.

There is clearly a range of interesting traditions here, dating at least to the eighteenth century, which need further study.

Herefordshire Leather (1912) 113. **Norfolk** *Folk-Lore* 40 (1929) 122–3. **Scotland** Kelly (1721); Henderson (1866) 6. **Northeast Scotland** Gregor (1874) 91. **Kintyre** Martin (1987) 184. **Angus** Laing (1885) 34. **Caithness** Rinder (1895) 52. **Ireland** *Folk-Lore* (1893) 359. **Isle of Man** Clague (1911) 177; Cashen (1912) 5. **Literary** Swift (1738).

back-formation

The standard way in which popular theories of origin are created is by back-formation, that is, taking a modern form of a superstition and extrapolating backwards into the past to invent an origin. In the absence of genuine information about the origins and development of a particular belief, the field is open for anyone to simply create an origin, combining the superstition as it appears in the present day and any current notions on the general nature of superstition. Based as they are on the current version, it is common for such origin stories to include what appear to be corroborative and legitimating details.

It need hardly be said that such stories are of little value to those who seek a genuine understanding of the history of superstitious belief, but they are of interest to the folklorist as examples of the way in which each generation reinterprets its traditional lore to suit its own purpose and world view. A very similar situation pertains in other fields – in particular, place-name studies, and folklore genres such as nursery rhymes, children's games, and calendar customs. In nursery rhymes, back-formed theories take a wider variety of forms, and show more clearly that theories follow the fashion of the time, whether for psychological explanations, political satires, mythology, the occult, or presumed ancient history. What they all have in common is a cavalier attitude to history. Those who propose and publish such explanations of superstitions take no account of the fact that the item itself may have changed dramatically in both form and meaning in its development, and that the modern form is not necessarily an accurate guide to the past. Nor do they recognize that few folkloric items can be proved to have a history of more than 300 years, and most even less, whereas it is common for the proposed origins to assume a history of at least a thousand or fifteen hundred years. In no other field than popular folklore would it be acceptable to assume a history centuries before the earliest evidence.

See also NARRATIVE.

baptism

see CHRISTENING.

bargaining

see BUYING AND SELLING.

barn-watching

A form of LOVE DIVINATION carried out, as so many were, on ST MARK'S EVE:

To see the vision of your future wife sit on a strike in the barn at midnight, when she will walk in at one door and out at the other. A man said that he once saw his future wife, a woman with black hair, in this way. Another man saw a pickaxe and a spade walk through the barn, which betokened that he would remain unmarried. In Derbyshire, this charm is tried on St. Mark's Eve.
                        Derbyshire Addy (1895) 73

This is the only example of this particular divination which has come to light, but it shares many elements with other St Mark's procedures, in particular CHAFF-RIDDLING.

basin upturned

see BUCKETS.

beans

see LUCKY BEANS; WART CURES: BEANS.

beards

Beards are often included in superstitions about when to cut or trim HAIR and FINGERNAILS.

bears

Several cures for WHOOPING COUGH involve riding or being close to particular animals, but one of the less well-known procedures was for the sufferer to ride on a bear's back – either as a cure, or to prevent a future attack:

The hooping-cough will never be taken by any child which has ridden on a bear. While bear-baiting was in fashion, a great part of the owner's profits arose from the money given by parents whose children had had a ride. The writer knows of cases in which the charm is said certainly to have been effectual.   Lancashire N&Q (1851)

Bears were surprisingly common in Britain. From medieval times to the middle of the nine-teenth century, bear-baiting was a popular pastime, and well into the twentieth century, travelling dancing-bears could be seen all over the country.

A belief that linked the breeding of LIONS with problems in human childbirth or the offspring of domestic animals, was occasionally also cited in relation to bears:

In Cheshire the superstition pertains to the bear and not to the lion. I have it recorded in my note-book that in 1878 my son lost a litter of pigs, and several of my neighbours were equally unfortu-nate. The misfortune was gravely attributed by my farm man to the supposition that 'bears must be breeding this year'. He further explained to me that bears only breed every seventh year, and that their breeding affects prejudicially the breeding of domestic animals.   Cheshire N&Q 6S:9 (1884)

Cheshire N&Q 6S:9 (1884), 337. England Addy (1895), 90. Lancashire N&Q 1S:3 (1851), 516.

beds: floorboards

It was formerly believed to be important to ensure that your bed was placed in line with the bedroom floorboards or beams rather than across them. Failure to observe this rule would at best mean a bad night's sleep, but at worst it would ensure that anyone dying in the bed would face a long and lingering process:

An old gossip in these parts, on being told by the mother of a dying child that her daughter's death was a very lingering one, went up to the sick chamber, and observing that the position of the bedstead was across the planks, instead of being parallel with them, assigned that as the reason for the patient's lingering death; so the bedstead's

beds

Beds are the locale of many of the fundamentals of human existence – birth, illness, death, dreams, sex, as well as sleep and rest – and given their importance in people's lives, it is no surprise that they were ruled by more superstitions than any other item of household furniture. Aspects covered by belief are many and various and are a curious mixture of the practical, the symbolic, and the magical. Close attention must be paid to the orientation of the bed itself as regards the floorboards, the door, and the points of the compass. Making the bed, getting up, and retiring for the night must all be done correctly. HORSESHOES and HOLED STONES are hung above the bed for protection; Bibles and other lucky items placed under the pillow. Pigeon and game FEATHERS must not be used in a feather bed, and the dying can be helped on their way by a form of EUTHANASIA called 'drawing the pillow'. A number of beliefs are concerned with where you are standing when you first hear the CUCKOO in spring, and if you are in bed at that time it indicates much illness, or even death, in the coming year. Many LOVE DIVINATION procedures culminate in the participants retiring to bed – often backwards or in silence – primarily because the object of the exercise is usually to dream of the future spouse. Herbal and magical prescriptions are recommended to cure BED-WETTING, as are others for CRAMP, RHEUMATISM, and so on.

See also CUCKOOS: WHERE STANDING.

---

position was altered, and it is said the poor girl's death was both speedy and painless.

Kent? N&Q (1879)

In common with several other bed superstitions, this one only appears from the mid nineteenth century and has only been collected in England, but its meaning remained stable well into the late twentieth century. Fitted carpets and plastered ceilings will have made the belief redundant anyway, as many people will be unaware of which way their bedroom floorboards run, even if they cared.

For other beliefs concerning a drawn-out death, or dying hard, as it was termed, *see* FEATHERS.

Kent? N&Q 5S:11 (1879) 125. **Somerset** [1923] Opie & Tatem, 25, *Folk-Lore* 34 (1923) 165. **Dorset** Udal (1922) 184. **Devon** *Athenaeum* (1846) 1069; *Devonshire Assoc.* 103 (1971) 268; *Devonshire Assoc.* 105 (1973) 217. **Cornwall** N&Q 4S:8 (1871) 322; Mayes (1978) 88. **Middlesex or Kent** N&Q 5S:11 (1879) 125, 414. **London** *Folk-Lore* 37 (1926) 367; [1953] Opie & Tatem, 25. **Norfolk** N&Q 5S:11 (1879) 125, 414. **Shropshire** Burne (1883) 282. **Unlocated** *Folk-Lore Jnl* 1 (1883) 196.

---

beds: getting up

Long-standing superstitions show great concern about how one gets out of bed in the morning, as this will affect one's fortune and temperament for the rest of the day. 'You got out of the wrong side of the bed this morning' is still regularly said to someone who is unaccountably grumpy. The basic notion of rising properly goes back at least to the sixteenth century, but its exact nature varies considerably from source to source. In the earlier versions it tends to be a concern with getting out of the right (as opposed to the left) side:

It is unfortunate to rise out of bed on one's left side. It is a common saying when evil befalls a person, who seems to himself have rushed to meet it, 'I did not rise on my right hand today'.

Highland Scotland Campbell (1900)

For others, it is getting out on to the right foot which mattered, and a third variation is to get in and out on the same side:

When getting out of bed always put the right foot on the floor first, otherwise you will be bad-tempered all day. Lincolnshire Rudkin (1936)

It was unlucky to get out of bed a different side from the one you got in. Wiltshire Wiltshire (1975)

The idea was already proverbial in the sixteenth century, appearing in two early plays – John Palsgrave's *Acolastus* (1540) and *Gammer Gurton's Needle* (1575).

Essex [1988] Opie & Tatem, 16. **Wiltshire** Wiltshire (1975) 87. **Lincolnshire** Peacock (1877) 18; Rudkin (1936) 20. **Yorkshire** Nicholson (1890) 44. **Newcastle** [1905] Peacock (1986) 70. **Wales** Trevelyan (1909), 329. **Highland Scotland** Campbell (1900) 230; Polson (1926) 127. **Unlocated** Gales (1914) 229–30; Igglesden (c.1932) 177. **General** W. Hawkins, *Apollo Shroving* (1627) 46, quoted Opie & Tatem, 16; Gaule, *Mag-astro-mances* (1652) 181; Brand (1810) 104. **Literary** John Palsgrave, *The Comedy of Acolastus* (1540); *Gammer Gurton's Needle* (1575) 2:1; Walter Scott, *Redgauntlet* (1824), Ch. 20; R.D. Blackmore, *Perlycross* (1894), Ch. 32.

beds: making, Fridays/ Sundays

Before the invention of sprung mattresses, beds needed a great deal more attention than they do in modern times. Feather beds in particular needed to be turned over and 'plumped up' every day, and 'turning the bed' was an onerous daily chore. A widespread superstition existed that it was unlucky to turn your mattress on a Friday, and some also said Sunday as well:

There were many superstitions about Friday. No bed was ever turned on Friday, and this custom brought a welcome release, a sign of contentment to all bed-makers . . . and, of course, no bed was turned on Sunday. 'It's Friday, we mustn't turn the bed today', said one, and they pushed and tossed the feathers in the great feather beds, thankful that they could be left. It took some strength to turn those beds, and to puff the feathers till the whole thing rose like a balloon. To get the bed to settle down into a horizontal position afterwards was not easy, for we were not allowed to flatten it violently.   Derbyshire [1890s] Uttley

As it was often young women – as housewives or maidservants – who made the beds, the predicted misfortune often took the form of being unlucky in love 'We shall turn away our sweethearts if we do' (**Herefordshire** Leather (1912)), while others promised bad dreams for the occupant of the bed, or even early death.

The mattress belief is only known from about 1835, and is reported from all over England but not, it seems, elsewhere in the British Isles. It presumably faded out with changes in the technology of bed manufacture. The broad connection of beds with the fundamentals of human life – birth, illness, dreams, death – is noted above, and in this case is combined with the long-standing belief that FRIDAYS are unlucky, and Sundays holy. There is also a distinct tendency in later superstitions for wordplay to influence the way beliefs are remembered. In this case the notion of turning the mattress becomes 'turning your luck' and 'turning away' your sweetheart.

Kent *Folk-Lore* 23 (1912) 354. **Sussex** Latham (1878) 11. **Hampshire** [1983] Opie & Tatem, 17. **Dorset** Udal (1922) 273. **Devon** N&Q 1S:4 (1851) 98; *Devonshire Assoc.* 81 (1949) 90. **Cornwall** *Folk-Lore* 34 (1923) 157; *Old Cornwall* 2 (1931–6) 39. **Wiltshire** *Wilts. N&Q* 1 (1893–5) 152; Wiltshire (1975) 86. **Berkshire** *Folk-Lore* 5 (1894) 338. **London** *Folk-Lore* 37 (1926) 366. **Essex** Ketteridge & Mays (1972) 141. **Hertfordshire** [1835] N&Q 5S:3 (1875) 424. **Oxfordshire** *Folk-Lore* 20 (1909) 218; *Folk-Lore* 34 (1923) 326. **Gloucestershire** *Folk-Lore* 34 (1923) 157. **Herefordshire** [c.1895] *Folk-Lore* 39 (1928)

386; Leather (1912) 114. **Northamptonshire** Sternberg (1851) 169. **Suffolk** *Folk-Lore* 35 (1924) 347. **Lincolnshire** Peacock (1877) 245. **Shropshire** N&Q 5S:3 (1875) 465; Burne (1883) 261–2; *Folk-Lore* 49 (1938) 232. **England** Addy (1895) 93, 114. **Derbyshire** Uttley (1946) 127–8. **Lancashire** N&Q 1S:6 (1852) 432. **Northumberland** Bosanquet (1929) 75. **Unlocated** N&Q 4S:10 (1872) 495; N&Q 7S:4 (1887) 246; Wright (1913) 215; N&Q 160 (1931) 427; Igglesden (c.1932) 99.

beds: making, other beliefs

The dominant belief about bed-making concerned a prohibition on turning the mattress on a Friday or Sunday (*see above*), but a great number of other beliefs on the subject have been recorded only once or twice in the nineteenth and twentieth centuries, including the following:

Turn your tye (i.e. feather-bed) from foot to head, then you'll never beg your bread.
                              Devon *Devonshire Assoc.* (1939)

If you wish your love to wed, turn your bed from foot to head.   Wiltshire Wiltshire (1975)

Should three people make a bed someone would die in it before the year was out.
        Wiltshire Wiltshire (1975); also Unlocated Wright (1913)

One should not sing when making a bed, else sleep will not be theirs.
                    Highland Scotland Macbain (1887/88)

[From a servant girl, about nineteen years old]
A bed maker who forgets to put the pillows in their places will not be married during the year of the occurrence.   Devon *Devonshire Assoc.* (1878)

To avoid night-mares, sleep with the open end of the pillow case pointing out of the bed. This enables horrid dreams to find an easy release.
                              Yorkshire Gill (1993)

[On getting up] *Beds should be made before leaving the room to prevent the next night being disturbed and restless.*
                    Watford Observer (11 Feb. 1994)

If you make your bed at bedtime, you will look fair in the morning.
                    East Anglia Forby (1830); Varden (1885)

In Scotland there is a belief that it is unlucky in making a bed to leave the work before it is completed. An interruption will cause the occupant of the bed to pass a sleepless night; or, it may be, some much worse evil will befall him.
                              Scotland N&Q (1892)

Did your mother never teach you girl? Now beat up all the feathers so there are no valleys or hummocks in the bed. Don't you know that the

devil could take possession of you if you can get
into the shape you left in the mattress when you
got up? Nothing would appease the old lady until
this was done.   Kent [1930s] Kent

A mother's bed must not be turned till a month
has elapsed after the birth of the baby.
                    Lancashire Lancashire Lore (1971)

An attendant was making a bed occupied by the
mother of a child born a few days previously.
When she attempted to turn it over, to give it a
better shaking, the nurse energetically interfered,
peremptorily forbidding her doing so till a month
after the confinement, on the ground that it was
decidedly unlucky; and said that she never
allowed it to be done till then on any account
whatever.   Lancashire N&Q (1852)

If you turn the bed, you must turn again in (to)
bed. That is, if you turn over the feather-bed or
mattress during your illness, you will not recover
at once, you must turn into bed again. Mrs.
Preston, a native of Rockbeare, over 70, gave this
as the cause of the slow recovery of the gardener's
wife, whom she was nursing, for during her absence
a sister had turned the mattress over and the
woman took cold.   Devon Devonshire Assoc. (1892)

Devon Devonshire Assoc. 10 (1878) 106; Devonshire
Assoc. 24 (1892) 51–2; Devonshire Assoc. 71 (1939) 130.
Kent [1930s] Kent (1977) 108. Wiltshire (1975) 86–7.
East Anglia Forby (1830) 415; Varden (1885) 114.
Yorkshire Gill (1993) 90. Lancashire N&Q 1S:6 (1852)
432; Lancashire Lore (1971) 49. Scotland N&Q 8S:2
(1892) 189. Highland Scotland Macbain (1887/88) 256.
Unlocated Wright (1913) 215. General Watford Observer
(11 Feb. 1994) 20.

beds: orientation

Tradition dictates that the orientation of one's
bed is important for health and a good night's
sleep. Unfortunately, there is no overall agreement as to which direction is best:

There is, I have been told, a folk-belief that it is
better to sleep lying north and south than lying
east and west; in the former position perhaps one
is supposed to roll over and over with the earth.
                    Unlocated N&Q 175 (1938)

A bed should point to the east and west, and not
to the north and south. Restlessness is caused by
placing the bed in the direction of north to south.
                    England Addy (1895)

The majority of informants recommend north/
south. The reason given sometimes is that the
earth rotates on an east-west axis and it is therefore more comfortable for us to roll over side-

ways than head over heels; others give the earth's
magnetic field as the reason, and maintain that
it is natural that our heads should thus point to
the north. This latter explanation was already
under discussion in the seventeenth century (see
Browne, Pseudodoxia Epidemica (1646)), as was
a completely different connotation:

Who to the north, or south, doth set his bed,
Male children shall beget.
                    Herrick, Hesperides (1648)

Wiltshire [1923] Opie & Tatem, 361. London [1953]
Opie & Tatem, 361. England Addy (1895) 90. Lancashire
Harland & Wilkinson (1882) 80–1. Ireland Wilde (1888)
201. Co. Longford Béaloideas 6 (1936) 265. Unlocated
N&Q 175 (1938) 476. General Browne Pseudodoxia
Epidemica (1646), Bk 2, Ch. 3. Literary Robert Herrick,
'Observation', Hesperides (1648).

beds: prayers at foot of

Two nineteenth-century references claim that it
is unlucky to say your prayers at the foot of the
bed, and it should be done at the side. No other
information is given.

Warwickshire Langford (1875) 11–12. Unlocated N&Q
2S:12 (1861) 491.

beds: pregnancy

see PREGNANCY: CHAIRS/BEDS.

beds: wetting

Children all over Britain believed – and no doubt
some still believe – that picking DANDELIONS
will cause you to wet the bed. The most widely
recommended cure for bedwetting was to eat
mice:

Children who cannot retain their water may be
cured by eating three roasted mice. The same dish
is also given for whooping cough. I have known
them given several times for both complaints,
and by respectable people.   Yorkshire N&Q (1852)

For full references, see MICE CURES: BEDWET-
TING
  Two writers give details of other less well-
known cures:

On day appointed for funeral of person of opposite sex, while the first part of service being read
in church child must urinate on open grave.
                    Sussex Latham (1878)

bees

The key characteristic of bees in the superstitions of Britain and Ireland is that they are very sensitive and censorious creatures. They are quick to take offence if not treated with respect, they know what is going on in the world of humans, they will not stay in a family which quarrels or swears, and they will not be bought and sold like domestic animals. Moreover, their behaviour is useful as an indicator of future events – settling on a dead branch is a death omen, and one flying into a house foretells the visit of a stranger.

In addition to these major beliefs, treated separately below, there were numerous others which have been recorded once or twice, any of which may have had a wider currency. It is no surprise to find that some believed that bees suddenly dying, or forsaking the hive, was taken as a death omen for one of the beekeeper's family:

If your bees fall sick and pine and die
One of your house will soon in churchyard lie.
Warwickshire Langford (1875)

Bees' abhorrence of quarrelling and swearing amongst their neighbours is well known, but they were also supposedly aware of the wider world picture:

It is a common saying that the bees are idle or unfortunate at their work whenever there are wars; a very curious observer and fancier says that this has been the case ever since the time of the movements in France, Prussia, and Hungary, up to the present time.   Hampshire N&Q (1855)

These bee-superstitions are living and flourishing. I believe it would be difficult to meet with any cottage beekeeper who did not honestly think that his insects were endued with knowledge and sagacity beyond that of the rest of the brute creation, and sometimes beyond that of mankind.   Shropshire Burne (1883)

It is lucky for bees to be kept in partnership.
Co. Durham Folk-Lore (1909)

It is never considered lucky to be the sole owner of bees. A man and woman, not man and wife, should be partners.
Northumberland Bigge (1860–62)

In removing a hive of bees, care must be taken not to carry them over any stream, for they will not live after crossing water.
Shropshire Burne (1883)

For much more material on bee lore in Britain and abroad, *see* Ransome (1937) and *Folk Life* 23 (1984–5) 21–48.

Hampshire N&Q 1S:12 (1855) 200–1. Warwickshire Langford (1875) 15. Shropshire Burne (1883) 233–7. Northumberland Bigge (1860–62) 91. Co. Durham Folk-Lore 20 (1909) 73.

. . . the child's first going alone to fix upon an ash-tree suitable for the purposes of this charm an ash-tree, and going afterwards upon another day, without indulging its intention, to gather a hand-ful of the ash-keys, which it must lay with left hand in hollow of right arm. Thus are they to be carried home and then they are to be burnt to ashes. The charm is completed by the child performing the same ceremony over the embers on the hearth.   Sussex Latham (1878)

A very similar use of an open grave is given for Lincolnshire by Rudkin, which was presumably designed to TRANSFER the problem to the occupant of the grave. She also prescribes the following:

Bedwetting – Egg-shell ground up and given to the child in milk or water will stop this habit.
Lincolnshire Rudkin (1936)

Sussex Latham (1878) 49. Lincolnshire Rudkin (1936) 28. Yorkshire N&Q 1S:6 (1852) 311–12.

bees: buying and selling

The sensitivity of bees to their surroundings is further reflected in restrictions on the way they change hands:

There is not one peasant, I believe in the village, who would sell you a swarm of bees. To be guilty of selling bees is a grievous omen indeed, than which nothing can be more dreadful. To barter bees is quite a different matter. If you want a hive, you may easily obtain it in lieu of a small pig, or some other equivalent. There may seem little difference in the eyes of enlightened persons between selling and bartering, but the superstitious beekeeper sees a grand distinction, and it is not his fault if you don't see it too.   Hampshire N&Q (1854)

If money must change hands, many informants explained that nothing less than gold would do, or the bees would take offence. Some beekeepers went even further, and frowned on the gift of a swarm:

Anyone who is thinking of taking up bee-culture must be warned against accepting as a gift a swarm of bees. Ill luck will follow if bees are given away. 'In Devon a few years ago, no Devonian would sell you a swarm of bees either, for money must not form part of the transaction. No, you must obtain your bees by barter; a sack of corn or a small pig was the usual equivalent for a May-time swarm.'   Devon *Devonshire Assoc.* (1933)

The basic belief was already well known in the eighteenth century, and lasted well into the twentieth.

Sussex Lucas (1904) 76; *Sussex County Mag.* 5 (1931) 122. **Hampshire** N&Q 1S:9 (1854) 446. **Somerset** [1923] Opie & Tatem, 17. **Devon** Brand 2 (1813) 202; N&Q 1S:2 (1850) 512; *Devonshire Assoc.* 65 (1933) 124. **Wiltshire** Smith (1874) 329. **Surrey** [1948] Opie & Tatem, 17. **Essex** N&Q 6S:4 (1881) 396. **Herefordshire** Leather (1912) 28. **Warwickshire** *Folk-Lore* 24 (1913) 240. **East Anglia** Forby (1830) 415; Varden (1885) 114. **Norfolk** *Norfolk Chronicle* (20 Dec. 1902). **Shropshire** Burne (1883) 233–7. **Cheshire** N&Q 2S:8 (1859) 242. **England** Addy (1895) 65. **Northern England** *Newcastle Weekly Chronicle* (11 Feb 1899) 7. **Yorkshire** Atkinson (1891) 126. **Montgomeryshire** *Bye-Gones* (6 Oct. 1886) 141. **Flintshire/Denbighshire** *Bye-Gones* (13 Oct. 1886), 143. **Northeast Scotland** Gregor (1881) 147. **Co. Wexford** *Folk-Lore Record* 5 (1882) 182. **Guernsey** MacCulloch MS (1864) 420–1; N&Q 6S:3 (1881) 517; De Garis (1975) 139. **General** Lupton (*c.*1720, 21st edn.) 217; W. Ellis, *Modern Husbandman* (1750) 182, quoted Opie & Tatem, 17; *Spectator* (18 Jan. 1902) 82.

bees: in house

One of many indications that a visitor was on the way was when a bee flew into the house. In most versions any bee would do, but for some it had to be something other than a normal hive bee:

Superstition abounded about bees. Some were lucky, others not. The Dummy Dors, bigger and noisier than a bumble bee, was especially dreaded. If one flew into the house it had to be avoided to ensure no harm was intended towards it. The Dummy was supposed to fore-tell the visit of a stranger. The length of time it stayed in the room would correspond to the duration of the stranger's stay.
    Essex [*c.*1920] Ketteridge & Mays

This notion was widely known across the south-ern half of England, but does not seem to have been reported much elsewhere, although one Scottish reference is clearly related:

If a bee flies into the house, good news may be expected soon, and if it be the first bee seen that season, it makes for wealth that it should be caught and put in a purse.
    Highland Scotland Polson (1926)

And in Irish tradition the bee is similarly welcome – 'It is very lucky for bees to come to the house' (Co. Longford *Béaloideas* (1936)).

No reference to these positive meanings has been found before the 1850s, but a very much earlier source (*c.*1050) states that dreaming of bees entering a house portends its destruction, and a handful of later sources are also quite clear that a bee in the house is a death omen:

The wild, or as we term him, the humble bee, is not without its share of superstitions which pertain to his more civilised brethren. The entrance of one into a cottage is deemed a certain sign of death.
    Northamptonshire N&Q (1850)

Southern England Jefferies (1879) Ch. 10. **Hampshire** [1962] Opie & Tatem, 47. **Devon** *Devonshire Assoc.* 61 (1929) 127. **Wiltshire** *Wilts. N&Q* 1 (1893–5), 60. **Berkshire** *Berks. Arch. Soc.* 1 (1889–91) 86. **Essex** [*c.*1920] Ketteridge & Mays (1972) 141–2. **Buckinghamshire** Henderson (1866) 92. **Oxfordshire** *Folk-Lore* 23 (1912) 357; [1920s] Surman (1992) 61. **Gloucestershire** *Folk-Lore* 12 (1902) 171; *Folk-Lore* 26 (1915) 210. **Herefordshire** Leather (1912) 28, 86. **Worcestershire** *Folk-Lore* 20 (1909) 344. **Northamptonshire** N&Q 1S:2 (1850) 165. **Bedfordshire** *Folk-Lore* 37 (1926) 77. **East Anglia** N&Q 4S:2 (1868) 221. **Suffolk** Fitzgerald (1887) 526; *Folk-Lore* 35 (1924) 350; Claxton (1954) 89. **Norfolk** [*c.*1870s] Haggard (1935) 18; *Norfolk Chronicle* (20 Dec. 1902); [1920s] Wigby (1976) 69. **Rutland** N&Q 5S:6 (1876) 462; N&Q 6S:2 (1880) 165; [1956] Opie & Tatem, 47. **Lincolnshire** Rudkin (1936) 20. **Shropshire** Burne (1883) 237. **England** Addy (1895) 65. **Highland Scotland** Polson (1926) 129. **Co. Longford** *Béaloideas* 6 (1936) 264. *Death omen:* **England** [*c.*1050] Cockayne 3 (1866) 169. **Somerset** [1923] Opie & Tatem, 47. **Worcestershire** *Folk-Lore* 20 (1909) 344. **Northamptonshire** N&Q 1S:2 (1850) 165. **Wales** Trevelyan (1909) 281.

bees: quarrelling owners

Several superstitions attest that bees are sensitive to their surroundings and to human behaviour. The most widespread is that they must be told about a death in the family (*see below*), but it was also maintained that they would not thrive in a quarrelsome family, and they objected to bad language:

An artisan I met on the rail, whom I put down as a Northumberland man, and who had pretty freely expressed his annoyance at the delay caused by the gate-money race traffic, concluded as he was about to leave the train, 'It wouldn't do to swear before bees, though. They'd pretty soon leave the place!'.

Northumberland N&Q (1899)

Kent N&Q 2S:12 (1861) 492. Hampshire N&Q 10S:2 (1904) 26–7. Oxfordshire *Gent. Mag.* (1855) 384–6. Herefordshire Leather (1912), 28. Northamptonshire N&Q 1S:2 (1850) 165. East Anglia Varden (1885) 114. Suffolk [1863] Chambers 1 (1878) 752. Shropshire Burne (1883) 233–7. Northumberland? N&Q 9S:3 (1899) 286.

bees: seafarers

A few sources report special beliefs about bees held by fishermen and sailors in various locations, but they do not seem to represent a unified whole. Until further examples are noted, it is impossible to say whether the differences are simply regional or whether they form a coherent pattern.

A bee lighting on a ship at sea is welcomed as a bringer of good luck.   Suffolk Gurdon (1893)

Sailors dislike a bee to appear in their boat, it is sure to be a witch.

Highland Scotland Macbain (1887/8)

To catch the first 'bumble-bee' seen in the spring and carry it out 'to the fishing' is considered a sure talisman for good luck. I was told this when, on seeing a 'bumble-bee' imprisoned in an inverted tumbler in a fisherman's cottage, I enquired the reason for its imprisonment.

Isle of Man N&Q (1880)

If a fisherman, on setting out, sees a humble bee flying in the same direction as he is going, he considers it a good omen, and that he is sure of a plentiful catch. If, however, the insect meets him it is quite the reverse. The ill-luck, however, may be averted by spitting thrice over the left shoulder.   Guernsey MacCulloch (1864)

Suffolk Gurdon (1893) 9. Highland Scotland Macbain (1887/88) 253. Guernsey MacCulloch (1864) 505–6. Isle of Man N&Q 6S:2 (1880) 224.

bees: settling

Rural dwellers took careful note of where swarming bees settled, and judged it lucky, or more usually unlucky, according to the place chosen. The most common belief was that it was a sure sign of death if they settled on a dead branch or hedge stake, especially if near the house:

Some years since the wife of a respectable cottager in my neighbourhood died in childbed. Calling on the widower soon after, I found that although deeply deploring an event which left him several motherless children, he spoke calmly of the fatal termination of the poor woman's illness, as an inevitable and foregone conclusion. On being pressed for an explanation of these sentiments, I discovered that both he and his poor wife had been 'warned' of the coming event by her going into the garden a fortnight before her confinement, and discovering that their bees, in the act of swarming, had made choice of a dead hedge stake for their settling place. This is generally considered an infallible sign of a death in the family, and in her situation it is no wonder that the poor woman should take the warning to herself; affording, too, another example of how a prediction may assist in working out its own fulfillment.   Sussex N&Q (1851)

This superstition was widely reported across England and Wales since its earliest appearance in John Gay's pastoral poem *The Shepherd's Week* in the early eighteenth century:

Swarm'd on a rotten stick the bees I spied
Which erst I saw when Goody Dobson died.

While the meaning of bees settling on dead wood was always the same, there was little agreement on other places:

If a swarm of bees takes possession of the roof of a house it portends death to the owner of it.

Dorset Udal (1922)

If bees make their nest in the roof of a house, none of the daughters in that dwelling will marry.

Sussex Latham (1878)

Bees swarming on roofs was a lucky sign.

Wales Jones (1930)

If they settle on the wall of a house, there will be a death in that house before long, and if on a person's head, his death is near at hand.

Shropshire Burne (1883)

If a bee alights on your head and stays there you will rise to be a great man in after years.

England Addy (1895)

Dead branch: Sussex N&Q 1S:4 (1851) 436; Latham (1878) 58. Dorset Udal (1922) 181. Somerset Tongue (1965) 137. Wiltshire Smith (1874) 329; [1922] Opie & Tatem, 20. Berkshire *Folk-Lore* 5 (1894) 336. East Anglia Varden (1885) 116. Lincolnshire N&Q 1S:8 (1853) 382; Peacock (1877) 20. Norfolk *Norfolk Chronicle* (20 Dec. 1902). Shropshire Burne (1883) 233–7. England Addy (1895) 65. Yorkshire Nicholson (1890) 136. Wales Trevelyan (1909) 281. Mid-Wales Davies (1911) 226. Anglesey *Folk-Lore* 19 (1908) 339. Literary John Gay,

Telling the bees was one of the most widely known superstitions connected with death in the nineteenth century. This engraving appeared in Scribner's Magazine *in May 1879.*

The Shepherd's Week (1714) Friday lines 107–8.
Other places: Sussex Latham (1878) 9, 33. **Dorset** Udal (1922) 181. **Suffolk** [1863] Chambers 1 (1878) 752. **Shropshire** Burne (1883) 233–7. **England** Addy (1895) 65. **Lancashire** *Lancashire Lore* (1971) 50. **Wales** Jones (1930), 178.

bees: souls

One or two references indicate a belief that people's souls can leave their body while asleep, usually taking the form of a bee:

I remember, some forty years ago, hearing a servant from Lincolnshire relate a story of two travellers who laid down by the road-side to rest, and one fell asleep. The other, seeing a bee settle on a neighbouring wall and go into a little hole, put the end of his staff in the hole, and so imprisoned the bee. Wishing to pursue his journey, he endeavoured to awaken his companion but was unable to do so, till, resuming his stick, the bee flew to the sleeping man and went into his ear. His companion then awoke him, remarking how soundly he had been asleep and asked what he had been dreaming of – 'Oh!', said he, 'I dreamt that you shut me up in a dark cave, and I could not awake until you let me out'. The person who told me the story firmly believed that the man's soul was in the bee.

Lincolnshire N&Q (1851)

It is not clear how widespread this belief was, although there is some indication that it was better known in Scotland.

See also SLEEP.

Lincolnshire N&Q 1S:3 (1851) 206. **Highland Scotland** Macbain (1887/88) 260.

bees: telling and mourning

By far the most common manifestation of the supposed sensitivity of bees to the doings of their human masters is the belief that they should be informed of any major change of circumstance in the owner's family, and in particular must be told of any death. Neglect of this obligation would lead to the bees themselves dying or leaving:

About thirty years ago, an old woman in my parish told my wife that her bees had died: a circumstance which she attributed to her having forgotten to tell her bees of the master's death . . . I mentioned it [recently] to my nurse, and asked her if she had ever heard of a similar custom. She said, 'Yes', and that she herself having lost her bees on the death of her first husband, was told by her neighbours that this had happened because she had neglected to tell the bees of her husband's death. She further said that in her village it was the custom, on the death of the master of a family, not only to inform the bees, but also to give them a piece of the funeral cake, together with beer sweetened with sugar.

Nottinghamshire? N&Q (1869)

The essence of the custom is this 'telling the bees', and often this is all that is recorded. In some cases there was a set routine which had to be followed – tapping gently on each hive, often with the house key, for example – and reciting a set phrase:

On the evening of the day Twister died, Edmund . . . saw Queenie come out of her door and go towards her beehives . . . She tapped on the roof of each hive in turn, like knocking at a door, and said, 'Bees, bees, your master's dead, an' now you must work for your missis'. Then seeing the little boy, she explained, 'I 'ad to tell 'em, you know, or they'd all've died, poor craturs'.

Oxfordshire [1880s] Thompson

Others prescribed a more elaborate process, not only informing the bees of the death, but inviting them to the funeral, placing black cloth on the hives, and making sure that they received some of the food and drink served to mourners.

When a bee-master dies tins containing funeral biscuits soaked in wine are put in front of the hives, so that the bees may partake of their master's funeral feast. Two kinds of funeral cakes are used, namely, biscuits and 'burying cakes', the latter only being given to the poor. The bees always have the biscuits, and not the 'burying cakes'. At Eyam in Derbyshire, a portion of the 'burnt drink' and of the three-cornered cakes used at funerals is given to the bees of the deceased bee-keeper. Sometimes pieces of black crape are pinned upon the hives. It is said that the bees must be told of their master's death, or they will all die. Derbyshire Addy (1895)

Another part of the custom, reported in many areas, was 'lifting' or 'turning' the hives, apparently to symbolize the bees' accompanying the funeral procession:

In North Shropshire it is very common, instead of – or as well as – telling the bees, to 'heave up' the hives, i.e. lift them a few inches from the stand and set them down again. This was one of the customs known to me at Edmond. 'At the funeral of one of my relatives', writes one of our best authorities on the Welsh (Oswestry) border, 'the bee-hive was "lifted" as the body was being carried from the house.' This was also the old custom at Worthen (on the western border, but south of the Severn) I imagine that the hive and the coffin are both to be "lifted" at the same moment. Shropshire Burne (1883)

Many keepers also told their bees of other major family events, such as weddings, when the hives were decorated and wedding food provided. Some even read letters from absent family members to them.

In one form or other, 'telling the bees' is reported from all over England, plus a few places in Wales and Ireland, but not, on current evidence, in Scotland. Considering its ubiquity in England in the nineteenth and twentieth centuries, it might be presumed that the custom of telling the bees has a long history, but at present this cannot be proved.

Opie and Tatem located the earliest reference, in P. Camerarius, *Historical Meditations* (1621), which comments on the belief that on the death of the master or mistress of the house, bees' hives should be moved elsewhere, and Brand (1813) quotes a newspaper from 1790 describing 'turning' the hives in a similar situation. But 'telling the bees', or dressing their hives for a funeral or wedding, does not appear until the first decades of the nineteenth century, and at present we have no grounds for believing it much older than that. A diligent search in European sources may shed further light on this question, as a similar custom certainly existed abroad. It would be no surprise to learn that the custom was still carried out amongst some modern-day beekeepers.

Southeast England N&Q 1S:1 (1850) 293. **Kent** Jesse (1834) 297–8; N&Q 4S:4 (1869) 507; [c.1880s] Kent (1976) 105–6. **Sussex** [1820] *Folk-Lore Record* 3 (1880) 136; Latham (1878) 69; *Sussex County Mag.* 5 (1931) 122; Ransome (1937) 221. **Hampshire** *Gent. Mag.* (1810) 309; N&Q 10S:2 (1904) 27. **Devon** *Athenaeum* (1846) 1018; N&Q 1S:5 (1852) 148; *Gent. Mag.* (1855) 384–6; [1874] *Folk-Lore* 26 (1915) 155; *Devonshire Assoc.* 8 (1876) 51; Hewett (1900) 53. *Devonshire Assoc.* 61 (1929) 126–7. **Cornwall** N&Q, 1S:12 (1855) 38; *Folk-Lore Jnl* 5 (1887) 193. **Somerset** *N&Q for Somerset & Dorset* 7 (1900–1) 207. **Wiltshire** N&Q 1S:4 (1851) 309; [1922] Opie &

Tatem, 21. **Berkshire** Lowsley (1888) 24. **Surrey** N&Q
1S:5 (1852) 413; N&Q 7S:10 (1890) 235.
Surrey/Sussex/Isle of Wight N&Q 1S:4 (1851) 309.
London [1984] Opie & Tatem, 19. **Essex** [1820s]
Atkinson (1891) 126–7; *Monthly Packet* 24 (1862) 434–7;
[c.1915] Mays (1969) 165; [c.1920] Ketteridge & Mays
(1972) 142. **Hertfordshire** *Folk-Lore Jnl.* 6 (1888) 146.
Buckinghamshire N&Q 1S:4 (1851) 308; N&Q 7S:10
(1890) 235. **Oxfordshire** N&Q 1S:4 (1851) 309; [1880s]
Thompson (1939) 87; *Folk-Lore* 34 (1923) 325; *Oxf. F L.
Soc. Ann. Record* (1950) 11. **Herefordshire** [1838]
Leather (1912) 123; Leather (1912) 28. **Worcestershire**
N&Q 7S:10 (1890) 177–8; Salisbury (1893) 72; Berkeley
& Jenkins (1932) 34. **Worcestershire/Shropshire** *Gent.
Mag.* (1855) 384–6. **Warwickshire** Jesse (1834) 297–8;
Langford (1875) 15. **Northamptonshire** *Folk-Lore* 3
(1892) 138; *Folk-Lore* 67 (1956) 110. **East Anglia** Varden
(1885) 116–17. **Suffolk** [1863] Chambers 1 (1878) 752;
Zincke (1887) 170–1; *Folk-Lore* 35 (1924) 349–50. **Norfolk**
Jesse (1834) 297–8; N&Q 1S:6 (1852) 480; [c.1870s]
Haggard (1935) 7; *Norfolk Chronicle* (20 Dec. 1902);
Folk-Lore 40 (1929) 123; [c.1912] Randell (1966) 94.
Rutland *Folk-Lore Jnl* 3 (1885) 379. **Lincolnshire**
Stamford Mercury (15 Apr. 1870) 6; Peacock (1877) 20;
Watkins (1886) 10; Rudkin (1936) 49. **Shropshire** Burne
(1883) 233–7, 299. **Cheshire** N&Q 2S:8 (1859) 242; N&Q
4S:10 (1872) 408. **England** Addy (1895) 65, 125.
Derbyshire N&Q 1S:4 (1851) 309; Addy (1895) 65;
[1950s] *Lore & Language* 5:2 (1986) 102.
Derbyshire/Nottinghamshire N&Q 7S:10 (1890) 235.
Nottinghamshire? 4S:4 (1869) 225–6. **Northern
England** [1850s] *Denham Tracts* 2 (1895) 213; N&Q
7S:10 (1890) 235; *Newcastle Weekly Chronicle* (11 Feb.
1899) 7. **Yorkshire** N&Q 1S:4 (1851) 309; N&Q 3S:5
(1864) 393; Addy (1888) xix; Atkinson (1891) 127–8;
Morris (1911) 233. *Folk-Lore* 43 (1932) 252. **Cumberland**
Gibson (1858) 106; Bulkeley (1886) 229. **Co. Durham**
Brockie (1886) 143–4; Leighton (1910) 52.
Northumberland Bigge (1860–62) 91. **Wales** Trevelyan
(1909) 281. **Mid-Wales** Davies (1911) 226.
Monmouthshire N&Q 1S:4 (1851) 309; *Folk-Lore* 15
(1904) 221. **N. Ireland** Foster (1951) 22. **Co. Kerry** [1986]
Opie & Tatem, 21. **Guernsey** MacCulloch MS (1864)
420–1; De Garis (1975) 139. **Unlocated** *Argus* (9 Sept.
1790) quoted Lean 2 (1905) 590; N&Q 7S:10 (1890) 126,
235; N&Q 11S:7 (1913) 388. **Literary** Rudyard Kipling,
Puck of Pook's Hill (1906), Ch. 9; W. Raymond, *Verity
Thurston* (1926), Ch. 15.

beetles

It should be noted that few of the sources which
quote superstitions distinguish between different
types of beetle, and that some of the apparent
inconsistencies in the following reports may be
explained by this fact. The dominant superstition in England was that killing beetles caused
rain:

*Rain-beetles were never killed by the village boys,
for that would make rain pour down, they said.*
 Derbyshire [c.1890s] Uttley

*A street urchin, on seeing one of the writers tread
on a large blackbeetle, remarked, 'Now we'll have
rain'.*
 Oxfordshire *Folk-Lore* (1915)

This was well known across most parts of
England, with occasional references from Wales
and Scotland, but no explanation for the belief
is given in any of the available sources. The earliest is 1852, and it was still being said in the 1980s,
but was presumably rare by then.

In some parts of Ireland and Scotland,
however, beetles were regarded as unlucky and
deliberately killed on sight. This destruction was
excused by reference to a traditional story about
the insect's betrayal of the Holy Family:

*The boys of Sutherland will never allow a beetle
to escape them; they stamp on the insect and cry,
'Beetle, beetle, you won't see tomorrow'. The
practice is without doubt connected with a legend
which may be heard in the counties, a legend of
special interest as a type of those curious Scottish
stories wherein New Testament history and
modern realism are interblent. Here it is: As they
fled into Egypt, Joseph and Mary and the child
Christ passed through a field where men scattered corn seeds. The Virgin said to the men,
'Should any ask of you if we have journeyed this
way, make answer, "A man, a woman, and a child
crossed the field as we sowed the corn"'. The men
promised to do her bidding. That night the grain
sprouted, grew rapidly, and ripened, so that next
day the labourers brought their sickles and began
to reap it. Now a band of soldiers came and questioned them: 'Have you seen a mother and child
on an ass with a man leading it, go this way?' The
men replied: 'As we sowed the corn which we now
reap, they passed'. When they heard these words,
the messengers of the king were about to turn
back, but a black beetle cried aloud: 'Yesterday,
yesterday, the corn was sown, and the son of God
passed through the field'.*
 Sutherland Rinder (1895)

The only English version so far found is
different in detail but serves the same purpose:

*Always kill a devil's-head beetle, as one of them
preceded Judas to the garden where our Lord was,
on the night before the crucifixion, and when
near our Lord it turned up its tail, thus discovering him to the betrayer.*
 Derbyshire *Folk-Lore Jnl* (1884)

These are typical of a range of stories which
relate how creatures helped or hindered Jesus'
flight (*see also* SPIDERS).

A few more miscellaneous beetle beliefs:

If you kill a fly or a blackbeetle, twenty flies or blackbeetles will come to the funeral [also said of other insects].   Unlocated N&Q (1878)

A blackbeetle can walk unharmed through fire.
                              Wales *Folk-Lore* (1934)

If you kill a beetle you will break a basin.
                    Norfolk *Norfolk Chronicle* (20 Dec. 1902)

White beetles in a house are called 'death-bringers'.   Wales Trevelyan (1909)

Clocks, or black beetles in a house were considered lucky; we have seen them carefully lifted by tongs or shovel and put out, because to kill them took away the luck.   Glasgow [c.1820] Napier

See also DEATHWATCH BEETLES.

Killing brings rain: Southern England Jefferies (1879) 167. **Cornwall** [1890s] *Old Cornwall* 1:12 (1930) 4. **Wiltshire** [1981] Opie & Tatem, 21. **Oxfordshire** *Folk-Lore* 26 (1915) 210. **Herefordshire** Leather (1912) 28. **Worcestershire** *Folk-Lore* 20 (1909) 344. **Cambridgeshire** *Folk-Lore* 25 (1914) 366. **Lincolnshire** Rudkin (1936) 14. **England** Addy (1895) 67. **Derbyshire** *Folk-Lore Jnl* 2 (1884) 280; [c.1890s] Uttley (1946), 136. **Yorkshire** N&Q 1S:6 (1852) 311–12; *Folk-Lore* 31 (1920) 319; Nicholson (1890) 136; Blakeborough (1898) 130. **Lancashire** Harland & Wilkinson (1873) 236. **Co. Durham** [1920s] Kirkup (1957) 20. **Glamorganshire** [1952] Opie & Tatem, 21. **Glasgow** [late 1940s] MacLeay (1990) 43.
Holy Family story: Highland Scotland Macbain (1887/88) 266. **Sutherland** Rinder (1895) 53–4. **Ireland** N&Q 4S:10 (1872) 183. Wilde (1888) 178. **Co. Tyrone** *Lore & Language* 1:7 (1972) 10.
Miscellaneous: Norfolk *Norfolk Chronicle* (20 Dec. 1902). Wales Trevelyan (1909) 283; *Folk-Lore* (1934). 161. **Glasgow** [c.1820] Napier (1864) 397. **Unlocated** N&Q 5S:10 (1878) 205.

---

beginnings and continuance

One of the most important underlying principles of superstition is that beginnings set the pattern of good or bad fortune for the future. In the most obvious cases it is a time period which is beginning – a new day, the start of spring, a new year. In others, it is a journey, a project, a business venture. Alternatively, it can be a new stage in life, a birth, a christening, a wedding. It is true for great and small – the coronation of the sovereign is watched as closely as the next-door baby's christening.

The character of the coming twelve months, for good or bad fortune, is foretold by the appearance of things on the morning of the new year. A trivial mishap, or the slightest instance of good luck, has now more than its usual significance, inasmuch as it predicts, in a general way, the course of events through the coming year.
                              Cornwall Couch (1871)

It is not always obvious that the principle is in operation because there are various ways of measuring time. The new year and the new day are obvious temporal markers, but for those who take notice of the phases of the moon, each new moon is the start of a new cycle, and for rural folk the traditional start of spring may be seeing the first lamb, or hearing the first cuckoo.

When you first hear the cuckoo take note how you are occupied, for what you are doing then will be your chief business during the year.
                              Sussex *Folk-Lore* (1914)

The notion of HANDSELLING is a specialized version of the beginning motif. The first money taken at market encourages further money later in the day. Furthermore, one must never put on a new coat without making sure that there is money in the pocket, otherwise it will continue to be empty throughout the coat's life.

Long ago when the people would open a new shop, the first man or woman in was to 'hansel' it. Another thing is that if a person bought a new bag or a new case or a new purse bag, the person that would have bought it for another person they would always put sixpence in it for good luck or for a 'hansel' because it was an old custom that when anybody would be giving a present of a purse it was the custom that they should put something in for luck.   Co. Wexford [1938] Ó Muirithe & Nuttall

The principle can also be seen at work in other superstitions. The avoidance of TURNING BACK when starting a journey is probably because this signals a bad beginning. The fear of MEETING certain people or animals when leaving home is sometimes a clear case, as is the custom of first footing (*see* NEW YEAR).

Sussex *Folk-Lore* 25 (1914) 369. Cornwall Couch (1871) 151. Co. Wexford Ó Muirithe & Nuttall (1999) 166.

---

bellows: on table

A number of superstitions forbid the placing of items on TABLES. The best known, and still quoted example, is new SHOES, but in the past bellows came a close second:

If a pair of bellows is put on a table, some great misfortune is sure to happen in the household.
                              Guernsey MacCulloch (1864)

In many cases it is simply 'very unlucky', but where a specific result is given it is usually, as with shoes, a quarrel or a parting:

For the following notes I am indebted to a simple serving-woman in Dublin: . . . If a pair of bellows be placed on a table, there will be a fight in the house.   Dublin N&Q (1869)

Without being able to say precisely why, it seems clear that the bellows and shoes interdiction are linked by both form and meaning, and many informants speak of both in the same breath. The two versions enter the documentary record at roughly the same time, although the first bellows reference predates the shoes by nearly thirty years, and the belief only lasts a hundred years or so, from about 1840 to the 1930s.

The bellows belief faded fast, just as bellows faded from the domestic scene, while the shoes version has retained a vigorous life to the present day.

Kent N&Q 4S:4 (1869) 507. **Dorset** Udal (1922) 274. **Somerset** [1923] Opie & Tatem, 22. **Devon** *Devonshire Assoc.* 9 (1877) 99; *Devonshire Assoc.* 15 (1883) 107; Hewett (1900) 54; N&Q 10S: 12 (1909) 66; *Devonshire Assoc.* 63 (1931) 129; *Devonshire Assoc.* 65 (1933) 124. **Cornwall** Hunt (1865) 241; [1890s] *Old Cornwall* 1:12 (1930) 4; *Old Cornwall* 2 (1931–6) 38. **Herefordshire** Leather (1912) 87, 118. **Shropshire** N&Q 4S:4 (1869) 307. **West Wales** Davies (1911) 216. **Highland Scotland** Polson (1926) 128. **Dublin** N&Q 4S:4 (1869) 505. **Guernsey** MacCulloch (1864) 506. **Unlocated** N&Q 4S:4 (1869) 213; N&Q 5S:10 (1878) 494. **Literary** *Mother Bunch's Golden Fortune-Teller* (c.1840) quoted Opie & Tatem, 21.

bells

see CLOCKS: STRIKING DURING CHURCH SERVICE; WEDDINGS: CLOCKS/BELLS.

bells: cures

see RINGWORM; SHINGLES.

Bible divination: dipping

One of several unofficial uses of the Bible for divination purposes involves opening the book at random and interpreting the first verse which meets the eye, to guide or predict future action or fate. The activity was often called 'dipping', and was typically carried out on the morning of NEW YEAR'S Day:

Opening the Bible on [New Year's Day] is a practice still in use in some parts of Somerset, and much credit is attached to it. It is usually set about with some solemnity before breakfast. The Holy Book is laid on the table unopened, and the parties who wish to consult it open it in succession. They are not allowed to choose any particular part of the book, but must open it at random. In whatever portion of the sacred volume this may happen to be, the inquirer is to place his finger on any chapter contained in the two open pages, but without perusing its contents. This part of Scripture is then read aloud, and commented on by the people assembled, and from it they form their conclusions as to the happiness or misery that will ensue during the coming year.   Somerset Poole (1877)

Dipping could also be done at other times – at the start of a journey or important enterprise, or in times of perplexity or doubt. Reported instances are all from nineteenth-century England, but there is no reason to think it was a strictly English custom, nor that it did not exist before and after that time.

Somerset Poole (1877) 9. **Oxfordshire** N&Q 2S:12 (1861) 303. **East Anglia** Forby (1830) 400–1. **Suffolk** N&Q 1S:4 (1851) 48. **Northamptonshire** Sternberg (1851) 171. **Yorkshire** Nicholson (1890) 85.

Bible and key divination

Two traditional divinatory procedures have a formality and complexity which distinguishes them from all others – the SIEVE AND SHEARS and the Bible and key. Both were widely practised and implicitly trusted, but the latter was much more common, in that its paraphernalia were easier to come by in a domestic setting. The Bible and key could be used for answering any question, but its two main purposes were to find STOLEN or lost property and for LOVE DIVINATION.

Many old people when they have lost anything, and suspect it to be stolen, take the fore-door key of their dwelling, and, in order to find out the thief, tie this key to the Bible, placing it very carefully on the eighteenth verse of the fiftieth psalm. Two persons must then hold up the book by the bow of the key, and first repeat the name of the suspected thief, and then the verse from the psalm. If the Bible moves, the suspected person is considered guilty; if it does not move, innocent. Mary Colling tells me she has very gravely seen this done, as an infallible test of finding out the truth.   Devon Bray (1838)

Most informants named a particular passage for the key to rest on, which was also recited, but there is no overall agreement on which one, and those chosen sometimes seem only tangentially relevant to the subject in question. Psalm 50:18, mentioned above, contains the words 'When thou sawest a thief, then thou consentedest with him, and hast been partaker with adulterers', which at least starts on the right lines. Ruth 4:4 is another verse recommended for the recovery of stolen goods: 'And I thought to advertise thee, saying buy it before the inhabitants and before the elders of my people. If thou wilt redeem it, redeem it; but if thou wilt not redeem it, then tell me that I may know, for there is none to redeem it beside thee'.

For love divination, Ruth 1:16 was the favourite piece: 'And Ruth said, Intreat me not to leave thee, or to return from following after thee, for whither thou goest, I will go; and where thou lodgest, I will lodge'. This appears to be relevant, if one ignores its original context, as Ruth is here talking to her mother-in-law rather than to her lover. Another popular passage was the Song of Solomon 8:6–7, which certainly seems to the point: 'Set me a seal upon thine heart, as a seal upon thine arm; for love is strong as death; jealousy is cruel as the grave; the coals thereof are coals of fire which hath a most vehement flame. Many waters cannot quench love, neither can the floods drown it, if a man would give all the substance of his house for love, it would utterly be contemned'.

The earlier references are all concerned with discovering thieves. The first is Mannyng's *Handlyng Synne* (1303), which talks of 'men turning the psalter', and Reginald Scot gives a good sceptical description in his *Discoverie of Witchcraft*, with the added details of written names:

Popish priests . . . do practice with a Psalter and a key fastened upon the 49 psalm, to discover a thief. And when the names of the suspected persons are orderlie put into the pipe of the key, at the reading of these words of the psalm . . . the book will wag, and fall out of the fingers of them that hold it, and he whose name remaineth in the key must be the thief. [Scot says the 49th Psalm, but he presumably means the 50th – 'When thou sawest a thief'.]   Scot (1584)

The practice is recorded many times in the sixteenth and seventeenth centuries. It is clear that procedures such as the sieve and shears and the Bible and key were of limited value as objective enquiries to find an unknown miscreant, but were an excellent way of confirming the suspicions already held by the grieved parties or their agents, precisely because they were open to manipulation, conscious or otherwise. Suspicions thus confirmed were sometimes correct anyway. It was also important for the culprits to believe in the efficacy of the ceremony, as they could often be persuaded to return stolen goods merely with the threat of having the key turned against them. It is obvious, however, that this system only operates effectively if criminal and victim live in the same community.

The Bible and key for the discovery of thieves continued to be used well into the late nineteenth century, but from about the 1830s reports of the love divination version gradually become the norm, and by the twentieth century it was the only one in use. There is also a gradual diminution in the degree of seriousness with which the procedure was treated, and in later years it was little more than a party game, although the use of the Bible still gave it some gravity:

[Fishing captain aged 63] *I don't remember when I first heard of this but I recall that it was often brought up in parties before I was twenty . . . Some cousin would say with a laugh, 'Let's see if you young courting couples are going to come together' (i.e. marry). Then a big key would be brought and all but its loop put into the Bible at the passage Ruth I 16. The Bible was then lashed up with twine to hold all firmly. Then my sweetheart and I had to put the tips of our right forefinger under the loop and so hold the Bible suspended between us, whilst we recited the passage in unison, repeating it after the cousin. This is the passage, I know it by heart, it is what Ruth said: 'Entreat me not to leave thee, or to return from following after thee; for whither thou goest, I will go; and where thou lodgest, I will lodge; thy people shall be my people, and thy God my God; where thou diest, will I die, and there will I be buried; the lord do so to me, and more also, if ought but death part thee and me'. Nobody was laughing while this was done. I think because the words are so beautiful and solemn. Whether it was nerves, or what, I don't know, but my sweetheart and I could never complete the passage before the Book seemed to slew and drop off. Yet we've been happily married forty-six years. Other people could succeed, but not we two.*

Devon *Devonshire Assoc.* (1952)

A serious limitation of procedures that involve naming names is the limited extent of their reach. While this may be quite acceptable for quasi-legal uses, few maids would willingly accept a system which condemned them to marrying only those they already knew, with no prospect of improvement. Other versions were therefore developed, such as announcing letters of the alphabet, and thereby hoping to reveal the lover's initials:

When I was [young], *right silly, I used to do these things with friends, girls together. I must have been about sixteen. The girl I worked beside, she used a Bible; this Bible was opened at a certain place and a big door key was put in, and string tied round. You each put a finger below the key and you said letters. It was supposed to move at a certain letter; it moved, but I don't know whether the other person was helping it move or not.*   Mull Bennett (1992)

Another use of the Bible and key was to identify and counter witchcraft:

For the removal of spells, the method is different; perhaps it was at one time a form of divination, used for the discovery of supposed witches, who had put on the spells. The key should be laid on two crossed sticks, one of 'witty' (mountain ash) and one of yew, both held potent against witchcraft. These are placed on the verses in the Bible beginning 'put on the whole armour' (Ephesians 6:13–15). These verses are to be read aloud nine times, and at each repetition a little tear is made in a piece of white paper. To break the spell, the paper is to be folded up, and sewn in the clothing of the person thought to be bewitched, without his or her knowledge.   Herefordshire Leather (1912)

See also CLERGYMEN: HEALING/DIVINING.

England Henderson (1866) 198; *Folk-Lore Jnl* 2 (1883) 156–7; Sussex Latham (1878) 31. **Hampshire** *The Times* (24 Jan. 1867) 9. **Devon** Bray (1838) 294; *Devonshire Assoc.* 17 (1885) 125; Hewett (1892) 29; Hewett (1900) 24; *Devonshire Assoc.* 84 (1952) 298–9, 300. **Cornwall** Couch (1871) 156. **Berkshire** Salmon (1902) 422–3; [1952] Opie & Tatem, 24. **Surrey** N&Q 1S:1 (1850) 413. **Oxfordshire** *Folk-Lore* 24 (1913) 80. **Gloucestershire** [1551] Thomas (1971) 254–5. **Herefordshire** Leather (1912) 65–6. **East Anglia** Forby (1830) 398–9. **Suffolk** Glyde (1866) 176; *Folk-Lore* 35 (1924) 352. **Norfolk** [c.1870s] Haggard (1935) 19–20; Fulcher Collection (c.1894). **Lincolnshire** Peacock (1877) 23; Swaby (1891) 90; Heanley (1902) 20. **Shropshire** *Folk-Lore Jnl* 1 (1883) 333. **Yorkshire** Blakeborough (1898) 128–9; Morris (1911) 228–9. **Lancashire** [c.1836] Cowper (1899) 318; N&Q 1S:2 (1850) 5. **Wales** Trevelyan (1909) 236; Davies (1911) 13–14. **Cardiganshire/Glamorgan** Jones (1930) 138. **Radnorshire**, Francis Kilvert, *Diary* (1 Feb. 1871). **Scotland** Henderson (1866) 195–6. **Western Scotland** Napier (1879) 106–7. **Ayrshire** [1963] Opie & Tatem, 24. **Mull** Bennett (1992) 91. **Shetland** [1846] Black (1903) 159. **N. Ireland** Foster (1951) 55. **Unlocated** Hone, *Year Book* (1832) 126–8. General Mannyng, *Handlyng Synne* (1303) lines 1092 (Fr.), 354 (Eng.); Scot (1584) Bk 16, Ch. 5; *Athenian Mercury* (1692) 3:22; Henderson (1866) 198. **Literary** Thomas Hardy, *Far from the Madding Crowd* (1874) Ch. 13.

bier-right

An ordeal in which a person, accused of murder, was required to approach the corpse and clear

himself on oath. Based on the idea that the victim's corpse will bleed when approached by the murderer.

See also CORPSE: BLEEDING.

birds: at window

A bird appearing at a window was widely interpreted as an ill omen, and if there was a sick person in the household it was taken as evidence that they would soon die:

Birds pecking at a window announce a death. The coincidences I have known in respect of this are certainly so remarkable as almost to justify the superstition. I was in a house, where at daybreak a large number of pigeons settled themselves along bedroom window ledges, making great pecking and noise, and awakening the inmates. About two hours later it was announced that the master of the house had died about the time referred to.   Berkshire Lowsley (1888)

The bird pecking on the window was the worst, but even birds simply alighting on the sill, or fluttering against the pane, was enough to unnerve people:

Of portents of death there are many . . . the hovering of birds round the house, or their resting on the window-sill, or flapping against the pane.
Co. Durham Leighton (1910)

Any bird acting in this way was an ill omen, but many people particularly feared robins in this context (*see* ROBINS: AT WINDOW for references).

Southern England Jefferies (1879) 152. **Sussex** *Sussex County Mag.* 13 (1939) 56–7. **Dorset** Udal (1922) 180. **Devon** Hewett (1900) 56. **Cornwall** *Folk-Lore Jnl* 5 (1887) 217; *Old Cornwall* 2 (1931–6) 39. **Berkshire** Lowsley (1888) 25; *Berks. Arch. Soc.* 1 (1889–91) 86. **Oxfordshire** [1880s] Thompson (1943) 319–20. **Gloucestershire** *Folk-Lore* 13 (1902) 172; *Folk-Lore* 34 (1923) 156. **Herefordshire** [c.1895] *Folk-Lore* 39 (1928) 392. **Worcestershire** *Folk-Lore* 20 (1909) 344. **East Anglia** Varden (1885) 116–17. **Shropshire** Burne (1883) 227. **England** Addy (1895) 68. **Northern England** Henderson (1866) 33. **Westmorland/Lancashire** [c.1939] *Folk-Lore* 64 (1953) 293. **Cumberland** Penfold (1907) 58. **Co. Durham** Leighton (1910) 51. **Glamorgan** Phillips (1925) 598. **Roxburghshire** Bennett (1992) 178. **Pembrokeshire** *Folk-Lore* 39 (1928) 173.

birds: dead

A handful of sources report a belief that finding a dead bird, or having one drop from the sky before you, is a bad omen:

birds

Birds feature widely in British superstitions, both in their own right and as adjuncts to other beliefs. One must be careful to dispose of any HAIR very carefully, because if birds get it they will weave it into their nests and you will suffer headaches. BIRD DROPPINGS are lucky when they fall on you, but BIRDS' EGGS are unlucky in the house. A wild bird in the house, or tapping at the window, means a death will follow soon, and any unusual behaviour exhibited by birds was ominous, especially if it appeared to single out a particular person:

When trouble is about to visit you a bird will come sighing or 'tweedling' about you so as to give you warning . . . When a man is in trouble a bird will always haunt him. He will see that bird wherever he goes. Yorkshire Addy (1895)

Similar worries were caused if they seemed to focus on one house:

In our district birds often give omens; A flock of birds flying over a house is an ill omen, unless indeed the birds are rooks, which are lucky.
Pembrokeshire *Folk-Lore* (1928)

People were particularly suspicious of large black or white birds. White birds often feature in death omen traditions which adhere to particular families. Edith Olivier, the Wiltshire author, provides an example which is more effective for its matter-of-fact tone:

Although Edith did not call herself 'psychic', inexplicable things did happen to her from time to time. On 16 August 1911, whilst returning from a picnic with the Wilton choirboys in a horse brake she saw two enormous white birds with very long wings pass overhead and fly north-west over the Hurdcott water-meadows. She had never seen such birds before and wondered whether they might be albatrosses. She forgot all about them when she arrived home and heard that the Bishop of Salisbury had just died. It was not until a day or two later that she suddenly recalled the story of the Bishop's birds told to her by Miss

Moberly, whose father had once been the Bishop of Salisbury. Wiltshire Middelboe (1989)

Particular species have their own traditions – but unlike most animal-based superstitions, there are numerous good luck as well as bad luck omens. Some birds were protected from harm – ROBINS, WRENS (some of the time), SWALLOWS, martins – while others, like the unfortunate YELLOWHAMMER, were killed on sight. Some were dreaded – OWLS hooting after dark, single MAGPIES – others, such as CUCKOOS, were welcomed if the circumstances were right.

The catalogue of other beliefs is almost endless, and a few examples must stand for all:

Unlucky if birds of the same name as the owner of a property (e.g. heron, finch, etc.) settle at that property. Kent Igglesden (c.1932)

Speedwell is called 'birds-eyes' . . . If you pluck birds-eyes, the birds will come and pluck out your eyes when you are asleep. Even if the windows are shut? Oh yes, they'd break the glass and get in. Essex *Monthly Packet* (1862)

To counteract the evil of seeing birds of ill omen – One should repeat seven times the following:

Clean birds by sevens, unclean birds by twos
The dove in the heavens, is the bird which I
    choose.

Devon Hewett (1900)

On falling in with a nest for the first time that year, if there be only one egg in it, or if there be an odd egg in it, that egg should be broken.
Highland Scotland Campbell (1900)

A flight of birds to the right of you is a good omen.
Wales Trevelyan (1909)

Kent Igglesden (c.1932) 77, 79. Devon Hewett (1900) 76; Devonshire Assoc. 64 (1932) 156. Essex *Monthly Packet* 24 (1862) 434–7. Wiltshire Middelboe (1989) 71. Norfolk Fulcher Collection (c.1894). Shropshire Burne (1883) 227. Yorkshire Addy (1895) 62, 67–8, 116. Wales Trevelyan (1909) 324–5. Pembrokeshire *Folk-Lore* 39 (1928) 173. Highland Scotland Campbell (1900) 237. Unlocated *Gent. Mag.* (1822) 311; N&Q 6S:12 (1885) 489.

[My] aunt thought it unlucky to find a dead bird on the path leading to the house.
Yorkshire *Folk-Lore* (1909)

Essex [1957] Opie & Tatem, 25. Yorkshire *Folk-Lore* 20 (1909) 79. Dumfriesshire [1957] Opie & Tatem, 25. Literary R. Lehmann, *Swan in the Evening* (1967) Pt 2, Ch. 5.

birds: droppings

Two somewhat contradictory superstitions feature bird droppings, or more precisely their effect when humans are on the receiving end. Despite the understandable annoyance of being hit by such a thing, it is often regarded as lucky:

I was on my way to an important meeting in London, and my shoulder was suddenly covered in bird's mess. My colleague, helping me to clear it off, remarked, 'I think it's meant to be lucky when that happens'.

London Steve Roud Collection (1992)

This notion has been current since at least the 1870s:

Sitting on the box of a coach the other day, in North Yorkshire, a youth who sat by me called my attention to certain droppings on his knee, just inflicted on him by a passing bird. 'It's a pity this isn't Easter Day,' said he, 'for we say in Cleveland that if a bird drops on you on Easter Day you'll be lucky all the year after'.

Yorkshire N&Q (1878)

It must be said that counting such an accident as lucky seems somewhat perverse, and even contrary to the way most superstitions seem to function, though the luck is perhaps some sort of compensation for one of life's little problems. On the other hand, birds dropping on you was formerly quoted as one of the traditional punishments for not wearing new CLOTHES at EASTER or WHITSUN:

On this day [Maundy Thursday] many rustics returning from Tombland fair may be observed to carry new hats, not on their heads, but in boxes, etc. They are worn for the first time on Easter Day; and by so doing, the bearer is secured from any birds dropping its 'card' upon him during the ensuing year. Indeed, it is very unlucky not to wear some new article of clothing on Easter Day.

Norfolk N&Q (1857)

Neither belief can be shown to be very old – 1878 for the lucky droppings, and 1857 for the birds' revenge, but while the latter has apparently sunk without trace, the former is still being quoted into the twenty-first century.

Lucky droppings: Somerset [1923] Opie & Tatem, 142. Surrey [1953 and 1988] Opie & Tatem, 142. London Steve Roud Collection, 1992. Yorkshire N&Q 5S:10 (1878) 287; [1964] Opie & Tatem, 142. Co. Tyrone *Lore & Language* 1:7 (1972) 11. Guernsey De Garis (1975) 137. Literary D. H. Lawrence, *The White Peacock* (1911) Pt 3, Ch. 1.
New clothes: Worcestershire *Folk-Lore* 26 (1915) 97. Norfolk N&Q 2S:4 (1857) 432. [1920s] Wigby (1976) 69. Shropshire Burne (1883) 217–18. Yorkshire N&Q 5S:10 (1878) 287; Nicholson (1890) 132. Lancashire Harland & Wilkinson (1873) 219; N&Q 5S:11 (1879) 54, 236. Co. Durham Leighton (1910) 57. Northumberland Bosanquet (1929) 79. Mid-Wales Davies (1911) 74. Anglesey N&Q 5S:11 (1879) 54, 236.

birds' eggs

Considering the widespread rural practice of 'birds-nesting' – which involved boys destroying every nest and egg they could find (with the exception of a few protected species such as ROBINS and SWALLOWS), and the equally popular pastime for both boys and adult naturalists to amass collections of eggs, it is odd to find a superstition that it was unlucky to bring birds' eggs into the house:

but, regarding those birds' eggs, we have a very foolish superstition here; the boys may take them unrestrained, but their mothers so dislike their being kept in the house, that they usually break them; their presence may be tolerated for a few days, but by the ensuing Sunday are frequently destroyed, under the idea that they bring bad luck, or prevent the coming of good fortune.

Gloucestershire Knapp (1830)

It was particularly dangerous when someone was sick:

At the same period [sixty years ago] it was deemed unlucky to have strings of birds' eggs in a house, especially in case of sickness. I can well remember my brothers and myself, our father being seriously ill, being compelled by our maiden aunt to remove our birds' eggs from the house, and hang them up in the garden.

Buckinghamshire N&Q (1890)

Although not commonly reported, references are widely enough spread to confirm its general existence, at least in England from the 1830s onwards, and, thanks to the collecting of Peter and Iona Opie, into the 1950s.

Sussex Latham (1878) 10. Cornwall [1890s] *Old Cornwall* 1:12 (1930) 4. Kent N&Q 4S:4 (1869) 114. Buckinghamshire [c.1830s] N&Q 7S:10 (1890) 235. Gloucestershire Knapp (1830) 224–5. Northamptonshire Sternberg (1851) 172; [1953] Opie & Tatem, 27. Lancashire N&Q 4S:5 (1870) 370. Unlocated Hone, *Year Book* (1832) 127.

birds: in house

A wild bird entering a house was a death omen to many people:

If a bird flies into your house, a death will follow within three days. I remember I had got the kitchen door open when I was cooking the dinner and this bird flew in the back door. I nearly went mad trying to get it out and in three days my

sister died suddenly, that was in 1953, so that
proved it was true.   Lincolnshire [1953] Sutton

Some sources specifically mention birds in the
chimney – again as a death omen. It is not clear,
however, whether the chimney itself was
significant or whether this was simply the way
the bird got into the room. As with several other
bird omens, the ROBIN was singled out as particularly unlucky in this context.

The fear of birds in the house normally
concerned only wild birds, but some took the
idea further and eschewed even caged birds,
while others even refused to have representations
of birds on china, wallpaper, and so on.

When I had a hardware shop I would never stock
cups, saucers, plates, dishes with a picture of a
bird on them as I knew I wouldn't be able to sell
them.   Yorkshire [1973] Opie & Tatem

Cornwall *Folk-Lore Jnl* 5 (1887) 217. **Sussex** *Sussex County*
Mag. 13 (1939) 56–7. **Dorset** Udal (1922) 180. **Essex** *Folk-*
Lore 64 (1953) 293. **East Anglia** Varden (1885) 116–17.
Norfolk [*c.1870s*] Haggard (1935) 18. **Lincolnshire** Sutton
(1992) 142. **Gloucestershire** *Folk-Lore* 13 (1902) 172.
Yorkshire *Folk-Lore* 21 (1910) 225; [1964] Opie & Tatem,
26; [1973] Opie & Tatem, 26. **Westmorland/Lancashire**
Folk-Lore 64 (1953) 293. **Lancashire** Corbridge (1964)
156–60. **Wales** Howells (1831) 65–6. **Monmouthshire**
[1954] Opie & Tatem, 26. **Western Scotland** Napier
(1879) 114. **Co. Offaly** N&Q 4S:11 (1873) 275. **Unlocated**
N&Q 1S:2 (1850) 435. **General** Browne *Pseudodoxia*
Epidemica (1646) Bk 1, Ch. 4.
Chimneys: **Devon** [*c.1915*] Lakeham (1982) 46.
Cornwall [1870s] Hughes (1934) Ch. 10.
Northamptonshire N&Q 1S:3 (1851) 4. **Shropshire**
[1811] N&Q 9S:8 (1901) 202–3. **Northern England**
[*c.1816*] Henderson (1866) 33. **Highland Scotland**
Polson (1926) 129. **General** Gaule (1652) 181.

birth

see BABIES.

birthday cakes

The ubiquitous current custom of presenting a
cake adorned with burning candles to a person
celebrating a birthday is so common as to
normally excite little comment, although it
appears to be a relatively recent importation. The
key elements today are that the number of candles
represents the age of the person whose birthday
is being marked, and that he or she must blow
them out (in one breath), and make a silent wish.
The exact time of introduction into Britain is not
clear, but three contributors to *Notes and Queries*
in 1901–2 describe it as a common German
custom, for example:

An English girl staying at a pension in Hanover,
where I also was a visitor some weeks since,
announced one morning that on the following
Thursday she would be eighteen years old. When
the day came our hostess presented her at break-
fast with a large sponge-cake, in which eighteen
lighted candles of various colours were stuck. This,
she said, is a common custom in Germany, but she
could not say how it originated or what was the
precise meaning of the candles, except that they
showed the person's age.   Germany N&Q (1901)

In the ensuing correspondence no one
mentions the practice being known in Britain,
although one claims it to be common in
America. The German custom differed from the
modern British form in that it had a larger
candle in the middle, called the *Lebenslicht*
(Light of Life), and it was this which the recipient should blow out – it being unlucky if
anyone else did so. Nevertheless, at least by the
time of the First World War, the custom had
reached Britain, and had already attained the
form in which we would recognize it today.
Diana Holman-Hunt, describing a birthday
about 1918, recorded:

'Oh what a lovely cake!' . . . 'You're welcome, miss,
I hope it eats well,' said Mrs. Hopkins . . . 'Aren't
the candles pretty?' asked Tilly. 'You must blow
them out together. When you cut the cake, you
have a wish.' 'I wish to play the gramophone,' I
said. 'Oh you mustn't tell or it won't come true,'
said Hannah, nervously stirring her tea.
                       Sussex? Holman-Hunt (1960)

Sussex? Holman-Hunt (1960) 19–20. **Germany** N&Q
9S:8 (1901) 344–5.

birth hour

With the exception of serious astrologers, few
would nowadays see any significance in the time
of day they were born, but a few beliefs have been
reported on the subject, and one superstition
concerning the 'chime hours' was apparently
quite widespread, at least in the nineteenth
century. Persons born during the 'chime hours'
are particularly sensitive to the supernatural –
they can see ghosts and spirits, and have other
'uncanny' gifts. Some say they are also immune
to the evil designs of witches.

A boy in this village once told the schoolmistress
very proudly that he had been born in the
'Chinese Hours' . . . His mother had meant to tell
him that his birth had fallen during the 'Chimes
hours'; accordingly he was gifted with second

sight, and could discern happenings hidden from the sight of lesser mortals.   **Suffolk** Evans (1965)

There is no agreed definition of the term 'chime hours', or how close to the hour one has to be born to qualify. Most sources list the hours of three, six, nine, and twelve, presumably on the strength of clocks which struck the quarters, but some name four, eight, and twelve. Of these, midnight is considered far and away the most powerful, and anyone born on the stroke of midnight is held to be particularly gifted. But to be even more 'psychic', midnight on certain key days, such as Christmas Eve, was required.

The earliest reference, and probably the best known, is the passage with which Dickens begins *David Copperfield*, but his hero's fate is complicated by the fact that the birthday was a FRIDAY, a generally unlucky day:

I record that I was born (as I have been informed and believe) on a Friday, at twelve o'clock at night. It was remarked that the clock began to strike, and I began to cry, simultaneously. In consideration of the day and hour of my birth, it was declared by the nurse, and by some sage women in the neighbourhood . . . first, that I was destined to be unlucky in life; and, secondly, that I was privileged to see ghosts and spirits.

Dickens, *David Copperfield* (1849)

There are a few indications of other beliefs, none of which seem to have been reported very often. Melton (1620), for example, commented, 'That if a man be born in the day time, he shall be unfortunate' and 250 years later,

An old inhabitant of Torrington lately stated to a friend of mine that 'children born by daylight never see ghosts'.   **Devon** *Devonshire Assoc.* (1877)

Few other examples have come to light.

Kent N&Q 3S:1 (1862) 223. **Devon** *Devonshire Assoc.* 9 (1877) 91. **Somerset** N&Q 1S:7 (1853) 152. **East Anglia** Varden (1885) 106. **Suffolk** *Folk-Lore* 35 (1924) 349; Evans (1965) 216. **Norfolk** Dew (1898) 77–81; N&Q 12S:1 (1916) 329. **Lincolnshire** *Folk-Lore* 10 (1899) 115. **England** Addy (1895) 119. **Lancashire** Harland & Wilkinson (1882) 105. **Co. Durham** Leighton (1910) 46. **Highland Scotland** Polson (1926) 4. **Unlocated** Melton (1620); N&Q 153 (1927) 154. **Literary** Charles Dickens, *David Copperfield* (1849) Ch. 1.

birthmarks and prenatal impressions

Birthmarks and other unusual physical characteristics of a new baby were explained by reference to the belief that strong influences on a pregnant woman could have a lasting effect. This influence could be any strong emotion, usually fear, or it could simply be the sight of something unusual or repellent. Birthmarks would usually take on the shape of whatever caused the emotion, but sometimes the influence could be much more profound:

Just before she was born, her father had some ferrets. He was nearly caught with them one day, and he ran home thinking he was followed, and threw the ferret into his wife's lap, telling her to hide it under her apron; but she was frightened, and fell right down on the floor, and the ferret ran away. Soon after, she had this little girl born, with red eyes, as red as flames, and white hair, as white as snow. She is married now and gets a lot of money by going about to fairs.

Essex [*c*.1830] Burnett (1975)

It was thus everybody's duty to ensure that pregnant women were protected from danger:

[26 June 1754, suffering from dropsy] Indeed so ghastly was my countenance, that timorous women with child had abstained from my house, for fear of the ill consequences of looking at me.

Fielding, *Journal of a Voyage to Lisbon* (1755)

An added danger was that if a pregnant woman's cravings or fancies were not satisfied, these too could mark the baby. Again, this was taken so much for granted that everyone around an expectant mother would be careful not to be the unwitting cause of a baby being marked:

It were a recognised part o' the daily round to go in and out of your neighbours two or three times every day. When a woman were expecting the neighbours 'ould take it on 'em to be interested and helpful. When the woman in question went in to see her neighbour, the neighbour 'ould say, 'If you see anything you want on my table yew take it, an' welcome', such store they set by having anything you fancied when you were carrying a baby.   **Huntingdonshire** [*c*.1890] Marshall

A well-known way to remove birthmarks was for the mother to lick it every day:

To cure them she, or some other woman should lick them all over with fasting spittle as soon as possible after birth, and go on doing it for periods which vary in different districts. A friend of mine was born with such a mark, and her mother told me she had cured it in this way. Certainly the treatment was successful, for no trace of the blemish now remains. This happened fifty years ago but the belief exists today also. About eighteen months ago in Berkshire I met three quite young and well-educated women who had done the same for their babies, and with equal success. I may say that not one of these women had heard of the traditional power of spittle, they had merely tried a well-known folk cure, and it had worked.

Berkshire *Folk-Lore* (1955)

Fasting SPITTLE was recommended for a wide range of other ailments. There were also more drastic remedies:

Having been born with marks of fruit on my face, the medical men considered that they were caused by aneurism, and required an operation which must have left me scarred for life . . . Our old nurse, Effie, had arrived at a different conclusion. She was convinced of the truth of the popular belief that a dead man's hand laid upon my cheek and brow would effectually remove the marks . . . An old man at last did die in one of the nearest cottages. I must have been taken there asleep, as no child would have forgotten it, had she been carried awake to the bed of a dead man and seen and felt his cold hand placed on her face; and I was old enough to have remembered it, for I have the most distinct recollection of being constantly stopped in our walks by the widow, who always examined my cheek in order to ascertain the state of her husband's body in the grave – as the marks, as she told my nurse, would certainly fade away as he turned into dust . . . Whatever the cause of the cure, the red marks faded away as I grew older, and in time disappeared.

Scotland *Reminiscences of Charlotte, Lady Wake* (1909)

The notion of maternal impression is found all over the world, and has been documented in virtually all ages. A well-known case is attributed to the Greek physician Hippocrates (*c.*460–*c.*370), in which he reputedly saved the honour of a princess who had borne a black child and was thus under sentence of death for adultery. He attributed the fact to the painting of a Negro which was hung in her rooms and was therefore in her sight throughout her pregnancy, and thus proved her innocence. Indeed, the biblical Jacob was operating on the same principle when he set up striped wooden rods before his flocks to increase the proportion of striped and speckled animals (Genesis 31:31–9).

The idea is still not completely exploded. In January 2002 an 86-year-old man phoned the present author at Croydon Library, asking about First World War Zeppelin raids. He said that as a child he had had very shaky hands, and his handwriting had been atrocious. His mother always said that this was because she was frightened by the Zeppelin raid when she was expecting him, and he believed her.

See also HARELIPS.

Hampshire [1778] White (1788) 200. Devon *Devonshire Assoc.* 67 (1935) 139; *Devonshire Assoc.* 120 (1988) 227. Berkshire *Folk-Lore* 66 (1955) 322–3. Surrey [2002] Steve Roud Collection. London [1754] Henry Fielding, *Journal of a Voyage to Lisbon* (1755); *Folk-Lore* 51 (1940) 116–7. Essex [*c.*1830] Burnett (1975) 57–8. Hertfordshire *Folk-Lore* 51 (1940) 116–7. Herefordshire Leather (1912) 78, 112. Huntingdonshire [*c.*1890] Marshall (1967) 171–2. Norfolk *Folk-Lore* 40 (1929) 122. Lincolnshire N&Q 10S:1 (1904) 431; Sutton (1992) 56, 163. Shropshire Burne (1883) 240–1; *Folk-Lore* 49 (1938) 229. Wales Jones (1930) 195–6. Cardiganshire Jones (1930) 198. Highland Scotland Macbain (1887/88) 253. Scotland *Reminiscences of Charlotte, Lady Wake* (1909) 34–5, quoted *Folk-Lore* 26 (1915) 93–4. N. Ireland Foster (1951) 64. Co. Tyrone *Lore & Language* 1:7 (1972) 9. Guernsey De Garis (1975) 6. General [1743] Thomas Bernard, *Comforts of Old Age* (1820) 105, quoted N&Q 10S:1 (1904) 430–1; Dr Quincy, *Lexicon Physico-Medicum* (1794) quoted N&Q 10S:1 (1904) 363; *Folk-Lore* 68 (1957) 414–15. General and International: Gould & Pyle (1900) 81–6; N&Q 10S:1 (1904) 362–3, 430–1, 493–4.

blackberries

The most widespread belief about blackberries is that the Devil ruins them on a certain date each year (*see below*). A few other miscellaneous beliefs have been noted, including several medicinal uses. The only one that seems to have been at all widely known is that horses, cats, and babies are often not well when the blackberries are ripe:

Baby's not well – it's blackberry time.

Devon *Devonshire Assoc.* (1959)

Cats are never very well at blackberry time. Horses also unwell at this time. A widespread belief.

Devon *Devonshire Assoc.* (1953)

There are dames in the country who, to cure the whooping cough, pass the afflicted child three times before breakfast under a blackberry bush, both ends of which grow into the ground. [compare BRAMBLES].

Unlocated Hone, *Year Book* (1832)

When people gather bilberries, blackberries, or other fruit, it is usual in Derbyshire to throw the first bilberry, or other fruit gathered, over one's head, and to say, 'Pray God send me good luck today'. Derbyshire Addy (1895)

Bramble-vinegar – that is vinegar made of blackberries: 'There's nothing afore bramble vinegar for a cough'. Lincolnshire Cole (1886)

Blackberry leaves for dysentery – Pick a double

handful. Put in a jug and steep in same way as elder and mint. **Devon** *Devonshire Assoc.* (1947)

Devon *Devonshire Assoc.* 79 (1947) 47; *Devonshire Assoc.* 85 (1953) 217; *Devonshire Assoc.* 91 (1959) 201. **Lincolnshire** Cole (1886) 20. **Derbyshire** Addy (1895) 141. **Unlocated** Hone, *Year Book* (1832) 126–8.

blackberries: Devil

An extremely widespread tradition concerning blackberries is that after a certain date each year they are at best no longer palatable and at worst poisonous. The date varies from place to place, but is often Michaelmas (29 September), 1, 10, or 11 of October. The latter dates would be Michaelmas day, OLD STYLE. Blackberries do indeed deteriorate rapidly late in the season, but the traditional explanation is that on that day the Devil goes round and spits on them, or wags his tail over them, puts his foot on them, and so on:

Bummel-kite – a bramble berry . . . I have often been admonished, by the 'good old folks', never to eat these berries after Michaelmas day; because the arch-fiend – 'huge in length, and floating many a rood' – was sure to pass his 'cloven foot' over them at that time. **Northern England** Brockett (1829)

Occasionally it was said that fairies or witches did the damage, but in the vast majority of cases it was believed to have been done by the Devil himself. Children in Galloway in the 1820s were threatened that if they failed to obey the injunction, 'worms will eat their ingangs' (Galloway Mactaggart (1824)).

This tradition has been noted from most parts of the British Isles, and is still heard, but does not seem to have been common before the early nineteenth century.

Kent *The Times* (12 Nov. 1973) 19. **Sussex** Latham (1878) 14. **Devon** *Devonshire Assoc.* 103 (1971) 268; *Devonshire Assoc.* 104 (1972) 267. **Cornwall** *The Times* (16 Nov. 1973) 21. **Essex** [1985] Opie & Tatem, 29. **Buckinghamshire** [1913] *Folk-Lore* 43 (1932) 108. **Oxfordshire** [1890s] Thompson (1945) 488. **Herefordshire** Leather (1912) 21. **Worcestershire** [1900] *Folk-Lore* 20 (1909) 343. **Warwickshire** Poole (1875) 85. **Northamptonshire** [1825] Clare (1993) 140. **Norfolk** *Folk-Lore* 37 (1926) 369. **Lincolnshire** Rudkin (1936) 40; [c.1940s] Sutton (1992) 128. **Staffordshire** Poole (1875) 85. **England** Addy (1895) 63. **Northern England** Brockett (1829) 53. **Yorkshire** Robinson (1855) 22. **Co. Durham** Brockie (1886) 115. Leighton (1910) 58. **Welsh Gypsies** Jarman (1991) 186. **Scotland** *Trans. Gaelic Soc. Inverness* 32 (1924) 37. **Galloway** Mactaggart (1824) 167. **Dumfriesshire** *Folk-Lore* 16 (1905) 454. **Ireland** Wilde (1852) 14. **Co. Wexford** [1938] Ó Muirithe & Nuttall (1999) 165. **Literary** D. H. Lawrence, *The White Peacock* (1911) Ch. 6.

blacksmiths

One of the regular nineteenth-century traditions concerning blacksmiths was that they would not work on Good Friday or, as some said, during the Christmas period, because of legends about the making of nails for the crucifixion (*see* GOOD FRIDAY: BLACKSMITHS). The other area of traditional belief in which blacksmiths regularly feature is that they were often resorted to for cures of certain ailments. The water in which the smith cooled hot metal had a curative reputation:

Another one for warts used forge water. When the blacksmith was shoeing horses he'd take the red-hot horseshoe out of the fire with pincers and he'd dip it into a barrel of water to cool it. The barrel would be there for maybe a year with the blacksmith using it every day. If you had warts on your hand you dipped it into the forge water. **Irish Travellers** [1940s] Joyce

The same water was also reputedly effective against consumption and CHILBLAINS. The blacksmith played a more direct role in cures for rickets and general weakness in children by passing his tools over the child, or even pretending to work on it:

Heart-grown, or Bewitched – a term applied to a sickly puny child, who does not grow. Such a child must be brought to a blacksmith of the seventh generation; this must be done before sunrise. The child is laid naked on the anvil, the smith raises the sledge hammer as if he were going to strike hot iron, but lets it come gently on the child's body. This is done three times, and the child always thrives after this. **Northumberland** Bigge (1860–62)

This procedure was already known in the seventeenth century, as recorded in Ralph Thoresby's *Diary* in 1691, and was reported regularly into the twentieth century.

See also HORSESHOES.

Gloucestershire *Folk-Lore* 22 (1911) 238. **Warwickshire** Bloom (c.1930) 28. **Bedfordshire** Marsom (1950) 184. **England** Addy (1895) 101. **Northern England** Henderson (1866) 151. **Yorkshire** R. Thoresby *Diary* (1 Apr. 1691). **Northumberland** Bigge (1860–62) 90. **Wales** Jones (1930) 143. **Banffshire** Gregor (1874) 269–70. **Galloway** Mactaggart (1824) 278. **Orkney** Brand (1703) 62–3. **Ireland** *Athenaeum* (17 Oct. 1846) 1068; Hickey (1938) 269; Logan (1981) 68. **Co. Longford** *Béaloideas* 6 (1936) 266. **Irish Travellers** [1940s] Joyce (1985) 16. **Isle of Man** Gill (1934) 36.

blade-bone divination

A form of divination, using the shoulder-blade of a sheep, or occasionally another animal, thoroughly cleaned, to predict future events.

In Lewis divination by means of the blade-bone of a sheep was practised in the following manner. The shoulder-blade of a black sheep was procured by the inquirer into future events, and with this he went to some reputed seer, who held the bone lengthwise before him and in the direction of the greatest length of the island. In this position the seer began to read the bone from some marks that he saw in it, and then oracularly declared what events to individuals or families were to happen. It is not very far distant that there were a host of believers in this method of prophecy.
                              Isle of Lewis *Folk-Lore* (1895)

There are two relatively distinct phases in the recorded history of blade-bone divination. The earliest sources speak of a general prognostication, of a serious nature, as summarized above. But from about the 1830s, a less serious LOVE DIVINATION procedure, which also used a bladebone, began to be reported, and this is treated separately (*see below*).

The earliest mention of the blade-bone procedure occurs in 1188, with a detailed description by Gerald of Wales. He writes of the Flemings, who had emigrated to Wales in the time of Henry I:

A strange habit of these Flemings is that they boil the right shoulder-blades of rams, but not roast them, strip off all the meat and, by examining them, foretell the future and reveal the secrets of events long past. Using these shoulder-blades they have the extraordinary power of being able to divine what is happening far away at this very moment. By looking carefully at the little indents and protuberances, they prophesy with complete confidence periods of peace and outbreaks of war, murders and conflagrations, the infidelities of married people and the welfare of the reigning king, especially his life and death.
        Wales Gerald of Wales, *Journey Through Wales* (1188)

Gerald continues with several examples of the bone's use. Other early writers also mention the procedure. Chaucer, for example, knew of it, as in the *Parson's Tale* (*c.*1395) he wrote of conjuration 'in the shoulder-bone of a sheep'. But it is difficult to sort out the literary from the popular traditions. It is clear that many of the earlier writers were quoting from Gerald of Wales, and

their testimony cannot therefore be taken as independent evidence of the existence of the custom. Caxton (1480), for example, cites the Flemings of West Wales, and Drayton (1622) refers to the 'Dutch made-English'. Nevertheless, from Sinclair's description in 1685 onwards, we find the divination described as prevalent in the Scottish Highlands, a new literary tradition is set up, and again the earlier writers are quoted by the later ones. Further sources need to be identified, and a close examination of the wording used, before the original can be sorted from the derivative.

Wales Gerald of Wales, *Journey Through Wales* (1188) Bk 1, Ch. 11; William Caxton, *Description of Britain* (1480); William Camden, *Britannia* (1586); Michael Drayton, *Poly-Olbion* 5 (1622) lines 263–8. **Scotland** Robert Kirk, *The Secret Common-Wealth* (1691/1976) Para 13; Pennant (1771) 118. *Folk-Lore Record* 1 (1878) 176–9. **Highland Scotland** G. Sinclair, *Satans Invisible World* (1685) 142; T. Insulanus, *Treatise on the Second Sight* (1763) 77; N&Q 3S:2 (1862) 484; Campbell (1900) 263–6. **Argyleshire** *Folk-Lore* 6 (1895) 157. **Morayshire** Shaw (1775) 249. **Hebrides** Pennant (1774) 280. **Isle of Lewis** *Folk-Lore* 6 (1895) 167. **Literary** Chaucer, *Parson's Tale* (*c.*1395) line 603. **Ireland** F. M. Misson, *Memoirs and Observations on his Travels through England* (1719) 152.

blade-bone: love divination

The ancient art of divination using the shoulderblade bone of an animal (*see above*) lasted from the twelfth century to the nineteenth, and was concerned with predicting general themes, including the life and death of the animal's owner. In contrast, from the mid nineteenth century onwards, a similar bone was used in a LOVE DIVINATION procedure designed to reveal a future spouse or to persuade a reluctant lover. The basic core varies little from version to version, involving piercing the bone with a knife, but other details vary. There was commonly a verbal CHARM and, as is usual in love divination, the bone was usually placed under the pillow. A simple version:

To dream of your sweetheart – take the bladebone of a rabbit and stick nine pins in it, and then put it under your pillow, and you will be sure to see the object of your affections.
                              Yorkshire N&Q (1852)

A more complex procedure:

To know if one's present fiancé will be true – Procure from a butcher a bladebone of a shoulder of lamb divested of all the meat. Borrow a penknife from an unmarried man, but do not say for what purpose it is required. Take a yard of white ribbon, and having tied it to the bone, hang it as high in your bedroom chimney as you can conveniently reach. On going to bed pierce the bone with the knife once, for nine successive nights, in a different place each night, repeat while doing so, the following:

> *'Tis not this bone I means to stick*
> *But my lover's heart I means to prick*
> *Wishing him neither rest nor sleep*
> *Till unto me he comes to speak*

At the end of the nine days your sweetheart will ask you to bind a wounded finger, or to attend to a cut which he will have met with during the time the charm was being used.

Devon Hewett (1900)

In contrast to the long history of the complex divination, the love version has not been found before the mid nineteenth century. Opie and Tatem identify the earliest printing in the *Everlasting Fortune-Teller* (1839), which already includes the charm rhyme, and may well be its original source.

Devon Hewett (1900) 69. **Norfolk** Varden (1885) 99; Fulcher Collection (*c*.1895). **Shropshire** N&Q 2S:12 (1861) 501. **Yorkshire** N&Q 1S:6 (1852) 312; Henderson (1866) 140–1; Addy (1895) 74. **Wales** Trevelyan (1909) 236–7; Davies (1911) 9. **Pembrokeshire** Sikes (1880) 303. **Ireland** N&Q 5S:7 (1877) 86. **Co. Limerick** *Folk-Lore* 19 (1908) 323. **Unlocated** Halliwell (1849) 224–5.

---

bleeding

Practical and herbal treatments for bleeding abound, including, for example, the application of puffballs, TOBACCO, turpentine, dry soil, comfrey, plantain, primrose leaves, and heliotrope, but the most commonly recommended traditional remedy was a spider's web:

When a knife slipped and a finger was cut, a clean spider's web was taken from the wall. It was easy enough to find a web in one of the corners of pantry or passage, for spiders have charmed lives. They were carried outside and not killed. The delicate film, like a grey bit of Valenciennes lace, was wrapped round the wound, and a white rag was bound over it. The bleeding was stanched, and quite soon the wound was healed.

Derbyshire [1890s] Uttley

Others said the blacker and thicker the web, the better it served. This remedy was clearly well known to the seventeenth-century dramatists, as both Shakespeare and Ben Jonson bear witness:

I shall desire you of more acquaintance, good Master Cobweb; if I cut my finger I shall make bold with you.

Shakespeare *A Midsummer Night's Dream* (*c*.1594)

Sweepes down no cobwebs here, But sells 'hem for cut-fingers. Jonson, *The Staple of Newes* (1624)

On the magical side, the most common remedy was to seek out a charmer who had the skill to staunch blood with a touch and the recitation of the requisite words (*see below*), but other methods were also recorded.

Remedy for staunching blood – Take a fine full-grown toad; kill him, then take three bricks and keep in a very hot oven until they are red hot. Take one out and place the toad upon it; when the brick is cold remove the toad; then take the other bricks and place the toad on them successively until he be reduced to powder. Then take the toad-ashes and sew them up carefully in a silk bag one-and-a-half inch square. When one is bleeding place this bag on the heart of the sufferer, and it will instantly stay the bleeding of the nose or any wound. Devon Hewett (1900)

A very similar procedure was described in the book *Most Excellent and Approved Remedies* (1652). In other cases, inanimate objects were believed to have power. A piece in the journal *Folk-Lore* for 1912 reports a Cambridgeshire woman who owned a 'bloodstone', which worked simply by proximity to the wound, as did a wooden cup in Cardiganshire, reputedly made from a piece of the true Cross (*Cassell's Saturday Jnl* (1893)).

See also NOSEBLEEDS.

Kent [1930s] Kent (1976) 21–2. **Devon** Henderson (1866) 136; *Devonshire Assoc.* 12 (1880) 101–2, 111; Hewett (1900) 81; [1931] *Devonshire Assoc.* 79 (1947) 47; *Devonshire Assoc.* 83 (1951) 74. **Cornwall** *Folk-Lore Jnl* 5 (1887) 203. **Wiltshire** Aubrey, *Miscellanies* (1696/1857) 139. **West Midlands** W. Midlands Fed. W. I.s (1996) 73–4. **Cambridgeshire** *Folk-Lore* 23 (1912) 349–50 **East Anglia** Hatfield (1994) 32–5. **Lincolnshire** Rudkin (1936) 26. **England** Addy (1895) 89. **Derbyshire** [1890s] Uttley (1946) 112. **Yorkshire** Nicholson (1890) 140. **Cardiganshire** *Cassell's Saturday Jnl* (1893). **N. Ireland** Foster (1951) 62. **Co. Carlow** *Béaloideas* 1 (1928) 327. **Co. Cavan** Maloney (1972) 71. **Guernsey** De Garis (1975) 140. **General** Lupton (1631) Bk 3, para. 84; *Most Excellent and Approved Remedies* (1652) quoted N&Q 1S:2 (1850) 510; *Salmon's London Dispensatory* (1676) quoted N&Q 11S:2 (1910) 194. **Literary** Shakespeare, *A Midsummer Night's Dream* (*c*.1594) 3:1; Ben Jonson, *The Staple of Newes* (1624) 2:4.

bleeding: charms

Verbal CHARMS were used in a wide range of medical situations, but if the number of recorded examples is any indication, bleeding was one of those problems which were thought particularly susceptible to this type of magical treatment. Certain people had a local reputation for skill as charmers, and at least a part of their skill resided in knowledge of the correct form of words to use. These words varied considerably, but there are identifiable groups within the corpus of traditional charms. The most common relates how Jesus was baptized in the river Jordan and commanded the water to stand:

Jesus was born in Bethlem
Baptized in the river Jordan
The water was wild and wood
But he was just and good
God spake, and the water stood
And so shall now thy blood.

Worcestershire Halliwell (1849)

Others refer to Jesus on the Cross, being pierced by a soldier's lance or by the crown of thorns. The third group conjures up a more obscure image of three virgins with knives, which echoes the 'three angels' often featured in charms for BURNS:

Three virgins came over Jordan's land
Each with a bloody knife in her hand
Stem, blood, stem – Letherly stand
Bloody nose (or mouth) in God's name mend.

Orkney N&Q (1854)

A fourth group involved the charmer simply reciting a piece from the Bible. The particular passage is not always identified (charmers, after all, needed to keep it a secret), but where it is named it is invariably Ezekiel 16:6:

And when I passed by thee and saw thee polluted in thine own blood, I said unto thee when thou wast in thy blood, Live; yea, I said unto thee when thou wast in thy blood, Live.

As with all charms taken from the Bible, the original context is immaterial, and the words need only be superficially relevant. In many of the recorded examples, it is clear that the charmers themselves were believed to have healing powers above and beyond knowledge of the requisite words. Some could even cure at some distance from the accident:

Old Ann had the power of 'stopping blood' – a most valuable accomplishment. When a school chum of mine got his foot cut badly with a broken bottle and the thing continued to bleed and bleed – well, the lad who was with him at the time – Johnnie C. – just ran as hard as his legs could carry him to Ann's cottage. Ann immediately 'did and said something' and assured the messenger that the bleeding had now stopped – which, as a matter of fact, it had!

Ross-shire [1890s] MacDonald

While it would have been safe enough to entrust minor cuts and nosebleeds to the ministrations of the charmer, for more serious wounds it must have taken great faith on the part of the sufferer to rely on such methods. It is impossible to calculate how often scenes like the following were enacted:

A farm labourer named Thos. Ryder, residing at Cornwood, a village in Devonshire, was sharpening his scythe on Tuesday, when he cut his wrist, and severed two of the arteries. His friends, instead of securing medical assistance, sent for a man and his wife who have a local reputation as 'charmers', and these people endeavoured to stop the flow of blood by the ceremony of 'charming'. Ryder, seeing how fruitless these efforts were, begged to be taken to the hospital at Plymouth, some eight miles off . . . Ryder died of loss of blood before he got there.

Devon *Daily Telegraph* (7 July 1887)

Devon: *Monthly Packet* 28 (1864) 443–7; Henderson (1866) 136–7; *Devonshire Assoc.* 17 (1885) 122; *Daily Telegraph* (7 July 1887) quoted in N&Q 7S:4 (1887) 67; Hewett (1892) 28; *Devonshire Assoc.* 32 (1900) 92; *Folk-Lore* 11 (1900) 217; Hewett (1900) 68; Crossing (1911) 143–4; *Devonshire Assoc.* 63 (1931) 130; *Devonshire Assoc.* 85 (1953) 218–19; *Devonshire Assoc.* 91 (1959) 200. **Devon/Cornwall** N&Q 1S:3 (1851) 259. **Cornwall** N&Q 2S:4 (1857) 25; Hunt (1865) 214; Couch (1871) 149; *Folk-Lore Jnl* 5 (1887) 203; *Jnl Royal Inst. Cornwall* 20 (1915) 126–7. **London** Samuel Pepys, *Diary* (31 Dec. 1664). **Gloucestershire** *Folk-Lore* 13 (1902) 173. **Herefordshire** [1804] Leather (1912) 73–4. **Worcestershire** Halliwell (1849) 210. **East Anglia** Forby (1830) 413; Varden (1885) 101. **Suffolk** Glyde (1866) 173. **Shropshire** [early 19th cent.] *Folk-Lore* 6 (1895) 202–4; Burne (1883) 183. **Lancashire** [1736–51] Cowper (1897) 371–2; N&Q 1S:3 (1851) 56; Harland & Wilkinson (1882) 77. **Cumberland** Dickinson (1875) 105. **Breconshire** *Folk-Lore* 24 (1913) 507. **Highland Scotland** Macbain (1887/88) 258. **Ross-shire** [1890s] MacDonald (1936) 58. **Orkney** Brand (1703) 61; N&Q 1S:10 (1854) 220–1; **Ireland** N&Q 7S:3 (1887) 414; Hickey (1938) 268. **Co. Carlow** *Béaloideas* 1 (1928) 327. **Co. Longford** *Béaloideas* 6 (1936) 257. **Isle of Man** Harrison (1869) 183; *Folk-Lore* 2 (1891) 294. **Guernsey** [*c.*1800] MacCulloch MS (1864) 395. **Unlocated** [15th cent.] N&Q 7S:4 (1887) 56; [1610] *Gent. Mag.* (1835) 31; *Athenian Mercury* 7 (10 May 1692); *Folk-Lore* 53 (1942) 126. **General** Scot (1584) Bk 12, Ch. 18; Black (1883) 79–80, 96–7.

blinked

A dialect word found in Scotland and Ireland, meaning 'bewitched' or 'overlooked':

Cow's milk is said to be blinked when it does not produce butter, in consequence of some supposed charm having been worked – a counter-charm is required to bring it right.

Co. Antrim Patterson (1880)

Not long ago in the Co. Donegal there was a famous blinker called 'Mag'. Nothing could pass her; everything she looked on came to grief, and in some cases at least, nearly instantaneously.

Co. Donegal *Folk-Lore Jnl* (1886)

Another meaning of the word, also found in England from the early seventeenth century, refers to milk, beer, wine, or other beverages which have turned sour, and it is likely that this latter usage reflects the idea that the drinks have been turned sour by someone with the EVIL EYE or other ill-wishing powers.

Co. Antrim Patterson (1880) 9. **Co. Donegal** *Folk-Lore Jnl* 4 (1886) 255–6. See also references in *Oxford English Dictionary; English Dialect Dictionary*.

blue beads

Folklorists in the 1920s and 1930s reported a contemporary custom of wearing necklaces of blue beads to guard against particular ailments such as bronchitis and colds:

A very common amulet is a string of special blue beads worn as a preventive of chest ailments both in London and in the country, and never under any circumstances removed. My wife showed such a string to a charwoman and asked if she knew anything about it, to which the woman replied 'No', after the suspicious fashion of those who think that you are 'getting at them' in some way. But later in the day she said, 'My Gladys wears a string like that you showed me', and, when questioned further – 'Do you ever take it off, say, when you wash her?' – replied very promptly, 'Oh no! then she'd catch cold'.

London Wright (1928)

Several of these reports concerned working-class Londoners, but others made it clear that the belief was also found in many other parts of England, always in the same basic form. Edward LOVETT, who made a particular study of the custom in London in 1914, reported that the necklaces were imported from Austria and were readily available, for a few pence, in local shops in 'lower class' districts, but were totally unknown in 'better areas'. He met numerous people who wore them, especially children.

The earliest reference so far found, quoted by Opie and Tatem, takes the record back to a few years before Lovett's investigations, with a report from a medical inspector in Wimbledon in 1909, who commented that 30 per cent of the children she inspected wore such a necklace. It is difficult to see how such a widespread custom escaped notice if it existed before this time, and we must therefore assume, provisionally, that it does not go back much beyond the turn of the twentieth century. Attempts to show that the blue beads are a direct descendant of much older notions of blue as a protective colour are not convincing. The colour does not appear often in recorded beliefs, except in isolated cases. Even G. F. Black, who was not normally averse to finding mystical connections, had to admit that 'it is remarkable that the mention of [the colour] in connection with folk-medicine is scanty' ((1883) 112). Nevertheless, Henderson prints an extract from the Scottish border country from about 1816, which could be potentially relevant if intermediate examples could be found:

Women who live on the banks of the Ale and Teviot have a singular custom of wearing round their necks blue woollen threads or small cords, till they wean their children. They do this for the purpose of averting ephemeral fevers.

Scottish Borders [*c*.1816] Henderson

The end of the custom is similarly mysterious, as reports cease in the 1930s, and no more is said of blue beads.

Cornwall *Old Cornwall* 1:9 (1929) 41. **Surrey** *The Hospital* (25 Dec. 1909) 351. **London** [1914] Lovett (1925) 81–4; *Folk-Lore* 37 (1926) 366; *Word-Lore* 3 (1928) 109; Wright (1928) 71. **Northumberland** [1914] Lovett (1925) 81–4. **Warwickshire** N&Q 160 (1931) 206. **Cambridgeshire** [1936] Porter (1969) 75. **Norfolk** *Folk-Lore* 40 (1929) 118. **Wales** [1914] Lovett (1925) 81–4. **Scottish Borders** [*c*.1816] Henderson (1866) 12–13.

blue clue/clew

see LOVE DIVINATION: BALL OF THREAD.

bones

see LUCKY BONES.

born feet first

In Scotland, people who were 'born feet first' were believed to have the power to cure various ailments, including SPRAINS:

Those who were born with their feet first possessed great power to heal all kinds of sprains, lumbago, and rheumatism either by rubbing the part or by trampling on it. The greater virtue lay in the feet. Those who came into the world in this fashion often exercised their power to their own profit.   Banffshire Gregor (1874)

This belief has only been reported a handful of times. One other reference prescribes a different meaning:

Child born feet first will later meet with accident and become lame, unless laurel leaves rubbed on its legs for half an hour within 4 hours of birth.
Unlocated Igglesden (c.1932)

Compare POSTHUMOUS CHILDREN; SEVENTH SONS.

Highland Scotland Macbain (1887/88) 252, 258.
Banffshire Gregor (1874) 271. Unlocated Igglesden (c.1932) 140.

boy's love

see SOUTHERNWOOD.

brambles

Several cures involve a sufferer being passed, or crawling through, the hole made in a split tree or a holed stone (*see* ASH TREES; STONES: HOLED), and a similar principle of TRANSFER-ENCE appears to be involved in a widespread custom using a bramble which is rooted at both ends, forming an arch. The operation was recommended most commonly for WHOOPING COUGH, but also for a variety of other ailments, including boils and RHEUMATISM:

The late Dr. Budd of North Tawton, my mother told me, once had a child brought to him with sore eyes. The said child was scratched all over, and he asked why. 'Well, us tried to cure 'un. Us drawed 'un dree times through a brimble bush backwards, and us got the old duck to quack dree times into the mouth of 'un, but that didn't cure 'un, so us brought 'un to 'ee.'
Devon Devonshire Assoc. (1956)

In some reports, if each end of the bramble was rooted in a different person's land, it was doubly effective. The operation was usually repeated a set number of times – three or nine being favourite – while the Lord's Prayer or other verbal charm was recited. The arched-bramble cure was already known in the early seventeenth century, and the earliest reference (Markham, 1607) recommends it for a horse which has been paralysed by a SHREW, although it is difficult to see how one could draw a horse through the bramble as instructed there. Long before that, however, the double-rooted bramble was believed to have curative powers. In the eleventh-century Saxon manuscript published in Cockayne's *Leechdoms*, a double-rooted bramble is said to alleviate dysentery if chopped up and drunk in milk.

A completely different set of traditions linked the bramble with love and marriage.

When thorns or brambles catch or cling to a girl's dress, they say a lover is coming.
Wales Trevelyan (1909)

The girls also look out secretly for a briar-thorn which has grown over into the ground, forming a loop. In the evening, late, this must be crept through three times in the devil's name, the briar cut and placed under the pillow without speaking a word, and the dream to follow will be of the future husband.   Co. Leitrim *Folk-Lore* (1894)

Cures: **Southern England** Jefferies (1879) 160. **Sussex** Latham (1878) 42–3; *Sussex County Mag.* 5 (1931) 122. **Devon** *Athenaeum* (1846) 1018; *Devonshire Assoc.* 9 (1877) 96; Crossing (1911) 144; *Devonshire Assoc.* 88 (1956) 257. **Cornwall** N&Q 1S:12 (1855) 37; Hunt (1865) 212, 215; Couch (1871) 166. **Herefordshire** [c.1895] *Folk-Lore* 39 (1928) 389; Leather (1912) 82. **Worcestershire** N&Q 1S:7 (1853) 104; Salisbury (1893) 69. **Warwickshire** N&Q 1S:7 (1853) 104. **Suffolk** *Gent. Mag.* (1867) 728–41. **Norfolk** Dew (1898) 77–81; *Folk-Lore* 40 (1929) 117; Haggard (1935) 16; *East Anglian Mag.* (Aug. 1935) 94. **Staffordshire** N&Q 1S:7 (1853) 104; Poole (1875) 81–2. **Shropshire** Burne (1883) 204–5. **Gwent** *Folk-Lore* 48 (1937) 53–4. **Co. Wexford** [1938] Ó Muirithe & Nuttall (1999) 97. **Unlocated** Hone, *Year Book* (1832) 127. **General** [c.1040] Cockayne (1865) 291–3; Gervase Markham, *Cavelarice, or The English Horseman* (1607) Ch. 7; Aubrey, *Remaines* (1686/1972) 261; Black (1883) 70. **Literary** Michael Drayton, *Nimphidia* (1627) lines 401–4; Charles Kingsley, *Alton Locke* (1850) Ch. 21.
Love and marriage: **Herefordshire** Leather (1912) 114. **Derbyshire** [1890s] Uttley (1946) 127. **Wales** Trevelyan (1909) 270. **Co. Leitrim** *Folk-Lore* 5 (1894) 195–7.

bread

Most of the staple domestic items like bread, FIRE, CANDLES, and so on, have dual roles which straddle the practical and symbolic worlds, making them the ideal breeding ground for superstition. Thus bread can be simply a basic food or can be seen as a symbol of food as an essential for life, and by extension a symbol of plenty. The way the bread behaves while being made can therefore take on an importance beyond the family diet: it can be blessed and used in official religious ritual, it can be presented to a newborn baby to ensure that it never lacks food, and it can play an essential part in WHOOPING COUGH cures. Bread baked on GOOD FRIDAY will take on the holy aspect of the day as it will never grow mouldy, it will be invaluable in cures for certain ailments, and so on.

The main bread superstitions have their own entries below, but a host of others have been reported from time to time, including the following:

Never sing while you are baking [compare SINGING]. Highland Scotland Macbain (1887/88)

If you bake bread when there is a corpse in the house it will not rise in the pancheon.
England Addy (1895)

It is unlucky to find a corn of wheat in a loaf of bread. England Addy (1895)

It is lucky to find three whole grains in a baked loaf. Wales Trevelyan (1909)

Two should never go to the oven if two are baking [compare TWO TOGETHER].
Suffolk *Folk-Lore* (1924)

If the bread you make rises well, your sweetheart is smiling on you.
Norfolk Fulcher Collection (c.1895)

Bread hung in a bag around a baby's neck will keep away the fairies. Welsh Gypsies Jarman (1991)

Omens are drawn from the appearance of the bread after baking. If four loaves (two on the Welsh border) adhere together on being taken out of the oven, it is a sign of a wedding; if five, of a funeral. Shropshire Burne (1883)

To cure a tongue-tied child, people took two loaves that had stuck together in the baking, and broke them loose over the sufferer's head.
Wales Trevelyan (1909)

A sick woman who had a fleshy growth over her eye was advised to steal some bread and cheese and, if possible to crumble them into the coffin of the first person who died in the village; but if she found it impossible to do this unobserved, she must then go to the first funeral and as the priest pronounced the words 'dust to dust', she was to perform the same ceremony; still unobserved, and she believed that as the stolen bread and cheese decayed, so would her growth vanish away.
Devon *Monthly Packet* (1864)

[Death token] *To take three loaves of bread from the oven at once is a sign of death within the year; or dropping a loaf in taking it from the oven.*
Herefordshire Leather (1912)

It is said that if a maid kneading up bread rub her 'doughy' hand over a boy's face, he will never have any whiskers. This belief seems to have been general in the county, for it is still known at Withington, and at Blakemere, in quite another district. Herefordshire Leather (1912)

Devon *Monthly Packet* 28 (1864) 443–7. Herefordshire Leather (1912) 118. Norfolk Fulcher Collection (c.1895). Suffolk *Folk-Lore* 35 (1924) 351. Shropshire Burne (1883) 276. England Addy (1895) 94, 122. Wales Trevelyan (1909) 316, 324. Welsh Gypsies Jarman (1991) 186. Highland Scotland Macbain (1887/88) 262.

bread: breaking

If a loaf broke apart, either in baking or when being sliced, it was considered an unlucky omen, but the exact meaning varied from person to person:

If bread, when being baked, breaks frequently a hungry stranger will come and eat it. Many cakes breaking are a sign of misfortune, by which the housewife is warned that 'something is making for her'. Highland Scotland Campbell (1900)

A funeral is foretold if, when dough is being shaped into loaves, a loaf splits across the top.
Herefordshire [c.1895] *Folk-Lore*

This is not one of the major bread superstitions, and, given the propensity for believers to worry about the meaning of any accidental occurrences in the domestic sphere, of fairly obvious symbolism. So far only noted from the 1860s onwards.

Berkshire *Folk-Lore* 5 (1894) 338. Herefordshire [c.1895] *Folk-Lore* 39 (1928) 391. Shropshire *The Times* (23 Jan. 1879); Burne (1883) 276. Northern England Henderson

(1866) 89. **Highland Scotland** Campbell (1900) 233.
Staffordshire Hackwood (1924) 149. **Caithness**
Sutherland (1937) 104.

bread: burning

It was regarded as particularly unlucky, even evil,
to burn bread. Even crumbs were included in the
prohibition:

*If a child threw crumbs in the fire the old-fashioned
mother lifted a warning finger and said 'If you
throw crumbs in the fire you are feeding the
devil'.*   Unlocated N&Q (1901)

This superstition is sometimes explained in
terms of thrift – don't waste food under any
circumstances – but an underlying factor is
probably the view which is reflected in other
beliefs, that bread is symbolic of food in general
and should therefore be treated with more
respect. This belief was more widespread than
the handful of references suggests, and although
first noted in the 1880s it was essentially a twentieth-century superstition, still being quoted in
the 1980s.

Devon *Devonshire Assoc.* 74 (1942) 103. **Wiltshire** [1923]
Opie & Tatem, 38. **Lincolnshire** Sutton (1992) 127.
Yorkshire [1982] Opie & Tatem, 38. **Scotland** *Folk-Lore*
45 (1934) 162. **Northern Scotland** *Folk-Lore Jnl* 7 (1889)
196. **Unlocated** N&Q 9S:8 (1901) 383.

bread: cutting

A handful of references reveal a strong belief, in
some households, that bread should be broken
rather than cut, following the biblical example:

*When quite a child, I was told that the reason
why it was more proper to break bread rather
than cut or bite it was because bread was broken
by Christ on the occasion of the Last Supper. At
some of the 'love feasts' as held in mid-Derbyshire
fifty years ago, the bread which was handed
round was first broken into small portions; in
some other parts of the county it was cut in small
cubes.*   Derbyshire N&Q (1902)

Some compromised by stipulating that only the
first loaf of a batch need be broken. On a more
prosaic level, a range of conditions covered how
one sliced a loaf, with fairly obvious symbolism:

[A domestic servant from Torquay, about
twenty years old] *said, when cutting bread and
butter, 'There! I haven't cut the loaf straight! I
shall have a crooked [= unfortunate] life!'*
                              Devon *Devonshire Assoc.* (1880)

*If you cut a loaf evenly, you will be successful and
rich.*   **Wales** Trevelyan (1909)

*Cut the topside of the loaf before you cut the
bottom; you will rise in the world.*
                              Unlocated N&Q (1861)

Breaking bread: **Essex** *Ralph Josselin's Diary* (23 Feb.
1650). **Derbyshire** N&Q 9S:9 (1902) 514. **Co. Durham**
N&Q 5S:6 (1876) 397.
Cutting bread: **Devon** *Devonshire Assoc.* 12 (1880) 111.
Herefordshire Leather (1912) 88. **Norfolk** Fulcher
Collection (c.1895). **England** Addy (1895) 96, 99. **Co.**
Durham N&Q 5S:6 (1876) 397. **Wales** Trevelyan (1909)
324. **Unlocated** Grose (1790) 45; N&Q 2S:12 (1861) 491.

bread: hole in loaf

There are many superstitions about relatively
trivial domestic occurrences or accidents,
including those which befall the family loaf. If a
loaf was found to have a hole in it (a 'hollow
loaf') this was interpreted as a grave or coffin,
and indicated that someone close to the family
would die soon.

*Then Granny cut me a slice of bread and butter
and told me to go to bed. She looked at the loaf
then and saw there was a big hole in the centre
of it. She dropped the knife and said, 'Dear me,
a coffin it is'. She went all white and trembly and
the others looked frightened too. Then they spoke
about the people they knew who were ill and
wondered which one was going to die.*
                              Wales [c.1870] Thomas

As is common with this type of superstition, a
refinement on size has been added:

*Some years ago, an old lady, a native of
Penshurst, Kent, explained to me that a 'very big
hole' in a loaf of bread signified that the owner
would shortly lose by death a near relative; but
that if the hole were but a medium-sized one, the
relative would be a distant one.*
                              Kent N&Q (1909)

This idea is reported widely, at least in England
and Wales, from about the 1870s, but there is no
sign of it before that date. Paradoxically, two
reports claim a very different meaning:

*The notion regarding the hollow loaf which
obtains in Pembrokeshire is precisely the reverse
. . . Down there they say it foretells a birth. More
than that, they say, 'Mrs. Baker is going to have
a child'.*   **Pembrokeshire** N&Q (1909)

Death: **Kent** N&Q 10S:12 (1909) 155. **Devon** *Devonshire
Assoc.* 8 (1876) 57. *Devonshire Assoc.* 12 (1880) 111.
Cornwall *Folk-Lore Jnl* 5 (1887) 216. N&Q 10S:12 (1909)

88. Wiltshire *Wilts. N&Q* 1 (1893–5) 61. Herefordshire *Folk-Lore* 37 (1926) 297. Worcestershire Berkeley & Jenkins (1932) 37. Warwickshire Bloom (*c.*1930) 44. Suffolk *Folk-Lore* 35 (1924) 350. Lincolnshire N&Q 10S:12 (1909) 155. England Addy (1895) 97. Nottinghamshire N&Q 10S:12 (1909) 155. Yorkshire N&Q 10S:12 (1909) 155. Lancashire [*c.*1915] Corbridge (1964) 156–60. Wales [*c.*1870] Thomas (1983) 26–7. Swansea [1955] Opie & Tatem, 38–9. *Pregnancy*: Hampshire [1966] Opie & Tatem, 39. Pembrokeshire N&Q 10S:12 (1909) 155.

bread: last piece

An odd sort of belief, which in some versions sounds more like a social cliché than a superstition:

When you offer someone the last slice of bread-and-butter, or the last cake, on the plate, you say 'Which will you have, a handsome husband or a thousand a year?' and the other person usually says 'A thousand a year, and then I'll get the handsome husband as well'.

Dorset [*c.*1935] Opie & Tatem

Each collected version differs slightly from the others, and such a lack of cohesion over so few references is unusual. Some simply predict a handsome partner or plenty of money, but not both; some say the food must be *offered* and not just *taken*, because in the latter case the taker will die unmarried. There is clearly some common origin just beyond reach of our knowledge, which will explain what this is all about – presumably a piece of Victorian popular culture. The earliest version only dates from the 1870s:

The person who takes the last piece of bread from a plate during any meal is favoured with a double omen; for he or she will either be blessed with a handsome partner, or die unmarried.

Lancashire Harland & Wilkinson (1873)

Rees (2001) reports that it is still being said in the twenty-first century.

Kent [1923] Opie & Tatem, 227. Dorset [*c.*1935] Opie & Tatem, 227. Essex [1964] Opie & Tatem, 227. Lincolnshire Swaby (1891) 89; Rudkin (1936) 18. Staffordshire [1954] Opie & Tatem, 227. Yorkshire *Folk-Lore* 43 (1932) 254. Lancashire Harland & Wilkinson (1873) 230. Northumberland Bosanquet (1929) 76. Argyllshire *Folk-Lore* 21 (1910) 89. Unlocated Rees (2001) 115–16.

bread: marking with a cross

Marking bread with a cross during the bread-making process was a widely-reported custom, in England at least, throughout the nineteenth and well into the twentieth century:

[From female servant aged forty] *In Shropshire we always make a cross on the flour after putting it to rise for baking, also on the malt in mashing up for brewing. It's to keep it from being bewitched.*   Shropshire N&Q (1875)

If dough (made into a loaf) was placed before the fire to make it rise, a cross was made on it to keep the Devil from sitting on it.

Oxfordshire *Folk-Lore* (1923)

In Yorkshire, this action was called 'Crossing the witches out'. In some reports there were restrictions on what could be used to make the mark – some stipulate a fork, others say the edge of a knife – but there is no consistency and most informants do not give this detail.

It is usually assumed that this tradition is a relic of pre-Reformation days, when making a sign of the cross would have been commonplace when preparing and eating food. This may be so, as the custom certainly existed in the seventeenth century – it is mentioned by both Herrick (1648) and Aubrey (1686). But the only evidence from before the mid seventeenth century is in negative form. For example, in the time of Henry III (1252) bakers throughout Essex and Hereford were forbidden by a royal mandate to mark the bread they sold with the sign of the cross (*Close Rolls*, 249) and the *Book of Common Prayer* of 1549 insisted that the bread used in the rite of Communion should be 'without any manner of print'.

Kent Aubrey *Remaines* (1686; 1972) 245. Somerset/Dorset *N&Q for Somerset & Dorset* 9 (1904–5) 113. Essex/Hereford *Close Rolls of Henry III*, quoted Opie & Tatem, 207. Oxfordshire *Folk-Lore* 34 (1923) 325. Gloucestershire N&Q 5S:5 (1876) 364; Hartland (1895) 52. Worcestershire Salisbury (1893) 72. Northamptonshire Sternberg (1851) 168. Shropshire N&Q 5S:3 (1875) 465; Burne (1883) 278. Staffordshire Hackwood (1924) 149. England Addy (1895) 79. Derbyshire N&Q 10S:9 (1908) 345. Northern England Brand 1 (1813) 131; [1850s] *Denham Tracts* (1895) 45. Yorkshire Carr (1828) 131; [1890s] Greenwood (1977); [1963] Opie & Tatem, 108. Lancashire N&Q 1S:3 (1851) 56; Harland & Wilkinson (1882) 72, 154. Co. Durham Leighton (1910) 45. Scotland Pennant (1771) 94. Literary, Robert Herrick, *Hesperides* (1648) 'Charmes'.

bread: upside down

A loaf of bread turned upside down on the table or in the oven, will bring ill luck, a death in the family, or even a shipwreck:

It is thought unlucky through the North to turn a loaf upside down, after helping oneself from it. Along the coast, they say, that for every loaf so turned a ship will be wrecked.

Northern England Henderson (1866)

If you turn a loaf of bread the wrong way you will turn someone out of the house.

Hampshire N&Q (1890)

This is one of the many English superstitions which suddenly appear in the first half of the nineteenth century, and by the turn of the twentieth are found all over the country. It was still being collected in the 1950s (**Hampshire**, Opie & Tatem), but is unlikely to have lasted much longer than that. The motif of upside down domestic items causing shipwrecks is quite common.

Kent *Folk-Lore* 23 (1912) 354. **Hampshire** N&Q 7S:9 (1890) 486; [1956] Opie & Tatem, 39. **Cornwall** Hunt (1865) 241; *Folk-Lore Jnl* 5 (1887) 190, 216; *Old Cornwall* 2 (1931–6) 40. **East Anglia** Forby (1830) 414; Varden (1885) 116–17. **Shropshire** Burne (1883) 276. **England** Addy (1895) 99. **Northern England** Henderson (1866) 89. **Yorkshire** Robinson (1861) 39; N&Q 10S:12 (1909) 155; *Folk-Lore* 21 (1910) 226. **Co. Durham** Brockie (1886) 214; Leighton (1910) 61. **Northumberland** Bigge (1860–62) 93. **Jersey** *Folk-Lore* 25 (1914) 246.

breakages

see THREE BREAKAGES.

bridges

A few references indicate a small range of superstitions concerning bridges, including two linked beliefs which were more widespread in the mid twentieth century than the number of recorded examples indicate. The first is that it is unlucky to talk while passing under a bridge. Igglesden is the first to mention it:

Bad luck to talk while passing under a railway bridge. Much observed during [First World] *War, especially by Welsh regiments.*

Wales Igglesden (c.1932)

This notion also holds good for railway tunnels, where it was said to be unwise to speak. The other belief is that it is unlucky to pass under a

bridge while a train is passing over it, or, in some cases, to cross over a bridge while a train passes underneath. The widespread nature of this notion was revealed by the research of Iona and Peter Opie in the 1950s, who quote examples from all over England, Wales, and Scotland:

In parts of Wales, I am told that this belief is held so firmly that buses will draw up to the side of the road when they see a train approaching.

Wales *Folk-Lore* (1954)

There are also many traditions about specific bridges which existed in the realms of custom or legend and thus fall outside the scope of this Guide. Some, however, include evidence of superstitious belief. As, for example:

There is . . . a firm belief among local schoolboys that anyone who walks under Copley Railway Bridge, wishes, and utters the name of a poet, will have his wish granted. But even here caution is necessary. On no account should Shakespeare be the chosen poet – 'Or he will shake his spear at you'. And most disheartening of all is the final warning that, 'If your wish doesn't come true in ten years, it never will'.

Yorkshire *Folk-Lore* (1932)

There was also a custom of railway passengers crossing the Forth Bridge tossing coins into the river (*Railway Mag.* (Mar. 1950)), although this may simply be a specific example of the wishing-well complex, by which people seem compelled to throw money into any piece of standing water.

One further extension of legend into superstition combines a belief about a particular bridge with the very widespread notion that WHOOPING COUGH and other respiratory diseases can be cured by breathing particular air (*see also* AIR CURES):

There was, it appears, a popular superstition among Chelsea folk some fifty years ago that seven currents of air met in the middle span of the bridge. A carpenter who is still living vividly remembers being taken by his mother to stand on the bridge on a bitterly cold March day, with his six brothers and sisters, who were all suffering from whooping-cough. It must have been a case of kill or cure; but in this instance the good woman's faith seems to have been justified, for all her seven children got over the whooping-cough and grew up hale and hearty.

London *Cornhill Mag.* (Apr. 1917)

It is clear from these examples that bridges can have an uncanny side to them in the popular imagination, but those beliefs quoted are all very recent, and nothing has been reported before the twentieth century. They show no evidence of any connection with the attributes of bridges usually stressed by popular writers on superstitions, which include religious allegory (souls crossing bridges to the afterlife, etc.), supposed foundation sacrifices, and narratives about the Devil being involved in helping to build them. In the latter, the international motif of the Devil claiming the first living being to cross a bridge, and being cheated out of his reward by the simple expedient of sending an animal over first, is widespread (*see* Aarne-Thompson motif S241.1). This may be seen as analogous to other beliefs concerning FIRSTS (e.g. the first person buried in a new graveyard), but this idea does not seem to have survived in the repertoire of British superstition.

Sussex [1954] Opie & Tatem, 321; Opie (1959) 213. **Hampshire** [1988] Opie & Tatem, 321. **London** *Cornhill Mag.* (Apr. 1917) 469. **Yorkshire** *Folk-Lore* 43 (1932) 255. **Lancashire** [1970s] Steve Roud Collection Sept. 2002. **Cumberland** [1957] Opie & Tatem, 321. **Co. Durham** [*c.*1938] Opie & Tatem, 321. **Wales** Igglesden (*c.*1932) 229–30; *Folk-Lore* 65 (1954) 160. **Monmouthshire** [1954] Opie & Tatem, 321. **Scotland** *Railway Mag.* (Mar. 1950) 150; *Folk-Lore* 65 (1954) 160. **Angus** Opie (1959) 213.

broadsides

Crudely printed single sheets, of various sizes, which were printed and sold cheaply in their millions in both town and country from the sixteenth to nineteenth centuries. Broadsides included a bewildering array of material, including ballads, moral tales, stories of monsters, scandals, last dying speeches of notorious criminals, religious controversies, political and social commentary, and instructions for telling fortunes – in robust, simple language, often embellished with woodcut illustrations. As popular literature, they are often useful evidence for superstitions, and one or two serve as valuable sources in their own right. The song 'Old Women's Sayings', for example, was published by various printers in the nineteenth century, and is a humorous list of current superstitions, which must have helped to keep them in circulation:

The first thing you will see
At the house of rich or poor
To keep the witches out
A horse shoe's o'er the door.
Bellows on the table
Cause a row both day and night
If there's two knives across
You are sure to have a fight.

A mid nineteenth-century tale which existed in several versions warns that fortune-telling may not be as safe and innocent as it is made out to be. *Fortune Telling and its Results* details how a group of girls went to a fortune-teller to ask about future husbands but were frightened out of their wits when a fearsome wraith, or the Devil himself, appeared before them (*see* Hindley (1871) for two versions).

On the other hand, a much-reprinted serious prose piece, under various titles, purporting to be a letter from Jesus Christ, was valued by many cottagers as a charm in itself, hung over the bed to help in childbirth (*see* SAVIOUR'S LETTERS).

See also CHAPBOOKS.

For a sampling of broadside types, see Charles Hindley, *Curiosities of Street Literature* (London: Reeves & Turner, 1871) and Leslie Shepard, *The History of Street Literature* (Newton Abbot: David & Charles, 1973).

brooches

Brooches were often included in the range of items which should not be given without reciprocal payment, however slight, for fear of 'cutting love':

A halfpenny was demanded from a friend giving you a brooch with a pin . . . The penalty for not doing this would be the loss of friendship.
                     Lancashire *Lancashire Lore* (1971) 6

The prohibition covers all things with sharp edges or points. *See* KNIVES: GIFT for full discussion and references.

brooms: across doorway

One of the ways recommended to identify a witch was to lay a broom across the doorway:

Overlooking – Many years ago, in my first curacy in Dorsetshire – on the borders of Wilts. – I went with the vicar one day to see a sick man, and we noticed a broom, or 'besom' lying across the door, so that it was necessary to remove it in order to enter. After conversation on other matters the vicar asked why that besom had been put there in such an unusual way across the door, and then it came out that the woman believed her husband had been 'overlooked', bewitched; that though she did not mind the doctor coming if he liked, yet that no good could be done to the sick man till she had found out the person who had overlooked him. This broom was placed there in the firm belief that if the person who had 'overlooked' her

brooms

Virtually all basic domestic items have had their superstitions, and brooms are no exception. The main ones are treated separately below, but following is a sample of the many minor ones:

If you set the broom in a corner, you will surely have strangers come to the house.

East Anglia Forby (1830)

It is said that if the handle come off the broom when sweeping, the servant will not get her wages. Herefordshire Leather (1912)

It is unlucky to lose a mop or a broom at sea.

Unlocated Jones (1880) and Devon Hewett (1900)

If a girl strides over a besom-handle she will be a mother before she is a wife. If an unmarried woman has a child, people say 'She's jumped o'er

t' besom' or 'She jumped o'er t' besom before she went t' church'. Mothers used to be particularly anxious that their daughters should not stride over a broom, and mischievous boys have been known to leave brooms on door-steps, and such like places, so that girls might accidentally stride over them. In Sheffield, a woman of loose habits is called a 'beesom' or 'besom'.

Yorkshire Addy (1895)

Never step over a broom if you are unmarried. You will bear a bastard child.

Somerset Tongue (1965)

Somerset Tongue (1965) 143. Devon Hewett (1900) 58. Herefordshire Leather (1912) 86. East Anglia Forby (1830) 414. Yorkshire Addy (1895) 102. Unlocated Jones (1880) 117.

husband came by, he or she would be obliged to take it up. 'Why,' said the vicar, 'how absurd; it was the merest chance that I did not take it up, instead of kicking it away'. 'Ah, sir,' said the woman, 'but you didn't take it up'. So the woman had the best of the argument.

Dorset Eddrup (1885)

Compare BROOMS: THROWN.

Western England Lea (1903) 1024. Dorset Eddrup (1885) 334. Lancashire Harland & Wilkinson (1873) 235.

brooms: in May

It was thought extremely unlucky to buy a broom in May, or to use one bought in that month:

Buy a broom in the month of May
Sweep one of the house away.

Devon Crossing (1911)

The idea was still going strong in the second half of the twentieth century:

The belief is surprisingly strong at the present time. The local representative of Kleen-e-ze . . . assures me that May is always his worst month. Many folk refuse flatly to buy a Kleen-e-ze brush on account of this superstition, and regard his innocent scepticism as little short of blasphemy. Occasionally he can circumvent the prejudice by pointing out that the order will not be delivered for three weeks, so that brushes arriving in May will have been ordered in April, or if the order is

given in May, the deadly brushes will not arrive till June. Even so, many people will not risk any part of the deal in May.

Devon *Devonshire Assoc.* (1954)

Occasionally, the same is said of Christmas. No reason is given for this belief in any of the sources to hand, although the month of MAY is also unlucky in other contexts. There is certainly some confusion between the implement 'broom' and the plant 'broom', and the latter shares the widespread prejudice against being brought into the house with the HAWTHORN. There is no sign of these broom beliefs before the mid nineteenth century.

Sussex Latham (1878) 52; Sussex County Mag. (1933) 210. Sussex County Mag. (1938) 309. Hampshire [1983] Opie & Tatem, 46. Devon Devonshire Assoc. 15 (1883) 107; Hewett (1900) 52; Crossing (1911) 136; Devonshire Assoc. 86 (1954) 297; Devonshire Assoc. 102 (1970) 271. Cornwall Couch (1871) 163. Wiltshire [1923] Opie & Tatem, 46. Herefordshire Leather (1912) 18–19. Suffolk N&Q 1S:2 (1850) 4; Zincke (1887) 179. Yorkshire [1982] Opie & Tatem, 46. Radnorshire [1953] Opie & Tatem, 45. Ireland N&Q 4S:8 (1871) 47. Unlocated N&Q 4S:1 (1868) 550.

brooms: thrown

A handful of references, from Scotland only, reveal a tradition that a broom thrown after a person or animal brought luck and broke any possible ill-wishing. The two contexts quoted are farms and fishing:

A besom was thrown after a new net when it first left the house, and also after the men starting on an expedition.
                            Northeast Scotland *Folk-Lore* (1939)

When an animal was led away to market the besom was thrown on it to ward all harm from witches.   Northeast Scotland Gregor (1881)

Brooms have been connected in the popular mind with witchcraft in many ways, one of which was that to lay a broom across a doorway prevented a witch from entering (*see above*), and this would seem to be related to the throwing motif described here. The motif of throwing for luck is also seen in the more widespread, and apparently much older, custom of throwing an old SHOE.

Northeast Scotland Gregor (1881) 188; *Folk-Lore* 50 (1939) 345. **Aberdeenshire** *Folk-Lore Jnl* 3 (1885) 308. **Banffshire** *Folk-Lore Jnl* 4 (1886) 16. **Galloway** Mactaggart (1824) 210.

bruises

Bruises have traditionally been treated with various plants, including houseleek, Madonna lily, comfrey root, common mallow, and goose grease or lard to make an ointment. Nevertheless, as with most other minor ailments, more magical methods have also been recorded.

To charm a bruise –
Holy chica! Holy chica!
This bruise will get well by-and-bye
Up sun high! Down moon low!

This bruise will be quite well very soon!
In the name of the Father, Son, and Holy Ghost, Amen.   Devon Hewett (1900)

A goodwife in this parish, who treats cuts and bruises very successfully with comfrey poultices is careful to apply red comfrey to a man's hurts and white comfrey to a woman's.
                            Shropshire Burne (1883)

Sussex [*c.*1900] Arthur (1989) 41–2. **Devon** Hewett (1900) 68; *Devonshire Assoc.* 83 (1951) 74. **Lincolnshire** Gutch & Peacock (1908) 119–20. **Norfolk** Randell (1966) 86. **Shropshire** Burne (1883) 190; *Folk-Lore* 6 (1895) 202–4. **Co. Longford** *Béaloideas* 6 (1936) 266. **Jersey** L'Amy (1927) 100. Various plant-based remedies in Vickery (1995) 51.

buckets

Fishermen, and other seafarers, have long had a horror of bad things happening to everyday items which could be seen symbolically as boats – particularly buckets and bowls:

No sailor will set out on a voyage if he finds his earthenware basin turned upside down in the morning when he is about to have breakfast. The boys sometimes turn their basins upside down purposely when they wish to have a day's play.
                            Yorkshire N&Q (1869)

It was also thought to be extremely unlucky to lose a bucket overboard while at sea. The symbolism is quite obvious, but the belief has not been found before the late nineteenth century.

Kent *Kent Messenger* (23 Aug. 1957) quoted Opie & Tatem, 46. **Lincolnshire** Rudkin (1936) 18. **Yorkshire** N&Q 4S:4 (1869) 131. **Co. Durham** Brockie (1886) 209. **Wales** Trevelyan (1909) 2. **General** Jones (1880) 117; N&Q 12S:1 (1916) 154.

burial

see CHURCHYARD.

burns/scalds

In addition to numerous traditional practical and herbal applications for burns, including turpentine, goose dung, baking soda, and buttermilk, and mashed potato, a few magical processes were also recommended. Reported mainly from Ireland was a notion that anyone who licked the underside of a NEWT or LIZARD acquired the ability to cure burns:

Anyone who licks a 'man-creeper' (newt) will ever after have the power of curing burns and scalds by licking them. Such a man's tongue, it appears, becomes incombustible. 'O that's perfectly true,' said a Meath man to me a short time ago. 'I have seen him set his tongue to the red iron. You could hear it hissing like bacon frying on the pan, and yet it wasn't burnt'.
                            Ireland *Folk-Lore* (1908)

Other cures fought fire with fire:

For erysipelas, burns, and inflammations of the eyes, the remedy was to strike fire by means of a stone or iron in 'front of the person'; or the sufferer was recommended to stand before a forge fire and allow the sparks to fall freely upon him.

To stir or blow a fire before the patient, so that the glow overspread his face, was a remedy for the same ailment. Wales Trevelyan (1909)

HOUSELEEK in another context protected a house from catching fire, so it is no surprise to find it used as a burn cure 'beaten up with cream . . . applied to burns to draw the fire out' (Lincolnshire *Folk-Lore* (1909)). Several other remedies for burns have been recorded, but in such scattered instances that it is difficult to ascertain how widely known they were:

In October 1910, a young friend of mine, then in lodgings in Liverpool had the misfortune to burn her hand. Her landlady – who held a post as char-woman in a neighbouring church, and who, as such, received gifts of old church linen – offered to bind up the wound with a piece of an old chalice veil; and she subsequently attributed the quick healing of the burn to the efficacy of her 'holy linen'. Liverpool Wright (1913)

Licking lizards/newts: Hebrides *Folk-Lore* 11 (1900) 448. Ireland *Folk-Lore* 19 (1908) 317; Hickey (1938) 269. Co. Cork [1937] Culloty (1993) 59. Co. Longford *Béaloideas* 6 (1936) 267. Co. Laoighis *Béaloideas* 9 (1939) 33. *Other cures*: Kent N&Q 4S:4 (1869) 507. Sussex [*c*.1900] Arthur (1989) 42. Norfolk [*c*.1920] Wigby (1976) 66; *Folk-Lore* 40 (1929) 118. Lincolnshire *Folk-Lore* 20 (1909) 489. Shropshire Burne (1883) 190. Liverpool Wright (1913) 236. Cumberland Penfold (1907) 56. Wales Trevelyan (1909) 317. Ireland [1730s] Logan (1981) 69; Wilde (1888) 82, 197. Co. Cavan Maloney (1972) 73. Co. Cavan/Co. Leitrim Logan (1965) 52; Logan (1963) 89–90. Unlocated *Folk-Lore* 66 (1955) 327.

---

burns: charms

The two everyday medical problems most commonly reported in the past as susceptible to cure by charming were BLEEDING and burns. It is in the nature of such CHARMS that the word-ing varies from person to person but that the core remains relatively constant, and the major-ity of recorded examples for the treatment of burns are variations on a theme of angels, frost, and fire. Samuel Pepys noted a basic version in his diary in 1664:

There came three angels out of the east;
The one brought fire, the other brought frost –
Out fire; in frost.
In the name of the Father and Son and Holy Ghost. Amen.
London Pepys, *Diary* (31 Dec. 1664)

The fire-and-frost motif, which is particularly apt for burns, has been remarkably long-lasting. It was already present in the earliest known version, recorded in 1568 in the corporation records of Sandwich, Kent. Occasionally there are more major deviations, as, for example, when the Virgin Mary replaces the angels:

A charm for burns – The Virgin Mary burnt her child with a spark of fire; out fire in frost, in the name, etc. Amen Herefordshire [1804] Leather

And there are a few cases where a completely different set of words was used:

Here come I to cure a burnt sore
If the dead knew what the living endure
The burnt sore would burn no more.
Shetland *New Stat. Acct Scotland* (1845)

These charms were thought effective when used by people with acknowledged curative abil-ities, but it is not clear how far it was thought that the words themselves had the power. The only other regularly reported element is that the charmer blows or breathes on the burn.

As with many of the charming cures, those for burns are reported from most parts of the British Isles, but there is a curious concentration of references in the English West Country. This may be an accident of collection rather than a true reflection of reality, but it would be interesting if further research could be brought to the subject to clarify the situation.

Kent [1568] William Boys, *Collections for an History of Sandwich in Kent* (1792) 690. Sussex Halliwell (1849) 211. Hampshire N&Q 1S:9 (1854) 446. Western England *Athenaeum* (1846) 1018. Devon *Pall Mall Gazette* (23 Nov. 1868); *Devonshire Assoc.* 18 (1886) 103; Hewett (1892) 28; Hewett (1900) 66; *Folk-Lore* 61 (1900) 217; Crossing (1911) 143; *Devonshire Assoc.* 63 (1931) 130; *Devonshire Assoc.* 65 (1933) 126–7; *Devonshire Assoc.* 96 (1964) 98; Lakeham (1982) 43. Devon/Cornwall N&Q 1S:3 (1851) 258. Cornwall N&Q 2S:4 (1857) 25; Hunt (1865) 213; Couch (1871) 149; *Folk-Lore Jnl* 5 (1887) 199–200. London Samuel Pepys, *Diary* (31 Dec. 1664). Gloucestershire *The Times* (31 Dec. 1849) 8. Herefordshire [1804] Leather (1912) 73. Worcestershire Salisbury (1893) 70. Worcestershire/Shropshire *Gent. Mag.* (Nov. 1855) 386. East Anglia Varden (1885) 101. Suffolk *Gent. Mag.* (1867) 728–41; Gurdon (1893) 18; N&Q 8S:3 (1893) 144. Norfolk N&Q 1S:6 (1852) 480. Shropshire [early 19th cent.] *Folk-Lore* 6 (1895) 202–4; Burne (1883) 183. Derbyshire [1890s] Uttley (1946) 119. Lancashire [1736–51] Cowper (1897) 371–2. Scotland Chambers (1842) 37. Shetland *New Stat. Acct. Scotland* (1845) 141. Orkney N&Q 1S:10 (1854) 220–21. Co. Tyrone *Lore & Language* 1:7 (1972) 10. Guernsey MacCulloch MS (1864) 395; Carey (1903) 395.

bus tickets

From the 1940s onwards, at least, children all over Britain keenly inspected the serial number on their bus or tram ticket, and brought several mathematical formulae to bear on it to test their luck and a range of future possibilities. The basic belief was that if the number added up to twenty-one the ticket was lucky and should be carefully saved:

Did you ever, I wonder, tally the numbers on a bus or caur-ticket to feel your heart fair loup on realising that the figures totalled a mystical twinty-wan? . . . Aye, a twenty-one bus or tram ticket was truly good fortune should you have taen a bit notion to someone of the opposite gender. If the serial number added up to the magical total, this itherwise dreich wee scrap of paper became a love-token, nae less, to be passed on, I understand, to the person on whom the affection was focused.

Glasgow [1940s] MacLeay (1990)

But there was more, as reported by Peter Opie:

and presents it to her boy friend. If he, in his turn, keeps it, or if he tears it in half and gives half back to her, it is a sign that he treasures her friendship; if on the other hand, he throws it away he throws away her love. But if the number does not add up to twenty-one as happens, I think, in thirty-five cases out of thirty-six, she divides the total by seven and uses the remainder to tell her fortune with our old friend:

> One for sorrow
> Two for joy
> Three for a letter
> Four for a boy
> Five for silver
> Six for gold
> Seven for a secret never to be told.

England/Scotland *Folk-Lore* (1954)

See MAGPIES for the more usual application of this rhyme.

The Opies reported a wide range of other techniques used by the children on the ticket number – 'If the numbers on the bus ticket add up to thirteen bad luck is forecast for the future', 'if the ticket has the figures 1, 2, 4, or 5 on it it means you are in love', '. . . the number 2158 means that a person will be married at 21, have five children, and earn £8 a week', and so on. It is not clear whether children still carry out these operations. If they do, the custom is certainly not as widespread as it was fifty years ago. Nevertheless, not a few adults still glance at the ticket number,

from force of habit, and feel pleased if it adds up to twenty-one.

England/Scotland *Folk-Lore* 65 (1954) 152–3. Glasgow [1940s] MacLeay (1990) 43, 45. **Numerous examples:** Opie (1959) 329–34; Opie & Tatem, 50.

butterflies

To modern minds it will come as a surprise that something as harmless and attractive as a butterfly could have sufficient negative reputation that several traditions dictated that it should be killed on sight. At the very least people were advised to kill the first one they encountered in the year, for luck:

they always chase and try to kill the first butterfly of the season; and, should they succeed, they will overcome their enemies.

Cornwall *Folk-Lore Jnl* 5 (1887)

The motif of the first sight of a particular species being significant is a commonplace of superstition (see also SNAKES and WASPS) but the meaning for butterflies varies from version to version:

If the first butterfly you see in the year is white, your bread will be white (i.e. good luck), but if brown, bread brown.

Gloucestershire Hartland (1895)

A range of other butterfly superstitions have been noted, almost all of them negative, but none of them have been recorded often enough for us to judge how widespread they were. The picture is further confused by the fact that although some traditions refer to particular types of butterfly, the reports do not give full details:

Some kinds of butterflies were called 'fever flies', and it was asserted that they carried germs of fever under their wings. A number of these seen flying together were carefully watched, and when they entered a house, it was a foretoken of malignant fever and death. Wales Trevelyan (1909)

Among children all coloured butterflies, such as the tortoise-shells, peacocks, fritillaries, etc. were called 'French', and the white ones were called 'English'. It was considered a duty imposed upon them to chase, and, if caught, to kill the 'French', sometimes even to torture them before doing so, while the 'English' butterfly, if caught, was treated kindly, indeed it was generally set free.

Montgomeryshire Hamer (1877)

Others are simply contradictory in all essentials:

To see three white butterflies together is lucky, so my old Grannie used to tell me.
Cambridgeshire Porter (1969)

Death omen – the sight of a trio of butterflies.
Northamptonshire N&Q (1851)

There is some indication of traditions which regard butterflies as either manifestations of the souls of the dead, or at least somehow connected with death:

Another elderly Cambridgeshire resident, in [1963], said that when she was a girl she was told by her mother, 'If you see a white butterfly you know that a baby or a little child has just died'. This belief, however, she thought might have been brought from Cornwall, where her mother lived until her marriage to a Cambridgeshire man.
Cambridgeshire? Porter (1969)

A child chasing a butterfly was chid by her companions saying. 'That may be the soul of your grandfather'.
Ireland Mason, *Parochial Survey of Ireland* (1819)

but again these are too few to permit any general theory of a coherent belief in the transmigration of souls. The striking fact of the documentary record as it stands is that there are no reports before the second decade of the nineteenth century, which is not a good base for building such theories. It is clear that further study of butterfly lore in Britain and Ireland is necessary.

See also MOTHS.

Good or indifferent: Gloucestershire N&Q 5S:5 (1876) 364; Hartland (1895) 51. **Cambridgeshire or Cornwall** Porter (1969) 49. **Suffolk** Fitzgerald (1887) 498; Gurdon (1893) 9. **Yorkshire** *Folk-Lore* 13 (1902) 432. **Montgomeryshire** Hamer (1877) 261. **Bad: Sussex** Lucas (1904) 76. **Western England** Manning (1837). **Cornwall** *Folk-Lore Jnl* 5 (1887) 214. **Northamptonshire** Hone, *Year Book* (1827) 339; N&Q 1S:3 (1851) 3–4. **Northern England** [c.1816] Henderson (1866) 33. **Wales** Trevelyan (1909) 323. **Aberdeenshire** *Folk-Lore Jnl* 7 (1889) 43. **Soul: Somerset** *N&Q for Somerset & Dorset* 3 (1892–3) 235–6. **Cambridgeshire or Cornwall** Porter (1969) 49–50. **Ireland** William Mason, *Parochial Survey of Ireland* (1819). **N. Ireland** Foster (1951) 15.

buying and selling

For the superstitious person, the business of buying and selling is a delicate situation fraught with the threat of displeasure which can turn into ill-wishing and retribution. This is especially true when selling animals which, even in the natural way of things, are subject to sudden illnesses and death – their bad points can be disguised, their history concealed, and any subsequent fault blamed on the seller. The three most widespread traditions involved in buying and selling, which are treated separately, are HANDSELLING, SPITTING on hands and money received, and the giving of LUCK MONEY:

When selling animals the bargain is not finally sealed until both parties spit on the palms and shake hands and buyer gives the seller back a luck-penny. Co. Tyrone *Lore & Language* (1972)

But there are many other traditional aspects to the situation which need attention. The potential problems start on the way to market, as who or what you MEET on the way determines your luck for that day. The usual things apply, including HARES, MAGPIES, and CROSS-EYED people, which all predict the worst.

Once there, the theory of handselling is that the first money taken is lucky and sets up good fortune for the day, but another belief – that it is unlucky to turn away the first offer of the day – complicates matters:

In the street market places, amongst the stall-keepers, it is reckoned to be nothing else than ruinous to turn away a 'first bid' for an article. It brings bad luck on the day's selling, and it is better to get the 'hansel' (as the first sale is called) over, even at a loss. In all such places, to the unlucky stall-keeper's exasperation, there are to be found mean folks who are known as hansel-hunters, and who are early in the field, and alert to take full advantage of the poor vendor's superstition. He, the vendor, is perfectly well aware of the paltry device to obtain goods at less than cost price; but though he may swear somewhat, it is rare that he will turn away a first bid, and 'chance' it. And when he has taken hansel money, he would as soon think of throwing it into the road, as putting it into his pocket without first 'spitting on it'. Unlocated Jones (1880)

The transaction itself involves a certain degree of trust but both sides must try to get advantage over the other. By praising an item too much, a seller is TEMPTING FATE and risking bad luck. If the buyer 'dispraises' the item, in order to lower the price, s/he must add a ritualistic phrase to make it clear that no ill-wishing is intended. Reginald Scot shows that this was already the case in the 1580s:

You shall not hear a butcher or horsecourser cheapen a bullock or a jade, but if he buy him not, he saith 'God save him'; if he do forget it, and the horse or bullock chance to die, the fault is imputed to the chapman.   Scot (1584)

But some unscrupulous people could trade even more directly on superstition:

A butcher . . . was reported to be the son of a witch. Whenever he wished to buy stock of the neighbours the latter were obliged to sell to him or the animals would surely die.
                    Glamorgan Trevelyan (1909)

The customs described were common all over the British Isles, in one variant or another, in addition to many local traditions, and more obscure beliefs reported irregularly, such as the following:

If a shopkeeper gives credit to his customers on Monday morning he will have no luck that week.
                    England Addy (1895)

Wear a pair of crossed pins under your lapel on

market day and you will get the better of every bargain.   Somerset [1907] Tongue

Even if you have no plans to sell an animal, you are still potentially subject to superstition:

If somebody offers you a price for an animal you haven't put up for sale, then take it because you won't get any more good out of the animal. It has been blinked and will die.
                    Co. Tyrone *Lore & Language* (1972)

See also WART CURES: BUYING AND SELLING.

Somerset [1907] Tongue (1965) 144. Cornwall Burne (1883) 208–9. Worcestershire Salisbury (1893) 64–5. Suffolk Fitzgerald (1887) 510. Lincolnshire Peacock (1877) 234. Shropshire Burne (1883) 208–9. England Addy (1895) 98. Derbyshire [1890s] Uttley (1946) 126. Yorkshire Robinson (1861) 296. Northumberland *Newcastle Weekly Chronicle* (4 Feb. 1899) 7. Wales Trevelyan (1909) 172, 327–9. Denbighshire *Bye-Gones* (12 Jan. 1887) 221. Glamorgan Trevelyan (1909) 214.

calendar

Much of the folklore of Britain was tied to the calendar in one way or another. Festivals and CALENDAR CUSTOMS took place on set days, and major beliefs clustered around fixed turning points such as New Year and saints' days, or less well-defined dates such as the start of spring, as measured by hearing the first CUCKOO. But even the official calendar had had its problems.

By the sixteenth century, the official calendar in Britain was, astronomically speaking, in a mess. The Julian system, on which all European calendars were based, was seriously flawed, and as time passed it became increasingly out of line with fixed points such as solstices and equinoxes. Pope Gregory XIII therefore introduced the Gregorian Calendar in 1582, which dropped ten days to bring it back in line with the sun. Over the next few years, most Catholic countries made the change, but Protestant nations were suspicious of what seemed to be a religious manoeuvre to wrong-foot them. For many years there were two calendars operating across the continent, and two dates for every point in time. Where international comparison was necessary, these were termed 'Old style' and 'New style'. As the advantages of the Gregorian system became apparent, most nations fell into line, but Britain was one of the last – holding out in complacent isolation until 1751. In that year Britain finally adopted the Gregorian calendar and deducted eleven days to achieve

synchronization (2 September was followed by 14 September). The 'loss' of these eleven days caused much consternation in the country from those who objected on religious grounds and those who did not understand, and many people decided to stick to the old calendar as much as they could. Thus, Britain had its own internal 'Old Style' dates, and there were two of each festival every year – for example, Christmas Day and Old Christmas Day eleven days later.

As time passed, there was gradual slippage towards the official dates, as there was in the twentieth century when customs which had previously taken place at Whitsun drifted to Spring Bank Holiday or May Day. Some traditionalists, however, stuck to the old ways, and a difference of eleven days should always be looked for when researching calendar customs and other popular festivals.

Nevertheless, for many people the official calendar was not the only way of calculating time. There were other cycles which were more important in everyday life. Obviously, the agricultural cycle played a dominant role in most rural communities, and this differed from area to area in response to the dominant crops grown, or the fundamental difference between pastoral and arable farming. Other seasonal trades had their own unofficial calendars, and the religious, university, legal, and business cycles provided a kaleidoscope of overlapping systems.

Highland Scotland Campbell (1900) 245–6. Fife N&Q 4S:6 (1870) 567. Co. Tyrone *Lore & Language* 1:7 (1972) 10, 12. Co. Longford *Béaloideas* 6 (1936) 264. Isle of Man Gill (1934) 172. Unlocated Jones (1880) 479. General Scot (1584) Bk 16, Ch. 8.

calendar customs

Customs which are carried out at a set time – usually once a year – are termed *calendar*, or *seasonal* customs, to distinguish them from others which are not date-based, such as life-cycle, family, and occupational customs.

Since the late nineteenth century, it has been the norm to assume that most traditional customs were designed to bring fertility, prosperity, or other direct benefit to the community, or to protect against evil spirits, or were themselves debased survivals of the ritual worship of forgotten deities. If this were true, virtually all calendar customs would be included under the definition of 'superstitions', in that they would be actions carried out to influence fortune or the future. But there is rarely any evidence of this. Whenever detailed scholarly studies of particular customs have been carried out they have almost invariably shown that their age has been grossly exaggerated and that assumptions of ritual origin are totally unsupported. Unfortunately, just as scholarship has begun to take a more reasoned approach to the subject, participants and organizers of many of the more widely known customs in Britain have taken the 'ritual origin' theories to heart and now quote them as established fact. This has the bizarre effect that, whatever the custom's history and development, if the participants now believe they are performing their custom to promote 'fertility' or 'luck', the prophecy fulfils itself as this becomes the new raison d'être.

As a general rule, calendar customs are excluded from this dictionary, unless there is evidence that a strong luck-bringing or other superstitious element has been present. Nevertheless, it is not always easy to make this theoretical distinction. In the same way as WEDDING customs, for example, are almost automatically given 'luck' overtones, many NEW YEAR customs are based on the strong principle that activities and actions carried out at the beginning of the year have resonance throughout the year, and custom and belief thus become impossible to disentangle.

There are numerous books on calendar customs – of varying quality – but for useful historical introductions *see*: Wright and Lones (1936–40), Banks (1937–41), Banks (1946), Hutton (1996), Simpson & Roud (2000), Owen (1987).

calendars

Given the fundamental fear in the superstitious mind of actions which TEMPT FATE, commercial products with dates – such as calendars and diaries – are an obvious problem. Occasionally recorded, but more widely known, is a set of linked beliefs which show this unease:

It is supposed to be unlucky to hang up a new almanac before the old year is out.
                                        Devon *Devonshire Assoc.* (1932)

Calendars received about Christmas time should not be hung on the wall till the new year, as it is unlucky to do so.   Birmingham *Folk-Lore* (1934)

Other versions extend the idea of the dangers of anticipation:

Reporter Jeremy Austin . . . is loathe to write special dates in his diary for fear that, once given substance, they will fail to materialise.
                        Hertfordshire *Watford Observer* (11 Feb. 1994)

Surprisingly, the earliest known references only come from the 1930s, but the underlying notions were still being cited into the twenty-first century.

I have been told that it is unlucky to cross off the day on your calendar until that day is over
        Hertfordshire Steve Roud Collection: Woman, aged 26
                                        (Jan. 2002)

Devon *Devonshire Assoc.* 64 (1932) 165. London [1983] Opie & Tatem, 53. Hertfordshire *Watford Observer* (11 Feb. 1994) 20; [2002] Steve Roud Collection. Birmingham *Folk-Lore* 45 (1934) 162. Yorkshire [1956] Opie & Tatem, 53. Monmouthshire [1946] Opie & Tatem, 53.

Candlemas (2 February)

The festival which celebrates the purification of the Virgin Mary, forty days after the birth of Christ. Candlemas was an important festival in the Catholic calendar, with candlelit processions as the central feature, but the day was downgraded and the hallowing of candles banned in the post-Reformation Protestant churches. The day survived in the traditional calendar, however, in various other ways. Numerous weather-lore beliefs and sayings focus on Candlemas Day, while the day was also regarded as the agreed end of the Christmas season, and therefore the time to take down CHRISTMAS DECORATIONS, until Twelfth Night took over that role.

In England there were also a number of

traditions which focused on the day's name and declared it as that on which candles could be dispensed with during working hours:

When I came out of church yesterday, after the usual service for the day, I was told by one of my servants that she formerly lived with a lady who always made it a rule to have tea by daylight for the first time on Candlemas Day – and, moreover, she said that on and after that day all shoemakers give up working by candle light. Unlocated N&Q 8S:5 (1894)

In terms of superstition, however, Candlemas only features in isolated cases. Two Scottish writers report beliefs in which the candles used on the day have special power:

The reciter says that he has frequently seen small bits of candles worn by people as a charm to keep mischief away. He believes they were the remains of candles that were set aside for that purpose at the time of Feill Bride (Candlemas). They sewed them in a convenient corner in the inside of their coats. Western Isles Banks (1939)

Sprinkled with holy water and blessed, these candles (of Candlemas) were supposed to possess the power of repelling evil spirits.
Scotland [1841] Banks

and a single reference from Devon hints at another aspect of the candle:

For a candle to drip at one side when carried in church at Candlemas, denotes a death during the year of some one dear.
Devon *Devonshire Assoc.* (1935)

Candlemas also features occasionally as one of those days (more commonly NEW YEAR and May Day) on which the incomings and outgoings of the house should be carefully monitored:

It was a custom not long ago to bring something into the houses on the morning of Candlemas Day before taking anything out.
Galloway [1897] Banks

Devon *Devonshire Assoc.* 67 (1935) 14. Norfolk N&Q 8S:6 (1894) 15. Scotland [1841] Banks (1939) 158. Western Isles Banks (1939) 158. Galloway [1897] Banks (1939) 158. Unlocated N&Q 8S:5 (1894) 449.
For weather and other Candlemas lore *see:* Banks (1939); Wright & Lones (1938) 118–29; Hutton (1996) 139–45.

candles: alone

Leaving a candle alight in an unoccupied room or a closet, invites a death in the family:

If a lighted candle is accidentally shut up in a pantry, it is a sure sign of death in the family soon. I asked Mrs. Z about this belief and she said, 'I went into my pantry and left a lighted candle there, and a month after my aunt died'.
Suffolk *Folk-Lore* (1924)

This is one of many minor candle superstitions reported a few times since the 1850s, but on present evidence curiously restricted to East Anglia. The example quoted by Enid Porter, collected in 1965, shows that the belief had successfully made the transition from candles to electric lights.

Cambridgeshire Porter (1969) 24. East Anglia Varden (1885) 116–17. Suffolk [1924] Opie & Tatem, 53; *Folk-Lore* 35 (1924) 350. Norfolk Fulcher Collection (c.1895). Unlocated N&Q 1S:12 (1855) 488.

candles: blue flame

A number of authorities comment on a candle flame burning blue, although various interpretations were made. In the earliest references, up to the late seventeenth century, the standard interpretation was that spirits or ghosts were near. Shakespeare alludes to this when, after a succession of ghosts has appeared to him, King Richard III observes, 'The lights burn blue. It is now dead midnight', and Melton, Grose, and others agree. In the early nineteenth century, the meaning still held good, but it could be the WRAITH of the lover, summoned in a LOVE DIVINATION procedure which affects the flame (*see* ST MARK'S EVE). The latest example, however (Dickinson (1899)), simply states that a blue flame is a death omen.

See also CANDLES: LOVE DIVINATION.

Yorkshire Carr (1824) 99. Cumberland Dickinson (1899) 'Deeth'. General Melton (1620); Grose (1787) 10. Literary, Shakespeare, *Richard III* (1594) 5:5; Daniel Defoe, *History of the Devil* (1726) Pt 2, Ch. 10; *Connoisseur* 59 (1755) 352; T. F. Forster, *Pocket Encyclopaedia* (1827) 36, quoted Opie & Tatem, 54.

candles: cures/protection

The material that candles were made of, whether tallow or wax, was sometimes recommended as an ingredient in cures:

Being afflicted two years since with a severe tertian ague, I was solicited, after the usual medical treatment had failed, by a lady to take as much of the snuff of a candle as would lie on a sixpence, made into an electuary with honey.

candles

As was natural in a candle-lit house, we had an intimate feeling for those soft yellow flames and the white candle. A spark flying from the flame meant a letter. A brightly glowing tip to the wick was a sweetheart in the candle. A tiny shred from the wick, falling into the cup of hot wax, was called a thief. A curl of wax rippling down the side of the candle was a winding-sheet.

Derbyshire [1890s] Uttley

As here indicated by the children's author Alison Uttley, the domestic candle was surrounded by a range of superstitions. Many were interpretations of the candle's behaviour – the burning of the flame, melting of the wax, refusal to burn or go out, and so on. Some were concerned with how and where the candles were placed – alone in a room, three in a room – while others called for candles to be used in spells and divinations. Several of these beliefs reached the pinnacle of superstition evolution when they became so well known as to become household phrases – 'a letter in the candle' and the 'winding sheet', in particular, were understood by virtually everybody in the nineteenth century, believers and non-believers alike, in the same way as 'cross your fingers' is understood in the modern world.

The main candle superstitions have their own entries below, but there was a host of others which were not so well documented, but had general currency when candles were in daily use. As ubiquitous domestic items, candles regularly took on the connotations of the situation in which they were found, whether in mainstream Christian ritual or in times of stress, such as in the room where a corpse was laid out. It was widely thought, for example, that it was wrong to leave a corpse in a room without a light, and the candles used for this purpose naturally became the focus of a variety of beliefs:

Often, when a candle has not been lighted in the chamber of the dead, have I heard a remonstrance couched in words like these – 'What a lack of respect' or 'Little do they care for the dead one'.

Somerset Poole (1877)

If, when a candle is burning beside a dead body, it falls out of the stick, it is a sign of another death within the twelvemonth.

Lincolnshire Peacock (1877)

Candles used in this way also acquired a reputation for healing and protection (*see* CANDLES: CURES). There was also the fairly obvious metaphor of the candle flame representing human life, which could be 'snuffed out' at any time:

If the wind blows out a candle on the altar, or lights grow dim in the chancel or around the pulpit, the clergyman or minister will soon die.

Wales Trevelyan (1909)

If a candle chance to be snuffed out, there will be one person more or less in the house before the morrow. Dublin N&Q (1869)

A selection of other less well-known candle beliefs follows:

If you light a candle from the flame of a fire you will end your days in the workhouse.

Lincolnshire Rudkin (1936)

For a candle to drip at one side when carried in church at Candlemas, denotes a death during the year of some one dear.

Devon *Devonshire Assoc.* (1935)

It is reputed to be bad luck to . . . take a lighted candle into the open air at Christmas.

Northern England N&Q (1868)

The candle must never be allowed to die out, or it brings death to some sailor out at sea.

Lincolnshire Swaby (1891)

If a farmer cuts a candle in two, something will go wrong with the cattle.

Berkshire *Folk-Lore* (1894)

Somerset Poole (1877) 24. **Devon** *Devonshire Assoc.* 67 (1935) 141. **Berkshire** *Folk-Lore* 5 (1894) 337. **Lincolnshire** Peacock (1877) 46; Swaby (1891) 92; Rudkin (1936) 21. **Derbyshire** [1890s] Uttley (1946) 128. **Northern England** N&Q 4S:2 (1868) 553. **Wales** Trevelyan (1909) 281. **Dublin** N&Q 4S:4 (1869) 505.

I complied; and, strange to say, a complete cure was effected. Norfolk N&Q (1851)

A similar cure was reported in the same journal five years later (**Lincolnshire** N&Q (1856)), and tallow was recommended for colds and

coughs (e.g. **Oxfordshire** *Oxf. FL Soc. Ann. Record* (1956)).

However, more interesting from a folkloric point of view are the long-standing beliefs that candles used in religious ceremonies (e.g. at CANDLEMAS), or in connection with rites for the dead, have special powers to cure ills and/or protect against ill-wishers.

The wick of a candle that had been burning in a dying man's room was supposed to be a certain cure for the goitre. It was rubbed on the affected part.   Wales Trevelyan (1909)

The ends of candles used at wakes are of great efficacy in curing burns.   Ireland Wilde (1888)

This notion has a long history. The authors of *Malleus Maleficarum* in 1486 described the protective properties of candle-wax – 'in the case of a blessed candle, although it is more appropriate to light it, the wax of it may be sprinkled about dwelling-houses' – and stated that blessed candles were effective against witches – 'by the lawful use of candles hallowed on Candlemas daie . . . are preserved from witchcraft'. The same passage was repeated by Scot a century later in his *Discoverie of Witchcraft* (1584).

See also CANDLEMAS.

Oxfordshire *Oxf. FL Soc. Ann. Record* (1956) 11–12. Worcestershire [*c.*1900] Knight (1960) 178–9. Norfolk N&Q (1851) 53. Lincolnshire N&Q 2S:1 (1856) 386. Wales Trevelyan (1909) 319. Ireland *Gent. Mag.* (1795) 201–3; Wilde (1888) 82. Dublin N&Q 4S 1 (1868) 51. General Sprenger & Kramer, *Malleus Maleficarum* (1486/1928) 89, 91; Scot (1584) Bk 12, Ch. 20.

candles: letter

The two leading superstitions about signs in the candle are the winding sheet (*see below*) and the bright spark which betokened the arrival of a letter.

A bright spark on the candle-wick indicates a letter coming to the house. The person towards whom it shines will receive it. The time of its arrival is determined by striking the bottom of the candlestick on the table. If the spark comes off on the first blow, it will be received tomorrow; if two blows are required, on the second day, and so on.   Cornwall Hunt (1865)

Further information could be gleaned by those who knew what to look for:

If a spark flies off the candle it is a sure sign of a letter in the morning. A spark on the wick means a letter for the one who first sees it, and a big glow like a parcel means money coming to you.
                          Suffolk *Folk-Lore* (1924)

In some houses, however, the spark foretold that a stranger would be visiting soon (*see below*). The letter and the winding sheet both

appear in the documentary record at the same time, in the *British Apollo* (1708), but both are quoted there as if they were already proverbial, and by the nineteenth century were household phrases.

Sussex Gales (1914) 231. Somerset Poole (1877) 42; Tongue (1965) 141. Dorset Udal (1922) 274. Devon *Devonshire Assoc.* 15 (1883) 107; Hewett (1900) 51. Cornwall Hunt (1865) 238; *Folk-Lore Jnl* 5 (1887) 220. Wiltshire *Wilts. N&Q* 1 (1893–5) 7–8. Shropshire Mitford (1830) 299; Lowsley (1888) 22. Oxfordshire [pre-1900] *Folk-Lore* 24 (1913) 91; *Folk-Lore* 34 (1923) 327. Gloucestershire *Folk-Lore* 12 (1902) 172. Suffolk *Folk-Lore* 35 (1924) 351. Norfolk Fulcher Collection (*c.*1895). Lincolnshire Peacock (1877) 241; Swaby (1891) 92. Shropshire Burne (1883) 275. Staffordshire Hackwood (1924) 147. England Addy (1895) 98. Derbyshire [1890s] Uttley (1946) 128. Yorkshire Nicholson (1890) 44; Gales (1914) 231. Lancashire Harland & Wilkinson (1882) 139. Wales Trevelyan (1909) 325. Dumfriesshire Shaw (1890) 13. Co. Longford *Béaloideas* 6 (1936) 264. Jersey *Folk-Lore* 25 (1914) 246. Unlocated Grose (1787) 68; Hone *Year Book* (1832) 126–8. General Foli (1902) 108. Literary *British Apollo* (7 Apr. 1708); Addison, *Spectator* (8 Mar. 1711); *Connoisseur* 59 (1755) 352; *Old Women's Sayings* (*c.*1835); Thomas Hardy, *The Trumpet-Major* (1880) Ch. 12.

candles: love divination

Several LOVE DIVINATION procedures call for the use of candles. In the most complex, maidens (usually) stuck PINS into the candle to force their sweethearts to pay attention:

[*Two servant-girls in the city of Durham*] *One of them, it seems, peeped out of curiosity into the box of her fellow-servant, and was astonished to find there the end of a tallow-candle stuck through with pins. 'What's that, Molly', said Bessie, 'that I see'd i' thy box?'; 'Oh,' said Molly, 'it's to bring my sweetheart. Thou see'st, sometimes he's slow a-coming, and if I stick a candle-end full o' pins it always fetches him.' A member of the family certifies that John was thus duly fetched from Ferryhill, a distance of six miles, and pretty often too.*   Co. Durham Henderson (1866)

This practice was often accompanied by a rhyme such as the following:

*It's not this candle alone I stick
But A.B.'s heart I mean to prick
Whether he be asleep or awake
I'd have him come to me and speak.*
                   Buckinghamshire Henderson (1866)

A more passive approach was to sit and watch a small candle:

On the eve of St. Mark or St. Agnes, place on the floor a lighted 'pigtail', a small farthing candle, which must have been previously stolen, or else the charm will not work. Then sit down in silence and watch it till it begins to burn blue, when the future husband will appear and walk across the room.   Yorkshire/Lancashire Wright (1913)

Again, the blue flame is regularly associated with the presence of 'spirits' (see CANDLES: BLUE FLAME).

A third approach was to interpret the molten wax while a candle burned, and, while some observers looked for winding sheets (*see below*) or coffin handles, girls looked for rings or sweethearts.

See also CANDLES: WEDDING.

Cornwall [1870] *Jnl Royal Inst. Cornwall* 20 (1915) 130–1. **Buckinghamshire** Henderson (1866) 139. **Lincolnshire** Rudkin (1936) 23. **Derbyshire** Uttley (1946) Ch. 11. **Yorkshire/Lancashire** Wright (1913) 261–2. **Lancashire** Harland & Wilkinson (1882) 140. **Co. Durham** Henderson (1866) 138. **Wales** Davies (1911) 10–11. **Literary** Oliver Goldsmith, *Vicar of Wakefield* (1766) Ch. 10.

candles: stranger/thief

In addition to the proverbial 'letter in the candle', some people predicted the coming of a stranger or a thief:

A tiny spark on one side denoted a letter to whoever was sitting opposite it. But a large speck, which made a channel down the side of the candle, meant thieves. 'There's a thief in the candle, take 'im out'.   Wiltshire *Wilts. N&Q* (1893–5)

Somerset [1923] Opie & Tatem, 56. **Wiltshire** *Wilts. N&Q* 1 (1893–5) 7–8. **Derbyshire** [1890s] Uttley (1946) 128. **General** Browne, *Pseudodoxia Epidemica* (1646) Bk 5, Para. 24; Gales (1914) 231.

candles: three

Three lighted lamps or candles in a room were held to be ominous, but there was sharp disagreement as to meaning. Many informants maintained that it meant a death, and they would immediately blow one out if they found three candles burning together. Others, however, claimed it meant a wedding, and were thus happy to leave them alight. Even in the earliest known example, in Kilvert's famous diary, the ambiguity of meaning is already evident:

Three candles were burning on the kitchen table, and the cook said that the person who was nearest to the shortest candle would be married first. Some people put it, 'Will die first'. It seems to be an old saying about three lighted candles together, but it was quite new to me.   Cornwall Kilvert, *Diary* (26 July 1870)

Leighton even says that in coastal areas of Northeastern England it meant a ship would be wrecked. On balance, the unlucky interpretation wins on points, but a lot more examples must be found before any firm conclusions can be reached. Further confusion is caused by a report from Devon, in 1880, that *four* candles, arranged in a square, foretold a wedding (*see* CANDLES: WEDDING).

It has been suggested, without any evidence being proffered, that the ominous meaning is based on the fact that three candles were traditional at funeral wakes, and also that this was the basis of a superficially similar belief about lighting THREE CIGARETTES.

Unlucky: **Cornwall** Francis Kilvert, *Diary* (26 July 1870); *Old Cornwall* 2 (1931–6) 38. **Herefordshire** Leather (1912) 87. **Co. Durham** Leighton (1910) 61. **Ireland** *Westminster Gazette* (3 Nov. 1893) 2; N&Q 10S:6 (1906) 509. **Literary** T. F. Powys, *Kindness in a Corner* (1930) 32, quoted Opie & Tatem, 55.
Wedding: **Cornwall** Francis Kilvert, *Diary* (26 July 1870); *Folk-Lore Jnl* 5 (1887) 215. **Lincolnshire** Rudkin (1936) 19.

candles: wedding

Signs in the candle flame can be interpreted in LOVE DIVINATION (*see above*), but the placing of candlesticks can also be said to predict an imminent wedding. The most common sign is the placing of three candles in a room, although this can also be read as meaning a death (*see* CANDLES: THREE), but in one detailed report from Devon, it was *four* candles which triggered the prediction of a wedding:

A nurse, about 50 years of age, a native of Cornwall, but long resident in South Devon, coming into a room in which I was sitting, at Torquay, in the summer of 1879, remarked, 'There'll be a marriage', and, on being questioned, directed attention to the following facts: – There were four candles burning on the same table; the candlesticks stood at the angles of a square, and those at the ends of one of the diagonals were a pair, in all respects alike; this was also the fact as regards those at the ends of the other diagonal, but the two pairs were unlike one

another. Moreover, the candles in one pair were
of the same height, but much shorter than those
in the other pair, which were also equally high.
In short, the candles, like the candlesticks, formed
two distinct pairs, and the entire group was
symmetrically arranged. Such an arrangement
the nurse assured me was commonly held to foretell the marriage of one of the company.

Devon Devonshire Assoc. (1880)

Occasional references seem to imply a superstition about snuffing candles and being
married, but without making it altogether clear
what was signified:

will be married next year. If you snuff out the
candle you certainly will.

Co. Durham Henderson (1866)

but poor cousin Nancy was ready to cry one time,
when she snuffed it [the candle] out and could
not blow it in again; though her sister did it at a
whiff.   Connoisseur (1755)

Devon Devonshire Assoc. 12 (1880) 109. Cornwall
Francis Kilvert, Diary (26 July 1870); Folk-Lore Jnl 5
(1887) 215. Lincolnshire Rudkin (1936) 19. Co. Durham
Henderson (1866) 85. Literary Connoisseur 59 (1755)
352.

candles: winding sheet

A particular shape created by the melting wax of
a candle was regarded as a death omen, and
widely known as a 'winding sheet', 'shroud', or,
occasionally, a 'coffin handle'. The precise
specification varies somewhat, but the general
drift is very similar:

Winding-Sheet – a little projection of wax or
tallow which, as the candle burns, gradually
lengthens and winds round upon itself. It is a sign
of the death of the person sitting opposite it.

Lincolnshire Peacock (1877)

A coffin handle in tallow, when it runs down and
forms a loop, is a sign of death to the person in
whose direction it points.

Somerset [1911] Tongue

The earliest reference so far located is in the British
Apollo (1708), but it is reported there as if it were
already proverbial. It was in the nineteenth
century that the belief became so well-known that
'winding sheet' became the generally accepted
word for such a formation, in the same way as the
spark on the wick was simply termed 'a letter' (see
above). Inevitably, the superstition faded during
the twentieth century, as candles were replaced by

other forms of domestic lighting, but in its day it
was one of the most widely known of all superstitions.

Kent Folk-Lore 23 (1912) 354. Sussex Sussex County Mag.
(1944) 84. Somerset [1911] Tongue (1965) 142. Dorset
Dorset Year Book (1961–2) 74–5. Devon Hewett (1900)
56. Cornwall Hunt (1865) 165. Wiltshire Smith (1874)
324; Wilts. N&Q 1 (1893–5) 7–8. Berkshire Folk-Lore 5
(1894) 337. Oxfordshire [1850s] Plowman (1919) 116;
[pre-1900] Folk-Lore 24 (1913) 88; Folk-Lore 24 (1913) 88.
Gloucestershire Folk-Lore 13 (1902) 172.
Worcestershire/Shropshire Gent. Mag. (1855) 386.
Warwickshire Langford (1875) 19. Bloom (c.1930) 44.
East Anglia Varden (1885) 117. Suffolk Chambers (1878)
52–3. Norfolk [c.1912] Randell (1966) 97. Lincolnshire
Gent. Mag. (1833) 590–3; Thompson (1856) 734; Peacock
(1877) 222, 276; Swaby (1891) 92. Derbyshire [1890s]
Uttley (1946) 128. Yorkshire Nicholson (1890) 44. Co.
Durham Leighton (1910) 51. Wales Trevelyan (1909)
281. Scotland Jamieson, Scottish Dictionary (Supp.,
1825) 'Dede-spale'; Henderson (1866) 33. Dumfriesshire
Shaw (1890) 13. Isle of Man [c.1850] Cashen (1912) 6.
Unlocated Grose (1787) 48; N&Q 6S:3 (1881) 449; N&Q
6S:4 (1881) 74; Gales (1914) 230–1. General British Apollo
(7 Apr. 1708). Literary Connoisseur 59 (1755) 352; Old
Women's Sayings (c.1835); Mrs Gaskell, Cranford (1853)
Ch. 9; Thomas Hardy, 'Standing by the Mantelpiece'
(1873) in Hardy (1928).

cards

If there is one area in which superstition is
particularly at home it must be in games of
chance, and it is no surprise that there is a wide
range of traditional beliefs and customs
concerned with card-playing.

Numerous ways of ensuring or improving
one's luck have been recorded, including sitting
CROSS-LEGGED, turning one's CHAIR, carrying
a piece of HANGMAN's rope, or, less commonly,
carrying a badger's tooth, sticking a pin into
one's jacket, or the following:

Thus at whist drives some women always carry
a coin issued in the year of their birth, some will
only mark the score with red pencils, some will
not wear black shoes.   General Hoggart (1957)

Certain cards have traditionally been regarded
as intrinsically unlucky. The ace of spades is
nowadays given prime place in this context, but
several other cards also had bad reputations:

From a Worcestershire farmer – 'There never was
a good hand at cards if the four of clubs was in
it'; 'Why?'; 'Because the four of clubs is an
unlucky card; it's the Devil's own card'; 'In what
way?'; 'It's the Devil's four-post bedstead'.

Worcestershire N&Q (1879)

It appears to be mainly black cards which were disliked:

To have a long succession of black cards (spades or clubs) dealt to a person while at play is prophetic of death to himself or some other member of the family.
Worcestershire/Shropshire *Gent. Mag.* (1855)

The idea behind the proverbial phrase 'Unlucky at cards, lucky in love' is at least as old as the mid eighteenth century, as both Swift (1738) and the *Connoisseur* (1755) both mention it. There has always been a degree of ambivalence about card-playing, and the potential moral dangers involved led to various stories about the results of playing on Sundays or other inappropriate times. A violent storm at sea could lead to packs of cards being thrown overboard, and an internationally known tale relates how the participants in a card game which continued after midnight on Saturday suddenly realized that they had an extra player, who turned out to be the Devil in disguise. Hence the sensible warning:

Always look at a man's foot before you play cards with him and don't play if he has a cloven foot.
Co. Tyrone *Lore & Language* (1972)

See also CROSSED LEGS: LUCK; CHAIRS: TURNING, UNLUCKY; HANGMAN'S ROPE: CURES.

Sussex Latham (1878) 32. Devon Hewett (1900) 51, 65. Cornwall *Folk-Lore Jnl* 5 (1887) 219. Worcestershire/Shropshire *Gent. Mag.* (1855) 385; N&Q 5S:12 (1879) 426. Birmingham [1784] N&Q 3S:8 (1865) 146. Suffolk *Folk-Lore Record* 3 (1880) 129; Fitzgerald (1887) 498. Lincolnshire *Gent. Mag.* (1832) 493. England Addy (1895) 94. Northern England Brockett (1829) 155. Yorkshire *Folk-Lore* 43 (1932) 254–5. Lancashire Harland & Wilkinson (1873) 236. Cumberland Dickinson (1875) 110–12. Northumberland Bigge (1860/62) 94. Western Scotland Napier (1879) 110. Highland Scotland Macbain (1887/88) 237–8. Ireland Wilde (1888) 205. Co. Tyrone *Lore & Language* 1:7 (1972) 12. Guernsey [*c.*1800] MacCulloch MS (1864) 394; De Garis (1975) 118–19. Unlocated Grose (1787) 60; N&Q 3S:1 (1862) 223; N&Q 4S:1 (1868) 193; N&Q 4S:12 (1873) 44; Igglesden (*c.*1932) 190. General *Gent. Mag.* (1796) 636; Knowlson (1910) 232–5; Hoggart (1957) Ch. 2; Opie & Tatem, 56–7. Literary Swift (1738) 213; *Connoisseur* 59 (1755) 352.

---

cast ne'er a clout till May is out

see CLOTHES: LEAVING OFF.

casting the heart

see HEART DISEASE: CASTING THE HEART.

caterpillars: cures

Many small creatures are sacrificed in the belief that they can cure human ailments if placed alive in a bag and worn around the neck of the sufferer until they die – SPIDERS and WOODLICE, for example, are given such treatment, and so are caterpillars.

There were numerous cures for whooping-cough of a superstitious character, practised extensively during the earlier years of this century, and some are still recommended. The following are a few of these . . . Find a hairy caterpillar, put it into a bag and hang it round the neck of the child. This will prove a cure.
Western Scotland Napier (1879)

The caterpillar cure is almost always for WHOOPING COUGH, and is presumably aimed at transferring the disease to the insect. Occasionally it is recommended for AGUE, which was similarly believed to be cured by the proximity of other insects.

As noted under SPIDERS: WHOOPING COUGH, these insect cures have a long history for ague, but are only recommended for whooping cough from the late nineteenth century. It appears that they have simply been extended from one disease to the other.

Sussex Latham (1878) 39. Devon *Devonshire Assoc.* 18 (1886) 104. Cornwall N&Q 9S:12 (1903) 126. Shropshire Burne (1883) 194. Northern England Henderson (1866) 110–13. Yorkshire Robinson (1855) 'Kincough'; Blakeborough (1898) 137. Lancashire N&Q 1S:3 (1851) 516. Co. Durham Brockie (1889) 221. Western Scotland Napier (1879) 95–6.

---

caterpillars: feared

Caterpillars were widely distrusted, and children, in particular, thought them poisonous:

When visiting at a farmhouse in the neighbourhood of Box, during the last summer, whilst walking in a field I picked up a very pretty hairy caterpillar (woolly bear). A little boy, who was with me at the time, cried out to me at once, 'Drop it, drop it, or it will kill you' and ran off in considerable fear.   Unlocated N&Q (1876)

Correspondence in *Notes & Queries* on this topic (N&Q 5S:7 (1877)) speculated that this tradition was based on the fact that some species of caterpillar can cause painful irritation to human skin if handled. But this hardly explains the particular fear, recorded from several places, that if the creature curled round your finger to make a ring, you would certainly die:

Some species of caterpillar were held in dread. If touched, and no one ever touched to find out, the furry one known as the 'Davel's Ring' was reputed to coil itself round the toucher's finger, and could only be removed by witchcraft.

Essex [*c*.1920] Ketteridge & Mays

A few other sources also report negative attitudes to the caterpillar:

The Irish always spit three times on the caterpillar when they see it creeping in order that it may not come that night to the house and sleep in the same bed with the person who has seen it.

Ireland N&Q (1873)

How now, fool! How now, caterpillar? It's a sign of death when such vermin creep hedges so early in the morning. Wily Beguiled (1606)

See also MOTHS.

Cornwall N&Q 5S:7 (1877) 53. Essex *Monthly Packet* 24 (1862) 434–7; [*c*.1920] Ketteridge & Mays (1972) 141. Oxfordshire *Folk-Lore* 34 (1923) 326. Ireland N&Q 4S:12 (1873) 469. Unlocated N&Q 5S:6 (1876) 462–3. General N&Q 5S:7 (1877) 53. Literary *Wily Beguiled* (1606).

caterpillars: lucky

Considering the general view of the caterpillar as poisonous and of evil portent (*see above*), it is surprising to find three reports which describe it as lucky, at least if you treat it correctly:

If you throw a black hairy caterpillar over your shoulder you have good luck.

Dumfries [1957] Opie & Tatem

Shropshire Burne (1883) 239. Yorkshire Blakeborough (1898) 130. Dumfries [1957] Opie & Tatem, 64.

cats and death

In many areas, when death occurred in a house, the family cats and DOGS would immediately be removed:

The household companions of dog and cat were rigidly excluded from the stricken house; indeed, it was not uncommon for the cat to be imprisoned beneath an inverted tub, for it was believed that if either of these animals should jump or cross over the dead body, the welfare of the spirit of the deceased would certainly be affected.

S.W. Scotland Wood (1911)

The reasons given for this exclusion are not always exactly the same. The rational explanation is that animals left with a corpse might maul it in some way, or worse. But this does not explain the very real fear evinced even when the body was already in its coffin or when the funeral procession was underway. If a cat or dog did succeed in jumping on to or over the corpse, it was immediately and unceremoniously killed.

The custom was already widespread in the eighteenth century, and is probably much older. Most examples are reported from Scotland and northern England, but elsewhere in England a different belief held sway which would seem to obviate the need for deliberate exclusion of cats as it maintained that they would not stay in a house where death was approaching or had recently occurred:

Cats were valuable, too, as able to forecast approaching death. When a person lay seriously ill at home and the family cat refused to stay indoors, then it was certain that the sick person would soon die. Cambridgeshire Porter (1969)

A number of beliefs like this centre on the ability of cats and dogs to predict a coming death, either by a natural but unexplained sense, or by a supernatural ability. DOGS HOWLING outside a house where a sick person lies, or a cat refusing to stay in such a house, are both seen as prime examples of these animals' uncanny abilities. In one instance, the pet's sense extended beyond the bounds of the house:

[22 Nov. 1930] She told me an odd thing. Bubbles, Mrs. Fawssett's cat, had been curled asleep on the rug, very much à la cat. Then suddenly he started up. His eyes glaring, his fur on end, made frantic efforts to get out and when he did rushed to Mrs. Fawssett's room which was empty as she'd been taken to Dr. Boyle's. Cecil was so impressed by this that he made a note of the time – a quarter past four – and this, as they learnt later, was the exact time that Mrs. Fawssett died.

Sussex Dudeney (1998)

See also DOGS.

Cats excluded: Cumberland [1962] Opie & Tatem, 64. Northumberland Henderson (1866) 43. Highland Scotland Pennant (1771) 69. Southwestern Scotland Wood (1911) 217. Aberdeenshire *Stat. Acct Scotland* 21 (1799) 147; [*c*.1890] Milne (1987) 2. Ross-shire *Folk-Lore Jnl* 6 (1888) 263. Orkney [1774] Black (1903) 216;

cats

According to superstition, cats were viewed with far more suspicion than affection in Britain, and numerous, sometimes contradictory, beliefs have existed side by side. It is certainly true to say that the range of cat beliefs has shrunk and been simplified over the years, and many have disappeared or been relegated to a few elderly or particularly superstitious people. Ask a British person nowadays about cat beliefs and they are likely to reply 'black cats are lucky', and perhaps that 'witches have black cats' and leave it at that.

The assumption that a witch's familiar will necessarily be a black cat is a relatively modern one:

Among quadrupeds the cat has long been looked upon with suspicion, a circumstance due no doubt to the belief that this was one of the forms in which witches were wont to masquerade.
Dumfriesshire Corrie (1890/91)

and is now irrevocably fixed by countless cartoon films and children's books. Witches are now as automatically connected with black cats as they are with pointed hats and broomsticks. Historically speaking, however, this was not so straightforward. In the great witchcraft trials of the seventeenth century and in stories about the more humble local village witches of later periods, the chosen companion could be any small animal, and cats only become the dominant species in the late nineteenth century.

What say you to this? that the witches have their spirits, some hath one, some hath more, as two, three, four, or five. Some in one likeness and some in another, as like cats, weasils, toads, or mise, whom they nourish with milk.
George Gifford, *A Dialogue of Witches and Witchcraft* (1603)

The idea that witches turn themselves into cats is equally problematic. Until the late nineteenth century at least, stories about witches turning themselves into other animals, especially HARES, greatly outnumber those of cats.

Without attempting to assign human characteristics to cats, it is reasonable to explain much of the distrust in which cats were held by reference to their naturally independent, even disdainful, demeanour, and their seemingly grudging acceptance of human contact and hospitality. Added to this their speed, cruelty,

and nocturnal habits, it is not surprising that they have excited a range of emotions in human hearts and minds. There are more superstitions about cats than any other domestic animals, and although dogs are also believed to have their 'uncanny' side (seeing ghosts and sensing danger and death), this is nothing compared to the range of beliefs about cats.

In addition to those beliefs given their own entries below, numerous superstitions have been reported only once or twice. A sample follows:

If a cat directly after wiping its face with its paw looks straight into your face you will be dead before that day twelvemonth.
Co. Cavan *Folk-Lore* (1908)

If a girl steps on the cat's tail, she will not be married in that year. Wales Trevelyan (1909)

If a cat crosses before you when you are going on a journey you needn't expect any luck that day.
Co. Longford *Béaloideas* (1936)

It is unlucky to tread on a cat's tail.
Devon Hewett (1900)

It is a strong belief that cat's tails should be cut so that they grow. The theory is that they have a worm at the tip which must be severed to ensure a luxuriant tail. Guernsey De Garis (1975)

Cats will not eat robins or swallows.
England Addy (1895)

Theatrical superstitions: Cat walking across stage very lucky. Unlocated Igglesden (c.1932)

It is said that the house cat can tell whether the soul of the dead person has 'gone to heaven or hell'. If immediately after death the house cat ascends a tree, the soul is 'gone to heaven'; if it descends, the soul is 'gone to hell'.
Wales Trevelyan (1909)

Cats, from no apparent cause, seeming shy, agitated, and traversing the house uttering cries, as if alarmed, is believed to forebode sudden and causeless strife between members of the families with whom they reside. The Mirror (10 Mar. 1832)

Devon Hewett (1900) 53. **England** Addy (1895) 67. **Wales** Trevelyan (1909) 270, 281. **Dumfriesshire** Corrie (1890/91) 80. **Co. Cavan** *Folk-Lore* 19 (1908) 318. **Co. Longford** *Béaloideas* 6 (1936) 263. **Guernsey** De Garis (1975) 130. **Unlocated** Igglesden (c.1932) 233–4. **General** *The Mirror* (10 Mar. 1832) 170–1.

Richard Gough, *Sepulchral Monuments* 2, Pt 1 (1786) 205. Northern **Ireland** Foster (1951) 21. **Literary** Charles Dickens, *Bleak House* (1853) Ch. 11.
Cats sense death: Sussex [1930] Dudeney (1998) 118. **Devon** N&Q 1S:2 (1850) 512. **Cambridgeshire** Porter (1969) 23, 52. **Northern England** [1850s] *Denham Tracts* 2 (1895) 74.

cats: babies

A set of linked beliefs about cats reveals a long-standing distrust of the animal and a potential danger to people with whom they share a house, and to human babies in particular. In modern times, the fear is often expressed that a cat will settle on the baby (for its warmth) and suffocate it. As the author's mother commented, 'You must never let the cat get on the pram – it'll smother the baby' (**London**, May 2002). For others a similar concern is couched in terms of the child's breathing in particles of cat hair. But in earlier times cats were accused of killing babies by 'sucking their breath away':

A child of eighteen months old was found dead near Plymouth; and it appeared, on the coroner's inquest, that the child died in consequence of a cat sucking its breath, occasioning a strangulation.
                                    Devon [1791] N&Q

This was the specific danger which particularly worried young parents, and was very widely believed, but a more general deleterious affinity between cats and babies was also often cited, and cats were frequently removed from a house when babies arrived:

[From a servant girl, aged about nineteen] *If a cat be kept in a house where there is a baby, one of them probably the baby, will die. The following fact has recently come to my knowledge. There was a kitten in the house of a Torquay tradesman when his second child was born. In a short time both the baby and the kitten were ill, when the nursemaid, to save the child, killed the kitten. The child recovered and is quite well.*
                        Devon *Devonshire Assoc.* (1878)

This notion was already well entrenched in the early seventeenth century, along with a general idea that a cat's breath could be poisonous to humans, and it is clear that breath – human or feline – is the unifying element in this range of beliefs.

See also CATS: UNHEALTHY FOR HUMANS.

Sussex Latham (1878) 18. **Somerset** [1922] Opie & Tatem, 61–2; **Devon** N&Q 3S:12 (1867) 185; *Devonshire Assoc.* 10 (1878) 107; *Devonshire Assoc.* 16 (1884) 123;

N&Q 3S:12 (1897) 185; Hewett (1900) 54. **Cornwall** N&Q 11S:2 (1910) 509; *Old Cornwall* 2 (1931–6) 39. **London** [1987] Opie & Tatem, 61; [2002] Steve Roud Collection. **Gloucestershire** *Trans. Bristol & Glos. Arch. Soc.* 53 (1931) 264. **East Anglia** Varden (1885) 107. **Suffolk** [1863] Chambers 2 (1878) 39. **Staffordshire** Hackwood (1924) 57. **Shropshire** Burne (1883) 212. **Northern England** *Newcastle Weekly Chronicle* (11 Feb. 1899) 7. **Yorkshire** *Leeds Mercury* (4 Oct. 1879). **Lancashire** N&Q 1S:3 (1851) 516; Harland & Wilkinson (1873) 219–20; Harland & Wilkinson (1882) 141. **Co. Durham** [1955] Opie & Tatem, 62. **Scotland** Jamieson, *Scottish Dictionary*, Supp. 1 (1825) 190. **Highland Scotland** Polson (1926) 6. **Unlocated** N&Q 2S:12 (1861) 500; *Daily News* (15 Dec. 1881) quoted by Lean 2 (1905) 113. **General** Topsell (1607) 106; *British Apollo* (24 Nov. 1708); *The Mirror* (10 Mar. 1832) 170–1. **Literary** Ben Jonson, *Masque of Queens* (1616); Thomas Middleton, *Anything for a Quiet Life* (1662) 5:1.

cats: behaviour

The idea that certain aspects of a cat's behaviour have meaning above and beyond its nature has a long history, and although there is not complete agreement over meanings, the general outline has remained remarkably constant for centuries. The most widespread has been the notion that when the house cat washes herself (cats are nearly always referred to as female), if she washes behind her ears it presages rain, or at least a change in the weather:

Watch the cat as she washes her face, and if she passes her paw over her ear it will rain tomorrow.
                        Co. Durham Leighton (1910)

It froze in the afternoon and the barometer still rising, but in the evening it thawed and some rain fell. I was saying before dinner that there would be an alteration of weather soon as I a long time observed one of our cats wash over both her ears – an old observation, and I must now believe it to be a pretty true one.
                Norfolk Woodforde, *Diary* (30 Jan. 1794)

Numerous writers refer in passing to this belief, confirming its widespread nature and turning it into something of a literary cliché,

True calendars, as pusses eare
Wash't o'rs, to tell what change is neare
                    Herrick, 'His Age . . .', *Hesperides* (1648)

and the meaning has remained relatively constant from at least 1507 to the late twentieth century.

Nevertheless, some have reported alternative meanings:

Cat washing behind its ears – the first person it looks up at will have a letter.
                        Devon *Devonshire Assoc.* (1959)

[From a servant girl, about nineteen years old]
The coming of a stranger may be expected if a
cat, when washing her face, puts her paw above
either of her ears.   **Devon** *Devonshire Assoc.* (1878)

This letter/stranger interpretation is much more
rarely reported than the dominant 'rain' theory,
and only from the mid eighteenth century, but
it, too, was still being quoted in the 1970s.

A third belief is that the cat sitting with her
back to the fire also predicts the weather – snow
or frost in some versions or, again, rain:

I have frequently heard it stated that if a cat sits
with its back towards the fire it is a sign that we
shall have some cold weather.

Devon *Devonshire Assoc.* (1886)

But the worst weather is predicted by a cat's
sudden unexplained activity – chasing its own
tail, much scratching of the furniture, for example – which means high winds or storms:

Sailors, I am informed on the authority of a naval
officer, have a great dislike to see the cat, on board
ship, unusually playful and frolicsome; such an
event, they consider, prognosticates a storm; and
they have a saying on these occasions that 'the cat
has a gale of wind in her tail'.

Unlocated Brand (1849)

Washing/Rain: **Somerset** [1922]Opie & Tatem, 59.
Devon *Devonshire Assoc.* 57 (1926) 111. **Wiltshire** *Wilts.*
N&Q 1 (1893–5) 104. **Berkshire** *Folk-Lore* 5 (1894) 337.
Herefordshire Leather (1912) 24, **Norfolk** James
Woodforde *Diary* (30 Jan. 1794), Fulcher Collection
(c.1895). **Lincolnshire** Thompson (1856) 735. **Shropshire**
Burne (1883) 212. **Derbyshire** *N&Q* 5S:7 (1877) 54.
Lancashire Harland & Wilkinson (1882) 141; [1984]
Opie & Tatem, 59. **Co. Durham** Leighton (1910) 56.
General *Gospelles of Dystaves* Pt 2, 22 (1507); Topsell
(1607) 105; Melton (1620); Thomas Wilsford, *Nature's*
Secrets (1638) 131; John Swan, *Speculum Mundi* (1643)
457; *Time's Telescope* (1825) 170. **General** Foli (1902) 108.
Literary Robert Herrick, 'His Age . . .', *Hesperides*
(1648); *Poetical Description of Beasts* (1773) 46, quoted
Opie & Tatem, 58; J. M. Barrie, *Sentimental Tommy*
(1896) 197.
Stranger/Letter: **Somerset** [1922] Opie & Tatem, 59.
Devon *Devonshire Assoc.* 10 (1878) 105; *Devonshire*
Assoc. 57 (1926) 110–11; *Devonshire Assoc.* 91 (1959) 200.
Glamorgan [1955] Opie & Tatem, 59. **Co. Wexford**
[1938] Ó Muirithe & Nuttall (1999) 162. **Guernsey** De
Garis (1975) 130. **Literary** *Connoisseur* 59 (1755) 352;
Revd S. Bishop, *Poems* 1 (1796) 116.
Back to the fire: **Devon** *Devonshire Assoc.* (1886), 105;
N&Q 10S:12 (1909) 66. **Berkshire** *Folk-Lore* 5 (1894)
337. **Norfolk** Fulcher Collection (c.1895). **Herefordshire**
Leather (1912) 24. **Lincolnshire** *Gent. Mag.* (1833) 590–3.
Shropshire Burne (1883) 212. **England** Addy (1895) 68.
Yorkshire *Leeds Mercury* (4 Oct. 1879). **Mid-Wales**
Davies (1911) 220. **N. Ireland** Foster (1951) 127. **Literary**
Connoisseur 59 (1755) 352.

Activity/Storms: **Somerset** [1922] Opie & Tatem, 58.
Worcestershire *Folk-Lore* 20 (1909) 344. **Lancashire**
N&Q 1S:3 (1851) 516; Harland & Wilkinson (1882) 141,
157. **Monmouthshire** [1954] Opie & Tatem, 58. **S.E.**
Ireland N&Q 3S:5 (1864) 236, 353. **Guernsey** De Garis
(1975) 130. **Unlocated** Brand 3 (1849) 188; *Chambers's*
Jnl (1873). **Literary** *Poetical Description of Beasts* (1773)
45, quoted Opie & Tatem, 58; Revd S. Bishop, *Poems* 1
(1796) 116.

cats: black

That black cats are lucky is now almost universally accepted in Britain. 'Good luck' cards bear
their pictures, lucky charms are on sale, and
brides are happy to meet one:

A well-known firm of soap manufacturers
recently used as an advertisement a charming
picture, obviously a photograph, of a family
wedding group standing on the church steps and
watching, with evident delight, a black cat walk-
ing up to the bride.   **Unlocated** *Folk-Lore* (1957)

The historical picture, however, is less straightforward, and there are plenty of references which

HERE'S ALL THE LUCK IN THE
WORLD, FROM THE SEASIDE!

Greeting-card manufacturers have routinely used
the black cat as a good-luck symbol since at least the
1920s. This example dates from the end of the
Second World War.

make it quite clear that for some the black cat was a far from good omen:

it is a very unfortunate thing for a man to meet early in a morning an ill-favoured man or woman, a rough-footed hen, a shag-haired dog, or a black cat. Unlocated Melton (1620)

[31 May 1797] Saw three black cats last night so did not go to market today fearing some evil, but it turned out well as Betty was taken with spasms and might have died had I not stayed at home and she is the best milker of all I have, this omen for ill brought nought but good.

Yorkshire Jeffrey (1923)

A crowing hen, a whistling girl, and a black cat are considered most unlucky. Beware of them in a house. Ireland Wilde (1888)

Even in specific circumstances, i.e. at sea, there is a lack of agreement. Writing of Yorkshire fishing communities, Jeffrey says: 'A stray black cat taking up her abode in a new house brings luck to the place, but its presence would not be tolerated on ship-board.' (**Yorkshire** Jeffrey (1923)), while at the same period, 'Westleton fishermen like to take both a black cat and a horseshoe to sea' (**Suffolk** *Folk-Lore* (1924)). Baker (1979), writing of the Navy in the twentieth century, comments: 'On British ships one black cat was lucky, two never' and goes on to describe what was claimed to be the last ship's cat in the Royal Navy, which left HMS *Hecate* in 1975.

Popular writers on superstition take it for granted that black cats are lucky. The better writers, however, come clean on their confusion, with comments such as: 'The superstitious beliefs about cats are so fragmented and various that it is difficult to make any sense of them' (Briggs (1980)). If such authorities are confused, it is hardly surprising to find contradictory statements, even in the same work, as, for example, John Nicholson's *Folk Lore of East Yorkshire* (1890). On page 43 Nicholson writes: 'Among unlucky things . . . to have a black cat, but lucky to meet one, and unlucky to meet a coloured one, especially yellow'; but on page 135, 'It is considered lucky to have a black cat, but unlucky to meet one'.

Some of the confusion can be explained by an awareness of the situational aspects of the cat/human interaction. Some informants indicate that there is a difference between owning and meeting a black cat, others are pleased or vexed depending on the position or orientation of the animal, and so on:

A black cat crossing one's path is a lucky omen. A black cat passing by a window foretells the arrival of a visitor. Guernsey De Garis (1975)

A number specifically mention doorways and houses, in particular that it is unlucky to drive a black cat from your door:

An Oxford landlady told us quite recently that she had driven away a black cat from her door shortly after she was married, some twelve years previously, and since then she had 'buried twenty-three relations'. Oxfordshire Wright (1913)

but

Unlucky to open a door to a black cat.
Devon N&Q (1909)

Another recurrent feature is the link between black cats and marriage:

In a house where a black cat is kept the spinster portion of its population will never lack plenty of sweethearts.

Whenever the cat of the house is black
The lasses of lovers will have no lack
Northern England [1850s] *Denham Tracts*

As in other areas of superstition, what we have mostly lost in the modern era is subtlety and variation.

The relative luckiness of black cats is not specifically mentioned until Melton's piece in 1620, and references before 1800 are almost nonexistent (although there are numerous reports which specify a black cat (or part of one) in a cure (*see* CATS: CURES USING). Contrasting this paucity of material with the plethora of references from the 1850s onwards, at least allows us to say that the belief was nowhere near as popular in the earlier period as it was later to become, and it seems to be a classic example of the growth of a superstition over time, which belies the assumption that later popularity can be read backwards and used to explain origins and development.

Sussex Latham (1878) 8. **Devon** N&Q 10S:12 (1909) 66. **Wiltshire** *Wilts. N&Q* 1 (1893–5) 315. **Essex** [c.1920] Mays (1969) 164; *Folk-Lore* 64 (1953) 294. **Oxfordshire** [pre-1900] *Folk-Lore* 24 (1913) 90; Wright (1913) 218; [1920s] Surman (1992) 62; *Oxon Folk-Lore Soc.* (1952) 9. **Herefordshire** [c.1895] *Folk-Lore* 39 (1928) 391; Leather (1912) 24. **Suffolk** *Folk-Lore* 35 (1924) 352. **Lincolnshire** Rudkin (1936) 16. **Shropshire** Burne (1883) 211–12. **Staffordshire** Poole (1875) 81. **England** Addy (1895) 68. **Nottinghamshire** N&Q 10S:8 (1907) 227. **Northern England** [1850s] *Denham Tracts* 2 (1895) 73; *Newcastle Weekly Chronicle* (11 Feb. 1899) 7. **Yorkshire** [1797] Jeffrey (1923) 140; *Leeds Mercury* (4 Oct. 1879);

Nicholson (1890) 43, 135; Blakeborough (1898) 127. **Lancashire** *Folk-Lore* 64 (1953) 294. **Westmorland** [*c*.1939] *Folk-Lore* 64 (1953) 294. **Co. Durham** Leighton (1910) 62. **Northumberland** Bosanquet (1929) 80. **Wales** Howells (1831) 67. **Mid-Wales** Davies (1911) 227. **Orkney** N&Q 10S:12 (1909) 483–4. **Ireland** Wilde (1888) 180. **N. Ireland** Foster (1951) 127. **Co. Wexford** [1938] Ó Muirithe & Nuttall (1999) 162. **Guernsey** De Garis (1975) 130. **Jersey** *Folk-Lore* 25 (1914) 246; L'Amy (1927) 98. **Royal Navy** Baker (1979) 84–8. **Unlocated** Melton (1620); *Chambers's Jnl.* (1873) 809; Igglesden (*c*.1932) 88–90; *Folk-Lore* 68 (1957) 418; *Folk-Lore* 73 (1962) 132. **General** Foli (1902) 107; Hoggart (1957) Ch. 2; Briggs (1980) 66; *Watford Observer* (11 Feb. 1994) 20.

cats: born in May

A widespread belief holds that cats born in May are unlucky, sickly, of little use as mousers, and prone to catching other creatures:

Kittens born in May will bring snakes into the house – They are also unlucky, apparently. Owing to the snake story the servant of a friend of mine was about to drown an entire family of kittens born in May, but owing to her remonstrance two were spared: one came to an untimely end, being murdered by her own pet dog and the other was eaten by a rat in its early infancy. On inquiry I find the snake legend obtains in my own kitchen. **Devon** *Devonshire Assoc.* (1901)

Although MAY is an unlucky month in other contexts, there is no clue as to why cats in particular are singled out in this way, although a few informants claim that other domestic animals, and even human children, born in the month are also unlucky and unlikely to thrive (see MAY: BABIES).

Available references show that the superstition was known in most parts of England, but evidence from elsewhere in the British Isles is lacking. This is unlikely to be a true reflection of reality. The superstition appears to spring into life, fully formed, all over the country in the 1850s, so it must have been around for at least a while before that time. Indeed, a verse from the early sixteenth century demonstrates that May kittens already had a bad reputation, but what happened to the belief between then and the 1850s is a mystery.

He seemed fader of all unthryftnesse,
Jagged and garded full ungay,
With a face filled with falsenesse
Berded lyke kitling of May.
Barclay, *Castle of Labour* (1506)

Sussex Latham (1878) 17. **Somerset** N&Q 1S:7 (1853) 152. **Devon** *Devonshire Assoc.* 11 (1879) 110; *Devonshire*

Assoc. 33 (1901) 128; N&Q 10S:12 (1909) 66; Crossing (1911) 135–6. **Cornwall** Hunt (1865) 237; *Folk-Lore Jnl* 5 (1887) 210; [1890s] *Old Cornwall* 1:12 (1930) 4; *Folk-Lore* 20 (1909) 488. **Wiltshire** *Wilts. N&Q* 1 (1893–5) 316. **Wiltshire/Devon** N&Q 1S:3 (1851) 20 **Herefordshire** Leather (1912) 24. **Huntingdonshire** N&Q 3S:8 (1865) 146. **Northern England** [1850s] *Denham Tracts* 2 (1895) 55. **Lancashire** N&Q 1S:3 (1851) 516. **Cumberland** *Folk-Lore* 40 (1929) 285. **Co. Durham** Brockie (1886) 121; *Folk-Lore* 20 (1909) 75; Leighton (1910) 62. **Northumberland** Bosanquet (1929) 80. **Unlocated** N&Q 1S:7 (1853) 152; *Folk-Lore* 68 (1957) 413. **Literary** Alex Barclay, *Castle of Labour* (1506) 2:5.

cats: cures using

Cats were used extensively in cures in the past for numerous human ailments. The most widely recorded use of a cat for medicinal purpose is to stroke an eyelid with its tail to cure a STYE. Other regular cures, for ERYSIPELAS, RINGWORM, and SHINGLES, for example, all used cat's blood, usually taken from the animal's ear or tail, and parts of a cat were also beneficial in other eye cures. The essentially magical nature of these cures is underlined by the fact that in most of them, a *black* cat was stipulated.

A very common cure for WHOOPING COUGH was for a few hairs from the patient's head to be placed between slices of bread and fed to a dog, in the conviction that the animal would take the cough away. Occasionally, a cat is stipulated in the dog's place (e.g. **Essex** *Folk-Lore* (1951)), but in an Irish reference, the roles are reversed:

Whooping Cough – Nine hairs from the tail of a black cat, chopped up and soaked in water, which is then swallowed, and the cough will be relieved.
Ireland Wilde (1888)

A regular feature of earlier medicine is the use of animals, cut open while still alive and placed on to ailing parts of the body. Again, PIGEONS and puppies were usually stipulated, but cats could also be used:

to cure swollen knee – kill a cat, split it lengthwise – bind it round knee while still warm and keep there as long as possible. A fowl answers quite as well. **Yorkshire** Nicholson (1890)

A few other isolated examples of the use of cats are as follows:

A cat's skin is a good remedy for toothache. You should keep a dried cat's skin and hold it to your cheek when your tooth aches.
England Addy (1895)

Raw cat's flesh as cure for asthma and consumption. **Unlocated** Igglesden (*c*.1932)

It is recommended by one white witch in my neighbourhood that you should cut off the cat's left ear, and drop three drops of its blood into a wineglass full of spring water. You then administer the remedy to the child who has measles.

Cornwall *Old Cornwall* (1931)

'Cast the cat o'er him' – It is believed that when a man is raving in a fever, the cat cast over him will cure him. The proverb is applied to them whom we hear telling extravagant things as they are raving.   Scotland Kelly, *Scottish Proverbs* (1721)

Cornwall *Old Cornwall* 2:1 (1931) 20. Essex *Folk-Lore* 62 (1951) 259–60. England Addy (1895) 89. Yorkshire Nicholson (1890) 139–40. Scotland Kelly (1721). Ireland Wilde (1888) 197. Unlocated Igglesden (c.1932) 204. General Topsell (1607) 106–7; W. Salmon, *London Dispensatory* (1678) 205; D. Turner, *Diseases of the Skin* (1726) 81–2.

cats: dreaming of

A few folklore collections specifically mention DREAMING of cats, and offer an interpretation apparently based on the spiteful side of feline character in their unanimous assessment:

To dream of cats is considered unlucky, denoting treachery and quarrels on the part of friends.

The Mirror (10 Mar. 1832)

Exactly the same attribution is also given in most popular DREAM BOOKS of the nineteenth and twentieth centuries.

Sussex Latham (1878) 13. England Addy (1895) 100. General *The Mirror* (10 Mar. 1832) 170–1.

cats: dying

It was considered very unlucky for a cat to die in the house. Some informants rationalized this feeling by reference to the love the family had for their pet, but this does not sit well with the reality in which ailing cats were taken outside, however tenderly, and left to die, or even simply drowned to avoid the promised ill fortune. Nor does it explain the 'bad luck' of failing to follow the dictates of the superstition:

It is a very unlucky thing to let a cat die in the house. Many a poor pet has been carried out into the back yard, by a kind housewife in canny Sunderland, and deposited tenderly on a mat, or a piece of old blanket to die.

Co. Durham Brockie (1886)

I have known cases where, when such a misfortune occurred, the family were thrown into great consternation, surmising what possible form of evil this omen portended to them. Generally when a cat was known to be ailing, the animal was removed from the house and placed in the coal cellar, or other outhouse, with plenty of food, and kept there until it either recovered or died.

Western Scotland Napier (1879)

Although quite widespread geographically, there is no evidence that the notion existed before the Victorian era.

Cornwall *Folk-Lore Jnl* 5 (1887) 195. Worcestershire *Folk-Lore* 20 (1909) 344. Shropshire Burne (1883) 212. Lancashire Harland & Wilkinson (1882) 141. Co. Durham Brockie (1886) 121. Western Scotland Napier (1879) 117–18.

cats: having a cold

A relatively widespread belief maintained that a family's health was to some extent dependent on the cat, and that if the latter showed symptoms of a cold (especially a sneeze or cough) the whole household would get it very soon:

It is firmly believed that if the cat coughs in the house every member of the family will in turn take the cough. Consequently, as soon as the feline pet begins to give indications of cold she must be removed from her snug position by the fire and given over to the tender mercies of the outer world.   Oxfordshire *Midland Garner* (1884)

Two isolated references hint at other meanings:

A cat sneezing is a sign of heavy rain.

Devon *Devonshire Assoc.* (1935)

If the cat sneezes the day before your wedding, you may expect great good fortune.

Northumberland *Folk-Lore* (1925)

Sussex Latham (1878) 10. Devon *Devonshire Assoc.* 67 (1935) 132. Wiltshire *Wilts. N&Q* 1 (1893–5) 152. Oxfordshire *Midland Garner* 1 (1884) 22. Shropshire Burne (1883) 212. East Anglia Forby (1830) 414. Suffolk Claxton (1954) 89. Northumberland *Folk-Lore* 36 (1925) 253. Unlocated Hone, *Year Book* (1832) 126–8. Literary *Connoisseur* 59 (1755) 352.

cats: moving house

Several traditional ways of convincing the family cat to stay in a new house have been documented, but by far the most often recommended, and still spoken of it not actually carried out, is 'buttering the feet':

To prevent a cat leaving a new house, butter her paws; she will not attempt to run away after that, say the wise. We had a cat who twice returned to the old homestead four miles away, though he was brought back fastened in a hamper, and in a closed carriage. An old woman advised me to butter his feet, whereupon Mr. Puss sat calmly down in front of the fire and licked it off. We had no more trouble; he never attempted to wander again.   Wiltshire *Wilts. N&Q* (1893–5)

Some suggest using cream or grease, but other remedies are also recommended, such as putting the cat in the oven (when cold), or:

In going to a new house, the cat should be put in through the window backwards; it is unlucky to let it walk in forwards. A woman complained of losing her cat, although she had buttered its feet when it came.   Herefordshire Leather (1912)

On the other hand, in some areas, particularly in Ireland, but also reported in England, it was considered unlucky to take the cat with you when you moved:

[According to] a simple serving-woman in Dublin: It is unlucky to take a cat with you when removing. In consequence of this belief cats often suffer terribly in Dublin.   Dublin *N&Q* (1869)

Kent [1930s] Kent (1977) 99. Sussex Latham (1878) 8. Devon *Devonshire Assoc.* 17 (1885) 122. Wiltshire *Wilts. N&Q* 1 (1893–5) 315. Herefordshire Leather (1912) 24. Suffolk Fitzgerald (1887) 498. Lancashire Harland & Wilkinson (1873) 219–20. Co. Durham Brockie (1886) 121. Unlocated *N&Q* 2S:5 (1858) 209.
Unlucky to take cat: Lincolnshire Watkins (1886) 11. England Addy (1895) 68. Dublin *N&Q* 4S:4 (1869) 505. Co. Longford *Béaloideas* 6 (1936) 264.

cats: nine lives

The notion that a cat has nine lives was already proverbial in the sixteenth century:

No wyfe, a woman hath nyne lyves like a cat,
    Heywood, *Proverbs* (1546)

It was quoted by dramatists and poets regularly throughout the seventeenth century and has remained in common parlance to the present day. It is not clear where the idea originated, although one early reference links it specifically with WITCHES:

A cat hath nine lives, that is to say, a witch may take on her a cat's body, nine times,
    Baldwin, *Beware the Cat* (1584)

but again it is not known whether Baldwin was quoting a genuine origin or was repeating a back-formed aetiological legend. No other known source corroborates the story, although it is possibly present in one of John Gay's *Fables*. In this poem a cat complains that because its owner has been thought a witch:

*And boys against our lives combine
Because, 'tis said, your cats have nine.*
    'The Old Woman and her Cats' (1727)

Selected references: Yorkshire *Leeds Mercury* (4 Oct. 1879). Lancashire N&Q 4S:6 (1870) 211. General Henry Fielding, *Journal of a Voyage to Lisbon* (1755). Literary Thomas Heywood, *Proverbs* (1546) Pt 2, Ch.4; William Baldwin, *Beware the Cat* (1584) line 114; Shakespeare, *Romeo and Juliet* (1595) 3:1; Davies of Hereford, *Humour's Heaven on Earth* (1609) 115; Thomas Dekker, *Strange Horse-Race* (1613); John Marston, *Dutch Courtezan* (1633); John Gay, *Fables* (1727) 'The Old Woman and her Cats'.

cats: overboard

Drowning a cat while at sea was held to be very unlucky by sailors, primarily because it brought on a storm; unless, of course, one needed some wind:

[11 July 1754] A most tragical incident fell out this day at sea. While the ship was under sail, but making, as will appear, no great way, a kitten, one of four of the feline inhabitants of the cabin, fell from the window into the water … [he was very surprised that the captain stopped the ship and the boatswain leapt overboard to save it] … The kitten at last recovered, to the great joy of the good captain; but to the great disappointment of some of the sailors, who asserted that the drowning of a cat was the very surest way of raising a favourable wind.
    Fielding, *Journal of a Voyage to Lisbon* (1755)

The notion is mentioned several times in the eighteenth century, and regularly since, but is considerably older, as shown in a Scottish witchcraft trial in 1590. The accused, Agnes Sampsoune, had wrecked a boat by baptizing a cat and throwing it in the sea.

Devon Hewett (1900) 59. Co. Durham Brockie (1886) 209. Scotland [1590] Pitcairn (1833) Pt 2, 237. Unlocated Henry Fielding, *Journal of a Voyage to Lisbon* (1755); N&Q 12S:1 (1916) 66; Grose (1790) 48; Brand (1813) 551–2; N&Q 1S:10 (1854) 26. General James P. Andrews, *Anecdotes* (1789) 225; Literary Frederick Marryat, *King's Own* (1830) Ch.6.

cats: shutting in

Cats being drowned at sea were reputed to create winds and storms (*see* CATS: OVERBOARD), but another treatment of the animal could also bring bad weather:

On telling the landlady's daughter I was leaving on the morrow, she laughingly threatened to put the cat under a pot to bring bad weather and force me to stay. She assured me it was a common practice among the sailor's wives.
Co. Limerick *Folk-Lore Jnl* (1883)

Charles Darwin's companions on the HMS *Beagle* in 1831 had the same idea. The cat could be enclosed in a cupboard, or cold oven, to the same effect. In other contexts, the oven could also be used to keep the cat from returning to the old home after moving house (*see* CATS: MOVING), for luck, or, in a mining community:

[c.1908] *Putting the cat in the oven at cavilling time was another strong superstition. The oven was cold, and the cat was kept in it till the lots for the cavills, or seams, were drawn. This is still done in some colliery villages. Apparently it is, or was until recently, so common that miners in Co. Durham seem amazed when one confesses ignorance of it. No one seems to know why it was done.*
Co. Durham *Folk-Lore* (1957)

Lancashire Harland & Wilkinson (1882) 140–1. Northumberland [1820s?] *Denham Tracts* (1895) 365. Co. Durham *Folk-Lore* 68 (1957) 425. Co. Limerick *Folk-Lore Jnl* 1 (1883) 330.

cats: unhealthy for humans

The specific health hazards for babies of cats in the house are covered separately (*see above*), but a number of references demonstrate a feeling that all cats are potentially harmful to human health, and they should not be handled or allowed to get too close. Very similar warnings were given in 1607 as in the nineteenth century:

That the breath of these animals is poisonous, that they can play with serpents and remain uninjured, whilst their fur communicates the infection of the venom of those reptiles, that they lend themselves readily to infernal agents and purposes, that certain portions of their bodies possess magical properties and were efficacious in the preparation of charmed potions, and that they are partly supernatural creatures, endowed with a power of bringing good or evil fortune

upon their possessors . . . was once devoutly believed by the illiterate, as it is partially at this very day.
The Mirror (10 Mar. 1832)

England Addy (1895) 90. Lancashire Harland & Wilkinson (1882) 141. General Topsell (1607) 106; *The Mirror* (10 Mar. 1832) 170–1.

cats: white

In a few recorded cases, white cats are specifically reported as unlucky, probably in contrast to the general luckiness of black cats, but possibly too because white examples of various animals (e.g. HARES) are viewed with suspicion.

I also have a little white cat, which I am begged to get rid of, as white cats are unlucky in a house, and everything had been going wrong since it came.
Middlesex N&Q (1889)

Devon *Devonshire Assoc.* 103 (1971) 269. Middlesex N&Q 7S:8 (1889) 464. Essex [c.1939] *Folk-Lore* 64 (1953) 294. Lancashire [c.1914] Corbridge (1964) 156–60.

cauls

Babies who are born with a section of the amniotic membrane, or caul, over their head and face have widely been regarded as being generally very lucky, and specifically immune from drowning throughout their life:

A close connection of mine born in Worcestershire in 1906 came into this world with a caul . . . The circumstances of his birth did not inspire his choice of a career, nor until after his third escape did he learn the old superstition about children being born with cauls preserved from drowning. It is undoubtedly a coincidence that he has had three narrow shaves from a watery death.
Worcestershire *Folk-Lore* (1950)

In most cases, this immunity only lasted while the fortunate one (or his/her family) kept the caul safe:

In Somerset, just before the 1939 war, I was told of a little boy who was born with a caul. This was carefully preserved at first, but when he was twelve months old, his mother was persuaded by some friends to throw it away. Very soon afterwards the child was drowned in a shallow pond. My informant, the boy's sister, thought this was merely a coincidence, though a curious one; but she said that almost everyone else in the village was quite sure that the accident would not have happened if only the caul had been kept.
Somerset *Folk-Lore* (1957)

Nevertheless, some families were more than willing to sell the caul because the immunity was thus transferred to the buyer, and many references record advertisements in newspapers and dock-side shop windows offering or requesting such items – particularly in times of war or other particular danger for sailors:

Sailors will still buy cauls when they can, and have been known to give as much as £20 for one. Even this fairly large sum hardly seems excessive if the buyer believes, as most do, that he is not only gaining safety for himself, but also for his ship, since no ship that contains a caul will sink at sea. In 1954 a Banbury woman told me that the midwife offered her £10 for her child's caul, which she wanted for a sailor friend. The mother refused the offer, preferring to keep the luck and the safety for her own little boy.

Oxfordshire *Folk-Lore* (1957)

An additional function of the caul is that if kept by the child's family it acts as an indicator of the well-being of its possessor when absent:

The mother had kept the caul stretched on a sheet of note-paper, and whenever her son was in danger it became wet and soft, but it remained dry and like a dried bladder so long as he was safe.   Hampshire N&Q (1899)

One was certainly thought sufficiently valuable to be included in the will of Sir John Offley, dated May 1658:

Item, I will and devise one jewell done all in gold enamelled wherein is a caul that covered my face and shoulders when I first came into the world, the use whereof to my loving daughter, the Lady Elizabeth Jenny, so long as she shall live: and after her decease the use likewise thereof to her son Offley Jenny during his natural life.

Staffordshire Hackwood (1924)

The belief certainly dates from before 1500 in Britain, was reported frequently right into the late twentieth century, and may still be current.

Other occasionally reported attributes of the caul include the belief that the person so born will always be a wanderer, and that s/he will be safe from the fairies.

Also called mask, baby's veil, silly-how, haly-hood.

Somerset [1905/1951/1961] Tongue (1965) 136; *Folk-Lore* 68 (1957) 412–13. Devon *Devonshire Assoc.* 10 (1878) 104–5; *Western Antiquary* 7 (1887–8) 61. Hampshire N&Q 9S:3 (1899) 26. Berkshire N&Q 10S:1 (1904) 26. London N&Q 11S:12 (1915) 239. Oxfordshire *Folk-Lore* 68 (1957) 412–13; East Anglia Varden (1885) 106–7.

Suffolk *Folk-Lore* 35 (1924) 349; *Folk-Lore* 56 (1945) 270. Norfolk Dew (1898) 77–81; *Folk-Lore* 40 (1929) 121–2. Warwickshire Bloom (c.1930) 18. Worcestershire *Folk-Lore* 61 (1950) 104. Shropshire Burne (1883) 285. Staffordshire Hackwood (1924) 57. Derbyshire [c.1890] Uttley (1946) 125. England Addy (1895) 120. Lincolnshire Peacock (1877) 51; Swaby (1891) 88. Yorkshire Nicholson (1890) 1; [1953] Opie & Tatem, 67. Lancashire *Lancashire Lore* (1971) 49. Co. Durham Leighton (1910) 46. Wales Trevelyan (1909) 265. West Wales Davies (1911) 218. Western Scotland Napier (1879) 32. Highland Scotland Polson (1926) 4. Argyllshire *Folk-Lore* 21 (1910) 90. Dumfriesshire Corrie (1890/91) 37. N. Ireland Foster (1951) 64. Co. Tyrone *Lore & Language* 1:7 (1972) 9. Co. Longford *Béaloideas* 6 (1936) 259. Connemara *Folk-Lore Jnl* 2 (1884) 257. Jersey *Folk-Lore* 38 (1927) 179. Guernsey De Garis (1975) 6. Unlocated Melton (1620) 46; Grose (1787) 60–1; N&Q 7S:2 (1886) 145. Literary Swift (1738); Thomas Hardy, *The Return of the Native* (1878) Bk 3, Ch. 7. General Browne, *Pseudodoxia Epidemica* (1672) Bk 5, Ch. 22, Para 17; *Gent. Mag.* (1796) 636; N&Q 9S:3 (1899) 78, 175.

celandine (*Ranunculus ficaria*)

No superstitions appear to have featured celandine, except in the field of folk cures. The plant has been recommended for various ailments, including WARTS, RINGWORM, cancer of the liver, jaundice, and, particularly, piles. Vickery comments that another name for the plant is *pilewort*, and that its supposed efficacy against piles arose because its root tubers resemble them.

Devon *Devonshire Assoc.* 81 (1949) 91. Norfolk *Folk-Lore* 40 (1929) 118–9. Lincolnshire [MS c.1680] Peacock (1877) 251. Various Vickery (1995) 61–2. General Hatfield (1994) numerous pages; Allen (1995) 95–6, 178; Baker (1996) 39.

chaff-riddling

A method of divination to ascertain who is to die in the coming year:

Another mode of divining into futurity ... called cauff-riddling ... The barn doors must be set wide open, a riddle and some chaff must be procured, and those who wish to pry into the future must go into the barn at midnight, and in turn commence the process of riddling. Should the riddler be doomed to die during the year, two persons will be seen passing by the open barn-doors carrying a coffin, in the other case nothing will be visible. Not many years ago two men and a woman went to a barn near Malton, in

Yorkshire, on St. Mark's Eve, to riddle cauff. All the requisite observances were attended to; the men took their turns, but nothing was seen; then the woman began to riddle. Scarcely had the chaff begun to fall on the floor when all saw the ominous pair of coffin-bearers passing by. There was a moment's pause; the men rushed out to look, but all had disappeared; there was no living creature in sight. The woman died within the year. This story was related to my informant by one who knew the persons concerned, and spoke of them by name. Yorkshire Henderson (1866)

see also ASH-RIDDLING for a very similar procedure in the house, and BARN-WATCHING.

Yorkshire Henderson (1866) 35–6; Nicholson (1890) 85.

chairs: falling over

Knocking over a chair as you rise from it seems an obvious candidate for superstitious meaning, but the few references which have survived do not provide an agreed meaning. For example:

If a chair falls as a person rises, it is an unlucky omen. Ireland Wilde (1888)

If a person in rising from table overturned his chair, this shewed that he had been speaking untruths. Western Scotland Napier (1879)

An older strand of meaning connects the chair with marriage, but it is unclear why:

As Miss rises, the chair falls behind her. Miss: Well, I shan't be lady mayoress this year. Neverout: No, miss, 'tis worse than that; you won't be married this year. Swift (1738)

echoed two centuries later in Ireland:

If a person fall off a seat he won't be married that year. Co. Longford *Béaloideas* 6 (1936)

Another specialist meaning was found in the nursing profession:

If a nurse knocks over a chair a new patient will soon be arriving. Unlocated Igglesden (*c.*1932)

If the chair over which the bedclothes are folded falls over, an emergency case will come into the ward. Daily Express (31 July 1958)

Western Scotland Napier (1879) 138. Ireland Wilde (1888) 204. Co. Longford *Béaloideas* 6 (1936) 260. Unlocated Igglesden (*c.*1932) 235; *Daily Express* (31 July 1958) 4, quoted Opie & Tatem, 68. Literary Swift (1738).

chairs: grave

Sitting in a chair immediately after someone has vacated it might still in some quarters evince a

chairs

All common domestic items have their share of beliefs, and chairs are no exception. They appear in many superstitions, although none of these is as widely known as those concerning TABLES. The following miscellaneous beliefs have only been found in one or two versions, although any of them may have been more widely known than our present knowledge admits:

Chairs have been seen to move about the rooms where people lay dying. Devon *Devonshire Assoc.* (1876)

We have wishing chairs here and there throughout the North Country. There is one at Finchale Priory; and he who seats himself in it, breathes a wish, and tells no one what it is, will possibly receive it. Co. Durham Brockie (1889)

[Milliners workshop, interwar years] *When a chair was passed over a table it foretold a row.* London Henrey (1955)

If the three-legged stool falls and lies upside down, you will be worried that day. Wales Trevelyan (1909)

If you sweep under a chair on which a woman is sitting, she will never marry. Lancashire *Lancashire Lore* (1971)

It is unlucky to sit next to an empty chair. Northumberland *Newcastle Weekly Chronicle* (4 Feb. 1899)

Devon *Devonshire Assoc.* 8 (1876) 57. **London** Henrey (1955) 97–8. **Lancashire** *Lancashire Lore* (1971) 51. **Co. Durham** Brockie (1886) 210. **Northumberland** *Newcastle Weekly Chronicle* (4 Feb. 1899) 7. **Wales** Trevelyan (1909) 329.

comment on the lines of 'You wouldn't jump into my grave so quick!' This connection with graves has been reported a handful of times since the eighteenth century, but the paucity of printed references certainly under-represents its widespread nature.

Neverout rises to pick up the [fallen] *chair, and Miss sits in his.* Neverout: *You wouldn't be so soon in my grave, madam.*   Swift (1738)

Even with so few examples, there is little agreement as to the exact nature of the grave connection. For Swift, and in the version remembered from the author's childhood (South London, 1950s), it is more a question of a breach of etiquette, whereas in others the sitter is either foretelling his own early death or, worse, wishing it upon the person who has just vacated the chair.

Devon *Devonshire Assoc.* 57 (1926) 130. **Wiltshire** *Wilts. N&Q* 1 (1893–5) 8; [1923] Opie & Tatem, 68. **Co. Tyrone** *Lore & Language* 1:7 (1972) 13. **Literary** Swift (1738).

chairs: pregnancy

see PREGNANCY: CHAIRS AND BEDS.

chairs: replacing

For those of us brought up to replace their chairs on rising from the table, it may be surprising to learn that in several mid twentieth-century references, this was considered an unfriendly act:

When having a meal with an acquaintance, do not push your chair under the table when you get up, or you will not come there again for a meal.   Lincolnshire Rudkin (1936)

The motif in question would seem to be the air of finality which the action entails. The geographical spread suggests that it was more widely known than is indicated by these few reports.

Devon *Devonshire Assoc.* 64 (1932); *Devonshire Assoc.* 165/77 (1945) 94. **Wiltshire** Wiltshire (1975) 84. **Lincolnshire** Rudkin (1936) 20. **Yorkshire** *Folk-Lore* 43 (1932) 254.

chairs: turning, lucky

When playing cards or other games of chance, a widespread notion is that one's luck can be improved by changing the situation or setting, in particular the chair in which one sits:

This odious chair, how came I stuck in't?
I think I never had good luck in't.
   Swift, *Journal of a Modern Lady* (1728)

The action varies between changing places and literally turning one's chair around:

'Turn your chair and turn your luck' – This is quite a common expression in Somerset. When people are playing cards or other games and have a run of bad luck they get up, turn themselves and their chair round, and sit down again in the hope that their luck will be changed.
   Somerset N&Q (1925)

In part this is a metaphoric action – 'changing' the luck by 'changing' the position – but for those more deeply imbued with superstition it may be that the natural ill-wishing of one's opponent in such competitive games may be confused by offering a moving target. The latter notion does not fit well other examples of 'ill-wishing', which are normally person- rather than place-specific, but one looks in vain for all-encompassing patterns in belief.

Somerset N&Q 148 (1925) 153. **Devon** Hewett (1900) 59. **Lincolnshire** *Gent. Mag.* (Dec. 1832) 493. **Shropshire** Burne (1883) 272. **England** Addy (1895) 94. **Unlocated** Igglesden (*c.*1932) 190. **Literary** Swift, *Journal of a Modern Lady* (1728); *Adventurer* (6 Mar. 1753) 6, quoted Opie & Tatem, 68.

chairs: turning, unlucky

The common superstition that to 'turn' or change your chair will break a run of bad luck at cards (*see above*), is contradicted by three reports which indicate that turning a chair was unlucky.

While talking thoughtlessly with a good woman, I carelessly turned a chair round two or three times; she was offended, and said it was a sign we should quarrel: and so it proved, for she never spoke friendly to me afterwards.
   Unlocated Hone, *Year Book* (1832)

With only three references, it is impossible to gauge how common this belief may have been, but the fact that they span nearly one hundred years argues for a wider distribution than that shown.

Staffordshire Hackwood (1924) 149. **Unlocated** Hone, *Year Book* (1832) 126–8; N&Q 148 (1925) 153.

chapbooks

Chapbooks were small paper-covered booklets, cheaply printed and often crudely illustrated, which poured in their millions from backstreet printing presses in London and other urban centres in Britain and Ireland, from the seventeenth to nineteenth centuries. They were sold by travelling rural chapmen, on stalls at markets, in urban streets and at fairs, in shops, and wherever else an outlet could be found. Along with BROADSIDES (single printed sheets), chapbooks made up the basic reading matter of the working and lower middle classes until they were gradually superseded in the Victorian era by newspapers, magazines, and more substantial cheaply printed books. An astonishing array of material reached the public through the chapbook trade, including traditional tales, songs, and children's rhymes, which earlier folklorists had presumed to be transmitted by oral tradition. The essential role of print in the dissemination of traditional material is only now being given its due attention.

The cover of a chapbook from c.1820. Superstitions and belief in fortune-telling were disseminated and perpetuated by countless popular publications such as this.

For the study of superstition, the key chapbook publications were DREAM BOOKS and fortune-telling guides, which were extremely popular:

It is quite astonishing to see the great demand there is, both in England and France, for dreambooks, and other trash of the same kind. Two books in England enjoy an extraordinary popularity, and have run through upwards of fifty editions in as many years in London alone, besides being reprinted in Manchester, Edinburgh, Glasgow, and Dublin. One is Mother Bridget's Dream-Book and Oracle of Fate; the other is the Norwood Gipsy. It is stated, on the authority of one who is curious in these matters, that there is a demand for these works, which are sold at sums varying from a penny to sixpence, chiefly to servant-girls and imperfectly-educated people, all over the country, of upwards of eleven thousand annually: and that at no period during the last thirty years has the average number sold been less than this. The total number during this period would thus amount to 330,000.

Mackay (1852) 295

The typical fare for these productions were lists of DREAM subjects and their meanings, elementary palmistry, TEA-LEAF READING, signification of MOLES on the body, telling fortunes with playing cards, by physiognomy, or the phases of the MOON, and so on. A regular feature was some form of impressive chart – such as a magic circle with numbers which could then be translated into predictive formulae. Occasionally, chapbooks specialized in one area, such as LOVE DIVINATION (*see* MOTHER BUNCH'S CLOSET) or simplified astrology, and their titles would often cash in on the fame of particular characters such as the NORWOOD GYPSIES.

Chapbook writers borrowed freely from each other's publications, and some key texts were simply reprinted, without acknowledgement, for decade after decade. Dating chapbooks and their contents is thus very difficult.

Leslie Shepard, *The History of Street Literature* (Newton Abbot: David & Charles, 1973); Roger Thompson, *Samuel Pepys' Penny Merriments* (London: Constable, 1976); John Ashton, *Chapbooks of the Eighteenth Century* (London: Chatto & Windus, 1882).

charms/charming

The word 'charm' has various meanings in modern English, but for present purposes it means a set of words which, when spoken or written down in the correct way, and with or without accompanying action by the charmer, have power in themselves to effect change or bring about action in the physical world. Thus a charm against bleeding will be expected to stop the flow of blood, a charm against a toothache to stop the pain. Charms can be curative, as in these examples, or protective – to prevent overlooking or ill-wishing when churning butter, for example. When written down and worn or carried about the person, the charm becomes an amulet, and charms could be handwritten or printed, as in the case of SAVIOUR'S LETTERS.

Written charms were also believed in as capable of effecting cures, or, at least, of preventing people from taking diseases. I have known people who wore written charms, sewed into the necks of their coats, if men, and into the headbands of petticoats if women . . . These talismans were so generally and thoroughly believed in, and so numerous and apparently well-attested were the evidences of their beneficial effects, that in years not long past, medical men believed in their efficacy, and promulgated various theories to account for it. Western Scotland Napier (1879)

Although the effectiveness of many charms relied on both words and the appropriate action, what was usually recorded was the action alone, as the charmer had an obvious incentive to keep the words to him/herself, and s/he thus mumbled or even simply thought them. The word 'charming' is thus sometimes used for cures which apparently have little or no verbal component.

In the neighbourhood of Stole Prior a charm was some time ago used by a labouring man for the removal of the thrush (or 'throcks' as it is locally termed). He would put his finger into his mouth and then into that of the child, rubbing the gums, while he mumbled out something terminating with 'Father, Son and Holy Ghost' then put down the child without speaking another word, and leave the house without eating or drinking.
Worcestershire/Shropshire *Gent. Mag.* (1855)

The most common problems for which charming was thought effective were TOOTHACHE, WARTS, AGUE, BURNS, THORNS, and BLEEDING.

For scalds/burns

> *There came two angels from the north*
> *One was fire and one was frost*
> *Out fire: In frost*
> *In the name of the Father, Son, and Holy Ghost*
> Sussex Latham (1878)

The vast majority were overtly Christian, sometimes detailing an incident in the lives of Jesus, Mary, or the disciples, or drawing on appropriate religious images such as the 'crown of thorns' when extracting a thorn, and so on. Although they usually directly invoked God in the form of 'In the name of the Father', they were not often addressed directly to God as prayers would be.

Cure for ague: When Jesus saw the cross, whereon his body should be crucified, his body shook, and the Jewes asked him had he the ague? He answered and said, 'Whosoever keepeth this in mind or writing shall not be troubled with fever or ague; so, Lord, help thy servant trusting in thee. Then say the Lord's prayer. This is to be read before it is folded, then knotted and not opened after'. Unlocated [1751] N&Q

While the charmer concentrated on such matters as warts and toothaches, there was little to lose, but more serious consequences could easily arise:

A SILLY SUPERSTITION: *A farm labourer named Thos. Ryder, residing at Cornwood, a village in Devonshire, was sharpening his scythe on Tuesday, when he cut his wrist, and severed two of the arteries. His friends, instead of securing medical assistance, sent for a man and his wife who have a local reputation as 'charmers', and these people endeavoured to stop the flow of blood by the ceremony of 'charming'. Ryder, seeing how fruitless these efforts were, begged to be taken to the hospital at Plymouth, some eight miles off . . . Ryder died of loss of blood before he got there.*
Devon *Daily Telegraph* (7 July 1887)

In most parts of Britain, at local level, there were amateur charmers who would undertake cures for free – indeed, it was forbidden to thank or pay them, but a 'gift' sometime later was always acceptable. But there were also many professional 'cunning men and women' who made a living from such activities. While certain people, such as SEVENTH SONS and POSTHUMOUS CHILDREN were said to have charming powers in themselves, they still had to learn the appropriate words, and other ordinary people could acquire power simply by being taught the words of the charm and the technique. A common tradition stated that men could only successfully pass on a charm to a woman, and vice versa.

The belief in charms was extremely widespread and long-lasting. The Christian church waged a continuing battle against their use, as most churchmen assumed that charms worked because the Devil or other spirits were behind them, despite their overtly godly tone. The pre-Reformation church had, indeed, sanctioned the use of verbal formulae and written prayers, but was never successful in teaching the mass of the people the difference between these and their own charms.

Mr. Ashmole told me, that a woman made use of a spell to cure an ague, by the advice of Dr. Napier; a minister came to her, and severely reprimanded her, for making use of diabolical help, and told her, she was in danger of damnation for it, and commanded her to burn it. She did so, but her distemper returned severely; insomuch that she was importunate with the Doctor to use the same again; she used it, and had ease. But the parson hearing of it, came to her again, and thundered hell and damnation, and frighted her so, that she burnt it again. Whereupon she fell extremely ill, and would have had it a third time; but the Doctor refused, saying that she had contemned and slighted the power and goodness of the blessed spirits (or Angels) and so she died.

Unlocated Aubrey, *Miscellanies* (1696)

Sussex Latham (1878) 35. Devon *Daily Telegraph* (7 July 1887) quoted N&Q 7S:4 (1887) 67. Worcestershire/Shropshire *Gent. Mag.* (1855) 133–9. Western Scotland Napier (1879) 91. Unlocated Aubrey, *Miscellanies* (1696/1857) 135–6; [1751] N&Q 1S:5 (1852) 413. Material on charms for specific ailments and problems are given under the appropriate entries. The following is a small selection of pieces of more general application. Felix Grendon, 'The Anglo-Saxon Charms', *Jnl American Folklore* 22 (1909) 105–237; A. R. Wright, 'Seventeenth Century Cures and Charms', *Folk-Lore* 23 (1912) 230–6, 490–7; Wilfrid Bonser, 'Anglo-Saxon Laws and Charms Relating to Theft', *Folk-Lore* 57 (1946) 7–11. Thomas R. Forbes, 'Verbal Charms in British Folk Medicine', *Papers of the Am. Phil. Soc.* 115 (1971) 293–316; Owen Davies, 'Healing Charms in Use in England and Wales 1700–1953', *Folklore* 107 (1996) 19–32. For charms in witchcraft, see Kittredge (1929), Robbins (1959) 85–8.

cheeks: burning

see EARS/CHEEKS BURNING.

chilblains

A variety of traditional cures for chilblains have been recorded, but three stand out as being the most widely known. The first is to treat them with holly:

An almost universal remedy recommended for chilblains is to thrash them with holly. Few of

those who prescribe this treatment have actually tried it themselves, but I once found a woman who claimed to have done so. She was very vague about the results and frankly I did not believe her.

East Anglia *East Anglian Mag.* (1953/4)

Despite the above writer's scepticism, it is clear from other reports that many people did try this remedy. Others believed in bathing the chilblains in urine, although they were often counselled to make sure it was fresh and 'their own':

In 1955 I was told that chilblains on hands or feet can be cured by dipping the afflicted members into the child's own urine every night and morning. 'There is an acid in it,' said my informant, 'that cures chilblains.' Unlocated *Folk-Lore* (1957)

The third was to rub the afflicted parts with snow. This was recommended as a preventative as well as a cure:

If a baby is taken out of doors when the first fall of snow which occurs after its birth is on the ground, and its feet well rubbed therewith, it will never have chilblains.

Herefordshire Leather (1912)

Other reported cures are to rub them with raw onions, goose grease, or the berries of the bittersweet (*Solanum dulcamara*) and, as with most minor ailments, they could be 'charmed away' by someone with the necessary skill:

A young woman . . . recently had [chilblains] charmed by a N. Devon farmer, whom she had contacted only by telephone.

Devon *Devonshire Assoc.* (1957)

Dorset Udal (1922) 179. Devon *Devonshire Assoc.* 12 (1880) 101; *Devonshire Assoc.* 79 (1947) 48; *Devonshire Assoc.* 89 (1957) 285–6. Surrey [1860s] Sturt (1927) 135–6. Oxfordshire *Midland Garner* 1 (1884) 22; [1920s] Harris (1969) 114; *Oxf. FL. Soc. Ann. Record* (1956) 13. Herefordshire Leather (1912) 78. Worcestershire [c.1900] Knight (1960) 180–4. West Midlands W. Midlands Fed. W.I.s (1996) 57. Midland England *Midland Garner* 1 (1884) 22. Bedfordshire Marsom (1950) 183. East Anglia *East Anglian Mag.* 13 (1953/4) 99; Hatfield (1994) 26–7. Suffolk Claxton (1954) 90. Norfolk [c.1920] Wigby (1976) 66–7; Randell (1966) 86. Lincolnshire Sutton (1992) 148. Staffordshire Poole (1875) 83. Yorkshire Blakeborough (1898) 135. Ireland Logan (1981) 68. Co. Cavan Maloney (1972). Co. Cork [1937/8] Culloty (1993) 59. Unlocated Igglesden (c.1932) 52; Raverat (1952) 57; *Folk-Lore* 68 (1957) 415.

child: posthumous

see POSTHUMOUS CHILD.

child: stepping over

see STEPPING OVER.

Childermas

see HOLY INNOCENTS' DAY.

chime hours

see BIRTH HOUR.

chimney sweeps

Several superstitions cluster round the figure of the chimney sweep. It was lucky to meet one in the street, one should always greet them, and they were particularly lucky to have at a wedding.

Sitting in front of two women on top of an omnibus yesterday I heard one remark in excitement to the other, 'Look there is a sweep!' and the other replied, 'Yes – and there are two more! We are in luck!' Then each speaker bade the sweeps good morning, and, as the omnibus bore them past the sweeps one remarked, 'We shall get something today – or perhaps we shall make some wonderful bargains at the sales. In our family we always say good morning to a sweep, the idea being that doing so ensures a present during the day'.   Unlocated *Folk-Lore* (1914)

Coach- and carriage-drivers in particular perpetuated the custom of greeting sweeps:

What is the origin of the custom among coaching men (amateur and professional), when driving four-in-hand or tandem, of lifting their hat to a chimney-sweep if they happen to meet one on the road?   Unlocated N&Q (1899)

A favourite theme of newspaper and magazine articles from the 1950s onwards was that sweeps could make as much money attending weddings as sweeping chimneys.

Not by mere chance was a sooty chimney-sweeper sauntering in front of Kensington Palace on the wedding morning of Prince Philip and Princess Elizabeth, thereby affording the excited bridegroom an opportunity to dash out from the royal apartments to wring his grubby hand for 'sweep's luck'.   England N&Q (1950)

Despite the fact that sweeps have almost disappeared from many people's everyday experience, there is still a feeling in many minds that sweeps

are lucky: a silhouette sweep figure can still appear on good luck charms and wedding cards, and they still do a good trade in wedding appearances.

There is no evidence at all that any of these traditions existed before the late Victorian period, and it seems reasonably certain that the connection with weddings is a twentieth-century phenomenon. But this has not prevented claims being made that the luck of the sweep is a survival from ancient times. See, for example, the letter in N&Q 195 (1950) 217, which confidently asserts that the lore of sweeps is based on the 'rites of Dionysus and fertility cults' of ancient Greece, on the strength of the fact that some of the characters in the supposed survivals of these rites in twentieth-century Greece had blackened faces. Others claim, with similar lack of foundation, that 'soot is associated with fertility, and the hearth is considered to have magical qualities' (*Sunday Telegraph* (28 Dec. 1997)).

A completely different origin theory was also available. It explained that a sweep once risked his life to stop the runaway horses of one of the King Georges. The saved sovereign adopted the habit of saluting every sweep he met – although that leaves us to wonder how many times the King came face to face with a chimney sweep.

England N&Q (1950) 168–70. **Sussex** *Brighton Gazette* (1 Sept. 1887), quoted N&Q 7S:4 (1887) 348. **Dorset** *Dorset Year Book* (1961–2) 73. **Surrey** [1953] Opie & Tatem, 71–2. **Oxfordshire** [1920s] Surman (1992) 60–1; *Oxon Folk-Lore Soc.* (1952) 9; *Oxf. & Dist. FL Soc. Ann. Record* (1955) 16. **London** [1920s] Poulsen (1988) 13; N&Q 167 (1934) 370. **Essex** [*c.*1917] Mays (1969) 164. **Lincolnshire** [1940s] Sutton (1992) 134. **Midland England** N&Q 8S:12 (1897) 148. **Staffordshire** [1954] Opie & Tatem, 72. **Yorkshire** N&Q 148 (1925) 425. **Co. Dublin** *Folk-Lore* 4 (1893) 362; *Folk-Lore* 71 (1960) 260. **Unlocated** N&Q 9S:3 (1899) 188; *Folk-Lore* 25 (1914) 382; *Folk-Lore* 68 (1957) 418. **General** N&Q 9S:3 (1899) 188; *Sunday Telegraph* (28 Dec. 1997) 17. Also examples of sweeps being thought lucky from Austria and Switzerland (N&Q 165 (1950) 168–70).

christening: baby must cry

A widespread belief concerning christening is that a baby should cry at the ceremony. This is taken as a sign that the Devil has been cast out and is therefore lucky, whereas it is unlucky if the baby remains silent. In the latter case it is also said the child will not live long – being too good for this world.

I was lately present at a christening in Sussex, when a lady of the party, who was a godmother of the child, whispered in a voice of anxiety. 'The

christening

The sacramental rite of baptism, by which a baby is admitted into the Church, has long been popularly believed to have wider meaning and usefulness. Thus, many parents thought that babies were at risk from fairies and witchcraft until they were protected by the religious ceremony, and kept the proposed name a tight secret until the officiating priest announced it. Similarly, ailing babies were confidently expected to get better after the christening, and even their temper was expected to improve. Various unofficial traditions grew around the ceremony – boys must be christened before girls, babies must cry to show that the Devil has been duly cast out, and so on. These are all covered in separate entries below, but a number of other less common beliefs indicate the importance of baptism in the popular mind.

The Welsh would never have a child baptized after a funeral, for they said it would not thus be prevented from following the dead to the grave during its infancy or early years. They disliked christening a babe on the anniversary of its brother's or sister's birth. If a babe holds its head up during the christening ceremony, it will live to be very old; if it allows its head to turn aside or sink back on the arm of the person who holds it, you may expect its early death. Christenings never take place on Friday in Wales. The child that is christened on Friday will grow up to be a rogue.

Wales Trevelyan (1909)

from the minister of a colliery village in the far north. 'I had not been in the parish long before I was struck with the circumstance that when a funeral took place there was almost sure to be a baptism party at the church at the same time, sometimes the baptism party arriving with the funeral party without the accustomed notice beforehand. On inquiry I found it to be a superstition in that part (I have not met with it elsewhere) that should a child be brought to the font at the same time that a body be committed to the ground, that whatever was "good" in the deceased person was transferred to the little child; that God did not allow any "goodness" to be buried and lost to the world, and that such goodness was most likely to enter a little child coming to the sacrament of baptism'.

Northern England *Folk-Lore* (1896)

If an infant is brought for baptism through the churchyard when a grave is open, it will die before the end of the year.

Devon *Devonshire Assoc.* (1927)

Children baptised after dark will see 'bokies' (ghosts).

Aberdeenshire *Folk-Lore* (1914)

If one of the sponsors at a christening looks into the font, the child will grow up like him.

Shropshire Burne (1883)

No person should 'stand for' (act as sponsor) two children in the same year. If they do not die they will always have misfortune.

Co. Longford *Béaloideas* (1936)

I am the most wretched fellow: sure some left-handed priest christened me, I am so unlucky: I am never out of one puddle or another.

Dekker, *Honest Whore Part 2* (1630)

Among other pleasant talke, he shewed hir how hee doubted that hee was not well christened; for, as hee said, hee used oftentimes to rise out of his bed in his sleepe, and going about the house, should doe as wist not what himselfe.

The Image of Idlenesse (1581)

At one christening, when a fine boy was presented for admission to the visible church, I was instructed on no account to wipe the baptismal drops from the baby's brow. It was laughingly added, in reply to the natural question, 'Why?' – 'It's an old freit'.

Angus Laing (1885)

Sussex Latham (1878) 11. Somerset Tongue (1965) 135. Devon *Devonshire Assoc.* 15 (1883) 107; Hewett (1900) 56; *Devonshire Assoc.* 59 (1927) 168. Cornwall *Folk-Lore Jnl* 5 (1887) 209–10. Herefordshire Leather (1912) 113. Worcestershire N&Q 7S:5 (1888) 46. Shropshire Burne (1883) 286. England Addy (1895) 120. Derbyshire N&Q 9S:5 (1900) 54. Northern England *Folk-Lore* 7 (1896) 280. Lancashire N&Q 1S:3 (1851) 516; *Morning Herald* (18 June 1860). Yorkshire Nicholson (1890) 2; N&Q 8S:9 (1896) 5. Cumberland N&Q 5S:6 (1876) 24. Co. Durham Brockie (1886) 180–1; Leighton (1910) 46. Northumberland Bosanquet (1929) 34. Wales Trevelyan (1909) 266–9. North Wales [early 18th cent.] *Archaeologia Cambrensis* 5S:2 (1885) 150. Scotland *Folk-Lore* 26 (1915) 213. Northeast Scotland Gregor (1874) 97–100. Western Scotland Napier (1879) 30–1. Angus Laing (1885) 17. Ayrshire N&Q 2S:3 (1857) 59. Dumfriesshire Corrie (1890/91) 38; N&Q 8S:4 (1893) 429. Aberdeenshire *Folk-Lore* 25 (1914) 349. Co. Wexford [1936] Ó Muirithe & Nuttall (1999) 182. Co. Laoighis *Béaloideas* 9 (1939) 32. Co. Longford *Béaloideas* 6 (1936) 258. Unlocated N&Q 6S:4 (1881) 494; N&Q 6S:5 (1882) 159; *Church Times* (17 Oct. 1899), quoted N&Q 9S:4 (1899) 518; N&Q 11S:10 (1914) 88; N&Q 182 (1942) 125, 179. General N&Q 9S:5 (1900) 54; *Folk-Lore* 68 (1957) 414. Literary *The Image of Idlenesse* (1581), quoted N&Q 3S:12 (1867) 185; Thomas Dekker, *Honest Whore Part 2* (1630) 3:2.

child never cried; why did not the nurse rouse it up?' After we had left the church, she said to her, 'Oh Nurse, why did not you pinch baby?' And, when the baby's good behaviour was afterwards commented upon, she observed, with a very serious air, 'I wish that he had cried'.

Sussex Latham (1878)

Many stories are told of nurses or mothers pinching the child to ensure that the lucky cry takes place.

The earliest reference dates from 1787, where the 'will not live' motif was already present. Similar fears were still being voiced nearly two hundred years later:

A Cambridge woman said in 1959 that she felt uneasy because her first grandchild, born that year, did not cry; she was afraid this meant he was not going to live long. She herself had had a sister who had died at the age of 3 and her mother had often said that this was because the baby had remained perfectly quiet throughout the christening.

Cambridgeshire Porter (1969)

It is most likely that the basic idea originated with official church baptismal procedures. Earlier forms of christening in the Anglican, and continuing forms in Catholic, churches, included an element of exorcism. The basic belief about crying being lucky is still being quoted today, even if not actually believed. This superstition is so well known in this form that it is surprising to find several references which give different interpretations – one or two of which say the opposite to the mainstream belief. None of these have been recorded on more than one or two occasions, so it is difficult to know how widely known, if at all, they were.

If a baby cries at its baptism it is a sign that it will be cross and peevish all its life.

Jersey *Folk-Lore* (1914)

A child who doesn't cry when the water is poured on him at baptism will have to face many difficulties in life, but he will face them bravely.

Co. Tyrone *Lore & Language* (1972)

In the East Riding they say that if a child screams at its christening it is resisting Satan . . . It is unlucky for children to cry whilst they are being baptized.

Yorkshire Addy (1895)

If the baby cries loudly at the christening, they say it will be a good singer.

Herefordshire Leather (1912)

If the baby cries when the water is poured on its head, it will die; if it does not cry, it will live.

Co. Wexford [1936] Ó Muirithe & Nuttall

Sussex Latham (1878) 11. **Somerset** Poole (1877) 30; [1923] Opie & Tatem, 72–3. **Dorset** Udal (1922) 178. **Devon** Hewett (1900) 56; *Devonshire Assoc.* 67 (1935) 139. **Cornwall** *Folk-Lore* 5 (1894) 338. *Jnl Royal Inst. Cornwall* 20 (1915) 129. **Herefordshire** Leather (1912) 113. **Warwickshire** Bloom (*c.*1930) 23. **Cambridgeshire** [1959] Porter (1969) 16. **East Anglia** Varden (1885) 108. **Norfolk** Dew (1898) 77–81. **Lincolnshire** *Gent. Mag.* (1832) 493; [c.1940s] Sutton (1992) 69. **Shropshire** Burne (1883) 286. **Yorkshire** Addy (1895) 120. **Lancashire** *Lancashire Lore* (1971) 49. **Co. Durham** *Folk-Lore* 20 (1909) 73. Leighton (1910) 47. **Highland Scotland** Macbain (1887/88) 254. Angus Laing (1885) 17. **Ireland** N&Q 1S:7 (1853) 97. **Co. Tyrone** *Lore & Language* 1:7 (1972) 9. **Co. Wexford** [1936] Ó Muirithe & Nuttall (1999) 182. **Jersey** *Folk-Lore* 25 (1914) 248. **Guernsey** De Garis (1975) 7. **Unlocated** Grose (1787) 51; Hone, *Year Book* (1832) 126–8; N&Q 1S:6 (1852) 601.

christening: boy or girl first

A widespread popular belief dictated that great care must be taken in christening babies to get them in the correct order:

The belief prevails still in some parts of the Perthshire highlands, that when a boy and girl are presented for baptism, the parents must be particular to let the boy be christened before the girl, otherwise the boy will grow up in life without a beard. An instance of this occurs to my recollection: Donald McNaughton and Isabella Stewart, in Strath Tay, were, by mistake, reversed in the presenting for baptism. The consequence usually attributed ensued in after life. The boy grew up without a hair on his chin, while the lassie grew to a woman, but with such a beard that she had regularly to keep it under.

Perthshire N&Q (1876)

This would seem to be simply an example of the expected sexism of organized religions and traditional societies, and this view is supported by an extract from Leofric's *Missal* of about 1050 which lays down the regulation for christening:

The priest receives them from their parents, and they are baptised first males, then females.

The picture is not quite so straightforward, however, as there are a few sources which say the opposite – girls should be christened before boys. The reason given in these is exactly the same as in those above:

If a boy and a girl were to be baptised together, the greatest care was taken to have the parents so placed that the minister must baptise the girl first. If there was the least suspicion of the minister reversing the order, great uneasiness was manifested, and if he did proceed to baptise the boy first, the girl was put forward, and when baptised first, a gleam of satisfaction lighted up the faces of the girl's friends. This procedure was followed under the belief that, if the boy was baptised before the girl, he left his beard in the water, and the girl would get it.

Northeast Scotland Gregor (1874)

A tentative line of development can be identified. Originally, it was official policy to christen boys first. The popular notion about beards, which is a metaphor for wider concerns about masculinity and femininity, was advanced to explain the male precedence. This was re-interpreted in some places with the introduction of the idea that the boys 'leave their beards in the water', and the traditional order was reversed to accommodate it.

This explanation, though reasonable, is unproven, primarily because apart from the extract from Leofric's *Missal*, we have no evidence of a concern with precedence before the very end of the eighteenth century. The chronological gap is too long to presume unbroken continuity.

A handful of references indicate a range of other concerns about the christening procedure, including further worries about relative position and about using the same water:

The water from one baby must not be used for another, or sins and the devil will be transmitted.   Devon *Devonshire Assoc.* (1935)

If there were three babies being christened at the same time, the central place was accounted the least favourable, for the middle child to be done, would not be expected to thrive.

Guernsey De Garis (1975)

Three women . . . were to have their babies – all girls – baptized on Whit Sunday. Each applied to have the baptism taken at a different time because they had heard it was unfortunate (unlucky) to baptize more than one girl in the same water.   Devon *Devonshire Assoc.* 30 (1898)

The good lady in question objected to the same water being used for the baptism of her child, which had done service for its two brethren-in-arms, on the ground that it was 'unlucky' for three boys to be baptized in the same water.

Devon *Devonshire Assoc.* (1883)

Boys first: Surrey N&Q 1S:10 (1854) 321. Worcestershire *Folk-Lore* 20 (1909) 346. Norfolk Dyer (1880) 179. Lincolnshire Swaby (1891) 89. Northern England N&Q 1S:2 (1850) 197. Yorkshire N&Q 3S:12 184–5. Co. Durham Leighton (1910) 46.

Northumberland/Cumberland Bulkeley (1886) 229–30. England/Scotland borders [*c.*1816] Henderson (1866) 9. Scotland N&Q 2S:1 (1856) 303. Highland Scotland Macbain (1887/88) 254. Dumfriesshire Corrie (1890/91) 38. Perthshire N&Q 5S:6 (1876) 323. Angus Laing (1885) 17. Orkney N&Q 10S:12 (1909) 483–4; *Stat. Acct Scotland* 15 (1795) 311. N. Ireland Foster (1951) 11. **Girls first:** Devon 10S:12 (1909) 66. Worcestershire N&Q 2S:1 (1856) 227. Northeast Scotland Gregor (1874) 99–100. Caithness Rinder (1895) 52. **Other beliefs:** Devon *Devonshire Assoc.* 15 (1883) 107–8; *Devonshire Assoc.* 30 (1898) 8; *Devonshire Assoc.* 59 (1927) 168; *Devonshire Assoc.* 67 (1935) 139. Worcestershire N&Q 5S:3 (1875) 424. West Wales Davies (1911) 216. Guernsey De Garis (1975) 7.

christening: cures

In the same way as baptism is believed to protect a newborn baby from evil-wishers (*see* CHRISTENING: NAMES), the rite was also believed to cure sick children – of both real diseases and character defects:

Children who are ill-tempered before baptism will be good-tempered after they have been baptized. They will also sleep better and thrive better. In this respect baptism acts as a charm.

England Addy (1895)

If any unchristened baby should be seized with convulsions, 'the only remedy is to baptize 'em', and the Edgmond mother sends for the parson instead of the doctor.   Shropshire Burne (1883)

Compare CONFIRMATION.

Herefordshire [*c.*1895] *Folk-Lore* 39 (1928) 388. East Anglia Forby (1830) 406; Varden (1885) 108. Shropshire Burne (1883) 192. England Addy (1895) 120. Lancashire N&Q 1S:3 (1851) 516. Co. Durham Leighton (1910) 47.

christening: names

The rite of baptism was popularly believed to do more than welcome the newborn baby into the church. Unbaptized children were seen to be in danger from witches, fairies, or others who might wish to harm them, because they did not yet have the protection afforded by God. In most places, such babies were kept indoors and protected as much as possible from harmful influences. One of these protective strategies was to keep the baby's name strictly secret until the christening:

Baptism was administered as early as circumstances would permit, and for various reasons. Without this sacrament the child was peculiarly exposed to the danger of being carried off or changed by fairies. It could not be taken out of the house, at least to any great distance, or into a neighbour's, till it was baptised. It could not be called by its name till after it was baptised. It was unlawful to pronounce the name, and no one would have dared to ask it. At baptism the name was commonly written on a slip of paper, which was handed to the minister. Death might come and take away the young one, and if not baptised its name could not be written in the 'Book of Life' and heaven was closed against it . . . There was an undefinable sort of awe about unbaptised infants, as well as an idea of uncanniness in having them without baptism in the house.

Northeast Scotland Gregor (1874)

It is not clear how widespread these fears were. The few clear references are relatively widely distributed geographically, but are mostly from a very restricted period of time. The number of references probably underestimates the belief's popularity.

Sussex Latham (1878) 11. **Devon** Hewett (1900) 55. **Co. Durham** Leighton (1910) 47. **Highland Scotland** Macbain (1887/88) 254; Polson (1926) 6–7. **Western Scotland** N&Q 2S:1 (1856) 303; Napier (1879) 30–1. **Northeast Scotland** Gregor (1874) 96–7. **Guernsey** De Garis (1975) 7.

christening piece

A widespread custom in Scotland dictated that the party returning from a christening should present the first person they meet with a 'christening piece' or 'bit', to ensure luck to the baby:

Going along one of the principal streets of Edinburgh lately on a Sunday afternoon, I met a very respectably dressed female with an attendant (nurse) carrying an infant. They stopped me, and the former presented to me a paper bag. On expressing my surprise, she said, 'Oh! Sir, it is the christening bit' and explained that it was an old custom in Edinburgh on going with a child to be baptised to offer a 'christening bit' to the first person they meet. Mine I found on getting home consisted of a biscuit, bit of cheese, and a bit of gingerbread. Edinburgh N&Q (1871)

The basic shape of the custom was remarkably stable, although details varied considerably. In some cases it was the first adult met, others allowed children to be the recipient, while many insisted that the piece be given to the first person of the opposite sex to the baby in question. The ingredients of the piece itself could also vary.

Bread and cheese was commonly quoted, but christening cake and various types of biscuit were also used. A small amount of money was also enclosed – some insisted on silver.

Apart from being the first person met, it was desirable that the recipient be an acceptably 'lucky' person, and if s/he knew the custom they would say something to bless the baby, and maybe walk a few yards with the party.

[Remembering c.1820] there were no such things as cabs to convey the baptismal party to the church. The baby was carried thither generally by an unmarried woman, and it being considered very unlucky for the mother to go out of the house or to visit a neighbour till the child was christened, this ceremony was generally performed upon the first or second Sabbath after the birth. The person who carried the child took with her bread and cheese, which were given to the first person she met. If the person receiving the gift did not turn and walk a short distance with the party, the child was not likely to live long. I have known people, who did not know this previously, being begged by the party carrying the baby to convoy them a short distance. Even the person carrying the baby had some little influence on its after welfare, in being lucky or unlucky; and if the person meeting her were known to be lucky, plain-soled, &c., all indicated good or bad fortune to the child in its after life.

Glasgow [c.1820] Napier

The basic requirement of a 'lucky' person were similar to those in many FIRST FOOTING customs.

Published references confirm this to be an overwhelmingly Scottish and Northern England custom, although there are, most intriguingly, a handful of references from Devon and Cornwall. The earliest reference is the one from Glasgow about 1820 quoted above, but it was clearly already an established custom at that time, and it was still going strong in the 1950s.

Cornwall Hunt (1865) 235; N&Q 4S:9 (1872) 47; *Old Cornwall* 1:12 (1930) 2. **Devon** *Western Morning News* (4 Jan. 1883) quoted N&Q 6S:7 (1883) 468. **Northern England** Brockett (1846) 90; [1850s] *Denham Tracts* 2 (1895) 43. **Co. Durham** N&Q 5S:10 (1878) 37–8, 216; *Folk-Lore* 20 (1909) 74. **Northumberland** Bigge (1860–62) 93; *Folk-Lore* 23 (1912) 354–5; *Folk-Lore* 36 (1925) 251, 256; Bosanquet (1929) 33–5. **Scotland** N&Q 2S:1 (1856) 303. **Highland Scotland** Macbain (1887/88) 254. **Western Scotland** Napier (1879) 32. **Northeast Scotland** Gregor (1874) 99. **Edinburgh** N&Q 4S:8 (1871) 506; N&Q 5S:10 (1878) 216, 278; N&Q 4S:8 (1871) 506. **Glasgow** [c.1820] Napier (1864) 394; N&Q 2S:3 (1857) 59; *Daily Mail* (21 Jan. 1961). **Kintyre** Martin (1987) 183. **Dundee** *Folk-Lore* 54 (1943) 308. **Midlothian** N&Q

5S:10 (1878) 398. **Fife** N&Q 4S:9 (1872) 130; *Daily Mail* (21 Jan. 1961).

christening: water

Water used in a christening was subject to a number of beliefs about how the ceremony was performed (*see* CHRISTENING: BOY OR GIRL FIRST), but it was also believed to have special properties – to cure and protect – for a wide range of problems.

Water preserved in fonts, was by the common people supposed to have a mystic virtue or secret power in it, to heal diseases, etc. wherefore there was a lock and key to most fonts, to prevent the water from being stolen.

Unlocated Grose (1787)

If an infant was baptised with water in which a little wine had been mixed, instead of pure water, it was supposed to act as a protection against midge-bites ever after.

Hebrides *Folk-Lore* (1900)

A cure for somnambulism was performed by pouring some of the baptismal water on the patient, while awake, but when occupied in conversation or otherwise, in so unexpected a manner as to cause a temporary shock. There are two females in my immediate neighbourhood who had been so treated within the last forty years. Hebrides *Folk-Lore* (1900)

Water that had been used in baptism was believed to have virtue to cure many distempers. It was a preventive against witchcraft and eyes bathed with it would never see a ghost.

Western Scotland Napier (1879)

Devon *Devonshire Assoc.* 67 (1935) 139. **Cornwall** Hunt (1865) 213. **Gloucestershire** N&Q 5S:1 (1874) 383; Hartland (1895) 53. **Herefordshire** Leather (1912) 113. **Wales** Trevelyan (1909) 268–9. **Northeast Scotland** Gregor (1874) 98–9. **Western Scotland** Napier (1879) 140. **Sutherland** *Folk-Lore* 11 (1900) 444–5. **Hebrides** *Folk-Lore* 11 (1900) 445. **Unlocated** Grose (1787) 51.

Christmas decorations: burning

Apart from the question of when exactly the decorations should be taken down (see below), there was also a sharp disagreement between those who believed that the plants should then be burnt and those who insisted they should not.

All decorations remained up till Candlemas, when they were taken down and burnt. I remember the cook setting fire to the kitchen chimney with them; it was one of the old-fashioned wide ones, and made a great blaze, but no one seemed to trouble about it.

Wiltshire *Wilts. N&Q* (1893–5)

Conversation with Mary (Housemaid): 'Miss – wants to know when you will take down the Christmas evergreens, Mary'. 'Oh, on Old Christmas Day, ma'am, to be sure, always'. 'Whom did you learn that from?' 'My mother, ma'am, she always did it.' 'And what shall you do with them? Burn them?' Mary (with horror) 'Oh no, ma'am, not burn them! Throw them away somewhere, carefully.' Cheshire *Folk-Lore* (1909)

Both sides maintained it would be dreadfully bad luck not to follow their rule, and those who were against burning often took the Christmas connection very seriously and said it was *sinful* to burn them. Others said it was bad luck to burn EVERGREENS at any time, while still others implied that it was unlucky to burn the decorations indoors, but all right to do so outside.

There is no discernible geographical pattern to explain the different views on burning. The pro-burning references cover most parts of England, as well as Wales and the Isle of Man. There are fewer sources from the anti-burning lobby, which has only one reference from Cornwall, and all the rest are north of a line from Shropshire to Lincolnshire. Two sources, however, from Shropshire and Cornwall, reveal that both views were present in their counties at the same time.

The chronological spread is perhaps more telling. The earliest anti-burning piece dates only from 1866, but there are references which mention burning right back to the eleventh century. On this evidence, it would seem that burning the Christmas evergreens was the norm until quite late in the nineteenth century, but this is a tentative hypothesis based on inadequate data. The burning could also serve another purpose:

If a sprig of Christmas holly is thrown on the fire and burns with a crackling noise, it is a sign of good luck; but, if it burns with a dull flame and does not crackle, it is a sign of a death in the family within the year.

Worcestershire [1900–1] *Folk-Lore*

Yes to burning: **Cornwall** *Folk-Lore* 20 (1909) 488–9; *Old Cornwall* 1:12 (1930) 22. **Wiltshire** *Wilts. N&Q* 1 (1893–5) 151. **Surrey** *Folk-Lore* 21 (1910) 224; [1988] Opie & Tatem, 76. **London** N&Q 1S:7 (1853) 152. **Oxfordshire** [1719/20] N&Q 9S:9 (1902) 217; [1920s] Surman (1992) 61. **Gloucestershire** *Folk-Lore* 13 (1902) 174. **Herefordshire** Leather (1912) 20. **Worcestershire**

[1900–1] *Folk-Lore* 343; *Folk-Lore* 20 (1909) 343. **Norfolk** Randell (1966) 99. **Shropshire** Burne (1883) 244–5. **England** Addy (1895) 111. **Yorkshire** [1960] Opie & Tatem, 76. **Wales** N&Q 9S:9 (1902) 86; Trevelyan (1909) 30. **Isle of Man** *Folk-Lore* 58 (1947) 239. **Unlocated** N&Q 8S:12 (1897) 173. **General** *The Exeter Book* (*c.*1070); N&Q 8S:12 (1897) 318. **Literary** Robert Herrick, *Hesperides* (1648) 'New Yeares Gift'; Thomas Hardy, *Winter Words* (1928) 'Burning the Holly'.
No to burning: **Cornwall** [1890s] *Old Cornwall* 1:12 (1930) 22. **Lincolnshire** Rudkin (1936) 39; [1940s?] Sutton (1992) 128. **Shropshire** Burne (1883) 244–5. **Cheshire** *Folk-Lore* 20 (1909) 488. **Staffordshire** *Folk-Lore* 20 (1909) 490. **Derbyshire** [1890s] Uttley (1946) 134. **Yorkshire** Henderson (1866) 88; Nicholson (1890) 41; *Folk-Lore* 21 (1910) 225. **Ayrshire** [1962] Opie & Tatem, 76. **Unlocated** N&Q 8S:11 (1897) 264.

Christmas decorations:
fed to cattle

A handful of reports indicate a custom of feeding evergreens used for Christmas decorations to the farm animals.

At Worthen, in the beginning of this century, the evergreens were disposed of in a remarkable manner; they were carefully carried to the cows' 'boosey' to be eaten by them. And at Edgmond, in much later years, it was customary to burn the holly, but to give the ivy to the milking cows.

Shropshire Burne (1883)

Christmas decorations

The putting up of Christmas decorations comes under the category of CALENDAR CUSTOMS, and only those elements which have taken on a superstitious aspect are included here. The main areas in which belief comes to the fore are: (1) which plants can be used and which, if any, forbidden; (2) when the decorations are put up; (3) when they are taken down; (4) what happens to them then, the key question being whether they should be burnt or not.

It should be noted that in all the references quoted here, the term 'Christmas decorations' refers solely to evergreens and other plants. Artificial decorations were not introduced until late Victorian times and do not seem to have gathered any beliefs of their own.

HOLLY and IVY have been the favourite plants for decoration for centuries, but many other evergreens were also used. MISTLETOE, too, was popular, at least since the early nineteenth century, when the kissing custom was first described, but the constant reiteration of dubious notions of sacredness and Druid connections have obscured its true history. Some plants had their own traditions:

It depends upon the kind of holly that comes into a house at Christmas which shall be master during the coming year, the wife or the husband. If the holly is smooth the wife will be master, if the holly is prickly, the husband will be the master. It is considered very unlucky for a house unless some mistletoe is brought in at Christmas.

Derbyshire N&Q 4S:8 (1871) 506

The question of the correct time for putting up and taking down decorations is covered in

An illustration from The Graphic, Christmas 1879, *showing a sailor fixing a bunch of holly to the masthead of his ship. Holly has been the staple element in Christmas decorations since at least early modern times.*

detail below, but the broad picture is one of major change a little over a century ago. Before that time they were put up just before Christmas (usually Christmas Eve), and left there for some time afterwards (often into February). Nowadays, they are put up some time before Christmas Day, but are taken down soon after (usually by Twelfth Night).

See CANDLEMAS.

This sounds like the sort of mixture of practicality and superstition which would appeal widely to farmers, but the few references so far found are all from the same region of England.

Worcestershire N&Q 1S:3 (1857) 343. **Shropshire** Burne (1883) 244–5; *Folk-Lore* 49 (1938) 233. **Yorkshire** Henderson (1866) 86.

Christmas decorations: plants

Holly and ivy have been the mainstay of Christmas decoration since at least the fifteenth and sixteenth centuries, when they are mentioned regularly in churchwardens' accounts (*see* examples in Wright & Lones 3 (1940)), although there are indications that ivy was later viewed with some suspicion:

In decorating the house with evergreens at Christmas, care must be taken not to let ivy be used alone, or even predominate, as it is a plant of bad omen, and will prove injurious.

Northamptonshire Sternberg (1851)

Other early records mention laurel, box, bay, rosemary (see, for example, the 1648 verse by Herrick, quoted under CHRISTMAS DECORATIONS: REMOVING), and there is no indication that any particular plant was deliberately avoided. Some later sources also question the inclusion of other plants:

If you bring yew into the house at Christmas, amongst the other evergreens used to dress it, you will have a death in the family before the end of the year.

East Anglia Forby (1830)

(*see also* YEW), but the most controversial is the MISTLETOE. The widespread notion that mistletoe is a 'pagan plant' and has always been excluded from churches at Christmas has no foundation, except in the sense that this is self-fulfilling prophecy, acted upon by many a credulous church official in relatively recent times. This idea seems to have started in the early nineteenth century and has been quoted as fact intermittently ever since, despite the fact that there is no evidence to support it and plenty to refute it:

Now with bright holly all your temples strow With laurel green and sacred mistletoe.

Gay, *Trivia* (1716)

It is likely that the notion was first floated by some antiquarian about 1800, just before the first published reference by John Brand, who had just discovered the reference to mistletoe-cutting Druids of Gaul by Pliny (*see* MISTLETOE).

London *Gent. Mag.* (1792) 432. **East Anglia** Forby (1830) 413. **Lincolnshire** Sutton (1992) 131. **Northamptonshire** Sternberg (1851) 163. **Derbyshire** N&Q 6S:4 (1881) 509. **General** Brand 1 (1813) 408. **Various** Wright & Lones 3 (1940) 243–7. **Literary** John Gay, *Trivia* (1716) Bk 2, lines 441–2.

Christmas decorations: putting up

In modern Britain, most people put up their decorations about a fortnight to a week before Christmas Day, although public displays are usually in place around 1 December. Few people would now wait until Christmas Eve, but in the past many believed that it was extremely unlucky to bring EVERGREENS into the house before that date. This is partly because any strong tradition pegged to a CALENDAR CUSTOM acquires beliefs about it being unlucky out of season, but also because HOLLY, the most important ingredient, was also thought unlucky in the house outside the Christmas period:

Early in December, 1905, I was carrying some fine holly through Chelford, and a group of women in the street commented on the ill-luck that would follow my taking it into the house before Christmas day. Gloucestershire *Folk-Lore* (1912)

Although fairly generally reported, we have no evidence that this concern over timing existed before the 1870s, and, as already mentioned, it certainly does not prevail widely nowadays.

Gloucestershire *Folk-Lore* 23 (1912) 455; Wright & Lones 3 (1940) 244. **Herefordshire** Leather (1912) 20, 92; [*c*.1895] *Folk-Lore* 39 (1928) 386. **Lincolnshire** [1940s] Sutton (1992) 131. **Rutland** N&Q 4S:12 (1873) 467. **Shropshire** *Bye-Gones* (22 Dec. 1897) 254; Vickery (1985) 37. **Derbyshire** [1890s] Uttley (1946) 134. **Glamorganshire** Vickery (1985) 36. **Guernsey** De Garis (1975) 118. **Unlocated** [1960] Opie & Tatem, 75.

Christmas decorations: removing

The norm for modern Christmas decorations is that they have to be removed on or before Twelfth Night, but for previous generations there was more scope for debate on the question.

The invariable custom among old-fashionable folks is to take down and scrupulously burn the decorations on the morning of 7 January, or the 8th if the 7th be a Sunday. The Epiphany, or Twelfth Day, is the last of the Christmas holiday, unless the morrow be a Sunday; and the decorations must be removed on the conclusion of Christmastide.   Unlocated N&Q (1897)

Various late Victorian authorities named other days close to Twelfth Night – New Year's Day and Old Christmas Day (6 Jan.) for example, but by far the most common before that time was CANDLEMAS Day (2 Feb.). This had been so since at least the mid seventeenth century. Robert Herrick alluded to Candlemas several times in his poems, including the famous lines:

*Down with the rosemary, and so
Down with the baies, and misletoe;
Down with the holly, ivie, all,
Wherewith ye drest the Christmas hall.*

Herrick, 'Ceremony upon Candlemas Eve' (1648)

Candlemas was being named as the proper time to remove Christmas decorations by some informants right up to the turn of the twentieth century. It demonstrates the power of custom that most people nowadays would recoil in horror from any suggestion that their Christmas decorations should stay up until February.

Whatever day was chosen for their removal, there was still the vital question of how to dispose of the evergreens. Some kept them to hand, and used them to make the fire to cook the pancakes on Shrove Tuesday, but others avoided burning them at all cost (*see above*). At the beginning of the season, many felt that it would be unlucky to bring evergreens into the house before Christmas Eve, and they were also very careful not to let any remain, in home or church, after the stipulated time:

If every scrap of Christmas decoration is not removed from the church before Candlemas-Day (2 Feb), there will be a death within a year in the family occupying the pew where a leaf or berry is left.   Suffolk Chambers (1864)

It is unlucky to keep Christmas holly about the house after Candlemas Day, as the Evil One will then come himself and pull it down.

Worcestershire [1900] *Folk-Lore*

This warning was also included in Robert Herrick's poem quoted above.

Caution must be advised, however, when comparing accounts of rules covering removal of decorations. They do not always make a distinction between *before* a date and *on* a date.

Twelfth Night: Sussex [1986] Opie & Tatem, 77. **Somerset** [1923] Opie & Tatem, 77. **Cornwall** [1890s] *Old Cornwall* 1:12 (1930) 22. **London** N&Q 1S:7 (1853) 152. **Essex** [*c.*1920] Ketteridge & Mays (1972) 143. **Oxfordshire** [1719/20] N&Q 9S:9 (1902) 217. **England** Addy (1895) 106. **Lincolnshire** Rudkin (1936) 39; [1940s] Sutton (1992) 131. **Derbyshire** [1890s] Uttley (1946) 134. **Yorkshire** Nicholson (1890) 41; [1982] Opie & Tatem, 77. **Wales** Trevelyan (1909) 30. **Literary** Thomas Hardy, *Winter Words* (1928) 'Burning the Holly'.
Candlemas: Wiltshire *Wilts. N&Q* 1 (1893–5) 151. **Herefordshire** Leather (1912) 20. **Worcestershire** [1900] *Folk-Lore* 20 (1909) 343. **East Anglia** Forby (1830) 415. **Shropshire** Burne (1883) 244–5. **Suffolk** Chambers (1864) 52–3. **Northumberland** *Newcastle Weekly Chronicle* (4 Feb. 1899) 7. **Wales** N&Q 9S:9 (1902) 86. **Literary** Robert Herrick, *Hesperides* (1648) 'Ceremony on Candlemas Eve'.
New Year: Cornwall *Folk-Lore* 20 (1909) 488–9. **Gloucestershire** *Folk-Lore* 13 (1902) 174 [*Old New Year's Day*]. **Yorkshire** *Folk-Lore* 43 (1932) 253.
Old Christmas Day: Cheshire *Folk-Lore* 20 (1909) 488. **Norfolk** Randell (1966) 99.
Others: Surrey *Folk-Lore* 21 (1910 224 [*No particular day*]. **Isle of Man** *Folk-Lore* 58 (1947) 239 [*Shrove Tuesday*]. **Devon** *Devonshire Assoc.* 104 (1972) 267. **Yorkshire** *Gent. Mag.* (1811) 423 [*Good Friday*]. **Northumberland** Bosanquet (1929) 74 [*12 January*]. **Various:** General N&Q 8S:12 (1897) 96, 318, 173, 514–15.

Christmas fly

see FLIES.

Christmas: mince pies

There is a distinct tendency for food which is customary at particular festivals to develop connotations of luck. This is true of both Christmas puddings and mince pies:

Mince pies, too, have their own magic; if you eat twelve of them, from twelve separate friends, during the twelve days of Christmas, you are promised a lucky twelve months to follow.

Wiltshire Wiltshire (1975)

The 'twelve separate friends' is more usually given as 'twelve different houses' – presumably it would be too easy to eat twelve of your own mince pies. This notion was widespread across England in the late nineteenth and twentieth centuries, but it has not been found before the 1850s. This was the period when Christmas was being drastically remodelled, and it is quite possible that it was a new fancy of the time. Nevertheless, according to a contributor to *Notes & Queries* in 1861 it was already ubiquitous by then:

Eating mince-pies in different houses – This saying is so well known that I need not relate it at length.   Unlocated N&Q (1861)

There is still a vague feeling in many people's minds that one should not refuse a mince pie at Christmas, and the saying is still quoted regularly as an excuse for mild festive overeating.

A few minor beliefs have also clustered around the mince pie – minor in that they have only been recorded a few times, but this may disguise more widespread superstitions. Along with many 'first things', children especially were encouraged to make a wish as they bit into their first mince pie, and in a handful of reports (Yorkshire, Co. Durham, Cardiganshire) it was stated that it was unlucky to cut a mince pie because it will cause strife or 'cut your luck'. Again, in common with other festive fare, it was bad luck to eat the special food outside the allotted time – in this case the Twelve Days of Christmas.

Lucky months: Hampshire [1960] Opie & Tatem, 249. Somerset [1923] Opie & Tatem, 248. Wiltshire Wiltshire (1975) 102. Essex [1985] Opie & Tatem, 249. Warwickshire Langford (1875) 11. Shropshire Burne (1883) 408; *Bye-Gones* (19 Jan. 1887) 228. Staffordshire Hackwood (1924) 49. England Addy (1895) 105. Derbyshire N&Q 6S:4 (1881) 509; [c.1890] Uttley (1946) 110. Northern England *Newcastle Weekly Chronicle* (11 Feb. 1899) 7. Cumberland/Westmorland [1850s] *Denham Tracts* (1895) 91. Co. Durham Leighton (1910) 59. Northumberland *Newcastle Weekly Chronicle* (8 Jan. 1887). Unlocated N&Q 2S:12 (1861) 491; N&Q 12S:8 (1921) 70; Igglesden (c.1932) 222.
Wishes: Somerset [1923] Opie & Tatem, 249. Oxfordshire [1920s] Surman (1992) 61. Derbyshire Uttley (1946) 110. Northumberland Bosanquet (1929) 22. Literary G. K. Chesterton, *New Poems* (1932) 'Some Wishes at Christmas'.
Other beliefs: Dorset Udal (1922) 51. Nottinghamshire [1987] Opie & Tatem, 249. Yorkshire [1966] Opie & Tatem, 249. Co. Durham [1986] Opie & Tatem, 249. Cardiganshire *Folk-Lore* 39 (1928) 174.

Christmas rose

see ROSES: LOVE DIVINATION.

Christmas: stirring cake/pudding

The custom of getting everyone in the household to stir the Christmas cake or pudding mix, at least in token terms, is still well known and widely practised.

When I was a child in the 1940s, we all had to help to make the Christmas cake. Mother used a large yellow mixing bowl and a big wooden spoon. We were called into the kitchen and had to stand on a chair to reach the bowl. You had to close your eyes and stir the mixture round three times, then you made a wish for what you wanted Santa to bring.

Lincolnshire Sutton (1992)

Various minor rules applied in different households – especially the number of times one must stir the mixture – but the wish is the essential feature. As with other Christmas food beliefs, this one is not recorded before the mid Victorian era, and it is quite feasible it was invented at that time as part of the 'Merrie England' Christmas which was then taking shape. The number of references given below grossly underestimates the popularity of the custom, at least in the twentieth century, but does indicate that this, along with many other Christmas beliefs, was a primarily English phenomenon.

Another belief, occasionally reported, is a seasonal extension of general superstitions concerned with BREAD-making:

If the Christmas pudding broke it was considered a very unfavourable omen. It meant the death of one of the heads of the household.

Wiltshire *Wilts. N&Q* 1 (1893–5)

Wiltshire *Wilts. N&Q* 1 (1893–5) 8, 151. Warwickshire Langford (1875) 11. West Midlands W. Midlands Fed. W. I.s (1996) 218. Lincolnshire Sutton (1992) 129. Shropshire Burne (1883) 277. Derbyshire N&Q 11S:2 (1910) 504. Yorkshire Nicholson (1890) 87–8. Northumberland Bosanquet (1929) 22. West Wales Davies (1911) 218. Unlocated N&Q 2S:12 (1861) 491.

church: porch watching

see PORCH WATCHING.

churches

Given their intimate connection with life and death, it is no surprise that the church and its churchyard became the focus for numerous beliefs and customs which extended, or even ran counter to, the official religion of the time. CHURCHYARDS were the site of many unofficial traditions, from cures to LOVE DIVINATIONS, and various magical procedures involved circling the church, peering in its windows, or watching in the PORCH to see who would die in the coming year. But even within the church itself there were still dozens of signs and omens to warn the superstitious in the congregation of coming bad, or occasionally good, events, and plenty more scope for divinations and cures. All the main events which take place in church, such as WEDDINGS, FUNERALS, and CHRISTENINGS, were fraught with hidden meaning, and items used, such as the sacrament wine, or the water from the font, could be used for cures. Even the fabric of the church, from its LEAD roof to the ALABASTER of its statues, could be used in this way, as well as the very dust from the floor:

An old woman of my acquaintance, who acted as the beadle or 'bobber' of a church, once brought to the bed of a dying person some of the sweepings from the floor of the altar, to ease and shorten a very lingering death.

Unlocated N&Q (1871)

The church CLOCK striking during a hymn or a wedding service was viewed with horror, and prognostications could be made from various other occurrences:

Whenever the priest makes a mistake in reading the prayers, the old people always look upon it as a sign of the death of one of the parishioners. I have often heard one old woman say, 'Passon made a slip t'marning. Wonder who 'twill be this week'.

Wiltshire N&Q (1886)

If the wind blows out a candle on the altar, or lights grow dim in the chancel or around the pulpit, the clergyman or minister will soon die. If the house candle gutters in a long length, it indicates a shroud or a coffin.

Wales Trevelyan (1909)

Unusual rattling of church door – before end of week it will be open to receive corpse.

Sussex Latham (1878)

Even something as innocuous as leaving the church could be cause for comment:

Just why church and chapel coming out at the same time should have been considered an ill omen is difficult to imagine. Only a week or two ago I was in conversation with a country woman who had recently lost her mother-in-law. She remarked to me, 'Funny thing, just before mother died, church and chapel come out together and she was the first t'see it'.

Dorset Dorset Year Book (1961–2)

And a new incumbent should be aware that every trivial thing he does might be ripe for interpretation:

I was a member of the congregation at a recent institution and induction service in a rather isolated Exmoor borderland parish church, and when the newly-inducted cleric tolled the bell, as the ceremony provides, heard a woman member of the congregation half audibly counting the strokes as the clergyman pulled the bell rope. He rang the bell five times, and in a tone of suppressed excitement the woman exclaimed 'five years' and whispered to a companion that it meant the clergyman would remain in the parish for that period.

Devon Devonshire Assoc. (1942)

Sussex Latham (1878) 51. Dorset Dorset Year Book (1961–2) 74. Somerset Tongue (1965) 145. Devon Devonshire Assoc. 9 (1877) 92; Hewett (1892) 28; Devonshire Assoc. 74 (1942) 104. Devon/Cornwall N&Q 1S:3 (1851) 259. Wiltshire N&Q 7S:2 (1886) 189; N&Q 8S:3 (1893) 209. Surrey N&Q 1S:3 (1851) 179. Essex [c.1917] Mays (1969) 164. Herefordshire [c.1895] Folk-Lore 39 (1928) 388. Worcestershire N&Q 8S:3 (1893) 209. Suffolk [1863] Chambers 1 (1878) 52–3. Norfolk N&Q 1S:6 (1852) 480. Liverpool Wright (1913) 236. Shropshire Burne (1884) 246–7. Yorkshire N&Q 1S:3 (1851) 220. Wales Trevelyan (1909) 281. Highland Scotland Macbain (1887/88) 254. Aberdeenshire Henderson (1866) 89. Banffshire Folk-Lore Jnl 1 (1883) 364. Ireland N&Q 1S:3 (1851) 268. Unlocated N&Q 4S:8 (1871) 505; Igglesden (c.1932) 230–1.

churching

Churching, or the occasion of the first visit to church by a new mother after the birth of her baby, has excited controversy for much of the last five hundred years. The basic problem has been whether the ceremonies carried out at the time should be viewed as 'purification' or 'thanksgiving'.

After the Reformation, the churching rite was roundly condemned by a range of reformers as being both Popish and an unacceptable relic of Jewish religion. The idea of purification was anathema to the increasingly vocal puritan sects, and mainstream churchmen responded by attempting to redefine the ceremony as one of thanksgiving rather than ritual cleansing. The debate rumbled on for centuries, and while the ceremony was kept in existence any reformer could use it as a stick to beat the establishment. On the other side, fundamentalists have also been able to quote the Old Testament, which makes it quite clear that mothers are unclean for a specified period:

If a woman have conceived seed, and born a man child: then she shall be unclean seven days; according to the days of the separation for her

*infirmity shall she be unclean . . . And she shall
then continue in the blood of her purifying three
and thirty days; she shall touch no hallowed
thing, nor come into the sanctuary, until the days
of her purifying be fulfilled. But if she bear a
maid child, then she shall be unclean two weeks.*

Leviticus 12:2–8

A more recent controversy has emerged among
historians who have debated the question of how
churching should be viewed historically. At one
extreme are those who see the whole business as
an aspect of patriarchal tyranny which seeks to
control and marginalize women at all times. At
the other end of the spectrum are those who
recognize that women enjoyed the period after
childbirth as a predominantly female time, and
regarded the churching itself as a time for
female-centred celebration.

Given this background of official ambivalence
and controversy, it is hardly surprising that there
were many unofficial superstitions surrounding
the time following a birth and the mother's activities and responsibilities. These were firmly
rooted in local tradition and were stringently
imposed, at least in the nineteenth century. The
most widespread rule was that the woman
should not leave her house until she had been
churched. If she did, she must not enter anyone
else's house, as she would bring bad luck to her
hosts:

*She must particularly refrain from entering
another woman's house, for she will certainly
bring misfortune of some kind, and if the second
woman is pregnant, she may cause a miscarriage.
The rector of a poor parish in Oxford told me that
this custom is rigidly observed there . . . The
ancient Judaic idea of uncleanness at such times
is not remembered by anyone, and would, indeed,
be hotly resented; but the notion lingers that
unchurched women are somehow dangerous and
bringers of bad luck.*

England *Folk-Lore* (1955)

Given the restrictive nature of this belief, it is
gratifying to read a story – probably apocryphal
– that Irish women circumvented the prohibition by placing pieces of their house thatch in
their hats so that they could claim to be still
'under their own roof' while out and about
(**Ireland** Varden (1885)).

On her way to the church for the ceremony,
the woman's behaviour was still prescribed by
superstition. She should not look at the sky or
even cross a road:

*A woman in this village, when going to church
for the first time after the birth of her child,*
*keeps to the same side of the road, and no
persuasions or threats would induce her to cross
it. She wears also upon that occasion a pair of
new boots or shoes, so that the mothers of large
families patronise greatly the disciples of St.
Crispin.*   **Hampshire** N&Q (1854)

There was also the astonishing idea that
unchurched women who broke these codes of
conduct were not even protected by the laws of
the land:

*It is an article in the vulgar creed that if a female
appears abroad, and receives either insults or
blows from any of her neighbours, previous to
the ceremony of churching, after giving birth to
a child, she has no remedy at law. Neither must
a mother enter the house of either friend, relative, or neighbour, till she has been churched. If
she is so uncanny, it betokens ill luck to the
parties visited.*

Northern England *Denham Tracts* (1895)

*My grandmother used to say, that if a woman
after childbirth crossed a cart or wheel rut before
she was churched, a man might shoot her, and he
could not be punished for it.*

Somerset N&Q (1873)

There is no clue in the official service laid
down in the Anglican *Book of Common Prayer* to
explain any of these popular beliefs, nor in the
verses of Leviticus, but there may be in the words
of Psalm 121 which, until the late seventeenth
century, were recited as part of the ceremony:
'The sun shall not smite thee by day, nor the
moon by night'. These may well have been interpreted as an injunction to stay at home.

The folkloric evidence does not shed much
light on the purification/thanksgiving debate.
Admittedly, the examples collected by folklorists
can easily be taken to demonstrate that notions
apparently based on the necessity for ritual separation followed by purification persisted into the
nineteenth and twentieth centuries. But the
material gives us no idea how typical these ideas
were. The collectors did not record how many
women took no notice of these restrictions, or
how many communities had very different traditions on the matter. This is the perennial problem of basing interpretation on research which
foregrounds the exotic at the expense of the ordinary. It is possible, however, that the folkloric
evidence supports neither camp, but suggests a
third interpretation. What seems clear from
some reports is that the women were viewed as
'unprotected' after childbirth, in the same way
unbaptized babies were liable to attack by fairies,
witches, and other ill-wishers until they received

the protection offered by the christening ceremony (*see* CHRISTENING: NAMES).

The ordinary women are hardly brought to look upon churching otherwise than as a charm to prevent witchcraft and think that grass will hardly ever grow where they tread before they are churched.   Wales [late 17th cent.] Edward Lhwyd

England *Folk-Lore* 66 (1955) 323. Sussex Parish (1875) 77. Hampshire N&Q 1S:9 (1854) 446. Somerset N&Q 4S:11 (1873) 341; Kettlewell (1927) 33. London *Folk-Lore* 51 (1940) 121; Willmott & Young (1957) 40. Herefordshire N&Q 1S:5 (1852) 293; Leather (1912) 113. West Midlands W. Midlands Fed. W. I.s (1996) 77. Warwickshire Bloom (*c.*1930) 24. Cambridgeshire *Folk-Lore* 25 (1914) 365. East Anglia Varden (1885) 108; *Folk-Lore* 50 (1939) 185. Suffolk Chambers (1878) 39. Lincolnshire N&Q 3S:9 (1866) 49–50; Peacock (1877) 57. Lincolnshire *Folk-Lore* 52 (1941) 75. Shropshire Burne (1883) 286. Staffordshire Hackwood (1924) 57. England Addy (1895) 93. Northern England *Denham Tracts* 2 (1895) 23. Yorkshire Young (1817) 883; *Folk-Lore* 51 (1940) 121. Lancashire *Lancashire Lore* (1971) 49. Co. Durham Leighton (1910) 47. Wales [late 17th cent.] Edward Lhwyd, 'Parochialia', supplement to *Archaeologia Cambrensis* 6S:11 (1911) 84. Montgomeryshire Hamer (1877) 258–9. Scotland Pennant (1776) 45–6; Jamieson, *Scottish Dictionary* (1808) 'Kirk'. Western Scotland Napier (1879) 33. Morayshire Shaw (1775) 230. Aberdeenshire *Stat. Acct Scotland* 21 (1799) 147. Angus Laing (1885) 34. Ireland Varden (1885) 108. Connemara [1830s] *Ulster Folklife* 37 (1991) 106. Jersey *Folk-Lore* 38 (1927) 179. Unlocated N&Q 3S:8 (1865) 500; N&Q 3S:9 (1866) 146; N&Q 8S:8 (1895) 154, 214, 408–9. General Vaux (1894) 84–8; N&Q 8S:6 (1894) 11, 276, 512; N&Q 8S:7 (1895) 436–7. Biblical Leviticus 12:2–8.
For differing historical views and extensive references, see Thomas (1971) 42–3, 68–9, and David Cressy, 'Purification, Thanksgiving and the Churching of Women in Post-reformation England', *Past and Present* 141 (1993) 106–41.

churchyard: first burial

Only a handful of references – oddly confined geographically to Scotland and the English West Country – document a belief that it was unfortunate to be the first person buried in a new churchyard:

In the same place [in Aberdeenshire] *there was great difficulty in bringing the new churchyard into use. No one would be the first to bury his dead there, for it was believed that the first corpse laid there was a teind to the Evil One. At last a poor tramp who was found dead in the road was interred, and after this there was no further difficulty. I have never heard of this superstition* [elsewhere] *except in Devonshire, where I know it to exist. The churchyard in St. John's Church in*

the parish of Bovey Tracey, South Devon, was long unused, the countrypeople declaring that the devil would seize the first body laid in it. At last a stranger was buried there, the servant of a visitor in the parish, after which interments began at once to take place
Aberdeenshire/Devon Henderson (1866)

As with the superstition about last burials, this belief would appear to be ancient, but it cannot at present be dated earlier than the late nineteenth century.

See also: CHURCHYARD: LAST BURIAL.

Aberdeenshire/Devon Henderson (1866) 89–90. Ayrshire *Folk-Lore Jnl* 3 (1885) 281. Somerset [1905–9] Tongue (1965) 147.

churchyard: last burial

A belief reported mostly in Ireland and Scotland, held that the last person buried in a churchyard had to undertake onerous tasks on behalf of those already buried, and led to unseemly haste and even pitched battles between rival funeral parties to get their loved one buried first. The tasks were usually to stand watch over the graveyard, or to fetch water for existing occupants:

The watch of the graveyard – The person last buried had to keep watch over the graveyard till the next funeral came. This was called Faire Chlaidh, *the graveyard watch, kept by the spirits of the departed.*   Highland Scotland *Campbell* (1900)

When two corpses come to the same graveyard the same day, the last to enter will be employed drawing water to wet the lips of all the souls in Purgatory. Two persons were to be buried at South Kilmurry the same day, and the relatives of one determined to be first. So they locked the gate and gave the key to the sexton with orders to let no one in. The two funerals arrived together, each trying to be first, but the gate was locked. The first tried to put their coffin over the ditch, but number two struck them, so they put down their coffin and went in search of the key. The moment their backs were turned the others threw their own coffin feet first over the wall, thus securing the entrée to the churchyard, and leaving the others to get in as best they could. They gave a wild cheer as they got it, the first intimation their rivals had of what happened (told to me by one present at the funeral).
Co. Cork *Folk-Lore* (1897)

The belief ran deep enough to arouse strong emotions. A fight which took place near Dublin, for example, described in *The Times* (28 July, 1835), led to a full-scale riot which resulted in the deaths of two mourners and serious injury of many more.

The only reference so far found from outside Scotland and Ireland is, oddly enough, from Somerset in 1941:

The last corpse buried must guard the graveyard, unless it is buried face downwards.

Somerset Tongue (1965)

On the surface, this superstition appears to have the hallmark of an ancient belief, but it can only be dated to the early nineteenth century, and the majority of references are from the late nineteenth and twentieth centuries.

See also FUNERALS; CHURCHYARD: FIRST BURIAL; FLOWERS: FROM CHURCHYARDS.

Somerset [1941] Tongue (1965) 148. **Highland Scotland** Campbell (1900) 242. **Argyllshire** N&Q 6S:10 (1884) 326. **Ireland** Wilde (1888) 213. **Dublin** *The Times* (28 July 1835) 5. **Co. Louth** *Belfast News-Letter* (1868) quoted in N&Q 4S:1 (1868) 361. **Co. Cork** *Folk-Lore* 8 (1897) 180. **Co. Kerry** *Folk-Lore* 31 (1920) 235. **Connaught** *Folk-Lore* 34 (1923) 337.

---

churchyards: north side

A widespread and persistent belief reported from the mid sixteenth to the late nineteenth centuries held that the northern section of a churchyard was unsuitable for the burial of respectable Christians and should be reserved for strangers, paupers, suicides, excommunicated persons, the unbaptized, and stillborn babies. It thus took on a sinister and 'unlucky' reputation and often remained unused for centuries.

I asked the sexton at Bradfield why, in a church-yard that was rather crowded with graves, there was no appearance of either mound or tombstone on the north side? His only answer was, 'It's mostly them 'at died i' t' workhus is buried at t' backside o' t' church'. An instance, but no expla-nation, of the prejudice entertained against the north side of churchyards.   Yorkshire N&Q (1851)

By the eighteenth century, this prejudice against a significant section of the churchyard was caus-ing problems in many country parishes:

Considering the size of the church, and the extent of the parish, the churchyard is very scanty; and especially as all wish to be buried on the south side, which is become such a mass of mortality that no person can be there interred without disturbing or displacing the bones of his ances-tors . . . At the east end are a few graves; yet none till very lately on the north side; but, as two or

three families of best repute have begun to bury in that quarter, prejudice may wear out by degrees, and their example followed by the rest of the neighbourhood.   Hampshire White (1788)

It was often believed that the ground to the north was 'unconsecrated', but there is no evidence that any particular area was ever officially omitted at the time of consecration. A lively correspondence in *Notes & Queries* in the 1850s, and again in 1899, brought to light numer-ous places where the prejudice had flourished, but also presented many examples of parishes in which it was apparently unknown, or where local factors conspired against it. In particular, corre-spondents pointed out that in places where the church was close to the southern boundary of the churchyard, or where the main approach from the local village was from the north, it was the southern side which was neglected and the north which was crowded with graves.

Nevertheless, since the majority of older Christian churches in Britain are aligned on an east-west axis and the main door is normally on the south side, the most plausible explanation for the custom is pragmatic rather than spiritual or magical. With a main door in the southern wall, parishioners will normally approach the church from the south, and the northern part of the churchyard is thus seen as, and was often called, the 'backside' of the church. Certainly, in Catholic times, it would be considered highly desirable to keep the memorials to the dead in constant view of churchgoers. In addition, the northern side would tend to be in the shadow of the church, and the southern side therefore sunnier – 'It would be so cold, sir . . . to be always lying where the sun would never shine on me' (Yorkshire N&Q (1851)), so the latter's character as the preferred side in local consciousness is understandable.

It is clear that this has operated as a self-rein-forcing circle – the ground which is popularly believed to be reserved for miscreants and strangers would be shunned by the families of deceased parishioners, and an already unpopu-lar and unpopulated area would be an obvious place to bury any corpse whose character or reli-gious standing was questionable.

Some writers have tried to prove a less obvious origin to the custom, and have assumed that there has always been a confirmed prejudice against the north. There are indeed sporadic references to the north being evil in Christian writing, but the notion does not seem to have been sufficiently widely known to found such a long-lasting and widespread tradition. Another ingenious expla-nation is from Matthew 25:33 – 'He shall set the sheep on His right hand, but the goats on His left' (**Southwest Scotland** Wood (1911)), but unfortunately left and right are relative to the way one is facing.

The prejudice against the north side was already widespread in the sixteenth century:

Syclik supersticion is amang thame, that will nocht berisch or erde the bodis of thair freindis on the north part of the kirk yard.

          Scotland J. Hamilton, *Catechisme* (1551)

Ann Ruter a singlewoman drowned herself and was buried the 4th day of July on the north side of the church.   **Yorkshire** [1597] Jupp & Gittings

Several N&Q correspondents stated that the prejudice against the northern section had broken down only a few decades before, i.e. around the 1820s and 1830s. As in Gilbert White's example above, the local breakthrough had usually been the result of a deliberate decision by a rector or a leading local family to break with custom, in the knowledge that others would follow. Nevertheless, a generalized dislike of the northern section, at least on the part of the poorer sections of the community, persisted in many places for a long time afterwards.

Kent [1930s] Kent (1977) 39–40. **Hampshire** White (1788) 287–8. **Western England** N&Q 1S:2 (1850) 55. **Somerset** Poole (1877) 27; Tongue (1965) 145–6. **Devon** N&Q 7S:8 (1889) 496–7; Vaux (1894) 132–3; *Devonshire Assoc.* 104 (1972) 268. **Cornwall** N&Q 148 (1925) 224. **Worcestershire** N&Q 1S:8 (1853) 207. **Worcestershire/Shropshire** *Gent. Mag.* (1855) 384–6. **Warwickshire** Bloom (c.1930) 47. **Bedfordshire** P. Samwaies, *Wise and Faithful Shepherd* (1657) 27, quoted Brand 2 (1849) 292–5. **East Anglia** Varden (1885) 118. **Norfolk** N&Q 7S:8 (1889) 496–7. **Suffolk** John Cullum, *History and Antiquities of Hawstead* (1784) 38; N&Q 7S:8 (1889) 496–7. **Lincolnshire** [1829] Gutch & Peacock (1908) 236; Peacock (1877) 58; N&Q 7S:8 (1889) 204. **Derbyshire** N&Q 148 (1925) 394. **Yorkshire** [1597] Jupp & Gittings (1999) 150; N&Q 1S:2 (1850) 126; N&Q 1S:3 (1851) 74–5; N&Q 1S:4 (1851) 309. **Lancashire** Harland & Wilkinson (1882) 275–6. **Northern England** [1850s] *Denham Tracts* 2 (1895) 38. **Co. Durham** Brockie (1886) 152; Leighton (1910) 64. **Wales** Brand 2 (1849) 292–5. **Glamorgan/Carmarthenshire** N&Q 1S:3 (1852) 113. **Scotland** J. Hamilton, *Catechisme* (1551) Pt 1, 22–3. **Southwest Scotland** Wood (1911) 240. **Shetland** Saxby (1932) 183. **Unlocated** N&Q 7S:8 (1889) 496–7. **General** *Gent. Mag.* (1802) 88; Brand 2 (1849) 292–5; N&Q 1S:2 (1850) 93, 189–90, 253–4; N&Q 7S:9 (1890) 53.

churchyard: treading on graves

It is hardly surprising that it was regarded as very unlucky to tread on a grave:

You should never, under any circumstances, walk upon a grave, or in any way tread upon it; it brings bad luck to do so, and is considered not only as a mark of disrespect to the person buried beneath your feet, but to all the dead that lie around.   **Lincolnshire** Gutch & Peacock (1908)

Pregnant women should be particularly careful in this respect:

A married woman should not walk upon graves, or her child will have a club-foot. If by accident she treads on a grave she must instantly kneel down, say a prayer, and make the sign of the cross on the sole of her shoe three times over.

                  Ireland Wilde (1888)

The few references given below do not adequately reflect the widespread nature of the fear of treading on a grave, which is still strongly felt by many people. It is certainly nothing new, as Theophrastus' *Superstitious Man* (c.319 BC) was also careful not to tread on a tombstone.

Hampshire [1989] Opie & Tatem, 181. **Lincolnshire** Gutch & Peacock (1908) 237. **Northern England** Brand 2 (1813) 8. **Wales** Trevelyan (1909) 266. **Scottish Borders** [c.1810] Henderson (1866) 4. **Banffshire** *Jnl Anthropological Inst.* 3 (1874) 267. **Ireland** Wilde (1888) 205. **Connaught** *Folk-Lore* 34 (1923) 337. **Literary** Samuel Taylor Coleridge, *The Three Graves* (1798). **Classical** Theophrastus, *Superstitious Man* (c.319 BC).

cigarette packets

One of several children's customs first brought to light by Iona and Peter Opie in their extensive research into childlore in the 1950s. In various parts of the country, children who found an empty cigarette packet of a certain brand covered it with their foot and spoke a rhyme. The wording of the rhyme varied with the brand: for 'Black Cat' it was:

Black cat, black cat, bring me luck
If you don't I'll tear you up,

while for Player's Navy Cut it was:

Sailor, sailor, bring me luck
Find a shilling in the muck.

Although apparently not recorded by folklorists before the 1950s, one of the Opies' informants claimed to remember carrying out a similar custom about 1910.

England/Wales Opie (1959) 222–3; Opie & Tatem, 82–3.

cigarettes

see THREE CIGARETTES.

clergymen: healing/divining

Despite centuries of Christian churches telling people that magic and religion are different things, many ordinary people were convinced that clergymen must have occult powers at their disposal. All that studying and learning, and their avowed role in keeping the Devil at bay, must count for something. Ministers were not only called upon to undertake exorcisms and to counter witchcraft, both of which, it could be argued, were in the ministers' natural province, but they were also expected to be able to cure ailments and even locate stolen property in the same way as the local CUNNING MAN purported to do:

I remember [c.1856–61] . . . hearing in the village of Churston Ferrers that a villager had, probably about the year 1830, lost £10, and fully believed that it had been stolen by a neighbour. He gave out that he would go, to find out the thief, to 'Parson Barter' of Cornworthy, on the other side of the Dart, who held that vicarage for seventy-one years . . . He told his story to Mr. Barter, and the old patriarch advised the man to go back to Churston, and give out that Mr. Barter says, if the money be not placed under a certain stone (which was specified) by a certain day, he was to come to Parson Barter again. That was enough; the money was found by its owner under the stone specified. I remember being told, in the same parish of Cornworthy, of which I was curate a little after Mr. Barter's death, by a poor old man, with whose loss of £20, the savings of his life, I was commiserating, that I could tell him who the thief was if I chose. Of course, I assured my poor friend of my readiness (if it were possible); and he said to me, 'You ginnelman that go up to college, find out the verses in the Bible to be repeated when you turn the key round'. My disclaimer of such ability had, I fear, but little effect on my poor friend, whom I visited several years afterwards in the Totnes workhouse; and he not only remembered his former conversation with me, but informed me that in the preceding week he had heard the master of the house read the verse that must be used in turning the key on a Bible to discover a thief, in one of the Psalms read to the inmates.
Devon *Devonshire Assoc.* (1885)

Suspended priests are considered capable of working cures by touch of the hand.
Aran Islands *Procs. Royal Irish Academy* (1892–3)

See Thomas (1971) for much more on this topic. *See also* BIBLE & KEY DIVINATION.

Devon Henderson (1866) 130; *Devonshire Assoc.* 17 (1885) 125. Northumberland Bigge (1860–62) 97. Dundee Henderson (1866) 129–30. Aran Islands *Procs. Royal Irish Academy* 3S:2 (1892–3) 819.

clergymen: unlucky

The ambivalence with which many people held clergymen and other ministers of religion is brought into focus by a number of beliefs which were widespread in FISHING communities all over the British Isles but particularly, it seems, in Scotland. It was extremely unlucky to meet a clergyman on the way to the boat, and it was also unlucky to take one on board with you, or to mention the word 'minister' while at sea:

One of the oldest [superstitions] seems to have a strong antipathy to the 'parson'. It was considered a most unlucky thing for a clergyman to enter a cottage when the 'gude mon' was baiting his lines, or to meet one on his way to the beach. To quote the words of one of the natives, 'I'd as soon meet the devil as the parson'. A fisherman would never go to sea after such a meeting.
Yorkshire N&Q (1875)

Another specific context in which a priest could be unwelcome was on the hunting field:

The huntsmen in the eighteenth and early nineteenth centuries thought it so unlucky to meet a parson that they turned home again with the hounds. If the parson was in the hunt, 'well and good', but it was 'bad to meet him'. He that wore the parson's left-off shoes or clothes would be unlucky.
Wales Trevelyan (1909)

And there were others:

To dream of a priest is bad; even to dream of the devil is better. Remember, also, either a present or a purchase from a priest is unlucky.
Ireland Wilde (1888)

Unlucky to have a minister first-foot you.
Orkney N&Q (1909)

No explanation for this antipathy has been suggested, but it is one of the few superstitions which can be definitely traced back to late medieval times. We have three clear references to the belief before 1300, and regular reports ever since. The earliest is by John of Salisbury in 1159, with the generalized: 'They tell us it is ominous to meet a priest or monk', and many add to the particular situations in which the meeting could be unfortunate:

It was counted ill luck to meet with a priest if a man were going forth to war or to tournament.
Schoolemaster (1583)

It is interesting to note that the specific connection with fishing is absent from the record until the 1870s, and even the specialized version of it being unlucky to carry a clergyman aboard ship does not appear until 1854.

Warwickshire N&Q 4S:2 (1868) 67. **Norfolk** Festing (1977) 28–9. **Yorkshire** N&Q 5S:3 (1875) 204. [1930s] Opie & Tatem, 83. **Co. Durham** Brockie (1886) 121. **Wales** Trevelyan (1909) 327–8. **Eastern Scotland** Anson (1930) 38. **Angus** [1954] Opie & Tatem, 83. **Caithness** Sutherland (1937) 104. **Orkney** Laing (1885) 72–3; N&Q 10S:12 (1909) 483–4. **Shetland** Edmonston (1809) 74; Tudor (1883) 166. [1963] Opie & Tatem, 249. **Ireland** Wilde (1888) 208. **Co. Kerry** Folk-Lore 31 (1920) 236. **Unlocated** N&Q 1S:10 (1854) 26. **General** John of Salisbury, *Policraticus* (1159) 50; Bartholomew of Exeter, *Penitential* (12th cent.); *Vices and Virtues* (c.1225) 29, quoted Opie & Tatem, 83; *Schoolemaster* (1583) Ch. 4, quoted Opie & Tatem, 83; Gaule (1652) 312; N&Q 1S:10 (1854) 26; Bullen (1899) 120. **Literary** Jonathan Swift, *Journal of a Modern Lady* (1728) lines 238–9.

clocks: falling/breaking

As with MIRRORS, the falling or breaking of a clock is ominous, but whereas the former is simply bad luck, the clock is usually a sign of death, either recently occurred or about to happen:

If a small clock or watch falls to the floor, there will be a death in the house.
Wales Trevelyan (1909)

A clock falling is a sign that the death of someone belonging to the family has taken place at the same moment.   Worcestershire Folk-Lore (1909)

Worcestershire *Folk-Lore* (1909). **Shropshire** Burne (1883) 280. **Yorkshire** Blakeborough (1898) 146. **Wales** Trevelyan (1909) 283.

clocks: opposite the fire

A small handful of references report the odd belief that it is unlucky to place a clock opposite a fire, saying, in two of the three cases, that it will put the fire out. The same is said about the sun, but whereas that belief makes some possible

scientific sense, it is difficult to see how the clock manages such a feat.

Somerset [1956] Tongue (1965) 142. **England** Addy (1895) 96. **Yorkshire** [1982] Opie & Tatem, 84.

clocks: stopped

The most widespread of the clock beliefs connects a stopped clock with death, but in two relatively distinct ways on the part of the clock – one in response to some mysterious power, and the other by the more prosaic intervention of a human being. In the former it is believed that a clock which stops of its own accord is a sign of the death of a family member occurring at that very moment, either at home or at a distance:

A relative, describing to me the death of a parent, said the clock stopped just at the time of his decease: adding, the nurses said it was a usual occurrence. On making enquiry, I was told, the clock went well previously, and had gone well since – nothing to account for the stopping.
Unlocated N&Q (1864)

Or, more dramatically:

A member of a household was lying ill in Sheffield eight or nine years ago. He was the head of the family, and with him were some of his nearest relations, his wife and the rest of the family being at their home some miles away. One night the weights inside the case of a grandfather clock in their house fell to the bottom of the case with a great clatter. The faces of the wife and children grew blank, and 'a great fear fell on them'. The next day a message came to say that the husband had died at the same time as the clock-weights fell. The clock remains with the weights at the bottom of the case, and I do not know if any member of the family will dare to set the old clock going again.   Yorkshire N&Q (1909)

The doomed person can be any member of the family, although a strong link seems to exist between the head of the household and the main clock in the house. On a higher level, several sovereigns are reputed to have left behind stopped clocks – George III, William IV, and Queen Victoria, for example. Folklorist Charlotte Burne commented drily:

I have heard of this belief only in respect of grandfather clocks. The small, cheap, modern mantelshelf clock does not seem to know its duty in this respect.   Shropshire Folk-Lore (1938)

All the references are nineteenth and twentieth century, and the only evidence that the belief existed even before the 1860s is an uncorroborated piece in *Notes & Queries* (1864) that describes a clock bearing a brass plaque that claims it stopped when George III died in 1820. Nevertheless the belief was sufficiently well known in Victorian times to inspire a tremendously popular song, 'Grandfather's Clock', written by Henry Clay Work in 1875.

The other version held that clocks *should be stopped* as a mark of respect when someone dies:

When the corpse is 'laid out', the death chamber is shrouded in white, the clock is stopped, and the looking-glass covered, to show that for the dead time is no more and earthly vanity departed.

Co. Durham Leighton (1910)

The stopped clock is linked with the covered MIRROR and ornaments in most accounts, and is either regarded as symbolic of time having stopped for the deceased, or simply as a mark of respect underlining the importance of their death to those left behind, and the need for the passing to be marked.

As with the other clock beliefs, this has not been found before the 1820s. The geographical distribution is, however, more interesting, with all the references concentrated in Northern England, Scotland and Ireland. The solitary London reference is unusual in that it concerns the clock outside a jeweller's shop being covered at the proprietor's death rather than being stopped.

Compare CLOCKS: STRIKING WRONG.

Clock is stopped by humans: London N&Q 5S:5 (1876) 510. **Yorkshire** Nicholson (1890) 5. **Cumberland** Penfold (1907) 60. **Co. Durham** Leighton (1910) 51; N&Q 146 (1924) 420. **Northumberland** *Newcastle Mag.* (Sept. 1825) quoted Opie & Tatem, 84. **Scotland** N&Q 1S:11 (1855) 215. **Dumfriesshire** Corrie (1890/91) 44. **Aberdeenshire** N&Q 3S:2 (1862) 483–4; [1890s] Milne (1987) 2. **Co. Longford** *Béaloideas* 6 (1936) 260. **N. Ireland** Foster (1951) 18.
Clock stops of own accord: **Somerset** Tongue (1965) 142. **Devon** *Folk-Lore* 23 (1912) 350; *Devonshire Assoc.* 68 (1936) 89; *Devonshire Assoc.* 91 (1959) 203. **Oxfordshire** [1880s] Thompson (1943) 319–20. **Warwickshire** Langford (1875) 15. **Suffolk** *Folk-Lore* 35 (1924) 350; [1953] Opie & Tatem, 85. **Shropshire** *Bye-Gones* (1 Jan. 1879); Burne (1883) 281; *Folk-Lore* 49 (1938) 225. **Yorkshire** N&Q 10S:11 (1909) 6; *Yorkshire Post* (4 Oct. 1961) 14. **Scotland** N&Q 10S:3 (1905) 124–5. **Unlocated** N&Q 3S:6 (1864) 27, 446. **General** N&Q 10S:3 (1905) 175.

clocks: striking during church service

A variety of beliefs are concerned with a clock striking while other, seemingly innocuous, events are taking place. The most common ones are concerned with church clocks. In several places, the notion was reported that if the clock chimes while a hymn is being sung inside the church, or while other specific parts of the church service are being performed, a death in the parish will soon follow:

During service in the church, if the church clock strikes whilst a hymn is being sung, the belief is that some parishioner will die within the week. So strong is this belief that the striking mechanism of the clock is always stopped during services in which hymns are sung.

Somerset N&Q (1889)

More specifically, it is particularly unlucky for a bride and groom if the clock strikes during their wedding ceremony:

I have several times been asked in this village to arrange a wedding at five minutes past the hour – 'so that we may not be in church when the clock strikes' is the reason given.

Worcestershire N&Q (1923)

See also WEDDINGS: CLOCKS/BELLS for further references.

In the domestic sphere, clocks striking are often just as ominous, but a few examples must stand for them all:

If a clock strikes at the same time as a bell rings, it is a sign of death.   Devon *Devonshire Assoc.* (1927)

It is unlucky to speak while the clock is striking.

Devon Hewett (1900)

If two clocks strike exactly at the same moment, a married couple will die in the village.

Wales Trevelyan (1909)

If two clocks are heard striking together . . . there will be a wedding in the district soon afterwards.

Oxfordshire *Oxf. & Dist. FL Soc. Ann. Record* (1952)

None of these beliefs are reported earlier than Victorian times. The fear of the chimes coinciding with the wedding service seems to be exclusively Northern English, whereas for the others there is a preponderance of Western England and Welsh examples.

Church service: **Sussex** 4S:5 (1870) 595–6 **Dorset** *Folk-Lore* 10 (1899) 480; Udal (1922) 182. **Somerset** N&Q 7S:7 (1889) *Folk-Lore* 34 (1923) 165. **Devon** *Devonshire Assoc.* 9

(1877) 99. Cornwall N&Q 5S:1 (1874) 204. Worcestershire N&Q (1923) 172. Lincolnshire Peacock (1877) 58. Shropshire Burne (1883) 296.
Miscellaneous: Devon *Devonshire Assoc.* 9 (1877) 99; Hewett (1900) 54; *Devonshire Assoc.* 59 (1927) 163. Oxfordshire *Oxf. & Dist. FL. Soc. Ann. Record* (1952) 6. Worcestershire *Folk-Lore* 20 (1909) 344. Shropshire Burne (1883) 280. Wales Trevelyan (1909) 283. Unlocated N&Q 2S:12 (1861) 492.

clocks: striking wrong

In addition to the fear of clocks striking while certain other events are taking place, or stopping for no apparent reason (*see above*), a clock striking the wrong time or otherwise misbehaving was also regarded as very unlucky, and was usually interpreted as a death omen:

I have often heard it said in the North Riding of Yorkshire, that, if a clock strike thirteen times instead of twelve, some member of the household will shortly die, or the death of some relative will be heard of.   Yorkshire N&Q (1892)

Striking THIRTEEN was the most commonly reported omen, and was rumoured to have happened when Marie Antoinette was executed (N&Q (1925)). The passing of public figures was often marked in this way – Queen Victoria, for example, warranted an impressive display:

At Whimpstone the writer once bought a 'grand-father' clock which had the reputation of striking wrongly; thirteen was the number specified when any member of the family died. Strangely enough, at the death of Queen Victoria the clutch failed to act and the clock certainly struck twenty-four.   Warwickshire Bloom (c.1930)

Sussex [1751] *Sussex Arch. Colls* 9 (1857) 191. Cornwall Rowse (1942) Ch. 2. London N&Q 8S:2 (1892) 86. Herefordshire Leather (1912) 118. Warwickshire Bloom (c.1930) 44. Northamptonshire Sternberg (1851) 171. East Anglia Varden (1885) 116–17. Nottingham N&Q 149 (1925) 157. Yorkshire N&Q 8S:2 (1892) 86. Wales Trevelyan (1909) 283. Isle of Man N&Q 149 (1925) 157. *Literary* Thomas Hardy, 'Premonitions' in Hardy (1925).

clothes: aprons

If a woman's apron came undone, or fell off, the standard response was that her sweetheart must be thinking of her:

[14 Sept. 1872] *My apron string got loose as I stood in the station yard, and again as I walk'd back I found it coming off again. So I thought: Well the saying must be true, that 'when your apron comes untied of itself your sweetheart's thinking about you' and I felt pretty sure M was thinking about me then.*   London [1872] Cullwick

This meaning was widely recorded from the 1860s to at least the 1950s. The same interpretation is sometimes attributed to a garter coming loose, but there are other meanings there which have a longer history (*see* CLOTHES: GARTERS). Other interpretations were also available for the loose apron, although these were rare compared to the dominant meaning reported above. They include: the wearer will have a baby this year (Wiltshire Wiltshire (1975)); she will encounter bad luck (Suffolk Gurdon (1893)); or ill-usage (Herefordshire [c.1895] *Folk-Lore*).

Women's aprons also feature in one or two other beliefs. It is still sometimes said that a girl who is careless enough to get her apron wet while doing housework will marry a drunkard (Yorkshire Gill (1993)), and that women can change their luck by turning their apron round (Yorkshire Gill (1993); Wiltshire Wiltshire (1975)). See also BLACKSMITHS for a tradition that their wives should not wear an apron on GOOD FRIDAY.

Sweetheart thinking of you: Cornwall *Folk-Lore Jnl* 5 (1887) 215. London [1872] Cullwick (1984) 243. Herefordshire Leather (1912) 114. Cambridgeshire *Folk-Lore* 25 (1914) 365. Lincolnshire Rudkin (1936) 19. Shropshire N&Q 5S:3 (1875) 465; Burne (1883) 270. England Addy (1895) 100. Derbyshire [1890s] Uttley (1946) 127. Co. Durham Leighton (1910) 60. Glamorganshire [1953] Opie & Tatem, 5. Co. Longford *Béaloideas* 6 (1936) 260. Unlocated N&Q 179 (1940) 302.
Other meanings: Wiltshire Wiltshire (1975) 85. Herefordshire [c.1895] *Folk-Lore* 39 (1928) 391. Suffolk Gurdon (1893) 135. Yorkshire Gill (1993) 94.

clothes: funeral/ mourning

Society had complex rules covering the wearing of mourning clothes, which changed over time but which were widely accepted as part of the general etiquette of the day. A few stray beliefs have also been recorded, which were no doubt much more widely known than is indicated by the few references noted here. For example:

It is very unlucky to wear anything new to a funeral. Boots are particularly unlucky.
          Co. Longford *Béaloideas* (1936)

Mourning clothes should only be worn for the time specified and then disposed of:

I seem to remember having been told by a Yorkshire woman that it is unlucky to keep mourning garments after the term for wearing them is over. A Cambridgeshire servant informs me that her mother enjoined her not to lay by some crape she was inclined to treasure, as if she did she would 'never have no more luck'.

Yorkshire N&Q (1880)

And obviously one should not anticipate the event:

If you put a widow's bonnet on you will become a widow yourself. England Addy (1895)

Warwickshire Bloom (*c*.1930) 43. England Addy (1895) 102. Yorkshire N&Q 6S:1 (1880) 212. Highland Scotland Macbain (1887/88) 262. Co. Longford *Béaloideas* 6 (1936) 261.

clothes

Clothes feature in a very wide variety of superstitions, old and new, trivial and deadly serious. Thus, Sylvia Lovat Corbridge (born 1906), remembering her childhood in Lancashire:

I would snatch a thread from a friend's dress because it would bring me a letter later in the day. On the rare occasions I wore anything green (even if it were only the leaf of the flower in my hat), I would solemnly put a piece of black material on my head when I came in, to make sure I would not wear mourning because, as everyone knew, 'black followed green' . . . If I put my underslip on inside out, then it must not be changed that day, unless I wanted to miss my chance of receiving an unexpected present. Lancashire [*c*.1920] Corbridge

And in the modern world:

Reporter Adam Parsons has a lucky football shirt he wears to support his favourite team, and various other colleagues admitted to possessing certain lucky items of clothing, even knickers in one case . . . [When dressing in the morning] If a button is missing malicious gossip will be about. Watford Observer (11 Feb. 1994)

Among other things, beliefs focus on how and when new clothes are worn, on chance happenings such as a garment being put on inside out, on the rituals of getting dressed in the morning, on the dress of special occasions such as weddings and funerals, the colour of clothes, the placing of items of clothing for curative or divinatory purposes, the making of new clothes, when clothes should be first worn and when left off, and so on.

The major clothes beliefs are treated separately, but out of a wide selection of less common superstitions, the following provide a representative sample:

My wife was recently told by an old Herefordshire woman that she should never iron the tail of a shirt, because by so doing she would be ironing the money out of it. Herefordshire Folk-Lore (1928)

If a servant burns her clothes on her back, it is a sign that she will not leave her place.

East Anglia Forby (1830)

If a girl's apron takes fire in front it is a sign of marriage. Fire on the side or the back is a sign of misfortune. Co. Longford *Béaloideas* (1936)

When walking a long journey if your feet are sore rub the feet of your stockings with soap.

West Wales Davies (1911)

If you stick a crooked pin in the lining of your coat, all the girls will have to follow you.

Somerset [1946] Tongue

Servants who go to their new places in black will never stay the year out.

Northamptonshire Sternberg (1851)

If a button was sewed on to a piece of new dress, or a single stitch put into it, on Sunday, the devil undid the work at night.

Northeast Scotland Gregor (1881)

See also BABIES' CLOTHES; BRAMBLES; CRAMP; GREEN; PETTICOATS; PINS; SHOES; STRAW BOATERS; THROAT CURES; TOOTHACHE; WEDDINGS.

Somerset [1907] Tongue (1965) 144; [1946] Tongue (1965) 143. Herefordshire Leather (1912) 114; *Folk-Lore* (1928) 183, 398–9. Northamptonshire Sternberg (1851) 173. East Anglia Forby (1830) 414; N&Q 4S:2 (1868) 221. Suffolk [1863] Chambers 1 (1878) 321–3. Norfolk Fulcher Collection (*c*.1895). Lincolnshire Peacock (1877) 268–9. Shropshire *Folk-Lore* 49 (1938) 229. Cheshire *Folk-Lore* 39 (1928) 398–9. England Addy (1895) 96, 105. Northern England [1850s] *Denham Tracts* 2 (1895) 48. Lancashire Harland & Wilkinson (1873) 236; [*c*.1920] Corbridge (1964) 156–60. Wales Jones (1930) 199. West Wales Davies (1911) 214, 218. Radnorshire Francis Kilvert, *Diary* (14 Oct. 1870). Highland Scotland Macbain (1887/88) 254, 262; Campbell (1900) 231. Northeast Scotland Gregor (1881) 31. Dumfriesshire Corrie (1890/91) 82. Ireland Wilde (1888) 211–12; N&Q 7S:12 (1891) 245–6. N. Ireland Foster (1951) 18. Co. Longford *Béaloideas* 6 (1936) 260. Unlocated Igglesden (*c*.1932) 218. Watford Observer (11 Feb. 1994) 20.

clothes: garters

In the days when women wore garters which were tied with ribbons, the fact of one coming undone was worthy of traditional comment, although the exact meaning was open to dispute. In some cases, it was said that her lover was thinking of her, which was also said of an apron coming untied (*see* CLOTHES: APRONS) and wrinkled stockings; this was probably in Swift's mind when he wrote in his satire on social life, *Polite Conversations* (1738), 'What, miss, are you thinking of your sweetheart? is your garter slipping down?'. To others, however, a loose garter meant that the woman's sweetheart or husband was unfaithful to her. The earliest reference does not assist us on meaning, as it simply states 'That it is naught [i.e. bad] for a man or woman to lose their hose garter' (Melton (1620)).

Cornwall Hunt (1865) 240; *Folk-Lore Jnl* 5 (1887) 215. England Addy (1895) 98. Shropshire Burne (1883) 270. Northumberland *Newcastle Weekly Chronicle* (4 Feb. 1899) 7. Wales Trevelyan (1909) 270. Argyllshire *Folk-Lore* 21 (1910) 89. Unlocated Melton (1620). Literary Swift (1738).

clothes: inside out

Accidental occurrences are almost always bad luck in British superstition, but one extremely widespread and long-lasting belief accounts it lucky to put an item of clothing on inside out or back to front, as long as it is done accidentally and not put right when discovered:

If you put anything on inside out you mustn't change it back. It's unlucky, d'ye see. I would feel like that now – the other day I wore my petticoat inside out all day 'cos I'd put it on wrong – I wouldn't change it.   Devon Lakeham (1982)

Some versions state that you will receive a present within a week, but most simply promise 'good luck'. Failure to follow the dictates of superstition brought ill luck:

A retired schoolmistress reports that a child in her class arrived at school one morning very distressed as she had fallen and broken her wrist. 'I put my pinafore on inside out, and changed it back,' she said, 'I didn't ought to have done it, did I?'
      Dorset *Dorset Year Book* (1961–2).

Most informants keep it simple, but a hierarchy of clothing items was possible:

'I knowed as I should see a great stranger today,' said an old woman at Pulverbatch to her landlord . . . 'for I put my flannel petticoat on wrong-side-out this morning'. A stocking (one, not both) wrong-side-out is even more lucky than a waistcoat or a petticoat, and the right stocking put on wrong-side-out on a Monday morning is a sign of a present to be received during the week.   Shropshire Burne (1883)

This lucky interpretation has been steadily reported with little alteration since at least the eighteenth century – 'in troth I am pleased at my stocking, very pleased at my stocking' exclaimed a superstitious character in Congreve's *Love for Love* (1695) when it was pointed out to him that it was inside out. But it is clear that other interpretations were available at various dates:

He that receiveth a mischance, will consider whether he . . . put on his shirt in the morning the contrary wyse.   Scot (1584)

To have good luck for the day one must rise on the right side of the bed, and, without making any mistake, put one's clothes on properly.
      Highland Scotland Polson (1926)

In addition, there were several situations in which deliberately turning one's clothes was recommended. It was a time-honoured way of breaking a spell which had been cast on you, or to confuse fairies who were trying to lead you astray on a journey. It could also be done to influence the weather at sea:

To this day there are fisher lassies who wear their chemises wrong side out when their sailor lads are away at sea and stormy weather threatens.
      Yorkshire Blakeborough (1898)

Accidental and lucky: Kent *Folk-Lore* 25 (1914) 367. Sussex Latham (1878) 8. Hampshire N&Q 7S:9 (1890) 486; [1988] Opie & Tatem, 87. Dorset Udal (1922) 274; *Dorset Year Book* (1961–2) 74. Devon *Devonshire Assoc.* 64 (1932) 157; *Devonshire Assoc.* 74 (1942) 103; N&Q 10S:12 (1909) 66; Lakeham (1982) 45. Wiltshire *Wilts. N&Q* 1 (1893–5) 103. Berkshire Mitford (1830) 301. *Folk-Lore* 5 (1894) 337. Surrey [1955] Opie & Tatem, 87. Essex [1920] Ketteridge & Mays (1972) 143. Oxfordshire [1920s] Surman (1992) 60; *Folk-Lore* 34 (1923) 326. Gloucestershire/Cornwall *Folk-Lore* 34 (1923) 156. Herefordshire Leather (1912) 86. Cambridgeshire *Folk-Lore* 25 (1914) 366. East Anglia Forby (1830) 415; Varden (1885) 112. Suffolk *Folk-Lore* 35 (1924) 352. Norfolk Fulcher Collection (*c*.1895). Lincolnshire *Gent. Mag.* (1833) 590–3; Thompson (1856) 735; Peacock (1877) 63; *Grantham Jnl* (22 June 1878). Shropshire Burne (1883) 270–1. Derbyshire [*c*.1890] Uttley (1946) 126. England Addy (1895) 100,

103. **Co. Durham** Henderson (1866) 84; **Brockie** (1886) 210; **Leighton** (1910) 59. **Wales** Trevelyan (1909) 324; **Jones** (1930) 142. **Highland Scotland** Polson (1926) 127–8. **Western Scotland** Napier (1879) 137. **Orkney** N&Q 10S:12 (1909) 483–4. **Co. Wexford** *Folk-Lore Record* 5 (1882) 83. **Jersey** *Folk-Lore* 25 (1914) 246; L'Amy (1927) 98. **Isle of Man** [*c.*1850] Cashen (1912) 29. **Unlocated** Grose (1787) 63; N&Q 2S:12 (1861) 491; *Chambers's Jnl* (1873) 809; N&Q 179 (1940) 245; N&Q 182 (1942) 78, 125; N&Q 183 (1942) 22. **General** *Gent. Mag.* (1796) 636; Brand (1810) 104; Hoggart (1957) Ch. 2. **Literary** William Congreve, *Love for Love* (1695) 2:1; *Connoisseur* 59 (1755) 353.

Deliberate or unlucky: **Devon** Bray (1838) 183. **Yorkshire** Robinson (1855) 'Smock-turning'; Blakeborough (1898) 152. **Co. Durham** Henderson (1866) 85. **Wales** Trevelyan (1909) 265. **Highland Scotland** Polson (1926) 129. **Banffshire** *Folk-Lore Jnl.* 4 (1886) 15. **Co. Cork** *Cork Constitution* (24 Jan. 1890) 3. **General** Scot (1584) Bk 11, Ch. 15; Howell, *Proverbs* (1659) 18.

clothes: leaving off

In the past, the decision when to stop wearing winter clothes was taken seriously. The ubiquitous phrase 'Cast ne'er [or Ne'er cast] a clout till May is out' still causes controversy as to whether 'May' refers to the month or the hawthorn plant, popularly called 'may'. Modern popular opinion appears to tend towards the plant, but this seems to be a relatively recent interpretation, and an examination of the phrase's history shows that it is definitely wrong. Many of the published references from the nineteenth century make this quite clear, as, for example: 'Never think to cast a clout until the month of May be out' (**Yorkshire** Robinson (1855)). Other cognate sayings about 'tucking' (short-coating) babies add further evidence – 'Tuck babies in May, you'll tuck them away' (**Cornwall** *Folk-Lore Jnl* (1887)) and 'Till April is dead, change not a thread' (**Devon** *Devonshire Assoc.* (1932)).

Admittedly, the earliest known reference in English, in Fuller's *Worthies of England* (1732), is ambiguous: 'Leave off not a clout, till May be out', but the capital letter on 'May' probably indicates the month. Further circumstantial evidence can be gleaned from a Spanish proverb from *c.*1627, reprinted in the *Oxford Dictionary of Proverbs* (1948 edn), 'Hasta Mayo no te quites el sayo' [Do not leave off your coat till May], from which it is conceivable that the English phrase was formed.

Other beliefs and sayings also focused on when to leave off wearing particular clothes. Sunday was usually thought best:

In the West of England, Sunday is reckoned to be the day for leaving off any article of clothing, as then those who divest themselves will have the prayers of every congregation in their behalf, and are sure not to catch cold. Devon Hewett (1900)

but GOOD FRIDAY and EASTER Sunday were also recommended for similar reasons.

Cast ne'er a clout: **Dorset** Udal (1922) 274–5. **Somerset** Elworthy (1886) 467. **Bedfordshire** [1986] Opie & Tatem, 242. **Yorkshire** Robinson (1855) 41. **Scotland** Henderson (1832) 154. **General** T. Fuller, *Worthies of England* (1732) No. 6193; Smith & Harvey (1948) 81; Vickery (1995) 170–1.
Tucking babies: **Somerset** [1923] Opie & Tatem, 242. **Hampshire** [1962] Opie & Tatem, 242. **Cornwall** *Folk-Lore Jnl* 5 (1887) 210.
Other beliefs: **Dorset** N&Q 5S:10 (1878) 23–4. **Devon** Hewett (1900) 45; *Devonshire Assoc.* 64 (1932) 165. **Co. Durham** Leighton (1910) 57.

clothes: left/right stocking first

see SHOES: PUTTING ON; TOOTHACHE: SHOES/STOCKINGS.

clothes: mending while wearing

It has been generally agreed, at least for the last 150 years, that to mend clothes while wearing them brings bad luck, although the exact nature of the misfortune varies considerably:

Bad luck is predicted by the following – to have your clothes mended on your back, for then you will be evil spoken of. East Anglia Varden (1885)

It is unlucky to mend your clothes on you, for then you will never grow rich.
Cornwall *Folk-Lore Jnl* (1887)

One informant clamed it meant you would have a drunken husband. Those versions which simply forecast bad luck often include memorable images such as the phrase 'you will sew sorrow to your back'. The earliest known example dates from 1850. The belief was clearly very widely known in the nineteenth and twentieth centuries, and is still heard today. The vast majority of reports are from England, but there is one each from Wales and Scotland, and two from Ireland.

Sussex Latham (1878) 12. **Hampshire** [1987] Opie & Tatem, 87. **Somerset** [1923] Opie & Tatem, 87. **Devon**

Crossing (1911) 137. *Devonshire Assoc.* 64 (1932) 157; *Devonshire Assoc.* 65 (1933) 124. **Cornwall** *Folk-Lore Jnl* 5 (1887) 220. **Wiltshire** *Wilts. N&Q* 1 (1893–5) 102. **Berkshire** *Berks. Arch. Soc.* 1 (1889–91) 86. **Oxfordshire** [pre-1900] *Folk-Lore* 24 (1913) 91. **Worcestershire** *Folk-Lore* 20 (1909) 346. **East Anglia** N&Q 4S:8 (1871) 322; Varden (1885) 113. **Suffolk** N&Q 1S:2 (1850) 4; [1953] Opie & Tatem, 87. **England** Addy (1895) 97. **Yorkshire** *Folk-Lore* 43 (1932) 253; [1972] Opie & Tatem, 87; Gill (1993) 93. **Co. Durham** Leighton (1910) 60. **Unlocated** Igglesden (*c.*1932) 174. **West Wales** Davies (1911) 216. **Argyllshire** *Folk-Lore* 21 (1910) 89. **Ireland** Wilde (1888) 212. **Literary** James Joyce, *Ulysses* (1922) (1960 edn) 910–11.

clothes: new, blessing

The widespread custom of HANDSELLING new clothes by putting money in the pocket (*see* CLOTHES: NEW, MONEY IN) was augmented by other customs carried out when the clothes were first worn. Two other responses were dictated by custom when you met a friend who was wearing new clothes for the first time. One was to bless the clothes and wish the wearer health, and the other was to pinch the wearer for luck:

It is proper to greet your friends with a pinch when they make their first appearance in new clothes. I have a lively childish remembrance of the 'Pinch you for your new frock', and of the action suited to the word, which decidedly lessened the pleasure of exhibiting one's new acquisition. The kindly saying of one dear old lady, 'I wish you health to wear it, strength to tear it, and money to buy another with', formed a much pleasanter reception than the pinching.
                                        Shropshire Burne (1883)

Recorded examples are widely separated, but remarkably similar in content. The earliest dates only from the late nineteenth century, and the custom does not seem to have lasted far into the twentieth century.

Somerset [1909] Tongue (1965) 144. **Shropshire** Burne (1883) 270. **Yorkshire** Nicholson (1890) 26. **Co. Durham** [1876] *Folk-Lore* 20 (1909) 79; Leighton (1910) 60. **Northeast Scotland** Gregor (1881) 31. **Highland Scotland** Campbell (1900) 231. **Co. Antrim** [*c.*1905] McDowell (1972) 129. **Unlocated** Wright (1913) 224.

clothes: new, Easter

There were several days in the year when custom dictated that everyone should wear new clothes or at least a new item of clothing. WHITSUN, NEW YEAR and Christmas day are sometimes mentioned in this context, but Easter was the most popular time:

[Easter] It is deemed essential by many people to wear some new article of dress, if only a pair of gloves or a new ribbon; for not to do so is considered unlucky; and the birds will be angry with you.
                                        Mid-Wales Davies (1911)

As mentioned here, the immediate penalty for failing to follow tradition in this respect was that the birds (usually rooks or crows) would 'dirty' on you, although others simply said that it was unlucky.

a correspondent whose early home at Kerry in Montgomeryshire . . . lay just in the homeward flight of the inhabitants of a large rookery, writes that in his childish days he used to look out anxiously for rooks on Easter Day, and run to shelter if he heard one cawing, in spite of his mother's habitual care to provide each of her family with some new garment for Easter wearing.
                                        Montgomeryshire Burne (1883)

Although reported widely in the nineteenth century, the custom was certainly not then a new one. Samuel Pepys wrote in 1662 of getting his wife new clothes 'against Easter', and as Mercutio says, 'Didst thou not fall out with a tailor for wearing his new doublet before Easter?' (*Romeo & Juliet* (1597)).

See also WHITSUN: NEW CLOTHES.

Hampshire Sikes (1880) 269. **London** Samuel Pepys, *Diary* (9 Feb. 1662). **Worcestershire** *Folk-Lore* 26 (1915) 97. **Northamptonshire** Sternberg (1851) 189. **East Anglia** Forby (1830) 414; Varden (1885) 112. **Norfolk** N&Q 2S:4 (1857) 432; [1920s] Wigby (1976) 69. **Suffolk** Claxton (1954) 89. **Lincolnshire** Thompson (1856) 735; [*c.*1920] Opie & Tatem, 131. **Shropshire** Burne (1883) 217–18. **England** Henderson (1866) 63. **Yorkshire** N&Q 4S:5 (1870) 595; N&Q 5S:10 (1878) 287; Nicholson (1890) 132. **Lancashire** Harland & Wilkinson (1873) 219; N&Q 5S:11 (1879) 236. **Cumberland** *Folk-Lore* 40 (1929) 284. **Co. Durham** Leighton (1910) 57. **Northumberland** Bosanquet (1929) 79. **Mid-Wales** Davies (1911) 74. **Anglesey** N&Q 5S:11 (1879) 54. **Montgomeryshire** Burne (1883) 217–18. **Dumfriesshire** [1957] Opie & Tatem, 131. **Co. Wexford** [1939] Ó Muirithe & Nuttall (1999) 167. **Literary** Thomas Lodge, *Wits Miserie* (1596) 14; Shakespeare, *Romeo & Juliet* (1597) 3:1.

clothes: new, first day worn

New, or even clean, clothes should be worn first on a Sunday, or at church, because that would bless them and make them last much longer. To ignore this rule was to court trouble:

You must be careful not to put on any new article of clothing for the first time on a Saturday, or some severe punishment will ensue. One person put on his new boots on a Saturday, and on Monday broke his arm.   Sussex Jefferies (1889)

Babies should also be promoted to toddler clothes, and children put into their summer outfits on a Sunday. One day which was particularly unlucky for anything new, including clothes, was HOLY INNOCENTS' DAY, as instructed by John Melton in 1620; 'it is not good to put on a new sute, pare ones nailes, or begin any thing on a Childermas day'.

Sussex Jefferies (1889) 85. **Dorset** N&Q 5S:10 (1878) 24. **Cornwall** *Folk-Lore Jnl* 5 (1887) 210. **Essex** [*c*.1920] Ketteridge & Mays (1972) 142. **Oxfordshire** [1985] Opie & Tatem, 86. **Highland Scotland** Shaw (1775) 242–3. **Western Scotland** Napier (1879) 137. **Ayrshire** [1962] Opie & Tatem, 86. **General** Melton (1620).

clothes: new, money in

A specialized application of the crucially important motif of BEGINNINGS has resulted in a widespread custom of HANDSELLING new clothes, on the grounds that money in the pocket, or given to the wearer, will ensure that luck and prosperity will continue to be associated with those clothes.

It was an old custom long ago with tailors to put either a penny or a half-penny in the pockets of the suit he would have made. Some say it was to hansel the suit. Others say that the person that would wear the suit would always have luck. Some used to put a halfpenny more in each pocket. They used to put a halfpenny in one pocket and a penny in another pocket and so on like that. Many people used not to go to a tailor that would not put something in the pockets of the suit.

Co. Wexford [1938] Ó Muirithe & Nuttall (1999)

Occasionally, the donor had to be aware of certain conditions:

A little lad who wears a new suit of clothes for the first time generally visits the neighbours' houses to show his finery and receive from them lucky pennies to put in his pockets. A custom akin to this is in vogue on the Borders, where no one will put on a new coat without first placing some money in the right-hand pocket. This ensures the pocket being always full; but if the unlucky wight should inadvertently put the cash in the left-hand pocket, he will never have any money as long as he wears the coat.

Yorkshire *Leeds Mercury* (4 Oct. 1879).

In other contexts, handselling has a much longer history, but references to this new clothes superstition have so far only been found back to the second half of the nineteenth century, but the idea was still being expressed in the 1950s. Many examples have been noted in Scotland and Ireland, once or twice in Wales, but in England only the northern counties are represented. It is likely that earlier references will come to light, and it will be interesting to note whether the geographical spread will remain as restricted as it seems at present.

Northern England Wright (1913) 225. **England** Addy (1895) 80. **Yorkshire** *Leeds Mercury* (4 Oct. 1879); Nicholson (1890) 2. **Co. Durham** Leighton (1910) 56, 59–60. **Wales** Trevelyan (1909) 324. **Northern England/Scotland Borders** Henderson (1866) 88. **Northeast Scotland** Gregor (1881) 31. **Fifeshire** [1952] Opie & Tatem, 188. **Co. Antrim** [*c*.1905] McDowell (1972) 129. **Co. Wexford** [1938] Ó Muirithe & Nuttall (1999) 167.

clothes: of the dead

Even in times of hardship, many people would not accept the clothes of anyone who had recently died, because it was generally believed that a dead person's clothes wore out very quickly:

The poor will not say thank you for clothes which belonged to anyone that has died. They believe that they will soon become rotten.

Herefordshire Leather (1912)

To be more explicit, it was believed that the clothes would rot as the body did. This notion was reasonably widely spread, but the first known reference only dates from the mid nineteenth century. Nevertheless, it was still being quoted in the 1980s.

A very different view of dead people's clothes was reported from Ireland:

When a man or woman dies, if the next of kin does not wish to wear the dead person's clothes himself, they must be given to some other relation. The recipient is bound to wear them to Mass on three consecutive Sundays and pray for the soul of the owner. It must be a complete set of clothes, shoes, shirt, hat and all, and if there is not a complete set, or if, for instance, the recipient could not wear the shoes of the dead person, then new ones must be bought and given in their stead. When Seumas died, his sons wouldn't wear his clothes because the coat was the cut-way style, old, heavy and stiff, so the clothes were given to Deaghan. Seumas was a good man and always

went to Mass, but Deaghan was not a church-
goer, and never went to Mass. However, when he
got the clothes, he had to go three Sundays
running, and he did, and what's more, he has
been every Sunday since – and that's months ago.
When Mary was dying she arranged for her
clothes to be given to her niece. The boots were
worn out, so the dying woman said: 'Be sure now
you buy good strong comfortable boots, and don't
be getting them small enough for the girl, but get
them fine and large for myself, the way I won't
be having my feet pinched in Heaven'. A priest
told me that he met a man going to Mass the other
day with his father's boots tied up in a red hand-
kerchief. The priest asked him why. He said he
could get no one to wear them, so he was forced
to take them to Mass the three Sundays himself.
                                    Co. Kerry *Folk-Lore* (1920)

Wiltshire *Wilts. N&Q* 1 (1893–5) 8, 58. Oxfordshire
[1986] Opie & Tatem, 88. Essex Varden (1885) 117.
Herefordshire Leather (1912) 89. Worcestershire *Folk-
Lore* 20 (1909) 346. Suffolk Chambers 2 (1878) 322.
Lincolnshire Gutch & Peacock (1908) 237. Derbyshire
[1890s] Uttley (1946) 126. Dumfriesshire Shaw (1890)
13. Co. Kerry *Folk-Lore* (1920) 234–5. Unlocated N&Q
2S:12 (1861) 492. General [1914–18 War] *Folk-Lore* 41
(1930) 256.

clothes: skirt hem

In accordance with the general principle that
untoward happenings to clothes are generally
thought lucky (*see* CLOTHES: INSIDE OUT), a
small number of sources report a belief that if a
woman's skirt hem is turned up, it means a present or a letter is on its way:

Lydia Milton, a native of Devonshire, told me in
April 1893 that in her native place it is said to be
lucky for a woman if, in putting on her dress, the
end of it turns up; she should not smooth it out,
but let it fall of its own accord, as it is a sign that
she is going to receive a present. The same applies
to a man in putting on his coat.
                                    Devon *Folk-Lore* (1915)

Two other skirt beliefs have occasionally been
noted in Wales:

If a bramble clings to the skirts of a young lady
some one has fallen in love with her; and the
same is said of a young man when his hat goes
against the branches of a tree.   West Wales Davies
(1911)

If in going out your skirt catches in the doorway,
it is a token of misadventure or misfortune.
                                    Wales Trevelyan (1909)

Devon [1893] *Folk-Lore* 26 (1915) 155; *Devonshire Assoc.*
57 (1926) 131. Hertfordshire *Folk-Lore* 25 (1914) 372–3.
Gloucestershire *Folk-Lore* 26 (1915) 210. Co. Durham
Leighton (1910) 60. Wales Trevelyan (1909) 270, 329;
Davies (1911) 217.

clothes: thread/pin left in

A belief only found once in the literature so far,
but probably more widely known:

A coat was sent home from the tailor's, out of
which he had not taken the basting-stitches. 'Ah'
someone exclaimed, 'that coat is not paid for . . .
and here's a pin left in, and that means the same'.
                                    East Anglia N&Q (1868)

This can be compared with a much more widespread notion that SHOES SQUEAKING means
they too are not paid for.

East Anglia N&Q 4S:2 (1868) 221.

clover

The four-leafed clover is one of the best-known
symbols of good luck in modern Britain, and has
been so for nearly five hundred years or more.
The modern belief is that to find and keep one
bestows luck and prosperity, and this has been
one of the main benefits right from the earliest
references:

That if a man walking in the fields, finde any
foure-leaved grasse, he shall in a small while after
finde some good thing.   Melton (1620)

But there were two other widely known connections which resulted in differing meanings. One
was a strong connection with love and marriage.
This is probably at the root of the allusion in
Robert Herrick's 'Nuptiall Song,' where he writes:

Glide by the banks of virgins then, and pass
The shewers of roses, lucky-four-leav'd grass.
                         Robert Herrick, *Hesperides* (1648)

The connection is much more explicit in a
widespread love divination procedure, which
works for either an 'even ash' (*see* ASH LEAF
DIVINATION) or the clover:

Even ash and four-leaved clover
You are sure your love to see
Before the day is over.
                                    New Forest Wise (1867)

Paradoxically, another love procedure calls for
a clover with *two* leaves, or 'clover of two'. When
a two-leafed clover is placed in the shoe, the next

person you meet of the opposite sex will be your future spouse (or will be of the same name as them).

The other useful attributes of a four-leafed clover are to protect against EVIL EYE and witchcraft, and to enable the possessor to see through any tricks and deceptions wrought by ill-wishers, fairies, or charlatans:

I remember a story which I heard when a boy, and the narrator of it I recollect spoke as if he were quite familiar with the fact. A certain man came to the village to exhibit the strength of a wonderful cock, who could draw, attached to its leg by a rope, a large log of wood. Many people went and paid to see this wonderful performance, which was exhibited in the back yard of a public house. One of the spectators present on one occasion had in his possession a four-leaved clover, and while others saw, as they supposed, a log of wood drawn through the yard, this person saw only a straw attached to the cock by a small thread. I may mention here that the four-leaved clover was reputed to be a preventative against madness, and against being drafted for military service. Western Scotland Napier (1879)

The general good luck and love connections with four-leafed clover are reported from at least the sixteenth century, Reginald Scot's *Discoverie of Witchcraft* (1584) being the first, but an earlier description appears in the Low Countries publication *Gospelles of Dystaves*, translated into English in 1507. The notion of conferring the ability to see through tricks is regularly reported only from the early nineteenth century onwards, but it was clearly well known across large parts of the British Isles. A possible earlier sighting was quoted by Vincent Lean (1905, 130) from the 'Legend of the Bischop of St. Andrews' (Dalyell, *Scottish Poems of the Sixteenth Century* (1801)), where a 'foure levit claver' was specified among the ingredients of sorcery.

General luck: Sussex *Sussex County Mag.* (1936) 824. Devon *Devonshire Assoc.* 63 (1931) 124. Essex [*c.*1920] Ketteridge & Mays (1972) 139; [1983] Opie & Tatem, 88. Oxfordshire [1920s] Surman (1992) 62. Norfolk [*c.*1870s] Haggard (1935) 19. England Addy (1895) 63. Wales Trevelyan (1909) 325. Dumfriesshire Corrie (1890/91) 83. Ireland Wilde (1887) 103. Guernsey De Garis (1975) 119. Unlocated *Chambers's Jrnl* (1873) 809. General Scot (1584) Bk 11, Ch. 13; Melton (1620). *Love and marriage*: New Forest Wise (1867) 179. Somerset [1923] Opie & Tatem, 88. Devon Hewett (1900) 25; Crossing (1911) 147; Wright (1913) 259. Cornwall Couch (1871) 155; Wright (1913) 259. Wiltshire *Athenaeum* (1846) 1142. Cambridgeshire N&Q 1S:10 (1854) 321; N&Q 165 (1933) 371. East Anglia Varden (1885) 109. Norfolk/Suffolk N&Q 1S:6 (1852) 601. Shropshire Wright

(1913) 259. Northern England *Denham Tracts* 2 (1895) 70–1. Yorkshire Nicholson (1890) 124; Blakeborough (1898) 130. Northumberland Wright (1913) 259. Wales Howells (1831) 67; Trevelyan (1909) 325. Highland Scotland Macbain (1887/88) 267. Guernsey [*c.*1800] MacCulloch MS (1864) 395. Unlocated N&Q 1S:2 (1850) 259; N&Q 165 (1933) 371. Literary Robert Herrick, *Hesperides* (1648) 'Nuptiall Song'.
Witches and trickery: Cornwall Hunt (1865) 101. Co. Durham Brockie (1886) 117; Leighton (1910) 45–6. Northumberland Oliver (1835) 106. Wales Jones (1930) 142. Western Scotland Napier (1879) 130, 133. Highland Scotland Macbain (1887/88) 267. Inverness-shire N&Q 2S:9 (1860) 381. Ireland Wilde (1888) 103. Isle of Man [*c.*1850] Cashen (1912) 75; Moore (1891) 152.

coal: lucky

A piece of coal has, for obvious reasons, been given a symbolic meaning in many contexts, especially those to do with hearth and home. Specific instances include giving a piece to occupants of a new house, to a newly married couple, in a Christmas stocking, and, most commonly, when carried by New Year FIRST FOOTERS.

When visiting someone who has just moved into a new house, never go with your two hands the one length. Always take something to hansel the house. Coal is the luckiest.
Co. Tyrone *Lore & Language* (1972)

Among the packages sent [recently] to a bride – an outfit of brooms and brushes and cleaning requisites – was one most carefully done up in silver paper which, on being opened, proved to be a piece of coal – for luck. London N&Q (1929)

Less easily explained was a widespread set of beliefs that a piece of coal was, in itself, a lucky object. If found, it should be picked up and thrown over the shoulder (some say spit on it first) or put on the nearest fire. Several writers record pieces of coal being carried in pockets and purses, again for luck, and Iona and Peter Opie discovered children taking pieces of coal into exams and adults taking a piece to driving tests. One particular group mentioned as being careful to carry a piece is fishermen:

They all went to sea with a bit of coal in the boat, most of them do now – at least the old fishermen, these proper fishermen's sons . . .
Norfolk Festing (1977)

and, according to newspaper reports, Victorian burglars (see Opie & Tatem, 89).

Although recorded from the 1870s onwards, these beliefs in coal as a lucky object appear to be much more common in the twentieth century and have only recently begun to die out.

Certainly, there are now plenty of children who hardly know what a piece of coal is, and its potential for symbolism will thus be severely weakened and finally disappear.

See also FIRE; FIRST FOOTING; MIDSUM-MER COAL.

Somerset Kettlewell (1927) 32. Devon [*c.*1915] Lakeham (1982) 47; [*c.*1915] *The Times* (7 Aug. 1954) 5; *Devonshire Assoc.* 57 (1926) 108; *Devonshire Assoc.* 102 (1970) 271. London N&Q 156 (1929) 319. Bedfordshire Marsom (1950) 183. Norfolk Festing (1977) 29. Lincolnshire Rudkin (1936) 16, 22. Yorkshire [1982] Opie & Tatem, 89. Cardiganshire [1953] Opie & Tatem, 89. Monmouthshire [1954] Opie & Tatem, 89. Scotland *Chambers's Jnl* (1873) 810. Co. Tyrone *Lore & Language* 1:7 (1972) 13. Various Opie (1959) 223, 226, 234, 271, 291.

cobwebs

see BLEEDING; SPIDERS.

cockerels: crow at door

The most widespread superstition in the nineteenth century about cocks was that one crowing directly at the door of the farmhouse betokened a visitor or, occasionally, news from afar:

If a cock crew in the morning with its head in at the door of the house, it was a token that a stranger

would pay the family a visit that day; and so firm was the faith in this that it was often followed by works, the house being redd up for the occasion. I remember lately visiting an old friend in the country, and on making my appearance I was hailed with the salutation, 'Come awa, I knew we would have a visit from strangers today, for the cock crowed thrice over with his head in at the door'.
Western Scotland Napier (1879)

The symbolism is fairly obvious, given the long-standing motif of a cock crowing as messenger. The belief is first recorded in Scotland about 1820 and is widely reported throughout the rest of the nineteenth, and the first half of the twentieth century. Cocks crowing were not always regarded in such a positive light (*see below*).

Cornwall N&Q 1S:12 (1855) 37; Couch (1871) 167. Somerset Tongue (1965) 50. Devon *Devonshire Assoc.* 57 (1926) 111; *Devonshire Assoc.* 59 (1927) 155; *Devonshire Assoc.* 71 (1939) 127–8. Devon/Cornwall N&Q 5S:1 (1876) 397. Somerset Poole (1877) 39. Wiltshire Wiltshire (1975) 105. Berkshire Lowsley (1888) 23; *Folk-Lore* 5 (1894) 337. Buckinghamshire Henderson (1866) 92. Worcestershire/Shropshire *Gent. Mag.* (1855) 385. Norfolk Fulcher Collection (*c.*1895). Shropshire N&Q 5S:6 (1876) 289; Burne (1883) 229. England Addy (1895) 66, 99. Derbyshire [1890s] Uttley (1946) 128. Yorkshire Nicholson (1890) 130; Morris (1911) 249. Lancashire N&Q 1S:3 (1851) 516; Harland & Wilkinson (1882) 156. Westmorland *London Saturday Jnl* (13 Mar. 1841) 131. Co. Durham N&Q 5S:6 (1876) 397; Leighton (1910) 62.

cockerels

Traditional views of the cockerel show some ambivalence; they are certainly uncanny at times, but good or bad by turn. They feature in a number of very widespread beliefs, mostly concerned with their role as messenger and when and where they crow – at the farmhouse door to predict a stranger, in the afternoon or at night to predict somebody's death, or sometimes for other purposes:

If a cock crows before midnight there is some news coming from the quarter in which he is looking; if his feet are warm it denotes good luck for the owner; if his feet are cold someone is to die.
Highland Scotland Macbain (1887/88)

The cock crows: Once for a wedding/Twice for a birth/Three times for sorrow/Four times for mirth.
Norfolk Fulcher Collection (*c.*1895)

Other aspects of cockerel behaviour have attracted much less attention. They feature in a CALEN-DAR CUSTOM for Shrovetide:

On Shrove Tuesday the unmarried girls made the pancakes, giving the first to the cock – the number of hens which joined him represented the number of years before she was married.
Lancashire *Lancashire Lore* (1971)

There is some confusion in Welsh accounts about whether a white cock was lucky or not, and cocks, black or white, were deliberately killed in Ireland on ST MARTIN'S DAY, and elsewhere, to CURE EPILEPSY.

Wiltshire *Folk-Lore* 12 (1901) 75; Wiltshire (1975) 104–5. Norfolk Fulcher Collection (*c.*1895). Lincolnshire Rudkin (1936) 20. England Addy (1895) 66. Lancashire *Lancashire Lore* (1971) 49, 51. Wales Trevelyan (1909) 328. Mid-Wales Davies (1911) 227. Montgomeryshire Hamer (1877) 267. Highland Scotland Macbain (1887/88) 261, 265; Campbell (1900) 257. Co. Longford *Béaloideas* 6 (1936) 264. Co. Wexford [1938] Ó Muirithe & Nuttall (1999) 162, 168.

Northumberland *Folk-Lore* 36 (1925) 253. **Mid-Wales**
Davies (1911) 227. **Montgomeryshire** Burne (1883) 229.
Western Scotland Napier (1879) 114. **Northeast
Scotland** Gregor (1881) 140. **Argyllshire** *Folk-Lore* 21
(1910) 90. **Caithness** Sutherland (1937) 104. **Glasgow**
[*c.*1820] Napier (1864) 397. **Ireland** Wilde (1888) 180.
Unlocated N&Q 6S:5 (1882) 46.

cockerels: epilepsy cure

A live cockerel was often killed in a cure for
epilepsy found in Scotland and Ireland.

*At Contin a boy took ill one day at school. Not long
after the schoolmaster called at the boy's home to
ask for the patient. He entered quite unexpectedly.
He found him in bed, and looking more narrowly
he saw a hole below the bed with a cock lying dead
in it. An old woman, a neighbour, was standing
near the bed with her hands stained with blood.*

Ross-shire *Folk-Lore* 11 (1900) 446

For full references, *see* EPILEPSY: COCKEREL
CURE.

cockerels: omens

A cock crowing at the wrong time, or in the
wrong way, was regarded as a bad sign – and
usually interpreted as predicting illness and
death. The wrong time was either at night or in
the afternoon, especially if repeated:

*A worthy laundress neighbour is in sore distress
– the cock has crowed on two or three nights at
nine o'clock. It is a sure sign of an early death in
her family, and that will be the dying hour. The
event happened exactly as fore-crowed, when she
lost her last daughter.* Unlocated N&Q (1868)

*Almost everyone in Shropshire knows that a cock
crowing at midnight is a sign of death. We are
told of a farmer's wife who killed her cock because
'he would crow at twelve at night'.*

Shropshire Burne (1883)

Alternatively, the crowing could simply coincide
with whatever was going on in the human world:

*So at the same instant that Mr. Ashton was going
to France, the cock happened to crow: at which
his wife was much troubled, and her mind gave
her, that it boded ill luck. He was taken at sea
and after tried and executed.*

Unlocated Aubrey, *Remaines* (1686)

*A mother who hears a cock crowing on the day her
baby is born is in for a spell of bad luck, consequently all cocks in ear-range are slaughtered . . .
it is associated with the denial in Scripture.*

Lancashire [1953] Opie & Tatem

The direction the cock is facing was taken as a
further clue to meaning.

*Not long ago a woman who heard the cock crow
towards midnight went out to see in what direction the bird looked, and returned to ask, 'Is there
anyone ill at the castle, as the cock was looking
that way?'. The laird was ill and died a few days
after.* Highland Scotland Polson (1926)

Thomas Hardy used the superstition very
effectively in his novel *Tess of the D'Urbervilles*
(1891); as the heroine Tess and her husband Angel
were leaving, after their afternoon wedding, a cock
settled on the fence and crowed – looking straight
at them. The onlookers sadly commented on their
prospects.

Broadly similar beliefs were recorded from all
parts of the British Isles. The earliest records in
British tradition appear in the sixteenth and
seventeenth centuries, but there are classical
antecedents, such as Petronius Arbiter (*c.*AD 65),
quoted by Opie and Tatem, and St John
Chrysostom's *Homilies on Ephesians* (*c.*AD 390).

Somerset Tongue (1965) 50. **Devon** *Devonshire Assoc.* 8
(1876) 57; [1900] *Devonshire Assoc.* 57 (1926) 111; Hewett
(1900) 55. **Dorset** Udal (1922) 180; *Dorset Year Book*
(1961–2) 74. **Cornwall** Hunt (1865) 166. **Essex** *Folk-Lore*
64 (1953) 293. **Buckinghamshire** Henderson (1866) 92.
Herefordshire Leather (1912) 25–6. **Lincolnshire** Swaby
(1891) 93; Gutch & Peacock (1908) 152. **Shropshire** Burne
(1883) 229. **England** Addy (1895) 66. **Northern England**
Newcastle Weekly Chronicle (11 Feb. 1899) 7. **Yorkshire**
Henderson (1866) 33; *Folk-Lore* 21 (1910) 226. **Lancashire**
[1953] Opie & Tatem, 90–1. **Cumberland** Penfold (1907)
58. **Co. Durham** Brockie (1886) 135; Leighton (1910) 51.
Wales Trevelyan (1909) 281. **West Wales** Davies (1911) 213.
Mid-Wales Davies (1911) 227. **Pembrokeshire** Davies
(1911) 62. **Neath** Phillips (1925) 597. **Montgomeryshire**
Hamer (1877) 257–8; Burne (1883) 229. **Highland
Scotland** Polson (1926) 17. **Northeast Scotland** Gregor
(1874) 133–4; Gregor (1881) 140. **Eastern Scotland** Anson
(1930) 38. **Aberdeenshire** *Folk-Lore Jnl* 6 (1888) 262.
Dumfriesshire Corrie (1890/1) 43. **Shetland** Saxby (1932)
183. **Ireland** Wilde (1888) 180. **N. Ireland** Foster (1951) 18,
131. **Co. Longford** *Béaloideas* 6 (1936) 260. **Guernsey** De
Garis (1975) 137. **Isle of Man** Cashen (1912) 6. **Unlocated**
R. Moresin, *Papatus* (1594) 21, quoted Opie & Tatem, 91;
Gaule, *Mag-astro-mances* (1652) 181. Aubrey, *Remaines*
(1686/1880) 196; N&Q 4S:1 (1868) 10; Kearton (1922)
63–4. **Literary** Thomas Hardy, *Tess of the D'Urbervilles*
(1891) Ch. 33.

cockerels: weather

In certain circumstances, a cock crowing foretold the weather, usually rain:

*Cock crowing, going to bed
Get up with a wet head (sign of rain)*

Berkshire *Folk-Lore* (1894)

The cock crowing on rainy weather is a sign of fair weather for the rest of the day.

Mid-Wales Davies (1911)

Devon/Cornwall N&Q 5S:1 (1876) 397. **Berkshire** *Folk-Lore* 5 (1894) 337. **Herefordshire** Leather (1912) 25–6. **Norfolk** Fulcher Collection (*c.*1895). **Mid-Wales** Davies (1911) 220. **Orkney** N&Q 10S:12 483.

coffee grounds

see TEA: LEAF READING.

coins

see MONEY: CROOKED/HOLED COINS.

combs

A comb is one of the many personal items which should not simply be picked up if you drop it.

If you drop a comb and let someone else pick it up for you; you will then have a surprise.

Lincolnshire Rudkin (1936)

When a comb has been dropped I have seen girls carefully tread on it before picking it up, but they could give no reason, except that it would be unlucky not to do so.

Herefordshire Leather (1912)

See also DROPPING THINGS.

Lincolnshire Rudkin (1936) 20. **Herefordshire** Leather (1912) 87.

comets

The idea that comets mark or predict great happenings has been common in many countries since at least the classical era, and was already known in eighth-century Britain:

Comets are long-haired stars with flames, appearing suddenly, and presaging a change in sovereignty, or plague, or war, or winds, or floods.

Northumberland Bede, *De Natura Rerum* (*c.*AD 725)

In contrast to STORMS, which could mark the passing of ordinary folk, providing they were sufficiently wicked, a comet was too important to be of concern to any but the great, as Shakespeare made clear:

When beggars die there are no comets seen;
The heavens themselves blaze forth the death of princes,   Shakespeare, *Julius Caesar* (1599)

a sentiment which was echoed centuries later by Thomas Hardy:

If 'tis a token that he's getting hot about the ways of anybody in this parish, 'tis about my Lady Constantine's, since she is the only one of a figure worth such a hint.   Hardy, *Two on a Tower* (1882)

It is clear that the omen was taken very seriously by very many people until recent times, although from the seventeenth century at least there are indications that the belief was failing to appeal to some intellectuals. Writers such as John Evelyn, who noted seeing a comet in his diary on 12 December 1680, were beginning to question whether a natural rather than superstitious explanation might be more appropriate. Nevertheless, coincidences such as the death of Edward VII and the appearance of Halley's comet in 1910 ensured that traditional beliefs continued to be cited well into the twentieth century, and are still well covered in the national press whenever a comet appears.

Devon Hewett (1900) 56. **Essex** [*c.*1920] Ketteridge & Mays (1972) 143. **Midland England** N&Q 10S:7 (1907) 129–30. **Northumberland** Bede, *De Natura Rerum* (*c.*AD 725) Ch. 24. **Wales** N&Q 10S:7 (1907) 196. **Scotland** *Complaynt of Scotland* 6 (1549). **General** *Gent. Mag.* 270 (1890) 464–72; Hazlitt (1905) 142; N&Q 11S:1 (1910) 448; N&Q 151 (1926) 224, 267. **Literary** Shakespeare, *Julius Caesar* (1599) 2:2; John Milton, *Paradise Lost* 2 (1667) 708; Daniel Defoe, *Journal of a Plague Year* (1722); Thomas Hardy, *Two on a Tower* (1882) Ch.13.

confirmation

Two popular superstitions attached themselves to the religious rite of confirmation, or being 'bishopped' as it was often called.

I am told that in the villages near here confirmation is considered a safe cure for rheumatism, and that consequently, old persons are in the habit of presenting themselves to the bishop from time to time, as often as they can get an opportunity, to receive the rite.   Lincolnshire N&Q (1884)

Religious items could also be utilized for the same complaint:

I have heard my father say that his grandmother – an excellent and pious woman – for whose memory he had the greatest respect – when she was troubled with rheumatism, took an extra sup of the Communion wine as a cure. This was probably less than eighty years ago.

Unlocated N&Q (1887)

The second superstition was more worrying for the worshipper, as it was largely beyond their control:

Though by the rubric the bishop is enjoined to lay his hand severally upon the head of every person brought to him for confirmation, a slovenly habit of confirming two at a time has added to the folk-lore of our land. It is considered very unlucky to receive confirmation from the bishop's left hand, those so unfortunate being 'doomed on the spot to single blessedness'.

East Anglia Varden (1885)

This belief was widely held, but at present cannot be traced earlier than 1852. A much earlier passage, however, in one of Thomas Dekker's plays, while not exactly the same superstition, shows that the unfortunate connection between the left hand and officiation at a religious ceremony has a much longer history:

I am the most wretched fellow: sure some left-handed priest christened me, I am so unlucky: I am never out of one puddle or another, still falling. Dekker, *Honest Whore Part 2* (1630)

Cures rheumatism: Sussex Latham (1878) 46. N&Q 7S:4 (1887) 534. Dorset *Dorset County Chronicle* (Jun 1888). Wiltshire *Wilts. N&Q* 1 (1893–5) 9. East Anglia Forby (1830) 406–7. Lincolnshire N&Q 6S:9 (1884) 346–7. Northern England N&Q 7S:4 (1887) 415. Yorkshire *Leeds Mercury* 4 Oct 1879. Unlocated N&Q 7S:4 (1887) 534.

Left hand unlucky: Somerset Poole (1877) 30. Tongue (1965) 145. Devon N&Q 1S:6 (1852) 601. Burne (1883) 269. Hewett (1900) 50, 55. Herefordshire Leather (1912) 80. East Anglia Varden (1885) 108. Lincolnshire *Grantham Jnl* (22 June 1878). Swaby (1891) 89. England Addy (1895) 95. Shropshire Burne (1883) 269. Lancashire Harland & Wilkinson (1873) 229–30. Co. Durham Brockie (1889) 206. General Opie (1959) 209. Literary Thomas Dekker, *Honest Whore Part 2* (1630) 3:2.

conjurers

see CUNNING MEN AND WOMEN.

Connoisseur, The

The Connoisseur was a short-lived humorous weekly periodical, in the tradition of the better-known *Spectator*, *Idler*, and *Rambler*, edited by 'Mr Town, Critic and Censor General' (i.e. Bonnell Thornton and George Colman, the elder). It lasted for 140 numbers, from January 1754 to September 1756. The two pieces reproduced below are particularly important as first-hand evidence of the existence of a number of superstitions and love divinations in the middle of the eighteenth century – a period for which we have little other solid information.

THE CONNOISSEUR No. 56 Thursday 20 February 1755, pp. 331–6

The idle superstitions of the vulgar are nowhere so conspicuous as in the affairs of love. When a raw girl's brain is once turned with a sweetheart, she converts every trifling accident of her life into a good or bad omen, and makes everything conspire to strengthen her in so pleasing a delusion. Virgil represents Dido, as soon as she has contracted her fatal passion for Aeneas, as going to the priests to have her fortune told. In like manner the lovesick girl runs to the cunning-man, or crosses the gipsy's hand with her last sixpence, to know when she shall be married, how many children she shall have, and whether she shall be happy with her husband. She also consults the cards, and finds out her lover in the Knave of Hearts. She learns how to interpret dreams, and every night furnishes her with meditations for the next day. If she happens to bring out anything in conversation which another person was about to say, she comforts herself that she shall be married before them; and if she stumbles as she is running up stairs, imagines she shall go to church with her sweetheart before the week is at an end. But if in the course of their amour she gives the dear man her hair wove in a true-lover's knot, or breaks a crooked ninepence with him, she thinks herself assured of his inviolable fidelity.

It would puzzle the most profound antiquary to discover what could give birth to the many strange notions cherished by fond nymphs and swains. The God of Love has more superstitious votaries, and is worshipped with more unaccountable rites than any fabulous deity whatever. Nothing indeed is so whimsical as the imagination of a person in love. The dying shepherd carves the name of his mistress on the trees, while the fond maid knits him a pair of garters with an amorous posey; and both look on what they do as a kind of charm to secure the affection of the other. A lover will rejoice to give his mistress a bracelet or a top-knot, and she perhaps will take pleasure in working him a pair of ruffles. These they will regard as the soft bonds of love, but neither would on any account run the risk of cutting love, by giving or receiving such a present as a knife or a pair of scissors. But to wear the picture of the beloved object constantly near the heart is universally accounted a most excellent and never-failing preservative of affection.

Some few years ago there was publickly advertised among the other extraordinary medicines whose wonderful qualities are daily related in the last page of our newspapers, a most efficacious love-powder, by which a despairing lover might create affection in the bosom of the most cruel mistress. Lovers have indeed always been fond of enchantment. Shakespeare has represented Othello as accused of winning his Desdemona by 'conjuration and mighty magic'; and Theocritus and Virgil have both introduced women into their pastorals using charms and incantations to recover the affection of their sweethearts. In a word, talismans, genii, witches, fairies, and all the instruments of magic and enchantment were first discovered by lovers, and employed in the business of love.

But I never had a thorough insight into all this amorous sorcery till I received the following letter, which was sent me from the country, a day or two after Valentine's Day, and I make no doubt but all true lovers most religiously performed the previous rites mentioned by my correspondent.

To Mr. Town

Dear Sir!   *Feb. 17, 1755*

You must know I am in love with a very clever man, a Londoner; and as I want to know if it is my fortune to have him, I have tried all the tricks I can hear of for that purpose. I have seen him several times in coffee-grounds, with a sword by his side, and he was once at the bottom of a tea-cup, in a coach and six, with two footmen behind it. I got up last May morning, and went in to the fields to hear the cuckoo; and when I pulled off my left shoe, I found a hair in it exactly the same colour with his. But I shall never forget what I did last Midsummer Eve. I and my two sisters tried the dumb-cake together: you must know, two must make it, two bake it, two break it, and the third put it under each of their pillows (but you must not speak a word all the time) and then you will dream of the man you are to have. This we did; and to be sure I did nothing all night, but dream of Mr. Blossom. The same night, exactly at twelve o'clock, I sowed hempseed in our back yard, and said to myself, 'Hempseed I sow, Hempseed I hoe, and he that is my true-love come after me and mow'. Will you believe me? I looked back and saw him behind me, as plain as eyes could see him. After that, I took a clean shift, and turned it, and hung upon the back of a chair; and very likely my sweetheart would have come and turned it right again (for I heard his step) but I was frightened, and could not help speaking, which broke the charm. I likewise stuck up two Midsummer Men, one for myself and one for him. Now if his had died away we should never have come together: but I assure you he blowed and turned to me. Our maid Betty tells me, that

if I go backwards without speaking a word into the garden upon Midsummer Eve, and gather a rose, and keep it in a clean sheet of paper, without looking at it, till Christmas Day, it will be as fresh as in June, and if I then stick it in my bosom, he that is to be my husband will come and take it out. If I am not married before the time comes about again, I will certainly do it, and only mind if Mr. Blossom is not the man.

I have tried a great many other fancies, and they have all turned out right. Whenever I go to lye in a strange bed, I always tye my garter nine times round the bed-post, and knit nine knots in it, and say to myself, 'This knot I knit, this knot I tye, to see my true love as he goes by, In his apparel and array, As he walks in every day.' I did so last holidays at my uncles, and so be sure I saw Mr. Blossom draw my curtains and tuck up the clothes at my bed's feet. Cousin Debby was married a little while ago, and she sent me a piece of bride-cake to put under my pillow, and I had the sweetest dream – I thought we were going to be married together. I have, many is the time, taken great pains to pare an apple whole, and afterwards flung the peel over my head, and it always fell in the shape of the first letter of his sirname or Christian name. I am sure Mr. Blossom loves me, because I stuck two of the kernels upon my forehead, while I thought upon him and the lubberly squire my pappa wants me to have: Mr. Blossom's kernel stuck on, but the other dropt off directly.

Last Friday, Mr. Town, was Valentine's day; and I'll tell you what I did the night before. I got five bay leaves and pinned four of them to the four corners of my pillow, and the fifth to the middle, and then if I dreamt of my sweetheart, Betty said we should be married before the year was out. But to make it more sure, I boiled an egg hard and took out the yolk, and filled it up with salt, and when I went to bed, eat shell and all, without speaking or drinking after it. And this was to have the same effect with the bay-leaves. We also wrote our lovers' names upon bits of paper, and rolled them up in clay, and put them into water; and the first that rose up, was to be our valentine. Would you think of it? Mr. Blossom was my man; and I lay a-bed and shut my eyes all the morning till he came to our house; for I would not have seen another man before him for all the world.

Dear Mr. Town, if you know any other ways to try our fortune by, do put them in your paper. My Mamma laughs at us, and says there is nothing in them, but I am sure there is, for several misses at our boarding school here tried them, and they have all happened true: and I am sure my own sister Hetty, who died just before

Christmas, stood in the church porch last Midsummer Eve to see all that were to die that year in our parish, and she saw her own apparition.

Your humble servant

ARABELLA WHIMSEY

THE CONNOISSEUR No. 59 Thursday 13 March 1755, pp. 349–54

Mr. Village to Mr. Town

Dear Cousin! March 3, 1755

I was greatly entertained with your late reflections on the several branches of magic made use of in the affairs of love. I have myself been very lately among the seers of visions and dreamers of dreams: and hope you will not be displeased at an account of portents and prognostics full as extravagant, though they are not all owing to the same cause, as those of your correspondent Miss Arabella Whimsey. You must know, Cousin, that I am just returned from a visit of a fortnight to an old aunt in the north: where I was mightily diverted with the traditional superstitions, which are most religiously preserved in the family, as they have been delivered down, time out of mind, from their sagacious grandmothers.

When I arrived, I found the mistress of the house very busily employed with her two daughters in nailing a horse-shoe to the threshold of the door. This they told me, was to guard against the spiteful designs of an old woman, who was a witch, and had threatened to do the family a mischief, because one of my young cousins laid two straws across, to see if the old hag could walk over them. The young lady herself assured me, that she had several times heard Goody Cripple muttering to herself; and to be sure she was saying the Lord's Prayer backwards. Besides, the old woman had very often asked them for a pin: but they took care never to give her any thing that was sharp, because she should not bewitch them. They afterwards told me many other particulars of this kind, the same as are mentioned with infinite humour by the Spectator; and to confirm them, they assured me, that the eldest Miss, when she was little, used to have fits, till the mother flung a knife at another old witch (whom the devil had carried off in a high wind) and fetched blood from her.

When I was to go to bed, my aunt made a thousand apologies for not putting me in the best room in the house, which she said had never been lain in, since the death of an old washer-woman, who walked every night, and haunted that room in particular. They fancied that the old woman had hid money somewhere, and could not rest till

she had told somebody; and my cousin assured me, that she might have had it all to herself, for the spirit came one night to her bed-side, and wanted to tell her, but she had not courage to speak to it. I learned also that they had a footman once, who hanged himself for love; and he walked for a great while, till they got the parson to lay him in the Red Sea.

I had not been here long, when an accident happened, which very much alarmed the whole family. Towser one night howled most terribly; which was a sure sign, that somebody belonging to them would die. The youngest Miss declared that she had heard the hen crow that morning; which was another fatal prognostic. They told me that just before uncle died, Towser howled so for several nights together, that they could not quiet him; and my aunt heard the death-watch tick as plainly as if there had been a clock in the room; the maid too, who sat up with him, heard a bell toll at the top of the stairs, the very moment the breath went out of his body. During this discourse, I overheard one of my cousins whisper the other, that she was afraid their mamma would not live long, for she smelt an ugly smell, like a dead body. They had a dairy-maid who died the very week after a hearse had stopt at their door in its way to church; and the eldest miss, when she was but thirteen, saw her own brother's ghost, (who was gone to the West-Indies) walking in the garden; and to be sure nine months after, they had an account, that he died on board the ship, the very same day, and hour of the day, that Miss saw his apparition.

I need not mention to you the common incidents, which were accounted by them no less prophetic. If a cinder popped from the fire, they were in haste to examine whether it was a purse or a coffin. They were aware of my arrival long before I came, because they had seen a stranger on the grate. The youngest Miss will let nobody use the poker but herself; because, when she stirs it, it always burns bright, which is a sign she will have a bright husband: and she is no less sure of a good one, because she generally has ill-luck at cards. Nor is the candle less oracular than the fire; for the squire of the parish came one night to pay them a visit, when the tallow winding-sheet pointed towards him, and he broke his neck soon after in a fox chase. My aunt one night observed with great pleasure a letter in the candle, and she hoped it would be from her son in London. We knew, when a spirit was in the room, by the candle burning blue; but poor cousin Nancy was ready to cry one time, when she snuffed it out and could not blow it in again; though her sister did it at a whiff.

We had no occasion for an almanack or the weather-glass, to let us know whether it would rain or shine. One evening I proposed to ride out with my cousins the next day to see a gentleman's house in the neighbourhood, but my aunt assured us it would be wet, she knew very well from the shooting of her corn. Besides, there was a great spider crawling up the chimney, and the black-bird in the kitchen began to sing: which were both of them as certain forerunners of rain. But the most to be depended on in these cases is a tabby cat. If the cat turned her tail to the fire, we were to have a hard frost: if she licked her tail, rain would certainly ensue. They wondered what stranger they would see, because Puss washed her foot over her left ear. The old lady complained of a cold, and her daughter remarked, it would go through the family; for she observed that poor Tab had sneezed several times. Poor Tab however once flew at one of my cousins; for which she had like to have been destroyed, and the whole family began to think she was no other than a witch.

It is impossible to tell you the several tokens by which they know whether good or ill luck will happen to them. Spilling of salt, or laying knives across, are everywhere accounted ill omens; but a pin with the head turned towards, or to be followed by a strange dog, I found were lucky. I heard one of my cousins tell the cookmaid that she boiled away all her sweethearts, because she had let her dishwater boil over. The same young lady one morning came down to breakfast with her cap the wrong side out; which the mother observing, charged her not to alter it all the day, for fear she should turn luck.

But, above all, I could not help remarking the various prognostics, which the old lady and her daughters used to collect from almost every part of the body. A white speck upon the nails made them as sure of a gift as if they had it already in their pockets. The eldest sister is to have one more husband than her the youngest, because she has one wrinkle more in her forehead, but the other will have the advantage of her in the number of children, as was plainly proved by snapping their finger-joints. It would take up too much room, to set down every circumstance which I observed of this sort during my stay with them: I shall there-fore conclude my letter with the several remarks on the rest of the body, as far as I could learn from this prophetic family: for as I was a relation, you know, they had less reserve.

If the head itches, it is a sign of rain. If the head aches, it is a profitable pain. If you have the tooth-ache you don't love true. If your eye-brow itches, you will see a stranger. If your right eye itches, you will cry; if your left you will laugh. If your nose itches, you will shake hands, kiss a fool, drink a glass of wine, run against a cuckold's door, or miss them all four. If your right ear or cheek burns, your left friends are talking of you; if your left your right friends are talking of you. If your elbow itches, you will change your bedfel-low. If your right hand itches, you will pay away money; if your left, you will receive. If your stom-ach itches, you will eat pudding. If your garter-ing place itches, you will go to a strange place. If your back itches, butter will be cheap when grass grows there. If your side itches somebody is wish-ing for you. If your knee itches, you will kneel in a strange church. If your foot, you will tread upon strange ground. Lastly, if you shiver, somebody is walking over the place of your grave.

I am, Dear Cousin, yours &c.

contemporary legend

A sub-genre of traditional NARRATIVE, which first attracted sustained scholarly attention in the 1970s, although it had been in existence for centuries. The key defining elements of contem-porary legends are that they are set in the modern everyday world and feature identifiable people, places, and situations rather than fantastic or vague settings. They are also told as *true* stories, and the localized details serve to support and legitimate to the point of disguising the fact that they are stories at all. They are thus closely akin to rumour, but have a more developed narrative format, and some writers have adopted the affectionate term 'FOAFtales' – Friend of a Friend tales – because they are often set at one remove from the narrator. This protects the teller against charges of lying if anyone challenges the story.

Many of the legends first identified in the 1970s are still active in Britain, from stories of fast-food chains (Chinese restaurants being closed by health inspectors because they found dogs in the freezer; customers being served a deep fried rat instead of chicken, and so on) to embarrassing moments (adulterous couples trapped in cars; people caught naked in inap-propriate situations; bizarre happenings while on holiday abroad). Some are funny, but many are disturbing or frightening – for example, people stealing other people's internal organs, deliberately infecting strangers with deadly diseases, and abducting children. New stories are regularly circulated, although these often turn out to be old stories adapted to modern settings. Moral panics, major disasters, and well-publi-cized crimes are always accompanied by a new rash of legends.

Such legends thrive particularly well among teenagers, and also within any closed group – especially those fundamentalist or ardent campaigning groups who have a strong sense of being a beleaguered minority. Legends are routinely used to highlight the shortcomings or evil doings of an opposing group, and are used to bolster a particular belief system.

Of all the narrative sub-genres, contemporary legends are particularly relevant to the study of superstitions because *belief*, or at least 'believability', plays such a central role. Superstitions are also found embedded in legends, and this plays an important role in their dissemination. Although most are easily recognizable, they are extraordinarily difficult to challenge in face-to-face social situations. Nevertheless, it is a safe bet that every one of us has unwittingly fallen victim to a few of these legends and consequently believes things which are in fact untrue.

Also called 'Urban myths'.

See Bennett and Smith (1993) for a bibliography of materials on contemporary legends.

coral

Necklaces made of coral were widely used as a way of helping to ease babies' TEETHING problems, but were also believed to be effective in countering witchcraft and the evil eye:

In this country coral beads were hung round the necks of babies, and are still used in country districts to protect them from an evil eye. Coral bells are used at present.

Western Scotland Napier (1879)

Reginald Scot provides evidence that this custom was widespread in his time:

The coral preserveth such as bear it from fascination or bewitching, and in this respect they are hanged about children's necks. But from whence that superstition is derived, and who invented the lie I know not, but I see how readily the people give credit thereunto, by the multitude of corals that way employed.

Scot (1584)

Other references mention that coral was a protection against other ailments, including epilepsy, and one, the so-called *Aristotle's Midwife* of the mid eighteenth century, describes its efficacy in childbirth.

The general regard for coral as both protective and curative is most probably derived from classical writers such as Pliny.

See also references under TEETHING.

Cornwall *Old Cornwall* 1:9 (1929) 41. **Warwickshire** Bloom (*c*.1930) 26. **England** Addy (1895) 81. **Lancashire** Harland & Wilkinson (1882) 262. **Western Scotland** Napier (1879) 36. **Unlocated** *The Mirror* 21 (1833) 421. **General** Scot (1584) Bk 13, Ch. 6; L. Lemnius, *Secret Miracles of Nature* (1658) 391; *Aristotle's Midwife* (*c*.1740) 52–3. **Literary** Robert Wilson, *Three Ladies of London* (1584). **Classical** Pliny, *Natural History* (AD 77) Bk 32, Ch. 11.

cork

In a handful of references, cork is recommended as a preventative against CRAMP. The writers vary considerably on where to put the cork – under the pillow, under the mattress, between the toes, around the wrist, and so on – but no one attempts to give any explanation for its efficacy. The belief suddenly springs into the record in the mid nineteenth century and was still being quoted in the later twentieth.

Devon N&Q 1S:2 (1850) 512. **Lincolnshire** N&Q 4S:5 (1870) 380. **England** Addy (1895) 91. **Yorkshire** *Folk-Lore* 20 (1909) 348. **Northumberland** *Sunday Post* (6 Jan. 1957). **Ireland** Logan (1981) 11. **Unlocated** N&Q 2S:12 (1861) 492; *Folk-Lore* 62 (1951) 268. **General** *Ladies Companion* (4 May 1850), quoted Opie & Tatem, 96.

cormorants (*Phalacrocorax carbo*)

One or two traditions about cormorants have been recorded, but this probably underestimates beliefs about the bird, at least in coastal areas.

Omens of good or bad luck are also derived from sea-birds. All depends on whether a gull or a cormorant is seen first, as, if a cormorant, no fish is to be expected that day.

Guernsey MacCulloch (1864)

Charles Swainson relates an incident in 1860 when a cormorant settled on the steeple of Boston (Lincs.) church and sat there until the next day, when it was shot by the caretaker of the church. This was taken as a grave omen, which was apparently confirmed shortly afterwards when news arrived of a major disaster – the loss of the *Lady Elgin*, with 300 passengers. It is not clear here whether the locals took fright because it was a cormorant or simply because of the unusual presence of a large bird. The latter is most likely. Other cormorant traditions are also given by Swainson.

Lincolnshire Swainson (1886) 142–3. **Guernsey** MacCulloch (1864) 506.

corns: cures

Various cures for corns have been recorded. One of the most common plant remedies was to wrap them in IVY leaves, and another was to rub them with the panacea of folk medicine, fasting SPITTLE, every morning. Another guaranteed method was to apply the paste made by dissolved mother-of-pearl buttons in lemon juice or vinegar.

I should like to say that, to my personal knowledge, this quaint remedy has been used for many years in Yorkshire. In Driffield, in the East Riding, also in Whitby thirty years ago, I knew several people who used it. As to its efficacy, I can speak favourably, having tried it with advantage to myself.   Yorkshire N&Q (1902)

Corns were also susceptible to more magical means of treatment:

Cure for corns – bare your foot to the new moon and say nine times, pointing to the foot, and the moon:

Corns down here
Narry waun up there.
   Cornwall *Jnl Royal Inst. Cornwall* (1915)

This runs counter to other widespread advice, that things such as corns should be cut or treated when the moon is waning, not waxing.

[A domestic servant from Great Torrington] told me that if people cut their corns when the moon was 'on its back', the corns would not grow as they otherwise would.
   Devon *Devonshire Assoc.* (1898)

Devon *Exeter Gazette* (17 May 1887); *Devonshire Assoc.* 30 (1898) 96. **Cornwall** *Jnl Royal Inst. Cornwall* 20 (1915) 128. **Wiltshire** *Wilts. N&Q* 1 (1893–5) 316. **Oxfordshire** *Folk-Lore* 34 (1923) 326; *Oxf. FL Soc. Ann. Record* (1956) 13. **Worcestershire** Salisbury (1893) 71. **Norfolk** [c.1920] Wigby (1976) 65; Randell (1966) 85. **Lincolnshire** N&Q 4S:1 (1868) 550. **Staffordshire** Hackwood (1924) 150. **Derbyshire?** N&Q 9S:9 (1902) 10. **Yorkshire** Nicholson (1890) 46; N&Q 9S:9 (1902) 158. **Highland Scotland** Polson (1926) 34. **Ireland** Logan (1981) 69. **Co. Cork** [1937] Culloty (1993) 62. **Unlocated** Hone, *Year Book* (1832) 126–8. **Literary** *Connoisseur* 59 (1755) 352.

corp criadhach (body of clay)

In Scotland, the clay image made to represent a victim in order to harm him/her by witchcraft. *See* EFFIGIES.

corpse: bleeding

The belief that the wounds of a murder victim's corpse will bleed anew if approached or touched by the murderer has a long history in European cultures, and features in medieval tales such as the *Nibelunglied* (*c.*1200) and Chrétien de Troyes' *Ywain* (*c.*1200) (Aarne-Thompson motif D1318.5.2). In Britain, the belief had official sanction in King James I's *Daemonology* (1597):

In a secret murder if the dead carcase be at any time thereafter handled by the murderer, it will gush out of blood, as if the blood were crying to heaven for revenge of the murder . . .

and it continued to be fully trusted as a genuine proof of guilt throughout the seventeenth century, when it was frequently commented on as an example of God's way of ensuring that murderers would not escape justice. It was also used regularly as a dramatic device by playwrights. The whole notion appears to have rapidly lost favour with the educated classes in the late seventeenth century, but it survived in the folk tradition until well into the twentieth century:

That such things had taken place was a belief amongst the folks where I was born. I can remember hearing a horrible tale of a man who was supposed to have murdered a relation somewhere in Derbyshire. He was accused of it, denied it, and began 'fendin' to prove that he was elsewhere. He was dragged into the stable where the body had been laid, and forced to bend and look down upon it. There was a rush of blood from the corpse; the man 'swounded' and, on coming round, confessed to the murder. Folks then were full of such beliefs in tales which had come down to them.   Derbyshire N&Q (1910)

An Irish peasant whom I met a few days ago told me that it is a very common belief in his country that the corpse bleeds afresh at the touch of the murderer. He said that he himself was fully convinced of its truth.   Ireland N&Q (1910)

Also known as *Bier-Right, Ordeal by Touch*, etc.

Cornwall Mayes (1978) 88. **Gloucestershire** *Glos. N&Q* 5 (1891–3) 157. **London** [1669] N&Q 11S:3 (1911) 35. **Hertfordshire** [1628/9] N&Q 11S:2 (1910) 391. **Derbyshire** N&Q 11S:2 (1910) 391. **Northern England** [1850s] *Denham Tracts* 2 (1895) 39; Henderson (1866) 40–1. **Orkney** [1629] Black (1903) 104. **Ireland** N&Q 11S:2 (1910) 498. **General** Lupton (1579) Bk 10, Para. 7; Scot (1584) Bk 13, Ch. 11; Bacon, *Sylva Sylvarum* (1627) 958; John Earle, *Micro-Cosmographie* (1628) Ch. 4; *Athenian Mercury* (16 May 1691); Grose (1787) 59; *Gent.*

Mag. (1796) 636; Brand 3 (1849) 231; Dyer (1883) 487; N&Q 11S:2 (1910) 391; N&Q 193 (1948) 239–40. Literary *The Nibelunglied* (ed. A. T. Hatto, 1965) 137, 365–6; Shakespeare, *Richard III* (*c.*1591) 1:2; Michael Drayton, *Idea, The Shepherd's Garland* (1593) 46; *Warning for Fair Women* (1599) 2; George Chapman, *The Widow's Tears* (1612) quoted Lean (1903) 646; Robert Heath, *Bleeding at the Nose at Clarastella's Approach* (1650) quoted Lean 2 (1903) 646; Charles Dickens, *Our Mutual Friend* (1865) Bk 1, Ch. 3.

corpse candles

A widespread omen of death, which takes the form of a light, like a ghostly candle flame, appearing shortly before a death in the neighbourhood – often the night before the event. These lights are variously described, but are most often blue, and in some accounts the size and brightness indicates whether a man, woman, or child is to die, or the number of the lights corresponds to the number of victims. In the normal form of the story, the light appears at the doomed person's house, and is then seen to make its way to the churchyard:

The belief in death-lights, or 'deed leets', once a common article of faith with many, is now confined to a very few, and these old persons. A death-light has been described to me as a 'blue lowe' about three feet high, which leaves the house the moment death has taken place and traverses the road that the funeral will follow. It enters the church under the door, and stands on the exact spot where the coffin will stand, flooding the building with light. Out of the church it eventually comes, and takes its way to the spot where the grave will be dug, and ends its career by sinking into the ground there.

Cumberland Penfold (1907)

A regular motif in the narrative is that the course of the light and the course of the subsequent funeral are so inextricably linked that one always follows the other, however erratic it may seem. In many cases, the light is seen to behave oddly, taking a detour across a field, for example, or standing motionless for a while at a particular spot. The reason is always explained when the funeral procession reaches that spot and has to make the same pause or detour because of some natural obstruction. Occasionally, the sequence is reversed, and a funeral cannot pass a spot because someone foolishly attempted to impede the course of a corpse light they had met a day or so previously. In many versions, however, it was extremely unwise to try to interfere with a corpse candle, as those who did so could themselves soon sicken and die. It was even dangerous to get in the way by accident.

Frequently, the candles simply mark the place of an accident rather than the funeral route, especially if the death is by drowning:

It is said, that some years ago when the coach which runs from Llandilo to Carmarthen, was passing by Golders Green (the property of the noble Earl Cawdor) three corpse candles were observed on the surface of the water, gliding down the stream which runs near the road; all the passengers beheld them, and it is related that a few days after, some men were crossing the river near there in a coracle, but one of them expressed his fear at venturing, as the river was flooded, and remained behind; the other three, possessing less discernment, ventured, and when about the middle of the river, lamentable to relate, their frail conveyance sank through the weight that was in it, and they were drowned.

Carmarthenshire/Pembrokeshire Howells (1831)

The corpse-candle omen is one of the superstitions which is most often recorded in the form of personal experience NARRATIVES, in which the tellers report purportedly real occurrences. As in all such examples, the tale validates and legitimizes the belief, and vice versa. The corpse candle is also one of the few death omens which has its own aetiological legend (at least in Wales):

The origin of the corpse-candle is supposed to date back to the fifth century. St. David, the patron of Wales, earnestly prayed that the people he loved, and among whom he toiled, should have some kind of warning to prepare them for death. In a vision he was told that through his intercession the Welsh would never again find themselves unprepared; for always before such an event the people in the land of Dewi Sant would be forewarned by the dim light of mysterious tapers when and where death might be expected. St. David apparently prayed particularly for south Wales, because it is said that corpse-candles are seen more vividly and frequently there than in North Wales.

Wales Trevelyan (1909)

The important point here is that the story highlights variation in the way death omens are perceived, and shows that major changes in popular perception have taken place. Whereas in modern times a death omen is viewed with horror, in certain religious contexts it can be seen as a welcome warning which provides notice of forthcoming events and the opportunity for the victim to prepare for a 'good death'.

Although not unknown in England and Ireland,

the belief was clearly strongest in Wales and Scotland.

The phenomenon appears under numerous names across the country, including: Fetch-lights, Dead man's candles, Dead-lights, *Canwyllau cyrph* or *Canwyll Corph* (Wales), and *Solus bais, Solus corp, Solus Spiorad* (Highland Scotland). Ordinary CANDLES were also believed to burn blue when a spirit was close by.

For a detailed account of the belief in Highland Scotland, see R. C. Maclagan, 'Ghost Lights of the West Highlands', *Folk-Lore* 8 (1897) 203–56.

Lincolnshire Peacock (1877) 69. Cumberland Bulkeley (1886) 229–30. Penfold (1907) 60–1. Northumberland Brand (1810) 110. Wales Grose (1787) 49–50; Trevelyan (1909) 178–9; [*c.*1870] Thomas (1983) 26–7. South Wales *Monthly Packet* 26 (1863) 676–85. Carmarthenshire/Pembrokeshire Howells (1831) 61–2. Carmarthenshire Brand (1810) 110; N&Q 5S:9 (1878) 65. Pembrokeshire *Folk-Lore* 39 (1928) 172. Carnarvonshire Rhys (1901) 274–5. Glamorgan Phillips (1925) 597. Monmouthshire *Blackwood's Mag.* (May 1818) 193–5. Highland Scotland *Folk-Lore* 8 (1897) 203–56. Northeast Scotland Gregor (1874) 133. Galloway Mactaggart (1824) 210. Dumfriesshire Corrie (1890/91) 42–3; Shaw (1890) 9. Caithness Rinder (1895) 56–7. Argyllshire *Folk-Lore* 7 (1896) 81; *Folk-Lore* 12 (1901) 343–4. Co. Clare *Folk-Lore* 21 (1910) 340.

corpse: eyes open

In the same way as a corpse remaining limp for some time after death was seen as a sign of another death coming soon (*see below*), it was regarded as a very bad sign if the eyes of a corpse would not close:

If after death the eyes of a corpse are open, it is gruesomely said to be looking for the next member of the family to die, i.e. another death will soon follow.   Herefordshire Leather (1912)

In an earlier report the open eyes were taken as a sign of a misspent life:

After the boddy hath been attended to in all its proper offices it be a good sign if the eyes do shut of themselves, if not then but a few years sen it was held to be the work of some evil spirits in some cases owing to a misspent life. In those days it was the common thing for to get or borrow a pair of leaden sigs (charms) from some wise dame or good neighbour, the like of those made by Betty Strother and others wise in such matters. They being magic made did ward off not openly from about the bed but from the room itself all the deamons of every sort and kind and did hold the een fast shutten so that neither witch or hellspell

could get aback of their power and cudgel them open again.   Yorkshire [1823] Home

Somerset [1923] Opie & Tatem, 98. Cornwall Mayes (1978) 88. Berkshire *Folk-Lore* 5 (1894) 337. Herefordshire Leather (1912) 119. Yorkshire [1823] Home (1915) 215–16.

corpse: limp

Anything untoward happening to a corpse is likely to be seen as ominous, and a body staying limp for longer than the usual time was taken as a sign that another death would soon follow.

Another very ordinarily spoken of [death-] sign was that if a corpse did not stiffen, but the joints remained limp and bendable, another death was sure to follow shortly. In the case of my grand-mother, aged eighty-eight, who was neither stiff nor cold the day she was buried, many were the solemn head-shakes and foretellings of what would follow. When an old relative, who had seen more than the allotted years of man, died six months later, many were the 'I told you so's' that went the round of the household.

Wiltshire *Wilts. N&Q* (1893–5)

The only significant variant reported is that it is sometimes specifically the neck which remains limp, and occasionally it is the body of a child which is stipulated. This superstition was widely reported from the mid nineteenth century and into the twentieth, from most parts of Britain and Ireland, but not, apparently, Scotland, and has remained remarkably constant in form and meaning. The earliest known mention is by Thomas Browne:

If a child dieth, and the neck becometh not stiff, but for many hours remaineth lythe and flaccid, some other in the same house will dye not long after.   Browne, *Pseudodoxia Epidemica* (1672)

It is odd that no references are known between Browne's and 1854. This may simply be an accident of history, but it is tempting to conclude that its absence in that period, contrasted with its commonness afterwards, argues at least that the superstition was not so widely known as it later became, or even that it was relaunched by somebody familiar with Browne's work.

Compare CORPSE: EYES OPEN.

Dorset N&Q 5S:6 (1876) 364; Udal (1922) 185. Somerset [1923] Opie & Tatem, 98. Tongue (1965) 136. Devon Hewett (1900) 21. Cornwall Hunt (1865) 241. Wiltshire *Wilts. N&Q* 1 (1893–5) 9–10. Worcestershire/Shropshire *Gent. Mag.* (1855) 385. Warwickshire Langford (1875) 19.

Cambridgeshire Porter (1969) 23. **East Anglia** Varden (1885) 117. **Suffolk** [1863] Chambers 2 (1878) 52–3; *Folk-Lore Record* 3 (1880) 129. **Norfolk** N&Q 1S:10 (1854) 88, 156; Swaby (1891) 94. **Lincolnshire** N&Q 4S:6 (1870) 130; Rudkin (1936) 16. **Cheshire** *Folk-Lore* 66 (1955) 324. **England** Addy (1895) 102. **Northern England** *Denham Tracts* 2 (1895) 49. **Yorkshire** Addy (1895) 102. **Lancashire** Harland & Wilkinson (1873) 228. **Cumberland** Penfold (1907) 60. **Wales** Trevelyan (1909) 282. **Ireland** N&Q 4S:6 (1870) 240. **Co. Wexford** *Folk-Lore Record* 5 (1882) 82. **General** Browne, *Pseudodoxia Epidemica* (1672) Bk 5, Ch. 23. **Literary** William Carleton, 'The Horse Stealers' in Carleton (1844); Thomas Hardy, 'Signs and Tokens' in Hardy (1917).

corpse: salt placed on

see SALT: PLACED ON CORPSE.

corpse: touching

In the time when most dead people were laid out in their home until the funeral, family, friends, and neighbours were expected to visit to 'pay their respects'. This involved viewing the body and, in many communities, touching it:

To visit a corpse without touching it is running a grave risk; indeed, I have been practically commanded to touch it. If you refuse, your rest will be disturbed for long afterwards with dreams of the deceased and of death.

Cumberland Penfold (1907)

Most references state that the touching is to prevent you 'dreaming about' the deceased, but it is clear from others that this is a euphemism for being 'haunted by' them. The touching itself was often ritualized, using thumb and forefinger, or the index finger; touching the chin, cheek, or temple, and so on. Sometimes a kiss was called for. Children were not exempted, and were often terrified:

my grandmother . . . placing my unwilling hand on the body of a dead child whose relations we were visiting. A mere infant at the time, seeing the dead child, and especially being forced to touch it, left a feeling of horror and dread that it took years to get free from.

Dumbartonshire *Folk-Lore* (1900)

Even if the touching was ostensibly to protect the living visitor, it clearly became an expected part of the ritual, and even adults report that they were unable to escape from the room without carrying it out:

Fifty years ago at funerals it was customary for a man to stand near the coffin and invite people to come and see the corpse. Most persons touched the corpse with a finger, but if any one moved away without doing so, the attendant said sharply, 'touch the corpse'.

Unlocated N&Q (1911)

The custom was clearly widespread, although all the references listed are from England and Scotland (plus one from the Channel Islands), and it lasted well into the twentieth century. The belief is surprisingly late in appearing, with the earliest clear reference only dating from 1787, and this merely states: 'Touching a dead body prevents dreaming of it'. But a story published in 1821, ostensibly set in 1725, is provided by Walter Scott and may be an early example of our superstition, or it may be a special case because of the betrothal motif:

[John Gow, the pirate, has been executed] – It is said that the lady whose affections Gow had engaged, went up to London to see him before his death, and that arriving too late, she had the courage to request a sight of his dead body; and then, touching the hand of the corpse she formally resumed the troth-plight which she had bestowed. Without going through this ceremony, she could not, according to the superstition of the country, have escaped a visit from the ghost of her departed lover, in the event of her bestowing upon any living suitor the faith which she had plighted to the dead.

Orkney Scott, *The Pirate* (1821)

Some authorities seek to connect this belief with the similar one in which a murdered corpse bleeds afresh if the murderer approaches it (*see* CORPSE: BLEEDING).

Dorset Udal (1922) 185. **Somerset** Poole (1877) 52; [1908] Tongue (1965) 136. **Devon** *Devonshire Assoc.* 12 (1880) 103; N&Q 11S:4 (1911) 95. **Berkshire** N&Q 2S:9 (1860) 380–1. **London** *Folk-Lore* 10 (1899) 254, 477; N&Q 11S:4 (1911) 434. **Oxfordshire** [pre-1900] *Folk-Lore* 24 (1913) 88. **Herefordshire** Leather (1912) 120. **Suffolk** *Folk-Lore* 35 (1924) 349. **Shropshire** *Folk-Lore* 49 (1938) 225. **Northern England** [c.1850s] *Denham Tracts* (1895) 59–60. **Yorkshire** Addy (1895) 123–4. **Lancashire** [c.1920] Blackburn (?1977) 21. **Northumberland** *Folk-Lore* 10 (1899) 253–4. **Cumberland** Penfold (1907) 60; *Folk-Lore* 31 (1920) 154. **Co. Durham** Leighton (1910) 51–2. **Scotland** [c.1816] Henderson (1866) 38; Maclean (1959) 198. **Dumbartonshire** *Folk-Lore* 11 (1900) 210. **Ross-shire** [1890s] MacDonald (1936) 65. **Orkney** [1725?] Walter Scott, *The Pirate* (1821) advertisement. **Channel Isles** N&Q 11S:4 (1911) 95. **Unlocated** Grose (1787); Hone, *Year Book* (1832) 126–8; N&Q 11S:4 (1911) 48, 95.

corpse: unburied on Sunday

It is an ominous sign if a corpse should be left unburied on Sunday, for this will mean that the death of another of the village community will occur 'before the week is out'. I have frequently heard this strange idea expressed with utmost sincerity and with a genuine belief in the inevitability of such a correlation of events.

Sussex *Sussex County Mag.* (1944)

No real reason is given for the belief, simply that it signifies a certain death to follow. On the present evidence, this seems to be a predominately English belief, with only one Welsh example from outside that area. Nor is there any evidence that it is older than the late nineteenth century. It appears to be connected to a similar belief, that it is a death omen to leave a GRAVE open on a Sunday.

See also DEATH: SUNDAY.

Hampshire *Folk-Lore* 61 (1950) 104; [1963] Opie & Tatem, 99. **Devon** *Devonshire Assoc.* 64 (1932) 165; *Devonshire Assoc.* 91 (1959) 202–3. **Sussex** N&Q 10S:1 (1904) 127; *Sussex County Mag.* (1944) 84. **Berkshire** *Berks. Arch. Soc.* 1 (1889–91) 60, 86, 106; *Folk-Lore* 5 (1894) 337; Salmon (1902) 423. **Buckinghamshire** [1914] *Folk-Lore* 43 (1932) 106. **Oxfordshire** [1986] Opie & Tatem, 99. **Gloucestershire** *Trans. Bristol & Glos. Arch. Soc.* 53 (1931) 264. **Worcestershire** Berkeley & Jenkins (1932) 35. **Warwickshire** Bloom (*c.*1930) 42–3. **Cambridgeshire** Porter (1969) 23. **Suffolk** [1877] Gurdon (1893) 29; *Folk-Lore* 35 (1924) 349. **Lincolnshire** [1894] Gutch & Peacock (1908) 150; Rudkin (1936) 15. **Wales** Trevelyan (1909) 282.

corpse's hand

see DEAD MAN'S HAND; HAND OF GLORY.

counting

A deep-seated principle of superstition is that one must not TEMPT FATE, and a visible confidence in the future must therefore be avoided lest it bring retribution in the form of bad luck or worse. In addition, there are vindictive beings, whether witches, fairies, bad neighbours, or rival tradesmen, who wish us harm at every turn, and it is best if these potential malefactors are prevented from obtaining too close a knowledge of our affairs. With these everyday problems in mind, there has long been an aversion to MEASURING, WEIGHING, and counting, in many walks of life:

All fishermen also know how unlucky it is to count one's fish until the catch has been landed, as, however freely they may be biting, counting them would invariably stop all sport for the day.

Guernsey MacCulloch (1864)

A Suffolk shepherd, for instance, will seldom willingly tell even his master the number of lambs born until the lambing-season is over for fear of bad luck.   Suffolk *Folk-Lore* (1943)

It is not good to count the cakes when done baking. They will not in that case last any time

Highland Scotland Campbell (1900)

Opie and Tatem supply early examples of this aversion to numbering too closely in both biblical (2 Samuel 24:10) and classical (Catullus, *Poems c.*50 BC) times, but their earliest British example is only from 1773 (John Byrom, *Miscellaneous Poems*). The latter implies a longer history by calling it a 'wise old saying'. The terse statement, 'They do not count their fish', appears in a Scottish manuscript of about 1699 (Campbell (1975)) and it is likely that other early references will be found. It is quite possible that the belief entered the British tradition direct from the Bible and classical literature in medieval times or later, but as the notion seems so basic to normal superstitious thinking it is equally possible that it had been here for much longer.

The references gathered below certainly underestimate the prevalence of the basic fear of counting, but they do show it to have been particularly strong in Scotland. It is still quite widespread – many card-players, for example, refuse to count their winnings while the game is still in progress. Counting also features in other beliefs – it was unlucky, for example, to count the STARS, but the one context where counting was obligatory was in cures, especially those for WARTS. *See also* COUNTING: STANDING STONES.

Suffolk Chambers 1 (1878) 322; *Folk-Lore* 54 (1943) 390. **England** Addy (1895) 101. **Highland Scotland** [*c.*1699] Campbell (1975) 63; Macgregor (1878) 128; Campbell (1900) 234. **Northeast Scotland** Gregor (1881) 200. **Perthshire** [1986] Opie & Tatem. **Outer Hebrides** N&Q 10S:10 (1908) 137. **Shetland** Tudor (1883) 173; Saxby (1932) 184. **Orkney** N&Q 10S:12 (1909) 483–4. **Guernsey** MacCulloch (1864) 506. **Literary** John Byrom, *Miscellaneous Poems* (1773). **Biblical** N&Q 10S:1 (1904) 457; N&Q 10S:9 (1908) 108.

counting: standing stones

A belief that it is unlucky to count the stones is found attached to many ancient megaliths around Britain:

When visiting the standing stones at Callernish he asked a peasant boy how many stones there were in the monument, but was told that no one knew for it was unlucky to count them. The lad looked as if he expected the ground to open when my friend replied that he had just counted them, and knew the exact number. Isle of Lewis N&Q (1908)

This is clearly related to an even more common legend that at places like Stonehenge and The Hurlers in Cornwall, it is impossible to count the stones accurately, as each attempt will result in a different number. Jennifer Westwood (1985) quotes several well-known writers who have attempted to refute this idea, including Charles II, John Evelyn, Celia Fiennes, and Daniel Defoe. Each one was confident they had recorded them correctly, but they all gave different numbers.

Compare COUNTING.

Kent *Folk-Lore* 57 (1946) 38–9. Isle of Lewis N&Q 10S:10 (1908) 137. **General** Grinsell (1976) various pages; Westwood (1985) 22, 67, 91, 311; *Folk-Lore* 85 (1974) 23–42; 86 (1975) 146–66.

couples

see ENGAGED COUPLES.

courting

A strong prejudice existed in nineteenth-century Lancashire against 'courting on a Friday', and anyone guilty of transgression in this respect was greeted with noisy disapproval strongly reminiscent of other social control customs such as rough music and ran-tanning (*see* Simpson & Roud (2000) 301):

Not long ago, I came across a man who was most industriously belabouring a frying-pan, exactly in the way country people do when bees are swarming. As it was not the season of the year for bees to swarm, I enquired what induced him to make that hideous noise. His reply was, that there was a woman down the lane courting on Friday, and that women guilty of this were always saluted in this manner. Lancashire N&Q (1868)

The unluckiness of FRIDAYS is well documented all over Britain, but this seems to be a particularly localized manifestation of the general principle. It has been suggested that it is a memory of the Catholic ban on any kind of pleasure on the day but, as it is not documented before the 1850s, this remains unproven. Two reports from elsewhere in the country show an awareness of a negative

connection between courting and Fridays, but with no hint of the community disapproval common in Lancashire: 'A man must never go courting on Friday' (**Angus Laing** (1885)); and 'Never court on a Friday or you'll never meet again' (**Oxfordshire** [1957] Opie & Tatem).

A handful of other beliefs about courting have been reported, but they are too miscellaneous to provide any recognizable pattern. They include elements such as: it is lucky to be followed by a stray dog; unlucky to accept a lock of hair; and, most surprisingly:

It is considered unlucky for a young man to present a copy of the Bible to his sweetheart. I heard this for the first time a few days ago.
Renfrewshire N&Q (1869)

Courting on Friday: Oxfordshire [1957] Opie & Tatem, 168. **Lancashire** N&Q 1S:3 (1851) 516; N&Q 4S:1 (1868) 362, 469; Harland & Wilkinson (1873) 223. Smith & Shortt (1890) 75; Ditchfield (1901) 199; N&Q 166 (1934) 241, 283. **Angus** Laing (1885) 22.
Other courting beliefs: Cheshire N&Q 6S:6 (1882) 386. **Dumfriesshire** Shaw (1890) 11. **Renfrewshire** N&Q 4S:4 (1869) 212. **Ireland** Wilde (1888) 203. **Unlocated** N&Q 2S:12 (1861) 491.

cradles/prams

In the domestic sphere, anything which touches upon the precarious health and welfare of babies is an obvious focus for superstition. Cradles and, later, prams, which inherited the same beliefs, are the subject of two widespread traditions, treated separately below, and several which have only been reported once or twice but which were probably more widely known in their time:

In Yorkshire, new parents were warned that a cradle must be paid for before the baby sleeps in it, otherwise it 'will end its days lacking the means to pay for its own coffin'.
Yorkshire Blakeborough (1898)

and if the mother wishes to ward off evil from the sleeping babe, she must never allow her hands to be idle while she rocks the cradle.
Lincolnshire Swaby (1891)

[1850s] *In all sales, either under distraint for rent or common debt, it is an ancient and invariable custom to leave the cradle unsold, and the original owner is at liberty to repossess it.*
Northern England *Denham Tracts* (1895)

[1936] *It is considered a very unlucky thing to put the first child in a new cradle, and it is said that the father or mother should not buy a cradle but that one of the relatives should provide it.*
Co. Wexford Ó Muirithe & Nuttall (1999)

*The first-born of a family should never be put in
a new cradle, or it will surely die. Any neighbour
will lend a cradle rather than see the rule broken.*
                                        Co. Longford *Béaloideas* (1936)

Lincolnshire Swaby (1891) 89. **Northern England**
Denham Tracts 2 (1895) 40. **Yorkshire** Blakeborough
(1898) 114–15. **Co. Wexford** Ó Muirithe & Nuttall (1999)
182. **Co. Longford** *Béaloideas* 6 (1936) 258.

cradles/prams: empty

It is very unlucky to rock an empty cradle, or
push an empty pram, although the predicted
consequences vary considerably. Two of these
consequences are indeed virtual opposites –
either it means that the cradle/pram will soon be
filled with a new arrival, or it means that the
current baby will die. The new-arrival theory is
the most widespread:

*'What a handsome cradle!' said a lady, going up
to an old carved oaken one one day in a cottage
at Berrington . . . 'Oh, but I suppose you won't
like me to touch it'. 'Eh, dear! no, ma'am,'
responded the good woman of the house; 'I've had
eleven already, and I've only been married fourteen years'; thus showing that she knew the belief
that if anyone should rock an empty cradle,
another child will soon come to occupy it.*
                                        Shropshire Burne (1883)

or, more succinctly:

*If you rock a cradle empty
Then you shall have babies plenty.*
                                        Sussex Latham (1878)

The notion that rocking an empty cradle will
cause the baby to die is less widespread, and has
also proved less durable.

*The cradle was never to be rocked unless the child
was in it; the penalty of neglecting this precaution would cause the child's death. The cradle was
always considered to be the property of the
youngest child.*   **Montgomeryshire** Hamer (1877)

The third idea is that it will cause the child to
suffer a headache or have other health problems.

*If a cradle were rocked when the child was not in
it, it was said to give the child a headache; but if
it so happened that the child was too old to be
rocked in a cradle, then this incident portended that its
mother would have another baby.*
                                        Western Scotland Napier (1879)

None of the meanings has been reported
before the nineteenth century, but the 'baby will

die' appears from the Scottish borders about
1816, while the 'new baby' is first mentioned in
the 1850s.

New baby: **Sussex** Latham (1878) 11. **Dorset** *Dorset Year
Book* (1961–2) 73. **Somerset** [1923] Opie & Tatem, 15.
Devon *Devonshire Assoc.* 91 (1959) 201. **Cornwall** *Folk-
Lore Jnl* 5 (1887) 210. *Jnl Royal Inst. Cornwall* 20 (1915)
129; *Old Cornwall* 1:9 (1929) 41. **Herefordshire** [*c.*1895]
Folk-Lore 39 (1928) 386. **East Anglia** Varden (1885) 107.
Norfolk Dew (1898) 77–81. **Suffolk** Chambers 2 (1878)
39. **Shropshire** Burne (1883) 286. **England** Addy (1895)
98. **Northern England** [1850s] *Denham Tracts* 2 (1895)
49. **Yorkshire** Henderson (1866) 10–11. **Lancashire**
Lancashire Lore (1971) 49. **Co. Durham** Henderson
(1866) 10–11; Leighton (1910) 47. **Radnorshire** [1953]
Opie & Tatem, 15. **Highland Scotland** Polson (1926) 6.
Orkney N&Q 10S:12 (1909) 483–4. **Unlocated** [*c.*1916]
Igglesden (*c.*1932) 143–4.
Baby will die: **Staffordshire** Poole (1875) 86. **East
Anglia** Varden (1885) 107. **Norfolk** Dew (1898) 77–81.
Wales Jones (1930) 199. **Montgomeryshire** Hamer
(1877) 259. **England/Scotland borders** [*c.*1816]
Henderson (1866) 10–11. **Highland Scotland** Polson
(1926) 6.
Headache/Health problems: **Co. Durham** Brockie
(1886) 180. **Wales** Trevelyan (1909) 267. **Western
Scotland** Napier (1879) 137–8. **Highland Scotland**
Macbain (1887/88) 254; Polson (1926) 6.

cradles/prams: new

Parents expecting their first baby are strongly
advised not to bring a new cradle or pram home
before the baby has actually arrived. To do so
would be to TEMPT FATE and thus risk the
baby's life:

*I was so proud when I got my Silver Cross pram
for my first. Mum and Nan had helped me pay it
off weekly. But even when I'd paid for it, I never
brought it home until I'd had the baby. You didn't
then. It was like a sort of superstition. Just in case.*
                                        London [1950s] O'Neill

There was no problem with later babies; one could
reuse the family pram or cradle ad infinitum:

*A new perambulator should not be brought into
the house before a birth. My maid, an
Oxfordshire girl, told me her sister had done this
in 1949, and lost her baby in consequence. This
superstition is so widespread that pram-selling
firms will always arrange to store the pram till it
is needed. (The tabu applies only to new peram-
bulators. It is quite permissible to use one which
is already in the house before pregnancy begins.)*
                                        England *Folk-Lore* (1955)

On the available evidence, the belief seems to
have been restricted to England, but it would be
surprising if this were actually the case. It also

cramp

Cramp is one of those conditions which are particularly susceptible to folk cures and preventative procedures. It is spectacularly painful but not life-threatening, some people can suffer regularly, while others are attacked only occasionally, it appears to have no definable cause, and, most importantly, it will normally go away of its own accord whatever the sufferer does.

Again, similar to other complaints such as NOSEBLEEDS, cures fall into definable categories, but with details specific to the ailment – such as a concentration on feet and beds: (1) carrying or wearing something believed to be effective (bones, rings, etc.); (2) placing items in the bed (e.g. cork); (3) protective actions (making the sign of a cross on the shoe); (4) verbal charms.

There is also a degree of overlap between conditions. Some sources, for example, suggest items more commonly recommended for RHEUMATISM and other ailments, such as carrying a POTATO in the pocket or wearing eelskin garters.

There are numerous items or procedures which are reported only once or twice; a sample follows.

Who so use to rub their fingers between their toes of their feet when they go to bed, especially when they smell most, and then to smell the same at their nose: it is a perfect remedy to put away the cramp. This was affirmed to me as a tried thing.
Lupton (1579)

Periwinkle placed under the mattress will prevent cramp in the limbs.
Lincolnshire Rudkin (1936)

A rusty sword standing by the bed-side is a remedy against cramp. Unlocated Grose (1787)

We used to put . . . an acorn in the bed for cramp.
Devon [c.1915] Lakeham

Devon [c.1915] Lakeham (1982) 48. Lincolnshire Rudkin (1936) 26. Unlocated Grose (1787) 55. General Lupton (1579) Bk 1, Para 83.

seems to be no older than the early twentieth century. Nevertheless, it was still being reported at the turn of the twenty-first. A contributor to the *Babyforum* Internet discussion list (May 2002) asked her fellow mums-to-be:

Has anyone bought their pram and had it in the house before their baby was born? We've just got ours and the lady in the shop asked us if we wanted them to keep it till after the birth as it was unlucky to have it in the house.

Two people who replied wrote that they took no notice of this superstition, but both had a relative (mother-in-law and sister respectively) who certainly did believe in it.

England *Folk-Lore* 66 (1955) 323. London [1950s] O'Neill (1999) 155; [1987] Opie & Tatem 316. Herefordshire Leather (1912) 113. Cambridgeshire Porter (1969) 17. Shropshire *Folk-Lore* 68 (1957) 503. Co. Durham [1984] Opie & Tatem 316.

cramp: bones

One of the most widespread ways of curing or preventing cramp was to carry a small bone in the pocket, usually the patella or knuckle bone of a sheep:

In the month of August last I met a gentleman, an extensive manufacturer in a southern district
of England, who showed me a small bone from the leg of a sheep, which he wore as a preventive of cramp. On being teased about it, he replied: 'I used to suffer most severely from cramp, but ever since I have worn this bone I have been entirely free from it, and I have now worn the bone for a long time.' Southern England N&Q (1870)

The efficacy of these bones was so widely known that they were commonly called 'cramp bones':

Cramp-bone – the patella of a sheep or lamb . . . it is carried in the pocket, the nearer the skin the better, of the credulous person, or laid under the pillow at night.
Suffolk Moor (1823)

Unlike several other cramp cures, this one is known to have been in regular use from at least the sixteenth century into the twentieth, although in the earliest reference the bone was used somewhat differently:

The little bone in the knee joynt of the hinder legge of an hare doth presently helpe the cramp, if you touch the grieved place therewith. Often proved . . . Lupton (1579)

and a second early reference is also to a hare's foot:

The bone also in a hare's foot mitigateth the crampe, as none other bone nor part else of the hare doth. Scot (1584)

A HARE'S foot was also carried for other ailments, most notably for RHEUMATISM and, according to Samuel Pepys, colic. Other animal parts could be used. At least one informant recommended the use of a MOLE'S foot in a similar way (Norfolk Folk-Lore 40 (1929), and another squirrels' teeth.

Although cramp affects the muscles rather than the bones or joints, the symbolism of a joint-bone being carried to help with the problem is quite understandable in the normal workings of superstitious cures.

See also HADDOCK.

Southern England N&Q 4S:6 (1870) 395. Kent Folk-Lore 25 (1914) 367. Western England Elworthy (1895) 437. Cornwall Folk-Lore Jnl 5 (1887) 201–2 Wiltshire Wilts. N&Q 1 (1893–5) 9, 152. Northamptonshire N&Q 1S:2 (1850) 36–7. Suffolk Moor (1823) 89–90; Gent. Mag. (1867) 728–41. Norfolk Folk-Lore 40 (1929) 119. Lincolnshire Gutch & Peacock (1908) 112. Co. Durham Folk-Lore Jnl 2 (1884) 158. Unlocated N&Q 4S:6 (1870) 299, 394–5; Black (1883) 154. General Lupton (1579) Bk 1, Para. 87; Scot (1584) Bk 13, Ch. 10. Literary Charles Dickens, Martin Chuzzlewit (1843–4) Ch. 46.

cramp: brimstone

A few references testify to the use of brimstone as a remedy for cramp – either carried about the person or placed in the bed.

Lancashire Harland & Wilkinson (1882) 75. Yorkshire Henderson (1866) 124. Unlocated Black (1883) 182.

cramp: charms

The use of verbal CHARMS to cure or prevent ailments was both widespread and ancient, and many minor problems, such as cramp, were thought to be conducive to such an approach. As early as 1620, John Melton included the cramp as one of the complaints which foolish and superstitious people believed could be dealt with in this way:

> that toothaches, agues, cramps, and fevers, and many other diseases may bee healed by mumbling a few strange words over the head of the diseased.   Melton (1620)

Two more or less standard forms of words for cramp charms have been recorded. Samuel Pepys wrote down the following lines:

> Cramp be thou faintless,
> As our lady was sinless,
> When she bare Jesus.
>
> London Pepys, Diary (31 Dec. 1664)

and almost exactly the same words were collected in the West Country in the 1840s (Athenaeum (1846)). The second, as remembered by Coleridge from his school days in the 1780s:

> The devil is tying a knot in my leg!
> Mark, Luke, and John, unloose it, I beg!
> Crosses three we make to ease us
> Two for the thieves, and one for Christ Jesus.
>
> London Coleridge, Table Talk (10 June 1832)

and again very similar words were noted in twentieth-century Staffordshire (Hackwood (1924)).

As with most charms of this type, the words and imagery are simple enough, and firmly Christian. No doubt, the cramp nearly always did cease after the lines were repeated a few times.

Devon/Cornwall Athenaeum (1846) 1018. Cornwall Couch (1871) 148. London Samuel Pepys, Diary (31 Dec. 1664); [1780s] Samuel Taylor Coleridge, Table Talk (10 June 1832). Staffordshire Hackwood (1924) 152. General Melton (1620).

cramp: cork

One of the substances traditionally recommended as a remedy for cramp, either placed in the bed or worn on the body:

> It is believed pretty generally in some parts of Lincolnshire that cork has the power of keeping off cramp. It is placed between the bed and the mattress, or even between the sheets; or cork garters are made by sewing together a series of thin discs of cork between two silk ribbons.
>
> Lincolnshire N&Q (1870)

> A friend of mine, a St John's Ambulance nursing sister who was recently called to lay out an old woman aged 100 told me she had 'corks' round her toes to 'keep away the cramp'.
>
> Unlocated Folk-Lore (1951)

None of the sources even hazards a guess as to why cork should be effective in this way. The earliest reference so far noted is 1850.

Devon N&Q 1S:2 (1850) 512. Lincolnshire N&Q 4S:5 (1870) 380; Black (1883) 199. England Addy (1895) 91. Yorkshire Folk-Lore 20 (1909) 348. Ireland Logan (1981) 11. Unlocated N&Q 2S:12 (1861) 492; Folk-Lore 62 (1951) 268.

cramp: draw cross

A further cure for cramp or 'pins and needles' in the foot (*see also* CRAMP: SHOES).

*When a foot has 'gone to sleep' I have often seen
people wet their forefingers in their mouths, stoop
and draw the form of a cross on it. This is said to
be an infallible remedy.*

Cornwall *Folk-Lore Jnl* (1887)

The earliest reference is provided by Samuel
Taylor Coleridge, remembering his school days
in the 1780s, in a version which apparently
combines the verbal charm (*see* CRAMP:
CHARMS) with the action of crossing the foot:

*Foot! foot! foot! is fast asleep!
Thumb! thumb! thumb! in spittle we steep
Crosses three we make to ease us
Two for the thieves, and one for Christ Jesus.*

London Coleridge, *Table Talk* (10 June 1832)

The use of the sign of the cross in cures and
remedies is widespread.

Cornwall Hunt (1865) 240; *Folk-Lore Jnl* 5 (1887) 202.
London [1780s] Samuel Taylor Coleridge, *Table Talk* (10
June 1832). Buckinghamshire N&Q 4S:4 (1869) 506.
Unlocated N&Q 6S:3 (1881) 449; N&Q 165 (1933) 245.

cramp/rheumatism cures: garters

Several of the traditional ways of preventing
cramp are shared with other ailments, particularly RHEUMATISM. In both cases, an eelskin
garter is recommended.

*For cramp our Durham remedy is to garter the left
leg below the knee. An eel's skin worn about the
naked leg is deemed a preventive too, especially by
schoolboys.* Co. Durham Henderson (1866)

In occasional instances it is a piece of tarred
string which should be worn, or carried in the
pocket.

Kent *Folk-Lore* 25 (1914) 367. Essex [*c.*1939] *Folk-Lore* 62
(1951) 263. Herefordshire Leather (1912) 78.
Bedfordshire Marsom (1950) 183. Huntingdonshire
[1880s] Marshall (1967) 221. Norfolk *Folk-Lore* 40 (1929)
116. Lincolnshire *Grantham Jnl* (22 June 1878).
Shropshire *Folk-Lore* 68 (1957) 503. Yorkshire
Blakeborough (1898) 140. *Folk-Lore* 21 (1910) 227. Co.
Durham Henderson (1866) 123. Leighton (1910) 53.
Northeast Scotland Gregor (1881) 145. Orkney Barry
(1808) 302. Unlocated Igglesden (*c.*1932) 206.

cramp: shoes

A widespread method of preventing cramp is to
place your shoes (and/or stockings) on the floor
or bed, in a prescribed manner, on retiring. The
most common advice is to place them in a T
shape or in a cross:

*A retired silversmith in Sheffield told me that
every night, before getting into bed, he crossed his
shoes in the shape of a T to keep the cramp off.*

Yorkshire *Folk-Lore* (1909)

Others simply advise the sufferer to place the
shoes soles uppermost. Given that much nocturnal cramp affects the feet, this preoccupation
with shoes and stockings is understandable, as
many cures rely on such a symbolic association.
But the same remedy was recommended for
other cramps as well:

*A short time ago she suffered much from cramp
in the stomach, and she complained to a neighbour of her pains. To her great delight the neighbour said that she knew a remedy for her ailment,
and one which she, the neighbour, had often
resorted to with complete success, and not only
did the proscription cure, but it also prevented
cramp. This was just the very thing which my
friend wished to procure. The wonderful remedy
was simple enough in all conscience, for it was –
'When you take your shoes off before going to bed,
place them with the top downwards before the
fire, and you will never suffer from cramp'. She
also added that sometimes she forgot to place her
shoes in the required position, but that her
husband, good kind man, always put them right
before he came to bed, and that by this kind
thoughtfulness and her own carefulness, she was
entirely free from her old enemy the cramp.*

Denbighshire *Bye-Gones* (20 Apr. 1887)

Similarly, it is not surprising to find making the
shape of a cross in such a procedure. Another
regular cramp cure (*see* CRAMP: DRAW CROSS)
uses similar symbolism of feet and crosses in a
rather different way.

On the available evidence, this practice was
restricted to England and Wales, and dates only
from the mid nineteenth century.

Kent *Folk-Lore* 25 (1914) 367. Devon *Devonshire Assoc.*
66 (1934) 83. Cornwall N&Q 1S:6 (1852) 601; *Folk-Lore
Jnl* 5 (1887) 202. London N&Q 4S:8 (1871) 505.
Worcestershire Salisbury (1893) 72. Northamptonshire
N&Q 1S:2 (1850) 36–7; Sternberg (1851) 168. Norfolk
Folk-Lore 40 (1929) 119. Shropshire Burne (1883) 191–2,
270. Yorkshire Henderson (1866) 124; *Folk-Lore* 20
(1909) 348. Lancashire N&Q 1S:3 (1851) 56; Harland &
Wilkinson (1882) 155. Welsh/English Gypsies Groome
(1880) 12–13. Welsh Gypsies Jarman (1991) 185.
Denbighshire *Bye-Gones* (20 Apr. 1887) 292. Unlocated
N&Q 2S:12 (1861) 492.

cramp: water

Another remedy for cramp, reported occasionally from England, involves a basin of water.

A cure for cramp in the night was to place a bowl of water under the bed. An old labourer at Holton told me he used to suffer dreadfully from cramp, but was cured in this way. He said, 'Nobody need ever have cramp'.
                              Oxfordshire *Folk-Lore* (1913)

Just how the water works is not explained.

Kent *Folk-Lore* 25 (1914) 367. Oxfordshire *Folk-Lore* 24 (1913) 89. Norfolk *Folk-Lore* 40 (1929) 119. Unlocated N&Q 2S:1 (1856) 386.

cream of the well

see NEW YEAR: FIRST WATER.

crickets

Crickets feature widely in superstition across Britain and Ireland, but there is no consensus as to their meaning, and even in the same geographical area there can be a wide divergence of opinion. The majority of references claim that the presence of crickets (typically by the kitchen hearth) is decidedly lucky:

A cricket singing on the hearth was a good omen, a token of coming riches to the family.
                              Western Scotland Napier (1879)

'It's merrier than ever tonight, I think.' 'And it's sure to bring us good fortune, John! It always has done so. To have a cricket on the hearth, is the luckiest thing in all the world!'
                              Dickens, *The Cricket on the Hearth* (1846)

By extension, it was widely considered unwise to kill a cricket:

[From a schoolboy's composition on 'Insects'] Crickets are those insects that sing behind the firegrate. Never kill crickets, for I tell yer I once killed a cricket while my mother was a mangling and I was rocking the baby by the side of the mangle, lookin in the fire, and then my mother began crying, saying baby would never have no luck. Then I cried, and then the baby started crying and wouldn't go to sleep. I'm sure I shant kill no more crickets, for I loves our baby more than yer think. London Barker (1889)

The penalty for this crime varies from general ill luck to certain death, but is often specific to the fact that the crickets will eat the clothes of the party responsible for the cruel deed.

In many instances, the cricket's very presence is seen as generally unlucky or even as an omen of death. All the seventeenth-century examples fall into this latter category, including the earliest known, in which the playwright John Webster brackets the cricket's chirp with the dreaded screech of an owl:

When screech-owls croak upon the chimney tops,
And the strange cricket i' the' oven sings and hops;
When yellow spots do on your hand appear,
Be certain that of a corse you shall hear.
                              Webster, *White Devil* (1612)

and he expressed similar sentiments a few years later, claiming that the singing of a cricket was sufficient to 'daunt' the 'whole man in us' (*Duchess of Malfi* (1623)).

Another strand of belief maintains that it is the departure of the crickets 'where they have bin many yeeres' (Melton (1620)), or their sudden proliferation, which is the sign of death.

In general, the historical trend has been from bad to good, with the earlier writers stressing the evil portent and the later ones the good fortune, but there is no simple chronological or geographical pattern, as will be seen by the references below. At least one writer (Hare (1952)) has claimed biblical precedent for the death omen: 'And the grasshopper shall be a burden, because man goeth to his long home' (Ecclesiastes xii:5). The occasional Irish reference indicates that there crickets were regarded almost as household sprites – old, wise, able to understand what was said about them, and liable to take offence. Speranza Wilde, in characteristically romantic mode:

Crickets are believed to be enchanted. People do not like to express an exact opinion about them, so they are spoken of with great mystery and awe. And no one would venture to kill them for the whole world. But they are by no means evil; on the contrary, the presence of the cricket is considered lucky, and their singing keeps away the fairies at night, who are always anxious, in their selfish way, to have the whole hearth left clear for themselves, so that they may sit round the last embers of the fire, and drink the cup of milk left for them by the farmer's wife, in peace and quietness. The crickets are supposed to be hundreds of years old. Ireland Wilde (1888)

Lucky to have: Cornwall N&Q 1S:12 (1855) 38; Couch (1871) 169. Wiltshire *Wilts. N&Q* 1 (1893–5) 9. Herefordshire Leather (1912) 28. Warwickshire Langford (1875) 11, 12. Northamptonshire N&Q 1S:3 (1851) 3. East Anglia Forby (1830) 414; Varden (1885) 113. Norfolk *Norfolk Chronicle* (20 Dec. 1902). Shropshire Burne (1883) 237–9. England Addy (1895) 68. Derbyshire N&Q 6S:4 (1881) 509. Yorkshire Nicholson (1890) 137. *Folk-Lore* 21 (1910) 22. Lancashire N&Q 1S:3 (1851) 516; Harland & Wilkinson (1882) 139. Wales Trevelyan (1909) 324–5. Pembrokeshire *Folk-Lore* 39 (1928) 173. Western Scotland Napier (1879) 114. Ireland Wilde (1888) 178. Unlocated N&Q 2S:12 (1861) 492. *General The Mirror* (17 Mar 1832) 180; *Illustrated London News* (27 Dec: 1851) 77. Literary Charles Dickens, *The Cricket on the Hearth* (1846) Ch. 1. Literary William Cowper, 'The Cricket' (written 1777).
Unlucky to have: Worcestershire/Shropshire *Gent. Mag.* (1855) 384–6. Shropshire Burne (1883) 237–9. General *The Mirror* (17 Mar. 1832) 180.
Unlucky to harm: Sussex Latham (1878) 13. *Sussex County Mag.* 23 (1949) 383. Somerset [1922] Opie & Tatem, 105. Wiltshire *Wilts. N&Q* 1 (1893–5) 9. London Barker (1889) 53. Warwickshire Langford (1875) 11, 12. Shropshire Burne (1883) 237–9. Yorkshire N&Q 1S:6 (1852) 311–12; Nicholson (1890) 137. Lancashire N&Q 1S:3 (1851) 516. South Wales *Monthly Packet* 26 (1863) 676–85. Dumfriesshire Corrie (1890/91) 80. Co. Leitrim *Folk-Lore* 5 (1894) 198. Connemara *Folk-Lore Jnl* 2 (1884) 261. Unlocated Grose (1787) 64. General *Gent. Mag.* (1796) 636.
Death omen: Sussex [1870] Hare (1952) 301. Oxfordshire *Folk-Lore* 24 (1913) 88. Herefordshire Leather (1912) 28. Shropshire Burne (1883) 237–9. England Addy (1895) 67–8. Ireland *Folk-Lore* 19 (1908) 318. Co. Mayo *Folk-Lore* 29 (1918) 310. Literary John Webster, *White Devil* (1612) 5:4; John Webster, *Duchess of Malfi* (1623) 2:3; Addison, *Spectator* (8 Mar. 1711); John Gay, *The Shepherd's Week* (1714) Friday lines 101–2. General Melton (1620); Igglesden (*c.*1932) 94–5.
Departure unlucky: Cornwall N&Q 1S:12 (1855) 38; Couch (1871) 169. Northamptonshire N&Q 1S:3 (1851) 3. East Anglia Forby (1830) 414. Norfolk *Norfolk Chronicle* (20 Dec. 1902). Shropshire Burne (1883) 237–9. Lancashire Harland & Wilkinson (1882) 139. Dumfriesshire *The Mirror* (17 Mar. 1832) 179. Shaw (1890) 13. Wales Trevelyan (1909) 281.
Miscellaneous: General Bourne (1725), Brand (1810) 97; White (1788) 231.

crossed eyes

Of the many people and animals which one was unlucky to MEET first thing in the morning or when starting on a journey, a person with crossed eyes was widely regarded as one of the worst, and the bad luck was intensified if it was a woman:

I had it from my father that to meet a squinting woman was reckoned of bad omen in Yorkshire, and if you met one when starting for any particular undertaking and it was Friday you might as well give it up, as it would be sure not to succeed.

The spell might be broken by spitting back over the left shoulder. Yorkshire N&Q (1882)

Miners and fishermen were particularly susceptible to such worries:

Omens ... known as Warnings: A collier would not descend the pit if on his way to work he encountered a cross-eyed woman or a one-legged man. Staffordshire Hackwood (1924)

In earlier references, it was people who appeared to have two pupils in their eye that were feared:

Women that have double apples in their eyes, or strayles; do every where hurt with their looking (which is called of some overlooking) ...
  Lupton (1579)

Many people would turn back after meeting an unlucky person, but some believed that they could ward off the evil luck with prompt action or gesture – SPITTING and crossing the fingers were recommended. Personal disability or deformity was routinely regarded as unlucky in the past, but there were exceptions. It was considered lucky to see and touch a HUNCHBACK, for example, and even the cross-eyed person was not universally shunned:

They believe in a 'lucky look' from a person who squints, but it must be one glance, and have done with it. Should the look be repeated, or even prolonged, the good turns to evil, and they will have 'bad luck'. At Billingsgate Market, and at Faringdon Market as well, may be found any morning a half-silly ragged boy with a squint, who picks up many a half-penny by dispensing 'lucky looks' amongst the itinerant fishmongers and greengrocers, ere they begin their daily 'round'. London Jones (1880)

It is lucky for a man to meet a squinting woman, unlucky to meet a squinting man, and vice versa for the other sex. England N&Q (1861)

The general antipathy to cross-eyed people was extremely widespread in the British Isles in the last two centuries, and in the 'two pupils' version has a very long history here. Many early writers mention it, such as Lupton (1579), Scot (1584), and Aubrey (1686), and even earlier by the Chester monk, Ranulf Higden, in his *Polychronicon* of about 1350. In this form it can be traced back to Pliny's *Natural History* (AD 77), and a clear connection with the traditions of the EVIL EYE:

Isoginus adds that there are people of the same kind among the Triballi and Illyrians, who also bewitch with a glance and who kill those they stare at for a longer time, especially with a look of anger, and that their evil eye is most felt by adults; and that what is more remarkable is that they have two pupils in each eye . . .

See also EVIL EYE.

England N&Q 2S:12 (1861) 491. Dorset Dorset Year Book (1954–5) 175. Devon Bray (1836) 176. Wiltshire Wiltshire (1975) 89. London Jones (1880) 479. Essex Ketteridge & Mays (1972) 140. Oxfordshire [1953] Opie & Tatem, 145; Oxf. & Dist. FL Soc. Annual Record (1955) 16. Worcestershire Folk-Lore 76 (1965) 148, quoting County Express (Stourbridge) (8 Aug. 1914). Worcestershire/Shropshire Gent. Mag. (1855) 385. Bedfordshire Folk-Lore 37 (1926) 77. Cambridgeshire Folk-Lore 25 (1914) 366; N&Q 176 (1939) 298. Norfolk Folk-Lore 40 (1929) 121–2; Randell (1966) 94. Staffordshire Hackwood (1924) 147. England Addy (1895) 97. Northern England Brockett (1829) 'Wall eyed'. Yorkshire N&Q 6S:6 (1882) 356–7; [1956] Opie & Tatem, 145; Observer Supp. (24 Nov. 1968) 10. Co. Durham Folk-Lore 68 (1957) 424; [1988] Opie & Tatem, 145. Wales Trevelyan (1909) 209, 327. Glamorganshire Morris (1979) 143–4. England/Scotland borders [c.1816] Henderson (1866) 37. Scotland Kelly (1721) 169; Chambers 2 (1864) 735. Highland Scotland Polson (1926) 129. Orkney N&Q 10S:12 (1909) 483. Unlocated Hone, Year Book (1832) 127. General Ranulf Higden, Polychronicon (c.1350); Lupton (1579) Bk 6, Para. 22; Scot (1584) Bk 16, Ch. 9; Aubrey, Remaines (1686/188.) 177. Literary Ben Jonson, Gypsies Metamorphosed 2 (1621) lines 1329–30. Classical Pliny's Natural History (AD 77) Bk 7, Ch. 2.

crossed fingers

Crossing the fingers is one of the most widely recognized luck gestures in modern Britain and Ireland, and it was no accident that the UK National Lottery adopted the symbol of the crossed fingers as their logo in the 1990s. In recent decades the gesture has had several different, but linked, meanings, depending on the context. We cross our fingers for luck and to enhance the chances of success in some venture, although we often simply say it rather than actually doing it:

she won't be getting married until next year when, crossed fingers, her lung will be clear.
                                    Ireland [1942] Lambkin

We are also advised to protect ourselves from harm when we have walked under a LADDER, seen two MAGPIES, or otherwise tempted fate. Children in the playground use the gesture, accompanied by an agreed truce word, to gain temporary respite during a chasing game. And we cross our fingers when telling a lie, in the hope that the gesture will negate such a misdeed, and protect us against the consequences.

Desmond Morris (1979) demonstrated that the gesture was virtually unknown elsewhere in Europe, apart from some parts of Scandinavia, and given its ubiquity in modern Britain, it is astonishing to learn that it does not seem to have been known before the late nineteenth century. The earliest clear reference dates from 1890: 'If you walk under a ladder, cross your fingers to avert bad luck' (**Hampshire** N&Q (1890)). As a good-luck gesture, crossing the legs (see below) has a much longer recorded history.

Similarly, well into the twentieth century a standard protective gesture against witches and for luck was to hold the thumb inside the clenched hand:

'Hinny, if ye ivver gan intiv a house, an' ye see a person there who has eyebrows meetin' each other, that person's a witch. An' you must be sure to cross yourself, and close the fingers of your left hand over your thumb; and that takes away her power. I always d'ed an' they can do nothing to us.' Such was the sage advice tendered to a young woman by an old crone, in the hearing of a friend of mine, a short time ago.   Co. Durham Brockie (1886)

See THUMBS for further references.

Sometime in the twentieth century, a popular explanation was circulated which is still regularly cited. It explained that, in the early days of Christianity, when followers were being persecuted, they used the crossed fingers as a secret gesture, to symbolize Christ's cross. Apart from the fact that the shape of crossed fingers bears no relation to the shape of the cross, the late appearance of the gesture and its restricted geographical spread combine to expose the explanation as a groundless guess.

Hampshire N&Q 7S:9 (1890) 486. Gloucestershire [1987] Opie & Tatem, 109. Hertfordshire Leather (1912) 88. Lincolnshire Rudkin (1936) 17–18. Co. Durham Brockie (1886) 216. Scotland Scottish Studies 3 (1959) 199. Aberdeenshire [1952] Opie & Tatem, 109. Ireland [1942] Lambkin (1992) 36. General Morris (1979) 15–24.

crossed legs: luck

In modern Britain, CROSSED FINGERS is the archetypal luck gesture, but it is not unusual to hear someone speak of crossing the legs as a duplication, an intensification of the crossed fingers, for extra power. It is unlikely that many people believe that crossing the legs alone would have the desired effect, unless in a situation (such as an exam) where crossing the fingers is impossible. On the present evidence, however, crossing the legs is considerably older than crossing the fingers, and the latter is a relative newcomer.

All the pre-twentieth-century references to leg-crossing for luck are concerned with the specific context of gambling – either lottery tickets or card-playing:

When one has ill luck at cards, 'tis common to say that somebody sits with his legges acrosse, and brings him ill luck.

Unlocated Aubrey *Remaines* (1686)

To obtain a clock at a raffle, sit crossed-leg and you will be sure to get it.

Northern England [1850s] Denham

Later references provide more variety, but in similar context:

[Milliner's workshop, interwar years] *If you have just finished a hat or a dress and the customer comes in to fit it, keep your legs crossed and there will be no complaints.*

London [*c*.1920s] Henrey

She asked a girl why she was sitting with her knees bumped up under the flap, and the girl said she did not think she would pass the exam unless she sat with her legs crossed.

Somerset [1953] Opie & Tatem

See also CROSSED FINGERS.

Somerset [1953] Opie & Tatem, 110. **London** [*c*.1920s] Henrey (1955) 97–8. **Lincolnshire** *Gent. Mag.* (Dec. 1832) 493. **Northern England** [1850s] Denham (1895) 299. **Northumberland** Bigge (1860–62) 94. **Co. Dublin** *Folk-Lore* 5 (1894) 283. **Unlocated** Aubrey, *Remaines* (1686/1880) 199; Grose (1787) 60. **General** *Gent. Mag.* (1796) 636. **Literary** *Westminster Drollery* (1671) 64; *Adventurer* (6 Mar. 1753) quoted in Opie & Tatem, 109–10.

crowing hen

see WHISTLING WOMAN.

crows: dirtying clothes

When custom dictated that new CLOTHES should be worn at EASTER or WHITSUN, it was often stated that the penalty for not doing so would be that the birds – often specifically crows – would retaliate by aiming their droppings at you:

'If they don't get a new suit at Easter', began one of our men visitors, 'Hush' said a shocked member of the W.I. – 'but we all know about the crows!'

Northumberland Bosanquet (1929)

Lancashire Harland & Wilkinson (1873) 219; *Lancashire Lore* (1971) 71. **Northumberland** Bosanquet (1929) 79.

crows: 'get out of my sight'

A traditional rhyme, chanted by children sent bird-scaring in the fields or by anyone bothered by the presence of crows:

Crow, crow, get out of my sight
Or else I'll eat thy liver and lights

I remember, as a child, sitting out of doors on an evening of a warm summer or autumn day, and repeating the crow charm to flights of rooks, as they winged home to their rookery. The charm was chanted so long as a crow remained in sight, the final disappearance of them being to my mind proof 'strong as Holy Writ' of the efficacy of the charm. Lancashire/Yorkshire N&Q (1851)

Staffordshire Poole (1875) 80. **England** Addy (1895) 68–9. **Lancashire** Harland & Wilkinson (1873) 219; Harland & Wilkinson (1882) 70. **Lancashire/Yorkshire** N&Q 1S:4 (1851) 53. **Yorkshire** Nicholson (1890) 132. **Montgomeryshire** Hamer (1877) 259.

crows: number seen

A single crow settling on or flying over a house was considered a bad omen (*see below*), but a group of crows could be good or bad, depending on the number seen:

About seeing crows on the road –
One crow sorrow
Two crows joy
Three crows a letter
Four crows a boy
Five crows silver
Six crows gold
Seven crows a secret
That must never be told.

Norfolk Fulcher Collection (*c*.1895)

This rhyme will be recognized as a version of the ubiquitous MAGPIE rhyme, and many informants reported that it was equally applicable to both birds. But crow beliefs show a wider variety of meanings, which go against the usual pattern:

If you see four crows in your path . . . it means a coming death to a relative.

East Anglia Varden (1885)

It is unlucky to see three crows together.

Devon *Devonshire Assoc.* (1926)

Devon *Devonshire Assoc.* 57 (1926) 112. **Wiltshire** *Wilts. N&Q* 1 (1893–5) 9. **Gloucestershire** *Folk-Lore* 12 (1902) 171. **Essex** Halliwell (1849) 171. **Herefordshire** Leather (1912) 26. **East Anglia** Varden (1885) 110, 113, 115. **Norfolk** Fulcher Collection (*c.*1895). **Shropshire** Burne (1883) 224. **England** Addy (1895) 68–9. **Derbyshire** *Folk-Lore Jnl* 2 (1884) 280. **Yorkshire** Robinson (1861) 300; *Folk-Lore* 43 (1932) 254. **Cardiganshire** *Folk-Lore* 39 (1928) 174. **Ayrshire** [1963] Opie & Tatem, 111. **Guernsey** De Garis (1975) 133. **Literary** D. H. Lawrence, *The White Peacock* (1911) Pt 1, Ch. 7.

crows: unlucky

In general, crows are not liked in British superstition, and although in certain limited circumstances they can be seen as lucky, in the vast majority of reports they are treated with suspicion. They were particularly feared if they seemed to be focusing their attention on a particular person or building, and this applied both to single birds and groups:

Even to this day a lingering superstition associates this bird with coming evil; and I have heard women working in the fields remark that such and such a farmer lying ill would not recover, for a crow had been seen to fly over his house but just above the roof-tree.   Wiltshire *Jefferies* (1878)

A community of crows gathered upon the roof of a farm homestead have often been regarded as a boding of ill to the unfortunate occupant, or someone belonging to his family, and neither reason nor argument would disabuse the farmers' minds of some impending calamity.
Co. Durham N&Q (1873)

Crows were also feared as omens of bad luck if one met a single bird on a journey or when setting out in the morning, in the same way as seeing a single MAGPIE. In common with most superstitions, the vast majority of reports simply take it for granted that crows are unlucky, and do not inquire into the reason, but occasionally there is an indication of an explanation:

We believed that a crow or rook carried a plague or brought a disease that could kill you, and that's why they are unlucky.   Lincolnshire [*c.*1930s] Sutton

However, this is likely to be a later rationalization rather than an indication of the original meaning. Some earlier references also distinguish between the bird's appearing and croaking on the left (bad) or the right (good) of the viewer.

The belief in the basic unluckiness of crows has a long history in Britain, and was mentioned by many leading literary figures, including Chaucer and Shakespeare, and before that in classical

times. Examples were still being quoted in the 1980s, and unless the ubiquitous magpie beliefs have entirely eliminated it, it is probably still held to this day.

Sussex Latham (1878) 52. **Somerset** Poole (1877) 40. **Devon** *Devonshire Assoc.* 91 (1959) 202. **Wiltshire** Jefferies (1878) Ch. 6. **Middlesex** [1984] Opie & Tatem, 112. **Essex** Mays (1969) 164. **Herefordshire** Leather (1912) 25. **Worcestershire** Berkeley & Jenkins (1932) 32. **Birmingham** [1987] Opie & Tatem, 112. **Northamptonshire** N&Q 1S:2 (1850) 164. **East Anglia** Varden (1885) 113. **Norfolk** Randell (1966) 94. **Lincolnshire** Swaby (1891) 84; [*c.*1930s] Sutton (1992) 142. **Shropshire** Burne (1883) 224. **Derbyshire** *Folk-Lore Jnl* 2 (1884) 280. **Yorkshire** *Folk-Lore* 21 (1910) 225. **Lancashire** Spencer (1966) 8. **Co. Durham** N&Q 4S:12 (1873) 394. **Wales** Howells (1831) 67; [*c.*1870] Thomas (1983) 26–7; Trevelyan (1909) 281, 325, 329. **Denbighshire** [1984] Opie & Tatem, 111. **Cardiganshire** *Folk-Lore* 39 (1928) 174. **Northeast Scotland** Gregor (1881) 136. **Highland Scotland** Macbain (1887/88) 265. **Aberdeenshire** *Folk-Lore* 25 (1914) 349. **Roxburghshire** Bennett (1992) 178. **Orkney** N&Q 10S:12 (1909) 483–4. **Guernsey** MacCulloch (1864) 504; Carey (1903) 506. **General** Gaule, *Mag-astro-mances* (1652) 181; Bourne (1725); Brand (1810) 96. **Literary** Chaucer, *Parliament of Fowls* (*c.*1380) line 363; Shakespeare, *Julius Caesar* (1599) 5:1; Samuel Butler, *Hudibras* (1664) Canto 2. **Classical** Pliny, *Natural History* (AD 77) Bk 10, Ch.14.

crows: white

Aberrations in nature were often treated with suspicion by superstitious people, and many people were particularly wary of a bird or animal which was unusually white.

A farmer at Longtown was ploughing, and was surprised to see a white crow come and perch on his plough; when he came home at night the bird followed him, and hovered about near his house. He went in and told his wife, remarking, 'That's not for nothin'; it's all up with me afore long'. The next night he was poisoned by a lodger in his house, who was afterwards hanged for the murder.   Herefordshire Leather (1912)

This farmer's interpretation of the event is based as much on the personal attention paid him by the bird as its colour, which mirrors the general beliefs in crows as omens (*see above*).

Herefordshire Leather (1912) 25. **Wales** Trevelyan (1909) 281–2. **Unlocated** Igglesden (*c.*1932) 75.

cuckoos: activity

In contrast to the cuckoo superstitions which are based on your situation or occupation when you

cuckoos (*Cuculus canorus*)

The cuckoo features widely in folklore in Britain and in the rest of Europe, in a variety of genres not covered by this dictionary, as well as in mainstream art-forms such as poetry and music. The bird has an essentially pastoral role in songs and poems as the key harbinger or personification of spring, appears in numerous weather predictions, and has traditional tales all of its own, such as the 'numskull' story of the villagers who try to prolong summer by building a wall to keep the cuckoo in. In proverbs and sayings, the cuckoo is synonymous with foolishness (as in the April 'gowk' or April Fool), and has bawdy connotations through the word 'cuckold', and its propensity for leaving offspring in other birds' nests. It was also the subject of various 'vulgar errors', which held, for example, that it turned into a hawk when it became older, that it hibernated in the winter, and that it regularly stole and sucked other birds' eggs, to keep its own voice clear. Many country people thought that there was only one cuckoo, which came every year.

It is therefore not surprising that the cuckoo also features in a number of superstitions. At first glance these seem reasonably varied, but nearly all are variations on a basic theme. The motif of BEGINNINGS is discussed fully elsewhere, but the majority of the beliefs listed below are firmly based on the idea that what you are doing or what your situation is at the beginning of a particular period will affect, for good or ill, the rest of that period. In this case it is spring which is the 'beginning' of the year, and it is no coincidence that some of these beliefs are mirrored at other key times, such as a NEW YEAR and the appearance of the new MOON. Some are relatively clear-cut – if you have money in your pocket at this crucial time, you will have money for the rest of the period in question, if you are in bed at the beginning, you will be ill (or die) before the year or season is over, and so on. Others are more symbolic – standing on a hard place will lead to having a hard time. As with most MEETING/hearing/seeing superstitions, these are passive, in the sense that you are stuck with how things are when the cuckoo decides to call; other beliefs are different in that they provide ways of deliberately affecting the future by prescribing an action to be carried out. The fact that 'laziness' is one fate which can be avoided appears to be an example of the basic PURITAN morality of superstition coming to the fore. The exception among the cuckoo beliefs is the divination by COUNTING the number of calls heard – translated into the years that will elapse before a death or a marriage.

For discussions of general cuckoo-lore, *see* Hardy (1879), Swainson (1886), and Armstrong (1958).

first hear the bird's call, this superstition instructs you to carry out certain actions as soon as you hear it:

A few days ago I noticed a person in this neighbourhood suddenly take to his heels and run rapidly round in a circle. When he had finished I asked him the reason of his singular act, when he told me he had heard the cuckoo for the first time this year, and that if he ran round in a circle as soon as he heard it, he would not be idle during the year.
Somerset N&Q (1856)

Another prescription, for a similar end, was to roll your friends on the ground, while a similar action could be an effective medical treatment:

In some parts of Wales the boys would roll their lazy companions in the grass when the cuckoo was first heard. This was to cure them of idleness. At one period the peasantry of Mid-Wales, when they heard the cuckoo for the first time in the season, rolled themselves three times in the grass, to insure freedom from back-ache, lumbago, and sciatica.
Wales Trevelyan (1909)

John Gay provides the earliest reference to the running, but he combines it with the hair-in-the-shoe LOVE DIVINATION. It is strange that no references have been found between 1714 and 1856, but these will presumably come to light one day. Those which have been reported are heavily weighted towards Southwestern England, with some in Wales and the Channel Islands. The only one outside this region is that reported by Addy from the Derbyshire area, which, like the Gay version, includes the hair motif.

Hampshire N&Q 11S:12 (1915) 288. **Somerset** N&Q 2S:1 (1856) 386; N&Q 5S:3 (1875) 424; [1904] Tongue (1965) 49–50. **Devon** Hewett (1900) 52; *Devonshire Assoc.* 63 (1931) 125; [1937] Tongue (1965) 49–50; *Devonshire Assoc.* 71 (1939) 128. **England** Addy (1895) 111. **Wales** Trevelyan (1909) 110. **Guernsey** MacCulloch (1864) 504; De Garis (1975) 135. **Literary** John Gay, *Shepherd's Week* (1714).

---

cuckoos: alighting

In addition to the direction from which one hears the first cuckoo (*see* CUCKOOS: DIRECTION

OF CALL), a number of traditions focus on where the bird alights to broadcast his call, and these include a higher proportion of gloomy predictions than is usual in cuckoo beliefs. As with swarming BEES, bad things will happen if the cuckoo alights on a dead branch:

If anyone be about to die suddenly, or to lose a relation, [the cuckoo] will light upon touchwood, or a rotten bough, and cuckoo. He foretold Mr Ward's fire at Irstead in 1844.

Norfolk *Norfolk Archaeology* (1849)

Similar consequences will occur if it alights on a roof or chimney. A cuckoo calling above one's head, however, may be good or bad, depending on where you are in the country:

If the cuckoo 'calls' as he's flying over the house there'll be a death before the year is past.

Norfolk Fulcher Collection (c.1895)

If the cuckoo cries three times in succession immediately above a person's head, it means good luck. Wales Trevelyan (1909)

East Anglia Varden (1885) 117. **Norfolk** *Norfolk Archaeology* 2 (1849) 301; Fulcher Collection (c.1895); [c.1920] Wigby (1976) 68. **Wales** Trevelyan (1909) 110. **Highland Scotland** Campbell (1900) 256. **Co. Antrim** [c.1905] McDowell (1972) 131.

cuckoos: direction of call

The direction from which you first hear the cuckoo's call is sometimes held as significant, although there is little agreement across the board on what each direction means. The most common prediction is based on the common right/left division:

If, on first hearing the cuckoo, the sounds proceed from the right, it signifies that you will be prosperous; or, to use the language of my informant, a country lad, 'You will go vore in the world'; if from the left, ill-luck is before you.

Cornwall N&Q (1855)

Others maintain that it is best if the bird is in front of you, as you will then go up in the world. A more direct correlation with direction is found in other beliefs which claim that the quarter from which you hear the cuckoo will be the one in which you will soon travel, or live, or from which your future lover will appear.

Somerset [1923] Opie & Tatem, 114. **Devon** Bray (1838) 326; Hewett (1900) 52; *Devonshire Assoc.* 65 (1933) 123. **Cornwall** N&Q 1S:12 (1855) 38. **Norfolk** Fulcher Collection (c.1895). **Lancashire** Harland & Wilkinson (1882) 143. **Dumfriesshire** Corrie (1890/91) 79. **Ireland**

Wilde (1888) 180–1; *Chambers's Jnl* (Oct. 1892) 684–5. **Co. Wexford** *Folk-Lore Record* 5 (1882) 82. **Unlocated** Igglesden (c.1932) 83.

cuckoos: empty stomach

A specific example of the notion that conditions prevailing at the BEGINNING will remain throughout is that to hear the first cuckoo while your stomach is empty predicts a hungry year to come. Only reported a handful of times since the 1870s, from Scotland only, but as the symbolism is quite obvious, it would be surprising if it were not more widespread. Maclean claims it was still common in 1959.

Scotland Maclean (1959) 198. **Highland Scotland** Macgregor (1878) 128. **Morayshire** *Folk-Lore Jnl* 7 (1889) 43.

cuckoos: fleas

One of the few cuckoo beliefs which seems to be outside the normal BEGINNINGS orbit links the bird's call with fleas:

To prevent fleas from entering the house – When you hear the first cuckoo in the spring, take some of the earth from the place on which your right foot is standing, and sprinkle it on the threshold of your front door; but speak of it to no one. Neither fleas, beetles, earwigs, or vermin of any sort will cross it. Devon Hewett (1900)

Fleas are more commonly connected with 1 March.

Somerset Tongue (1965) 49–50. **Devon** Hewett (1900) 75. **General** *A Book of Dreams and Other Things Useful to Know* (1784) quoted N&Q 3S:8 (1865) 146.

cuckoos: lucky/protected

Despite the potential for bad luck inherent in some of the superstitions surrounding it, the cuckoo was generally regarded as a lucky bird and was thus one of a select few birds traditionally protected from harm:

Cuckoo and swift – A labouring man from Hampshire tells me that in his part of the country it is considered very unlucky to kill either of these birds. Hampshire *Folk-Lore Jnl* (1883)

Its position as harbinger of spring probably accounts for this generally favourable reputation. In some cases, there is more to it than simple good luck:

To see a cuckoo before the bird cries is a token that you will be able to find out hidden secrets in the season. To catch a cuckoo without killing it and let it go again means remarkable prosperity.

Wales Trevelyan (1909)

but this contrasts strangely with the experience of a Norfolk boy at the same period:

When I was about eight I found a young cuckoo one day in a hedge betty's nest, and thinking I was doing well, took it home. As soon as my parents saw it, though, they rushed me out of the house with it, taking great care not to touch the birds themselves, while my father shouted at me: 'Sluther yew off, bor, and put it back where it came from; we don't want any ill-luck in this house'. So off I ran, and as soon as I was gone my mother went into the garden, picked some rosemary, thyme, lavender, and other strong-smelling herbs and brushed them all round the downstair room to clean them from the Devil.

Norfolk [c.1909] Randell

This may simply be regional variation, but more examples will need to be gathered before we can be sure.

Compare other protected birds, such as ROBINS, WRENS, SWALLOWS.

Hampshire *Folk-Lore Jnl* 1 (1883) 394. **Norfolk** [c.1909] Randell (1966) 94. **Lincolnshire** Thompson (1856) 735. **Wales** Trevelyan (1909) 108, 110. **Connemara** *Folk-Lore Jnl* 2 (1884) 258. **Ireland** Wilde (1888) 177.

cuckoos: money

The most common of the cuckoo superstitions and the one with the clearest symbolism. In keeping with other BEGINNINGS beliefs, such as those on seeing a new MOON, it is held to be very important to have money in your pocket when you hear the first cuckoo of the year. In many references one is strongly advised to turn the money over, SPIT on it, or otherwise draw attention to it by jingling or shaking. Obviously, the failure to have money at this time means a poor year ahead.

When the cry of the cuckoo is heard for the first time in the season, it is customary to turn the money in the pocket, and wish. If within the bounds of reason, it is sure to be fulfilled. In reference to the pecuniary idea respecting the cuckoo, the children sing: Cuckoo, cuckoo, cherry tree/Catch a penny and give it to me.

Northamptonshire N&Q (1850)

This is little different to the earliest known reference:

And now take this advice from me,
Let money in your pockets be,
When first you do the cuckow hear,
If you'd have money all the year.

Poor Robin's Almanack (1763)

The similarity to the new moon superstition – which involved turning your money over at the first sight of a new moon to ensure future prosperity – is striking, but it is surprising that the cuckoo belief first appears as late as the 1760s when both the new moon belief and other cuckoo beliefs were being recorded 200 years or so before that time. On available evidence, the cuckoo belief could well be simply an adaptation of the new moon superstition.

Its geographical spread is also puzzling. According to the documentary record, this belief was common across England and Wales, and known in the Channel Islands, but surprisingly absent from Scotland and only one example from Ireland.

Sussex Latham (1878) 9–10; *Sussex County Mag.* 5 (1931) 122. **Somerset** Poole (1877) 40; Tongue (1965) 49–50. **Wiltshire** Smith (1874) 329. **Oxfordshire** *Midland Garner* 1 (1884) 19. **Herefordshire** Leather (1912) 26. **Northamptonshire** N&Q 1:2 (1850) 164. **Bedfordshire** *Folk-Lore* 37 (1926) 77. **Lincolnshire** *Gent. Mag.* (1832); *Grantham Jnl* (22 June 1878); Swaby (1891) 92. **Shropshire** Burne (1883) 219–21. **England** Addy (1895) 113. **Northern England** Henderson (1866) 72–3. **Yorkshire** N&Q 1S:6 (1852) 311–12; Nicholson (1890) 131; Blakeborough (1898) 130; *Folk-Lore* 43 (1932) 254. **Lancashire** [c.1880] Spencer (1966) 4; Harland & Wilkinson (1873) 219; Harland & Wilkinson (1882) 139, 143; *Lancashire Lore* (1971) 71. **Co. Durham** Leighton (1910) 62–3. **Wales** Trevelyan (1909) 109. **Mid-Wales** Davies (1911) 222. **Denbighshire** [1984] Opie & Tatem, 113. **Radnorshire** [1953] Opie & Tatem, 113. **Montgomeryshire** Hamer (1877) 260. **Co. Wexford** *Folk-Lore Record* 5 (1882) 82. **Guernsey** De Garis (1975) 135. **Unlocated** *Poor Robin's Almanack* (1763) April; Brand (1810) 442n; N&Q 1S:5 (1852) 293; N&Q 1S:11 (1855) 416.

cuckoos: number of calls

The oldest of the cuckoo beliefs involves counting the number of calls one hears, and prognosticating from them how many years one still has to live:

Whoever heard the cuckoo and observed its successive notes, could, from its song, anticipate the number of years he had to live.

This, the oldest reference, as quoted by Opie and Tatem, comes from a fourteenth-century manuscript, but by the mid nineteenth century, a rhyme had been composed which takes something of the sting out of the prediction, especially when chanted by children:

The children cry out

> *Cuckoo, cuckoo, true answer give*
> *How many years have I to live*

as many times as the bird says 'cuckoo' after the question is asked will be the number of years left to live.   Wales Trevelyan (1909)

Thoughts of death are diminished further when cherries are introduced:

> *Cuckoo, cherry tree*
> *Come down and tell me*
> *How many years I have to live*

Each child then shook the tree – and the number of cherries which fell betokened the years of its future life.

Yorkshire *Athenaeum* (1846)

Much more recent is the idea that the number of calls indicates how many years until one's marriage. Obviously, the essential difference between death and marriage is that one would wish that the interval before the latter be short, while the time before death to be long. As the number of calls is likely to be quite numerous, those concerned with marriage have an opt-out clause which casts doubt on the cuckoo's accuracy:

Girls ask:

> *Cuckoo, cuckoo, on the tree*
> *How long before I wedded be*

If in answer the cuckoo calls more than three or six times, the girls say the bird is bewitched.

Wales Trevelyan (1909)

A third variation, rarely reported, predicts the number of lucky months in the next year.

Years till death: Sussex Arundel MS (14th cent.) quoted Opie & Tatem, 112. **Norfolk** Fulcher Collection (*c*.1895). **Yorkshire** *Athenaeum* (1846) 863; **Yorkshire/Northamptonshire** Hardy (1879) 86–8. **Lancashire** Harland & Wilkinson (1873) 218. **Wales** Trevelyan (1909) 109. **Scotland** *Glasgow Herald* (Oct. 1859). **Unlocated** Henderson (1866) 72. **General** Werenfels (1748) 6. **Literary** Abraham Cowley, *Love's Riddle* (1638) 5:1.
Years till marriage: **England** Swainson (1886) 116. **Somerset** [1923] Opie & Tatem, 112. **Norfolk** Fulcher Collection (*c*.1895). **Staffordshire** *Folk-Lore* 28 (1917) 452. **Wales** Trevelyan (1909) 109. **Unlocated** *Spectator* (18 Jan. 1902) 82.
Lucky months: **Somerset** [1954] Tongue (1965) 49–50. For European analogues: Hardy (1879); Swainson (1886) 109–22.

cuckoos: occupation

A further aspect of the BEGINNINGS principle: a few references report that whatever you are doing when you hear the first cuckoo will be your main occupation or interest for the coming year.

Sussex *Folk-Lore* 25 (1914) 369. **Berkshire** Lowsley (1888) 22. **Herefordshire** Leather (1912) 26. **Norfolk** Fulcher Collection (*c*.1895). **Radnorshire** [1953] Opie & Tatem, 113.

cuckoos: shoe divination

Most of the cuckoo superstitions are concerned with affecting future prosperity by controlling the situation at the BEGINNING of the season. This one, however, is designed as a form of LOVE DIVINATION – to ascertain the colour of your future lover's hair:

The women say that if you remove the shoe from your foot when you first hear the cuckoo, you will find on your stocking a hair resembling in colour that of your future husband in life.

Wales Trevelyan (1909)

Some versions include extra stipulations, paralleled in other cuckoo superstitions, such as having to run as fast as you can before checking your shoe, or that the hair will be found under, rather than in, your shoe.

The love divination theme is constant throughout all the references from *Mother Bunch's Closet* (1685) onwards, but the earliest description translates the hair colour into a straightforward colour scheme for good or bad luck. It is also the only one which requires you to see, rather than hear, the bird:

When you first see the cuckowe, mark well where your right foot doth stand; for you shall find there an hair. Which if it be black, it signifies that you shall have very evil luck all that year after. If it be white then it signifies very good luck; But if it be grey then indifferent.

Unlocated Lupton (1579)

Somerset Tongue (1965) 49–50. **Herefordshire** Leather (1912) 63. **Norfolk** Fulcher Collection (*c*.1895). **Shropshire** Burne (1883) 219–2. **England** Addy (1895) 78, 111. **Yorkshire** *Yorkshire Post* (11 May 1957) 6. **Lancashire** Harland & Wilkinson (1873) 218. **Wales** Trevelyan (1909) 109. **Northeast Scotland** Gregor (1874) 102. **N. Ireland** Foster (1951) 33. **Co. Longford** *Béaloideas* 6 (1936) 265. **Co. Antrim** [*c*.1905] McDowell (1972) 131. **Co. Wexford** *Folk-Lore Record* 5 (1882) 82. **Unlocated** Lupton (1579) Bk 10, Para. 80; [1771] *N&Q* 5S:3 (1875) 285–6. **Literary** *Mother Bunch's Closet Newly*

Broke Open (1685) 6. John Gay, *The Shepherd's Week* (1714); *Connoisseur* 56 (1755) 333–4; *Poor Robin's Almanack* (1765).

Béaloideas 6 (1936) 260. **Unlocated** N&Q 11S:12 (1915) 250.

cuckoos: where standing

In keeping with the principles of BEGINNINGS AND CONTINUANCE, a widespread set of beliefs maintain that where you are when you first hear the cuckoo is symbolic of where you will be for the rest of the year. Thus, to be in bed indicates future illness or even death:

If anyone hears the cuckoo's first note when in bed, there is sure to be illness or death to him or one of his family.

Norfolk *Norfolk Archaeology* (1849)

Even being caught bending can be interpreted as ominous:

If one is stooping, and looking towards the ground when one hears the cuckoo for the first time, it signifies a death before she comes again.

Co. Longford *Béaloideas* (1936)

Not quite so obvious is the notion that you should be standing on grass, rather than a hard surface like a road, or sometimes the distinction is made between grass and bare earth. Either way, the penalty for not being on grass varies from general bad luck to death:

In many parts of Wales it is asserted that if when you hear the cuckoo for the first time you are standing on grass or any green leaves, you will certainly live to hear the bird next season; but if you are standing on a roadway, or on the earth, or even upon stone, you will not live to hear the cuckoo when it comes next. **Wales** Trevelyan (1909)

The symbolism in this case is sometimes explained as a 'hard' surface leads to a 'hard' life.
 The particular slant on cuckoo lore represented by this set of beliefs only enters the documentary record in the mid nineteenth century, but was well reported in the twentieth. The symbolism also has a higher level of sophistication than older examples, and on present evidence it should probably be seen as a relatively late extension of the earlier 'hearing the first cuckoo' superstitions.

Somerset [1923] Opie & Tatem, 113; Tongue (1965) 49–50. **Wiltshire** Jefferies (1878) Ch. 4. **East Anglia** Varden (1885) 116–17. **Norfolk** *Norfolk Archaeology* 2 (1849) 301; Fulcher Collection (c.1895). **England** Addy (1895) 111. **Yorkshire** [1982] Opie & Tatem, 114. **Northumberland** Neville (1909) 110. Bosanquet (1929) 78. **Wales** Trevelyan (1909) 109–10, 282. **Co. Longford**

cunning men/women

Cunning men or women were widespread names for those local characters who professed to be expert in the occult sciences of discovering and countering witchcraft, divining the future, and so on, and whose services were at the disposal of anyone with the money to buy them. The terminology was elastic and possibly regional. Such people could also be called wise men and women, conjurers, wizards, white witches, healers, charmers, or simply witches, depending on a combination of local usage, their own specialisms and reputation, and the opinion of the beholder.

The expression 'cunning' is one I have never heard in North Herefordshire; they say 'clever' instead, or call the diviner the 'conjurer'.

Herefordshire Leather (1912)

Under any name, cunning men and women were a regular feature of village and small town life for centuries. Admittedly, in any community there would have been people, especially in the upper echelons of local society, who knew nothing of such goings-on, but the majority of the populace would be well aware of who claimed powers in what context, and who could be paid for occult assistance when necessary. Even into the late nineteenth century, belief in witchcraft was not a minor aberration but a major element in community life.

Coupled with the witch is the 'wise woman', a common figure in eighteenth century Suffolk who survived well into living memory when various 'rustic oracles' of more than merely local reputation were still consulted. Thus, an elderly farm-bailiff, telling the writer of a family quarrel in a village near Diss some forty years ago, mentioned that one party 'went to a woman near Lowestoft' to help him locate money of which he thought himself robbed. My informant, incidentally, seemed to think such an act needed neither explanation nor apology.

Suffolk *Folk-Lore* (1943)

The standard fare for the average cunning man or woman would include fortune-telling, by various means, the location of lost or stolen property, love magic (whereby recalcitrant lovers could be brought to heel), the identification of spells cast upon the client and his/her goods, and measures to counter them, and magical healing techniques.

Gross superstition – A case was brought before the Plymouth bench of magistrates on Tuesday, showing the extent to which superstition lingers in Devon. The prisoner was Mary Catherine Murray, respectably dressed, aged about 50, and the charge was that of imposing upon Thomas Rendle by means of a piece of parchment called a 'charm'. The prosecutor is a labourer living at Modbury who out of the small earnings of about 10s. a week had managed to scrape together a few pounds. His wife was taken ill, and he thought she was 'ill-wished'. Hearing of the powers of the prisoner, who lived at 18 William Street, Plymouth, and whose reputation as a healer of those bewitched had spread as far as Modbury, he went and consulted her. She said his wife would have to go and see the planets, and gather certain herbs in the churchyard for 21 nights. The prisoner charged him one guinea for her advice, and afterwards received from him £3 for powders and a 'skin'. The skin was to be worn round the neck, and must be put on for the first time on a Sunday. The powders were to be burnt in the fire – one in the morning and the other in the evening, beginning also on the Sunday; and there was also some medicine in bottles. When the last powder was burnt, the prisoner ordered that the 91st psalm should be read. The prisoner expressed her belief in her powers and she was remanded, bail being refused.   Devon The Times (13 Dec. 1867)

Much of our information about such activities in the nineteenth century comes from narratives collected by folklorists, which are often good stories, but in themselves already traditional and filtered, and the characters already semi-legendary. An alternative view is gleaned from local newspapers, which tend to focus on court cases but give a more accurate picture of who and what was involved. It must be understood that the modern romantic view of these local practitioners as harmless eccentrics possessed of secret herbal knowledge which modern civilization foolishly ignores is seriously misleading. Countless people were tricked into spending their life savings on charms and nostrums, were persuaded that a neighbour had bewitched them, were bullied and frightened by people whose main expertise was to identify and profit from human weakness.

The word 'cunning', meaning 'knowledgeable' and 'skilful', was widely used in various contexts in Middle English, at least from the early fourteenth century onwards. It did not start to acquire its present-day negative overtones of craftiness and deviousness until the turn of the seventeenth century. 'Cunning man' was already being used as a synonym for 'local wise man' in the fourteenth century, and it was still common in the seventeenth: 'A cunning man did calculate my birth, and told me that by water I should die' (Shakespeare, 2 Henry VI (1593) 4:1); 'Going in disguise to that conjurer and to this cunning woman' (Ben Jonson, Silent Woman (1609) 2:1).

The references given below include material on practitioners under all their various names, and not just those called 'cunning'.

Devon The Times (13 Dec. 1867) 10; N&Q 5S:6 (1876) 144; Devonshire Assoc. 11 (1879) 105; Devonshire Assoc. 26 (1894) 82–3; Devonshire Assoc. 86 (1954) 301. Gloucestershire Folk-Lore 16 (1905) 169–70. Herefordshire Leather (1912) 57–61, 71. Worcestershire/Shropshire Gent. Mag. (1855) 384–6. Suffolk Folk-Lore 54 (1943) 390. Lincolnshire The Times (30 Mar. 1850) 6; N&Q 1S:6 (1852) 145. Staffordshire [16th cent.] Poole (1875) 72; [1820] Poole (1875) 83. Shropshire Gough (1601–7) 46. Derbyshire N&Q 10S:11 (1909) 6. Yorkshire Dawson (1882) 197–202. Cumberland [1817–18] Dickinson (1875) 106–9. Montgomeryshire Davies (1938) 158–70. Merioneth Jnl Merioneth Hist. & Record Soc. 3 (1957–60) 280–3. Aberdeenshire Folk-Lore 25 (1914) 348. Ireland Wilde (1888) 209. Jersey Folk-Lore 25 (1914) 244–5. Major studies Davies (1997); Davies (1999).

cursing

The ability to curse someone effectively has presumably been part of the stock-in-trade of every aspiring witch, wizard, and CUNNING MAN or woman in all ages and cultures, and much of their power over their neighbours and customers must have depended on their reputation in this area. This power would also necessarily require secrecy, as there would be no market for their services if everyone could do the same thing. Descriptions of people casting curses or being cursed are replete with circumstantial detail, but they lack essential information about the curse itself, and in particular they describe actions but do not reveal the accompanying verbal charms. They are thus more satisfying as narratives than for imparting specific information about the processes involved:

A Gipsy's curse – At the beginning of April, 1929, a gipsy called at a farm near here (South Molton) and asked the farmer's daughter to buy something from her basket. The young lady refused, and the gipsy then begged for some cider which was also refused, as also was a glass of milk the woman asked for, but she offered the gipsy a glass of water. The woman took it, but without drinking she said something, poured the water on the ground and handed back the glass. Someone who knew a good deal about gipsies said it was done to bring ill-luck. My daughter asked a gipsy at Crediton, 'Why did the gipsy take the water if she did not mean to drink it?' The woman asked eagerly, 'where was that done? It is the worst gipsy curse there is.' The young lady was engaged to be married, house furnished and wedding day fixed, but on the day their banns were to have been called, her fiancé's dead body was taken into the church, after he had suffered a very brief illness.   Devon *Devonshire Assoc.* (1931)

Clearly, such stories assume that the listener or reader finds cursing credible.

A curious incident took place once at Penallt. A woman and her daughter had been turned out of their house, which had made them furious. Soon afterwards the older woman died, and while her corpse was being carried to church the daughter suddenly drew a slipper from under her apron and struck with it three times at the coffin, exclaiming as she did so, 'Mother, I'm here, fulfilling your commands!', and with that she threw the slipper into an orchard close by belonging to those people who had turned them out. And for long after that the farm never prospered and no one could stay there, though by this time the curse appears to have been removed, as the present inhabitants are doing well.

Monmouthshire *Folk-Lore* (1905)

Certain curses were available to all and sundry, and apparently needed no more special power than the necessary degree of anger and spite. Scorned lovers, for example, had opportunity for revenge at the wedding of their former sweethearts. Ella Leather reported an incident in which a jilted girl confronted her ex-lover as he left the church with his new bride and threw a handful of rue at him, saying 'May you rue this day as long as you live':

My informant said this caused a good deal of talk at the time, and he was told that the curse would come true, because the rue was taken direct from the plant to the churchyard and thrown 'between holy and unholy ground', that is between the church and churchyard.

Herefordshire Leather (1912)

If anyone at a marriage repeats the benediction after the priest, and ties a knot at the mention of each of the three sacred names on a handkerchief, or a piece of string, the marriage will be childless for fifteen years, unless the knotted string is burnt in the meantime.

Aran Islands *Procs. Royal Irish Academy* (1891–3)

A number of the descriptions include the motif that a curse uttered lightly, or performed badly, rebounds upon the curser:

Any person can pray that his enemy be dead, if he wishes to repeat Psalm 109 ['Hold not thy peace, O God of my praise . . .'] every night and morning for a whole year. If he misses one night or morning, he must certainly die himself.

Wales Trevelyan (1909)

See below for two widespread methods of cursing using stones: 'turning the stones' and the 'fire of stones'. See also WEDDINGS: CURSING.

Devon *Devonshire Assoc.* 8 (1876) 53; *Devonshire Assoc.* 24 (1892) 54; Hewett (1900) 82; Devonshire Assoc. 63 (1931) 130. **Herefordshire** [c.1895] *Folk-Lore* 39 (1928) 390; Leather (1912) 89, 115. **Wales** Trevelyan (1909) 282. **Denbighshire** *Bye-Gones* (26 Jan. 1887) 233. **Monmouthshire** *Folk-Lore* 16 (1905) 66. **Morayshire** N&Q 1S:11 (1855) 239. **Ireland** Power (1974) *passim.* **N. Ireland** St Clair (1971) 60–3. **Aran Islands** *Procs. Royal Irish Academy* 3S:2 (1891–3) 818.

cursing: fire of stones

A powerful procedure, usually carried out by tenants forced to leave a farm against their will, involved placing a curse on the land by building a fire of stones:

The modus operandi is extremely primitive, simple, and original; how far it is effective it is difficult to say. The plaintiff (if I may use the term) collects from the surrounding fields as many boulders as will fill the principal hearth of the holding he is being compelled to surrender. These he piles in the manner of turf sods arranged for firing; and then, kneeling down, prays that until the heap burns, may every kind of sweat, bad luck, and misfortune attend the landlord and his family, to untold generations. Rising, he takes the stones in armfuls and hurls them here and there, in loch, pool, bog-hole or stream, so that by no possibility could the collection be recovered.

Co. Fermanagh *Jnl Royal Hist. & Arch. Association of Ireland* (1875)

Some details vary, but the essential core is the same. In some accounts the stones are left in the fireplace, to increase the dramatic effect. The incoming occupant will be in no doubt as to what has been done. Sometimes an eggshell full of water was placed on top of the stones to suggest that the ill luck would last until the stones boiled that water.

Examples have been noted from various parts of Ireland, and one or two from Scotland. Although curses such as this have an archaic feel, there seems to be no record of this one before the 1820s, as reported in the supplement to Jamieson's Scottish dictionary. It was still being talked about, if not actually carried out, in Ireland in the later twentieth century.

Scotland, Jamieson, *Dict. of the Scottish Language* (Supp.) (1825). Ireland *Folk-Lore* 5 (1894) 282. Wood-Martin 2 (1902) 58; St Clair (1971) 60–2. N. Ireland Foster (1951) 122. Co. Monaghan *California Folk-Lore Quarterly* 2:4 (1943) 309–14. Co. Fermanagh *Jnl of the Royal Hist. & Arch. Association of Ireland* (July 1875) quoted N&Q 5S:5 (1876) 223; *Folk-Lore* 5 (1894) 3–4. Major treatment Fionnuala Williams, 'A Fire of Stones Curse', *Folk Life* 35 (1996–7) 63–73.

cursing: turning the stones

'Turning the stones' was a way of inflicting a potent curse on anyone you wished to harm. The method was widely reported in parts of Ireland, although it is more often referred to than described:

Near Black Lion, at the extreme north of Co. Cavan, there is a cursing stone. It is a large horizontal slab, with twelve or thirteen bullans or basins cut in it, and in each bullan save one, there is a large round stone. The curser takes up one of the stones and places it in the empty basin – and so on, one after another, till have been gone over. During the movement he is cursing his enemy, and if he removes all the stones without letting one of them slip (no easy operation on account of their form), his curses will have effect, but not otherwise. If he lets one slip, the curses will return on his own head. Co. Cavan *Folk-Lore* (1894)

Power (1974) claims that the custom is 'very ancient indeed', although he offers no evidence to support his assertion. A couple of reports from Devon show that it was also known and feared there.

Devon N&Q 5S:5 (1876) 363; *Devonshire Assoc.* 8 (1876) 53. Ross-shire *Folk-Lore* 49 (1938) 88–9. Ireland Power (1974) 29–33. N. Ireland Foster (1951) 118–19. Co. Clare *Folk-Lore* 22 (1911) 50–60. Co. Cavan/Co. Donegal *Folk-Lore* 5 (1894) 3–4.

cutlery

see KNIVES; SPOONS.

cuttlefish

Ground and powdered cuttlefish were used in cures, both medicinal and magical:

Ringworm was the work of a witch, and was cured by means of seaweed poultices and powdered cuttlefish sprinkled on the sore place. This, with stone, gravel, affections of the spleen, and gripes, were singled out for exorcism of a special kind. The same method was followed in cases of tumour, fistula, whitlow, cancer, 'king's evil' or scrofula, and boils of all kinds.
Wales Trevelyan (1909)

In Shetland, it was used both for drying ink on letters and curing bad eyes in sheep.

Wales Trevelyan (1909) 319. Shetland *Folk-Lore* 49 (1938) 90.

daffodils: death omen

Robert Herrick's poem 'Divination by a Daffodil' belies the cheerful image of the flower as a welcome sign of spring:

When a daffodil I see,
Hanging down his head t'wards me,
Guess I may, what I must be:
First I shall decline my head;
Secondly I shall be dead;
Lastly, safely buried.

It appears to be the drooping head of the flower which triggers the gloomy prognostication. The general existence of the belief is confirmed by a version from the Derbyshire area collected by S. O. Addy in the 1890s, and another by A. S. Macmillan in Wiltshire in 1923.

Wiltshire [1923] Opie & Tatem, 115. England Addy (1895) 63. Literary Robert Herrick, *Hesperides* (1648) 'Divination by a Daffodil'.

daffodils: effect on poultry

The main superstition about daffodils, which they share with PRIMROSES, is the idea that they are closely linked with goslings and chicks:

My friend had been out for a walk in the meadows, near the river; along its banks the daffodils are very abundant. He picked one and put it in the button-hole of his coat. When he got back to the farm-house he pulled out the flower and laid it on the table. Soon after a servant came into the room and saw the flower, and at once exclaimed, 'Who brought in this daffodil? Did you, Mr. G.? We shall have no ducks this year!'. My friend enquired the reason for such a superstition, but he could get no satisfactory answer; only that it

A German illustration from 1895 shows children blowing dandelion seeds to make a wish or to tell the time – a widely spread and still prevalent belief.

was so . . . I am informed that a single flower is unlucky for the ducklings; but if a handful is brought in, it is in their favour, and the season will be fortunate.   **Devon** *Devonshire Assoc.* (1877)

Geese themselves were apparently aware of this problem:

[A Cornish farmer's wife] *in 1880 declared 'that if a goose saw a Lent lily (daffodil) before hatching its goslings it would, when they came forth, destroy them.'*   **Cornwall** *Folk-Lore Jnl* (1887)

This idea is only reported from the nineteenth century onwards, and is probably based on nothing more than the coincidences of colour and time of year between the plant and the young birds.

Devon *Devonshire Assoc.* 9 (1877) 88–9, quoting *Daily Western Times*; *Devonshire Assoc.* 11 (1879) 109; **Devon** *Devonshire Assoc.* 64 (1932) 154. **Cornwall** *Folk-Lore Jnl* 5 (1887) 193; *Old Cornwall* 10 (1929) 42. **Herefordshire** Leather (1912) 17. **Isle of Man** Clague (1911) 177; [1982] Vickery (1995) 99.

daisies

see PETALS.

dandelions (*Taraxacum officinale*)

Dandelions have been recommended as a cure for numerous ailments, including WARTS, eczema, indigestion, jaundice, and liver disease:

For liver complaints we dug up dandelion roots with a one-tined fork specially made by the blacksmith for the purpose, washed, dried, and roasted them in the oven, then crushed them to a powder with a bottle, and after pouring boiling water over them, half a teaspoonful to a large cup, we added milk and sugar, when we had it, and drank the beverage for breakfast as coffee . . . We also ate the young dandelion leaves in early spring when there was no other green salad about, sometimes bleaching them, by covering them with an old sack. This was supposed to be a blood-cleanser.

Worcestershire [*c.*1900] Knight

Dandelion was also used to treat diseases of the urinary tract and to clean the kidneys and the bladder, which presumably gave rise to the extremely widespread children's belief that picking dandelions caused BED-WETTING:

Buttercups and daisies were our first favourites [for flower chains], dandelions being shunned somewhat, because . . . the handling them was supposed to induce 'undesirable consequences at night'. In fact, we called dandelions in Derbyshire 'pisabeds'.   Derbyshire N&Q (1901)

The plant had similar local names all over the country.

Bed-wetting: Essex [1917] Mays (1969) 165. Hertfordshire [1979] Vickery (1995) 102. **Worcestershire** Knight (1960) 182. **Northamptonshire** N&Q 9S:7 (1901) 511. Derbyshire N&Q 9S:8 (1901) 70. **Yorkshire** Nicholson (1890) 123. **Dyfed** [1983] Vickery (1995) 102. **Fife** [1930s] Vickery (1995) 102. **Ireland** Logan (1981) 37–8. **Belfast** [1950s] Vickery (1995) 103. **Guernsey** De Garis (1975) 119. For use in general herbal cures, *see* Logan (1981); Hatfield (1994); Vickery (1995).

dandelions: seeds

Children all over the British Isles have blown the seeds off the dandelion to tell the time, to answer simple questions such as how many years until marriage, or to play the game of 'she loves me, she loves me not'. The earliest reference so far found is from the 1830s:

The flower-stalk must be plucked carefully, so as not to injure the globe of seeds, and you are then to blow off the seeds with your breath. So many puffs as are required to blow every seed clean off, so many years it will be before you are married.
                                    East Anglia Forby (1830)

Worcestershire [1991] Vickery (1995) 103. **East Anglia** Forby (1830) 423–4; Varden (1885) 109. **Nottinghamshire** [1920s] Vickery (1995) 103. **Northern England** Brockett (1829) 72. **Yorkshire** Nicholson (1890) 123. **Gwynned** [1991] Vickery (1995) 103. **Montgomeryshire** Hamer (1877) 261. **Dumfriesshire** Corrie (1890/91) 83. **Elgin** [1940s] Vickery (1995) 104. **Co. Offaly** [1985] Vickery (1995) 103. **Guernsey** De Garis (1975) 119.

dates (food)

John Aubrey reported the use of date stones in curing human stones:

I have learned that dates are an admirable medicine for the stone, from old Captain Tooke of K— Take six or ten date-stones, dry them in an oven, pulverize and scarce them; take as much as will lie on a six-pence, in a quarter of a pint of wine fasting, and at four in the afternoon; walk or ride an hour after; in a week's time it will give ease, and in a month cure. If you are at the Bath, the Bath water is better than white wine to take it in.   Aubrey, *Miscellanies* (1696/1857) 61

The symbolic nature of using pulverized and powdered stones to treat other stones is obvious.

days: unlucky

The notion that particular days are lucky or unlucky is, presumably, universal. In antiquity, the Egyptians, Jews, Greeks, and Romans all had complex systems which either identified specific unlucky days or laid out a whole year and assigned each day as either lucky or unlucky. These notions were certainly known in Britain in Saxon times, and medieval calendars also identified days as good or bad. Since at least the turn of the fifteenth century, unlucky days were called 'Egyptian days', either because it was thought that the system used for calculating them went back to Egyptian times or because they were believed to be connected with events such as the ten plagues of Moses and other biblical phrases where the adjective 'Egyptian' was used to denote gloom and misery. From about the same time, they were also termed 'dismal days' – the word dismal being derived from the Latin *dies mala* (bad day), with which the days were marked on medieval calendars. Unlucky days were also called 'Cross days'.

As an example of the list of unlucky days, the following is from a manuscript *Kalendar* of the time of Henry VI (1422–61):

These underwritten be the perilous days, for to take any sickness in, or to be hurt in, or to be wedded in, or to take any journey upon, or to begin any work on, that he would well speed. The number of these days be in the year 32; they be these: – January 1, 2, 4, 5, 7, 10, 15; February 6, 7, 18; March 1, 6, 8; April 1, 11; May 5, 6, 7; June 7, 15; July 5, 19; August 15, 19; September 6, 7; October 6; November 15, 16; December 15, 16, 17.
                                    Chambers (1878)

These lists, when compared, seem to bear little relationship to each other, although, to be fair, if they were calculated on forthcoming astronomical features they would indeed be different each year. However, there is no reason to think that they were any more scientific than the daily horoscope predictions in a modern tabloid newspaper. But they were certainly taken literally by many:

Regarders of times, as they are which will have one time more lucky than another: to be born at one hour more unfortunate than at another: to take a journey or any other enterprise in hand, to be more dangerous or prosperous at one time than another: as likewise, if such a festival day fall upon such a day of the week, or suchlike, we shall have such a year following: and many other such like vain speculations, set down by our astrologians, having neither footing in God's word, nor yet natural reason to support them; but being grounded only upon the superstitious imagination of man's brain.

Mason, *Anatomie of Sorcerie* (1612)

Ordinary people will have known little of the 'science' of astrology, but a simplified and popular form was filtered down to them via the ALMANACS which sold in their hundreds of thousands each year. These cheap publications also provided data on the phases of the MOON, which were also taken into account when planning many aspects of daily life, especially on the farm.

Apart from those unlucky days set by almanac and calendar makers, there seems to have been little structure to the days individuals regarded as unlucky or lucky. As indicated elsewhere, FRIDAYS have generally been regarded as unlucky since at least the medieval period, and GOOD FRIDAY was singled out for gloom in some contexts. Nowadays, of course, FRIDAY 13TH is widely feared, but this can only be traced back to Victorian times. The only other day which was widely regarded as unlucky was HOLY INNOCENTS' DAY or Childermas (28 Dec.), and those who took this seriously also regarded the day of the week on which it fell as suspect for the rest of the year.

The antiquarian John Aubrey was interested in the topic, and he devoted a chapter to 'Day fatality' in his *Miscellanies* (1696), in which he discussed the way particular dates seem to be significant to individuals and to nations; however, his thoughts on the matter are anything but convincing. His method is to list events which had happened on a certain date, and then stand back in awe of the coincidence of it all. He was particularly fascinated by people who had been born and had died on the same date in the year and, as he translated their deaths into a 'good thing' (going to meet their maker), he declared this to be their lucky date. Most other attempts to prove the reality of individual lucky and unlucky days are similarly unconvincing.

Perthshire *Stat. Acct. of Scotland* 5 (1793) 82; James Mason, *Anatomie of Sorcerie* (1612) 85; Melton (1620) 56; Aubrey, *Miscellanies* (1696/1857) 1–24; Brand 2 (1849) 44–51; Chambers (1878) 41–2.

dead man's hand: butter-making

A specialist use of a corpse's hand, by which a person can steal his/her neighbour's butter:

Butter is taken by means of 'a dead hand'. In every case it is a woman who uses the hand, which she has cut off a corpse in the graveyard. Before sunrise she milks the neighbours' cows into a bottle – even one 'strig' will do – she takes the milk home and puts it thro' her own supply. Before commencing to churn she waves the 'dead hand' around outside the churn and commands her neighbours' butter to come. She mentions each name separately and repeats the process for each person. They get no butter then as she has all theirs. In several cases cows of people whose butter was taken went mad and calves died.

Co. Longford *Béaloideas* (1936)

This description is closely related to the HAND OF GLORY, which was also used for nefarious purposes. This belief is mostly reported from Ireland, from the late nineteenth century onwards, but an earlier reference from Shetland may be relevant. In a seventeenth-century witch trial in Shetland, it was claimed that Barbara Thomasdochter offered help 'to one who churned in vain':

She wald gif her sum thing gif she wald heild it, that wald do hir guid: and oppnit hir pwrs and tuik ane bone furth therof, quhilk wes the bone of ane manes finger great at the ane end and small at the uther, of twa insh lang or therby, and bad hir steir hir milk with it and she wald get hir profeit [She would give her something if she would hide it, that would do her good: and opened her purse and took a bone forth thereof, which was the bone of a man's finger great at the one end and small at the other, of two inches long or thereby, and bade her stir her milk with it and she would get her profit].

Shetland [1616] Dalyell

The principle seems the same as that of the dead hand quoted above, although in this case it was later explained that it was a seal's bone.

See also DEAD MAN'S HAND; HAND OF GLORY.

Shetland [1616] Dalyell (1834) 264. **Ireland** Wilde (1888) 81; Jenkins (1977) 39–40. **Co. Cavan** Murphy (1973) 34. **Co. Wexford** *Folk-Lore Record* 5 (1882) 81. **Co. Longford** *Béaloideas* 6 (1936) 262.

dead man's hand: cures

A widespread belief held that a certain cure for wens, goitre, scrofula, tumours, and other swellings or skin complaints was to stroke the affected place with a corpse's hand. In most cases, the hand of an executed criminal, or a SUICIDE was preferred:

A hanging at Newgate Prison in 1814. The dead man's hand is pressed against a sick woman to effect a cure.

Cure for a wen – The body of a suicide who hanged himself in Heselden Dene was laid in an outhouse awaiting the coroner's inquest. The wife of a pitman at Castle Eden Colliery, suffering from a wen in the neck, following the advice given her by a 'wise woman' went alone, and lay all night in the outhouse with the hand of the corpse on her wen. She was assured that the hand of a suicide was an infallible cure. The shock to the nervous system was such that she did not rally for some weeks, and eventually died from the wen. This happened about the year 1853, under my own cognizance.

Northumberland Tristram (1860/62)

In the days of public hanging (abolished 1868), the hangman carried on a lucrative trade charging people for the use of the dead hand, and there was often a queue of afflicted persons willing to pay for the privilege.

Wens – After a criminal is dead, but still hanging, his hand must be rubbed thrice over the wen. Many persons are still living who in their younger days have undergone the ceremony, always, they say, attended with complete success. On execution days at Northampton, numbers of sufferers used to congregate round the gallows, in order to receive the 'dead-stroke' as it is termed. At the last execution which took place in the town, a very few only were operated upon, not so much in consequence of decrease of faith, as from the higher fee demanded by the hangman.

Northamptonshire N&Q (1850)

The principles at work here are not clear, as the belief is open to a number of interpretations, all of them speculative and lacking in solid evidence. At first glance, it is difficult to find any reason why the hand of a dead person, and more particularly someone who has been executed or has committed suicide, should have the power of healing. By deconstructing the belief and taking one aspect at a time, a number of parallels can be drawn, but none are totally satisfactory in explaining the superstition. The simplest suggestion, backed by one or two references, is that this is an example of the widespread belief in the TRANSFERENCE of disease. Where the report states that 'as the hand moulders' the affliction will disappear, the above principle is being invoked, but references to this notion are not common enough to warrant the conclusion that this is the real basis of the belief.

The idea that certain people have the power of a 'healing touch' is a commonplace in popular and religious tradition. Kings and queens, for example, 'touched' people suffering from the King's Evil, or SCROFULA. Further down the social scale, the belief in SEVENTH SONS and their ability to heal by touch was widespread, and even many humble WART-charmers did little more than touch the warts and mumble a few words. In all these cases, however, the power is inherent in a special person, usually from birth, while he or she is still alive.

Of possible relevance, too, are the hands of holy men which continued to heal the sick and work miracles after their death – men, for example, such as St Oswald of Northumbria (d. 642) and Father Arrowsmith. The latter was a reputedly martyred Catholic priest, executed for his faith in Lancashire in 1628, whose preserved right hand continued to bring about cures right up to the late nineteenth century (see Harland & Wilkinson (1882) 158–63). These were the hands of dead men, but their inherent power clearly lay in the goodness of their owners which could transcend even death.

There are also many precedents in which things associated with the dead are believed to have healing powers – coffin handles and nails, pieces of wood from a GALLOWS or gibbet, moss or teeth taken from human SKULLS, and pieces of the HANGMAN'S ROPE. The latter brings us closer to the dead man's hand in terms of being concerned with people who have been executed. The question that remains unanswered is how or why the act of death turned the ordinary being into a healing one, and in particular why the violent death by execution or suicide was often singled out as conferring this posthumous distinction.

The belief is well attested in the British Isles from at least the 1590s onwards and was very widely reported well into the twentieth century, although by the latter time it was passing rapidly into memory culture. Exactly the same belief was known in classical times, as reported, for example, by Pliny:

We are assured that the hand of a person carried off by premature death cures by a touch scrofulous sores, diseased parotid glands, and throat affections. Natural History (AD 77)

Indeed, this description is so close as to pose the question whether it was introduced to Britain by sixteenth-century scholars such as Scot, who were keen on classical sources.

Among the numerous minor variations in Britain, one or two should be noted. Standard cures for WHOOPING COUGH often involved bread and butter being eaten by the sufferer or fed to a dog, but a handful of cures combine the bread with the dead man's hand motif:

If a woman have the king's evil, put a piece of bread and butter in the hand of a man that has been killed, and make her eat it out of the hand. If a man [be thus afflicted] it must be a woman's hand. Shropshire Burne (1883)

No doubt the sufferer would need to be even more desperate than those who would mount the scaffold for a cure, but many would regard the following as even worse, even if the impracticability involved probably ensured that it was never actually carried out:

If you wish to avoid pregnancy for one year, you must place your hand into a new made grave and open up the coffin. Find the dead man's hand and hold it for two minutes. This will keep you from becoming pregnant for one year. Lincolnshire [1930s] Sutton

The attempted cure could also have directly disastrous results, as, for example when the hand belonged to a man who had died of typhoid, which then effectively wiped out the whole family of the sufferer (The Times (16 Dec. 1870)).

The dead man's hand should be distinguished from the HAND OF GLORY, a severed corpse's hand, by which burglars sought to send their victims into a deep sleep or which was used to make butter by magical means.

For foreign analogues and connections between death and healing, see Folk-Lore 7 (1896) 268–83.

Kent [1819] Brand 3 (1849) 277. Sussex Latham (1878) 48. Dorset Udal (1922) 185. Somerset Aubrey, *Remaines* (1686/1880) 198; Aubrey, *Miscellanies* (1696/1857) 125; Poole (1877) 52; [1950] Tongue (1965) 136. Devon The Times (16 Jan. 1851) 7; *Devonshire Assoc.* 12 (1880) 102–3; *Devonshire Assoc.* 66 (1934) 83. Cornwall N&Q 2S:8 (1859) 489; Hunt (1865) 164; *Folk-Lore Jnl* 5 (1887) 203–5; *Jnl Royal Inst. Cornwall* 20 (1915) 126. Essex [1939] Folk-Lore 62 (1951) 262. Oxfordshire N&Q 1S:6 (1852) 145; [pre-1900] *Folk-Lore* 24 (1913) 88. Herefordshire Duncomb (1804) 56; Leather (1912) 82, 84. Warwickshire [1845] Brand 3 (1849) 278. Northamptonshire N&Q 1S:2 (1850) 36. Cambridgeshire [1899] *Folk-Lore* 79 (1968) 232; Porter (1969) 11. East Anglia Varden (1885) 104. Suffolk Glyde (1866) 175; *Gent. Mag.* (1867) 728–41; The Times (16 Dec. 1870) 4; *Folk-Lore* 56 (1945) 270. Norfolk *Folk-Lore* 40 (1929) 119. Lincolnshire Stamford Mercury (26 Mar. 1830) 3; Swaby (1891) 91; *Folk-Lore* 7 (1896) 268; Rudkin (1936) 27; [1930s] Sutton (1992) 92. Shropshire Burne (1883) 202. Staffordshire Poole (1875) 84. Lancashire Harland & Wilkinson (1873) 226. Cumberland Folk-Lore 20 (1909) 216. Co. Durham [1853] Brockie (1886) 221–2; Leighton (1910) 53. Northumberland Tristram (1860/62) 98. Highland Scotland Macbain (1887/88) 258. Galloway Mactaggart (1824) 463. Ireland Wilde (1888) 82; Hickey (1938) 269.

Co. Longford *Béaloideas* 6 (1936) 266. **Unlocated** [1759] N&Q 1S:6 (1852) 144–5; Grose (1787) 56; N&Q 3S:3 (1863) 262. **General** Scot (1584) Bk 12, Ch. 14; Browne, *Pseudodoxia Epidemica* (1672 edn) Bk 5, Ch. 23, Para. 9; [1777] Brand 3 (1849) 276; *Gent. Mag.* (1796) 636; Brand (1810) 107. **Classical** Pliny *Natural History* (AD 77) Bk 28, Para. 11.

deafness

see EARACHE.

death: clothes

see CLOTHES: OF THE DEAD.

death: doors open (1)

Two superstitions link death with open doors – the first when a person is dying, and the second at the time of the funeral. They are sometimes confused in the literature, but should be seen as relatively distinct beliefs.

It was widely believed that, as near as possible to the time of someone dying, all windows and doors, or at least the windows of the death room, or main door of the house, should be opened wide:

In the very moment of death all the doors and windows that were capable of being opened were thrown wide open, to give the departing spirit full and free egress, lest the evil spirits might intercept it in its heavenward flight.
Northeast Scotland Gregor (1881)

As here, the usual reason given is to avoid impeding the flight of the dead person's spirit, but it is also part of a more complex belief concerned with ensuring an 'easy death'. In many instances, it is recorded that closed doors and windows, and locks of cupboards, boxes, and so on, actually impede or even prevent the natural course of death taking place, and failure to see to these details causes the unfortunate one to 'die hard':

When a curate in Exeter I met with the following superstition, which I do not remember to have seen noticed before. I had long visited a poor man, who was dying of a very painful disease, and was daily expecting his death. Upon calling one morning to see my poor friend, his wife informed me that she thought he would have died during the night, and consequently she and her friend unfastened every lock in the house. On my inquiring the reason, I was told that any bolt or lock fastened was supposed to cause uneasiness to, and hinder the departure of the soul, and

consequently upon the approach of death all the boxes, doors, &c.in the house were unlocked.
Devon N&Q (1850)

The opening of windows and doors seems a relatively straightforward practice, given the basic Christian belief that the soul leaves the body at the time of death, and can be seen both as literal and symbolic for the easing of the soul's transition. Undoing locks, however, appears less obvious. It has been suggested that it was believed that evil spirits could lurk in locked drawers and the like, but it is not clear if this was really a widespread notion. Perhaps there is no rational explanation. In the same context of 'dying easy', see also other seemingly inexplicable notions such as not allowing pigeon or game FEATHERS in the bedding, and not placing BEDS across the direction of a beam or floorboards.

The custom of opening doors and windows is presumed to be ancient, but the earliest clear reference so far found dates only from the early nineteenth century, in Walter Scott's novel *Guy Mannering*, published in 1815:

And wha ever heard of a door being barred when a man was in the dead-thraw? – how d'ye think the spirit was to get awa through bolts and bars like thae?

Walter Scott also provides a different aspect of the open door. In the introduction to the ballad *Young Benjie*, published 1806, he maintained that, with a corpse in the house, the front door must never be left ajar but opened wide or left closed. Leaving it ajar was an integral part of an occult ceremony designed to make the corpse speak, and failure to observe the rules ran the risk of this taking place unplanned. Again, it is not clear how widespread this belief was, if at all.

Sussex Latham (1878) 60. **Dorset** Udal (1922) 184. **Somerset** *The Times* (4 Sept. 1863). **Devon** Bray (1838) 293–4; *Athenaeum* (17 Oct. 1846) 1069; N&Q 1S:1 (1850) 315–6. **Cornwall** *Folk-Lore Jnl* 5 (1887) 208. **Oxfordshire** *Oxf. & Dist. FL Soc. Ann. Record* (1950) 12. **Cambridgeshire** *Folk-Lore* 19 (1908) 337. **Worcestershire** N&Q 1S:1 (1850) 350; Berkeley & Jenkins (1932) 36. **Warwickshire** Langford (1875) 14; N&Q 170 (1936) 231. **England** Addy (1895) 123. **Northern England** N&Q 1S:1 (1850) 467. **Yorkshire** Nicholson (1890) 5. **Co. Durham** N&Q 170 (1936) 231. **Wales** Trevelyan (1909) 275. **West Wales** *Folk-Lore* 19 (1908) 108. **England/Scotland Border** [c.1916] Henderson (1866) 36. **Highland Scotland** *Folk-Lore Jnl* 3 (1885) 281; Macbain (1887/88) 254. **Southwestern Scotland** Wood (1911) 216. **Northeastern Scotland** Gregor (1881) 206. **Caithness** Rinder (1895) 56. **N. Ireland** Foster (1951) 18. **Co. Kerry** *Folk-Lore* 4 (1893) 351. **Co. Tyrone** *Lore & Language* 1:7 (1972) 8. **Literary** Walter Scott, *Minstrelsy of the Scottish Border* 2 (1806) 215–17; Walter Scott, *Guy Mannering* (1815) Ch 27.

death: doors open (2)

The second belief which connects death with an open door is concerned with the time that the coffin leaves the house for its final journey:

A few days ago the body of a gentleman in this neighbourhood was conveyed to the hearse, and while being placed in it, the door of the house, whether from design or inadvertence I know not, was closed before the friends came out to take their places in the coaches. An old lady, who was watching the proceedings, immediately exclaimed, 'God bless me! they have closed the door upon the corpse; there will be another death in that house before many days are over'. She was fully impressed with this belief, and unhappily this impression has been confirmed. The funeral was on Saturday, and on the Monday morning following a young man, resident in the house, was found dead in bed, having died under the influence of chloroform, which he had inhaled, self-administered to relieve the pain of toothache or tic-douloureux. Yorkshire N&Q (1850)

Superstition dictated that the door be left open until the mourners return, and if necessary a neighbour was asked to house-sit for the duration. This belief does not seem to have had a long history, as its first recorded instance is only from 1850 and the last is from the mid twentieth century. It is likely that it was finally made obsolete by the major shift in funeral custom, since the coffin now rests at the funeral parlour rather than in the home of the deceased. Although reported from most parts of England, it seems to have been confined to that country alone.

Charlotte Burne also recorded a superstition that dictated that a body leaving the house to be buried must be carried through the front door or 'there would certainly be another death in the house within a short time' (Shropshire Burne (1883)). This accords with other general beliefs about front DOORS.

England *Folk-Lore* 66 (1955) 325. Sussex Latham (1878) 57–8. Isle of Wight IOW Fed. W. I.s (1994) 99. Somerset [1923] Opie & Tatem 117. Devon *Folk-Lore* 20 (1909) 229. Wiltshire Wilts. *N&Q* 1 (1893–5) 58. Berkshire N&Q 2S:9 (1860) 380–1. Warwickshire N&Q 7S:11 (1891) 305; Bloom (*c*.1930) 43. Herefordshire Leather (1912) 118. Shropshire Burne (1883) 304. England Addy (1895) 124. Yorkshire N&Q 1S:2 (1850) 259. Co. Durham N&Q 146 (1924) 420. Unlocated N&Q 2S:12 (1861) 492.

death knocks

A specialized version of the DEATH SOUND, which precedes and announces a forthcoming death, is an unexplained knocking at the door, window, sick person's bed-head, or anywhere else in the house. In some cases it is a single sudden sound, but in the classic examples it is three measured knocks and therefore not amenable to naturalistic explanation. Sometimes the sound is repeated three times during the night, or on three successive nights:

[My grandmother] *had many other experiences such as three knocks which were premonitions of death. One night she was in bed in her cottage in Tiree and she heard three knocks at the door but when she got up to answer it there was nobody there. This happened three times that night and in the end she thought it must have been the wind. In the morning, however, she heard the three knocks again, so she went to the door where she found her neighbour whose husband had just died, coming for help.* Mull Bennett (1992)

If there is a sick person in the house, the 'call' is usually for them, otherwise it is taken to be an announcement of a relative's or neighbour's imminent demise. Further sounds, such as voices, can also be added:

R—'s mother knew that there was 'something going to happen him' and publicly stated her belief because three successive nights there was a distinct rap at the door, and a voice on each occasion asking for R—. Northumberland N&Q (1870)

As with other death sounds, the knocks can be seen as symbolic supernatural signs or can be interpreted more literally as real knocks simply projected forward in time as a warning:

At Gollanfield, near Inverness, a father, mother, brother and sister were one autumn evening at family worship, and, while the father was engaged at prayer, a loud knock was heard at the door, but by the mother and daughter only. The father and brother declared that they heard nothing. When they opened the door nobody was to be seen, though it was not then dark. A fortnight after that a horseman knocked at the door with the end of his whip – a knock exactly similar to that heard before. Only the mother and daughter were in at the time. There they found a man who came to tell them of an intimate friend's death. Highland Scotland Polson (1926)

The three knocks was first recorded by John Aubrey in 1696 and, although only rarely reported in the eighteenth century, numerous examples are available from the nineteenth and twentieth, from most parts of the British Isles.

Sussex *Sussex County Mag.* 13 (1939) 56–7. **Dorset** Udal (1922) 183. **Berkshire** Salmon (1902) 423. **Somerset** [1923] Opie & Tatem, 220. **Gloucestershire** *Folk-Lore* 13 (1902) 172. **London** [1986] Opie & Tatem, 220. **Huntingdonshire** [1880's] Marshall (1967) 246. **Shropshire** Burne (1883) 296. **Suffolk** *Gent. Mag.* (1867) 307–22. **Lincolnshire** *Folk-Lore* 19 (1908) 467–8. **Northamptonshire** Sternberg (1851) 171. **Lancashire** *Lancashire Lore* (1971) 50. **England** Addy (1895) 98. **Derbyshire** N&Q 12S:7 (1920) 168. **Yorkshire** *Leeds Mercury,* 4 Oct. 1879; [1963] Opie & Tatem, 220. **Northern England** Brockett (1829) 93. **Cumberland** Penfold (1907) 58. **Northumberland** Bigge (1860–62) 92; Henderson (1866) 33; N&Q 4S:6 (1870) 240. **Co. Durham** Brockie (1886) 203; Leighton (1910) 51. **Wales** Trevelyan (1909) 280. **Montgomeryshire** Hamer (1877) 257. **Northeastern Scotland** Gregor (1881) 203. **Western Scotland** Napier (1879) 57. **Highland Scotland** Polson (1926) 19–20. **Mull** Bennett (1992) 182. **Glasgow** [*c.*1820] Napier (1864) 395. **Caithness** Rinder (1895) 56–7. **Dumfriesshire** Corrie (1890/91) 43. **N. Ireland** Foster (1951) 18. **General** *Gent. Mag.* (1796) 636; **Unlocated** Grose (1787) 47.

death: mirrors covered

see MIRRORS: COVERED AT DEATH.

death: plants in mourning

A handful of nineteenth-century references report a West Country belief that houseplants, and sometimes other living things such as caged birds, should be put into mourning on the death of an occupant:

Mary observed in the cottage window several beautiful plants, each having a small piece of black crape or riband tied around it. She inquired what might be the reason of their being so decorated. When the poor woman told her, with a sigh, that she had very lately buried her husband, and if she had not put the plants into mourning they would have died too . . . [The widow said] the question was natural enough for one who came from a town, but the custom was the usual thing in the country. Devon Bray (1838)

The idea is clearly related to the ubiquitous beliefs concerning 'telling the BEES', which often include instructions to decorate their hives with black ribbon and give them a share of the funeral food. The relatively late appearance of the plant superstition, and its severely restricted geographical distribution, suggest that it was simply a local extension of the bee belief to the notion that all living elements within the household are potentially affected by a death and must therefore partake in the mourning.

Devon Bray (1838) 295; *Devonshire Assoc.* 12 (1880) 113. **Cornwall** N&Q 1S:12 (1855) 38; *Folk-Lore Jnl* 5 (1887) 193.

death: salt placed on corpse

see SALT: CORPSE.

death sounds

A wide range of sounds have been interpreted as death omens, and their key elements are that they are sudden, and not easily explained by natural causes. It is clear that to those who believe that death can be announced in advance, or even those who are simply susceptible to possible supernatural phenomena, something so unexpected and invisible is a particularly evocative combination, and it is hardly surprising that numerous traditions have grown up on the subject. The most common are given separate entries.

Death warning sounds can be separated into several categories. First are those which are simply sudden, unexpected, unexplainable noises around the house or its vicinity which can be interpreted as omens. Second are more specific noises which are deemed to be natural sounds of what will happen after the person is dead, but appearing out of their proper timeframe. Thus, sounds of coffins being manufactured or placed on chairs, funeral carts, people gathering (footsteps, voices) for the funeral, and so on. Knocking on the door or the rattling of windows are included in the category of 'natural sounds', but with an extra dimension: the dead are being 'called' away – symbolically combining the material knock and the spiritual 'call'. A third category includes a range of sounds which are neither random nor naturalistic but are traditionally known, and therefore expected, in the community.

In the category of random crashes and bangs, any suitably alarming sounds could be interpreted as death signs, especially in retrospect:

Mr. L. of Maryport told me that in his own house, once when his father died and again when an uncle died, they heard a loud noise of broken glass, as if a heavy chandelier had fallen. They had no glass of any kind broken.
Cumberland *Folk-Lore* (1909)

Clearly, the situation of the hearers and a suitable context are major factors in deciding whether or not sounds become interpreted as omens. Most are reported as occurring in the evening stillness or at night, and a common motif is that only certain persons can hear them. The latter is sometimes explained by the fact that only certain people are sensitive to such things, but in some stories it is only those directly involved who experience them (*see* DEATH KNOCKS for an example). In some situations, however, others could join in:

Such sounds were heard at any time during night or day. Night, however, was the usual time when they were heard. They were heard first by one, and could not be heard by a second without taking hold of the one that first heard them. This was the case with all the sights and sounds that prognosticated death, and lasted for any length of time. Northeast Scotland Gregor (1881)

Pre-echoes of funeral sounds to come can also take various forms:

On another occasion she heard banging coming from the kitchen, so she went to investigate the noise. It appeared to come from two kitchen chairs, as she heard a bang on one chair, and then a bang on the other. The next day a neighbour came to borrow two chairs to lay a coffin on. Mull Bennett (1992)

The third category includes the Scottish 'dead-drap':

Another omen was the 'dead-drap'. Its sound resembled that of a continued drop of water falling slowly and regularly from a height, but it was leaden and hollow . . . Northeast Scotland Gregor (1874)

And the Welsh *Cyhiraeth*:

The Cyhiraeth was a doleful cry proceeding from the home of a sick person, and traversing the way leading to the place of interment. Sometimes it assumed a sad, wailing sound, heard at a distance. Occasionally it sounded like a smothered shriek, or a rushing noise resembling the whirring of birds' wings, or a flight of starlings. When heard on the seashore it foretokened wrecks. If the moaning passed up and down among the houses in a hamlet or village, it indicated epidemics. Wales Trevelyan (1909)

One further relevant category is suggested by the belief that major crimes, such as particularly horrid murders, could be announced by uncanny sounds. Gregor quotes an example from 1797:

Shortly before the deed was committed a sound was heard passing along the road the two men were seen to take in the direction of the place at which the murder was perpetrated. So loud and extraordinary was the sound that the people left their houses to see what it was that was passing. To the amazement of everyone nothing was to be seen, though it was moonlight, and moonlight so bright that it aroused attention. Aberdeenshire Gregor (1881)

See also DEATH KNOCKS; DEATHWATCH BEETLE; FURNITURE CREAKING; SECOND SIGHT.

Huntingdonshire [1880s] Marshall (1967) 246. Worcestershire *Folk-Lore* 28 (1917) 312. Buckinghamshire [1910] *Folk-Lore* 43 (1932) 105–6. England Addy (1895) 98. Cumberland *Folk-Lore* 20 (1909) 216. England/Scotland borders [1816] Henderson (1866) 83. Wales Howells (1831) 65; Trevelyan (1909) 284–5. Carmarthenshire Howells (1831) 57. Carnarvonshire/Denbighshire *Bye-Gones* (9 Mar. 1887) 265. Northeast Scotland Gregor (1874) 132–3; Gregor (1881) 203–6. Aberdeenshire Gregor (1881) 203. Mull Bennett (1992) 182. Co. Tyrone *Lore & Language* 1:7 (1972) 8. Co. Mayo *Folk-Lore* 29 (1918) 309–10. Co. Kerry *Folk-Lore* 19 (1908) 318. Literary *Connoisseur* 59 (1755) 351.

death sounds: cart

One of the regular death sound omens was the hearing of a cart which cannot be seen, especially if it seems to stop at your door:

I must not omit to mention, however, that a most terrific source of alarm still retains its influence over the superstitious in some parts of this county, in the visionary death-cart. Before the demise of any individual, this tremendous machine is heard to rattle along the streets like a whirlwind. Every heart beats with dismal apprehension at the ominous sound. The father of a family feels an involuntary shudder pervade his frame; children hide their faces in their mother's lap, who herself exhibits too many evident symptoms of alarm to afford any comfort to her terrified offspring; while the more experienced, with a significant shake of the head, exclaim, 'Ah poor —! he'll die before morning!' referring to some person whose indisposition is known; and each endeavours to avert the omen from himself by fixing the application on his neighbour; although he secretly fears, at the same time, that the affliction will assuredly fall on some devoted member of his own family. Lincolnshire *Gent. Mag.* (1832)

Lincolnshire *Gent. Mag.* (1832) 494; Peacock (1877) 83. Pembrokeshire *Folk-Lore* 39 (1928) 172. Dumfriesshire Shaw (1890) 10.

death: Sunday

Two related superstitions link death with Sundays. Many people had a horror of a grave being dug and left open over a Sunday, and most sextons would go to some lengths to avoid this happening. The details of the predicted result varied from place to place, but always involved inevitable further deaths:

Unlucky for a grave to be left open on a Sunday because in that case one of the same family will die within the year.   Devon N&Q (1909)

Almost everywhere in England it is considered dangerous to delay a funeral over the weekend and still more dangerous to leave a grave open over Sunday. Such a grave is said to yawn for a second corpse. A curious story was told to me some years ago about a funeral which took place in Devon in 1932. This funeral was arranged for a Monday, and the sexton insisted in digging the grave on the previous Saturday. The Senior Churchwarden of the parish tried to persuade him to wait till Monday morning, or at least to cover the open grave with planks and turf, but through obstinacy, the man refused, and the grave remained open throughout Sunday. On the funeral day my informant and the Churchwarden were waiting in the church for the procession to arrive, when the latter turned to say something to his companion and then, without warning, fell dead in the centre aisle. His death was apparently caused by some unsuspected heart-trouble, but many of the parishioners openly ascribed it to the grave left yawning on a Sunday.   Devon Folk-Lore (1955)

It does not take too great a stretch of the imagination to see how an open grave could be seen as 'yawning' for another body, although the choice of Sunday as the ominous day is less obvious. One would have thought that the holy nature of Sunday would have negated any evil implications in this context, as in a Welsh belief:

In Cardiganshire, it is believed that he who dies on Sunday is a godly man.
                               West Wales Davies (1911) 216

In a similarly widespread belief, it was simply the presence of a corpse in the house over Sunday which was feared:

If a body is lying dead in a village on a Sunday, there will be a death in the same parish almost immediately.   Wales Trevelyan (1909)

An unusual number of deaths occurred in a small Sussex village last year, the last of which

happened on a recent Saturday night. A villager thereupon presaged another death within the month, because the corpse would of necessity lie unburied 'over a Sunday', and she justified her prediction by referring to the last two deaths, the latter of which followed the earlier within a month, the earlier one also having 'lain over the Sunday'.   Sussex N&Q (1904)

Neither version seems particularly old, as they both first appear in the 1870s, and although they show a reasonably wide geographical spread, they seem to be restricted to England and Wales.

   See also CORPSE: UNBURIED ON SUNDAY; THREE DEATHS.

Grave open: Devon N&Q 10S:12 (1909) 66; *Devonshire Assoc.* 64 (1932) 165; [1932] *Folk-Lore* 66 (1955) 324–5; *Devonshire Assoc.* 68 (1936) 89; *Devonshire Assoc.* 104 (1972) 268. **Gloucestershire** *Glos. N&Q* 1 (1881) 43; Hartland (1895) 52. **Warwickshire** Langford (1875) 14. **East Anglia** Varden (1885) 117. **Suffolk** Chambers (1878) 52–3. **Nottinghamshire** [1965] Opie & Tatem, 181. **Corpse unburied:** Sussex N&Q 10S:1 (1904) 127. **Hampshire** *Folk-Lore* 61 (1950) 104; [1963] Opie & Tatem, 99. **Devon** *Devonshire Assoc.* 64 (1932) 165; *Devonshire Assoc.* 91 (1959) 202–3. **Berkshire** *Berks. Arch. Soc.* 1 (1889–91) 60, 86, 106; *Folk-Lore* 5 (1894) 337; Salmon (1902) 423. **Buckinghamshire** *Folk-Lore* 43 (1932) 106. **Oxfordshire** [1986] Opie & Tatem, 99. **Gloucestershire** *Trans. Bristol & Glos. Arch. Soc.* 53 (1931) 264. **Warwickshire** Bloom (c.1930) 42–3. **Cambridgeshire** Porter (1969) 23. **Suffolk** [1877] Gurdon (1893) 29; *Folk-Lore* 35 (1924) 349. **Lincolnshire** *Horncastle News* (9 June 1894); Rudkin (1936) 15. **Wales** Trevelyan (1909) 282.

deathwatch beetle

The sound of certain wood-burrowing insects of the *Anobiidae* family, such as the *Xestobium rufovillosum*, who make an audible clicking or ticking sound, has long been regarded as a warning of approaching death and has been reported from all over Britain and Ireland since the late seventeenth century.

Few ears have escaped the noise of the Dead-watch, that is, the little clicking sound heard often in many rooms, somewhat resembling that of a watch; and this is conceived to be of an evil omen or prediction of some person's death, wherein notwithstanding there is nothing of rational presage or just cause of terror unto melancholy and meticulous heads.
          Browne, *Pseudodoxia Epidemica* (1672)

The belief has indeed been so common as to have been proverbial from the time of its first known mention, and has remained remarkably consistent throughout its history. Writers often simply list the belief with other well-known omens, such as a howling DOG, without comment, as though further explanation were unnecessary:

there is no end to the stories or ravens or death-watches either; both are firmly believed in.

Essex *Monthly Packet* (1862)

As with other domestic insect noise omens such as those of CRICKETS, even the believers were usually aware of the natural basis of the sounds – they knew they were made by real insects. But the meaning was nevertheless supernatural, especially if heard in a house where sickness already reigned, or where the sound had not been noticed before. The earliest known reference is in John Wilkins's *An Essay Towards Real Character* (1668):

Sheathed winged insects . . . that of a long slender body, frequent about houses, making a noise like the minute of a watch . . . Death watch.

Several other pre-1700 writers mention it, and numerous eighteenth- and nineteenth-century authors do the same. Well-known literary references include Gay, Goldsmith, and Swift. The latter, in a satirical poem on William Wood written in 1725, prescribes a prosaic way to avoid the Deathwatch's prediction:

But a kettle of scalding hot water injected,
Infallibly cures the timber affected;
The omen is broke, the danger is over;
The maggot will dye, and the sick will recover.

Swift, *Wood, an Insect* (1735) (written 1725)

How the insects know about the approaching death is of course never explained, but in most cases it is assumed that the death will take place in the house in which the Deathwatch gives its timely warning. But two examples published in 1882 extend its power to distance-warning:

In the first example my friend said that he remembered quite well, when a little boy of about nine years of age, hearing one evening a strange ticking sound, for which there was no natural means of accounting. He exclaimed (though he cannot now recall how he first heard the word) 'There's the death tick!'. His playmates stopped their game and anxiously listened to the sound with him. His father, who was a hundred miles away, and whom he did not know to be ailing, died that evening.

Unlocated N&Q (1882)

The popular name is particularly evocative. Most writers comment on its derivation by analogy from the ticking of a watch, but the term also cleverly includes added connotations of the word 'watch' as in the custom of 'watching' over the recently dead, and inferences of the insect not simply predicting death, but 'bearing witness'. Other terms listed by the *English Dialect Dictionary* include *Death-Tick*, and *Death-Warner*.

Anyone who has heard the noise will testify to the eerie nature of the sound, late at night, in an otherwise quiet room, and even now it takes little imagination to construe a supernatural meaning, however fleeting the impression may be.

Compare DEATH SOUNDS.

Sussex Latham (1878) 57. **Devon** *Devonshire Assoc.* 18 (1886) 105. Hewett (1900) 21, 57. **Cornwall** N&Q 1S:12 (1855) 37. **Southern England** Jefferies (1879) 168. **Wiltshire** Smith (1874) 324; *Wilts. N&Q* 1 (1893–5) 152–3. **Essex** *Monthly Packet* 24 (1862) 434–7. **Oxfordshire** [1850s] Plowman (1919) 116; [1880s] Thompson (1943) 319–20; *Midland Garner* 1 (1884) 22; *Folk-Lore* 24 (1913) 88. **Warwickshire** Bloom (*c.*1930) 42. **Lincolnshire** Cole (1886) 30; Swaby (1891) 93. **Staffordshire** Poole (1875) 81. **Yorkshire** Nicholson (1890) 137. **Co. Durham** Brockie (1886) 144. **Wales** Trevelyan (1909) 281. **West Wales** Davies (1911) 213–14. **Western Scotland** Napier (1879) 56. **Glasgow** [*c.*1820] Napier (1864) 395. **Dumfriesshire** Corrie (1890/1) 42. **Co. Mayo** *Folk-Lore* 29 (1918) 309. **Unlocated** N&Q 6S:6 (1882) 385–6; Grose (1787) 51. **General** John Wilkins, *An Essay Towards Real Character* (1668) 2.5.2, 127; Browne, *Pseudodoxia Epidemica* (1672) Bk 2, Ch. 7; Bourne (1725); R. Baxter, *Worlds of Spirits* (1691) 203; *Athenian Mercury* (18 Jul 1691); *Gent. Mag.* (1796) 636. **Literary** John Gay, *The Shepherd's Week* (1714) Friday, lines 101–2; Swift, *Wood, an Insect* (1735) (Written 1725); *Connoisseur* 59 (1755) 351.

diaries

see CALENDARS.

dog-bites

Several of the principles which underlie folk cures can be seen clearly at work in traditional responses to dog-bites, rabies, and hydrophobia. Until the twentieth century, there was a very real fear of mad dogs and the harm they could do if they bit humans or other animals. The danger of such animals was drummed into children from an early age, and the cry of 'mad dog' in a village could cause real panic. Even if the dog which bit you was not rabid at the time of the assault, it was essential that it be killed immediately, in case it developed the disease at a later date:

[A footman has been bitten by a lady's dog] *The fellow, whether really alarmed for his life, or insti-gated by the desire of revenge, came in and bluntly demanded that the dog should be put to death; on the supposition, that if ever he should run mad hereafter, he, who had been bit by him, would be infected.*   Smollett, *Humphry Clinker* (1771)

This is an example of the principle of a SYMPA-THETIC connection set up between the dog and the victim. A traditional way of disposing of the dog was by drowning. If the dog were already infected, the principle of LIKE CURES LIKE was brought into play. The animal's liver or heart was taken out, cooked, and fed to the victim:

At an inquest held on the 5th inst. at Bradwell, Bucks., on the body of a child of five years of age, which had died of hydrophobia, evidence was given of a practice almost incredible in civilised England. Sarah Mackness stated that at the request of the mother of the deceased, she had fished the body of the dog by which the child had been bitten out of the river, and had extracted the liver, a slice of which she had frizzled before the fire, and had then given it to the child to be eaten with some bread. The dog had been drowned nine days before. The child ate the liver greedily, drank some tea after-wards, and died in spite of this strange specific.
Buckinghamshire *Pall Mall Gazette* (12 Oct. 1866)

Hair from the dog could also be plastered on the wound or fed to the patient, which is presum-ably the origin of the phrase 'the hair of the dog that bit you' still used today (*see* DOGS: HAIR). Parts of (healthy) dogs were widely used in other traditional cures.

A further option was a written CHARM:

To cure the biting of a mad dog, write these words in paper: Rebus Rubus Epitepscum, and give it to the party, or beast bit, to eat in bread &c. A gentleman of good quality, and a sober grave person, did affirm that this receipt never fails.
Unlocated Aubrey, *Remaines* (1686)

Write this on a piece of cheese, and give it to the dog:

> *Fuary, gary, nary*
> *Gary, nary, fuary*
> *Nary, fuary, gary.*
>   Herefordshire [1804] Leather

The medical use of stones was also widespread and of long history, and these were often recom-mended for dog-bites. Soft stones could be powdered and administered directly on the wound, taken internally, or rubbed on a wound to 'extract the poison' (*see also* ALABASTER). 'Mad-stones' such as these underwent something of a revival in the nineteenth century, and W. G. Black comments, 'we are accustomed to see occasionally

in the newspapers accounts of wonderful stones which cure hydrophobia' (*Folk Medicine* (1883) 144). They were much sought-after:

[The stone] came to my father's possession on the death of his uncle, Rev. David Bowen of Waunifor, about the year 1847. In those days and for many years afterwards, mad dogs were very 'fashionable', a summer never passing without one hearing of a great many people having been bitten, and, consequently, a great many people called at Gilfachwen for a dose of the Llaethfaen, and whether it had curative or preventive powers or not, none of the patients were ever known to be attacked with hydrophobia. People who been bitten would travel immense distances in order to get the stone.   Wales Davies (1911)

Herbal remedies were many and various, including application of tobacco leaves, and the following example from Ireland:

For the bite of a mad dog – Six ounces of rue, four ounces of garlic, two ounces of Venice treacle, and two ounces of pewter filings. Boil for two hours in a close vessel, in two quarts of ale, and give a spoonful fasting each morning till cure is effected. The liquor is to be strained before use.
Ireland Wilde (1888)

For all this battery of preventative methods and cures, should a person finally develop hydrophobia there was a widespread belief, especially in Ireland, that the disease was incur-able and so terrible for both the sufferer and his/her family that the only humane course of action was to kill the victim immediately. Smothering between two feather beds (ticks) was the traditional method recommended, and it was further believed that this was a perfectly lawful action in such circumstances. It is doubt-ful whether this was often carried out, if at all, but stories of it happening were widely dissem-inated and it has direct parallels in beliefs about other situations where mercy-killing was believed to be legal (*see* ANIMAL INFESTATION; EUTHANASIA). See Ballard (1986) for examples and discussion.

See also DOGS.

Sussex [*c*.1790] Allen (1995) 58–60; Latham (1878) 43. Devon *Exeter Gazette* (17 July 1879). Essex *Ralph Josselin's Diary* (19 Aug. 1655). Buckinghamshire *Pall Mall Gazette* (12 Oct. 1866). Herefordshire [1804] Leather (1912) 74. Lincolnshire Peacock (1877) 163. Yorkshire Henderson (1866) 127–8; Nicholson (1890) 135; Blakeborough (1898) 139. Lancashire Harland & Wilkinson (1873) 225. Co. Durham Henderson (1866) 127–8; Leighton (1910) 53. Wales Davies (1911) 287–9; *Folk-Lore* 30 (1919) 157. Welsh Gypsies Jarman (1991)

dogs

Dogs do not feature so widely in British superstitions as do CATS, although they certainly have a traditional 'uncanny' side. The one area in which they score over cats is that of supernatural beings – black dogs and other doglike bogies being common. Real dogs are believed to be sensitive to the supernatural. They can see ghosts and anticipate death, and their behaviour can be interpreted to predict future luck, good or bad. A dog howling was one of the most widespread death omens, but dogs had other methods of prediction:

Dogs scratching holes in the earth were looked upon by country folk as digging graves, and it was confidently expected that a death would surely follow in the locality. So great was the belief in this omen, that I have heard of persons who would follow a dog and fill up the holes it had made. Wiltshire *Wilts. N&Q* (1893–5)

They must never be allowed to jump over a dead body (*see* CATS AND DEATH). They also feature in cures, both as active and passive agents:

The Blackburn magistrates had a gruesome case before them the other day. A youth of the name of William Heaton was caught red-handed, as it were, decoying a valuable dog from its home for the purpose of killing it and rendering it down to fat. It appears that dog-grease, as it is called, has attained considerable local notoriety as a cure for rheumatism. As a result, the killing of canine waifs and their transformation into ointment has developed into a small industry Blackburn way. It transpired in evidence that Heaton's father had carried on the calling for years. This ointment, which is popularly supposed to have extraordinary curative powers, it was stated, is sold at 1s 6d per pound. Lancashire *Folk-Lore* (1903)

In other instances, dogs were cut open and the warm carcase applied to a sick person's body in the same way as PIGEONS and other animals.

See also DOG-BITES; DOGS: HOWLING; DOGS: HAIR; DOGS: LUCKY/UNLUCKY; DOGS: SALIVA CURES; WHOOPING COUGH.

Wiltshire *Wilts. N&Q* 1 (1893–5) 152. Lancashire *Folk-Lore* 14 (1903) 85–6.

185. Cardiganshire [1802] N&Q 11S:6 (1912) 234–5. Highland Scotland Macbain (1887/88) 258. Northeast Scotland Gregor (1881) 127. Banffshire Gregor (1874) 272. Ireland *Folk-Lore Jnl* 3 (1885) 282; Wilde (1888) 201–2, 207; Logan (1981) 11–12; Ballard (1986) 83–6. N. Ireland Foster (1951) 59. Unlocated Aubrey, *Remaines* (1686/1972) 260; N&Q 7S:8 (1889) 238. General Black (1883) 144–7. Literary Tobias Smollett, *Humphry Clinker* (1771) 111.

dogs: hair

Dog hairs were used in a number of folk cures, especially WHOOPING COUGH and for DOG-BITES. The latter is an example of the principle of LIKE CURES LIKE and is still very much alive in the phrase 'the hair of the dog that bit you' – meaning that the thing which caused the problem is the best cure or means of relief. In the popular mind this is firmly wedded to the idea that another drink is the best way to cure a hangover, but it has a much wider relevance and can be used metaphorically in many situations. The saying was already proverbial in the mid sixteenth century, being included in Heywood's *Proverbs* (1546) as 'A heare of the dog that bote us last night', where it already referred to a hangover.

London Opie & Tatem, 121. Lancashire Harland & Wilkinson (1873) 225. Literary John Heywood *Proverbs* (1546) Pt 1, Ch. 11; Swift (1738).

dogs: howling

The idea that a dog howling is an omen of death is so commonly reported that it has almost reached the status of cliché in folklore writing:

The mournful howling of a dog, termed in Welsh Udo, during the night, especially if close to the house of a sick person, was deemed a presage of death. The writer has many times heard it stated by those who knew the dog that an old dame living in Pen dre (top of the town) had an aged terrier, which seemed gifted with the faculty of foretelling death, as there was scarcely a person who died without 'old Pal's' dog having his howl in the street. Montgomeryshire *Hamer* (1877)

Many writers simply include the howling dog in their list of omens without further comment, but where details are included the most common are that the howling must occur at night and be directly outside a particular house for it to be taken seriously.

Dogs are said to sit down and howl before the door when any one is about to be sick, or die. A death is considered certain if the dog returns as often as driven away. Dogs are hence considered to be somehow acquainted with the spirit world . . . The life of a dog is sometimes said to be bound up with that of its master or mistress. When either dies, the other cannot live. The whining of a favourite dog is considered by many to betoken calamity to which it belongs.   Lancashire Harland & Wilkinson (1882)

The notion that dogs can sense supernatural beings, such as ghosts, which humans cannot has also long been a commonplace of popular belief, and the howling omen is most likely an extension of this belief. Certainly, anyone who has heard a dog howling in the night hardly needs to wonder at the origin of the belief.

For Shakespeare and other early writers, a howling dog was not necessarily a symbol of death but a certain omen of evil – along with owls, crows, and the like:

The owl shrieked at thy birth – an evil sign;
The night-crow cried, aboding luckless time;
Dogs howled, and hideous tempests shook down
*   trees;*
The raven rooked her on the chimney's pot;
And chattering pies in dismal discords sung.

Shakespeare, *3 Henry VI* (*c.*1592)

The earliest reference in English is found in the *Gospelles of Dystaves* (1507), but that describes the tradition of the Low Countries rather than Britain, and it is not till the seventeenth century that a clear example is found in this country: 'That dogs . . . by their howling portend death and calamities is plain by history and experience' (A. Ross, *Arcana Microcosmi* (1651) quoted in Opie & Tatem, 121). The belief was still being quoted in the later twentieth century.

Dorset Udal (1922) 181. Somerset [1912] Tongue (1965) 136. Devon *Devonshire Assoc.* 8 (1876) 57; *Devonshire Assoc.* 103 (1971) 268. Cornwall N&Q 1S:12 (1855) 37; Hunt (1865) 166; [1870s] Hughes (1934) Ch. 10; Couch (1871) 167. Wiltshire *Wilts. N&Q* 1 (1893–5) 9, 58. Berkshire Lowsley (1888) 22. London [1863] Cullwick (1984) 117. Essex [*c.*1939] *Folk-Lore* 64 (1953) 293. Oxfordshire [1850s] Plowman (1919) 116; *Folk-Lore* 24 (1913) 88. Herefordshire Leather (1912) 24. Worcestershire *Folk-Lore* 4 (1893) 258. Worcestershire/Shropshire *Gent. Mag.* (Oct. 1855) 386. Midland England *Midland Garner* 1 (1884) 23. Warwickshire Langford (1875) 16, 19. Northamptonshire N&Q 1S:3 (1851) 3–4. Cambridgeshire Porter (1969) 23, 53. East Anglia Forby (1830) 415; Varden (1885) 116–17. Suffolk [1863] Chambers (1878) 52–3; *Folk-Lore* 35 (1924) 350. Norfolk *Norfolk Archaeology* 2 (1849) 302–3; [*c.*1870] Haggard (1935) 17; *Norfolk Chronicle* (20 Dec. 1902). Lincolnshire *Gent. Mag.* (1833) 590–3; Thompson (1856) 735; Swaby (1891) 93. Shropshire Burne (1883) 211; *Folk-Lore* 49 (1938) 224. Staffordshire Poole (1875) 81; Hackwood (1924) 147. Derbyshire [1890s] Uttley (1946) 128–9. Northern England *Denham Tracts* 2 (1895) 55. Yorkshire [1823] Home (1915) 215; N&Q 4S:1 (1868) 193; Nicholson (1890) 42; Blakeborough (1898) 127.

Lancashire N&Q 1S:3 (1851) 516; Harland & Wilkinson (1882) 142. Cumberland Penfold (1907) 59. Co. Durham Brockie (1886) 127; Leighton (1910) 51. England/Scotland borders [*c.*1816] Henderson (1866) 32. Wales Howells (1831) 67; Trevelyan (1909) 283. West Wales Davies (1911) 213. Montgomeryshire Hamer (1877) 256. Pembrokeshire *Folk-Lore* 39 (1928) 173. Glamorgan Phillips (1925) 598. Scotland Laing (1885) 86; Maclean (1959) 198. Western Scotland Napier (1879) 56. Highland Scotland Macbain (1887/88) 254, 265; Polson (1926) 17. Northeast Scotland Gregor (1874) 134; Gregor (1881) 126. Aberdeenshire *Folk-Lore Jnl* 6 (1888) 263. Dumfriesshire Shaw (1890) 13; Corrie (1890/91) 42. Glasgow [*c.*1820] Napier (1864) 397. Aberdeenshire *Folk-Lore Jnl* 6 (1888) 263. Ireland N&Q 3S:5 (1864) 353. N. Ireland Foster (1951) 18. Co. Mayo *Folk-Lore* 29 (1918) 309. Isle of Man [*c.*1850] Cashen (1912) 6. Unlocated Grose (1787) 47. Hone *Year Book* (1832) 126–8; Igglesden (*c.*1932) 88. General Alexander Ross, *Arcana Microcosmi* (1651) 218–19; *Gent. Mag.* (1796) 636; *The Mirror* (10 Mar. 1832) 171. Literary Shakespeare, *3 Henry VI* (*c.*1592) 5:6; Addison, *Spectator* (8 Mar 1711); *Connoisseur* 59 (1755) 351; *Old Women's Sayings* (*c.*1835); Charles Dickens, *Martin Chuzzlewit* (1844) Ch. 19.

dogs: lucky/unlucky

The general behaviour of dogs was watched for signs of good or bad luck, but again it was not reported as frequently as the behaviour of cats. To be followed in the street by a strange dog, or for one to come into your house, was generally regarded as lucky:

They have also the following adage,
*   Ci dwad a chath du,*
*   Si yn cadw'r gofid maes o'r tu*

which being translated signifies, that a strange dog that comes to your house and stays voluntarily, and a black cat, will keep away all care and trouble from the house.   Wales Howells (1831)

Good fortune was predicted for one of my sisters, because a strange dog followed her when she was a babe in arms.

Lincolnshire *Grantham Jnl* (22 June 1878)

The first clear reference to this belief is in the *Connoisseur* of 1755, but Opie & Tatem quote a related belief from about 1700 that it is evidence of forthcoming ill-fortune if your own dog will not follow you.

Nevertheless, in certain circumstances, a dog's appearance was not welcome. A dog crossing the path of a funeral party, or coming between bride and groom during the wedding ceremony, is occasionally cited as very unlucky. According to Charles Igglesden, it is 'bad luck if a dog enters room in which cards are being played', but this is a typical example of his type of writing on superstitions – he does not say on whom the bad luck will fall, and in a game of cards the players cannot *all* be unlucky.

Lucky: Sussex Latham (1878) 8. Somerset [1923] Opie & Tatem, 121. Devon *Devonshire Assoc.* 57 (1926) 111. East Anglia N&Q 4S:11 (1873) 341. Lincolnshire *Grantham Jnl* (22 June 1878). Wales Howells (1831) 67. Western Scotland Napier (1879) 121. Ireland N&Q 4S:4 (1869) 212. Co. Wexford *Folk-Lore Record* 5 (1882) 83. Unlocated *Chambers's Jnl* (1873) 809. General *The Mirror* (10 Mar. 1832) 171. Literary *Connoisseur* 59 (1755) 353.
Unlucky: Unlocated Igglesden (*c.*1932) 190. Highland Scotland Macbain (1887/88) 254. Orkney N&Q 10S:12 (1909) 483–4. Dublin 4S:4 (1869) 505.

dogs: saliva cures

The belief that dog saliva has a curative effect on human wounds is known in many parts of the world and has been a standard part of British folk medicine for centuries:

The tongue of a dog is believed to possess curative properties, and I have seen people allow their dogs to lick their cuts 'to clean them'.
N. Ireland Foster (1951)

The belief has biblical sanction, as in Luke 16:21 where the dogs came and licked the sores of Lazarus. Allen (1995) claims that the healing power of dog saliva has now been proved as scientific fact.

Sussex Allen (1995) 58–60. England Addy (1895) 89. Northeast Scotland Gregor (1881) 127. Highland Scotland Macbain (1887/88) 258. Shetland Tudor (1883) 169. N. Ireland Foster (1951) 126. General Black (1883) 148–51.

donkeys: hair cures

Given the story that the donkey got its cross-shaped back markings for service to Jesus Christ (*see above*), it is not surprising that hairs from this cross were considered particularly beneficial in cures. Donkeys were particularly associated with WHOOPING COUGH:

When I had the whooping-cough in Cornwall sixty-four years ago my nurse cut a lock of hair from the cross on the back of a she-neddy, and I wore it around my neck in a little bag until I recovered.
Cornwall *Devonshire Assoc.* (1917)

The same procedure was also believed to be effective against child convulsions, to assist in TEETHING, and sometimes for bronchitis or measles. In a few instances the donkey's hair was actually fed to the sufferer, which reverses the more widespread whooping-cough cure of giving some of the patient's hair to a dog to eat:

Another family, some years back were in the same neighbourhood cured of the whooping-cough by a donkey's hair, which was dried on the baking iron of the open hearth, reduced to powder, and administered to them. There are very various ways of doing this, one is between thin slices of bread and butter.
Cornwall *Folk-Lore Jnl* (1887)

Both the wearing round the neck and the 'bread and butter' are very common motifs in such cures.

The donkey-hair cure was reasonably widespread in the nineteenth and earlier twentieth century, but was not as commonly reported as the procedure of passing the child over and under the animal's body (*see below*). The first recorded reference is in 1851, although as the basic belief in the donkey's cross is at least two hundred years older (*see above*), it is quite likely to have been in operation some time before that first date.

Sussex Latham (1878) 38. Cornwall *Folk-Lore Jnl* 5 (1887) 211; *Cassell's Saturday Jnl* (1893); *Devonshire Assoc.* 49 (1917) 75. Kent/Essex N&Q 6S:12 (1885) 205. Essex [*c.*1939] *Folk-Lore* 62 (1951) 259–60. Gloucestershire N&Q 5S:1 (1874) 204; Hartland (1895) 52. Herefordshire Leather (1912) 81, 83. Suffolk *Gent. Mag* (1867) 728–41. Norfolk Dew (1898) 77–81. Shropshire Burne (1883) 192, 203. Staffordshire Poole (1875) 83. Lincolnshire Swaby (1891) 91. Welsh Gypsies Jarman (1991) 186–8. Ireland N&Q 1S:6 (1852) 600. Unlocated N&Q 1S:7 (1853) 105; N&Q 6S:4 (1881) 357.

donkeys: passing under cures

One of the most widespread of the many cures for WHOOPING COUGH was to pass the suffering child under the belly of a donkey and over its back, a requisite number of times:

On Thursday, a travelling candyman and rug-gatherer, with a cart drawn by an ass, drew up in front of a row of houses known as Pirrat's Tow, a little off the highway at Maryhill, Glasgow. Two children living in this quarter are suffering from whooping cough. After a short conversation with the proprietor of the ass, the mothers of the two children took up a position one on each side of the animal. One woman then took one of the children and passed it below the ass's belly to the other woman, the child's face being towards the ground. The women on the other side caught hold of the child, and, giving it a gentle somersault, handed it back to the other woman over the ass, the child's face being turned towards the sky. The process having been repeated three times, the child was taken away to the house, and then the second child was similarly treated. While this was

going on two other children were brought to undergo the magical cure. In order that the operation might have its due effect, the ass must not be forgotten, and at the close of the ceremony each mother must carry her child to the head of the animal, and allow it to eat something, such as bread or biscuits, out of the child's lap. This proceeding having been performed in turn by the four mothers, the prescribed course was concluded. When it began there were not many people present, but before it was finished quite a crowd of spectators had gathered. From inquiries made yesterday morning, and again last night, it seems the mothers are thoroughly satisfied that their children are the better of the enchantment.
Glasgow *Edinburgh Evening News* (14 May 1887)

In some cases, added details are given – it must be a female donkey, a man and woman must do the passing, the donkey must be fed certain food while the ceremony is carried out, and so on. The number of times the child is passed also varies, with three and nine being the most common, but in none of the documented cases was an accompanying verbal CHARM reported. The majority of instances prescribe this cure for whooping cough, but a significant number also mention the same procedure as effective for other childhood ailments such as measles, rickets, thrush, consumption, and scarlet fever.

It is difficult to find an even remotely rational explanation for this procedure. Given the widespread belief in the blessed nature of the donkey,

donkeys

In common parlance, the donkey is characterized as stubborn, stupid, and totally unglamorous, but it features in a positive light in several superstitions and cures. At the root of this positive reputation is the fable which explains that the black markings on the donkey's back and shoulders form a cross, which first appeared after it bore Jesus Christ into Jerusalem (or, in some versions, the Holy Family on their way to the stable):

[Circus worker] *Anna said that the donkey was God's animal. She said her nan had taught her that. She said that it had a cross on its back.*
England [1990s] Stroud

One result of this cross is:

The devil can turn himself into every animal except a donkey which has a cross on its back.
Co. Tyrone *Lore & Language* (1972)

Donkeys are thus said to be generally lucky to have around, their shoes are sometimes said to be as efficacious as HORSESHOES in a protective context, and they figure in widespread cures for WHOOPING COUGH and other childhood diseases. The two most common cures are passing the patient over and under the donkey and utilizing hairs from the animal's back (for both *see below*), but a range of others have been reported less frequently. The sufferer can be cured, for example, simply by riding on the donkey's back, often facing backwards towards its tail, or by drinking ass's milk.

Cures for the hooping cough, still practised in the Midland counties. The one is that a boy thus afflicted should ride for a quarter of a mile upon a female donkey, a jackass being substituted when the patient is a girl. This remedy I know to have been tried in good faith at Great Burton, in Lincolnshire, only last year. Lincolnshire (1872)

The special place of the donkey in popular Christian tradition is also reflected in a few references which claim that donkeys kneel at Easter in the same way as cattle do at Christmas (*see:* ANIMALS KNEELING), and in others such as the following:

Innocents Day (28 Dec) . . . All donkeys have a day's holiday and an extra feed. This is particularly noticeable in the Clovelly district, but it is observed also in Cornwall and at Tavistock. It has reference to the Blessed Virgin Mary's flight into Egypt. Most Nonconformist owners still observe this custom, and believe that, if omitted, bad luck will follow. Devon *Devonshire Assoc.* (1935)

England [1990s] Stroud (1999) 25. Devon *Devonshire Assoc.* 57 (1926) 111; *Devonshire Assoc.* 67 (1935) 142. Cornwall *Folk-Lore Jnl* 5 (1887) 210. Worcestershire Dyer (1880) 153; Berkeley & Jenkins (1932) 37. Worcestershire/Shropshire *Gent. Mag.* (Oct. 1855) 385. Lincolnshire N&Q 4S:10 (1872) 24. Shropshire Burne (1883) 204–5, 209; Gaskell (1894) 266–7. Yorkshire Nicholson (1890) 134; Morris (1911) 238–9. Co. Durham Brockie (1886) 124–5. Mid-Wales Davies (1911) 229. Scotland Laing (1885) 87. Banffshire Gregor (1874) 270. Ireland *Gent. Mag.* (1865) 701; Wilde (1888) 207. N. Ireland Foster (1951) 130–1. Co. Wexford *Folk-Lore Record* 5 (1882) 83. Co. Longford *Béaloideas* 6 (1936) 262, 265. Co. Leitrim/Co. Cavan *Folk-Lore* 15 (1904) 338. Co. Tyrone *Lore & Language* 1:7 (1972) 12. General Browne, *Pseudodoxia Epidemica* (1646) Bk 6, Ch. 11; Grose (1787) 67.

and the cross on its back (*see above*), cures which involve riding the animal or using its hair make perfect sense within the normal terms of folk cures. Similarly, it has been suggested, not very convincingly, that the donkey's braying is sufficiently like a child in the throes of whooping cough to suggest a LIKE CURES LIKE connection. These factors may explain the connection between the disease and the animal, but why this is translated into passing the child over and under the animal remains a mystery. An alternative explanation is that this is a specialized example of other cures that involve passing the patient through or under other objects (*see* BRAMBLES; STONES, HOLED; ASH TREES). Unfortunately, the bramble cure for whooping cough is just as inexplicable, while the passing of children through a split tree is normally to cure rupture and includes the essential SYMPATHETIC element of binding the tree up afterwards.

Nevertheless, the belief was very widely known and acted upon, particularly in England and Ireland, but it cannot be shown to be very old. The two earliest references come hard on each other's heels in the 1820s, and reports then appear regularly until the mid twentieth century, when they disappear.

Sussex Latham (1878) 47. Devon [1847] N&Q 3S:1 (1862) 503; Hewett (1900) 79; *Devonshire Assoc.* 60 (1928) 124; *Devonshire Assoc.* 66 (1934) 83; *Devonshire Assoc.* 91 (1959) 199. Cornwall Hunt (1865) 218–19. *Folk-Lore Jnl* 5 (1887) 211. London N&Q 1S:12 (1855) 260. Suffolk Gurdon (1893) 20. Lancashire N&Q 1S:3 (1851) 516; Harland & Wilkinson (1873) 226; Harland & Wilkinson (1882) 75. Yorkshire N&Q 7S:4 (1887) 176; Nicholson (1890) 141; Blakeborough (1898) 137; Morris (1911) 247. Co. Durham Brockie (1886) 221; Leighton (1910) 53. Northumberland Bigge (1860–62) 89. Western Scotland Napier (1879) 95–6. Glasgow *Edinburgh Evening News* (14 May 1887), quoted N&Q 7S:4 (1887) 5. Ireland Wilde (1888) 197. Co. Down *Down Recorder* (16 Jan. 1897) quoted in *Ulster Folklife* 17 (1971) 94; *Down Recorder* (26 Sept. 1908) 3, quoted N&Q 10S:10 (1908) 326. Co. Leitrim Folk-Lore 5 (1894) 199. Co. Wexford N&Q 3S:1 (1862) 446–7. Co. Cork Folk-Lore 8 (1897) 179–80; [1937/8] Culloty (1993) 59. Co. Cavan/Co. Leitrim Logan (1963) 91–2. Co. Longford *Béaloideas* 6 (1936) 265. Belfast N&Q 8S:11 (1897) 206. Unlocated [c.1880s] Igglesden (c.1932) 175.

donkeys: with cattle

Many farmers in the nineteenth and twentieth centuries kept a GOAT to run with their cattle and horses, believing them to have a beneficial and calming effect. Some authorities mention donkeys in exactly the same way:

A donkey, or more rarely a goat, may often be seen in the fields with a herd of cattle. Various reasons are given for this; that it is lucky, that it prevents mischance among the cattle, that it keeps them contented, also that it insures fertility. Others declare that it is only because donkeys and goats eat some kind of herbage that is not good for the cows. Herefordshire Leather (1912)

This has all the hallmarks of an old custom, but the earliest reference dates only from 1799, and for goats is even later (1840s).

Wiltshire *Farmer's Weekly* (5 Oct. 1973) 117, quoted Opie & Tatem, 123. Berkshire/Worcestershire N&Q 11S:2 (1910) 534. Oxfordshire *Oxf. & Dist. FL Soc. Ann. Record* (1959) 7. Worcestershire N&Q 9S:5 (1900) 360; Archer (1972) 18. Herefordshire Leather (1912) 23. Yorkshire/Co. Durham Samuel Taylor Coleridge *Notebooks* [Nov. 1799] (ed. Coburn, 1957).

doors

A number of superstitions focus on doors – usually house doors, but sometimes of other buildings, such as churches. The most common of these is that it is unlucky to enter and leave a building by different doors (*see below*). Many others have been reported once or twice, particularly a concern that important events, such as WEDDING parties, new babies, and the first time you enter a new house, should always be by the front door. A selection of other miscellaneous beliefs follow:

Unlucky to depart from house and leave 'thruf-oppen deears' (doors open through the house), the back door must be closed before the front is. Yorkshire Nicholson (1890)

If several people are sitting in a room and the door opens of itself, the one who first closes it will be the first to die. Herefordshire Leather (1912)

An old lady from Ipplepen says – If the door-bell rings or the knocker is used at the same time as the clock strikes, there'll be anger in the house. Devon *Devonshire Assoc.* (1877)

Children were punished if they swung on a door. The explanation is that 'this blew up a gale for those at sea'. Cordelia Jones remembers that 'if stood by a door chatting, you must never idly swing it'. Yorkshire Gill (1993)

See also DEATH: DOORS OPEN; DEATH KNOCKS; FIRST FOOTING; HORSESHOES; HOUSES; KEYS; THUNDER AND LIGHTNING; WEDDINGS: DOORS.

Somerset [1923] Opie & Tatem, 124. **Devon** *Devonshire Assoc.* 9 (1877) 99. **Herefordshire** Leather (1912) 119. **Suffolk** Chambers 1 (1878) 322. **Shropshire** Burne (1883) 304. **Yorkshire** Nicholson (1890) 43; Gill (1993) 90. **Ireland** N&Q 7S:10 (1890) 126.

doors: enter and leave by same

One of the regular door beliefs cautioned against entering and leaving by different doors:

If anyone called at the house, mother always made them go out of the same door. You couldn't come in at the back door and leave at the front, that would bring bad luck. Lincolnshire [*c.*1930s] Sutton

This belief has not been found earlier than the mid nineteenth century, but it was still being said in the 1980s and it was almost certainly more widespread than the few references listed here indicate. A specialized version concerned the bride and groom on their wedding day (*see* WEDDINGS: DOORS).

Cornwall [1985] Opie & Tatem, 124. **Lincolnshire** [*c.*1930s] Sutton (1992) 140; Sutton (1992) 69. **Yorkshire** N&Q 1S:6 (1852) 311; [1961] Opie & Tatem, 124; Gill (1993) 90.

dragon's blood

see LOVE DIVINATION: DRAGON'S BLOOD.

drawing the pillow

see EUTHANASIA.

dream books

Dream books were publications designed to please those who believed that dreams were prophetic and who wished to interpret their hidden meanings. They were thus aimed at the lower rather than the educated classes, were written accordingly, and were sold cheaply by itinerant merchants in rural areas and in local shops and stalls in towns.

Dreams are reckoned as omens of great importance, but the current interpretations are of a very contradictory character. The saying that dreams always go by 'contrairies' is heard in company of stories of literal fulfilments; and the penny 'Dream-book' or 'Napoleon's Book of Fate' ... is yet a highly valued authority. East Anglia Varden (1885)

In addition to dream interpretations, many dream books included other fortune-telling material – how to read cards, tea leaves, moles, basic astrology, palmistry, and so on. They share many of the characteristics of other popular literature such as CHAPBOOKS and ALMANACS. They were cheaply printed in huge numbers, were usually anonymous (or pseudonymous), and the compilers shamelessly copied and stole from each other. Few were dated, and their bibliography is fraught with difficulty.

An excellent nineteenth-century example was the NORWOOD GYPSY, which appeared in several guises, but there were many others, with titles such as *Zadkiel's Dream Book*, *The Royal Dream Book and Fortune Teller*, *Imperial Dream Book*, *Raphael's Book of Dreams*, and *Everybody's Dream Book*.

Dream books were extremely popular, but it is unclear how lasting was their effect on traditional beliefs about dreams. The published folklore collections contain a range of traditional dream meanings but in nothing like the numbers which appear in the books and there is apparently little correlation between the two genres at the level of individual meanings. However, there is certainly scope for a major study of the genre. Their direct descendants, dictionaries of dreams, are still in print and still sell well.

Southern England Jefferies (1879) 109. **East Anglia** Varden (1885) 115. **General** Mackay (1852) 295.

dreams

The idea that dreams foretell the future, or report what is happening many miles away, is obviously not restricted to Britain and Ireland nor to the modern period. The subject is too broad, and examples too numerous, to do more than sketch a few lines of inquiry.

A recurrent theme in British sources is 'dreams go by contraries' so that to dream of a wedding, for example, signifies a death. This notion was already current in the classical era, as clearly stated in Apuleius' *Golden Ass* (*c.*AD 150), and was evident in many references in Britain since at least the fifteenth century (see Opie & Tatem, 126).

The Saxon manuscript of dream prognostications of *c.*1050 published by Cockayne (1866) provides a long list of meanings, including a number which appear to be based on the principle of opposites; but the latter are a minority, and the rest are either too obscure for classification or definitely based on obvious similarities rather than contrasts:

To see the dead betokens bliss. To kiss the dead beto-
kens a life to live . . . To weep in dreams betokens
bliss . . . To see blood drop from one's side betokens
harm . . . To suffer annoyance from a snake be-
tokens sight of an enemy.   Cockayne (1866)

The opposites theme was reiterated time and
again, but it is quite clear that it was not always
followed. Nearly all of the recorded 'prophetic
dreams', although couched in symbolic terms,
were interpreted literally, and the DREAM BOOKS
are full of meanings which are clearly not
governed by the rule of opposites. It is difficult
to avoid the conclusion reached by Hannah
More in her moralistic tale about Tawney Rachel,
a swindling fortune-teller:

Rachel was also a famous interpreter of dreams
. . . She had a cunning way of getting herself off
when any of her prophecies failed. When she
explained a dream according to the natural
appearance of things, and it did not come to pass,
then she would get out of that scrape by saying
that this sort of dreams went by contraries.
                                    More (c.1810)

There are many interpretations of specific items
and situations appearing in dreams, but only a
handful turn up often enough to be definitely
labelled 'traditional'. Dreaming that you lose your
teeth is one of those (see TEETH: DREAMING OF),
of CATS is another, and dreaming of fruit out of
season meant 'trouble without reason' (Cornwall
Folk-Lore Jnl (1887)). Another regularly reported
motif is dreaming of eggs:

It is believed to be very unlucky to dream of eggs,
especially spoiled eggs, and is thought to be a sign
of a death in the family of the dreamer. A short
time ago a Herefordshire lady sent her maid to
gather eggs before breakfast, remarking that she
had been dreaming that they had been forgotten
and were all spoiled. Later in the day she had
occasion to tell the same maid of the death of a
relative, news of which had come by the morn-
ing's post. 'Yes, ma'am', was the unexpected reply,
'cook was saying how it would be when she heard
of your dream about the eggs all spoiled'.
                           Herefordshire Leather (1912)

As already indicated, many prophetic dreams
that are reported in the literature are couched in
symbolism that is easily understood – at least
once the outcome is known. They are normally
told as simple tales and are all the more convincing for it:

Over fifty years have elapsed since Mrs. A.
received this symbolic intimation of trouble to
come, but it has always been a tradition in the

family. She dreamt she was walking with her two
little girls, K. and M., in a beautiful wood full of
violets which she could smell as well as see.
Suddenly two men sprang out from behind the
trees, snatched up M., and made off with her.
Mrs. A. ran after them and begged them to give
her back the child, and take K. instead; for she
felt that one of them had to be taken. They did
as she asked, and the dream ended. Neither of the
children was known to be unwell at the time, but
K. died that day week.   Isle of Man Gill (1963)

Various strategies existed to find out whether
a dream would come true or to make sure it
would if you wished it so. The most frequently
reported was that a Friday's dream told on a
Saturday morning was bound to come true (*see*
FRIDAYS: DREAMS) and a 'dream three times
repeated' was also assured (**Shropshire** Burne
(1883)). Similarly, 'The first part of any one's first
dream on the eve of All Hallows will certainly
come true' (**Derbyshire** N&Q (1871)), and
Speranza Wilde advised:

Never tell your dreams fasting, and always tell
them first to a woman called Mary.
                                    Ireland Wilde (1888)

Dream interpretations were available to all in
specialist publications termed 'Dream books'
(*see above*).

Sussex Latham (1878) 13–14, 58. **Dorset** [1888] Udal
(1922) 276. **Devon** *Devonshire Assoc.* 66 (1934) 78.
Cornwall Henderson (1866) 290–1; *Folk-Lore Jnl* 5
(1887) 214; *Old Cornwall* 2 (1931–6) 40. **Wiltshire** *Wilts.
N&Q* 1 (1893–5) 61. **Berkshire** Mitford (1830) 299.
Oxfordshire [pre-1900] *Folk-Lore* 24 (1913) 91.
Gloucestershire *Folk-Lore* 34 (1923) 157. **Herefordshire**
Leather (1912) 118, 257. **Warwickshire** Langford (1875)
19. **Huntingdonshire** [c.1920] Marshall (1967) 246. **East
Anglia** Varden (1885) 110, 115. **Suffolk** Glyde (1866) 175.
Norfolk Fulcher Collection (c.1895). **Lincolnshire**
Grantham Jnl (22 June 1878); Gutch & Peacock (1908)
165. **Shropshire** Burne (1883) 263–4. **England** Addy
(1895) 69, 93–102. **Derbyshire** N&Q 4S:8 (1871) 506.
Northern England Henderson (1866) 287–98. **Yorkshire**
Nicholson (1890) 44–5. **Lancashire** Halliwell (1849) 184;
Harland & Wilkinson (1882) 139–40; Harland &
Wilkinson (1873) 228. **Cumberland** Penfold (1907) 58.
Co. Durham *Folk-Lore* 20 (1909) 73. **England/Scotland
borders** [c.1816] Henderson (1866) 83. **Highland
Scotland** Macbain (1887/88) 259; Polson (1926) 19.
Western Scotland Napier (1879) 142. **Dumfriesshire**
Shaw (1890) 13. **Aberdeenshire** *Folk-Lore* 49 (1938) 91.
Orkney N&Q 10S:12 (1909) 483–4. **Ireland** Wilde (1888)
208. **Co.** Longford *Béaloideas* 6 (1936) 260–1. **Co.
Tyrone** *Lore & Language* 1:6 (1972) 6. **Jersey** *Folk-Lore*
25 (1914) 246. **Isle of Man** [1850] Cashen (1912) 28; Gill
(1963) 397. **Unlocated** Melton (1620); Hone, *Year Book*
(1832) 126–8; Henderson (1866) 288–90; N&Q 160
(1931) 8. **General** [c.1050] Cockayne 3 (1866) 199–215.

Aubrey, *Miscellanies* (1696/1857) 49–69; Timbs (1860) 65; Foli (1902) 108; Hoggart (1957) Ch. 2. **Literary** Oliver Goldsmith, *The Vicar of Wakefield* (1766) Ch. 10; Hannah More, *Tawney Rachel* (c.1810).

drinking glass ringing

An occasionally reported superstition which maintains that if a drinking glass is accidentally struck and 'rings', it must be stopped immediately or a sailor at sea will be drowned:

Have you ever noticed the effect upon a dinner-party should anyone hit a glass and make it ring? Nothing less than an interruption in conversation – a momentary silence – relieved only when the culprit placed a finger on the rim 'to save a sailor from drowning'.   Unlocated Igglesden (c.1932)

The superstition is not reported in any of the major nineteenth-century collections, and only enters the documentary record in 1909. There is no reason to suspect that it is much older than that, and nor has there been any plausible explanation to its meaning.

Kent [1923] Opie & Tatem, 173. **Somerset** *Folk-Lore* 21 (1910) 224. **Devon** *Devonshire Assoc.* 61 (1929) 128. **Unlocated** N&Q 10S:12 (1909) 310; Igglesden (c.1932) 26; N&Q 172 (1937) 334; [1970] Opie & Tatem, 173.

dropping things

A number of superstitions centre on the idea that it is unlucky to drop certain everyday items, and a regular motif is that it is particularly unfortunate to pick them up yourself, or to say thank-you to whoever does it for you. In the case of domestic cutlery, the incident signifies a visitor, and in other contexts a recurrent motif is to tread on the item before picking it up to avoid bad luck. *See* COMBS; GLOVES; KNIVES; PARCELS; SCISSORS; SOAP; UMBRELLAS/WALKING STICKS; WEDDINGS: RINGS. Dropping can also be compared to other accidental events such as SPILLING and items FALLING.

drowned bodies: locating

A number of traditional methods were recommended to help locate the bodies of drowned people. Details varied, but the two basic principles involved were floating some special item on the water in the belief that it would pause where the body lay and causing concussion with guns or drums. The most favoured substance for

floating was a loaf of bread, loaded with a quantity of quicksilver:

On January 24, 1872, a boy named Harris fell into the stream at Sherborne, Dorsetshire, near Darkhole Mill and was drowned. The body not having been found for some days, the following expedient was adopted to discover its where-abouts. On January 30 a four-pound loaf of best flour was procured, and a small piece cut out of the side of it, forming a cavity, into which a little quicksilver was poured. The piece was then replaced and tied firmly in its original position. The loaf thus prepared was then thrown into the river at the spot where the boy fell in, and was expected to float down the stream until it came to the place where the body had lodged, when it would begin to eddy round and round, thus indicating the sought-for spot. An eyewitness of this experiment from whom I received this account a few days after it happened, told me that no satisfactory result occurred on this occasion.   Dorset N&Q (1878)

The same bread procedure, but without the quicksilver, was recommended as early as 1581 in Thomas Hill's *Natural and Artificial Conclusions*, although he was probably quoting a European original. It remained widespread in Britain and was still being suggested by locals faced with drowning tragedies in the mid twentieth century.

Others recommended an apple, a bundle of straw, or a lighted candle, the latter with disastrous results:

A short time since, a little boy fell into the river Tamar, a few miles from Devonport, and was drowned. The watermen being unable to find the body, the mother was advised to stick a candle in a wooden bowl, and set it afloat, with a recommendatory prayer to St. Nicholas, and that the bowl would then stop over the corpse. This nonsensical experiment she put in practice, but the current drifted the candle against a boat-load of hay, which took fire, and the flames communicated to her house on the bank of the river, consuming it to ashes.   Devon *The Times* (25 Oct. 1826)

The use of guns or loud drums was reputed to 'burst the gall bladder' of the victim, which caused the body to float.

A few weeks ago, while an English merchantman was unloading off one of the Black sea ports – near Batoum, I think it was – a man was swept overboard by a heavy sea and drowned. The body disappeared; but two days afterwards certain Russian guns on shore happened to fire a salute. 'That'll bring him up!' said a seaman on board. 'Not yet,' said another, 'wait till the fourth day'.

On the fourth day the Russian guns fired again; and, during the firing, the drowned man's corpse rose to the surface, not far from the ship. 'I was one of them that saw him rise, and helped to haul him aboard,' said the sailor who told me all this, a trustworthy man. 'You see, sir,' he added, 'it's the gunfiring bursts the gall inside the corpse, and then it rises; but it must be on the fourth day'.

N&Q (1879)

This was also a widespread belief, although the detail of the 'fourth day' is unusual. It was more commonly believed that, left to its own devices, the body would rise after nine days – again because the gall bladder would have burst.

Other traditional beliefs about drowning included the idea that females floated face down, and males face up, as described by Pliny (*Natural History* (AD 77). This was current in Britain at least as early as the mid seventeenth century – Thomas Browne devoted much space to refuting it (*Pseudodoxia Epidemica* (1672)) – but it was still widely believed in the late Victorian era (N&Q (1868); N&Q (1870)).

Another 'vulgar error' on the theme maintained that if the body floated, it must have been dead before putting in the water because the body of an accidental drowning or suicide sank immediately. A piece in *Notes & Queries* reports a trial at Hertford Assizes in 1699 where this fact was the main evidence in a prosecution for murder (N&Q (1934)).

See also DEAD MAN'S HAND – sometimes stipulated as of a drowned man.

Bread: Dorset N&Q 5S:9 (1878) 111. Devon *Devonshire Assoc.* 39 (1907) 107. Wiltshire *The Times* (18 Apr. 1856) 12. Berkshire *Gent. Mag.* (1767) 189; N&Q 1S:4 (1851) 48–9; N&Q 5S:9 (1878) 478. Middlesex N&Q 7S:11 (1891) 345. Worcestershire N&Q 5S:6 (1876) 323. Lincolnshire Rudkin (1936) 21. Cheshire *Folk-Lore* 64 (1953) 429. Staffordshire [1972] Opie & Tatem, 34. England Addy (1895) 77. Lancashire N&Q 5S:9 (1878) 478. Yorkshire N&Q 1S:6 (1852) 311–12; N&Q 5S:9 (1878) 8; *Sheffield Daily Telegraph* (18 Aug. 1890). Co. Durham Henderson (1866) 43–4; Leighton (1910) 52. Scotland/Northern England N&Q 5S:9 (1878) 516. Ireland N&Q 7S:11 (1891) 345. General Thomas Hill, *Natural and Artificial Conclusions* (1581). **Other floating items:** Devon *The Times* (25 Oct. 1826) 2. Suffolk Chambers 1 (1878) 322; Varden (1885) 117. Ireland *Folk-Lore* 4 (1893) 357, 360. **Guns or drums:** England *Daily Telegraph* (10 Sept. 1878) quoted N&Q 5S:10 (1878) 276. Wiltshire *The Times* (18 Apr. 1856) 12. Norfolk *Suffolk Times & Mercury* (4 Nov. 1892). Lancashire N&Q 5S:9 (1878) 478. Northern England [1850s] *Denham Tracts* 2 (1895) 72. Co. Durham Henderson (1866) 43–4; Brockie (1886) 203. Scotland/Northern England N&Q 5S:9 (1878) 516. General N&Q 5S:11 (1879) 119. **Others:** Pliny, *Natural History* (AD 77) Bk 7, Ch. 17; Browne *Pseudodoxia Epidemica* (1672) Bk 4, Ch. 6; N&Q 4S:2 (1868) 9; N&Q 4S:5 (1870) 517; N&Q 167 (1934) 336–7; N&Q 167 (1934) 297.

drowning

Unbelievably callous as it may seem to modern ears, there was a widespread set of beliefs in coastal areas throughout the nineteenth century that it was extremely unwise to save a drowning person or even to pull a body from the water:

It is told how a man not only declined to put off his boat to rescue another drowning close inshore, but took the oars out so as to prevent it being used for this purpose; how three men stood and looked at their neighbour drowning before their eyes, and then turned around and walked homewards; how another pulled past a floating woman, and paid no heed. These things happened within forty years, and many other similar cases in every district of the country.

Shetland Laurenson (1879/80)

Three linked reasons were quoted for this refusal to act in aid of those in distress. In the first it was stated that the person you have saved will necessarily be your enemy and at a future date will harm or even kill you:

'Are ye mad?' said he, 'you that have lived sae lang in Zetland, to risk the saving of a drowning man? Wot ye know, if ye bring him to life again, he will be sure to do you some capital injury.'

Walter Scott, *The Pirate* (1822)

A second thread to the belief is that the sea will not be cheated, and if you save someone it will later take you instead. The third maintained that whoever pulled someone from the water was henceforth liable for their upkeep, or for their burial if already dead:

At a coroner's inquest recently held at Hebburn on the body of a man drowned in the Tyne, several witnesses who were questioned as to why they did not get the body out of the river when they found it, gave as their reason the strange belief that that if they had done so they would have been responsible for its burial.

Co. Durham N&Q (1934)

These notions reveal a deep strain of fatalism which seems endemic to many fishing and seafaring beliefs and traditions. Allied superstitions include those that maintain that our fate is mapped out before us, and certain signs distinguish those who are destined to be hanged or drowned:

[An old nurse] *believed also, that those destined to be drowned at sea came into the world with a slight indenture on the forehead which gradually filled up, until, when the allotted number of days had passed, it was indistinguishable.*

Caithness Rinder (1895)

The refusal to save a drowning person appears to have all the hallmarks of an ancient belief, but the earliest clear reference so far found dates only from the Walter Scott novel quoted above, although there is a slightly confusing passage in *Twelfth Night* which possibly refers to it. In the play, Antonio has saved Sebastian from the sea:

Antonio: *If you will not murder me for my love, let me be your servant.*
Sebastian: *If you will not undo what you have done, that is, kill him whom you have recovered – desire it not.*   Shakespeare, *Twelfth Night* (1601)

On the other hand, in coastal communities the ever-present threat of sudden death by drowning resulted in other, more understandable, beliefs:

Wishing the body home – When I was at Westward Ho in 1936–7 I was told of an Appledore custom that when a body was lost at sea relatives sat in the house with drawn blinds and 'wished the body home'. I am not certain how this was to be achieved. There is a point on the Northern Burrows where bodies are said to be thrown up; it is a matter of currents at sea. A visitor committed suicide when I was at Westward Ho and as I heard of it then I do know that the body was washed up at the point in question and I went with a relative to the mortuary to identify it. The first time it was actually someone else from Bideford, but the second, two days later, at the same spot was the expected body.

Devon *Devonshire Assoc.* (1963)

See also CAULS.

Devon Hewett (1900) 58; *Devonshire Assoc.* 95 (1963) 98. Wiltshire [1923] Opie & Tatem, 127. England Addy (1895) 97. Co. Durham N&Q 167 (1934) 276. Highland Scotland Campbell (1900) 231. Caithness Rinder (1895) 52–3, 58. Aberdeenshire *Folk-Lore Jnl* 3 (1885) 184. Shetland Laurenson (1879/80) 713–4. Western Ireland *Listener* (9 Oct. 1958) 554. N. Ireland Foster (1951) 54. Guernsey Igglesden (c.1932) 200. General N&Q 161 (1931) 164, 230, 337–8. Literary Shakespeare, *Twelfth Night* (1601) 2:1; Walter Scott, *The Pirate* (1822) Ch. 7.

dumb cake

One of the most widely reported of the complex LOVE DIVINATION ceremonies, designed to reveal the participants' future husbands. Details vary, but the key elements are that silence must be preserved throughout the operation, and that the ingredients and preparation must be a cooperative effort between those taking part.

The making of the dumb-cake, however, differs only in one particular throughout the riding. Some hold that those engaged in its preparation must stand on something upon which they have never stood before, no two persons standing on a similar thing, e.g. a box-lid, a newspaper, etc. Others altogether ignore this canon in the ritual. Therefore I must leave my fair readers to decide which formula they will adopt, in case they decide to make a dumb-cake for themselves. As to the actual preparation it must be begun after eleven o'clock p.m., on the eve of St. Agnes, and either three, five, or seven maidens may take part. In the making of a dumb-cake, each must take a handful of flour and lay it on a sheet of clean paper (this must be pretty large), bearing in mind that from the moment the first hand is dipped in the flour not a word must be uttered whilst the cake-makers remain in that room, or the spell will be broken. Having each laid a handful of flour on the sheet of paper, all add a small pinch of salt, water being also added, all taking part in working the same into dough, every one kneading and assisting in rolling the same into a thin cake sufficiently large for each to mark her initials in fairly large letters thereon. All must now lend a hand in lifting it on to a tin, and in carrying into the fire, in front of which it must be laid. Having seated themselves as far from the fire as possible, each will in turn rise, cross the room, and turn the cake round once – not over, as it must be left inscribed side uppermost. All this having been accomplished before twelve strikes, remain quietly seated; for, a few minutes after midnight, the husband of the maiden who is to be married first will appear and touch her initials, often leaving his fingermark on the same. So there can be no doubt about it.   Yorkshire Blakeborough (1898)

In other versions, the girls eat the cake, still in silence, retire to bed backwards, and dream of their husbands. The operation has always to be timed to finish at twelve midnight, but the prescribed night varies – Christmas Eve, ST AGNES'EVE, ST MARK'S EVE, and HALLOWE'EN are the most common – all of which are standard love-divination nights.

The earliest three references all occur in 1685–6, and the procedure is mentioned regularly from that time onwards, into the early twentieth century. All parts of the British Isles are represented, including the Isle of Man and the Channel Islands, except, on the present evidence, Ireland. Earlier versions tend to include nastier ingredients, such as soot and urine, presumably to test the girls' resolve, and explain why many of the recipes stipulate the thimble or eggshell as the unit of measurement required.

As is usual with this type of divination, there are risks involved:

Those that are to die unmarried neither see or hear anything; but they have terrible dreams, which are sure to be of new-made graves, winding-sheets, and church-yards, and of rings that will fit no finger, or which, if they do, crumble into dust as soon as put on.

Northamptonshire Sternberg (1851)

And there are other obstacles to success:

[From a woman between seventy and eighty] When I was a girl, I had no more sense than to make dumb-cake with the other lasses on Hallow-E'en. Three of us made it with a virgin-egg (that is, the first egg laid by a pullet), flour, and a little water – not more than a spoonful. We mixed the cake, and baked it on a shovel over the fire, without speaking; but just as the fire was lit, the shovel fell backwards with a clatter, and awakened master, who slept in the room above. Down he came to see what the noise below-stairs was, and we ran and hid in the dairy; so the spell was broken, and the cake was no good.

Lincolnshire [c.1830s] Folk-Lore

Oxfordshire Aubrey, *Remaines* (1686/1972) 207–8; *Folk-Lore* 24 (1913) 79. **Herefordshire** [1856] Leather (1912) 257; Leather (1912) 61–2. **Northamptonshire** [1825] Clare (1993) 138; Sternberg (1851) 187–8. **East Anglia** Forby (1830) 408; Varden (1885) 123. **Lincolnshire** [c.1830s] *Folk-Lore* 2 (1891) 512. **Yorkshire** Young (1817) 881; Henderson (1866) 70; Addy (1888) xxv; Blakeborough (1898) 73–5; Morris (1911) 230–2. **Northern England** Brockett (1829) 103. **Cumberland** *Folk-Lore* 40 (1929) 285. **Co. Durham** Henderson (1866) 70. **Wales?** Gomme Collection, Corres. Gertrude Hope (1 Mar. 1893). **South Wales** *Monthly Packet* 26 (1863) 676–83. **Highland Scotland** G. Sinclair, *Satan's Invisible World Discovered* (1685) 141. **Guernsey** MacCulloch MS (1864) 410–11. **Isle of Man** Moore (1891) 125. **Unlocated** Grose (1790) 55; [c.1830] N&Q 7S:9 (1890) 67. **Literary** *Mother Bunch's Closet Newly Broke Open* (1685); *Connoisseur* 56 (1755) 334.

Duncan, Helen (1897–1956)

Billed as 'the last witch in Britain', Helen Duncan was a spiritualist medium who was the last person to be charged under the WITCHCRAFT ACT OF 1736. Duncan had been a practising medium for many years, specializing in the materialization of ectoplasm at her séances, and had previously been denounced as a fraud and convicted as such in 1933. She was brought into the national spotlight in 1944 in a case which still excites passion in spiritualist quarters. Duncan was pursuing her profession in the key naval town of Portsmouth at a particularly sensitive point in the War, not long before the allied invasion of Europe. She had revealed in her séances certain 'secret' facts about losses at sea, which she always maintained proved her spiritualist powers beyond a doubt, whereas the police held the more prosaic view that she must have an illegal source of information and thus prosecuted her to remove her from the scene. The use of the 1736 Act was unusual, as other such cases would normally have been brought under section IV of the Vagrancy Act (1824); use of the older statute is taken by many as evidence that the authorities would stop at nothing to silence her. She was found guilty and sentenced to nine months in prison. She died in 1956, soon after another police raid on one of her meetings. The case quite naturally excited a great deal of interest, and for believers spiritualism itself had been put on trial. It has remained a major cause célèbre. Helen Duncan is viewed as a martyr to the cause, and efforts to obtain a posthumous pardon for her still continue. As with all good conspiracy theories, tales of secret service involvement, the sympathy of the Prime Minister Winston Churchill, and other secret goings-on, abound.

Helen Duncan's case was a major catalyst in the repeal of the 1736 Act and its replacement by the FRAUDULENT MEDIUMS ACT OF 1951, which remains in force today.

See Gaskill (2001 a, b) and numerous websites.

eagle-stone

The *Aetite*, or eagle-stone, was a naturally formed hollow stone with a loose nucleus, which thus moved and rattled when shaken. Its name reflects the belief that it could only be found in an eagle's nest, and it was firmly believed that the eagle-stone had a most powerful beneficial effect on human childbirth. Details of use varied, but typically it was bound to a woman's left arm during pregnancy to help prevent abortion, but when her time came it was tied on the thigh to promote a quick and easy birth.

Aetites, called the eagles stone, tied to the left arm or side; it brings this benefit to women with child, that they shall not be delivered before their time. Besides that, it brings love between the man and the wife. And if a woman have a painful travaile in the birth of her child, this stone tied to her thigh, brings an ease and light birth; but you must take it away quickly after the birth. Lupton (1579)

The eagle-stone was well known to classical writers, and numerous early European writers extolled its virtues. In Britain, it was widely known and believed in, at least from the sixteenth to the eighteenth centuries, and while most writers mention its efficacy, only a few cast any degree of doubt. Eagle-stones were much sought after, and anyone who possessed one was expected to lend or hire it out to any woman in need of it. They were often housed in a bag, with tapes or strings for easy attachment.

It is so useful that my wife can seldom keep it at home, and therefore she hath sewed the strings to the knitt purse in which the stone is, for the convenience of the trying it to the patient on occasion, and hath a box to put the purse and stone in.   Unlocated [1676] Jones

It is hardly surprising that this symbolically 'pregnant' stone would come to be regarded as useful in childbirth, but other traditions claim its efficacy for neutralizing poison and detecting theft.

Selected references only: **Worcestershire** [1643] *Gent. Mag.* (1855) 384–6. **Norfolk** N&Q 6S:3 (1881) 327. **Staffordshire** Hackwood (1924) 151. **Unlocated** [1676] Jones (1880) 388. **General** Lupton (1579) Bk 2, Para. 52; Browne *Pseudoxia Epidemica* (1669) Bk 2, Ch. 5, Para. 9. **Classical** Pliny, *Natural History* (AD 77) Bk 10, Para. 4.
Major treatments: Forbes (1966) 64–71; Barb (1950); Bromehead (1947).

earache/deafness

Various items are recommended to cure earache and deafness, but by far the most widely used was a hot onion:

For earache a small baked onion was inserted in the affected ear, although we cringed and protested, 'Not too hot, Mother, please'.
Worcestershire [c.1900] Knight

For Deafness – Three or four drops of onion-juice at lying down, and stop it with a little wool.
Wesley (1768)

Other substances placed in the ear were SNAIL juice (prick the snail first), warm HEDGEHOG fat, hot TOBACCO smoke, hot EEL oil, whisky, hot salt, and even a hot currant:

My mother's remedy for earache is to heat a currant by holding it on a hatpin in a candle flame, wrap it in muslin and put it in the ear.
Bedfordshire *Marsom* (1950)

Two sources describe the use of ASH sticks:

I had a sort of runny ear when I was a child . . . My father got a cure from an old travelling woman. He took a piece of ash stick and put one end in the fire; the stick had to be green, not dry or rotten. When the heat got at the stick, drops of water came out the other end, they weren't hot, they were freezing cold, little drops with bubbles in them. Three drops were put in my ear so many times a week, and it was completely cured.
Irish Travellers [1940s] Joyce

Similar description for Sussex, *c.*1900, in Arthur (1989).

Onions: **Sussex** [c.1900] Arthur (1989) 42; *Sussex Life* (Jan. 1973) 35. **Worcestershire** [c.1900] Knight (1960) 182. **Huntingdonshire** [1880s] Marshall (1967) 221. **Cambridgeshire** Porter (1969) 81. **Suffolk** *East Anglian Mag.* 13 (1953/4) 395. **Lincolnshire** Sutton (1992) 149. **Co. Cavan** Maloney (1972) 74. **Co. Wexford** Ó Muirithe & Nuttall (1999) 100. **Unlocated** N&Q 11S:11 (1915) 117. **General** Wesley (1768) 58.
Other cures: **Sussex** [c.1900] Arthur (1989) 42. **Oxfordshire** [1920s] Harris (1969) 114. **Gloucestershire** N&Q 4S:4 (1873) 500; *Glos. N&Q* 1 (1881) 43; Hartland (1895) 51. **Worcestershire** Berkeley & Jenkins (1932) 33, 36. **Bedfordshire** Marsom (1950) 183. **Norfolk** *Folk-Lore* 40 (1929) 119; [c.1920] Wigby (1976) 66. **Lincolnshire** Peacock (1877) 82; Gutch & Peacock (1908) 119. **Welsh Gypsies** Jarman (1991) 187. **Radnorshire** Francis Kilvert, *Diary* (18 Oct. 1870). **Scotland/England** N&Q 5S:9 (1878) 65. **Co. Longford** *Béaloideas* 6 (1936) 266. **Co. Cork** [1937] Culloty (1993) 61–2. **Irish Travellers** [1940s] Joyce (1985) 17.

earnest money

see GOD'S PENNY.

ears/cheeks: burning

An ITCHING or tingling sensation in certain parts of the body has long been held significant in various ways, but the feeling in the ear or cheek is by far the most widespread and oldest of these beliefs, and is the only one still heard on a regular basis. The basic meaning has remained remarkably constant for centuries, although certain details vary considerably:

Most people are familiar with the notion that when the right ear tingles some person is speaking well of one, but should the sensation be in the left ear then the opposite is the case.
Dumfriesshire Corrie (1890/91)

The designation of right for good and left for bad is generally agreed, but is far from universal, as a significant minority of authorities report the opposite, including John Melton in 1620. Others sidestep the issue by contrasting mundane with desirable, rather than good with bad:

[From a servant girl, about nineteen years old]
If your right ear burn, your mother is thinking of you; if your left ear, you are occupying your lover's thoughts.   Devon *Devonshire Assoc.* (1878)

Many versions continue – 'but left or right is good at night'. A number of small extensions to the belief have also been recorded, including ways to stop the slanderer. Pinching your ear, biting your finger, cutting a piece off your apron, or tying a knot in it, will all make the talker bite their tongue, or develop a stammer. In some cases, of course, one may not wish to stop the talk:

Right cheek, right cheek, why do you burn?
Cursed be she that doth me any harm
If she be a maid, let her be staid
If she be a widow, long let her moan
But if she be my own true love – burn, cheek, burn.

Warwickshire Langford *(1875)*

Chaucer is the first to mention the belief in Britain (*Troilus and Criseyde* (c.1374)), and it has been regularly recorded ever since in a wide variety of contexts in almost every quarter of the British Isles. It is still routinely expressed today, even if not meant literally, in such phrases as 'Your ears must have been burning last night' when reporting to someone that they had been talked about in their absence. The belief is of even older vintage, however, and it is one of the few where the examples from classical times are genuinely similar in meaning to the modern ones. Pliny, for example, wrote, circa AD 77, 'according to an accepted belief absent people can divine by the ringing in their ears that they are the object of talk' (*Natural History* Bk 28, Ch. 5).

A closely related belief, sometimes confused with this one, is that a ringing in the ear constitutes a death omen or, at least, presages news (*see* EARS: RINGING).

Hampshire N&Q 7S:10 (1890) 7. [1988] Opie & Tatem, 131. Dorset Udal (1922) 276. Somerset Poole (1877) 41–2; [1905/1960] Tongue (1965) 138. Devon *Devonshire Assoc.* 10 (1878) 105; *Devonshire Assoc.* 12 (1880) 111; Hewett (1900) 59. Cornwall N&Q 1S:12 (1855) 38; Hunt (1865) 237; Couch (1871) 169; *Folk-Lore Jnl* 5 (1887) 219. Wiltshire N&Q 7S:10 (1890) 137; *Wilts. N&Q* 1 (1893–5) 58–9. Berkshire Lowsley (1888) 23. Essex [1953] Opie & Tatem, 131. Buckinghamshire [1911] *Folk-Lore* 43 (1932) 109. Worcestershire/Shropshire *Gent. Mag.* (Oct. 1855) 385. Shropshire Burne (1883) 269–70. Warwickshire Langford (1875) 23. Suffolk *Folk-Lore* 35 (1924) 352.

Lincolnshire *Gent. Mag.* (1833) 590–3; Thompson (1856) 735. *Grantham Jnl* (22 June 1878); Swaby (1891) 93; Rudkin (1936) 19. Liverpool? N&Q 7S:10 (1890) 137. Staffordshire Poole (1875) 79; Hackwood (1924) 149. England Addy (1895) 95, 98, 101. Yorkshire N&Q 1S:6 (1852) 311–12; Nicholson (1890) 44. Lancashire N&Q 1S:3 (1851) 55; Harland & Wilkinson (1882) 153. Northern England [c.1850s] *Denham Tracts* 2 (1895) 36. Co. Durham Henderson (1866) 85; Brockie (1886) 211; Leighton (1910) 60. Northumberland *Folk-Lore* 36 (1925) 253. Bosanquet (1929) 81. Wales Trevelyan (1909) 325, 328. Western Scotland Napier (1879) 137. Dumfriesshire Shaw (1890) 12–13; Corrie (1890/91) 82–3. Aberdeenshire *Folk-Lore* 25 (1914) 350. Orkney N&Q 10S:12 (1909) 483–4. Ireland Wilde (1888) 206. Co. Meath/Co. Tipperary *Folk-Lore* 15 (1904) 461–2. Co. Tyrone *Lore & Language* 1:7 (1972) 11. Jersey *Folk-Lore* 25 (1914) 246. L'Amy (1927) 98. Literary Chaucer, *Troilus and Criseyde* (c.1374) Bk, 2 lines 1021–2; Swift (1738); *Connoisseur* 59 (1755) 354; *Illustrated London News* (27 Dec. 1851) 779. Unlocated Hone, *Year Book* (1832) 126–8. General Scot (1584) Bk 12, Ch. 16; Melton (1620) 45. Browne, *Pseudodoxia Epidemica* (1672) Bk 5, Ch. 22; Aubrey, *Remaines* (1686/1972) 221; Grose (1787) 59–60; Brand (1810) 101.

---

ears: ringing

A ringing in the ear can have more than one meaning. Since the eighteenth century at least it has been taken as a death omen, or at least a sign of bad news on the way:

'What a night of horrors!' murmured Joseph Poorgrass, waving his hands spasmodically, 'I've had the news-bell ringing in my left ear quite bad enough for a murder, and I've seen a magpie all alone!'   Hardy, *Far from the Madding Crowd* (1874)

A later interpretation, however, was more cheerful:

A short time since, a young lady, a parishioner of mine, said suddenly, in my hearing, to another lady present, 'Give me a number!'. The lady she addressed was talking at the time, and did not notice the request at once; she was almost immediately told it was too late. The young lady then gave us the following explanation. She had a 'singing' in her ears; when this occurs to one, one should at once ask for a number, and at once get it, one should then count the letters of the alphabet till one comes to the number given; the corresponding letter will be the initial letter of the name of the person one is destined to marry.
Oxfordshire N&Q 3S:8 (1865)

The ominous meaning is first reported by Defoe in the early eighteenth century and was still being quoted, in milder form, in the mid twentieth. The divinatory number procedure is only known from 1865 onwards, but was still current when Opie and Tatem were carrying out their research in the 1980s.

A third interpretation, apparently reported only from Ireland, gives a religious slant:

A singing in your ear is a sign that there is a soul in Purgatory calling for a prayer.

Co. Wexford [1938] Ó Muirithe & Nuttall

Wiltshire *Wilts. N&Q* 1 (1893–5) 58–9. Surrey [1959] Opie & Tatem, 130. Middlesex [1984] Opie & Tatem, 130. Oxfordshire N&Q 3S:8 (1865) 494. Wales Trevelyan (1909) 325. West Wales Davies (1911) 214, 218. Western Scotland Napier (1879) 57. Mull Bennett (1992) 182. Co. Wexford [1938] Ó Muirithe & Nuttall (1999) 162. Co. Longford *Béaloideas* 6 (1936) 260. Literary Thomas Hardy, *Far from the Madding Crowd* (1874) Ch. 8.

Easter

In addition to the widespread Easter traditions of the sun dancing (*see below*), and the need to wear new clothes (*see* CLOTHES, NEW: EASTER), a few other stray beliefs can be noticed:

In former times people had such respect for this day that many kept their children unbaptised till Easter Sunday, and many old men and old women went to church to receive the Communion who were hardly to be seen in the Lord's House on any other Sunday during the year.

Mid-Wales Davies (1911)

Unless you have duck for dinner on Easter-day, you'll never pay your debts.

Devon *Devonshire Assoc.* (1878)

Most of the beliefs about the donkey in this country are traceable to Christian origins, the belief that donkeys kneel at the moment of sunrise on Easter morning, for instance, that they bray three times at sunrise on Good Friday. [see also ANIMALS KNEELING]   N. Ireland Foster (1951)

If anyone looks into St. Austin's Well the first thing on Easter morning he will see the faces of those who will die within the year. [compare PORCH WATCHING]   Dorset *Folk-Lore* 10 (1899)

See also GOOD FRIDAY; CLOTHES.

Dorset *Folk-Lore* 10 (1899) 480. Devon *Devonshire Assoc.* 10 (1878) 107. Mid-Wales Davies (1911) 74. N. Ireland Foster (1951) 130–1.

Easter: sun dances

The most widespread Easter belief was that the when the sun rises on Easter Sunday, it dances 'for joy':

On Easter Sunday, people at Castleton, Derbyshire, used to climb the hill on which the castle is built, at six o'clock in the morning, to see the sun rise. On this day the sun is said to dance for joy at his rising. On the Wednesday before Easter Sunday a Derbyshire man said, 'I think the sun will hardly be able to contain himself till Sunday'. In Derbyshire they say that the sun spins round when he sets on Easter Sunday, and people go out to see this spinning.   Derbyshire Addy (1895)

There are some major variations. In some reports, participants put out buckets of water or gathered at strategic bodies of water to see the sun dance's reflection – which is, of course, likely to enhance the chance of success. In others it is the Lamb of God which they hope to see within the sun.

To this pool the people used to come on Easter morning to see the sun dance and play in the water and the angels who were at the Resurrection playing backwards and forwards before the sun.

Radnorshire Francis Kilvert, *Diary* (14 Oct. 1870)

In answer to those who say they cannot see the performance, believers have two replies – either the watcher lacks faith, which is the standard reply to all doubters of supernatural phenomena the world over, or that the Devil always attempts to obscure the wondrous sight.

The notion was clearly already well known in the mid seventeenth century, as Sir John Suckling used the image in his description of a girl dancing at a wedding:

*But oh! She dances such a way –
No sun upon an Easter day
Were half so fine a sight*

Suckling, *Ballade Upon a Wedding* (1646)

But even in that century, there were those who doubted the literal truth of the phenomenon. Thus, Sir Thomas Browne:

We shall not, I hope, disparage the Resurrection of our Redeemer, if we say the sun doth not dance on Easter day.

Browne, *Pseudodoxia Epidemica* (1672)

Similarly, the *Athenian Mercury* of 16 May 1691 calls it an 'old, weak, superstitious error'. Nevertheless, it was still being said well into the twentieth century.

Sussex Parish (1875) 'Holy-Sunday'. Somerset *Folk-Lore* 5 (1894) 339; [1910] Tongue (1965) 140. Devon N&Q 3S:5 (1864) 394; Henderson (1866) 63–4; *Devonshire Assoc.* 8 (1876) 57–8. Cornwall Couch (1871) 153;

Western Antiquary 3 (1883) 91. **Lincolnshire** Watkins (1886) 11. **Shropshire** Burne (1883) 335; *Folk-Lore* 49 (1938) 233. **Derbyshire** Addy (1895) 55. **Northern England** Brockett (1829) 296; Henderson (1866) 81. **Yorkshire** *Monthly Packet* 25 (1863) 549–51; Morris (1911) 224. **Northumberland** Bigge (1860–62) 92. **Mid-Wales** Davies (1911) 74. **Radnorshire** Francis Kilvert, *Diary* (17 Apr. 1870; 14 Oct. 1870). **Ireland** Hone, *Every-Day Book* 1 (1827) 211; *Gent. Mag.* (1865) 703; N&Q 156 (1929) 116; Danaher (1972) 74–5. **Co. Laoighis** *Béaloideas* 9 (1939) 31. **Co. Wexford** Kennedy (1867) 195; [1939] Ó Muirithe & Nuttall (1999) 167. **Isle of Man** Moore (1891) 109. **General** Browne, *Pseudodoxia Epidemica* (1672) Bk 5, Ch. 22; *Athenian Mercury* (16 May 1691); Bourne (1725) 188. **Literary** John Suckling, *Ballade Upon a Wedding* (1646).

---

eclipses

Natural phenomena such as COMETS, SHOOTING STARS, and major STORMS have each had traditions and beliefs attached to them, usually of an ominous kind. Nothing particular is reported of eclipses, but a general feeling of fear and doom was widespread:

An eclipse of the sun was looked on as an omen of coming calamity. In 1597, during an eclipse of the sun, it was stated by Calderwood that men and women thought the day of judgment was come. Many women swooned, the street of Edinburgh was full of crying, and in fear some ran to the kirk to pray. I remember an eclipse about 1818, when about three parts of the sun was covered. The alarm in the village was very great, indoor work was suspended for the time, and in several families prayers were offered for protection, believing that it portended some awful calamity; but when it passed off there was a general feeling of relief

           Western Scotland Napier (1879)

Devon Hewett (1900) 56. **Essex** [*c.*1920] Ketteridge & Mays (1972). **Northumberland** Jnl of John Aston, (22 May 1639), in *Six North Country Diaries* (1910) 12. **Western Scotland** Napier (1879) 141.

---

eels

Eels feature in several beliefs, the most widespread being that they are generated spontaneously from horse hairs in water (*see* HORSE HAIRS: ANIMATED) and in cures for cramp and warts (*see* CRAMP/RHEUMATISM CURES: GARTERS; WART CURES: EELS). They were also recommended for deafness and EARACHE:

Old James Jones was breaking stones below Pentwyn. He told me how he had once cured his deafness for a time by pouring hot eel oil into his

ear, and again by sticking into his ear an 'ellern' (elder) twig, and wearing it there night and day.

           Radnorshire Kilvert, *Diary* (18 Oct 1870)

Many communities disliked and distrusted eels, and certainly would not eat them:

Eels are detested, on account of their resemblance to serpents, and many people decline to eat them. If the following be said to an eel, it will make itself into a knot:

    Eelie, eelie cast your knot
    And you'll get into a water yet.

      Northern England *Newcastle Weekly Chronicle*
                (11 Feb. 1899)

The same rhyme was also recorded in Cornwall (*Old Cornwall* 1:8 (Oct 1928) 39). Another popular misconception about eels was that they formed themselves into massive knots that could only be untied by thunder, often mentioned by seventeenth-century writers, including Shakespeare:

I warrant you mistress, thunder shall not so awake the beds of eels.   Shakespeare, *Pericles* (1608)

Eels and thunder: Literary Shakespeare, *Pericles* (1608) Sc. 16;S.S., *The Honest Lawyer* (1616); T. Adams, *Works* (1629) 346.
Eels inedible: English Gypsies N&Q 1S:3 (1851) 221. **Northern England** *Newcastle Weekly Chronicle* (11 Feb: 1899) 7. **Orkney** [1774] Low (1879) 58.
Eels and deafness: Radnorshire Francis Kilvert, *Diary* (18 Oct. 1870). **Scotland/England** N&Q 5S:9 (1878) 65.

---

effigies

The idea that someone can be harmed by an ill-wisher mistreating an image made in his/her likeness has a long history, and is found in most human cultures. This 'image magic' is widely reported in Britain and Ireland, and although there are variations on the basic theme, the degree of similarity is remarkable considering its longevity and wide distribution.

The key variables of the custom can be categorized as follows: (1) the materials used; (2) fashioning the image; (3) the inclusion of something of the victim or christening it with the victim's name; (4) mistreating it – usually with pins or nails, but also twisting or malforming – to cause illness or discomfort; (5) accompanying rituals or words; (6) destroying the effigy – burning, melting, dissolving, burying, rotting.

The two most common materials were wax and clay, probably because the operator had the choice to destroy them quickly or slowly, as required:

The belief in 'casting ill' on one was prevalent. This power of casting ill was not in the possession of all; yet few districts of the country were without one or more who were dreaded as possessing it. To such no one would be foolhardy enough to have denied a request, however much it would have cost to grant it. There were two modes of working ill on a person. In the one mode a small figure in human shape was made of wax and placed near the fire in such a position as to melt very slowly. As the figure melted the person represented by it wasted away by lingering disease. In the other the figure was made of clay, stuck full of pins and placed on the hearth among the hot ashes. As the figure dried up and crumbled into powder slow diseases burned away the life of the hapless victim. Banffshire Gregor (1874)

Other materials could be used, to the same effect:

Burying the sheaf: *The person working the charm first goes to the chapel and says certain prayers with his back to the altar; then he takes a sheaf of wheat, which he fashions like the human body, sticking pins in the joints and the stems and (according to one account) shaping a heart of plaited straw. This sheaf he buries in the name of the devil near the house of his enemy, who he believes will gradually pine away as the sheaf decays, dying when it finally decomposes. If the operator of the charm wishes his enemy to die rapidly he buries the sheaf in wet ground where it will soon decay; but if, on the other hand, he desires his victim to linger in pain he chooses a dry spot where decomposition will be slow. In the case alluded to above it is said that the woman who worked the charm was discovered by the relatives of her victim, who was ill, coming by night to pour water on the sheaf to hasten its decay.* Co. Louth *Folk-Lore* (1895)

There are records of the use of such effigies for malevolent purposes in Britain from the tenth century onwards, and numerous condemnations in early laws and penitentials (see Kittredge (1929)). Early examples were usually documented because they were aimed at harming the sovereign or others of the ruling classes and were thus treated as high treason. There is no doubt that kings and queens until the seventeenth century took such matters very seriously. One of the key ways to link the image and the victim was to enact some sort of ceremony naming the effigy after its human counterpart. A significant feature in several of the early cases was that the perpetrator managed to find a corrupt priest to christen the image, and this added considerably to its power.

The scholarly word for the process is 'invultuation' or 'invultation' (for discussion of use and derivation, see *Notes & Queries* 8S: 11 (1897) 107, 236, 314, 395). It is more commonly called 'image magic', or, in Scotland, the *corp criadhach* (various spellings, but meaning 'body of clay').

Vultivoli *are they who, for the purpose of working upon the feelings of men, fashion in a somewhat soft substance (as wax or clay) images of those whose natures they are striving to distort.*
John of Salisbury, *Policraticus* (1159/1938) 41–2.

The same procedures could be carried out with a live FROG or TOAD replacing the man-made image:

When my Aunt Silvina ran off with another man, Will Solomon, her husband went off to a cunning man. He told Bob to buy a pennyworth of new pins, then to find a toad and stick all the pins in its back and belly, till it looked like a hedgehog. Next he was to go and dig a hole at the foot of a grave where one of Will Solomon's kinsfolk was buried, and there at midnight he was to bury the cup with the toad covered up in it by a piece of slate. The wise man told him, too, to go in five weeks' time and dig up toad and cup, and if he didn't do that he was safe to go mad himself; but if it was all done right, Will Solomon would go off his head. So poor silly Bob did everything the wise man bade him, except that he made a mistake in not finding the right grave, neither did he go there to raise the cup at twelve o'clock, as the man had told him. Which was the cause of my cousin going off his head, and died so at Caernarvon.
Welsh/English Gypsies Groome (1880)

Another variation on the same theme was to use a photograph:

This tale [of using photograph of ill-wisher] *seems to be a modern version of the ancient method of making a wax image of one's enemy, and then melting it before a fire. Psalm 68, verse 2, probably refers to the same practice:*
Cornwall *Old Cornwall* (1931)

The words which the ill-wishers used to accompany their image-work are not usually recorded, but the Psalm mentioned above certainly seems ideal for the job:

As smoke is driven away, so drive them away; as wax melteth before the fire, so let the wicked perish in the presence of God. Psalms 68:2

Images could also be made for purposes other than direct harm, including the promotion of love, or at least infatuation. At village level, local witches and cunning men and women were always available to help to persuade a reluctant lover, but again the best-documented cases are those involving the rich and famous. Indeed, it seems that whenever anyone powerful wished to disentangle themselves from a previous marriage or liaison, they could claim that they had been bewitched:

The infatuation of Edward III for Alice Perrers . . . was of course ascribed to occult arts . . . Alice, it seems, had in her service a friar who professed to be a physician but was in fact a sorcerer. He made figures of wax, representing king Edward and Alice, and, operating with these and using powerful herbs and charms, he had brought the king completely under her control.

England Kittredge (1929)

England Kittredge (1929) 105. **Hampshire** Groome (1880) 13. **Devon** Baring-Gould (1900) 186; Duncan (1953) 121–2. **Cornwall** *Old Cornwall* 2:1 (1931) 21. Derbyshire Addy (1895) 79; N&Q 10S:2 (1904) 205–6. **Yorkshire** [1951] Opie & Tatem, 208. **Highland Scotland** N&Q 5S:7 (1877) 163. **Banffshire** Gregor (1874) 266–7. **Dumfriesshire** Cromek (1810) 282. **Glasgow** *Folk-Lore Jnl* 2 (1884) 219–20. **Ross-shire** [1890s] MacDonald (1936) 63. **Welsh/English Gypsies** Groome (1880) 14–15. **Co. Louth** *Folk-Lore* 6 (1895) 302. **General** John of Salisbury, *Policraticus* (1159/1938) 41–2; *Malleus Maleficarum* (1486) 135; Scot (1584) Bk 12, Ch. 16; James I *Daemonologie* (1597) 44. Aubrey, *Remaines* (1686/1880) 61; N&Q 8S:11 (1897) 107; **General** N&Q 10S:2 (1904) 272. **Literary** James Hogg, *Mountain Bard* (1807); Thomas Hardy, *The Return of the Native* (1878) Bk 5, Ch. 7; Thomas Hardy, *The Mayor of Casterbridge* (1886) Ch.27.
Major studies: Kittredge (1929) 73–103; Robbins (1959) 530–3.

eggs: after sunset

A minor egg superstition prohibited taking eggs into, or out of, the house after sunset:

A farmer's wife, in Rutland, was promised a 'setting' of ducks' eggs by the wife of another farmer, who sent the eggs at nine o'clock in the evening. 'I cannot imagine how she could have been so foolish,' said the first-named, when she mentioned the matter to me on the following day. I inquired as to the foolishness and was told that ducks' eggs brought into a house after sunset would do no good, and would never be hatched.

Rutland N&Q (1876)

In other versions, the bad luck fell on the occupants of the house, and even egg-sellers refused to trade after dark. No explanation, rational or otherwise, is offered in any recorded versions. The earliest known reference is from 1853, but Opie and Tatem show that it was still being said

in the 1980s. Apart from one reference from Scotland, all the rest come from a relatively restricted area of England.

Wiltshire Wiltshire (1975) 105. **Lincolnshire** N&Q 1S:8 (1853) 382; Watkins (1886) 12. **Rutland** N&Q 5S:6 (1876) 24. **England** Addy (1895) 55. **Nottinghamshire** N&Q 1S:7 (1853) 7–8. **Yorkshire** N&Q 4S:4 (1869) 131; Jeffrey (1923) 138; [1983] Opie & Tatem, 134. **Scotland** *People's Friend* (8 Nov. 1882) 712. **Unlocated** Igglesden (*c.*1932) 83.

eggs: Good Friday

see GOOD FRIDAY: EGGS.

eggs: love divination

see LOVE DIVINATION: EGGS.

eggs: setting an odd number

'Why does every old woman hold it as an indispensable rule to set her hen upon an odd number of eggs?' asked a correspondent to the *Gentleman's Magazine* in 1796. Unfortunately, no one wrote in to explain why, but he was correct in his assessment, and the custom was widely reported throughout the nineteenth and twentieth centuries:

It's a strange queer thing, but an even number o' eggs (12 instead of 11 or 13) never hatches nowt but stags (cockerels).

Lincolnshire Rudkin (1936)

When placing a sitting of eggs under a hen, 13 is a lucky number. If you have not got this quantity of eggs you must place an odd number to have any success with the hatching.

Guernsey De Garis (1975)

The idea that odd NUMBERS are lucky and even ones unlucky is a general rule in British superstitions, but many informants agreed that THIRTEEN was the best number for eggs, and this is contrary to the general rule which holds this the unluckiest number of all. It is noticeable, however, that the earlier references all simply recommend an odd number, and it is only from the 1880s onwards – the same time as thirteen was beginning to be generally quoted as unlucky – that thirteen is singled out as desirable.

The earliest British reference is provided by Aubrey (1686), who states, commenting on classical sources, 'And our house-wives, in setting of their egges under the hen, do lay an odd number'; Aubrey also quotes Pliny, who devoted many pages to the lore and care of poultry, saying, 'An odd number should be put under the hen' (*Natural History* (AD 77)).

Somerset Tongue (1965) 145. Herefordshire Leather (1912) 26. Warwickshire *Folk-Lore* 26 (1915) 97. Northamptonshire N&Q 1S:2 (1850) 164. Cambridgeshire Porter (1969) 37. East Anglia Varden (1885) 114. Lincolnshire Swaby (1891) 92; Rudkin (1936) 21. Shropshire Burne (1883) 262–3. England Addy (1895) 66. Lancashire *Lancashire Lore* (1971) 51. Co. Durham Brockie (1886) 210; Leighton (1910) 62. Montgomeryshire *Bye-Gones* (22 Sept. 1886) 122. Highland Scotland Macbain (1887/88) 262. N. Ireland Foster (1951) 131. Guernsey De Garis (1975) 137. Jersey *Folk-Lore* 25 (1914) 247. General Aubrey *Remaines* (1686/1880) 194; Grose (1787) 68; *Gent. Mag.* (1796) 636; N&Q 192 (1947) 193. Classical Pliny, *Natural History* (AD 77) B1 10, Ch.75.

eggshells: burning

The theory of a SYMPATHETIC connection between objects which were once connected but have now been separated is demonstrated by a number of domestic beliefs. If you burn milk, for example, your cows will cease to produce, and on the same principle, if you burn eggshells your hens will stop laying:

Well two years ago I had four hens laying at Christmas time – when eggs are worth having. And two gentlemen who were snipe shooting came in for breakfast. I boiled four eggs for them, two a-piece. When they'd finished what do you think they did? Threw the shells in the fire . . . I didn't think anything about it at the time, but the next morning there wasn't a single egg laid – nor one the next day, nor the next week . . . Never throw an eggshell in the fire.

Sussex Igglesden (*c.*1932)

The notion was not universal, however. The stronger tradition that eggshells should be destroyed to stop witches using them for boats (*see below*) led some people to advise burning as the best way to ensure their complete destruction.

The shells of geese and ducks are always thrown on the fire, lest witches should find them and use them for coracles on their nocturnal trips to the opposite coast.   Wales Trevelyan (1909)

The sympathetic principle is well attested from the sixteenth century onwards, but this particular superstition about burnt eggshells has not been found earlier than 1853.

Sussex Igglesden (*c.*1932) 81–2. Dorset Udal (1922) 276. Wiltshire Wiltshire (1975) 104. Essex [*c.*1920] Ketteridge & Mays (1972) 143. Worcestershire Salisbury (1893) 72. Warwickshire Langford (1875) 14. Lincolnshire N&Q 1S:8 (1853) 382. England Addy (1895) 66. Yorkshire N&Q 6S:4 (1881) 307. Lancashire *Lancashire Lore* (1971) 51. Wales Trevelyan (1909) 115. N. Ireland Foster (1951) 132.

eggshells: witches

Witches like to use eggshells as boats, to go to sea and wreck real ships, and for this reason anyone who eats a boiled egg must be careful to break the shell afterwards:

As soon as a Devonian has eaten a boiled egg, he thrusts a spoon through the end of the shell, opposite the one at which it was begun to be eaten. When I enquired why this was done, the reply given was: 'Tu keep they baggering witches vrom agwaine to zay in a egg-boat'. It is supposed that the witches appropriate the unbroken shells to sail out to sea to brew storms.

Devon Hewett (1892)

This custom is reported with little variation across Britain, although in areas where fairies are more feared than witches it is they whose machinations must be foiled:

People ought to remember that egg-shells are favourite retreats of the fairies, therefore the judicious eater should always break the shell after use, to prevent the fairy sprite from taking up his lodgement therein.   Ireland Wilde (1888)

In Britain, the idea of witches using shells as boats goes back at least to the 1580s, as attested by Scot's *Discoverie of Witchcraft*, and has been regularly reported ever since. Most of the later informants imply that witches used the shells in some direct way to go to sea, and why they did not simply get their own eggs for such uses is not explained. However, at the root of the superstition may be the notion that the eggs were used symbolically – placed in a tub of water to represent ships, and the tub then agitated to cause a real storm at sea.

Wells Parish Register: December 1583 – Perished upon the west coast, coming from Spain, Richard Waller [and thirteen others] whose deaths were brought to pass by the detestable working of an execrable witch of Kings Lynn, whose name was Mother Gabley, by the boiling or rather labouring of certain eggs in a pail full of cold water, afterward approved sufficiently at the arraignment of ye said witch.

Norfolk *Norfolk Archaeology* (1859)

There is some evidence that an earlier version held that witches would simply prick the unbroken shells, in the same way as they would a wax image, to do mischief to whoever had eaten the egg. That is what worried egg (and snail) eaters in classical times:

There is indeed nobody who does not fear to be spell-bound by imprecations. A similar feeling makes everybody break the shells of eggs or snails immediately after eating them, or else pierce them with the spoon that they have used.

Pliny, *Natural History* (AD 77)

And it seems that this fear was adopted in Britain by sixteenth and seventeenth century scholars such as John Aubrey.

Kent [c.1903] Opie & Tatem, 136. Sussex Latham (1878) 10. Devon Hewett (1892) 27. Somerset N&Q 1S:7 (1853) 152. Norfolk [1583] *Norfolk Archaeology* 5 (1859) 87; *Folk-Lore* 40 (1929) 121–2. Lincolnshire *Gent. Mag.* (1832) 494; N&Q 4S:5 (1870) 516; Swaby (1891) 92. Lancashire Harland & Wilkinson (1882) 68; [c.1915] Corbridge (1964) 156–60. Wales Trevelyan (1909) 115. Ireland Wilde (1888) 203–4. N. Ireland Foster (1951) 132. General Scot (1584) Bk 1, Ch. 4; Aubrey, *Remaines* (1686/1880) 193; Grose (1787) 68. Classical Pliny, *Natural History* (AD 77) Bk 28, Ch. 4.

elbows: itching

One of a set of beliefs which claim a significance for the ITCHING of particular parts of the body, although this one often has a feel more proverbial than prognosticatory. From the mid seventeenth century, the meaning is usually given as 'you will (or should) change your bedfellow'. In this sense it turns up in literary guise from James Howell's *Paroimiographia* (1659) onwards and in later folklore collections from all over Britain.

The meaning of earlier references is, however, more obscure. Scot (1584) includes 'tingling' of the elbow in a list of 'an innumerable multitude of objects, whereupon they prognosticate good or bad lucke', while Thomas Nash (1599) uses the phrase 'elbows itch for joy', which is echoed in other references, including that of Robert Burns (c.1800). Shakespeare also refers twice to elbows in less than clear contexts:

Borachio: *Conrade, I say.*
Conrade: *Here, man, I am at thy elbow.*
Borachio: *Mass, an my elbow itched, I thought there would a scab follow.*

Shakespeare, *Much Ado About Nothing* (c.1600)

Of fickle changelings and poor discontents Which gape and rub the elbow at the news Of hurly-burly innovation.

Shakespeare, *Henry IV Part 1* (1598)

Two other references give different meanings:

They say that if . . . the inside of your elbow itches it is a sure sign that someone will be coming to the house; or the outside of your elbow, that someone will soon be leaving,

Co. Meath/Co. Tipperary *Folk-Lore* (1904)

and Opie & Tatem provide one in which an itch on the right elbow means simply good luck, and on the left bad luck (Somerset (1923)).

Bedfellows: Sussex *Sussex County Mag.* 5 (1931) 122. Cornwall N&Q 1S:12 (1855) 38. Shropshire Burne (1883) 270. Western Scotland Napier (1879) 138. Ireland Wilde (1888) 206. General James Howell, *Paroimiographia* (1659) 12; *Illustrated London News* (27 Dec 1851) 779. Literary Swift (1738); *Connoisseur* 59 (13 Mar 1755). *Others*: Somerset [1923] Opie & Tatem, 137. Yorkshire N&Q 1S:6 (1852) 602. Co. Meath/Co. Tipperary *Folk-Lore* 15 (1904) 461–2. General Scot (1584) Bk 11, Ch. 13. Literary Thomas Nash, *Lenten Stuffe* (1599) 165; Shakespeare, *Henry IV Part 1* (1598) 5:1. Shakespeare, *Much Ado Nothing* (c.1600) 3:3; [c.1619?] Furnivall (1874) 7–9; Philip Massinger, *The Virgin Martyr* (1622) 3:3; [c.1800] Robert Burns, 'To Colonel De Peyster'.

elbows: knocking

Much more rare than the 'itching elbow' superstitions, a few references report beliefs to do with banging one's elbow:

My aunt (aged seventy, of a Norfolk family) exclaimed, when a friend knocked her funny bone, 'that will stop you singing!', and on my asking her meaning, said, 'Have you never heard the saying, "If you knock your funny bone you'll never sing again"?'

Norfolk N&Q (1899)

Another meaning, still heard in conversation, but not apparently included in folklore collections, is that if you knock one elbow, you should immediately knock the other 'for luck', or to break the spell of bad luck. Opie & Tatem give three versions of the latter.

Hampshire [1984] Opie & Tatem, 137. London [1987] Opie & Tatem, 137. Norfolk N&Q 9S:3 (1899) 469; [1958] Opie & Tatem, 137.

elder: cures

Despite its dubious reputation in many other beliefs, the elder tree was the most widely used plant in folk medicine. Every part was used – flowers, leaves, berries, bark, and the wood itself; it was made into ointments, infused as tea, made

elder (*Sambucus nigra*)

The elder is without doubt the hardest plant to classify in terms of its superstitions and traditions. On the one hand it is widely regarded as extremely useful in the prevention and cure of ailments as diverse as EPILEPSY and saddle sores, and is sometimes reported as generally protective, while on the other it was widely feared and treated with suspicion. Compare, for example, the following:

The elder tree is a sacred tree and should be planted as near as possible to the back door, the most used entrance in the home. It is credited with being a very good protection against witchcraft. Guernsey De Garis (1975)

The elder was regarded with considerable awe. In South Wales it was deemed very dangerous to build any premises in or near the spot where an elder-tree stood. Wales Trevelyan (1909)

This is not simply a geographically based difference, as positive and negative attributes are reported from nearly all quarters:

In Cambridgeshire the elder was associated with witchcraft. Elderly residents of Crishall recalled in 1958 that because witches were supposed to have a particular liking for the tree it should never be touched, cut, sawn, or in any way tampered with after dark. Paradoxically, however, some inhabitants of the same village

said that the elder tree afforded protection against lightning and that it was particularly lucky to have a tree growing in or near a farmyard because it kept away evil spirits and promoted fertility among the stock. Cambridgeshire Porter (1969)

Elders were everywhere connected with fairies and witches, although it was not always clear in what way. It was also reputed to be the tree on which Judas Iscariot hanged himself, and it was believed to have provided the wood for the Crucifixion. Furthermore, it must never be cut down, or the wood burned; it must never be used to make cradles; a wound inflicted with an elder spike was bound to prove fatal; and the tree would 'bleed' if cut.

It has proved impossible to reach an adequate synthesis of elder beliefs, because the evidence is patchy and contradictory, and all that can be said is that elder was generally agreed to be 'uncanny'. There is a curious sense that the negative and positive feelings stemmed from the same basic notions and may have depended largely on the general disposition of the informant. Further research into elder beliefs would be most welcome.

Cambridgeshire Porter (1969) 61. Wales Trevelyan (1909) 103. Guernsey De Garis (1975) 116.

into wine, powdered, boiled, or used straight – as when elder twigs were stuck into ears to cure earache. It was recommended for a bewildering variety of ailments, including toothache, earache, rheumatism, jaundice, burns, coughs and colds, gout, adder and mad-dog bites, freckles, and pimples.

Most of these cures can be viewed as purely herbal, but in many other cases there are strong 'magical' or superstitious elements. These are especially clear in the use of elder sticks in WART cures, and the wearing of elder necklaces.

Take a green sprig of elder-wood and a penknife. Touch one of the warts with the point of the knife, and then cut a snip or notch in the sprig or stick of elder. When you have touched all the warts, one by one, with the point of the knife, and cut as many snips in the elder sticks as there are warts on the patient's body, bury the stick in the ground. Then as the stick decays the warts will decay also. England Addy (1895)

Most of the standard elements of wart cures are here – touching the warts, counting them,

burying the item – and the method differs little from version to version. This process was well known in seventeenth-century England, and lasted well into the twentieth century. A very similar description had appeared much earlier in the *Gospelles of Dystaves* (1507), but as this was translated from a Low Countries original, it is not direct evidence for the practice in Britain at the time.

Pieces of elder were also threaded on to necklaces and worn to alleviate TEETHING problems, EPILEPSY, or WHOOPING COUGH:

For epilepsy – Take nine pieces of young elder twig; run a thread of silk of three strands through the pieces, each piece being an inch long. Tie this round the patient's neck next the skin. Should the thread break and the amulet fall, it must be buried deep in the earth and another amulet made like the first, for if once it touches the ground the charm is lost. Ireland Wilde (1888)

These prescriptions often include difficult details, for example the tree must grow in a churchyard, or even 'the elder must come from plants seeded by birds in the pollard tops of willows and must be cut by the father at full moon' (**Warwickshire** Bloom (c.1930)).

The earliest known English prescription for a cure involving elder occurs in a manuscript of *c.*AD 950, and is magical. It is strongly reminiscent of many later wart cures with its throwing-over-the-shoulder motif:

For fellons [whitlows] take, to begin, a hazel or an elder stick or spoon, write thy name thereon, cut three scores on the place, fill the name with blood, throw it over thy shoulder or between thy thighs into running water.   Cockayne (1864)

Warts: **Somerset** N&Q 1S:2 (1850) 150; Poole (1877) 52–3. **Berkshire** Salmon (1902) 420. **London** N&Q 1S:11 (1855) 7–8. **Herefordshire** Leather (1912) 83. **Northamptonshire** N&Q 1S:2 (1850) 36–7. **Suffolk** *Folk-Lore* 35 (1924) 356–7. **Derbyshire** [1890s] Uttley (1946) 114–15. **England** Addy (1895) 88. **West Wales** Davies (1911) 282. **Monmouth** [1954] Opie & Tatem, 422. **Co. Longford** *Béaloideas* 6 (1936) 266. **Unlocated** Opie (1959) 315. **General** Francis Bacon, *Sylva Sylvarum* (1627) 264; W. Langham, *The Garden of Health* (1633).
Necklace: **Warwickshire** Bloom (c.1930) 25–6. **Shropshire** Burne (1883) 194–5. **Ireland** Wilde (1888) 199.
Miscellaneous: **Sussex** Latham (1878) 39; *Sussex Life* (Jan. 1973) 34. **Gloucestershire** Hartland (1895) 55. **Herefordshire** Leather (1912) 80. **Cambridgeshire** Porter (1969) 88. **Suffolk** *Folk-Lore* 35 (1924) 356. **Norfolk** [c.1920] Wigby (1976) 65–6. **Shropshire** Burne (1883) 184, 200. **Wales** Trevelyan (1909) 316. **Radnorshire** Francis Kilvert, *Diary* (18 Oct. 1870). **Ireland** Wilde (1888) 197. **Co. Cork** [1937] Culloty (1993) 59. **Guernsey** De Garis (1975) 116. **General** [c.950] Cockayne 2 (1864) 105; Nicholas Culpeper, *English Physician Enlarged* (1653) 110–11; Browne, *Pseudodoxia Epidemica* (1672) Bk 2, Ch. 7; Black (1883) 192; Hatfield (1994) various pages; Vickery (1995) 118–26; Baker (1996) 52–6.

elder: immune from lightning

One of the positive attributes of the elder was that it was immune from LIGHTNING strikes, so it was safe to shelter underneath it and good to plant near any building:

Speaking to some little children one day about the danger of taking shelter under trees during a thunderstorm, one of them said that it was not so with all trees, 'For,' said he, 'you will be quite safe under an eldern-tree, because the cross was made of that, and so the lightning never strikes it'.   **Suffolk** Chambers (1878)

Other informants linked this immunity from lightning with the notion that elder must not be

burnt, or that it was under the protection of witches. *See below* for the tradition that the Cross was made of elder wood, and *above* for discussion of the ambivalent nature of traditions about the tree.

Essex [c.1920] Ketteridge & Mays (1972) 138. **Cambridgeshire** Porter (1969) 61. **East Anglia** Varden (1885) 113. **Suffolk** Chambers 2 (1878) 322. **Lincolnshire** *Stamford Mercury* (19 July 1861). **Co. Longford** [1991] Vickery (1995) 121. **Unlocated** N&Q 10S:8 (1907) 315.

elder: Judas and Cross traditions

Two different traditions about the elder, both with biblical connotations, were regularly quoted in explanation of the beliefs about its bad reputation, the fear of burning it, and its freedom from lightning strikes (*see above and below*). On the one hand, it was widely reputed to be the tree on which Judas Iscariot hanged himself, but on the other it was the wood out of which the Cross was made:

It was unlucky to stand under an elder tree when the sun was setting, because the elder tree was supposed to be the tree upon which Judas hanged himself. The person who did so would be bewitched.   **Oxfordshire** *Folk-Lore* (1923)

I was visiting a poor parishioner the other day, when the following question was put to me: 'Pray, sir, can you tell me whether there is any doubt of what kind of wood our Lord's cross was made? I have always heard that it was made of elder, and we look carefully into the faggots before we burn them, for fear that there should be any of this wood in them'.   **Unlocated** N&Q (1853)

Both stories are apocryphal in that they do not appear in official Christian writings but are formed by the common process in which homely details are added to biblical stories in popular tradition. The tree's Judas connection appears to have the longer history of the two. There are two conflicting versions of Judas' death in the Bible; in one (Matthew 27:3–10), he hangs himself, but we are not told how or where. The tradition that it was an elder tree was certainly current in England by the mid fourteenth century, when *Piers Plowman* was written:

*Judas he japed with the Jewen silver
And sithen on an eller hanged hym after.*
          Langland, *Piers Plowman* (c.1366–c.1399)

About the same time, Sir John Maundeville claimed to have seen the very elder tree, in his fictional *Voiage and Travaille*. Both Marlowe and Shakespeare mention the tradition in passing, and the legend was still widely known when the nineteenth-century folklorists were amassing their great collections.

The tradition linking the elder with the Cross appears much later, being noted only from the 1850s onwards, but was still being collected in the second half of the twentieth century. The elder was not the only tree which was claimed as providing the wood for the cross. A different tradition explains that it was the aspen – hence its appearance of quivering, in remorse.

Judas Iscariot: Cornwall *Old Cornwall* 1:9 (1929) 40. **Oxfordshire** *Folk-Lore* 34 (1923) 326. **Cambridgeshire** Porter (1969) 61. **Suffolk** Moor (1823) 119. **Lincolnshire** [*c.*1940s] Sutton (1992) 135. **Yorkshire** [1985] Vickery (1995) 119. **Ireland** [1916] Vickery (1995) 119. **Isle of Man** Moore (1891) 152. **Unlocated** N&Q 10S:8 (1907) 211–12. **Literary** William Langland, *Piers Plowman* (*c.*1366–*c.*1399) B-text, Passus 1, lines 67–8; Sir John Maundeville, *The Voiage and Travaille* (*c.*1366; 1725 edn) 112; Christopher Marlowe, *The Jew of Malta* (*c.*1590) 4:4; Shakespeare, *Love's Labour's Lost* (1598) 5:2. **The Cross: Devon** *Devonshire Assoc.* 103 (1971) 268. **Cambridgeshire** Porter (1969) 61. **Suffolk** Chambers 2 (1878) 322. **Shropshire** *Folk-Lore* 49 (1938) 232. **England** N&Q 10S:8 (1907) 131. **Derbyshire** Addy (1895) 63. **Unlocated** N&Q 1S:7 (1853) 177; N&Q 10S:8 (1907) 211–12, 315.

elder: negative attributes

In addition to numerous beliefs about the elder, good and bad, which are given separate entries, there are many which were reported more rarely but which contribute to the general impression of fear and loathing of the plant, in a variety of contexts. This negative view was expressed in various parts of the country, and concerned every aspect of the plant.

It was believed that children laid in a cradle made in whole or part of elderwood, would not sleep well, and were in danger of falling out of the cradle.   Western Scotland Napier (1879)

The same thing was still being said in Lincolnshire in the 1940s (Sutton (1992)).

No labourer in the fields ever dared to fall asleep under the elder, because the leaves were thought to give off a deadly scent which, if inhaled for any length of time, sent the sleeper into a coma from which he would never awaken.
Cambridgeshire Porter (1969)

Animals and children must not be struck with elder sticks, or their growth will be stunted, and elder flowers were included by some in the long list of FLOWERS that were unlucky to bring indoors:

Elderberry flowers – these were never allowed in the rooms of Fenland houses, because they were supposed to attract snakes and vipers. These reptiles were numerous in the undrained fens and their habit of coiling up in the roots of elder trees made the flowers unpopular with the superstitious.   Cambridgeshire Porter (1969)

*Hawthorn bloom and elder flowers
Will fill a house with evil powers.*
Warwickshire Langford (1875)

Reasons for this uneasiness about the elder are not often provided, but where they are stated, reference is made to the usual Cross and/or Judas legends (*see above*), or simply to vague connections between the tree and witches or fairies. Even the medicinal properties of the tree, so widely acknowledged, are compromised in certain contexts:

A few days ago a gamekeeper . . . was chasing some fowls from a spinney to the roost, when he tripped up on an elder-bush, a spike of which entered his hand. It is a popular superstition that a wound from the elder is fatal, and it proved so in this case. The wound was promptly dressed, and an operation was performed a few days later at Cambridge Hospital, but he died in that institution yesterday from tetanus.
Bedfordshire *Folk-Lore* (1905)

Essex [*c.*1920] Ketteridge & Mays (1972) 138. **Oxfordshire** *Folk-Lore* 34 (1923) 326. **Worcestershire** Berkeley & Jenkins (1932) 34. **Warwickshire** Langford (1875) 15. **Bedfordshire** *Folk-Lore* 16 (1905) 100. **Cambridgeshire** Porter (1969) 43, 61. **Lincolnshire** *Lincs. N&Q* (1889) 56; *Saga Book of the Viking Club* 3 (1901) 55; [*c.*1940s] Sutton (1992) 135. **Shropshire** *Folk-Lore* 49 (1938) 232. **Wales** Trevelyan (1909) 103. **Western Scotland** Napier (1879) 126–7. **Unlocated** Brand (1813) 588. **General** Vickery (1985) 60–4; Vickery (1995) 118–26.

elder: prevents saddle sores

One particular aspect of the elder, which must have had more relevance in past times than in the present day, is that it was particularly useful in preventing saddle sores. The rider simply had to carry a piece of elder in his/her pocket or hand. This notion was recorded a number of times between the mid seventeenth and mid nineteenth centuries and was clearly in general circulation:

It is a rustic idea ... that a sprig of elder, in which there is a joint, worn in one of the lower pockets, will operate as a charm against this galling inconvenience.   **Northern England** Brockett (1829)

Wiltshire Aubrey, *Remaines* (1686/1880) 178. **Northern England** Brockett (1829) 21. **General** W. Coles, *The Art of Simpling* (1656) 68; R. Flecknoe *Diarium* (1656) 65; Browne, *Pseudodoxia Epidemica* (1672) Bk 2, Ch. 8; *Athenian Mercury* (19 July 1692).

elder: prohibition on burning

One of the most widespread results of the uncanny reputation which elder wood enjoyed was the belief that it must not be burned. At best, this action would be extremely unlucky, but many believed it brought disharmony, ague, or even death into the house:

Only a few weeks ago a young fellow in my village told me with some amusement, that he was helping an old woodman to clean up and burn rubbish left in a wood after the timber had been felled and taken away. The lad put a piece of elder on the bonfire, but the old woodman 'got in a regular taking' said the boy; "'e took the stick o' elderwood and 'e pitched it down the woodside, as far as 'e could see, and 'e says to me, "D'ye want someone to die in your house within the year, you unlucky lad."' The boy thought it was a great joke, but the older people in the place are expecting a death in the house within the year, or at least a misfortune as the elderwood was not actually burned.
Shropshire Folk-Lore (1938)

Other predicted results included 'it rouses the witches' and 'the Devil would come down the chimbley'. The reasons given for this were that the tree was used to make the Cross, or that Judas hanged himself on it (*see above*).

The prohibition on burning elder was widely known in most parts of Britain and Ireland, but in contrast to some other elder superstitions it does not seem to have been noted before about 1830. It was still being cited in the late twentieth century and is probably still followed by some rural people.

Hampshire [1930s] Goodland (1963) 89. **Somerset** Tongue (1965) 142. **Devon** *Devonshire Assoc.* 57 (1926) 109; *Devonshire Assoc.* 103 (1971) 268; *Devonshire Assoc.* 104 (1972) 267. **Cornwall** *Old Cornwall* 1:9 (1929) 40. **Essex** [*c.*1920] Ketteridge & Mays (1972) 138. **Oxfordshire** [1950s] Vickery (1995) 119. **Gloucestershire** Hartland (1895) 54–5. **Herefordshire** Leather (1912) 19. **Worcestershire** [1900] *Folk-Lore* 20 (1909) 343.

Warwickshire *Folk-Lore* 55 (1944) 41. **East Anglia** Forby (1830) 414; Varden (1885) 113. **Suffolk** Claxton (1954) 89. **Norfolk** Chadwick (1960) 86. **Lincolnshire** Rudkin (1936) 18. **Shropshire** Gaskell (1894) 267; *Folk-Lore* 49 (1938) 224–5, 232. **Staffordshire/Shropshire** Burne (1883) 243–4. **Derbyshire** Addy (1895) 63. **Nottinghamshire** Joseph Wright, *English Dialect Dictionary* 2 (1900) 245; *Folk-Lore* 23 (1912) 356. **Yorkshire** [1982] Opie & Tatem, 137. **Wales** Trevelyan (1909) 103–4. **Dyfed** [1984] Vickery (1995) 119. **Western Scotland** Napier (1879) 126–7. **Co. Kildare** [1984] Vickery (1995) 119. **Isle of Man** [*c.*1975 & 1992] Vickery (1995) 119. **Unlocated** N&Q 1S:7 (1853) 177.

elder: protective

Despite the widespread fears about cutting down or burning elders, and warnings against planting them near your house, a number of traditions cast the tree in a distinctly positive light – protecting houses and people against witchcraft, the fairies, or simply against bad luck.

It was used as a charm for protecting houses and gardens from the influence of sorcery and witchcraft, and even at the present time, an elder tree may be observed growing by almost every old cottage in the Island. Its leaves, like those of the Cuirn [rowan], were picked on May-eve, and affixed to doors and windows to protect the house from witchcraft.
Isle of Man Moore (1891)

A very similar tradition about elder leaves was reported by W. Coles in *The Art of Simpling* (1656). Other parts of the tree also had magical properties:

Elder berries, gathered on St. John's Eve, would prevent the possessor suffering from witchcraft, and often bestowed upon their owners magical powers. If the elder were planted in the form of a cross upon a new-made grave, and if it bloomed, it was a sure sign that the soul of the dead person was happy.
Western Scotland Napier (1879)

Carrying a branch of elder could also be beneficial, in a similar way to that more commonly reported for the ROWAN:

The elder-tree is supposed to have the virtue of protecting persons, bearing a branch of it, from the charms of witches and wizards.
Scotland Grose (1787)

References to the evil nature of the elder outnumber the positive ones, although if the medicinal properties are added, the balance tips the other way. Broadly speaking, it appears that the reports of definitely positive attributes for elder come from Scotland, Northern England, and the Isle of Man, but further research would be necessary before this impression can be confirmed or denied. The picture here is again unclear because of the confused nature of the evidence. Many informants were clearly unsure about the tree and an attempted overview necessarily reflects this ambivalence.

Dorset [1991] Vickery (1995) 121. **Northern England** Brockett (1829) 55; [1850s] Denham (1895) 325. **Co. Durham** Brockie (1886) 114–15. **Scotland** Grose (1787) 59; Webster (1978) 342. **Western Scotland** Napier (1879) 126–7. **Glasgow** [1820s] Napier (1864) 394. **Ireland** [1984] Vickery (1995) 121. **Isle of Man** Moore (1891) 152; Killip (1975) 35–6. **General** W. Coles, *The Art of Simpling* (1656) 66–7, quoted Opie & Tatem, 138; Vickery (1995) 118–26.

elder: repels flies

One of the benign properties of elder was that it was good for keeping flies, midges, wasps, and other insect pests at bay:

When inspecting a slaughter-house a summer or two ago, I commented on the absence of flies, and was told this was due to a large elder bush growing some ten feet away, and that branches of elder hung in any building would keep away flies.
Cornwall *Jnl Royal Inst. Cornwall* (1915)

This was one explanation for elders being planted near houses, and branches of elder were also tied to horses' harnesses for the same reason.

Sussex *Sussex Life* (Jan. 1973) 34. **Kent** [1930s] Kent (1977) 92–3. **Cornwall** *Jnl Royal Inst. Cornwall* 20 (1915) 123. **Essex** [1989] Vickery (1995) 122. **Oxfordshire** Vickery (1995) 122. **Midland England** N&Q 11S:12 (1915) 489. **Cambridgeshire** Vickery (1995) 122. **Lincolnshire** Rudkin (1936) 27. **Northumberland** [1988] Vickery (1995) 122.

elephants: lucky

Meeting an elephant was regarded as lucky:

[Lucky things for wedding to meet] . . . *and so, rather curiously, is an elephant. The odds against encountering an elephant on the way to an English wedding would seem to be fairly high, yet the superstition is well known. I was once at a marriage at Morecambe when the bridegroom did meet such a beast as he drove to church, and afterwards received numerous congratulations on his singular good fortune.*   Lancashire *Folk-Lore* (1957)

See also ORNAMENTS.

Westmorland [c.1939] *Folk-Lore* 64 (1953) 294. **Lancashire** *Folk-Lore* 68 (1957) 418.

elf shot

It is generally agreed that the theory of medicine prevalent in the early Middle Ages, as evidenced by surviving manuscripts, was almost entirely based on classical and Christian sources. Very little can be shown to have survived from earlier periods of either Anglo-Saxon or British history. One exception to this rule is the concept of illness being caused by direct malevolent action by supernatural beings – elves or fairies – commonly called being 'elf shot'. This could happen to humans, but was most common in large farm animals – particularly horses and cattle:

The stone arrow heads of the old inhabitants of this island, are supposed to be weapons shot by fairies at cattle, to which are attributed any disorders they have: in order to effect a cure, the cow is to be touched by an elf-shot, or made to drink the water in which one has been dropped.
Hebrides Pennant (1771)

Cures usually involved soaking these arrowheads in water and giving the patient the water to drink. A regular alternative was to place silver money – if possible coins with crosses on them – into water, and to give this 'silver water' to the patient. As befitted a disease with a supernatural cause, elf shot could only be diagnosed by a local CUNNING MAN or recognized healer. A regular method of diagnosis was to measure the afflicted animal several times, and if the animal was found to be getting smaller, a confident diagnosis could be made:

Prehistoric flints, found in the fields, were carried or worn as amulets to protect animals and people from being 'elf shot'. This cigarette card dates from 1923.

unfortunate state of being 'elf-shot'. This disease manifested itself in two ways; an extensive swelling of the stomach or a hole (which only the cow doctor could find) somewhere in the skin. The particular incident I am going to refer to was a case of swelling . . . when the animal was pointed out to [the cow doctor] *he proceeded to measure her from the tip of the tail to the nose. He did this three times. Placing the tip of her tail against his elbow and proceeding in forearm lengths (cubits) all the way up her back to the nose. Finally pronouncing solemnly, 'Aye, she's elf-shot'. He then retired to the farm-house where he demanded a jug of spring water. He then took from his pocket a small purse and extracted some petrified reeds and pieces of stick, often found in boulder clay, and known locally as fairy stones. These he placed in the jug of water and left the whole lot to 'brew' on the table in the kitchen. My grandmother, preparing to make some tea, moved the jug thoughtlessly out of the way and was roundly cursed for her pains, the cow doctor having to repeat the preparation as she had apparently broken the 'charm'. The potent mixture at last having been pronounced ready, the 'doctor' and his admirers adjourned to the byre where the unfortunate cow was impatiently awaiting his attention. The water was then sprinkled on her nose, and a drop put in each ear, and my grandfather was warned to send for him the following morning if there was no improvement. This, funnily enough, was not necessary . . .* [Asked how he knew the cow to be elf-shot, the cow doctor claimed] *'she was getting shorter every time I measured her'.*

Co. Fermanagh *Ulster Folklife* (1961)

The idea was certainly current in many areas throughout the nineteenth and well into the twentieth century.

Nevertheless, the history and development of this belief is still unclear, and we are faced with several unsolved problems. The condition of being elf-shot is mentioned in a matter-of-fact tone in a number of medieval Saxon manuscripts (*see* Cockayne (1865)). But the next available reference turns up in the 1660s. So the first problem is the question of what happened in the intervening six or seven hundred years? Is it safe to assume the existence of a direct tradition, surviving from generation to generation over that time, without any documentary evidence?

The second problem is concerned with distribution. Experts on medieval medicine such as Bonser and Singer agree that the elf-shot concept is a survival of the Teutonic heritage of England,

and was brought to its shores by Anglo-Saxon invaders and settlers. But the distribution of the belief in later years is predominantly in Scotland and Ireland, which, broadly speaking, are not known for their Teutonic roots. Obviously, if a continuous thread of tradition had continued over the intervening centuries, there was plenty of time for the idea to spread northwards and westwards from England, but there is no evidence of this taking place. Further work clearly needs to be carried out.

Although the concept of being elf-shot is clearly the same in Saxon and modern times, the cures prescribed in the Anglo-Saxon manuscripts are very different from those reported in later sources. The classic tenth-century Saxon prescription is as follows, which bears almost no relation to the activities of the Fermanagh cowdoctor described above.

If a horse is elf shot, then take the knife of which the haft is horn of a fallow ox, and on which are three brass nails, then write upon the horse's forehead Christ's mark, and on each of the limbs which thou may feel at; then take the left ear, prick a hole in it in silence; this thou shalt do; then take a yerd, strike the horse on the back, then will it be hole. And write upon the horn of the knife these words: 'Benedicite omnia pera domini, dominum'. Be the elf what it may, this is mighty for him to amends.   Cockayne 2 (1865)

See also RED THREAD.

Bristol? [1940s] Opie & Tatem, 140. **Staffordshire** Hackwood (1924) 150. **Northern England** Brockett (1829) 108. **Yorkshire** Robinson (1855) 'Awfshots'. **England/Scotland Borders** [*c.*1816] Henderson (1866) 149. **Scotland** Allan Ramsay, Poems (1721) 224; *Trans. Royal Soc. Edinburgh* 1:2 (1749) 68; Dalyell (1834) 22–3, 352–8; Keightley (1850) 351–2. **Highland Scotland** [*c.*1699] Campbell (1975) 66. **North East Scotland** Gregor (1881) 184. **Caithness** *Folk-Lore* 16 (1905) 335–6. **Galloway** Mactaggart (1824) 195–8, 210. **Hebrides** Pennant (1771) 94–5. **Ireland** C. Vallency, *De Rebus Hibernicis* (1783) 4:13, plate 11; Wood-Martin 1 (1902) 41–2. **N. Ireland** Foster (1951) 119. **Northwest Ireland** *Folk-Lore* 17 (1906) 200–10. **Co. Donegal** *Folk-Lore Jnl* 4 (1886) 255–6. **Co. Fermanagh** *Ulster Folklife* 7 (1961) 73–4. **Unlocated** *Folk-Lore* 73 (1962) 282–3. **General** [10th cent.] Cockayne 2 (1865) 290–1; Browne *Pseudodoxia Epidemica* (1669) Bk 2, Para. 5, Sec. 10; Literary Raymond (1934) 70–1.
Major historical studies: Cockayne (1864–6); Singer (1919–20); Bonser (1926a,b); Grattan & Singer (1952); Bonser (1963).

elm

Elm trees do not appear to have acquired much of a reputation in traditional belief in Britain and Ireland, and only isolated sources refer to it at all. One reference describes a protective use usually associated with ROWAN or ELDER:

Quite recently, I talked with an old lady in Ross-shire who showed me a small piece of elm twig she had carried for ten years in the pocket of her skirt as a protection for her cow against the evil eye of an unfriendly neighbour. When I smiled, and urged it was ridiculous to believe either in the evil eye or the efficacy of a bit of elm as a precaution, she retorted that before she had resorted to the elm twig two cows in succession had 'gone wrong' on her – one in the udder, and the other took fits – and I might laugh as I liked but she would carry her elm twig!   Ross-shire MacDonald (1936)

Another describes the imprisonment of a shrew, again usually associated with the ASH:

The little shrew or sherrow mouse was sometimes accused of running over cattle when lying down and hurting them. The remedy was to go to a tree that was prepared for the purpose, get some twigs and boil them, and wash the affected part with water. The tree was prepared by making a hole, putting in a living shrew and closing the hole on it. There were two old elm trees in the parish since my remembrance, which were good for the 'sherrow crope'.   Devon *Devonshire Assoc.* (1934)

A specific elm tree is reported as providing a family death omen:

A large elm tree near Credenhill Court is called the 'Prophet Elm'. It is said to foretell each death in the family of the Eckleys, who formerly owned the place, by flinging off a limb.
Herefordshire Leather (1912)

For the use of elm in folk medicine, *see* Vickery (1995) 126–7.

Devon *Devonshire Assoc.* 66 (1934) 74. Herefordshire Leather (1912) 20. Ross-shire MacDonald (1936) 64.

engaged couples

Several different superstitions involved couples who were engaged to be married, but they all seem to be based on the same fear of TEMPTING FATE. In each case, failure to obey the dictates of tradition would result in their never getting married. Some couples, for example, avoided posing for a PHOTOGRAPH together:

According to a Brighton beach photographer the objection of an engaged couple to have their portraits taken together has again come into vogue. The superstition is that if the couple are photographed together the engagement will be broken off.   Sussex Igglesden (c.1932)

Similarly, an engaged couple should not walk together when leaving someone else's wedding, nor should a girl allow another to try on her engagement ring. These beliefs are only reported from late nineteenth- and twentieth-century sources, but one which is certainly older held that engaged couples must never both stand as godparents for the same child:

In some parts of Cornwall it is considered a sure sign of being sweethearts if a young man and woman 'stand witness together', i.e. become godfather and godmother of the same child. But not in all, for I remember once hearing in Penzance a couple refuse to do so, saying it was unlucky. 'First at the font, never at the altar'.
Cornwall *Folk-Lore Jnl* (1887)

Opie & Tatem record an example of this latter superstition dating from 1800.

Sussex Igglesden (c.1932) 149–50. Hampshire N&Q 7S:9 (1890) 486. Somerset Tongue (1965) 135. Cornwall *Folk-Lore Jnl* 5 (1887) 210. Surrey [1960] Opie & Tatem, 141. London *Folk-Lore* 37 (1926) 366. Essex [1983] Opie & Tatem, 141. Worcestershire N&Q 7S:5 (1888) 46. Lancashire N&Q 7S:5 (1886) 133. Unlocated [c.1800] Opie & Tatem, 140; N&Q 6S:12 (1885) 144; Wright (1913) v.

ephialtes

see NIGHTMARES.

epilepsy: cockerel cure

To cure someone of epilepsy, it is necessary to locate the exact spot on which the first seizure took place and carry out certain actions on that spot:

A friend of mine told me quite recently, that when he was a boy in the Shawbost School, early in the sixties, one of his class-fellows, as he sat beside him at the writing-desk, took a fit of epilepsy. On the following day, his father and a man well-known to the writer, of local fame for curing that dreadful malady, came to the school-house. They opened the floor at the very spot at which the boy had the fit, and placed a living black cock, with clippings of the patient's hair and nails, in the

epilepsy

Also called *falling sickness* or, simply, *fits*.

It is hardly surprising that an alarming disease such as epilepsy, which was completely beyond the skill and comprehension of medical practitioners for most of human history, should have attracted a number of magical cures. It was widely thought that those who suffered epileptic fits were possessed by evil spirits, bewitched by someone wishing them ill, or even that they were 'touched by God':

Though there are many old remedies for this disease, there are few modern ones. Probably doctors can relieve the disease more effectually than they used to do. There is still great reluctance to touch a person in a fit. The fit is supposed to be a visitation of God, and man must not interfere. Norfolk *Folk-Lore* (1929)

These supernatural explanations had been around for a very long time, being held by all the early civilizations for which we have evidence, and it was not until the 1850s that practitioners of medical science began to agree that the cause of the problem lay with a brain malfunction and took steps to find practical remedies. Superstitious cures, however, lasted well into the twentieth century.

In the traditions of Britain and Ireland, two common cures were wearing a silver ring made from sacrament money, and killing a black or white cockerel on the site of the first attack. Each of these has its own entry. Numerous other cures have been reported, most of which have close parallels elsewhere in folk medicine. For example, the disease was thought amenable to CHARMS:

A young farmer from the neighbourhood of Torrington called on me and asked me to tell him what was contained in a bag which he had worn round his neck since infancy, and which a white witch had given his mother as a preventative against fits. After cutting open several outer cases, well-worn and sweat-stained, I came upon the original inner one, which contained a number of pieces of paper, each bearing one word. Piecing them together I found they formed the following sentences: 'Sinner, Jesus died for thee' (thrice repeated), 'Therefore flee that sin'. At the man's request these pieces were reinserted in their several bags, and my maidservant sewed them up again, and he, replacing the charm round his neck once more, went on his way rejoicing, being now in a position to tell a neighbour, whose child had also fits, that was a certain cure for them. Devon *Folk-Lore* (1908)

Other cures included MOLES' blood, a piece of HANGMAN'S ROPE, roasted MOUSE liver, and SWALLOW-stones. In more than one report we are warned not to come between the sufferer and the fire, or the disease would come to us. Another remedy reported in several versions involved the hair off a DONKEY's back:

Help with teething, keep away fits & convulsions – Take a few hairs from the dark cross on donkey's back, sew them up in black silk bag, hung round child's neck. Gloucestershire Hartland (1895)

Another regular remedy was to use LEAD from the parish church or for the patient to go to a church at night time and perform certain actions:

And the very old custom of going into the church at night whilst the chimes are playing twelve o'clock, in order to creep three times under the communion table to be cured of fits, is still held in repute. The present sexton, Mr. James Cole, has been applied to in such cases to unlock the church door. Devon Bray (1838)

See also CORAL; ELDER.

Sussex Latham (1878) 25. Dorset *Folk-Lore* 11 (1900) 112. Devon Bray (1838) 291; *Devonshire Assoc.* 9 (1877) 92; *Devonshire Assoc.* 10 (1878) 102; Hewett (1892) 28; *Folk-Lore* 19 (1908) 341–2; *Devonshire Assoc.* 66 (1934) 83. Devon/Cornwall N&Q 1S:3 (1851) 259. Cornwall *Cornishman* (Dec 1881). New Forest Wise (1867) 177. Surrey N&Q 1S:3 (1851) 179. Gloucestershire N&Q 4S:11 (1873). Hartland (1895) 52. East Anglia Varden (1885) 103. Norfolk *Folk-Lore* (1929) 116. Lincolnshire *Folk-Lore* 7 (1896) 268; Rudkin (1936) 26. Yorkshire Blakeborough (1898) 135. Lancashire Harland & Wilkinson (1882) 75. Westmorland/Lancashire [*c.*1939] *Folk-Lore* 62 (1951) 262. Wales Trevelyan (1909) 318. West Wales Davies (1911) 283. Highland Scotland Macbain (1887/88) 258–9; Polson (1926) 29–30. Banffshire Gregor (1874) 269. Ireland N&Q 1S:1 (1850) 349; Wilde (1888) 199; *Folk-Lore* 8 (1897) 389. Co. Cavan Maloney (1972) 74. Co. Cavan/Co. Leitrim Logan (1965) 52–3. Co. Meath *Folk-Lore* 19 (1908) 316. Unlocated N&Q 2S:4 (1857) 487; N&Q 6S:4 (1881) 357; *Cassell's Saturday Jnl* (1893). General [1661] N&Q 1S:4 (1851) 52–3; [1697] *Folk-Lore* 23 (1912) 235.

opening made, covered it over, adjusted the floor to its usual level, and left the cock there. My friend said that he was in school with the boy for some time thereafter, and never saw or heard of his taking another fit.   Hebrides *Folk-Lore* (1900)

The procedure is remarkably consistent across the known versions, and the only real difference in other accounts is that sometimes a white cock is stipulated. The key characteristic which distinguishes this cure from most others is that it is focused on the place where the disease first showed itself rather than attempting to tackle the symptoms as they later appear. This approach is reasonably easy to account for, since traditional explanations of the malady include possession by an evil spirit, or ill-wishing by an enemy. In this context, of the two variables, time and place, it is *place* that is most important, whereas the linear sequence of time – as in so many superstitions – is of less importance. There is indeed no illogicality in carrying out such a remedy *after* the attack if one believed that a *sympathy* still existed between the locus and the victim.

Killing a cockerel in this way is often described as a 'sacrifice' or 'offering', but this terminology is misleading. Both words imply a transitive action, that there is something or someone to which the offering is made, which does not seem to be the case. It should be seen more on the lines of an 'exorcism'. In numerous other counter-witchcraft procedures, animals, or parts of them such as the heart, are utilized. They are often roasted, buried, or have pins stuck into them, and the inclusion of the patient's nail and hair clippings is also a standard motif in both casting and countering spells. In this case, as the cockerel is buried, it is also quite possible that the principle of TRANSFERENCE is in operation – the disease has been transferred to the bird, and as the latter rots away the disease will fade with it. None of the sources claim that this is the process that is being invoked, but analogy with other cures – such as WARTS – makes it possible.

This remedy is widely reported from Scotland and Ireland, but not, as yet from England and Wales. The wanton killing of the bird is usually assumed to be a mark of its great antiquity, but at present it cannot be dated earlier than the mid nineteenth century.

Scotland *Folk-Lore* 29 (1918) 86. **Highland Scotland** Macbain (1887/88) 258–9; Polson (1926) 29–30. **Northeast Scotland** Gregor (1881) 140. **Caithness** Sutherland (1937) 106–7. **Banffshire** Gregor (1874) 269. **Ross-shire** [1890s] MacDonald (1936) 61–2; *Folk-Lore* 11 (1900) 446. **Hebrides** *Folk-Lore* 11 (1900) 446; N&Q 166 (1934) 96. **Skye** N&Q 166 (1934) 138. **Lewis** *Folk-Lore* 6 (1895) 167. **N. Ireland** Foster (1951) 62–3. **Co. Down** *Ulster Folk-Lore* 7 (1961) 71.

epilepsy: sacrament money cure

A complex cure for epilepsy, which relied on the idea that items made holy by contact with official church ceremonies would be especially effective:

On a recent Sunday a farm labourer stood in the porch of the parish church of a village on the banks of the Tamar and collected half-a-crown in coppers from different members of the congregation, the thirtieth donor giving the half-crown and taking the twenty-nine pence as a climax to the weird ceremony. From the consecrated coin thus quaintly acquired the labourer has manufactured a silver ring which he will wear as an infallible remedy for epilepsy.

West Country *Southern Daily Mail* (22 Jan. 1903)

In some versions, the sufferer actually gives money in exchange for a silver coin from the collection, but more usually s/he stands in the doorway of the church after the service and is given pennies by fellow-worshippers as they leave. By these methods, the sufferer very neatly gains the wherewithal to purchase a ring, with no cost to him/herself, and also gains the sanction of the official church. Those in a more elevated social position collected silver sixpences rather than pennies.

In many cases there are further rules that cover the collection. For example, female sufferers must collect from unmarried men, and vice versa, and there must be no spoken thanks, or even a direct request. In the latter case, the whole thing had to be planned in advance by some other interested party, and several of the published accounts were written by clergymen who had been asked to co-operate in such schemes.

A variant of the procedure involves visiting selected people in their homes to ask for a contribution.

Twenty years ago, after we settled in this place, we were surprised by a visit from a farmer, a respectable-looking man, from Ilsington, a village about six miles off. With a little hesitation he introduced himself, and told us that his son had long been a sufferer from the falling-sickness, that medical care had utterly failed, and as a last resource he had been advised to collect seven sixpences from seven maidens in seven different parishes, and have them melted down into a ring for the lad to wear. 'I can't tell you,' he went on, 'how many miles I have travelled on this business, for the villages hereabouts are far apart. So hearing a family of ladies had settled here, I thought I would come up the hill, to see if one among them had a heart kind enough to help my poor Bill'. The appeal was irresistible; the sixpence was given, and the simple-hearted countryman went away full of gratitude, but not daring to utter it for fear of breaking the spell.   Devon Henderson (1866)

This cure was reported from most parts of England in the nineteenth and earlier twentieth centuries, but not elsewhere in the British Isles, it seems. The earliest report, however, is much older, being found in an account book of 1754 which reads: 'A poor woman at Barton, who had fits, towards buying a silver ring, 1d' (Lincolnshire Henderson (1866)). The wearing of rings to cure or prevent ailments is a commonplace of folk medicine, see also, for example, CRAMP.

Sussex Latham (1878) 39. Dorset *Folk-Lore* 11 (1900) 112. West Country N&Q 5S:6 (1876) 144–5; *Southern Daily Mail* (22 Jan. 1903). Devon N&Q 1S:10 (1854) 321; *The Times* (7 Mar. 1854) 8; [1837] *Devonshire Assoc.* 59 (1927) 166; Henderson (1866) 114–15; *Devonshire Assoc.* 12 (1880) 101; N&Q 6S:4 (1881) 106, 396; *Folk-Lore* 19 (1908) 340–2. Cornwall *Folk-Lore* 5 (1887) 206; *Cassell's Saturday Jnl* (1893). Wiltshire N&Q 5S:4 (1875) 508; [1876] Eddrup (1885) 330–1. Berkshire Igglesden (*c*.1932) 206. Essex N&Q 1S:6 (1852) 50; [*c*.1939] *Folk-Lore* 62 (1951) 262. Oxfordshire *Folk-Lore* 34 (1923) 326. Gloucestershire N&Q 2S:1 (1856) 331. Herefordshire N&Q 5S:5 (1876) 97; Havergal (1887) 46; [*c*.1895] *Folk-Lore* 19 (1928) 387; Leather (1912) 79. Worcestershire/Shropshire *Gent. Mag.* (1855) 385. Northamptonshire N&Q 1S:8 (1853) 146. Huntingdonshire [1861] Saunders (1888) 272–3. East Anglia Varden (1885) 103. Suffolk N&Q 1S:2 (1850) 4. Norfolk N&Q 1S:4 (1851) 53. Lincolnshire [1754] Henderson (1866) 115; *Gent. Mag.* (1832) 493. Lincolnshire *Grantham Jnl* (22 June 1878); Watkins (1886) 11. Shropshire Burne (1883) 192–3. Yorkshire Henderson (1866) 113–14; Blakeborough (1898) 139. Co. Durham Brockie (1886) 223; Leighton (1910) 53. Unlocated Chambers 1 (1878) 732; N&Q 6S:4 (1881) 357.

erysipelas (St Anthony's fire/wild fire/the rose)

An acute streptococcal disease, in which the main visible symptoms are bright-red, painful lesions which typically spread across the skin of the face or legs. In most cases the infection regresses after one or two weeks, but may return to the same site after months or even years. In the elderly, or other weakened patients, the condition can lead to complications such as pneumonia and can thus prove fatal, but modern antibiotics deal effectively with it.

The highly visible symptoms, and the fact that it often seems to go away by itself, given time, make it an ideal candidate both for folk medicine aimed at treating the symptom rather than the cause, and for superstition-based treatments such as verbal CHARMS. The range of treatments is wider than with most conditions, but they readily fall into patterns across the genre. The verbal charms are characteristically simple, Christian-based, and invoke the symbolism of fire as appropriate to the popular perception of the disease:

For St. Anthony's Fire – The fire of earth is hot, and the fire of hell is hotter; but the love of Mary is above all. Who will quench the fire? Who will heal the sick? May the fire of God consume the Evil One! Amen.   Ireland Wilde (1888)

For wildfire
　　Christ, he walketh over the land
　　Carried the wildfire in his hand
　　He rebuked the fire, and bid it stand
　　Stand, wildfire, stand (three times repeated)
　　In the name of etc.
                Cornwall *Folk-Lore Jnl* (1887)

Fire is also used symbolically in a cure from Wales:

For erysipelas, burns, and inflammations of the eyes, the remedy was to strike fire by means of a stone or iron in 'front of the person'; or the sufferer was recommended to stand before a forge fire and allow the sparks to fall freely upon him. To stir or blow a fire before the patient, so that the glow overspread his face, was a remedy for the same ailment.
                Wales Trevelyan (1909)

The redness of the infection also suggests a connection with blood, and a number of references report the use of blood, either of a SEVENTH SON or a member of a particular family whose blood was believed to have curative powers:

A most notable form of treatment is the use of Keogh's blood. The cure is possessed by a family called Keogh who live near Two Mile House in County Kildare. In making this cure, a male member of the family rubs some of his own blood on the infected area and this quickly cures it. This cure is widely known in Counties Wicklow, Kildare and Carlow, and everybody believes in its usefulness.   Ireland Logan (1981)

Black (1883) lists the Walches, Keoghs, and Cahills as families having this facility. In a number of references, the blood should be taken from a black CAT, usually from its ear, in common with some cures for RINGWORM.

In the category of natural cures, butter, fresh cow dung, wool, milk, and various plants are featured. But the wool and milk, in particular, must be of a special kind:

S. Courtier gave me an excellent cure for the erysipelas, of which there are three sorts. Take the wool from under the left ear of a black sheep and the milk of a red cow. The wool is dipped in the milk every morning and used as a lotion, and you say a prayer. C. said it saved one woman from having her leg cut off.

Devon [1908] *Devonshire Assoc.*

A further characteristic of the disease is that the area of infection is surrounded by a palpable raised margin, and this appears to be the basis of a cure (again in common with some cures for ringworm) which involved writing the patient's name at the edge, reputed to stop it spreading further.

Compare RINGWORM; SHINGLES.

Devon *Devonshire Assoc.* 15 (1883) 100; [1908] *Devonshire Assoc.* 57 (1926) 121; *Devonshire Assoc.* 64 (1932) 162. **Cornwall** Couch (1871) 149; *Folk-Lore Jnl* 5 (1887) 199–202. **Worcestershire** Salisbury (1893) 70. **Cumberland** Penfold (1907) 54. **Co. Durham** N&Q 6S:4 (1881) 510. **Wales** Trevelyan (1909) 317. **Pembrokeshire** *Archaeologia Cambrensis* 89 (1934)183–4. **Highland Scotland** Henderson (1866) 117–18; Polson (1926) 32. **Ireland** Black (1883) 140; Wilde (1888) 194; *Folk-Lore* 8 (1897) 387–9; Hickey (1938) 268; Logan (1981) 70. **N. Ireland** Foster (1951) 57. **Co. Carlow** N&Q 1S:2 (1850) 259; *Béaloideas* 1 (1928) 327. **Co. Wicklow** *Folk-Lore* 4 (1893) 360. **Co. Kerry** *Folk-Lore* 4 (1893) 350; *Folk-Lore* 19 (1908) 316; *Folk-Lore* 31 (1920) 236. **Co. Donegal** *Folk-Lore* 4 (1893) 350. **Co. Longford** *Béaloideas* 6 (1936) 266. **Guernsey** MacCulloch MS (1864) 402–3.

euthanasia

Unofficial euthanasia has no doubt always existed, whatever the view of the official religion of the time. Two traditional methods are regularly mentioned in the literature, one of which, 'drawing the pillow', was certainly practised, while the other, smothering, is apocryphal. Removing the pillow from under a dying person's head was widely seen as an act of mercy, to help the patient on their way and relieve their suffering:

A doctor told me he had come across two instances where the death of a person, who was too slow in dying, was hastened by removing the pillow and allowing the sick person's head to fall back. On one occasion he reproached the old woman who had done it, and told her it was murder. 'Oh no, sir, it's not murder, it's what we call "drawing the pillow"'.

Norfolk *Folk-Lore* (1929)

This practice was often linked with the notion that people could not die if their bed or pillow contained pigeon or game feathers. Removing the pillow, or removing the patient from the bed entirely, was seen as a way of ensuring that the release was not prolonged unnaturally (*see* FEATHERS: IN BEDDING).

Most of the reports are from the nineteenth and twentieth centuries, but the method was certainly well known in the seventeenth, and probably long before:

*And in his next fit we may let him go,
'Tis but to pull the pillow from his head,
And he is throttled: it had been done before,
But for your scrupulous doubts.*

Jonson, *Volpone* (1607)

'Smothering' was a standard motif in ANIMAL INFESTATION stories, and also as the prescribed method for certain conditions such as hydrophobia and also for 'monstrous' births. The legendary nature is brought out well in stories such as the following:

I remember the wildest rumours used to run through our street. I was never allowed out to play with other children, so it was not from them I heard these things. I always listened intently to grown-ups talking, and sometimes another tenant would drop in with the air of one who had great tidings to tell, and one would hear the strangest stories of a baby born a few doors away with a horse's head, or with two heads, or of some monster up at the hospital being born with ten legs. Always the grown-up would shake her head wisely and say, 'Of course, they'll smother it'.

Cornwall [early 1900s] Smith

An interesting motif in the animal infestation stories is that the hospital authorities were just waiting for the King's permission to smother the victim, as if this was simply the way such things were done.

Drawing the pillow: Warwickshire [*c.*1932] Hewins (1985) 41. **Norfolk** [*c.*1870s] Haggard (1935) 6–7; *Folk-Lore* 40 (1929) 124. **Unlocated** H. Woolley, *Queen-Like Closet* (1684) Supp 2. **General** Fynes Moryson, *Itinerary* (1617) Pt 3, 1:34. **Literary** Ben Jonson, *Volpone* (1607) 2:6; Shakespeare, *Timon of Athens* (*c.*1607) 4:3. ***Smothering:*** **Cornwall** [early 1900s] Smith (1954). **London/Surrey** *Folk-Lore* 37 (1926) 78–80. **Lancashire** Naughton (1988) 141–2. **Ireland** Ballard (1986) 83–6.

even numbers

see NUMBERS: ODDS AND EVENS.

evergreens

The main domestic use of evergreens is for CHRISTMAS DECORATIONS, and opinion has been sharply divided on the question of whether the plants used in this way should be burnt when taken down. A few other sources indicate a belief that evergreens should not be burnt at any time of year:

If you burn green
Your sorrow's soon seen.

Co. Durham Leighton (1910)

Judging by the paucity of references, and their relatively late date, this is probably a simple extension of the Christmas decoration superstition.

Norfolk Randell (1966) 99. **Lincolnshire** [1940s?] Sutton (1992) 128. **England** Addy (1895) 63. **Derbyshire** *Folk-Lore Jnl* 2 (1884) 280. **Co. Durham** Leighton (1910) 62. **Northumberland** Bosanquet (1929) 74. **General** Hoggart (1957) Ch. 2.

evil eye

The notion that certain people can harm other humans, animals, and even inanimate objects, simply by looking at them, is found in many cultures throughout the world but is not, it seems, universal (*see* Dundes (1981)). It has certainly been extremely widespread in Europe at least since classical times, and it also has biblical sanction. The best-known European evil-eye beliefs flourished around the Mediterranean – in particular Italy and Greece – but there was also a strong tradition in northern Europe, in which Britain and Ireland shared, which differed markedly from its southern counterpart. In contrast to the Mediterranean model, the evil eye in Britain is in many respects simply a part of the general belief in WITCHCRAFT. Several of the vernacular terms for ill-wishing or witchcraft demonstrate the importance of eyes in the business of bewitchment – for example, overlooking, blinking, and eye-biting. Casting a spell by looking at something or someone was simply one of the weapons in the witch's arsenal.

Witches could acquire this power as part of their (somewhat vaguely defined) 'pact with the Devil', but on the other hand there were many reports of people who had simply inherited it or had acquired it innocently enough:

In a district of North Antrim there is living at the present time a family, members of which are thought to possess the power to 'blink' cattle. No one will show them young animals, nor indeed any animal if they can avoid it. Other neighbours are taken to see the new foal or the litter of young pigs, but never a member of this family. I have been in houses when one of them was seen approaching, and warnings were immediately issued, 'Don't be mentioning the wee pigs' or, 'Don't say a word about the new horse we bought'. I have often wondered if they know that they are suspected of being witches, or if they think that it is the neighbours who behave oddly. Unfortunately, it is not a subject about which one can enquire easily. One cannot say, 'I'm told you have the Evil Eye. What do you think about it?' In this particular instance, the Evil Eye is believed to be hereditary. A woman, whose daughter was marrying into the family, told me that she would as soon see her marrying the Devil himself and, from her point of view, there was little difference for, according to local tradition, the Devil was the god of these people . . . This family is believed to have fairy associations, and they tend to be red-haired and small. N. Ireland Foster (1951)

A child born on May Day will have an evil eye. The seventh daughter of a seventh daughter always has an evil eye.

Co. Longford *Béaloideas* (1936)

If a child has been weaned, and again given the breast, the people say it will have an ill-eye.

Co. Leitrim *Folk-Lore* (1894)

Indeed, there are stories of people who were mortified to find that they had the power, and who always made sure they avoided causing damage by carefully regulating where their gaze fell. The first glance each morning was the most dangerous:

Though also some are of so venomous a constitution, by being radicated in envy and malice, that they pierce and kill (like a cockatrice) whatever creature they first set their eye on in the morning. So it was, with Walter Graham, some-

time living in the same parish, wherein now I am, who killed his own cow, after commending its fatness, and shot a hare with his eye, having praised its swiftness (such was the infection of an evil eye).

Scotland Kirk, *Secret Commonwealth* (1691)

Where the evil eye was used deliberately to do harm, it could fall on anyone who displeased the possessor, but certain areas of life seemed particularly prone to attack – babies, new animals, milking, and butter-making:

Several examples are recorded of men and women in the island who had the power of the evil eye. The power was so strong that if, when milking, they but glanced at the milk in the pail, it would turn sour before it reached the dairy. If a witch had a grudge against a farmer's wife and should cast her evil eye on the churn, when churning was in progress, no butter would come; a fact known to me.   Jersey *Folk-Lore* (1914)

Where babies and farm animals were concerned, the overriding emotional context was usually envy – anything which might incite another's envy was at risk. In the same context, people were careful not to praise things – if they praised their own they were TEMPTING FATE; if they praised others' they were suspected of wishing ill in the guise of honeyed words.

You must bless the baby in praising it for there is danger from one's evil eye. The evil eye is peculiarly apt to fall on babies.

Highland Scotland Macbain (1887/88)

A number of protective measures and remedies were available, although again these were the same as were used for other types of ill-wishing. HOLED STONES, HORSESHOES, RED THREAD, pieces of ROWAN, and SILVER WATER were all recommended, but there is no sign of the elaborate system of gestures, amulets, and protective icons which are characteristic of Mediterranean and Middle Eastern traditions.

The phrase 'evil eye' occurs regularly in English at least from AD 1000 (*OED*), but it is not always clear whether it refers to supernatural power or to a more generalized description of a facial expression or vindictive mood. James I certainly referred to the occult power when he used the term in his *Daemonologie* (1597), but Reginald Scot, writing a few years earlier, in the 1580s, calls it 'eye-biting':

The Irishmen addict themselves wonderfully to the credit and practice hereof; insomuch as they affirm, that not only their children, but their

cattle, are (as they call it) eybitten, when they fall suddenly sick, and term one sort of their witches eybiters; yea and they will not stick to affirm, that they can rime either man or beast to death.

Ireland Scot (1584)

In Scotland, 'ill eye' and 'canny eye' were also widely used.

Widespread fears of meeting a person with CROSSED EYES, and one with a double pupil in their eye, are clearly related to the evil-eye tradition and provide another route of development from classical sources such as Pliny's *Natural History* (AD 77).

See also CORAL.

Somerset Folk-Lore 24 (1913) 302–3; Folk-Lore 66 (1955) 328. Gloucestershire Hartland (1895) 53. Norfolk Folk-Lore 40 (1929) 129–33. Lincolnshire Rudkin (1936) 23. Northern England Brockett (1829) 109–10. Yorkshire N&Q 1S:1 (1850) 429. Lancashire/Yorkshire Harland & Wilkinson (1882) 69. Northumberland Bigge (1860–62) 94. Cardiganshire Folk-Lore 37 (1926) 163–7. Scotland Kirk (1691); Chambers's Jnl (1950) 308–11. Highland Scotland [c.1699] Campbell (1975) 66; Macbain (1887/88) 242–4, 269. Western Scotland Maclagan (1901) passim, Polson (1932) 173–80. Perthshire Folk-Lore 8 (1897) 92. Galloway Mactaggart (1824) 278. Banffshire Gregor (1874) 267. North Uist Folk-Lore 68 (1957) 486–8. Orkney [1643] Dalyell (1834) 5. Ireland Scot (1584) Bk 3, Ch. 15; Wilde (1888) 141, 194. N. Ireland Foster (1951) 87–9. Co. Longford Béaloideas 6 (1936) 259. Co. Leitrim Folk-Lore 5 (1894) 199. Jersey Folk-Lore 25 (1914) 245. Classical Pliny, Natural History (AD 77) Bk 7, Ch. 2. For major studies see Maclagan (1901); Elworthy (1895); Gifford (1958); Dundes (1981); Lykiardopoulos (1981).

eyebrows

Eyebrows which meet across the bridge of the nose have generally been held to be indicative of the character, or general fortune, of the person who bears them. The majority of references treat this feature as a very bad thing, but some disagree completely and claim it a very fortunate sign. The earliest reference is unequivocal:

They whose haire of the eye-browes doe touch or meet together, of all other are the worst. They doe shew that hee or shee is a wicked person, and an enticer of servants, and given to unlawfull and naughty acts which Iohannes Indagnies saith, hee hath observed in old women being witches, which were led to bee burned, whose eye-browes were such. As Thaddeus Hageccius hath also noted.

Lupton (1579)

Many others agree with this assessment – echoing the connection with witches and general deceitfulness, while some specify that those with meeting eyebrows will be hanged, or at best drowned. A handy couplet sums up another aspect:

Trust not the man whose eyebrows meet
For in his heart you'll find deceit.

Unlocated N&Q (1878)

and the belief is presumably behind Shakespeare's phrase 'But in faith, honest as the skin between his brows' (*Much Ado About Nothing* (*c.*1598)).

Lupton's mention of Johannes Indagine (*c.*1467–1537) and Thaddeus Hagecius (or Hajek) (1525–1600) connects the belief with the Europe-wide world of scholarship and enquiry into natural science taking shape at the time. Indagine's *Introductiones Apotelesmaticae* (or *Chiromantia*), first published in Frankfurt in 1522, was an immensely influential treatise on chiromancy, physiology, and astrology, which attempted to explain cosmic influence on human behaviour and personality, and was often reprinted and translated into English and other major languages. Hajek was a Czech astronomer and alchemist. These connections, and the absence of earlier references in Britain, make a foreign origin quite possible.

Despite the early references from the sixteenth and early seventeenth centuries, the notion is strangely absent from the documentary record until it appears again in the nineteenth, but from then it is quoted regularly and was still being collected in the 1980s. Its influence may have been strengthened in the twentieth century by popular fortune-telling books, many of which included a negative view of meeting eyebrows in their sections on physiognomy; for example:

Eyebrows that meet and seem to run almost in a straight line right across the face are signs of a hasty temper, easily aroused to violence, in some cases from the most trivial cause.

Madame Fabia, *The Book of Fortune-Telling* (London: *Daily Express*, 1925)

Eyebrows that meet over the nose are sometimes, though not always, a sign of bad temper.

Allied Newspapers, *Fortune-Telling for Everyone* [n.d]

Nevertheless, from at least the 1850s, some have believed the exact opposite:

The current saying in the South of England is 'It is good to have meeting eyebrows, you will never have trouble'.   Southern England N&Q (1878)

Persons whose eyebrows meet are deemed specially fortunate as being lucky in all their undertakings.   Yorkshire Nicholson (1890)

There seems no way to reconcile these opposing notions. The 'unlucky' belief wins convincingly in terms of longevity and geographical spread, but the 'lucky' references are sufficiently numerous to rule out simple individual misunderstanding – even if two of the three Durham citings are copied from the first, which is quite likely.

Unlucky: Lincolnshire *Folk-Lore* 20 (1909) 217. Lancashire Harland & Wilkinson (1873) 225. Co. Durham Brockie (1886) 216; [1985] Opie & Tatem, 144. Northumberland [1850s] *Denham Tracts* (1895) 325. Wales Trevelyan (1909) 209. Dumfriesshire Shaw (1890) 13. Aberdeenshire/Dumbartonshire *Folk-Lore* 6 (1895) 395. Literary Shakespeare, *Much Ado About Nothing* (*c.*1598) 3:3; *Sir Giles Goosecap* (1606) 2:1; Edna O'Brien, *Girls in their Married Bliss* (1964) Ch. 1. Unlocated N&Q 5S:10 (1878) 288. General Lupton (1579) Bk 6, Para. 99.
Lucky: Southern England N&Q 5S:9 (1878) 65. Yorkshire Nicholson (1890) 45. Co. Durham Henderson (1866) 84; Brockie (1886) 210; Leighton (1910) 60. Unlocated N&Q 1S:7 (1853) 152.

eyelashes

A simple wishing custom to be undertaken when an eyelash comes out:

If an eyelash falls out, put it on the back of the hand, and wish, and the wish will come true.

Worcestershire *Folk-Lore* (1909)

Details vary, but the outline remains very similar:

When an eyelash falls out its owner puts it on the tip of her nose, wishes, and blows at it; should she blow it off, she will have her wish

Cornwall *Folk-Lore Jnl* (1887)

Cornwall *Folk-Lore Jnl* 5 (1887) 214. Essex [1953] Opie & Tatem, 144. England Addy (1895) 93. Shropshire Burne (1883) 268. Worcestershire *Folk-Lore* 20 (1909) 346.

eyes

see CROSSED EYES.

eyes: itching

One of a set of superstitions concerned with ITCHING on a particular part of the body; an itching eye usually means laughter or tears, depending on the eye involved:

A twitching in the eyelid is lucky; but you must not say when it comes nor when it goes. Right eye itching, a sign of laughter; but left over right, you'll cry before night.

Cornwall *Folk-Lore Jnl* (1887)

A regular extension to the belief explains that if either eye itches it is fortunate at night: 'Left or right/Brings good at night' (Hone, *Year Book* (1832)), but with no indication why. The same phrase is sometimes used of EAR or cheek burning.

The majority of later references follow the general right/good, left/bad pattern of other beliefs, although occasionally the meanings are reversed. It is noticeable, however, that all the seventeenth- and eighteenth-century versions cite the left eye as good and the right as bad, and there seems to have been a reversal in meaning over time, which in turn may suggest that the relative attributes usually assigned to right and left are less stable and long-lasting than is often assumed.

The belief is certainly as old as the early seventeenth century, as Shakespeare has Desdemona say, 'Mine eyes doth itch, Doth that bode weeping?' and it is reported sporadically into the twentieth century. There are also classical analogues, as in, 'My right eye itches now, and shall I see my love?' (Theocritus, *Idylls* (*c.*275 BC) 3).

Somerset [1923] Opie & Tatem, 143. Cornwall *Folk-Lore Jnl* 5 (1887) 219. Shropshire Burne (1883) 270. Yorkshire Nicholson (1890) 44. Wales Trevelyan (1909) 325. Welsh Gypsies Jarman (1991) 184. Western Scotland Napier (1879) 137. Jersey *Folk-Lore* 25 (1914) 246. Unlocated Grose (1787) 60; Hone, *Year Book* (1832) 126–8; Gales (1914) 234. Literary Shakespeare, *Othello* (1604) 4:3; *Connoisseur* 59 (1755) 353; *Old Women's Sayings* (*c.*1835).

falling

Any everyday item suddenly falling can be interpreted as ominous, but certain things are singled out in specific superstitions. *See*: CHAIRS: FALLING OVER; PICTURES: FALLING.

Falling can also be compared to DROPPING and SPILLING things.

falling sickness

see EPILEPSY.

fasting spittle

see SPITTLE.

fate

see TEMPTING FATE.

feathers: in bedding

A very widely reported belief held that the presence of pigeon or game-bird feathers in a pillow or mattress of a dying person prevented death occurring quickly, and caused them to 'die hard', or endure a drawn-out death.

There is a strong superstition in this parish that a person cannot die comfortably upon a pillow in which there are any pigeons' feathers. A few months ago a case occurred of an old woman who was dying 'very hard', as the saying is, when a neighbour suggested that probably there were pigeons' feathers in the pillow. It was immediately changed for one that was known to contain none, and the patient became quiet at once and did not very long survive.

Berkshire *Berks. Arch. Soc.* (1889–91)

Although there are variations in the particular birds to be avoided, versions of the superstition are remarkably similar and are often supported by purportedly true anecdotes concerning instances known to the narrator.

The wife of a Sussex clergyman was told by a rural sick-nurse that never did she see anyone die so hard as old Master Short, and at last she thought (though her daughter said there were none) that there must be game feathers in the bed and she tried to pull it from under him, but he was a heavy man, and she could not manage it alone, and there was no one with him but herself, and so she got a rope, and tied it round him, and pulled him off the bed, and 'he went off in a minute quite comfortable, just like a lamb'.

Sussex *Midland Garner* (1884)

Taking somebody out of bed and putting them on the floor, or removing the pillow from under their head, to help them 'die easy', were both standard ways of showing compassion for the old and terminally ill, and existed independently of the feathers belief (*see* EUTHANASIA). In these narratives, however, they often provide a touch of unconscious humour, not lost on the folklorists who noted them down. 'He went off like a lamb' being almost a punch line in such reports:

Dearee me, sir, you see there was partridge feathers in the bed, and folks can't die upon geame feathers no-how, and we thought as how he never would go, so we pulled the bed away, and then I just pinched his poor nose tight with one hand and shut his mouth close with t'other, and, poor dear! he went off like a lamb.   Kent N&Q (1881)

The earliest clear reference dates from 1710, with a letter published in the *British Apollo* requesting information, and from then on the belief was noted regularly until well into the twentieth century, from all over Britain except, apparently, Scotland. This is just the sort of motif to have appealed to seventeenth-century dramatists, and its apparent absence from their plays could be taken as tentative evidence that it did not exist much before the first reference noted here. The superstition makes its most famous appearance in Emily Brontë's novel *Wuthering Heights* (1847): 'Ah they put pigeons' feathers in the pillows – no wonder I couldn't die!'

See also BEDS; PIGEONS.

England Wright (1913) 277. **Kent** N&Q 6S:4 (1881) 236. **Sussex** Latham (1878) 59; *Midland Garner* 2 (1884) 2. **Dorset** Udal (1922) 184. **Devon** *Devonshire Assoc.* 10 (1878) 104; *Devonshire Assoc.* 71 (1939) 128. **Cornwall** N&Q 1S:12 (1855) 38; Couch (1871) 168. **Surrey** N&Q 1S:5 (1852) 413. **Berkshire** *Berks. Arch. Soc.* 1 (1889–91) 105–6. **Oxfordshire** *Midland Garner* 1 (1884) 19. **Gloucestershire** N&Q 2S:12 (1861) 500. **Herefordshire** Leather (1912) 119–20. **Warwickshire** Bloom (*c.*1930) 44; N&Q 165 (1933) 189. **Northamptonshire** N&Q 1S:2 (1850) 164–5; Sternberg (1851) 160. **East Anglia** *East Anglian Mag.* 13 (1953/4) 99. **Suffolk** *Folk-Lore Record* 3 (1880) 129; Gurdon (1893) 9, 136. **Norfolk** N&Q 5S:11 (1879) 414; *Folk-Lore* 40 (1929) 122. **Lincolnshire** Thompson (1856) 736. **Shropshire** Burne (1883) 231; *Folk-Lore* 49 (1938) 225; **Staffordshire** Poole (1875) 86. **Derbyshire** *Athenaeum* (1846) 1299; N&Q 10S:12 (1909) 514. **Nottinghamshire** N&Q 23 (1912) 356. **Yorkshire** [1823] Home (1915) 214; *Athenaeum* (1846) 1299; Robinson (1861) 298; *Leeds Mercury* (4 Oct. 1879); Addy (1888) xix–xx; Nicholson (1890) 5, 130; Addy (1895) 123; N&Q 10S:12 (1909) 287; Morris (1911) 237–8. **Lancashire** *Athenaeum* (1846) 1117. **Cumberland** *Athenaeum* (1846) 1299; Gibson (1858) 106; Penfold (1907) 57; *Folk-Lore* 40 (1929) 281. **Co. Durham** Brockie (1886) 130–1; *Folk-Lore* 20 (1909) 72; Leighton (1910) 51. **Northumberland** Neville (1909) 114–15. **Wales** Burne (1883) 231. **Mid-Wales** Davies (1911) 226. **Glamorgan** *Athenaeum* (1846) 1299. **Monmouthshire** *Athenaeum* (1846) 1299. **Co. Mayo** *Athenaeum* (1846) 1299. **Sligo** *Athenaeum* (1846) 1299. **Unlocated** *British Apollo* (25 Jan. 1710) 309; Grose (1787) 69; *Folk-Lore* 64 (1953) 429. **General** *Gent. Mag.* (1796) 465, 636. **Literary** Emily Brontë, *Wuthering Heights* (1847) Ch.12.

feet: cures applied to

A standard cure for fevers and other ailments in the seventeenth century was to apply pigeons (or, less frequently, small animals), split in half while still alive, to the soles of the feet. This was based on the theory that the feet and head were intimately connected, and the pigeon would draw the fever out. This treatment had lost favour with the medical profession by the eighteenth century, but lived on in folk medicine into the twentieth:

The lung of a sheep still warm was formerly applied to the soles of the feet of a child suffering from pneumonia. It was spoken of as the best possible remedy by those using it; the idea seems to be that the healthy lung of the sheep could draw the disease from the lungs of the patient.
Herefordshire Leather (1912)

Even when live animals were not used, the principle of treating the feet was still evident:

One Oxfordshire farmer's wife rubbed home-prepared goose-grease on her children's chests and feet whenever they had coughs, and preferred it to any bought liniment. She said she always kept some by her, and many young mothers came to her for it. It is widely believed that any lotion or ointment used for coughs must be applied to the soles of the feet as well as, and at the same time as, to the chest, or it will not work.
Oxfordshire Folk-Lore (1957)

A woman, when suffering from pain in her cheek, applied a mustard poultice to her instep, in the expectation of being freed from the pain.
Suffolk Gent. Mag (1867)

See also CHILBLAINS; CORNS; PIGEONS: CURES.

Oxfordshire *Folk-Lore* 68 (1957) 415. Herefordshire Leather (1912) 80. Suffolk *Gent. Mag* (1867) 728–41.

feet: itching

One of the set of beliefs about ITCHING on particular parts of the body:

The itching of the foot is supposed to indicate that the person experiencing it will shortly walk on strange ground.   Dumfriesshire Corrie (1890/91)

The meaning is remarkably constant from version to version, although one Welsh report adds a little variety:

Itching of the soles of your feet is a token that you will have good news, or an invitation to a dance. If your feet itch, you will soon tread on strange ground.   Wales Trevelyan (1909)

The earliest known version is in the humorous *Connoisseur* article published in 1755, whereas several of the other itching beliefs — HANDS, EYES, NOSES, and EARS — are a good deal older. Nevertheless, given a pre-existing belief that itching is significant, the 'strange ground' meaning is quite straightforward and obvious, and it could thus be much older.

Sussex *Sussex County Mag.* 5 (1931) 122. Somerset Tongue (1965) 138. Cornwall N&Q 1S:12 (1855) 38; Couch (1871) 169. London *Folk-Lore* 37 (1926) 365. Essex [1953] Opie & Tatem, 167. Buckinghamshire Uttley (1946) 136. Herefordshire Leather (1912) 88. East Anglia Varden (1885) 113. Norfolk Fulcher Collection (*c.*1895). Shropshire Burne (1883) 270. England Addy (1895) 100. Yorkshire Robinson (1861) 300; Nicholson (1890) 44. Dumfriesshire Corrie (1890/91) 83. Co. Durham Henderson (1866) 85; Brockie (1886) 211; Leighton (1910) 60. Wales Trevelyan (1909) 325. West Wales Davies (1911) 218. Western Scotland Napier (1879) 137–8. Orkney N&Q 10S:12 (1909) 483–4. Co. Longford *Béaloideas* 6 (1936) 265. Jersey *Folk-Lore* 25 (1914) 246; L'Amy (1927) 98. Literary *Connoisseur* (13 Mar. 1755).

feet: lucky/unlucky

In the superstitious world of luck good and bad, a lucky or unlucky 'foot' can mean the style of someone's foot per se, or a person who one meets at the start of a journey, or someone who arrives the house, as in FIRST FOOTING.

I will not speak of ridiculous friets, such as our meeting with a lucky or unlucky foot, when we are going about important business.

Highland Scotland Sinclair (1685)

The unfortunate person may have gained this reputation because of something other than his/her feet:

A person with red hair is by some looked upon as having an 'ill fit' ... If a fisherman meets one that has the reputation of having an 'ill fit', he makes some excuse for turning and walking a few steps with him or her to turn away the ill luck.

Banffshire *Folk-Lore Jnl* (1885)

The turning and walking ploy is to avoid the consequences of simply MEETING the person face to face. The two attributes of feet which were believed to be particularly unlucky were flatness and bareness.

In some districts, special weight is attached to the 'first foot' being that of a person with a high-arched instep, a foot that 'water runs under'. A flat-footed person would bring great ill-luck for the coming year.

Northern England Henderson (1879)

A bare-footed woman is almost as bad as a witch.

Scotland *Edinburgh Mag.* (Nov. 1818)

It is possible that a barefoot person symbolized poverty, but the prejudice against flat feet is inexplicable. Fear of meeting a bare-foot woman is first mentioned by Nigel de Longchamps in his *Mirror of Fools* (1180), but the flat-footed were apparently safe until the early seventeenth century. They were both still being avoided in the mid twentieth century. These concerns with feet are almost entirely restricted to Scotland, Isle of Man, and Ireland.

See also FEET: RIGHT OR LEFT.

Northern England Henderson (1866) 87; Henderson (1879) 74. Scotland *Edinburgh Mag.* (Nov. 1818) 412; Jamieson, *Scottish Dict. Supp.* (1825) 'Platch'. Eastern Scotland Anson (1930) 38. Northeast Scotland Gregor (1881) 198. Highland Scotland Sinclair (1685) 141. Morayshire Shaw (1775) 232. Glasgow [*c.*1820] Napier (1864) 397. Banffshire Stat. Acct Scotland 14 (1795) 541; *Folk-Lore Jnl* (1885) 308. Aberdeenshire [*c.*1700] Opie & Tatem, 166. Orkney N&Q 10S:12 (1909) 483. Dublin N&Q 4S:2 (1869) 505. Isle of Man *Folk-Lore* 3 (1892) 79; *Folk-Lore* 52 (1941) 269. Unlocated Chambers 2 (1878) 635; Jones (1880) 117. General Nigel de Longchamps, *Mirror of Fools* (1180); R. Bernard, *Guide to Grand-Jury Men* (1627) 14:183.

feet: right or left

The general rule of right/good, left/bad, was translated into a concern with which foot was used first when setting out from home, or entering another:

If you enter another man's house, with your 'skir' [left] foot foremost, you draw down evil on its inhabitants. If, therefore, you have carelessly done so, you must avert the mischief by going out, and making your entrance a second time with the right foot foremost.

Northern England Henderson (1866)

Recorded examples of this belief are only spasmodic, but there is no doubt that it was generally known and followed by many from at least the seventeenth century and probably earlier. It was certainly known in classical times, and Opie & Tatem quote Petronius' *Satyricon* (*c.*AD 65), and St John Chrysostom (*c.*AD 390), who wrote: 'I myself in coming out set forth with the left foot foremost and this . . . is a token of misfortune'.

Woodruff (1967) indicates that it was also a habit of some actors to enter on to the stage with their right foot first. It was also generally considered essential that one got out of bed each morning on to the right foot (*see* BEDS: GETTING UP).

Several other traditions focused on which shoe or stocking was put on first. In general, the right was the lucky one, but in some contexts the left was specifically recommended (*see* SHOES: PUTTING ON; TOOTHACHE: SHOES/STOCKINGS).

Devon Hewett (1900) 51. England Addy (1895) 94. Northern England Henderson (1866) 86–7. Co. Durham Leighton (1910) 60. Scotland *Scotsman* (9 May 1962) 11. General Gaule, *Mag-astro-mances* (1652) 181. Classical Petronius, *Satyricon* (c.AD 65) Ch. 30; St John Chrysostom, *Homilies on Ephesians* (c.AD 390) Ch. 12. Theatrical Woodruff (1967) 110.

feet: toes

A handful of references indicate beliefs about the state of people's toes, but there is little real agreement on meaning.

A woman whose second toe is longer than her big toe will be boss in the house . . . A person with webbed feet will never be drowned.
                Co. Tyrone *Lore & Language* (1972)

If the second toe is longer than the first – the muckle tae – in a man he is unkind to his wife. My informant told me she knew two men who had this peculiarity in the structure of the toes, and they were harsh to their wives.
                Aberdeenshire *Folk-Lore* (1895)

If your toes are joined together by a web you will be lucky.   England Addy (1895)

In 1951 I was told in Gloucestershire that a baby born with an extra toe or finger will always be lucky.   Gloucestershire *Folk-Lore* (1957)

. . . when the two toes next the great toe lie close together it is looked upon as a sign of riches.
                Dumfriesshire Corrie (1890/91)

Gloucestershire *Folk-Lore* 68 (1957) 413. England Addy (1895) 95. Aberdeenshire *Folk-Lore* 6 (1895) 397. Dumfriesshire Corrie (1890/91) 37. Co. Tyrone *Lore & Language* 1:7 (1972) 12. Unlocated N&Q 5S:9 (1878) 286, 476.

ferns: cut stalk

A small set of beliefs centre on the idea that if you cut a fern stalk horizontally you will see a significant letter. In the most common version, it is a form of LOVE DIVINATION:

Other ways of discovering the name of the lover are: Cut through the stem of a bracken fern, and the veins will show the letter.
                Norfolk Wright (1913)

Less common, but more serious, was the idea that the initial is always a C:

The bracken [witches] *also detest because it bears on its root the letter C, the initial of the holy name of Christ, which may plainly be seen on cutting the root horizontally.*   Scotland [c.1816] Henderson

This particular version of the fern belief has only been reported once or twice, but the desire to find comforting religious symbols in the vegetable world is much more common – as witnessed, for example, by the 'Allah in the aubergine' stories of the 1980s. An Irish slant noted in 1865 claimed the letter to be the initial of the name of the chief who owned the land (*Gent. Mag.* (1865)).

A third possibility is that the shape is a representation of an oak tree – the one in which King Charles hid, some say, although why this should be is not stated.

Love divination: Sussex Latham (1878) 31. Cornwall *Folk-Lore Jnl* 5 (1887) 215. East Anglia Forby (1830) 415; Varden (1885) 109. Norfolk Wright (1913) 259.
Jesus Christ/Chief: Scotland [c.1816] Henderson (1866) 190; [c.1909] *Sunday Express* (17 June 1979) 4. Ireland *Gent. Mag.* (1865) 703.
Oak tree: Surrey N&Q 1S:7 (1853) 152. London Vickery (1995) 44.

ferrets

One of the many animals involved in nineteenth-century cures for WHOOPING COUGH:

A boy came into my kitchen the other day with a basin containing a gill of new milk, saying his mother hoped I would let my son's white ferret drink half of it, and then he would take the other half home to the bairn to cure its cough. I found the boy had been getting milk in the village for some days, and thus giving our ferret half of it.
                Co. Durham Henderson (1866)

The details are remarkably constant across Ireland and some parts of England, although it is only reported from the 1860s onwards. This cure is slightly different to the norm. In most whooping cough cures the idea is to pass the disease on to the unwitting animal, but in this case the ferret drinks the milk first. It is thus clear that the animal is playing an active role by bestowing something curative to the sufferer. What that something is, however, is never explained.

Suffolk *Gent. Mag.* (1867) 728–41; *Folk-Lore* 35 (1924) 356. Norfolk Dew (1898) 77–81; *Folk-Lore* 40 (1929) 117.

Shropshire *Folk-Lore* 49 (1938) 228. **Co. Durham** Henderson (1866) 112–13; Leighton (1910) 53. **Co. Longford** *Béaloideas* 6 (1936) 265. **Co. Cork** [1937/8] Culloty (1993) 59. **Co. Leitrim** *Folk-Lore* 5 (1894) 199. **Co. Kerry** *Folk-Lore* 4 (1893) 351.

fighting

Two stray beliefs about fighting, the first of which makes more sense than the second:

Unlucky to fight on board ship – the ship will sink within 24 hours.   Orkney N&Q (1909)

To make peace between men who are fighting – Write on the circumference of an apple the letters H A O N and throw it in the midst of the combatants.   Guernsey [c.1800] MacCulloch MS

Orkney N&Q 10S:12 (1909) 483–4. Guernsey [c.1800] MacCulloch MS (1864) 395.

fingernails: babies'

An extremely widespread superstition prohibited the cutting of a baby's fingernails and hair before it had reached a certain age – usually a year:

It was considered very unlucky to weigh a baby or cut its nails before it was twelve months old. If this was done it would never grow strong and well; the prejudice still exists, and district nurses are looked upon with scant favour for bringing ill-luck on the infant. The nails, if cut, make the child light-fingered; they should be bitten, not cut.   Warwickshire Bloom (c.1930)

As in this example, it was permissible for the mother to bite the nails off, and in most cases the consequence of ignoring this injunction was that the child would grow up to be a thief. This was taken quite seriously, at least by some:

My niece tells me that, in conversation with a poor woman in a village near Bath mention was made of the inmates of a neighbouring reformatory. The poor woman assigned as a reason for their propensity to pilfer and steal, that their mothers must have cut their nails before they were a year old. She always bit her babies' nails, otherwise they would turn out thieves.   Bath N&Q (1865)

It is difficult to hazard any logical explanation for this. Certainly, the cutting and disposal of fingernails and hair were subject to several beliefs (*see* HAIR: DISPOSAL), as were other body parts such as TEETH, at the heart of which was the possibility that witches, fairies, or other

ill-wishers could use such personal material in their spells against you. However, this is simply an argument for careful disposal, and would be just as relevant whether the nails were cut or bitten. A number of superstitions involve the notion that witches and fairies can't abide metal, and some authorities have used this as the reason for the prohibition of scissors when cutting a baby's fingernails. Again, this falls at the first hurdle – if the metal were a protection against ill-wishing, it would be logical to use it in this context rather than ban it.

The basic superstition has been noted from all parts of the British Isles, and was apparently extremely well known from Victorian times onwards, although the first known references are only from the 1850s. It is unlikely to have been brand new at that time, considering that by 1851/2 it was already reported from the Orkneys to Dorset.

Sussex Latham (1878) 11. **Hampshire** [1986] Opie & Tatem, 275. **Dorset** N&Q 1S:4 (1851) 53–4; N&Q 6S:6 (1882) 416; Hewett (1900) 51, 56; Udal (1922) 178, 282. **Devon** *Devonshire Assoc.* 59 (1927) 168; *Devonshire Assoc.* 60 (1928) 125; *Devonshire Assoc.* 105 (1973) 213. **Cornwall** *Folk-Lore Jnl* 5 (1887) 207–8; *Jnl Royal Inst. Cornwall* 20 (1915) 129; *Old Cornwall* 1:9 (1929) 41; *Old Cornwall* 2 (1931–6) 39. **Wiltshire** *Wilts. N&Q* 1 (1893–5) 103, 153. **London** [1982] Opie & Tatem, 275. **Oxfordshire** N&Q 6S:6 (1882) 249. **Bath** N&Q 3S:8 (1865) 146. **Gloucestershire** *Folk-Lore* 26 (1915) 210. **Herefordshire** Leather (1912) 113. **Worcestershire** Salisbury (1893) 71. **Warwickshire** Bloom (c.1930) 27. **East Anglia** Varden (1885) 107. **Norfolk** Dew (1898) 77–81. **Lincolnshire** Swaby (1891) 88; N&Q 1S:6 (1852) 71. **Shropshire** Burne (1883) 285. **Staffordshire** Poole (1875) 85. **England** Addy (1895) 102. **Derbyshire** N&Q 6S:6 (1882) 416; *Midland Garner* 1 (1884) 23; [1890s] Uttley (1946) 125. **Nottinghamshire** N&Q 6S:6 (1882) 416. **Northern England** [1850s] *Denham Tracts* 2 (1895) 24. **Yorkshire** Nicholson (1890) 43; *Folk-Lore* 71 (1960) 261. **Lancashire** Harland & Wilkinson (1873) 221; Harland & Wilkinson (1882) 141; *Lancashire Lore* (1971) 49. **Co. Durham** Brockie (1886) 183; Leighton (1910) 48. **Northumberland** Bigge (1860/62) 93; Bosanquet (1929) 33–4. **West Wales** Trevelyan (1909) 267; Jones (1930) 199. **West Wales** Davies (1911) 218. **Montgomeryshire** Hamer (1877) 258. **Scotland** N&Q 6S:6 (1882) 416. **Western Scotland** Napier (1879) 139. **Dumfriesshire** Corrie (1890/91) 38. **Orkney** N&Q 1S:6 (1852) 311–12. **Co. Antrim** [1905] McDowell (1972) 129–30. **Guernsey** Carey (1903) 506; De Garis (1975) 8. **Unlocated** N&Q 6S:6 (1882) 416; N&Q 2S:12 (1861) 500; N&Q 9S:5 (1900) 375; Igglesden (c.1932) 101, 140.

fingernails: cut on certain days

The idea that finger- (and toe-) nails should be cut only on certain days was extremely wide-spread in British tradition, and has a recorded history of over four hundred years. Details vary to a certain extent, but the strict prohibition of nail-cutting on Fridays and Sundays is almost universal, while the day singled out for lucky paring is most often Monday:

An Irishman told me, with great solemnity, he would rather cut his ear off than cut his nails on a Friday.   Ireland Igglesden (c.1932)

If you cut your nails on Monday morning before breakfast you will receive a present before the week is out. Cut them at all on Friday and dire misfortune will follow.   Hampshire N&Q (1890)

Never cut hair on Friday or trim nails on Sunday:

Friday hair, Sunday shorn
You'll go to devil
Afore Monday morn.

Yorkshire Nicholson (1890)

The well-known rhyme, still often quoted, which enumerates each day of the week, is a relative newcomer, reported only from 1830 onwards. It varies little from version to version, which suggests a primarily literary rather than oral tradition:

Cut them on a Monday, you cut them for
*   health*
Cut them on a Tuesday, you cut them for
*   wealth*
Cut them on Wednesday, you cut them for news
Cut them on Thursday, a new pair of shoes
Cut them on Friday, you cut them for sorrow
Cut them on Saturday, see your true-love
*   tomorrow*
Cut them on Sunday, the devil will be with you
*   all the week.*

East Anglia Forby (1830)

Occasionally, the rhythm is changed, but the content is similar:

Monday health
Tuesday wealth
Wednesday for good fortin
Thursday losses
Friday crosses
And Saturday signifies northin.

Northamptonshire N&Q (1861)

Several references to nail-cutting have survived from the sixteenth and early seventeenth centuries, which attest to the belief's wide currency at that time. Some of these simply state that certain days are unlucky without specifying them – 'young folks beware on what day they par'd their nayles' (Nashe (1594)), but most are unambiguous and the belief was clearly already well entrenched. It continued to be proverbial throughout the seventeenth and eighteenth centuries:

Ha! thou'rt melancholy, old Prognostication, as melancholy as if thou hadst spoilt the salt, or pared thy nails of a Sunday.

Congreve, *Love for Love* (1695)

The idea that FRIDAY is an unlucky day for most activities is extremely widespread, as is the notion that Sunday should be kept clear of anything which is unnecessary or could be construed as 'work'. But the singling out of fingernails (and hair) is not satisfactorily explained by these general prohibitions. It is perhaps more instructive to examine these beliefs in the context of other fingernail superstitions. Many of the other fingernail beliefs are reported a long time after this one, but the acceptance that fingernails could be used in cures, and by witches and other ill-wishers in their spells, is found in British sources just as early as the Friday/Sunday prohibitions. It thus seems likely that we have here a combination of two existing beliefs – (1) be careful with your nail-cuttings, and (2) Fridays and Sundays are to be treated with care.

One or two authorities warn against cutting the nails on the other universally unlucky day, HOLY INNOCENTS' (Childermas) DAY:

That it is not good to put on a new suit, pare ones nails, or begin any thing on a Childermas day.

Melton (1620)

Confusingly, however, GOOD FRIDAY is singled out as a good day for cutting your nails:

Cut all your nails before twelve o'clock on Good Friday, but never cut them on any other Friday in the year, and you will not have toothache.

Worcestershire *Folk-Lore* (1909)

A concern for good and bad days for cutting fingernails, beards, and hair was already widespread in classical times. Ausonius (c.AD 390), for example, wrote that one must cut nails on a Tuesday, beards on Wednesdays, and hair on Friday.

Compare: HAIR: CUTTING

Kent N&Q 1S:6 (1852) 432. Sussex Latham (1878) 11:
Hampshire N&Q 7S:9 (1890) 486. Dorset *Dorset
County Chronicle* (June 1888). Somerset *Folk-Lore* 5
(1894) 338. Devon N&Q 1S:3 (1851) 462; *Devonshire
Assoc.* 10 (1878) 105; *Western Antiquary* 2 (Oct. 1882) 114;
Hewett (1900) 45, 54; N&Q 10S:12 (1909) 66; Crossing
(1911) 134–5; *Devonshire Assoc.* 66 (1934) 75; *Devonshire
Assoc.* 67 (1935) 142; *Devonshire Assoc.* 105 (1973) 213.
Cornwall *Folk-Lore Jnl* 5 (1887) 212; *Old Cornwall* 2
(1931–6) 40. Essex [*c.*1920] Ketteridge & Mays (1972)
141. Hertfordshire *Athenaeum* (1848) 142. Herefordshire
Folk-Lore 26 (1915) 210. Worcestershire/Shropshire
Gent. Mag. (Oct. 1855) 385. Worcestershire *Folk-Lore* 20
(1909) 346. Midland England *Midland Garner* 1 (1884)
23. Warwickshire Langford (1875) 11, 15.
Northamptonshire N&Q 2S:12 (1861) 491. East Anglia
Forby (1830), 410–11. Norfolk Fulcher Collection
(*c.*1895). Shropshire Burne (1883) 259–61. Cheshire
Folk-Lore Jnl 7 (1889) 24. England Addy (1895) 114.
Yorkshire Nicholson (1890) 141–2. Lancashire N&Q
1S:3 (1851) 55; N&Q 4S:6 (1870) 211; Harland &
Wilkinson (1873) 236; Harland & Wilkinson (1882) 68,
153. Co. Durham Brockie (1886) 183; Leighton (1910) 48.
Northumberland/Westmorland *Denham Tracts* 2 (1895)
344. Eastern Scotland Anson (1930) 40. Western
Scotland Napier (1879) 139. Dumfriesshire Shaw (1890)
11. Orkney N&Q 10S:12 (1909) 483–4. Ireland Igglesden
(*c.*1932) 101. Co. Antrim [1905] McDowell (1972) 129–30.
Guernsey Carey (1903) 506 Unlocated Hone, *Year Book*
(1832) 126–8; *Gent. Mag.* (Nov. 1855) 504; *Western
Antiquary* 2 (Oct. 1882) 114; N&Q 160 (1931) 427.
General Thomas Nashe, *Terrors of the Night* (1594) E4;
Melton (1620); Browne, *Pseudodoxia Epidemica* (1672)
Bk 5, Ch. 22 Para: 10; Aubrey, *Remaines* (1686) 194;
Illustrated London News (27 Dec. 1851) 779. Literary
Thomas Lodge, *Wit's Miserie* (1596); William Congreve,
Love for Love (1695) 3:1. Classical Ausonius *Eclogues*
(*c.*AD 390) 26.

---

fingernails: gifts

The small white specks which sometimes appear
on the fingernails were widely believed to be
significant and to betoken a forthcoming gift. So
widespread was this notion that the specks were
simply called 'gifts' in everyday language.

*Gifts on the nails – Small white specks on the nails
are sure indications that those who are so fortunate as to have them, will in some way or other be
better for them; though perhaps not literally in the
matter implied by the name. And some sagacious
old women are very shrewd in explaining, from
their number, size, position, &c.in what manner
they will be.*   East Anglia Forby (1830)

Children, especially, were pleased to see the
marks appear:

*I well remember, when a boy, how a school-mate
speculated on the appearance of a 'gift' on his
thumb, as to what the gift would be; for he
certainly believed there was one in store for him.*

*How delighted he was when a letter was received,
saying his uncle was coming to visit his widowed
mother, and bring a watch for him.*
                              Yorkshire Nicholson (1890)

Further information could be gleaned by which
finger the mark appeared on:

*On the thumb, sure to come
On the finger, sure to linger
[Counting from the thumb]
A friend, a foe, a letter to write
And a journey to go.*
                              Wiltshire *Wilts. N&Q* (1893–5)

Several seventeenth-century writers refer to
such marks on the nails as predictive, in terms
which show that the belief was already proverbial by that period. Ben Jonson is the earliest, in
the play *The Alchemist* (1610), and Thomas
Browne was sceptical about their meaning in his
Pseudodoxia Epidemica (1652). John Melton
(1620), however, provides a clue to wider nail
beliefs '. . . to have yellow speckles on the nails of
one's hand is a great sign of death'.

Kent Igglesden (*c.*1932) 228–9. Sussex Latham (1878) 32.
Hampshire [1969] Opie & Tatem, 273. Devon Hewett
(1900) 51; Crossing (1911) 134–5. Cornwall Couch (1871)
169; *Folk-Lore Jnl* 5 (1887) 213. Wiltshire *Wilts. N&Q* 1
(1893–5) 149. Berkshire Lowsley (1888) 22. Oxfordshire
[pre-1900] *Folk-Lore* 24 (1913) 90. Warwickshire
Langford (1875) 22. Northamptonshire Baker (1854)
'Gifts'; N&Q 2S:12 (1861) 491. East Anglia Forby (1830)
410–11; Varden (1885) 107. Suffolk Moor (1823) 'Gifts'.
Norfolk Fulcher Collection (*c.*1895). Staffordshire
Hackwood (1924) 149. Northern England Brockett
(1829) 132. Yorkshire Nicholson (1890) 42. Co. Durham
Brockie (1886) 184. Wales Jones (1930) 199. West Wales
Davies (1911) 216. Scotland *Folk-Lore* 6 (1895) 396.
Aberdeenshire *Folk-Lore* 6 (1895) 397. Dumfriesshire
Corrie (1890/91) 37. Forfarshire [1950] Opie & Tatem,
273. Orkney N&Q 10S:12 (1909) 483–4. Co. Tyrone *Lore
& Language* 1:7 (1972) 12. Unlocated N&Q 149 (1925)
107, 122. General Browne *Pseudodoxia Epidemica* (1650)
Bk 5, Ch. 12; Melton (1620) 45; *British Apollo* (7 Apr.
1708). Literary Ben Jonson, *The Alchemist* (1610) 1:3;
Connoisseur 59 (1755) 353.

---

fingernails: spells

see HAIR: SPELLS.

---

fingers

The most widespread beliefs about fingers are
given separate treatment (*see below* and FINGER-
NAILS; CROSSED FINGERS), but a variety of
other beliefs and customs have also been

collected on the subject. As with many other body features, the size and shape of a person's fingers could reveal major character traits. Long fingers, for example, were believed to show a disposition to thieving:

If the forefinger is equal in length to the second finger, or longer than it, the person will not hesitate to steal. One of my informants knew a man who had this peculiarity in the fingers. When a child was born in the district the women present at the birth examined the new-born's fingers, and if there was no such malformation the remark was made that the fingers were not like So-and-So's.   Aberdeenshire *Folk-Lore* (1895)

But there was little agreement about crooked fingers:

Crooked fingers indicate a crabbed disposition.   Aberdeenshire *Folk-Lore* (1895)

One with crooked little fingers will be rich before death.   Hebrides *Folk-Lore* (1895)

Even clasped hands are indicative:

If a person habitually and without intent clasp the hands interlacing the fingers, so that the right thumb is over the left, it shows that he or she has a strong will. If the left is over the right, a weak will. I think there is the same idea about crossing the legs, but I am not sure.   Co. Dublin *Folk-Lore* (1894)

Children seem to be especially fond of little fingers, as they featured in several of their customs. If two people say the same thing at the same time they should link little fingers and make a wish (*see* TALKING) and after a quarrel they can link fingers and chant something on the lines of 'Make up, make up, never do it again'. Correspondence in *Notes and Queries* in 1876 discussed a phrase 'Pinching by the little finger':

When I was a boy, I remember often pinching and being pinched. Boys pinched the little finger of girls, and vice versa, to see whether they could keep a secret or not. If anyone screamed out under the operation, it was a sign that the person so pinched could not keep a secret, and vice versa. Of course boys pinched harder than girls, and so the latter were deemed unworthy of confidence. I believe the like operation was performed by lovers to try each other's constancy.   N&Q (1876)

It is suggested that this custom may help explain two obscure references in Shakespeare (*Henry IV Pt 1* 2:3 and *Winter's Tale* 1:2) which refer to fingers and truth, and pinching fingers, respectively.

Gloucestershire *Folk-Lore* 68 (1957) 413. **England** Addy (1895) 78, 93. **Wales** Trevelyan (1909) 328. **Aberdeenshire** *Folk-Lore* 6 (1895) 396. **Dumbartonshire** *Folk-Lore* 6 (1895) 396. **Hebrides** *Folk-Lore* 6 (1895) 396. **Co. Dublin** *Folk-Lore* 5 (1894) 283. **General** N&Q 5S:6 (1876) 108, 214, 337–8.

fingers: good/bad

It was thought by many in the nineteenth and even for much of the twentieth century that the forefinger, or index finger, of the right hand was poisonous, and must never be used in any medical treatment:

The forefinger of the right hand is considered by the common people as venomous, and consequently is never used in applying anything to a wound or sore.   Northern England [1850s] *Denham Tracts*

Sources vary on which was the best finger to use instead: some recommend the middle finger, while others insist on the ring finger.

Salves and ointments should not be applied with the first finger, but with the middle or longest finger.   England Addy (1895)

The ring-finger is the healing finger because it has been blessed.   Somerset Tongue (1965)

In much older tradition, as evidenced from a manuscript from the fifteenth century in Cambridge University, each finger had a name and supposed character. The ring finger was called 'lecheman' (= leechman, or doctor), but the index finger was called 'towcher' (= toucher), and no mention is made of any bad qualities.

Somerset N&Q 1S:7 (1853) 153; Kettlewell (1927) 32–3; [1912/1957] Tongue (1965) 138. **Cornwall** *Jnl Royal Inst. Cornwall* 20 (1915) 131. **Shropshire** Burne (1883) 185. **Staffordshire** [1891] *Folk-Lore* 20 (1909) 221. **England** Addy (1895) 90. **Northern England** [1850s] *Denham Tracts* 2 (1895) 24. **Yorkshire?** [1988] Opie & Tatem, 149. **Lancashire** Harland & Wilkinson (1882) 75. **General** [15th cent.] MS Camb. Univ. Lib. Ff. v. 48, f.82v., quoted Opie & Tatem, 149; Browne *Pseudodoxia Epidemica* (1646) Bk 4, Ch. 4; Brand 3 (1849) 177–8.

fingers: joints cracking

Occasional references indicate a divinatory procedure which involved cracking the joints of someone's fingers:

We pulled each finger and the number of joints that cracked meant one had that number of sweethearts.   Sussex [*c.*1915] Opie & Tatem, 149

In some the cracks predict the number of babies one would have in the future. Although recorded only a few times, this divination game is quite long-lived: it was already in circulation in the 1750s, and was still being reported two hundred years later.

Sussex [*c*.1915] Opie & Tatem, 149. Yorkshire *Folk-Lore Jnl* 6 (1887) 85. Unlocated Opie (1959) 328. Literary *Connoisseur* 59 (1755) 353; *Old Women's Sayings* (*c*.1835).

fire: cinders falling from

One of several superstitions regarding the behaviour of the domestic fire, which claims to predict good or bad fortune:

A cinder thrown out of the fire is eagerly examined, and if it is long and hollow, is called a coffin; if it is round, it is said to be a purse.
                                    Yorkshire *Leeds Mercury* (4 Oct. 1879)

The earliest known reference is in 1727, but the belief is clearly already well known at that time by the proverbial way in which it is mentioned:

Last night (I vow to heav'n 'tis true)
Bounce from the fire a coffin flew
Next post some fatal news shall tell.
                    Gay, 'The Farmer's Wife and the Raven' (1727)

Another eighteenth-century treatment of the theme is similarly terse:

The girls themselves had their omens . . . purses bounced from the fire.
                    Goldsmith, *The Vicar of Wakefield* (1766)

The basic belief is remarkably stable over the years, although occasionally a third shape (oval) is held to resemble a cradle and to predict a birth, or the sound the cinder makes is significant: noiseless (funeral) or clinking sound (money). As in other falling or spilling superstitions, note was often taken of who the cinder flew towards as they would be the one for whom the omen was destined.

The geographical spread of references is overwhelmingly English, with only one each from Wales and Scotland. However, some Irish examples indicate that cinders from their fires meant a stranger:

If a burning ember falls out of the fire you'll have either an insleeper or an outsleeper. (An insleeper is a visitor who spends the night in the house and an outsleeper is a member of the household who spends the night elsewhere and not under the family roof.)   Co. Tyrone *Lore & Language* (1972)

When a coal falls someone is coming. Spit on it and he can do no harm, or put it back in the fire and he will go astray.
                    Co. Longford *Béaloideas* (1936)

Wiltshire *Wilts. N&Q* 1 (1893–5) 8, 59. Berkshire Mitford (1830) 299; Lowsley (1888) 22. Somerset [1923] Opie & Tatem, 83. Herefordshire [1804] Leather (1912) 65. Worcestershire/Shropshire *Gent. Mag.* (Oct. 1855) 385. Warwickshire Bloom (*c*.1930) 44. East Anglia Varden (1885) 113. Suffolk [1863] Chambers 2 (1878) 52–3. Lincolnshire *Gent. Mag.* (1833) 590–3; Peacock (1877) 66; Swaby (1891) 92. Staffordshire Hackwood (1924) 147. Northern England Brockett (1829) 76. Yorkshire *Leeds Mercury* 4 Oct. 1879; Nicholson (1890) 43–4. Lancashire Harland & Wilkinson (1882) 139. Co. Durham N&Q 5S:6 (1876) 397; [1984] Opie & Tatem, 83. Wales Trevelyan (1909) 283. Western Scotland Napier (1879) 138–9. Co. Longford *Béaloideas* (1936) 263. Co. Tyrone *Lore & Language* (1972) 11. Unlocated Grose (1787) 48, 68. Literary John Gay, 'The Farmer's Wife and the Raven, *Fables* (1727); *Connoisseur* 59 (1755) 351; Oliver Goldsmith, *The Vicar of Wakefield* (1766) Ch. 10; *Illustrated London News* (27 Dec. 1851) 779.

fire: poker

On the boundary between superstition and vulgar error lie beliefs such as the following:

If the fire does not burn well, and you want to 'draw it up', you should set the poker across the hearth, with the fore part leaning across the top bar of the grate, and you will have a good fire – if you wait long enough . . . I have seen the thing done scores of times.   Suffolk Chambers (1878)

While some in the past maintained hotly that it is a scientific fact that this stratagem works, with an explanation involving split draughts, others are equally sure that it was practised to keep 'witches' or other 'evil powers' away, by forming a cross between the vertical poker and the horizontal bars of the grate. Either way, the custom was certainly common:

I have seen it done in private houses, and very frequently in the public rooms of country inns. Indeed, in such public rooms it was the common practice when the servant put on a fire, that after sweeping up the dust she placed the poker in this position, and left the room. Probably she had no idea why she did it, but merely followed the custom.   Western Scotland Napier (1879)

The 'witches' explanation was already in place for our earliest reference in 1731, and Boswell reports a conversation with Johnson in 1779 in which the latter is clearly aware of the superstition. We thus have the unusual situation of having the customary action and the explanation in place right from the start of the documentary record, referring to a previous time, and we thus have little option but to believe it. Quotations in Opie and Tatem show the custom alive and well in the 1980s.

A more recent explanation, that the poker works against evil forces because it is made of IRON, has little merit when one considers that the whole grate would already be made of metal and would presumably not need any addition.

Hampshire [1983] Opie & Tatem, 313. **Somerset** [1904–7] Tongue (1965) 142; [1923] Opie & Tatem, 313. **Surrey** Mrs Thrale, *Diary* (1778). **London** Boswell, *Life of Samuel Johnson* (10 Oct. 1779). **Bedfordshire** *Folk-Lore* 37 (1926) 77. **Suffolk?** Chambers 1 (1878) 104–5. **Norfolk** *Folk-Lore* 26 (1915) 210. **Yorkshire** Nicholson (1890) 86; *Folk-Lore* 26 (1915) 210. **Lancashire** Harland & Wilkinson (1873) 238. **Co. Durham** [1980] Opie & Tatem, 313. **Western Scotland** Napier (1879) 136. **Unlocated** Brand 3 (1849) 310; Wright (1913) 230; Igglesden (*c.*1932) 176. **General** *Round About the Coal-Fire* (1731) 22.

---

fire: poking

Part statement of social etiquette and part superstition, it was previously a common saying that one should never poke another person's fire – unless you knew them very well:

You must be a seven years' friend of the house before you dare stir the fire.

Unlocated N&Q (1880)

we do not like strangers to stir our fires. This would only be done by a person of long-standing acquaintance, and is usually prefaced by the remark, 'May I poke your fire? I've known you seven years, I think'. And even though the hostess might assent, she would still think it not very good manners on the part of the other person.

Co. Durham *Folk-Lore* (1960)

The 'seven years' rule is often quoted, and occasionally extended to 'or been drunk with him three times'. The belief is only reported from England and Wales and, although reasonably widespread, does not appear to date back further than the late nineteenth century. Nevertheless, other ideas about poking the fire have been documented once or twice, including one which is diametrically opposed to that quoted above:

It is good luck for a stranger to poke the house fire.

Worcestershire *Folk-Lore* (1909)

It is difficult to know whether the relative rarity of the following superstitions in the documentary record is an accident or reflects the true state of affairs, but they do serve to show that treatment of the domestic fire was a serious business:

Arrived at her new place, a maid's first care, if she would have luck there, must be to light a fire . . . or to poke or mend a fire.

Shropshire Burne (1883)

When you go to a new house, poke the fire for luck.

England Addy (1895)

Stir the fire with the tongs stirs up anger.

Somerset *Folk-Lore* (1894)

If you go to see a neighbour and find that she is poking the fire as you enter, it is a sign that you are not welcome.

Herefordshire Leather (1912)

One situation when it was permissible, even expected, for a visitor to stir the fire was when it was part of a NEW YEAR first footing or guising custom (eg. **Shropshire** Burne (1883)).

Wiltshire *Grantham Jnl* (22 June 1878); Wiltshire (1975) 85. **Berkshire** *Folk-Lore* 5 (1894) 338. **Somerset** *Folk-Lore* 5 (1894) 338. **Herefordshire** Leather (1912) 86. **Worcestershire** *Folk-Lore* 20 (1909) 345. **Lincolnshire** Rudkin (1936) 20. **Shropshire** Burne (1883) 274, 317. **England** Addy (1895) 93. **Co. Durham** *Folk-Lore* 71 (1960) 254. **West Wales** Davies (1911) 216. **Northeast Scotland** Gregor (1881) 30. **Unlocated** N&Q 174 (1938) 103, 142; N&Q 6S:1 (1880) 55.

---

fire: soot on grate

Some superstitions are so familiar to all that they become well-known sayings in their own right. Such, for example, was the 'Letter in the candle' (*see* CANDLES: LETTER), and the 'Stranger on the bar':

If a piece of soot clings to the bar of a grate it is a sign that a stranger may be expected; and if it hangs down a long flake you can ascertain what day the stranger will come by clapping your hands close to it until it falls off by reason of the current of air thus created, whilst repeating at each stroke a day of the week.

Dorset Udal (1922)

In some cases, there was more to it:

The popular lines as I have known them all my life are:

If the stranger on the bar goes in the fire
Your friend will come nigher;
If the stranger goes in the ash,

Your friend will come none the less;
If the stranger goes up the chimney,
Your friend will come, but you'll not see
*   him (her).*

The rule is to wait and see; but if the 'stranger'
takes much time over deciding which way to
dispose itself, you may 'waft' it with your hands
and say:

Stranger mine, come to me;
If not mine, flee a-wee!

A littler stranger is a child; a medium one, a lady,
and a big one a man. Two together on a bar are
a sign of a married couple, or that there will be
a wedding in the family if both fly away together,
but if separately, the wedding will not be 'yet a
while'. Lasses, especially country lasses, used to
make much of the 'stranger on the bar'; and if
'wafting' with the hands did not make it budge,
the end was hastened by using the apron.

Unlocated N&Q (1910)

First mentioned in the mid eighteenth century
and lasting well into the twentieth, but presumably now the victim of smokeless fuels and the
demise of the domestic open fire.

Dorset Udal (1922) 286. **Somerset** [1923] Opie & Tatem,
151. **Essex** [1983] Opie & Tatem, 151. **Wiltshire** Wilts.
N&Q 1 (1893–5) 59. **Herefordshire** Leather (1912) 86.
Worcestershire/Shropshire Gent. Mag. (Oct. 1855) 385.
East Anglia Varden (1885) 113. **Lincolnshire** Thompson
(1856) 734; Swaby (1891) 92. **Staffordshire** Poole (1875)
86; Hackwood (1924) 149. **Derbyshire** [1890s] Uttley
(1946) 128. **Northern England** Brand (1777) 94; N&Q
4S:2 (1868) 553. **Yorkshire** Leeds Mercury (4 Oct. 1879);
Nicholson (1890) 86–7; Folk-Lore 21 (1910) 227.
Lancashire Harland & Wilkinson (1882) 139.
Glamorgan Phillips (1925) 598. **Western Scotland**
Napier (1879) 140–1. **Glasgow** [c.1820] Napier (1864)]
397. **Dumfriesshire** Shaw (1890) 13; Corrie (1890/91) 83.
Isle of Man Gill (1934) 36. **Unlocated** Grose (1787) 68;
N&Q 11S:1 (1910) 415. **Literary** Connoisseur 59 (1755)
351.

fire: two together

Several superstitions warn against two people
doing the same thing together. The most widespread of these is WASHING HANDS, but minor
versions include making up a fire:

It is very unlucky for two persons to kindle a fire,
as they will inevitably quarrel.

Shropshire Burne (1883)

Compare TWO TOGETHER.

Southern England [1981] Opie & Tatem, 156.
Shropshire Burne (1883) 275.

first animal seen: head or tail

A widespread belief says that when you see the
first young of certain species in the spring, it is
lucky if they are facing you, but unlucky if you
see their tail first. This can apply to any domestic or farm animal, but was mostly said of lambs
and foals.

See SHEEP: FIRST LAMB SEEN; HORSES:
FIRST FOAL SEEN.

first animal seen: killed

It was a tradition to kill the first example of
certain species that were seen in the year. The
usual reason for this is that one would thereby
overcome, or be free from, one's enemies for the
coming year.

See BUTTERFLIES; SNAKES; WASPS.

first footing (New Year)

First footing is regarded as the archetypal
Scottish custom but in fact it was previously
common in England and parts of Wales as well.
Nevertheless, it was taken more seriously in
Scotland than elsewhere and continued to
operate there while virtually dying out in other
parts. 'First footing' can also be applied to other
situations which involve 'firsts', such as MEET-
ING someone first thing in the morning, and it
can also refer to Christmas rather than New
Year.

The basic tenet of the custom is that the first
person who enters the house in the New Year
brings either good or bad luck for the next twelve
months, depending on whether or not s/he
conforms to the local idea of being 'lucky', and
whether s/he performs the expected tasks.

Each community had its own rules for the
custom, and these varied widely within a basic
broad format. Indeed, it seems to be the case that
many households had their own individual ways
of proceeding, but the long-term trend has
definitely been towards homogeneity.

Elements of the first-footing custom can be
assigned to one of four main categories: (1) positive personal characteristics of the first footer,
which were sought after; (2) negative personal
attributes, which should be avoided; (3) symbolic
gifts which were carried into the house; and (4)

Many customs and superstitions, such as first footing, were so well known that they needed no explanation when used in publications such as Punch.

symbolic actions carried out by him/her, or the occupants of the house.

Most accounts stress some physical aspect of the first footer, and the modern positive stereotype is a 'tall dark-haired man', but this was not always the case. Dark hair is definitely the most often quoted attribute, but it was certainly not universal, even in Scotland, and a small minority of descriptions say a fair- or red-haired man was preferred:

The Lucky Bird – the first man that comes to the house, if he be fair, especially if he has a red head, brings luck; if he be dark-haired is unlucky. This was so much observed in the Bradford and Huddersfield district that a red-haired man was sometimes hired to come round. A woman or black-haired man are unlucky.

Yorkshire *Folk-Lore* (1894)

Again, despite the wide variety of acceptable or desirable physical attributes, almost all agree that a woman would be bad luck. There are a few exceptions to this rule, but they are a tiny minority. Some sources indicate ambivalence, or at least differing views on this question:

In most places throughout West Wales, even at the present day, people are very particular as to whether they see a man or a woman the first thing on New Year's morning. Mr. Williams in

his 'Llen-Gwerin Sir Gaerfyrddin' says that in parts of Carmarthenshire in order to secure future luck or success during the coming year, a man must see a woman and a woman a man. And the Rev. N. Thomas, Vicar of Llanbadarn Fawr, informed me that he has met people in his parish who consider it lucky to see a woman first. As a rule, however, the majority of people both men and women deem it lucky to see a man, but unlucky to see a woman.

Wales Davies (1911)

The seriousness with which some householders took this matter is demonstrated in many accounts of specific instances, such as the following extract reporting a case at Mansfield Police Court. A man was charged with assaulting a young woman on New Year's Day, and the following explanation for her being out of doors at the time was given:

The young woman attended the midnight service at the parish church, and returned home a few minutes past twelve o'clock; but the mother, believing in the superstition that it is unlucky for a female to enter the house on New Year's morning before a man, told the daughter that neither her father nor brother had yet come home, and she was to wait until they came to enter the house first. The girl, in consequence, went for a stroll, the morning being moonlight, and returned to the house five times, but, as her father and brother had not returned, the mother kept the door locked. For the sixth time she went for a walk along the streets, this being about a quarter to one o'clock, when the prisoner met and assaulted her.

Nottinghamshire N&Q (1890)

Apart from colour of hair, and sex, other negative characteristics of the first footer are numerous. A representative list given in Banks 2 (1939), taken from a variety of late nineteenth-century Scottish sources, includes people who are pious and sanctimonious, flat-footed, barefooted, stingy, lame, who have a blind eye, who are midwives, ministers, doctors, gravediggers, thieves, who have met with an accident on the way, and who are carrying a knife or a pointed tool. Despite the apparently bewildering variety of attributes to avoid, the underlying principles are clear. The first footer must be whole, socially acceptable, and lucky, to guarantee those desirable qualities for the house for the forthcoming year.

The next key point of first footing is that the person must not arrive empty-handed. The overwhelming importance of bringing something into the house before anything is taken out at this time of year is treated below (*see* NEW YEAR: INWARD AND OUTWARD). As the first person to enter, the first footer must be careful not to break this rule. A wide variety of items were carried, but most of them carried symbolic weight by being staples of life such as food, drink, heat, or light:

It was very important, too, that the qualtagh *on New Year's Day, should bring some gift, as if he or she came empty handed, misfortunes would be sure to ensue.*   Isle of Man Moore (1891)

In Durham, the first foot must bring in a piece of coal, a bit of iron, and a bottle of whiskey.
  Co. Durham *Newcastle Weekly Chronicle* (11 Feb. 1899)

Sometimes, instead of a whisky-bottle, the first-foot carries shortbread, oatcakes, 'sweeties', and last, but not least, sowens . . . it used to be customary to bring water from the well and peats from the stack.
        Aberdeenshire *Folk-Lore* (1895)

Symbolic actions are not always reported, but in many cases there were set things that the first footer should do. They nearly always have to wish everyone a happy New Year, sometimes have to cut a special cake, stir the fire, or visit every room in the house. Some households stipulate that the first footer should enter by the front door and leave by the back, which is directly opposed to how it would be at other times of the year (*see* DOORS).

The main job of the First Foot is, of course, to 'Cut the cake'. A round cake is preferred to any other shape, placed, if possible, on a round table. He wishes prosperity to all while plunging the knife into the cake. All present are expected to eat a piece, however small, so that the chain of luck will not be broken. The First Foot is not immune from hazards. If he should stumble on entering the house, ill-luck will follow him, as it will if he 'breaks the cake', that is does not make a clean cut. And woe betide him if, on cutting the cake, he breaks the cake-stand! He is doomed to die within the year. As a child, I remember the awful silence which once followed such a catastrophe at a First-Footing. The superstition must have gained ground enormously in our family when, a few months later, the unhappy First Foot died suddenly.
        Co. Durham *Folk-Lore* (1960)

Few people left the matter to chance, and most householders who believed in the custom arranged beforehand for someone who fitted the ideal to come along soon after midnight. Some knew exactly who to expect:

The old folk go off to bed but many of the young ones will not be there for hours yet. Each girl is expecting the first-foot from her sweetheart, and anxious to be the first to open the door to him, and many a quiet stratagem is sometimes spent in the endeavour to outwit her, and get the old grandmother, or some dooce serving-lass to be the first to met the kiss-expecting lover. Quieter folks will put off their first footing until morning, but in nearly all Scottish families the first-foot is looked upon as a matter of no little importance, and notes will be compared among the neighbours in country villages as to who was their first-foot-luck or ill-luck, according to the character of the visitor.
        Scotland *All the Year Round* (31 Dec. 1870)

The biggest mystery about New Year first-footing is that it cannot be traced before the mid nineteenth century, and even if we allow some earlier references which refer to similar first-foot customs on Christmas Day, the documentary record still only reaches back to about 1804/5. It is not at all unusual for CALENDAR CUSTOMS to have a much shorter history than has been assumed, but given the popularity and wide geographical distribution of first footing, it is surprising that earlier descriptions have not been found. The central motif of good/bad luck being predicted by a person met in the morning or at the start of a journey certainly goes back much further, and a tentative suggestion is that the New Year custom is simply a specialized version of the former belief, which was later incorporated into a calendar custom.

Some time before that date there had been long-running confusion over exactly when the New Year commenced. Scotland officially adopted 1 January as the start of the year in 1600, but England, Ireland, and Wales did not do so until 1752 (*see* CALENDAR). Until that date in the latter countries, the official and religious new year started on 25 March, but unofficially there had been a long slow process of adoption of 1 January as the de facto New Year's Day. Samuel Pepys, for example, labelled 1 January 1666 as New Year's Day in his Diary, almost a century before it was officially recognized.

The geographical distribution is interesting. Clearly, with such a widely practised custom, the listing given here is more than usually tentative, but it is clear from this list that first footing was strongest in Scotland and northern England – particularly Yorkshire and Lancashire. Ireland hardly appears at all. Nevertheless, of the five references so far found from before 1850, two are from Scotland, two from Herefordshire, and one from the Isle of Man.

Devon N&Q 10S:12 (1909) 66; [1920s] *Devonshire Assoc.* 91 (1959) 202. Wiltshire *Wilts. N&Q* 1 (1893–5) 105. Surrey [1893] *Folk-Lore* 26 (1915) 162. London [1872] Cullwick (1984) 189, 262. Bristol N&Q 10S:5 (1906) 94–5. Gloucestershire *Folk-Lore* 7 (1896) 90; *Folk-Lore* 13 (1902) 174; *Folk-Lore* 37 (1926) 371. Herefordshire Duncomb (1804) 59; [1821] Leather (1912) 109. Worcestershire/Shropshire *Gent. Mag.* (1855) 384–6. Worcestershire N&Q 2S:3 (1857) 343; N&Q 5S:3 (1875) 6–7; Salisbury (1893) 72; Berkeley & Jenkins (1932) 33. Suffolk *Folk-Lore* 35 (1924) 352. Norfolk Randell (1966) 99. Lincolnshire Watkins (1886) 12; Swaby (1891) 94; Rudkin (1936) 41. Leicestershire Billson (1895) 70. Shropshire [*c.*1830] *Folk-Lore* 20 (1909) 222; N&Q 2S:4 (1857) 25; N&Q 5S:3 (1875) 465; Burne (1883) 159; *Bye-Gones* (12 Jan. 1887) 223; *Folk-Lore* 49 (1938) 231–2. Staffordshire [1891] *Folk-Lore* 20 (1909) 222. England Addy (1895) 106–7. Derbyshire N&Q 10S:5 (1906) 45. Nottinghamshire *Jnl. Brit. Arch. Assoc.* 8 (1853) 231; N&Q 7S:10 (1890) 5. Northern England Brockett (1829) 118–9; [1850s] *Denham Tracts* 2 (1895) 24; *Illustrated London News* (2 May 1857); N&Q 4S:5 (1870) 89; Williamson (1962) 9. Yorkshire Young 2 (1817) 879; N&Q 1S:6 (1852) 311–12; N&Q 1S:11 (1855) 105; Robinson (1861) 266; Henderson (1866) 55–6; N&Q 5S:9 (1878) 477–8; N&Q 7S:10 (1890) 516; Nicholson (1890) 20; *Folk-Lore* 5 (1894) 341; Addy (1895) 105–6; Blakeborough (1898) 71; *Folk-Lore* 11 (1900) 220; Gutch (1901) 230; Home (1905) 259; Morris (1911) 218; *Folk-Lore* 43 (1932) 253; Kitchen (1940) ch. 15; [1957] Opie & Tatem, 159; *Observer Supp.* (24 Nov. 1968) 10. Yorkshire/Lancashire N&Q 4S:5 (1878) 118. Lancashire N&Q 1S:3 (1851) 56, 516; *Illustrated London News* (2 May 1857) 416; N&Q 2S:4 (1857) 25; N&Q 4S:7 (1871) 299–300; Harland & Wilkinson (1873) 225; Harland & Wilkinson (1882) 155, 214–15; *Folk-Lore* 7 (1896) 90; *Folk-Lore* 11 (1900) 220; *Folk-Lore* 21 (1910) 224. Cumberland Bulkeley (1886) 231. Co. Durham Henderson (1866) 55–6; *Newcastle Weekly Chronicle* (11 Feb. 1899) 7; *Folk-Lore* 20 (1909) 73; Leighton (1910) 56; *Folk-Lore* 71 (1960) 252, 254. Northumberland Bigge (1860–62) 92; Henderson (1866) 55–6; Heslop (1892) 286; Balfour (1904) 64; *Folk-Lore* 36 (1925) 255; Bosanquet (1929) 74; [1982] Opie & Tatem, 161. Wales Trevelyan (1909) 325–30; Davies (1911) 62–4. Breconshire Francis Kilvert, *Diary* (20 Oct. 1870). Pembrokeshire Sikes (1880) 254–5; Davies (1911) 62–4. Carmarthenshire Davies (1911) 62–4. Cardiganshire Davies (1911) 62–4. Montgomeryshire Hamer (1877) 252–4. Scotland J. Nichol, *Poems* 1 (1805) 33, quoted Opie & Tatem, 159; Jamieson, *Scottish Dictionary* 1 (1825) 408; *All the Year Round* (31 Dec. 1870) 110. Highland Scotland Macbain (1887/88) 250. Renfrewshire [1986] Opie & Tatem, 159. Fifeshire Simpkins (1912) 146. Angus Laing (1885) 70; [1954] Opie & Tatem, 160. Aberdeenshire *Folk-Lore* 6 (1895) 395. Edinburgh Gomme Collection: Corres. Gertrude Hope (1 Mar. 1893). Caithness Sutherland (1937) 104. Hebrides McPhee (1970) 9. Isle of Skye *Folk-Lore* 34 (1923) 90. Orkney N&Q 10S:12 (1909) 483–4; Banks (1946) 41. N. Ireland Foster (1951) 36. Co. Tyrone *Lore*

& Language 1:7 (1972) 7. Isle of Man Train 2 (1845) 115; Moore (1891) 102–3. Unlocated N&Q 2S:2 (1856) 325–6; N&Q 10S:5 (1906) 45. General *Punch* (1 Jan. 1881) 310; Hoggart (1957) Ch.2.
For major studies of New Year customs *see*: Banks 2 (1939) 73–118; Wright & Lones 2 (1938) 1–50; *Folk-Lore* 3 (1892) 253–64; *Folk-Lore* 4 (1893) 309–21.

firsts

The overwhelming importance of BEGINNINGS in superstition results in a widespread concern with *firsts*. If the beginning of a time period, a journey, project, or venture is so important to its later success, the superstitious person is keen to maximize his/her chances by following certain procedures and looks for signs to indicate how things will turn out. S/he must get out of bed in the right way, put on a certain shoe or stocking first, take the first step over the threshold with the right foot, and so on.

These are matters under his/her control, but outside the house there is much more scope for mischief. Hopefully, the first person met will not have undesirable attributes, such as CROSSED EYES, or RED HAIR; the first money received at the market (the HANDSEL) should be spat on for luck, and the CUCKOO must first be heard when you have money in your pocket. In addition, the first lamb or foal seen in spring must be facing you to be lucky, the first fruit of the season should be greeted with some little ceremony, and the first sight of the new MOON, or the first MINCE PIE of the day, with a wish.

Many things discovered for the first time in the year had the property of bestowing a wish, we said. So off we started, wishing with the first snowdrop we saw, with the first primrose we found, with the first strawberry we ate.

Derbyshire [1890s] Uttley (1946) 135

fishing: forbidden words

One of the best-known superstitions of fishermen and their families is that they had (and still have in some cases) a number of words which they refuse to use while at sea, or while engaged in other important aspects of their trade, such as mending nets. These words, if uttered, were thought to bring bad luck to the fishing trip or to the boat, and were thus habitually avoided. The words varied somewhat from place to place, but the most common were pig, hare, rabbit, church/kirk, minister, salmon, egg, cat, and rat.

fishing industry

It is no exaggeration to state that fishing communities have been the most superstitious of all, and especially the fishermen themselves. A huge range of superstitions have been reported from the industry all over the British Isles. Many of these are also reported from non-fishing communities and they follow the general principles that other people's beliefs do, but there are also a fair number that are unique to them.

The reason that is normally given for the extra-superstitious nature of fishing communities is that the men face such dangers, and are at the mercy of the elements, day after day, that their beliefs seek to compensate for the perceived lack of control over their own fate. There is no doubt a lot of truth in this, and other workers in dangerous situations, such as miners, have traditionally shown a similar heightened awareness of luck, good and bad. But there is also a sense that superstition, like all shared tradition, thrives best where there is a strong, tightly knit community which is inwardly rather than outwardly focused. As discussed under FISHING: FORBIDDEN WORDS, there is a strong sense that superstitions which provide rules covering the trivia of everyday life function as markers of who is in and who is out of the group. Fishermen from fishing families will know the rules, outsiders will not. Youngsters will thus be particularly keen to learn them, in order to prove themselves fit for membership.

In addition to those superstitions treated separately below, out of dozens reported only a handful of times, a sample demonstrates the range involved.

Fishermen, like others, have a horror of TEMPTING FATE:

Fishermen count it as unlucky to be asked the number of their catch.   Orkney N&Q (1909)

Fishermen count it as unlucky for anyone to wish them good luck as they are putting out.
Orkney N&Q (1909)

Their beliefs reveal a keen sense of the symbolic action which translates into bad luck aboard ship. Thus they avoid turning buckets upside down, and anything to do with water must be carefully controlled:

Fishermen's womenfolk say: 'Never wash on the day your man go away, or you wash him away.'
Suffolk *Folk-Lore* (1924)

Fishermen count it as unlucky for anyone to throw water on a person going to the fishing.
Orkney N&Q (1909)

At times, the symbolism seems to rely on little more than a verbal pun:

No fisherwife would dream of winding wool by candle-light – to do such a wicked thing would be tantamount to winding the husband overboard.   Yorkshire Blakeborough (1898)

Harmful, if not fatal, results are believed to follow the utterance of certain words at sea. The salmon is ever a 'fine bit fish', and swine, minister, kirk, hare, and numerous other words are solemnly interdicted.   Caithness Rinder (1895)

We don't mention pigs. We call 'em Grecians, jacks, four-legged dinners, 'owt but a pig. But the odd thing about Staithes people is that while they won't speak of pigs almost every fishing family keeps one. They tell endless stories: about the man who was working on his lines when a smallholder friend came in and spoke of the sow and litter he'd just lost. 'That's done it,' said the fisherman.
Yorkshire *Observer Supp.* (24 Nov. 1968)

Although reported from most coastal parts of the British Isles, the overwhelming majority of descriptions are from Scotland and northern England. A regularly reported antidote to anyone using a banned word was for the hearer to touch some metal, and say 'cold iron' to emphasize the fact – an action known to ward off ill-luck or evil in many communities (*see also* TOUCHING IRON):

Once, when speaking to one of these fishermen in her kitchen, she was interrupted by the entrance of an old woman, reputed to be a witch. The fisherman's consternation was great, and he made it exceedingly emphatic by uttering the words 'Cauld iron!' and effecting at the same time a successful dash towards an iron hook fixed in the ceiling.   Eastern Scotland N&Q (1906)

According to published reports, great store was placed by traditional fishermen on strict obedience to these rules about forbidden words and actions, and the breaking of any interdiction could result in the loss of a day's fishing or at least a period of depressed morale amongst the crew. But it must be admitted that from the outside the apparently deliberate complication

The natural world was scoured for omens:

Omens of good or bad luck are also derived from sea-birds. All depends on whether a gull or a cormorant is seen first, as, if a cormorant, no fish is to be expected that day. All fishermen also know how unlucky it is to count one's fish until the catch has been landed, as, however freely they may be biting, counting them would invariably stop all sport for the day. Guernsey MacCulloch (1864)

But the fear of particular birds could also be symbolic:

Question: Why is it considered bad luck to carry a box of Swan Vestas aboard a boat or ship? Answer: [On] fishing boats: I was given a dressing-down for carrying Swan Vestas while at sea and was told that the swan on the box is held to represent the unfortunate albatross from Coleridge's epic poem The Rime of the Ancient Mariner. In some cases the skipper will throw the matches over the side, circle them three times and return to port.
Northumberland *Daily Mail* (21 Apr. 1994)

It is no surprise that sharks were not liked:

When a shark was observed in the wake of a ship, its appearance was held to indicate the approaching death of someone on board, for the dread monster was believed to possess supernatural foreknowledge of the coming of the last enemy.
Orkney Laing (1885)

There were dozens of beliefs about how the fish were caught, or not caught, and especially about the first of the catch:

If a fisherman lost the first fish as he was hauling his line in, or if the first fish was caught by the stern-most man in the boat, it was considered unlucky. If the first herring caught in the boat for the season had a roe, it was lucky; if it was a milt herring it was unlucky. To go out third boat on the first day of the season, especially, but also at any time, was unlucky. Isle of Man Cashen (1912)

But it is difficult to see the rationale behind certain types of cake being avoided:

Richard Ferguson, fisherman, of the Salerie, tells me that there is a great objection against taking currant cake with them when they go a-fishing, it is sure to bring them bad luck. Guernsey MacCulloch (1864)

The fishermen of both North and South Cornwall believe that saffron brings bad luck, and that saffron-cake carried in a boat spoils the chance of a catch. Cornwall *Folk-Lore* (1908)

See also PINS: FISHING BOATS; SHOES: THROWING; COUNTING.

Cornwall *Folk-Lore* 19 (1908) 108. Suffolk *Folk-Lore* 35 (1924) 351. Yorkshire Blakeborough (1898) 147. Northumberland *Daily Mail* (21 Apr. 1994) 58. Orkney Laing (1885) 76–7; N&Q 10S:12 (1909) 483. Isle of Man Cashen (1912) 29. Guernsey MacCulloch (1864) 506.

of everyday life by such restrictions is even more inexplicable than other superstitions which seem to have no rational basis. The evidence for the belief is copious but inconsistent and patchy, and solid conclusions are difficult to reach. Faced with such a dilemma, many people have turned to Frazer's *Golden Bough*, which indeed has a great deal to say about 'tabooed words'. He presents numerous examples of forbidden names from around the world, and he places them in certain categories – names of gods, names of kings and sacred persons, names of the dead, personal names, names of relations, and so on. This is not applicable here, as the commonest forbidden words in Britain do not fit these categories, but it has led many an unwary writer to presume that any forbidden word must necessarily be connected with the sacred world of our ancestors and the milieu of gods and tribal totems.

Frazer does, however, provide a final category of 'common words tabooed', which commences with Scottish fishermen and then tours the globe for other examples in his quest for elucidation of the 'savage mind'. Many of the words found are the names of dangerous animals, and his conclusion is summed up with the sentence, 'The avoidance of common words seems to be based on a fear of spirits and a wish to deceive them or elude their notice' (p. 416). This may explain why, as Frazer reveals, the Siamese dared not utter the proper words for tiger or crocodile, but is not obviously applicable to a Fifeshire fisherman refusing to say 'rabbit'.

Nevertheless, examples of euphemisms for something feared are certainly known across Britain and Ireland – as when people refer to the fairies as 'the Good People', or use one of the many nicknames for the Devil. To say the name of something conjures it up – 'talk of the Devil, and you will see his horns' – or attracts its attention. If it could be shown that these forbidden words all represent unlucky things in their own right, it would provide a simple explanation – for example, rabbits are unlucky things to meet, so even saying the word could bring bad luck.

In these islands the fishermen never talk of rats as such, but when these animals are spoken of the name used is 'cold iron'. They believe that rats can understand human speech, and they dislike being gossiped about, and are apt to take revenge upon anyone speaking of them by gnawing their fishing gear, sea-boots, etc., but all is safe if 'cold iron' is the name used.

Co. Galway *Spectator* (10 Aug. 1907)

Many problems still remain. Most of the commonly reported restricted words are names of items which are unlucky in some context or other – it is unlucky to meet a hare or pig; unlucky to carry a minister on board – but many informants imply that numerous other everyday words were also banned, although having said this they nearly all quote the same few words. In addition, there are numerous contradictions – pigs may have been unlucky to meet in the morning and may be unlucky to mention at sea, but many fishing families still kept a pig and were happy to eat it when its time came. Ministers were unlucky on board, but most fishermen still went to church.

It is possible that, having got used to the rule of not uttering certain words at sea, it was easy to extend the list to further heighten the difference between life 'on land' and life 'at sea'. But this is to pile hypothesis upon hypothesis.

Customary actions which are so incomprehensible to onlookers function at more than one level. Regardless of origin, or even of belief, there is a sense that superstitions like these act as effective markers to label insiders and outsiders in the community. 'Real' fishermen and their families understand the traditional restrictions, and need no guidance on how to navigate them successfully. 'Outsiders' will always be at a loss, at a disadvantage, and their lack of status within the group quite obvious to those already inside. It is one of the functions of tradition to provide the basis for such distinctions between 'them' and 'us', conscious or otherwise.

Supporters of pagan and mythic origins to these superstitions must also face another problem. With the exception of HARES, there are no reports of forbidden words in this context before the nineteenth century.

Devon Hewett (1900) 58; N&Q 147 (1924) 159–60. Cornwall N&Q 8S:10 (1896) 393. Yorkshire N&Q 5S:3 (1875) 204; Blakeborough (1898) 147; Jeffrey (1923) 128; *Observer Supp.* (24 Nov. 1968) 10; Gill (1993) 48–50. Co.

Durham Brockie (1886) 121; [1986] Opie & Tatem, 308. Northumberland Neville (1909) 109–10; *Folk-Lore* 36 (1925) 252, 256. Northeast Scotland Gregor (1881) 129; Anson (1965) 102. Eastern Scotland N&Q 10S:6 (1906) 230; Anson (1930) 38–40. Berwickshire Anson (1930) 38. Fifeshire Ramsay (1861) 31–2; [*c*.1884] Anson (1930) 43; *Folk-Lore* 75 (1964) 39. Aberdeenshire *Daily News* (3 Dec. 1892) quoted N&Q 8S:3 (1893) 245; [1952] Opie & Tatem, 308; [1963] Opie & Tatem, 249. Banffshire *Folk-Lore Jnl* 4 (1886) 13. Caithness Rinder (1895) 57–8. Orkney Teignmouth 1 (1836) 286; Laing (1885) 72–3; N&Q 10S:12 (1909) 483. Shetland Edmonston 2 (1809) 74; Tudor (1883) 166. Co. Galway *Spectator* (10 Aug. 1907) 190. Isle of Man [*c*.1850] Cashen (1912) 27; Rhys 1 (1901) 345. Guernsey *Folk-Lore* 38 (1927) 181–2. Jersey *Folk-Lore* 38 (1927) 178–9.

fishing: knife in mast

A handful of references refer to a custom of sticking a knife into the mast of a fishing vessel; either for 'good luck' or for the more immediate assistance of a wind:

When the wind falls you should stick a knife in the mast and a breeze will come. Some men on beginning a voyage drive the point of a knife into the mast, and as long as it remains there the voyage will prosper.　　　　Shetland Saxby (1932)

Oddly enough, Speranza Wilde says exactly the opposite: 'To stick a penknife in the mast of a boat when sailing is most unlucky' (Ireland Wilde (1887)).

Co. Durham [1980] Opie & Tatem, 228. Shetland Fergusson (1884) 169; Saxby (1932) 192. Orkney N&Q 10S:12 (1909) 483. Ireland Wilde (1887) 114.

fishing: meeting unlucky things

The bad luck entailed in MEETING or seeing unlucky people or things at the start of the day or a journey is one of the basic motifs of superstition, and is reported in numerous contexts. The feeling was particularly strong in certain communities, at least from the nineteenth century onwards, such as mining and fishing. The most commonly cited ill omens were: WOMEN in general, but especially those with RED HAIR, people with CROSSED EYES, CLERGYMEN, HARES, RABBITS, and PIGS.

To meet a hare, when one was going to fish, was in some districts thought to be a disaster only equalled by meeting a red-haired woman.

N. Ireland Foster (1951)

Only a few weeks ago the writer visited a small fishing village on the Galway coast, and just before getting on his car to return home was chatting to the landlady of the little inn. A strapping young fisherman, who was walking down the road towards the harbour suddenly stopped, climbed over the fence, and made his way to his boat across the fields. The writer observed to his hostess that the young fellow must have mistaken him for a process-server with a writ for him. She laughed rather derisively, and said: 'It's not you at all, sir, he's afraid of, but me! He's just going fishing, and would not pass me by if you gave him the fill of his hat of gold!' She said that his action was not exceptional, and that any of the other men would have done the same thing. It seems curious, as nothing could have appeared less sinister than the rosy-cheeked, plump, jolly-looking woman herself.

Co. Donegal/Galway *Spectator* (10 Aug. 1907)

As with most other fishing superstitions, these were generally reported across the British Isles, but most commonly from Scotland, Ireland, and northern England.

Cornwall N&Q 8S:10 (1896) 393; *Old Cornwall* 10 (1929) 40–1. **Suffolk** *Folk-Lore* 56 (1945) 269. **Yorkshire** N&Q 4S:4 (1869) 131; N&Q 5S:2 (1874) 184; N&Q 5S:3 (1875) 204; Nicholson (1890) 46; Blakeborough (1898) 146–7; *Observer Supp.* (24 Nov. 1968) 10. **Northumberland** Neville (1909) 109–10; *Folk-Lore* 36 (1925) 252, 256. **Eastern Scotland** Anson (1930) 38. **Highland Scotland** Macbain (1887/88) 255, 265. **Fifeshire** N&Q 10S:10 (1908) 330. **Caithness** Sutherland (1937) 104. **Orkney** N&Q 10S:12 483. **Shetland** Low (1879) 162; *Gent. Mag.* (1882) 358. **N. Ireland** Foster (1951) 129–30. **Co. Donegal** *Spectator* (10 Aug. 1907) 190. **Co. Galway** *Spectator* (10 Aug. 1907) 190. **Guernsey** MacCulloch (1864) 505–6.

fishing: shedding blood

A handful of reports from Scotland reveal a belief that it was lucky to shed blood at the New Year:

At Burghead there existed the superstition that a fisherman should never go to sea after the New Year until he had shed blood. The first person who should draw blood in a quarrel was held to have fulfilled this obligation.

Eastern Scotland Anson (1930)

Those who had no quarrel to settle, beat their wives instead.

Northeast Scotland N&Q 4S:11 (1873) 10. **Eastern Scotland** Anson (1930) 42. **Banffshire** *Folk-Lore Jnl* 3 (1885) 14.

fishing: turning sunwise

A number of everyday actions were required to be carried out in a certain direction if bad luck was to be avoided. The direction previously called 'sunwise' was preferred – what would be called 'clockwise' in modern parlance. Fishing communities in Scotland were particularly keen to observe this rule:

In going to sea they turn the boat in the direction of the sun's course. To move in the opposite way would be considered improper if not dangerous.

Shetland *New Stat. Acct Scotland* (1845)

Martin Martin first noticed this on his trip to the Western Isles in 1695 (published 1703) and it was reported regularly from then until well into the twentieth century.

See also SUNWISE.

Devon Hewett (1900) 58. **Aberdeenshire** *Daily News* (3 Dec 1892) quoted N&Q 8S:3 (1893) 245. **Sutherland** [1962] Opie & Tatem, 384. **Caithness** Rinder (1895) 58. **Hebrides** McPhee (1970) 150. **Lewis** Martin (1703) 16. **Shetland** *New Stat. Acct Scotland* (1845) 141, 143. **Orkney** *Stat. Acct Scotland* 7 (1791–9) 560; Barry (1808) 348; Teignmouth 1 (1836) 286; N&Q 10S:12 (1909) 483. **Isle of Man** [*c*.1850] Cashen (1912) 27; Gill (1934) 185.

fishing: unlucky/lucky days

The general feeling that it is very unlucky to start anything new on a FRIDAY is strongly represented in the fishing industry by an extreme unwillingness to set sail on that day, or to do anything new:

I wouldn't start in a new boat on a Friday, and I'd never start a new fishing then – changing from lobsters to fishing with lines. One man put his pots in on a Friday and nothing went right. One of his mates left him and at the end he was drownded.

Yorkshire *Observer Supp.* (24 Nov. 1968)

[At Westleton] *the fishermen say:*
A Friday's sail
Always fail

Suffolk *Folk-Lore* (1924)

Other unlucky days are mentioned less often, but include HOLY INNOCENTS' DAY (Childermas), Christmas Day, and Old Christmas Day. Lucky days are also mentioned infrequently, but Saturday, Monday, and Sunday were occasionally identified as fortunate, especially the latter if the men could get the fishing boats blessed first.

The fear of misfortune on Friday goes back at least to medieval times, but the first report specific to the fishing industry refers to the Orkney Islands in the late eighteenth century.

See also FRIDAYS: UNLUCKY.

Somerset [1904–57] Tongue (1965) 139. **Devon** *Folk-Lore* 24 (1913) 237. **Suffolk** *Folk-Lore* (1924) 347; *Folk-Lore* 56 (1945) 269. **Norfolk** Festing (1977) 29. **Yorkshire** N&Q 5S:3 (1875) 204; *Observer Supp.* (24 Nov. 1968) 10. **Co. Durham** Brockie (1886) 209. **Northeast Scotland** Gregor (1881) 149. **Eastern Scotland** Anson (1930) 40–2. **East Lothian** N&Q 1S:5 (1852) 5. **Orkney** *Stat. Acct Scotland* 7 (1791–9) 560; Laing (1885) 72; N&Q 10S:12 (1909) 483–4. **Shetland** Tudor (1883) 166. **Isle of Man** [*c.*1850] Cashen (1912) 27. **Unlocated** Marryat 1 (1872) 37. **General** *Gent. Mag.* (1823) 16–17; Bullen (1899) 119–20. **Literary** Wood (1899) 232.

fleas

see CUCKOOS: FLEAS.

flies

A number of superstitions about flies have been recorded, but none are widely reported, and they seem contradictory. A fly in the house out of season, especially at Christmas or New Year, was lucky and left unmolested:

what about the Christmas fly? Is there anywhere in England where it is thought to be the height of good luck to have an ordinary house-fly hovering around the house between Christmas and New Year?   Co. Durham *Folk-Lore* (1960)

This seems to be mainly restricted to northern England and Scotland in the twentieth century. On the other hand:

If flies come into the house at an unseasonable time of year, it portends death.
   Staffordshire *Folk-Lore* (1909)

Bluebottle flies were called 'fever flies' or 'death flies' and were supposed to bring fever or death to the person on whose body they alighted. When a persistent bluebottle could not be got rid of from a bedroom, people said the occupant of the apartment would either have the fever or die within the year.   Wales Trevelyan (1909)

A third possibility was that a fly falling into your drink was lucky:

Amongst our deep sea fishermen there is a most comical idea, that if a fly falls into the glass from which any one has been drinking, or is about to

drink, it is considered a sure and true omen of good luck to the drinker, and is always noticed as such by the company.   Renfrewshire N&Q (1855)

Christmas fly: **Sussex** *Sussex Express* (9 Jan. 1970) 10. **Cumberland** [1948] Opie & Tatem, 164. **Northeast England** [1987] Opie & Tatem, 164. **Co. Durham** *Folk-Lore* 71 (1960) 255. **Northumberland** Bosanquet (1929) 80. **Argyllshire** [1960] Opie & Tatem, 164.
Death: **Oxfordshire** *Folk-Lore* 24 (1913) 88. **Staffordshire** *Folk-Lore* 20 (1909) 220. **Wales** Trevelyan (1909) 323.
In glass: **Somerset** [1923] Opie & Tatem, 164. **Renfrewshire** N&Q 1S:11 (1855) 488. **Aberdeenshire** *Aberdeen Weekly Free Press* (29 Oct. 1898) 3. **Unlocated** *Chambers's Jnl* (1873) 809.

flower of the well

see NEW YEAR: FIRST WATER.

flowers: from churchyards

Flowers are connected with death in popular tradition in many different ways. Not only have they formed an integral part of funerals for centuries, but various varieties have the reputation of predicting or even causing death if brought indoors. In some cases, houseplants were decorated with black on the death of one of the family (*see* DEATH: PLANTS IN MOURNING). Another tradition, which was undoubtedly more widespread than is apparent from the handful of references listed below, was that flowers in churchyards should not be removed. This applied to flowers growing, and also those bought for placing on the grave:

It is considered unlucky to pluck a flower that is growing on a grave. Persons doing so will experience death or disaster in their own families before a year has passed.
   Wales Trevelyan (1909)

At one cemetery in South London plants are sold at the lodge for placing on the graves. I bought one as I went out on my way home, and I noticed that the seller seemed surprised. I was afterwards told that it was very unlucky to bring a plant or a flower home from a cemetery.
   London *Folk-Lore* (1926)

Devon *Devonshire Assoc.* 66 (1934) 86–7. **Cornwall** *Folk-Lore Jnl* 5 (1887) 213; *Old Cornwall* 2 (1931–6) 40. **London** *Folk-Lore* 37 (1926) 366–7. **Norfolk** *Folk-Lore* 37 (1926) 371. **Wales** Trevelyan (1909) 283. **Connaught** *Folk-Lore* 34 (1923) 236. **Unlocated** Uttley (1957) Ch. 2.

flowers: picking up

It was considered very unwise to pick up a flower found in the street, even by children who were not overly squeamish about what else they picked up:

[Remembering childhood in Chelsea in 1920s] *It was not a rare occurrence, particularly near the stall at the top of our street or in the Fulham market, to see a cut flower lying on the ground, and if one of the younger children went to touch it, the rest of us dragged him back gasping 'pick up a flower, pick up a fever'.*

London [1920s] Gamble

Or, more graphically:

Pick up flowers, pick up sickness
Pick up sickness, fall down dead.

Buckinghamshire [1913] *Folk-Lore*

This belief was noted mainly from children, or from people remembering their childhood, although it is clear that some adults believed it as well and cautioned their children accordingly. As with other flower beliefs, it has been suggested that this horror of chance-found flowers reveals a strong connection in people's minds between flowers with funerals. Also in line with most flower superstitions, this one has not been found before the turn of the twentieth century

See also PETALS.

Sussex [*c.*1915] Opie & Tatem, 163–4. Devon *Devonshire Assoc.* 57 (1926) 110. London [1920s] Gamble (1979) 89; *Folk-Lore* 37 (1926) 366. Buckinghamshire [1913] *Folk-Lore* 43 (1932) 108. Essex [1983] Opie & Tatem, 163–4. Suffolk [1947] Opie & Tatem, 163–4. Gwynedd [1983] Vickery (1995) 137.

flowers: red

Although a handful of beliefs centre on red flowers, such as roses, it does not seem to be their colour which causes concern but other situational factors, such as the petals falling:

To scatter the leaves of a red rose on the ground is unlucky, and betokens an early death.

Jones (1880)

In the context of red and white flowers together, however, there is very widespread superstition (*see below*).

See also ROSES: LOVE DIVINATION

General Jones (1880) 528; Vickery (1995) 308–9; Opie & Tatem, 325.

flowers: red and white together

The mixing of red and white flowers in the same vase is widely considered to be unlucky, or even an omen of death. The addition of even one flower of any other colour breaks the spell, and the placing of red and white blooms in separate vases in the same room is also quite acceptable. It appears to be the mixing that causes the unease.

One almost universal flower tabu forbids a mixed bunch of red and white flowers to be taken into hospital. I found this superstition amongst nurses from Northumberland to Somerset, and in every case the reason was the same. It means a death in the ward. This belief is not confined to nurses. In 1954 a Banbury florist flatly refused to sell some red and white gladioli to a customer because the latter told him they were for a hospital patient.

England *Folk-Lore* (1955)

This avoidance is particularly common in hospitals, but is also widely followed in other contexts, and many people avoid the combination even in their homes when no sickness is present. As with many current superstitions, the exact meaning of the belief is difficult to pin down. In all cases the combination of the flowers is seen as 'unlucky' in some way, but while to some it is a sign of a death to come, others regard it as an invitation to, or even a cause of, that death. One family, at least, believed that the hospital staff would use the flowers as a sign:

The family of a friend of mine went to visit their mother in hospital in Galashiels. When they got there they were very upset to see a vase of red and white flowers placed on the locker beside her bed. They complained to the sister, and told her that they would rather be told that the hospital thought that their mother was going to die, instead of having them dropping hints. They thought that the red and white flowers indicated that the hospital had given up hope with their mother.

Borders [1985] Vickery

The most often quoted reason for the ban is that red and white flowers represent 'blood and bandages'. Given this association, the avoidance is understandable outside the hospital environment, as people do not, after all, wish to be reminded of sickness and death in their homes; but why thinking of 'blood and bandages' should be avoided in their proper context of a hospital ward is not at all clear. It is likely that this

supposed connection is a BACK-FORMED explanation, probably based on the earlier red and white
stripes on the pole used to advertise barbers' shops,
for which the same explanation used to be given,
with a similar lack of real evidence.

The superstition is still very widely known and
followed. Hospital staff avoid putting red and
white together to avoid upsetting patients, even if
they do not themselves believe: 'I know not to put
red and white flowers together,' said a young nurse
asked about superstitions by the writer in October
2001. Many florists are similarly careful in making
up arrangements and bouquets. The superstition
does not, however, appear to be very old at all,
and is an example of a belief which has actually
gained considerable ground during the twentieth
century. The earliest reference so far located is in
the *Sunlight Almanac* for 1896, where it is claimed
that to dream of red and white flowers is a prediction of death. The belief is not listed in the main
regional folklore collections, nor in the nineteenth-century books on plant-lore, and a search
of a number of Victorian and Edwardian DREAM
BOOKS also failed to locate relevant examples.
There are, however, numerous beliefs about the
unluckiness of white flowers, both individual
species and in general (*see below*), from earlier
periods. Some of these are otherwise identical to
those in the *Sunlight Almanac*, as, for example, 'to
dream of white flowers has been supposed to prognosticate death' (Dyer (1889) 106), and it is
conceivable that the ban on red and white flowers
has grown from avoidance of the white.

England *Folk-Lore* 66 (1955) 324. Dorset *Folk-Lore* 89
(1978) 158. Devon *Devonshire Assoc.* 104 (1972) 267.
London [1953] Opie & Tatem 164. Oxfordshire [1920s]
Surman (1992) 62. Cambridgeshire Porter (1969) 43.
Lancashire *Lancashire Lore* (1971) 6. Cumbria [1986]
Opie & Tatem 164. Borders [1985] Vickery (1995) 307.
Fife Bennett (1992) 185. General *Sunlight Almanac*
(1893) 333. Also several other examples from England,
Wales, Ireland, and Scotland, in the 1980s in Vickery
(1995) 306–9.

flowers: white

A number of species of white flowers are considered unlucky, particularly if brought into the
house, but some people have clearly decided that
all white flowers should be shunned:

*I have heard from a social worker in London that
it is most unlucky – almost offensively unlucky,
in fact – to give any white flowers, even those not
native to England, like white chrysanthemums,
to sick people. Apparently some implication that,
being white, they would be suitable for the
funeral, is involved. The people to whom these*
*particular white chrysanthemums were given
were quite young, moderately well educated,
typical Londoners, and yet superstitious on this
point – which they said was well known to everyone.*   London N&Q (1931)

The notion that white flowers are for funerals
seems to be the general consensus, and they are
thus felt unsuitable for everyday use and, it is
believed, may even bring about a death. As is the
case with red and white flowers together, the
general aversion to white flowers is relatively well
reported through most of the twentieth century,
but there is little evidence of such a belief before
that time. Interestingly, the first reference for
white flowers and the first for red and white are
both concerned with dreams:

*To dream of white flowers has been supposed to
prognosticate death.*   Dyer (1889)

See also FLOWERS: RED AND WHITE;
HAWTHORN; LILAC; SNOWDROPS. For funeral
flowers *see* Vickery (1995) 143–9.

London N&Q 160 (1931) 195; Davies (2000) 197–8
Buckinghamshire [1990] Vickery (1995) 396. Shropshire
[1981] Opie & Tatem, 443. Warwickshire [1974] Vickery
(1995) 395. Norfolk [1984] Vickery (1995) 395.
Nottinghamshire [1983] Vickery (1995) 395. Unlocated
The Times (15 Feb. 1966) 12. General Dyer (1889) 106;
Lynd (1922) 161.

foot

see FEET.

foxes

Foxes feature surprisingly little in the superstitions of Britain and Ireland. While scattered
references include fox beliefs, they do not indicate any coherent view of the animal or provide
any clue to how it was generally viewed. They are
also remarkably recent.

*A black fox... was regarded as a messenger of death
... If you see a wandering fox in the morning, you
will have a good day.*   Wales Trevelyan (1909)

It is lucky to see a fox at night.
                 Herefordshire [c.1895] *Folk-Lore*

*If bitten by a fox, you will certainly die within
seven years.*   Lincolnshire Watkins (1886)

*If a fisherman from the Claddagh saw a fox
before he intended to go fishing, he went home
without putting to sea.*   Galway Power (1974)

Two informants reported a strange injunction not to think of a fox while cutting your FINGERNAILS, as this would be unlucky. This must have been quite difficult once the idea was suggested (**Sussex** Latham (1878); **Devon** *Devonshire Assoc.* (1934)).

A fox's tongue was prized in folk medicine, particularly in Ireland, as it was believed to have strong 'drawing power' to remove THORNS, needles, and so on:

If a needle stuck in a person's hand or in any other part of the body it was supposed it could be got out by means of a fox's tongue. When a fox is killed the tongue is cut out and preserved. It is just like the skin of a rotten banana only that it is tough like leather.

Co. **Cork** [1937/8] Culloty

And one source describes a cure for WHOOPING COUGH attempted in Oxfordshire which involved the patient drinking milk given to a fox to drink. This is more usually said of FERRETS.

Thorn removal: Yorkshire *Folk-Lore* 8 (1897) 387. Co. Cork [1937/8] Culloty (1993) 62. **Co. Louth** *Folk-Lore* 19 (1908) 317. **Co. Leitrim** *Folk-Lore* 5 (1894) 199. **Co. Donegal** *Folk-Lore* 4 (1893) 351.
Miscellaneous: Sussex Latham (1878) 8. **Devon** *Devonshire Assoc.* 66 (1934) 75. **Oxfordshire** N&Q 2S:12 (1861) 303. **Herefordshire** [*c.*1895] *Folk-Lore* 39 (1928) 391. **Lincolnshire** Watkins (1886) 11. **Wales** Trevelyan (1909) 282, 324. **Galway** Power (1974) 85.

Fraudulent Mediums Act 1951

The Fraudulent Mediums Act (Ch. 33) of 1951 finally took the concept of witchcraft off the statute book by repealing the WITCHCRAFT ACT OF 1736. The latter had been used as late as 1944 in the prosecution and conviction of a spiritualist medium, HELEN DUNCAN, and had long been seen as anachronistic. Publicity surrounding the Duncan case was a major catalyst, but the spiritualist movement had numerous influential supporters, including MPs and members of the House of Lords, who had been steadily lobbying Parliament since at least 1930. Other societal changes had also been moving in the same direction, such as the widespread popularity of newspaper astrology.

The new Act concentrated on the protection of the public from obvious trickery and deception, with phrases such as 'fraudulent devices' and 'intent to deceive' and specifically excluded practices carried out by amateurs and solely for entertainment. Prosecutors needed hard evidence of deliberate deception for profit to obtain conviction.

This Act remains in force. In 1996, Lord Lester of Herne Hill submitted a question to the government, asking 'Whether the Fraudulent Mediums Act 1951 is obsolete and should be repealed'. In reply (10 Dec. 1996), Baroness Blatch, Minister of State for the Home Office, stated 'The Fraudulent Mediums Act 1951 remains in force. Although there have been few recent prosecutions, the Act provides a safeguard to deal with those who exploit the credulity of others'.

An Act to repeal the Witchcraft Act 1735, and to make, in substitution for certain provisions of section four of the Vagrancy Act 1824, express provision for the punishment of persons who fraudulently purport to act as spiritualistic mediums or to exercise powers of telepathy, clairvoyance or other similar powers. Be it enacted by the King's most Excellent Majesty, by and with the advice and consent of the Lords Spiritual and Temporal, and Commons, in this present Parliament assembled, and by the authority of the same as follows:

1. *(1) Subject to the provisions of this section, any person who –*

    (a) with intent to deceive purports to act as spiritualistic medium or to exercise any powers of telepathy, clairvoyance or other similar powers, or

    (b) in purporting to act as a spiritualistic medium or to exercise such powers as aforesaid, uses any fraudulent device, shall be guilty of an offence.

    (2) A person shall not be convicted of an offence under the foregoing subsection unless it is proved that he acted for reward; and for the purposes of this section a person shall be deemed to act for reward if any money is paid, or other valuable thing given in respect of what he does, whether to him or any other person.

    (3) A person guilty of an offence under this section shall be liable on summary conviction to a fine not exceeding fifty pounds or to imprisonment for a term not exceeding four months or to both such fine and such imprisonment, or on conviction on indictment for a term not exceeding five hundred pounds or to imprisonment for a term not exceeding two years or to both such fine and such imprisonment.

    (4) No proceedings for an offence under this

section shall be brought in England and Wales except by or with the consent of the Director of Public Prosecutions.
(5) Nothing in subsection (1) of this section shall apply to anything done solely for the purpose of entertainment.
2. The following enactments are hereby repealed, that is to say
(a) the Witchcraft Act 1735, so far as still in force and
(b) section four of the Vagrancy Act 1824, so far as it extends to persons purporting to act as spiritualistic mediums or to exercise any powers of telepathy, clairvoyance or other similar powers, or to persons who in purporting so to act or to exercise such powers, use fraudulent devices.
3. (1) This Act may be cited as the Fraudulent Mediums Act 1951.
(2) This Act shall not extend to Northern Ireland.   Davies (1999) 71–8.

freets

A Scots and Northern Irish term for superstitions. Used, for example, by John Mactaggart in his *Scottish Gallovidian Encyclopedia* (1824) as the local word in the 'South of Scotland' for 'Superstitious observances, with respect to good or bad, more commonly bad; the greater part of which now-a-days, though they be observed are not paid great attention to'. He then gives a useful list of examples, covering cattle care, funerals, love divination, rhymes, and sayings. Patterson (1880) also gives *freety*, as used in Antrim and Down for 'Having a belief in charms or omens, as, for example: 'We're no *freety* about here'.

Mactaggart (1824) 210–12. Patterson (1880) 40.

Fridays: dreams

One of the few exceptions to the rule that anything to do with Friday is doomed or unlucky, Friday dreams are special:

If you have a pleasant dream on a Friday, be sure and tell it to someone on Saturday:

> Friday's dream on Saturday told
> Is sure to come true, be it never so old.
>   Foli (1902)

The rhyming couplet has helped to keep the belief in general circulation, although minor

changes in the second line have threatened its literal meaning in some versions – often coming out as 'if it's ever so old' or suchlike. Occasionally it is 'improved':

A Friday night's dream on a Saturday told Is sure to come true 'ere 'tis nine days old.
>   Somerset [1907] Tongue

One report that goes completely against the trend may indicate a different thread of tradition, or may simply be an individual variation – 'Unlucky to tell Friday's dream on a Saturday' (Orkney N&Q (1909)).

Another view of dreams on Friday is represented by some LOVE DIVINATION procedures, which specify the day:

Repeat this rhyme on three consecutive Friday nights and you will dream of future husband on third night:

> Tonight tonight is Friday night
> Lay me down in dirty white
> Dream who my husband is to be
> Lay my children by my side
> If I am to live to be his bride.
>   East Anglia Varden (1885)

It is quite possible that the potency of this procedure rests on the 'Friday's dream' belief, but the historical record on this point is inconclusive, and the love divination belief may have come first. The 'Friday's dream' notion is first found in Hone's *Year Book* (1832), whereas much earlier references seem to be more directly concerned with love. Consider, for example, Thomas Overbury's 'Milkmaid' (1615): 'A Friday's dream is all her superstition: that she conceals for fear of anger', and more clearly: 'I fasted Friday, had my dream, and dreamt of none but perfect him' (*Palace Miscellany* (1733)). Further early examples are needed to clarify this relationship.

Somerset [1907] Tongue (1965) 140. **Dorset** [1888] Udal (1922) 276. **Wiltshire** [1964] Opie & Tatem, 125. **East Anglia** Varden (1885) 109. **Lincolnshire** *Grantham Jnl* (22 June 1878). **Unlocated** Hone, *Year Book* (1832) 126–8; Chambers (1878) 41–2. **General** Foli (1902) 108. **Literary** Thomas Overbury, *Characters* (1615) 'Milkmaid'; 'Progress of Matrimony', *Palace Miscellany* (1733) 32, quoted Opie & Tatem, 125.

Friday 13th

The belief that Friday 13th is an especially unlucky day is one of the widest known superstitions in Britain today, and is erroneously assumed to be of great antiquity. The only one of the superstitions regarding the number thirteen which can be traced back further than Victorian times is that it is very unlucky to have THIRTEEN AT TABLE, or in a company, which first appears in the 1690s. The notion that THIRTEEN is a generally unlucky number has not been found earlier than 1852. FRIDAYS, however, have been regarded as unlucky since medieval times.

It is quite certain that the fear of Friday 13th is a combination of the pre-existing thirteen at table and unlucky Friday, and that this hybrid belief was created in late Victorian times. The first concrete reference to Friday 13th is from 1913:

I have met a 'coach' of fine mental capacities, which had been carefully cultivated, who dreaded the evil luck of Friday the 13th.

Unlocated N&Q (1913)

But what may be a point in the development of Friday 13th is provided by a piece from *Notes & Queries* in 1873:

Thirteen at Dinner: I apprehend that there is no doubt that this notion has reference to the Last Supper, at which thirteen were present. Some, I believe, have carried it to the extent of disliking that number at all times; but the commoner form limits it to Friday. Not that there is any ground of fact for this, for the Last Supper was on the fifth, not the sixth, day of the week. Sailors are held somewhat superstitious and I know an eminent naval officer who, though I do not know that he acted on it earlier in his life, actually would walk out of the room when the conjunction happened on a Friday, after the death of his wife and daughter, both of which events were preceded by the said conjunction.

Unlocated N&Q (1873)

It is not quite clear which particular 'conjunction' this writer means, but it seems to be thirteen at table and Friday rather than the date. It does show, however, that Fridays and thirteens were beginning to be connected in the 1870s.

The idea that Friday 13th is an ancient superstition is so ingrained that the assertion that it is no older than Victorian times is frequently met with disbelief, even anger, but the evidence is overwhelming.

Historical research into folklore topics is bedevilled by the problem of negative evidence. To put it simply, we cannot be sure that a belief or custom did not exist at a particular time simply because a written reference to it has not been found. Nevertheless, with a belief such as Friday 13th, we are on much safer ground than usual, for the obvious reason that it concerns a particular calendar date, and there is no short-

age of date-based material. From the seventeenth century onwards, the printing presses poured forth ALMANACS – publications whose whole *raison d'être* was to provide information about dates, including lucky and unlucky ones. None of them single out Friday 13th. Since before Samuel Pepys's time, people have kept detailed diaries and journals, scores of which have been published and are generally available – those before the twentieth century do not mention Friday 13th being unlucky. Our sixteenth- and seventeenth-century dramatists, great and small, wrote tragedies full of omens – dogs howl, owls shriek, ravens, comets, and thunderstorms predict disaster – but no tragedy happens on Friday 13th. And so on.

Even in the later nineteenth and early twentieth centuries, the belief does not seem to be nearly as widely known as today. The Victorian folklore collectors rarely mention it, and even popular turn-of-the-century books on superstitions often omit it. T. Sharper Knowlson, for example, devotes a section of his *Origins of Popular Superstitions and Customs* (1910) to the unlucky nature of Fridays, and another to thirteen at the table, but does not connect the two. The same situation applies in the USA, where the Friday 13th superstition is today as strong as it is in Britain. For example, the article 'The Thirteen Superstition among the Fair Sex' (*Belford's Magazine* (1891)) printed letters from well-known American women. They all interpreted the title as referring to thirteen at table – none of them mentions Friday 13th even those who admit to being superstitious and who were careful not to organize dinner parties with thirteen guests.

Nowadays even non-believers can hardly fail to be aware of the date on that day. Popular and local newspapers regularly run features whenever the day occurs, and list the dreadful things reported to have happened. News bulletins do not disdain to mention it, and the quality newspapers help by mixing more serious reporting with material verging on the fatuous:

Researchers have found from a study of accident figures on the southern section of the M25 that the risk of being admitted to hospital as a result of a crash increased by a factor of 50 per cent on Friday the 13th . . . There were 1.4 per cent fewer vehicles on [that section] on Friday the 13th . . . this could mean at least 1.4 per cent of the population are sufficiently superstitious to alter their behaviour and refrain from driving on motorways on Friday the 13th. Are people's perceptions and beliefs self-fulfilling – if you believe something enough will it in fact happen to you?

Daily Telegraph (17 Dec. 1993)

The article finishes, however, with:

This week, Liverpool was blacked out by a power failure on the 13th minute of the 13th hour on the 13th day of the month.

No attempt is made here to list all the twentieth-century published references to Friday 13th.

Unlocated N&Q 4S:11 (1873) 330; N&Q 11S:8 (1913) 434; *Daily Telegraph* (17 Dec. 1993) 8, quoting the *British Medical Journal.* **Various** Opie & Tatem, 169. **USA** 'The Thirteen Superstition among the Fair Sex', *Belford's Magazine* (May 1891) 801–16.

Fridays: unlucky

Across the whole British Isles, Friday has long had the reputation of being the unluckiest day of the week, and there were numerous traditional restrictions and prohibitions about what should or should not be done on the day. In accordance with the general superstitious fear of bad BEGINNINGS, particular concern was felt about starting anything on a Friday – a new journey, business project, job, or marriage:

My wife recently wanted a fresh servant, and advertised for one in a local newspaper. A girl, a native of Devonshire, applied for the situation, and appearing to be in every way suitable, she was engaged, and asked to come on a given date. That date happened to be on a Friday, but the girl positively refused to enter on a new situation on a Friday. She said she would 'rather give up the place'. We had to submit, and she came to our house on a Saturday. Devon N&Q (1900)

People would not move house ('Friday flit, short sit'), and fishermen would not set sail:

'I suppose you'd liked to say that you won't go out on a Friday!' 'That's just it,' said Jack. 'You are superstitious, Captain Tanerton,' mocked the broker. 'I am not,' answered Jack, 'but I sail with those who are. Sailors are more foolish on this point than you can imagine; and I believe – I believe in my conscience – that ships, sailing on a Friday, have come to grief through their crew losing heart. No matter what impediment is met with – bad weather, accidents, what not – the men say at once it's of no use, we sailed on a Friday. They lose their spirit, and their energy with it, and I say, Mr. Freeman, that vessels have been lost through this, which might have otherwise been saved. I will not go out of dock tomorrow; and I refuse to do it in your interest as in my own'. Wood (1899)

In the domestic sphere, fingernails and hair should definitely not be cut.

Friday cut and Sunday shorn
Better never have been born
Lancashire N&Q (1870)

See FINGERNAILS: CUT ON CERTAIN DAYS for full references.

As late as the 1950s, this superstition still had strong influence in many quarters:

The Amusement Caterers' Association in reply to a query arising from a report in The Times *(2 May 1951) of a meeting of showmen 'to hear what could be done to overcome the fact that a Friday would be the first day on which visitors would be admitted to the fun fair' stated . . . it is quite true to say that, especially among the older showmen and amusement caterers, there is a superstition that it is unlucky to open on a Friday, but, so far as we know, it is dying out as the newer generations come into the business. The feeling, however, has been strong enough to encourage showmen of Battersea Park to stage the reported unofficial opening (or 'dress rehearsal') on Thursday next when, as you have read, several thousand children will be invited to the amusement park as guests of the concessionaires.*
London *Folk-Lore* (1951)

Numerous minor beliefs also clustered around the day: 'Adam and Eve ate the forbidden fruit on a Friday' (**Sussex** Latham (1878)); 'A Crow would not carry a straw to its nest on a Friday' (**Orkney** N&Q (1909)); 'Criminals are very superstitious – there are fewer burglaries on Fridays' (**Unlocated** Igglesden (c.1932)); 'If people marry on Friday they will 'lead a cat-and-dog life', that is, they will quarrel' (**England** Addy (1895)); and many others.

There is little doubt that this belief has simple Christian roots. The medieval Catholic church promoted Friday across Europe as a day of penance and abstinence in commemoration of Christ's death on the day.

In a large class of our population few would yet defy evil fate by beginning a journey or any important undertaking, or marrying, on a Friday; on which day Lancashire, like other sailors, have a strong repugnance to beginning a voyage. This day of the week is regarded of evil augury, because it was the day (Good Friday) when our Saviour's blood was shed.
Lancashire Harland & Wilkinson (1882)

The unluckiness of Fridays is well documented since the late fourteenth century, when Chaucer wrote 'And on a Friday fell all this mischance' in the *Nun's Priest's Tale* (*c.*1390). In the last century or so, the rise of FRIDAY 13TH as unlucky has all but eclipsed the idea that all Fridays are suspect.

See also COURTING; FINGERNAILS: CUT ON CERTAIN DAYS; FISHING: UNLUCKY/LUCKY DAYS; FRIDAY 13TH; GOOD FRIDAY.

England N&Q 4S:5 (1879) 74–5. **Kent** N&Q 166 (1934) 241. **Sussex** Latham (1878) 13. **Dorset** [1888] Udal (1922) 279, 287. **Somerset** [1923] Opie & Tatem, 169; Tongue (1965) 139. **Devon** Bray (1838) 287; N&Q 1:4 (1851) 98; N&Q 9S:6 (1900) 454; Hewett (1900) 54–5; *Devonshire Assoc.* 33 (1901) 127; Crossing (1911) 135; *Folk-Lore* 24 (1913) 237; *Devonshire Assoc.* 60 (1928) 126. **Cornwall** Couch (1871) 164; [1890s] *Old Cornwall* 1:12 (1930) 4; *Old Cornwall* 2 (1931–6) 40. **Wiltshire** *Wilts. N&Q* 1 (1893–5) 104. **London** *Folk-Lore* 62 (1951) 405. **Essex** Ketteridge & Mays (1972) 141. **Oxfordshire** [*c.*1850s] Plowman (1919) 117; *Folk-Lore* 34 (1923) 326. **Herefordshire** Duncomb (1804) 58; [*c.*1895] *Folk-Lore* 39 (1928) 386. **Worcestershire** Salisbury (1893) 71–2. **Worcestershire/Shropshire** *Gent. Mag.* (1855) 384–6. **Midland England** N&Q 1S:1 (1850) 451. **East Anglia** Forby (1830) 415; Varden (1885) 113. **Suffolk** *Gent. Mag.* (1867) 728–41; *Folk-Lore* 35 (1924) 347; *Folk-Lore* 56 (1945) 269; Claxton (1954) 89. **Norfolk** N&Q 2S:4 (1857) 432; Festing (1977) 29. **Lincolnshire** *Gent. Mag.* (1833) 590–3; Thompson (1856) 735; *Grantham Jnl* (29 June 1878); Swaby (1891) 91; Gutch & Peacock (1908) 156. **Shropshire** Burne (1883) 259–61; *Folk-Lore* 49 (1938) 232. **Staffordshire** [1890/1] *Folk-Lore* 20 (1909) 221–2. **England** Addy (1895) 94, 113–14, 121. **Derbyshire** [1890s] Uttley (1946) 128; [1982] Opie & Tatem, 169. **Yorkshire** N&Q 4S:4 (1869) 131; N&Q 6S:6 (1882) 356–7; Blakeborough (1898) 146; Morris (1911) 218–19; *Folk-Lore* 43 (1932) 255; *Observer Supp.* (24 Nov. 1968) 10. **Lancashire** N&Q 4S:6 (1870) 211; Harland & Wilkinson (1873) 223; Harland & Wilkinson (1882) 139; N&Q 166 (1934) 283; Corbridge (1964) 156–60. **Westmorland** *London Saturday Jnl* (13 Mar. 1841) 130. **Cumberland** *Folk-Lore* 40 (1929) 278. **Co. Durham** Brockie (1886) 209; Leighton (1910) 61. **Northumberland** Bigge (1860/62) 92; Bosanquet (1929) 75. **Northumberland/Westmorland** [1850s] *Denham Tracts* 2 (1895) 344. **Mid-Wales** Davies (1911) 215. **Radnorshire** [1953] Opie & Tatem, 169. **Northern England/Scotland** Brockett (1829) 132. **Northeast Scotland** Gregor (1881) 149. **Eastern Scotland** Anson (1930) 40. **Highland Scotland** Macbain (1887/88) 272. **Dumfriesshire** Shaw (1890) 11–12. **Glasgow** N&Q 4S:5 (1879) 74–5. **Argyllshire** *Scotsman* (6 Sept. 1900) quoted N&Q 9S:6 (1900) 265–6. **Banffshire** *Stat. Acct Scotland* 14 (1795) 541. **Orkney** Barry (1808) 348; Laing (1885) 72; N&Q 10S:12 (1909) 483–4. **Ireland** Wilde (1888) 212–14. **Co. Wexford** [1938] Ó Muirithe & Nuttall (1999) 162. **Co. Antrim** [*c.*1905] McDowell (1972) 130. **Co. Tyrone** *Lore & Language* 1:7 (1972) 7. **Isle of Man** [*c.*1850] Cashen (1912) 27. **Unlocated** Grose (1787) 65; T. Wilkinson, *Wandering Patentee* 2 (1795) 263; *The Times* (19 Nov. 1825) 2; Hone, *Year Book* (1832) 126–8; Halliwell (1849) 159; *Gent. Mag.* (Nov. 1855) 504; Marryat 1 (1872) 37; N&Q 9S:6 (1900) 373; N&Q 160 (1931) 427; Igglesden (*c.*1932) 98–9, 102. **General** *Gent. Mag.* (1823) 16–17; Chambers (1878) 41–2. Bullen (1899) 119–20. **Literary**

Chaucer, *Nun's Priest's Tale* (*c.*1390) line 3341; (*c.*1390) line 3341; John Gay, 'The Farmer's Wife and the Raven', *Fables* (1727); Hannah More, *Tawney Rachel* (*c.*1810) 7; Charles Dickens, *David Copperfield* (1849); R. S. Surtees, *Mr Facey Romford's Hounds* (1865) Ch. 60; Wood (1899) 232, 343. Theatrical Igglesden (*c.*1932) 233–4.

frogs

Frogs and toads are often regarded as inter-changeable in many traditions (*see* TOADS), but where toads were often seen as ugly and poisonous, frogs were viewed in a more positive light. They were widely used in cures for human ailments (*see below*), but surprisingly few other superstitions about them have survived. Even those which are recorded are often off-shoots of beliefs about other creatures, such as the following:

To injure or kill a frog is very unlucky, and it is commonly believed that if anyone throw hair out of doors after combing his head, the toads will take it to their holes, and the person from whose head it came will have a headache (some say the toothache) as long as he lives [usually said of birds, see HAIR: DISPOSAL].

Staffordshire Poole (1875)

In and about the kiln I learned that if you smash a frog with a stone, no matter how hard you hit him, he cannot die till sunset [usually said of SNAKES].

Sussex Jefferies (1889)

Eye diseases – Catch a live frog, and lick the frog's eyes with the tongue. The person who does so has only to lick with the tongue any diseased eye, and a cure is effected [usually said of LIZARDS].

Banffshire Gregor (1874)

Sussex Jefferies (1889) 85. Staffordshire Poole (1875) 86. Banffshire Gregor (1874) 271.

frogs: cures

Frogs were recommended in a wide range of medicinal contexts, but the method of using the animal varied considerably. For ailments affecting the throat and respiratory organs, such as THRUSH and WHOOPING COUGH, the frog was held in front of the patient's mouth:

To cure the thrush – Take a living frog, and hold it in a cloth, that it does not go down into the child's mouth; and put the head into the child's mouth till it is dead; and then take another frog, and do the same.

Unlocated Aubrey, *Miscellanies* (1696)

In some versions, the frog was then let go, or hung up in the chimney and allowed to die. In these cases it is clear that the disease has been transferred to the frog, rather than the frog's breath being thought therapeutic.

A widespread cure for a range of diseases involved wearing frog's or toad's legs in a bag round the neck:

A charm for fits was a leg of a frog sewn up in a heart-shaped woollen bag with some incantations. The patient dared not open the bag or the efficacy would be void.   Devon *Devonshire Assoc.* (1934)

Another method was to swallow small live frogs, or make them into a soup, recommended for consumption, whooping cough, and other ailments:

An old lady, now dead, told my husband before the War that, when a girl of thirteen or fourteen years old and living at Clapham, she used to go out in the early morning with a delicate boy of the same age and help him to catch young frogs at a pond. Three of these he had been told to swallow alive each day, to avoid consumption, and he did it.   London *Folk-Lore* (1926)

All these methods were also used in conjunction with other creatures, such as SPIDERS and MICE, and were widely known in folk medicine. Frogs were also often interchangeable with TOADS in these cures.

Breathing/Sucking: Cornwall *Jnl Royal Inst. Cornwall* 20 (1915) 130. **Essex** *Folk-Lore* 70 (1959) 414. **Herefordshire** Leather (1912) 82. **Midland England** *Midland Garner* 1 (1884) 23. **East Anglia** Varden (1885) 105. **Suffolk** *Gent. Mag.* (1867) 728–41. **Norfolk** Dew (1898) 77–81; *Folk-Lore* 40 (1929) 117; Haggard (1935) 16. **Lincolnshire** N&Q 3S:9 (1866) 319. **England** Addy (1895) 92. **Yorkshire** Nicholson (1890) 141; Blakeborough (1898) 136–7. **Unlocated** Aubrey, *Miscellanies* (1696/1857) 137–8.
Swallowing: Essex [*c.*1939] *Folk-Lore* 62 (1951) 259–60. **London** *Folk-Lore* 37 (1926) 367–8. **Norfolk/Lincolnshire** *Folk-Lore* 40 (1929) 116–17. **Norfolk** Fulcher Collection (*c.*1894). **Shropshire** *Folk-Lore* 49 (1938) 229. **Yorkshire** Blakeborough (1898) 145. **Berwickshire** N&Q 2S:4 (1857) 145.
Wearing round neck: Devon *Devonshire Assoc.* 66 (1934) 83. **Worcestershire/Shropshire** *Gent. Mag.* (1855) 384–6. **Shropshire** Burne (1883) 194. **Unlocated** N&Q 1S:12 (1855) 487.
Miscellaneous: Northamptonshire N&Q 1S:2 (1850) 36–7. **Lincolnshire** Sutton (1992) 146. **Shropshire** *Folk-Lore* 49 (1938) 229. **England** Addy (1895) 67. **Co.** Wexford [1938] Ó Muirithe & Nuttall (1999) 100. **General** Kenelm Digby, *Discourse on Sympathy* (1658) 76–7.

frostbite

One of the regularly reported cures for CRAMP was also adaptable for the prevention of frostbite:

This custom of wetting one's forefinger and making a cross on the toe of one's boot, is an old one in N.W. Durham and S. Northumberland. I have known of it for sixty years. It is fast becoming obsolete, only old persons (generally women) now do it. It was always more common in winter months, and was considered 'a charm' against frostbite. There was a rhyme connected with it

> *Christ-cross*
> *Keep away*
> *The frost bite*
> *Every day.*
>   Co. Durham/Northumberland
>   *N&Q* 166 (1934) 121–2

full moon

see MOON.

funerals: clothes

see CLOTHES: FUNERAL/MOURNING.

funerals: meeting

One of the most common motifs in superstition is that MEETING or seeing a particular person, animal, or thing is portentous. Almost all these things, from HARES and black CATS, to single MAGPIES and squinting WOMEN, are decidedly bad luck, and it is therefore hardly surprising that meeting such a reminder of human mortality as a funeral procession is regarded as at best unlucky, and most often as a sign of death.

For a funeral to cross your path betokens either an approaching death in your family or a coming sorrow.   Warwickshire Langford (1875)

A number of ways are suggested for counteracting the evil influence of the encounter. Taking off your hat is recommended both as a mark of respect and a counter-charm, but the most regularly reported method was to turn and accompany the procession for a short time, thus, presumably, breaking the *meeting* part of the omen. In some communities, this was not regarded as optional, and was as important for those in the procession as for those meeting it:

funerals

It hardly needs stressing that funerals have changed dramatically in Britain over the last hundred years, and one major consequence of these changes has been that people's personal contact with death has been minimized and placed at one remove. The potential for superstition and individual belief has thus narrowed considerably. In general, corpses are not kept in the home, friends and neighbours are not expected to visit and 'view the body', the coffin is not carried through the parish on bearers' shoulders, nor is it followed by mourners on foot. As cremation becomes increasingly more common, there is no graveside service, and the burial is more likely to be in a municipal cemetery than a church graveyard.

Every part of the time between death and final burial was formerly governed by a mixture of religion, law, etiquette, fashion, tradition, and superstition. The main funeral superstitions have their own entries, but there are numerous others which have been reported less frequently but which may have been more widely known in the past. A selection follows, with a longer piece, from Northern Ireland, to demonstrate some of the niceties involved.

If the parish clerk is asked at a churchyard for change by the undertaker or other person in paying the funeral fees, it is believed that there will be a second death in the family of the deceased within a year.

Herefordshire Havergal (1887)

Unlucky for a dog to cross the path of a funeral party – the relatives of the deceased will never prosper till the dog has been killed.

Orkney N&Q (1909)

Extremely unlucky for anyone to run after a funeral. However late a person may happen to be . . . he should always walk, never run, or fatal consequences will at no distant date befall the unfortunate individual. Dorset Udal (1922)

It is often quoted in Pilling that if there are two funerals in a week there will be three in a fortnight. Lancashire *Lancashire Lore* (1971)

On no account should there be an odd number in the funeral party, or soon the dead will call for a companion. Lincolnshire Rudkin (1936)

Never wear new clothes at a funeral.

Highland Scotland Macbain (1887/88)

A funeral procession moving too fast is a sign that another funeral will soon follow.

West Wales Davies (1911)

[In the funeral procession] a man and a woman together all along the line in pairs, always an even number, never an odd number or the odd one out would soon join up with the dead person to make a pair. Lincolnshire [1930s] Sutton

In the funeral preparations there is also a code of behaviour which must be observed. When the coffin has been resting on chairs and is removed, the chairs must be knocked over or, if it had been laid on a bed, the bed must be shaken up. The coffin must always be taken out of the house feet-foremost, and it must be carried for a part of the journey to the graveyard on the shoulders of relatives and friends. The shortest distance for carrying is until the procession is out of sight of the home. There is a certain etiquette attached to carrying. The nearest blood relatives come first, insofar as height will permit, for obviously four men of roughly equal height are required. The rule must be strictly observed if family feuds are to be avoided. In-laws come after blood relatives, then friends and neighbours, and it is a delicate task to arrange these in correct order of precedence. It is considered to be altogether wrong to take short-cuts with a funeral, and care must be taken to avoid gaps in the procession, for a gap in a funeral is believed to be a sign that another death will occur shortly after. It is indecent for a funeral to hurry unless it is known that there is to be another burial in the same graveyard around the same time. In such a case it is essential to arrive first, for there is a belief that the last person to be buried must wait on the others in the graveyard. I once heard a woman ask her husband when he returned from her father's burial, if they had arrived at the burying-ground before another funeral. When she heard that they had, she sighed with relief and said, 'Thank God! I wouldn't have liked to think of my Da waiting on the like of thon!' It is unusual for women to attend funerals in Ulster. It is thought to be 'not their place'. In North Antrim I have never known women to sit down to the after-funeral meal with the men. In some old graveyards, Inishmurray for instance, the men are buried on one side and the women on the other.

N. Ireland Foster (1951) 22–3

Dorset Udal (1922) 187. Lincolnshire [1930s] Sutton (1992) 173; Rudkin (1936) 15. Lancashire *Lancashire Lore* (1971) 54. Herefordshire Havergal (1887) 46. West Wales Davies (1911) 214. Highland Scotland Macbain (1887/88) 262. Orkney N&Q 10S:12 (1909) 483–4. N. Ireland Foster (1951) 22–3.

We met a funeral, with a long array of mourners and attendants: in all kinds of vehicles – cars, carts, and waggons – and attired in all sorts of costume . . . On nearing the procession our carman stopped, drawing up to the side of the road. A man, who appeared to be the conductor of the ceremony, advanced; and with native politeness . . . asked that we would be good enough to allow [our] car to follow the procession; adding that it was a custom with which we might not be acquainted. This was done, and after our car had followed some hundred paces, he thanked us, and said that would do; and we then observed that he resumed his place at the head of the procession.   Galway N&Q (1862)

Research among British children carried out by Iona and Peter Opie in the 1950s revealed a range of things which must be done when you see a funeral, including the commonplace SPIT-TING and CROSSED FINGERS, and holding the collar until you see a dog or a bird (*compare* AMBULANCES).

For obvious reasons, it was particularly unlucky for a wedding party to meet a funeral, and organizers would go to great lengths to avoid this happening:

It is a very bad sign for a bridal party to see or meet a funeral. In 1952 one of my friends went to a burial in Reading. She arrived too early at the church, and found the sexton in a state of great agitation because a wedding had just been held there, and the wedding party were still in the churchyard, taking photographs. He said it would be most unlucky if the funeral procession should arrive before the bride and groom had gone. Eventually he spoke to the best man who at once grasped the position and hustled his party away just in time.   Unlocated *Folk-Lore* (1957)

The force of this belief has been severely weakened by developments in the way funerals are carried out. As indicated above, the modern carborne funeral has removed much of the personal aspect of the procession, and although a few older people may remove their hat briefly as a funeral cortège goes by, those not personally involved take little notice of its passing.

Hampshire N&Q 7S:9 (1890) 486; [1973] Opie & Tatem, 171. Essex [1953] Opie & Tatem, 171. Oxfordshire [pre-1900] *Folk-Lore* 24 (1913) 90; [1920s] Surman (1992) 60–1; *Oxf. & Dist. FL. Soc. Ann. Record* (1955) 16. Midland England *Midland Garner* 1 (1884) 23. Warwickshire Langford (1875) 11; Bloom (*c.*1930) 46. Shropshire Burne (1883) 296. Lincolnshire *Gent. Mag.* (1833) 590–3. Derbyshire Addy (1895) 124. Northern England [1850s] *Denham Tracts* 2 (1895) 39. Yorkshire

N&Q 1S:6 (1852) 311–12; Blakeborough (1898) 102. Co. Durham Leighton (1910) 52. Northumberland *Folk-Lore* 36 (1925) 252. English/Scottish Border [*c.*1816] Henderson (1866) 27. Western Scotland Napier (1879) 51. Angus Laing (1885) 21; [1954] Opie & Tatem, 171. Aberdeenshire [1952] Opie & Tatem, 171. Shetland Low (1774) 162. Ireland Wilde (1888) 83, 211, 213. Southern Ireland N&Q 1S:2 (1850) 226. Co. Cork [1937/8] Culloty (1993) 123. Galway N&Q 3S:1 (1862) 503–4. Co. Longford *Béaloideas* 6 (1936) 260–1. Various Opie (1959) 215. Unlocated Grose (1787) 62; *Folk-Lore* 68 (1957) 418.

funerals: next death

A handful of references testify to a belief which was probably more widespread, and which extends the bad luck of meeting a funeral (*see above*) to predict the sex of the next person to die in the parish. If the person met was male, the next death would be male, and so on. This could also be combined with the particular misfortune predicted by a meeting between a wedding party and a funeral procession:

To meet a funeral either in going to or coming from marriage was very unlucky. If the funeral was that of a female, the young wife would not live long; if a male, the bridegroom would die soon.   Western Scotland Napier (1879)

Somerset [1923] Opie & Tatem, 170. Lincolnshire Rudkin (1936) 15. Northern England [1850s] *Denham Tracts* 2 (1895) 49. Western Scotland Napier (1879) 51.

funerals: rain

'Happy is the bride the sun shines on' is still a well-known saying, but equally common in previous times was the corollary concerning funerals:

In Wales they say 'Blessed are the dead that the rain rains on'.   Wales Trevelyan (1909)

It was generally believed that the soul of the deceased was thereby benefited, but how this was meant to work is not altogether clear. Some took it symbolically – the heavens were weeping in sympathy – but most sources do not explain, and it may simply be that rain for sorrow, and sunshine for joy, is a 'natural' human reaction. The idea was widely known and believed:

It 'ud ha' been better luck if they'd ha' buried him I' the forenoon when the rain was fallin'; there's no likelihoods of a drop now.

Eliot, *Adam Bede* (1859)

The earliest reference to the belief is in the play *The Puritan* (1607), four decades before the earliest known for the Happy Bride, but it is quite feasible that they came into being at the same time. The rain belief has not lasted so well, and is probably close to being forgotten in most circles.

See also WEDDINGS: SUN SHINES ON.

Sussex [1862] Hare (1952) 171. Hampshire [1964] Opie & Tatem, 98. Cornwall Hunt (1865) 235–6. Oxfordshire [pre-1900] *Folk-Lore* 24 (1913) 88. Warwickshire Langford (1875) 16. Norfolk N&Q 2S:8 (1859) 300; Fulcher Collection (*c*.1894). Lincolnshire Thompson (1856) 735. Shropshire Burne (1883) 296. England Addy (1895) 123. Co. Durham Leighton (1910) 52. Wales *Archaeologia Cambrensis* 4S:3 (1872) 332; Trevelyan (1909) 282. Scotland/England borders [*c*.1816] Henderson (1866) 27. Co. Longford *Béaloideas* 6 (1936) 261. Unlocated Brand (1777) 53; Grose (1787) 62. Literary W. S. *The Puritan* (1607) 1:1; George Eliot, *Adam Bede* (1859) Ch.18.

funerals: right of way

A widespread LEGAL ERROR held that the passage of a corpse over any land creates an inviolable right of way:

The belief that the carrying of a corpse over a private footpath or bye-road legalizes the same as a public highway prevails also in Glamorganshire. An instance thereof came under [my] *observation last month. It being suggested that the body of an infant, three months old, should be carried by the way of an ancient footpath, across some fields to the church, the grandfather of the child refused to do so, though the journey to the graveyard would have been thereby much shortened.*

Glamorganshire N&Q (1873)

As with all such legendary material, this belief was well-entrenched in people's minds, and no amount of argument could shift it. Most of the reports are in NARRATIVE form and include piquant details of funerals having to cross rivers on rafts or go miles out of their way because some landowner or bridge-keeper refused them admittance. The question of tolls is sometimes included. In one variant, the funeral crossing a toll bridge is supposed to 'free the bridge forever' for everyone. In another it is maintained that the way to prevent the right of way being created is for the landowner to charge the funeral a toll, and that, purportedly, creates the right to charge a toll in future. The toll paid is often nominal, in the form of pins.

Needless to say, no basis for this belief has been found in modern English law, although C. H.

Cooper (N&Q 1S:3 (1851)) and William Weeks (*Folk-Lore* 39 (1928)) argue a case for an origin in the breakdown of a customary practice from pre-enclosure times. Citing the *Book of Homilies* (1562), they identify the practice of leaving baulks of uncultivated land between the arable strips, some of which must be 'broad and sufficient bier balk to carry the corpse to the Christian sepulchre'. The author of the *Book* complains that men have been ploughing too close and reducing the width of these baulks, and funerals are forced to go 'farther about in the high streets'. In many places, these bier baulks survived enclosure as customary corpse-roads or church-ways, over which parishioners claimed the right to carry their dead to the churchyard. This situation, it is argued, was transmuted in popular tradition into the notion that it was the carrying of the corpse which created the right of way, rather than the other way round.

Cooper also cites a much earlier case which has all the hallmarks of the nineteenth-century examples. About the year 1270, when the funeral of the Bishop of Exeter's chaplain was forced by bad weather to change its route, it was refused passage across a neighbouring gentleman's land: 'He, being advertised of such a burial towards in his parish, and a leech way to be made over his land, without his leave or consent therein', called his tenants to support him in blocking the bridge over which the procession needed to pass to enter his property. In the ensuing fracas, the coffin ended up in the lake. It is not clear whether the 'gentleman' was justified in protecting his rights or acting on legend and local belief like his Victorian successors, but it is hoped that if other examples come to light the question can be laid to rest once and for all. Apart from the one instance in Glamorganshire, all the reported cases are from England.

England *Folk-Lore* 39 (1928) 82–3. Sussex N&Q 5S:10 (1878) 49. Somerset N&Q 1S:9 (1854) 536. Cornwall N&Q 4S:11 (1873) 285–6. Surrey N&Q 1S:11 (1855) 194; [1910] *Folk-Lore* 38 (1927) 82–3; *Folk-Lore* 61 (1950) 104. London N&Q 1S:3 (1851) 477. Essex *Folk-Lore* 70 (1959) 414–15. Buckinghamshire N&Q 4S:11 (1873) 433. Oxfordshire *Folk-Lore* 38 (1927) 82–3; *Folk-Lore* 66 (1955) 325–6. Gloucestershire *Trans. Bristol & Glos. Arch. Soc.* 53 (1931) 264. Worcestershire N&Q 4S:11 (1873) 285–6; Berkeley & Jenkins (1932) 36. Warwickshire Bloom (*c*.1930) 48–9. Northamptonshire N&Q 1S:11 (1855) 254. Norfolk N&Q 1S:4 (1851) 240; *Folk-Lore* 50 (1939) 72. Cheshire N&Q 4S:11 (1873) 374. Derbyshire N&Q 4S:11 (1873) 213. Lancashire *Folk-Lore* 39 (1928) 393; *Lancashire Lore* (1971) 50. Yorkshire Addy (1888) xxiv. Co. Durham Leighton (1910) 52. Glamorganshire N&Q 4S:11 (1873) 374. Unlocated N&Q 1S:4 (1851) 124; Igglesden (*c*.1932) 193. General N&Q 1S:3 (1851) 507, 519; N&Q 4S:12 (1873) 96, 158;

N&Q 5S:10 (1878) 197; *Folk-Lore* 38 (1927) 82–3; *Folk-Lore* 39 (1928) 284–5, 393–8; *Folk-Lore* 40 (1929) 196–7.

funerals: seen through glass

In common with two other superstitions, it was felt to be particularly unlucky to see a funeral though a window:

It is unlucky to look at a funeral procession through a window, or to stand in the door to do so. One must go right outside. My informant was reproved by her father for attempting to do so.
Aberdeenshire *Folk-Lore Jnl* (1888)

See also MOON: SEEN THROUGH GLASS; GLASS: SEEN THROUGH.

Hampshire [1973] Opie & Tatem, 171. Herefordshire Leather (1912) 119. Highland Scotland Macbain (1887/88) 255. Aberdeenshire *Folk-Lore Jnl* 6 (1888) 263. Northeast Scotland Gregor (1874) 148. Co. Tyrone *Lore & Language* 1:7 (1972) 8. Co. Antrim [1987] Opie & Tatem, 171.

funerals: sunwise

A number of activities which involved movement were traditionally carried out, whenever possible, in a clockwise direction, or 'with the sun'. The two most commonly described were the turning of FISHING boats, and funerals approaching the graveyard:

Many persons in this neighbourhood consider it very bad luck if, when a body is taken to be buried, the funeral procession proceeds to the churchyard by a way which will make them meet the sun in its course. They call this going to be buried 'the back way'; and I know of people who would do almost anything over a funeral rather than not follow the sun.
Nottinghamshire N&Q (1877)

This is usually assumed to be a relic of sunworship, but this is highly unlikely, and there is no evidence to support the assertion.
See also SUNWISE.

Herefordshire [1838] Leather (1912) 123. Nottinghamshire N&Q 5S:8 (1877) 182. Yorkshire Henderson (1866) 45. Co. Durham Leighton (1910) 52. Inverness *Scottish Studies* (1959) 197. Morayshire Shaw (1775) 230. Isle of Lewis *Folk-Lore* 6 (1895) 168. Connemara *Folk-Lore* 4 (1893) 358. Co. Kerry *Folk-Lore* 31 (1920) 235. Unlocated N&Q 5S:8 (1877) 182.

fungus

A single source includes the superstition 'Never kick fungi with your foot, or you will have bad luck for seven years'. It is not clear whether this was more widely known or simply an individual fancy. The 'seven years' motif is presumably borrowed from mirror beliefs.

Worcestershire [1900] *Folk-Lore* 20 (1909) 343.

furniture creaking

It would perhaps be thought that the occasional noises made by old-fashioned furniture would be too common to excite much comment, but, like the much more common DEATHWATCH sound, creaking furniture was counted by some as ominous. At best it meant rain, at worst the death of someone in the house:

Any creaking of the chairs and tables in a house is looked upon as a sure sign of the death of one of the family. My informant told me that, not long ago, her mother entered a house in which was lying a young woman sick. She heard some creaking among the chairs or tables during the time she was in the house. On returning home she mentioned the fact, and at the same time made the remark that it was the warning of the death of the girl. The girl died not long after.
Aberdeenshire *Folk-Lore Jnl* (1888)

The few examples span little more than twenty years, but they are widely spread geographically, which would argue for the belief being more widely known than the documentary record indicates.
See also CHAIRS.

Wiltshire Wilts. *N&Q* 1 (1893–5) 104. Berkshire Lowsley (1888) 23. Wales Trevelyan (1909) 328. Highland Scotland Macbain (1887/88) 262. Aberdeenshire *Folk-Lore Jnl* 6 (1888) 262–3.

gallows/gibbets

A piece of wood taken from a public gallows or gibbet was used as a cure either for AGUE or TOOTHACHE. The earlier references, the first of which appears in the writings of Thomas Browne in 1650, refer to the ague:

The chips or cuttings of a gibbet or gallows, on which one or more persons have been executed or exposed, if worn next the skin, or round the neck, in a bag, will cure the ague, or prevent it.
Unlocated Grose (1787)

For toothache, the piece of wood was rubbed on the tooth or gum. Local legends often grew up around the sites of gibbets, particularly, it seems, in the North of England, which were often named after the last person to hang there, or a particularly famous occupant. Gibbets were disused from 1832, but often lingered on in lonely remote places:

At the head of Esthwaite Lake, near where the road crosses the beck, between the town and Colthouse, once stood a gibbet (named in parish registers in 1672) of which inhabitants can still remember the stump standing. Within the memory of man there was a common belief that a fragment torn from the rotting fragment of this gallows, and placed in an aching tooth, formed a sure cure.   Lancashire Cowper (1897)

Toothache, in particular, appears to have attracted several gruesome cures, as other specifics for the problem included biting a tooth out of a skull.

See also HANGMAN'S ROPE; DEAD MAN'S HAND; SKULLS.

Ague: General Browne, *Pseudodoxia Epidemica* (1650/6th edn 1672) Bk 5, Ch. 23; Grose (1787) 57; *Gent. Mag.* (1796) 636; Brand (1810) 107.
Toothache: Lancashire Cowper (1897) 372–3. Co. Durham Brockett (1829) 291. Northumberland Henderson (1866) 113.

---

gardens: cattle straying into

Three references record a belief that cattle straying into a domestic garden is unlucky for the occupants:

A bad omen seems to be drawn from an ox or cow breaking into a garden. Though I laugh at the superstition, the omen was painfully fulfilled in my case. About the middle of March, 1843, some cattle were driven close to my house; and, the back door being open, three got into our little bit of garden, and trampled it. When our schooldrudge came in the afternoon, and asked the cause of the confusion, she expressed great sorrow and apprehension on being told – said it was a bad sign – and that we should hear of three deaths within the next six months. Alas! in April we heard of dear J—'s murder, a fortnight after, A—died, and tomorrow, August 10th, I am to attend the funeral; of my excellent son-in-law. I have just heard of the same omen from another quarter. But what is still more remarkable is, that when I went down to Mr.—'s funeral, and was

mentioning the superstition, they told me that, while he was lying ill, a cow got in the front garden, and was driven out with great difficulty.
                         Unlocated N&Q (1850)

The paucity of recorded examples makes it difficult to judge how widespread this belief really was, but it was clearly not simply an individual fancy.

Somerset [1923] Opie & Tatem, 103. **England** Addy (1895) 97. **Unlocated** N&Q 1S:1 (1850) 258.

---

garlic

The widespread idea that garlic is generally protective against evil is largely the result of the vampire industry, and was imported in the late nineteenth century from mid European lore by popular novels and later popularized by films. Nevertheless, there are some indications that the plant was used protectively in Ireland:

and cloves of wild garlic are planted on thatch over the door, for good luck.
                         Ireland *Gent. Mag.* (1865)

Garlic was much more commonly used in cures, in a similar way to ONIONS, for a wide range of ailments including tuberculosis and other lung complaints, WHOOPING COUGH, piles, cuts, and poisonous bites. In Ireland, garlic was thought to be particularly effective if planted on GOOD FRIDAY. Seventeenth-century compilers of herbals, such as Nicholas Culpeper, included garlic in their medicinal writings, but again onions seem to have been more favoured. Hatfield (1994) and Vickery (1995) detail many more recent uses.

East Anglia Hatfield (1994) various pages; **Ireland** N&Q 1S:1 (1850) 349; *Gent. Mag.* (1865) 700; Logan (1981) various pages. **General** N&Q 10S:11 (1909) 173. N&Q 11S:12 (1915) 246; Vickery (1995) 150–1.

---

garters

see CLOTHES: GARTERS; CRAMP; LOVE DIVINATION: GARTER SPELLS.

---

gasworks

One of the many cures for WHOOPING COUGH and other respiratory diseases, which involved making the sufferer inhale particular fumes or pungent odours:

When my sister had whooping cough very badly, I had to take her each day to stand on the little bridge over the stinking effluent from the gasworks. She objected, but if we went home too soon we were sent back again. It was supposed to have a curative effect. All I can say is, I didn't get whooping cough.
Isle of Wight IOW Fed. W. I.s (1994)

The use of gasworks in this way can only date from the introduction of commercial gas in the early nineteenth century, but a similar effect was looked for from older industrial sites such as LIME KILNS as well as naturally occurring ozone such as at the seaside.

See also AIR CURES.

Isle of Wight IOW Fed. W. I.s (1994). Surrey *Croydon Advertiser* (4 Jan. 2002) 18. London [*c.*1918] Rolph (1980) 194. Bedfordshire Marsom (1950) 182. Worcestershire *Folk-Lore* 68 (1957) 503. Norfolk *Folk-Lore* 40 (1929) 117. Lancashire Harland & Wilkinson (1873) 226. Yorkshire Blakeborough (1898) 136. Westmorland/Lancashire [*c.*1939] *Folk-Lore* 62 (1951) 259–60. Northern England Henderson (1866) 110–13. Co. Durham Brockie (1886) 221. Dublin Logan (1981) 44.

gates/stiles

A surprisingly wide range of beliefs feature gates and stiles, although none are particularly commonly reported, nor do they seem to hang together in any logical way. In some the gate or stile is simply the commonplace locale, but in others it takes a more central role. Several sources warn that two people should not cross a stile or gate together:

Not long since, I saw a party of little girls passing through the turnstile beside the churchyard gate at Eccleshall, one of whom was urgent with her companions only to go through the stile one at a time. 'One at once!' she cried distractedly, tugging at the skirts of those who pressed forward too fast, 'One at once! It's bad luck, it's bad luck!'
Shropshire Burne (1883)

This is perhaps comparable to the notion that it is unlucky to pass someone on the STAIRS, or may be compared to a number of other beliefs which warn against two people doing things together.

Two sources report an important choice between using a gate and stile:

Go thro' a gate when there's a stile hard by You'll be a widow before you die,
Cornwall *Folk-Lore Jnl* (1887)

but another Cornish version (Hazlitt (1907)) says it the other way round. Another source simply states 'To say GOODBYE over a stile brings bad luck' (Worcestershire *Folk-Lore* (1895)).

Stiles also feature in a range of cures, as a way of TRANSFERRING an ailment to another:

When I was suffering from ague a few years ago, I was strongly advised to go to a stile – one of those which are placed across footpaths – and to drive a nail into that part over which foot passengers travel in their journeys,
Suffolk *Gent. Mag.* (1867)

although an apparently analogous practice is less easy to explain:

A superstitious practice of sticking pins in a stile whenever a corpse is taken over it prevails in these parts.
Kent *Gent. Mag.* (1824)

This may perhaps be related to a widespread belief that carrying a corpse along any path creates a right of way over that land for evermore. One suggested way to avoid this happening was to charge a toll, however nominal, such as a pin (*see* FUNERALS: RIGHT OF WAY).

The gate or stile features as the locale for several LOVE DIVINATION customs. One group which features the new MOON is first reported in the seventeenth century, but turns up in almost exactly the same form in the twentieth:

At the first appearance of the new moon after new year's day (some say any other new moon is as good) go out in the evening, and stand over the spars of a gate or stile, looking at the moon and say:

> *All hail to the moon, all hail to thee*
> *I prithee good moon reveal to me*
> *This night who my husband (wife) must be*

You must presently after go to bed. I know two gentlewomen that did thus when they were young maids, and they had dreams of those that married them.
Unlocated Aubrey, *Miscellanies* (1696)

A Derbyshire version explains that the questioner climbs the gate to get as near to the moon as possible. In a second group, all from the late nineteenth century, the gate or stile has a more prominent part to play:

A girl must go to a five-barred gate and make nine notches in it, and when she does the last she must stand on one of the bars of the gate, and call the name of a young man three times; if any answer comes to the last call then she will marry him. This must be done at a 'chime hour'.   Norfolk Fulcher Collection (*c.*1895)

In a Herefordshire version, the supplicant cuts one notch every night for eight nights, and on the ninth his future wife will appear to cut the ninth, while in Shropshire it was three notches a night for nine nights. Both were to be undertaken at midnight.

Lastly, the stile features in a practice which usually takes place on first hearing the CUCKOO, but in this case is another new moon ceremony:

When you first see the new moon in the new year, take your stocking off from one foot, and run to the next stile, when you get there between the great toe and the next, you will find a hair, which will be the colour of your lover's.

Devon N&Q (1851)

Kent *Gent. Mag.* (1824) 28–33. Sussex *Folk-Lore Record* 1 (1878) 30. Devon N&Q 1:4 (1851) 99; N&Q 10S:12 (1909) 66; *Devonshire Assoc.* 103 (1971); *Devonshire Assoc.* 108 (1976). Cornwall *Folk-Lore Jnl* 5 (1887); Hazlitt (1907) 123. Herefordshire *Folk-Lore* 6 (1895) 304; Leather (1912) 87. Worcestershire *Folk-Lore* 6 (1895) 305; *Folk-Lore* 20 (1909) 345. Suffolk *Gent. Mag.* (1867) 728–41. Norfolk Fulcher Collection (*c.*1895). Shropshire Burne (1883) 177, 276. Derbyshire N&Q 10S:1 (1904) 252. Unlocated Aubrey, *Miscellanies* (1696/1857) 132–3.

geese: cures

Geese and goose products were recommended for a range of human ailments. Goose-grease was applied for bruises, aches and pains, sprains, colds and coughs (smeared on the chest and feet for the last two ailments). Goose dung was also recommended surprisingly often – taken internally, for example, for JAUNDICE, and externally for baldness and burns. Addled goose eggs were even used to counter adder-bites.

An Irish cure which appears to be based on the idea of TRANSFERENCE of disease was prescribed for the treatment of THRUSH:

Thrush was a common and painful complaint. It showed itself first on the tongue then on both sides of the mouth until the entire mouth was covered with white blisters. It became dangerous when it attacked the palate as it could suffocate a child . . . Keep a gander fasting for twenty four hours. Then put the gander's bill into the child's mouth and cause the gander to screech.

Co. Cork Culloty (1993)

For thrush: Co. Cork [1937] Culloty (1993) 58–9; *Folk-Lore* 8 (1897) 180. Ireland Hickey (1938) 269. *Other cures:* Devon *Devonshire Assoc.* 83 (1951) 74. Oxfordshire *Oxf. FL Soc. Ann. Record* (1956) 11–12; *Folk-Lore* 68 (1957) 415. Lincolnshire Peacock (1877) 26. Shropshire Burne (1883) 189–90. Yorkshire Nicholson (1890) 140, 143. Ireland Logan (1981) 124, 158. Co. Wexford Ó Muirithe & Nuttall (1999) 163. Co. Cork

geese

In addition to the relatively well-known specific beliefs covered in the following entries, a few other superstitions about geese have been noted less frequently.

If a goose begins to sit on her eggs when the wind is in the east, she will sit five weeks before she hatches.   East Anglia Forby (1830)

which is presumably related to the following, which indicates a wider distribution:

[From schoolboys' compositions on local superstitions] *Unlucky to let a goose sit on eggs when a west wind is blowing.*   Devon N&Q (1909)

Marie Trevelyan included more goose-related beliefs in her collection of Welsh folklore than the other authors put together, including:

Geese cackling and making much noise at midnight, or any unusual hour after going to roost, are said to portend theft and robbery on the premises. When they turn back home after starting out, a stranger may be expected . . . A grey goose straying into a neighbour's yard is a token of slander. When flocks of geese or ducks or fowls desert their homes, death is coming among the inmates . . . If geese, fowls, or ducks wander far, and seek new abodes among strangers, there is danger of a fire in their old haunts . . . If a goose lays one soft and one hard egg, or two eggs in a day, it means misfortune to the owner.

Wales Trevelyan (1909)

It is not clear whether Welsh tradition was particularly rich in goose-lore, or whether Ms Trevelyan was especially fond of them.

Devon 10S:12 (1909) 66. East Anglia Forby (1830) 414. Cumberland *Folk-Lore* 40 (1929) 285. Wales Trevelyan (1909) 114–5, 281, 323, 328. Ireland N&Q 6S:3 (1881) 163.

[1937] Culloty (1993) 59. **Guernsey** [1589] *Channel Islands Ann. Anth.* (1972–3) 21.

geese: flowers/catkins

A widespread superstition forbade anyone to bring PRIMROSES or DAFFODILS indoors, for fear of bad luck and a disastrous effect on chicks or goslings belonging to the household. A similar ban on another yellow plant was reported from Herefordshire and Shropshire:

But the strongest condemnation of all lights on willow catkins. The soft round yellowish blossoms are considered to resemble young goslings, and are accordingly called in various localities 'goosy goslins', 'gis an' gullies' or 'geese and gullies'. Whatever the name be, however, the ban on the blossom is the same. No vegetable goslings may be brought into the house, for if they be, no feathered goslings will be hatched; and from one quarter, in the Clee Hills, we learn that the same effect will be produced if any spring flowers are brought into the house while the geese are sitting.

Shropshire Burne (1883)

Herefordshire [*c.*1895] *Folk-Lore* 39 (1928) 386; Leather (1912) 17. **Shropshire** Burne (1883) 248.

geese: Michaelmas

One of the strongest traditional associations in the English festival calendar of the past was Michaelmas (29 September) and the eating of roast goose – stronger even than the modern connection between Christmas and turkey. Everyone who could afford it ate goose at Michaelmas, and although the origin of the association is not known, the custom had been in place since at least the fifteenth century. As with most festive food, a superstition developed that it was lucky to eat the food prescribed for the season, and in the case of the Michaelmas goose it was said that it was a positive way to ensure money for the next twelve months:

Pray tell me whence the custom'd proverb did commence, that who eats goose on Michael's Day, shan't money lack his debts to pay?

British Apollo (22 Oct. 1708)

This reference shows the belief already in place in the early eighteenth century, and it was still being said with no change in the twentieth, although by then Michaelmas was starting to pass each year without anyone taking any notice.

West Country Kendall (1944) 173. **Somerset** [1923] Opie & Tatem, 179. **East Anglia** Forby (1830) 414. **Norfolk**

Wright & Lones 3 (1940) 84. **Nottinghamshire** *Jnl Brit. Arch. Assoc.* 8 (1853) 236. **General** *British Apollo* (22 Oct. 1708); Grose (1787) 70; J. Brady, *Clavis Calendria* 2 (1812) 179–80; Jane Austen, *Letters* (11–12 Oct. 1813); [1839] Baron-Wilson 1 (1886) 163–4. For general Michaelmas customs *see* Wright & Lones 3 (1940) 80–90; Banks 3 (1941) 86–97.

German bands

From late Victorian times until the outbreak of the First World War, a regular feature of village and town life was the visit of groups of German musicians playing popular tunes and collecting money from the locals. 'German bands' were so well known that the name was adopted as rhyming slang for 'hand'. It was widely said that the playing of these bands brought rain.

Oxfordshire *Folk-Lore* 20 (1909) 490. **Yorkshire** *Folk-Lore* 20 (1909) 348.

glass: seen through

Two references report what may have been a fairly widespread LEGAL ERROR, that things seen through glass cannot be sworn to:

I have recently come across a case in which it was believed that it was not legal to swear to something that had been seen through glass. I have heard of the idea before, but a few days since a man consulted me about his wife. He had been told that a woman, looking through the partly opened door of his house, had seen a man in a compromising situation with his wife. I advised him nothing could be done unless he brought the witness to my office, and I found that her story was reliable, and I could get a 'signed' statement from her. A day or two afterwards he met me and said he would pursue the matter no further, as he found that what the woman said she saw was seen by her by looking through the window. He then added, 'You can't swear to what you see through glass. It's not legal. You know that very well!' He evidently considered he had stated such a well-known legal proposition that, as a lawyer, I must recognize its force at once.

Lancashire Folk-Lore (1920)

No theory of origin for such a belief has been put forward.

Two other superstitions involve the prohibition of seeing the new MOON or a FUNERAL through glass.

Shropshire Burne (1883) 282. **Lancashire** *Folk-Lore* 31 (1920) 237–8.

gloves

Several superstitions concern gloves, but none of them have been recorded a great number of times, nor are any particularly old. In common with other everyday items such as UMBRELLAS and CUTLERY, it is unlucky to drop a glove, but the misfortune can be diverted if someone else picks it up for you:

My Welsh-born mother-in-law dropped her gloves and I picked them up for her. She said, 'Oh that's good luck – as long as I don't say the Ta word' (i.e. as long as I don't say 'thank you').

Wales/England [Nov. 2001] Steve Roud Collection

This fear of dropping a glove has only been recorded from the 1920s onwards, although the above example shows it is still current. A second set of beliefs, which may be related to the first, maintains that it is unlucky to pick up a glove that you see lying in the road:

If you find a left-hand glove, leave it lying where it is, or it will bring sorrow.

Worcestershire *Folk-Lore* (1909)

A third superstition concerns gloves as gifts:

A tradition recorded in Oxfordshire within the last few years is that gloves make an unlucky gift between friends, foretelling a parting of the ways for the two people concerned. This idea cuts across the generally accepted notion that gloves are appropriate offerings from a lover.

Oxfordshire Radford (1971)

From the available evidence, this last would seem a purely twentieth-century invention, but a piece in the *Welcome Guest* of 1862, identified by Opie & Tatem, makes it clear that some superstition on the subject already existed at that time. In speaking of giving gloves as a present, it explicitly says that 'notions about luck are all exploded'.

Dropping: Middlesex [1984] Opie & Tatem, 174. Essex [*c*.1917] Mays (1969) 164. Oxfordshire [1920s] Surman (1992) 60–1. Lincolnshire Rudkin (1936) 18. Wales/England [2001] Steve Roud Collection. Neath Phillips (1925) 597.
Finding: London *Folk-Lore* 37 (1926) 366. Worcestershire *Folk-Lore* 20 (1909) 346. Northumberland *Folk-Lore* 36 (1925) 252.
Gift: Hampshire [1969] Opie & Tatem, 174. Middlesex [1984] Opie & Tatem, 174. Oxfordshire Radford (1971) 171. Suffolk [1953] Opie & Tatem, 174. General *Welcome Guest* (17 May 1862) 304.

goats

Goats feature surprisingly little in the superstitions of Britain and Ireland; such beliefs as have been recorded are scattered and contradictory, and no consistent overall view seems possible. The only belief which was widely agreed was that keeping a goat with cattle and horses was beneficial (*see below*). Considering the centuries-old propensity for portraying the Devil as a goat, which still survives in countless films and book illustrations, there seems to be little in traditional belief about goats to reflect this idea. A handful of reports suggest an affinity, but in a very mild, almost homely, fashion:

A superstition prevails both in England and Scotland that goats are never to be seen for twenty-four hours together, owing to their paying Satan a visit once during that period to have their beards combed. The Mirror (10 Mar. 1832)

A sample of other beliefs, none of which have been recorded very often, reveals a mixture of positive and negative attributes:

A strip of sheep or goatskin suspended from the collar of a horse will avert the evil eye.

Lincolnshire Rudkin (1936)

A young bride shouldn't drink goat's milk. It could make her barren.

Co. Tyrone *Lore & Language* (1972)

What is the origin or fundamental idea of the superstition belonging to the folk-lore of Wales to the effect that it brings luck to a bride if the first thing she sees on coming out of a church after her wedding is a tethered goat?

Wales N&Q (1915)

Goat's milk was also a cure [for consumption], *and if possible it had to be drunk on the hillside in the morning.* Highland Scotland Polson (1926)

Lincolnshire Rudkin (1936) 23. **Northern England** *Newcastle Weekly Chronicle* (11 Feb. 1899) 7. **Wales** N&Q 11S:12 (1915) 181. **Scotland** *Scottish Studies* 7 (1963) 201–8, 8 (1964) 213–7, 9 (1965) 182–8. **Highland Scotland** Polson (1926) 30–1. **Co. Cork** *Folk-Lore* 8 (1897) 179. **Co. Tyrone** *Lore & Language* 1:7 (1972) 8. **General** *The Mirror* (10 Mar. 1832) 170.

goats: with cattle

A widespread custom found among farmers in Britain and Ireland was to keep goats among their cattle because, it was believed, the cows benefited in various ways from their presence:

It is still a generally received opinion, that one of these animals kept about an inn or farmstead is not only conducive to the health of the other domestic animals, but also brings good luck to the owner.

Northern England [1850s] *Denham Tracts*

Apart from being generally 'lucky', goats were reputed to have a calming effect on the cattle and also, more specifically, to prevent abortion in the cows:

The practice of keeping a goat among a herd of cows to prevent abortion is by no means confined to Leicestershire. It must be a Billy goat, and the more it stinks the better. How the charm works nobody knows. Since I introduced a he-goat among my shorthorns, abortion has ceased. Previously it was very troublesome.

Gloucestershire N&Q (1910)

Precisely how this works is never clear. Some farmers believed that the goats ate certain 'herbs' which were noxious to cattle, but no one has been able to identify which particular plants these might be. Others claimed that the smell of the goats was somehow protective, or that they actually attract diseases to themselves and thus prevent infection of the cows. In addition, the goat was reputed to kill adders:

The custom of keeping a goat with a herd of cattle has been prevalent in North-West Durham for the past forty years to my knowledge. What the reason or effect was, or is, I cannot say, but one farmer in Satley parish, whose farm was the haunt of adders, always kept a Billy-goat on it, while he lived there, to go with his cattle and sheep, for he believed the goat killed and ate the reptiles, and so prevented them from doing any damage to his stock by 'stinging' them. I used to doubt the killing and eating part of the business, until one day I saw Mr. Goat kill an adder by jumping on it and mangling it, and then bite it to pieces.

Co. Durham N&Q (1917)

In one Scottish source, the reputed cure is more explicit:

in the 1920s when my parents proposed keeping a milk-goat, the farm manager protested strenuously that if this were done everyone would think that our pedigree Highland herd (not used for milk) was suffering from tuberculosis and that the goat had been brought in to cure them. In deference to his feelings the idea was given up.

Argyll *Scottish Studies* (1965)

Goats were believed to have a similarly beneficial effect on horses, and were regularly kept in stables. The earliest reference so far found is in this context:

Some may think it all a fable, When I say that in the stable I'm a doctor, and my scent does many maladies prevent.   *Riddle-Book* (c.1840)

There is no doubt that the practice was widespread and literally believed, and it has the hallmarks of an old custom. Nevertheless, despite numerous descriptions, the earliest datable source remains stubbornly about 1840, and even those later writers who refer to their own history do not take us back beyond that point. We thus have no grounds to assign it to an earlier period. Similar claims were made, less commonly, for DONKEYS, but the earliest reference there is still only from 1799.

One or two references are explicit that goats were a protection against the evil eye, witches, and so on. This is strange, considering the close connection between goats, witches, and the Devil in the popular mind (but see GOATS, *above*) that would seem to imply that goats would attract witches rather than repel them.

Southern England N&Q 9S:5 (1900) 52. **Dorset** *Folk-Lore* 28 (1917) 451. **Devon** *Devonshire Assoc.* 86 (1954) 297–8; *Devonshire Assoc.* 88 (1956) 254. **Berkshire** N&Q 11S:2 (1910) 534; *Folk-Lore* 44 (1933) 218. **London** *Folk-Lore* 44 (1933) 218. **Oxfordshire** *Oxf. & Dist. FL Soc. Ann. Record* (1959) 7. **Gloucestershire** N&Q 11S:2 (1910) 534; *Farmers Weekly* (9 Nov. 1973) 93. **Herefordshire** *Leather* (1912) 23. **Worcestershire** N&Q 11S:2 (1910) 534. **Norfolk** [c.1912] Randell (1966) 90. **Lincolnshire** N&Q 9S:5 (1900) 248–9. **Leicestershire** N&Q 11S:2 (1910) 466, 534; N&Q 12S:1 (1916) 16. **Shropshire** *Folk-Lore* 49 (1938) 232; *Folk-Lore* 68 (1957) 503. **Northern England** [1850s] *Denham Tracts* 2 (1895) 75. **Yorkshire** *Folk-Lore* 26 (1915) 213. **Manchester** *Manchester Courier* (29 Jan. 1866). **Co. Durham** N&Q 12S:3 (1917) 310. **Wales** Jones (1930) 142. **Montgomeryshire** Hamer (1877) 261. **Argyll** *Scottish Studies* 9 (1965) 183. **N. Ireland** N&Q 9S:5 (1900) 359–60; Buckley (1980) 21. **Co. Tipperary** *Folk-Lore* 30 (1919) 239. **Guernsey** De Garis (1975) 125. **Jersey** *Folk-Lore* 25 (1914) 247. **Unlocated** N&Q 3S:9 (1866) 330; N&Q 11S:11 (1915) 500. **Literary** *Riddle-Book* [c.1840] 12, quoted Opie & Tatem, 174; George Eliot, *Middlemarch* (1872) Bk 4, Ch. 39. **Virginia** N&Q 9S:5 (1900) 52.

God's penny

A number of customs and beliefs surrounded the action of handing over money in the process of BUYING AND SELLING, on which the success of the transaction, and the future luck of the participants, largely depended. The seller was expected, for example, to give back to the purchaser a small sum for luck, which was thus called LUCK MONEY or a 'luck penny', even though it could be substantially more than that. A different principle was covered by the 'God's penny', which was given in advance of payment, as a binding deposit or promise. Similarly, 'earnest money' (often called 'arles' or 'earls') was paid to servants when they were hired, by which both sides agreed to stick to the bargain made.

Although the God's penny changed hands for business rather than superstitious reasons, it had its roots in belief. In earlier times it had been customary, at least in theory, to put this money to a charitable purpose and thus invoke divine blessing, an echo of which was still resonating in the mid nineteenth century:

[On sharing out the fishing boat's takings] *If it should happen that there were any odd shillings – which there often was – the money would be reserved for the poor, the aged, the widow or the fatherless. They believed that their luck depended upon remembering the poor, They called the odd money 'God's portion' and it had to be used accordingly.* Isle of Man [*c.*1850s] Cashen

But the terminology can also be unclear, with the terms 'God's penny', 'luck money' and 'earnest money' often used apparently indiscriminately. Both God's penny and earnest money had been in use since at least the thirteenth or fourteenth centuries (*see* numerous examples in *OED*), but luck money appears to be a much later concept.

Isle of Man Cashen (1912) 39–41. **General** N&Q 9S:11 (1903) 358; Snell (1911) 232–8.

gold

see STYE CURES.

Goldfinches (*Carduelis carduelis*)

It is a common belief in Lincolnshire that redcaps, i.e. goldfinches, frequently poison their captive young. I remember as a child hearing great lamentation made in a cottage-garden, when it was discovered that the nestlings confined in a cage hanging in an apple-tree had all been 'poisoned by the old birds', who visited them with food. Lincolnshire N&Q (1895)

Replies in the same journal confirmed the existence of the same belief in Derbyshire and France.

Lincolnshire N&Q 8S:8 (1895) 155. **Derbyshire** N&Q 8S:8 (1895) 293. **France** N&Q 8S:8 (1896) 89.

Good Friday: blacksmiths

One of the categories of worker reported as unwilling to work on Good Friday is BLACK-SMITHS:

Blacksmiths will not light their fires on Good Friday. If necessity compels them to do anything in the shop, they will not bring fire in, but will make it by striking a piece of iron till it becomes red hot. Northumberland Bigge (1860–62)

The symbolism is more obvious in another aspect of the work:

A friend who passed his boyhood in the north of Durham informs me that no blacksmith throughout that district would then drive a nail on that day; a remembrance of the awful purpose for which hammer and nails were used on the first Good Friday doubtless held them back. Co. Durham Henderson (1866)

Other versions of the prohibition on the making or use of nails on this day also included the blacksmith's wife. She used her apron to fan the flames when the bellows refused, or carried the nails in her apron to the executioners (Aarne-Thompson motif V211.2.3.0.2). As a result, some nineteenth-century blacksmiths' wives refused to wear an APRON on Good Friday.

As with many other Good Friday traditions, this does not seem to date back before the mid Victorian era.

Co. Durham Henderson (1866) 61; N&Q 5S:10 (1878) 23 [same as Henderson]; Leighton (1910) 56. **Northumberland** Bigge (1860–62) 92. **Lincolnshire** *Saga Book of the Viking Club* 3 (1902) 8. **Aberdeenshire** Pratt (1858) 20. **Caithness** Calder (1842) 233.

Good Friday: born on

The ambivalence shown elsewhere in Good Friday beliefs is further reflected in conflicting notions concerning those who are born on the day. Whereas some are quite clear that such people are unfortunate:

The birth of a child on that day is very unlucky – indeed a birth on any Friday of the whole year is to be deprecated as a most unfortunate circumstance: Wales Sikes (1880)

others are more positive:

Unlucky to be born on a Friday, unless it happened to be Good Friday. Lancashire N&Q (1870)

Good Friday

Popular traditions and beliefs about Good Friday reveal a long-standing underlying ambivalence about the meaning of the day in the minds of the people. In the eyes of the official religion, the commemoration of the death of its founder would clearly be a day set aside from all others as one of mourning, fast, prayer, and penitence. But for very many individuals, the day has long been far from gloomy. The confusion is certainly not helped by the term *Good* Friday, in common use since the thirteenth century, and originally meaning *Holy* or *God's* Friday. The notion that the day was 'good' because Christ's sacrifice opened to us the gates of everlasting life was a distinction which was lost on many English-speaking folk.

Established churches have always attempted to control the way people spend their leisure time: by example, by sermon, by threat, and by legislation. The long-running battle over Sunday observance is the most obvious example in Britain, but tension also focused on Good Friday, which, as it falls in springtime, was clearly an ideal day for fun and frolic, playing marbles, skipping, and gardening. In the early nineteenth century, before the introduction of Bank Holidays, Good Friday and Christmas Day were the only two days which were almost universally granted as holiday to working people, and rural workers, in particular, regarded Good Friday as the ideal time to plant their potatoes and to get forward on their gardens and allotments. They naturally resented being told to do no work on the day.

In popular superstition, therefore, we find the day treated as good or bad, almost at random. Thus, bread baked on Good Friday is lucky and cures all ills, but 'He who bakes or brews on Good Friday will have his house burnt down before the end of the year' (**Northamptonshire** Sternberg (1851)). Similarly, 'Potatoes must always be planted on Good Friday' (**Devon** *Devonshire Assoc.* (1972)), but 'Potatoes must not be dibbled on Good Friday or bad crop will follow' (**Unlocated** Igglesden (*c*.1932)).

The picture is further complicated by the widespread fear of FRIDAY as the unluckiest day of the week. It is likely that this reputation itself came about in pre-Reformation Britain by extension from Good Friday, but as it became widespread in its own right, it in turn strengthened the original negative reputation of Good Friday. This connection between all Fridays and Good Friday is often made by informants:

One of the assistants at the bathing machines assured me that most accidents happened on Fridays, especially on Good Fridays. He had never worked on Good Fridays for many years,

nor would he ever do so again. He then gave a long series of misfortunes, fatal accidents, etc. which had happened on Fridays in his own experience.   Yorkshire N&Q (1869)

The most widespread beliefs about Good Friday have their own entries, but there are many others, such as a belief that 'It is unlucky to shed blood on Good Friday' (**Co. Longford** *Béaloideas* (1936):

a story told me years ago by a former servant, which I recollect made a deep impression on me at the time . . . She told me how her father one Good Friday tried to kill a pig, notwithstanding the traditional unluckiness of the day; but in vain, as the pig would not die, and he was at length compelled to abandon the attempt for that day.   Devon *Devonshire Assoc.* (1883)

One notable characteristic of Good Friday prohibitions is the frequency with which they are explained and supported by stories based on apocryphal events which took place when Christ was on his way to Calvary. The ban on washing, for example, and the reluctance of blacksmiths to use nails, and their wives to wear aprons, are explained in this way. Occasional references indicate what was probably a wide range of other stories, such as the following:

'my mother always told me not to pour anything down the sink till after three o'clock on Good Friday'. 'Why not?' asked the puzzled parson. 'Because the gutters of Jerusalem was running with our Lord's blood up till three o'clock; you must never pour anything down the sink till after three o'clock on Good Friday.'
                    Birmingham [1925] *Folk-Lore*

One continuing puzzle over Good Friday traditions and beliefs is the apparently late date at which they start to be recorded. As far as the written record goes, most of them seem to be no older than the nineteenth century. This is unlikely to be entirely true, but further research is necessary before any firm conclusions can be reached.

Compare ASCENSION DAY.

Devon *Devonshire Assoc.* 15 (1883) 107; **Devon** *Devonshire Assoc.* 104 (1972) 267. **Birmingham** [1925] *Folk-Lore* 51 (1940) 297–8. **Northamptonshire** Sternberg (1851) 189. **Yorkshire** N&Q 45:4 (1869) 131. **Ireland** Danaher (1972) 70–2. **Co. Longford** *Béaloideas* 6 (1936) 264. **Unlocated** Igglesden (*c*. 1932) 101–2. For calendar customs and general Good Friday activities, *see* Wright & Lones 1 (1936) 68–84; Banks 1 (1937) 34–7; Danaher (1972) 70–2; Owen (1987) 82–4.

In some people's eyes, Good Friday shares the attribute of Christmas Day and the CHIME hours that anyone born at that time will have the power to see spirits and will be generally receptive to the supernatural. Another reference states that they will never be afraid. Taken as a whole, there are so few references, and so little agreement, that no generalization about the meaning can be made.

Lincolnshire N&Q 8S:10 (1896) 92. **England** Addy (1895) 114. **Lancashire** N&Q 4S:6 (1870) 211. **Wales** Sikes (1880) 267. **Literary** Walter Scott, *Marmion*, Canto 3, note G.

Good Friday: bread

Undoubtedly the most widespread of Good Friday beliefs concern the special food associated with the day – bread, buns, and eggs. The basic tradition is that bread and buns baked on the day never grow mouldy but remain edible for ever, and similarly, eggs laid on Good Friday never go bad. They also have considerable power in the medicinal sphere, and were thus routinely kept in many a home for use during the coming year.

Calling at a cottage one day, I saw a small loaf hanging up oddly in a corner of the house. I asked why it was placed there, and was told that it was Good Friday bread; that it would never grow mouldy (and on inspecting it I certainly found it very dry) and that it was very serviceable against some diseases, the bloody flux being mentioned as an example. Suffolk *Gent. Mag.* (1867)

Typically, the bread was hung up in a bag or simply on a string from the kitchen ceiling. This was not simply the traditional place for it: the position helped to ensure that it was kept dry and aired. When it was needed, a few COBWEBS would not have put anyone off, as these in themselves were considered to have medicinal properties (*see also* SPIDERS).

In some of our houses the Good Friday bun may be seen hanging by a string to the bacon-rack; slowly diminishing until the return of the season replaces it by a fresh one. It is of sovereign good in all manner of diseases afflicting the family or the cattle. I have more than once seen a little of this cake grated into a warm mash for a sick cow. Cornwall Couch (1871)

The bread was particularly effective for stomach and bowel complaints, and WHOOPING COUGH, but everything is recommended for the latter. Numerous other complaints are mentioned as susceptible to treatment with

Good Friday bread, ranging from hiccups to cholera, and, as above, many farmers used it to dose ailing cattle. The main characteristic of the bread is that it must be hard – 'hard as a stone' is the usual description – and dry, and being hung up in a kitchen would ensure that it stayed this way. When it was needed for medicinal purposes it was typically grated into water, or pieces were broken off and soaked ready for use. Occasional references indicate its additional use as a poultice.

Most accounts simply mention 'bread' made on the day, in small loaves, but there is evidence of traditions of specially made cakes, apart from the modern hot cross buns, which probably varied from region to region:

It is many years ago since I saw a Good Friday cake hung up in a house. It used to be a round thin cake of about six inches across, said to be good for stomach complaints. This was always renewed on Good Friday. Devon *Devonshire Assoc.* (1934)

and in Hone's *Every-Day Book* (1827) it is described as a 'hard biscuit-like cake of open cross-work'. But in later times, ordinary bread or cakes baked on the day were the norm, provided they were dry enough, and eventually the belief in its efficacy even embraced buns made by the local baker:

It was formerly quite a general custom to bake on Good Friday, in order to have some of the bread, marked with the cross, to keep for the rest of the year as medicine, chiefly for intestinal troubles, in 'dumb animals or Christians'. I have known many people in Weobley who did this; now-a-days they are content to keep a baker's hot cross bun. Herefordshire Leather (1912)

Good Friday bread was also held to have protective properties, most commonly against fire, but also in some coastal areas against shipwreck. Its presence in the kitchen also assured good luck in baking throughout the coming year. In Ireland, water collected from holy wells on Good Friday was thought particularly beneficial.

In common with other Good Friday beliefs, there is a short legend to explain why baked products should have so much power on this day, although it is not often quoted in the literature, and it is thus difficult to assess how widely known it really was:

As our Blessed Lord was carrying His cross on his way to His crucifixion, a woman who had been washing came out of the house and threw her dirty water over the Saviour; another woman

*who was standing near with some freshly baked
bread said to her, 'Why do you treat that poor
man like that, One who never did you any harm?'
and she gave our Blessed Lord a loaf, which He
ate, and said 'from henceforth blessed be to the
baker, and cursed be the washer'.*

Herefordshire Leather (1912)

The 'washing' part of the story is more widely
reported (*see* GOOD FRIDAY: WASHING).

The history of the belief in the potency of
Good Friday bread is unclear. Certainly it was
extremely well known and widely reported
throughout the nineteenth century, and was
already in circulation in the mid eighteenth
century, but before that the record is blank,
apart from a very early reference identified by
Opie and Tatem. In a letter to Bishop Wulfsige,
written around the year 1001, English Abbot
Aelfric refers to priests keeping 'the sacrament
consecrated on Easter Day the whole year long
for sick men'. If this tradition remained active
from medieval times to the eighteenth century,
it is a mystery why it does not seem to be
mentioned by anyone. Similarly, if the belief
was re-introduced after a long lapse, it is
difficult to see why, or how. Such re-introduc-
tions are normally taken from classical texts. A
parallel custom of keeping pieces of soul-bread
for luck is of little help in this respect, as it, too,
is not reported before the nineteenth century.

Compare ASCENSION DAY.

Sussex *Athenaeum* (1846) 1142; N&Q 4S:6 (1870) 68;
Henderson (1879) 82. **Somerset** *Athenaeum* (1847) 95;
Folk-Lore 31 (1920) 244. **Dorset/Somerset** *N&Q for
Somerset & Dorset* 9 (1904–5) 113. **Dorset** N&Q 3S:8
(!865) 146; *Folk-Lore* 11 (1900) 112. **New Forest** Wise
(1867) 177. **Devon** Hewett (1900) 77; *Devonshire Assoc.*
60 (1928) 125; *Devonshire Assoc.* 66 (1934) 88. **Cornwall**
Couch (1871) 153; *Western Antiquary* 3 (1883) 91; *Folk-
Lore Jnl* 5 (1887) 202; *Cassell's Saturday Jnl* (1893).
Wiltshire Francis Kilvert, *Diary* (10 Feb. 1874); Smith
(1874) 328. **Berkshire** Salmon (1902) 423. **Oxfordshire**
Athenaeum (1847) 95; *Oxf. FL Soc. Ann. Record* (1956)
12. **Gloucestershire** *Folk-Lore* 13 (1902) 173.
Herefordshire [c.1895] *Folk-Lore* 39 (1928) 388; Leather
(1912) 78–9, 84–5. **Worcestershire** Salisbury (1893) 70;
Folk-Lore 26 (1915) 95; Berkeley & Jenkins (1932) 36.
Warwickshire N&Q 3S:3 (1863) 262–3. **East Anglia**
Forby (1830) 402–3; Varden (1885) 103. **Suffolk** *Gent.
Mag.* (1867) 728–41; Chambers 1 (1878) 322. **Norfolk**
Fulcher Collection (c.1895). **Lincolnshire** N&Q 4S:10
(1872) 24; Sutton (1992) 132. **Midlands** Henderson
(1879) 82. **Worcestershire/Shropshire** *Gent. Mag.* (1855)
384–6. **Shropshire** Burne (1883) 191, 333–4. **Staffordshire**
Athenaeum (1847) 95; Hackwood (1924) 149. **Derbyshire**
N&Q 10S:9 (1908) 345. **Yorkshire** N&Q 4S:5 (1870) 595;
Henderson (1879) 82; Sutton (1992) 132. **Lancashire**
Harland & Wilkinson (1882) 226. **Co. Durham** Brockie
(1886) 221. **Wales** Sikes (1880) 267. **Ireland** Danaher

(1972) 71–2. **Unlocated** *Athenaeum* (1846) 1142. **General**
Hone, *Every-Day Book* 1 (1827) 202.

Good Friday: eggs

Less well attested than the belief in Good Friday
bread (*see below*), some references report that
Good Friday eggs are also special:

*In Suffolk, eggs laid on Good Friday are also kept
with the greatest care by the farmers' wives, who
maintain that they will never go bad, and that a
piece of such an egg gives immediate relief to a
person suffering from colic.*

Suffolk Henderson (1879)

One of the lesser beliefs about Good Friday
bread was that its presence in the house
prevented fire, whereas the egg helped put it out:

*It is a very old belief that with the eggs laid on
Good Friday any fire can be extinguished, simply
by throwing the said egg into the heart of it.*

Somerset [1923] Opie & Tatem

Somerset [1923] Opie & Tatem, 178. **Northamptonshire**
N&Q 1S:2 (1850) 164. **Suffolk** Henderson (1879) 82.
Western Scotland Napier (1879) 114. **Unlocated** N&Q
12S:9 (1921) 489; Igglesden (c.1932) 102. **General** N&Q
12S:9 (1921) 489; N&Q 12S:12 (1923) 17.

Good Friday:
hair/fingernails

A handful of references indicate beliefs in the
beneficial effects of cutting FINGERNAILS and
HAIR on Good Friday, even though these activities are usually strictly avoided on FRIDAYS. The
activity is especially good for TOOTHACHE:

*In conversing yesterday with an old bedridden
man in this parish, fast approaching fourscore
and ten, I said to him, 'Why, Benjamin, you have
wonderfully good teeth for your time of life. I
suppose you have never suffered much from
toothache.' 'Well then, Sir, I'll tell you how it was,'
said the old gentleman, 'I used to suffer very
much from toothache many years ago, till a
neighbour told me how to cure it. I got up on
Good Friday before the sun rose, and cut all the
nails on my hands and my feet, and wrapped it
all up in a bit of writing paper, and put it in my
pocket, and I've never had the toothache since.'*

Gloucestershire N&Q (1867)

Devon *Devonshire Assoc.* 63 (1931) 131. **Gloucestershire**
N&Q 3S:11 (1867) 233–4. **Worcestershire** *Folk-Lore* 20
(1909) 346. **Co. Longford** *Béaloideas* 6 (1936) 266.

Good Friday: washing

One of the most widespread prohibitions on Good Friday behaviour was the ban of WASHING. Various calamities could be the result of such a sinful act: clothes washed or hung out to dry would be found spattered with blood, soap suds would turn red, the family would be dreadfully unlucky, or someone would die because you 'washed them away'. As with other Good Friday beliefs, this is backed up with a simple story about Christ:

An old woman of the North Riding once asked a friend of mine whether it was wrong to wash on Good Friday. 'I used to do so,' she said, 'and thought no harm of it, till once, when I was hanging out my clothes, a young woman passed by (a dressmaker she was, and a Methodist); and she reproved me, and told me this story. While our Lord Jesus was being led to Calvary, they took him past a woman who was washing, and the woman "blirted" the thing she was washing in His face; on which He said, "Cursed be every one who hereafter shall wash on this day". And never again,' added the old woman, 'have I washed on Good Friday'. Now it is said, in Cleveland, that clothes washed and hung out to dry on Good Friday will become spotted with blood.   Yorkshire Henderson (1866)

Although reported fairly often, the belief is found in a surprisingly restricted area – all the known references are from English locations – and the earliest is only from 1836.

See WASHING for other days on which it is prohibited. See also ASCENSION DAY.

Somerset *Folk-Lore* 31 (1920) 244. **Somerset/Dorset** *Folk-Lore* 31 (1920) 244–5. **Devon** Bray (1836) 286; Hewett (1900) 54; Crossing (1911) 134–5. **Berkshire** *Folk-Lore* 5 (1894) 337; Salmon (1902) 423. **Oxfordshire** *Folk-Lore* 34 (1923) 327–8. **Worcestershire** *Gent. Mag.* (1855) 384–6; Berkeley & Jenkins (1932) 34. **Warwickshire** Bloom (*c.*1930) 40. **Birmingham** [1925] *Folk-Lore* 51 (1940) 297–8. **Lincolnshire** Sutton (1992) 132. **Staffordshire** Hackwood (1924) 149. **England** Addy (1895) 114. **Yorkshire** N&Q 3S:3 (1863) 363; Henderson (1866) 62–3.

Good Friday: weaning babies

The beneficial nature of actions undertaken on Good Friday are reflected in a handful of references which reveal a belief that children should be weaned on that day, and that it was also a good time to dress them in lightweight clothes for the spring:

Good Friday is the best day of all the year to begin weaning children, which ought if possible to be put off till that day.   Lancashire N&Q (1851)

Although only reported a few times, the geographical spread of the references suggests a more widely known belief. As usual with the minor Good Friday traditions, it seems to date only from the mid nineteenth century.

Hampshire Yonge (1898) 175. **Devon** Hewett (1900) 50. **Cheshire** Wright & Lones 1 (1936) 81. **Lancashire** N&Q 1S:3 (1851) 516. **Co. Durham** Leighton (1910) 57.

Good Friday: work

Given the nature of Good Friday as the key day for Christian mourning, it is not surprising that there was a general feeling that, like a sort of super-Sunday, no work should be done on the day:

Ole Jimmy Emery, the farmer, sent him to work on a Good Friday, and Ole Jimmy's best horse ran the pole of a cart into that's chest, and died. Ole Jimmy he used to send the men to work out of the way on a Good Friday . . . but the old parson, he say 'God Almighty, he can see you wherever you go, that's no use a-hidin'. That were a judgment on you for workin' on Good Friday'. Ole Jimmy never let anyone work on a Good Friday again. 'I don't want to lose another horse' says he. Poor Ole Jimmy. That wouldn't do to let him see you a-doin' anything on a Good Friday after that!
Norfolk *Folk-Lore* (1926)

Nevertheless, this prohibition is only included in a handful of folklore collections, and evidence for its existence is remarkably thin. It is possible that collectors thought of it more as orthodox religion than superstition. Certain categories of work, however, were more specifically reported, but again not widely. Some blacksmiths, fishermen, and miners, for example, had a particular aversion to following their trades on this day, although by all accounts they were happy enough to do other 'work' on the day. In the domestic sphere WASHING was particularly frowned upon, although baking was not, and other activities, such as sewing, occasionally prohibited. There was also some ambivalence about people working on their gardens or allotments on the day (*see below*). The picture is slightly clouded by an overlap with the general feeling that any FRIDAY was an unlucky day to start any enterprise or project.

Devon *Devonshire Assoc.* 68 (1936) 93–4; Wright & Lones 1 (1936) 84. **Norfolk** *Norfolk Archaeology* 2 (1849) 296; *Folk-Lore* 37 (1926) 370. **Lincolnshire** Sutton (1992) 132–3. **England** Addy (1895) 114. **Derbyshire** Cox (1907) 363. **Yorkshire** N&Q 4S:4 131–2; Sutton (1992) 132–3. **Ireland** Danaher (1972) 70–2.

Good Friday: work on the land

The ambivalent nature of Good Friday beliefs is shown most clearly in the realm of work on the land and the planting of crops, where completely opposite advice is given.

I learn from a clergyman familiar with the North Riding of Yorkshire, that great care is there taken not to disturb the earth in any way; it were impious to use spade, plough, or harrow. He remembers, when a boy, hearing of a villager, Charlie Marston by name, who shocked his neighbours by planting potatoes on Good Friday, but they never came up.   Yorkshire Henderson (1866)

Many people then begin to till their gardens, as they believe, to use their own words, that all things put in the earth on Good Friday will grow 'goody', and return to them with great increase.
                        Devon Bray (1838)

Unfortunately, it is not simply a geographical north-south divide, as positive attitudes to the day are found in each region, although the strongest prohibitions are all found in Scotland and Northern England. The ambivalence also existed in Irish tradition:

Usually no work was done on the land on Good Friday . . . Most farmers would, however, plant a small quantity of grain or potatoes on this blessed day, thus invoking a blessing of the crops.
                        Ireland Danaher (1972)

POTATOES and PARSLEY are singled out as suited for Good Friday planting, but all growing things were thought susceptible to the influence of the day, and were often expected to 'come up double'.

The prohibition on agricultural activity was supported by a general ban on work on Good Friday (*see above*), but there was also a strong feeling that the land in particular should be undisturbed, and a focus on the tools used is a regular feature:

There was hardly any belief that had a stronger hold on the Highlander's mind than that on no account whatever should iron be put into the ground on this day. So great was the aversion of

doing so that the more superstitious extended the prohibition to every Friday. As a matter of course no ploughing was done, and if a burial to take place, the grave was opened on the previous day, and the earth was settled over the coffin with a wooden shovel. Commonly, however, ploughing was abstained from only on Good Friday.
                Highland Scotland Campbell (1902)

Somerset *Folk-Lore* 31 (1920) 244. **Dorset** *Folk-Lore* 11 (1900) 112. **Devon** Bray (1838) 286; Hewett (1900) 50; *Devonshire Assoc.* 104 (1972) 267. **Surrey** N&Q 5S:3 (1875) 424. **Essex** *Monthly Packet* 24 (1862) 434–7. **Oxfordshire** *Folk-Lore* 34 (1923) 326. **Worcestershire** *Folk-Lore* 26 (1915) 95–6. **Lincolnshire** Heanley (1902) 8; Gutch & Peacock (1908) 190. **Derbyshire** [1890s] Uttley (1946) 134–5. **Yorkshire** Henderson (1866) 61–2; Morris (1911) 218–19 **Highland Scotland** Campbell (1902) 262. **Ireland** Danaher (1972) 70–1. **Unlocated** Igglesden (*c.*1932) 101–2. **Literary** George Eliot, *Adam Bede* (1859) Ch. 18.

goodbye

A small set of beliefs surround the everyday act of saying goodbye to someone, each of them apparently designed to avoid *finality* as that tempts fate to fulfil the prediction. Watching people until they are out of sight is thus forbidden:

It is unlucky to watch anyone out of sight; if you do so you will never see that person again.
                Northern England Henderson (1866)

People seeing off ships should be particularly careful in this respect. Saying goodbye more than once is also to be avoided:

We must not say goodbye again, as I don't want to bring misfortune to you and I don't want it on myself.   Devon *Devonshire Assoc.* (1942)

And remember it is unlucky to say goodnight three times to the girl you love, without returning to the house and starting the whole thing over again, but one doesn't mind that. When parting with friends for any length of time, never say goodbye without adding that you hope to see them again, and never watch the parting ones out of sight – it is most unlucky.
                Yorkshire Blakeborough (1898)

Other variations are that one should not say goodbye at a crossroads, GATE or stile (you will be parted from your friends), nor among graves (for obvious reasons).

Of these parting beliefs, the 'watching out of sight' has been the strongest, in terms of the number of times recorded, and it was still being said in the 1980s. But none of them have been found in any source before the 1860s.

Dorset [1953] Opie & Tatem, 300. Somerset [1923] Opie & Tatem, 300. Devon *Devonshire Assoc.* 74 (1942) 103. Cornwall *Old Cornwall* 2 (1931–6) 39. Herefordshire Leather (1912) 87. Worcestershire *Folk-Lore* 6 (1895) 305; [1895] *Folk-Lore* 20 (1909) 346. East Anglia Varden (1885) 113. Northern England Henderson (1866) 88. Yorkshire Blakeborough (1898) 133; [1982] Opie & Tatem, 300. Radnorshire [1953] Opie & Tatem, 299–300. Perth [1954] Opie & Tatem, 300. Aberdeenshire *Folk-Lore* 25 (1914) 350. Unlocated N&Q 6S:7 (1883) 8; N&Q 153 (1927) 137; Igglesden (*c.*1932) 114–5. Literary Wood (1899) 10.

goose

see GEESE.

gooseberries

Gooseberries do not feature often in superstition, although see BRAMBLES for cures for WHOOPING COUGH which involve crawling or being passed under gooseberry bushes.

The gooseberry thorn comes into its own in Ireland, however, as a regular cure for STYES:

A treatment which is practised in many parts of Ireland is the use of a twig of a gooseberry bush with nine thorns. All the other thorns are broken off the twig until only nine remain and care is taken to ensure that each thorn points in the direction opposite to the thorn next to it. Each thorn is pointed at the stye and an Our Father, a Hail Mary and a Gloria are said each time. The ritual is repeated daily for nine days to complete the cure. Ireland Logan (1981)

One other Irish reference includes a gooseberry thorn in a WART cure:

To cure warts . . . A wedding-ring is procured, and the wart touched or pricked with a gooseberry thorn through the ring. Ireland N&Q (1850)

and a solitary English reference indicates a connection between the bush itself and its owner:

At Hartlebury it is believed that, if a gooseberry or currant bush dies or shrivels up when covered with fruit, there will be a death in the family of the owner before the year is out.
Worcestershire [1891] *Folk-Lore*

Worcestershire [1891] *Folk-Lore* 20 (1909) 343. Ireland N&Q 1S:1 (1850) 349; Wilde (1888) 198; Logan (1981) 58. Co. Wexford N&Q 3S:1 (1862) 446–7; [1938]

Ó Muirithe & Nuttall (1999) 97, 100. Co. Longford *Béaloideas* 6 (1936) 267. Co. Cavan Logan (1963) 89. Co. Leitrim/Co. Offaly Vickery (1995) 154–5. Co. Londonderry *Folk-Lore* 4 (1893) 356.

gout

It is little surprise that gout has attracted numerous folk cures, including straight herbal remedies such as groundsel and elder leaves, and gargling with carrot juice, but others have magical elements, as 'Gout was often attributed to the malicious work of witches' (Wales Trevelyan (1909)).

For gout take a nail from a dead man's boot and bury it a foot deep in earth under an ash or oak.
Wales Trevelyan (1909)

To relieve gout – remove legs from a spider, wrap it in deerskin and apply to the foot.
[17th cent.] Igglesden (*c.*1932)

See also HORSERADISH.

Essex Mays (1969) 165. East Anglia Hatfield (1994) 75. Norfolk [*c.*1920] Wigby (1976) 65–6. Wales Trevelyan (1909) 226, 317–18, 321. General [1619] N&Q 4S:8 (1871) 23; *A Closet for Ladies and Gentlewomen* (1636) quoted *Bye-Gones* (20 Apr. 1887) 294; [17th cent.] Igglesden (*c.*1932) 204; Black (1883) various.

green

Apart from black, with its funeral associations, green is the only colour to be consistently regarded as unlucky across the British Isles. The strongest prohibition focused on clothes, and it was widely believed that wearing green would surely lead to wearing black:

I have a young servant from a small village near Staines who wished to buy a new green gown. Her mother has positively forbidden it, 'as death in the family is sure to follow the wearing a green gown'. Middlesex N&Q (1889)

[Remembering a childhood in Lancashire (born 1906)] On the rare occasions I wore anything green (even if it were only the leaf of the flower in my hat, I would solemnly put a piece of black material on my head when I came in, to make sure I would not wear mourning because, as everyone knew, black followed green.
Lancashire Corbridge (1964)

The colour was particularly unlucky for WEDDINGS, which was summed up in the oft-quoted phrase, 'Green is forsaken and yellow is foresworn'. The dislike of the colour also manifested itself in other areas in the twentieth century. Green cars were proverbially difficult to sell, and many everyday items came under the ban:

A chemist giving orders for hot-water bottles said, 'For heaven's sake don't send any more green ones. Folk don't want them. Superstition I suppose. I've still ten left'.

Unlocated *Folk-Lore* (1962)

A visitor at a north Devon home expressed horror at seeing the table laid with a green cloth – and a white cat in the room as well.

Devon *Devonshire Assoc.* (1971)

This superstition is usually presumed to be ancient, but there is no evidence to support this idea. The earliest reference is from the end of the eighteenth century, although the wording implies that it was already well entrenched:

[Describing a wedding procession] *Every other colour . . . about her gown and hat, except forsaken green, which I was glad to perceive was not worn by any of the throng.*

Yorkshire *Gent. Mag.* (1793)

The belief does not seem to feature in the prolific writings of the seventeenth- and eighteenth-century dramatists, where one would certainly expect to find it if it did exist at that time, nor in any earlier published material. There are numerous mentions of green clothing, without any perceptible hint of a bad reputation.

A number of informants stated that the reason for green's bad reputation was that it was the favourite colour of the fairies, and they resented mortals wearing it. This notion reads like a modern invented origin, because there is little evidence that the fairies were particularly partial to green, but it was already in circulation in Scotland in the early nineteenth century (**Perthshire** Graham (1806)), and by the twentieth century it had become the orthodox explanation. Further research in pre-eighteenth-century literature may turn up some earlier references, but on present evidence it remains a superstition of relatively recent coinage. The fear of green remained strong well into the second half of the twentieth century but, although not totally dead, is now rapidly losing its hold.

See also WEDDINGS.

Devon *Folk-Lore* 27 (1916) 307; N&Q 147 (1924) 159–60; *Devonshire Assoc.* 103 (1971) 269. **Somerset** Tongue (1965) 135, 150. **London** Henrey (1955) 97–8; *Folk-Lore* 66 (1955) 298–9; *Observer Supp.* (24 Nov.

1968) 12–13. **Middlesex** N&Q 7S:8 (1889) 464. **Essex** [*c.*1917] Mays (1969) 164. **Oxfordshire** [1880s] Thompson (1939) 102–3. **Cambridgeshire** Porter (1969) 24. **Norfolk** [*c.*1920] Wigby (1976) 68. **Lincolnshire** N&Q 147 (1924) 112; [1930s–1950s] Sutton (1992) 144–5. **England** Addy (1895) 121. **Shropshire** Burne (1883) 289. **Staffordshire** *Folk-Lore* 28 (1917) 452. **Northern England** Henderson (1866) 21; Henderson (1879) 35. **Yorkshire** *Gent. Mag.* (1793) 300; N&Q 9S:8 (1901) 121; Morris (1911) 227–8; *Folk-Lore* 43 (1932) 255; [1982] Opie & Tatem, 182. **Lancashire** [*c.*1915] Corbridge (1964) 156–60; *Lancashire Lore* (1971) 6. **Glamorgan** *Folk-Lore* 73 (1962) 133. **Perthshire** Graham (1806) 107; Chambers (1826) 286; Chambers (1842) 35; N&Q 147 (1924) 112. **Highland Scotland** Macbain (1887/88) 271; N&Q 9S:8 (1901) 193. **Ireland** Lynd (1922) 162–3. **Co. Tyrone** *Lore & Language* 1:7 (1972) 8. **Guernsey** De Garis (1975) 8. **Unlocated** N&Q 9S:8 (1901) 193; N&Q 182 (1942) 125, 179; *Folk-Lore* 73 (1962) 132. **General** *Folk-Lore* 64 (1953) 427. **Literary** Walter Scott, *Lady of the Lake* (1810) note to canto 4, stanza 13.

groundsel (*Senecio vulgaris*)

Groundsel is used extensively in folk medicine as a cure for many ailments, including WARTS, AGUE, RHEUMATISM, cuts, TEETHING troubles, boils and carbuncles. Most of these are herbal remedies, in that the plant itself is believed to have medicinal properties, but sometimes a touch of magic creeps in:

To cause a wart to disappear we understand that it should be rubbed with groundsel, the weed to be afterwards thrown over the sufferer's head. It should then be buried by another person, and as it rots so will the wart.

Devon Crossing (1911)

Dorset Vickery (1995) 163–4. **Devon** Crossing (1911) 143; [1931] *Devonshire Assoc.* 79 (1947) 47. **Cornwall** Deane & Shaw (1975) 123. **Midland England** *Midland Garner* 1 (1884) 23. **East Anglia** Hatfield (1994) 75. **Norfolk** [*c.*1920] Wigby (1976) 65; Randell (1966) 85; Vickery (1995) 163. **Unlocated** N&Q 2S:4 (1857) 487; N&Q 4S:12 (1873) 469.

guessing

Four twentieth-century reports indicate a superstition about people who are 'good guessers'. They cover a wide geographical area, which suggests that they were better known than is reflected by the paucity of references, but the restricted timescale makes it difficult to judge just how widespread it was. The references, such as they are, are quoted in full below. The last one contradicts the others, which may simply be a mistake on the part of the collector or may indicate a genuine variation. It is difficult to hazard any reason for such a belief.

Good guessers never marry.

Gloucestershire *Folk-Lore* (1923)

If a girl can always guess the right quantities of things, either in making cakes or puddings or other dishes, it is a sign that she will never marry.

London *Folk-Lore* (1926)

Those who can always guess the time accurately will never be married.

Co. Durham Leighton (1910)

Good guessers will marry soon.

Ireland or Canada *Folk-Lore* (1923)

London *Folk-Lore* 37 (1926) 365. Gloucestershire *Folk-Lore* 34 (1923) 157. Co. Durham Leighton (1910) 60. Ireland or Canada *Folk-Lore* 34 (1923) 157.

---

gunpowder

Gunpowder features as an ingredient in some folk cures for the itch, strangury, as a blood purifier, and as an abortifacient:

Babies were not welcomed in our family. I have heard my mother say on more than one occasion in her middle age that if she had to live her life again and knew as much as she did then she wouldn't have had one of us. She told me she even took gunpowder to get rid of me, mixing it to a paste in a soapdish on her washstand every night.

Yorkshire [1890] Burnett

A single reference also records its use in CURS-ING:

Cursing by aid of gunpowder – At Widecombe a short time since a person was seen in the act of calling down a curse on another in the following manner. She spread the ashes of a hearth fire, and placed a train of gunpowder in a circle the size of a dinner-plate, pronouncing, as she ignited it, the name of the devoted person who had offended her in some way, and then exclaimed that now the old wretch was suffering.

Devon *Devonshire Assoc.* (1876)

See also RISING OF THE LIGHTS.

Devon *Devonshire Assoc.* 8 (1876) 53; *Devonshire Assoc.* 67 (1935) 138. Worcestershire [1760] *Country Life* (6 Nov 1958) 1061. Yorkshire [1890] Burnett (1982) 90. Wales *Country Life* (3 July 1958) 28.

haddock (*Gadidae*)

On the strength of the markings found on both fish, the haddock and the JOHN DORY were both claimed to be the very fish that Peter caught, at the behest of Jesus, to find the 'tribute money' (Matthew 17:27):

In North Devon the haddock is reputed to be the fish from which the tribute money was taken. The fish boy from Appledore calls the attention of his customers to the peculiar patches to be found on the shoulder of this fish as proof of its genuineness, but he attributes the marks to Christ, not to Peter, saying 'You can see they are real haddocks because they have the marks of Jesus Christ's finger and thumb on them'.

Devon *Devonshire Assoc.* (1931)

It has frequently been pointed out that both fish are salt-water species and cannot therefore have been found in the Sea of Galilee, but legend cares nought for such niceties. The association of animal markings with sacred events in the past is a regular motif in folklore, and this one can be compared with the origin of the cross on the DONKEY's back.

The haddock also provided some people with bones to ward off CRAMP and TOOTHACHE:

For toothache – Carry in your pocket the two jaw-bones of a haddock; for ever since the miracle of the loaves and fishes these bones are an infallible remedy against toothache, and the older they are the better, as nearer the time of the miracle.

Ireland Wilde (1888)

Devon *Devonshire Assoc.* 63 (1931) 126. Cambridgeshire *Folk-Lore* 25 (1914) 366. England Addy (1895) 67. Co. Durham Brockie (1886) 137–8. Scotland Laing (1885) 87. Ireland Wilde (1888) 196. Unlocated Pennant, *British Zoology* (1768); Grose (1787) 68.

---

hag-riding

When horses were found sweating, exhausted, and frightened in their stables in the morning, it was automatically assumed that they had been 'hag-ridden'. The most widespread method of protection was to hang up a stone with a natural hole in it – thus often called a 'hag-stone':

Another source of protection against witches, evil spirits and nightmare is the hanging up of a stone with a natural hole in it. The writer has in his possession several holed stones which have been used in this way. One was taken from a stable at West Bradford, near Clitheroe, where it had been suspended over a horse's stall for more than twenty years. It is about six inches long, and has been apparently picked out of the bed of a stream. It has a small hole, evidently worn by the water at one end. The farmer from whom it was obtained said his father and grandfather believed that such stones kept away the nightmare, and they used to say that before they hung such stones over the horses' stalls it was not an uncommon thing on going into the stable in the morning to find the horses, which had been left all right overnight, all in a sweat and reeking – like horses that had been over-ridden – and in a state of fear and trembling. This was supposed to be caused by their having been ridden by the witches during the night. This sort of thing never happened after the horses were protected by the suspended stones. A Clitheroe friend tells the writer that when a lad he often used to hear persons living at Wiswell, Whitewell, and other places in the district, speak of going into the shippon in the morning and finding the cows sweating and in a state of fear, with two of them 'sealed up' together, instead of separately, as they were left overnight; and it was a very common thing in those days to hang up perforated stones in the shippons and also over the hay baulks to keep away the evil influence of the witches. The Rev. Mr. Doxey, formerly curate of Whalley, had one of these stones, which he obtained from a farmer at Wiswell Moor, who had it suspended over his bed to protect him from nightmare and witchcraft. The writer knew an old lady at Clitheroe who used to keep a holed stone hanging on the wall in her bedroom.   Lancashire Weeks (1910)

Another method was to ensure the presence of IRON, which also deterred witches:

Hang up hooks, and sheers to scare
Hence the hag, that rides the mare,
Till they be all over wet,
With the mire, and the sweat:
This observ'd, the manes shall be
Of your horses, all knot-free.
                                          Herrick (1648)

The juxtaposition of notions of night attacks and witches or evil spirits have wrought a fusion between the hag-riding attacks on animals in stable and byre, and nightmares, which were predominately aimed at humans in their beds.

See also NIGHTMARES; STONES: HOLED.

Hertfordshire Folk-Lore 66 (1955) 416–17. Bedfordshire N&Q 10S 7 (1907) 26. Norfolk Folk-Lore 40 (1929) 124; Haggard (1935) 16. Suffolk N&Q 1S:4 (1851) 53; Glyde (1866) 175; Gent. Mag. (1867) 307–22, 728–41; Evans (1965) 206–7, 211–12. Northern England Brand (1810) 107. Yorkshire Monthly Packet 25 (1863) 549–51; Nicholson (1890) 87. Lancashire N&Q 1S:3 (1851) 56; Harland & Wilkinson (1882) 72, 154; Weeks (1910) 107–9. Co. Durham Folk-Lore 20 (1909) 74; Leighton (1910) 46. Northumberland Neville (1909) 111–12. Guernsey Carey (1903) 507; De Garis (1975) 125. Unlocated Aubrey, Miscellanies (1696/1857) 140; Grose (1787) 57–8. General Gent. Mag. (1796) 636; Dent (1964) 46–8, 68–78. Literary Herrick (1648) 'Another Charme for Stables'.

hag-stones

see STONES: HOLED.

hair: character test

It was generally believed that certain characteristics of a person's hair would reveal elements of their general character. The most widespread example is the distrust of RED-HAIRED people, but for others, curly hair was also suspect. Such hair was seen as a sign of pride, whether naturally curly or revealed when tested in a traditional way:

Curly hair is a sign of pride. Nurse-maids teach their charges to draw a hair sharply between the nails of the fore-finger and thumb, to discover by its 'crinkling' or the reverse, whether the owner is of haughty temperament; and the writer of this note has more than once been saluted by unmannerly children with the cry 'Co'ly locks, my wo'd is n't she prood'.
                        Lincolnshire Gutch & Peacock (1908)

This tradition does not show much stability, as several other interpretations were possible, such as those given in the two later examples, printed by Opie & Tatem from Dorset and Glasgow, respectively. In the first the induced curl means the girl is flirtatious, and in the other the number of curls reveals the number of husbands she will have. Yet another explanation is given by Addy:

To find out whether you will be rich or poor, take a single hair from your head, and draw it between your wetted first finger and thumb. If it curls you will be rich, if not you will be poor.
                                          England Addy (1895)

The general distrust of the curly means that straight hair is often imbued with good qualities, as in the following advice from a farmer to his young labourer in the 1830s:

hair

Two parts of the body which are routinely removed are hair and nails, and on the principle of SYMPATHETIC connection, it was believed that what happened to them after removal could still vitally affect the body itself. Hair and nails could thus be used for good or evil – in cures or witchcraft – and beliefs about them are often interchangeable or combined. Many of the following superstitions reflect this concern for the fate of cut hair, or for the times and situations in which it should be removed.

See also FINGERNAILS; RED HAIR; WIDOW'S PEAK.

If ever you choose a young woman, look out for one whose hair lies straight on her head, for she'll be sure to have a good temper.

Essex? Burnett (1975)

Dorset [1935] Opie & Tatem, 185. **Essex?** [1830s] Burnett (1975) 57. **Lincolnshire** Gutch & Peacock (1908) 165. **Shropshire** Burne (1883) 268. **England** Addy (1895) 86–7. **Northeast Scotland** Gregor (1881) 26. **Glasgow** [1957] Opie & Tatem, 185. **Dumfriesshire** Shaw (1890) 13.

hair: cures

As noted above, one of the basic principles of superstition held that what happened to hair which had been removed still affected the body. This could be exploited in cures. A widespread remedy for WHOOPING COUGH, for example, was to take a hair from the afflicted child, place it between two slices of bread, and give them to a dog to eat. This is a clear example of the TRANSFERENCE principle of disease, with the hair simply acting as the personal agent. The following examples of other cures were reported less often:

The crown of the head is shaved, and the hair hung upon a bush ... in firm belief that the birds carrying it away to their nests will carry away the cough along with it.

Northern England Henderson (1866)

Clippings of the hair and nails of a child tied up in a linen cloth and placed under the cradle will cure convulsions. Ireland Wilde (1888)

See also FINGERNAILS.

Northern England Henderson (1866) 111. **Morayshire** Shaw (1775) 248. **Banffshire** *Jnl Anthropological Institute* 3 (1874) 269. **Ireland** Wilde (1888) 101. **General** Lupton (1579) Bk 4, Para. 46.

hair: cutting

The most widespread beliefs about hair cutting are covered in other entries. The strongest was that the cutting should be done at the growing, not the waning of the moon (*see* MOON: HAIR/NAILS) and another was that children's hair and fingernails must not be cut until they are at least 12 months old (*see* FINGERNAILS: BABIES').

The third group of superstitions concerning hair cutting is concerned with days on which it is not acceptable to carry out the operation. As with fingernails, FRIDAY and Sunday were the days most often prohibited:

It was considered unlucky either to cut the hair on a Friday or shave the beard on a Sunday; hence the warning rhyme:

> *Friday cut and Sunday shorn*
> *Better never have been born.*
> Lancashire N&Q (1870)

but some Irish informants report that Monday, too, was shunned:

A man whose hair is cut on a Monday will go bald. Hence a kind of comic imprecation used in Kerry: 'the shearing of Monday on you'.

Co. Kerry *Folk-Lore* (1908)

To complicate matters, the occasional reference states that cutting hair on GOOD FRIDAY is beneficial.

See also GOOD FRIDAY: HAIR/FINGERNAILS; HAIR: DISPOSAL.

Kent Igglesden (*c.*1932) 99. **Cornwall** *Old Cornwall* 2 (1931–6) 40. **England** Addy (1895) 114. **Yorkshire** Nicholson (1890) 141–2. **Lancashire** N&Q 4S:6 (1870) 211. **Highland Scotland** Macbain (1887/88) 256. **Co. Kerry** *Folk-Lore* 19 (1908) 319. **Co. Longford** *Béaloideas* 6 (1936) 266.

hair: disposal

Removable parts of the body, such as hair and fingernails, had to be carefully guarded and were subject to a range of prohibitions. Many people were in deadly earnest in their concern for where any strands of their hair ended up:

*It was once believed that witches had the power
to draw to them any person whose hair had fallen
into their hands, and wise-women in the country used to advise girls to obtain a lock of hair of
the man they wished to marry.*
                              N. Ireland Foster (1951)

Not only could witches use nail and hair clippings in their ill-wishing or controlling spells,
but a very widespread concern was to keep hair
out of the way of birds:

*Hair, too, should be carefully burnt. It is unlucky
to throw it out of doors, as birds may weave it
into their nests, and then the person to whom it
belonged will suffer from headache. This has once
been a very general superstition, but I doubt
whether it is still much respected.*
                              Shropshire Burne (1883)

But there is sharp disagreement about the
wisdom of burning hair. While the English
sources recommend it as the surest way of
destroying the hair, most Irish writers view such
behaviour with alarm:

*It is most unlucky to burn any of your hair, as on
the Last Day you will have to collect it so as to
appear with the whole of it as God created you.*
                              Co. Cavan Folk-Lore (1908)

Considering the widespread habit of giving
and keeping locks of hair of loved ones, children,
and so on, it is surprising to find a handful of
reports which specifically warn against this
tendency:

*Parents should not keep locks of the children's
hair if they wish them to live.*
                              England Addy (1895)

Sussex Latham (1878) 44. Devon *Devonshire Assoc.* 63
(1931) 126. Cornwall *Old Cornwall* 2 (1931–6) 39.
Wiltshire *Wilts. N&Q* 1 (1893–5) 60. London *Folk-Lore*
37 (1926) 367. Herefordshire Leather (1912) 88.
Northamptonshire Sternberg (1851) 166. Shropshire
Burne (1883) 268. Staffordshire Poole (1875) 86.
England Addy (1895) 93, 142. Yorkshire *Folk-Lore* 20
(1909) 348. Scotland *Folk-Lore* 45 (1934) 162. Highland
Scotland Macbain (1887/88) 256; Campbell (1900)
236–7. Western Scotland Napier (1879) 114.
Dumfriesshire Shaw (1890) 11. Renfrewshire N&Q 2S:1
(1856) 386–7. Glasgow [c.1820] Napier (1864) 397.
Hebrides McPhee (1970) 150. Ireland N&Q 3S:10 (1866)
146; Wilde (1888) 206; *Folk-Lore* 19 (1908) 319. N.
Ireland Foster (1951) 60, 93. Co. Longford *Béaloideas* 6
(1936) 263. Co. Cavan *Folk-Lore* 19 (1908) 319. Co.
Tyrone *Lore & Language* 1:7 (1972) 10. Isle of Man
Moore (1891) 145.

hair: divination

A simple form of divination aimed at ascertaining whether a long life still lies ahead is to take
note of how your hair burns when thrown on
the fire:

*If a person's hair burn brightly when thrown into
the fire, it is a sign of longevity; the brighter the
flame, the longer the life. On the other hand, if it
smoulder away, and refuse to burn, it is a sign of
approaching death.*
                              Co. Durham Henderson (1866)

All the sources agree that blazing is good, smoul-
dering is bad, but occasionally extra elements are
added, such as:

*If the hair, when thrown on the fire, will not burn,
it is a sign the person will be drowned.*
                              Highland Scotland Campbell (1900)

Hair also features strongly in a range of LOVE
DIVINATION practices, from the simple hope of
finding a hair in your shoe when you hear the
first CUCKOO, to being the active ingredient in
complex procedures such as the following:

*Two young unmarried girls must sit together in
a room by themselves, from twelve o'clock at
night till one o'clock the next morning, without
speaking a word. During this time each of them
must take as many hairs from her head as she is
years old, and, having put them into a linen cloth
with some of the herb true-love [moon-wort], as
soon as the clock strikes one, she must burn every
hair separately, saying:*

> *I offer this my sacrifice*
> *To him most precious in my eyes*
> *I charge thee now come forth to me*
> *That I this minute may thee see*

*Upon which her first husband will appear, and
walk round the room, and then vanish. The same
event happens to both the girls, but neither sees
the other's lover.*   Unlocated Halliwell (1849)

Nevertheless, not all people would dare to burn
human hair (*see* HAIR: DISPOSAL). See also
WIDOW'S PEAK.

London *Folk-Lore* 37 (1926) 365. Lincolnshire Rudkin
(1936) 21. Shropshire Burne (1883) 268. Herefordshire
Leather (1912) 88. England Addy (1895) 100. Yorkshire
Addy (1888) xxiii. Lancashire N&Q 1S:3 (1851) 55;
Harland & Wilkinson (1882) 153; [c.1915] Corbridge
(1964) 156–60. Co. Durham Henderson (1866) 84;
Brockie (1886) 211; *Folk-Lore* 20 (1909) 73; Leighton
(1910) 48. Highland Scotland Campbell (1900) 237.
Hebrides McPhee (1970) 150. Unlocated Halliwell
(1849) 215–16.

hair: double crown

A handful of twentieth-century references demonstrate beliefs about children born with 'double crowns', or where hair parts in two places on the head, but there is no agreement on basic meaning. For example:

A child born with a double crown will live to be a hundred.   Norfolk *Folk-Lore* (1929)

A double whorl in the hair of a child means that it will live to see two kings crowned, or that it will be 'a great wanderer'.   Aberdeenshire *Folk-Lore* (1914)

A child with two crowns to its head will be lucky in money matters.   Wales Trevelyan (1909)

The wide geographical spread suggests a better-known belief than is indicated by the paucity of references.

Wiltshire *Folk-Lore* 12 (1901) 75. **Norfolk** *Folk-Lore* 40 (1929) 122. **Liverpool** [1954] Opie & Tatem, 184. **Wales** Trevelyan (1909) 265. **Angus** [1950] Opie & Tatem, 184. **Aberdeenshire** *Folk-Lore* 25 (1914) 349. **Literary** J. Lehmann, *Whispering Gallery* (1955) 334.

hair of the dog that bit you

see DOGS: HAIR.

hair: spells

A regular motif in the casting of malevolent personal spells was to include something of intimate connection to the proposed victim, and hair and fingernail clippings were regarded as ideal. Shakespeare was aware of the danger:

Some devils ask but the parings of ones nail.
    Shakespeare *Comedy of Errors* (1590)

and so were many people well into the twentieth century:

hair and nail trimmings should be carefully destroyed, because if birds pick them up you might have a 'sore head' or 'sore hands'. The older belief was that witches made use of such things to work evil. They could be mixed with the wax for an image which, melted slowly before a fire, would cause the person represented to waste away. If pins were stuck into the waxen image the victim would have pains at the places where they penetrated.   N. Ireland Foster (1951)

Pieces of hair and nails often turn up in surviving examples of WITCH BOTTLES and other receptacles in which the ingredients of witchcraft were placed:

In a remote part of the Highlands, an ignorant and malignant woman seems really to have meditated the destruction of her neighbour's property by placing in a cow-house, or byre as we call it, a pot of baked clay containing locks of hair, parings of nails and other trumpery. The formidable spell is now in my possession.
    Highland Scotland Scott (1830)

It should also be noted, however, that hair and nails of the victim were also widely used in counter-charms as well as in offensive witchcraft.

Scotland [1590] Pitcairn 1, Pt 2 (1833) 201. **Highland Scotland** Scott (1830) Letter 8. **Western Scotland** Napier (1879) 39. **N. Ireland** Foster (1951) 93. **General** Merrifield (1987) *passim*. **Literary** Shakespeare *Comedy of Errors* (1590) 4:3.

hair: swallowing

It used to be firmly believed by many that if you swallowed a long hair it would 'wind around your heart' and kill you. George Sturt reported that the danger extended to other similar materials:

It was dangerous to chew string or to bite cotton instead of taking scissors to it, for, if swallowed, string or cotton might wind round your heart and kill you.   Surrey [1860s] Sturt

The belief was more widespread in the nineteenth and twentieth centuries than is indicated by the paucity of references, and was clearly not new even then:

If I trust her, as she's a woman, let one of her long hairs wind about my heart, and be the end of me; which were a piteous lamentable tragedy, and might be entituled, 'A fair warning for all hair-bracelets'.   Middleton, *The Witch* (c.1615)

Surrey [1860s] Sturt (1927) 134–5. **Northamptonshire** Sternberg (1851) 172. **Co. Durham** Leighton (1910) 48. **Unlocated** N&Q 8S:10 (1896) 47. **Literary** Thomas Middleton, *The Witch* (c.1615) 4:1.

hairpins

Various minor accidents occurring to female apparel, such as APRON strings or GARTERS coming untied, stockings wrinkling, and so on, were interpreted as 'your lover is thinking of you'. Hairpins were also occasionally mentioned in the same context:

A hair-pin falling out of the hair is a sign, say the maids, that 'some one' wants to speak to you.

Shropshire Burne (1883)

Judging by the paucity of references, a relatively shortlived superstition.

Somerset [1923] Opie & Tatem, 186. **Lincolnshire** Rudkin (1936) 19. **Shropshire** Burne (1883) 270. **Yorkshire** [1956] Opie & Tatem, 186.

hairy arms

A number of miscellaneous beliefs or sayings about personal appearance existed in the nineteenth century, which were concerned, for example, with TEETH that were wide apart, EYEBROWS meeting, and the like. One example maintained that those with hairy arms were destined to be wealthy:

Ladies with overmuch down, gentlemen with overmuch hair upon their arms and hands, carry about them nature's own guarantee that they are born to be rich some day.

Unlocated *Chambers's Jnl* (1873)

The meaning remained remarkably constant from version to version, except the one quoted by Sternberg which insisted that 'Hairy persons always go to heaven'.

Midland England N&Q 1S:1 (1850) 451. **Warwickshire** Langford (1875) 14. **Northamptonshire** Sternberg (1851) 171. **Staffordshire** Hackwood (1924) 149. **Lancashire** Harland & Wilkinson (1873) 225. **England** Addy (1895) 101. **Hebrides** *Folk-Lore* 6 (1895) 396. **Unlocated** Hone, *Year Book* (1832) 126–8; *Chambers's Jnl* (1873) 810.

Hallowe'en (31 October)

Hallowe'en is probably the most misrepresented and misunderstood festival in the traditional calendar. The widespread notion that the day (or rather the night) is a pre-Christian pagan celebration of the dead is not historically correct, but is now so well-entrenched as to be immovable. Certainly, the festival on the 1 November, called *Samhain*, was by far the most important of the four quarter days in the medieval Irish calendar, with tribal gatherings and feasts, and a sense that this was the time of year when the physical and supernatural worlds were closest and magical things could happen. But however strong the early evidence is in Ireland, in Wales it was 1 May and New Year which took precedence, in Scotland there is hardly any mention of 1 November until much later, and in Anglo-Saxon

England even fewer mentions. Even without the latter, Samhain's importance has been extrapolated from the Irish evidence and thus overemphasized for the rest of the British Isles:

It must be concluded, therefore, that the medieval records furnish no evidence that 1 November was a major pan-Celtic festival, and none of religious ceremonies, even where it was observed.

Hutton (1996) 362

On the other hand, it was a very important time of year in the Catholic church. Hallowe'en is the Eve of All Hallows or All Saints (1 November) which, along with All Souls (2 November), constitute Hallowtide. These festivals were confirmed at these dates from about AD 800 to 1000, but later gradually coalesced around the night of 31 October/1 November, and All Souls took the highest profile. The key element was that this was the time for commemoration of the departed faithful, and in particular the day when prayers could be said and bells could be rung, to get souls out of purgatory and into heaven. The connection between the dead and this time of year was thus a Christian invention. The reforming Protestant churches abolished these notions, but they continued in Catholic areas and in the popular mind and tradition.

Nevertheless, when folklore records began to be recorded in the eighteenth and nineteenth centuries, the overwhelming features of Hallowe'en were divination (usually LOVE DIVINATION) and games. Few of these are reported as happening solely at this season, but those concerned with seasonal plants – apples, nuts, cabbages – are more in evidence than at other times.

Beyond the modern obsession with witches' hats and brooms, our view of the traditional Hallowe'en is heavily influenced by the catalogue of divinations so entertainingly provided by Robert Burns in his Hallowe'en (1786) poem (*see below*), and his basic accuracy is confirmed by other sources. A generation later, Hugh Miller (1835) set out to complete the picture by describing the games, tricks, and practical jokes which also took place on the night. Kevin Danaher's description of the night in Ireland paints a very similar picture, as do other Irish authorities:

Fortune-telling has a place in all Hallowe'en parties, and the fortunes are usually concerned with love and marriage. Girls used to veil mirrors and hope to see the face of a future husband when the veil was removed at midnight. Young men pulled cabbage-stalks, kale-runts. And from their size and the amount of earth which adhered to them they foretold whether their future wives would be tall or short, rich or poor. I saw this done

'Hallowe'en' (Robert Burns)

Robert Burns' poem 'Hallowe'en' was first published in 1786 in his collection *Poems Chiefly in the Scottish Dialect*. It rapidly became the major source of information about eighteenth-century Hallowe'en customs in Scotland, and it influenced not only scholars and later writers but it also served as a model for anyone interested in keeping an 'old time' festival themselves.

The testimony of poets and novelists cannot always be relied on, nor taken literally when describing such matters – their business is primarily artistic rather than documentary. But a few, such as Robert Burns, Walter Scott, and Thomas Hardy, have a high reputation among historians and folklorists and can be trusted, as far as we know, to paint a true and accurate figure. Stanzas marked * have notes by Burns explaining the action (*see below*).

1 *Upon that night, when fairies light*
On Cassilis Downans dance,
Or owre the lays, in splendid blaze,
On sprightly coursers prance;
Or for Colean the rout is taen,
Beneath the moon's pale beams;
There, up the Cove, to stray and rove,
Amang the rocks and streams
To sport that night:

2 *Amang the bonie winding banks,*
Where Doon rins, wimplin, clear;
Where Bruce ance ruled the martial ranks,
An' shook his Carrick spear;
Some merry, friendly, country-folks
Together did convene,
To burn their nits, an' pou their stocks,
An' haud their Hallowe'en
Fu' blithe that night.

3 *The lassies feat an' cleanly neat,*
Mair braw than when they're fine;
Their faces blythe fu' sweetly kythe
Hearts leal, an' warm, an' kin':
The lads sae trig, wi' wooer-babs
Weel-knotted on their garten;
Some unco blate, an' some wi' gabs
Gar lasses' hearts gang startin
Whyles fast at night.

4* *Then, first an' foremost, thro' the kail,*
Their stocks maun a' be sought ance;
They steek their een, an' grape an' wale
For muckle anes, an' straught anes.
Poor hav'rel Will fell aff the drift,
An' wandered thro' the bow-kail,
An' pow't, for want o' better shift,
A runt, was like a sow-tail,
Sae bow't that night.

5 *Then, straught or crooked, yird or nane*
They roar an' cry an' throu'ther;
The vera wee-things, toddlin, rin
Wi' stocks out-owre their shouther:
An' gif the custock's sweet or sour,
Wi' joctelegs they taste them;
Syne coziely, aboon the door,
Wi' cannie care, they've plac'd them
To lie that night.

6* *The lasses staw frae 'mang them a',*
To pou their stalks o' corn;
But Rab slips out, an' jinks about,
Behint the muckle thorn:
He grippet Nelly hard an' fast;
Loud skirl'd a' the lasses;
But her tap-pickle maist was lost,
Whan kiutlin in the fause-house
Wi' him that night.

7* *The auld guid-wife's weel-hoordet nits*
Are round an' round divided,
An' monie lads' an' lasses' fates
Are there that night decided:
Some kindle couthie, side by side,
An' burn thegether trimly;
Some start awa wi' saucy pride,
An' jump out-owre the chimlie
Fu' high that night.

8 *Jean slips in twa, wi' tentie e'e;*
Wha 'twas, she wadna tell;
But this is Jock, and this is me,
She says in to hersel:
He bleez'd owre her, an' she owre him,
As they wad never mair part;
Till fuff! he started up the lum,
And Jean had e'en a sair heart
To see't that night.

9 *Poor Willie, wi' his bow-kail runt,*
Was burnt wi' primsie Mallie;
An' Mary, nae doubt, took the drunt,
To be compar'd to Willie:
Mall's nit lap out, wi' pridefu' fling,
An' her ain fit, it burnt it;
While Willie lap, an' swoor by jing,
'Twas just the way he wanted
To be that night.

10 *Nell had the fause-house in her min',*
She pits hersel an' Rob in;
In loving bleeze they sweetly join,
Till white in ase they're sobbin;
Nell's heart was dancin at the view;
She whisper'd Rob to leuk for't:
Rob, stownlins, prie'd her bonie mou,
Fu' cozie in the neuk for't,
Unseen that night.

11* But Merran sat behint their backs,
Her thoughts on Andrew Bell;
She lea'es them gashing at their cracks,
An' slips out by herself:
She thro' the yard the nearest taks,
An' to the kiln she goes then,
An' darklins grapit for the bauks,
And in the blue-clue throws then,
      Right fear't that night.

12 An' ay she win't, an' ay she awat —
I wat she made nae jaukin;
Till something held within the pat,
Guid Lord! but she was quakin!
But whether 'twas the Deil himself,
Or whether 'twas a bauk-en',
Or whether it was Andrew Bell,
She did na wait on talkin
      To spier that night.

13* Wee Jenny to her graunie says,
'Will ye go wi' me, graunie?
I'll eat the apple at the glass,
I gat frae uncle Johnie';
She fuff't her pipe wi' sic a lunt,
In wrath she was sae vap'rin,
She notic't na an aizle brunt
Her braw, new, worset apron
      Out thro' that night.

14 'Ye little skelpie-limmer's-face!
I daur ye try sic sportin,
An seek the Foul Thief onie place,
For him to spae your fortune:
Nae doubt but ye may get a sight!
Great cause ye hae to fear it;
For monie a ane has gotten a fright,
An' liv'd an' died deleeret,
      On sic a night.

15 'Ae hairst afore the Sherra-moor,
I mind't as weel's yestreen —
I was a gilpey then, I'm sure
I was na past fifteen:
The simmer had been cauld an' wat,
An' stuff was unco green;
An' ay a rantin kirn we gat,
An' just on Halloween
      It fell that night.

16* 'Our stibble-rig was Rab M'Graen,
A clever, sturdy fallow;
His sin gat Eppie Sim wi' wean,
That lived in Achmacalla;
He gat hemp-seed, I mind it weel,
An' he made unco light o't;
But monie a day was by himsel,
He was sae sairly frighted
      That vera night'.

17 Then up gat fechtin Jamie Fleck,
An' he swoor by his conscience,
That he could saw hemp-seed a peck;
For it was a' but nonsense:
The auld guidman raught down the pock,
An' out a handfu' gied him;
Syne bad him slip frae 'mang the folk,
Sometime when nae ane see'd him,
      An' try't that night.

18 He marches thro' amang the stacks,
Tho' he was something sturtin;
The graip he for a harrow taks,
And haurls at his curpin;
And ev'ry now and then, he says,
'Hemp-seed I saw thee,
An' her that is to be my lass
Come after me, an' draw thee
      As fast this night.

19 He whistl'd up Lord Lenòx' March,
To keep his courage cheery;
Altho' his hair began to arch,
He was sae fley'd an' eerie;
Till presently he hears a squeak,
An' then a grane an' gruntle;
He by his shouther gae a keek,
An' tumbl'd wi' a wintle
      Out-owre that night.

20 He roar'd a horrid murder-shout,
In dreadfu' desperation!
An' young an' auld come rennin out,
An' hear the sad narration:
He swoor 'twas hilchin Jean McCraw,
Or crouchie Merran Humphie —
Till stop! She trotted thro' them a';
An' what was it but grumphie
      Asteer that night?

21* Meg fain wad to the barn gaen,
To winn three wechts o' naething;
But for to meet the Deil her lane,
She pat but little faith in;
She gies the herd a pickle nits,
An' twa red-cheekit apples,
To watch while for the barn she sets,
Inhopes to see Tam Kipples
      That vera night.

22 She turns the key wi' cannie thraw,
An' owre the threshold ventures;
But first on Sawnie gies a ca'
Syne bauldly in she enters:
A ratton rattle'd up the wa',
An' she cry'd, L—d preserve her!
An' ran thro' midden-hole an' a',
An' pray'd wi' zeal and fervour
      Fu' fast that night.

They hoy't out Will, wi' sair advice;
They hecht him some fine braw ane;
It chanc'd the stack he faddom't thrice,
Was timmer-propt for thrawin:
He taks a swirlie, auld moss-oak
For some black gruesome carlin;
An' loot a winze, an' drew a stroke,
Till skin in blypes cam haurlin
    Aff's nieves that night.

24* *A wanton widow Leezie was,*
As cantie as a kittlin;
But och! that night, amang the shaws,
She gat a fearfu' settlin!
She thro' the whins, an' by the cairn,
An' owre the hill gaed scrievin,
Whare three lairds' lands met at a burn,
To dip her left sark-sleeve in
    Was bent that night.

25 *Whyles owre a lin the burnie plays,*
As thro' the glen it wimpl't;
Whyles round a rocky scaur it strays,
Whyles in a wiel ir dimpl't;
Whyles glitter'd to the nightly rays,
Wi' bickerin, dancin dazzle;
Whyles cookit underneath the braes,
Below the spreading hazel
    Unseen that night.

26 *Amang the brachens, on the brae,*
Between her an' the moon,
The Deil, or else an outler quey,
Gat up an' gae a croon:
Poor Leezie's heart maist lap the hool;
Near lav'rock-height she jumpit,
But mist a fit, an' in the pool
Out-owre the lugs she plumpit
    Wi' a plunge that night.

27* *In order, on the clean hearth-stane,*
The luggies three are ranged;
And ev'ry time great is taen
To see them duly changed:
Auld uncle John, wha wedlock's joys
Sin Mar's-year did desire,
Because he gat the toom dish thrice,
He heav'd them on the fire
    In wrath that night.

28 *Wi' merry sangs, an' friendly cracks,*
I wat they did na weary;
An unco tales, an' funnie jokes –
Their sports were cheap an' cheery;
Till butter'd sow'ns, wi' fragrant lunt,
Set a' their gabs a-steerin;
Syne, wi' a social glass o' strunt,
They parted aff careerin
    Fu' blythe that night.

[Only those of Burns' notes which appertain to the divinations are given here.]

[Hallowe'en] is thought to be a night when witches, devils, and other mischief-making beings are all abroad on their baneful, midnight errands; particularly those aerial people, the fairies, are said, on that night, to hold a grand anniversary.

Stanza 4 'Their stocks maun a' be sought ance' The Wrst ceremony of Hallowe'en is, pulling each a 'stock' or plant of kail. They must go out, hand in hand, with eyes shut, and pull the Wrst they meet with: its being big or little, straight or crooked, is prophetic of the size and shape of the grand object of all their spells – the husband or wife. If any 'yird' or earth, stick to the root, that is 'tocher' or fortune; and the taste of the 'custoc', that is, the heart of the stem, is indicative of the natural temper and disposition. Lastly, the stems, or to give them their ordinary appellation, the 'runts' are placed somewhere above the head of the door; and the Christian names of people whom chance brings into the house are, according to the priority of placing the 'runts', the names in question.

Stanza 6 'To pou their stalks o' corn' They go to the barnyard, and pull each, at three several times, a stalk of oats. If the third stalk wants the 'tap-pickle', that is, the grain at the top of the stalk, the party in question will come to the marriage bed anything but a maid.

Stanza 7 'The auld guid-wife's weel-hoordet nits' Burning the nuts is a favourite charm. They name the lad and lass to each particular nut, as they lay them in the Wre; and according as they burn quietly together, or start from beside each other, the course and issue of the courtship will be.

Stanza 11 'And in the blue-clue throws then' Whoever would, with success, try this spell, must strictly observe these directions: Steal out, all alone, to the kiln, and, darkling, throw into the 'pot' a clue of blue yarn; wind it in a new clue oV the old one; and, towards the latter end, something will hold the thread: demand 'Wha hauds?', i.e. 'who holds?' and answer will be returned from the kiln-pot, by naming the Christian name and surname of your future spouse [*see* LOVE DIVINATION: BALL OF THREAD].

Stanza 13 'I'll eat the apple at the glass' Take a candle, and go alone to a looking-glass; eat an apple before it, and some traditions say you should comb your hair all the time; the face of your conjugal companion, to be, will be seen in the glass, as if peeping over your shoulder [*see* APPLES: MIRROR DIVINATION].

Stanza 16 'He gat hemp-seed, I mind it weel'
Steal out, unperceived, and sow a handful of hemp-seed, harrowing it with anything you can conveniently draw after you. Repeat, now and then, 'Hemp-seed I sow thee, hemp-seed I sow thee; and him (or her) that is to be my true love, come after me a pou thee'. Look over your left shoulder, and you will see the appearance of the person invoked, in the attitude of pulling hemp. Some traditions say, 'Come after me and shaw thee', that is, show theyself; in case, it simply appears. Others omit the harrowing, and say, 'Come after me and harrow thee' [*see* HEMP SEED DIVINATION].

Stanza 21 'To winn three wechts o' naething'
This charm must likewise be performed unperceived and alone. You go to the barn, and open both doors, taking them oV the hinges, if possible: for there is danger that the being about to appear, may shut the doors, and do you some mischief. Then take that instrument used in winnowing the corn, which in our country dialect we call a 'wecht' and go through all the attitudes of letting down corn against the wind . . . repeat it three times, and the third time, an apparition will pass through the barn, in at the windy door, and out at the other, having both the Wgure in question, and the appearance of retinue, marking the employment or station in life.

Stanza 23 'It chanc'd the stack he faddom't thrice'
Take an opportunity of going (unnoticed) to a 'bear-stack' and fathom it three times round. The last fathom of the last time, you will catch in your arms the appearance of your future conjugal yoke-fellow.

Stanza 24 'Whare three lairds' lands met at a burn'
You go out, one or more (for this is a social spell) to a south-running spring, or rivulet, where 'three lairds' lands meet', and dip your left shirt-sleeve. Go to bed in sight of a Wre, and hang your wet sleeve before it to dry. Lie awake, and, some time near midnight, an apparition, having the exact Wgure of the grand object in question, will come and turn the sleeve, as if to dry the other side of it [*compare* LOVE DIVINATION: WASHING SHIFT].

Stanza 27 'The luggies three are ranged'
Take three dishes, put clean water in one, foul water in another, and leave the third empty; blindfold a person, and lead him to the hearth where the dishes are ranged; he (or she) dips the left hand; if by chance in the clean water, the future (husband or) wife will come to the bar of matrimony a maid; if in the foul water, a widow; if in the empty dish it foretells, with equal certainty, no marriage at all. It is repeated three times, and every time the arrangement of the dishes is altered [*see* THREE DISHES DIVINATION].

at a Hallowe'en party a few years ago. The burning of nuts is still practised. Couples place nuts in pairs on the hearth and from their behaviour they draw conclusions about their own future love-life. Bowls of water, one clean and one dirty, and an empty bowl, tell whether the future partner will be rich or poor, or if there will be no future partner. The young people are in turn blindfolded and led to the bowls. The one they touch indicates their fate.

N. Ireland Foster (1951)

In England, the festival remained far less prominent in the traditional calendar, although the closer one gets to Scotland the higher its profile. It was one of several nights in the year when LOVE DIVINATION procedures were thought particularly effective:

[On Hallowe'en] *The following story is true. A young girl hired at a farm in the Hesket district was persuaded to try 'evening the weights', i.e. to go at midnight into a barn where the doors faced east and west, and to make a true or swinging balance on a weighing machine. Upon her return, she was asked by her mistress (who had been instrumental in her trying the charm), if she 'saw owt'.*

'Nobbut t' maister,' was the lassie's reply, 'He come in a yeh door and out at t'udder'. 'Be gud ta my bairns, then,' said her mistress. Not long afterwards the mistress died, and the master eventually married the girl, who kept her promise and treated her step-children the same as her own.　　　　Cumberland *Folk-Lore* (1929)

The divination could also be aimed at predictions other than love:

There was in some places another weird ceremony in going round the church at midnight, and look in through the keyhole in order to see the spectral forms, or to hear a spirit calling the names of all those who were to die in the neighbourhood during the year; that is during the

coming twelve months from that date [compare
PORCH WATCHING].   Mid-Wales Davies (1911)

See also ANIMALS KNEELING.

Selected references only: **England** Wright & Lones 3
(1940) 107–20. **Cumberland** *Folk-Lore* (1929) 285. **Wales**
Owen (1987) 133–5. **Mid-Wales** Davies (1911) 77.
Scotland Miller (1835/1994) 60–72; Banks 3 (1941)
108–75. **Ireland** Danaher (1972) 200–27. **N. Ireland**
Foster (1951) 27. **General** Hutton (1991) 176–83; Hutton
(1996) 360–85; Opie (1959) 268–76.

Hand of Glory

The Hand of Glory was known in various forms
across Europe from at least the Middle Ages
onwards. It was the severed hand of a murderer
(or other executed criminal) which, once
prepared with appropriate occult rites and ingredients, could be used for various nefarious
purposes. In some European traditions possession of the hand bestowed invisibility and other
powers, but in the British stories it was more
usually used to induce sleep while thieves made
away with people's goods. The hand was
anointed with fat (often gruesomely human fat)
and the fingers lighted like candles or, alternatively, the hand was simply made to hold a
candle. Once the candle, or fingers, were lit,
everyone in the house (except the burglar) would
fall into an enchanted sleep.

The history of the Hand of Glory in Britain
is complicated by the free use of continental
material by many authorities, and the constant
repetition, often inaccurately copied and unat-
tributed, of a limited number of stories. One of
the versions given by William Henderson (*see
below*) has not been so frequently reprinted as
the others, and can be given in full to give the
flavour of them all:

*One dark night, when all was shut up, there
came a tap at the door of a lone inn in the
middle of a barren moor. The door was opened,
and there stood without, shivering and shaking,
a poor beggar, his rags soaked with rain, and his
hands white with cold. He asked piteously for a
lodging, and it was cheerfully granted him: there
was not a spare bed in the house, but he could
lie on the mat before the kitchen-fire, and
welcome. So this was settled, and everyone in
the house went to bed except the cook, who from
the back kitchen could see into the large room
through a pane of glass let into the door. She
watched the beggar and saw him, as soon as he
was left alone, draw himself up from the floor,*

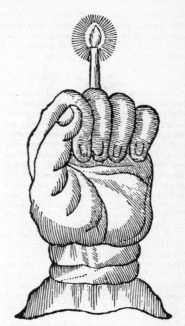

*A number of descriptions exist of how the Hand
of Glory functioned. This comes from a French
publication, Petit Albert.*

*seat himself at the table, extract from his pocket
a brown withered human hand, and set it
upright in the candlestick. He then anointed the
fingers, and applying a match to them, they
began to flame. Filled with horror, the cook
rushed up the backstairs, and endeavoured to
arouse her master and the men of the house. But
all was in vain – they slept a charmed sleep; so
in despair she hastened down again, and placed
herself at her post of observation. She saw the
fingers of the hand flaming, but the thumb
remained unlighted, because one inmate of the
house was awake. The beggar was busy collecting the valuables around him into a large sack,
and having taken all he cared for in the large
room, he entered another. On this, the woman
ran in, and seizing the light tried to extinguish
the flames. But this was not so easy. She blew at
them, but they burnt on as before. She poured
the dregs of a beer-jug over them, but they
burned up the brighter. As a last resource, she
caught up a jug of milk, and dashed it over the*

four lambent flames, and they died out at once. Uttering a loud cry, she rushed to the door of the apartment the beggar had entered, and locked it. The whole family was roused, and the thief easily secured and hanged. This tale is told in Northumberland.

Northumberland Henderson (1866)

There are four strands to Hand of Glory material in Britain, which interweave at times, but which can be separated for analysis. First there was an 'antiquarian tradition' – eighteenth- and nineteenth-century antiquarians and folklorists who identified and described the Hand of Glory from foreign and British sources. Some of this material was couched in terms of narratives of the Hand's use, and these stories were picked up and reprinted by editors of folk tales, which formed the second, 'folk tale', strand. Third, there was a literary tradition, whereby novelists and poets in the nineteenth and twentieth centuries incorporated the Hand of Glory theme into their works, more or less based on the traditional tales, but adapted for their own artistic purposes. The fourth strand is the most difficult to tease out, but comprises a handful of reports which show that the Hand, or something similar, was known in Britain apparently independently of the sources already described, from at least the fifteenth century to within living memory.

The three key publications in the 'antiquarian tradition', from which nearly all others derive, are Francis Grose (1787), John Brand (1849), and William Henderson (1866). Grose printed a description of how to make a Hand of Glory, without naming a source, but later writers have identified it as translated from *Secrets merveilleux de la magie naturelle et cabalistique de Petit Albert* (1704, or earlier), or 'Little Albert' as it was colloquially known. Many years later, Brand quoted from Grose, and added a story of a burglary, in County Meath, from the *Observer* of 16 Jan. 1831. Henderson (1866) gave the fullest account, from a variety of sources: (1) the version from Co. Meath (1831); (2) what he calls his 'Stainmore story', dated 1790–1800, collected by Charles Wastell in spring 1861 from an old woman named Bella Parkin; (3) a version contributed by Sabine Baring-Gould, translated from Martin Del Rio's study of witchcraft entitled *Disquisitionum magicarum libri VI* (1599); (4) another Northumberland version (reproduced above); (5) brief references to a Belgian version (using a murderer's foot instead of a hand, and a thief's finger in the village of Alveringen – the latter from Benjamin Thorpe's *Northern Mythology* (1851); (6) another descrip-

tion translated from Colin de Planey, *Dictionaire Infernal* (1818).

The story which Henderson calls his Stainmore story was subsequently reprinted in numerous folk-tale and folklore collections (listed below) and is now also presented on innumerable Internet sites. The best known of the literary adaptations are also listed below.

This leaves us with the other sources that reveal a long history for the Hand superstition in Britain and Ireland. The earliest is found in the report of a coroner's inquest in Maidstone, Kent, in 1440 which was told:

Take . . . the arm of a dead man that has lain in the earth nine days and nine nights, and put in the dead hand a burning candle, and go to a place wherever thou wilt and though there be therein an hundred people, they that sleep shall sleep and they that wake shall not move whatever you do,

Kent [1440] *Bull. Inst. Hist. Research*

and two hundred years later, the antiquarian John Aubrey wrote:

a story that was generally believed when I was a schoolboy (before the civil warres) that thieves, when they broke open a house, would putt a candle into a deadman's hand: and then the people in the chamber would not awake.

Wiltshire Aubrey, *Remaines* (1686)

A number of sources indicate the belief had a strong presence in Ireland. In 1863, one James Hagan was charged with beating his wife, Sarah. She had hidden his prize possession, a 'dead man's finger' and could not find it again. It was claimed it would enable him to rob any premises without being detected by its occupants (**Co. Antrim** *The Times* (19 Sept. 1863)). The tradition was still alive in Ireland in the 1970s, when Michael J. Murphy collected tales of sleep-inducing lighted candles in dead hands, from storytellers in Counties Down, Armagh, and Louth (Murphy (1973)).

Stories of the Hand of Glory can be seen as part of a series of other traditions. Other DEAD MEN'S HANDS were recommended for cures and for magical assistance in making butter, and there were holy hands of dead saints and martyrs like Father Arrowsmith (*see* Harland & Wilkinson (1882) 158–63) which performed miracles. Other tales included motifs of substances which conferred invisibility or induced sleep, and many other witchcraft traditions involved candles. A human hand, reputedly used as a Hand of Glory, is one of the most popular items in Whitby Museum, Yorkshire.

The derivation and history of the name 'Hand of Glory' is itself confused. First used in English around 1707, it is a mis-translation of the medieval French *maindegloire*, meaning a 'mandrake'. But the name 'Hand of Glory' is too evocative to be confined to such a grisly past, and it has now been appropriated by jewellery makers who market silver or pewter pendants in the shape of hands, on the Internet. In Aug. 2002, one was advertised with the suggestion that it should be worn 'for tranquillity and good health, and peace of mind', for only $4.95. A very far cry from the original.

Kent [1440] *Bull. Inst. Hist. Research* 36 (1963) 86–7. Wiltshire Aubrey, *Remaines* (1686/1880) 103. Shropshire *Folk-Lore* 20 (1909) 219–20. Lancashire N&Q 4S:6 (1870) 211; *Ashton-under-Lyne Reporter* (22 Apr. 1905) quoted *FLS News* 17 (1993) 15. Northumberland Henderson (1866) 200–5. Ireland *Gent. Mag.* (1865) 702; Wilde (1888) 81–2, 201; Murphy (1973) 33–4; Jenkins (1977) 39–40. Co. Antrim *The Times* (19 Sept. 1863) 8. Co. Meath [1831] Brand 3 (1849) 278–9. General *City Press* (31 May 1893) quoted in N&Q 8S:4 (1893) 47; Robbins (1959) 241. France Grose (1787) 73–5. Correspondence in *FLS News* 17 (1993) 15; 19 (1994) 11; 20 (1994) 9; 21 (1995) 6. *See also* comprehensive international bibliography in Kittredge (1929) 463–4. *Folk tale collections*: Sidney Hartland, *English Fairy and Other Folktales* (1890) 196–9; Katharine M. Briggs, *A Dictionary of British Folk-Tales Pt B Folk Legends* 2 (1970) 534–7; E. & M. A. Radford, *Encyclopaedia of Superstitions* (1971) 179–80; Neil Philip, *Penguin Book of English Folktales* (1992) 199–200. *Literary adaptations*: Robert Southey, *Thalaba the Destroyer* (1801) Bk 5; Walter Scott, *The Antiquary* (1816) Ch. 17; Richard Barham, *Ingoldsby Legends* (1840) 'The Nurse's Story'; W. Harrison Ainsworth, *Rookwood* (1857) Bk 1, Ch. 2; Sabine Baring-Gould, *Red Spider* (1887) Ch. 24; R. Blakeborough, *The Hand of Glory* (1924) Ch. 1.

handkerchiefs

A few miscellaneous traditions centre on the humble handkerchief, and although none is widely recorded, some can be shown to be astonishingly long-lasting.

It is very unlucky, I am told, to put your clean handkerchief into your pocket folded up. It should always be opened before being put into that receptacle. Is this idea confined to the Midlands?
Midland England *Midland Garner* (1884)

Almost exactly the same thing was said by a thirteen-year old boy from Forfar (**Angus** Opie & Tatem) and a woman in the *Daily Express*, both in 1954.

Many people still claim that tying a knot in your handkerchief helps you to remember something, but this in itself is not always sufficient:

Some years ago I mentioned to a friend that, though I often tied a knot in my handkerchief in order to remember something, I generally forgot what the thing was I had wanted to remember. 'Oh!' said he, 'you should whisper "rabbits" three times into the knot as you tie it. Then you'll remember'. I have met other persons acquainted with this custom, but not very many, and I have no evidence that it belongs to any particular part of the country. In order to avoid raising false hopes, I may say that I have not personally found the formula at all infallible
Gloucester *Saturday Westminster Gazette* (5 Apr. 1919)

That the knotting is no recent innovation is demonstrated by a reference from the thirteenth-century work of advice to women about how to become religious recluses:

a man ties a knot in his girdle to remember a thing; but our Lord, in order never to forget us, made a mark of piercing in both His hands.
Ancren Riwle (c.1230)

Handkerchiefs also featured in some cures, as the medium through which a disease could be transferred:

The following instance occurred a short time since. At the close of the funeral of a man who in a fit of insanity had laid violent hands upon himself, a woman advanced and threw a new white pocket handkerchief on the coffin. I am told that the belief is that as, in the grave of a suicide, the handkerchief decays, so will any disease the depositor may have. Devon N&Q (1874)

A similar description appeared in the *Journal of the Royal Institute of Cornwall* (1915). A belief noted from a Co. Durham woman in 1984 that held it was unlucky to borrow a handkerchief because it meant 'borrowing tears' (Opie & Tatem), echoes a phrase in William Drummond's *Poems* (*c.*1614): 'Ah, napkin, ominous present of my deare. Gift miserable'.

Devon N&Q 5S:1 (1874) 204. Cornwall *Jnl. Royal Inst. Cornwall* 20 (1915) 126. Gloucester *Saturday Westminster Gazette* (5 Apr. 1919) 26. Midland England *Midland Garner* 2 (1884) 26. Co. Durham [1984] Opie & Tatem, 187. Angus [1954] Opie & Tatem 187. Unlocated *Ancren Riwle* (*c.*1230); *Daily Express* (13 Aug. 1954) 4, quoted Opie & Tatem, 187. Literary William Drummond, *Poems* (*c.*1614).

hands: itching

The dominant symbolism of hands in the superstitions of Britain and Ireland is money – coming in or going out, depending on the context. Added to this is a range of beliefs concerning ITCHING as predictive of future events:

If the right hand itched, it signified that money would shortly be received by it; and if the left hand itched, that money would shortly have to be paid away.   Western Scotland Napier (1879)

This idea was very widely known, and remarkably stable in meaning across virtually all versions. An additional rhyme, apparently dating from the mid nineteenth century, gave further information:

Rub it on wood
It's sure to be good
Rub it on brass
It'll come to pass.

Norfolk Fulcher Collection (c.1895)

The meaning is already in place when John Melton included it in his list of superstitions in 1620. A few years earlier, Shakespeare had given evidence of a slightly different meaning of the 'itchy palm'. While still involving money, his interpretation involved avarice and corruption:

Let me tell you, Cassius, you yourself
Are much condemned to have an itching palm
To sell and mart your offices for gold
To undeservers.

Shakespeare, *Julius Caesar* (1599)

Both meanings can still be heard.

Sussex *Sussex County Mag.* 5 (1931) 122. **Hampshire** [1987] Opie & Tatem, 186. **Somerset** Tongue (1965) 138. **Devon** Hewett (1900) 77; *Devonshire Assoc.* 59 (1927) 158. **Cornwall** N&Q 1S:12 (1855) 38; Couch (1871) 169; *Folk-Lore Jnl* 5 (1887) 219. **Wiltshire** *Wilts. N&Q* 1 (1893–5) 60. **London** *Folk-Lore* 37 (1926) 365; *Observer Supp.* (24 Nov. 1968) 8. **Midland England** N&Q 1S:1 (1850) 451. **Warwickshire** Langford (1875) 14. **East Anglia** Varden (1885) 113. **Suffolk** *Folk-Lore Record* 1 (1878) 240. **Norfolk** Fulcher Collection (c.1895). **Lincolnshire** *Gent. Mag.* (1833) 590–3; Rudkin (1936) 19. **Shropshire** Burne (1883) 240–1, 269. **Staffordshire** Hackwood (1924) 148–9. **England** Addy (1895) 92, 100. **Yorkshire** N&Q 1S:6 (1852) 311–12; Nicholson (1890) 44; [1965] Opie & Tatem, 186. **Lancashire** *Lancashire Lore* (1971) 71. **Co. Durham** Henderson (1866) 85; Brockie (1886) 211; Leighton (1910) 60. **Northumberland** Bosanquet (1929) 79. **Wales** Trevelyan (1909) 325. **West Wales** Davies (1911) 218. **Welsh Gypsies** Jarman (1991) 184. **Western Scotland** Napier (1879) 138. **Dumfriesshire**

Shaw (1890) 12; Corrie (1890/91) 83. **Caithness** Sutherland (1937) 104. **Orkney** N&Q 10S:12 (1909) 483–4. **Ireland** Wilde (1888) 206. **Co. Tyrone** *Lore & Language* 1:7 (1972) 11. **Co. Longford** Béaloideas 6 (1936) 265. **Jersey** *Folk-Lore* 25 (1914) 246; L'Amy (1927) 98. Unlocated Melton (1620); *Chambers's Jnl* (1873) 810; Gales (1914) 234. Literary Shakespeare, *Julius Caesar* (1599) 4:3; Swift (1738); *Connoisseur* 59 (1755) 354; *Old Women's Sayings* (c.1835).

handsel

As a noun, a handsel (or hansel) is an auspicious inauguration or first use, and as a verb it is the giving or using of something in that capacity.

Any new item of clothing with a pocket must have money in it to hansel it.   Yorkshire Nicholson (1890)

The key to understanding the concept of handselling is to realize the overwhelming importance of BEGINNINGS in all superstitious thought. Whatever enterprise you are engaged in, whatever period of time you are entering, whatever new piece of clothing you are wearing, whatever item you are using for the first time – if it starts well it will continue well, or, more to the point, if it starts lucky it will always be lucky. The new coat is handselled by a tailor putting a coin in the pocket before the customer wears it. A baby is handselled by giving it a coin. The first money taken in the day by a market trader or itinerant trader is their handsel.

'Tis common use in London, and perhaps over great part of England for apple-women and oyster-women &c.and some butchers, to spit on the money which they first receive in the morning, which they call good handsell.

London Aubrey, *Remaines* (1686)

Nearly two hundred years later, Victorian servant Hannah Cullwick recorded in her diary in 1867:

The old gentleman said goodbye and thank'd me for what I had done for him, and put half-a-crown in my hand. His was my hansell and of course I hoped to see a good many more come and go before the end o' the season, and so I spit on the half-a-crown for luck, same as you see the hawkers do with their'n.

London [1867] Cullwick

SPITTING on money was common in other contexts as well, but is so often part of the handsel transaction that it is impossible to separate them.

Both the word 'handsel' and the concept of luck in gift or transaction has been in common use in English since at least 1200 and has roots in similar old Scandinavian words for money, although in the latter the connotation of luck, or first use, does not appear to be present. See *Oxford English Dictionary* for numerous examples of its use since 1200. Because of the combination of luck and money-gift, some writers conflate 'handsel' with LUCK MONEY, but these are quite different concepts and are best treated separately.

Dorset Udal (1922) 281. Devon *Devonshire Assoc.* 12 (1880) 112; Hewett (1900) 52. London Aubrey, *Remaines* (1686/1972) 247; [1867] Cullwick (1984) 65. Lincolnshire *Gent. Mag.* (1833) 590–3. Shropshire Burne (1883) 272–3. Staffordshire Hackwood (1924) 148. Northern England Brockett (1829) 146–7. Derbyshire N&Q 9S:6 (1900) 273–4. Yorkshire Nicholson (1890) 2, 43. Co. Durham Brockie (1886) 216; Leighton (1910) 61. Northumberland Bosanquet (1929) 74. Wales Trevelyan (1909) 329; Wales *Folk-Lore* 37 (1926) 174. Mid-Wales Davies (1911) 215. Ireland N&Q 4S:1 (1868) 193; [1890s] Uttley (1956) 126. N. Ireland Foster (1951) 10. Co. Wexford [1938] Ó Muirithe & Nuttall (1999) 166–7. Co. Antrim [c.1905] McDowell (1972) 129. Connemara *Folk-Lore* 4 (1893) 358. Jersey *Folk-Lore* 25 (1914) 247. Unlocated Grose (1787) 64; N&Q 3S:7 (1865) 432–3; Jones (1880) 479.

hangman's rope: cures

Various items connected with executions and suicides enjoyed a reputation for being lucky or valuable for their curative powers, including pieces of the GALLOWS and the touch of a DEAD MAN'S HAND. A piece of hangman's rope was also believed to cure a variety of ailments:

A charm for a headache – Tie a halter about your head, wherewith one hath been hanged.
Scot (1584)

A piece of the rope with which a criminal has been hanged is good against epilepsy.
Lincolnshire *Folk-Lore* (1896)

The range of ailments so treated also included the AGUE, King's Evil (SCROFULA), and bad eyes. Some held that it should be the rope used by a suicide:

Fits can be cured by procuring a strand from a rope with which a man has hung himself, and wearing it always around the neck.
Lincolnshire Rudkin (1936)

No attempt at explanation is given in any of the sources quoted, and it defies logical inquiry. But the belief was certainly widespread, and had been current in Britain at least since the sixteenth century, as indicated by the piece from Scot,

quoted above. Long before that, it was included in Pliny's *Natural History* (AD 77) and, given the immense popularity of that work with educated British readers from medieval times onwards, is likely to be the ultimate source.

Devon *Devonshire Assoc.* 85 (1953) 218. Cornwall *Folk-Lore Jnl* 5 (1887) 205; *Cassell's Saturday Jnl* (1893). Bristol Scot (1584) Bk 12, Ch. 14; [1752] Brand 2 (1813) 583. London Aubrey, *Remaines* (1688/ 1880) 198. Lincolnshire *Folke-Lore* 7 (1896) 268; *Folk-Lore* 44 (1933) 202; Rudkin (1936) 26. Northumberland Brand 3 (1849) 276–7. General Scot (1584) Bk 12, Ch. 14; *Gent. Mag.* (1796) 636. Classical Pliny, *Natural History* (AD 77) Bk 28, Para. 12.

hangman's rope: lucky

A piece of hangman's rope has curative powers (*see above*) but was also regarded as a lucky thing to possess:

The instrument by which the unfortunate put an end to its life was eagerly sought after, as the possession of it, particularly the knot of the rope, if death was brought about by hanging, secured great worldly prosperity. The notion about the knot of a rope by which one was hanged did not attach simply to a suicide's rope, but to a criminal's.
Northeast Scotland Gregor (1874)

Such an item was particularly prized by card-players:

It is held by certain gamesters that a bit of a hangman's rope is a charm for success at cards. It cost eight pounds – they're very difficult to get now.
N&Q (1868)

These few examples are noticeably fewer and more recent than those which claim the rope as curative. Exactly the same belief was also reported from nineteenth-century **Russia** (*Folk-Lore Record* 3 (1880) 137) and **France** (*Folk-Lore* 7 (1896) 269–70).

Devon Hewett (1900) 52, 65. Northeast Scotland Gregor (1874) 150. General N&Q 4S:1 (1868) 193.

harelips

Many people in the past, and not a few in the present, were convinced that antenatal influences on an expectant mother could have a marked effect on the baby in the womb. BIRTH-MARKS were often explained by reference to the mother being frightened or otherwise impressed with a strong emotion caused by a particular sight or occurrence. The most widely known example of this belief is that if a pregnant woman met a hare her child would be born with a hare-lip (cheiloschisis) or cleft palate.

If a woman in an 'interesting condition' sees a hare in her path, she must immediately stop and make three rents in her under garment, or the child will be hare-shorn – i.e. have a cleft upper lip.   Warwickshire Langford (1875)

For the woman to tear her shift or skirt was widely accepted as the only way to prevent the tragedy, unless the hare were dead:

When a hare is killed the person, before carrying it home, is careful to remove the tail. If he does not do so and meets a pregnant woman while carrying the hare, her baby will be born with a hare lip.   Co. Cavan Logan (1963)

The earliest reference to the term *harelip* in the OED is 1567, and it is clear that not only the cause but also the remedy were already well known at that period. Lupton devotes a paragraph of his *Thousand Notable Things* (1579) to advising pregnant women to be prepared by leaving part of their dress unstitched, or even deliberately torn, just in case they meet the animal on their walks. The presumed connection between hares and harelips is still well-known, and was given a boost by its inclusion in Mary Webb's novel *Precious Bane*, first published in 1924.

See also BIRTHMARKS.

Warwickshire Langford (1875) 20; Bloom (*c.*1930) 17. Suffolk Glyde (1866) 177. Shropshire Burne (1883) 212–13. Northern England *Newcastle Weekly Chronicle* (11 Feb. 1899) 7. Montgomeryshire Burne (1883) 212–13. Northeast Scotland Gregor (1881) 129. N. Ireland Foster (1951) 129–30. Co. Antrim Evans & Thomson (1972) 220. Co. Cavan Logan (1963) 90–1. Co. Longford *Béaloideas* 6 (1936) 259. General Lupton (1579) Bk 2, Para. 6, Bk 4, Para. 15; N. Homes *Daemonologie* (1650) 60. Literary Mary Webb, *Precious Bane* (1924).

hares: fire prediction

One of the minor beliefs about hares was that it was a bad omen if it ran through a village, since it predicted a fire:

It is generally believed in Hertfordshire that if a hare enters a town or village an outbreak of fire will shortly occur. It is said that several of the great conflagrations which have taken place were foretold in this way.   Hertfordshire N&Q (1909)

Some informants stated that a fire would certainly occur in any building in which the hare took shelter. Although reported fairly regularly, this does not seem to be a widespread or old belief. All recorded examples are from the southern half of England, and the earliest only dates from 1851. Nevertheless, it was still being quoted in the second half of the twentieth century.

Evans and Thomson (1972) point out the unusual behaviour of hares faced by a fire in the wild. Their informants claimed that hares will tend to try to escape by running *through* the fire, rather than away from it as most other animals do. This possibly sets up a connection in the country person's mind between hares and fire, but does not really explain the superstition, and no other plausible one has been suggested.

Devon *Devonshire Assoc.* 18 (1886) 105; *Devonshire Assoc.* 39 (1907) 109. Essex [*c.*1939] *Folk-Lore* 64 (1953) 293. Middlesex N&Q 10S:11 (1909) 458. Hertfordshire N&Q 10S:11 (1909) 310. Worcestershire Salisbury (1893) 72. Northamptonshire N&Q 1S:3 (1851) 3–4; N&Q 10S:11 (1909) 413.
Bedfordshire/Huntingdonshire/Cambridgeshire Gomme Collection (Letter, F. Atkinson, 30 Sept. 1892). Cambridgeshire Porter (1969) 54. Suffolk Evans & Thomson (1972) 126. Midland England *Midland Garner* 1 (1884) 23.

hares: witches

It was common knowledge, for centuries, that witches could turn themselves into hares. Many folklore collections have a version of a tale about hunters trying to shoot or catch a hare which continually eludes them, until it is finally injured and seen to enter a nearby house. When the men get into the house they find an old woman with the same injuries as had been inflicted on the hare.

One day they were a long time looking for a hare. At last they found a fine fat one under a bush on the mountain. A little boy on the hill nearby shouted 'Run, grannie, run, the hounds be after thee!'. By that they knew she was a witch. She ran to a little cottage and disappeared through the keyhole, but as she went through one of the hounds bit her leg. The door was locked and they could not get in at first. When they opened it they found a very old woman sitting by the fire doctoring a wound in her leg [Aarne-Thompson motif G211.2.7.].   Herefordshire Leather (1912)

The little boy is an unusual motif, but the rest is standard. Another version also tells of a hare which evades all attempts to shoot it, until a huntsman loads his gun with silver bullets, with the same ending as above.

It is a striking characteristic of traditional British witches that they usually turned them-

hares

Hares have a strangely mixed reputation in the traditions of Britain and Ireland. They are consistently described as unlucky, unfit to eat, uncanny, and as witches in disguise, but newborn children were fed on hares' brains, and numerous people carried a hare's foot for luck or to cure or prevent disease. The documentary record for hare beliefs is unusually full, and a significant number are mentioned by medieval writers. Some have lasted well into living memory.

Meeting a hare was very unlucky, especially for a pregnant woman, whose baby would be born with a 'harelip' if she did not take immediate protective action such as tearing her shift. Hares were one of several animals which fishermen dreaded seeing on the way to their boats, or while they were mending their nets, and the word 'hare' must not be spoken while at sea, at the risk of serious bad luck.

A Wick fishing crew went in ordinary course to the Stornaway fishing. Their nets and other equipment were stored in the hold of the boat. On spreading out their nets after their arrival in Stornaway, to their dismay, they found a hare's foot among the nets. The least evil that this foreboded was a blank season, so far as the capture of fish was concerned, but it might well be the forerunner of still greater calamities such as the loss of life. So great was their faith in this supposed omen of evil that they picked up their nets, sailed back to Wick, and lost the Stornaway fishing for that season. Someone, no doubt, put the hare's foot among the nets, perhaps with malicious intent, or it may be as a joke, not realising that it would be taken so seriously to heart.
                              Caithness Sutherland (1937)

The unluckiness of the hare is clearly related to, and possibly originates from, numerous stories in which witches turned themselves into hares.

Popular errors also abounded. The hare was believed to be so timid that it did not shut its eyes, even when asleep, and it was also believed to change its sex every year. In literary parlance it was regularly termed the 'melancholy hare', and its meat was thought to have the same effect on humans:

*Madam, will your ladyship have any of this hare?
No, Madam, they say 'tis melancholy meat.*
                              Swift (1738)

Many people would not eat hare meat under any circumstances, perhaps following biblical precedent (Deuteronomy 14:7–8), but that source also proscribes coneys, which the British would understand as rabbits, and these were certainly not avoided:

No Norfolk labourer will take a hare as a gift, although they are very fond of rabbits.
                              Norfolk *Folk-Lore* (1926)

Nevertheless, hare's brains were deemed suitable for newborn babies:

If the new-born infant seemed restless and made a sucking movement with its lips, it was supposed to show a desire for something its mother had not been able to supply. In Warwickshire this something took the form of hare's brains reduced to jelly. It was an ordinary custom on the Alscot estate to send a deputation to the lady of the manor to beg a hare's head for the purpose; this custom was kept up to the last thirty years. There is also an Ilmington record which carries us back more than a century. Warwickshire Bloom (c.1930)

The problem remains of how to interpret Caesar's early references to Britons not eating hares:

Hares, fowl, and geese they think it unlawful to eat, but rear them for pleasure and amusement.
                              Caesar, *The Conquest of Gaul* (54 BC)

This has been interpreted to mean that these creatures were 'sacred' or 'holy' to the Britons, but there is no evidence in the wording to support this interpretation.

New Forest Wise (1867) 177. **Warwickshire** Bloom (c.1930) 19–20. **Norfolk** *Folk-Lore* 37 (1926) 370–1. **Yorkshire** Blakeborough (1898) 136. **Caithness** Sutherland (1937) 102. **Co.** Kerry *Folk-Lore* 4 (1893) 352. **Guernsey** De Garis (1975) 128. **General** *Folk-Lore Jnl* 1 (1883) 84–90. *Baily's Mag.* (Oct. 1915) 169–74. Evans & Thomson (1972) *passim*. **Literary** Swift (1738) 143. **Classical** Caesar, *The Conquest of Gaul* (54 BC) Bk 5, Para. 12.

selves into small and relatively harmless creatures – hares, cats, mice, and the like – and the height of their mischief when thus transformed was to milk cows illicitly:

It has been a frequent complaint, from old times, as well as in the present, that certain hags in Wales, as well as in Ireland and Scotland, changed themselves into the shape of hares, that, sucking teats under this counterfeit form, they might stealthily rob other people's milk.
                              Gerald of Wales, *Topographica Hibernica* (1184)

This is the earliest known mention of witch-hares, but the notion was recorded regularly right up to the twentieth century. The close connection between witches and hares may have contributed to the hare's uncanny reputation and beliefs about it being unlucky to meet the animal at the start of a journey (*see below*).

Somerset Tongue (1965) 71–2. Devon Bray (1838) 277. Herefordshire Leather (1912) 52. Northern England Henderson (1866) 165. Yorkshire Atkinson (1891) 81–90. Wales Ranulphus Higden, *Polychronicon* (*c.*1350); Trevelyan (1909) 212. Scotland [1662] Scott (1830) 171. Ireland Ranulphus Higden, *Polychronicon* (*c.*1350); Wilde (1888) 201. Co. Limerick William Camden, *Britannia* (1586). Isle of Man N&Q 1S:5 (1852) 341; Rhys 1 (1901) 309. Unlocated *Spectator* (14 July 1711). General Gerald of Wales, *Topographica Hibernica* (1184) Bk 2, Ch. 19; Kittredge (1929) 179, 497–8; Evans & Thomson (1972) 142–77. Literary John Clare, *Shepherd's Calendar* (1827) lines 194–6.

hares/rabbits: forbidden words

Across the British Isles, fishermen and their families believed that certain animals and people were unlucky to meet on their way to their boats, or to see while engaged in important tasks on which their livelihood depended. In most cases, it was forbidden to even mention them by name while at sea. Hares and rabbits were most commonly included is this category of unlucky beasts:

To say to a fisherwoman that there was a hare's foot in her creel, or to say to a fisherman that there was a hare in his boat, aroused great ire, and called forth strong words. The word 'hare' was never pronounced at sea. To have thrown a hare, or any part of a hare, into a boat would have stopped many a fisherman in by-gone days from going to sea; and if any misfortune had happened, however long afterwards, it was traced up to the hare.   Northeast Scotland Gregor (1881)

Most of the beliefs in forbidden words can only be traced back to the nineteenth century, but the hare is the exception. It was already known at the turn of the seventeenth, as Richard Carew described:

Now from within harbour we will launch out into the deep, and see what luck of fish God shall there send us, which (so you talk not of hares or such uncouth things, for that proves as ominous to the fisherman as the beginning of a voyage on the day when Childermas day fell, doth to the mariner).
Cornwall Carew (1602)

Even earlier, the hare was 'the animal that no one dare name' in a thirteenth-century manuscript from Shropshire. Most forbidden word beliefs are found predominantly in Scotland, but the hare has a much wider geographical base.

See also FISHING: FORBIDDEN WORDS.

Kent *Morning Post* (9 June 1919) 3. Dorset [1953] Opie & Tatem, 193; *Daily Express* (20 Nov. 1963) 10. Devon Hewett (1900) 58. Cornwall Carew (1602/1969) 50; N&Q 8S:10 (1896) 393. Norfolk [1981] Opie & Tatem, 193. Shropshire [late 13th cent.] MS Digby 86, quoted Opie & Tatem, 192. Yorkshire N&Q 5S:3 (1875) 204. Banffshire *Folk-Lore Jnl* 4 (1886) 14; Anson (1965) 131. Northeast Scotland Gregor (1881) 129. Caithness Rinder (1895) 57–8; Sutherland (1937) 102. Guernsey De Garis (1975) 128. Unlocated N&Q 12S:1 (1916) 66.

hares/rabbits: meeting

The good or bad luck which attached to MEETING particular animals or people at the beginning of a journey is a common motif in superstition, and the animal most often singled out is the hare (or occasionally the rabbit):

If a person on going to his work, or while going on an errand, were to see a hare cross the road in front of him, it was a token that ill luck would shortly befall him. Many under such circumstances would return home and not pursue their quest until the next meal had been eaten, for beyond that the evil influence did not extend.
Western Scotland Napier (1879)

The vast majority of informants claimed that meeting a hare was a powerfully bad omen in itself, but a few distinguished between whether the animal approached from the right (good) or left (bad), while others stated that meeting the hare was all right, it was only if it actually crossed your path that it was unfortunate.

It is unusual to have more than one confirmation of the existence of a belief in the medieval era, but both John of Salisbury (1159) and Nigel de Longchamps (1180) show that it was already well known in Britain in the twelfth century.

The general association between hares and witches in British superstition is well known, and this may possibly be at the root of the fear of meeting one. The belief was found in every quarter of the British Isles, and is unusually well documented into the late twentieth century. The string of references show clearly that it was extremely well known, widely believed, and remarkably stable in meaning, considering its longevity.

Sussex Latham (1878) 56. **Dorset** [1953] Opie & Tatem, 191. **Devon** [c.1918] *Devonshire Assoc.* 100 (1968) 366. **Essex** *Folk-Lore* 64 (1953) 293–4. **Herefordshire** Leather (1912) 23. **Northamptonshire** N&Q 1S:3 (1851) 3–4. **East Anglia** Varden (1885) 113. **Suffolk** *Folk-Lore* 35 (1924) 350. **Norfolk** *Folk-Lore* 40 (1929) 121–2; Evans & Thomson (1972) 215. **Shropshire** Burne (1883) 212–13, 274. **Northern England** *Newcastle Weekly Chronicle* (4 Feb. 1899) 7. **Yorkshire** N&Q 5S:3 (1875) 204; Nicholson (1890) 134. **Cumberland** Gibson (1858) 106. **Westmorland/Lancashire** *Folk-Lore* 64 (1953) 293–4. **Northumberland** Neville (1909) 109–10. **Wales** Howells (1831) 67; Trevelyan (1909) 327. **Pembrokeshire** Davies (1911) 62. **Caernarvonshire** Evans & Thomson (1972) 214–15. **Scotland** *Edinburgh Mag.* (Nov. 1818) 412; N&Q 2S:4 (1857) 25. **Highland Scotland** Macbain (1887/88) 265; Campbell (1900) 254. **Northeast Scotland** Gregor (1881) 129. **Western Scotland** Napier (1879) 117. **Dumfriesshire** Shaw (1890) 12; Corrie (1890/91) 81. **Glasgow** [c.1820] Napier (1864) 397. **Galloway** Mactaggart (1824) 210. **Ireland** Wilde (1888) 211. **N. Ireland** Foster (1951) 129–30. **Connemara** *Folk-Lore Jnl* 2 (1884) 258. **General** John of Salisbury, *Policraticus* (1159); Nigel de Longchamps, *Mirror for Fools* (1180); Scot (1584) Bk 11, Ch. 15; George Gifford, *Subtill Practises of Devills* (1587) C2; Melton (1620); Thomas Cooper, *The Mystery of Witch-craft* (1617) 137; Aubrey, *Remaines* (1686/1972) 217; Bourne, *Antiquitates Vulgares* (1725); Brand (1810) 96. **Literary** George Wither, *Abuses Stript an Whipt* (1613) 2:1; John Webster, *Duchess of Malfi* (1623) 2:3; Walter Scott, *The Pirate* (1822) Ch. 24.

hare's/rabbit's foot: cures

The carrying of a hare's or rabbit's foot was a well-known cure for a variety of ailments, including RHEUMATISM and CRAMP:

The bone also in a hare's foot mitigateth the crampe, as none other bone nor part else of the hare doth.   Scot (1584)

Samuel Pepys carried one for colic:

So homeward, in my way buying a hare and taking it home – which arose upon my discourse today with Mr. Batten in Westminster-hall – who showed me my mistake, that my hares-foot hath not the joint to it, and assures me that he never had his cholique since he carried it about him, for I no sooner handled his foot but my belly begin to loose and to break wind.
London Samuel Pepys, *Diary* (20 Jan. 1665)

In later reports, it was also one of the myriad cures for WHOOPING COUGH. These descriptions of the curative properties of hares' feet predate any references to them being carried as lucky amulets (*see below*), but are probably taken direct from classical sources in the sixteenth century. Pliny, for example, wrote that:

Gouty pains are alleviated by a hare's foot, cut off from the living animal, if the patient carries it about continuously on the person.
Pliny, *Natural History* (AD 77)

Compare CRAMP: BONES; MOLES: FEET.

Sussex Latham (1878) 39. **London** Samuel Pepys, *Diary* (31 Dec. 1664; 20 Jan. 1665). **Northamptonshire** N&Q 1S:2 (1850) 36–7. **East Anglia** Varden (1885) 104. **Suffolk** Evans & Thomson (1972) 234. **Staffordshire** Poole (1875) 81–2. **Northumberland** *Newcastle Weekly Chronicle* (4 Feb. 1899) 7. **Unlocated** Igglesden (c.1932) 146. **General** Scot (1584) Bk 13, Ch. 11. **Classical** Pliny, *Natural History* (AD 77) Bk 28, Ch. 62.

hare's/rabbit's foot: lucky

A rabbit's foot is a well-known lucky amulet in the present day, but its history is strangely difficult to pin down. The earliest reference links a hare's foot with protection:

[My mother] also carries a hare's foot in her pocket, to guard against attacks in that quarter [by witchcraft] by day.
Westmorland Hone, *Table Book* (1827)

But there are no more references until well into the twentieth century, when it is always a rabbit's foot which is valued. Given its current reputation as a 'lucky charm', it is strange that so few historical references have come to light. This is in complete contrast to the United States, where it is probably the most widely known amulet of all. It is likely that the current awareness of the rabbit's foot in Britain today is an introduction from North America, in the post-Second-World-War era.

Sussex Woodford (1968) 60. **Yorkshire** [1982] Opie & Tatem, 194. **Lancashire** *Reveille* (2 Oct. 1953) 2, quoted Opie & Tatem, 194. **Westmorland** Hone, *Table Book* (1827) 338. **Co. Durham** [1982] Opie & Tatem, 194. **Glamorganshire** Evans & Thomson (1972) 170. **Unlocated** Igglesden (c.1932) 146. **Theatrical** Granville (1952) 179.

hawthorn: blossoms unlucky

The most widely known, by a very wide margin, of the many unlucky FLOWERS beliefs held that it was very unwise to bring hawthorn or 'may' blossom into the house. At best it was unlucky, but in many minds it was an omen, or even a cause, of a coming death in the family:

Hawthorn was never brought into the house during the month of May. Indeed it was never taken into our rooms. There was a strong feeling against it in every cottage and farmhouse, for it was a portent of death in that year.

Derbyshire [1890s] Uttley

The dread was expressed in a number of local sayings, which show much more variety than is usual with the genre:

*Hawthorn bloom and elder flowers
Will fill a house with evil powers.*

Warwickshire Langford (1875)

May in – coffin out.

Unlocated Igglesden (c.1932)

*If you draw may into the house,
You draw the head of the house out.*

Essex *Folk-Lore* (1910)

Some informants claimed more specific deaths would result from hawthorn blossoms indoors – children were told that their mother would die if they ignored the prohibition, while others thought a child would die. Many of the people who acted on this superstition claimed that the blossom 'smelled like death', or, more specifically, like the plague, and did not even like it outdoors:

I have found it a popular notion among . . . country cottagers, that the peculiar scent of the hawthorn is 'exactly like the smell of the Great Plague of London' . . . I am not aware that the powerful perfume of the gorse has ever been compared to anything connected with death; but I happen to know that it produces in many people so overpowering a sensation of faintness and sickness that they cannot, with comfort, pass by the flowering gorse bushes without covering their mouths and noses with a handkerchief.

Unlocated *Gent. Mag.* (1866)

This assessment of the flower goes back to at least the early seventeenth century, long before the Great Plague of the 1660s. In the earliest reference known to us, Francis Bacon wrote that the plague had a scent 'of the smell of a mellow apple and (as some say) of May flowers (*Sylva Sylvarum* (1627)).

Certainly, the flowers of some species of hawthorn decay rapidly when picked and emit a pungent smell. The popular assessment that this 'smells like death' is more than simply a superstitious fancy, however, as science confirms a connection:

More recently it has been shown that trimethylamine, one of the first products formed when animal tissues start to decay, is present in hawthorn flowers.

Vickery (1995) 169

Other popular explanations also existed. One is that the superstition arose at the Reformation because may blossom was popular in Catholic churches for decorating statues of the Virgin Mary. It was therefore forbidden and branded as evil by the new Anglican Church. This explanation was still being quoted in the mid twentieth century (e.g. **Lincolnshire** Sutton (1992)), but is not supported by history. The strong connection between Mary and the month of May only started in the eighteenth century, in Italy, and it came to Britain and Ireland some time later. May devotions were not introduced until the nineteenth century (*see* Vickery (1995)). Another explanation is that Christ's 'crown of thorns' was made from the hawthorn.

For comprehensive summaries of hawthorn beliefs *see* Vickery (1985) 16–26, and (1995) 166–72.

Kent Foster (1951) 110. **Sussex** *Sussex County Mag* 13 (1939) 57. **Somerset** Tongue (1965) 222. **Devon** [1874] *Devonshire Assoc.* 15 (1883) 107; *Devonshire Assoc.* 57 (1926) 109; *Devonshire Assoc.* 61 (1929) 126; *Devonshire Assoc.* 63 (1931) 124; *Devonshire Assoc.* 103 (1971) 268. **Hampshire** [1923] Opie & Tatem, 243. **Essex** *Monthly Packet* 24 (1862) 434–7; *Folk-Lore* 21 (1910) 224. **Buckinghamshire** [1912] *Folk-Lore* 43 (1932) 109. **Oxfordshire** [c.1918] Thompson (1943) 228; [1920s] Harris (1969) 125. **Herefordshire** Leather (1912) 17. **Worcestershire** [1900] *Folk-Lore* 20 (1909) 343; Berkeley & Jenkins (1932) 34, 37. **Warwickshire** Langford (1875) 15. **Cambridgeshire** Porter (1969) 62. **East Anglia** N&Q 4S:1 (1868) 550; Varden (1885) 117. **Suffolk** N&Q 1S:2 (1850) 5; N&Q 4S:1 (1868) 550; Zincke (1887) 179–80; *Folk-Lore* 54 (1943) 390; Claxton (1954) 89; [1983] Opie & Tatem, 243. **Norfolk** [c.1912] Randell (1966) 97. **Lincolnshire** N&Q 7S:2 (1886) 215; Rudkin (1936) 17; Sutton (1992) 126. **Shropshire/Staffordshire** Burne (1883) 243–4. **Derbyshire** N&Q 7S:2 (1886) 215; [1890s] Uttley (1946) 134. **Yorkshire** Addy (1895) 63. **Lancashire** [c.1915] Corbridge (1964) 156–60; *Lancashire Lore* (1971) 6, 66. **Cumberland** *Folk-Lore* 40 (1929) 285. **Co. Durham** Leighton (1910) 62. **Wales** Jones (1930) 181. **Cardiganshire** *Folk-Lore* 55 (1944) 162. **N. Ireland** Foster (1951) 110–11. **Ireland** *Gent. Mag.* (1865) 700; Wilde (1888) 206. **Co. Meath** *Folk-Lore* 15 (1904) 460. **Co. Tyrone** *Lore & Language* 1:7 (1972) 11. **Guernsey/Alderney** MacCulloch MS (1864) 413; Carey (1903) 507; De Garis (1975) 117. **Unlocated** *Gent. Mag.* (1866) 73. N&Q 7S:1 (1886) 158; Igglesden (c.1932) 63. **General** Francis Bacon, *Sylva Sylvarum* (1627) sect. 912; N&Q 7S:2 (1886) 215.

hay carts

A cartload of hay would seem to be too common a sight in rural areas to excite much notice, but an odd set of beliefs held it to be unlucky, or lucky, depending on the informant:

A load of hay met with upon the road means bad luck, but you can overcome this misfortune by the vulgar habit of spitting. A load of straw has the reverse effect and good luck will follow the passer-by. Sussex *Sussex County Mag.* (1944)

Good luck superstitions – To meet a load of hay. Worcestershire Berkeley & Jenkins (1932)

If there is a consensus, it is that it is lucky or neutral to see the front, but unlucky to see the back of the vehicle, a motif which is recorded in a number of other contexts, from lambs in spring (*see* SHEEP) to NUNS. It is even more strange that this superstition appears to have sprung into existence in the twentieth century, without precedents, and was still being quoted in the 1980s:

I hate following a load of hay in my car. I'm constantly looking for one coming in the other direction. I think they cancel each other out. Somerset [1983] Opie & Tatem

Sussex *Sussex County Mag.* 18 (1944) 261. **Somerset** [1983] Opie & Tatem, 194. **Essex** [1953] Opie & Tatem, 194. **Worcestershire** Berkeley & Jenkins (1932) 34. **Wales** Igglesden (*c.*1932) 106. **Glamorganshire** [1952] Opie & Tatem, 194; Morris (1979) 144. **Monmouthshire** [1954] Opie & Tatem, 194.

headaches

It is to be expected that a problem such as a headache will have attracted numerous folk cures and home remedies, and there are therefore many prescriptions in the published folklore literature. Two stand out as reported more widely, however: a piece of HANGMAN'S ROPE and a SNAKESKIN.

I remember once to have seen, at Newcastle-upon-Tyne, after a person executed had been cut down, men climb up upon the gallows and contend for that part of the rope which remained, and which they wished to preserve for some lucky purpose or other. I have lately made the important discovery that it is reckoned as cure for the headache. Northumberland Brand (1849)

The connection between death and the cure of headaches has not been explained, but has been present in British tradition since at least the sixteenth century when Reginald Scot wrote of it in his *Discoverie of Witchcraft*. In classical times, Pliny also wrote of this same headache

cure, and it is likely that this was the direct source used by Scot and his contemporaries or immediate predecessors.

Two other examples continue the theme of the use of items associated with death:

Moss growing on a human skull, if dried, powdered, and taken as snuff, will cure the headache. Grose (1787)

The corner of a sheet that has wrapped a corpse is a cure for a headache if tied round the head. Ireland Wilde (1888)

The other widespread magical cure was to wear a snakeskin around the head, usually worn inside the hat, for convenience:

[From an old gardener] *Snakes seem pretty nigh exterminated now in Suffolk, but when I wer a boy there wer a few, and the avel of a snake – we used not to say skin, but snake's avel, we used – that wer said to be a sure cure for the head-ache as a boy, and I found a snake's avel and wore it in my hat nigh upon a year, until it dropped to powder, and I lost the head-ache; I don't know if it wer the snake's avel, or if I out-grew the head-ache.* Suffolk Gurdon (1893)

The snakeskin cure cannot boast such a long history as the hangman's rope, but it was certainly known in the late seventeenth century, as indicated by John Aubrey's description. See SNAKES: SKINS for other cures.

Other remedies include vinegar on the temples: vinegar and brown paper (best known for its appearance in the nursery rhyme 'Jack and Jill' from the early nineteenth century); fresh parsley; buttercups; and camomile.

There are also traditions linking headaches with POPPIES.

Hangman's rope: Herefordshire Leather (1912) 79. **Northumberland** Brand 3 (1849) 276–7. **Unlocated** Grose (1787) 56. **General** Scot (1584) Bk 12, Ch. 14; *Gent. Mag.* (1796) 636. **Classical** Pliny *Natural History* (AD 77) Bk 28, Para. 12.
Snakeskin: Sussex Aubrey, *Remaines* (1686/1880) 18. **Wiltshire** Jefferies (1878) Ch. 2. **Oxfordshire** *Oxf. FL Soc. Ann. Record* (1956) 13. **Worcestershire** Salisbury (1893) 70. **Cambridgeshire** N&Q 2S:1 (1856) 386. **Suffolk** Gurdon (1893) 23–4. **Norfolk** [*c.*1870s] Haggard (1935) 15–16. **Lincolnshire** [1850] Peacock (1877) 131; N&Q 1S:8 (1853) 382.
Miscellaneous: Devon *Devonshire Assoc.* 79 (1947) 47. **Bedfordshire** Marsom (1950) 182. **Norfolk** [*c.*1920] Wigby (1976) 66–7. **Lincolnshire** Peacock (1877) 131. **Wales** Trevelyan (1909) 321. **Ireland** Logan (1981) 49–52. **N. Ireland** Foster (1951) 60. **Co. Wexford** [1938] Ó Muirithe & Nuttall (1999) 97. **Co. Longford** *Béaloideas* 6 (1936) 266. **Co. Cavan** Maloney (1972) 75.

heart disease: casting the heart

A number of ill-defined medical problems and conditions, such as a person becoming suddenly listless or depressed, were put down to heart problems. The difficulty was to ascertain whether the condition was caused by physical heart disease or by witchcraft. Molten lead in cold water was at the core of two related procedures aimed at a correct diagnosis. The witchcraft detection technique is reported in early sources:

There are some who can distinguish such illnesses by means of a certain practice, which is as follows. They hold molten lead over the sick man, and pour it into a bowl of water. And if the lead condenses into some image, they judge that the sickness is due to witchcraft. And when such men are asked whether the image so formed is caused by the work of devils, or is due to some natural cause, they answer that it is due to the power of Saturn over lead, the influence of that planet being in other respects evil, and that the sun has a similar power over gold.
                                   Malleus Maleficarum (1486)

A knacke to know whether you be bewitched, or no – It is also expedient to learne how to know whether a sicke man be bewitched or no: this is the practice thereof. You must hold molten lead over the sicke bodie, and powre it into a porrenger full of water; and then, if there appeare upon the lead, anie image, you may know the partie is bewitched.   Scot (1584)

The procedure for heart disease, called 'casting the heart', began to be reported in the early eighteenth century, and in this form appears to have been exclusive to the Scottish Highlands and Islands, although a similar procedure using oatmeal instead of lead was known in Ireland and Wales (see HEART DISEASE: OATMEAL CURE). Details vary, but the molten lead and water were always the basis of the ceremony, and descriptions often brought out the belief that insanity was caused by a 'displaced' heart:

Heart disease was regarded as a serious thing, and the diagnosis for it was special. The patient was made to kneel on the floor by the fire, a sieve was placed on his head, and in the sieve was a large bowl filled with water. Into this bowl molten lead was poured through iron – the finger hole of a scissor blade or key was often used – and it was thought that one of the pieces of lead was sure to assume shape of a heart. If this rough shape had

within it a scallop or hole – then heart disease was a certainty, and the lead was to be melted again and poured into the water over and over again, until a neatly shaped piece bearing some resemblance to a heart was produced with no hole and no scallop, and only then was the patient considered cured. This cure is also resorted to in the case of nervousness succeeding a scare.   Highland Scotland Polson (1926)

The heart-shaped piece would then be worn inside the patient's clothing to complete the cure. It was also believed that a displaced heart could be caused by a sudden shock:

Mental derangement may occur from a sudden terror; a person is then said to be a cochall a' chridhe – his heart out of its shell or place. Then some wise person was called in to turn the heart back in its place.
                              Highland Scotland Macbain (1887/88)

Highland Scotland Macbain (1887/88) 259, 260; Polson (1926) 27–28, 33. Caithness Rinder (1895) 59. Banffshire Gregor (1874) 267–8. Orkney/Shetland Brand (1703) 62. Shetland [1774] Low (1879) 82; [c.1820] Black (1903) 150; Hibbert (1822/1891) 274; Spence (1899) 156–7. General Sprenger & Kramer, *Malleus Maleficarum* (1486) 87; Scot (1584) Bk 12, Ch. 18.

heart disease: oatmeal cure

A number of ailments were traditionally thought to be caused by problems of the heart, and there were several ways of diagnosing and curing them. A Scottish method, using molten lead, is described above (HEART DISEASE: CASTING THE HEART), but in Wales and Ireland a somewhat similar procedure used oatmeal:

Heart-disease may be cured by means of a powerful charm known only to a few, which is put in practice as follows: The patient sits on a low stool, having a cup full of dry oatmeal in his hand or on his knee. The operator, standing over him, takes hold of a lock of hair on his crown and gradually raises it up. At the same he walks round the patient and repeats the charm. If the patient really has the disease, the meal in the cup will sink as the hair is raised until it has almost disappeared. The charm should be worked before sunrise on three successive mornings, and the patient should be fasting. What remains over of the meal should be burnt. My informant said that her mother had seen this cure practised.
                                  Co. Cavan *Folk-Lore* (1908)

Pembrokeshire *Archaeologia Cambrensis* 89 (1934) 185. Co. Cavan *Folk-Lore* 19 (1908) 315–16. Co. Cavan/Co. Leitrim Logan (1963) 91.

heart-eaten

A form of ill-wishing based upon envy or spite:

When a man has deeply coveted but failed to obtain an animal, such as a cow or a horse, he is sometimes said to have 'heart-eaten' it. A heart-eaten being, it is said, will not prosper. A farmer near Bradfield wished to purchase a cow from a neighbour, but did not succeed in doing so. Shortly afterwards the owner of the cow told him that she had 'picked' her calf. 'Well, I didn't heart-eat her,' the farmer said.

Yorkshire Addy (1888) xxii

hedgehogs

It was very widely believed, in past centuries, that hedgehogs sucked milk from cows' udders as the cattle lay in the fields, and they were thus killed on sight by farmers and their workers:

D.G.A. told that her father is perfectly certain that, when a cow is asleep at night, a hedgehog will sometimes milk her dry.

Buckinghamshire [1918] *Folk-Lore*

Cows giving bloody milk was taken as particular evidence of a hedgehog's involvement:

In the morning the bullock gave bloud, her bag swelled and so continued bloud on that bigge till Oct 17; wee found ye hedge hog in ye field Oct 4 and kild it.

Essex Ralph Josselin, *Diary* (27 Sept. 1660)

The earliest documentary records show that the belief was the basis of official policy from Tudor times, and it probably existed before that time. Churchwardens' accounts from Ecclesfield, for example, quoted in N&Q (1851), show that regular payments were being made for dead hedgehogs, along with other vermin, from at least 1590 to the 1740s. While educated Victorian writers tried hard to eradicate this erroneous belief, it proved remarkably durable, and was still being claimed as true in many parts of the country well into the twentieth century.

Another story, even more unlikely than the idea of milk-stealing, is that hedgehogs steal fruit which has fallen from the tree by rolling on to it and thus sticking it to their spines to be carried back to their homes. In an early version in the Anglo-Norman *Bestiary* by Philip de Thaun (*c*.1120), quoted by Hazlitt (1905), the hedgehog climbs trees to knock the fruit – in this case grapes – to the ground first.

A few other more mundane traditions involving hedgehogs can be noted. The fat or oil of a cooked hedgehog was used for various ailments, including EARACHE and eczema (Oxfordshire *Oxf. FL Soc. Ann. Record* (1956) 13. **Worcestershire** Berkeley & Jenkins (1932) 36. **Norfolk** *Folk-Lore* 40 (1929) 119), while the flesh could be eaten instead of the more usual fried MOUSE for WHOOPING COUGH (*Gent. Mag.* (1779) 395). Hedgehogs, like SHREWS, were believed by some to have the power to disable farm animals by biting them (Lincolnshire Peacock (1877) 134; Watkins (1886) 10–11). The jawbone of a hedgehog could be carried in the pocket to ward off RHEUMATISM (Lincolnshire Gutch & Peacock (1908) 107) and TOOTHACHE (Wigtonshire *Folk-Lore* 26 (1915) 208–9).

Sucking cows: **Devon** *Devonshire Assoc.* 15 (1883) 99; [*c*.1918] *Devonshire Assoc.* 100 (1968) 366. **Wiltshire** Smith (1874) 329. **Essex** Ralph Josselin, *Diary* (27 Sept. 1660). **Buckinghamshire** [1918] *Folk-Lore* 43 (1932) 108. **Herefordshire** Leather (1912) 23. **Northamptonshire** N&Q 1S:3 (1851) 3–4. **Suffolk** N&Q 12S:5 (1919) 105. **Lincolnshire** *Folk-Lore* 28 (1917) 325–6. **Northern England** [1850s] *Denham Tracts* 2 (1895) 57. **Yorkshire** [1821] *Folk-Lore* 45 (1934) 159–60; N&Q 1S:4 (1851) 390; Nicholson (1890) 133. **Co. Durham** N&Q 6S:8 (1883) 32; Leighton (1910) 62. **Unlocated** *Gent. Mag.* (1779) 351; N&Q 6S:7 (1883) 309. **General** *The Mirror* (17 Mar. 1832) 179; N&Q 12S:5 (1919) 304.

hemp seed divination

One of the best known of the old LOVE DIVINATION ceremonies, reported regularly from 1685 onwards, in more or less the same format.

Another way in which a girl may catch a sight of her future husband is by going out into the churchyard on Midsummer Eve with a handful of hempseed, which she throws behind her without looking back, and as she do so, she says:

> *Hemp-seed I scatter/Hemp-seed I sow*
> *He that is my true love/Come after me and mow*

Then she runs away; but as she goes, she will, if she is bold enough to turn her head, see the wraith of her lover pursuing her with a scythe.

Somerset Poole (1877)

If, however, she is to die an old maid, she will be pursued by a coffin, or perhaps hear a bell. The conjuring of the future lover's WRAITH places this rite into a high level category of love divination, and the midnight, outdoor (often churchyard) setting ensured a high degree of nervous tension for the participants who, if traditional accounts are accurate, often became too frightened to carry it out to its end. When carried out by a group of girls in unison, the ritual may be only play-frightening, as in the case presented in Thomas Hardy's novel *The Woodlanders*, where the other villagers know that the ceremony is being tried, and gather to watch. The young men of the village position themselves to 'be seen' by the girls at the appropriate moment, or to intercept them in their inevitable headlong flight. On the other hand, stories are told about how serious consequences can come to young people who get involved in such goings-on:

The well-known 'sowing hempseed' over the left shoulder, walking round the churchyard at midnight in order to see one's future husband, must last have happened in Northleigh nearly a hundred years ago. Three girls crept out of their beds and went down to the churchyard on Christmas Eve. The eldest went first and performed the rite duly, but saw nothing. She died a spinster at the age of 83. The next oldest then started, but after a few minutes began shrieking terribly, saying that a coffin was following her, and got into a dreadful state. A few months later she died. Of course the third did not take her turn, and the rite was absolutely forbidden and no one has since been known to go through it.   Oxfordshire *Folk-Lore* (1929)

The raising of wraiths or spirits is always a dangerous game. What will happen to a girl who does not run fast enough to escape the wraith's scythe is not usually spelled out.

The overall structure remains remarkably constant, although details vary to a certain degree. The proper day for its practice is most often cited as Midsummer, but Hallowe'en, Christmas Eve, St Mark's, Valentine's Day, and St Agnes' Eve, are also mentioned. Occasionally, other types of seed are mentioned – barley, rape, lint, butter-dock, and even fernseed – but again the structure remains the same.

The early history of the ritual is puzzling. It springs apparently fully-formed into the documentary record in the late seventeenth century, and is reported regularly ever since, all over Britain and Ireland, and is so well known that its name is almost proverbial. Given that, it is strange that it does not appear to be mentioned in the works of the seventeenth-century playwrights and poets. It is just possible, of course, that the author of the *Mother Bunch* chapbook invented the whole thing, but the fact that it turns up, with different wording, in Aubrey's *Remaines* manuscript a year or so later argues against this idea. Again, although the rite fits into the general pattern of love divination ceremonies, no reason for the use of hemp seed, as such, has been found. Earlier slang and dialect references to hemp abound, but none seem at all relevant to love or marriage, and indeed the strongest slang connection is with the hangman's rope.

Sussex Latham (1878) 33. **Somerset** Poole (1877) 16. **Dorset** Hone, *Year Book* (1832) 588. **Devon** N&Q 3S:2 (1862) 62; Hewett (1892) 29; Crossing (1911) 147–8. **Cornwall** Couch (1871) 156. **Wiltshire** *Wilts. N&Q* 1 (1893–5) 155. **Berkshire** Salmon (1902) 422. **Oxfordshire** *Folk-Lore* 24 (1913) 79; *Folk-Lore* 34 (1923) 324; *Folk-Lore* 40 (1929) 382–3. **Herefordshire** Leather (1912) 61. **Warwickshire** Langford (1875) 18. **East Anglia** Forby (1830) 407–8; Varden (1885) 123. **Norfolk** [c.1820s] Henderson (1879) 104–5. **Shropshire** *Bye-Gones* (30 Nov. 1887) 463; Gaskell (1894) 264. **England** Addy (1895) 84–5. **Derbyshire** *Jnl Brit. Arch. Assoc.* (1851–2). **Lancashire** *Lancashire Lore* (1971) 49. **Wales** *Archaeologia Cambrensis* 4S:3 (1872) 334. **South Wales** *Monthly Packet* 26 (1863) 676–85. **Scotland** Robert Burns, footnote to poem 'Hallowe'en' (1786). **Caithness** Rinder (1895) 54. **Co. Longford** *Béaloideas* 6 (1936) 268. **Jersey** *Folk-Lore* 25 (1914) 248. **Guernsey** De Garis (1975) 22. **Unlocated** Aubrey, *Remaines* (1686/1880) 95; Halliwell (1849) 215. **Literary** *Mother Bunch's Closet Newly Broke Open* (1685); John Gay, *The Shepherd's Week* (1714); *Connoisseur* 56 (1755) 334; Thomas Hardy, *The Woodlanders* (1887) Ch. 20.

hen: crowing

see WHISTLING WOMAN/CROWING HEN.

hens

see WHISTLING WOMAN/CROWING HEN.

hernia

The most commonly recommended cure for hernia was to pass the sufferer through a tree (usually an ash) which had been split for the purpose:

A sapling ash is split, and the patient is passed, naked, through it three times at daybreak, each time with its face turned to the rising sun. The tree is then bound up tightly, and as the tree grows together again and the bark heals, the child recovers. This is also said to be a sovereign remedy for rickets, but in both cases seems to be only available on behalf of young children.
          East Anglia Varden (1885) 103

See ASH TREES for further examples and references.

hiccups

Although there are numerous prescriptions for curing the hiccups, it is strange that there seems to be very little in the way of other beliefs concerning them – in stark contrast to that other involuntary affliction the SNEEZE, for which the time, the duration, and the number all have definite meanings in numerous versions. There is the general statement 'When a child suffers from hiccough, he is said to be thriving' (**Wales** Trevelyan (1909)), and occasionally we are told something more:

When anyone happens to sneeze he is asked 'What's kirn hae ye been at?' A hiccough is also looked upon as an evidence of theft, but not necessarily of the same specific character.
                              Dumfriesshire Corrie (1890/91)

Regular motifs in hiccup cures include specific instructions for breathing, drinking, repeating a rhyme, prayer, or other formula, and making a sign of the cross. The annoying habit of trying to shock people out of the hiccups by making them jump is clearly not new:

A sudden fright cures the hiccough. We often used to jump out on each other, as children, when we had them, to make the one troubled with them to start violently; the cough was generally gone when we had recovered our tempers, which were always much ruffled in the operation. Sitting on the stairs and counting so many numbers, whilst holding the breath with the fingers placed in a certain position was another cure.
                              Wiltshire *Wilts. N&Q* (1893–5)

I am not troubled with the hickup, gentlemen,
You should bestow this fright on me.
                              Shirley, *Lady of Pleasure* (1637)

Other early sources imply that rather than a shock being meted out, some people opted for telling the sufferer some feigned ill news, or even falsely accusing them of some wrong-doing.

A traditional remedy was to recite a special rhyme – usually a set number of times:

Hickup-snickup, stand up, stick up
One drop, two drops – good for the hiccup (three times)   **Northern England** Brockett (1829)

Hecup, hecup
Three drops in a tea-cup (nine times)
                              Lincolnshire *Grantham Jnl* (22 June 1878)

This probably explains the line in *Twelfth Night*, when Sir Toby Belch, after an evening of carousing suddenly says 'Sneck up!' Another regular motif is to make a cross with a wetted finger – often involving a shoe, which is probably derived from a CRAMP cure:

To cure the hiccough – Wet the forefinger of the right hand with spittle, and cross the front of the left shoe or boot three times, repeating the Lord's Prayer backwards.   Cornwall Hunt (1865)

Drinking water is also prescribed, usually involving some complexity such as drinking out of the wrong side of the cup, or a certain number of sips, or grating some GOOD FRIDAY bread into the glass:

[Girls' school, 1876] Cure for hiccough. Stop your ears and take three (or nine) sips of water.
                              Co. Durham *Folk-Lore* (1909)

Sussex Latham (1878) 44–5. **Cornwall** Hunt (1865) 240; *Folk-Lore Jnl* 5 (1887) 202; *Cassell's Saturday Jnl* (1893). **Wiltshire** *Wilts. N&Q* 1 (1893–5) 316. **Gloucestershire** *Folk-Lore* 34 (1923) 157. **Worcestershire** *Folk-Lore* 20 (1909) 346. **Suffolk** Moor (1823) 167. **Lincolnshire** *Grantham Jnl* (22 June 1878). **Northern England** Brockett (1829) 153. **Lancashire** N&Q 4S:6 (1870) 211. **Co. Durham** [1876] *Folk-Lore* 20 (1909) 77. **Wales** Trevelyan (1909) 265. **Northeast Scotland** Gregor (1881) 49. **Dumfriesshire** Corrie (1890/91) 83. **Unlocated** Halliwell (1849) 208. **General** Robert Burton, *Anatomy of Melancholy* (1651) Pt 3, Sect. 2, Mem. 5, Sub. 2; Richard Bradley, *Family Dictionary* (1727); Thomas Birch, *Life of the Honorable Robert Boyle* (1744) 83; **Literary** Shakespeare, *Twelfth Night* (1602) 2:3; James Shirley, *Lady of Pleasure* (1637) 3:2.

holly: cures

see CHILBLAINS.

holly: dominant partner

The different between male (prickly) and female (smooth) holly allows a variation on the common theme of who will be the dominant partner in the marriage:

Part of the holly [at Christmas] should be of the smooth kind, and part prickly; and if this was so affairs in the house would go on through the coming year in an even prosperous way. Both kinds should, however, come in together. Should the prickly be first in the house, then the master would absolutely rule throughout the year; should the smooth come in first, then the wife would be mistress and master too. I have known of women who have made quite sure about the holly by gathering it on the previous day, and bringing it in the next morning as soon as it was fairly light.   Derbyshire N&Q (1881)

holly (*Ilex aquifolia*)

Holly was far and away the most popular plant for CHRISTMAS DECORATIONS, and is mentioned in that context in early records, such as the Churchwarden's Accounts, St Laurence, Reading (1505): 'Payed to Mackrell for the holy bush agayne Christmas'. Similarly, John Stow (1598) reported an occurrence at Christmas 1444 when a 'tempest of thunder and lightning', brought about by a malignant spirit, brought down a street decoration of holly and ivy.

As such, it came under various prohibitions covering decorations – in particular not being brought into the house before Christmas Eve, disagreements about whether or not it should be burnt afterwards, and differentiation between male and female varieties.

Outside the Christmas season, holly was held in a generally positive light, although unlucky to bring into the house. It was thought unlucky to cut it down or otherwise harm it:

about fifteen years ago two holly trees were cut down in the parish. Locals protested violently, saying this would produce poltergeist havoc.
Devon *Devonshire Assoc.* (1971)

and it was also thought to be immune from lightning strikes, and to protect against the harmful activities of witches:

Pieces of holly along with rowan were placed inside over the door of the stable to prevent the entrance of the nightmare.
Aberdeenshire *Folk-Lore Jnl* (1889)

The earliest reference to holly being protective seems to be John Aubrey (1686).

Holly was also widely recommended as a cure for CHILBLAINS.

Hampshire [1963] Opie & Tatem, 200; [1975] Opie & Tatem, 200. **Devon** *Devonshire Assoc.* 63 (1931) 124; *Devonshire Assoc.* 103 (1971) 268. **Surrey** [1987] Opie & Tatem, 200. **London** John Stow, *A Survey of London* (1598). **Essex** [c.1915] Mays (1969) 164; Hatfield (1994) 27. **Cambridgeshire** Porter (1969) 62. **Suffolk** Evans (1956) Ch. 24. **Lincolnshire** Rudkin (1936) 15. **Derbyshire** N&Q 6S:4 (1881) 509. **Northumberland** Henderson (1866) 78–9. **Montgomeryshire** Burne (1883) 195–6. **Aberdeenshire** *Folk-Lore Jnl* 7 (1889) 41. **Guernsey** MacCulloch MS (1864) 410. **Unlocated** Aubrey, *Remaines* (1686/1972) 231; N&Q 10S:5 (1906) 167. **Various** Vickery (1995) 180–2.

This tradition has only been recorded twice, in Victorian Derbyshire, and without further examples it is impossible to gauge how popular it was.

Derbyshire N&Q 4S:8 (1871) 506; N&Q 6S:4 (1881) 509.

holly: protected

A number of references indicate a tradition that holly should not be uprooted or in any way harmed:

There is a field with a holly tree standing somewhere near the centre. The field would be much easier to farm if the tree were removed; but the farmer will not have it touched as he believes that cutting down a holly-tree is always followed by bad luck.
Suffolk Evans (1956)

This belief was probably much more widespread than the few examples recorded below. One informant offered a reason, but again it is not known whether this was widely believed or simply a local explanation:

If hung in the hall, holly would ward off witches, but it should never be cut or burnt because,

believed to be the tree on which Christ was crucified, Christ's blood and tears would flow with the sap.
Essex [c.1920] Ketteridge & Mays

Hampshire [1975] Opie & Tatem, 200. **Devon** *Devonshire Assoc.* 91 (1959) 200; *Devonshire Assoc.* 98 (1966) 88. **Surrey** [1987] Opie & Tatem, 200. **Essex** Ketteridge & Mays (1972) 138–9. **Suffolk** Evans (1956) Ch. 24.

holly: unlucky indoors

It is not always easy to separate traditions about holly per se, from those about CHRISTMAS DECORATIONS and general EVERGREENS, but certainly there were many who disliked bringing holly into the house at any time other than Christmas:

Holly and ivy are used for decorating at Christmas, and it is very unlucky to bring holly into the house before; all evergreens must be taken down and burnt before Candlemas Day.
Herefordshire Leather (1912)

There is a tendency, noticeable in many CALENDAR CUSTOMS, but especially at Christmas, for items closely associated with a particular festival to be supported by traditions about good luck (e.g. lucky to eat mince pies), and also ill luck if used outside the allotted time. But in the case of holly, which has protective qualities if left outside the house (*see above*), there seems to be a different, but at present ill-defined, impetus at work. Some people confused the word 'holly' with 'holy':

Holly was never brought into the house before Christmas Eve, but it was stored under a roof near. Neither was holly or mistletoe burned on the house-fire. After Twelfth Night there must be no trace of leaf or berry left indoors. It was a holy decoration, not to be used for secular purposes.
                                    Derbyshire [1890s] Uttley

On the other hand, in some parts, 'holy holly' was the variegated variety with white-spotted leaves:

The white spots are where Mary, when she was nursing the Baby, spilt some of the milk on the leaves.   **Devon** *Devonshire Assoc.* (1931)

It is noticeable that there is no sign of this unlucky side to holly before the late nineteenth century.

Devon N&Q 10S:12 (1909) 66; *Devonshire Assoc.* 57 (1926) 109–10; *Devonshire Assoc.* 63 (1931) 124. **Oxfordshire** [1920s] Harris (1969) 125. **Herefordshire** [c.1895] *Folk-Lore* 39 (1928) 386; Leather (1912) 20. **Worcestershire** [1900] *Folk-Lore* 20 (1909) 343. **Shropshire** Burne (1883) 244–5. **Rutland** N&Q 4S:12 (1873) 467. **Derbyshire** [1890s] Uttley (1946) 134. **Yorkshire** *Folk-Lore* 21 (1910) 225. **Wales** Jones (1930) 181. **Guernsey** De Garis (1975) 118. **General** Hoggart (1957) Ch. 2.

holly wood

Holly and ivy are often linked, and even confused, in traditional thought. A handful of sources, for example, report a tradition that WHOOPING COUGH can be cured by the patient drinking from a vessel made of IVY WOOD, and one makes the same claim for the holly:

It is said by the inhabitants of the forest of Bere, East Hants., that new milk drunk out of a cup made of the wood of the variegated holly is a cure for the hooping cough.   **Hampshire** N&Q 1S:4 (1851) 227

Holy Innocents' Day
(28 December)

In the Christian churches, the day dedicated to the first-born children massacred by Herod (Matthew 2:1–18). Also known as Childermas

Day. To commemorate that awful event, the day was a 'dismal' day (*see* DAYS: UNLUCKY), with muffled peals of bells and, despite falling within the twelve days of Christmas, a subdued and penitential air.

The official religious background is reflected in superstitions surrounding the day, which was generally considered very unlucky:

No salting of pork or even killing of a pig, and no nails or hair cut, or trouble ensues. All donkeys have a day's holiday and an extra feed. This is particularly noticeable in the Clovelly district, but it is observed also in Cornwall and at Tavistock. It has reference to the Blessed Virgin Mary's flight into Egypt. Most Nonconformist owners still observe this custom, and believe that, if omitted, bad luck will follow.
                              Devon *Devonshire Assoc.* (1935)

If anything was started on the day, it would never be finished or would go disastrously wrong, fishermen refused to leave harbour, and, in the home, no major housework was attempted and in particular no WASHING done. The latter would be certain to result in a death in the family.

Not only was the day itself unlucky, but the day of the week on which it fell would also be unlucky for the coming year, and in some communities that day would be referred to as a 'cross' day all year. The earliest references are from the early seventeenth century, with Carew's description of Cornwall in 1602, and Melton's attack on superstitions in his *Astrologaster*:

That it is not good to put on a new sute, pare ones nailes, or begin any thing on a Childermas day.
                                                    Melton (1620)

And even in the late twentieth century a few people still remembered not to wash on the day.

Somerset [1923] Opie & Tatem, 70. **Cornwall** Carew (1602) 32; Couch (1871) 163; *Old Cornwall* 2 (1931–6) 39; [1985] Opie & Tatem, 70. **Devon** *Devonshire Assoc.* 59 (1927) 172; *Devonshire Assoc.* 67 (1935) 142; [c.1915] Lakeham (1982) 46. **Gloucestershire** Hartland (1895) 53. **Herefordshire** Duncomb (1804) 58; Leather (1912) 110. **East Anglia** Forby (1830) 404–5. **Shropshire** Burne (1883) 408. **Northern England** Brockett (1829) 67. **Yorkshire** Young (1817) 880. **Northumberland** N&Q 1S:12 1855) 201. **Aran Islands** *Procs. Royal Irish Academy* 3S:2 (1891–3) 820. **Co. Clare** N&Q 4S:12 (1873) 185. **General** Melton (1620); R. Holme, *Academy of Armory* 3 (1688) 131; Aubrey, *Miscellanies* (1696/1857) 3. **Literary** Addison, *Spectator* (8 Mar. 1711).

holy stones

see STONES: HOLED.

---

honeysuckle (*Lonicera periclymenum*)

The honeysuckle, or woodbine, is one of the many plants which some people regarded as unlucky to bring indoors. Usually, no reason was given for a flower being unlucky, but Enid Porter provided an interesting explanation in this case:

The flower was never brought into a Fenland home where there were young girls; it was thought to give them erotic dreams. If any was brought indoors, then a wedding would follow.
Cambridgeshire Porter (1969)

The plant was also occasionally reported as useful in cures, including jaundice (Co. Leitrim/Co. Cavan Vickery (1995)) and headaches (East Anglia Hatfield (1994)).

Essex [*c.*1920] Ketteridge & Mays (1972) 138. Cambridgeshire Porter (1969) 45. East Anglia Hatfield (1994) 39–40. Cheshire Vickery (1995) 188. Dyfed Vickery (1995) 188. Scotland Vickery (1995) 188. Co. Leitrim/Co. Cavan Vickery (1995) 188. General Baker (1996) 79.

---

horse hairs: animated

An extremely widespread and tenacious belief held that horse hairs placed in water would turn, after a certain time, into live eels (or, less commonly, snakes or worms). This notion was certainly current in the sixteenth century – Churchward's *Discourse of Rebellion* (1570) and Harrison's *Description of England* (1587) refer to it, and it is possibly the basis for Shakespeare's lines in *Antony & Cleopatra*:

Much is Breeding
Which, like the courser's hair, hath yet but life
And not a serpent's poison.

Despite regular debunking by rationalists and scientists over the years, the belief continued to be prevalent all over Britain and Ireland at least to the end of the nineteenth century and probably into the twentieth. A number of writers report that in their childhood they were firmly convinced of the absolute truth of the notion, and claim to have tried out the experiment (or to have known others who had done so) to their own satisfaction. Nevertheless, the belief's longevity cannot simply be attributed to the credulity of youth. Many writers claim that most working-class adults were firmly convinced:

Every [English] *peasant I ever spoke to on the subject has absolutely affirmed that horsehairs turn into eels,*   Various N&Q (1886)

and even some well educated writers showed extreme reluctance to let go of the belief in adulthood. Southey and Wordsworth were convinced of its truth, for example, and Cobbett referred to it as a 'notoriously true' fact.

Several rational explanations have been suggested – for example that baby eels burrow into hollow horse hairs, or that water lice clinging to hairs give them the appearance of life. The most likely, however, is simply that small hair-like water creatures, such as *Gordius aquaticus*, were assumed to have been generated from horse hairs.

Correspondents in N&Q (1886–7) also claimed the belief was widespread in Germany, Russia, and the USA.

England N&Q 7S:2 (1886) 24, 230. Cornwall N&Q 7S:2 (1886) 110–11. Worcestershire Salisbury (1893) 78. Midland England N&Q 7S:2 (1886) 110–11. Derbyshire N&Q 7S:2 (1886) 230–1; N&Q 2S:7 (1859) 98. Northern England [1850s] *Denham Tracts* 2 (1895) 29. Cumberland [1813] *Life and Correspondence of Robert Southey* 4 (1850) 35. Co. Durham Brockie (1886) 138–9; Leighton (1910) 49. Northumberland N&Q 7S:2 (1886) 111. Scotland N&Q 2S:7 (1859) 18; N&Q 7S:2 (1886) 24, 230. Galloway Mactaggart (1824) 312. Roxburghshire N&Q 7S:2 (1886) 110. Dumfriesshire Corrie (1890/91) 81. Orkney [1774] Low (1879) 58. Co. Down/Co. Antrim N&Q 7S:2 (1886) 294. General Churchward, *Discourse of Rebellion* (1570), quoted N&Q 7S:2 (1886) 24; Harrison (1587) 320–1; *The Holy State* (1642), Bk 2, Ch. 6, Sec. 4, p. 71, quoted N&Q 7S:2 (1886) 110; Swinnock, *Christian Man's Calling* (1668), quoted N&Q 2S:6 (1858) 322; Cobbett (1830) 'Across Surrey'; N&Q 2S:7 (1859) 18–19. Literary Shakespeare, *Antony & Cleopatra* (1608) 1:2; USA *Popular Science Monthly* (July 1886).

Horseman's Word

In many arable farming areas in the nineteenth century, the workers who handled the horses were the acknowledged aristocrats of the agricultural workforce, who possessed skills which their employers could not match nor easily do without. The horsemen were proud of their status and jealous of their rights, and in northeast Scotland one result was a semi-secret trade society called the Horseman's Word. This was partly modelled on the Freemasons, but also on a previous trade organization called the Miller's Word. Members of the Horseman's Word had to undergo initiation ceremonies which often parodied religious rites, had to swear oaths of secrecy and brotherhood, and generally behaved as all men-only, working-class social groups did, and do.

Members encouraged outsiders in the idea that the horsemen possessed secret magical charms and procedures for controlling horses, but it is clear that what was really shared, apart from drink and comradeship, was genuine skills rather than magic potions. The society also functioned to a certain degree as a trade union, and young horse-workers were keen to be accepted into its ranks.

Records of the Horseman's Word in England are almost entirely confined to the eastern counties, particularly Suffolk. In contrast to the Scottish evidence, reports from England are vague concerning any organized fraternity, and if such existed at all it was a much weaker organization than in Scotland. Emphasis here was on a supposed magical rite which the novice had to undertake to become a member of the secret society and to obtain the magical item – a frog or toad's bone – which would be the basis of his power (*see* TOADS/FROGS: MAGIC BONE). This ceremony explains why skilled horse-workers were often called 'toadmen'. Nearly all the evidence is in the form of traditional narratives, reporting specific instance in which, typically, the horseman demonstrates his skill in the face of opposition or disbelief from his employers, the police, or other figures of authority, often in mundane everyday settings:

A farmer had a horseman who couldn't pass a pub. So he told the policeman at B— to look out for him: if he ever saw the horses standing outside a pub, to get the horseman out of it and send him home. One day the policeman saw this farmer's horses standing outside The Fox. He went inside and said to the horseman: 'You better get back to the farm.' 'Yes, I will: when I'm ready.' 'If you don't get going now I'll take the wagon and the horses back myself.' 'Right, in that case I'll be here till stop-tap.' The policeman went out and tried to lead the horses back to the farm. But he couldn't get them to move an inch. He returned to the pub and told the horseman: 'I can't shift 'em.' 'No more you will. They'll go when I'm ready', and he quietly finished his drink and took the horses home without further trouble. Suffolk Evans (1960)

Basic skills included 'drawing' a horse, working successfully with untrained or dangerous animals, working horses without reins or commands, and, as in this story, rendering horses immobile. As suggested, the horse-handling skills were a combination of experience and body language,

but some authorities suggested that the men used secret concoctions of herbs which acted on the animal's acute sense of smell. But the real mystery which featured in many of the stories was the power of the 'word' – the supposed magical charm which could be whispered in the horse's ear, and which was imparted to members of the fraternity only.

Long before the formation of the Horseman's Word societies, certain individuals had reputations as uncannily good horse-handlers, and some of the earlier references identify these as 'whisperers'. The earliest concerns John Young, a Sussex 'horse courser' in 1648, who could 'tame the fiercest bull, or the wildest horse, by whispering in its ear' (Méric Casaubon, *Treatise Proving Spirits* (1672)). Another seventeenth-century example demonstrates that the immobilization motif was already in force:

In Renfrewshire, Thomas Lindsay, a young lad apprehended on a charge of witchcraft, in 1664, boasted that he would for a halfpenny make a horse stand still in the plough, at the word of command by turning himself widdershins or contrary to the course of the sun.
Grant, *Narratives of the Sufferings of a Young Girl* (1698)

Dalyell also relates the story of another 'whisperer' in the south of Ireland, named Sullivan, about 1800, who was 'celebrated for the remarkable control which he could exercise immediately over vicious horses'.

Sussex [1648] Méric Casaubon, *Treatise Proving Spirits* (1672) 107, quoted Dalyell (1834) 445. **Cambridgeshire** *Folk-Lore* 64 (1953) 424–6; Porter (1969) 55–9. **Suffolk** Evans (1960) 204–39. **Northeast Scotland** Carter (1979) 154–6. **Renfrewshire** [1664] Francis Grant, *Narratives of the Sufferings of a Young Girl* (1698) 41, quoted Davidson (1956) 71. **Ireland** [c.1800] Dalyell (1834) 445. **General** *Gwerin* 1:2 (1956) 67–74; Evans (1979); *Fortean Times* 83 (1995) 39–40; Hutton (1999) 61–4.

horseradish (*Armoracia rusticana*)

Horseradish was believed to be effective in curing a number of ailments, particularly by people on the eastern side of England, including, among others, lumbago, catarrh, cuts, GOUT, headaches, and TOOTHACHE. For the latter, it was applied in a surprising manner:

To cure the toothache, place a poultice of finely-scraped horseradish on the wrist of the right hand, if the tooth aching be on the left side of the mouth; if on the right side the poultice must be

horses

Horses feature in a wide range of superstitions and traditions, which reflects the vital part they have played in human life in the past. Foals feature with other young farm animals, such as lambs, in beliefs that it is lucky if you see the first one in the spring facing you, but unlucky if you see its tail first. White horses, too, were lucky if you carried out certain little ceremonies, or counted one hundred of them. Piebald horses had curative powers, but their riders were even more important, as they could invariably tell worried parents how to cure their children's WHOOPING COUGH. How the riders knew is not explained. Workers with horses were often reputed to have strange powers, and some were believed to be organized in secret societies (*see* HORSEMAN'S WORD). There are also very strong traditions in veterinary medicine and weather lore, and it was widely believed that horses thrived best if a GOAT or DONKEY were kept with them.

Horses and cows, as the most valuable animals in the farm economy, were particularly prone to witchcraft and ill-wishing. Spite focused largely on a cow's milk yield, but the main evidence of horses being bewitched was their refusal to work. Witches could make horses stand stock still and refuse to budge until released – a power which was also credited to those who knew the Horseman's Word. But horses were far more intelligent than cows and, together with dogs and cats, were thought to be sensitive to ghosts and other supernatural forces. The fact that horses could easily be 'overlooked' (bewitched) meant that one had to be particularly careful when BUYING AND SELLING them.

It is very unlucky to refuse a good offer for a horse. If you do, some accident will befall the animal shortly afterwards.　　　Shropshire Burne (1883)

Horses were believed to have been HAG-RIDDEN when they were found wild-eyed and exhausted, their coats matted with sweat as if they had been ridden hard all night, even though the stable door was locked all the time. STUMBLING was long regarded as a bad omen, especially when starting on a journey, but earlier writers show that a horse stumbling was particularly feared. John Melton included it in his list of superstitions in 1620, and a few years later John Webster included it with other well-known omens:

How superstitiously we mind our evils!
The throwing down salt, or crossing of a hare,
Bleeding at nose, the stumbling of a horse,
Or singing of a cricket, are of power
To daunt whole man in us.

Webster, *Duchess of Malfi* (1623)

Horses seem particularly susceptible to being whispered to. Again, some of the 'secret' methods of the Horseman's Word involved whispering:

To tame a horse – Whisper the Creed in his right ear on a Friday, and again in his left ear on a

placed on the left wrist, and the pain at once ceases.　　　Lincolnshire N&Q (1868)

The plant was also reputed to be an antidote to hard-boiled eggs, which were widely believed to be indigestible and dangerous to eat. In 1718, the Revd John Thomlinson recorded a story in his diary about a man who bet his whole estate that he could 'eat two eggs after every dinner for a year and never drink till an hour after', but he died in the attempt. Thomlinson continued:

He was opened, and a hard thing about his heart – which his relation kept – made a cane head of it, lying near some radishes it dissolved – he laid the same wager with the doctor for the same estate, and won it, the eating of radishes dissolved the eggs.

Diary of the Revd John Thomlinson (1 Apr. 1718) in
Surtees Society 118 (1910)

Cambridgeshire *Folk-Lore* 69 (1958) 118; Porter (1969) 12. **East Anglia** Hatfield (1994) various. **Lincolnshire** N&Q 4S:1 (1868) 550; N&Q 10S:2 (1904) 446–7. **England** (various) Vickery (1995) 197.

horses: first foal seen

An extremely widespread belief holds that the first new lamb you see in spring should be facing you for luck (*see* SHEEP: FIRST LAMB SEEN) and exactly the same was said of foals, although much less often:

Take notice how the first foal of the year that you see stands. If it is with the head towards you, good luck will be yours through the year; if the tail is towards you, bad luck.　　　Suffolk Gurdon (1893)

The basic principle of BEGINNINGS is in operation here, as spring was one of the most important symbolic times for the testing of good or bad luck for the year. As with the lamb version, the earliest reference to the foal belief is only in 1826.

An interesting variant was reported from Glasgow, on the same principle:

The first plough seen in the season, or the first met when going upon any business, if the horses'

Wednesday. Do this weekly until he is tamed; for so he will be.   Ireland Wilde (1888)

Despite many wild theories, and taken as a whole, there is not the slightest evidence that any of these beliefs is a survival of an ancient horse-worship cult, if such a thing ever existed in Britain. Apart from the lucky HORSESHOE, none of the main horse beliefs have been found before the nineteenth century. Out of dozens of other reported beliefs and traditions, the following is a representative sample:

At Weobley it is still believed that horses and cattle do not eat on Saints' Days. An old man said lately to his master, 'Be it a saant's daay, mais-ter? Them cattle 'anna touched a bent all daay'.
          Herefordshire *Folk-Lore* (1912)

A mare in foal must never assist in drawing a corpse to the grave. If she be permitted to do so, she and her foal, or a member of her owner's family, will die within the ensuing twelvemonth.
          Lincolnshire Gutch & Peacock (1908)

You must never yoke or work a horse on Good Friday. It is lucky to take a horse through your house.   England Addy (1895)

Whitsuntide is a most unlucky time; horses foaled then will grow up dangerous and kill some one.   Ireland Wilde (1888)

If a horse stood and looked through a gateway or along a road where a bride or bridegroom dwelt, it was a very bad omen for the future happiness of the intending couple. The one dwelling in that direction would not live long. If a horse neighed at the door of a house, it boded sickness to some of the inmates.
          Western Scotland Napier (1879)

Devon *Devonshire Assoc.* 15 (1883) 99; *Devonshire Assoc.* 85 (1953) 217; *Devonshire Assoc.* 88 (1956) 257; *Devonshire Assoc.* 92 (1960) 371–2; *Devonshire Assoc.* 98 (1966) 89; *Devonshire Assoc.* 100 (1968) 366. Herefordshire Leather (1912) 23; *Folk-Lore* 23 (1912) 351–2. Warwickshire Bloom (*c.*1930) 42. Northamptonshire Sternberg (1851) 166. East Anglia Forby (1830) 415. Norfolk N&Q 1S:6 (1852) 480. Lincolnshire Peacock (1877) 54, 232; Gutch & Peacock (1908) 152; Rudkin (1936) 23, 27. Shropshire Burne (1883) 208. England Addy (1895) 69, 114. Derbyshire [1890s] Uttley (1946) 128–9; Addy (1895) 132. Yorkshire N&Q 1S:6 (1852) 602; N&Q 4S:2 (1868) 557; *Leeds Mercury* (4 Oct. 1879). Wales Trevelyan (1909) 317, 323. Scotland *Edinburgh Mag.* (Nov. 1818) 412; Chambers (1826) 284; N&Q 9S:7 (1901) 193. Highland Scotland Polson (1926) 31–2. Western Scotland Napier (1879) 114. Galloway Mactaggart (1824) 210–11. Ireland Wilde (1888) 140–1, 193, 202. N. Ireland Foster (1951) 59. Co. Longford *Béaloideas* 6 (1936) 265. Guernsey [*c.*1800] MacCulloch MS (1864) 396. Unlocated N&Q 1S:2 (1850) 515; Igglesden (*c.*1932) 107. General Melton (1620). Literary John Webster, *Duchess of Malfi* (1623) 2:3.

heads are turned towards you, it is lucky; if going from you ill luck.   Glasgow [*c.*1820] Napier

Worcestershire/Shropshire *Gent. Mag.* (1855) 384–6. Suffolk Gurdon (1893) 136. Welsh border Burne (1883) 215. Anglesey N&Q 6S:2 (1880) 258. Highland Scotland Chambers (1826) 284; Macbain (1887/88) 265. Caithness Sutherland (1937) 104. Dumfriesshire Corrie (1890/91) 80. Glasgow [*c.*1820] Napier (1864) 396–7.

horses: piebald

The most common superstition concerning the piebald horse was the strange belief that a sure cure for WHOOPING COUGH could be obtained by asking the rider of such a horse to recommend something, and following his instructions to the letter. The piebald also shares with the white horse the attribute that it is lucky to meet one, provided certain precautions were taken:

To meet a piebald horse was lucky. If two such horses were met apart, the one after the other,

and if then the person who met them were to spit three times, and express any reasonable wish, it would be granted within three days.
          Western Scotland Napier (1879)

In different versions, SPITTING was a regular feature, while some said you had to avoid seeing the horse's tail, or carry out more complex feats:

I never heard of luck connected with meeting white horses; but I remember a tradition of my childhood that if you could touch a piebald horse with a man on it, accidentally met, or else curtsey nine times backwards, whatever you wished for while doing so would come to pass. It required some dexterity to perform either feat unremarked while taking a constitutional in Hyde Park.
          London N&Q (1882)

Nevertheless, references to white horses in this context outnumber those to piebalds over two to one. The first concrete description of the lucky piebald horse was the Scottish reference quoted above, published in 1879. But the 1882 London reference, also quoted, is set in the writer's childhood and must therefore be at least a decade or two earlier. Again, this is about the same time the white horse beliefs appeared on the scene.

Compare HORSES: WHITE/GREY.

Somerset [1950] Opie & Tatem, 306. London [1965] Opie & Tatem, 306. Essex [1983] Opie & Tatem, 306. Oxfordshire *Folk-Lore* 42 (1931) 293; *Oxf. & Dist. FL Soc. Ann. Record* (1955) 16. London N&Q 6S:6 (1882) 357. Cambridgeshire Porter (1969) 53. Norfolk Randell (1966) 94. Lincolnshire Rudkin (1936) 22. England Addy (1895) 101. Shropshire Burne (1883) 208. Yorkshire Blakeborough (1898) 131. Lancashire/Westmorland [c.1939] *Folk-Lore* 64 (1953) 294. Northumberland Bosanquet (1929) 80. Western Scotland Napier (1879) 120–1. Unlocated N&Q 11S:3 (1911) 217–8; Wright (1928) 65; Igglesden (c.1932) 108.

horses: white/grey

A very widely reported belief and accompanying action was carried out, mainly by children, in response to seeing a white (or grey) horse. Descriptions could be couched in positive or negative terms, probably depending a great deal on the temperament of the individual, as in 'White horses are unlucky, unless you do so-and-so', or 'White horses are lucky if you do so-and-so':

It was considered unlucky to meet a white horse, and to avert this bad luck, spitting was considered the necessary remedy. Hence the expression 'Spit for a white horse'.

Montgomeryshire Hamer (1877)

If you meet a white horse, cross your thumbs and wish; the wish will certainly come true. Or bend down and make a cross on your shoe with your finger, then you will have a present.

Herefordshire Leather (1912)

Some had a rhyme:

*White horse, white horse
Hung upon a tree
White horse, white horse
Bring luck to me*

Devon *Devonshire Assoc.* (1959)

The most common actions for averting bad luck were SPITTING, sometimes three times, often 'over the finger', or making the shape of a cross with spittle on the shoe.

Documentary evidence for this belief only starts about 1850, but one informant, writing from Devon in 1852 (N&Q 1S:6) described the custom in his 'own boyhood', so this may well

put it back into the 1830s or beyond. It was collected in most parts of England and Wales, less often in Scotland, but so far not in Ireland.

Another children's custom, noted much more rarely, was to count the white horses seen, and make a wish when you reached one hundred. For children's author Alison Uttley, who grew up in Derbyshire in the 1890s, the target was even more complicated:

White horses brought us luck, the village children said. We used to count them and save them up, as children now count cars. A hundred white horses, a blind man, a chimney sweep, and a fiddler together brought the power of making a wish. To make a wish that would really come true was something much desired. Each day we looked out of the train window on the way to the grammar school and counted the white horses we saw in the fields and roads. The same horse must not be counted twice, and it took several weeks to make an original hundred . . . When we had made the wish we began again.

Derbyshire [c.1890s] Uttley

A number of other white-horse beliefs have been recorded once or twice, including the following: to dream of a white horse meant a death or a wedding (**Shropshire** Burne (1883) 264); white horses could be fairy horses (**Guernsey** De Garis (1975) 125); grey is an unlucky colour for a racehorse (**Unlocated** N&Q 6S:9 (1884) 266); to buy grey horses is unlucky (**Welsh Gypsies** Jarman (1991) 185); and two Irish references indicate that it was bad luck for a funeral to meet someone on a white horse (**Ireland** Wilde (1888) 213. **Co. Longford** *Béaloideas* 6 (1936) 260.)

Compare HORSES: PIEBALD.

Kent *Folk-Lore* 25 (1914) 367. Devon? N&Q 1S:6 (1852) 193; Hewett (1900) 50; *Devonshire Assoc.* 57 (1926) 111; *Devonshire Assoc.* 61 (1929) 126; *Devonshire Assoc.* 91 (1959) 200. Essex [c.1939] *Folk-Lore* 64 (1953) 294. Oxfordshire N&Q 6S:6 (1882) 9; [1920s] Harris (1969) 125. Gloucestershire [1956] Opie & Tatem, 445. Herefordshire Leather (1912) 23, 61. Warwickshire Langford (1875) 11 Midland England N&Q 1S:1 (1850) 451. Birmingham N&Q 6S:6 (1882) 178. Suffolk *Folk-Lore* 35 (1924) 350. Derbyshire [c.1890s] Uttley (1946) 131. Lincolnshire Cole (1886) 167; Rudkin (1936) 18; Sutton (1992) 144. Shropshire Burne (1883) 208. England Addy (1895) 80, 102. Yorkshire Henderson (1866) 86; N&Q 6S:6 (1882) 178; Nicholson (1890) 43 [1949] Opie & Tatem, 445. Lancashire [c.1939] *Folk-Lore* 64 (1953) 294. Westmorland [c 1939] *Folk-Lore* 64 (1953) 294. Wales Jones (1930) 143. Mid-Wales Davies (1911) 215. Montgomeryshire Hamer (1877) 260–1. Carmarthenshire [1985] Opie & Tatem, 445. Orkney N&Q 10S:12 (1909) 483–4. Guernsey De Garis (1975) 125. Unlocated N&Q 3S:7 (1865) 432–3.

horses: white legs

Good or bad luck in a horse can depend on how many white 'stockings' appear on its legs, and a commonly quoted rhyme lays down the rules:

One white leg buy a horse
Two white legs try a horse
Three white legs look about a horse
Four white legs go without a horse.
Unlocated N&Q (1882)

The wording varies from version to version, but they all agree on the progression from one to four and good to bad. No published account gives any reason for this prejudice against white feet. A slightly confusing description, published in *Notes & Queries* in 1877, indicates a more complex prescription, but it has not yet been possible to confirm this from any other source:

It is very lucky to own a horse whose fore legs are both equally 'white stockinged', but if one fore and one hind leg on the same side are white, it is unlucky. It is unlucky when one leg only of the four is 'white stockinged', but if opposite legs, as off fore and near hind, are white, very lucky.
Unlocated N&Q (1877)

All the references listed date from a restricted period, 1875–1901.

Devon? *Western Antiquary* 9 (1889–90) 190. **Warwickshire** Langford (1875) 22. **Derbyshire** N&Q 6S:6 (1882) 357. **Unlocated** N&Q 5S:7 (1877) 64; N&Q 6S:6 (1882) 357; N&Q 6S:5 (1882) 427; N&Q 9S:7 (1901) 111.

horseshoes

The horseshoe is without doubt the most instantly recognizable graphic symbol of good luck in Britain and Ireland today. Horseshoe shapes appear routinely on good-luck cards, confetti and other wedding paraphernalia, brooches, charm bracelets and other jewellery, advertisements, and anywhere that the concept of luck needs to be graphically represented. We all understand it at a glance, and it is challenged only in the good-luck context by the SHAM-ROCK, CLOVER, and CROSSED FINGERS.

Historically speaking, there are two aspects to horseshoe superstitions. Everybody knows that it is lucky to nail a horseshoe to your door, and many still do so, but less well known today is the notion that it is lucky to *find* a horseshoe. Indeed, many of the earlier references make it clear that it is only a shoe that has been accidentally found

that is worth nailing to the door or keeping for luck:

Horse-shoes that are found by the owner have ten times the power of those acquired in other ways, while one that is bought is useless.
Unlocated *Folk-Lore* (1942)

Some even maintain that the found shoe must still have some nails in it:

I picked up a horseshoe the other day and brought it home, and was struggling to remove two ill-clenched nails when Mrs. Wrightson assured me it was very lucky to find a horseshoe nail, so I let them be.
Yorkshire [1965] Opie & Tatem

Many thought it was lucky to carry the shoe, or something associated with it, around with them:

As a preventative against being bewitched you must carry some nails (the contents of one shoe) from a stallion's foot in your pocket. These must be constantly carried about, never omitting to take them with you when changing garments.
Norfolk Fulcher Collection (c.1895)

The earliest reference to the luck of finding a horseshoe dates from a late fourteenth century manuscript (C. R. Rypon MS Harl. 4894, quoted Opie & Tatem 203–4) – two hundred years before the first mention of nailing shoes up for protection, and on this evidence it is quite possible that the latter was simply a development of the former.

There were other ceremonies which could be carried out when you found your shoe:

If you see a horse-shoe, or a piece of old iron, on your path, take it up, spit on it and throw it over your shoulder, framing your wish at the same time. Keep the wish secret, and you will have it in time.
Northern England Henderson (1866)

The earliest reference to nailing a shoe on the door appeared in the late sixteenth century:

to shew you how to prevent and cure all mischiefs wrought by these charms and witchcrafts . . . One principal way is to nail a horse shoe at the inside of the outmost threshold of your house, and so you shall be sure no witch will have power to enter thereinto. And if you mark it, you shall find that rule observed in many country houses.
Scot (1584)

This meaning of a barrier to witches remained remarkably constant until the late nineteenth century when it began to degenerate into the colourless 'for luck' meaning it has for most people today. Other regularly reported sites for

The horseshoe regularly served as a good-luck symbol on greetings cards from at least the First World War onwards (this example is c.1920). In almost every case, the shoe was shown with its points downwards.

protective horseshoes include stables, fishing-boats, cradles, and milk-churns:

Country wenches, when they experience any peculiar difficulty in making butter, will sometimes drop into the churn a horse-shoe heated, believing the cream to be spell-bound, and that this operation will destroy the charm.

Gent. Mag. (1823)

There has been continued controversy about the right way to hang the horseshoe for at least three hundred years. There is no definitive answer, as both ways have had their stalwart defenders. Not all sources give attention to this detail, and when they do their description is not always clear to the present generation, who know so little about horse's feet and the way they were shod. Many refer to the heel(s) and toe of the shoe – the heel being the open prongs. The earliest known description, in J. Blagrave's *Astrological Practice* (1671) maintained that the heel must be upwards, and, on balance, the majority of subsequent writers have agreed. This is certainly the most common way up nowadays,

but is still far from universal. As this was being written a horse-box drove past the editor's house, and emblazoned on its side was a local stable's logo, including prominent horseshoes with the prongs pointing downwards. Similar graphical imagery from the past confirms that the symbol was regularly displayed with prongs down, especially when the design included an illustration within the shoe. In the editor's collection of early twentieth-century postcards from Britain, France, and USA, the horseshoe is incorporated into many birthday, Christmas, and good-luck greetings. In every case the prongs are downwards.

Some informants claimed that particular groups preferred different effects, but there does not seem to have been any consistency:

Gipsies hang the shoe with its points (the heel) upward, in cup-form, 'to catch the good luck', but grooms generally hang it toe upward, in roof-form, to ward off bad luck.   England? N&Q (1905)

The only people who, by custom, nailed the horse-shoes point downwards, were the blacksmiths in their forges. At least one former forge in St. Pierre du Bois still has the horse-shoes hanging in this fashion.   Guernsey De Garis (1975)

I have seen them where they have been nailed to the doors of cow-houses, barns, and stables, but most frequently on the inside fittings of the majority of the boats lying on the sea beach at the various watering-places that be-gem our coast. The favourite – that is to say the most convenient spot in a boat, is at the bow, inside the stem. I once asked a sailor and fisherman why he put a horse-shoe in his boat. He smiled and said 'It was to keep out the witches'. I do not recollect having seen a shoe with the points upwards. I have been told that it must be an old half worn-out shoe, and certainly not a new one, as that would not possess the charm.

Unlocated *Western Antiquary* (1889–90)

In jewellery, horseshoes appear mostly with the two points downwards. I possess two lockets, one with a pearl and turquoise horseshoe, and the other with a diamond horseshoe, given to me about thirty-eight years ago. I also have a coral horseshoe brooch, bought at the first Italian Exhibition in London – all three have the points turned down. I always understood they were symbols of good luck.   N&Q (1905)

In the debate whether the shoe should be hung with prongs up or down, the champions of the 'up' position have long used the mnemonic, first floated in the nineteenth century, that the luck runs out of the ends if they point downwards. This, however, is countered by saying that with the prongs upwards, the Devil sits in the shoe. A third explanation is rarely heard in the present day, but was previously popular. It says that the horseshoe shape is effective because the Devil/witches 'travel in circles' and therefore keep having to turn back when they meet the open end of the shoe. This idea of their 'travelling in circles' appears in no other context and was presumably invented for this explanation alone.

No remotely convincing reason for the faith in horseshoes has been forthcoming, although plenty of unconvincing ones have been proposed. During the nineteenth century it was suggested that the practice was a survival of the worship of Isis in ancient Egypt whose symbol was a crescent moon, and this hypothesis is still regularly repeated as given fact. How such a custom survived the intervening thousands of years between Egypt and its first mention in Britain, or made the journey here from north Africa without showing up in the intervening years, is not explained. As we have seen, the horseshoe makes an excellent graphical symbol, and even if the written record had failed to record its existence, one would have thought a picture or artefact might have done so. It also leaves one to wonder, if the horseshoe was meant to represent the crescent moon, why the sideways orientation is never seen.

Another theory maintains that the shoe represents a horned God, although which one is not clear. Again, if the shoe represents the Devil, it is surely more likely to attract than repel witches. Other suggestions include a remnant of pre-Christian horse-worship, or a trade symbol for grooms, blacksmiths, and gypsies. It goes without saying that there is no shred of evidence to support such ideas.

One problem with such origin theories is that we have no way of knowing what particular attribute of the horseshoe first attracted the attention of the superstitious. Was it the shape, or its connection with the horse, or merely the fact that it is a readily obtainable object made of IRON? Iron has certainly been regarded as protective in a range of beliefs, and indeed many of the descriptions of superstitions based on finding horseshoes or nails make it clear that it is the metal which is lucky to find.

England? N&Q 10S:3 (1905) 90; [1981] Opie & Tatem, 203. **Sussex** Timbs (1860) 145; Latham (1878) 9, 24. **Dorset** Folk-Lore 89 (1978) 158. **Devon** Bray 3 (1838) 255; Western Antiquary 11 (1891–2) 45; Devonshire Assoc. 24 (1892) 52; Hewett (1900) 49; Devonshire Assoc. 66 (1934)

82. **Cornwall** Polwhele (1826) 610; Hunt (1865) 240; Couch (1871) 147; Western Antiquary 3 (1883) 91; Folk-Lore Jnl 4 (1886) 226; N&Q 1S:11 (1955) 498. **Wiltshire** Wilts. N&Q 1 (1893–5) 317. **Berkshire** Lowsley (1888) 23; [1901] Folk-Lore 26 (1915) 154; Wright (1913) 233. **London** Aubrey, Remaines (1686/1972) 231–2; Aubrey, Miscellanies (1696/1857) 140–1; Gent. Mag. (1855) 504; Napier (1879) 139; Hazlitt (1905) 331. **Essex** [c.1920] Ketteridge & Mays (1972) 139; [1983] Opie & Tatem, 203. **Worcestershire/Shropshire** Gent. Mag. (1855) 385. **Worcestershire** Salisbury (1893) 71. **Northamptonshire** Sternberg (1851) 169; [1904] Folk-Lore 26 (1915) 158. **East Anglia** Varden (1885) 112. **Suffolk** Gent. Mag. (1867) 318; Folk-Lore 35 (1924) 352. **Norfolk** Norfolk Archaeology 2 (1849) 305–6; [c.1870] Haggard (1935) 16; Fulcher Collection (c.1895); Folk-Lore 26 (1915) 210; East Anglian Mag. (Aug. 1935) 95. **Lincolnshire** Gent. Mag. (1832) 494; Gent. Mag. (1833) 590–3; Heanley (1902) 20; Good (1900) 107; Rudkin (1936) 17; Sutton (1992) 140. **Shropshire** Burne (1883) 204; N&Q 10S:3 (1905) 91. **England** Addy (1895) 71–2, 97. **Derbyshire** Addy (1895) 73. **Northern England** Brockett (1846); Henderson (1866) 81; Denham Tracts 2 (1895) 62, 213. **Yorkshire** Monthly Packet 25 (1863) 549–51; N&Q 5S:9 (1878) 65; Addy (1888) xix, xxii; Nicholson (1890) 87; Atkinson (1891) 71–2; Blakeborough (1898) 158; Folk-Lore 20 (1909) 348; Folk-Lore 43 (1932) 255; [c.1900] Greenwood (1977); [1952] Opie & Tatem, 204; [1965] Opie & Tatem, 204; [1982] Opie & Tatem, 204. **Lancashire** N&Q 1S:3 (1851) 56; Harland & Wilkinson (1882) 72, 139, 154. **Co. Durham** Brockie (1886) 210; Leighton (1910) 46, 54; [1986] Opie & Tatem, 203. **Northumberland** Neville (1909) 110–11; Bosanquet (1929) 77. **Wales** Bye-Gones (1873) 220; Trevelyan (1909) 267, 324–5; Folk-Lore 20 (1909) 95. **Mid-Wales** Davies (1911) 215. **Scotland** Kelly (1721) 348; N&Q 2S:4 (1857) 25; Hazlitt (1905) 331. **Western Scotland** Napier (1879) 139. **Highland Scotland** Macbain (1887/88) 261. **Dumfriesshire** Corrie (1890/91) 76. **Glasgow** [1940s] MacLeay (1990) 45. **Fifeshire** [1952] Opie & Tatem, 203. **Aberdeenshire** Folk-Lore Jnl 6 (1888) 265. **Galloway** Mactaggart (1824) 210. **Orkney** Laing (1885) 73; N&Q 10S:12 (1909) 483–4. **Ireland** Gent. Mag. (1865) 700–1; Wilde (1888) 181. **N. Ireland** Foster (1951) 47, 90. **S.E. Ireland** N&Q 3S:5 (1864) 353. **Co. Longford** Béaloideas 6 (1936) 262–4. **Co. Laoighis** Béaloideas 9 (1939) 32. **Jersey** Folk-Lore 25 (1914) 248; L'Amy (1927) 99. **Guernsey** De Garis (1975) 125. **Isle of Man** [c.1850] Cashen (1912) 27; Moore (1891) 152–3. **Unlocated** [late 14th cent.] C. R. Rypon MS Harl. 4894, quoted Opie & Tatem 203–4; Gent. Mag. (1813) 431; Chambers's Jnl (1873) 809; N&Q 5S:9 (1878) 65; Western Antiquary 9 (1889–90) 81; N&Q 10S:3 (1905) 9; N&Q 10S:3 (1905) 91; N&Q 10S:8 (1907) 210; Folk-Lore 53 (1942) 97. **General** Scot (1584) Bk 12, Ch. 18; J. Blagrave, Astrological Practice (1671) 138, quoted Opie & Tatem, 203; Gent. Mag. (1822) 482; Gent. Mag. (1823) 16–17, 412; N&Q 10S:3 (1905) 91, 315. **Literary** Samuel Butler, Hudibras (1664) Pt 2, Canto 3; William Congreve, Love for Love (1695) 3:4; John Gay, Fables (1727) 'The Old Woman and her Cats'; Connoisseur 59 (1755) 350; Goody Two-Shoes (1766) quoted Opie & Tatem, 203; Tobias Smollett, Humphry Clinker (1771) 299; Walter Scott, Redgauntlet (1824) Ch. 12; Mitford 4 (1824–32) Ch. 33; Old Women's Sayings (c.1835).

houseleeks (*Sempervivum tectorum*)

Succulent perennial herb with leaves forming a tight rosette, and with pink flowers, which grows commonly on walls and the roofs of houses. As with many herbs, it has extensive traditional medicinal uses but also at least one widespread magical belief: that it provides protection against thunderstorms and LIGHT-NING strikes:

The presence of a houseleek plant on the roof of a house is still believed by some Cambridgeshire people to provide an excellent protection against lightning. Between 1951 and 1962 three instances have been recorded of families moving from old or condemned dwellings to new council houses and carefully taking with them houseleeks to place on the roofs of their new homes.

Cambridgeshire Porter (1969)

This idea was already in full force in the mid sixteenth century, with two writers noticing it in 1562:

groweth in mountaynes and hylly places, some use to set it upon theyr houses.

Turner, *A New Herball* (1562)

Old writers . . . held an opinion supersticiously, that in what house so ever it groweth, no lyght-nyng or tempest can take place to doe any harme.

Bullein, *Defence Against Sickness* (1562)

It is never explained how or why the house-leek manages to ward off the lightning, but a clue may be provided by the fact that in the early herbals one of the plant's main attributes is that it is a cooling agent:

Our ordinary houseleek is good for all inward heats as well as outward, and in the eyes or other parts of the body; a posset made with the juice of houseleek is singularly good in all hot agues, for it cooleth and tempereth the blood and spirits, and quencheth the thirst.

Culpeper, *The English Physician* (1653)

It is still being cited as good for burns, St Anthony's fire (ERYSIPELAS), cuts, insect bites and stings, and numerous other conditions, into the present day.

On roofs: Kent N&Q 4S:4 (1869) 507. Sussex Latham (1878) 13; *Sussex County Mag.* 23 (1949) 383. Cambridgeshire Porter (1969) 69. Suffolk Moor (1823) 177–8. Lincolnshire Gutch & Peacock (1908) 23. Derbyshire Uttley (1946) 119. Yorkshire Nicholson (1890) 124; Addy (1895) 62. Co. Durham Brockie

(1886) 117. Ireland *Ulster Folklife* 15/16 (1970) 25. Co. Cavan/Co. Leitrim Logan (1965) 52. Co. Mayo *Folk-Lore* 58 (1947) 278. Unlocated Brand (1810) 241. General W. Bullein, *Defence Against Sickness* (1562) 37; William Turner, *A New Herball* Pt.2 (1562); Nicholas Culpeper, *The English Physician* (1653) 79; Thomas Hill, *Natural and Artificial Conclusions* (1670) n. 139. Literary Thomas Deloney, *The Pleasant History of the Gentle Craft* (1648) Pt 1, Ch.4; Thomas Hardy, *Far from the Madding Crowd* (1870) Ch. 9. *Cures [selected references]:* Bedfordshire Marsom (1950) 183. Norfolk *Folk-Lore* 40 (1929) 119. Lincolnshire *Folk-Lore* 20 (1909) 489; Rudkin (1936) 27. Shropshire Wright, *English Dialect Dictionary* 5 (1904) 444; *Folk-Lore* 49 (1938) 230. Derbyshire Uttley (1946) 119. Ireland *Ulster Folklife* 15/16 (1970) 25. Guernsey [1589] *Channel Islands Ann. Anth.* (1972–3) 19. *See also* Vickery (1995) 197–9, for other medicinal uses.

housemartins

see SWALLOWS.

houses: corner

Three sources indicate a prejudice against corner houses:

The superstition that corner houses are unlucky is very common in Herefordshire. I once resided next to a corner house, and was frequently congratulated on having escaped that unenviable position, while, if I had been in any way unfortunate, my friends would exclaim, 'No wonder – living next to a corner house'.

Herefordshire N&Q (1875)

These references confirm one another, and show that the belief lasted at least a hundred years, but it is a mystery why no one else seems to have reported it, and there is no hint as to why corner houses were believed to be unlucky.

Herefordshire N&Q 5S:4 (1875) 216. Co. Durham [1947] Opie & Tatem, 97. Literary Charles Dickens, *Dombey and Son* (1848) Ch. 51.

houses: moving in

A number of superstitions focus on the act of moving into a new house. Clearly many people felt that this important step needed special attention and measures to promote good luck, but the recorded beliefs are quite diverse, and only hold together at the broadest level. The newcomers should not enter empty-handed but must carry certain items with them:

houses

Numerous superstitions are concerned with particular aspects of houses, and what goes on in them, and these are all treated separately. Creatures coming into the house, such as BEES or BIRDS, or SNAKES, had particular meaning, as did COCKERELS crowing at the door, and certain birds' nests (especially HOUSEMARTINS and SWALLOWS) should be left unmolested if they were attached to the house. A whole range of FLOWERS must not be brought in, or only under certain circumstances, such as HAWTHORN, PRIMROSES, SNOWDROPS, and DAFFODILS. People were cautioned about entering and leaving by different DOORS, or seeing things like the new MOON through a WINDOW, but doors and windows would be opened in STORMS or when there was a DEATH in the house. Nobody should open an UMBRELLA, or shoulder a SPADE, in the house, and there were several beliefs about what could be done on the STAIRS.

Moving house should never be undertaken on a FRIDAY, and pets such as CATS and DOGS had to be treated in certain ways when moving, or again when there was a death in the house. FIRES, BEDS, and other furniture had their own superstitions, and the house itself could be unlucky if numbered THIRTEEN. The plant HOUSELEEK should be encouraged to grow on the roof, as it protected the house from lightning, and various trees such as HOLLY and ROWAN are lucky if planted near the house. You may wish to nail a HORSEHOE to the door, or hang a holed STONE somewhere for protection against the EVIL EYE. You will certainly hope that the previous occupiers have not CURSED the house with a fire of stones. You may even be the possessor of a human SKULL, which causes havoc if anyone tries to take it from the premises. Numerous other beliefs have reported once or twice; a representative sample is given below.

If a house does not like new tenants they won't be able to stay long. Houses are lucky to some people. Always send a cat in first into a new house. If the house is unlucky the cat won't stay.
Somerset [1905–12] Tongue

Our Summercourt correspondent witnessed an amusing affair on Thursday morning. Seeing a crowd in the street, he asked the reason, and found that a young lady was about to perform the feat of throwing a pig's nose over a house for good luck! This is how it was done. The lady took the nose of a pig, that was killed the day before, in her right hand; stood with her back to the house, and threw the nose over her head, and over the house, into the back garden. Had she failed in the attempt her luck was supposed to be bad.
Cornwall *Folk-Lore Jnl* (1887)

Another of the Pendle Forest charms inspected by the writer was as follows: 'Omnes spiritu laudet domnum moson habent dusot praheates exurgrat disipentur inimicus'. It is marked on the back 'For the house' and was intended to be placed over the door to protect the house and its inmates. It is on a very small piece of paper in an illiterate hand. The formula was evidently at one time Latin, but, having been copied over and over

A box of coal and a plate of salt should be the first things taken into an empty house, before moving any furniture. At Eastnor, people leaving a house were warned that they must leave bread and salt behind them; if this were not done it would mean ill-luck for those leaving and for the next tenants.
Herefordshire Leather (1912)

Visitors should similarly always bring something on their first visit. As well as the obvious food, light, and warmth, others recommended more symbolic items:

the pair were safely married and set out for their future home, the bride being cautioned by her sister to be sure to carry a Bible about her when she went into her new house.
Staffordshire *Folk-Lore* (1897)

or particular luck-bringing actions:

A friend tells me that she went recently to see a mother and daughter who were moving into a new flat. She found them busy strewing salt in the rooms. They explained that it was lucky and that they always salted the dwelling into which they moved.
Unlocated *Folk-Lore* (1934)

There are several related principles at work here, all concerned with the overriding principle of ensuring luck at the BEGINNING of this new phase of life. For some, it is clearly a form of HANDSELLING the house, ensuring prosperity by making sure that it is not empty at the beginning. For others, it seems to be akin to the FIRST FOOTING at New Year, where symbolic gifts ensure good luck, or the principle of OUTGOING/INCOMING to make sure that material goods and prosperity in the future flow in faster than out. These principles explain the insistence on incomers entering first with staples such as coal or bread, and the gifts from visitors, but other ideas are also at work in some reported cases. The suggestion that the newcomers carry a Bible again by a series of ignorant persons who did not know the meaning of what they were writing, it has at length become nothing but an unmeaning jargon. The last three words were evidently intended for the opening words of Psalm lxviii, 'Exurgat Deus, et dissipentur inimici ejus' (Let God arise and let His enemies be scattered).

Lancashire Weeks (1910)

'Aye, shour, we're removin', home' said a shipmaster's wife in Bishopwearmouth, as she stood at the door of her domicile one day, with her household goods around her; 'folks say it's all them unlucky houses. My hoosband was three times shipwrecked in our first house. Then we removed; but we had ney sooner getting into the next house than he was browt on shore in the life-boat. Aw's shour I hope we'll hev better luck in the house we're gan tey.'

Co. Durham Brockie (1886)

If a horse neighed at the door of a house, it boded sickness to some of the inmates.

Western Scotland Napier (1879)

If two bells ring at the same time in the house, they say someone is going to leave before the year is out. Kent Folk-Lore (1912)

If an occupied house be left empty, and you see it lit up bright at night, it is a sign of sickness or trouble. (Mrs. X saw it lately at her opposite neighbour's house and much trouble followed for the neighbour.) Suffolk Folk-Lore (1924)

Never hang anything on a door handle. If you do, someone is sure to leave.

London Folk-Lore (1926)

If a wife spills water she may expect the house to be full of visitors ere it dries; but if her daughter does this, she knows that her lover is thinking of her. A very strange belief is that if water be taken with soup the drinker will cough in his grave.

Highland Scotland Polson (1926)

The other day an old woman here heard two girls talking about doing some spring cleaning and having their rooms papered. 'What,' said she, 'papering your rooms in January? Then we'll have snows after all'. And, sure enough, we had snow, after three weeks of delightful, bright sunny weather. Orkney N&Q (1908)

If the parlour bell rings while the clock is striking, it is a sign of scolding.

Unlocated N&Q (1861)

It is lucky to take a horse through your house.

England Addy (1895)

Kent Folk-Lore 23 (1912) 354. Somerset [1905–12] Tongue (1965) 141. Cornwall Folk-Lore Jnl 5 (1887) 195. London Folk-Lore 37 (1926) 367. Suffolk Folk-Lore 35 (1924) 350. England Addy (1895) 69. Lancashire Weeks (1910) 105–7. Co. Durham Brockie (1886) 214. Highland Scotland Polson (1926) 128. Western Scotland Napier (1879) 114. Orkney N&Q 10S:9 (1908) 210. Unlocated N&Q 2S:12 (1861) 492.

in hand is clearly protective and can be seen as an orthodox Christian blessing or a superstition, but several sources recommend the sprinkling of SALT in each room, for luck, which is harder to explain but may be a ritual 'purification'.

Other symbolic actions were recommended or proscribed, as, for example, the following specialist version of not entering and leaving a house by different DOORS:

A friend taking possession of a new house, for instance, brought back a piece of ritual which had lain forgotten at the back of my mind for many years. She must not walk in at the front door and out at the back to admire her new garden, I told her, for that would mean she would never settle. I persuaded her to go outside again and enter for a second time before she opened the back door. Lancashire Corbridge (1964)

For others, it was quite simple:

When you go to a new house, poke the fire for luck. England Addy (1895)

The recorded examples are geographically quite widespread, but not in sufficient quantity to suggest really well-known beliefs. It is surprising that none can be found before the 1860s.

Sussex [1984] Opie & Tatem, 205. Herefordshire Leather (1912) 24, 86–7. Worcestershire [1914] Folklore 76 (1965) 148. Cheshire N&Q 4S:3 (1869) 359. Staffordshire Folk-Lore 8 (1897) 91. England Addy (1895) 93. Yorkshire [1981] Opie & Tatem, 205. Lancashire Harland & Wilkinson (1873) 236; Corbridge (1964) 156–60. Co. Durham Folk-Lore 20 (1909) 217; [1985] Opie & Tatem, 205. Pembrokeshire Cambrian N&Q 1 (1902) 39. Cardiganshire Folk-Lore 37 (1926) 174. Co. Clare Folk-Lore 22 (1911) 203. Co. Tyrone Lore & Language 1:7 (1972) 13. Unlocated Folk-Lore 45 (1934) 267.

hunchbacks

A handful of references from 1899 to the 1930s report a tradition that it was lucky to touch a hunchback's hump, although the belief was probably much more widespread than is indicated by these few examples, and the earliest indicate a longer history back into the nineteenth century at least. Like CHIMNEY SWEEPS, people with deformed backs were apparently not averse to capitalizing on superstition by being in the right place at the right time:

There is nothing new in the story of Lord Torrington and his friends, when leaving for the front, treating the little hunchback newsboy at the Paddington bookstall as a mascot, and rewarding him for allowing them to touch him. Years ago a hunchback used always to take his stand outside Waterloo Station on race-meeting days, and there must be many who remember paying twopence to rub him on the back on their way to Sandown and elsewhere.   London *Observer* (6 Sept. 1914)

Devon *Devonshire Assoc.* 67 (1935) 133. **London** *Observer* (6 Sept. 1914) 5. **Theatrical** Booth (1933) 97. **General** *The People* (11 June 1899).

hydrangeas (*Hydrangea macrophylla*)

One of the many plants which are regarded by some as unlucky:

Writing from Edinburgh to a popular Sunday newspaper (12 Dec 1956), a woman states that she has a potted hydrangea in her house; that a visitor told her it would bring ill-luck, and that in fact several misfortunes have occurred since she got it. She asks if anyone else has heard of this 'hydrangea superstition', in which she personally seems not to believe.   Edinburgh *Folk-Lore* (1957)

Other reports indicate the more specific belief that the flower affects marriage prospects:

By the way, the hydrangea ill-luck ... is feminine only. If you plant hydrangeas near your house, your daughters will not marry.
    Somerset *Folk-Lore* (1957)

This superstition has not been reported very often, and some writers in the 1950s and 1960s took it to be a recently coined belief. Ketteridge and Mays report its existence in the 1920s, but it is unlikely to be earlier than the twentieth century. It is still believed in some quarters.

Somerset *Folk-Lore* 68 (1957) 435; **Surrey** Vickery (1995) 200; **London** [1968] Opie & Tatem, 206. **Essex** [*c*.1920] Ketteridge & Mays (1972) 138. **Cambridgeshire** Porter (1969) 45; Vickery (1995) 200. **Edinburgh** *Folk-Lore* 68 (1957) 297. **General** Baker (1996) 81.

hydrophobia

see DOG-BITES.

ill eye

see EVIL EYE.

image magic

see EFFIGIES.

incubus

see NIGHTMARES.

ink

see WRITING.

invultuation or invultation

Scholarly word for the act of making or using effigies or images of people or animals for use in spells and other acts of witchcraft. For discussion of use and derivation, see *Notes & Queries* 8S:11 (1897) 107, 236, 314, 395.
    See EFFIGIES.

Irish charms

Across England, but mainly in the northern counties, certain items hailing from Ireland were believed to have special powers. 'Irish stones' were treasured for curing snakebite and other poisons, and sticks from Irish trees, or even teeth from Irish cattle, were believed to have similar curative effect. The origin is presumably the well-known story that St Patrick banished all snakes and venomous things from Ireland, but the belief was already current in Britain in the early eighth century, as evidenced by Bede, from Northumbria, who wrote of Ireland thus:

There are no reptiles, and no snake can exist there; for although often brought over from Britain, as soon as the ship nears land, they breathe the scent of its air, and die. In fact, almost everything in this isle confers immunity to poison, and I have seen folk suffering from snakebite have drunk water in which scrapings from the leaves of books from Ireland have been steeped, and that this remedy checked the spreading poison and reduced the swelling.

> Bede, *History of the English Church and People*
> (AD 731)

In later traditions, it was believed that spiders would not survive on Irish wood, and that Irish earth would keep out snakes and toads:

The cloisters [of Durham Cathedral] *are ceiled with Irish oak, so that they never harbour dust or cobwebs.*   Co. Durham Leighton (1910)

At Goodrich Castle . . . the cellars were floored with Irish earth, so that no toad could live there; and the timber was also believed to be brought from Ireland, in order to avoid the annoyance of cobwebs.   Herefordshire Leather (1912)

Some parts of Shetland and Orkney have a similar reputation for being lethal to snakes and other unpleasant creatures (*see* Black (1903) 12–20).

Sussex N&Q 199 (1954) 543. Herefordshire Leather (1912) 25. Yorkshire *Folk-Lore* 81 (1970) 143. Co. Durham Leighton (1910) 64. Northumberland Bede, *History of the English Church and People* (AD 731) Bk 1, Ch. 2; *Folk-Lore* 81 (1970) 220–1. Northumberland/Co. Durham *Folklore* 80 (1969) 262–5. General N&Q 200 (1955) 86; Davies (1998) 48–9.

iron

see also TOUCHING IRON.

iron: finding

Finding and picking up a piece of metal in the road was regarded as lucky, especially if it was a HORSESHOE. What was done with the metal once it was found varied from person to person; some took it home, or carried it about with them for luck:

Picking up scraps of iron – I knew this custom as a regular thing in Derbyshire when a lad, and have known many others in various places do the same. One I know who had quite a collection of odd nails – horseshoe nails mostly – and bits of iron.   Derbyshire N&Q (1905)

while others actually thought it was unlucky to take old iron into the house. Some went through a little ritual, similar to that used when picking up things in the street:

Pick up the iron in the right hand, spit on it, and throw it over the left shoulder. You must on no account see where it falls, or you will lose the good luck which your action is supposed to bring . . . The spitting is omitted by very refined persons, and I am not aware that their luck has suffered.
> Unlocated N&Q (1905)

The idea that it is lucky to find a horseshoe was so well known that it effectively eclipsed the idea that finding any piece of iron was fortunate, even though the latter may have been the basis of the former. Iron has a very positive reputation in British superstition (*see below*), but it is not clear why. In other contexts, including as a horseshoe, it had protective qualities – against fairies and witches – and this may explain why it was lucky to find it.

The earliest reference to finding iron is in the same source as that for the lucky horseshoe, the Harleian manuscript of the late fourteenth century which says 'iron nails are among the lucky finds' (quoted in Opie & Tatem) and is mentioned regularly in seventeenth-century sources.

Cambridgeshire *Folk-Lore* 25 (1914) 365. East Anglia Varden (1885) 112. Lincolnshire *Grantham Jnl* (29 June 1878). Derbyshire N&Q 10S:3 (1905) 397. Northern England Henderson (1866) 81. Yorkshire Nicholson (1890) 46. Lancashire Harland & Wilkinson (1882) 139. Cumberland Gibson (1858) 106. Co. Durham Brockie (1886) 210. Glasgow [1940s] MacLeay (1990) 45, 47. Co. Longford *Béaloideas* 6 (1936) 264. Unlocated N&Q 1S:5 (1852) 293; *Chambers's Jnl* (1873) 809; N&Q 10S:3 (1905) 348, 397–8. General [late 14th cent.] C. R. Rypon MS Harl. 4894, quoted Opie & Tatem, 210; James Mason, *Anatomie of Sorcerie* (1612); Thomas Cooper, *Mysterie of Witchcraft* (1617) 137; Nathaniel Homes, *Daemonologie* (1650) 60.

iron: protects

It was generally agreed that both witches and fairies disliked iron, and could be kept at bay by its presence. The most widespread manifestation of this belief was the HORSESHOE at the door, but various other strategies were adopted to capitalize on the protective qualities of the metal. Iron was regularly deposited in places thought particularly vulnerable to ill-wishing, such as the stable or the dairy, or at times of danger such as childbirth or at sea.

And a piece of iron should be sewn in the infant's clothes, and kept there till after the baptism.
> Ireland Wilde (1888)

In 1942 a farmer near Bungay was informed by a villager that iron under the doormat was a certain protection against witches.
> Suffolk *Folk-Lore* (1943)

The earliest clear reference is in one of Robert Herrick's short poems, written while he was living in Devon, which advised the reader to hang up metal tools like shears to keep the horses from being HAG-RIDDEN:

Hang up hooks, and sheers to scare
Hence the hag, that rides the mare,
Till they be all over wet,
With the mire, and the sweat:
This observ'd, the manes shall be
Of your horses, all knot-free.

Herrick (1648) 'Another Charme for Stables'

This antipathy to iron felt by witches and fairies has never been satisfactorily explained, but was widely known, at least from the seventeenth to mid twentieth centuries. A Victorian explanation which still appears regularly in popular works on superstition is that when the use of iron was first discovered most people were so in awe of it that they regarded it as a sacred substance. This was, of course, pure speculation, with no shred of evidence, nor even any probability, to support it. The idea that a superstition can have lasted, virtually intact, from the beginning of the Iron Age to the present day is hardly credible. An allied notion, used to explain why the use of iron was forbidden in certain contexts (*see above*), maintained that the belief in the uncanniness of iron has survived from a previous, stone-using race who were conquered by an invading iron-wielding race; however, this is equally unfounded. In this scenario, the vanquished race have presumably become the witches and fairies of tradition.

Hampshire N&Q 10S:7 (1907) 157. **London** Lovett (1928) 21. **Essex** *Observer Supp.* (24 Nov. 1968) 18. **Worcestershire** *Folk-Lore* 20 (1909) 345. **Cambridgeshire** [*c*.1850] *Folk-Lore* 16 (1905) 187. **Suffolk** *Folk-Lore* 54 (1943) 390. **Northern England** Henderson (1866) 194. **Yorkshire** N&Q 5S:10 (1878) 266. **Anglesey** *Folk-Lore* 29 (1918) 158–9. **Highland Scotland** Kirk (1691); Macbain (1887/88) 269. **Skye** *Folk-Lore* 34 (1923) 92. **Orkney** *Stat. Acct. Scotland* 15 (1795) 311. **Shetland** Reid (1869) 24. **Ireland** Wilde (1888) 203. **Co. Derry** *Folk-Lore* 4 (1893) 355. **Literary** Herrick (1648) 'Another Charme for Stables'.

itching

A sudden or persistent itch on any part of the body has long been held to have significance. The meanings given for some are well known and surprisingly stable over time, while for others there is little agreement. The meaning is often relatively 'logical' – itching of the foot means you will tread on strange land, of the ear, someone is talking of you – but others are less clear, such as a nose itch signifying you will meet a stranger or kiss a fool (or the other way round). At times there seems to be an element of parody – 'If your stomach itches, you will eat pudding. If your back itches, butter will be cheap when grass grows there'.

The most common ones are as follows (*see* separate entry for each one):

Hand – you will give or receive money.
Ear – someone is talking about you.
Foot – you will tread on strange ground.
Eye – you will cry or laugh.
Knee – you will kneel in a strange church.
Elbow – you will have a strange bedfellow.
Nose – you will be kissed, cursed, run into a gatepost, or shake hands with a fool.

Itching beliefs are used to great effect in the humorous pieces in the *Connoisseur* 59 (1755) 353, and *Old Women's Sayings* (*c*.1835).

ivy leaf: cures

Ivy leaves were recommended by many herbalists and amateur healers, for a variety of ailments, but the most regularly cited use is for the treatment of corns:

An ivy leaf tied around a soft corn is said to cure it – if the treatment can be continued for long enough. A more elaborate treatment is to soak the feet in a strong solution of washing soda. This is repeated daily for several days until the pain of the corn is relieved. If these methods are not successful, a handful of ivy leaves should be put to steep in a pint of vinegar in a tightly corked bottle for forty-eight hours. The liquid is then poured off and still kept tightly corked. When required, it is applied carefully to each corn, taking care to see that the preparation does not get on the skin – it is very painful.

Ireland Logan (1981)

Most other corn remedies are less complex. Ivy could also be taken internally:

He'd bruise the ivy leaves and berries and a-swish them round and round in his tea. 'Take a sip of that, me gal', he'd say, offering me his steaming billy-can, 'They'll never have the rheumatics if thee drink ivy-leaf tea'.

Warwickshire [*c*.1910] Stewart

Devon *Devonshire Assoc.* 88 (1956) 257. **Herefordshire** Leather (1912) 79. **West Midlands** W. Midlands Fed. W. I.s (1996) 72–3. **Warwickshire** [*c*.1910] Stewart (1971) 76. **East Anglia** Hatfield (1994) various pages. **Norfolk**

ivy (*Hedera helix*)

Ivy has something of a mixed reputation in the superstitions of Britain and Ireland. Many people have happily used it for years, along with other evergreens, for Christmas decorations, and there are old traditions about the holly (male) and the ivy (female). But many people in the nineteenth and twentieth centuries regarded it as unlucky and would not bring it into the house, even at Christmas:

The cook gave in her notice, just before Christmas, and I couldn't think why. Finally she said she couldn't work in a house where there was that ivy. It was for my Christmas decorations, but I threw it out.   **London** [1969] Opie & Tatem

In decorating the house with evergreens at Christmas, care must be taken not to let ivy be used alone, or even predominate, as it is a plant of bad omen, and will prove injurious.
                  Northamptonshire Sternberg (1851)

No reason is usually given, although there is more than a hint that ivy is associated with old buildings and graveyards. The following quotations also highlight this ambivalence, but as both have only been recorded once, it is difficult to determine how widespread either one was, if at all:

Anyone who wishes to dream of the devil; should pin four ivy-leaves to the corners of his pillow.
                Cornwall *Folk-Lore Jnl* (1887)

Ivy should be hung over the bed on New Year's Eve, whilst the occupant of the bed is asleep, so that the ivy is the first thing seen on awaking on New Year's morning.   **Lincolnshire** Rudkin (1936)

It is noticeable that these traditions are all very recent.

See also HOLLY.

Cornwall *Folk-Lore Jnl* 5 (1887) 213. **Devon** *Devonshire Assoc.* 105 (1973) 214. **London** [1969] Opie & Tatem, 213. **Essex** [*c.*1920] Ketteridge & Mays (1972) 138. **Herefordshire** Leather (1912) 20. **Northamptonshire** Sternberg (1851) 163. **Lincolnshire** Rudkin (1936) 42. **Shropshire** *Folk-Lore* 49 (1938) 233. **Yorkshire** [1959] Opie & Tatem, 213. **Co. Durham** [1946] Opie & Tatem, 213. **Unlocated** Folkard (1884) 60. **Various** Vickery (1995) 202–4.

[*c.*1920] Wigby (1976) 65. **Highland Scotland** Polson (1926) 34. **Ireland** [1730s] Logan (1981) 69; *Folk-Lore* 8 (1897) 388. **Co. Cork** Culloty (1993) 62. **Various** Vickery (1995) 202–4.

---

ivy leaves: divination

Two very different divinatory procedures involving ivy leaves have been recorded, but neither very often. One version involved placing leaves in water on a key night of the year:

The following Hallowe'en charm was practised recently, to satisfy a morbid desire to know if any member of the family would die during the coming year. An ivy leaf was taken for each one and placed in a bowl of water, to remain all night. The leaves were marked, so that each person knew his or her own, and it was believed that any to die soon would have a coffin marked on the leaf in the morning.   **Herefordshire** Leather (1912)

Essentially the same procedure was described by Lupton in 1579, as one of his *Thousand Notable Things*, but he stated that New Year's Eve was the correct time, and a version from Cornwall (*Folk-Lore Jnl* (1886)) recommended Twelfth Night. It is surprising to find a custom so unchanged after three hundred years – especially as there is no sign of it in between times.

The other ivy leaf procedure was a LOVE DIVINATION. Many such divinations use plant leaves or flowers in a very similar way.

To see her future husband, she put an ivy leaf in her pocket. The first man she met out of doors whilst carrying it would be the man she was to marry.   **Oxfordshire** *Oxon Folklore Soc.* (1952)

The only thing missing from this version is the accompanying words, which were usually on the lines of 'Ivy, ivy, I pluck thee, In my bosom I lay thee'.

What may be simply a more complex version of the above, or a different belief altogether, was recorded from Co. Leitrim in the 1890s:

The boys gather ten ivy leaves, without speaking, and throw away the tenth. They must not be brought into the house until bedtime, when they are placed in the right sock, and this, again, under the pillow, saying these words only:

> *Nine ivy leaves I place under my head*
> *To dream of the living and not of the dead*
> *If ere I be married or wed unto thee*
> *To dream of her tonight, and her for to see*
> *The colour of her hair, and the clothes that*
>   *she wears*
> *And the day she'll be wedded to me*

Sometimes yarrow leaves are used instead of ivy.
                Co. Leitrim *Folk-Lore* (1894)

These love versions seem to have been most common in Scotland, and have not been reported before the 1890s. It is difficult to determine whether there is any connection with the older beliefs concerned with health and death.

Leaf in water: Cornwall [*c.*1845] *Folk-Lore Jnl* 4 (1886) 125. **Herefordshire** Leather (1912) 65. **General** Lupton (1579) Bk 10, Para. 87.
Love divination: Oxfordshire *Oxon Folklore Soc.* (1952) 6–7. **Scotland** *Weekly Scotsman* (Xmas number 1898) 7, quoted Opie & Tatem, 213. **Dumfriesshire** [1957] Opie & Tatem, 214. **Dunbartonshire** [1940s] Vickery (1995) 202. **Angus** [1905] Rodger (1948) 29. **Co. Leitrim** *Folk-Lore* 5 (1894) 195–7.

ivy wood

A handful of references indicate a tradition that bowls and drinking vessels made out of ivy wood were useful for curing WHOOPING COUGH:

Drinking-cups made from the wood of the common ivy, and used by children affected with this complaint, for taking therefrom all they require to drink, is current in the county of Salop as an infallible remedy; and I once knew an old gentleman (now no more), who being fond of turning as an amusement, was accustomed to supply his neighbours with them, and whose brother always supplied him with the wood, cut from his own plantations. It is necessary, in order to be effective, that the ivy from which the cups are made should be cut at some particular change of the moon, or hour of the night, etc., which I am now unable to ascertain.
                            Shropshire N&Q (1853)

Available references show that this belief was in circulation at least from the 1750s to the early twentieth century, but without further examples it is difficult to estimate how widely known it was. Ivy often gets linked with HOLLY in tradition, and a stray report claims that milk drunk from a cup made of holly wood is also a sure cure for whooping cough (**Hampshire** N&Q 1S:4 (1851) 227).

Herefordshire Leather (1912) 82. **Shropshire** N&Q 1S:7 (1853) 128. **General** W. Ellis, *Modern Husbandman* 7 (1759) 179, quoted Opie & Tatem, 214.

jackdaws (*Corvus monedula*)

Jackdaws mostly get a bad press in British superstition. In most reports the appearance of a jackdaw was seen as at best unlucky, and often as the sign of impending death or disaster:

A stonemason of Clifton, relating to me an accident that occurred to one of the workmen at the suspension-bridge over the Avon, at the time when the river was simply spanned by a single chain, dwelt on the fact that a solitary jackdaw had been noticed by many of the workmen perched upon the centre of the chain, and had by them been regarded as a precursor of ill luck.
                        Gloucestershire N&Q (1873)

One or two informants claimed a more positive interpretation of the bird's appearance:

In the Fens, in the last century, the jackdaw was by no means considered a bird of ill omen; in fact if a bride saw one on her way to her wedding it meant that her married life would be happy and prosperous.   Cambridgeshire Porter (1969)

Jackdaws are also occasionally treated like MAGPIES:

I was walking with a friend through a wood when we came in sight of several jackdaws. My friend at once raised his hat, and upon seeing my look of surprise he laughingly exclaimed, 'Always take your hat off to the jackdaws'.
                        Gloucestershire *Glos. N&Q* (1890)

Jackdaw beliefs are reported far less often than those for other birds such as MAGPIES and CROWS, and all but one of the references are from the mid nineteenth century onwards. The exception is a passage in William of Malmesbury's *Kings of England* of 1042, in which a woman who hears a jackdaw chattering loudly grows pale and declares that some dreadful calamity is about to befall her.

England William of Malmesbury, *Kings of England* (1042) 2:24. **Devon** *Devonshire Assoc.* 57 (1926) 112. **Gloucestershire** N&Q 4S:12 (1873) 395; *Glos. N&Q* 4 (1890) 471. **Northamptonshire** N&Q 1S:3 (1851) 3–4. **Cambridgeshire** Porter (1969) 38–9. **Northern England** *Newcastle Weekly Chronicle* (11 Feb. 1899) 7. **Lancashire** Harland & Wilkinson (1882) 142–3. **General** Swainson (1886) 81–2.

jaundice

The common medical condition caused by an excess of bilirubin in the blood, which manifests itself in yellow skin and whites of the eyes. The most common forms of jaundice usually clear up by themselves or with relatively simple treatment, although there are forms (popularly called 'black jaundice') which can be fatal if untreated. The fact that the condition had such obvious symptoms and would probably cure itself, made it a favourite with local curers and charmers, and a range of folk cures have been recorded. The most obvious feature of these cures was a high proportion of yellow ingredients, on the simple premise of LIKE CURES LIKE: charlock, saffron, buttercups, yellow iris, dandelions, and even cheese with words written on it; also wearing a yellow ribbon or holding a yellowhammer were said to be efficacious. The urine of the patient was also utilized in various ways:

Jaunders was usually treated by some village quack who declared that he possessed an unfailing remedy; one of these consisted of the patient's urine flavoured with sugar, to which a little saffron had been added.

Warwickshire Bloom (c.1930)

Other regular ingredients, taken internally, were sheep droppings and goose dung (specifically 'the green end'), live spiders, woodlice, and other small creatures, and some of these cures are recorded as far back as the sixteenth century. It is not surprising that folklorist Charlotte Burne, in uncharacteristically squeamish mood, was prompted to write:

but the curing process, so far as it was known to her neighbours, is better forgotten – remedies for jaundice are apt to be somewhat disgusting.

Shropshire Burne (1883)

Sussex Latham (1878) 45. Dorset N&Q 1S:10 (1854) 321. Devon *Devonshire Assoc.* 66 (1934) 83. Cornwall *Folk-Lore Jnl* 5 (1887) 207. Wiltshire Eddrup (1885) 332–3. Herefordshire Leather (1912) 80. Warwickshire Bloom (c.1930) 28. Norfolk *Folk-Lore* 40 (1929) 119. Lincolnshire Peacock (1877) 26. Gutch & Peacock (1908) 117. Shropshire Burne (1883) 184–5, 199. Staffordshire Black (1883) 56. Lancashire Cowper (1897) 373–4. Cumberland Gibson (1858) 107; Penfold (1907) 56. Co. Durham *Folk-Lore* 20 (1909) 72. Northumberland *Folk-Lore* 36 (1925) 257. Wales Trevelyan (1909) 227–8, 312; *Archaeologia Cambrensis* 79 (1924) 28. Carmarthenshire *Folk-Lore* 23 (1912) 481–2. Pembrokeshire *Bye-Gones* (22 June 1887) 326–7. Highland Scotland Polson (1926) 32. Banffshire Gregor (1874) 270. Shetland Brand (1703) 108. Ireland Logan (1981) 45–8. Ulster *Folk-Lore* 8 (1897) 387. Co. Cork [1937/8] Culloty (1993) 61. Co. Cavan Maloney (1972)

75. Guernsey [1589] *Channel Islands Ann. Anth.* (1972–3) 21. Unlocated Aubrey, *Miscellanies* (1696/1857) 138. General *New London Dispensary* (1676) quoted Peacock (1877) 26.

jays (*Garrulus glandarius*)

Jay traditions focus mainly on the feathers, which were popular for hat decorations, although some held that they were unlucky if brought into the house:

If you have a jay's feather in your hat you'll never be without a penny in your pocket.

Lancashire *Lancashire Lore* (1971)

Do not bring jay's feathers into the house or you will never get a moment's peace from noise.

Somerset [1906] Tongue

Similar things are said, more commonly, about PEACOCK feathers.

George Wither, writing in 1613, indicates that the jay may have been an evil omen in his time. He lists omens such as NOSEBLEEDS and SALT being spilled, and continues:

Or if the babbling fowl we call a jay,
A squirrel or a hare, but cross the way.

Wither, *Abuses Stript an Whipt* (1613)

As usual with isolated references, without independent confirmation it is difficult to assess whether he means the jay specifically or is simply implying that superstitious people who are 'seduced with this foolish vanity' will baulk at anything crossing their way. He also mentions squirrels, which are not generally known as bad omens, and hares, which most definitely are.

Somerset [1906] Tongue (1965) 151. New Forest Wise (1867) 176–7. Lancashire *Lancashire Lore* (1971) 51. Wales Jones (1930) 181. General and foreign Swainson (1886) 75. Literary George Wither, *Abuses Stript an Whipt* (1613) 2:1.

John Dory (*Zeus faber*)

The HADDOCK and the John Dory have the distinction of being the fish that Peter caught to find the tribute money (Matthew 17:27):

'That's a John Dory, me dear. See them black marks? Look like finger-marks, don't 'em? An' they do say that they be finger-marks. He made 'em, that night, ye know, when they was fishin', ye know, an He took some an' cooked 'em all ready for 'em, an' ever since, they say, that ivery

*John Dory as comes out o' the sea have got His
finger-marks on 'un'.*

Oxfordshire Thompson (1939)

This cannot be strictly true, as the Dory is a salt-
water fish, and would not therefore be found in
the Sea of Galilee.

Devon [1797] *Devonshire Assoc.* 65 (1933) 123–4;
Devonshire Assoc. 63 (1931) 126. **Oxfordshire** Thompson
(1939) 120. **General** *The Mirror* (31 Mar. 1832) 212.

joints cracking

see FINGERS: JOINTS CRACKING.

kail, pulling

see LOVE DIVINATION: CABBAGE.

keys

Keys feature in two widespread beliefs, both
treated separately, the BIBLE AND KEY divination and as a cure for NOSEBLEEDS. In addition
to these, there are a number of other uncommon
superstitions which feature house keys, but they
are too disparate to allow any synthesis.

Dropping a key was seen as a sign of bad luck,
or at least a removal, as indicated by Thomas
Hardy:

*'I hope nothing is wrong about mistress,' said
Maryann . . . 'but an unlucky token came to me
indoors this morning. I went to unlock the door
and dropped the key, and it fell upon the stone
floor and broke into two pieces. Breaking a key is
a dreadful bodement. I wish mis'ess was home.'*

Hardy, *Far from the Madding Crowd* (1874)

In another context, keys could bring protection,
although it is more likely to be the fact that they
are made of IRON which brought the beneficial
effect:

*If a newly-born infant cries, three keys should be
placed in the bottom of the cradle.*

Wales Trevelyan (1909)

An odd custom involving keys was described
as still existing at Lynn harbour in the early
1890s:

*I have seen groups of women, no doubt the wives
and sweethearts of the sailors, assembled on the
quay, watching for the arrival or departure of a
ship, in the crew of which one or all might have*

*an interest. Each carried in her hand a key, gener-
ally apparently the key of the house-door; and if
she was watching for a vessel expected 'up with
the tide', she would, by inserting one finger in the
bow of it, and placing a finger of the other hand
in the angle of the wards and the stem, continue
turning the key towards herself until the vessel
arrived, or until the tide turned and its coming
was, for a time, hopeless. The object of the winding motion was to bring the vessel home.*

Norfolk *Folk-Lore* 4 (1893)

The women who were watching the departure of
a ship turned the key in the opposite direction,
to wish the ship good luck.

Somerset [1923] Opie & Tatem, 216. **Norfolk** *Folk-Lore*
4 (1893) 391–2. **Lincolnshire** (Irish man) *Folk-Lore* 25
(1914) 381–2. **Yorkshire** Nicholson (1890) 87; **Yorkshire**
Gill (1993) 90. **Co. Durham** N&Q 5S:6 (1876) 397.
Wales Trevelyan (1909) 265–6. **Ireland** Wilde (1888)
201–2, 207. **General** Henderson (1866) 198. **Literary**
Thomas Hardy, *Far from the Madding Crowd* (1874)
Ch. 23.

kingfishers (*Alcedo atthis*)

A persistent notion about the kingfisher is that
if suspended by a string in a house, it will act as
an effective weather-vane:

*I have once or twice seen a stuffed bird of this
species hung up to the beam of a cottage ceiling,
and imagined that the beauty of the feathers had
recommended it to this sad pre-eminence, till, on
enquiry, I was assured that it served the purpose
of a weather vane, and, though sheltered from the
immediate influences of the wind, never failed to
show every change by turning its beak to the
quarter whence the wind blew. It was also
pretended that the lifeless skin had the power of
averting of thunder, augmenting hidden treasure, bestowing grace and beauty on the person
who carries it, and renewing its plumage each
season of moulting.*

General Smith (1807)

This belief was already current in the sixteenth
century, as included in Lupton's *Thousand
Notable Things*, and both Marlowe and
Shakespeare refer to it in their plays. It was still
to be found in the twentieth century – Edward
LOVETT discovered one so suspended in a Sussex
cottage in the 1920s.

Two reports, in the same book of Somerset lore,
link the bird with drowning, but as these beliefs
are otherwise unrecorded it is difficult to assess
their meaning or whether they were more widely
known: [1920] 'A kingfisher's feathers will drown

your beasts if you keep it', [Schoolchildren, 1906–12] 'A kingfisher's feather will keep you from drowning' (**Somerset** Tongue (1965)).

Sussex Lovett (1928) 26. **Somerset** [1906/1920] Tongue (1965) 151. **Unlocated** Potter & Sargent (1973) 294. **General** Lupton (1579) Bk 10, Para. 96; Browne, *Pseudodoxia Epidemica* (1646) Bk 3, Para. 10; Smith (1807) 88. **Literary** Christopher Marlowe, *Jew of Malta* (1592) 1:1; Shakespeare, *King Lear* (1606) 2:2.

King's Evil

see SCROFULA.

knees

The knee has not attracted much notice in British superstition, although it is one of the many parts of the body on which an ITCH can be significant. Reginald Scot (1584) mentions tingling in the knee as one of the innumerable ways people prognosticate good or bad luck, but neglects to say what this particular sign means. From the 1870s to the 1930s, however, there is a handful of references from various English locations, which maintain that an itching knee means that you will kneel in a strange church. This was probably formed by analogy from the more commonly reported FEET itching which means you will soon tread on strange soil. One further meaning is reported:

If somebody rubs her knee when telling you a story, the story is a lie.

Co. Tyrone *Lore & Language* (1972)

Sussex *Sussex County Mag.* 5 (1931) 122. **Cornwall** Couch (1871) 169. **Devon** *Devonshire Assoc.* 10 (1878) 106. **Co. Tyrone** *Lore & Language* 1:7 (1972) 11. **General** Scot (1584) Bk 11, Ch. 13.

knives: crossed

An extremely widespread superstition maintains that knives (or occasionally knife and fork) laid across each other are very unlucky and presage at best a quarrel and at worst a death:

The sight of accidentally crossed knives upon our luncheon table today caused a distinct shudder to run through my wife and grown-up daughters . . . The nearest one made a grab at the offending cutlery and at once carefully placed the knives parallel. Further, she almost simultaneously exclaimed, with evident concern, 'Crossed knives! dear me, how very unlucky'. This belief is general throughout Devonshire.   Devon N&Q (1902)

The superstition is well reported across the whole of England, but much less frequently in the other parts of the British Isles. It has attracted several explanations which are more sensible than most modern theories on the origins of superstitions, but which have still not explained the matter convincingly. For a start, it appears to contradict two widespread motifs. Elsewhere in superstitious tradition, the sign of the cross in always beneficial and protective, and so too is metal. Nevertheless, as the most commonly predicted result is a quarrel, and occasional informants state that other edged tools such as sickles must also not be crossed, it has been argued that the symbolism here invoked is the 'crossed swords' of battle. It has also been suggested that before the Reformation it was normal to place one's cutlery in a cross form (despite the fact that forks were not generally used until the late seventeenth century), as a pious protection and benediction of the meal. As with all such back-formed origin theories, this sounds plausible enough, but is at best unproven. Another nineteenth-century explanation was that the crossed knives were branded as superstitious and therefore banned by the revolutionaries of the French Revolution. This can be readily discounted, as a number of references predate that event by many decades.

The picture is further clouded by disagreements over the etiquette of knife handling at the table. Modern middle-class British table-manners dictate that knife and fork be placed together, side by side, to signify that one has finished eating, while if they are laid down somewhat apart it signals that the meal continues. But this was once far from universal:

In the Midland counties, when I was a lad, we used to leave our knife and fork crossed on our plate when we desired a second 'help' and side by side when we did not.

Midland England N&Q (1903)

[Fifty years ago] To leave the knife and fork side by side, in certain grades of provincial society, was an indication to the waiter that no more was required; on the other hand, a crossed knife and fork was a silent call for another helping.

Unlocated N&Q (1902)

Amongst the village folk in the Westmorland dales the knife and fork were always crossed on the plate, and the latter pushed a little away to indicate the repast was finished; not to do so was considered ill-bred sixty years ago. When more food was required the knife and fork were retained in one hand whilst it was being supplied.

Westmorland N&Q (1902)

knives

In superstition, as in real life, knives are tricky things, and can have both negative and positive attributes in different contexts. While their sharpness can be dangerous – physically as well as symbolically – it can also be protective. In the symbolic sphere, the most common superstition was that to give a knife, or any sharp object, would cause a rift between the giver and the recipient, because it would 'cut love'. The remedy was for the recipient to 'pay' a nominal fee, to break the bad luck. Knives should never be placed across each other, or be used in a STORM, be allowed to fall, be picked up in the street, or placed edge upwards (unless one is trying to counter the effects of EPILEPSY). Nor should one stir with a knife or toast bread on one.

On the other hand, a knife stuck into a mast or door lintel is good luck, and placed in a cradle protected a baby from evil influences. It could also be spun on the table to find out future chances in love and marriage. Nevertheless, the negative beliefs outnumber the positive in both number and popularity. Many of the knife beliefs can be seen as a combination of superstition, etiquette, tradition, and commonsense safety.

Compare with other sharp objects, such as SCISSORS; PINS; BROOCHES.

Margaret Visser also points out that this aspect of the etiquette of knife and fork differs sharply from country to country across Europe, and has changed over time. There is disagreement whether a crossed knife and fork was also included in the prohibition to cross knives. Although later writers assumed this to be the case, nineteenth-century authorities contradict it.

Indeed, at the present time, the combination of etiquette, religion and superstition is impossible to unravel, and the earliest reference adds another element. The ban on crossed knives was already well known in the early eighteenth century, as Addison, Gay, and the writer of the *Connoisseur* article all make unambiguous mention of the belief. The only earlier reference, as discovered by Opie and Tatem, is not so clear, and introduces the notion of witchcraft:

Some marks of witches altogether unwarrantable, as proceeding from ignorance, humor, superstition . . . are . . . the sticking of knives across, &c.

Gaule, *Select Cases of Conscience Touching Witches* (1646)

Sussex Latham (1878) 12. Hampshire N&Q 7S:9 (1890) 486. Dorset Udal (1922) 280–1. Somerset [1923] Opie & Tatem, 219; Kettlewell (1927) 32; Tongue (1965) 143. Devon Hewett (1900) 54; N&Q 9S:9 (1902) 14–15; *Devonshire Assoc.* 70 (1938) 116. Cornwall Hunt (1865) 241; *Old Cornwall* 2 (1931–6) 38. Wiltshire *Wilts. N&Q* 1 (1893–5) 61. Berkshire Mitford (1830) 299; Lowsley (1888) 23; *Folk-Lore* 5 (1894) 338. London [1920s] Gamble (1979) 89. Essex [c.1920] Ketteridge & Mays (1972) 142; [1964] Opie & Tatem, 219; [1982] Opie & Tatem, 219. Oxfordshire Surman (1992) 61. Herefordshire Leather (1912) 87. Worcestershire Salisbury (1893) 71. Worcestershire/Shropshire *Gent. Mag.* (1855) 385. Warwickshire Langford (1875) 11; Hewins (1985) 93. Northamptonshire Sternberg (1851)

172. Midland England *Midland Garner* 1 (1884) 23; N&Q 9S:11 (1903) 156. East Anglia Varden (1885) 113. Suffolk *Folk-Lore* 35 (1924) 350. Norfolk Fulcher Collection (c.1895). Lincolnshire Swaby (1891) 93; Good (1900) 108; Sutton (1992) 139. Shropshire Burne (1883) 279. Staffordshire Hackwood (1924) 149. England Addy (1895) 95, 99. Derbyshire *Folk-Lore Jnl* 2 (1884) 280. Yorkshire N&Q 1S:6 (1852) 311–12; *Leeds Mercury* (4 Oct. 1879); Addy (1888) xxi; Nicholson (1890) 42; *Folk-Lore* 43 (1932) 253; Gill (1993) 94. Lancashire [1920s] Corbridge (1964) 156–60; *Lancashire Lore* (1971) 6, 66. Westmorland N&Q 9S:10 (1902) 254. Co. Durham Leighton (1910) 61; N&Q 9S:9 (1902) 357. Northumberland Bosanquet (1929) 76. Wales Davies (1911) 217–18. Monmouthshire [1985] Opie & Tatem, 219. Highland Scotland Polson (1926) 128. Co. Wexford [1938] Ó Muirithe & Nuttall (1999) 162. Jersey *Folk-Lore* 25 (1914) 246. Unlocated Grose (1787) 65; N&Q 9S:9 (1902) 14, 357; N&Q 9S:10 (1902) 74. General John Gaule, *Select Cases of Conscience Touching Witches and Witchcraft* (1646) 75–6; N&Q 9S:9 (1902) 357; N&Q 9S:10 (1902) 74; Hoggart (1957) Ch. 2; Visser (1991) *passim*. Literary Addison, *Spectator* (8 Mar. 1711); John Gay, 'The Farmer's Wife and the Raven', *Fables* (1727); *Connoisseur* 59 (1755) 353; *Old Women's Sayings* (c.1835).

knives: dropped

If a knife is accidentally dropped, a visitor will soon arrive:

If you drop a knife, it means that a man is coming to the house. The gas-man and a friend arriving almost immediately after this announcement on the occasion of such accident, fulfilled it to the great satisfaction of the speaker.

Devon *Devonshire Assoc.* (1926)

In most cases, a knife means a man coming, a dropped fork means a woman, and a spoon either a child or a fool, although occasional informants give knife for woman and fork for man. The size can also be significant:

Should anybody drop a knife, a male visitor was coming – the size of the knife telling how tall the visitor. If our carving knife fell to the floor my aunt invariably remarked 'the rector' (a very tall big man) who often then came.

Wiltshire Wiltshire (1975)

and the direction in which the item points can also be brought in to predict the direction from which the visitor will come, or who in the family s/he will come to see.

The notion of the dropped knife was extremely widespread, being noted all the way from Cornwall to the Orkneys. The earliest mention is from Shropshire in 1873, and there are several other examples before the turn of the century, but the superstition did not seem to reach its full popularity until well into the twentieth century.

Of the three main knife superstitions (knives as gifts, crossed knives and dropped knives), this is the one which does not rely on the dangerous sharp edge as its main feature. Other aspects of a dropped knife, which are not nearly so commonly reported, include the fact that the person who dropped it should not pick it up (a common motif, *see* DROPPING THINGS), and a specialist version of the visitor theme: 'If a girl let her knife fall, her lover and future husband is coming' (**Wales** Trevelyan (1909)).

Somerset Tongue (1965) 143. Dorset Udal (1922) 280–1. Devon Devonshire Assoc. 57 (1926) 130; Devonshire Assoc. 71 (1939) 127–8; Devonshire Assoc. 91 (1959) 200. Cornwall Old Cornwall 2 (1931–6) 38. Wiltshire Wilts. N&Q 1 (1893–5) 61; Wiltshire (1975) 85. London Folk-Lore 37 (1926) 366; Observer Supp. (24 Nov. 1968) 8. Essex [c.1917] Mays (1969) 164. Oxfordshire Folk-Lore 20 (1909) 219. Herefordshire Leather (1912) 86. Bedfordshire Folk-Lore 37 (1926) 77. Cambridgeshire Folk-Lore 25 (1914) 364. Suffolk Folk-Lore 35 (1924) 351. Norfolk Fulcher Collection (c.1895). Lincolnshire Rudkin (1936) 18; [c.1940s] Sutton (1992) 139. Shropshire Bye-Gones (28 May 1873) 171; N&Q 5S:3 (1875) 465; Burne (1883) 279. Staffordshire Folk-Lore 28 (1917) 452; Hackwood (1924) 149; [1954] Opie & Tatem, 218. England Addy (1895) 99. Derbyshire [1890s] Uttley (1946) 128. Yorkshire Folk-Lore 21 (1910) 226; Gill (1993) 94. Co. Durham [1984] Opie & Tatem, 218. Wales Trevelyan (1909) 270. Highland Scotland Polson (1926) 128. Argyllshire Folk-Lore 21 (1910) 89. Caithness Sutherland (1937) 104. Orkney N&Q 10S:12 (1909) 483–4. Co. Wexford Folk-Lore Record 5 (1882) 83; [1938] Ó Muirithe & Nuttall (1999) 162. Unlocated Igglesden (c.1932) 173.

knives: edge upwards

Knives placed with their edge upwards were believed by some to be ominous, but for others were beneficial:

In Portesham, and elsewhere, as a cure for epilepsy, a knife if placed on its back, edge up, under the patient's bed, to cut the charm.

Dorset Folk-Lore (1900)

It is unlucky to put a knife on the table with edge upwards. Cornwall Old Cornwall (1931–6)

I would never have a knife stand with its sharp edge up. I would always put it flat, or the fairies'd cut their feet. I'd think, 'There's another poor fairy with its feet cut'.

Hampshire [1983] Opie & Tatem

Hampshire [1983] Opie & Tatem, 218. Dorset Folk-Lore 11 (1900) 112. Somerset [1923] Opie & Tatem, 218. Cornwall Old Cornwall 2 (1931–6) 38.

knives: finding

Finding a knife is unlucky:

To find a knife on the road or in a field is also supposed to be a very bad omen. This superstition is very general in all parts of Wales.

Wales Davies (1911)

Some specify a disappointment instead of general bad luck. As with other knife beliefs, this appears to be simply a manifestation of the symbolic fear of sharp things, and is especially close to the idea that a knife as a gift cuts love or friendship (*see below*). This superstition appears first in Grose's collection of 1787, a hundred years before many of the other minor knife beliefs, but does not seem to have lasted well in the twentieth century.

Somerset [1923] Opie & Tatem, 218. Northamptonshire Sternberg (1851) 169. Wales Davies (1911) 217–18. Galloway Mactaggart (1824) 210. General Grose (1787) 63.

knives: gift

An extremely widespread superstition dictates that one must never make a gift of a knife or pair of SCISSORS to another, unless the recipient pays for it with a trifle.

When I was a boy (some sixty years ago), a cutler made me a present of a pocket knife, and within the past week one was given me from a Christmas tree. In both cases I was asked for a halfpenny in exchange. Unlocated N&Q (1912)

Failure to reciprocate would mean that the gift would 'cut the love' between the parties and cause a parting or argument. Knives and scissors are the most commonly cited, but the prohibition covers all sharp objects, including even brooches and, in some people's eyes, pins and needles. The belief was so widely known that it was invoked even on formal occasions:

An old superstition was perpetrated at Hanley yesterday. A presentation of cutlery was made by the employees of a local firm to the principal. Before the gathering dispersed the recipient gave each employee a new halfpenny as a symbol of a continuance of the happy relationship existing between the employers and employees, or, to use a localism 'so as not to cut the friendship'.

Glasgow *Glasgow Evening Citizen* (3 Feb. 1912)

There are also many reports of occasions when a dignitary (not excepting the reigning sovereign) has been expected to pay the toll when handed the ceremonial scissors to cut the ribbon to open a new building or project. The fact that everybody understood the symbolism involved could indeed be turned to advantage:

When lads and lasses gave their sweethearts scissors or knives, great care was taken that something should be passed in return – a kiss, a handkerchief, or a small coin. This custom was 'thought much of', and now and then a lass would give a knife, and refuse anything in return, on purpose to cut love. But I never knew a lad to do so.

Unlocated N&Q (1912)

This is one of the few truly satisfying superstitions for the researcher. The meaning has remained remarkably constant from earliest references to the present, and there is no need to guess because it is made explicit in many of the reports. There are abundant examples from all over the British Isles, with no suspicious gaps in the documentary record and from all segments of society. There is also evidence that it functioned at various levels, as these cultural items often do: as literary device, shared joke, confidence between intimates, as well as straightforward superstition. As young Dorothy Osborne could write to her estranged lover in 1654:

Did not you say once you knew where good French tweeses were to bee had? Send me a payer, they shall cutt noe love.

Bedfordshire [1654] Hart (1968)

and over 300 years later, a 23-year-old light-heavyweight boxer could assert:

If you give a safety-pin never give it direct or it'll sever your friendship. Always pin it on his jacket.

London *Observer Supp.* (24 Nov. 1968)

The origin, of course, is still unknown, but it is interesting to note that the three earliest examples – 1611, 1619, 1620 – are so close to each other that we can assume either that it was already well known at that time, or perhaps was fashionably new.

Kent [1983] Opie & Tatem, 345. Sussex Latham (1878) 12. Dorset Udal (1922) 280–1, 285. Somerset [1960] Tongue (1965) 143. Devon Hewett (1900) 54. Cornwall *Old Cornwall* 2 (1931–6) 39. Wiltshire *Wilts. N&Q* 1 (1893–5) 61. London *Observer Supp.* (24 Nov. 1968) 8. Essex [c.1920] Ketteridge & Mays (1972) 143. Oxfordshire [1920s] Surman (1992) 61. Worcestershire *Worcester Herald* (10 Apr. 1858); *Folk-Lore* 20 (1909) 345. Worcestershire/Shropshire *Gent. Mag.* (Oct. 1855) 385. Bedfordshire [1654] Hart (1968) 149. Suffolk Wright (1928) 67. Lincolnshire *Gent. Mag.* (1833) 590–3; Peacock (1877) 151; Good (1900) 108; [c.1940s] Sutton (1992) 139. Shropshire Burne (1883) 279. England Addy (1895) 99. Yorkshire N&Q 1S:6 (1852) 311–12; Robinson (1861) 299; *Leeds Mercury* (4 Oct. 1879); Nicholson (1890) 46; *Folk-Lore* 43 (1932) 253; Gill (1993) 94. Lancashire *Lancashire Lore* (1971) 6. Co. Durham Henderson (1866) 88; Brockie (1886) 212; Leighton (1910) 61. Northumberland Bosanquet (1929) 76. Wales Davies (1911) 217–18. Scotland Wright (1928) 67. Western Scotland Napier (1879) 138. Highland Scotland Polson (1926) 128. Northeast Scotland Gregor (1881) 31. Glasgow *Glasgow Evening Citizen* (3 Feb. 1912). Dumfriesshire Shaw (1890) 12. Argyllshire *Folk-Lore* 21 Aberdeenshire [1952] Opie & Tatem, 345. (1910) 89. Co. Longford *Béaloideas* 6 (1936) 264. Guernsey Carey (1903) 506. Unlocated Grose (1787) 63; Hone, *Year Book* (1832) 126–8; Halliwell (1849) 222; *Gent. Mag.* (1855) 504; N&Q 11S:5 (1912) 91, 157; Gales (1914) 230; Igglesden (c.1932) 209. General Melton (1620); *Illustrated London News* (3 Dec. 1851) 779; Foli (1902) 107; Hoggart (1957) Ch. 2. Literary F. Davison, *Poetical Rapsodie* (1611) 6; *Two Wise Men and All the Rest Fools* (1619) 7:3; John Gay, *The Shepherd's Week* (1714) Tuesday, line 102; Swift (1738); *Connoisseur* 56 (1755) 332; Mrs. Ewing, *Mrs Overtheway's Remembrances* (1894) 35.

knives: sharpening

A handful of references explain that it is unwise to sharpen a knife after sunset (or after supper):

To sharpen a knife after sunset warned that an enemy or a thief would enter your house.

Wiltshire Wiltshire (1975)

The invitation to thieves and burglars is a regular feature of this superstition, but the connection is unfortunately never explained. One report states that it is unlucky to sharpen a knife on a Sunday (**Cornwall** [1890s] *Old Cornwall*).

Cornwall [1890s] *Old Cornwall* 1:12 (1930) 4. **Wiltshire** Wiltshire (1975) 85. **Lincolnshire** Watkins (1886) 12; Swaby (1891) 93. **England** Addy (1895) 102.

knives: spinning

A knife spinning round on the table can be good or bad, depending on whether it was deliberate or accidental:

If a knife turns round and stops with its point towards me (say when I'm washing up and put it on the table) I always dodge to one side out of its way.   Lancashire [1985] Opie & Tatem

In this context, it means death, or at least bad luck, to whoever the blade points to. On the other hand, many people deliberately spin a knife as a mild form of divination, or as a game:

To find out whether your husband will have light or dark hair, take a table knife with a white haft and spin it round on the table. If it stops with the blade towards you your husband will be a dark-haired man, if with the haft he will be a light-haired man.   England Addy (1895)

Neither meaning is well documented in published works, but both were certainly widespread in the twentieth century. Nor can they be shown to be very old, as the earliest reference for each appears in the same 1895 book. The practice of spinning something (a knife or wine bottle, for instance) is still widely done at dinner parties as a game or to decide minor points such as who will get the last after-dinner mint.

The fear of the blade pointing to you accidentally may be connected to the idea that picking up a PIN in the road is all right, as long as it does not point towards you. Another context for the way the knife points is provided by the belief that letting a knife fall means a visitor is coming (*see* KNIVES: DROPPED).

Hampshire [1987] Opie & Tatem, 219. **Dorset** [1935] Opie & Tatem, 219. **Warwickshire** [1982] Opie & Tatem, 219. **England** Addy (1895) 82, 99. **Nottinghamshire** [1987] Opie & Tatem, 219. **Lancashire** [1985] Opie & Tatem, 219.

knives: stirring with

The principle of the knife being symbolically as well as physically dangerous appears to be at the root of a relatively recent superstition which warns that it is unlucky to stir anything with a knife:

If you stir with a knife
You stir up strife.
     Norfolk Fulcher Collection (*c*.1895)

This has only been reported since the 1890s, but during the twentieth century it was more widely known than is indicated by the few references gathered here. There are still many people who know the rhyme even if they do not believe or follow its advice.

Hampshire [1962] Opie & Tatem, 219. **Somerset** [1923] Opie & Tatem, 219; [1960] Tongue (1965) 143. **Devon** *Devonshire Assoc.* 32 (1900) 66. **Gloucestershire** [1984] Opie & Tatem, 219. **Buckinghamshire** [1907] *Folk-Lore* 43 (1932) 110. **Norfolk** Fulcher Collection (*c*.1895). **Highland Scotland** Polson (1926) 128.

knives: stuck in masts, doorposts, bedheads

Sticking a knife into wood was the basis of several superstitious customs, although none were reported very frequently. A knife in the mast was a way of bringing luck to a fishing trip in Shetland and Orkney, although Speranza Wilde counted it as unlucky in Ireland. In the domestic sphere, a similar custom had a protective purpose:

In a lot of the old houses in them days you would see the blade of a knife driven in the door posts or the lintel of the door – they used to say that kept the witches away.   Norfolk [*c*.1870] Haggard

Alternatively, it could be used in LOVE DIVINATION:

A knife thrust violently into the post at the foot of the bed – accompanied with the following rhymes –

  It's not this post alone I stick,
  But (lover's name) heart I wish to prick;
  Whether he be asleep or awake,
  I'd have him come to me and speak

is supposed to bring the sulkiest of lovers back to his mistress.   East Anglia Varden (1885)

East Anglia Varden (1885) 99. **Norfolk** [*c*.1870] Haggard (1935) 16. **Co. Durham** [1980] Opie & Tatem 218. **Shetland** Saxby (1932) 192. **Orkney** N&Q 10S:12 (1909) 483. **Ireland** Wilde (1888) 211.

knives: toasting with

One must never toast bread on the end of a knife. To do so brings bad results, although these vary – 'If you toast with a knife, you'll never be a wife', or 'you'll be poor all your life', or 'no luck all your life'. No explanation is forthcoming.

Somerset [1923] Opie & Tatem, 220. England Addy (1895) 101. Highland Scotland Polson (1926) 128. Unlocated Igglesden (c.1932) 173.

knots

see LOVE DIVINATION: GARTER SPELL; THREAD/STRING.

ladders

The prohibition against walking under a ladder is one of the most widespread superstitions of modern Britain. It is unlikely that any adult does not know it – even if they do not believe it – and it is routinely acted upon even by many who profess not to be superstitious. The fact that it is one of the few well-known beliefs to have a genuine pragmatic value ensures that believers

WHO SAID IT WAS UNLUCKY TO WALK UNDER A LADDER?

Well-known beliefs often receive humorous treatment, as in this postcard from c.1916.

and sceptics alike have an interest in observing it:

a friend of mine, who objected on principle to such superstitious nonsense, had a paint-brush dropped right on his head while passing under a ladder in Cornhill. He has since been a devout believer in the ill-luck of the proceeding.

London N&Q (1866)

a frame of mind gently spoofed by the magazine *Punch*:

It is considered unfortunate by some people to go underneath a ladder. These are the people on whom workmen have dropped pots of paint and molten lead. Others consider it unfortunate to pass outside a ladder. These are they who have stepped off the pavement into the road and have been run over by traction-engines.

Punch (1 Jan. 1881)

Several predicted results of walking under ladders have been given. The earliest reference states simply that 'it may prevent your being married that year', and although this is not the most commonly cited result in later years, it was still being claimed by some informants in late Victorian times:

Some few years ago I was walking with some friends along the streets of a considerable Midland town, when we reached a ladder reared against a house. We were a party of four; a young lady and a gentleman walking in front, a married lady and myself following. The two former walked straight on, unheeding. I, from force of habit, almost mechanically stepped into the roadway, and my companion followed me, exclaiming as she did so in horrified tones, 'Oh, Grace has walked under a ladder! Don't tell her, don't tell her!' 'Why not?' I asked innocently. 'What, don't you know? She'll never be married now!'

Shropshire Burne (1883)

Later references predicted that the careless pedestrian would end up on the gallows, which is presumably linked to one of the supposed origins of the superstition (*see below*). Nevertheless, the majority of historical sources, and virtually everyone in modern times, simply state 'it is unlucky'.

There are also several traditional ways of avoiding the ill luck. SPITTING is one (often specifically between the rungs of the offending ladder, or a set number of times), and CROSS-ING your fingers is another; both of which are regularly used in other protective contexts. More modern prescriptions include details such as

'Don't speak till you see a four-legged animal', or, as in this ungentlemanly example, do not speak first:

If you must pass under a ladder, cross your fingers and wish. The unsophisticated spit; and if you are walking with someone wait for him to speak first, and any ill luck that may be coming will fall on his head.   Co. Durham Leighton (1910)

In popular tradition, there are three main contenders for the origin of the ladder superstition. The one which appears to be the most modern, and is certainly the most obtuse, is that the ladder, floor, and wall form a triangle, and as Christians revere the Trinity, walking through would be disrespectful. This explanation, which sounds like one of the fanciful origin-explanations invented by journalists in the 1970s, was in fact already in circulation by the early 1930s. It is suggested, for example, by Charles Igglesden in 1932. There is not the slightest shred of evidence to support it, and it can be dismissed unreservedly. The other two at least have the distinction of being plausible and fitting with what we know of the workings of superstition in general. One is that each ladder is symbolic of the ladder raised to take Jesus Christ off the Cross, under which, some say, the Devil lurked, either glorying in his triumph or attempting to prevent Jesus' removal. A contributor to *Notes & Queries* points to paintings as, if not the source, at least proof that the superstitious dislike of ladders has a solid Christian basis. The last is that in some designs of gallows (depicted in many popular prints), a ladder is shown leaning at an angle, up which those about to die must climb. However, none of these suggestions is supported by the earliest reference, which specifically claims the action as detrimental to matrimonial opportunities, with which the crucifixion gallows would seem to have nothing in common.

The belief is so ubiquitous nowadays that it is difficult to imagine a time when it was not so well known. But in later Victorian times, it appears that some were unaware of its significance. That excellent observer of Oxfordshire village life, Flora Thompson, specifically states that she did not come across the belief in her youth, and Polson, writing of Highland Scotland at the turn of the twentieth century, commented, 'Neither was it thought unlucky to walk under a ladder'. The role of 'fashion' in the rise and fall of superstitious belief is always underestimated, but the documentary record suggests that the ladder belief, from a slow start in the later eighteenth century, took time to achieve its total market penetration in the late twentieth.

Hampshire N&Q 7S:9 (1890) 486. **Dorset** Udal (1922) 28. **Somerset** N&Q 155 (1928) 209–10. **Devon?** N&Q 1S:6 (1852) 193; Hewett (1900) 53; Crossing (1911) 136; *Devonshire Assoc.* 57 (1926) 131. **Cornwall** *Old Cornwall* 2 (1931–6) 40. **Wiltshire** *Wilts. N&Q* 1 (1893–5) 103. **London?** *Gent. Mag.* (1855) 504; N&Q 3S:9 (1866) 460; Igglesden (*c.*1932) 45–7. **Essex** Mays [*c.*1917] (1969) 163. **Oxfordshire** [1850s?] Plowman (1919) 117; [1890s] Thompson (1943) 488; [1920s] Surman (1992) 60. **Herefordshire** Leather (1912) 88. **Worcestershire/Shropshire** *Gent. Mag.* (1855) 385. **Warwickshire** Langford (1875) 11. **Bedfordshire** *Folk-Lore* 37 (1926) 77. **East Anglia** Varden (1885) 113. **Lincolnshire** *Gent. Mag.* (1833) 590–3; *Grantham Jnl* (29 June 1878). **Shropshire** Burne (1883) 283. **England** Addy (1895) 93. **Derbyshire** *Folk-Lore Jnl* 2 (1884) 280. **Yorkshire** Morris (1911) 238; *Folk-Lore* 43 (1932) 253; Nicholson (1890) 43. **Lancashire** Harland & Wilkinson (1873) 229; [*c.*1916] Corbridge (1964) 156–60; *Lancashire Lore* (1971) 66. **Cumberland** N&Q 6S:6 (1882) 357. **Co. Durham** Leighton (1910) 61. **Northumberland** Bosanquet (1929) 77. **West Wales** Davies (1911) 218. **Scotland** Maclean (1959) 198–9. **Highland Scotland** Polson (1926) 127. **Co. Wexford** [1938]. **Co. Dublin** *Folk-Lore* 4 (1893) 363. **Co. Longford** *Béaloideas* 6 (1936) 263; Ó Muirithe & Nuttall (1999) 162. **Jersey** L'Amy (1927) 98. **Unlocated** Grose (1787) 63; *Punch* (1 Jan. 1881) 310; N&Q 155 (1928) 172, 209, 247; *Watford Observer* (11 Feb. 1994) 20. **General** N&Q 3S:9 (1866) 391; Hone, *Year Book* (1832) 126; N&Q 11S:3 (1911) 217–8.

lad's love

see SOUTHERNWOOD.

ladybirds (*coccinellidae*)

The ladybird is the one insect which has received a consistently positive press in British belief and custom. It was generally thought to be lucky, and was protected from harm – in the same way as ROBINS were in the bird realm – and also featured in a love-divination procedure designed to predict the direction of the future lover's home. The latter was first reported by John Gay in 1714, and lasted well into the twentieth century:

This lady-fly I take from off the grass
Whose spotted back might scarlet red surpass
Fly, lady-bird; north, south, or east or west
Fly where the man is found that I love best.
            John Gay, *The Shepherd's Week* (1714)

It could also help predict the wedding day:

Bisha-bisha-barny-bee
Tell me when my wedding be
If it be tomorrow day
Spread your wings and fly away

*Should the insect fly away the wedding will take
place soon, if it only move and open its wings as
if it would fly, then the lover is thinking of the
girl, and the marriage will take place at a more
distant date.*   Norfolk Fulcher Collection (*c.*1895)

From at least the 1850s onwards, it was considered very unlucky to harm a ladybird, and unspecified, but dire, consequences would follow if anyone was foolish enough to ignore this warning. On the other side of the matter, finding a ladybird could be regarded as lucky:

*The ladybird is very, very lucky particularly if it
comes on you. I remember one coming on me
before a tennis match and being overjoyed.*
Edinburgh [1920s] Opie & Tatem

The insect had numerous local names – including lady-bug, bishop barnabee, lady-cow, and God almighty's cow – and all the different strands of belief could be accompanied by a rhyme which was recited as the ladybird settled on the hand, or when it was seen. The rhyme is still widely known, but it varies considerably across the country. A consistent theme is the house on fire and children:

*Lady-cow, lady-cow, fly thy ways home
Thy house is on fire, thy children are gone
All but one, and he is Tum* [Tom]
And he lies under the grindelstun [grindstone].
Shropshire Burne (1883)

See Opie (1951) for British and foreign versions. Yet another strand of tradition linked the insect with weather:

*The ladybird is considered an accomplished
meteorologist, and is addressed in a Welsh verse
by children thus:*

  *Little speckled cow
  Will there be rain or fair weather
  If there'll be rain, fall down
  If fair weather, fly away*

*And according as the ladybird spreads its wings,
or falls from the finger, the augury is determined.*
South Wales *Monthly Packet* (1863)

Somerset [1923] Opie & Tatem, 226. **London** Barker (1889) 52–3. **Essex** [*c.*1880] *Folk-Lore* 49 (1938) 33. **Herefordshire** Leather (1912) 64. **Worcestershire/Shropshire** *Gent. Mag.* (Oct. 1855) 385. **East Anglia** Forby (1830) 25. **Suffolk** *Folk-Lore Record* 3 (1880) 129. **Norfolk** N&Q 1S:1 (1849) 131–2; Fulcher Collection (*c.*1895). **Shropshire** Burne (1883) 237–8; Gaskell (1894) 267. **Northern England** *Newcastle Weekly Chronicle* (11 Feb. 1899) 7. **Lancashire/Yorkshire** N&Q

1S:4 (1851) 53; Harland & Wilkinson (1882) 70–1. **Yorkshire** N&Q 1S:1 (1849) 132. Nicholson (1890) 137. **Co. Durham** [1940] Opie & Tatem, 226. **South Wales** *Monthly Packet* 26 (1863) 676–85. **Breconshire** *Folk-Lore* 24 (1913) 517. **Scotland** *Edinburgh Mag.* (Oct. 1818) 326–7; Chambers (1842) 43. **Western Scotland** Napier (1879) 117. **Edinburgh** [1920s] Opie & Tatem, 226. **General** Opie (1951) 263–4. **Unlocated** Grose (1787) 64; Igglesden (*c.*1932) 93–4. **Literary** John Gay, *The Shepherd's Week* (1714) Thursday, lines 83–6.

lambs

see SHEEP.

lapwings (*Vanellus vulgaris*)

Also called *peewit*. In British and European tradition, the lapwing does not enjoy a positive reputation but is associated with pride, deceit, and the potential for misfortune:

*I was informed that the country people regard
these birds with much dislike, believing that the
cry they made was – 'bewitch'd, bewitch'd' –
and shrank from them in consequence, fearing
that some witchery and evil were connected
with them. A lady resident in the parish
informed me that her son caught a young
lapwing in the meadows, and showing it to the
wife of the parish clerk was earnestly advised
by her not to keep it, because if he did some
accident or misfortune would be sure to
happen. Mr. Custance tells me that the rustic
belief is that the peewits are departed spirits,
who still haunt the earth, in consequence of
something that troubles them.*
Herefordshire [1856] Leather

Devon *Devonshire Assoc.* 100 (1968) 366. **Herefordshire** [1856] Leather (1912) 256. **General and foreign** Swainson (1886) 183–7.

larks

see SKYLARKS.

last comer

In Thomas Hardy's novel *The Return of the Native*, he describes a superstition about the 'last comer' being lucky. The character Christian is being persuaded to take the last available ticket in a lottery:

'You'll anyhow have the same chance as the rest of us,' said Sam. 'And the extra luck of being the last comer,' said another. 'And I was born wi' a caul, and perhaps can be no more ruined than drowned?' Christian added, beginning to give way.

This belief is apparently not confirmed by any other source. Hardy has an excellent reputation with folklorists because he regularly used folklore material in ways faithful to the tradition and did not normally invent things simply to fit the story. It would be no surprise if other versions of the belief are discovered in due course. The second part of the quotation is also accurate (*see* CAULS).

Literary Thomas Hardy, *The Return of the Native* (1878) Bk 3, Ch. 7.

laughing

The well-known proverb 'sing before breakfast and you'll cry before supper' is occasionally given as 'laugh before breakfast . . .' (*see* SINGING). On the same PURITAN principle, other occasional reports warn against laughter in certain contexts, and there seems to have been a general unease about inordinate merriment in many minds:

It is wrong to laugh before saying one's prayers in the morning, or after saying them at night.
Lincolnshire Gutch & Peacock (1908)

If you laugh very heartily, or laugh till the tears come, you will have trouble afterwards.
England Addy (1895)

The latter is sometimes expressed, cheerfully, as 'Laugh till you cry, sorrow till you die'.

Suffolk [*c*.1880] Opie & Tatem, 228. Lincolnshire Gutch & Peacock (1908) 160, 164. England Addy (1895) 95. Northeast England [1987] Opie & Tatem, 228. General Gaule, *Mag-astro-mances* (1652) 181.

laurel
(*Prunus laurocerasus*)

A recent LOVE DIVINATION procedure reported from various parts of southern England involved pricking a name on a laurel leaf:

When a girl wished to be sure her lover was true she pricked his name on a laurel leaf. If the prickmarks turned pink, it was a sign that he would marry her, but if not, he would desert her.
Oxfordshire *Oxon Folk-Lore Soc.* (1952)

The detail missing in this account is that the leaf was placed in the clothing near the heart. One of Roy Vickery's correspondents explained that when they placed the leaf inside their vest, the warmth brought out the name clearly.

Occasional reports describe other uses of laurel leaves:

A child born feet first will later meet with accident and become lame, unless laurel leaves rubbed on its legs for half an hour within 4 hours of birth.
Unlocated Igglesden (*c*.1932)

The spotted laurel is said to have been spotted ever since some of the milk from the Virgin Mary's breast fell upon it, as she suckled the infant Christ.
Herefordshire Leather (1912)

A stye in the eye is called in Guernsey 'un laurier', and is to be cured by bathing the eye with an infusion of laurel leaves or 'lauriers'.
Guernsey MacCulloch (1864)

Devon [1993] Vickery (1995) 212. Oxfordshire *Oxon Folk-Lore Soc.* (1952) 6. Herefordshire Leather (1912) 19, 63. Cambridgeshire [1952] Vickery (1995) 212. Norfolk Fulcher Collection (*c*.1895). Northamptonshire [1992] Vickery (1995) 212. Guernsey MacCulloch (1864) 505. Unlocated Igglesden (*c*.1932) 140.

lavender

Lavender does not feature widely in the traditions of Britain and Ireland, and only two references have come to light which include references to the plant. The first is impossible to assess without knowing where the author got his information:

Lavender keeps away all evil.
Unlocated Igglesden (*c*.1932)

The second is more interesting in that it connects with other plants which are sensitive to the sex of the human owner:

On my wife mentioning that we were going to plant some lavender in the garden, a message was sent from an old woman to warn us that it must be planted by the man of the house.
Kent *Folk-Lore* 30 (1919)

Kent *Folk-Lore* 30 (1919) 317. Unlocated Igglesden (*c*.1932) 63.

lead

see also HEART DISEASE: CASTING THE HEART.

lead: church roof

A handful of West Country references demonstrate a belief that lead taken from a church could be used medicinally:

Mr. Bray received, as clergyman of the place, the following letter: 'Rev sir, I should take it as a great favour if your Honour would be good enough to let me have the key of the churchyard tonight, to go in at twelve o'clock, to cut off three bits of lead about the size of half a farthing; each from three different shuts (spouts), for the cure of fits.'

                                        Devon Bray (1838)

This belief is one of several which relies on the idea that items connected with a church have a special quality, and has parallels in other 'cures' such as those which utilize ALABASTER scraped from church statues, and the collection of communion pennies, a much more widespread cure for EPILEPSY.

Devon Bray (1838) 291; Devonshire Assoc. 10 (1878) 102.
Devon/Cornwall N&Q 1S:3 (1851) 259.

lead: love divination

A widespread LOVE DIVINATION procedure involved pouring molten lead into cold water and interpreting the shapes it formed, which would indicate the trade of the future husband:

On New Year's Day unmarried girls melt lead and pour it into a bucket of water. It then assumes various shapes, such as a hammer, and from this they divine the trades or occupations of their future husbands.   England Addy (1895)

A less complex, and therefore more common, version involved the use of egg-whites in the same way. As with other divinations, NEW YEAR, HALLOWE'EN and MIDSUMMER were the favourite times for operation, but the procedure could be carried out at any time.

A more romantically fulfilling result was reported from an Irish woman remembering her Victorian childhood, although it is not clear whether this was a general tradition or simply a one-off development within her family circle:

When we were children Hallow Eve was always an occasion for practising mysterious rites, the end and aim of each being to foretell the future. The first thing always was to get an old iron spoon, filled with lead in scraps; this was held over a hot fire till it melted. Then a key, which must be the hall-door key, was held over a tub of cold water, and the hot lead was poured through the wards of the key. The lead cooled in falling through the water, and when it had all settled in the bottom of the tub, the old nurse proceeded to read its surface. I don't know whether there was originally one especial story of the 'willow pattern' description, but I do know that the many I have heard all bore a family likeness. There was always a castle or a tower here, and a narrow window there, and a knight riding to the door to deliver a beautiful lady who was imprisoned there. And of course the lady was the round-eyed child who was listening with bated breath, and who was eventually to marry the said knight.

                    Co. Leix Folk-Lore (1893)

Devon *Western Antiquary* 9 (1889–90) 14.
Herefordshire Leather (1912) 63. **England** Addy (1895) 80. **Lancashire** Harland & Wilkinson (1882) 104; Wright (1913) 260. **Wales** Trevelyan (1909) 229. **Co. Leix** *Folk-Lore* 4 (1893) 361–2. **Guernsey** MacCulloch MS (1864) 410. **General** *Everlasting Fortune-Teller* (1839) 11, quoted in Opie & Tatem, 229.

leather

see SHOES: CHRISTMAS; SHOES: BURNING.

leaves falling

A predominately children's belief holds that it is lucky to catch a leaf which is falling from a tree:

I could never restrain the impulse to dart among the shower [of autumnal leaves] *and catch a falling leaf. As a small boy I had whimsically been taught that there was magic in a falling leaf, if you caught it before it touched the ground.*

                    Sussex [1930s] Murray (1948)

Most authorities state that you will have a happy month for each one caught, and they agree that the leaf must not touch ground. It is more widely known than is indicated by the few published references, and is still passed on, at least in England, from parents to small children on autumnal walks. Not recorded before the late nineteenth century.

Sussex Latham (1878) 9; [1930s] Murray (1948) 179–80. Oxfordshire [1880s] Thompson (1943) 314. Lincolnshire Rudkin (1936) 39. Northamptonshire [1986] Opie & Tatem 230. Cheshire [1948] Opie & Tatem 230. Radnorshire [1953] Opie & Tatem 230.

left

see SUNWISE.

left twin

A person that has outlived its twin was called a 'left twin', in the sense of 'left behind'. Such a one was believed to have certain powers, particularly in the way of curing diseases such as THRUSH.

legal errors

A small number of quasi-superstitions exist in which an erroneous assertion is made that the belief is enshrined in British law, and on the pattern of the older term 'Vulgar errors', these are hereby labelled 'Legal errors'.

For example, it has been claimed that one cannot swear to what one has seen through glass, that the carriage of a corpse down a path or across a piece of land establishes a legal right of way, that it is treason to place a stamp upside down on an envelope, and that butchers and surgeons cannot sit on juries trying murder cases.

As with other folklore genres which involve belief, such as CONTEMPORARY LEGEND, these notions are firmly fixed in many people's minds, who will often become quite angry if challenged or contradicted. Nevertheless, no trace of them has been found in British laws, common or otherwise.

See GLASS: SEEN THROUGH; FUNERALS: RIGHT OF WAY.

life-cycle customs

Traditional activities which take place at key points in an individual's life – birth, baptism, coming of age, marriage, death, and so on. Also called *rites of passage*. These are distinguished from other categories of custom, such as those which take place at a set time of year (CALENDAR CUSTOMS), in a particular occupation, or sporadically for specific ends, such as 'rough music', designed to express community disapproval.

Depending on the point in the life which is being marked, life-cycle customs normally include both a celebratory element, looking backwards to the past, and an anticipatory element which faces the future. Where the latter contains actions or words designed to influence future luck or prosperity, the custom is deemed

sufficiently 'superstitious' to be included in this Guide. Otherwise, they are excluded.

lightening before death

The belief that a dying person will suddenly become quite lucid and articulate and apparently perfectly well, for a short time just before death, is termed 'lightening before death'. Shakespeare refers to it in *Romeo and Juliet*:

How oft when men are at the point of death
Have they been merry? Which their keepers call
A lightning before death.

Other early writers use it as a proverbial phrase, and as a metaphor for an old man being unaccountably merry. The notion lasted well, and folklore collectors found it still current in some areas in the later nineteenth century.

Shropshire Burne (1883) 297. **Northern England** [1850s] *Denham Tracts* 2 (1895) 59. **Literary** Shakespeare, *Romeo and Juliet* (1597) 5:3; S. Daniel *Civil Wars* (1609) 7:93. **General** Thomas Cogan, *Haven of Health* (1596) 135.

lightning

In earlier reports of superstitions about storms, it is clear that the thunder was more feared than the lightning, and this is reflected in many beliefs.

Some of the old cottage folk are still positive that it is not the lightning but the thunder that splits the trees; they ask if a great noise does not make the windows rattle, and want to know whether a still greater one may not rive an oak. They allow, however, that the mischief is sometimes done by a thunder-bolt.
                        Southern England Jefferies (1879) 387

It is probably true, however, that over time lightning has gradually become accepted as the more dangerous component, but in many superstitions it is not possible to separate them. Entries on lightning beliefs are therefore subsumed under THUNDER & LIGHTNING headings.

See also ASCENSION DAY: LIGHTNING.

like cures like

Simila similibus curantur or 'like cures like' is a useful portmanteau term covering three linked concepts in the sphere of folk medicine. In one sense it signifies the notion that the thing which causes a malady is the best means of cure or relief. So, for example, a traditional cure for a DOG-BITE is to eat a piece of the liver of the dog that bit you. The second is less precise, and is concerned with physical similarities between an illness and the item supposed to cure it. Thus, yellow objects often feature in cures for JAUN-DICE, a red thread around the neck helps with a NOSEBLEED, and remedies connected with fire and blood were recommended for ERYSIPELAS.

The third concept is the 'doctrine of signa-tures' which was influential with herbalists from the fifteenth century, when it was described by Paracelsus, until the seventeenth century. The doctrine held that God, in his infinite wisdom, would not have placed the burden of illness and accident on humans without also supplying remedy and cure. Thus, plants had something physical about them which indicated what they would be useful for. Although Vickery (1995) doubts whether this doctrine ever penetrated deeply into popular consciousness, it was welcomed by some compilers of published herbals as a neat way of endowing their herbal theories with a Christian legitimacy.

lilac (*Syringa vulgaris*)

Like many other sweet-smelling flowers, lilac is widely regarded as an unlucky plant to bring indoors, especially white-flowered varieties:

'Don't yew dare bring that in, 'cos I 'on't hev it. Tha's unlucky tew hev in housen, laylock allus wor!' Chris's aunt gave vehement emphasis to the belief she shared with most village folk, that white lilac was unlucky if taken into the house.
Essex [*c.*1920] Ketteridge & Mays

This seems a predominantly southern English belief, although Vickery (1995) gives one exam-ple from Co. Roscommon, and no references have yet come to light from before the early twentieth century. It is still widely believed.

See also FLOWERS: WHITE.

England (various) Vickery (1985) 70–4; Vickery (1995) 220. Devon *Devonshire Assoc.* 61 (1929) 126; *Devonshire Assoc.* 74 (1942) 103. Essex Ketteridge & Mays (1972) 138. Oxfordshire Harris (1969) 125. Herefordshire Leather (1912) 20. Co. Roscommon Vickery (1995) 220. General Baker (1996) 89–90.

limekilns

Various types of industrial fumes, as well as natural airs, have widely been believed to be efficacious in the treatment of WHOOPING COUGH and other respiratory diseases. Patients were treated to regular trips to the local GASWORKS or limekiln:

Cure for whooping cough . . . in carrying the patient through the smoke of a limekiln. Children have lately been brought from some distance to the limekilns at Hawkwell near Stamfordham and passed backwards and forwards.
Northumberland Henderson (1866)

See also AIR CURES.

Staffordshire Poole (1875) 81–2. Lancashire Harland & Wilkinson (1873) 226. Co. Durham Brockie (1886) 221. Northumberland Bigge (1860/62) 89; Henderson (1866) 110–13.

lions: human fertility

Presumed connections between nature and human fertility take several forms, but one of the oddest is the belief that the time when certain animals give birth to their young is very danger-ous for women who are about to do the same. The animals in question were occasionally BEARS and ELEPHANTS, but most frequently lions:

Several women attended by a local midwife having died in child-bed, a neighbour of this woman assured me that she was not to blame for these occurrences, because this was 'the Lion-year'. My informant explained to me that every seven years 'the lioness' had a litter of young, and that if anything went wrong with either mother or cubs on this occasion, many lying-in women died during the year; that 'the' lioness had just cubbed, and that one of her off-spring was dead, this being the sole cause of the deaths in the midwife's practice. She also said that she recol-lected a similar occurrence seven years previ-ously, with like results. I find on enquiry that this belief is general in the district.
Yorkshire N&Q (1884)

Most informants named seven years as the natu-ral cycle involved, but for others it was three years. Some farm animals, particularly pigs it seems, were similarly affected. The belief was sustained by stories which circulated every time a travelling menagerie came to the area, as was another aspect of the same connection between large mammals and human babies (see LIONS: PREGNANT WOMEN).

The earliest reference only dates from the 1870s, but it was still being said in the 1950s.

Sussex Henderson (1879) 23–4. **Somerset** Elworthy (1895) 76. **Middlesex?** N&Q 7S:9 (1890) 385–6. **Midland England** N&Q 5S:2 (1874) 306. **Northamptonshire** Folk-Lore Jnl 3 (1885) 283. **Shropshire** Burne (1883) 286. **Cheshire** N&Q 6S:9 (1884) 337. **Derbyshire** Newcastle Weekly Chronicle (9 Feb. 1895). **Yorkshire** N&Q 6S:9 (1884) 266–7; N&Q 7S:10 (1890) 13. **Inverness-shire** Folk-Lore 62 (1951) 327.

lions: pregnant women

The presumed connection between human childbirth and certain animals is described above, but a different tradition also linked lions and tigers with human pregnancy, by the belief that the animals could not stand to be approached by a pregnant woman:

One year when the [wild beast] *show were on at Ramsey there were quite a bit of excitement. The lions suddenly begun to git so troublesome that it seemed they'd break out o' their cages. They roared and snarled and pounded their bars, that the men had to come a-running with their red hot bars, but even then they couldn't quieten 'em. Then the manager came out and announced that he would have to ask the lady who was expecting a child who was in the tent, to leave. He said he knowed what the matter was, because lions could allus smell a woman as was expecting, and then they allus behaved like this, though he ha'n't ever knowed 'em to be quite so bad afore. Well there were a poor young woman there as were like to have a child soon. When she found the lions a-roaring at her and everybody a-blaming her and pushing her outside the tent, she were so frightened and upset that she fainted right away. I remember my mother and her neighbours a-talking about it, and if I remember aright, they blamed her a bit for ever going to a wild beast show in such a state. Of course they thought such an experience would mark the child, and that it 'ould be born with a lion's mane, or something like that.*

Huntingdonshire [c.1890] Marshall (1967)

This belief was mentioned in Smollett's novel *Humphry Clinker* (1771) and then a handful of times in the late nineteenth century, but the latter informants made it clear that it was widely known at the time.

Huntingdonshire [c.1890] Marshall (1967) 171. **Yorkshire** N&Q 6S:9 (1884) 319. **Literary** Tobias Smollett, *Humphry Clinker* (1771) 140.

lions: ruling monarch

The royal menagerie in the Tower of London was formed in 1235 (or perhaps 1204) and lasted until 1835, when the surviving animals were moved to the Zoological Gardens. In its time the menagerie was very popular with sight-seeing Londoners and visitors, and since at least the year 1288 the collection usually included one or more lions, which were the centre of attraction. At some point the lions in the Tower became associated in the public mind with the ruling sovereign, and the king's death was thought to be preceded by the death of one of the animals:

The king has been ill. It was generally thought he would have died . . . for the oldest lion in the Tower, much about the king's age, died a fortnight ago.   Letter from Lord Chesterfield to his son
(21 Nov. 1758)

It is not clear when this tradition first started, but it is mentioned by several eighteenth-century writers as a common belief of the period.

London Joseph Addison *Free-Holder* (1 June 1716); John Strype, *Stow's Survey of London* 1 (1720) 119; [21 Nov. 1758] *Letters written by Lord Chesterfield to His Son* (1889); Chambers 2 (1878) 595; N&Q 8S:7 (1895) 145.

lizards

Lizards were viewed with suspicion by many people across Britain. It was unlucky if one crossed your path, and dangerous to get too close to one:

The lizard is a vicious animal, always trying to get down people's throats; it will even try to steal into houses where children are that it may get down their throats.

Connemara *Folk-Lore* (1884)

Nevertheless, if one had the courage, one could acquire a tongue that could heal burns:

The lizard, in Irish 'airc luichair', which being literally translated means 'the pig of the rushes' is said to possess curative powers under certain circumstances. When caught, the person who is anxious of having the curative power communicated to him takes the lizard in his hand, licks the creature all over – head, feet, belly, legs, sides, tail; and the tongue of the person who thus licks the airc luichair is said to possess the power, ever afterwards, of taking the sting and pain out of a burn.   Ireland N&Q (1873)

See also ANIMAL INFESTATION; NEWTS.

Somerset [1922] Opie & Tatem, 232. **Herefordshire** [*c*.1895] *Folk-Lore* 39 (1928) 391. **Yorkshire** Blakeborough (1898) 137. **Wales** Trevelyan (1909) 312. **Dumfriesshire** Corrie (1890/91) 81. **Ireland** N&Q 4S:12 (1873) 469; Hickey (1938) 269. **Co. Laoighis** *Béaloideas* 9 (1939) 33. **Connemara** *Folk-Lore* 2 (1884) 261.

lost property, locating

see STOLEN GOODS.

love divination: acorns

see ACORNS.

love divination: apples

Several relatively distinct love-divination procedures utilize apples in some form or other. The apple can be eaten while looking into a mirror, an unbroken apple peel can be thrown over the shoulder and interpreted as the first letter of a name, apple pips can be placed in a fire or otherwise manipulated to reveal a future spouse or love affair, or pins can be stuck into the fruit and placed under the pillow with appropriate spoken charm.

See APPLES: MIRROR DIVINATION; APPLES: PEEL DIVINATION; APPLES: PIN DIVINATION; APPLES: PIP DIVINATION.

love divination: ash leaf

see ASH LEAF DIVINATION.

love divination: ball of thread

A love divination procedure involving a ball of thread or yarn, best known in the description supplied by Robert Burns in a footnote to his 'Hallowe'en' poem, but also reported from Ireland, and England:

The Blue-clue *– Whoever would, with success, try this spell, must strictly observe these directions. Steal out, all alone, to the kiln, and, darkling, throw into the pot a clew of blue yarn; wind it in a new clew, off the old one; and towards the latter end, something will hold the thread; demand 'Wha hauds?', i.e. Who holds? and answer will be returned from the kiln-pot, by naming the Christian and surname of your future spouse.*

Scotland Burns, *Hallowe'en* (1786)

Most other reports do not specify the colour of the thread, and some relate that the thread should be thrown out of the girl's bedroom window. Some also add to the frisson provided by undertaking a 'magic' ritual that requires the recitation of the Paternoster, backwards. Needless to say, if no answer comes, the inquirer will die an old maid, but alternatively she is free to interpret this occurrence as evidence that she did not carry out the ritual properly. Informants also hinted at the possibilities offered to real young men, rather than their WRAITHS, to be in the right place at the right time to make sure their names were spoken.

A similar, but more down-to-earth, practice is reported from Wales:

When spinning of yarn or flax was general in Welsh homesteads, the girls stretched the first piece of yarn or thread they spun on Christmas Eve or the day of twelfth Night outside the door of the house. The first man who passed over it would bear the same Christian name as the future husband. Wales Trevelyan (1909)

Derbyshire N&Q 4S:9 (1872) 135. **Wales** Trevelyan (1909) 235; Davies (1911) 8–9. **Scotland** Robert Burns, fn. to 'Hallowe'en' (1786). **Northeast Scotland** Gregor (1874) 104. **Dumfriesshire** Shaw (1890) 12. **Ireland** Charles Vallencey, *Collectanea de Rebus Hibernicis* 3 (1783) 459–60. *Gent. Mag.* (1865) 701–2. [Some accounts show signs of unacknowledged borrowing from each other.]

love divination: blade-bone

A relatively complex divinatory procedure, using the shoulder-blade of a lamb:

To know if your present sweetheart will marry you let an unmarried woman take the bladebone of a shoulder of lamb, and borrowing a penknife, without on any account mentioning the purpose for which it is required, stick it through the bone when she goes to bed for nine nights in different places, repeating the following lines each time:

> *'Tis not this bone I mean to stick*
> *But my love's heart I mean to prick*
> *Wishing him neither rest nor sleep*
> *Until he comes to me to speak*

According at the end of nine days, or shortly afterwards, he will ask for something to put to a wound he will have met with during the time he was thus charmed. Unlocated Halliwell (1849) 224–5

See BLADE-BONE for further discussion and references.

love divination in 1714

From John Gay, *The Shepherd's Week* (1714)

John Gay's *The Shepherd's Week* is a series of six mock-heroic eclogues in the tradition of Virgil and others, first published in 1714. Gay's characters are shepherds and milkmaids in a contemporary English, rather than classical, pastoral landscape, parodied with gentle humour. In the extract reproduced below, Hobnelia is worried that the affections of her favourite, Lubberkin, have wandered, and she lists all the love divination procedures she has tried – which all confirm that Hobnelia and Lubberkin are meant for each other. All of the ceremonies described have been reported elsewhere, which confirms their accuracy, and in several cases Gay's is the earliest record we have of these particular superstitions.

Thursday; or, The Spell

Hobnelia, seated in a dreary vale,
In pensive mode rehears'd her piteous tale;
Her piteous tale the winds in sighs bemoan,
And pining Echo answers groan for groan:
'I rue the day, a rueful day I trow,
The woful day, a day indeed of woe!'
When Lubberkin to town his cattle drove,
And maiden fine bedight he hapt to love;
The maiden fine bedight his love retains,
And for the village he forsakes the plains.
Return, my Lubberkin! these ditties hear,
Spells will I try, and spells shall ease my care.
  With my sharp heel I three times mark the
    ground,
  And turn me thrice around, around,
    around.
When first the year I heard the cuckoo sing,
And call with welcome note the budding spring,
I straightway set a running with such haste,
Deborah that won the smock scarce ran so fast;
Till spent for lack of breath, quite weary grown,
Upon a rising bank I sat adown,
Then doff'd my shoe; and, by my troth, I swear
Therein I spied this yellow frizzled hair,
As like to Lubberkin's in curl and hue,
As if upon his comely pate it grew.
  With my sharp heel I three times mark the
    ground,
  And turn me thrice around, around,
    around.
At eve last midsummer no sleep I sought,
But to the field a bag of hempseed brought;
I scatter'd round the seed on every side,
And three times in a trembling accent cried,
'This hempseed with my virgin hand I sow,
Who shall my true-love be, the crop shall mow'.
I straight look'd back, and if my eyes speak
    truth,

With his keen scythe behind me came the
    youth.
  With my sharp heel I three times mark the
    ground,
  And turn me thrice around, around,
    around.
Last Valentine, the day when birds of kind
Their paramours with mutual chirpings find,
I early rose, just at the break of day,
Before the sun had chas'd the stars away;
A-field I went, amid the morning dew,
To milk my kine (for so should housewives do)
The first I spied, and the first swain we see,
In spite of fortune, shall our true-love be.
See, Lubberkin! each bird his partner take,
And canst thou then thy sweetheart dear
    forsake?
  With my sharp heel I three times mark the
    ground,
  And turn me thrice around, around,
    around.
Last May-day fair I search'd to find a snail
That might my secret lover's name reveal;
Upon a gooseberry-bush a snail I found,
For always snails near sweetest fruit abound.
I seiz'd the vermin, home I quickly sped,
And on the hearth the milk-white embers
    spread:
Slow crawl'd the snail, and if I right can spell,
In the soft ashes mark'd a curious L:
Oh! may this wondrous omen lucky prove!
For L is found in Lubberkin and love,
  With my sharp heel I three times mark the
    ground,
  And turn me thrice around, around,
    around.
Two hazel-nuts I threw into the flame,
And to each nut I gave a sweetheart's name;
This with the loudest bounce me sore amaz'd,
That in a flame of brightest colour blaz'd:
As blaz'd the nut so may thy passion grow,
For 'twas thy nut that did so brightly glow.
  With my sharp heel I three times mark the
    ground,
  And turn me thrice around, around,
    around.
As peascods once I pluck'd, I chanc'd to see
One that was closely fill'd with three times
    three,
Which when I cropp'd, I safely home convey'd,
And o'er the door the spell in secret laid:
My wheel I turn'd, and sung a ballad new,
While from the spindle I the fleeces drew;
The latch mov'd up, when who should first
    come in,
But, in his proper person – Lubberkin!

I broke my yarn, surpris'd the sight to see,
Sure sign that he would break his word with
   me.
Eftsoons I join'd it with my wonted sleight;
So may again his love with mine unite!
      With my sharp heel I three times mark the
         ground,
      And turn me thrice around, around,
         around.
This lady-fly I take from off the grass,
Whose spotted back might scarlet red surpass.
Fly, lady-bird; north, south, or east, or west,
Fly, where the man is found that I love best.
He leaves my hand; see to the west he's flown,
To call my true-love from the faithless town.
      With my sharp heel I three times mark the
         ground,
      And turn me thrice around, around,
         around.
This mellow pippin which I pare around,
My shepherd's name shall flourish on the
   ground:
I fling the unbroken paring o'er my head,
Upon the grass a perfect L is read;
Yet on my heart a fairer L is seen
Than what the paring marks upon the green.
      With my sharp heel I three times mark the
         ground,
      And turn me thrice around, around,
         around.
This pippin shall another trial make;
See from the core two kernels brown I take;
This on my cheek for Lubberkin is worn,
And Boobyclod on t'other side is borne:
But Boobyclod soon drops upon the ground,
A certain token his love's unsound;
While Lubberkin sticks a firmly to the last;
Oh! were his lips to mine but join'd so fast!

      With my sharp heel I three times mark the
         ground,
      And turn me thrice around, around,
         around.
As Lubberkin once slept beneath a tree,
I twitch'd his dangling garter from his knee;
He wist not when the hempen string I drew;
Now mine I quickly doff of inkle blue;
Together fast I tie the garters twain,
And while I knit the knot repeat this strain;
Three times a true-love's knot I tie secure,
Firm be the knot, firm may his love endure.
      With my sharp heel I three times mark the
         ground,
      And turn me thrice around, around,
         around.
As I was wont, I trudg'd last market-day
To town, with new-laid eggs preserv'd in hay.
I made my market long before 'twas night;
My purse grew heavy, and my basket light.
Straight to the 'pothecary's shop I went,
And in love-powder all my money spent:
Behap what will, next Sunday, after prayers,
When to the alehouse Lubberkin repairs,
These golden flies into his mug I'll throw,
And soon the swain with fervent love shall
   glow.
      With my sharp heel I three times mark the
         ground,
      And turn me thrice around, around,
         around.
But hold – our Lightfoot barks, and cocks his
   ears,
O'er yonder stile see Lubberkin appears.
He comes! he comes! Hobnelia's not betray'd,
Nor shall she, crown'd with willow, die a maid.
He vows, he swears, he'll give me a green gown;
Oh dear! I fall adown, adown, adown!

love divination:
cabbage/kail stalks

A well-known love-divination procedure which
owes its main fame to its inclusion in Robert
Burns's famous poem 'Hallowe'en'. Burns
himself provided an explanatory footnote:

*The first ceremony of Hallowe'en is, pulling each
a stock, or plant of kail. They must go out, hand
in hand, with eyes shut, and pull the first they
meet with; its being big or little, straight or
crooked, is prophetic of the size and shape of the
grand object of all their spells – the husband or
wife. If any 'yird', or earth, stick to the root, that
is 'tocher' or fortune, and the taste of the 'custoc',
that is the heart of the stem, is indicative of the
natural temper and disposition. Lastly, the
stems, or to give them their ordinary appellation, the 'runts' are placed somewhere above the
head of the door; and the Christian names of
the people whom chance brings into the house,
are, according to the priority of placing the
'runts', the names in question.*

Scotland Burns, *Hallowe'en* (1786)

Details vary a little, but the main shape of the
procedure remained remarkably stable for at
least 150 years. The divination was not unknown
in England, but was more commonly reported
from Scotland and Ireland, and it is quite possibly Scottish in origin. Burns's poems were so

widely read and admired that it is feasible that his books contributed greatly to the dissemination of this particular divination method. Foster attests to its survival in Ulster in the mid twentieth century:

Fortune-telling has a place in all Hallowe'en parties, and the fortunes are usually concerned with love and marriage . . . Young men pulled cabbage-stalks, kale-runts. And from their size and the amount of earth which adhered to them they foretold whether their future wives would be tall or short, rich or poor. I saw this done at a Hallowe'en party a few years ago.   N. Ireland Foster (1951)

Herefordshire Leather (1912) 64. England Addy (1895) 84. Derbyshire N&Q 4S:9 (1872) 135. Scotland Robert Burns, n. to 'Hallowe'en' (1786); *People's Friend* (1 Nov. 1882) 693. Highland Scotland Polson (1926) 146–7. Northeast Scotland Gregor (1874) 102. Dunbartonshire [1952] Opie & Tatem. N. Ireland Foster (1951) 27. Co. Leix *Folk-Lore* 4 (1893) 362. Co. Longford *Béaloideas* 6 (1936) 268.

love divination: candles

see CANDLES: LOVE DIVINATION.

love divination: clover

see CLOVER.

love divination: coal

see MIDSUMMER COAL.

love divination: cuckoos

A number of love-divination procedures could be carried out on hearing the first cuckoo in spring:

If a girl sit down when she first hear the cuckoo in the spring, and take off her shoe and stocking from the left foot, she will find a hair between the big toe and the next. This will match the hair of the man she will marry.
Herefordshire Leather (1912)

Girls ask:

Cuckoo, cuckoo, on the tree
How long before I wedded be

If in answer the cuckoo calls more than three or six times, the girls say the bird is bewitched.
Wales Trevelyan (1909)

See CUCKOOS for further discussion and references.

Herefordshire Leather (1912) 63. Wales Trevelyan (1909) 109.

love divination: dragon's blood

'Dragon's blood' is a reddish-brown resin, or powder, made from various trees from countries including Indonesia and the Canary Islands. It had several industrial uses in the manufacture of varnish and as a dye, but herbalists also sold it for use in medicinal and therapeutic contexts. In Britain it was reputed to have particular effect in love divinations, and was recommended in various procedures:

A friend of mine, a retired chemist, informs me that he has sold in the course of business quantities of Dragon's-blood, generally in three-penny-worths, and sometime six-pennyworths; but so much as this is only used in desperate cases – where the lover has fallen off very much in his attention to his fair one.   Devon *Devonshire Assoc.* (1877)

The usual method was to throw it into the fire while certain words were recited:

If your lover forsakes you buy two pennyworth of dragon's blood, and burn it on the fire. Whilst it is burning repeat these lines

'Tis not this blood I wish to burn
But [William's] heart I wish to turn
May he neither sleep nor rest
Till he has granted my request

The same charm can be practised by throwing twelve pins into the fire at midnight and repeating similar lines.   England Addy (1895)

Descriptions of the physical effect of burning dragon's blood vary, but one source describes it as giving off a 'strong herbal spicy fragrance' which will have added to its effect. Dragon's blood can still be bought on the Internet.

Devon *Devonshire Assoc.* 9 (1877) 93–4. Herefordshire Leather (1912) 64. Norfolk Randell (1966) 115. Staffordshire *Folk-Lore* 20 (1909) 221. England Addy (1895) 80. Wales Trevelyan (1909) 237.

love divination: egg whites

The white of an egg – usually stipulated as the first egg laid by a hen – when broken into a tumbler of water, was expected to form shapes which would reveal the trade of the inquirer's future husband.

There were the servants, Budd the cook and the merrymaking among the girls in the kitchen; putting the white of an egg in a glass of water to stand outside on Midsummer's Day to see the shape of your future husband; Budd declaring that hers would be a sailor – she could see the riggings.   Cornwall [1880s] Rowse

As with the similar procedure with molten LEAD, this process allows a high degree of individual interpretation and calls for certain powers of imagination. Some people specialized in such fortune-telling:

But all these portents, good though they be, are as nothing compared with the 'reading of glasses'. The first requisite in order to have one's future told in this way is to find a woman with 'a familiar spirit', by which is meant a woman well up in the foibles and dispositions of young folk who seek her, and possessed of a vivid imagination and a good 'gift of the gab' to give it utterance. When she has got a dozen youngsters round her, she is willing enough to make them happy. First she makes them cast lots as to the order in which their fortunes are to be read, for, of course, the fortunes would all be wrong if they came up in the wrong order. They are then supplied with a tumbler or wine glass which they fill with clean water. She next cracks an egg and lets a few drops fall into the glass, and, after watching the surface bubbles and the long streaks for some time, she reads such fortunes as: 'The person whose glass this is will go a long journey, and come back laden with money. He will lose his present sweetheart, but will again go on another long voyage, and afterwards come home with a beautiful wife'.
                    Highland Scotland Polson (1926)

Many sources do not stipulate a particular time of year for this divination, but a significant number describe MIDSUMMER as the proper time.

The simplicity of the procedure has ensured that it remained remarkably stable from the earliest reference published in *Illustrious Providences* in 1686, and noted by John Aubrey the same year, to the latest, reported in 1956 (Opie & Tatem. 135).

English Gypsies Crabb (1831) 40–1. Cornwall Couch (1871) 155. [1880s] Rowse (1942) 78–9. Wright (1913)

260. Devon *Devonshire Assoc.* 9 (1877) 89–90; *Western Antiquary* 9 (1889–90) 14; Crossing (1911) 149. East Anglia Varden (1885) 110. Northern England Henderson (1866) 81. Co. Durham Brockie (1886) 135. Cumberland Gibson (1858) 105. Highland Scotland Polson (1926) 148–9. Ross & Cromarty Miller (1835) 117. Unlocated J. Mather, *Illustrious Providences* (1684) 288, quoted Opie & Tatem, 135; Aubrey, *Remaines* (1686/1880) 133; Aubrey, *Miscellanies* (1696/1857) 130; [1956] Opie & Tatem, 135.

love divination: eggs eaten

Several love-divination procedures involved eating unpalatable things – the DUMB CAKE, for example, or raw herrings (*see below*) – presumably on the premise that the more difficult the procedure the more powerful its prediction will be.

St. Agnes Fast – To procure a sight of a future husband – Eat nothing all day till going to bed, boil as many hard eggs as there are fasters, extract the yoke, fill the cavity with salt, eat the egg, shell and all, then walk backwards to bed, uttering this invocation to the saint:

> *Sweet St. Agnes work thy fast*
> *If ever I be to marry man*
> *Or man be to marry me*
> *I hope him this night to see.*
>   Northumberland Bigge (1860–62)

This divination was not so well known as the dumb cake, but certainly lasted from the seventeenth to late nineteenth centuries. Accounts differ little in essence. John Aubrey was the first to publish a description, and he, characteristically, was inclined to believe it:

Mrs. Fines of Albery in Oxfordshire did thus; she dream't of an ancient grey, or white-hair'd man and such a shape, which was her husband. This I heard from her owne mouth at Ricot, before the Earl of Abington.
                    Oxfordshire Aubrey, *Remaines* (1686)

Oxfordshire Aubrey, *Remaines* (1686/1972) 208. Herefordshire Lees (1856) 297; Leather (1912) 62. East Anglia Varden (1885) 109. Norfolk Fulcher Collection (c.1894). England Addy (1895) 82. Yorkshire Morris (1911) 229–30. Northumberland Bigge (1860–62) 95–6; Henderson (1866) 70–1. Wales Sikes (1880) 304; Davies (1911) 11. Literary *Connoisseur* 56 (1755) 335.

love divination: ferns

see FERNS: CUT STALK.

love divination: garter spell

A species of love divination in which a girl tied her garter in knots, or round the bedpost, on going to bed, in the usual hope of seeing her future husband in a dream:

To obtain a sight of her future husband, when a young girl sleeps in a strange bed, she observes the ceremony of tying her garter round the bed-post in nine distinct knots, carefully repeating some potent incantation.　　　　Lincolnshire *Gent. Mag.* (1832)

The recited words were very similar to those used in other love divination customs, and other details can be observed, such as approaching the bed backwards, placing the SHOES in a T, and so on.

Put three knots on the left garter, and at every knot say:

> *This knot, this knot, this knot to see*
> *The thing I never saw yet*
> *To see my love in his array*
> *And what he walks in every day*
> *And what his occupation*
> *This night may I in my dream see*
> *And if my love be clad in green*
> *His love for me it is well seen*
> *And if my love be clad in grey*
> *His love for me is far away*
> *And if my love is clad in blue*
> *His love for me is very true*

Go to bed, place the knotted garter under your pillow, and you will see your future husband in a dream.　　　　Co. Longford *Béaloideas* (1936)

The garter was probably singled out for this divination because of its semi-private associations. The process was first mentioned in the humorous article in the *Connoisseur* in 1755, and was later reported a fair number of times, from various parts of the country.

Devon Hewett (1900) 69–70. **Oxfordshire** *Folk-Lore* 24 (1913) 79–80; *Oxon* Folk-Lore Soc. (1952) 7–8. **Lincolnshire** *Gent. Mag.* (Dec. 1832) 493. **Shropshire** Burne (1883) 27. **Radnorshire** N&Q 8S:10 (1896) 214; *Folk-Lore* 6 (1895) 202–4. **Co. Longford** *Béaloideas* 6 (1936) 268. **Unlocated** Grose (1787) 53–4. **Literary** *Connoisseur* 56 (20 Feb. 1755) 331–6.

love divination: gates/stiles

see GATES/STILES.

love divination: hair

see HAIR DIVINATION.

love divination: hemp seed

see HEMP SEED DIVINATION.

love divination: herrings

Herrings could be used in two different love-divination procedures. The first can be compared to others in which something unpleasant had to be eaten, such as the DUMB CAKE and eating eggshells of salt (*see above*), to make the future lover appear in a dream:

When a young woman wishes to know what trade or occupation her future husband is to be, she takes a red herring, and eats it whole, head, tail, fins, and all; and then she goes off to bed in the dark, without speaking a word. If she utter a single sound by the way, the spell is broken. So it is common to lay all sorts of impediments in her road, so as to provoke her to speak, or utter some sudden exclamation. If she passes the ordeal successfully, as soon as she falls asleep she dreams of the sweetheart whom she is to make a happy man of.　　　　Co. Durham Brockie (1886)

A more simple procedure is to throw the herring against the wall:

in a herring, a small silvery-coloured glutinous membrane, of perhaps an inch and a half in length . . . I recollect seeing, not many years ago, the woman servants in my father's kitchen [in Belfast] divining by means of this little membrane, and ascertaining thereby the characters, physical at all events, of their future husbands. The mode of operation was very simple: it consisted merely in throwing the little object from a distance of two or three yards against a whitewashed wall, where from its soft and glutinous nature it adhered, and it depended on the way in which it rested, if stretched out quite straight, curved, very crooked, or all in a little heap, whether the future husband would be tall and handsome, or small and ugly, or perhaps one of the many gradations between these two extremes. Of course each person desiring the omen had to throw for herself, and if I recollect right, could only use the membrane of the herring which she had herself eaten.
　　　　Belfast N&Q (1873)

Neither of these divinations is found before the nineteenth century.

Lincolnshire *Folk-Lore* 2 (1891) 512. **Co. Durham** Brockie (1886) 138. **Northumberland** Bigge (1860–62) 95–6; Henderson (1866) 71. **Co. Longford** *Béaloideas* 6 (1936) 268. **Belfast** N&Q 4S:11 (1873) 274. **Dumfriesshire** Shaw (1890) 12. **Galloway** Mactaggart (1824) 430.

love divination: ivy leaves

see IVY LEAVES: DIVINATION.

love divination: knives

see KNIVES: STUCK IN MASTS, DOORPOSTS, BEDHEADS.

love divination: laurel

see LAUREL.

love divination: lead shapes

A well-known procedure which hoped to reveal details of future love-life:

The future husband's occupation may be revealed on New Year's Eve by pouring some melted lead into a glass of water, and observing what form the drops assume. If they resemble scissors, they point to a tailor; if they depict a hammer, then they foretell a carpenter, and so on.   **Lancashire** Wright (1913) 260

For further description and full references, *see* LEAD: LOVE DIVINATION.

love divination: mirrors

The most common love divination using a mirror involved eating an apple while looking at yourself (*see* APPLES: MIRROR DIVINATION), but one variant omits that key element and focuses instead on the spine-tingling possibilities of candlelight and reflections:

If a maiden sits before her looking glass in her bedroom, at midnight on St Mark's Eve, with a candle in a far corner of the room, giving only a dim light, and repeats these lines:

Come lover, come lad
And make my heart glad
For husband I'll have you
For good or for bad

she will presently see the shadow of her future husband appear in the glass.
  Norfolk Wright & Lones 2 (1938) 187.

Midnight on ST MARK'S EVE was a regular time for such divinations.

love divination: names

A love-divination procedure designed to reveal the name of the future spouse:

On Christmas Eve take three little slips of paper, and write on each the name of a man you like, put each paper into a bread-ball, and throw them into a glass of water, the ball which floats to the top will contain the desired one's name.
  Norfolk Fulcher Collection (*c.*1895)

One of the problems here is that the names are restricted to people that the inquirer already knows, leaving no room for future development, so to speak. Some versions solve this by requiring only a letter of the alphabet on each piece of paper:

Another St. Thomas' Eve love charm is to cut out in paper all the letters of the alphabet and having, on going to bed, placed them in a basin of water underneath the bedstead, in the morning when you look under the bed you will see floating on the surface of the water the letters which represent the initials of your lover.
  Guernsey De Garis (1975)

The time of year also varies from version to version, including all the main love-divination festivals: Christmas Eve, Valentine's Eve, Midsummer, and St Thomas's Eve. This simple divination has been in circulation since at least the 1750s, but has only been reported sporadically since, and only from England and the Channel Islands.

A different approach to names in this context is shown in Joseph Strutt's *Manners and Customs* (1776, 180). Here, the names were written on paper, which was then burnt. The ashes were gathered and placed under the pillow, for the inquirer to 'dream on'.

Somerset Poole (1877) 16–17. **Dorset** Hone, *Year Book* (1832) 588. **Devon** Crossing (1911) 148–9. **Berkshire** Wright (1913) 260. **East Anglia** Varden (1885) 109. **Norfolk** Fulcher Collection (*c.*1895). **Shropshire** Burne (1883) 179. **Guernsey** MacCulloch MS (1864) 409–10; De Garis (1975) 21. **Unlocated** Grose (1790) 55; Halliwell (1849) 225.

love divination: new moon

At the first sight of the new moon, those who wish to find out about their future love-life have two main options. If they can catch the first new moon in the New Year, so much the better. The first is to appeal direct to the moon:

Should a girl wish to ascertain what will be the personal appearance of her future husband she must sit across a gate or stile and look steadfastly at the first new moon that rises after New Year's Day. She must go alone and must not have confided her intention of doing so to anyone, and when the moon appears it is thus apostrophized:

> *All hail to thee, moon! All hail to thee*
> *I pray thee, good moon, reveal to me*
> *This night who my husband must be*

I know of no recent instance of this charm being tried, but I hear that the new January moon is still watched by our Sussex maidens, who, shiv-ering with cold and fear, see the likeness of the future husband come.
> Sussex *Folk-Lore Record* (1878)

The second method was to look at the moon through a handkerchief or reflected in water:

Indeed some persons are content with securing the year's good luck on this occasion, and take little heed of after moons. There is, moreover, an often-practised form of divination by the first new moon in the year; namely, by looking at it through a new silk handkerchief, which of course confuses the vision. As many moons as the inquirer sees, so many years will it be before he or she is married. At Worthen the same thing has been practised by counting the reflections in a pail of water, and at Pulverbatch we hear of the reflections in a looking-glass cunningly placed.
> Shropshire Burne (1883)

See MOON: DIVINATION for further discussion and references.

Sussex *Folk-Lore Record* (1878) 30. **Shropshire** Burne (1883) 256–9.

An illustration from Pearson's Royal Magazine, 1901, *depicting a love-divination procedure at new moon.*

love divination: nuts

A simple form of love divination, carried out mainly at HALLOWE'EN, but sometimes on ST MARK'S EVE.

At Hallowe'en chestnuts are roasted. Two are placed before a hot fire and named after two young people in whom you are interested. If the chestnuts burn steadily side by side they will marry and live happily ever afterwards; should either burst or jump away, the match will not come off.
> Sussex *Folk-Lore* (1914)

This divination was well known all over the British Isles with little variation from at least the early eighteenth century. Burns's poem is the most famous example:

> *The aul guid-wife's weel-hoordet nits*
> *Are round an' round divided,*
> *An' moonie lads an' lasses fates*
> *Are there that night decided:*
> *Some kindle, couthie, side by side,*
> *An' burn thegither trimly;*
> *Some start awa', wi' saucy pride,*
> *An jump out owre the chimlie.*
> Scotland Burns, *Hallowe'en* (1786)

although John Gay had used the theme over seventy years earlier in his *Shepherd's Week* pastoral (1714).

One significant variation was reported in

some areas in the nineteenth century. A couplet was recited as the nuts were placed in the fire, which appears to hope for the opposite reaction to the more normal one described above:

If he loves me pop and fly
If he hates me let and die.

Sussex Latham (1878)

The same procedure could be carried out with APPLE PIPS, PEAS, and PLUMS.

Sussex Latham (1878) 30; *Folk-Lore* 25 (1914) 36; [c.1915] Opie & Tatem, 289. Suffolk *Bye-Gones* (1 June 1887) 317. Lincolnshire Peacock (1877) 162. Derbyshire [1890s] Uttley (1946) 124. Cheshire *Bye-Gones* (1 June 1887) 318. Yorkshire Nicholson (1890) 86. Wales Davies (1911) 13. Denbighshire *Bye-Gones* (19 Jan. 1887) 227. Scotland Robert Burns, 'Hallowe'en' (1786). Northeast Scotland Gregor (1874) 105. Ireland Brand 1 (1813) 302; *Gent. Mag.* (1865) 701; N&Q 4S:1 (1868) 361. N. Ireland Foster (1951) 27. Co. Leix *Folk-Lore* 4 (1893) 362. Unlocated Chambers 1 (1878) 550. Literary John Gay, *The Shepherd's Week* (1714).

love divination: onions

A love divination procedure which involved pins, onion, and pillows:

Girls used to have a method of divination with a St. Thomas's onion, for the purpose of ascertaining their future partners. They peeled the onion, wrapped it up in a clean handkerchief, and then placing it under their heads, said the following lines

Good St. Thomas, do me right
And let my true love come tonight
That I may see him in the face
And him in my kind arms embrace

which was considered infallible for procuring a dream of the beloved one.

Unlocated Halliwell (1849) 224

See ONIONS: DIVINATION for further details and references.

love divination: peas

A well-known love divination which was triggered by finding nine peas in one pod:

If in shelling green peas she finds a pod containing nine, and lays it on the threshold of the kitchen door, the first male to cross it will be either husband or sweetheart.

East Anglia Varden (1885) 109

See PEAS for further description and references.

love divination: prepared meal

One of the more complex of love-divination procedures, designed to make the lover's WRAITH appear:

Watching the Supper – In the extracts from the Hull Advertiser of 1796 . . . is one referring to girls watching their supper on St. Mark's Eve. Old persons used to speak of this as a common practice in houses where there were several female servants. Supper was laid just before midnight, in the kitchen-place, the girls sitting away from the table. As the clock struck midnight 'the shadow' of one or more of the girls' future husbands or sweethearts would come in, and sit down on one of the chairs. My mother had seen tables thus set out in the kitchen of her father's farmhouse about one hundred years ago.

Yorkshire [1796] N&Q

Details vary little from version to version, although some mention that the door must be left open to admit the wraith, and the possibility of a spectral coffin entering the room, which signifies death in the coming year. The earliest example found is in Bovet's *Pandaemonium* (1684), where he describes essentially the same procedure taking place on Midsummer Eve.

Compare LOVE DIVINATION: WASHING SHIFT OR SHIRT.

Somerset Poole (1877) 15–16. Lincolnshire Peacock (1877) 211; Penny (1915) 75. Yorkshire *Hull Advertiser* (14 May 1796) 3, quoted N&Q 11S:3 (1911) 305. Wales Sikes (1880) 302. Angus Laing (1885) 71. General R. Bovet, *Pandaemonium* (1684) 221. Literary Thomas Hardy, *Under the Greenwood Tree* (1872) Pt 1, Ch. 8.

love divination: roses

see ROSES: LOVE DIVINATION.

love divination: sage

see SAGE: LOVE DIVINATION.

love divination: shoes in a T shape

A simple, but widespread, love-divination procedure involved placing the shoes into a certain shape, and saying the requisite rhyme:

Another method of obtaining in your dreams a vision of your lover is to place your boots and shoes on the floor directly below the spot where your head generally reposes, in the shape of a T, and when in bed repeat the following quatrain:

> *I've put my shoes in the form of a T*
> *Hoping my true love to see*
> *Let him be young, or let him be old*
> *Let him come and visit me.*

Jersey *Folk-Lore* (1914)

Descriptions vary very little, except in the length of the rhyme, which seems infinitely extendable:

> *I pin my garters to the wall*
> *And put my shoes in the shape of a T*
> *In hopes my true love for to see*
> *Not in his apparel not in his array*
> *But in the clothes he wears every day*
> *If I am his bride to be*
> *If I am his clothes to wear*
> *If I am his children to bear*
> *I hope he'll turn his face to me*
> *But if I am not his bride to be*
> *If I am not his clothes to wear*
> *If I am not his children to bear*
> *I hope he'll turn his back to me*

Oxfordshire *Folk-Lore* (1913)

In common with many love-divination beliefs, this one is not known before the mid nineteenth century.

Dorset Halliwell (1849) 217. Devon Crossing (1911) 148–9. Cornwall *Old Cornwall* 1:2 (Oct. 1925) 35–6. Oxfordshire *Folk-Lore* 24 (1913) 79–80; *Oxon Folk-Lore Soc.* (1952) 7–8. Herefordshire Leather (1912) 62–3. England Addy (1895) 85. Wales Davies (1911) 9. Pembrokeshire Sikes (1880) 303. Jersey *Folk-Lore* 25 (1914) 247–8.

love divination: snails

see SNAILS: DIVINATION.

love divination: turnips

see TURNIPS: LOVE DIVINATION.

love divination: washing shift or shirt

A complex love-divination procedure designed to bring a future lover's WRAITH into the inquirer's sight:

Maidens anxious for husbands keep watch on Christmas Eve. She who wishes for a sight of her future spouse washes out her chemise, hangs it before the fire to dry, and waits in solemn silence until midnight, when he will come in and turn the linen. This ceremony is observed in some places on New Year's Eve.

East Anglia Varden (1885)

Some details vary considerably, but the core of the ceremony – wetting or washing an item of clothing, setting it to dry, the lover appearing to turn it – is constant in virtually all versions. When it took place indoors, the doors were usually opened, and the enforced silence is also a regular motif.

Accounts of this procedure are sometimes couched in morally neutral terms, simply describing what lovesick girls used to get up to, but others are clearly told as warnings not to meddle with things outside their control. As with other procedures designed to conjure up wraiths, this one could go seriously wrong, and a number of narratives tell of girls who get more than they bargained for. The lover may turn out to be violent or worthless, or the girl may see a coffin, which predicts her husband's or her own early death:

On Hallowe'en or New Year's Eve a border maiden may wash her sark, and hang it over a chair to dry, taking care to tell no one what she is about. If she lie awake long enough, she will see the form of her future spouse enter the room and turn the sark. We are told of one young girl, who, after fulfilling this rite, looked out of bed and saw a coffin behind the sark; it remained visible for some time, and then disappeared. The girl rose up in agony, and told her family what had occurred, and the next morning she heard of her lover's death. In another instance the young woman is said to have seen her lover at first, but his image quickly vanished, and was replaced by a coffin. She was shortly afterwards married to the man, but he soon died and left her a widow.

Northern England Henderson (1866)

As will be seen from these examples, there is no stability in the date chosen for carrying out the rite – Christmas Eve, New Year's Eve, Midsummer Eve, St Mark's Eve, Hallowe'en – all are mentioned by different informants, but all are regular nights for other love-divination routines.

The earliest record for this procedure is in 1685 and, unusually, we have two versions from the same year. While the two reports describe essentially the same activity, they could not be further apart in moral tone. While G. Sinclair was worried that the girl in his version did not realize the wraith was really the Devil, the writer of the chapbook entitled *Mother Bunch's Closet* clearly believed the procedure was a bit of harmless fun. The two reports show that the divination was either already well known at the time or, perhaps, simply 'in fashion'. It is certainly recorded regularly from then on, and no part of the British Isles is without a documented version.

Compare LOVE DIVINATION: PREPARED MEAL.

Sussex Latham (1878) 33. **Devon** [c.1850s] *Devonshire Assoc.* 108 (1976) 188–9. **Wiltshire** *Wilts. N&Q* 1 (1893–5) 155. **East Anglia** Varden (1885) 130. **Suffolk** [c.1820] Gurdon (1893) 98–9; *Folk-Lore* 35 (1924) 352–3. **Norfolk** Fulcher Collection (c.1895). **England** Addy (1895) 88. **Northern England** Henderson (1866) 79. **Yorkshire** Addy (1888) xxv; Blakeborough (1898) 83–4. **Wales** Davies (1911) 10. **South Wales** *Monthly Packet* 26 (1863) 676–85. **Carmarthenshire** Howells (1831) 62–3. **Northeast Scotland** Gregor (1874) 104. **Highland Scotland** G. Sinclair, *Satan's Invisible World* (1685) 141–2. **Dumfriesshire** Corrie (1890/91) 39. **Shetland** [1893] Black (1903) 161. **Shetland** Saxby (1932) 178. **Ireland** C. Vallencey, *De Rebus Hibernicis* 3 (1783) 459–60; *Gent. Mag.* (1865) 701; Wilde (1888) 110. **Literary** *Mother Bunch's Closet Newly Broke Open* (1685); *Connoisseur* 56 (1755) 334; Robert Burns, *Tam Glen* (1790). **General** *Poor Robin's Almanack* (1770) Apr.

love divination: wedding cakes

The symbolic nature of superstition regularly leads to everyday items taking on extra connotations, and it is therefore no surprise that various parts of the wedding procedure, such as the cake and the ring, have taken on love-divinatory roles. A number of procedures existed, for example, which involved placing pieces of wedding cake under the pillow, in the promise that the sleeper would dream of their future spouse. In the simplest version, the cake was merely placed there with no ceremony, but a widespread method involved the new bride's WEDDING RING – thus duplicating the 'love' connection:

They made Agnes take off her ring, and I passed a great many pieces of cake through it for the benefit of those unmarried friends who wished to dream on it.

New South Wales (Scottish) [1844] Boswell

Further complexities were also possible, by adding elements well known from other love divinations:

Most girls have had pieces of wedding cake given them to 'dream on' which they put under their pillows before going to bed, but at Northleigh a girl went through quite a ceremony when doing so. She took a piece of wedding cake, which must consist of both cake and icing, the cake representing the man and the icing the girl, and got into bed backwards, repeating the while the following lines:

> *I put this cake under my head*
> *To dream of the living and not of the dead*
> *To dream of the man that I am to wed*
> *Not in his best or Sunday array*
> *But in clothes he wears every day*

On no account must the girl speak after repeating this rhyme, as, if she said a word, it would prevent her from dreaming of her future husband.   Oxfordshire *Folk-Lore* (1923)

Versions of the wedding cake procedure were already well known in the eighteenth century, being first mentioned in the *Palace Miscellany* of 1733, and appearing in the *Connoisseur* of 1755, in Grose in 1787, and in other publications. It was clearly well known at the time, but it is not certain whether this was because it had already become traditional or whether it was simply new and fashionable. It lasted well into the twentieth century, and it would also be no surprise to learn that some modern girls still put wedding cake under their pillow.

Devon *Devonshire Assoc.* 60 (1928) 119. **Berkshire** Lowsley (1888) 24; Wright (1913) 260. **Oxfordshire** [1920s] Surman (1992) 60–1; *Folk-Lore* 34 (1923) 324–5; *Oxon Folk-Lore Soc.* (1952) 7. **East Anglia** Varden (1885) 109–10. **Lincolnshire** *Gent. Mag.* (1832) 492; *Grantham Jnl* (22 June 1878); Swaby (1891) 91. **Staffordshire** Opie & Tatem, 435. **Derbyshire** [1890s] Uttley (1946) 124. **Northern England** Brand 1 (1813) 32. **Co. Durham** *Folk-Lore* 20 (1909) 74. **Northumberland** Bosanquet (1929) 37. **New South Wales** (Scottish) [1844] Boswell (1965) 94. **Western Scotland** Napier (1879) 51. **Ireland** Wilde (1888) 203. **Co. Tyrone** *Lore & Language* 1:7 (1972) 8. **Unlocated** *Gent. Mag.* (1765) 231; Grose (1787) 54. **Guernsey** De Garis (1975) 22. **General** *Gent. Mag.* (1796) 636. **Literary** *Palace Miscellany* (1733) 30; *Connoisseur* 56 (1755) 335; Charles Dickens, *Pickwick Papers* (1837) Ch. 28.

love divination: wraiths

see WRAITHS.

---

love divination: yarrow

Two forms of LOVE DIVINATION utilize the plant yarrow. In the simpler form, the yarrow is merely plucked and placed under the pillow, with appropriate rhyme, to 'dream on':

Go into the fields at the time of the new moon and pluck a piece of herb yarrow; put it when going to bed under your pillow, saying:

> *Good night, fair yarrow*
> *Thrice good night to thee*
> *I hope before tomorrow's dawn*
> *My true love I shall see*

If you are to be married your sweetheart will appear to you in your dreams.

Cornwall *Folk-Lore Jnl* (1887)

Where and how the plant is found varies from version to version, with some informants stipulating that it grow on 'a young man's grave', while others – especially Irish versions – insisting that the procedure should be carried out on May Day or Hallowe'en.

The second version – often combined with elements of the first – relies on the reputation of the plant to cause NOSEBLEEDS:

Another plant of omen is the yarrow . . . called by us yarroway. The mode of divination is this; you must take one of the serrated leaves of the plant, and with it tickle the inside of the nostrils, repeating each time the following lines: Yarroway, yarroway, bear a white blow/If my love love me, my nose will bleed now. If the blood follows this charm, success in your courtship is held to be certain.

East Anglia Forby (1830)

This version from East Anglia is the first clear example of the yarrow used for love divination, although the connection with nosebleeds dates at least from John Gerard's *Herball* of 1597. There is also earlier evidence of its use in other divinatory contexts, which are unfortunately not always made clear. Thomas Killigrew, for example, includes it in his list of failed lovers' tokens and procedures:

And what becomes of all our vows in Croydon? the bowed two-pence and the garter, which was given with tears because the present spoiled the pair, nor the charms of Valentine, plucked daisies, nor yarrow, St. Ann's Vision, nor her fast, nor ground-willow under her lover's head charms now.

Killigrew, *Thomaso* (1663)

And in a witchcraft trial in Orkney, in 1616, poor Elspeth Reoch was charged with plucking 'ane herb called melefour' [i.e. yarrow], which would cure distemper and give powers of prediction (*Maitland Club Miscellany* 2 (1834–47) 189).

Yarrow love divinations are well reported across Ireland and the southern half of England, but only rarely elsewhere.

See also NOSEBLEED: YARROW; YARROW.

Sussex Latham (1878) 32. **Devon** N&Q 1:4 (1851) 99; Crossing (1911) 147. **Cornwall** *Folk-Lore Jnl* 5 (1887) 215. **Cambridgeshire** [1989] Vickery (1995) 407. **Eastern England** Halliwell (1849) 223–4; **East Anglia** Forby (1830) 424; Wright (1913) 258; **Suffolk** *Folk-Lore Record* 1 (1878) 156. **Dumfriesshire** Corrie (1890/91) 39. **Ireland** Wilde (1888) 104. **Co. Leitrim** *Folk-Lore* 5 (1894) 195–7. **Belfast** [1991] Vickery (1995) 407. **Co. Donegal** *Folk-Lore Jnl* 2 (1884) 90. **Co. Wicklow** [1870] *Folk-Lore Record* 1 (1878) 157. **Dublin** N&Q 4S:4 (1869) 505. **Co. Longford** *Béaloideas* 6 (1936) 268–9. **Literary** Thomas Killigrew, *Thomaso* Pt 2 (1663) 4:2.

Lovett, Edward (1852–1933) [collector and writer]

Edward Lovett was one of the few folklorists of the Victorian/Edwardian era that took an interest in modern superstitious practices, and he was even rarer in that he collected material in London and other urban areas. By profession he was a clerk at the Bank of Scotland in London, rising to the position of Chief Cashier by his retirement in 1912, but in the evenings and at weekends he was an avid, even obsessive, collector of folklore and folklife material. He hoped to be able to found a folklife museum, and his house in Croydon, Surrey, contained a vast amount of material, including, reputedly, one hundred mangles. He was also a champion of alpine plants for the suburban garden and published articles on that topic. The two main areas for which he is remembered are dolls, of which he amassed one of the best historical collections ever made, and superstition and magic.

From an early age, Lovett was fascinated by people's belief in amulets, herbal cures, and 'magical' practices. For him, the term 'magic' encompassed beliefs in everyday objects which he found all around him and which he loved to collect: strings of BLUE BEADS worn against bronchitis, phials of mercury carried to ward off RHEUMATISM, calves' teeth to help with babies'

TEETHING, and torn playing cards, for luck. He made particular studies of the many and various forms of lucky CHARM carried by the First World War soldiers, and the superstitions of FISHER-MEN. In the pursuit of objects and information, he prowled the backstreets, markets, and dock-yards of London, asking questions, buying arte-facts, swapping cheap mass-produced dolls for the homemade affairs carried by children in the slums, and discussing cures, beliefs, and customs with anyone who would listen. Chance meetings on the train or when out for a walk would often yield interesting material, and his writings are full of charming little vignettes:

One of my herbalist friends once informed me that two Stratford-by-Bow girls came into his shop one day and asked for a 'pennorth of tormentil' [Potentilla tormentilla]. A week later both girls returned for more, so he asked them what they wanted it for. The girls hesitated, when the younger said to the other, who had asked for the stuff: 'Oh! Tell him, Jess, I don't mind'. The elder girl then told the herbalist that her sister had been 'chucked' by her 'young man'. Whereupon she consulted an old woman who was 'wise', and that this old woman had told her to get some 'tormentil' root and to burn it at midnight on a Friday; this would so torment and worry the young man that he would soon return

FOR
GOOD LUCK TO ALL TRAVELLERS

(Actual Size)
A. W. GAMAGE, Ltd., Holborn, London, E.C.
BENETFINK & CO., Ltd., Cheapside, E.C.

Superstitions collector Edward Lovett hoped to cash in on a fashion for car mascots by producing this somewhat fanciful example c.1912.

to his lone sweetheart. My herbalist friend told me that the girls came for three successive weeks and then stopped.
                    Magic in Modern London (1925) 9

Lovett's empirical research formed the basis for numerous lectures, which were often in popular demand, especially during the First World War. He also had major exhibitions at a number of venues, including the Crystal Palace, Wellcome Historical Medicine Museum, and the Whitechapel Art Gallery.

As with most of his contemporaries Lovett is at his best in the empirical sphere, when he is describing what he found and what people said and did, and this information is extremely valu-able, but his theorizing has not stood the test of time. Again, he was typical of his generation in that he would pull in 'evidence' from anywhere in the world and any time in history to support what he was saying at the moment, implying that all beliefs can be traced back to classical times and beyond. This is apparently based on the implicit notion that all superstition and magic are the same, and this is where he crosses the line between researcher and practitioner/believer. His approach is summed up by an object which he produced about 1912 and offered for sale through Gamage's of London. It is a 16 cm. high polished brass horseshoe, called 'The Lovett Motor Mascot', which would be 'Good Luck to All Travellers', for 15/-. The brochure explains:

This mascot is, by far, the most powerful one that has ever been devised, consisting as it does of five of the most widely recognised types of amulet in existence, some of which have been in use for more than two thousand years.

The symbols are crescent moons, the wheel of a sun chariot, and a swastika, and the blurb mentions Babylon, Egypt, Greece, Rome, and a handful of ancient deities, but steers clear of anything overtly Christian. What is interesting is that this object was clearly not aimed at the poor, but at the still very select motor-owning classes.

Lovett's life would be almost a complete mystery but for one biographical account, a 53-page typescript, lodged in the Horniman Museum, written by James D. Sage, of New York. Sage's account is undated and names no sources, but he clearly had contact with members of Lovett's family (Lovett had two sons and, prob-ably, a daughter), and provides a fair amount of detail, albeit in somewhat romanticized form.

Although his papers have not survived, many museums hold objects from Lovett's extensive collections, including the Cuming Museum (London), Horniman Museum (London), Science Museum (London), Imperial War Museum (London), Museum of Childhood (Edinburgh), Pitt Rivers Museum (Oxford), and the National Museum of Wales (Cardiff). Most of his public pronouncements were in lecture form, but these were widely printed in local and national newspapers, and he often had these reports printed up as offprints. Catalogues to some of his exhibitions have also survived. Apart from this ephemeral material – which desperately needs bringing together and analysing – he published two more substantial booklets, the first of which is particularly useful for superstition research: *Magic in Modern London* (1925), and *Folk-Lore and Legend of the Surrey Hills and the Sussex Downs and Forest* (1928).

Collection of material at Croydon Local Studies Library; James Sage, *Lovett* (typescript held by Horniman Museum); Tecwyn Vaughan Jones, 'The Lovett Collection', *International Toy & Doll Collector* 12 (1982) 20–2; Short obituaries: *The Times* (10 Aug. 1933) 12; *Croydon Advertiser* (12 Aug. 1933) 5; *Croydon Times* (16 Aug. 1933) 7; National Museum of Wales, *Handbook to the Exhibition of the Lovett Collection of Dolls* (Cardiff, 1914).

luck money

One of several traditions which covered the exchange of money (*see* BUYING AND SELLING), the 'luck penny' or 'luck money' was given back to the buyer once s/he had paid the purchase price, 'for luck'.

A few years ago I sold a venerable carriage, which had for long encumbered our coachhouse to a young innkeeper in East Lancashire for wedding and funeral purposes. In handing me the money he asked me 'for something back for luck' in such a serious and formal manner, that I felt that here was a survival of some ancient ceremony, and that I ought not to attempt to escape from taking part in it. When he received my florin he held it in the palm of his hand with some solemnity, and then ceremoniously covered it with saliva before putting it in his pocket.   Lancashire N&Q (1903)

The amount given back was covered by loose, but locally understood, customary rules, but was also sometimes subject to bargaining as part of the agreed purchase price.

In the buying and selling of cattle old customs are still observed. No one will buy an animal unless a 'luck penny' is given by the seller. 'Penny' is

misleading, the money often runs into pounds and is as much a subject for barter as is the price of the animal.   N. Ireland Foster (1951)

For the superstitious, who took the notion of luck seriously, the return of the money ensured a lucky transaction and minimized the risk of either side's ill-wishing the item sold, out of disgruntlement or spite. This was particularly important when buying and selling animals. For many others, however, it was simply a customary bonus, especially if the buyer were acting on behalf of an employer or other third party, because the discount of the 'luck money' would rarely be passed on.

The system was widely practised and deeply entrenched but it was open to abuse, and by the later nineteenth century many farmers, businessmen and manufacturers began to campaign against it as anachronistic. At best they regarded it as an unwarranted tax on business transactions, and at worst a system of unofficial bribery.

A considerable proportion of the disputes arising from the sale of agricultural produce spring, in one way or another, from this absurd custom of luck-money, which nine-tenths of the farmers wish to see abolished altogether.
                    Lincolnshire N&Q (1877)

Nevertheless, the idea of luck money persisted in many places well into the twentieth century.

See also GOD'S PENNY.

England N&Q 5S:8 (1877) 376–7. Dorset Udal (1922) 281. Devon *Devonshire Assoc.* 12 (1880) 112. Wiltshire N&Q 5S:8 (1877) 37–8. London N&Q 9S:11 (1903) 196. Northamptonshire N&Q 9S:11 (1903) 196. Lincolnshire N&Q 5S:7 (1877) 488; Peacock (1877) 261. England Addy (1895) 99. Shropshire Burne (1883) 272–3. Cheshire Bridge (1917) 144. Northern England Brockett (1829) 193. Yorkshire N&Q 5S:6 (1876) 6; Robinson (1876) 'Luck penny'; Nicholson (1890) 27. Lancashire N&Q 9S:11 (1903) 127. Westmorland *Daily Telegraph* (8 June 1964). Wales Trevelyan (1909) 329. Montgomeryshire *Daily Express* (15 May 1962) 4, quoted Opie & Tatem, 233. Scotland Jamieson, *Scottish Dictionary* (1808) 'Luck-penny'. Edinburgh *Edinburgh Evening Courant* (28 Oct. 1805) 3. Galloway Mactaggart (1824) 324. N. Ireland Foster (1951) 125. Co. Tyrone *Lore & Language* 1:7 (1972) 12.

lucky beans

The beans and seeds of several tropical plants are regularly brought to the western coast of Britain by the Gulf Stream from their native lands in the Caribbean and South America. The larger of these have been prized as 'lucky beans' at least since the early seventeenth century, when

Richard Carew described their use in his *Survey of Cornwall*:

The sea strand is also strewed with sundry fashioned and coloured shells . . . With these are found, moreover, certain nuts, somewhat resembling a sheep's kidney, save that they are flatter; the outside consisteth of a hard dark coloured rind, the inner part of a kernel void of any taste, but not so of virtue, especially for women travailing in childbirth, if at least old wives' tales may deserve any credit.   Cornwall Carew (1602)

Later sources explain that they were worn as amulets to ward off witchcraft, or simply for 'good luck'. Roy Vickery (1995) indicates that they can still be bought in gift shops, but nowadays they are imported in bulk rather than gathered on the seashore.

Also called Molucca beans, sea-beans, and Virgin Mary's nuts.

Cornwall Carew (1602/1969) 44. London [1986] Opie & Tatem, 258. Scotland Scott 2 (1802) 172. Western Scotland Martin (1703) 38–9. Major study Vickery (1995) 337–40.

lucky bird

'Lucky bird' was the name given to the New Year first footer in the Yorkshire area. See FIRST FOOTING (NEW YEAR).

lucky bit

see TONGUE: LUCKY BIT.

lucky bones

A T-shaped bone found in a sheep's head was often termed a 'lucky bone', and carried or worn as an amulet:

The Lucky bone – as its name indicates, is worn about the person to produce good luck; and is also reckoned an excellent protection against witchcraft. It is the bone taken from the head of a sheep, and its form, which is that of the T cross, may have, perhaps, originated the peculiar sanctity in which it is held.
          Northamptonshire Sternberg (1851)

The handful of reports of this 'lucky bone' are all from the northern counties of England from the 1850s onwards, but correspondents to *Notes & Queries* in the 1860s claimed that in Cornwall a small pig's bone served a similar purpose, and described a newspaper advertisement inserted by a 'travelling quack' in July 1764:

I advise the poor gratis, at the Cock, in Church Lane, and I do give twopence for the little round bone in a pig's skull; it lies inside between the eye and ear.   Unlocated N&Q (1866)

See also WISHBONES.

Cornwall N&Q 3S:9 (1866) 146. Northamptonshire Sternberg (1851) 154. England Addy (1895) 87. Northern England [1850s] *Denham Tracts* 2 (1895) 58. Yorkshire Jeffrey (1923) 141. Northumberland Heslop (1894) 'Lucky-byen'; Bosanquet (1929) 78. Unlocated [1764] N&Q 3S:9 (1866) 59.

Macbeth

see THEATRE.

magnets

A few reports claim that magnets are good for CRAMP or RHEUMATISM:

A retired nurse still attending occasional private patients in Worthing told me she had learnt from one of them an infallible way of preventing sudden cramps during the night. All one need do is to put a magnet in the bed, near the foot of it. She added, 'It stands to reason that it works well, because, after all, a cramp is only a form of magnetism, isn't it? So of course a magnet will cure it'.   Sussex *Folk-Lore* (1965)

One can still buy 'magnetic bracelets' which are alleged to counter aches and pains in chemists' and other shops throughout the land.

Sussex *Folk-Lore* 76 (1965) 61–2. Wiltshire Wiltshire (1975) 43. Staffordshire Poole (1875) 83.

magpies: averting bad luck

For those who believe that it is unfortunate to see a magpie, a number of traditional strategies are available to avert the bad luck. These protective procedures usually comprise one or two elements from four basic categories: 1) SPITTING; 2) making the sign of the cross; 3) showing respect by bowing, raising the hat, or speaking politely to the bird; 4) reciting defiant words.

Some, if they do but hear a magpie chatter, wet the forefinger with spittle and therewith make the sign of the cross on the shoe . . . At Pulverbatch they spit on the ground three times and say,

magic in London (1920)

Incantations and spells are often woven within sound of the rumble of London's motor-omnibuses.

The scene is a little shop of a herbalist in the East End. A mother brings her child, whose leg has been scalded by boiling water spouting from a kettle. The herbalist – an old man with a white beard – blows his breath three times on the blisters of the scald, and says:-

'Here come I to cure a burnt sore
If the dead knew what the living endure
The burnt sore would burn no more'.

The next visitor may be a young girl, who wants a charm to bring back and retain the wandering affections of her lover. She is told that she could not do better than to give him secretly in a cup of tea a potion brewed from the roots of the tormentilla – a little yellow flower of the grasslands. The herbalist is a bit of a wag. He cautions the girl to be careful not to administer the potion by mistake to the cat, or the poor animal would die of her unrequited affections!

In a cosmopolitan city like London most of the superstitious survivals of the world are to be found. Superstitions were certainly revived during the war. There was a remarkable vogue in fortune telling and a demand for charms and amulets which brought good luck or preserved the wearer from danger. In this way, what are called the lower and uneducated classes stretched out their hands gropingly to try to get in touch with the supernatural, just as the better and more

intelligent ranks of society availed themselves of the spiritualists 'mediums' for the same purpose.

A 'BOOMING' TRADE

The herbalist does a large trade in cures for various diseases. For cuts and bruises he has an ointment made of the leaves of the elder – the tree upon which, legend has it, Judas hanged himself. He has decoctions of the nettle for chest complaints, and of the dandelion for impurities of the blood. Much of this branch of his business has little or no relation to superstition. The remedies he provides are, to some extent, derived from folklore, and have the recommendation of success, as well as of age, behind them. Of quite a different class is the necklace of blue beads which is said to ward off bronchitis. The depth of human credulity is still more exhibited by a stone having a natural hole through it, which averts bad dreams – unpleasant things in themselves and forecasts of evils to come. The more gruesome an object is the more efficacious it appears to be. There is hardly anything that a coffin-ring got out of a grave will not accomplish: and next to that in efficacy is a stone which has been bitten by a mad dog.

The belief in particular charms rises and wanes, according to circumstances. At one time nearly all seafarers regarded a child's caul as a sure protection from drowning. Then it fell entirely out of fashion. During the German submarine menace as much as £5 would be given for one in the East-end. Now that the safety of the ocean highways has been restored it would be hard to find a sailor who would accept a present of a child's caul. London *The Times* (12 Apr. 1920).

Devil, devil, I defy you
Magpie, magpie, I go by thee

A north Shropshire friend takes off his hat, spits 'in the direction of the bird or birds' and says, 'devil, devil, I defy thee'. Other West Salopians . . . say a man should take off his hat (and a woman drop a curtsey) and say a prayer.
                                   Shropshire/Staffordshire Burne (1883)

Speaking and bowing to magpies was quite a common thing and to this day I still nod my head and politely say 'Good morning, sir' when I catch sight of one.   Oxfordshire Harris (1969)

Sussex Latham (1878) 8–9. Devon N&Q 1S:2 (1850) 512; N&Q 7S:3 (1887) 414–15; Crossing (1911) 136; *Devonshire Assoc.* 66 (1934) 74. Cornwall Hunt (1865) 236–7. Wiltshire Uttley (1946) 131–2. Berkshire N&Q 3S:9 (1866) 59. Oxfordshire Harris (1969) 125. Worcestershire Berkeley & Jenkins (1932) 35.

Warwickshire Langford (1875) 14. Bedfordshire *Folk-Lore* 37 (1926) 77. Lincolnshire *Gent. Mag.* (1833) 593; N&Q 1S:8 (1853) 38; Rudkin (1936) 17. Shropshire/Staffordshire Burne (1883) 223–4. Cheshire N&Q 4S:12 (1873) 327. Staffordshire Poole (1875) 80. Yorkshire N&Q 7S:3 (1887) 414–15; Addy (1888) xviii–xix, Atkinson (1891) 71. Yorkshire/Lancashire N&Q 3S:9 (1866) 187; Harland & Wilkinson (1882) 144. Westmorland *London Saturday Jnl* (13 Mar. 1841) 130–1; Denham Tracts 2 (1895) 20. Co. Durham Brockie (1886) 129–30; Leighton (1910) 63. Mid-Wales Davies (1911) 225. Scotland N&Q 7S:3 (1887) 414–15. Co. Dublin *Folk-Lore* 5 (1894) 283; *Folk-Lore* 4 (1893) 362. Unlocated N&Q 1S:10 (1854) 224; Igglesden (c.1932) 53–4. General *Watford Observer* (11 Feb. 1994) 20.

---

magpies: evil omen

The general dislike of the magpie in Britain and Ireland has already been noted. In particular, the

magpies

In general, magpies get a mixed press in the superstitions of Britain and Ireland. In many traditions they are very unlucky to meet, and are sometimes regarded as outright death omens. In other beliefs, however, they are neutral – such as forecasting the arrival of a stranger – and in the ubiquitous rhyme ('One for sorrow') they have good connotations when they appear in certain numbers. Nevertheless, overall they are disliked and feared. This bad reputation remains largely unexplained. On the European continent, where numerous negative magpie beliefs have also been recorded, the bad reputation is sometimes explained by the belief that witches regularly turned themselves into magpies, but this explanation hardly ever appears in the British Isles.

Some writers, however, refer to the magpie as being called 'the Devil's bird', and some assert that it has 'a drop of the Devil's blood', a claim which is more often made of the YELLOWHAMMER.

[The magpie] *was sometimes called 'the devil's bird' and was believed to have a drop of the devil's blood in its tongue. It was a common notion that a magpie could receive the gift of speech by scratching its tongue, and inserting into the wound a drop of blood from the human tongue.* Northeast Scotland Gregor (1881)

Attempts to explain the beliefs by reference to the magpie's colour have not been convincing. It is true that many black birds are generally treated with caution – RAVENS, for example, and CROWS, which share some of the specific traditions of the magpie. But colour alone does not provide sufficient explanation. Blackbirds and rooks are not feared, nor, for that matter, are black CATS. And the magpie's dual colouring is the same as the piebald HORSE, which in Britain is always given a favourable character.

Traditional legends which seek to explain the magpie's character are most probably post-facto creations.

A north-country servant thus accounted for the unluckiness of the 'pyet' to her master, the Rev. H. Humble. 'It was,' the girl said, 'the only bird which did not go into the ark with Noah; it liked better to sit outside, jabbering over the drowned world'. Co. Durham Brockie (1886)

Noah's Ark is a favourite setting for fables which explain the characteristic of specific species. Another story explains that the magpie is black and white because it was the offspring of the dove and the raven, the first two birds sent out by Noah as the flood neared its end, and it was not baptized during the Flood (Aarne-Thompson motifs A2382.1 and A2542.1.1). For continental analogues to magpie traditions, *see* Swainson (1886) 75–81.

Co. Durham Brockie (1886) 129–30. Northeast Scotland Gregor (1881) 138.

meeting of a single magpie is almost universally regarded as a bad omen. In some versions it means death, in others simply bad luck, but either way the bird is to be avoided, or the planned undertaking abandoned. The most common modern form of this aversion is couched in terms of how many birds are seen together, usually in the rhyme 'One for sorrow' (*see below*), but the versions discussed here are those where only one or two magpies are mentioned, although the distinction is not always clear.

A single magpie crossing your path is esteemed an evil omen, and I once saw a person actually tremble and dissolve into a copious perspiration, when one of these birds flitted chattering before him. Lincolnshire *Gent. Mag.* (1832)

The underlying premise of these beliefs is clear, but there is wide variation in the detail, and the overall pattern is confused. Some versions require specific behaviour on the part of the bird – it is bad if it hops towards you, or flies from your left, or if you see it in the morning. Others worry if it approaches the house:

The magpie is another bird of evil omen, and its chattering near a dwelling is supposed to foretell the decease of one of the inmates. Dumfriesshire Corrie (1890/91)

I was recently told by a native of Morayshire that it is there believed, to the present day, that magpies flying near the windows of a house portend a speedy death to some inmate. Morayshire N&Q (1876)

Nevertheless, a very few reports go against the trend and ascribe good things to the magpie:

A tree with a magpie's nest in it is never known to fall. The perching of a magpie on the roof of a house is regarded as a good sign, a proof of that house being in no danger of falling. Sussex Latham (1878)

The earliest reference in English is found in the *Gospelles of Dystaves* (1507), but this is a translation of a Belgian book and is thus not clear evidence. Certainly, by Shakespeare's time the magpie shared attributes with other ill-boding signs. He writes that 'chattering pies in dismal discords sung' in a passage which includes shrieking owls, ravens, howling dogs, and hideous tempests (*3 Henry VI*). From then on the unluckiness of magpies is reported only sporadically until the deluge of references to the number rhyme take over from the late eighteenth century. Specific procedures for counteracting the birds' evil influence do not appear in the record until relatively late (*see below*).

Kent [1930s] Kent (1977) 148. Sussex Latham (1878) 8–9. Devon Bray (1838) 292; N&Q 10S:12 (1909) 66. Lincolnshire *Gent. Mag.* (1832) 593. Northern England Henderson (1866) 95. Northumberland Bosanquet (1929) 80–1. Wales Jones (1930) 178. Montgomeryshire Hamer (1877) 259. Scotland *Edinburgh Mag.* (Nov. 1818) 412; Jamieson, *Scottish Dictionary* (1825) 'pyat'. Highland Scotland Polson (1926) 18. Morayshire N&Q 5S:6 (1876) 144. Aberdeenshire Laing (1885) 84. Dumfriesshire Corrie (1890–91) 43. Guernsey MacCulloch (1864) 504. General Gaule, *Mag-astromances* (1652) 181; Bourne (1725) 71. Literary Shakespeare, *3 Henry VI* (1595) 5:6; Thomas Hardy, *Far from the Madding Crowd* (1874) Ch. 8.

---

magpies: 'one for sorrow'

The idea that the significance of meeting or seeing magpies is dependent on the number of birds seen is without doubt one of the best-known superstitions in Britain today. This is mainly because of the catchy rhyme, of which almost everyone can recite at least the first two lines. The belief is listed in all the major collections of the nineteenth and early twentieth centuries, although often only in passing, precisely because it was so well known. The rhyme exists in numerous versions, but there is evidence of standardization in recent decades, as people now rely more on books of nursery rhymes than on local or family tradition for their folklore. A relatively 'standard' version:

One for sorrow
Two for joy
Three for a girl
And four for a boy
Five for silver
Six for gold
Seven for a secret never to be told.

South London (author's family)

Another common version:

One for sorrow
Two for mirth
Three for a wedding
Four for a birth
Five for heaven
Six for hell
Seven you'll see the de'il himsell.

Lincolnshire Swaby (1891)

Nevertheless, a close examination of a large number of versions shows that there is far less variation than is apparent at first sight. Similar symbolism occurs again and again but in a different order. There is certainly no definable pattern which can be discerned in the attributes assigned to individual numbers, except for 'one', which is almost always bad (*see below*). Indeed, the pattern is clearly dictated by the exigencies of rhyme and rhythm rather than any intrinsic belief in the numbers themselves. In addition, the basic structure is invariably based on contrasting couplets, usually, but not necessarily, Good or Bad, e.g. Joy/Sorrow, Wedding/Death, Boy/Girl. The rhyme scheme is normally ABCB, so if number two is 'joy', number four is likely to be 'boy', and therefore three is 'girl'. Similarly, if two is 'mirth', four is likely to be 'birth' (or perhaps 'death'), and so on.

Another complicating factor is a kind of 'slippage' – the same couplets can move up or down the scale, again giving only superficial variation. So, for example, two Scottish versions which are almost identical on the verbal scale give very different meanings to each number, simply by starting at a different point:

Ane's joy   *Twa's joy,*
Twa's grief   *Three's grief*
Three's a marriage   *Four's a wedding*
Four's death   *Five's death*
Northeast Scotland   **Scotland** Laing (1885)
Gregor (1881)

Many versions stop at four, but there is a definite rhythmic satisfaction in continuing to seven. As seven gets twice as many syllables as the others, the result is simply the four-line verse which is the bedrock of traditional song and poetry in the English language. Few versions continue after seven, but when they do they simply repeat the pattern.

As indicated, the rhyme was known all over the British Isles, but England and Scotland provide the bulk of the references. On present evidence, the rhyme is not often reported from Wales, and as the magpie was a relative latecomer to Ireland, the belief is less well known there:

Magpies are rare in the more northerly parts of Ulster, I never saw one when I was a child, and the old rhyme 'One for sorrow' is not known to older people in North Antrim and Derry though it is well-known in most other parts. It is surprising how many people dislike seeing a single magpie.   N. Ireland Foster (1951)

The overwhelming majority of reports deem a single magpie to be a bad omen, but a handful of references indicate that for some the opposite was the case, sufficient at least to rule out a simple mistake on the part of the collectors. Perhaps there was more variation on this point than is reflected in the literature. Indeed, a survey of superstitions launched in 1939 and reported in 1953, based on information from Westmorland, Lancashire, and Essex, indicated a substantial minority for a positive interpretation:

To see one magpie is lucky (6 respondents)
To see one magpie is unlucky (12 respondents)
                            Folk-Lore 64 (1953)

The idea that the number of magpies seen is significant cannot be shown to be anywhere near as old as other magpie beliefs. The first two references are both from the same decade of the late eighteenth century, but they already show wide variation, which may perhaps indicate a longer lineage:

One for sorrow
Two for mirth
Three for a wedding
And four for death
            Lincolnshire (c.1780) quoted Opie & Tatem

It is unlucky to see, first one magpie, and then more; but to see two, denotes marriage or merriment; three a successful journey; four an unexpected piece of good news; five you will shortly be in a great company.   Unlocated Grose (1787)

Similar things were also said of CROWS.

Sussex Latham (1878) 8–9; *Sussex County Mag.* 13 (1939) 57–8. Somerset Poole (1877) 38; [1890] Tongue (1965) 46. Devon Bray (1838) 291–2; *Devonshire Assoc.* 21 (1889) 116; Hewett (1892) 26; Hewett (1900) 55; Crossing (1911) 136; *Devonshire Assoc.* 121 (1989) 245. Cornwall N&Q 1S:12 (1855) 37; Hunt (1865) 236–7; Couch (1871) 167; [c.1872] Rowse (1942) 44; N&Q 7S:3 (1887) 414. Wiltshire Smith (1874) 329. Berkshire Mitford (1830) 298–9; Lowsley (1888) 24. Essex [c.1939] *Folk-Lore* 64 (1953) 294; Ketteridge & Mays (1972) 140. Oxfordshire *Folk-Lore* 24 (1913) 88. Herefordshire Leather (1912) 26. Worcestershire Berkeley & Jenkins (1932) 35. Warwickshire Langford (1875) 14; N&Q 7S:3 (1887) 188; *Folk-Lore* 55 (1944) 72. Northamptonshire N&Q 1S:3 (1851) 3–4; N&Q 7S:3 (1887) 188. Cambridgeshire

Porter (1969) 39. Norfolk Randell (1966) 94. Lincolnshire (c.1780) quoted Opie & Tatem, 235; *Gent. Mag.* (1833) 593; Swaby (1891) 93–4; Rudkin (1936) 16–19. Shropshire/Staffordshire Burne (1883) 223–4. Staffordshire Poole (1875) 80. England Addy (1895) 66. Derbyshire [c.1890s] Uttley (1946) 151. Nottinghamshire Addy (1895) 66; Rudkin (1936) 19. Northern England [1850s] *Denham Tracts* 2 (1895) 19–20. Yorkshire N&Q 3S:9 (1866) 187; N&Q 7S:3 (1887) 414–15; Addy (1888) xviii–xix; Blakeborough (1898) 130; *Folk-Lore* 43 (1932) 254. Lancashire Halliwell (1849) 167–8; N&Q 3S:9 (1866) 187; Harland & Wilkinson (1873) 219; Harland & Wilkinson (1882) 143–5; [c.1939] *Folk-Lore* 64 (1953) 294. Westmorland *London Saturday Jnl* (13 Mar. 1841) 130–1; [c.1939] *Folk-Lore* 64 (1953) 294. Co. Durham N&Q 4S:12 (1873) 394; Brockie (1886) 129–30; *Folk-Lore* 20 (1909) 73; Leighton (1910) 63. Northumberland *Folk-Lore* 36 (1925) 253; Bosanquet (1929) 80–1. Pembrokeshire *Folk-Lore* 39 (1928) 173. Scotland Chambers (1826) 285; Chambers (1870) 340–1; Laing (1885) 84. Highland Scotland Macbain (1887/88) 265. Western Scotland Napier (1879) 113–14. Northeast Scotland Gregor (1881) 138. Glasgow [c.1820] Napier (1864) 396. Ayrshire N&Q 2S:4 (1857) 486. Galloway Mactaggart (1824) 212. Ireland *Gent. Mag.* (1865) 700; N&Q 7S:3 (1887) 298; Wilde (1888) 177, 180. Co. Dublin *Folk-Lore* 4 (1893) 363. Co. Mayo *Folk-Lore* 29 (1918) 310. Co. Leitrim *Folk-Lore* 5 (1894) 197–8 Co. Antrim [c.1905] McDowell (1972) 131. N. Ireland Foster (1951) 132. Jersey *Folk-Lore* 25 (1914) 246; L'Amy (1927) 99. Guernsey De Garis (1975) 133. Unlocated Grose (1787) 62; N&Q 1S:5 (1852) 293; *Chamber's Jnl* (1873) 809; N&Q 7S:3 (1887) 414; Igglesden (c.1932) 53–4.

magpies: predict news

Probably as an offshoot of the predicted stranger (*see below*), two references claim that a magpie announces news in some form:

If a magpie chatter twelve times near a house expect a letter soon.
            Co. Longford *Béaloideas* (1936)

A magpie hopping near a dwelling-house was the unfailing indication of the coming of good news, particularly from a far country
            Northeast Scotland Gregor (1881)

Northeast Scotland Gregor (1881) 138. Co. Longford *Béaloideas* 6 (1936) 264.

magpies: predict stranger

The oldest of the magpie superstitions, by some considerable margin, is that the sound of a chattering magpie denotes the coming of a stranger:

When a magpie chatters on a tree by the house it declares the coming of a stranger thither that night.   Unlocated Aubrey, *Remaines* (1686)

The earliest known reference dates from 1159, and a number of subsequent authors confirm this meaning as generally known. It is reported rarely, however, after the sixteenth century. This timespan overlaps with that of the more common belief in the magpie as death omen (*see above*), and it is tempting to say that the latter superstition replaced the former, but this remains unproven. Indeed, it is also possible that the two beliefs were totally independent. It is interesting to note, for example, that the 'stranger' belief invariably stresses the sound made by the magpie (i.e. its chattering), while the other superstitions are almost always concerned with seeing or MEETING the bird, or simply with its presence.

Angus Jamieson, *Scottish Dictionary Supp.* (1825) 'pyat'. **General** John of Salisbury, *Policraticus* (1159); Mannyng, *Handlyng Synne* (1303) lines 355–60; Scot (1584) Bk 9, Ch. 3; N. Homes, *Daemonologie* (1650) 59; Aubrey, *Remaines* (1686/1972) 218; Brand (1777) 93.

magpies: protected from harm

Despite being generally mistrusted and disliked, the magpie is protected, in some people's minds, by the belief that it should not be harmed. The misfortune for ignoring this can be general, or specific:

To have shot a magpie was the certain way of incurring all manner of mishaps.
                        Northeast Scotland Gregor (1881)

It is unlucky to kill a magpie or rob its nest, because if either are done they will kill all your chickens and geese. I have seen people abused, and even pelted, for shooting a magpie at a village.   **Connemara** *Folk-Lore Jnl* (1884)

Kent Igglesden (*c.*1932) 54. **Northeast Scotland** Gregor (1881) 138. **Highland Scotland** Campbell (1900) 249. **Connemara** *Folk-Lore Jnl* 2 (1884) 258. **Unlocated** Grose (1787) 62.

mail van

Research by Iona and Peter Opie in the 1950s discovered a handful of children's beliefs concerned with mail vans. Some reported it as lucky to see, others that it was unlucky to see the back of one (Swansea), while others vied to touch the crown on the side (Scotland). A note in the *Daily Mirror* (31 October 1974) revealed: 'A saying we had [in Suffolk] as youngsters after seeing a Royal Mail van was "Royal Mail, touch the ground, the first boy you speak to you love". We would then spend ages avoiding boys we did not like!'

Various Opie (1959) 218; Opie and Tatem (1989) 236–7.

mandrake (*Mandragora officinarum*)

Although it does not normally grow in Britain, the mandrake has long been surrounded by powerful traditions and beliefs in this country as elsewhere in Europe. Its distinctive form is often claimed to resemble a human being, and since biblical times it has been believed to aid with human conception (Genesis 30:14–16), in addition to possessing many other magical and curative powers. As recorded by Shakespeare and others of his generation, it was believed that it shrieked when pulled out of the ground:

Shrikes like mandrakes torn out of the earth, that living mortals hearing them, run mad.
            Shakespeare, *Romeo & Juliet* (1597)

In later tradition, it was still unlucky to interfere with:

In December 1908, a man employed in digging a neglected garden half a mile from Stratford-on-Avon, cut a large root of white bryony through with his spade. He called it a 'mandrake', and ceased work at once, saying that it was 'awful bad luck'. Before the week was out, he fell down some steps and broke his neck.
                Warwickshire *Folk-Lore* (1913)

Nevertheless, it still had a formidable reputation as a curative well into the twentieth century. Edward Lovett, the great documenter of London superstitions, found that it was still familiar to herbalists in the 1920s. After discussing earlier beliefs about aphrodisiac properties, he commented:

Today I know several places in London where mandrake can be bought, and I have two or three records of these little figures being fixed to the bed-head 'for good luck'. I regret to say, however, that the mandrake has lost its romance. I have seen it very frequently cut up and sold in penny slices. I tried to find out if there was a scrap of romance left. There was not! The vendor said, 'It cures everything'.   **London** Lovett (1925)

In Britain, white bryony (*Bryonia dioica*) was used as a substitute, and indeed was believed by many to be a mandrake.

Wiltshire *Folk-Lore* 45 (1934) 192. **London** Lovett (1925) 73–4. **Warwickshire** *Folk-Lore* 24 (1913) 240. **Lincolnshire** Rudkin (1936) 28–9. **Northumberland** *Newcastle Weekly Chronicle* (11 Feb. 1899) 7. **Unlocated** Grose (1787) 68. **General** [*c*.1050] Cockayne 1 (1864) 249; Gerard, *Herbal* (1597) 280–2; Topsell (1607) 424; Browne, *Pseudodoxia Epidemica* (1646) Bk 2, Ch.6; *Folk-Lore* 73 (1962) 257–69; Vickery (1995) 230, 393–4; Opie & Tatem, 237–8. **Literary** Shakespeare, *Romeo & Juliet* (1597) 4:3; Thomas Scot, *Philomythie* A vii r (1610/1616) quoted in Lean 2 (1905) 651; John Webster, *Duchess of Malfi* (1623) 4:2.

marriage: dominant partner

see HOLLY; PARSLEY; ROSEMARY; WEDDINGS.

marriage: lucky

see MOON: MARRIAGE.

marriage bones

see WISHBONES.

marriages

see WEDDINGS.

May: babies born in

It was commonly believed that kittens born in May were unlucky, no use as mousers, and brought snakes into the house. It was thus not at all uncommon for all kittens born in the month to be unceremoniously drowned (*see* CATS: BORN IN MAY). A similar belief spilled over into the human sphere, and held that babies born in May were sickly and unlucky:

May-born babies, like May kittens, are said to be weakly and unlikely to thrive. Whenever any misfortune befell my grandmother, who died in 1925, she never failed to remind us that she had been born in May. Unlocated *Folk-Lore* (1957)

I used to be quite upset as a child when people said to me, when they heard that my birthday was in May, 'Oh you're a May kitten – you should have been drowned'.
Co. Durham [1986] Opie & Tatem

This belief is not reported as often as that concerning May kittens, and seems a primarily

English superstition, although it was known in Scotland (e.g. Banks 2 (1939) 204). The solitary Irish reference is different to the others, and is probably unrelated to them: 'A child born on May Day will have an evil eye' (Co. Longford *Béaloideas* (1936)).

As noted under CATS, it is unclear why May has been singled out as such an unlucky month.

Somerset [1923] Opie & Tatem, 241. **Cornwall** Hunt (1865) 237. *Folk-Lore Jnl* 5 (1887) 210; *Old Cornwall* 2 (1931–6) 39. **Herefordshire** Leather (1912) 24. **Yorkshire** Addy (1895) 116. **Co. Durham** Leighton (1910) 46; [1986] Opie & Tatem, 241. **Co. Longford** *Béaloideas* 6 (1936) 259. **Unlocated** N&Q 1S:7 (1853) 152; *Folk-Lore* 68 (1957) 413.

May: clothes

see CLOTHES: LEAVING OFF.

May: washing blankets

It is very unlucky to wash blankets during the month of May. A Devon woman, born in 1903, still held to the belief in the 1980s:

I don't wash blankets in May and neither does any of my family – or else you defy superstition. If mine isn't done in April then they have to wait till June. Devon Lakeham (1982)

At best, the blankets will shrink and be useless, but some thought that 'You'll wash the head of the house away', or:

Wash blankets in May
You'll soon be under clay.
Oxfordshire [1920s] Harris

There are a number of superstitions pertaining to WASHING, and in particular several which forbid any washing on specific days, most notably GOOD FRIDAY and NEW YEAR, but this superstition is different in that it refers to a whole month, and to a specific item. Similarly, MAY is an unlucky month in many other respects, including the domestic sphere (*see* also BROOMS: IN MAY), but even in combination these do not fully explain the blanket superstition. It certainly seems to be of recent origin, as there are no reports yet from before 1913, but it was better known than is suggested by the few references given below, and was still being quoted in the late twentieth century. The geographical spread is restricted to southern England.

Somerset [1923] Opie & Tatem, 242. **Devon** *Devonshire Assoc.* 102 (1970) 271; Lakeham (1982) 46; [1987] Opie &

Tatem, 242. **Buckinghamshire** [1913] *Folk-Lore* 43 (1932) 110. **Oxfordshire** [1920s] Harris (1969) 124. **Unlocated** Igglesden (*c.*1932) 99.

May dew: complexion

The best-known feature of May dew is that it is excellent for the complexion – in particular for the removal of freckles – and some said the effect of one bathing lasted all year:

Washing the face with dew gathered on the morning of the first day of May kept it from being tanned by the sun and becoming freckled.
Northeast Scotland Gregor (1881)

It was still being recommended in the late twentieth century:

We were told by other women, 'Wash your face in the May dew, it's good for your skin and will bring good luck'.   Lincolnshire Sutton (1992)

The earliest clear reference is as late as the seventeenth century, and occurs in Samuel Pepys's *Diary*. He describes how his wife, Elizabeth, got up early to gather the dew:

After dinner, my wife away down with Jane and W. Hewer to Woolwich in order to a little ayre, and to lie there tonight and so to gather May dew tomorrow morning, which Mrs. Turner hath taught her as the only thing in the world to wash her face with, and I am contented with it.
London Pepys, *Diary* (28 May 1667)

She went out again on 10 May 1669, but on that occasion he was worried about her being up and about so early. It is worth noting that Elizabeth Pepys clearly believed in the efficacy of the dew throughout May rather than being restricted to the first of the month as was later the case. The wording of Pepys's diary entry could be taken to confirm that the idea of May dew for the complexion was new to him, and as we have no earlier description in Britain it is quite possible that it was a new fashion, probably introduced from the Continent, but research into European analogues would be necessary before this could be tested.

The early history of the custom is unfortunately confused by imprecise reading of primary sources. There are numerous references, going back at least as far as Chaucer's time, to the custom of 'going a-Maying', in which parties would go out to the woods to fetch green boughs to decorate their homes and public buildings. It is often assumed that these trips included bathing in the dew, but this is unwarranted.

London Samuel Pepys, *Diary* (28 May 1667 and 10 May 1669). **Oxfordshire** Harris (1969) 114–5. **Lincolnshire** Sutton (1992) 133. **Shropshire** Burne (1883) 190. **Yorkshire** Nicholson (1890) 142. **Wales** Trevelyan (1909) 312. **Northeast Scotland** Gregor (1881) 151. **Fifeshire** [1952] Opie & Tatem, 246. **Perthshire** Henderson (1879) 85–6. **Edinburgh** Hone, *Every-Day Book* 2 (1827) 305–6. **Angus** Laing (1885) 70. **Ireland** Wilde (1888) 206. **Co. Longford** *Béaloideas* 6 (1936) 264. **New South Wales** (Scottish) Boswell (1965) 165. **Various** Opie (1959) 255–6. **Unlocated** *Morning Post* (2 May 1791). **General** Foli (1902) 108.

May dew: cures

Dew collected on May Day also had something of a medicinal reputation, being recommended for a variety of ailments, including sore eyes, gout, and weakness of the bones:

I knew a little idiot boy whose mother (fancying it was weakness of the spine which prevented him from walking) took him into the fields nine mornings running to rub his back with May-dew.
Shropshire Burne (1883)

Cornwall N&Q 1S:2 (1850) 475. **Wiltshire** Aubrey, *Natural History of Wiltshire* (1691/1847) 73. **Shropshire** Burne (1883) 190. **Wales** N&Q 9S:7 (1901) 141. **Northern Scotland** Jamieson, *Scottish Dictionary* (1808) 'Rude'. **General** Francis Bacon, *Sylva Sylvarum* (1626) Para. 781.

May dew: wishing

A relatively minor belief concerning May dew was that while gathering it for cosmetic purposes (*see above*), there was an opportunity to make a wish:

On the first day of May girls went to wash their faces in the dew and wish before sunrise – while doing this they name some lad and wish in their own mind that he may become their sweetheart, and they get their wish.
Ross & Cromarty Banks (1939)

Cumberland [1957] Opie & Tatem, 245. **Stirlingshire** Hone, *Every-Day Book* 2 (1827) 343. **Aberdeenshire** [1957] Opie & Tatem, 245. **Ross & Cromarty** Banks 2 (1939) 224.

measuring babies

The entrenched fear of TEMPTING FATE manifested itself in new parents' minds in an extreme reluctance to WEIGH or measure the baby, at least until it was of a certain age:

neither at birth nor at baptism will a Highland mother allow her child to be weighed or measured, as that is very unlucky. She is, however,

quite pleased that the medical officer should do so when the youngster goes to school.
Highland Scotland Polson (1926)

In some minds, there was the added incentive that it suggested measuring for a coffin, and in a Welsh example:

If you measure a child for garments in the first six months of its life, it will often want clothes.
Wales Trevelyan (1909)

These notions came under increased attack from post-Second-World-War improvements in health care, and rapidly died out, at least in women of child-bearing age, from about the 1960s.

See also WEIGHING; COUNTING.

Cornwall *Jnl Royal Inst. of Cornwall* 20 (1915) 129; *Old Cornwall* 1:9 (1929). **Wales** Trevelyan (1909) 268. **Highland Scotland** Macbain (1887/88) 254; Polson (1926) 6. **Guernsey** De Garis (1975) 7.

measuring: cures

A number of traditional cures involve measuring the patient:

An old custom with regard to consumption died out in the middle of the nineteenth century. Old women who were skilful in making herb-tea, ointments, and decoctions of all kinds, professed to tell for certain when a person was consumptive. This was by measuring the body. They took a string and measured the patient from head to feet, then from tip to tip of the outspread arms. If the person's length was less than his breadth, he was consumptive; if the width from shoulder to shoulder was narrower than from the throat to the waist, there was little hope of cure. The proper measure was made of yarn.
Wales Trevelyan (1909)

Similar procedures were available for a range of problems, from headache to jaundice, and also formed part of the traditional treatment of cattle who had been ELF-SHOT.

All the recorded examples are from Wales and Ireland.

Wales Trevelyan (1909) 317; *Archaeologia Cambrensis* 79 (1924) 28. **Cardiganshire** *Folk-Lore* 37 (1926) 173. **Co. Clare** *Folk-Lore* 22 (1911) 57. **Co. Longford** *Béaloideas* 6 (1936) 266. **Co. Fermanagh** *Ulster Folklife* 7 (1961) 73–4.

meeting

A large number of superstitions revolved around the concept of *meeting* some person or animal

which was held to have some intrinsic meaning and significance. In most cases this is a clear case of the overwhelming importance of the motif of BEGINNINGS, combined with the inherent ill-luck of the person or thing met with. For example, CROSS-EYED people were often regarded with suspicion, so meeting one was unlucky. The range of unlucky people and things is, however, very large, including: WOMEN, CLERGYMEN, RED-HAIRED people, bare-footed or flat-footed people, PIGS, HARES, single MAGPIES, and black CATS.

He that receiveth a mischance will consider whether he met not a cat or a hare when he went first out of his doors in the morning. Scot (1584)

The vast majority of these beliefs are negative, but a few lucky omens existed, such as (for some) black cats, CHIMNEY SWEEPS, the right number of magpies. Many people had a range of attributes by which they judged a person:

They consider the looks of the first person they see. If he has a good countenance, is decently clad, and has a fair reputation, they rejoice in the omen. If the contrary, they proceed with fears, or return home, and begin their journey a second time. **Scotland** Pennant (1776)

In some contexts, the first person met was deliberately singled out, presumably to leave the matter in the hands of providence, such as when a christening party was instructed to give the CHRISTENING PIECE, of food and money, to the first person they encountered on the way back from church. In other traditions, it is not simply the meeting which counts, but other contributing factors, such as whether the animal crosses your path and, if so, whether from right to left.

Scotland Pennant (1776) 47. **General** Scot (1584) Bk 11, Ch. 15.

mice cures: bed-wetting

The second most common problem for which cooked mouse was recommended was bed-wetting in children:

An old woman lately recommended an occasional roast mouse as a certain cure for a little boy who wetted his bed at night. Her own son, she said, had got over this weakness by eating three roast mice. I am told that the Faculty employ this remedy, and that it has been prescribed in the Oxford infirmary.
Unlocated N&Q (1850)

mice

Mice do not feature strongly in British superstitions, except in the sphere of folk medicine. They were formerly used extensively in cures, most commonly for BED-WETTING and WHOOPING COUGH, but also for a range of other ailments (*see below*). Where mice do appear in beliefs, they usually share key characteristics with RATS. The two main superstitions in this category are that rats or mice gnawing a person's clothes, or a sudden influx of rats or mice into a building, are both taken as death omens. As rats are more commonly cited in these contexts, the entries appear under their own heading rather than here.

A single reference reports that it is unfortunate if a mouse cross your path – a notion which is sometimes cited for other small animals such as SHREWS and WEASELS:

In going a journey, if a mouse runs across one's path he must kill it, and success will attend him; if he fails in this, that day's work will also be a failure. Highland Scotland Macbain (1887/88) 265

See also RATS/MICE.

There is little agreement on how the mouse should be prepared – fried, roasted, boiled, powdered, or baked in a pie are all recommended by various informants. Surprisingly, this use of a cooked mouse can be shown to be very much older than that for the WHOOPING COUGH. It was highly commended, for example, by Thomas Lupton in 1579:

A flaine mouse rosted, or made in powder and drunke at one time, both perfectly helpe such as cannot hold or keepe their water, especially if it be used three dayes in the order. This is very true, and often proved. Lupton (1579)

and was repeatedly printed in seventeenth century works before being collected from all over the country by nineteenth and twentieth century folklorists. Exactly the same cure was well-known in classical times, and it is likely that it entered the British tradition when Lupton and others lifted it directly from Latin sources, such as Pliny's *Natural History* (AD 77), which simply states 'Incontinence of urine in babies is checked by giving in their food boiled mice' (Bk 30, Ch. 47). It was still being described, if not actually recommended, well into the twentieth century.

See also BEDS: WETTING for other cures.

Somerset [1923] Opie & Tatem, 268. London *Folk-Lore* 37 (1926) 367. Oxfordshire [1890s] Thompson (1943) 488; N&Q 1S:2 (1850) 435. Warwickshire Bloom (c.1930) 27–8. Lincolnshire [1920s] Opie & Tatem, 268; Rudkin (1936) 28. Yorkshire N&Q 1S:6 (1852) 311–12; Nicholson (1890) 142. Lancashire Harland & Wilkinson (1882) 75. Wales Trevelyan (1909) 319; Jones (1930) 144. Co. Tyrone *Lore & Language* 1:7 (1972) 10. Unlocated N&Q 1S:2 (1850) 435. General Lupton (1579) Bk 1, Para. 40; Topsell (1607) 515; Richard Lovell, *Panzoologicomineralogia* (1661); N&Q 1S:4 (1851) 52–3.

mice cures: whooping cough

A classic cure for WHOOPING COUGH was to feed the sufferer a cooked mouse:

the husband of one of my informants was induced, when a boy, by his parents, to eat a flayed and toasted mouse, on the representation that it was a little bird. Suffolk *Folk-Lore* (1924)

Different informants prescribe different ways of preparing the mouse – fried, boiled, roasted, powdered, or in a pie, and occasionally there is the added detail that the mouse must be alive at the start of the cooking. In some cases, the patient had to eat mice several times – one a day for three days was common, but in at least one extreme case, three a day for three days was recommended.

This same remedy was also recommended for a range of other problems, including jaundice, croup, fits, stammering, and even smallpox, but by far the most common references are for whooping cough and BED-WETTING.

As with many other whooping cough cures, this one cannot be shown to be older than the mid eighteenth century, in contrast to references to bed-wetting, which occur from the 1570s and even before that in classical sources. As no one has yet come up with any plausible link between the mouse and the whooping cough to explain its popularity, it seems likely that a 'successful' cure was simply transferred to this illness; this process appears to have happened with other whooping cough cures.

Surprisingly, the remedy was still being recommended in the mid twentieth century. The survey of beliefs from Lancashire, Westmorland, and Essex, published in the 1951 issue of *Folk-Lore*, reported that the cooked mouse cure was still known to numerous respondents, and Gwen Raverat also provides evidence of its continued existence:

And even in the year 1947 a fried mouse was earnestly recommended to me as a cure for whooping cough. Unlocated Raverat (1952)

Whooping cough: Sussex [1734] Allen (1995) 114–16. Essex [*c.*1939] *Folk-Lore* 62 (1951) 259–60. Buckinghamshire N&Q 1S:1 (1850) 397. Oxfordshire *Oxf. FL Soc. Ann. Record* (1956) 12. Gloucestershire N&Q 4S:11 (1873) 500; *Glos. N&Q* 1 (1881) 43. Herefordshire Leather (1912) 79. Warwickshire Bloom (*c.*1930) 27–8. Suffolk *Gent. Mag.* (1867) 728–41; Gurdon (1893) 20; *Folk-Lore* 35 (1924) 356; Claxton (1954) 90. Norfolk N&Q 1S:2 (1850) 197; Dew (1898) 77–81; [*c.*1920] Wigby (1976) 66; *Folk-Lore* 40 (1929) 117; Haggard (1935) 16; *East Anglian Mag.* (Aug. 1935) 94. Leicestershire/Northamptonshire N&Q 1S:2 (1850) 4. Shropshire Burne (1883) 212. Lincolnshire Peacock (1877) 170. Nottinghamshire N&Q 4S:2 (1868) 220. England Addy (1895) 91. Yorkshire *Monthly Packet* 25 (1863) 549–51. Westmorland/Lancashire [*c.*1939] *Folk-Lore* 62 (1951) 259–60. Wales Trevelyan (1909) 319. Northeast Scotland Gregor (1881) 127. Banffshire Gregor (1874) 270. Unlocated *Gent. Mag.* (1779) 395; N&Q 1S:2 (1850) 510; Raverat (1952) 57. General N&Q 1S:2 (1850) 510.
Other ailments: Kent Igglesden (*c.*1932) 206. Sussex Latham (1878) 49. Suffolk *Gent. Mag.* (1867) 728–41; [1958] Opie & Tatem, 268. East Anglia Varden (1885) 104. Shropshire [1905] *Folk-Lore* 49 (1938) 229. Yorkshire Nicholson (1890) 142. Wales Trevelyan (1909) 319. Unlocated Chambers 1 (1878) 732. General Richard Lovell, *Panzoologicomineralogia* (1661). Literary Beaumont & Fletcher, *Knight of the Burning Pestle* (1613) 3:2.

Michaelmas
(29 September)

see BLACKBERRIES; GEESE.

midsummer coal

A belief in a magical coal which can only be found on Midsummer's Eve or Day was reported a number of times in the sixteenth and seventeenth centuries, and has the feel of a CONTEMPORARY LEGEND of the time. The power of the coal varies, as does the plant under which it can be found:

It is certainly and constantly affirmed that on Midsummer Eve ... there is found, under the root of mugwort, a coal which saves or keeps them safe from the plague, carbuncle, lightning, the quartain ague, and from burning, that bears the same about them: and Mizaldus, the writer hereof,

saith, that he doth hear that it is to be found the same day under the root of plantain, which I know to be of a truth, for I have found them the same day under the root of plantain, which is especially and chiefly to be found at noon.
Lupton (1579)

By John Aubrey's time, the coal was for LOVE DIVINATION:

The last summer, on the day of St John the Baptist, 1694, I accidentally was walking in the pasture behind Montague House, it was 12 o'clock. I saw there about two or three and twenty young women, most of them well habited, on their knees very busy, as if they had been weeding. I could not presently learn what the matter was; at last a young man told me, that they were looking for a coal under the root of a plantain, to put under their head that night, and they should dream who would be their husbands: It was to be sought for that day and hour.
Aubrey, *Miscellanies* (1696)

No more is heard of this magical coal, but a curious echo is found in a belief collected in 1923 and printed in Opie & Tatem:

On Midsummer day between 10 and 12 take a live coal from the fire and bury it in the garden without speaking to anyone, and you'll be lucky all the year.

Lupton (1579) Bk 1, Para. 59; Thomas Hill, *Natural and Artificial Conclusions* (1650) 146; *Practice of Paul Barbette* (1675) 7; Aubrey, *Miscellanies* (1696) 131.

midsummer men

A well-known and long-standing LOVE DIVINATION procedure in which two plants are picked, named for two potential or existing sweethearts, and placed side by side. Their relative positions are later checked and the chances of future happiness judged:

On Midsummer Eve there is a custom at Cwmcarvon to make a little mound of clay shaped like a grave and put in it pieces of valerian ('midsummer men' they call it about here) naming one for each member of the household. In the morning some are found lying right down – these are those destined to die within the year, those drooping will be ill during the year, and so on. To prophesy the course of true love, two 'midsummer men' should be taken and named, say one for Tom and one for Jane. These should be stuck in clay and put over the lintel of the door. In the morning you will be able to tell how things stand. If Jane leans to Tom and Tom stands straight or leans away, Jane loves him in vain, and vice versa. If both stand straight they do not care for each other, and if they bend over and touch they will marry within the year.

Monmouthshire *Folk-Lore* (1905)

Details vary, but the basic shape of the custom is always the same. The most common plant used is the orpine (*Sedum telephium*), which is often called 'Midsummer Men' in consequence. Orpine is particularly suited to this type of treatment as it flowers in July and remains fresh long after being gathered.

'Midsummer Men' seem to have been proverbial from an early date. Brand (1849) describes a gold ring discovered in Yorkshire in 1801 which bore a device of two orpine plants, bending towards each other, surmounted by a true-love knot, and he estimates the ring to be of the fifteenth century. Vickery (1995), however, advises caution, as the ring cannot now be located and the plants may have been mis-identified. The Belgian botanist Rembert Dodoens includes the orpine in his pioneering *Niewe Herball* (in Flemish, 1554; English translation, 1578) and comments that country people 'delight much' in setting it around the house on Midsummer Eve, but he does not actually mention the divinatory aspect. A century later, however, John Aubrey provides the first definite description:

Also I remember the mayds (especially the cooke-mayds and dairy-mayds) would stick up in some chinkes of the joists or &c.Midsomer-men, which are slips of orpins: they placed them by paires, sc. one for such a man the other for such a mayd his sweetheart, and accordingly as the orpin did incline to, or recline from the other; that there would be love, or aversion; if either did wither death. Unlocated Aubrey, *Remaines* (1686)

The tradition lasted well into the twentieth century.

Sussex [1920s] Simpson (1973) 123. Wiltshire Hone, *Table Book* (1827) 842–3; Francis Kilvert, *Diary* (11 June (1874). Berkshire Salmon (1902) 422. Herefordshire Leather (1912) 64. Shropshire Burne (1883) 242. Monmouthshire *Folk-Lore* 16 (1905) 65. Unlocated Aubrey, *Remaines* (1686/1972) 214; *Connoisseur* (20 Feb. 1755). General Dodoens, *Niewe Herball* (1578); Brand 1 (1849) 330; Vickery (1995) 270–1. Literary Hannah More, *Tawney Rachel* (*c*.1800).

midsummer rose

see ROSES: LOVE DIVINATION.

mince pies

see CHRISTMAS: MINCE PIES.

mirrors

see also APPLES: MIRROR DIVINATION.

mirrors: baby seeing itself

Not as well known as some of the other 'mirror' superstitions, the idea that it is unlucky for a baby to see itself in a mirror was reasonably widespread from the mid nineteenth to the later twentieth century, but is probably forgotten now. The period of prohibition varied from four months to two years, or before the child could walk, or talk, or had teeth. Similarly, the consequence varies from general bad luck to contracting rickets, becoming cross-eyed, or have a hard time teething. The earliest references date only from the 1850s, and are not very informative:

It is also considered highly injurious to let a child look in [a mirror] before it is a year old.

Northamptonshire Sternberg (1851)

A child must not be suffered to look in a glass before it is twelve months old.

Northern England [1850s] *Denham Tracts*

One variant adds a detail:

A young woman here has been troubled because her baby might see itself in the looking-glass at the back of her sideboard before it was a year old. Her mother, a native of Nottinghamshire, long resident in Lincolnshire, said by way of comfort – 'Just seeing itself by chance does not count. It is showing the baby its own reflection which is unlucky.' Lincolnshire *Folk-Lore* (1909)

The 'uncanny' nature of mirrors, and the PURITAN streak of superstition which frowns on people spending too much time in front of the glass are noted in entries for other mirror beliefs, but these do not satisfactorily explain the prohibition on babies seeing their own reflection. It could perhaps be argued that allowing the baby to be reflected is a form of TEMPTING FATE, but this is tenuous at best.

Devon N&Q 10S:12 (1909) 66; *Devonshire Assoc.* 59 (1927) 168–9; *Devonshire Assoc.* 60 (1928) 125; *Devonshire Assoc.* 104 (1972) 267; *Devonshire Assoc.* 105 (1973) 214. Cornwall *Jnl Royal Inst. Cornwall* 20 (1915) 129; *Old Cornwall* 1:9 (1929); *Old Cornwall* 2 (1931–6)

39. **Wiltshire** *Wilts. N&Q* 1 (1893–5) 103. **Herefordshire** Leather (1912) 113. **Warwickshire** Bloom (c.1930) 19. **Northamptonshire** Sternberg (1851) 172. **Suffolk** [1953] Opie & Tatem, 253. **Lincolnshire** *Grantham Jnl* (22 June 1878); *Folk-Lore* 20 (1909) 218; **Shropshire** Burne (1883) 286. **England** Addy (1895) 102. **Northern England** [1850s] *Denham Tracts* 2 (1895) 48. **Wales** Trevelyan (1909) 268. **Highland Scotland** Polson (1926) 127; Macbain (1887/88) 254. **Yorkshire** Nicholson (1890) 43. **Dumfriesshire** Corrie (1890/91) 38. **Guernsey** De Garis (1975) 8. **Unlocated** Igglesden (c.1932) 139–40.

mirrors: breaking

One of the most common superstitions in Britain today, the idea that breaking a mirror means bad luck, is widely known to believers and non-believers alike. First references date from the late eighteenth century and are very similar in content:

To break a looking-glass is accounted a very unlucky accident.   Unlocated Brand (1777)

To break a looking-glass is extremely unlucky; the party to whom it belongs will lose his best friend . . . Breaking a looking-glass betokens a mortality in the family.   Unlocated Grose (1787)

The belief is well documented through the nineteenth and twentieth centuries, although most of the references continue to simply state the bare essentials with no elaboration. Unspecified bad luck or death of a family member is the usual consequence, but the specific 'seven years bad luck', so common nowadays, only appears from 1851 onwards. Occasionally, the breaking glass is seen as a sign of an event rather than an omen:

This instance I can vouch for. A group of persons stood discussing the state of a sick friend, when one of the number accidentally knocked down a glass, and shattered it into fragments. '— is dead,' said one. 'It is a death notice,' said another. Such it turned out; the person died in the same hour.   Unlocated N&Q (1893)

The broken mirror still has power to upset people:

In February 1996 a young woman who was hurriedly packing her possessions (on the break-up of her marriage), heard the mirror on the inside of her vanity-case break. She burst into tears, saying 'As if I didn't have enough troubles – now I'm going to have seven years!'   Sussex Steve Roud Collection

A rational, but unconvincing, explanation is that looking-glasses were expensive and cherished

items in the past, and so the bad luck was simply economic. The underlying reasoning may perhaps hinge on the fact that, as mirrors reflect the faces of their owners, the 'personality' of the object and the person become inextricably linked. The breaking of one thus presages the 'breaking' of the other. On the surface, this may seem far-fetched, but it is given some support by the existence of cognate older beliefs regarding portraits (*see* PICTURES). This explanation does not suit all cases, however. In the example given above concerning the 'long-distance' warning of someone's death, it is not the dead person's mirror which broke, but someone else's, and a direct link can hardly have been present. The premise must therefore be that from a belief based on the sympathy between a person and their mirror, the broken mirror took on a wider signification and came to mean bad luck all round. This is not completely satisfying, but is the best we have for now.

Sussex Latham (1878) 51; *Sussex County Mag.* 5 (1931) 122; [1996] Steve Roud Collection. **Somerset** Poole (1877) 41. **Devon** *Devonshire Assoc.* 8 (1876) 57; Hewett (1900) 54. **Cornwall** N&Q 1S:12 (1855) 38; Hunt (1865) 236; *Old Cornwall* 2 (1931–6) 39. **Wiltshire** *Wilts. N&Q* 1 (1893–5) 103. **Surrey** [1984] Opie & Tatem, 250. **Essex** *Folk-Lore* 43 (1932) 110. **East Anglia** Varden (1885) 113. **Suffolk** *Folk-Lore* 35 (1924) 351. **Norfolk** Fulcher Collection (c.1895). **Warwickshire** Langford (1875) 11. **Northamptonshire** Sternberg (1851) 172. **Shropshire** Burne (1883) 281. **Staffordshire** Poole (1875) 79. **England** Addy (1895) 94. **Yorkshire** Robinson (1861) 296; Nicholson (1890) 43; *Folk-Lore* 21 (1910) 227; *Folk-Lore* 43 (1932) 253; *Yorkshire Post* (5 May 1960) 7; [1982] Opie & Tatem, 250. **Co. Durham** Leighton (1910) 62. **Northumberland** Bosanquet (1929) 77. **West Wales** Davies (1911) 216. **Pembrokeshire** [c.1880] *Archaeologia Cambrensis* 85 (1930) 206. **Highland Scotland** Polson (1926) 127. **Western Scotland** Napier (1879) 137. **Orkney** N&Q 10S:12 (1909) 483–4. **Ireland** *Gent. Mag.* (1865) 700. **N. Ireland** Foster (1951) 18. **Co. Wexford** [1938] Ó Muirithe, & Nuttall (1999) 162. **Co. Longford** *Béaloideas* 6 (1936) 263. **Jersey** *Folk-Lore* 25 (1914) 246; L'Amy (1927) 98. **Unlocated** Brand (1777) 91; Grose (1787) 48, 61; N&Q 1S:12 (1855) 488; N&Q 2S:12 (1861) 490; N&Q 8S:4 (1893) 243–4; Igglesden (c.1932) 212. **General** Foli (1902) 107. **Literary** Tennyson, 'The Lady of Shalott' (1832) lines 115–7; **Literary** Thomas Hardy, 'Honeymoon time at an Inn' (1917).

mirrors: covered at death

When death occurs in a house, there have been a number of traditionally sanctioned customs which should be carried out. One of these is covering any mirrors or pictures in the room (or the whole house), a practice which was sometimes extended to all ornaments:

The custom of covering, not looking-glasses only, but various articles in the apartment where the corpse is laid, was, and is even yet, a well-known custom in Scotland. When a death takes place, another custom is to stop the clock, or clocks, if there be several in the house. Different individuals have different whims ('frets' they call them); for example, I have heard of persons turning the face of a looking-glass to the wall on the occurrence of a death, while some turn the face of a portrait of the deceased in like fashion, should there chance to be one in the house.

Glasgow N&Q (1888)

Only one reference is known from the eighteenth century:

Funeral ceremonies in Orkney are much the same as in Scotland. The corpse is laid out after being stretcht on a board till it is coffined for burial. I know not for what reason they lock up all the cats of the house, and cover all looking glasses as soon as any person dies.

Orkney Gough, *Sepulchral Monuments* (1786)

but the custom is well documented in the nineteenth and first half of the twentieth centuries.

In the majority of instances where a reason is stated, the fear is expressed that anyone looking into a mirror at such a time, even if only accidentally, will see either an unspecified apparition or the dead person looking over their shoulder – clearly something to be avoided. Some informants offer a more symbolic interpretation that for the dead 'all vanity is over', or that they are beyond all everyday needs:

This custom is prevalent here in Wales: but the reason does not seem very apparent. A lady who is wont to drape in white the mirrors, and put ornaments, etc., away in the room where the departed lies, tells me it is done out of respect for the dead, who are no longer in need of such accessories.

Wales N&Q (1888)

In the available sources, the fear of an 'apparition' is first mentioned as late as the 1860s.

The geographical spread is also puzzling. There is a distinct preponderance of references from Scotland and Northern England, two late references for Wales, and even later ones for Ireland. Southern England is only represented by one reference each in Devon and Wiltshire.

See also PICTURES.

Devon Henderson (1866) 41. **Wiltshire** N&Q 7S:5 (1888) 73. **Warwickshire** Henderson (1866) 41. **Shropshire** Burne (1883) 299. **Yorkshire** Nicholson (1890) 5. **Cumberland** Penfold (1907) 60; *Folk-Lore* 31 (1920) 154.

Northern England [1850s] *Denham Tracts* 2 (1895) 73; Henderson (1866) 41. **Co. Durham** [1850s] N&Q 146 (1924) 420; Brockie (1886) 203; Leighton (1910) 51. **Wales** N&Q 7S:5 (1888) 73; Trevelyan (1909) 282. **Scotland** N&Q 1S:11 (1855) 215; [1958] Opie & Tatem, 251. **Dumfriesshire** Corrie (1890/91) 44. **Glasgow** N&Q 7S:5 (1888) 73. **Orkney** Richard Gough, *Sepulchral Monuments* (1786) Pt 1, 205. **N. Ireland** Foster (1951) 14. **Co. Armagh** [1940s] Opie & Tatem, 251.

mirrors: thunder and lightning

In a STORM, shiny or reflective objects or surfaces that might attract lightning must be covered or put away:

At the first sign of a thunderstorm Mum had taught us to cover up the looking-glass and the water-jug with cloths, otherwise it was a direct invitation to have the house struck by lightning.

London [1920s] Gamble

The belief is reported regularly through the twentieth century, from various parts of England, at least up to the 1980s. But its earlier history is not so easy to determine. The first known mention is in correspondence in *Notes & Queries* published in 1900, but contributors there claimed to have known the idea for more than fifty years previously:

In my boyhood, fifty or more years ago, the habit mentioned was almost universally adopted by the maidservants at my native place three miles from Tamworth, in South Staffordshire. The landlady of the house in Paddington where I now have rooms also informs me that she (a Londoner pure bred) has done the same ever since she was a girl, and that she inherited the habit from her mother, who was, however, a Kentish woman.

Staffordshire/London N&Q (1900)

It is clear that the belief was more widespread than the available documentation suggests. The belief in a link between lightning and reflective surfaces is not surprising, although its apparently restricted geographical spread and relatively late appearance are. Mirrors were also covered in times of sickness and death.

See also THUNDER AND LIGHTNING: REFLECTIVE SURFACES.

Kent [1930s] Kent (1977) 93. **London** N&Q 9S:6 (1900) 131; [1920s] Gamble (1979) 89; [1985] Opie & Tatem, 251. **Essex** [c.1917] Mays (1969) 163. **Hertfordshire** N&Q 9S:6 (1900) 7. **Cambridgeshire** Porter (1969) 69. **Suffolk** Evans (1965) 218. **Lincolnshire** Sutton (1992) 139. **Staffordshire** [1850s] N&Q 9S:6 (1900) 131. **Derbyshire**

[1890s] Uttley (1946) 132. **Derbyshire** *Daily Express* (10 Aug. 1954). **Yorkshire** Gill (1993) 94. **Lancashire** [*c*.1915] Corbridge (1964) 156–60; *Lancashire Lore* (1971) 66. **Unlocated** [1850s] N&Q 9S:6 (1900) 131.

mistletoe (*Viscum album*)

In AD 77, Pliny the Elder wrote his famous description of Druids, stating that they revered mistletoe growing on an oak as their most sacred plant, and harvested it with a golden sickle. This short piece is responsible for more disinformation in British folklore than almost any other. Whatever its merits in itself, it has been repeated, ad nauseam, by countless British writers, and has been used as the basis for innumerable flights of fancy about Druids and the ancient origins of our customs and beliefs. This situation led plant-lore expert Roy Vickery to write, in some exasperation it seems:

More nonsense has been written about mistletoe than about any other British plant.

Vickery (1995)

This Druid preoccupation with the plant is always assumed to be the basis of our modern custom of kissing under the mistletoe at Christmas, and also as the reason for the (erroneous) idea that as mistletoe is a 'pagan' plant, it has always been banned from Christian churches. Stating a succinct case against such popular notions which have become entrenched by constant repetition and elaboration is very difficult, because it is the whole premise and chain of thought which is in question as well as the individual facts. To put it simply: Pliny was writing about the Gauls, not the British. We do not know where or from whom he got his information. Classical authors, however reliable they may be in other respects, are at their shakiest, and most gullible, when describing foreign peoples and their lands (see, for example, Caesar's delightful description of the elk in his *Conquest of Gaul*, Bk 6, Ch. 4). There is no hint anywhere else to support Pliny's report. There is no other mention of the sacred nature of mistletoe in Britain until antiquarians start reading and believing Pliny, some 1,500 years later. Even if Pliny's description was accurate, there is no evidence that the practice continued into historical times, or had any influence on later lore. Modern mistletoe beliefs are reported almost exclusively from England – not the Celtic areas where, we are told (but we do not believe), the Druid traditions continue to have resonance. And so on.

There is no discernible connection between this description and the dominant British mistletoe tradition of kissing at Christmas, first reported in 1813, and how the supposed sacred mistletoe of the Druids got transformed into this excuse for boys and girls to indulge in Christmas horseplay is rarely considered.

Keeping our feet planted on more solid ground, apart from the Christmas kissing, the mistletoe does not make much of an appearance in British traditions. It had something of an international reputation in cures, much of which was again copied from Pliny by literate herbalists. Otherwise, its lore is almost entirely to do with its role in CHRISTMAS DECORATION:

It is considered very unlucky for a house unless some mistletoe is brought in at Christmas.

Derbyshire N&Q (1871)

If you want to have extra good luck to your dairy, give your bunch of mistletoe to the first cow that calves after New Year's Day.

Yorkshire Henderson (1866)

If you hang up mistletoe at Christmas, your house will never be struck by lightning.

Staffordshire [1891] *Folk-Lore*

The notion that it was banned from churches was questioned by a writer in the *Gentleman's Magazine* of 1792. He quotes John Gay's poem 'Trivia' (1716) as evidence of the plant's use, and also his own experience in the London area:

Since his time I remember to have seen a large bough of this plant suspended under the arch of an entrance into the chancel of a church within the Bills of Mortality. London *Gent. Mag.* (1792)

Devon N&Q 4S:10 (1872) 495; *Devonshire Assoc.* 57 (1926) 110; *Devonshire Assoc.* 91 (1959) 200; *Devonshire Assoc.* 104 (1972) 267. **Surrey** *Gent. Mag.* (1827) 483–6. **London** *Gent. Mag.* (1792) 432; [1863] Cullwick (1984) 145. **Berkshire** Mitford (1828) 53. **Herefordshire** Leather (1912) 19, 79. **Worcestershire** N&Q 1S:3 (1857) 343; [1900] *Folk-Lore* 20 (1909) 343; *Folk-Lore* 72 (1961) 321. **Lincolnshire** [1930s & 1950s] Sutton (1992) 131. **Norfolk** [*c*.1870s] Haggard (1935) 16. **Shropshire** Burne (1883) 246. **Staffordshire** [1891] *Folk-Lore* 20 (1909) 220. **Derbyshire** N&Q 4S:8 (1871) 506; N&Q 6S:4 (1881) 509. **Yorkshire** Henderson (1866) 86; Blakeborough (1898) 69. **Wales** Trevelyan (1909) 171. **Montgomeryshire** Burne (1883) 246. **Unlocated** Igglesden (*c*.1932) 69–70. **General** Irving (1820) Bk 2, 63; Nares (1822) 'Misseltoe'; Dyer (1889) 288–9; Hatfield (1994) 31, 90–1; Vickery (1995) 240–3. Baker (1996) 99–101. **Literary** John Gay, *Trivia* (1716) Bk 2 lines 441–2. John Clare, *The Shepherd's Calendar* (1827) 94; Charles Dickens, *Pickwick Papers* (1837) Ch. 28. **Classical** Pliny, *Natural History* (AD 77) Bk 16, Ch. 95.

mistletoe: kissing under

The dominant belief about mistletoe, and one of the central customs of Christmas, was that anyone who stood under it could not refuse to be kissed. It was already widespread in the early nineteenth century, as John Brand (1813), Washington Irving (1820), and John Clare (1827) all describe it in their works:

The shepherd now no more afraid,
Since custom doth the chance bestow,
Starts up to kiss the giggling maid
Beneath the branch of mistletoe
That 'neath each cottage beam is seen,
Clare, Shepherd's Calendar (1827)

and it has continued to the present day. It has been suggested that this is a survival of a classical belief recorded by Pliny (AD 77) that mistletoe promotes conception in females if they carry a piece with them, but it is difficult to see how this survived the intervening 1,800 years without being noticed elsewhere, unless it was re-introduced to British tradition directly by translation of Pliny's works.

A number of minor variations have been recorded, but not frequently:

If [Christmas] mistletoe be not burned all couples who have kissed beneath it will be foes before the end of the year.   Unlocated Igglesden (c.1932)

Lasses were sure of good luck if they were kissed under the mistletoe. If it was discovered that they had not so been kissed, the young men swept them down with a brush or besom.
Derbyshire N&Q (1881)

Berkshire Mitford 3 (1828) 53. **London** [1863] Cullwick (1984) 145. **Worcestershire** *Folk-Lore* 72 (1961) 321. **Lincolnshire** [1930s & 1950s] Sutton (1992) 131. **Derbyshire** N&Q 6S:4 (1881) 509. **Yorkshire** Blakeborough (1898) 69. **Unlocated** Igglesden (c.1932) 69–70. **General** Brand 1 (1813) 408; Irving (1820) Bk 2, 63; Nares (1822) 'Misseltoe'. **Literary** John Clare, *The Shepherd's Calendar* (1827) 94; Charles Dickens, *Pickwick Papers* (1837) Ch. 28. **Classical** Pliny, *Natural History* (AD 77) Bk 24, Para. 6.

---

moles: cures

In addition to the widespread custom of carrying a mole's foot as a preventative or cure for various complaints (*see below*), the animal was also used for other medicinal purposes. Several sources report a belief that if you catch a live mole and then let it die in your hand, you will henceforth have healing powers:

To make a sonsy hand; i.e. a healing hand – hold a mole in your hand till it expires.   Grose (1790)

This is reminiscent of other accounts in which SEVENTH SONS, as babies, were confirmed in their considerable powers by allowing worms to die in their hand.

Moles' blood was considered particularly powerful, being prescribed for a range of ailments, including EPILEPSY:

Epilepsy – Another remedy is to cut the tip off the nose of a live mole, and let nine drops of its blood fall upon a lump of sugar, which is then administered to the patient.   East Anglia Varden (1885)

Essentially the same cure was published in Woolley's *Queen-Like Closet* (1684). Other cures are reported once or twice, but were probably more widespread:

A bit of moleskin worn on the chest was believed to cure asthma.   Wales Jones (1930)

The poor mole could also be used more directly, in the same way as PIGEONS and other creatures were:

In white-swelling of the knee, the cure is affected by slitting open a live puppy and binding it, while quivering, upon the peccant member. A mole, too, is sometimes vivisected and applied in like manner to the neck for curing wens.
Gloucestershire N&Q (1873)

Sussex Allen (1995) 176. **Devon** *Devonshire Assoc.* 15 (1883) 99–100; *Devonshire Assoc.* 100 (1968) 366. **Cornwall** [1953] Opie & Tatem, 256. **Berkshire** Salmon (1902) 422. **Gloucestershire** N&Q 3S:10 (1866) 24–5; N&Q 4S:11 (1873) 500. **Herefordshire** Leather (1912) 84–5. **Worcestershire** N&Q 3S:12 (1867) 197. **East Anglia** Varden (1885) 103. **Wales** Jones (1930) 143. **Banffshire** Gregor (1874) 271. **General** H. Woolley, *Queen-Like Closet* (1684) 14; Grose (1790) 45.

---

moles: feet

Parts of various animals are reputed to have curative powers if carried about the person, including the feet of HARES or RABBITS, and LUCKY BONES (mostly from sheep). On the same principle, moles' feet were regularly carried, or worn round the neck, to prevent TOOTHACHE, or to relieve RHEUMATISM:

Cure for toothache . . . A mole-trap must be watched, and the moment it is sprung, and whilst the poor mouldwarp is in extremis, but before life is extinct (for on this latter condition the success of the charm depends), his hand-like paws are to

moles

Many small animals were used extensively in folk medicine, but the material indicates that the mole was regarded as something special. It is not clear why.

Classical writers valued the mole highly:

It should be unique evidence of fraud that they look upon the mole of all living creatures with the greatest awe, although it is cursed by Nature with so many defects, being permanently blind, sunk in other darkness also, and resembling the buried dead. In no entrails is placed such faith; to no creature do they attribute more supernatural properties, so that if anyone eats its heart, fresh and still beating, they promise powers of divination and of foretelling the issue of matters in hand. They declare that a tooth, extracted from a living mole and attached as an amulet, cures toothache. (Pliny, *Natural History*, Bk 30, Para. 7)

This is not to argue an unbroken tradition in Britain stretching from Roman times to modern times, but given the immense influence of classical writings on the educated classes of Britain and Europe from medieval times onwards, it is quite possible that our beliefs were engendered by them.

[About fifty years ago] There was a great deal of mole-trapping done then, as the skins were much in demand, and the old people would draw attention to the fore feet of these little animals. The story was told that long ago there was a lady who was very proud and arrogant, who lived only for fine clothes and the adornment of her person. For her pride the fairies turned her into a mole, condemned forever to burrow in the dark ground.
Devon *Devonshire Assoc.* (1968)

See also PURSES.

Devon *Devonshire Assoc.* 100 (1968) 366. **Berkshire** Salmon (1902) 422.

be cut off, and worn by the patient. A dexter paw must be used should the offending tooth be on the right side of the jaw, and the contrary . . . I have seen a mole's paw mounted in Silver in London.
Staffordshire/Shropshire N&Q (1854)

Nearly all informants agree that the mole must be alive when its feet are taken, and many say that the charm will only work if the mole is then set free to die in its own time.

The belief was clearly well known, at least in England, in the nineteenth century, and it lasted well into the twentieth. An entry in Thomas Naish's diary, for 18 Oct 1723, shows that it is much older, and was also used to counteract children's convulsions:

My son Thomas had two convulsive fitts this day: and for remedy I hanged two wonts [moles] feet about his neck upon the pitt of his stomack, cut off alive, by which means we think that my son John was cured of the same distemper last Whitsuntyde was three year, he having had no fitt since that time.
Wiltshire *Diary of Thomas Naish* (1965)

Sussex Latham (1878) 40. **Devon** *Devonshire Assoc.* 100 (1968) 366. **Wiltshire** *Diary of Thomas Naish*, 18 Oct. 1723 (1965) 79. N&Q 3S:5 (1864) 393. **Gloucestershire** N&Q 4S:11 (1873) 500. *Folk-Lore* 13 (1902) 173. **Herefordshire** Havergal (1887) 46; N&Q 3S:12 (1867) 197. **Norfolk** *Folk-Lore* 40 (1929) 116, 119. **Lincolnshire** Rudkin (1936) 27. **Shropshire** Burne (1883) 193, 214. **Staffordshire/Shropshire** N&Q 1S:10 (1854) 6.

Westmorland/Lancashire [*c.*1939] *Folk-Lore* 62 (1951) 262. **Welsh/English Gypsies** Groome (1880) 13.

moles: omens

The appearance of moles in the garden would seem to be too common an occurrence for comment, but a handful of sources report various beliefs that moles can be seen as unlucky, or even as omens of death, simply by showing their presence:

If a mole burrows under the washhouse or dairy, the mistress of the home will die within the year. If a molehill be found among the cabbages in the garden, the master of the house will die before the year is out. If any person saw a white mole, he might expect his own death.
Wales Trevelyan (1909)

Moles near the house were also interpreted as ominous, or if their hills formed a certain pattern:

I remarked to my neighbour that there were molehills all along the bank at the bottom of our garden, and he said, 'Oh then we'll hear of a move for someone soon, and if they throw them up in a circle round the house, it means a death'.
Hampshire [1987] Opie & Tatem

Hampshire [1987] Opie & Tatem, 256. **Somerset** [1922] Opie & Tatem, 256. **Herefordshire** [*c.*1895] *Folk-Lore* 39

(1928) 391; Leather (1912) 24. **Worcestershire** *Folk-Lore* 20 (1909) 344. **Wales** Trevelyan (1909) 280–1. **Highland Scotland** Campbell (1900) 256.

moles (on body)

'Various and ridiculous are the superstitions concerning moles on different parts of the body,' commented John Brand in 1777, and a number of later collectors noted isolated meanings, often contradictory:

If you have a mole under your left arm you will be wealthy. If you have a mole at the back of your neck you will be beautiful.   England Addy (1895)

Mole on the neck, trouble by the peck.
                    Gloucestershire *Folk-Lore* (1923)

A mole at the back of the neck marks out the bearer of it as in danger of hanging.
                    Co. Durham Henderson (1866)

'Prognostications by moles' were a regular feature of popular DREAM BOOKS and fortune-telling publications of the nineteenth and twentieth centuries, and these provided a whole list of meanings – usually the same list, as the compilers of these books lifted freely from each other. These published versions do not, on the whole, coincide with those collected in the field, and we are not justified in presuming that the latter are surviving fragments of a unified traditional scheme.

Devon N&Q 5S:2 (1874) 184. **Gloucestershire** *Folk-Lore* (1923) 156. **Herefordshire** *Folk-Lore* 39 (1928) 391. **East Anglia** Varden (1885) 104. **Shropshire** Burne (1883) 267. **England** Addy (1895) 94. **Co. Durham** Henderson (1866) 85. **Unlocated** Igglesden (c.1932) 140–3. **General** Brand (1777) 95.

molucca beans

see LUCKY BEANS.

'Monday's child'

see BABIES: 'MONDAY'S CHILD'.

money: crooked/holed coins

Coins which have been defaced in certain ways have long been regarded as lucky pieces across Britain, and have been widely carried or worn to ensure good fortune, or protect against bad luck.

From the early nineteenth century onwards, many reports focus on coins with holes in them:

Mr. Hooley [famous financier] *asserts himself free from superstition, but in point of fact he has one fad. Believing in the luck-bringing qualities of threepenny pieces with holes pierced in them, he gave his bankers a standing order to collect them for him, and used to give some to his friends, always carrying a lot of loose ones in his pocket.*   Cambridgeshire [1899] *Folklore*

The exact denomination does not seem to matter, although sixpences are mentioned more often than other coins. Long before the holed coin came to prominence, however, it was bent coins which were prized – often referred to as 'bowed' or 'crooked'. At least as early as the mid sixteenth century, bowed coins were being given to people by well-wishers 'for luck', and the practice was well known enough to be mentioned in passing by contemporary writers – 'And what becomes of all our vows in Croydon? The bowed two-pence and the garter,' wrote Thomas Killigrew in his play *Thomaso* in 1663. Two hundred years later the custom was still going strong:

A bent coin is often given in the west of England for luck. A crooked sixpence is usually selected by careful grandmothers, aunts and uncles, to bestow as the 'handselling' of a new purse.
                    Western England N&Q (1854)

Even earlier, in the medieval period, bent coins were regularly offered to saints to accompany a vow, mark a pilgrimage, or request a cure. See Finucane (1977) for examples.

Kent [1557] N&Q 1S:10 (1854) 505. **Hampshire** [1987] Opie & Tatem, 106. **Western England** N&Q 1S:10 (1854) 505. **Dorset** Morsley (1979) 305. **Devon** Hewett (1900) 50. **Wiltshire** [1923] Opie & Tatem, 106. **Surrey** [1953] Opie & Tatem, 93. **London** Lovett (1925) 13–14. **Cambridgeshire** *Folklore* 79 (1968) 232, quoting *St Neots Advertiser* (25 Mar. 1899). **East Anglia** Varden (1885) 112. **Staffordshire** Hackwood (1924) 148. **Shropshire** Burne (1883) 272. **Derbyshire** Addy (1895) 80. **England** Addy (1895) 100. **Northern England** [1850s] *Denham Tracts* (1895) 72; Henderson (1866) 146. **Yorkshire** Robinson (1861) 300. **Lancashire** Harland & Wilkinson (1873) 227. **Co. Durham** Leighton (1910) 45–6. **Northumberland** Bigge (1860/62) 94. **Wales** Trevelyan (1909) 324. **Northeast Scotland** Gregor (1881) 31. **Highland Scotland** Polson (1926) 130. **Aberdeen** [1952] Opie & Tatem, 106. **Guernsey** Carey (1903) 507. **Unlocated** Hone, *Year Book* (1832) 127. **General** Finucane (1977) 94–5. **Literary** Thomas Killigrew, *Thomaso* (1663) 2:4; Hannah More, *Tawney Rachel* (c.1810) 9.

money: crown coins

A curious belief, reported only from the 1950s and 1960s, held that it was unlucky to receive a five-shilling piece, or 'crown', although informants claimed it was current some years earlier:

It was almost impossible to change a crown in a public house before the war because superstition had it that the barmaid who accepted it would be the first person to lose her job.

Unlocated *The Times* (23 Oct. 1954)

A similar superstition existed in the THEATRE:

in the entertainment world, in which there was a superstition that a five-shilling piece taken at a theatre box-office meant that the show would close down, or that some bad luck would befall a member of the cast.

London *Sunday Times* (5 Jan. 1958)

London *Sunday Times* (5 Jan. 1958) 4. Unlocated *The Times* (22 Oct. 1954) 9; *The Times* (23 Oct. 1954) 7; *Daily Telegraph* (28 Sept. 1963) 8; *Daily Telegraph* (2 Oct. 1963) 14.

money: finding

To many people it may seem strange that finding money could have been regarded as unlucky, but such a belief is well attested from the sixteenth century until well into living memory.

Faith friend . . . 'tis ill luck to keep found money, we'll go spend it in a pottle of wine.

Greene, *Art of Coney-Catching* (1591)

The earlier references simply state that finding, and keeping, money was unlucky, but later informants discriminate between circumstances, and suggest protective strategies. For many, a sixpence was particularly unlucky (unless crooked, *see above*):

A sixpence is regarded by many as the most unlucky coin that can be found. Many people absolutely refuse to pick up a sixpence which has been lost. An instance is given in which some person picked up this unlucky coin in the road, and no end of illness followed on the daring act.

Cumberland Penfold (1907)

Others argued that it was all right if the coin lay with head, rather than tail, upwards. There was also the universal method for avoiding bad luck when accepting money – to spit on it:

Any coin should be spat upon if found, or received for slight value, or in any way unexpectedly come by. To do so averts ill luck.

Cornwall *Jnl Royal Inst. Cornwall* (1915)

Cornwall *Jnl Royal Inst. Cornwall* 20 (1915) 130. **Bedfordshire** [1957] Opie & Tatem, 259. **Lancashire** Harland & Wilkinson (1873) 227. **Cumberland** Penfold (1907) 57. **Wales** Trevelyan (1909) 324, 326, 329. **West Wales** Davies (1911) 215. **Co. Tyrone** *Lore & Language* 1:7 (1972) 7. **General** R. Greene, *Art of Coney-Catching* (1591); Melton (1620); *Athenian Mercury* (1691); N&Q 11S:3 (1911) 217.

money: new purse

A group of related beliefs dictate that one should never allow a purse, money-box, coat-pocket, or other receptacle for money to be empty. In some cases it is a clear example of HANDSELLING, based on a belief in the luck of the *first* use of an item, or the symbolic BEGINNING of its life. One must therefore be particularly careful when giving a purse as a present:

Another thing is that if a person bought a new bag or a new case or a new purse bag, the person that would have bought it for another person they would always put sixpence in it for good luck or for a 'hansel' because it was an old custom that when anybody would be giving a present of a purse it was the custom that they should put something in for luck.

Co. Wexford [1938] Ó Muirithe & Nuttall (1999)

Even after the newness has worn off, it continues to be unlucky to allow any receptacle to be empty, or it will remain so. Older references, however, show a darker reason for continued poverty. An empty purse or pocket is at risk of being occupied by the Devil himself:

The deuille may daunce in crosslesse purse when coyne hathe tooke his tyde,

Drant, *Horace* (1566)

which is based, it has been suggested, on the fact that early coins bore crosses on one side, and it was these which kept the Devil at bay. The basic idea was still being quoted over 300 years later:

At an inquest held lately at Roydon, Essex, on the body of a man found on the line, a police constable stated that all the money he found on deceased was one halfpenny, whereupon one of the jury said, 'They say that's to keep the devil out'.

Essex N&Q (1882)

The notion could even be extended to cover the whole house:

I was told, the other day, of a nobleman, who has now been dead for several years, that, on leaving his various houses in town and country, he placed some pieces of silver and copper in a drawer in the house, as he considered it very unlucky to return to a house in which there was not any money. It was a part of this folk-lore that the drawer in question must not be locked. I am told that, when he returned to the house, one of his first acts was to examine the drawer to see if his deposit for luck remained intact; and that he always found this to be the case. This was not to be wondered at, as I am told that the housekeeper who was left in charge, being aware of her master's peculiarity, removed the money from the open drawer as soon as he had quitted the house, and replaced it before his return.   Unlocated N&Q (1876)

The prohibition against giving an empty purse or wallet can still be heard regularly today.

See also CLOTHES: NEW, MONEY IN; HANDSEL.

Sussex N&Q 6S:6 (1882) 17. Somerset [1923] Opie & Tatem, 188. Middlesex [1984] Opie & Tatem, 189. London Steve Roud Collection, 2001. Essex N&Q 6S:5 (1882) 408. Lincolnshire Rudkin (1936) 21. Highland Scotland Macbain (1887/88) 262. Aberdeenshire [1952] Opie & Tatem, 188–9. Co. Wexford [1938] Ó Muirithe & Nuttall (1999) 166. Unlocated N&Q 5S:6 (1876) 24. Literary Thomas Drant, *A Medicinable Morall, that is the Two Bookes of Horace his Satyres* (London, 1566) 1:3, quoted N&Q 6S:6 (1882) 17.

money-spider/money-spinner

see SPIDERS: MONEY-SPIDERS.

monkey-puzzle tree (*Araucaria araucana*)

A modest set of beliefs surround the peculiar tree nicknamed the monkey-puzzle. Since at least the 1930s, children have believed that one must not say a word in its vicinity:

The writer was told in Caterham, Surrey, in 1953, where a handsome monkey puzzle stood in front of the then council offices, that one should never speak while passing the tree, or otherwise attract its attention, lest some misfortune follow.
                                        Surrey Baker (2001)

Versions of this superstition have been noted in various parts of England and in Scotland, and it was clearly much more widespread than the few published references imply.

A different belief, reported in Essex in the 1920s, linked the Devil with the tree:

The monkey-puzzle tree with its dark green spiked leaves – one of which grew in the parson's garden – was believed to be more puzzling to the Devil than to monkeys. Sunday school children who lagged in learning, or played hookey, had but to climb this tree and the Devil, if not parsons and parents, would never catch them.
                        Essex Ketteridge & Mays [*c*.1920]

And in Cambridgeshire:

It was an old Fenland belief that if a monkey puzzle tree was planted on the edge of a grave-yard it would prove an obstacle to the Devil when he tried to hide in the branches to watch a burial. Many elderly Cambridgeshire people believe the tree is an unlucky one.
                            Cambridgeshire Porter (1969)

These associations with the Devil may well explain the children's fear of speaking near the tree, or 'attracting its attention', although if the tree generally 'puzzled' the Devil it would logically be a lucky one. The Fenland story is also a statutory lesson to those who assume that stories of devils and churchyards are necessarily ancient. The monkey-puzzle was only introduced to Britain, from Chile, in the 1790s.

Surrey [1953] Baker (1996) 102; [1960] Opie & Tatem, 260. Essex [*c*.1920] Ketteridge & Mays (1972) 139. Cambridgeshire [1930s] Vickery (1995) 245; Porter (1969) 63. Angus [1954] Opie & Tatem, 260.

months: saying 'rabbits'

A strange but widespread custom which exists mainly in the domestic setting of a family. It involves marking the first day of the month, and sometimes the night before, by saying out loud 'rabbits' or 'hares', and thereby ensuring a wish or good luck through the coming month. Details vary considerably, but the broad outline is always recognizable:

To say 'rabbits' before going to sleep on the last night of the month and 'hares' when you awake in the morning is to be lucky all month.
                                    Essex [*c*.1939] *Folk-Lore*

On the first of each month as soon as you realise it is the first, say 'White rabbits, white rabbits, white rabbits'. This will ensure luck for the rest of the month.   Co. Tyrone *Lore & Language* (1972)

On the first day of the month, the one who can say 'rabbits' first can wish a wish.
                            Northumberland Bosanquet (1929)

The almost universal rule is that whatever words are prescribed for the last night must be the last thing said, and those for the morning must be the first. In some families it is the first to say it who gets the wish, while others more diplomatically promise a lucky month for everyone who keeps within the rules.

The earliest concrete dating for the custom is found in a correspondence which appeared in the *Saturday Westminster Gazette* in March and April 1919. The first writer simply asks for details, and others reply from various parts of England stating that their families already carry out the custom every month. One writer claims to have known it for about twenty-five years, but it is clear that the custom was not by any means universally known at that time, and many regarded it as relatively new.

The basic principle involved is most probably simply the marking of another BEGINNING within the cycle of months, but no plausible suggestion as to why it is rabbits and hares has been suggested.

It has certainly been more widely known than is suggested by the few references listed below, and is still current.

Sussex [1984] Opie & Tatem, 192. Dorset *Dorset Year Book* (1961–2) 76. London [1941] Hodgson (1976) 107. Essex [c.1939] *Folk-Lore* 64 (1953) 293. Suffolk [c.1915] Opie & Tatem, 192. Yorkshire *Folk-Lore* 31 (1920) 319. Co. Durham [1982] Opie & Tatem, 192. Northumberland Bosanquet (1929) 78. Radnorshire [1953] Opie & Tatem, 192. Co. Tyrone *Lore & Language* 1:7 (1972) 7; *Devonshire Assoc.* 105 (1973) 213, contributions from: Dorset/Devon/Surrey/Leicestershire/Yorkshire; *Saturday Westminster Gazette* (1 Mar. 1919) 19, (15 Mar. 1919) 23, (22 Mar. 1919) 23, (29 Mar. 1919) 23, (5 Apr. 1919) 26, contributions from: Oxfordshire/Cambridgeshire/Isle of Wight/Yorkshire/London/Ireland.

moon: births and deaths

A handful of references indicate a range of beliefs which link the phase of the moon with human births and deaths. None of them seems to be more than occasionally reported, and they do not appear to constitute a coherent scheme, apart from the basic idea that to be born during the waxing was better than at the waning:

One born in the spring of the moon shall be healthy; in that time of the wane, when the moon is utterly decayed, the child when born cannot live, and in the conjunction, it cannot long continue.   Scot (1584)

They may represent more generally known superstitions which have simply escaped documentation. Indeed, given the strength and popularity of other moon beliefs, and the strong traditional links between the tide and human life, it would be surprising if this were not so.

A child born when the moon is new will be very eloquent. Those born at the last quarter will have excellent reasoning powers. Girls born while the moon is waxing will be precocious . . . If a man dies exactly at the time of the new moon, he will take away all the family luck with him.
                                    Wales Trevelyan (1909)

A popular notion amongst old folks is, that when a boy is born on the waning moon the next birth will be a girl, and vice versa. They also say that when a birth takes place on the growing of the moon the next child will be of the same sex. A child born in the interval between the old and new moons is fated to die young.
                                    Cornwall *Folk-Lore Jnl* 5 (1887)

Victorian novelist Thomas Hardy uses what he claims to be a well-known proverb – 'No moon, no man' – to illustrate the character of poor Christian Cantle:

'Do ye really think it serious, Mister Fairway, that there was no moon?' 'Yes, no moon, no man, 'tis one of the truest sayings ever spit out. The boy never comes to anything that's born at new moon. A bad job for thee, Christian, that you should have showed your nose then of all days in the month'.   Hardy, *The Return of the Native* (1878)

Somerset [1923] Opie & Tatem, 261. Dorset Udal (1922) 178. Cornwall Dyer (1878) 41; *Folk-Lore Jnl* 5 (1887) 208. Shropshire *Folk-Lore* 49 (1938) 225. Wales Trevelyan (1909) 267, 282. Angus Jamieson, *Scottish Dictionary* (1808) 'Mone'. General Scot (1584) Bk 9, Ch. 2; Francis Bacon, *Sylva Sylvarum* (1627) Para. 897. Literary Thomas Hardy, *The Return of the Native* (1878) Pt 1, Ch. 3.

moon: bowing to

One of the most widespread practices on seeing the new moon was to bow or curtsey to it:

When living, a few years ago, in Ayrshire, our housekeep used to make obeisance several times to the new moon when she observed it, looking very solemn the while. And when I asked her why she did so, she replied that by so doing she would be sure to get a present before the next moon appeared. She wished me (then a very young girl) to do so too, and when I told her it was all nonsense, she 'fired up' and said her mother had done so, and she would continue to do so. I rather think this is no uncommon practice, for our previous servant did the same thing, and neither of them was older than about forty or fifty.

Ayrshire *Scotsman* (27 Dec. 1889)

The form of the obeisance varies considerably – bowing or curtseying are by far the most common, but nodding, raising the hat, and kissing the hand are also reported. The number of stipulated times can also be any odd number from one to nine. This bowing motif is very often combined with other elements of 'new moon' belief, such as making a wish or reciting a rhyme to divine future partners (*see below*), but the most common direct result of paying one's respect is that you will get a present, or find something nice, before the next new moon:

It was a prevalent belief that if a person catching the first glimpse of new moon were to instantly stand still, kiss their hand three times to the moon, and bow to it, that they would find something of value before that moon was out.

Western Scotland Napier (1879)

Unusually, the earliest references show that the custom was already widespread by the seventeenth century, providing evidence from Ireland, Scotland, and England. Camden's *Britannia* (c.1566) describes how in Limerick 'when they first see her after the change they commonly bow the knee, and say the Lord's Prayer', and antiquarian John Aubrey (born in Wiltshire in 1626) commented that:

In Scotland (especially among the Highlanders) the women do make a curtsey to the new-moon; I have known one in England doe it . . . When I was a boy before ye civill warres 'twas the fashion to kisse ones hand and make a legge.

Aubrey, *Remaines* (1686)

To 'make a leg' means to bow. The custom was not reported widely in the eighteenth century but, as with other new moon beliefs, was extremely widespread in the nineteenth and lasted well into the late twentieth. It is probably still done by some people.

Reading the mass of examples, the overall impression is of 'paying respect' rather than 'worshipping' and few of the direct reports use language to suggest the latter interpretation, except where collectors have introduced their own slant. There is indeed no evidence that these actions are a remnant of moon worship as the cultural survivalists would like to believe. Nevertheless, without suggesting a direct line of descent, it must be acknowledged that earlier peoples had apparently similar procedures for

greeting the moon – the biblical Job (31:26–7), for example, speaks of kissing one's hand when beholding the moon, and Psalm 81 (verse 3) exhorts, 'Blow up the trumpet in the new moon'. Similarly, in classical times, Horace (*Odes* 3:23) wrote, 'if thou lift thy hands to heaven when the moon is new', but the potential meaning of these is beyond the scope of the present work.

Kent [c.1903] Opie & Tatem, 280. Sussex Latham (1878) 10. Somerset [1957] Tongue (1965) 140. Devon *Devonshire Assoc.* 9 (1877) 91; *Devonshire Assoc.* 15 (1883) 107; Hewett (1892) 27; *Devonshire Assoc.* 60 (1928) 111; *Devonshire Assoc.* 63 (1931) 123. Cornwall *Old Cornwall* 2 (1931–6) 39. Wiltshire Aubrey, *Remaines* (1686/1880) 36–7; *Wilts. N&Q* 1 (1893–5) 61. Essex *Monthly Packet* 24 (1862) 434–7; [c.1920] Ketteridge & Mays (1972) 140. Oxfordshire [1920s] Harris (1969) 124–5. Warwickshire *Folk-Lore* 55 (1944) 72. Cambridgeshire Porter (1969) 59. Suffolk Chambers 1 (1878) 203–4. Norfolk Fulcher Collection (c.1895). Lincolnshire Rudkin (1936) 21–2; [1946] Opie & Tatem, 280. Shropshire Burne (1883) 256–9. England Addy (1895) 59. Derbyshire *Folk-Lore Jnl* 2 (1884) 280; [c.1890s] Uttley (1946) 133. Yorkshire [1973] Opie & Tatem, 280. Westmorland/Lancashire *Folk-Lore* [c.1939] 64 (1953) 296–7. Co. Durham Leighton (1910) 56; Northumberland Neville (1909) 110; Bosanquet (1929) 78–9. Wales *N&Q* 10S:12 (1909) 406–7. West Wales Davies (1911) 218. Cardiganshire *Folk-Lore* 39 (1928) 174. Scotland Aubrey, *Remaines* (1686/1880) 36–7. Western Scotland Napier (1879) 98. Ayrshire *Scotsman* (27 Dec. 1889) 7. Glasgow [c.1820] Napier (1864) 397. Ireland C. Vallencey, *De Rebus Hibernicis* (1770) Ch. 13. N. Ireland Foster (1951) 54. Co. Limerick William Camden, *Britannia* (1586). Jersey *Folk-Lore* 25 (1914) 247. Unlocated *Spectator* (18 Jan. 1902) 82.

moon: divination

The first sight of a new moon is one of those BEGINNING points around which LOVE DIVINATION customs have traditionally clustered. In some cases it is the first new moon of the year, but quite commonly any new moon would do. There were two main categories of divination.

In the first, the supplicant addresses her/himself directly to the new moon, either making a wish or reciting a traditional rhyme, which varies only in the details, hoping that s/he will later dream of their future spouse. The custom can be quite simple:

The young women of the Lowlands, on first observing the new moon, exclaim as follows:

New mune, true mune, tell unto me
If [naming favourite lover] be my true love
He will marry me

*If he marry me in haste, let me see his
    bonnie face
If he marry me betide, let me see his bonnie
    side
Gin he marry na me ava, turn his back and
    gae awa.*

Scotland Chambers (1826)

or can be elaborated in terms of both action and
placing of the participant. Several informants
state that one should be 'as close to the moon as
possible', which usually entails climbing stile or
GATE. Some elements have been borrowed from
other key love-divinatory times, such as the
following which is more commonly carried out
on hearing the first CUCKOO:

*When you first see the new moon in the new year,
take your stocking off from one foot, and run to the
next stile, when you get there between the great toe
and the next, you will find a hair, which will be the
colour of your lover's.*   **Devon** N&Q (1851)

An added element, apparently unique to
Ireland, involved a knife:

*At new moon it is not uncommon to point with
a knife, and after invoking the blessed Trinity, to
say: New moon, true moon, be true now to
me/That I ere the morrow my true love may see.
The knife is then placed under the pillow, and
silence strictly observed, lest the charm should be
spoilt.*   **Dublin** N&Q (1869)

The second main method is to view the moon
indirectly, either through some piece of material
– a new silk handkerchief is often stipulated – or
reflected in a pail of water or a mirror. The effect
of the operation is that if more than one moon
is seen, the number will represent how many
years the viewer must wait before marriage:

*You should look through a new silk handkerchief
at the first new moon in the year, and as many
moons as you saw would be years before you'd be
married, or turn your back and look at it in the
looking-glass, and count the same as with the silk
handkerchief.*   **Northumberland** Bosanquet (1929)

The refraction method is only reported from
the early nineteenth century onwards, but
remained popular throughout the twentieth.
Addressing the moon in rhyme, however, was
already well known in the mid seventeenth
century, as recorded by John Aubrey (1686) and
by the compiler of the chapbook *Mother Bunch's
Closet Newly Broke Open* (1685), and decades
before, it seems to be the gist of a passage in the
play *Cupid's Whirligig*:

*I think an ill star reigned when I was born: I
cannot have as much as a suitor. This master
Miccome, that you forsooth so much scorn, I
could find in my heart to pray nine times to the
moon and fast three St. Agnes Eves so that I might
be sure to have him to my husband.*

Cupid's Whirligig (1607)

Direct address: **Sussex** *Folk-Lore Record* 1 (1878) 30.
Somerset Tongue (1965) 140. **Devon** N&Q 1S:4 (1851)
99; Hewett (1900) 71. **Berkshire** Hone, *Year Book* (1832)
126–8; N&Q 10S:1 (1904) 175–6. **Oxfordshire** *Folk-Lore*
20 (1909) 343. **Herefordshire** Leather (1912) 64.
Lincolnshire N&Q 10S:1 (1904) 125. **Derbyshire** N&Q
10S:1 (1904) 252. **Scotland** Chambers (1826) 287.
Western Scotland Napier (1879) 98. **Galloway**
Mactaggart (1824) 211. **Ireland** N&Q 10S:1 (1904) 175–6;
Wilde (1888) 185, 205–6. **Co. Meath/Co. Tipperary** *Folk-
Lore* 15 (1904) 461. **Dublin** N&Q 4S:4 (1869) 505.
Unlocated Aubrey, *Miscellanies* (1696/1857) 36–7, 132–3;
Halliwell (1849) 159–60; N&Q 10S:1 (1904) 252. *Literary*
Cupid's Whirligig (1607) quoted Lean 2 (1903) 374;
Thomas May, *The Old Couple* 1 (1658) quoted Lean 2
(1903) 373; *Mother Bunch's Closet Newly Broke Open*
(1685).

Refraction: **Northamptonshire** [1825] Clare (1993) 140.
Norfolk Fulcher Collection (*c*.1895). **Lincolnshire**
Watkins (1886) 12. **Leicestershire** N&Q 1S:7 (1853) 153.
Shropshire Burne (1883) 256–9. **England** Addy (1895)
81–2. **Derbyshire** N&Q 4S:8 (1871) 506. **Northern
England** [1850s] *Denham Tracts* (1895) 280–1. **Yorkshire**
Young (1817) 881; N&Q 1S:7 (1853) 177; Henderson
(1866) 86; Nicholson (1890) 86. **Lancashire** *Lancashire
Lore* (1971) 49–50. **Northumberland** Hone, *Every-Day
Book* 1 (1825) 755; Bosanquet (1929) 78. **Mid-Wales**
Davies (1911) 215.

moon: growing plants

Belief in the intimate connection between the
moon's cycle and living things on earth is also
manifested in strict instructions to farmers and
gardeners to pay heed to the time for planting
seeds and harvesting certain crops:

*Rule for planting – Everything below ground (i.e.
tubers, etc.) on a waning moon; everything above
ground (green vegetables) on a waxing moon.*
        Devon *Devonshire Assoc.* (1961)

More specialist tasks, such as grafting fruit trees,
were also ruled by the same principle.

*One must always graft at the waxing of the moon;
or, even better, three or four days before the
waxing, for as many days as there are [to the
waxing] so much time the tree will have to
prepare to bear its fruit.*
        Guernsey [1589] *Channel Islands Ann. Anth.*

These ideas are not so widely reported in the
folklore literature as the belief in the connection

between the moon's phase and the killing of animals (see MOON: PIG-KILLING), but they were certainly just as widespread and with a similarly long history. The same ideas were held in classical times. Moreover, as horticulture is still largely in the hands of ordinary people rather than professionals, the strictures on planting have lasted longer than those on animals, and are probably still followed in some quarters.

Hampshire [1984] Opie & Tatem, 264. Somerset [c.1949] Tongue (1965) 140. Devon N&Q 1S:10 (1854) 156; *Devonshire Assoc.* 9 (1877) 91; *Devonshire Assoc.* 93 (1961) 112. Essex [c.1920] Ketteridge & Mays (1972) 140. Bedfordshire *Folk-Lore* 37 (1926) 77. Cambridgeshire Porter (1969) 59. East Anglia Tusser, *Five Hundred Points of Good Husbandry* (1573) Ch. 33. Norfolk Randell (1966) 93. England Addy (1895) 55. West Wales Davies (1911) 218. Pembrokeshire Lockley (1957) 41. Forfarshire [1954] Opie & Tatem, 263–4. N. Ireland Foster (1951) 54. Guernsey [1589] *Channel Islands Ann. Anth.* (1972–3) 27. General A. Fitzherbert, *Boke of Husbandrye* (1523) 8; Scot (1584) Bk 9, Ch. 2; Werenfels (1748) 6. Classical Pliny, *Natural History* (AD 77) Bk 18, Para. 75.

---

moon: hair/nails

The idea that the moon's waxing and waning directly affects the growing and shrinking of earthly living things is extended to apply to humans in beliefs which cover the cutting of hair and, less commonly, fingernails and corns. Hair should be cut when the moon is waxing, to ensure subsequent growth:

My mother-in-law in her youth always had her hair cut every month as the moon was growing, never when on the wane. She is now 77, with a wealth of dark hair reaching below her waist, and she attributes it to the care and attention given in early days and cut at the time mentioned.

Kent N&Q (1922)

Conversely, nails and corns, whose growth is to be retarded, should be cut when the moon is on the wane:

[A domestic servant from Great Torrington] told me that if people cut their corns when the moon was 'on its back', the corns would not grow as they otherwise would.

Devon *Devonshire Assoc.* (1898)

The idea has a long history. Opie and Tatem identify the earliest known British example in a letter from Arabella Stewart, an eleven-year-old girl, to her grandmother, enclosing the 'endes of my heare, which was cut the sixt day of the moone'. The belief is also well known abroad,

and was already in vogue in classical times:

Similarly, the emperor Tiberius kept to the period between two moons even in having his hair cut. Marcus Varro advises the plan of having one's hair cut just after full moon, as a precaution against going bald. Pliny, *Natural History* (AD 77)

Documentary evidence shows that it lasted in Britain well into the twentieth century. Opie and Tatem quote a Hampshire hairdresser in 1987 who believed it to be scientific fact.

Kent N&Q 12S:11 (1922) 14. Sussex N&Q 6S:6 (1882) 416. Hampshire [1987] Opie & Tatem, 262. Dorset *Procs. Dorset Nat. Hist. & Ant. Field Club* 35 (1914) 83–4; Udal (1922) 279–80. Devon N&Q 1S:4 (1851) 98–9; *Devonshire Assoc.* 9 (1877) 91; *Devonshire Assoc.* 12 (1880) 112; *Devonshire Assoc.* 15 (1883) 107; *Devonshire Assoc.* 30 (1898) 8; *Devonshire Assoc.* 63 (1931) 124. Cornwall *Jnl Royal Inst. Cornwall* 20 (1915) 128; *Old Cornwall* 2 (1931–6) 39–40. Berkshire *Folk-Lore* 5 (1894) 338. Oxfordshire *Folk-Lore* 34 (1923) 326. Herefordshire [c.1895] *Folk-Lore* 39 (1928) 384–5. Worcestershire [1900] *Folk-Lore* 20 (1909) 342. Worcestershire/Shropshire *Gent. Mag.* (1855) 385. Suffolk Evans (1965) 213. Shropshire Burne (1883) 256–9. England Addy (1895) 59. Lancashire [1717] N&Q 12S:10 (1922) 93; Harland & Wilkinson (1882) 141. Co. Durham Leighton (1910) 48. Wales Jones (1930) 198. West Wales Davies (1911) 218. Jersey *Folk-Lore* 25 (1914) 247; L'Amy (1927) 98–9. Unlocated [1587] Opie & Tatem, 262; N&Q 6S:9 (1884) 366; N&Q 12S:10 (1922) 238; *Folk-Lore* 38 (1927) 37. General *British Apollo* (17 Apr. 1710). Classical Pliny, *Natural History* (AD 77) Bk 16, Ch. 76.

---

moon: marriage

The positive attributes generally assigned to the waxing moon, and the avoidance of undertaking new enterprises while it is waning, was extended to apply to marriage:

All weddings in Shetland must commence with the new moon, otherwise the marriage will be an unlucky one. Shetland Reid (1869)

Given the widespread nature of belief in the growing new moon, it would seem likely that its application to weddings would also be generally found, but virtually all the recorded instances come from Orkney and Shetland, where it was clearly very strong.

Wales Trevelyan (1909) 270–1. Scotland Dalyell (1834) 285. Orkney *Stat. Acct Scotland* 7 (1791–9) 560; *Stat. Acct Scotland* 15 (1791–9) 311; Barry (1808) 348; *New Stat. Acct Scotland* (1845) 143; N&Q 10S:12 (1909) 483–4. Shetland Reid (1869) 60–2.

moon: moonlight dangerous

The supposed connection between the moon and insanity, encapsulated in the word 'lunacy', has a very long history, and is now a cliché of popular culture. Nevertheless, many people, even in relatively recent times, took the idea quite seriously:

Two instances have been recorded between 1961 and 1963 of the effect of the full moon on persons suffering from mental illness. In both cases the symptoms of the patient – acute depression in one, restlessness and agitation in the other – were said by other members of the family to become more marked at the time of a full moon.

Cambridgeshire Porter (1969)

Moonlight also featured in a range of other beliefs – always with a negative and dangerous reputation. Humans sleeping in moonlight were said to be, at best, subject to bad luck and bad dreams, and at worst prone to stammering, blindness, paralysis, and idiocy. To avoid this fate, some children were taught a protective rhyme:

Very few mothers will suffer the full moon to shine in at the bedroom windows when their children have retired to rest; for the popular opinion is, that her rays will cause the sleepers to lose their senses. Should children observe the moon looking into their rooms, they are taught to endeavour to avert her influence by repeating the words:

*I see the moon
The moon sees me
God bless the priest
That christened me.*

Lancashire Harland & Wilkinson (1873)

Moonlight was also believed to accelerate putrefaction in raw meat, and particularly fish:

My . . . servant, a seafaring girl, tells me that she was once made very ill by eating mackerel which had been made poisonous by the moon shining on it – 'that will turn any fish to poison,' she said.

Unlocated N&Q (1894)

These notions were widely held by sailors and travellers who had experienced moonlight in the tropics, but were also believed as scientific fact by many at home:

That the light of the moon accelerates putrefaction is more than an unfounded popular opinion. I have heard it repeatedly asserted by observant and sober-minded naval officers as a

fact, established by experience in tropical climates. Their constant testimony was, that when there is no moon the fresh meat is hung over the stern of the ship at night for coolness; but if this is done when the moon shines, the meat becomes unfit to eat.

N&Q 1S:2 (1851)

Essex [c.1920] Ketteridge & Mays (1972) 140. Cambridgeshire Porter (1969) 59. Norfolk *East Anglian Mag.* (Aug. 1935) 94. Derbyshire [c.1890s] Uttley (1946) 133. Lancashire Harland & Wilkinson (1873) 238. Co. Durham [1982] Opie & Tatem, 265. Northeast Scotland Gregor (1881) 152. Ireland N&Q 10S:1 (1904) 395. N. Ireland Foster (1951) 54. Various N&Q 12S:11 (1922) 311, 355, 397, 437–8, 494; 12S:12 (1923) 34–5. Unlocated N&Q 8S:5 (1894) 449. General N&Q 1S:4 (1851) 332; Smyth (1867) 483. Literary N&Q 1S:4 (1851) 273, 355.

moon: pig-killing

It was a matter of common knowledge for centuries that animals must be slaughtered during the waxing of the moon, or the meat would be at best inferior and at worst downright bad. As pigs were the animals most commonly killed at home rather than in professional butchers' premises, the majority of recorded beliefs focus on them:

[Attempting to book local pig-killer] On my questioning him as to his impending engagements, he made various references to the moon, that, to me, were unintelligible. At last he spoke plainly: 'I tell you what it is, guv'nor. If you don't want to lose your pig, you won't let me kill him when the moon's a-going off. Better wait till she's getting near the full'. On consulting the almanac I found that this arrangement would not be altogether convenient, and I suspected that he was putting me off to suit his own business; I, therefore, pressed him to come 'at the end of the moon'. He reluctantly consented, but argued that the pig would not weigh so much by many pounds as if it were killed towards the full of the moon. 'You kill him now, guv'nor, and weigh him; and then kill him at the full o' the moon, and you'll see the differ'. I, in my turn, argued that this was an impossibility . . . 'Does this only apply to pigs?' – 'No, guv'nor, it holds good with all beasts'.

Unlocated N&Q (1875)

The analogy is quite simple. The moon in its 'growing' phase, results in meat that 'grows' (or at least does not shrink) in the cooking:

A pig must not be killed when the moon is waning, or the bacon will 'boil out', that is it will shrink in boiling instead of 'plimming up' (or becoming plump) as good bacon should do.

Worcestershire Salisbury (1893)

As with other new-moon beliefs, the notion of size is also translated into good and bad, and other elements of animal husbandry were also ruled by the same cycle:

Old-fashioned shepherds never dock lambs' tails when the moon is southing, that is, on the wane. If they do the lambs will die.

Oxfordshire *Oxf. & Dist. FL Soc. Ann. Record* (1959)

The usuall and best time for geldinge of lambs is aboute the middle or 20th of June, the moone beinge four or six dayes past the full.

Yorkshire Best, *Rural Economy* (1641)

It is because of the implicit belief in its effect on animals and plants that rural dwellers needed to be aware of the moon's phases at all times, and kept the sale of ALMANACS so high for so long. The belief is well documented from the sixteenth century across the British Isles, but it does not seem to have much survived the era of home pig-killing which ended in the second half of the twentieth. Those who buy their pork at the supermarket know little of when and how it was killed.

Sussex Latham (1878) 11. Somerset [1946–9] Tongue (1965) 140. Devon *Devonshire Assoc.* 15 (1883) 107; *Devonshire Assoc.* 17 (1885) 122; *Devonshire Assoc.* 60 (1928) 112; *Devonshire Assoc.* 63 (1931) 123. Cornwall *Old Cornwall* 2 (1931–6) 40. Essex [c.1920] Ketteridge & Mays (1972) 140. Hertfordshire [1835] N&Q 5S:3 (1875) 424. Oxfordshire *Oxf. & Dist. FL Soc. Ann. Record* (1959) 7. Gloucestershire *Trans. Bristol & Glos. Arch. Soc.* 53 (1931) 264. Herefordshire [c.1895] *Folk-Lore* 39 (1928) 384–5; Duncomb (1804) 60. Worcestershire Salisbury (1893) 77. Warwickshire N&Q 1S:8 (1853) 146; N&Q 4S:8 (1871) 505. Bedfordshire *Folk-Lore* 37 (1926) 77. Huntingdonshire [c.1950] Opie & Tatem, 263. Cambridgeshire [1959] Porter (1969) 59. East Anglia Forby (1830) 404. Suffolk Chambers 1 (1878) 203–4. Norfolk Randell (1966) 95. Lincolnshire Watkins (1886) 10; Rudkin (1936) 51. Leicestershire N&Q 4S:8 (1871) 505. Shropshire Burne (1883) 256–9. England Addy (1895) 60. Derbyshire N&Q 5S:4 (1875) 184; [c.1890s] Uttley (1946) 133; N&Q 11S:2 (1910) 504. Yorkshire Henry Best, *Rural Economy* (1641); [1920s] Kitchen (1940) Ch. 2. Lancashire Harland & Wilkinson (1873) 224. Northumberland Neville (1909) 109. Highland Scotland [1529] Dalyell (1834) 286; Macbain (1887/88) 271–2. Northeast Scotland Gregor (1881) 151. Orkney *Stat. Acct Scotland* (1791–9) 560; Barry (1808) 348; *New Stat. Acct Scotland* (1845) 143; N&Q 10S:12 (1909) 483–4. Jersey *Folk-Lore* 38 (1927) 178. Guernsey De Garis (1975) 127. Unlocated N&Q 1S:10 (1854) 7–8; N&Q 5S:3 (1875) 84. General *Husband-Man's Practice* (1673) H8, quoted Opie & Tatem, 262.

moon: pointing at

A relatively widely reported nineteenth-century superstition prohibited any pointing at the moon, on the basic grounds of being disrespectful:

A lady, upwards of seventy years of age, informs me that when a child on a visit to her uncle at Ashburton, she was severely scolded by one of the servants, for pointing her finger at the moon. The act was considered very wicked, being an insult; and no one knew what evil instances it might call down.   Devon *Devonshire Assoc.* (1879)

Descriptions are normally couched in terms of pointing as a breach of Victorian good manners, and some informants commented that they had been brought up to regard pointing at anything or anybody as unacceptably rude. A different story is occasionally given, which cites the 'man in the moon' as the reason for not pointing, and the following example also includes another regular motif that it is the number of times one points that matters:

Fifty years ago it was held to be unlucky to point at the moon and count the stars. Derbyshire girls and boys 'dared' each other to do it. To point at the moon properly it was necessary to get as near to it as possible, and gates, fences, and walls were mounted before the pointing was begun. They might point six times without ill effect, but at the seventh 'you would be struck blind'. This pointing seemed to have some connexion with 'the man in the moon', so far as talk went, who had been sufficiently punished for his sin without being pointed at. Amongst the folk to point the finger at anyone was an offensive action at all times, and was always resented. The more daring children evaded the probable consequences by 'hooking the finger' at the seventh pointing, going through the motion, but not having the forefinger extended. It was bad luck to 'count out' the stars up to one hundred, and 'you might be struck down dead' for it. Generally, the counting stopped at ninety-nine, only a few venturing beyond 'in fear and trembling'. Mothers used to say, 'Don't point at moon!' 'Don't count stars!' Except that in pointing the 'man in the moon' was taken into consideration, reasons why the stars should not be counted were not given.

Derbyshire N&Q (1902)

The first published account only dates from 1851, but the Devonshire example quoted above must refer to a time before the 1820s. Similar beliefs about pointing at STARS and RAINBOWS also date from around the same period. All references are from England, and the belief does not seem to have lasted well in the twentieth century.

A completely different angle on moon-pointing is offered by another description, which combines the regular divination rhyme (see MOON: DIVINATION) with a knife motif:

For the following notes I am indebted to a simple serving-woman in Dublin: At new moon it is not uncommon to point with a knife, and after invoking the blessed Trinity, to say: New moon, true moon, be true now to me/That I ere the morrow my true love may see. The knife is then placed under the pillow, and silence strictly observed, lest the charm should be spoilt.

Dublin N&Q (1869)

Sussex N&Q 6S:4 (1881) 407–8. Somerset [1956] Tongue (1965) 140. Devon *Devonshire Assoc.* 11 (1879) 110. Northamptonshire Sternberg (1851) 170. Shropshire Burne (1883) 258. England Addy (1895) 56, 97. Derbyshire [c.1890s] Uttley (1946) 133; N&Q 9S:9 (1902) 357–8. Lancashire N&Q 6S:4 (1881) 407–8. Dublin N&Q 4S:4 (1869) 505.

moon: right shoulder

One of several stipulations about how you should see the new moon is that it must be over your right shoulder:

A new moon seen over the right shoulder is lucky, over the left shoulder unlucky, and straight before prognosticates good luck to the end of the moon.

Devon N&Q (1851)

This follows the general, but not invariable, pattern of right is good, left is bad, found in British superstitions. The stipulation about shoulders does not usually stand alone, but, like the ban on seeing the moon through glass, is a prerequisite for other moon beliefs:

Bow three times when you see the new moon, and wish; if you see it for the first time over your right shoulder you will get your wish.

Cardiganshire *Folk-Lore* (1928)

This belief is reported from most parts of the British Isles except, on present evidence, Scotland, but this is unlikely to be a true picture. Although regularly reported in the Victorian period and after, like most moon superstitions it is only recorded from the 1830s onwards.

Kent *Folk-Lore* 25 (1914) 367. Sussex Latham (1878) 8. Dorset Udal (1922) 281. Somerset [1923] Opie & Tatem, 282. Devon Bray (1838) 294; N&Q 1S:4 (1851) 98–9; Hewett (1892) 27; Hewett (1900) 49, 55. Oxfordshire N&Q 3S:2 (1862) 485. Northamptonshire Sternberg

(1851) 170. East Anglia Forby (1830) 415. Suffolk Claxton (1954) 89. Lincolnshire Thompson (1856) 735. Westmorland/Lancashire *Folk-Lore* 64 (1953) 299. Northumberland *Folk-Lore* 36 (1925) 253. Wales N&Q 10S:12 (1909) 406–7. Glamorgan Phillips (1925) 598. Cardiganshire *Folk-Lore* 39 (1928) 174. Co. Longford *Béaloideas* 6 (1936) 264. Jersey *Folk-Lore* 25 (1914) 247; L'Amy (1927) 98–9.

moon: seen empty-handed

A few late nineteenth-century references report a belief that it is unlucky to see the new moon for the first time empty-handed, presumably on the same principle that one must have money at that time to ensure future riches.

It was unlucky to see the new moon for the first time through a window, or with empty hands. To have something in the hand on the first sight of the new moon was lucky, and indicated a present before the moon had waned.

Northeast Scotland Gregor (1881)

The same principle of 'something in the hand' is included in NEW YEAR customs such as first footing. As applied to the new moon, it is mainly reported from Scotland.

England Addy (1895) 59. Highland Scotland *People's Friend* (13 Sept. 1882) 580. Northeast Scotland Gregor (1881) 151. Orkney N&Q 10S:12 (1909) 483–4.

moon: seen through glass

One of the two major superstitions regarding how or where the new moon is first seen dictates that it is very bad luck to see it through glass:

Many Cambridgeshire people still consider it unlucky to see a new moon for the first time through glass, although few, if any, now go to the length of taking the precautions to avoid doing so which their grandparents, in many instances, took. An elderly Cambridge man recalled in 1958 that when he used to stay with his grandmother in Ely when he was a boy, he remembers being told by her to stand by an open kitchen window to warn her of an appearance of a new moon so that she could join him and see it from the doorstep and not through a window.

Cambridgeshire Porter (1969)

The penalty for ignoring this interdiction is usually cited as generally 'very bad luck', but some informants specified that the result would be that you would 'break glass' during that moon. Less common, but still reported in significant numbers, was the idea that it was also unlucky to see the moon 'through trees'.

If the moon you see
Neither through glass or tree
It shall be a lucky moon to thee.

Jersey Folk-Lore (1914)

It is not entirely clear why viewing through glass was counted as so significant, although similar prohibitions were reported, much less commonly, in other contexts. It was believed, for example, that it was bad luck to see a FUNERAL through a window, and that what is seen through glass is not permissible as evidence in court (*see* LEGAL ERRORS). The only clue which emerges from the mass of references to the new-moon belief is an impression, and it is no more than that, that it is somehow *disrespectful* to the moon not to see it face to face.

Informants disagreed over the obvious question of what to do with spectacles. Some carefully removed them before looking at the sky, while others were more pragmatic:

[Remembering childhood, born 1914] *Our mother had a lot of warnings: . . . Her favourite one was: Never look at the new moon through glass! She went spare if one of us did that. Dad used to have to go outside, tell her if it was shining. 'Yes,' he said, 'it is'. Then she said, 'Don't look out the winder, there's a new moon'. 'What about me glasses Mam when I goes out?' 'Spectacles don't count'.*   Warwickshire Hewins (1985)

An added complication is provided by the fact that some moon divination customs specifically require the moon's reflection to be viewed in a mirror (*see* MOON: DIVINATION). It seems that in this context the danger only lies in seeing *through* glass, not *in* it.

The superstition was extremely widespread in the nineteenth and twentieth centuries, and most regional folklore collections include versions. It has not, however, been found before 1830, and it is quite likely it did not exist before about 1800.

Kent/Sussex N&Q 4S:11 (1873) 141. Sussex Latham (1878) 11. Dorset Udal (1922) 281; *Dorset Year Book* (1961–2) 73. Devon N&Q 6S:5 (1882) 15; *Devonshire Assoc.* 15 (1883) 107; Hewett (1892) 27; Hewett (1900) 55; *Devonshire Assoc.* 63 (1931) 123. Cornwall Hunt (1865) 236; *Old Cornwall* 2 (1931–6) 39. Wiltshire *Wilts. N&Q* 1 (1893–5) 61. Berkshire Mitford (1830) 301; Lowsley (1888) 24. London N&Q 6S:5 (1882) 15. Essex [*c*.1920] Ketteridge & Mays (1972) 140; *Folk-Lore* 64 (1953) 296. Oxfordshire N&Q 3S:2 (1862) 485; [*c*.1920s] Surman (1992) 61; Harris (1969) 124–5. Worcestershire Salisbury (1893) 71. Worcestershire/Shropshire *Gent. Mag.* (1855)

385. Midland England *Midland Garner* 1 (1884) 23. Warwickshire Langford (1875) 12; [*c*.1924] Hewins (1985) 93. Northamptonshire Sternberg (1851) 170. Cambridgeshire Porter (1969) 59. East Anglia Varden (1885) 113. Suffolk Chambers 1 (1878) 203–4; Fitzgerald (1887) 505. Norfolk Fulcher Collection (*c*.1895); [*c*.1912] Randell (1966) 99; [*c*.1920] Wigby (1976) 68. Suffolk *Folk-Lore* 35 (1924) 350. Lincolnshire Good (1900) 108. Rutland N&Q 4S:11 (1873) 53. Shropshire [1860s] Burne (1883) 256–9. England Addy (1895) 59. Derbyshire [*c*.1890s] Uttley (1946) 133. Yorkshire Blakeborough (1898) 130; Atkinson (1891) 71. Lancashire Harland & Wilkinson (1882) 149. Cumberland Gibson (1858) 105–6. Westmorland/Lancashire *Folk-Lore* 64 (1953) 296. Co. Durham Brockie (1886) 215; Leighton (1910) 56. Northumberland Neville (1909) 110; *Folk-Lore* 36 (1925) 253; Bosanquet (1929) 78–9. Wales N&Q 10S:12 (1909) 406–7. West Wales Davies (1911) 218. Pembrokeshire *Archaeologia Cambrensis* 85 (1930) 206. Western Scotland Napier (1879) 98. Northeast Scotland Gregor (1881) 151. Orkney N&Q 10S:12 (1909) 483–4. N. Ireland Foster (1951) 54. Co. Longford *Béaloideas* 6 (1936) 263. Jersey *Folk-Lore* 25 (1914) 247; L'Amy (1927) 98–9. Unlocated N&Q 2S:12 (1861) 491; N&Q 10S:12 (1909) 518. General *Punch* (1 Jan. 1881) 310.

moon: turn your apron

A handful of nineteenth-century references report the idea that women should 'turn their aprons' when they first see the new moon:

A schoolfellow of mine always took off her apron and turned it, curtseying three times to the moon, repeating at the same time a rhyme, which I have forgotten.   Wiltshire *Wilts. N&Q* (1893–5)

As in this example, the action is usually part of the much more common obeisance of bowing or curtseying to the new moon (*see* MOON: BOWING TO) and wishing, and turning money. The significance of the apron is not clear, but can be compared to another belief, that women can 'change their luck' by turning their aprons round (*see* CLOTHES: APRONS).

Wiltshire *Wilts. N&Q* 1 (1893–5) 61. Northern England [1850s] Denham Tracts 2 (1895) 24. Cumberland Gibson (1858) 105–6. Dumfriesshire Corrie (1890/91) 82.

moon: wart cures

A recurrent element in WART cures is the stipulation that the operation must take place at a particular phase of the moon, or actually in moonlight:

I was told of another remedy by a farmer whose sister's warts had been supposed to have been removed by the following means. It was the night of the new moon; indeed it was necessary that so it should be for the efficacy of the means used. The young woman had on no account to look at the moon, but someone had to go out and observe in which quarter of the heavens she was, and then come and lead the patient out into the garden, whereupon she had to stoop down and rub the warts all over with the soil without attempting to look at the quarter where the moon lay, and return to the house at once. I was assured that in this case the operation was a complete success.

Yorkshire Morris (1911)

The moon is thus an integral part of the prescription, usually combined with other regular elements such as SNAILS or plants, but the timing varies considerably from version to version. In some it is the full, in others the new, moon, and so on. Where the new moon is stipulated, the instructions apparently abrogate the general rule that if you wish something (i.e. the wart) to *decrease*, the operation should be carried out at the *waning* of the moon. Those which specify the full moon are probably following this general rule, especially in cases where the moonlight itself appears to be the primary active agent in the cure:

Another way is to pretend to wash your hands in an empty bowl out of doors, keeping your face fixed on the full moon for two succeeding nights. On the third night the warts will have gone.

England Addy (1895)

This pretended washing is mentioned twice in the 1650s, in terms which imply that it is already a generally known and accepted cure, and the moon continued to be an element in wart cures at least into the 1950s. It also has classical antecedents:

Warts are removed by those who, after the twentieth day of the month, lie face upwards on a path, gaze at the moon with hands stretched over their head, and rub the wart with whatever they have grasped. Pliny, *Natural History* (AD 77)

Devon *Devonshire Assoc.* 57 (1926) 121; *Devonshire Assoc.* 84 (1952) 297. **Cornwall** *Folk-Lore Jnl* 5 (1887) 200; *Jnl Royal Inst. Cornwall* 20 (1915) 124. **Cambridgeshire** *Folk-Lore* 64 (1953) 425. **Shropshire** *Folk-Lore* 49 (1938) 226–8. **England** Addy (1895) 89. **Yorkshire** Morris (1911) 248. **Highland Scotland** Polson (1926) 34–5. **Glasgow** [*c.*1820] Napier (1864) 397. **General** Thomas Browne, *Pseudodoxia Epidemica* (1650) Bk 5 Ch. 23 Para. 9; K. Digby, *Late Discourse* (1658) 43. **Classical** Pliny, *Natural History* (AD 77) Bk 28, Para. 12.

moon: weather

Weather-lore is not covered by this Guide, but beliefs connecting the time of the new moon and future weather are so numerous, and were such an integral part of moon-lore, that they must be mentioned, even if only in passing. Apart from innumerable general predictions about the appearance, colour, brightness, etc. of the moon, the most regularly reported superstition was that a new moon on Saturday (some say Friday) was bad:

A Saturday moon, if it comes once in seven years, comes too soon.

and especially so if followed by a full moon on Sunday:

On Saturday new, on Sunday full Was never good, and never wull.

East Anglia Forby (1830)

The general unluckiness of FRIDAY is well known, but it is unclear why Saturday is thus singled out, being, in most other contexts, a usually lucky day.

Selected refs only: Devon N&Q 5S:6 (1876) 364; *Devonshire Assoc.* 15 (1883) 107. Surrey [1793–5] N&Q 5S:10 (1878) 23. Essex [*c.*1920] Ketteridge & Mays (1972) 140. East Anglia Forby (1830) 416–17. Suffolk Chambers 1 (1878) 203–4. Lincolnshire *Gent. Mag.* (1833) 590–3. Yorkshire *Leeds Mercury* (4 Oct. 1879). Galloway Mactaggart (1824) 212. Unlocated Halliwell (1849) 159; N&Q 1S:2 (1850) 515.

Mother Bunch's Closet

A copy of an anonymous seventeenth-century CHAPBOOK entitled *Mother Bunch's Closet Newly Broke Open*, printed in London in 1685, survives in the Samuel Pepys collection in Magdalene College, Cambridge. In the book, Mother Bunch undertakes to teach young women how to get husbands, by reciting a number of LOVE DIVINATION procedures, including the St Thomas ONION, DUMB CAKE, HEMP SEED, WASHING SHIFT, and addressing the new MOON, as well as the importance in such matters of specific nights such as ST AGNES and MIDSUMMER eves. The chapbook is particularly important because in many cases it provides us with the earliest datable reference to these superstitions and a valuable insight into how such material came to be circulated. The complete text was reprinted by G. L. Gomme for the Villon Society in 1885, together with a 1780 continuation, *The History of Mother Bunch of the Weste.*

moths

A number of scattered reports indicate that moths, like BUTTERFLIES, were not particularly liked in the past. Apart from the idea that a persistent moth indicated news on its way (*see below*), moths were believed to bring fever, or to be connected with evil in some way or another:

Certain flying moths that become very trouble-some in some years were called 'fever moths', and were supposed to carry disease in their wings. When these moths infested a house, people said somebody would die of fever therein.

Wales Trevelyan (1909)

Moths were called 'witches', and were looked upon with a sort of indefinable dread, as being very uncanny.   Northeast Scotland Gregor (1881)

Clothes moths are called 'ghosts', and every time one is killed, there is the danger of injuring a rela-tive.

Northern England *Newcastle Weekly Chronicle* (11 Feb. 1899)

Somerset N&Q 1S:3 (1851) 133. New Forest Wise (1867) 177. Wiltshire Smith (1874) 324. London N&Q 1S:12 (1855) 201. Shropshire Burne (1883) 239. Yorkshire [1823] Home (1915) 215; N&Q 1S:3 (1851) 220. Northern England *Newcastle Weekly Chronicle* (11 Feb. 1899) 7. Wales Trevelyan (1909) 322–3. Northeast Scotland Gregor (1881) 147. Kilkenny N&Q 1S:1 (1850) 349.

moths: predict letter

A reasonably widespread superstition main-tained that a moth flying around a person or a room predicted a letter or some news:

A moth hovering around one is a sign of good news; that is, of a letter bearing such, or of some coming in any other way. At Hartland we say the moth foretells a letter in the post – whether the news expected is good or bad.

Devon *Devonshire Assoc.* (1932)

The meaning is constant across all the recorded versions, although occasionally it means the imminent arrival of a stranger (*compare* BEES: IN HOUSE).

Somerset [1922] Opie & Tatem, 266. Devon *Devonshire Assoc.* 64 (1932) 157. London *Folk-Lore* 37 (1926) 364. Worcestershire/Herefordshire N&Q 6S:6 (1882) 186. Welsh Gypsies Jarman (1991) 184. Monmouthshire [1954] Opie & Tatem, 266. Renfrewshire N&Q 4S:4 (1869) 212. Argyllshire *Folk-Lore* 21 (1910) 90.

mourning: clothes

see CLOTHES: FUNERAL/MOURNING.

mourning paper

In the days when black-edged notepaper was an integral part of the bereavement ritual for a family in mourning, it was regarded by some as very unwise to keep such paper in the house at other times, as TEMPTING FATE to supply another death:

an Irish lady, with whom she lived, burnt a quan-tity of black-edged paper which remained after some time of mourning had elapsed, rather than incur the risk of hoarding it. Such stationery being part of the 'pomp and circumstance' of modern grief-showing, is, no doubt, to be sacrificed on the same principle as the clothes; that being, I suppose, that a house must be purged of every symbol of sorrow, lest like should attract like.   Ireland N&Q (1880)

Although recorded here in only three late instances, the general principle of not keeping items closely associated with death around the house is more widely known, and this belief was probably of more general currency, at least in Victorian and Edwardian times.

Compare CLOTHES: FUNERAL/MOURNING.

Aberdeenshire *Folk-Lore* 25 (1914) 350. Ireland N&Q 6S:1 (1880) 55, 212.

mouse

see MICE.

mushrooms

A handful of sources record a belief that mush-rooms are shy:

We have, in Ireland, a strange idea that mush-rooms never grow after they have been seen.

Ireland *Athenaeum* (1846)

Roy Vickery also reports that mushrooms grow best where horses are kept, as they thrive on stal-lions' semen.

East Anglia Varden (1885) 114. Suffolk [1863] Chambers 1 (1878) 322. Yorkshire Vickery (1995) 251. Ireland *Athenaeum* (1846) 1069.

Napoleon's *Book of Fate*

One of the most popular of the oracle-style fortune-telling books, the *Book of Fate, formerly in the Possession of Napoleon, the Late Emperor of France*, was first published in London in 1822, purportedly translated from the German by Herman Kirchenhoffer. The book was an immediate success, and within a few years had run through a dozen editions. It was regularly reprinted in Britain and North America throughout the nineteenth and twentieth centuries, and is still in print today. Kirchenhoffer's introduction claimed it as an ancient text, discovered in a mummy's tomb by one of the scientists accompanying Napoleon on his 1798 Egyptian campaign. He further claimed that Napoleon himself had used the manuscript extensively in planning his military and political career, until it was lost in the chaos after his defeat at the Battle of Leipzig (1813), with only a translation surviving. The story thus claims both a suitably romantic and remote origin and a link to Napoleon (and his first wife Marie-Rose, 'Josephine') who were fast gaining a reputation for having had an avid interest in all things occult. The story of the book's origins, however, contains numerous inconsistencies, and it has also proved impossible even to identify Kirchenhoffer himself. There is no evidence to suggest that the *Book of Fate* is anything other than an early nineteenth-century fabrication. Nevertheless, its admirers claim that it works well, and it is often claimed as a simplified, Western-style I Ching.

The book works on a fixed oracle principle, offering thirty-two possible questions (for example, 'Inform me of any or all particulars relating to the woman I shall marry'; 'Have I any or many enemies?'; 'Will my intended journey be prosperous or unlucky?'). The inquirer starts by marking short lines on a piece of paper, without counting them. These are translated into a series of stars and numbers, which are again translated into one of thirty-two hieroglyphs (sun, moon, castle, wheatsheaf, etc.), which then leads to the specific answer.

Richard Deacon, *Napoleon's Book of Fate: Its Origins and Uses* (Secaucus: Citadel, 1977).

narrative

The basic format for a superstition is 'if you do this, that will happen', or 'if you see/meet this, that will happen'. So, for example, 'if you walk under a ladder, you will have bad luck', or 'if you see two magpies, you will get good luck'. Alternatively, a superstition might involve a simple statement: 'seventh sons can cure people', 'witches turn themselves into hares'. These are the building blocks of superstition, and are passed on from person to person, from generation to generation, in this simple didactic form. However, beliefs often circulate in a more developed form, in which they are 'narrativized' or embedded within a story. This narrative format not only serves to make the basic superstition more interesting and memorable, but it also helps to legitimize and strengthen the belief, and many of the examples quoted in this book show signs of having passed through this process. *Localization* is a well-known principle in folklore study, and is one of the processes in play here. Stories, songs, and other narrative forms accrue local details which function to ground the item in the shared experience of teller and listener. The items themselves are thus legitimated, and the basic belief supported, by this 'evidence' and this appeal to history and custom. Who can question some occurrence when one is being assured that it happened to Uncle Fred?

There are many people still who can stop bleeding by just saying 'something'. A man here stopped a wound bleeding only a week or so before the account was given to me. His wife said he was sent for in the middle of the night to a friend of his because a blood vessel had burst inside his head, and he stayed the blood before the doctor came. He also stopped the bleeding from a bad cut in a boy's foot quite lately. The foot was stretched out on a stool before him and he just put his hands out over it and said something – of course, not allowing any of the standers-by to hear what he said. The wound was then streaming, so that the blood ran over the floor, but the flow ceased and the wound only wept a little after the words were spoken. The same man can also prevent a thorn festering.

Devon *Folk-Lore* 11 (1900) 217

Good stories are formulaic, rounded, satisfying, and believable.

The aetiological legend is another narrative form which the investigator of superstition must be able to recognize. As stories, aetiological legends are characteristically shorter than those already discussed and are less satisfying as narratives, for example: 'Saying "bless you" goes back to the plague, because sneezing was the first symptom of the disease, and if you sneezed you would probably die'; 'At the battle of Agincourt, the French were so frightened of the English archers that when they captured one they chopped off the first two fingers of his right hand so that he could no longer draw a bow. The bowmen who had not been mutilated taunted the French by holding up their two fingers and jeering, and this was the start of the offensive V-sign gesture'.

Aetiological legends seem to be a relatively recent phenomenon, engendered by Victorian folklorists who declared that mundane folklore had interesting ancient roots, and enthusiastically continued by popular writers and journalists ever since.

See also BACK-FORMATION.

needles

Needles feature in a few scattered beliefs, usually as spillovers from more common superstitions regarding PINS seen on the floor, and SCISSORS being dropped:

If a pair of scissors, a knife, or a needle falls to the floor and sticks in an upright position, an unexpected guest will arrive ere long . . . A needle broken in two while sewing brings good fortune to the wearer of the article sewn; if in three pieces an offer of marriage.   Argyllshire *Folk-Lore* (1910)

For needles stuck in hands, etc., *see* THORNS.

Somerset [1923] Opie & Tatem, 279. **Wales** Trevelyan (1909) 324. **Glamorgan** [1957] Opie & Tatem, 279. **Argyllshire** *Folk-Lore* 21 (1910) 89. **Dumfriesshire** [1957] Opie & Tatem, 279.

ne'er cast a clout till May is out

see CLOTHES: LEAVING OFF.

nettles

The application of a dock leaf has been recommended for a nettle sting for at least 650 years, and remains almost universally known. Many people are still convinced that docks and nettles always grow in close proximity simply for human convenience. In the past, however, the dock leaf itself was only one half of the cure, as it was also necessary to recite a certain CHARM to make it effective. Many people still know versions of the charm, although it is now usually regarded simply as a rhyme for children rather than an essential part of the cure. The words of the rhyme vary considerably, but nearly always follow a similar simple pattern. Either they

simply demand relief in a rhythm which is a regular characteristic:

Nettle in, dock out
Dock in, nettle out
Nettle in, dock out
Dock rub nettle out.

Northumberland N&Q (1876)

or they introduce an element of bribery:

Out nettle
In dock
Dock shall have
A new smock.

Cornwall Hunt (1865)

This rhyme was already proverbial in Chaucer's time, as when Troilus protests that he cannot simply switch his love to another: 'But kanstow playen raket, to and fro, Nettle in, dok out, now this, now that?' (*Troilus and Criseyde* (*c.*1374)); similarly, in the sixteenth century it still meant an unsettled state of mind: 'For in one state they twain could not yet settle, but wavering as the wind, in dock out nettle' (Heywood, *Proverbs* (1546)) and a very similar sentiment is found in the play *Ralph Roister Doister* (1566).

Other aspects of nettle lore are outside our scope, as the plant is regularly recommended as food, and for a wide range of ailments, including RHEUMATISM, to purify the blood, and pleurisy. See Hatfield (1994) and Vickery (1995) for some of these aspects of nettles. Nevertheless, a few references indicate more than simple herbal properties for the plant, for example:

To prove whether a sick person will live or die, place a handful of nettles under his pillow. If they keep green, the invalid will recover; if they turn colour, he will surely die.   Wales Trevelyan (1909)

In our district at least, the medicinal virtue of the nettle lay in its being 'unspoken', i.e. no one must speak to the gatherer of it, and collected at the hour of midnight.   Scotland *Folk-Lore Jnl* (1884)

Sussex Latham (1878) 45; *Sussex County Mag.* 5 (1931) 122. **Cornwall** N&Q 1S:12 (1855) 37; Hunt (1865) 215; Couch (1871) 166; *Folk-Lore Jnl* 5 (1887) 213. **Devon** [1820s] *Athenaeum* (1846) 1018. **Wiltshire** Akerman (1842) 15–16. **Surrey** [1860s] Sturt (1927) 136. **Essex** [*c.*1915] Mays (1969) 165. **Shropshire** Burne (1883) 184. **Worcestershire** Salisbury (1893) 71. **Huntingdonshire** N&Q 1S:3 (1851) 368. **Lincolnshire** Gutch & Peacock (1908) 118. **Lancashire** Harland & Wilkinson (1873) 227. **Derbyshire** [*c.*1890s] Uttley (1946) 112. **England** Addy (1895) 92. **Yorkshire** Nicholson (1890) 125. **Northern England** Brockett (1829) 99; [1850s] *Denham Tracts* 2 (1895) 71; Henderson (1866) 17. **Co. Durham** Brockie (1886) 117; Leighton (1910) 49. **Northumberland** N&Q 1S:3 (1851) 133; N&Q 5S:6 (1876) 462; **Cumberland**

[1957] Opie & Tatem, 279. **Wales** Trevelyan (1909) 281. **Scotland** *Folk-Lore Jnl* 2 (1884) 377–8. **Dumfriesshire** Corrie (1890/91) 83. **N. Ireland** Foster (1951) 61. **Ireland** Logan (1981) 67–8. **Unlocated** Halliwell (1849) 223. **Literary** Chaucer, *Troilus and Criseyde* (*c.*1374) Bk 4, lines 460–1; John Heywood, *Proverbs* (1546) 140; *Ralph Roister Doister* (1566) 2:3.

newts

Several erroneous beliefs existed about the newt, including the widespread idea that it was poisonous, and even spat fire:

About twenty-five years ago several children were busy catching newts from a pond to bring to school. A farmer who saw them rated them soundly, assuring them they were poisonous and would spit fire at them.

Devon *Devonshire Assoc.* (1935)

Further beliefs also connected them with fire:

It is said that the newt will not burn when placed in the fire.

Northern England *Newcastle Weekly Chronicle* (11 Feb. 1899)

and a particularly strong belief in Ireland held that this immunity could be transferred to humans:

Anyone who licks a 'man-creeper' (newt) will ever after have the power of curing burns and scalds by licking them. Such a man's tongue, it appears, becomes incombustible. 'O that's perfectly true,' said a Meath man to me a short time ago. 'I have seen him set his tongue to the red iron. You could hear it hissing like bacon frying on the pan, and yet it wasn't burnt'. **Ireland** *Folk-Lore* (1908)

Newts were also prone to getting inside human bodies:

It is believed that if anyone swallows an 'asgill' (newt) when drinking water it will grow inside him and he will pine away and die.

Shropshire *Folk-Lore* (1938)

See also ANIMAL INFESTATION.
NB: It is not always clear whether writers are referring to newts or LIZARDS.

Devon *Devonshire Assoc.* 67 (1935) 133. **Surrey** N&Q 13S:1 (1923) 172. **Essex** [*c.*1939] *Folk-Lore* 64 (1953) 294. **Herefordshire** [*c.*1895] *Folk-Lore* 39 (1928) 391. **Worcestershire** *Folk-Lore* 20 (1909) 347. **Lincolnshire** Watkins (1886) 11. **Shropshire** *Folk-Lore* 49 (1938) 230. **Northern England** Brockett (1829) 11; *Newcastle Weekly Chronicle* (11 Feb. 1899) 7. **Yorkshire** Nicholson (1890) 127. **Co. Durham** Brockie (1886) 142. **Ireland** *Folk-Lore* 19 (1908) 317. **Co. Meath/Co. Tipperary** *Folk-Lore* 15 (1904) 460. **Co. Cork** [1937/8] Culloty (1993) 59.

New Year: activities

The heightened feeling of New Year as a specially powerful BEGINNING is manifest in the idea that whatever you are engaged in at that time will dominate your life for the next twelve months:

There is still a widespread superstition that whatever one is doing when the church bells ring in the New Year, one will be doing the same most of the year. Few people, therefore, go to bed, for obvious reasons and even the old and infirm prefer to sit up. Black was never worn on New Year's Eve; to wear it was to invite death in the New Year. Women already in mourning often tied on a white apron. There is still a good deal of prejudice against wearing black at this time.

Co. Durham *Folk-Lore* (1960)

Other informants warned against breaking things, lending money, and crying. This notion was much more widespread than is suggested by the few references listed. Similar fears of continuance surround other beginning times, such as when you hear the CUCKOO for the first time in spring.

Perhaps allied to these beliefs was the idea that one should never allow a project to straddle the New Year:

Another curious belief was that work commenced in the old year should upon no account be left unfinished till the new, else its resumption would be attended by disastrous consequences.

Dumfriesshire Corrie (1890/91)

England Addy (1895) 105. **Derbyshire** [*c.*1890s] Uttley (1957) Ch. 2. **Co. Durham** *Folk-Lore* 71 (1960) 254. **Isle of Man** Moore (1891) 103. **Renfrewshire** [1986] Opie & Tatem, 283. **Dumfriesshire** Corrie (1890/91) 82.

New Year: fire and light

A cluster of beliefs centred on the domestic fire at Christmas and New Year. Householders were urged to keep the fire burning all night, and they believed that it was bad luck for the family for the coming year if it was allowed to go out. In addition, a widespread prohibition against allowing fire to leave the house, under any circumstances, was reported:

If any householder's fire does not burn through the night of New Year's Eve, it betokens bad luck

New Year

The importance of BEGINNINGS is one of the fundamental principles of superstition in Britain and Ireland, and is thus documented throughout this Guide. Beliefs cluster round the beginning of the day, of a journey, of spring, of a marriage, of a life, and so on. The New Year is an obvious addition to this list, and is still regarded as a key turning-point, even by those who claim to be non-superstitious. The feeling of a new beginning pervades our cultural and personal responses to the season, and even if we only make vague assessments of the previous year, and resolutions about the next, we are playing the same game. As Pliny asked, nearly 2,000 years ago, 'Why on the first day of the year do we wish one another cheerfully a happy and prosperous new year?' (*Natural History* (AD 77) Bk 28, Ch. 5).

For those who are prone to superstition, almost anything which happens at New Year can be taken as ominous, and activities which if they occurred at other times in the year would be regarded as simple customs, can take on a potential luck-enhancing role. A similar situation pertains with WEDDINGS, where, because of the nature of the celebration, any minor custom can become essential to follow because it would be 'unlucky' to do otherwise.

The character of the coming twelve months, for good or bad fortune, is foretold by the appearance of things on the morning of the new year. A trivial mishap, or the slightest instance of good luck, has now more than its usual significance, inasmuch as it predicts, in a general way, the course of events through the coming year. Cornwall Couch (1871)

It is not easy to reach an accurate synthesis of New Year beliefs and customs in the past. While underlying principles are remarkably constant, details vary considerably across Britain and Ireland, and even in a single county there can be sharp disagreement over essential details such as the preferred colour of the hair for the 'first footer'. Confusion also reigns over nomenclature. The generic term 'letting' or 'bringing' in the New Year can cover a variety of activities designed to mark the turn of the year, and 'first footing' in Scotland could mean the New Year custom of the first person to enter the house, or the first person met – at any time of year – in the morning or at the start of a journey.

There is also great potential for confusion over dates. In addition to the two New Years, old and new, provided by the change of CALENDAR in 1752, there is another historical problem of different dates for the new year. The official new year started on 25 March in England, Ireland, and Wales until 1752, but in Scotland it was set at 1 January from 1600. There is also considerable overspill from Christmas, and forward spillage to Handsel Monday (the first Monday in the year). Mrs Banks's description of the latter sums up the problem:

The rites [of Handsel Monday] *resemble those quoted for New Year's Day, for, owing to the change of style, this day was in many parts of Scotland observed on January 12th, later 13th, which day then fell together with Handsel Monday, and popular customs were transferred to this old time holiday. Where the New Year observances had been banned they were transferred to the later date.* Scotland Banks 2 (1939)

These are real difficulties when looking at the historical record, but in the modern period most of these discrepancies and local variations have been lost, and few would attempt to argue that New Year's Day is anything but 1 January.

The very noticeable differences between the

during the ensuing year; and if any party allow another a live coal, or even a lighted candle, on such an occasion, the bad luck is extended to the other party for commiserating with the former in his misfortunes. Lancashire N&Q (1851)

This prohibition was also extended to ashes, with even more direct consequences:

At Coniston it is believed that no light should be taken outside the house from Christmas Eve to the New Year, and that, for the same period, the ashpit under the kitchen fire must not be emptied lest a death should follow speedily.
Lancashire *Folk-Lore* (1910)

Keeping the fire burning is a further clear example of the simple motif that whatever happens, good or bad, at the turn of the year will effect the household in the coming months. The refusal to let fire leave the house can also be seen as part of the general reluctance to take anything out on New Year's Day, but to ensure that things were brought in (*see* NEW YEAR: INWARD AND OUTWARD). This would certainly explain the extension of the prohibition to include ashes. A prosaic explanation would add that, in midwinter, fire is so important to comfort and survival that it is no surprise that any cottager's mind was focused on it.

relative importance placed on Christmas and New Year by the English and the Scots is also rapidly losing ground. In the past, the difference was extremely pronounced, and is an excellent example of how political and religious conditions can affect the everyday world of custom and usage. The difference in dating has already been mentioned, but further divergence took place in the mid seventeenth century, with the rise to power of Puritan sects in both countries. In the 1640s, Christmas was banned both in England and Scotland, but while it was reinstated in England on the restoration of the monarchy, it was again proscribed by the church in Scotland in 1688, and the celebrations of the people in the two countries consequently diverged.

A basic separation is made in this book between CALENDAR CUSTOMS and superstitions, with the former being excluded. As already indicated, the distinction in the case of New Year is problematic, as any custom at this period can be viewed as luck-bringing. To keep the discussion to manageable proportions and impose some order on chaos, a crude distinction is made between the following aspects:

First footing – The belief that the first person to enter the house on New Year's Day should be a certain type of individual, selected for their personal characteristics. 'First footing' beliefs at other times are discussed under the main entry MEETING.

Letting in the New Year – Householders opening door or windows, sometimes bringing something into the house themselves.

Inwards and outwards – Manifestations of the idea that things should be brought *into* the house before anything is allowed out. This is also often an implicit element of *first footing*. *Guisers, singers, and other visitors who stay outside the*

house are not included in this Guide as being defined as CALENDAR CUSTOMS rather than superstitions.

Dozens of New Year superstitions have been reported once or twice, and it is always difficult to determine which were rare and which were widely known but were simply missed by the collectors. Most follow the same pattern as the widespread beliefs discussed below, and the same motifs of beginnings and continuance are in evidence.

Should one of your children fall sick when on a visit at a friend's house, it is held to be sure to entail bad luck on that family for the rest of the year, if you stay over New Year's Day. Persons have been known to travel sixty miles with a sick child rather than run the risk.
Lancashire Harland & Wilkinson (1882)

On New Year's Day you should get the newest pin you can and drop it in the water, 'because it is the blood of Christ'. I can get no explanation of this saying. Gloucestershire *Folk-Lore* (1902)

There is a saying in the neighbourhood of Cusop and Hay that, if a tramp calls on New Year's morning, every knock he gives at the door will be a happy month for the occupants of the house. This applies only to men.
Herefordshire *Folk-Lore* (1913)

[Going up before down] *This also extends to New Year's Day. The moment after midnight has struck, and the New Year begins, you must rise – be it on a stair, a chair, or anything – or misfortune will pursue you in the coming year.*
Guernsey *Folk-Lore* (1927)

Cornwall Couch (1871) 151. Gloucestershire *Folk-Lore* 13 (1902) 174. Herefordshire *Folk-Lore* 24 (1913) 238–9. Lancashire Harland & Wilkinson (1882) 138–9. Scotland Banks 2 (1939) 118. Guernsey *Folk-Lore* 38 (1927) 179.

But this explanation alone does not quite satisfy all the evidence. Similar prohibitions against fire leaving the house have been reported, albeit less frequently, for other days in the year – notably May Day – and in other circumstances, such as when there was a sick person or unbaptized child in the house. These examples have been reported from Irish informants. The Revd Walter Gregor implied that in Scottish fishing communities the removal of fire at any time was unwise:

It is accounted unlucky to give fire out of house, so much so that one would not enter a house, and light his pipe at the fire, and walk out. Luck would leave the house. Banffshire *Folk-Lore Jnl* (1885)

The fire is here treated as if symbolic of the 'luck of the house'. Serious commentary on these fire beliefs has been seriously hampered in the past by the assumption that they are relics of a fire festival devoted to pagan gods, but if this could be set aside, further study might help to shed some new light on the topic.

An added dimension is provided by another Scottish source, which points out that witches could gain power over the household if allowed to take fire out:

On New Year's day fire should not be given out of the house on any consideration to a doubtful person. If he is ill-disposed, not a beast will be alive next New Year. A suspected witch came on this day to a neighbour's house for fire, her own having gone out, and got it. When she went away a burning peat was thrown into a tub of water. she came a second time and the precaution was again taken.   Highland Scotland Campbell (1900)

Devon *Devonshire Assoc.* 66 (1934) 88; *Devonshire Assoc.* 105 (1973) 213. **Herefordshire** Fosbroke (1821) 59. **Worcestershire** *Folk-Lore* 20 (1909) 345. **Lincolnshire** Swaby (1891) 94. **Shropshire** Burne (1883) 401–2. **Yorkshire** *Gent. Mag.* (1811) 424; Young 2 (1817) 880; *Yorkshire Post* (31 Dec. 1964) 4. **Lancashire** N&Q 1S:3 (1851) 56; N&Q 3S:1 (1862) 482; N&Q 3S:2 (1862) 484; Harland & Wilkinson (1882) 155, 214; *Folk-Lore* 21 (1910) 224. **Northern England** [1850s] *Denham Tracts* 2 (1895) 24. **Co. Durham** *Folk-Lore* 71 (1960) 254. **Northumberland** [1850s] *Denham Tracts* (1895) 340. **Welsh Gypsies** Jarman (1991) 185. **Scottish borders** [*c.*1816] Henderson (1866) 54. **Eastern Scotland** Anson (1930) 42. **Highland Scotland** Macbain (1887/88) 269. **Glasgow** [*c.*1820] Napier (1864) 396. **Banffshire** *Folk-Lore Jnl* 3 (1885) 309.

New Year: first water

The firm conviction that the special character of New Year's Day is reflected in the natural world led to at least four different customs based on the first water collected on that day. The most widespread of these, variously known as the cream, flower, crop, or ream of the well, held that whoever succeeded in getting the first water from any well would be lucky in some way – usually in love:

The maiden who, on New Year's morning, first draws a pailful of water from the village well is accounted singularly fortunate. She has, in truth, secured the 'flower o' the well', and will be happy for the succeeding year. The lassies often sing this couplet:

The flower o' the well to our howse gaes
And the bonniest lad'll be mine.

Caithness Rinder (1895)

The custom was therefore almost exclusively confined to females. In some versions, the water had similar qualities to MAY DEW:

It was formerly the custom in Herefordshire farmhouses for the servants to sit up to see the New Year in, and at midnight to rush for the 'cream o' the well', the first water drawn from the well in the year, which was thought to be beautifying and lucky. The maid who succeeded in getting it would take it to the bedroom of her mistress, who would give her a present for it. 'My missus always had the cream o' the well to wash

in on New Year's morning,' said Mrs. M—, 'and she always put a shilling under the basin for me too'.   Herefordshire Leather (1912)

The custom is mostly recorded from Scotland and Northern England, but there are several references from the Welsh border. It was probably much more widespread than the handful of references suggests. The earliest clear reference to it appears in one of the Revd James Nicol's Scottish poems in 1804, with lines very similar to the Caithness example quoted above. But long before that, the West Country poet Robert Herrick may have referred to the idea in 1648 when he wrote that 'Perilla' should 'bring Part of the creame from that Religious Spring' to wash his body after death. Nearly all the descriptions stress the competitive nature of the custom, and a different slant was offered by a correspondent to *The Times*:

Whoever drank first would be 'master' throughout the year. From my recollection of an old woman who used to practise this with her husband, I should say she was generally the first to reach the well.

Herefordshire *The Times* (19 Feb. 1926)

The other 'first water' customs are much more regionally confined. In South Wales, a house-visiting custom centred on children collecting 'New Year water', which would bring luck to those sprinkled with it:

On New Year's morning the children go round the streets calling at the houses to offer all New Year's water, which they bring with them in cups, with sprinklers of sea spurge . . . a penny or two is expected before the sprinkling is given. No doubt if asked, the object would be called 'for luck'.

Pembrokeshire *Country Life* (14 Jan. 1944)

In Scotland, water gathered on New Year's Day was combined with the notion that the first items brought into the house were symbolic of prosperity for the coming year:

An informant in the parish of New Machar (Mr. Wm. Porter) tells me that his parents are still living, and that they can recollect that in the beginning of the present century it was customary to go out and bring grass and water into a house on New Year's morning before anything was taken out. This was to ensure plenty of food for man and beast in the ensuing year.

Aberdeenshire *Folk-Lore* (1893)

In some cases, it was water and peat. On dairy farms, the water and grass fed to the cows helped to make them produce creamy milk.

In fishing communities in Scotland, the first water was drawn from the sea:

It was a custom to go to the sea and draw a pailful of water, and take it along with a little seaweed to the house on the morning of New Year's Day.   Banffshire *Folk-Lore Jnl* (1886)

Cream/Flower of the well: **Herefordshire** Duncomb (1804) 206; Leather (1912) 91; *The Times* (19 Feb. 1926) 20. **Northern England** *Newcastle Weekly Chronicle* (11 Feb. 1899) 7. **Northumberland** *Archaeologia Aeliana* 8 (1880) 67. **Monmouthshire** *The Times* (12 Feb. 1926) 8. **Scotland** Nicol (1805) 80; Hampson 1 (1841) 129–30; Haliburton (1894) 29. **Northeast Scotland** Banks 2 (1939) 100. **Aberdeenshire** *Folk-Lore* 4 (1893) 316. **Caithness** Rinder (1895) 59–60. **Literary** Robert Herrick, *Hesperides* (1648) 'To Perilla'. *Calender custom*: **South Wales** *Athenaeum* (1848) 142. **Pembrokeshire** *Bye-Gones* (1888) 138; *Country Life* (14 Jan. 1944) 77. *Water and grass*: **Scotland** N&Q 4S:10 (1872) 408. **Aberdeenshire** *Folk-Lore* 4 (1893) 316; Banks 2 (1939) 100. *Sea-water*: **Banffshire** *Folk-Lore Jnl* 4 (1886) 17; [mid 19th cent.] Anson (1965) 78.

New Year: inward and outward

The deep-felt need to set a good precedent at New Year, which underlies many of the superstitions of the day, is manifest in a concern about the inward and outward flow of concrete items which symbolize such intangibles as luck and prosperity. There was thus a widespread feeling that nothing should be taken out of the house before something was brought in. This is the one of the main points of many versions of FIRST FOOTING, but where that custom does not take place, or where householders feel in need of even more assurance, further steps have to be taken to ensure that the balance of incomings and outgoings remains firmly in favour of the former. For some, this idea was confined to certain staples such as money:

My mother (died 1928, aged 46), whose early years were spent in Cornwall, always put a small sum of money (it was always silver) out of the house before midnight and took it in again some time on New Year's Day – not necessarily just after midnight. When I asked her why she did it, she said she had always been told it would insure that during the year just beginning, her incomings would be more than her outgoings.   Devon *Devonshire Assoc.* (1959)

The other key staple, fire (and ashes), has its own entry (*see* NEW YEAR: FIRE AND LIGHT). Many people took the principle to its logical conclusion and forbade all outgoings, however mundane:

It happened that, when a boy, I spent Christmas . . . I remember accompanying the mistress of the house to her kitchen on New Year's Eve, when she called together all her servants, and warned them, under pain of dismissal, not to allow anything to be carried out of the house on the following day, though they might bring in as much as they pleased. Acting on this order, all ashes, dish-washings, or potato-parings, and so forth, were retained in the house till the next day, while coals, potatoes, firewood, and bread were brought in as usual, the mistress keeping a sharp look-out on the fulfilment of her orders.   Northern England Henderson (1866)

It is clear that those who believed such things were concerned to keep the control of New Year ins and outs in their own hands and to manipulate fate as much as they could. The quoted example is one of many which describe householders hiding money or other objects outside the house on New Year's Eve so that it could be brought in, in triumph, after midnight. Others were even more ingenious:

To ensure luck to herself during the present year, and also to the house where for the time she lives, the servant of one of my neighbours tied a piece of string to a lump of coal just before midnight of the old year, laid the string across the doorsill, and afterwards, as the clock at the church was striking the hour of twelve, opened the door. As soon as the last stroke sounded, she pulled the piece of coal into the house, in this way making sure that something came into the house before anything was taken out of it. This bringing in ensured good luck all the year. If anything had gone out first – herself, for instance – the year would bring bad luck more or less of a serious nature.   Unlocated N&Q (1906)

One solitary reference, which may therefore simply be an individual fancy, shows how the same principle can have a quite different result:

It is lucky to pay money on the first of January, as it ensures the blessing of ready cash for all payments throughout the year.   Devon Hewett (1900)

Somerset [1923] Opie & Tatem, 284. **Devon** Hewett (1900) 50; *Devonshire Assoc.* 87 (1955) 355; *Devonshire Assoc.* 91 (1959) 202. **Cornwall** *Western Antiquary* 3 (1883) 91. **Herefordshire/Worcestershire** N&Q 6S:6 (1882) 186. **Lincolnshire** Brand 1 (1849) 15; Good (1900) 108; Rudkin (1936) 41. **Nottinghamshire** *Jnl Brit. Archl. Assoc.* 8 (1853) 231; N&Q 5S:6 (1876) 534. **Derbyshire**

N&Q 10S:5 (1906) 45. **Northern England** [1850s]
Denham Tracts 2 (1895) 24; Henderson (1866) 57.
Yorkshire Young 2 (1817) 880; [1982] Opie & Tatem,
284, 285. **Cumberland** Bulkeley (1886) 231. **Co. Durham**
Leighton (1910) 56. **Dumfriesshire** Corrie (1890/91) 82.
Aberdeenshire *Folk-Lore* 4 (1893) 316. **Ireland** Wilde
(1888) 212. **N. Ireland** Foster (1951) 36. **Isle of Man**
Train 2 (1845) 115. **Unlocated** Brand 1 (1849) 20; N&Q
10S:5 (1906) 45; N&Q 11S:10 (1914) 505.

New Year: letting in

In many homes, the central symbolic focus of the
turning of the year took the form of physical steps
to 'let the New Year in'. In most cases it was simply
a question of opening doors or windows:

*As the clock struck twelve, it was customary to
open the back door first, to let the old year out;
then, the front door was opened, to let the new
year in.*   Herefordshire Leather (1912)

Sometimes, however, it could take some attributes of INWARD/OUTWARD flow traditions (*see
above*):

*When you open the door first thing in the morn-
ing on New Year's Day to let the New Year in, then
you walk out of the house a little way with some
money in your left hand, and then you turn
round and you change the money over from the
left hand to the right and go indoors again; by
doing this, you'll have money to spend all the year
and will have some given you, too.*
                    Devon *Devonshire Assoc.* (1934)

There was also a crossover with FIRST FOOT-
ING; in some households tradition insisted that
the first footer enter the house by one door and
leave by another.

Devon *Devonshire Assoc.* 64 (1932) 165; *Devonshire
Assoc.* 66 (1934) 88; *Devonshire Assoc.* 91 (1959) 201–2.
Wiltshire *Wilts. N&Q* 1 (1893–5) 105. **Herefordshire**
Leather (1912) 89. **Warwickshire** [1987] Opie & Tatem,
284. **Eastern England** N&Q 4S:1 (1868) 193. **Sutherland**
[1953] Opie & Tatem, 284.

New Year: new clothes

Another specific example of the notion that
one's situation on New Year's Day will affect the
rest of the year is reflected in the idea that you
should always have new clothes to wear:

*Always wear something new on New Year's Day
and you will have plenty of new clothes all the
year. (The informant believed firmly in this, and
went to considerable trouble to change her charge
into a new frock accordingly.)*
                    Gloucestershire *Folk-Lore* (1923)

The good luck will naturally be enhanced if the
new clothes have money in the pockets. Other
days on which new clothes should be worn are
EASTER and WHITSUN.
  See also CLOTHES: NEW.

Devon *Devonshire Assoc.* 57 (1926) 127. **Gloucestershire**
Folk-Lore 34 (1923) 155. **Northern England** Henderson
(1866) 55. **Co. Durham** Leighton (1910) 56. **Highland
Scotland** Macbain (1887/88) 262. **Unlocated** Hone, *Year
Book* (1832) 126–8.

New Year: washing clothes

New Year's Day was one of the days of the year
when WASHING was prohibited in many households, for fear it would cause a death in the family:

*On New Year's day one of our maids (not a
Devonshire one) was going to do the family washing, when our West-country girl exclaimed in
horror*

*Pray don't 'ee wash on New Year's day
Or you'll wash one of the family away*

*On inquiry I find the belief widely spread here-
abouts, that if the year commences in domestic
circles with a washing day, one of the occupants
of the house is washed out (i.e. dies) during the
year.*   Devon N&Q (1896)

A general dislike of doing domestic work on
New Year's Day (and GOOD FRIDAY) is often
recorded, with particular emphasis placed on
washing and, sometimes, cleaning in general:

*Some persons will not even permit any dishes,
plates, etc. to be cleaned on the first day of the
year.*   Devon N&Q (1877)

Reported examples are overwhelmingly from
southern England, with a particular concentration in the West Country. But Alec Gill showed
that the superstition was also believed in fishing
families in Hull, and this was probably so elsewhere in seagoing communities. At first glance,
the superstitions reported by Gill seem based
mainly on ghastly puns – in addition to 'washing one of the family away', he reports that family
members 'Never shook a mat on that day because
that would shake a man overboard' and 'Don't
peg out clothes or someone will "peg out" in the
family'. Nevertheless, the seriousness with which
such beliefs can be held is demonstrated by his
description of one family's continued memory
of the loss of a loved one at sea in 1933:

*When news came through of her beloved
brother's loss, Ivy's thoughts immediately sprang*

*back to New Year's Day. She had broken the strict
taboo and done her family washing that day. This
superstition played guiltily on her mind – she had
washed her brother Arthur out of her family . . .
Sixty years after the loss of their Uncle Arthur,
nieces Dorothy and Betty . . . never wash on New
Year's Day.*   Yorkshire Gill (1993)

In common with the other major New Year
superstitions, there is no indication that this fear
of washing is older than the mid nineteenth
century, and indeed it seems to have been most
widespread in the twentieth.

Sussex *The Times* (22 May 1934) 15. **Hampshire** [1969]
Opie & Tatem, 286. **Dorset** Udal (1922) 287. **Somerset**
[1923] Opie & Tatem, 286. **Devon** N&Q 5S:7 (1877) 26;
N&Q 8S:9 (1896) 46; *Devonshire Assoc.* 33 (1901) 128;
Crossing (1911) 134–5; *Devonshire Assoc.* 72 (1940)
115–16; *Devonshire Assoc.* 98 (1966) 88; *Devonshire Assoc.*
105 (1973) 213; *Devonshire Assoc.* 118 (1986) 246.
Cornwall *Old Cornwall* 2 (1931–6) 39. **Worcestershire**
The Times (22 May 1934) 15. **Yorkshire** Gill (1993)
105–6. **Guernsey** De Garis (1975) 69.

nightingales (*Luscinia megarhynchos*)

The nightingale's popular song, and its appearance each year in spring, contribute to a generally positive image in Britain and Ireland, and it
is often linked with the CUCKOO in traditional
belief: 'You should always wish when you hear
the first cuckoo or nightingale' (Igglesden
(*c.*1932)). A belief noted by A. S. Macmillan in
Somerset in 1923 maintains that it is best to hear
your first nightingale before the first cuckoo, as
that 'foretells success in love'. Almost the same
wording occurs in John Milton's poem 'To the
Nightingale' (1629), and in the absence of other
traditional versions, we must suspect direct literary borrowing on the part of Macmillan's
informant or in the chain of transmission before
them. The idea has even deeper literary roots.
Milton probably got it from the early fifteenth
century courtly poem 'The Cuckoo and the
Nightingale' (previously ascribed to Chaucer,
but now agreed to be by Clanvowe). In that
poem, the narrator has a dream in which the
cuckoo and nightingale debate the subject of
love. While the cuckoo laughs at love and its
human victims, the nightingale praises it. The
poem includes the lines:

*I thought how lovers had a tokening
And among them it was a common tale
That it were good to hear the nightingale
Rather than the lewd cuckoo sing.*

A completely different view is provided by an
example from Shropshire, which shows how
context and timing are so important in analysis
of superstition:

*Recently at Newport, Shropshire, a pair of
nightingales built for the first time near the
canal, and people used to collect at night to listen
to them singing. People now say that it would be
a good thing if they never returned, because bad
luck, including seven deaths, occurred in the
neighbourhood as a result of their sojourn.*
                                    Shropshire *Folk-Lore* (1914)

Somerset [1923] Opie & Tatem, 287. **Shropshire** *Folk-
Lore* 25 (1914) 372. **Unlocated** Igglesden (*c.*1932) 83.
Literary Sir T. Clanvowe, 'The Cuckoo and the
Nightingale' (*c.*1403); John Milton 'To the Nightingale'
(1629) lines 5–7. **General and foreign** Swainson (1886)
18–22.

nightjars (*Caprimulgus europaeus*)

Isolated references indicate a dislike or fear of
the nightjar, although without further evidence
it is difficult to assess how widespread this was.
Ruth Tongue, collecting from farm children
around 1904, reported a definite negative image
for the bird:

*A nightjar is even more sinister than an owl. It is
a witch in disguise and sucks the cows' milk. It
can only be shot with a silver sixpence.*
                                    Somerset [1904] Tongue

Swainson confirmed the belief about sucking
milk from cows, which, he says, was found in the
south of England and some parts of Ireland. He
also reprints a belief from Yorkshire that night-
jars embody the souls of unbaptized children,
'doomed to wander forever in the air'.

Somerset [1904] Tongue (1965) 48. **General and foreign**
Swainson (1886) 96–8.

nightmares

The current meaning of 'nightmare' as simply a
bad dream obscures an earlier, more specific
meaning, and also a historical confusion with a
different phenomenon otherwise called HAG-
RIDING. The original 'nightmare' referred to a
distressing night-time condition whereby a
sleeper feels a huge weight on his/her chest,
suffocating and immobilizing at the same time.
This was presumed to be an attack by an evil
creature called an incubus or, in Old English, a

'maere' or 'mara'. The similarity in words, and the metaphor of being 'ridden' by the spirit, suggested a connection with real 'mares', and the night-maere became a nightmare.

A further step connects this spirit-riding with the phenomenon of witches riding real horses during the night and leaving them sweating and exhausted in their stables in the morning (*see* HAG-RIDING).

Various methods were recommended for keeping the nightmare at bay, all of which were also used in other protective contexts. A stone with a hole, or 'hag-stone' (*see* STONES: HOLED), which was more often used against hag-riding, was popular, as was ensuring that something made of IRON was nearby. Placing the shoes or stockings in a certain position on going to bed was a third option:

A flint-stone with a hole in it hung over the bed's head will prevent nightmare; or place your boots when taken off 'coming and going' – that is, the heel of the one beside the toe of the other.

East Anglia Varden (1885)

As a contribution to the folk-lore of night-hags, I may mention that I used to hear from my father of a woman in Hampshire who was accustomed to hang a scythe over her children's bed. When asked the reason, she replied, 'It's to keep the hags from riding the childer by nights'.

Hampshire N&Q (1907)

In an early account, Thomas Blundeville of Norfolk states that the nightmare results from bad digestion rather than supernatural causes, but then relates a 'fonde foolishe charme' in which his contemporaries believed. This involved a holed stone hung over the sufferer, with an accompanying written CHARM, which is not one of the common ones:

In nomine patris, &c.
Saint George our Ladyes Knight
He walked day so did he night
Untill he hir found
He hir beate and he hir bounde
Till truly hir trouth she him plyght
That she woulde not come within the night
There as Saint George our Ladyes Knight
Named was three tymes, Saint George.

Blundeville, *The Fower Chiefest Offices belonging to Horsemanship* (1564)

The nightmare was also called by the Greek-based word *ephialtes*.

Hampshire N&Q 10S:7 (1907) 157. **East Anglia** Varden (1885) 103. **Suffolk** N&Q 15:4 (1851) 53; *Folk-Lore* 56 (1945) 270. **Yorkshire** N&Q 5S:10 (1878) 266. **Wales**

Trevelyan (1909) 324. **Shetland** Edmonston & Saxby (1888) 186–7. **General** Thomas Blundeville, *The Fower Chiefest Offices belonging to Horsemanship* (*c.*1565) quoted N&Q 6S:1 (1880) 54; Culpeper, *The Complete Herbal and British Physician* (1656) 296; Brand (1777) 324. **Major studies:** Hufford (1982); Davies (1996–7).

Northern Lights

see AURORA BOREALIS.

Norwood Gypsies

Only seven miles south of the City of London stands Norwood, traditionally the place where Surrey bordered Kent but now where five London boroughs meet. As the name suggests, the area had always been heavily wooded and enjoyed a reputation for wild and dangerous country, the haunt of Gypsies, vagabonds, and outlaws. It is not known when the Gypsies settled in the area, but as early as 1668, Samuel Pepys recorded a visit:

This afternoon, my wife and Mercer and Deb went with Pelling to see the Gipsys at Lambeth and have their fortunes told; but what they did, I did not enquire. (11 Aug. 1668)

and the Norwood Gypsies became so widely known in the eighteenth and nineteenth centuries that the very phrase became synonymous with fortune-telling. Like Elizabeth Pepys, hundreds of eighteenth- and nineteenth-century London girls made the trip to Norwood to have their fortunes told, and painters, poets, and musicians helped to create a national reputation which must have made the trade a lucrative one for the locals. Dozens of nineteenth-century CHAPBOOKS were issued with titles such as *The Original Norwood Gipsy or the Fortune-Teller's Guide*, or *The Circle of Fate, or True Norwood Gipsy*, and so on, while J. A. Fisher's pantomime *The Norwood Gipsies* (1777) brought them to the London stage, Samuel Howell's poem 'Norwood' (1820) to the poetry-reading public, and various published engravings helped to enhance their image. These are the Gypsies of the romantic imagination – wild and free, mysterious and enigmatic, possessing occult powers which house-dwellers could tap into; safe enough to visit but with just the right amount of danger to provide a frisson of fear.

One character in particular became nationally known in her time: Margaret Finch, purportedly the Gypsy Queen, who died in 1740, at the reputed age of 108 or 109: She was succeeded in popular affection by her niece Bridget. Gypsies

nosebleed cures

A nosebleed is an ideal candidate for folk and superstitious cures; it is impressively real, not life-threatening, and will normally stop of its own accord given a little time. As such, there are scores of traditional remedies, many of which overlap with methods of curing other types of BLEEDING (e.g. the use of COBWEBS), while others are unique to this problem. As with traditional cures for most ailments, three categories of remedy can be identified: placing substances on or in the site of the problem (the nose), placing substances or operating elsewhere on the body, and verbal charms or prayers. Many remedies are herbal, others patently magical, and some of indeterminate nature. A few, such as the cold key down the back, are known to almost everybody, while others appear to be found in isolated cases, and may even be specific to certain families. The most widespread are identified in their own entries, below.

Most nosebleed cures are characterized by being short and simple. Of those which recommend, quite logically, placing something in the nostril, less common examples include fresh pig dung (**Devon** *Devonshire Assoc.* (1880)), nettle juice (Chamberlain (1981)), and the plant called 'Red Roger' (**Co. Down** *Folk-Lore* (1897)). In the second, indirect, category, a survey of beliefs and cures carried out in the 1940s in Westmorland and North Lancashire included in addition to the more common cures, the eating of sour raisins, the fastening of a string round the finger, or the taking of horehound (**Westmorland/Lancashire** *Folk-Lore* (1951)).

Occasional references describe the use of a 'bloodstone' – a stone which, usually from its red markings, is reputed to stop bleeding:

A lady near Cromer has a 'blood stone' (possibly an agate or a piece of serpentine) which she lends to persons who suffer from excessive nose-bleeding.

It is worn round the neck in a bag. One man wore a similar stone for forty years, and his nose bled the first day he left it off.
Norfolk *Folk-Lore* (1929) and **Cambridgeshire** *Folk-Lore* (1912)

John Aubrey provides a seventeenth-century remedy, reportedly used on royalty:

To staunch bleeding: Cut an ash of one, two, or three years growth, at the very hour and minute of the sun's entering into Taurus: a chip of this applied will stop it; if it is a shoot, it must be cut from the ground. Mr. Nicholas Mercator, astronomer, told me that he had tried it with effect. Mr. G.W. says the stick must not be bound or holden; but dipped or wetted in the blood. When King James II was at Salisbury, his nose bled near two days, and after many essays in vain, was stopped by this sympathetick ash, which Mr. William Nash, a surgeon in Salisbury, applied.
Wiltshire Aubrey, *Miscellanies* (1696)

And one from the sixteenth century:

If a spider be put in a linen cloth a little bruised and holden to the nose that bleeds (but touch not the nose therewith, but smell to the same) by and by the blood will stay, and the nose will leave bleeding. This is very true for the venomous spider is to the contrary, and such an enemy to man's blood, that the blood draws back, and shuns the spider presently. A marvellous thing.
Lupton (1579)

Devon *Devonshire Assoc.* 12 (1880) 101–2. **Wiltshire** Aubrey, *Miscellanies* (1696/1857) 139. **Cambridgeshire** *Folk-Lore* 23 (1912) 349–50. **Norfolk** *Folk-Lore* 40 (1929) 124. **Westmorland/Lancashire** [*c*.1939] *Folk-Lore* 62 (1951) 261. **Co. Down** *Folk-Lore* 8 (1897) 387. **Unlocated** Chamberlain (1981) 238. **General** Lupton (1579) Bk 8, Para. 88.

---

stayed in the area for most of the nineteenth century, but their influence waned from 1800 when enclosure and, later, extensive building gradually civilized the neighbourhood. Ironically, it was at this same time, from the 1820s to 1860s, that the 'Norwood Gypsies' name became so popular in chapbooks.

See also CHAPBOOKS; DREAM BOOKS.

Coulter (1996) 11–13. Material held in London Borough of Croydon, Local Studies Library.

nosebleed cures: charms

For reasons stated above, nosebleeds are particularly susceptible to unorthodox healing procedures, and it is little surprise that various verbal CHARMS have been recorded. These formulae follow the basic pattern of other charms; especially those designed to stop BLEEDING from wounds and in other contexts. Where the actual words are recorded, almost all of them are overtly Christian, being either short prayers or narrative vignettes concerning the doings of Christ or the Disciples:

Charm for staunching bleeding of the nose – Jesus Christ was born in Bethlehem, baptized in the river Jordan; the water was wild in the wood, the child Jesus was meek and also good. He spoke and the water stood, and so shall your blood, in the name of the Father, and of the Son, and of the Holy Ghost.   Devon *Devonshire Assoc.* (1889)

For stopping haemorrhage, as spitting of blood, bleeding from the nose, bleeding from a wound, &c., the following charm must be solemnly repeated once, twice, or oftener, according to the urgency of the case, by some old man or woman accounted more sagacious than their neighbours. It must not be repeated out loud, nor in the presence of any one but the patient:

> *Three virgins came over Jordan's land*
> *Each with a bloody knife in her hand*
> *Stem, blood, stem – Letherly stand*
> *Bloody nose (or mouth) in God's name mend.*
>   Orkney N&Q 1S:10 (1854)

The idea of being able to charm away nosebleeds and other minor ailments is ancient, and was still being reported well into the twentieth century.

See also BLEEDING: CHARMS.

Dorset *Procs. Dorset Nat. Hist. & Ant. Field Club* 35 (1914) 82. Devon *Devonshire Assoc.* 21 (1889) 113; Hewett (1900) 80. Worcestershire Salisbury (1893) 69. Yorkshire [17th cent.] Gutch (1901) 168–9. Lancashire [1296–1346] MS *Liber Loci Benedicti de Whalley*, quoted in Black (1883) 76, and Harland & Wilkinson (1882) 77. Northumberland Bigge (1860–62) 89–90; Henderson (1866) 120–1. Orkney N&Q 1S:10 (1854) 220–1.

---

nosebleed cures: key down back

Within living memory, and to the present day, the most common folk cure for a nosebleed has been to put a cold key down the back of the sufferer:

Nosebleeding was cured by the great key of the house door. The sufferer lay down on the settle among the cushions and the big ice-cold iron key, which shone like silver with its constant handling, was placed next his skin. Like a block of ice it lay on the spine. If the bleeding continued too long we were laid on the hearthrug, with the key for company and, as it grew warm, it was removed and another equally large and cold key took its place.   Derbyshire [1890s] Uttley

Other details for added effectiveness emerge in some accounts. A piece of paper under the

tongue helps, for example; moreover, if the key has previously been placed in the Bible its power is enhanced. Attempts to explain the key's effectiveness in a rational way are not convincing, from the simple 'cools the blood' theory to the more complex:

the application of the cold metal is generally successful, as it causes a stoppage of the bleeding by acting in a reflex manner on the nerves, and producing contraction of vessels distributed in the neighbourhood of these nerves.
   Black (1883)

Despite its widespread nature, the key method may not be very old, as available references only start in the mid nineteenth century and informal research indicates that it is rapidly losing its hold in modern Britain. Younger people, when asked about nosebleeds, are markedly less likely to offer the key remedy than their elders.

Cornwall *Folk-Lore Jnl* 5 (1887) 203. Wiltshire *Wilts. N&Q* 1 (1893–5) 61. Essex [c.1939] *Folk-Lore* 62 (1951) 261. Gloucestershire *Folk-Lore* 16 (1905) 169–70. Worcestershire Salisbury (1893) 69. Bedfordshire Marsom (1950) 184. Cambridgeshire Porter (1969) 83–4. Lincolnshire Heanley (1902) 20; Rudkin (1936) 27. Staffordshire [c.1855] N&Q 4S:7 (1871) 91; Poole (1875) 84. Derbyshire [1890s] Uttley (1946) 113. Yorkshire Nicholson (1890) 140. Lancashire Harland & Wilkinson (1873) 226. Westmorland/Lancashire [c.1939] *Folk-Lore* 62 (1951) 261. Glasgow [1940s] MacLeay (1990) 48. Ireland Logan (1981) 87. Co. Cork [1937/8] Culloty (1993) 62. Unlocated N&Q 3S:12 (1867) 119. General Black (1883) 184.

---

nosebleed cures: red thread

A widespread motif in folk cures is that LIKE CURES LIKE, and the colour red often features in remedies for BLEEDING. In the case of nosebleeds, a RED THREAD, most often of silk, is placed around the sufferer's neck:

In 1931 an old man living in Cambridge showed a silk cord which he had worn round his neck for years as a safeguard against nose bleeding.
   Cambridgeshire Porter (1969)

In many cases, the thread is knotted, and a regular stipulation is that the knots must be tied by someone of the opposite sex to the patient – again, these are regular cure motifs:

To cure bleeding from the nose – Wear a skein of scarlet silk round the neck, tied with nine knots down the front. If the patient is a male, the silk

*should be put on and the knots tied by a female,
and vice versa.* Suffolk Glyde (1866)

As in the case of the 'key' cure (*see above*),
despite being widely reported, the red thread
remedy for a nosebleed cannot be shown to be
older than mid Victorian times, although as a
cure for other ailments it is considerably older.
Nor has it lasted as well as the key, having
apparently faded from view in the middle of the
twentieth century.

Sussex N&Q 3S:12 (1867) 42. Essex [c.1939] *Folk-Lore* 62
(1951) 261. Worcestershire Salisbury (1893) 69.
Northamptonshire N&Q 1S:2 (1850) 36–7.
Cambridgeshire [1931] Porter (1969) 84. East Anglia
Varden (1885) 103. Suffolk Glyde (1866) 173; [1877]
Gurdon (1893) 23. Norfolk [c.1870s] Haggard (1935) 15;
Folk-Lore 40 (1929) 118. Lincolnshire Rudkin (1936) 27.
Rutland N&Q 4S:10 (1872) 83. Wales Sikes (1880) 251.
Unlocated N&Q 2S:12 (1861) 492; Black (1883) 111.

nosebleed cures: toads

TOADS feature widely in British folk medicine,
and it is no surprise to find them in a few recipes
to cure nosebleeds. As elsewhere, the toad (or
parts of it) can be placed in a bag which is worn
on a string round the neck, or it can be taken as
a powder:

*To cure bleeding of the nose – Take one or two
fine old toads, place them in a cold oven, increase
the heat until sufficiently fierce to cook the toads
and reduce them to a brown crisp mass. Remove
from the oven and beat them to a powder in a
stone mortar. Place the powder in a box, and use
as snuff.* Devon Hewett (1900)

Such 'cures' were regularly prescribed from at
least the seventeenth century, but, fortunately,
appear to have died out completely.

Devon Hewett (1900) 76. Northamptonshire N&Q 1S:2
(1850) 36–7. Yorkshire [17th cent.] Gutch (1901) 169.
General *Most Excellent and Approved Remedies* (1652)
quoted in N&Q 1S:2 (1850) 510.

nosebleed: love

In addition to the notion that sudden nosebleeds
are literally ominous, writers in the sixteenth and
seventeenth centuries clearly felt a connection
between a nose bleeding and love, friendship,
and hate:

*Even from my childhood, never fell from hence
One crimson drop, but either my greatest enemy
Or my dearest friend was near.*
Heywood, *Fair Maid of the West* (1631)

The idea appears to be that the bleeding was
occasioned by great passion, or even sexual
desire:

*Both damsels and wives use many such feats:
I know them that will lay out their fair teats
Purposely, men to allure into their love,
For it is a thing that doth the heart greatly
    move.
At such sights of women I have known men,
    indeed,
That, with talking and beholding, their noses
    will bleed.*
Wager, *Repentance of Mary Magdalene* (1567)

These attributes of the nosebleed do not seem
to have outlasted the seventeenth century.

Literary Lewis Wager, *Repentance of Mary Magdalene*
(1567); J. Grange, *Golden Aphroditis* (1577); Thomas
Lodge, *Rosalynde: Euphues Golden Legacy* (1592); *A
Warning for Faire Women* (1599); Richard Tarlton, *News
out of Purgatorie* (1630) 101; Thomas Heywood, *Fair
Maid of the West* (1631) 2:4; Richard Braithwait, *Boulster
Lecture* (1640) 130. References given in N&Q 6S:6
(1882) 536; N&Q 6S:7 (1883) 238–9; Lean 2:1 (1903)
288–90.

nosebleed: omen

The idea that a sudden nosebleed, especially if
only one or two drops, was an omen was a
commonplace of sixteenth- and seventeenth-
century literature:

*My nose bleeds
One that were superstitious, would count
This ominous: when it merely comes by chance.*
Webster, *Duchess of Malfi* (1623)

and Samuel Pepys testifies that it was also known
in everyday situations:

*but it was an ominous thing methought, just as
he was bidding me his last adieu, his nose fell a-
bleeding, which run in my mind a pretty while
after.* London Pepys, *Diary* (6 July 1667)

In general, it was thought an automatically
bad sign, although Melton (1620) distinguishes
the right (bad) and left (good) nostril. Opie and
Tatem identify the earliest mention as 1180, by
Nigel de Longchamps, but it is 400 years later
that regular references start to appear. Despite its
early popularity, the superstition is rarely
reported after 1700, although one or two references indicate that it had not entirely disappeared even by Victoria's reign:

*Three drops of cold blood falling from the nose
was the sure indication of the death of one very*

nearly related to the one from whose nose the blood fell.   Northeast Scotland Gregor (1874)

London Samuel Pepys, *Diary* (6 July 1667). **Staffordshire** Poole (1875) 79. **Northeast Scotland** Gregor (1874) 135. **Unlocated** Melton (1620) 46; Aubrey, *Miscellanies* (1696/1857) 79; *British Apollo* (30 Dec. 1709); Grose (1787) 47. **General** Nigel De Longchamps, *Mirror for Fools* (1180) quoted Opie & Tatem, 287; George Gifford, *Subtill Practises of Devilles* (1587); Thomas Nashe, *Terrors on the Night* (1594); R. Bernard, *Guide to Grand-Jury Men* (1627); J. Banks, *Island Queens* (1684) 31–2. **Literary** George Wither, *Abuses Stript an Whipt* (1613) 2:1; Thomas Deloney, *Thomas of Reading* (1623) Ch. 11; John Webster, *Duchess of Malfi* (1623) 2:3; John Ford, *The Lover's Melancholy* (1629) 5:1; Thomas Heywood, *Fair Maid of the West* (1631) 2:4, 2:5.

nosebleed: yarrow

A curious collection of beliefs connects the plant YARROW (*Achillea millefolium*) with nosebleeds in widely varying contexts. Yarrow was commonly used in cures for other BLEEDING, and also for LOVE DIVINATIONS. As a cure for nosebleeds, the plant is simply held to the nose, placed in the nostril, or prepared in other ways:

My grandparents (b. 1856 and 1858) put yarrow in boiling water, and then over the nose for nosebleed.   Gloucestershire Vickery (1995)

To stop nosebleed, smell the flower of the yarrow – called locally 'nosebleed'.
          Lincolnshire Rudkin (1936)

On the other hand, a piece of yarrow up the nostril is reputed to *cause*, rather than cure, a nosebleed:

The common people in order to cure the headache, do sometimes thrust a leaf of it up their nostrils, to make their nose bleed.
          Scotland Lightfoot, *Flora Scotia* (1777)

This is also the basis of a love-divination procedure, reported three times from East Anglia, although it is possible that two of these sources were simply reprinting this earliest one:

Another plant of omen is the yarrow . . . called by us yarroway. The mode of divination is this; you must take one of the serrated leaves of the plant, and with it tickle the inside of the nostrils, repeating each time the following lines:

Yarroway, yarroway, bear a white blow
If my love love me, my nose will bleed now.

If the blood follows this charm, success in your courtship is held to be certain.
          East Anglia Forby (1830)

The widespread popular term for the yarrow, 'nosebleed', can thus be explained either by its curative or causative attributes.

See also BLEEDING; LOVE DIVINATION; YARROW.

Love divination: East Anglia Forby (1830) 424; Varden (1885) 109. **Eastern England** Halliwell (1849) 223–4. **Nosebleed cure:** Gloucestershire [*c*.1900?] Vickery (1995) 407. **Lincolnshire** Rudkin (1936) 26. **Scotland** J. Lightfoot, *Flora Scotia* (1777) quoted Vickery (1995) 407. **Highland Scotland** Polson (1926) 28–9.

noses: blue vein

It was generally thought to be unlucky to be born with a marked blue vein across the nose, and in many cases it was predicted that the child would not live long or would be drowned:

A fond mother was paying more than ordinary attention to a fine healthy-looking child, a boy about three years old. The poor woman's breast was heaving with emotion, and she struggled to repress her sighs. Upon inquiring if anything was really wrong, she said, 'the old lady of the house had just told her that the child could not live long, because he had a blue vein across his nose.'
          Cornwall Hunt (1865)

This is the first known reference to this meaning, which contrasts sharply with a much earlier definition:

And if a little vein appear between the eyes and the nose of a wench, they say that it signifieth virginity, and in a man, subtiltie of understanding; and if it appear great and black, it signifieth corruption, heat, and melancholy in women, and in man, rudeness and default of wit; but that vein appeareth not always.
          The Shepherd's Kalendar (1503)

Devon Hewett (1900) 55; *Devonshire Assoc.* 60 (1928) 125. **Cornwall** Hunt (1865) 238. *Folk-Lore Jnl* 5 (1887) 208. **Suffolk** *Folk-Lore* 35 (1924) 349. **England** Addy (1895) 96. **Unlocated** *Folk-Lore* 68 (1957) 413. **Literary** *The Shepherd's Kalendar* (1503) quoted in Lean 2 (1903) 291.

noses: itching

Most of the beliefs concerned with ITCHING are relatively stable in meaning – for example, itching HANDS mean money coming in or out, and itching EARS mean someone is talking about you. An itching nose, however, can have a wide variety of meanings. The most commonly cited has an air of parody about it, and certainly provides scope for humorous treatment in everyday occurrence:

But should your nose itch you would either be kissed, cursed, vexed, would run against a gatepost, or shake hands with a fool (my uncle invariably held out his hand if anyone rubbed their nose).   Wiltshire Wiltshire (1975)

If your nose itches, they declared, you will be kissed cussed and vexed or shake hands with a fool. My mother used to say she would shake hands with herself and get it over, but another Dorset woman I know holds out her hand to her husband, who invariably waves it aside saying emphatically, 'No, I bain't'.
    Dorset *Dorset Year Book* (1961–2)

Other informants gave meanings which include elements of the above, and may simply be reduced versions: 'Nose itches – you will soon be angry' (Yorkshire Nicholson (1890)); 'When your nose itches you will be vexed' (Unlocated Hone, *Year Book* (1832)); 'If the nose be itchy you will quarrel with a woman' (Co. Longford *Béaloideas* (1936)).

Others, however, maintain that it means news, a letter, or a stranger: 'We shall ha' guests to day, I lay my little maidenhead; my nose itches so' (Dekker, *The Honest Whore* (1604) is the earliest documented reference on the subject), or:

If your nose itch you'll hear some news, left side – bad; right side – good news; or you will be kissed by a fool.   Norfolk Fulcher Collection (*c.*1895)

Another set of reports gloss the itchy nose as ominous of imminent drunkenness.

Examining the earliest references does not much clarify the situation. Dekker's 'stranger' meaning, quoted above, contrasts with the second earliest, in Melton's *Astrologaster* of 1620, 'That when a mans nose itcheth, it is a signe he shall drinke wine'. The 'multiple' meaning first occurs in the eighteenth century and lasted well into the first half of the twentieth, but then seems to have given way to simpler versions. It can be argued that the meanings for itches on other parts of the body such as hands, eyes, and feet are directly symbolic, but that for a nose there is nothing usable that is obviously applicable – 'if your nose itches you will smell a bad smell' would be pointless. The way is thus open for general meanings such as 'stranger' and 'letter'.

Long version: Dorset *Dorset Year Book* (1961–2) 73. Devon Hewett (1900) 58; *Devonshire Assoc.* 64 (1932) 157. Cornwall *Folk-Lore Jnl* 5 (1887) 219. Wiltshire *Wilts*

N&Q 1 (1893–5) 149; Wiltshire (1975) 89–90. Berkshire Lowsley (1888) 23. Oxfordshire [pre-1900] *Folk-Lore* 24 (1913) 90. Warwickshire Langford (1875) 14. Lincolnshire Rudkin (1936) 21. Shropshire Burne (1883) 270. Staffordshire Hackwood (1924) 149. England Addy (1895) 100. Co. Durham Henderson (1866) 84–5. Unlocated Igglesden (*c.*1932) 228. General *Illustrated London News* (27 Dec. 1851) 779; Foli (1902) 107. Literary Swift (1738); *Connoisseur* 59 (1755) 353–4.
Vexed or angry: Lincolnshire *Grantham Jnl* (22 June 1878). Yorkshire Nicholson (1890) 44. Co. Durham [1985] Opie & Tatem, 288. Glamorganshire [1954] Opie & Tatem, 288. Western Scotland Napier (1879) 137. Co. Longford *Béaloideas* 6 (1936) 265. Jersey *Folk-Lore* 25 (1914) 245–6; L'Amy (1927) 98. Unlocated Hone, *Year Book* (1832) 126–8. Literary *Old Women's Sayings* (*c.*1835).
Drink: Co. Durham Leighton (1910) 60. Welsh Gypsies Jarman (1991) 184. Co. Meath/Co. Tipperary *Folk-Lore* 15 (1904) 461–2. General Melton (1620).
News, letter, stranger: Devon *Devonshire Assoc.* 10 (1878) 105. Worcestershire/Shropshire *Gent. Mag.* (1855) 385. Middlesex [1984] Opie & Tatem, 288. Norfolk Fulcher Collection (*c.*1895). Hebrides McPhee (1970) 150. Unlocated N&Q 6S:9 (1884) 247. Literary Thomas Dekker, *The Honest Whore* (1604) 2:1.

number 666

On the authority of the Bible, the number 666 is the 'number of the Beast':

16 And he causeth all, both small and great, rich and poor, free and bond, to receive a mark in their right hand, or in their foreheads. 17 And that no man might buy or sell, save he that had the mark, or the name of the beast, or the number of his name. 18 Here is wisdom. Let him that hath understanding count the number of the beast: for it is the number of a man: and his number is Six hundred threescore and six.

Book of Revelations 13:16–18

Ever since the Bible became generally available, these verses have fascinated people and prompted them to attempt to unravel the mysterious language. In London in 1666 – clearly a date which would increase interest in the topic – Samuel Pepys recorded in his diary that he found a book by Francis Potter entitled *An Interpretation of the Number 666*, published in 1642, 'mighty ingenious' (16 Feb. 1665/6; 10 Nov. 1666).

The main manifestation of this concern in the realm of modern superstition is more down to earth, in that the number is believed to be extremely unlucky in all contexts. Fortunately, unlike the number thirteen, which is a common house-number, the beast's number does not occur often in everyday life. One exception is in car-registration numbers, and the popular press occasionally run pieces which show that any car thus encumbered brings dreadful luck to its owner. Consider poor Mr Quinn, whose car registration was HFR 666S and whose woes were detailed in 'Devil Plate has Wrecked my Life', with the sub-heading 'Wife died, burgled twice, and garage burnt' (*Sun* (26 Apr. 1993)). It has since been reported that no more 666 numberplates are being issued. In another context, the local council of the London Borough of Croydon was asked by relatives to renumber grave 666 in a local cemetery (*Croydon Advertiser* (3 Dec. 1993)).

Attempts to decode the number 666 have continued and greatly increased in recent years, using a variety of alpha-numeric systems, and many have succeeded in proving that the number refers to the Roman Catholic Church, the Pope (individually and Popes collectively), Napoleon, the American government, any recent American president one cares to name, communism, the Soviet Union, and Adolf Hitler. Interested readers are invited to carry out a search on the Internet (try '666 beast') and they will get more information on the subject than anyone could possibly need. For a synopsis of similar nineteenth-century views, *see* Jones (1880) 280–89.

For those who are happy to accept 'the beast' as Satan, the text of verses 16 and 17 offers ample scope for concern. The text has been ingeniously identified as referring to the invention of bar codes, and there is a widespread conspiracy theory that all bar codes have a secret 666 encoded in them, and that 'the government', under the control of the Devil, is planning to implant everybody with microchips that are similarly encoded. It is not clear what will happen once we all have this 'mark' on us, but it will be very bad. Again, an Internet search provides ample evidence of the wide-ranging international nature of this hypothesis, including the basic assumption that anyone who questions the reality of such theories is by definition part of the conspiracy.

numbers: odds and evens

Various superstitions include numbers, but there does not seem to have been any systematic numerology in British traditional lore. The most general rule was that odd numbers were lucky, even numbers unlucky:

A friend and I were visiting an old woman of 82 years, who was suffering from rheumatism. The latter asked me to give her seven drops of oil of juniper from a bottle standing near. From curiosity I asked, 'Supposing it was six or eight drops,

would that make much difference, Mrs. Lee?' She answered: 'Aw, me dear, that wouldn't never du; it must be odd numbers to have any vartue'.
Devon *Devonshire Assoc.* (1927)

[Diary entry of Edith Olivier] *I rather dread 1928. Don't like years with even numbers.*
Wiltshire Middelboe (1989)

This preference for odd numbers was well established even by Shakespeare's time:

Prithee, no more prattling; go; I'll hold. This is the third time. I hope good luck lies in odd numbers. Away, go! They say there is divinity in odd numbers, either in nativity, chance, or death. Away!
Shakespeare, *The Merry Wives of Windsor* (1597)

and was also prevalent in classical times (e.g. Pliny, *Natural History* (AD 77)). Individual odd numbers, especially three and seven, and to a lesser extent five and nine, occur regularly in a positive light in other beliefs and cures, but again this is not an invariable rule – bad luck comes in THREES, lighting THREE CIGARETTES from one match is fatal, THIRTEEN is generally unlucky, and so on.

It should also be remembered that numerous everyday items which have positive overtones come in even numbers: twelve apostles, ten commandments, four evangelists, four elements, four points of the compass, and so on. And in certain contexts, odd numbers were carefully avoided, particularly at wedding feasts and funerals:

If at a funeral an odd person enters the churchyard gate, another member of the family of the individual buried will die within the year. That is, suppose there should be eight couples walking in the procession and one person alone, as there must be if seventeen attend the funeral. Woman attending her aunt's funeral remarked to another: 'There are seventeen came in at the gate. One of the children ought to have been kept home. You'll see someone else of my family will die within the twelvemonth'. This was on the 15th February. On the 14th February the following year another aunt died, and again an odd person attended the funeral. My informant called the attention of the acquaintance to whom she had made the prophecy to its fulfilment, and added, 'This year another of the family will die'. In the following December her own mother died. This was told in all seriousness by the woman herself.
Devon *Devonshire Assoc.* (1917)

Odd numbers preferred: Devon *Devonshire Assoc.* 49 (1917) 70; *Devonshire Assoc.* 59 (1927) 162. **Surrey** N&Q

1S:7 (1853) 153. **Wiltshire** Middelboe (1989) 68. **England** Addy (1895) 80, 95, 128. **Yorkshire** N&Q 1S:6 (1852) 311–12. **West Wales** Davies (1911) 216. **Scotland** Maclean (1959) 198. **Highland Scotland** Macbain (1887/88) 270. **Unlocated** Grose (1787) 68–9; *Chambers's Jnl* (1873) 809; N&Q 6S:1 (1880) 193–4. **General** Werenfels (1748) 8. **Literary** Spenser, *Faerie Queen* (1590) Bk 3, Canto 50; Shakespeare, *The Merry Wives of Windsor* (1597) 5:1; S. Lover, *Rory O'More* (1826). **Classical** Pliny, *Natural History* (AD 77) Bk 27, Ch. 5.
Odd numbers avoided: **Devon** *Devonshire Assoc.* 49 (1917) 77–8. **Essex** [1983] Opie & Tatem, 292. **Herefordshire** Leather (1912) 114. **Lincolnshire** *Folk-Lore* 44 (1933) 191. **Yorkshire** Robinson (1861) 300. **Highland Scotland** Macgregor (1878) 128–9. **Unlocated** *Chambers's Jnl* (1871); Lean 2 (1904) 564. **Literary** More (c.1810) 11.

nuns

Among the many inexplicable superstitions of the twentieth century, it was widely held to be good or bad luck to see or meet a nun, depending on the circumstances of the encounter. For some, it was seeing a nun's back that was unlucky:

My son Jim has never had more than two days' work in the last seven weeks. Yesterday, as we was in the front garden, I see two nuns walking up the road. 'Do you see those two nuns?' I says, 'That's lucky. You'll have some work tomorrow. Come inside and don't look at their backs'. Sure enough, he got some work today.

London *Folk-Lore* (1926)

In some fishing communities, seeing a nun in the morning promised bad luck equal to meeting a RED-HAIRED or CROSS-EYED woman. But some argued that it predicted (or caused) bad weather:

[80-year-old fisherman] *We wouldn't have a woman near the boat, and if two nuns came walking along the front together that meant a two-reef breeze, three of them, you got a three-reef breeze. That was a good bit of wind.*

Norfolk *Festing* (1977)

Iona and Peter Opie found a vigorous tradition of nun beliefs among children, across the whole British Isles, in their fieldwork in the 1950s, and these traditions probably still exist in the minds of adults who grew up at that time.
Compare CLERGYMAN: UNLUCKY.

Somerset [1905] Tongue (1965) 145. **London** *Folk-Lore* 37 (1926) 364; [1985] Opie & Tatem, 288. **Norfolk** Festing (1977) 28–9. **Yorkshire** *Observer Supp.* (24 Nov. 1968) 10. **Swansea** Opie (1959) 218. **Edinburgh** Opie (1959) 218.

nutmegs

Nutmegs were very popular in folk medicine, for a wide variety of ailments. They could be carried whole, in pocket or bag, to counter problems such as lumbago, rheumatism, headache, or they could be grated and sprinkled on food or into drink to be taken internally. The latter was such a widespread fashion in the nineteenth century that pocket-sized nutmeg graters, in various shapes, were available in their thousands for women to carry about with them (*see* Newman (1943) for illustrations). Newman also gives details of numerous published herbals from the sixteenth to the eighteenth centuries which all recommended nutmeg for digestive problems and flatulence.

A different tradition is hinted at in a comment by one of Swift's characters:

(Miss, searching her pocket for a thimble, brings out a nutmeg) O miss, have a care; for if you carry a nutmeg in your pocket, you'll certainly be married to an old man.

Swift (1738)

but, unfortunately, the quip is not explained.

Hampshire [1966] Opie & Tatem, 289. **Devon** *Devonshire Assoc.* 16 (1884) 123; [c.1915] Lakeham (1982) 48; *Devonshire Assoc.* 67 (1935) 138; *Devonshire Assoc.* 91 (1959) 199. **Oxfordshire** [1920s] Harris (1969) 113. **Lincolnshire** Rudkin (1936) 27. **Shropshire** *Folk-Lore* 49 (1938) 229. **Yorkshire** [1957] Opie & Tatem, 289. **Unlocated** Igglesden (c.1932) 206; *Folk-Lore* 61 (1950) 36. **Literary** Swift (1738); Charles Dickens, *Martin Chuzzlewit* (1843–4) Ch. 46. **Major study:** L. F. Newman, 'Some Notes on the Nutmeg Graters Used in Folk-Medicine' *Folk-Lore* 54 (1943) 334–7.

nuts

Nuts feature in a small range of beliefs and customs, often with an underlying connection with love and marriage. A widespread saying was that 'a good year for nuts is a good year for babies'. This could be taken literally as one of the strange coincidences of nature, but an alternative explanation was that young people traditionally used going out into the woods to gather nuts as a cover for amorous encounters (*see* BABIES: NUTS).

While out nutting, many thought it lucky to find a cluster of five or seven, but particular store was set on finding a 'double nut' – one with two kernels. It was generally fortunate to find one, and some people carried them in their pockets 'for luck', or to ward off TOOTHACHE. However, one must never eat both kernels, and there were various traditional rules on how to proceed. Some advised throwing one kernel over the shoulder and making a wish, while others insisted that the feast should be shared:

Hazel – We observed a ceremony on cracking a double nut . . . Nobody who cared for 'what was what' ever thought of eating both kernels: the owner would pass one to a friend, and each would munch his share in solemn silence, wishing a wish which had to be kept secret in order to be realised.

Lincolnshire *Grantham Jnl* (22 June 1878)

Games and divinations involving nuts were particularly popular at HALLOWE'EN. A well-known LOVE DIVINATION custom involved naming two nuts for potential lovers, placing the nuts in the fire, and predicting the couple's future relationship by the behaviour of the nuts. The same procedure could be used to bring general good fortune:

In Nottinghamshire on All-Hallows Eve nuts are thrown into the fire, and wishes are expressed in secret. If the nut blazes the wish will be granted, but not if it 'dies away'.

Nottinghamshire Addy (1895)

The obvious symbol of two-joined-as-one could easily be combined with the traditional love connection to take on a deeper significance.

A doubled nut was always considered fortunate; and I have one now in my possession which was carried in an old lady's pocket for years: it is well polished by the constant friction. It was picked in Norridge Wood, near Warminster, given her, when a young woman, by her sweetheart; but luck did not follow that giving; the grave parted the lovers, though the nut still lies unbroken.

Wiltshire *Wilts. N&Q* (1893–5)

But a Shropshire girl revealed a local belief in 1953 when she explained that if you eat both kernels you will have twins (Opie & Tatem, 290).

Devon *Devonshire* Assoc. 9 (1877) 101. Wiltshire *Wilts. N&Q* 1 (1893–5) 61. Buckinghamshire *Midland Garner* 2 (1884) 27. Northamptonshire Sternberg (1851) 163. Lincolnshire *Grantham Jnl* (22 June 1878). Shropshire Burne (1883) 243; [1953] Opie & Tatem, 290. England Addy (1895) 85. Nottinghamshire Addy (1895) 82. Derbyshire Uttley (1946) 127. Lancashire Harland & Wilkinson (1873) 230. Wales Trevelyan (1909) 325. Western Scotland Napier (1879) 136. Dumfriesshire Corrie (1890/91) 83. Ireland *Gent. Mag.* (1865) 701.

nutting

Trips to the countryside to gather nuts in the appropriate season were popular outings for young and old, but a widespread set of beliefs associated 'going nutting' with love, sex, and childbirth (*see* NUTS and BABIES: NUTS). The moral dangers of 'going nutting' were therefore well understood in rural communities, but particularly strong warnings were given about the dangers of nutting on Sundays, and this prohibition was backed up by traditional localized NARRATIVES:

a youth of this neighbourhood went into the woods to pick nuts on a Sunday; and the devil, pleased to see him so employed instead of going to church, kindly gave him assistance, and pulled down the bushes for him. The lad thought himself highly favoured, till he perceived the cloven foot; when he instantly quitted the wood, but soon after died.

Devon Bray (1838)

There was also a particular day in the year, usually Holy Rood Day (14 September), on which the Devil gathered nuts, and this day was therefore to be avoided by mortals (*compare* BLACKBERRIES). This notion was already in circulation in the seventeenth century, as *Poor Robin's Almanack* for 1670 warns the unwary that they might meet a 'tall man in black with cloven feet' on that day.

Sussex N&Q 4S:9 (1872) 57–8; Latham (1878) 14. Devon Bray (1838) 285. Surrey *Folk-Lore* 26 (1915) 161. Northamptonshire [1825] Clare (1993) 140. East Anglia Forby (1830) 418. Yorkshire N&Q 3S:2 (1862) 343. Unlocated *Poor Robin's Almanack* (1670).

oak-apples

A close examination of an oak-apple will give clues to the coming year:

If on Michaelmas Day there be found a certain little worm in the oak apple the year will then certainly be very pleasant and seasonable; if there be found a spider it will be a barren year and there will be great scarcity of all things; if a fly it is a sign of a moderate season, if there be nothing at all found in it, it is a sign that very sore diseases shall reign all that year.

Gaffarel, *Unheard-of Curiosities* (1650)

Very similar words are given in several sources, which argues for a literary rather than a traditional transmission. Trevelyan is the only folk-lore collector who hints at any folk tradition about oak-apples:

A worm in it was a sure sign of poverty.

Wales Trevelyan (1909)

Kent Rembert Dodoens, *Herball* (1578) 746. **Wales** Trevelyan (1909) 101. **General** Lupton (1579) Bk 3, Para. 7; Jacques Gaffarel, *Unheard-of Curiosities* (1650) 79, quoted in N&Q 6S:2 (1880) 286; *Athenian Oracle* (1710) Supp. 476.

oaks

In some folklore genres, the oak has an important role. In England, for example, it was central to celebrations on Oak Apple Day (29 May), founded to commemorate the restoration of the monarchy in 1660. But in other folklore, including superstition, the oak does not make a strong showing and is far less important than many other species such as the ELDER, ASH, and ROWAN. Examples of oak-lore follow, but many of them are uncommon or even isolated examples, and cannot be used as evidence for widespread veneration or regard for the tree.

The oak features in a well-known weather prediction:

The opening of the leaves of oak and ash in spring is still carefully watched because of belief in the old rhyme:

   If the oak is out before the ash
   There will be a splash (fine summer)
   If the ash is out before the oak
   There will be a soak (wet summer)

It is also said that if the oak be out first, there will be a good year of hops.

Herefordshire Leather (1912)

In folk medicine, the oak was used to cure TOOTHACHE, in a method which presumably transferred the pain to the tree:

To cure the tooth-ache – Take a new nail and make the gum bleed with it, and then drive it into an oak. This did cure William Neal's son, a very stout gentleman, when he was almost mad with the pain, and had a mind to have pistolled himself. Unlocated Aubrey, *Miscellanies* (1696)

Similarly, for WHOOPING COUGH a piece of hair, or nail-clippings, of the sufferer were pinned to, or placed under, the bark of an oak.

Oaks were also thought to be dangerous to be near during a STORM, and a traditional rhyme that recommends which trees to seek or avoid, begins:

Beware of an oak
It draws the stroke.

Sussex Latham (1878)

Charlotte Burne described villagers taking home pieces of a lightning-struck oak to protect their homes from a similar fate (**Staffordshire** *Folk-Lore* 7 (1896)).

The solitary oak's majestic appearance and long-standing presence in many rural communities resulted in a number of legends and names (e.g. 'gospel oak') adhering to specific local trees. In many cases, the oak has little more than a bit part, as the locale for the story's action, for example. But in some the tree itself is the central focus.

Despite attempts by popular writers to build oak traditions into a grand survival of Druid reverence or Norse mythology, there is no evidence of such connections. One regular assertion is that the oak was sacred to Thor, the god of thunder, and the acorn-shaped wooden toggles on roller-blinds are a survival of this connection – placed there to protect the house from lightning. This is repeated often as established fact (e.g. Radford (1971) 253), and is only mentioned here as an example of how folklore research is open to fatuous and unsubstantiated inventions which rapidly become part of popular orthodoxy by dint of repetition.

For various aspects of oak-lore, *see* Vickery (1995) 260–4. For some individual local legends, *see* Westwood (1985).

See also ACORNS; OAK-APPLES.

Sussex Latham (1878) 43. **Hampshire** N&Q 6S:10 (1884) 18; *Folk-Lore* 61 (1950) 104. **Wiltshire** N&Q 1S:10 (1854) 505. **Essex** [*c.1920*] Ketteridge & Mays (1972) 142. **Hertfordshire** N&Q 1S:6 (1852) 5. **Herefordshire** Leather (1912) 20, 82–33. **Staffordshire** Folk-Lore 7 (1896) 381. **Yorkshire** N&Q 4S:1 (1868) 193. **Western Scotland** Napier (1879) 131. **Unlocated** Aubrey, *Miscellanies* (1696/1857) 138.

od

A term coined about 1850 by Baron von Reichenbach (1788–1869) to name the hypothetical force which was believed to be at work in animal magnetism, mesmerism, crystals, and other pseudo-scientific phenomena. In humans, the force streamed from the fingertips of suitably sensitive persons. The idea that a ring suspended on a thread would oscillate meaningfully had already been around for centuries before this attempted 'scientific' explanation: *see* PENDULUM DIVINATION.

odd numbers

see NUMBERS: ODDS AND EVENS.

'Old Women's Sayings'

A song published on BROADSIDE by a number of nineteenth-century printers, the earliest being John Pitts and James Catnach. Broadsides are notoriously difficult to date accurately, as all the printers simply stole each other's songs as a matter of course, but from various clues we can hazard a guess at c.1835 for the earliest sheets bearing versions of this song. The wording on each sheet is almost identical.

Draw near and give attention
And you shall hear in rhyme
The old women's saying
In the olden time.
High and low, rich and poor
By daylight or dark
Are sure for to make
Some curious remark
With some foolish idea
Your brains they will bother
For some believes one thing
And some believes another.

Chorus:
These are odds and ends
And superstitious ways
The signs and tokens
Of my grandmother's days.

The first thing you will see
At the house of rich or poor
To keep the witches out
A horse-shoe's o'er the door;
Bellows on the table
Cause a row by day or night

If there's two knives across
You are sure to have a fight;
There's a stranger in the grate
Or if the cat should sneeze
Or lay before the fire
It will rain or freeze.

A cinder with a hole
In the middle, is a purse
But a long one from the fire
Is a coffin – which is worse;
A spider ticking in the wall
Is the death-watch at night
A spark in the candle
Is a letter, sure as life;
If your right eye itches
You'll cry till out of breath
A winding-sheet in the candle
Is a sure sign of death.

If your left eye itches
You will laugh outright
But the left or the right
Is very good at night;
If your elbow itch
A strange bedfellow found
If the bottom of your foot itch
You'll tread on fresh ground:
If your knee itch you'll kneel
In a church, that's a good 'un
And if your belly itch
You'll get a lot of pudden.

If your back should itch
I do declare

old style dates

The official calendar in use in Britain was altered in 1752, by Act of Parliament, to reconcile the differences between the Julian and Gregorian calendars. Under this new law, September 1752 was shortened by eleven days, with the 2nd being followed by the 14th. Many people at the time were unhappy about the change and refused to recognize the new calendar in calculating the dates of festivals and seasonal customs. They therefore celebrated Christmas Day on 6 January and created alternative dates throughout the year. These became known as 'old style' dates. This duplication had a profound effect on the shape of the traditional year, and many anomalies apparent in later years were created at that time. See CALENDAR for further details.

one for sorrow

see MAGPIES: ONE FOR SORROW.

onions: caning

see SCHOOLCHILDREN: CANING.

onions: cures

Onions were, and still are, treasured for a wide range of cures – from rubbing on WASP stings to rheumatism, chilblains, toothache, baldness, and others:

Other virtues claimed for the onion are that it
expels catarrh from the system; stimulates the
digestive organs; softens the skin, and clears the

Butter will be cheap
When the grass grows there;
If the dog howl at night
Or mournfully cry
Or if the cock should crow
There will somebody die;
If you stumble up stairs
Indeed I'm no railer
You'll be married to a snob
Or else to a tailor.

A speck on your finger nail
Is a gift that's funny
If your hand itch in the middle
You will get some money;
Spilling of the salt
Is anger outright
You will see a ghost if the doors
Should rattle in the night;
If your sweetheart
Dreams of bacon and eggs
She'll have a little boy
That has got three legs.

The cat washing her face
The wind will blow
If the cat licks her foot
It is sure for to snow;
Put your gown or your jacket
On, inside out
You will change your luck
And be put to the route [sic]
If your nose itches
You'll get vexed till you jump

If your great toe itch
You'll get a kick in the rump.

If a girl snaps one finger
She'll have a child it seems
And if she snaps two
She's sure to have twins;
And if she snaps eight
Nine, ten, or eleven
It's a chance if she don't
Have twenty and seven;
If you lay with your head
Underneath the clothes
You'll have an ugly old man
What has got no nose.

If you see a star shoot
You'll get what you wish
If a hair gets in your mouth
You'll get as drunk as a fish;
If your little toe itch
You'll be lost in a wave
If you shiver there's somebody
Going over your grave;
If you go under a ladder
You'll have bad luck and fall
And some say bad luck
Is better than none at all;
So to please outright
I have told you in rhyme
The great superstition
Of the olden time.

Old Women's Sayings (c.1835)

complexion; induces sound, refreshing sleep; promotes a healthy appetite; preserves the teeth.
Unlocated N&Q (1915)

Indeed, somewhat alarmingly, it was predicted:

Families which do not eat onions become extinct in the third generation. Unlocated N&Q (1915)

They were also widely recommended for EARACHE and colds:

[Remembering his childhood] *Onions, too, played a great part in keeping us fit for the arduous battle for survival that we were fighting. A basinful of hot onion broth on getting into bed at night, with a topcoat thrown across the bed, generally meant leaving the cold between the sheets in the morning. For earache a small baked onion was inserted in the affected ear, although* we cringed and protested, 'Not too hot, Mother, please'. Worcestershire [c.1900] Knight

Published herbals, since at least the sixteenth century, have generally agreed with these diverse traditions about the effectiveness of onions.

Hampshire [1920s] Hampshire Fed. W. I.s (1994) 76, 133. Essex Folk-Lore 70 (1959) 414. Worcestershire [c.1900] Knight (1960) 182. Northamptonshire Northampton Herald (3 Feb. 1911) quoted N&Q 11S:12 (1915) 209. Bedfordshire Marsom (1950) 183. Midland England Midland Garner 1 (1884) 22. Norfolk Norwich Mercury (26 Aug. 1775) quoted in Morsley (1979) 84. Lincolnshire N&Q 10S:2 (1904) 447. N. Ireland Foster (1951) 60. Co. Cavan Maloney (1972) 73. Unlocated N&Q 11S:11 (1915) 117; N&Q 11S:12 (1915) 150, 167–8, 246, 406. General N&Q 11S:11 (1915) 117.

onions: divination

Two forms of LOVE DIVINATION known since at least the sixteenth century featured the humble onion. In the more common version, which usually took place on St Thomas's Eve (20/21 December) the onion was simply put under the girl's pillow, while a simple verse was recited, or the onion was first stuck with pins:

On St. Thomas's Eve there used to be a custom among girls to procure a large red onion, into which, after peeling, they would stick nine pins, and say:

> *Good Saint Thomas do me right*
> *Send me my true love this night*
> *In his clothes and his array*
> *Which he weareth every day*

Eight pins were stuck round one in the centre, to which was given the name of the swain – the 'true love'. The onion was placed under the pillow on going to bed, and they were certain to dream of or see in their sleep the desired person.
>   Derbyshire N&Q (1871)

In this 'pillow' form, the custom is first described in the CHAPBOOK *Mother Bunch's Closet Newly Broke Open* (1685), but more than a century before that maids were placing onions in selected places, naming each for a man of their acquaintance and waiting to see which 'sprouted first':

In these same dayes young wanton gyrles, that meete for marriage be
Doe search to know the names of them that shall their husbandes bee
Four onyons, five, or eight they take and make it every one
Such names as they do fansie most, and best do think upon
Thus neere the chimney them they set, and that same onyon than
That firste doth sproute, doth surely beare the name of their good man.
>   Naogeorgus, *The Popish Kingdom* (1570)

Exactly the same procedure was still in use in Welsh farmhouses around 1900, as reported by Marie Trevelyan. An added detail in a London version is interesting, but inexplicable:

In buying onions always go in by one door of the shop, and come out by another. Select a shop with two doorways. These onions, placed under your pillow on St. Thomas's Eve, are sure to bring visions of your true-love, your future husband.
>   London N&Q (1853)

See also LOVE DIVINATION: ONIONS; PINS.

London N&Q 1S:7 (1853) 152. **Northamptonshire** [1825] Clare (1993) 140. **Derbyshire** N&Q 4S:8 (1871) 506; *Long Ago* 2 (1873–4) 26. **Wales** Trevelyan (1909) 235. **Unlocated** Halliwell (1849) 224; N&Q 4S:10 (1872) 24. **General** Naogeorgus, *The Popish Kingdom* (1570); Robert Burton, *Anatomy of Melancholy* (1651) Pt 3, sect. 2, memb. 3. **Literary** *Mother Bunch's Closet Newly Broke Open* (1685); John Clare, *St. Martin's Eve* (1831).

onions: germs

A widespread and firm belief, which may not yet be totally dead, held that peeled or cut onions have the power to draw germs and infections to them from the surrounding atmosphere, an idea which resulted in the onion being regarded by different people as lucky or unlucky. For some, the onion draws dangerous germs to the house, and onions must never therefore be left lying around:

My mother never allowed a cut onion in the house; the part unused was always thrown away. I have heard her say they 'bred sickness'.
>   Wiltshire *Wilts. N&Q* (1893–5)

On the other hand, this quality could have a more positive side:

One belief upholds the qualities of a sliced onion as a kind of disinfectant. The onion is cut up and stood in an old tin plate. Then you place it in the room where the sick child sleeps, the onion draws the complaint into itself, and when the child is better care must be taken to see that the onion is properly burnt.
>   Suffolk Evans (1965)

This was also believed to work on a much larger scale. Several stories, which bear all the hall-marks of CONTEMPORARY LEGENDS, tell how particular groups of people were found to be immune to outbreaks of cholera, the plague, measles, and other major epidemics, simply because they had onions hanging in their homes:

The virtues of the onion were never more plainly demonstrated than during the great cholera epidemic in London in 1849. Saffron Hill was practically free, although the surrounding neighbourhood suffered severely. The Board of Health investigated, and discovered that it was due to the fact that all the cholera-proof houses were occupied by Italian organ-grinders who consumed huge quantities of onions, which were hanging in strings from the ceilings of their rooms. When this was made known Londoners just reeked of onions!
>   *Daily Chronicle* (26 July 1915)

Many of the numerous applications of onions in folk medicine have a very long history (*see* ONIONS: CURES; EARACHE/DEAFNESS), but this specific belief in the drawing-power of onions has so far only been documented since the mid nineteenth century.

Sussex [1936] *Sussex Life* (Jan. 1973) 35. **Hampshire** [1958] Opie & Tatem, 294; [1986] Opie & Tatem, 294. **Cornwall** *Old Cornwall* 2 (1931–6) 38. **Wiltshire** *Wilts. N&Q* 1 (1893–5) 61, 155–6; [1923] Opie & Tatem, 294. **London** N&Q 11S:12 (1915) 101. **Essex** N&Q 7S:11 (1891) 387. **Herefordshire** Leather (1912) 21. **Worcestershire/Shropshire** *Gent. Mag.* (1855) 385. **Warwickshire** [1915] Bloom (*c.*1930) 29–30. **Suffolk** Evans (1965) 218. **Lancashire** *Folk-Lore* 20 (1909) 489. **Wales** Jones (1930) 181. **Western Scotland** Napier (1879) 127–8. **General** N&Q 7S:11 (1891) 475. *Epidemics*: **Sussex** *Sussex Life* (Jan. 1973) 35. **London** *Daily Chronicle* (26 July 1915). **Cheshire** N&Q 167 (1934) 356; Vickery (1995) 265–6.

---

opals

Since the mid nineteenth century at least, opals have been regarded as unlucky – especially for engagement rings – and white opals in particular were said to be associated with widowhood and tears. This assessment of the stone certainly holds good from 1869, when a correspondent asked in *Notes & Queries*:

Can any of your readers inform me what is the origin of a superstition, which appears to be very generally believed in 'good society', as to opals being unlucky? N&Q (1869)

Soon after this, a story entitled 'The Opal Ring', which appeared in the Christmas number of Charles Dickens's magazine *All the Year Round* in 1874, included an opal as one of those cursed stones which wreak havoc as it passes from hand to hand. But the key point for present purposes is that characters in the story openly refer to superstitions regarding all opals as unlucky. In further correspondence in *Notes & Queries* in 1875, some writers confirmed the stone's unlucky reputation, but others questioned it – and cited classical and continental authors to show that the opal had been much valued previously. The idea was thus mooted that the popular view of the opal had changed dramatically some time in the earlier nineteenth century, but this is based more on comparison with classical sources than with old British traditions. It was also suggested that Sir Walter Scott's novel *Anne of Geierstein* (1829), which featured an opal, was largely responsible for the opal's bad reputation, but this is also unlikely. The opal in that story was worn by a half mortal/half 'fairy' female, and mirrored her emotional state by flashing and changing colour. She disappeared in mysterious circumstances when some holy water was accidentally sprinkled on the opal. The gem is thus magical and mysterious, but not unlucky. Further research into the subject is necessary before this episode in the gem's history can be clarified. Certainly, it was still being condemned as unlucky in the 1970s and after.

In previous times, opals had other associations, including being useful in detecting poisons and, according to a passage by Ben Jonson, they appear to have had magical qualities in conferring invisibility:

Why were you seene?
Because indeed I had
No med'cine, Sir, to goe invisible:
No ferne-seed in my pocket; Nor an opal
Wrapt in a bay-leafe, i' my left fist,
To charme their eyes with.

Jonson, *The New Inne* (1631)

London *The Mirror* (3 Sept. 1970) 16. **Oxfordshire** *Folk-Lore* 24 (1913) 90. **England** Addy (1895) 93. **General** N&Q 4S:3 (1869) 59; N&Q 5S:3 (1875) 429, 475; N&Q 5S:4 (1875) 56, 97; *Fortnightly Review* (July 1884) 85; *Young Ladies Jnl* 35 (1890) 4, quoted Opie & Tatem, 294; Igglesden (*c.*1932) 71; **Unlocated** N&Q 167 (1934) 458; N&Q 168 (1935) 30. **Literary** Jonson, *The New Inne* (1631) 1:6; *All the Year Round* (Christmas 1874) 1–48.

---

ordeal by touch

see CORPSE: BLEEDING

---

ornaments

Many British homes in the past sported china ornaments of various shapes and sizes, and the prime purpose of these was decorative and aesthetic. A few reports indicate other motives, but as these seem to be isolated examples, it is difficult to assess how widespread they really were:

China dogs, too, so often seen upon the mantel-shelf of the Dorset cottage, were supposed to counteract the evil spells of any 'overlooked'.

Dorset *Dorset Year Book* (1954–5)

To ward off bad luck in the 1950s, my mum used to hang the plaster of Paris ducks on the wall in order of size so the biggest was the last in line.

Lincolnshire [1950s?] Sutton

One belief about the placing of ornaments was widely reported from the mid twentieth century onwards, and is still known:

*It is a superstition in my family ... that any orna-
ment which has a face should be so placed that
it is facing the door by which one normally enters
the room. I am not sure whether it is so that one
can see its face – or it can see yours. Not to do so
is considered unlucky, and it was suggested that
the death of my father in 1967 was affected (or
portended) by an ornament being accidentally
turned round some weeks earlier. I presume that
the very common ornament of a few years ago,
the carved black elephant, either caused a general
superstition to be attached to a particular ornament, the elephant, or a particular superstition
to become generalised.*

London/Essex *Folk-Lore* (1970)

This is most commonly said of ornamental
ELEPHANTS, and seems to have sprung up in the
1940s. One informant had it the other way
round:

*If you had an ornamental elephant, you had to
put it on your mantelpiece with its tail facing the
door.*   **Lincolnshire** [1950s?] Sutton

It is just possible that this belief is an extension
of the widespread older superstitions about
seeing lambs and other farm animals for the first
time in spring, with their heads rather than tails
towards you (*see* SHEEP: FIRST LAMB SEEN).

See also ELEPHANTS: LUCKY.

England *Folk-Lore* 80 (1969) 308. **Kent** [1984] Opie &
Tatem, 139. **Somerset** [1940] Tongue (1965) 143. **Dorset**
Dorset Year Book (1954–5) 175. **London/Essex** *Folk-Lore*
81 (1970) 144. **Lincolnshire** [1950s?] Sutton (1992) 141.
Unlocated *Woman's Own* (4 Apr. 1957) 7.

orpine

see MIDSUMMER MEN.

outgoing/incoming

Care about the balance between outgoings and
incomings in the domestic sphere was one of the
fundamental principles of superstition, especially when combined with the important motif
of BEGINNINGS. Traditional rules covered
tangible basics such as food, drink, fire, and so
on, which took on a symbolic role at these key
times, but were also concerned with intangibles
such as luck. Keeping the 'luck of the house' is
one of the phrases used to explain these traditional prohibitions. In some cases, this was translated into a fear of letting anything out of the
house at the key time – even the dust swept from

the floor. In others, it was certain items only
which were forbidden to leave the house – FIRE,
for example. In the majority of FIRST FOOTING
customs, there was simply a concern to ensure
that key items came *in* before anything went *out*,
so that the same positive inward flow would
continue throughout the coming year. The two
most important times in this context were
Christmas/NEW YEAR and, in Ireland especially,
May Day.

owls

Owls were generally disliked and feared, and
their screech was a proverbial death omen –
especially if there was a sick person in the house:

*When a screech-owl is heard crying near a house,
it is an indication of death on the premises. When
a barn-owl alights on a house, hoots, and then
flies over it, an inmate will die within the year.*

Wales Trevelyan (1909)

*Before my grandfather died, two owls came and
hooted at the bottom of our garden for several
nights, and I think there must be something in it.*

Shropshire Burne (1883)

This interpretation of the owl has a very long
literary history, from Chaucer's *Parliament of
Fowls* (c.1380) 'The oule eke, that of deth the bode
bringeth', to numerous writers of the sixteenth
and seventeenth centuries for whom the owl,
RAVEN, and howling DOG were the stock motifs
signalling horror and tragedy – instantly recognized by audiences and readers:

*With that the scritch owle cried piteously, and
anone after the night raven sate croking hard by
his window. Iesu have mercy upon me (quoth
hee) what an ill favoured cry doe yonder carrion
birds make, and therewithall he laid him downe
in his bed, from whence he never rose againe.*

Deloney, *Thomas of Reading* (1623)

Owls were also identified with witches. In
literary productions they often provided one of
the ingredients in the witches' cauldrons (e.g.
Macbeth), and in later traditional beliefs they
had a more direct connection:

*Owls are in Cambridgeshire regarded as birds of
ill omen. In the Fens they were thought to be
witches in disguise and were, if possible, shot on
sight.*   **Cambridgeshire** Porter (1969)

*The old wives say that a cow will give bloody milk
if it is frightened by an owl, and will fall sick and
die if touched by it.*   **Shetland** Saxby (1874)

Nevertheless, other traditions painted a less
threatening picture:

Mrs. Collins also told me the following story, which accounts for Ophelia's saying, 'They say the owl was a baker's daughter'. It was this. Our Lord went to a baker's shop to ask for something to eat, and the woman there began making Him a cake. But each time she put a handful of flour into the pan, she took some out saying, 'Oo-ooh, that's too much, Oo-ooh, that's too much'. And He said to her:

'Owl thou art and owl thou shalt be
And all the birds of earth shall peck at thee'.

'And if you come to look at the owl,' said Mrs. Collins, 'it has more the face of a Christian than a bird'. A variant of this story, also told in Berkshire, is that the woman was turned into an owl, and condemned always to be poor, and get her food at night.　　　　　Berkshire Salmon (1902)

Sussex Latham (1878) 54. Somerset Poole (1877) 40; Tongue (1965) 47. Cornwall [1870s] Hughes (1934) Ch. 10. Wiltshire Smith (1874) 325; Wilts. N&Q 1 (1893–5) 58. Berkshire Berks. Arch. Soc. 1 (1889–91) 86; Folk-Lore 5 (1894) 337. Berkshire Salmon (1902) 421. Essex Ketteridge & Mays (1972) 140. Oxfordshire Folk-Lore 24 (1913) 88. Gloucestershire Folk-Lore 13 (1902) 172. Herefordshire Leather (1912) 25. Warwickshire Langford (1875) 19. Northamptonshire N&Q 1S:2 (1850) 164. Cambridgeshire Porter (1969) 23, 39. Suffolk [1863] Chambers 1 (1878) 52–3. Norfolk Randell (1966) 98. Shropshire Burne (1883) 226; Folk-Lore 49 (1938) 224. England Addy (1895) 70. Northern England Brockett (1829) 161. Yorkshire [1823] Home (1915) 214; Blakeborough (1898) 130–1, 136. Lancashire Harland & Wilkinson (1882) 139. Wales Howells (1831) 67; Trevelyan (1909) 281. West Wales Davies (1911) 213. Mid-Wales Davies (1911) 224. Pembrokeshire Folk-Lore 39 (1928) 173. Monmouthshire Bye-Gones (18 Sept. 1872) 86. Dumfriesshire Corrie (1890/91) 43. Shetland Saxby (1874) 51. N. Ireland Foster (1951) 18. Guernsey Carey (1903) 502; De Garis (1975) 134. Unlocated Grose (1787) 47; Ruskin (1887) 363. General Bourne (1725) 70–1; Gent. Mag. (1796) 636; White (1788) 143. Literary Chaucer, Parliament of Fowls (c.1380) line 343; Shakespeare, Midsummer Night's Dream (1595) 5:1; Shakespeare, 3 Henry VI (1595) 5:6; John Marston, Antonie & Mellida (1602) 3:3; Shakespeare, Macbeth (1606) 2:2; John Webster, White Devil (1612) 5:4; Samuel Rowlands, More Knaves Yet (1612); John Marston, Insatiate Countess (1613) 4; Thomas Deloney, Thomas of Reading (1623) Ch. 11; John Webster, Duchess of Malfi (1623) 4:2; Addison, Spectator (8 Mar. 1711); Thomas Hardy, 'Premonitions', in Hardy (1925). International & classical: Swainson (1886) 125–8.

parcels

One of the many everyday items which superstition dictates should be picked up by someone else if you drop it:

In 1930 I dropped my umbrella in a train and was told by a country-woman in the compartment that I must not pick it up myself or I should have bad luck. In 1932 I dropped a parcel and was told by another country-woman the same thing.
　　　　　Devon Devonshire Assoc. (1933)

See also DROPPING THINGS.

Devon Devonshire Assoc. 65 (1933) 124.

parsley: Devil

According to tradition, parsley is in league with the Devil somehow:

When parsley is sown it goes nine times to the Devil before it comes up. Only the wicked can make parsley grow.　　　　　England Addy (1895)

The Devil motif is usually simply a metaphor for the slowness with which the plant grows in some areas, but the story varies from place to place:

Parsley is a decidedly uncanny herb. It is, I believe, a fact that in some situations it is extremely difficult to grow it from seed, and there is a common popular idea that it must be sown nine times before it will come up. The old saying on the subject at Worthen is that 'parsley must be sown nine times, for the devil takes all but the last'; varied at Pulverbatch to 'it goes to the devil nine times, and very often forgets to come back again'.　　　　　Shropshire Burne (1883)

Like the other parsley beliefs, this one is not found before the later nineteenth century, but seems quite widespread in the twentieth, at least in England.

Sussex Simpson (1973) 113. Somerset [1923] Opie & Tatem, 298. Devon Devonshire Assoc. 64 (1932) 155. Wiltshire Wilts. N&Q 1 (1893–5) 102. Warwickshire Folk-Lore 55 (1944) 72. Shropshire Burne (1883) 248–9. England Addy (1895) 63. Lancashire N&Q 4S:6 (1870) 211; Various Vickery (1995) 274.

parsley: giving

One of the lesser-known parsley traditions is that it is unlucky to give or receive the plant:

Last year his grandfather gave my friend's mother some, which she planted. The latter was telling her washerwoman of this, when the woman exclaimed, 'Oh, ma'am, you have not taken the parsley? Then your father will die within the year'. Unfortunately, this prediction was verified, so, doubtless, the woman is more than ever convinced of the truth of her absurd superstition.
　　　　　Hampshire N&Q (1873)

parsley

A surprising number of different superstitions have been recorded about parsley, of such a disparate nature that it is difficult to see how they are connected. Despite being valued in numerous cures, and being the subject of semi-humorous notions about who is master in the household, parsley also had evil connotations connecting it with the Devil, and was said to be serious bad luck if transplanted:

Someone gave me a root of parsley and a neighbour said it was unlucky. Anyway, I tossed my head and thought 'so what'. Not long after my husband died. So that's the last I will grow.

Dorset Vickery (1995)

The main beliefs are detailed below. In folk medicine, parsley was recommended for a variety of ailments, including sore eyes, kidney complaints, water stoppage, headache, the complexion, and various gynaecological problems.

Devon [1933] *Devonshire Assoc.* 79 (1947) 47; *Devonshire Assoc.* 84 (1952) 296–7. **Dorset** Vickery (1995) 272–5. **Herefordshire** Leather (1912) 21. **Worcestershire** [*c.*1900] Knight (1960) 180–1. **Wales** Trevelyan (1909) 316. **N. Ireland** Foster (1951) 61. **General** Vickery (1995) 272–5.

This is the earliest reference to the belief, but it was still being quoted in the late twentieth century. It is possible that this idea grew from the much more common belief that transplanting parsley was to court death (*see below*). There was, of course, an alternative strategy:

Parsley should never be taken as a gift, but it is very lucky to steal some. **Guernsey** Carey (1903)

Hampshire N&Q 4S:11 (1873) 341. **Somerset** Kettlewell (1927) 32. **Essex** [1957] Opie & Tatem, 298. **Yorkshire** *Yorkshire Post* (29 Jan. 1960) 6. **Glamorganshire** [1954] Opie & Tatem, 298. **Guernsey** Carey (1903) 506.

parsley: pregnancy

A few references indicate a connection between parsley and human pregnancy, but there are diametrically opposed opinions about the plant's effect. It either helps to cause a pregnancy, or can be used as an abortifacient:

If a young woman sows parsley-seed she will have a child. **Lincolnshire** Rudkin (1936)

When a woman wants a baby, she should go out and pick some parsley.
Oxfordshire [1951] Opie & Tatem

Parsley is believed to prevent a pregnancy . . . it is sometimes eaten as a salad by young married women who do not desire to have a family.
Cambridgeshire *Folk-Lore* (1939)

A somewhat similar confusion exists with lettuce.

Causes: **Surrey** N&Q 171 (1936) 33. **Oxfordshire** [1951] Opie & Tatem, 299. **Lincolnshire** Rudkin (1936) 22. ***Prevents:*** **London** [1982] Opie & Tatem, 299.

Cambridgeshire *Folk-Lore* 50 (1939) 187; *Folk-Lore* 69 (1958) 112. **General** *Aristotle's Last Legacy* (1707) 1906.

parsley: sowing

There are various traditions reported from southern England about how and when parsley should be sown. It was one of the plants which were traditionally sown on GOOD FRIDAY, to ensure good growth and good luck:

If you plant parsley on Good Friday it will come up double. **Essex** *Monthly Packet* (1862)

and other conditions also helped:

A woman sowing parsley seed on Sunday morning explained that it always grew better if sown when the church bells were ringing . . . Parsley must be sown by a woman.
Devon *Devonshire Assoc.* (1931)

These religious connotations do not sit well with the more dominant beliefs that transplanting parsley caused a death in the family, and that the plant was ruled by the Devil (*see above and below*).

Sussex Simpson (1973) 113. **Somerset** *Folk-Lore* 31 (1920) 244; Kettlewell (1927) 34. **Devon** *Devonshire Assoc.* 63 (1931) 125; *Devonshire Assoc.* 64 (1932) 154–5, 165; *Devonshire Assoc.* 105 (1973) 214. **Surrey** N&Q 5S:3 (1875) 424. **Essex** *Monthly Packet* 24 (1862) 434–7. **General** Vickery (1995) 273–4.

parsley: transplanting

The most commonly reported superstition about parsley was that it was considered extremely unlucky to transplant it. It could be grubbed up completely, but not moved, as it would risk someone's illness or even death:

A little girl, playing about, moved some roots of parsley from one part of the garden to another, and her aunt coming and seeing what had been done, said to the mother, 'Why did you let Annie do this? you will surely have a death in the family'. Sure enough, Annie herself soon fell ill and died. Years elapsed, and the coincidence had been forgotten, until one day the mother saw the gardener bringing some roots of parsley, and then, remembering the superstition, she sent her husband to prevent him. The man, however, said it was nonsense, and persisted in planting them, and before long the husband died. This was told me by one of the family, who are very respectable people, and firmly believe in it.

Shropshire Burne (1883)

This was a widespread belief, at least across southern England and the Channel Islands, but no indication is ever given as to why the plant had such a dangerous reputation. It is perhaps tempting to compare it with another parsley tradition – that the plant goes nine times to the Devil and back before it sprouts. But the latter is a jocular allusion to how difficult it can be to get parsley to grow, and is never connected with the death omen. The other parsley beliefs are even less helpful.

A farmer's daughter told me that parsley seed should be planted with a spoon to stop the electricity of the body running out. Her father said he would not transplant parsley for a hundred pounds.   Devon *Devonshire Assoc.* (1940)

Somerset Poole (1877) 41; [1906 & 1950] Tongue (1965) 136. Dorset *Folk-Lore* 89 (1978) 158; Devon N&Q 4S:4 (1869) 506; *Western Antiquary* 2 (Oct. 1882) 114; Hewett (1900) 57; *Devonshire Assoc.* 39 (1907) 108; *Devonshire Assoc.* (1940) 115; *Devonshire Assoc.* 104 (1972) 267; Cornwall/Devon *Devonshire Assoc.* 9 (1877) 90. Surrey *Sunday Times* (6 Mar. 1955) 2. London/Surrey N&Q 1S:7 (1853) 153. Essex [1986] Opie & Tatem, 299. Oxfordshire Brand 3 (1849) 113. Gloucestershire Hartland (1895) 54. Warwickshire *Folk-Lore* 24 (1913) 240. Shropshire Burne (1883) 248–9. Jersey L'Amy (1927) 98. Unlocated Igglesden (c.1932) 69; Various Vickery (1995) 274–5.

parsley: woman is master

One of several indications that the woman is master in the house is that parsley grows well in the garden:

Where parsley grows in the garden, the missis is master.   Shropshire Burne (1883)

Where the parsley grows strongly, the woman wears the trousers. Somerset [1987] Opie & Tatem

For other beliefs concerning mastery in the home, see ROSEMARY: WIFE IS MASTER.

Sussex *Sussex County Mag.* (1937) 571. Somerset [1987] Opie & Tatem, 298. Devon *Devonshire Assoc.* 63 (1931) 125; *Devonshire Assoc.* 71 (1939) 130; *Devonshire Assoc.* 105 (1973) 214. Cambridgeshire Porter (1969) 47. Shropshire Burne (1883) 248. Monmouthshire *Folk-Lore* 16 (1905) 67. General Vickery (1995) 273.

parting

see GOODBYE.

passing through

A regular motif in certain cures, especially of children, was to pass the patient through or under some special object. The most common examples include passing through a split ASH tree, under an arched BRAMBLE which was rooted at both ends, through a holed STONE, a coiled ROPE, or over and under a DONKEY. These curative operations are probably best seen as examples of TRANSFERENCE of the ailment, although in many superstitions involving a split ash tree, it is the later growing together of the tree which effects the cure.

pavements

Avoiding stepping on the cracks between the paving stones, or on cracked stones, is well known as a children's game (called 'broken biscuits' in the author's South London childhood), but for some it was a much more serious business:

Before long I was whizzing through the streets, darting nimbly round solid citizens, and making a point of not stepping on any join in the pavement, as if my life depended on it, each crack a chasm into hell.   London [1943] Hughes

Various results were predicted: you will marry a black man and have a black baby, bears or snakes will chase, bite, or eat you, you will get your sums wrong, you will break your mother's best crockery, and so on.

An apparently more modern worry about pavements was reported in the 1998 Superstitions Survey carried out under the auspices of the Folklore Society. Two or three respondents quoted their own childhood belief in the need to avoid 'three drains' on the pavement. These were any place where three drains, manhole covers, etc., appeared together in a row; it was unlucky to tread on them. This belief still exists, as shown by the following note the author made in August 2002:

Walking through a local shopping centre in Croydon this morning, behind a man, mid to late twenties I would guess, and I noticed he was weaving from side to side as he walked. I realised that he was deliberately avoiding stepping on the sets of three access hatches set in the pavement, which appeared in front of each shop. I was pretty sure he was doing this, and it was confirmed by the last one, for which he misjudged the distance and had to make a smart jump sideways to avoid treading on it. He then looked round sheepishly to see if anyone was looking.

The earliest reference, identified by Opie & Tatem, is to London about 1890.

London [c.1890] Opie & Tatem, 300; [1920s] Gamble (1979) 89; [1943] Hughes (1994) 101–2; Steve Roud Collection (7 Aug. 2002). Gloucestershire [1954] Opie & Tatem, 300. Lincolnshire Sutton (1992) 124. Yorkshire Folk-Lore 43 (1932) 254. Cardiganshire [1953] Opie & Tatem, 300. Glamorganshire [c.1910] Opie & Tatem, 300. Aberdeenshire [1952] Opie & Tatem, 300. General Watford Observer (11 Feb. 1994) 20. Literary A. A. Milne, When We Were Very Young (1924) 'Lines and Squares'. Various Opie (1959) 220–2.

peacocks

From the mid nineteenth century to recent times, many have regarded peacocks' feathers as unlucky, and refuse to have them in the house or handle anything made with them:

I recently heard a harrowing story of a certain poor woman, a strong believer in this superstition, who to her horror received a Christmas present of a box of chocolates with a picture of the noxious birds upon the cover. True to her convictions, she mortified her flesh and defied the devil by throwing the whole lot into the dust-bin.
                              Yorkshire Folk-Lore (1932)

General bad luck is usually cited as the result of ignoring this superstition, but one specific which is sometimes given is that the presence of the feathers have adverse links with matrimony:

until the other day I had not heard that so long as they were kept the daughters of the house would have no suitors for their hands in marriage.
                              Unlocated N&Q (1893)

More than with other superstitions, there seems to have been a distinct division in society between those who believed and those who did not. In Victorian times, peacock feathers were fashionable in fans, hats, and common as household arrangements, at all levels of society. A number of informants report how they were suddenly confronted with angry people when they innocently appeared sporting the offending article:

Some eight or ten years ago a gentleman well known to me went to call on a baronet, an intimate friend of his. Unfortunately for him, he had the eye of a peacock's feather in his hat. When the lady of the house saw it, she snatched it from him, and threw it out of the hall door, 'rating' him as if he had been guilty of some great moral offence.
                              Unlocated N&Q (1893)

The general dislike of the peacock and its feathers is also reported as a theatrical superstition. Igglesden relates an incident in which Shakespearian actor Henry Irving (1838–1905) insisted that a member of the audience discard her peacock feather fan, and Peter Bull was reported as saying 'Anything to do with peacocks is fatal. I put on a play called "Cage me a Peacock", which lost me every penny I had' (Observer Supp. (24 Nov. 1968)).

The superstition suddenly springs, fully-fledged, into the documentary record in the mid 1860s, and there is no reason to believe it much older than that in this form. However, two further ideas, published by Lupton (1660), which link the bird's cry with rain (e.g. Nicholson (1890)) and death, both lasted long enough to be reported occasionally in Victorian times:

A Devonshire friend tells me of peacock-screaming being considered to forebode death (just the same as a dog howling), and a notable instance of the fact actually happened a few months ago in his own house.
                              Devon Folk-Lore Jnl (1883)

Sussex Sussex County Mag. 13 (1939) 57. Somerset Tongue (1965) 151. Devon Folk-Lore Jnl 1 (1883) 227; Hewett (1900) 55; Devonshire Assoc. 64 (1932) 156. Cambridgeshire N&Q 6S:3 (1881) 339. Norfolk [1884] Hope-Nicholson (1966) 170; Fulcher Collection (c.1894). Lincolnshire Watkins (1886) 11. Shropshire Burne (1883) 230; Gaskell (1894) 264. Staffordshire Burne (1883) 230. Derbyshire N&Q 3S:9 (1866) 187. England Addy (1895) 93. Nottinghamshire Burne (1883) 230. Yorkshire Nicholson (1890) 132; Folk-Lore 43 (1932) 254. Northern England N&Q 3S:9 (1866) 109. Co. Durham Leighton (1910) 62. Wales Trevelyan (1909) 328; Jones (1930) 181. Scotland N&Q 6S:3 (1881) 339. Highland Scotland Polson (1926) 128. Unlocated N&Q 3S:8 (1865) 332; Folk-Lore Jnl 1 (1883) 93; N&Q 8S:4

(1893) 426, 531; Igglesden (c.1932) 85, 234–5. **General** Foli (1902) 107. **Theatrical** *Observer Supp.* (24 Nov. 1968).

---

pearls

Many people nowadays regard pearls as somehow unlucky, and 'pearls mean tears' is a well-known saying, but the history of this belief has been difficult to document. It has certainly been known, but perhaps not widely, for a hundred years or so. Opie & Tatem print three twentieth-century references and Vincent Lean quotes a Durham divorce court case of 1885 where it was cited. The indefatigable contributor to *Notes & Queries* 'St. Swithin' (Mrs Gutch) also refers to it as generally known in 1897. Nevertheless, most of the main popular books on superstitions published in the twentieth century do not mention it at all.

A connection between pearls and tears seems to have been a commonplace in the seventeenth century. In John Webster's *Duchess of Malfi*, for example, the connection is quite explicit when the Duchess reports a dream that her coronet turned into pearls and Antonio comments 'My interpretation is, you'll weep shortly; for to me the pearls do signify your tears', and Thomas Killigrew wrote in similar vein in his play *The Parson's Wedding* (1663). All these early references concern dreaming about pearls rather than wearing them, but the bulk of nineteenth- and twentieth-century DREAM BOOKS are unanimous in declaring that to dream of pearls is very fortunate and means a successful marriage or business venture. Further research is certainly necessary.

General N&Q 8S:11 (1897) 146; [1885] Lean 2 (1905) 90; Opie & Tatem, 301. **Literary** Thomas Killigrew, *The Parson's Wedding* (1663) 2:5; John Webster, *Duchess of Malfi* (1623) 3:5.

---

pears

APPLES feature widely in superstition, but pears are rarely mentioned. The belief that fruit and blossom appearing on a tree at the same time indicates misfortune is said of pear trees as well as other fruit (*see* APPLES: BLOSSOM):

The blossoming of a pear tree at an unseasonable time is another sure sign of death during the year. Our pear-tree blossomed last autumn, and we were accordingly warned of coming misfortune, but in this case the omen was at fault. This same superstition still exists in Devon and many other parts of England.

Oxfordshire/Devon *Midland Garner* (1884)

Two stray references report beliefs which have not been reported elsewhere:

If a girl walk backwards to a pear tree on Christmas Eve, and walk round it three times, she will see the spirit or image of the man who is to be her husband.   England Addy (1895)

Mr. Lee informs us of a pear-tree in Wyre forest, the fruit of which is now hung up in the houses of the peasantry as a protection against witchcraft.   Worcestershire/Shropshire Gent. Mag. (1855)

Hampshire Yonge (1892) 270. **Oxfordshire/Devon** *Midland Garner* 1 (1884) 22. **Herefordshire** Leather (1912) 20. **Worcestershire/Shropshire** *Gent. Mag.* (1855) 384–6. **England** Addy (1895) 84.

---

peas

A LOVE DIVINATION custom, which remained remarkably stable from the seventeenth into the twentieth century, held that a pod containing nine peas should be placed above a doorway (sometimes on the threshold instead) and that the first eligible man that walked through would be the girl's future lover or, at least, would bear the same name as this desired being. First recorded in a letter from Dorothy Osborne to William Temple (22 July 1654):

I could not forbeare layeing a peascod with nine pease in't under the doore yesterday and was informed by it that my husbands name should bee Thomas, how doe you like that? But what Thomas I cannot image.
Bedfordshire Hart (1968)

and, similarly,

A pod containing nine peas was often put over the door to tell the fortune; the first man entering after it had been so placed would be your sweetheart, or, at least, his name would begin with the same letter.
Wiltshire *Wilts. N&Q* (1893–5)

In a few cases, nine peas in a pod is simply reported as 'lucky' or, if thrown over the shoulder, guarantees a wish will come true.

Peas could also be used in WART CURES, and roasted in the fire as a LOVE DIVINATION instead of the more commonly used NUTS.

Divination: **Somerset** [1923] Opie & Tatem, 302. **Devon** [1910] *Folk-Lore* 28 (1917) 313. **Wiltshire** *Wilts. N&Q* 1 (1893–5) 315–16. **Herefordshire** Leather (1912) 61. **Bedfordshire** Hart (1968) 195. **East Anglia** Forby (1830) 424; Varden (1885) 109. **Suffolk** Brand 2 (1849) 99; N&Q 1S:2 (1850) 4. **England** Addy (1895) 83. **England/Scotland borders** [c.1816] Henderson (1866)

83. **Scotland** N&Q 2S:4 (1857) 25 **Galloway**
Mactaggart (1824) 384. **Co. Cavan** Folk-Lore 19 (1908)
323. **Unlocated** N&Q 5S:10 (1878) 494. **Literary** John
Gay, The Shepherd's Week (1714) Thursday, lines
69–72; History of Mother Bunch of the Weste
(c.1780) 29.
Nine peas lucky: **Sussex** Latham (1878) 9.
Northamptonshire Sternberg (1851) 163. **Derbyshire**
Uttley (1946) 134. **Yorkshire** Nicholson (1890) 89.

pendulum divination

A traditional method of divination, for various
purposes, was to suspend a ring or sometimes
another metal object such as a needle or coin by
a thread to interpret the way it moved. In the
earliest versions, it was claimed simply that one
could accurately determine the time:

You shall know what it is a clocke, if you hold
between your finger and your thumbe a thread
of six or seven inches long, unto the other end
whereof is tied a gold ring, or some such thing in
place; in such sort as upon the beating of your
pulse, and the moving of the ring, the same may
strike upon either side of a goblet or glasse.

Scot (1584)

The same process was later used as a parlour
game, to determine whether one was to be
married, how many years till the wedding, and
to answer other similar questions. The alleged
basis for this phenomenon was called OD by
Baron von Reichenbach in 1850. To the present
day it is also used to determine the sex of unborn
babies and unhatched eggs (*see* PREGNANCY:
PENDULUM DIVINATION).

Sussex Folk-Lore Record 1 (1878) 31. **London** [1955] Opie
& Tatem, 303. **Northern England** Henderson (1866) 82.
Lancashire N&Q 1S:3 (1851) 517. **General** Scot (1584) Bk
16, Ch. 5; Melton (1620) 45; Pictorial Juvenile Mag. 2
(1853) 158, quoted Opie & Tatem, 302.

peonies

A curious set of almost incompatible beliefs have
clustered around the peony over the years. In the
late nineteenth century it was connected with
death:

On the death of a friend in the summer, an old
lady, a relative, who was on a visit of condolence
to the widow, went quietly into the garden and
counted the flowers on the peonies. On her
return, after remarking that a dog was howling
before the door but a short time before when she
was there, and that it was generally accounted a
sign of death, said she had counted the flowers on

the peonies in the garden, and there was an odd
number on each plant, which was a sure sign of
a death in the house before the year was out.

Unlocated N&Q (1873)

This is confirmed by a note in the Fulcher
Collection of Norfolk folklore in the Folklore
Society: 'An uneven number of peony blossoms
on a plant is a sign of a death in the family in
whose garden it grows'. But at a similar period,
beads made from peony roots were hung around
children's necks to help with teething and
prevent convulsions. (**Sussex** Folk-Lore Record
(1878)).

This latter application appears to be in line
with a long tradition of protective uses of the
plant when worn round the neck as an amulet.
It was detailed in Lupton's Thousand Notable
Things of 1579, where it was recommended
against epilepsy and falling sickness. Much of
Lupton's material was taken from European
sources, but the further references listed below
demonstrate its acceptance into British tradition. One of the medieval manuscripts published
by Cockayne recommended the peony for
cramps, quiverings, and control of rough
weather.

Sussex Folk-Lore Record 1 (1878) 44. **Norfolk** Fulcher
Collection (c.1895). **Unlocated** N&Q 4S:12 (1873) 469.
General [c.1050] Cockayne 1 (1864) 303; Lupton (1579)
Bk 4, Para. 100; Robert Burton, Anatomie of Melancholy
(1621) Pt 2, Sect. 5; Francis Bacon, Sylva Sylvarum
(1627) Para. 966; J. Parkinson, Theatrum Botanicum
(1640); E. Darwin, Loves of Plants (1791) 90.

petals

One of the simplest and most widely known
forms of LOVE DIVINATION is to pluck the
petals from a flower while reciting 'She loves me,
she loves me not'. However widely known these
words are today, this is not the only form of
words which can be found in this context:

Gathering a daisy, she commences plucking the
petals off, saying with each one, 'Does he love me
– much – a little – devotedly – not at all', and the
last petal settles the question.

Wales Trevelyan (1909)

and other rhymes can also be used, such as the
ubiquitous TINKER TAILOR. None of these
rhymes can be traced before the nineteenth
century, but the connection between love and
daisies was current much earlier. Evidence
comes, for example, from Thomas Killigrew's
play Thomaso (1663), where 'plucked daisies' is

'Does she love me? Yes, I know – 'cos the petals of the daisy told me so.' An early twentieth-century illustration.

Surrey [1959] Opie & Tatem, 303. **Herefordshire** *Folk-Lore* 23 (1912) 352. **East Anglia** Varden (1885) 114. **Suffolk** Chambers 1 (1878) 321–3. **Western Scotland** Napier (1879) 137.

photographs

The supposed close connection between a photograph or portrait and its human subject is reflected both in the belief that a PICTURE falling is a bad omen and in a sense of unease which many people in the past reportedly felt about having their photograph taken:

> To the present day they [gypsies] *fear – or affect to fear – the taking of their photographs . . .* 'No, *doctor, I ain't going to have you take my photygraph no more. I've had nought but ill-luck since you took me last year,' said a handsome old Romany woman. 'I'm sorry for that,' I said, 'because I've got some packets of your favourite 'Nosegay' baccy with me, that I meant to give you if . . .' 'Oh well, doctor,' she hastened to add, 'seeing as how 'tis you.'*

Sussex *Sussex County Mag.* (1939)

Reports of this belief are spread across England, Scotland, and Ireland, but do not seem to have appeared before the mid nineteenth century. It is tempting to argue that this dating reflects the invention and rise of photography, and therefore the gradual spread of access to personal photography across the populace. But the first reference, from Cambridgeshire Gypsies in 1851, describes a violent objection to being sketched:

> I know there's a fiz [charm] in it. There was my youngest, that the gorja drawed out on Newmarket heath, she never held her head up after, but wasted away, and died; and she's buried in March churchyard.

Cambridgeshire *Illustrated London News* (13 Dec. 1851)

Some variations are recorded. In one version it is young babies who should not be photographed, apparently on the same basis as the widespread belief that infants under one year of age should not be shown their own reflection in a MIRROR. One Cornish informant maintained that an effective way of breaking a spell cast upon you is to obtain a photograph of the ill-wisher, write their name across the face of the picture, and burn it (*Old Cornwall* (1931)).

See also ENGAGED COUPLES.

Sussex *Sussex County Mag.* 13 (1939) 57. **Devon** *Devonshire Assoc.* 60 (1928) 125; *Devonshire Assoc.* 90

included in a list of love-related items such as a bent COIN, valentines, and YARROW.

See FLOWERS: RED.

Dorset Hone, *Year Book* (1832) 587–8. **Wales** Trevelyan (1909) 97. **Monmouthshire** [1986] Opie & Tatem, 115. **General** Igglesden (*c*.1932) 64. **Literary** Thomas Killigrew, *Thomaso* (1663) 4:11.

petticoats

If a woman's petticoat hang below her dress they say, 'Your father likes you more than your mother'. **Herefordshire** *Folk-Lore* (1912)

Exactly the same belief has been reported, from various parts of the country, a handful of times since 1863. It is usually explained that a mother should be more attentive to the details of her daughter's dress than to allow such a situation to arise.

A different connotation, reported only in Opie and Tatem, quotes a Surrey woman as saying in 1959:

If any of the staff are showing a petticoat they are accused of husband hunting.

The petticoat is also one of the items of clothing, like stockings, prone to be put on inside out. *See* CLOTHES: INSIDE OUT.

(1958) 246; *Devonshire Assoc.* 104 (1972) 268. **Cornwall** *Old Cornwall* 2:1 (1931) 21. **Wiltshire** [*c.*1910] *Folk-Lore* 27 (1916) 308. **London** *Folk-Lore* 37 (1926) 366. **Cambridgeshire** *Illustrated London News* (13 Dec. 1851) 715, also in Groome (1880) 336–8. **Essex** [*c.*1916] Mays (1969) 163–4. **Highland Scotland** Macbain (1887/88) 270. **Western Scotland** Napier (1879) 142. **N. Ireland** Foster (1951) 14. **Connemara** N&Q 149 (1925) 92.

pictures: above door or bed

Much less common than the superstition about a picture falling down (*see below*) is a belief that it is unlucky to hang a picture above a door or a bed, reported only a handful of times in the twentieth century. No reason is given, but Igglesden specifically names it as a theatrical superstition.

Lincolnshire Rudkin (1936) 17. **Co. Durham** [1984] Opie & Tatem, 305. **Northumberland** Bosanquet (1929) 77. **Unlocated** Igglesden (*c.*1932) 233–4.

pictures: falling

The sudden falling of a picture from the wall has been widely regarded as ominous, but although the broad pattern is similar, details vary from case to case. The strongest notion is that if the picture is a portrait then the person portrayed is definitely not long for this world:

A picture falling from the wall presages misfortune; should it be a portrait, of which the original is still alive, it portends his death. I was once staying with a friend in this parish when the portrait of the master of the family fell down; he was depressed and unwell for days on account of the accident, but he lived for some years after.

Devon *Devonshire Assoc.* (1928)

In other cases, a distinction is made between whether the glass is broken in the fall – if so, a death is expected soon in the family, if not, simple bad luck is predicted. An added condition of 'unnatural causes' was also sometimes invoked:

A picture frame had fallen, and the belief that this presaged a death was mentioned. But D.G.A. *said that the picture should have fallen without an obvious reason – to betoken a death – whereas in this case the string had broken.*

Buckinghamshire [1927] *Folk-Lore*

The earliest references are from the seventeenth century, commencing with Heylin's *Life*

of William Laud (1668) in which Laud finds a portrait of himself fallen flat on the floor and wonders if it is an omen. The second known reference, in the *Athenian Mercury* (1692), also refers to portraits of kings and great men, and it seems clear that in this older version of the belief, it is the close connection between the living person and his/her portrait which is the central motif – bad things happening to a portrait presage bad things happening to the real person. In contrast, the generalized 'falling picture means bad luck' occurs much later, appearing only from the late nineteenth century, and is apparently based simply on the principle of 'accidental happenings'. Nevertheless, a general ambivalence about portraits is evident in some people's reluctance to have their PHOTOGRAPH taken. Pictures also get included in beliefs concerning MIRRORS and other shiny objects which were covered when there was a death in the house, or during a STORM.

Devon *Devonshire Assoc.* 60 (1928) 119–20; *Devonshire Assoc.* 91 (1959) 203; *Devonshire Assoc.* 104 (1972) 268. **Essex** [*c.*1915] Mays (1969) 164. **Buckinghamshire** [1927] *Folk-Lore* 43 (1932) 110. **Oxfordshire** [1880s] Thompson (1943) 319–2. **Warwickshire** Bloom (*c.*1930) 42. **Lincolnshire** Rudkin (1936) 19. **Yorkshire** Nicholson (1890) 42; Blakeborough (1898) 127. **Lancashire** [*c.*1912] Corbridge (1964) 156–60. **Northumberland** Bosanquet (1929) 77. **Highland Scotland** Macbain (1887/88) 270. **N. Ireland** Foster (1951) 18. **Co. Tyrone** *Lore & Language* 1:7 (1972) 7. **Co. Longford** *Béaloideas* 6 (1936) 260. **Unlocated** Igglesden (*c.*1932) 201, 232.

pigeons: craving for

An odd sort of belief held that the last thing an invalid craved to eat was pigeon, and if they did so it was taken as a sure indication that they were dying:

On applying the other day to a highly respectable farmer's wife to know if she had any pigeons ready to eat, as a sick person had expressed a longing for one, she said, 'Ah, poor fellow! is he so far gone? A pigeon is generally almost the last thing they want; I have supplied many a one for the like purpose.'

Lancashire N&Q (1851)

This has only been recorded irregularly since the 1850s, but enough times and on a wide enough geographical spread to confirm its independent existence. No reason for the belief has been suggested, although the regular interpretation of the bird as a death omen (*see below*) may be at its root.

pigeons

Pigeons have a largely negative reputation in British traditional belief. They were widely feared as death omens if they alighted near a home, they were said to be the last thing a dying invalid requested to eat, and they were extensively used in last ditch attempts to save dying people. It was also widely believed that pigeon feathers in a mattress prevented anyone 'dying easy' in that bed, and condemned the sufferer to a prolonged and difficult passing (*see* FEATHERS: IN BEDDING).

A reported saying, 'He who is sprinkled with pigeon's blood will never die a natural death', has a literary rather than a popular history. It appears to have originated with a story, first printed by John Aubrey in his chapter on 'Omens', concerning a bust of King Charles I:

The bust of King Charles I, carved by Bernini, as it was brought in a boat upon the Thames, a strange bird (the like whereof the bargemen had never seen) dropped a drop of blood, or blood-like upon it; which left a stain not to be wiped off.   Aubrey, *Miscellanies* (1696)

In later versions, the blood comes from a pigeon which has been attacked by a hawk, and the indelible mark forms round the bust's throat, thus predicting Charles' death by beheading (*see* N&Q (1889–90)). Nevertheless, Black points out that pigeon's blood, far from being thought poisonous, was elsewhere recommended as a cure for eye complaints (Black (1883)).

A few miscellaneous beliefs are as follows:

For pigeons to roost on the roof of a newly married couple foretells felicity, also a long family.   Devon *Devonshire Assoc.* (1935)

An old coachman at Minehead about 1893 used to say that stolen pigeons would never mate, but if they were sent home, even after two years they would mate again. He also said that a swallow-tailed pigeon brings luck, particularly if it is a white one.   Somerset [1893] Tongue

Survey results included: For toothache: Carry a pair of pigeon's feet in your pocket.
           Westmorland/Lancashire [c.1939] *Folk-Lore*

There is a country belief that pigeon meat has a dramatically binding effect on the human constitution.   Kent [1930s] Kent

For general notes on pigeon lore, *see also* Swainson (1886) 168–9.

Kent [1930s] Kent (1977) 5. Somerset [1893] Tongue (1965) 48. Devon *Devonshire Assoc.* 67 (1935) 132. Westmorland/Lancashire [c.1939] *Folk-Lore* 62 (1951) 262. General Black (1883) 163; Swainson (1886) 168–9. *King Charles story*: Aubrey, *Miscellanies* (1696/1857) 41; N&Q 7S:8 (1889) 468; 7S:9 (1890) 13–14, 77.

Southern England Jefferies (1879) 152. Lancashire N&Q 1S:3 (1851) 517. Wales *Folk-Lore* 30 (1919) 157. Mid-Wales Davies (1911) 226.

pigeons: cures

A recurrent theme in folk medicine is the use of live animals, skinned, dismembered, or simply cloven in two, which are applied to the sick or wounded person in one way or another. In many of these cases, the implication is that the animal provides both natural healing heat and acts beneficially by *drawing* the sickness out of the patient's body. Live pigeons were the creatures cited most often to suffer and serve in this way, and there are numerous reports of their use from the seventeenth to nineteenth centuries. What seems strange to modern thought is that for much of this period the pigeon was actually applied to the sufferer's feet, even in cases of general fever or problems with the head. This was because it was believed that the feet and head were physiologically closely linked.

Samuel Pepys twice mentioned the treatment, in a matter-of-fact way:

(21 Jan. 1668) News from Kate Joyce that if I would see her husband alive, I must come presently . . . and find him in his sick bed . . . but his breath rattled in his throat and they did lay pigeons to his feet while I was in the house; and all despair of him.

and, writing of the Queen's current illness:

(19 Oct. 1663) It seems she was so ill as to be shaved and pigeons put to her feet.

The implication is usually that the pigeons were the last resort, and administered when the patient was *in extremis*. The treatment was sufficiently well known to become a literary cliché in seventeenth-century writing – 'I would sooner eat a dead pigeon taken from the soles of the feet of one sick of the plague than kiss one of you fasting' (Webster, *Duchess of Malfi* (1623)), and both Congreve (1695) and Otway (1681) use a similar image in their plays.

In the cases already cited, the unfortunate bird was sliced in half for use, but in other situations it was used whole:

Bite of a viper or a rattle-snake – Apply the anus of a pigeon to the wound. Sometimes two are needful.   Wesley (1768)

Again, the principle of *drawing out* is clearly at work. The implication in some accounts, such as the one following, is that the disease was actually TRANSFERRED to the bird, and the bird's disposal therefore warranted careful consideration:

A cure for any disease was the following – Two live pigeons were taken, ripped up, and tied to the soles of the patient's feet, sometimes wrapped in cloths to prevent the bed from being soiled. At times they were left uncovered fluttering on the patient's feet. A near relative in the early morning, or 'atween the sin and the sky' removed the pigeons and carried them to a place over which the dead and the living did not cross, that is, to the top of a precipice, and left them. Some who have gone through this rite are still alive.
                                    Banffshire Gregor (1874)

Cornwall Polwhele (1826) 607. London Samuel Pepys, *Diary* (19 Oct. 1663; 21 Jan. 1668). Essex *The Times* (21 Oct. 1835) 7. Lincolnshire N&Q 9S:6 (1900) 306–7. Staffordshire Hackwood (1924) 150. Derbyshire *Derby Mercury* (30 Nov. 1797) quoted Morsley (1979) 144. Banffshire Gregor (1874) 266. General *The English Huswife* (1615); James Primrose, *De Vulgi Erroribus in Medicina* (1638); Wesley (1768) 125; N&Q 4S:4 (1869) 505–6. Literary John Webster, *Duchess of Malfi* (1623) 2:1; Thomas Otway, *The Souldier's Fortune* (1681) 1:1; William Congreve, *Love for Love* (1695) 4:15. French analogues: Black (1883) 163–4; N&Q 151 (1926) 136.

pigeons: death omens

The pigeon's reputation as a death omen has been largely forgotten, but in the nineteenth and early twentieth centuries it was widely regarded with suspicion and horror right across the British Isles:

It is unlucky for a pigeon to settle on the house. Send it off! If it comes down I'll wring its neck. One settled on the wash-house where I was working, and the woman's old man died.
                                    London *Folk-Lore* (1926)

In some reports it was specifically a white or black pigeon that was feared, or it was the particular circumstances of its appearance, such as perching near the window of a room where someone lay sick. These are all standard motifs

found in other bird omens, but in many cases the pigeon needed only to alight on the house to cause the fear.

In the earliest version, from Richard Gough's *History of Myddle*, the omen has a formality which stamps it as a recurrent family omen:

It is observed that if the chief person of the family that inhabits this farm do fall sick, if his sickness be to death, there comes a pair of pigeons to the house about a fortnight or a week before the person's death, and then go away. This I have known thrice do three several times. First, old Mr. Bradocke, fell sick about a quarter of a year after my sister was married, and the pair of pigeons came thither, which I saw.
                                    Shropshire Gough (1601–7)

England *Folk-Lore* 10 (1899) 248–9. Somerset Tongue (1965) 48–9. London *Folk-Lore* 37 (1926) 364. Herefordshire Leather (1912) 25; *Folk-Lore* 39 (1928) 391. Worcestershire [1895] *Folk-Lore* 28 (1917) 312. Warwickshire Langford (1875) 12. Suffolk *Folk-Lore* 35 (1924) 350. Lincolnshire N&Q 1S:8 (1853) 382; Watkins (1886) 11; Rudkin (1936) 16. England Addy (1895) 66, 96. Derbyshire N&Q 7S:12 (1891) 86. Shropshire Gough (1601–7) 30–1. N&Q 7S:12 (1891) 86. Northern England *Newcastle Weekly Chronicle* (11 Feb. 1899) 7). Yorkshire Henderson (1866) 34; *Leeds Mercury* (4 Oct. 1879); Nicholson (1890) 130. Lancashire N&Q 7S:12 (1891) 213. Co. Durham *Folk-Lore* 20 (1909) 72. Wales Trevelyan (1909) 282. Glamorgan Phillips (1925) 598. Radnorshire [1953] Opie & Tatem, 309. Co. Leitrim *Folk-Lore* 5 (1894) 198. Guernsey De Garis (1975) 137. Unlocated N&Q 2S:12 (1861) 492.

pigeons: witchcraft

Pigeons' hearts were sometimes used as an integral part of WITCHCRAFT spells, either as counter-magic or in a love charm:

In November of the year 1861, I was sent for by a parishioner, the wife of a small farmer, who complained that she had been 'scandalised' by her neighbours opposite, who accused her of witchcraft. These neighbours had lost two horses during the last year, and consulted 'Black Willie' at Hartlepool, who assured them they had been bewitched. Following his advice they adopted the following means for discovering the witch. Having procured a pigeon and tied its wings, every aperture to the house, even to the keyholes, was carefully stopped, and pins run into the pigeon while alive by each member of the family, so as to pierce its heart. The pigeon was then roasted, and a watch kept at the window during the operation. The first person who passed the door would be the guilty person. This neighbour had the misfortune to be the first person who passed the window, and the family are firmly convinced she had exercised the 'evil eye', though she is a comely matron not yet fifty years old. This happened in a village close to the Tees.

Northumberland Tristram (1860–62)

If your lover has forsaken you, and you want to bring him back to you, take a live pigeon, pluck out its heart, and stick pins therein. Put the heart under your pillow, and your lover will return to you.   England Addy (1895)

The hearts of other creatures were similarly used in other versions, and there is no indication whether the pigeon was held to have any special characteristic or was simply relatively easy to obtain in such circumstances.

Herefordshire Leather (1912) 64. **England** Addy (1895) 79. **Northamptonshire** Sternberg (1851) 185. **Northumberland** Tristram (1860–62) 98. **Guernsey** De Garis (1975) 137.

---

pig: forbidden word

see FISHING: FORBIDDEN WORDS.

pigs: killing

The killing of the family pig was an immensely important event for the future economy of the household, and it was clearly necessary to get it right and leave little to chance. The killing itself and the subsequent preparation of the meat were skilled practical tasks, but there were a few superstitions which also helped in the process. An extremely widespread belief dictated that the pig be killed at the waxing of the moon or the meat would be spoilt (*see* MOON: PIG-KILLING for fuller discussion).

Pigs which are killed between eight and ten of the clock in the morning will weigh more and be in better condition than they would be if killed at a later time of day.   England Addy (1895)

There were also strong local traditions covering who should receive parts of the meat as a courtesy or reward for assistance, and fine distinctions between relatives and neighbours were reflected in who received which particular cuts. Another superstition covered this area:

It is but neighbourly to send a dish of pig's fry ('pig-fare' as the term is) to a friend; but the dish must on no account be washed when it is returned. It must be left soiled, else the bacon will not cure. So with the 'beestlings' (the milk of the

first three milkings after a cow has calved) the pail must never be washed, or the cow will 'go dry'.   Lincolnshire Watkins (1886)

There was also the general restriction on the activities of menstruating women:

No woman was ever allowed to touch the meat [of a pig] during her monthly period otherwise it would go bad, and I know families who, to this day, will only kill a pig when the moon is on the wax and when the wife is not menstruating.

Norfolk Randell (1966)

Norfolk Randell (1966) 95. **Lincolnshire** Watkins (1886) 10; Sutton (1992) 129. **England** Addy (1895) 67, 99.

pigs: meeting

A number of superstitions exist which include the basic motif that it is unlucky to MEET certain people or animals first thing in the morning, or when starting a journey. HARES and single MAGPIES were commonly cited in this context, and CROSS-EYED people or women were also avoided. Also commonly reported as unlucky were pigs:

A friend recently informed me that at Preston Pans the . . . following superstitious observation exists among the fishermen of that place. If, on their way to their boats, they meet a pig, they at once turn back and defer their embarkation. The event is an omen that bodes ill for their fishery.

East Lothian N&Q (1852)

In the earliest reference, the matter was somewhat more complex:

If, going a journey or business, a sow crosses the road, you will probably meet with a disappointment, if not a bodily accident, before you return home. To avert this, you must endeavour to prevent her crossing you; and if that cannot be done, you must ride round on fresh ground. If the sow is attended with her litter of pigs, it is lucky, and denotes a successful journey.

Unlocated Grose (1787)

Fishermen were particularly prone to these restrictions on who or what could be met, and they included 'pig' in the list of words which they refused to utter while at sea (*see* FISHING: FORBIDDEN WORDS). The other context in which pigs could be especially unlucky was if met by a wedding party:

It is very unlucky for swine to cross in front of a wedding party. The bridegroom, as well as the

pigs

Pigs featured in a fair number of superstitions in their own right, as well as being prone to witchcraft and ill-wishing as all farmyard animals were. The most widespread belief concerned the need to observe the phases of the moon and ensure that the animal was slaughtered when the moon was waxing and not when it was waning (*see* MOON: PIG-KILLING). Pigs were also unlucky to MEET when setting out from home, and FISHERMEN were careful not to say the word 'pig' while out at sea (*see below* for further references).

When the men of Holy Island are going out to fish, they do not suffer anyone to mention a pig or a priest. Our informant saith, he was threatened to be thrown overboard, as Jonah was of old, if he dared to go on with a story he had begun about a pig being able to see the wind. The men believed they would catch no fish if he did not hold his tongue, or that the boat would be swamped. Co. Durham Brockie (1886)

It is still often said that pigs can 'see the wind' (*see* PIGS: WEATHER), but another 'vulgar error' – that they cannot swim, because their trotters cut their throats if they try – is less often heard nowadays.

Taken in total, it seems that pigs were regarded as uncanny in many communities in a rather undefined way, which may simply reflect the animal's appearances in the Bible. There was the story of the Gadarene swine of Mark 5: 11–15 and

Luke 8:32–3 was well known, while Deuteronomy 14:7–8 declares the animal unclean.

We don't kill a pig every day, but we did a short time since; and after its hairs were scraped off, our attention was directed to six small rings, about the size of a pea, and in colour as if burnt or branded, on the inside of each fore leg and disposed curvilinearly. Our labourer informed us with great gravity, and evidently believed it, that these marks were caused by the pressure of the devil's fingers, when he entered the herd of swine which immediately ran violently in the sea.
Unlocated N&Q (1853)

But these biblical stories do not seem sufficient to explain the range of beliefs collected in the last 200 years. It is also noticeable that none of the pig superstitions are documented before the mid eighteenth century, and most are only found from the nineteenth onwards.

Pig products were used in folk medicine, although not particularly widely. Pig's blood could be used, like many other animals' blood, to cure WARTS, and pig fat was used as a base for many ointments and other concoctions. Pig dung also had its uses:

To stop bleeding, fresh pigs' dung is used occasionally in my neighbourhood. At Mamhead a farmer's son having sustained a severe incised wound in the palm of the hand, the farmer followed a pig about the farm-yard till the animal parted with sufficient dressing. The son's

bride, has been known to turn back, instead of proceeding to church, when such an occurrence happened. This was, of course, before the days when actions for breach of promise became fashionable. Hence the old adage, 'The swine's run through it'.*
Scotland/England borders [*c.*1816] Henderson

This superstition has been reported occasionally from southern England and Wales, but the overwhelming majority of references are from the northern counties of England and Scotland. No sensible reason for this fear of pigs has been put forward, although it is true to say that the various pig-related superstitions suggest that the animal was regarded as somewhat uncanny in a general way (*see above*). It is noticeable that neither the 'pig-meeting' nor the 'pig-saying' beliefs have been found before the eighteenth century, whereas similar fears about hares are

demonstrably centuries older. It is quite possible that the notion of the unluckiness of meeting a pig was formed directly by extension of the hare belief, but this is mere speculation.

Somerset [1923] Opie & Tatem, 307. **Southwest England** Elworthy (1895) 31. **Northern England** *Newcastle Weekly Chronicle* (11 Feb. 1899) 7. **Northumberland** Neville (1909) 109–10; *Folk-Lore* 36 (1925) 252, 256. **Yorkshire** N&Q 4S:4 131–2. **Wales** Trevelyan (1909) 327. **Scotland/England borders** [*c.*1816] Henderson (1866) 21. **Western Scotland** Napier (1879) 120. **Highland Scotland** Campbell (1900) 254; Polson (1926) 129. **Fife** Ramsay (1861) 30–1. **East Lothian** N&Q 1S:5 (1852) 5. **Aberdeenshire** *Folk-Lore Jnl.* 3 (1885) 282. **Orkney** N&Q 10S:12 (1909) 483–4. **Unlocated** Grose (1787) 61–2. **General** *The Mirror* (10 Mar. 1832) 171.

hand was then immediately covered with this, and wrapped up in a cloth. A farmer's son residing at Exminster had an attack of bleeding at the nose. The farmer laid the boy on his back, and filled his nostrils with the unsavoury medicament. A cure was in both cases affected.

Devon *Devonshire Assoc.* (1880)

Epilepsy – Take three drops of sow's milk.

Ireland N&Q (1850)

Victorian island matrons used to rub the scalp with an unguent made of unsalted pork rind. It was said of one lady who lived to the age of 78 that when she died her hair was as golden as when she was a young girl because she used this treatment regularly. **Guernsey** De Garis (1975)

Some examples of other beliefs, reported only once or twice:

Swine are sometimes said to give their master warning of his death by giving utterance to a certain peculiar whine, known and understood only by the initiated in such matters.

Northamptonshire N&Q (1851)

It is very unlucky to put a pig into a new home head first; it must be put in backwards.

Devon *Devonshire Assoc.* (1926)

About fifty years ago my father knew an Inishowen man who mixed written charms with his pigs' food. The charms were supplied by a local wise-man. **N. Ireland** Foster (1951)

Should you be troubled by unexplained illness and death amongst your pigs you should bury the poor victims toes upwards, and the trouble will cease. **Gloucestershire** *Folk-Lore* (1902)

Upwards of thirty years ago an old man who lived in north-west Lincolnshire told me that collars made of Deadly Nightshade, if fastened around the necks of pigs which were suffering from witchcraft, would at once make them quite well. The name he gave the plant was not nightshade but 'shady-night'. **Lincolnshire** N&Q (1911)

At Norton, if a pig's hock is hung up in the house, and whitewashed every time the house is whitewashed, the cattle of the farmer will be protected, it is said, against disease. **Yorkshire** Addy (1888)

If you eat pig's marrow you will go mad.

Warwickshire Langford (1875)

Devon *Devonshire Assoc.* 12 (1880) 101–2; N&Q 147 (1924) 159–60; *Devonshire Assoc.* 57 (1926) 111. **Cornwall** *Folk-Lore Jnl* 5 (1887) 195. **Gloucestershire** *Folk-Lore* 13 (1902) 172. **Worcestershire** [c.1900] Knight (1960) 180–1. **Worcestershire/Shropshire** *Gent. Mag.* (1855) 384–6. **Warwickshire** Langford (1875) 14. **Northamptonshire** N&Q 1S:3 (1851) 3–4. **Bedfordshire** *Folk-Lore* 37 (1926) 77. **Norfolk** [1870s] Haggard (1935) 19. **Lincolnshire** Cole (1886) 93; N&Q (1911) 427. **Yorkshire** Addy (1888) xxi. **Co. Durham** Brockie (1886) 121. **Scotland** *Yorkshire Post* (11 Aug. 1924) quoted N&Q 147 (1924) 112. **Northeast Scotland** Gregor (1881) 129. **Ireland** *Athenaeum* (1846) 1068; N&Q 1S:1 (1850) 349; Wilde (1888) 199. **N. Ireland** Foster (1951) 59. **Guernsey** De Garis (1975) 127. **Unlocated** N&Q 1S:7 (1853) 281.

pigs: weather

It was commonly reported that bad weather could be predicted from watching pigs' behaviour:

In all parts of Ulster pigs enjoy the reputation of being able to see the wind. They are said to behave in a peculiar fashion before and during a storm, which may be because they are sensitive to atmospheric changes, but quite a number of country people believe that they see the wind and are afraid. **N. Ireland** Foster (1951)

The idea that they can 'see the wind' is still commonly stated, although presumably not literally believed. According to one tradition, it would be easy enough to test the notion:

If you wash your eyes with sow's milk you will see the wind as red as fire.

Welsh Gypsies Jarman (1991)

England Addy (1895) 67. **Northern England** *Newcastle Weekly Chronicle* (11 Feb. 1899) 7. **Lancashire** Harland & Wilkinson (1873) 224. **Welsh Gypsies** Jarman (1991) 185. **Northeast Scotland** Gregor (1881) 130. **N. Ireland** Foster (1951) 125. **Guernsey** De Garis (1975) 127. **Unlocated** Hone, *Year Book* (1832) 126–8. **General** *The Mirror* (10 Mar. 1832) 171.

pins and needles

see CRAMP.

pins: finding

Since at least early Victorian times, we have been exhorted in a very well-known rhyme not to pass by and leave a pin on the floor or in the street:

See a pin and pick it up
All the day you'll have good luck

pins

The humble pin features in a wide range of beliefs, both as central character and in walk-on parts, but its reason for being there varies from case to case.

In some, the pin's pointed nature symbolizes attack or defence. Pins were used extensively in witchcraft, both for harming (e.g. sticking pins in EFFIGIES) and for counter-spells (sticking pins in the heart of a bewitched animal to get back at the witch or placing them in WITCH BOTTLES). Its sharpness makes a pin dangerous to find if pointing towards you, and dangerous to give to someone, in case it 'cuts love' (*see also* KNIVES: GIFT).

Pins can take on the attributes of a particular occasion: when they are taken from a bride's dress they can carry the power to help bring on another wedding. In dressmaking and tailoring, they can be good or bad, depending on the situation. They can be stuck into ONIONS as part of LOVE DIVINATION ceremonies or pointed at WARTS to help cure them, but they must not be taken on to a fishing trawler.

Pins are also symbols of insignificance – things are 'not worth a pin'. If one must give or leave something, a pin is the most nominal thing there is, a gesture. This is probably the reason behind the throwing of pins into wells.

See a pin and let it lay
You will have bad luck all day

or

See a pin and let it lie
In the evening you will cry.

Lincolnshire Rudkin (1936)

The wording of the third and fourth lines varies considerably, but the thrust is always the same. As noted above, it is difficult to know which attribute of the pin is in play at any given time, but in this case the meaning seems to be simply that of thrift – take care of the pennies and the pounds will look after themselves. Samuel Pepys recorded in his *Diary* for 2 Jan. 1668, 'I see your majesty do not remember the old English proverb, "He that will not stoop for a pin, will never be worth a pound"', and more recently, a Welsh proverb maintains, '*Gwell plygu at bin, na phlygu at ddim*' (It is better to bend down for a pin, than to bend down for nothing) (West Wales Davies (1911)).

The first known appearance of the rhyme is in 1842, in Halliwell's collection of nursery rhymes, so it was presumably already widely known at that time, and it is still regularly quoted today. Nevertheless, it is flatly contradicted by another, less common, maxim: 'Pick up a pin and you pick up poverty' (Norfolk Fulcher Collection (*c.*1895)) or 'Pick up pins, pick up sorrow' (Shropshire Burne (1883)). To complicate matters further, some sources claim that a pin is only lucky if its head is towards you:

If you see a pin on the floor with the point towards you, do not lift it or you will have great 'sharpness' and disappointment; but if the pin's head is towards you, lift it, and you will have good luck and never want for a pin.

Co. Meath/Co. Tipperary Folk-Lore (1904)

This variation is in line with beliefs about other sharp-edged finds, such as KNIVES, and is much older than the common rhyme. It is mentioned, for example, in Congreve's play *Love for Love* (1695).

Finally, certain pins are intrinsically bad:

But a yellow, crooked pin must on no account be picked up, or the tidy person who removes it from the floor will die an old maid. Often have I heard the warning given, not to touch 'the nasty thing'.

Sussex Latham (1878)

Sussex Latham (1878) 33. Hampshire [1987] Opie & Tatem, 311. Devon Hewett (1900) 49, 56. Cornwall *Folk-Lore Jnl* 5 (1887) 220. Wiltshire *Wilts. N&Q* 1 (1893–5) 62. Surrey Sturt (1927) 138–9. London Samuel Pepys, *Diary* (2 Jan. 1668); [*c.*1924] Steve Roud Collection (2002). Essex [*c.*1917] Mays (1969) 163–4; [1983] Opie & Tatem, 310–11. Oxfordshire [1920s] Surman (1992) 60–1. Suffolk *Folk-Lore* 35 (1924) 351–2. Norfolk Fulcher Collection (*c.*1895). Lincolnshire Rudkin (1936) 16–17; [*c.*1940s] Sutton (1992) 137. Shropshire Burne (1883) 279–80. Staffordshire [1956] Opie & Tatem, 310. Derbyshire [1890s] Uttley (1946) 135–6. Derbyshire? [*c.*1849] N&Q 10S:12 (1909) 518. Northumberland Bosanquet (1929) 77. West Wales Davies (1911) 216–17. Galloway Mactaggart (1824) 210. Angus [1954] Opie & Tatem, 310. Dumfriesshire Corrie (1890/91) 82. Orkney N&Q 10S:12 (1909) 483–4. Ireland *Gent. Mag.* (1865) 700. Co. Longford *Béaloideas* 6 (1936) 264. Co. Meath/Co. Tipperary *Folk-Lore* 15 (1904) 462. Unlocated Halliwell (1842) 98; N&Q 4S:10 (1872) 408; *Chambers's Jnl* (1873) 809; N&Q 10S:3 (1905) 397; Igglesden (*c.*1932) 209. Literary William Congreve, *Love for Love* (1695) 3:1.

pins: fishing boats

A handful of references, identified by Opie and Tatem, report that it was unlucky to take pins aboard fishing boats:

To have a pin about you on board ship is considered very foolish. But no one can tell me why.
Yorkshire Jeffrey (1923)

All three are from the eastern seaboard of England, and from a restricted period. It is not known how widespread the belief was.

Suffolk *The People* (5 June 1887) 5. **Lincolnshire** [.890s] Opie & Tatem, 312. **Yorkshire** Jeffrey (1923) 141.

pins: giving and lending

The sharpness of the pin seems to be at the root of a range of prohibitions regarding giving or lending them.

Many north country people would not, on any account, lend another a pin. They will say, 'You may take one, but mind, I do not give it'.
Northern England Henderson (1866)

Others stipulate that you must not say 'thank you' for a pin. Some sources make it clear that the fear here is the same as accepting any sharp objects as gifts – they will 'cut love', or cause quarrels (*see* KNIVES: GIFT).

Nevertheless, the three references from the eighteenth century make it clear that the real worry then was that the recipient might put themselves into a witch's power:

This very old woman had the reputation of a witch. There was not a maid in the parish that would take a pin of her, though she should offer a bag of money with it.   *Spectator* (14 July 1711)

Somerset [1923] Opie & Tatem, 310. **Cornwall** *Folk-Lore Jnl* 5 (1887) 220. **London** *Observer Supp.* (24 Nov. 1968) 8. **Herefordshire** Leather (1912) 86. **England** Addy (1895) 100. **Northern England** Henderson (1866) 88. **Yorkshire** [1981] Opie & Tatem, 310. **Literary** *Spectator* (14 July 1711); *Connoisseur* 59 (1755) 350; Hannah More, *Tawney Rachel* (*c.*1797) 7. **Unlocated** N&Q 11S:5 (1912) 157.

pins: wedding

Many of the items associated with WEDDINGS have taken on a 'lucky' aspect, and pins used in wedding dresses are no exception:

A bride, on her return from church, is often robbed of all the pins about her dress by the single women present, from the belief that whoever possesses one of them will be married in the course of a year.   Sussex Latham (1878)

They are even reputed to be lucky in other contexts:

A dressmaker of her acquaintance always keeps the pins she uses when making a wedding-dress, and gives them to her friends for use in picking out horses before betting in a horse-race.
Unlocated *Folk-Lore* (1962)

Although only recorded a few times, these beliefs were quite well known, at least in the later nineteenth and twentieth centuries. They may, indeed, be much older. Opie & Tatem reprint a piece describing the marriage of Mary Queen of Scots in 1565: 'She suffreth them that stood by, everie man that coulde approche to take owte a pyn [from her wedding gown]'.

Sussex Latham (1878) 32. **Wales** Trevelyan (1909) 270–1. **Unlocated** *Folk-Lore* 73 (1962) 134. **General** *Woman* (14 Mar. 1959) 6.

plums

Not only do people count their plum stones to the rhyme of TINKER TAILOR, they can also use a variation of the LOVE DIVINATION procedure usually carried out with NUTS:

Let a girl take the stone out of a plum, throw the stones in the fire, and say these words

If he loves me crack and fly
If he hates me burn and die

Then let her mention the name of her sweetheart. If he loves her the stone will crack and fly out of the fire. If he does not love her it will quietly burn to ashes.   England Addy (1895) 84

pneumonia

Pneumonia was one of those diseases thought conducive to remedies applied to the soles of the feet.

See FEET: CURES APPLIED TO.

pointing

Several superstitions forbid people to point at things. The most common items protected in this way are celestial objects such as the MOON, the STARS, RAINBOWS, and THUNDER AND LIGHTNING, but there was also a belief that it was unlucky to point at a ship:

Novices in the Manx fisheries have to learn not to point to anything with one finger, they have to point with the whole hand, or not at all.
Isle of Man Rhys (1901)

The reasoning here is not clear. In the celestial sphere, there is a strong undertone that it is disrespectful to point, but this is not obviously applicable to ships. An alternative view, that the bad luck resides in TEMPTING FATE by drawing attention to something so vulnerable to the whims of fortune, does not seem to apply because pointing with the whole hand is permitted.

Norfolk Radford (1971) 192. **Northeastern Scotland** Gregor (1881) 200. **Isle of Man** Rhys 1 (1901) 346. **Unlocated** Igglesden (*c*.1932) 117.

porch watching

'Watching' in the church porch was a superstitious custom which was widely known and talked about, if not actually often practised:

St. Mark's Eve . . . the watching in the church porch. It was, and in some places is, believed that any one watching for one hour before and one hour after midnight in the church porch would learn who in the parish would die in the coming year. As the clock struck the hour of midnight a procession would pass into the church, infants unable to walk would roll in, those who were to be very sick, but recover, would come out again, after a stay corresponding to the duration of their illness, but those who were to die would not appear again. Those who were to be married during the same period also put in an appearance; they walk in couples and speedily reappear. If the watcher falls asleep, he will die himself during the year.   East Anglia Varden (1885)

The proper night for the custom varies from account to account, with Christmas Eve, NEW YEAR, MIDSUMMER, and HALLOWE'EN being mentioned on occasion, but the majority took place on ST MARK'S EVE (24/25 April). This is in line with many other divinatory practices in England, although it is not known exactly why this day was considered particularly conducive to such matters. Full details of what happens in the porch are not always given, but the commonest form, as above, is that all the parishioners' WRAITHS appear in procession and enter the church. Those who are to live are then seen leaving. Occasionally, those about to die are seen in their shrouds, and wedding couples appear in some versions.

Wirt Sikes recounted a Welsh version which relied on sound rather than sight:

Listening at the church door in the dark, to hear shouted by a ghostly voice in the deserted edifice the names of those who are shortly to be buried in the adjoining churchyard, is a Hallow E'en custom in some parts of Wales. In other parts the window serves the same purpose. There are said to be still extant, outside some village churches, steps which were constructed in order to enable the superstitious peasantry to climb to the window to listen.   Wales Sikes (1880)

Many of the published reports provide excellent examples of NARRATIVE superstition. While some of the sources simply describe what will happen if one watches in the porch, many relate stories of people who have actually carried it out, told in the form of a true tale. The telling of such tales, in localized versions and with named local characters, supplied the same frisson as ghost stories and other supernatural fare, and also added a veneer of believability to the belief. In the developed narrative form, one of two motifs usually appears in addition to the core of the watching itself. In one, the watcher does not fall asleep but sees their own wraith, falls in a faint, and never recovers his/her full wits. In the other, the person who has 'watched' is thereafter treated with caution by the rest of the community on account of the illicit information s/he possesses, in the fear that they will use this knowledge as blackmail or to upset anyone who crosses them.

The custom certainly dates at least from the turn of the seventeenth century, and the essential elements are already in place in the first known reference:

Katherine Foxegale, of Walesbie, presented 26 July at East Retford. 'For watchinge upon Saint Markes even at nighte laste in the church porche to presage by divelishe demonstracion the deathe of somme neighbours within this yeere.'
    Nottingham [1608] *Thoroton Soc. Trans.*

It was reported frequently right up to the early twentieth century, but most of the later references are couched in terms of what 'used to be done'. The geographical distribution is interestingly uneven, although it may, as usual, be distorted by the accident of collecting activity. Wales and Scotland are represented, but the vast majority of descriptions are from East Anglia, Midland and Northern England.

Dorset *Folk-Lore* 10 (1899) 481. **Devon** Bray (1838) 127–8; N&Q 3S:2 (1862) 62; *Devonshire Assoc.* 9 (1877) 90–1. **Gloucestershire** *Folk-Lore* 13 (1902) 174. **Northamptonshire** [1825] Clare (1993) 138–9; Sternberg (1851) 187–9. **Cambridgeshire** [1812] Porter (1969) 109–11. **East Anglia** Forby (1830) 407–8; Varden (1885) 123. **Norfolk** *Norfolk Archaeology* 2 (1849) 295. **Lincolnshire** [1634] Gervase Hollis, Lansdowne MS, quoted in Wright & Lones 2 (1938) 190; *Stamford*

Mercury (15 Apr. 1870); Peacock (1877) 211–12; N&Q 7S:8 (1889) 388; Swaby (1891) 94; Heanley (1902) 43; Rudkin (1936) 40. **Nottingham** [1608] *Thoroton Soc. Trans.* 30 (1926) 112. **Northern England** Brockett (1829) 323. **Yorkshire** Brand 1 (1813) 166; Young (1817) 882; Hone, *Every-Day Book* 2 (1827) 275–6; Brand 1 (1849) 92–3; Henderson (1866) 34–5; Baring-Gould (1874) 15–18; Addy (1888) xxiv-xxv; Nicholson (1890) 84–5; Blakeborough (1898) 79–81; Morris (1911) 225–6; *Folk-Lore* 25 (1914) 376. **Lancashire** Harland & Wilkinson (1873) 229; N&Q 7S:8 (1889) 388. **Co. Durham** Leighton (1910) 51. **Northumberland** Henderson (1866) 34–5. **Wales** Sikes (1880) 214–15; Howells (1931) 58. **Scotland** *John O'Groats Jnl* (15 Dec. 1911); Banks 3 (1941) 16. **Unlocated** Grose (1787) 52; Tyack (1899) 58–9. **Literary** *Connoisseur* 56 (1755) 336. For major studies and additional examples, *see* Wright & Lones 2 (1938) 189–92; Menefee (1989).

posthumous child

A child born after the death of his/her father was termed a 'posthumous child' and in some traditions s/he was expected to have healing powers in a similar way to the more well-known SEVENTH SON:

A posthumous child, by putting its hand on a tumour, could charm it away.

Wales Trevelyan (1909)

THRUSH was one of the ailments often cured by a posthumous child blowing into the mouth of the sufferer.

Sussex *Sussex County Mag.* 5 (1931) 122; Allen (1995) 154–5. **Cornwall** N&Q 1S:12 (1855) 37; *Devonshire Assoc.* 9 (1877) 96. **Cheshire** *Folk-Lore* 66 (1955) 326–7; *Folk-Lore* 68 (1957) 413. **Yorkshire** Blakeborough (1898) 161; Morris (1911) 247. **Wales** Trevelyan (1909) 225. **Ireland** Hickey (1938) 269; Logan (1981) 53. **Co. Kerry** *Folk-Lore* 19 (1908) 316. **Co. Cork** *Folk-Lore* 8 (1897) 180. **Co. Donegal** *Folk-Lore* 4 (1893) 351.

potatoes

A widely practised cure for RHEUMATISM involved the simple process of carrying a potato in the pocket:

Your readers will scarcely believe it, but I have heard of a man who belongs to what he would consider the educated classes, and who nevertheless wears a potato in each of his trousers' pockets as a cure for rheumatism. As the vegetables diminish in size, he believes that they are absorbed into his system, and conceives that he is much benefited thereby.

Unlocated N&Q (1868)

The only significant variation is that some people said you must steal the potato for it to be effective – a familiar motif probably borrowed from the very common raw meat WART CURE. Potatoes were also used by some to cure their warts. The rheumatism cure was widely reported in the late nineteenth and throughout the twentieth century, and is probably still in use by some people, but it has not been found before the late 1860s.

In many rural areas, farm-workers traditionally planted their potatoes on Good Friday, although there was a contrary belief that no work at all on the land was allowed on that day (*see* GOOD FRIDAY: WORK ON THE LAND). Potatoes also featured in a variety of other home remedies, including the following:

A black eye could be cured by the application of a slice of uncooked potato.

Highland Scotland Polson (1926)

This is a cure for a whitlow. Put the finger into the boiling potato water three times, when the potatoes are boiling on the fire.

Co. Wexford [1938] Ó Muirithe & Nuttall

For a small burn, my grandmother used to slice a potato up and put the slices on it, or, if it were a bad 'un, she'd scoop out the insides of the tater, mash it, like, and put that all over the spot.

Sussex [*c.*1900] Arthur

Rheumatism: Sussex Parish (1875) 95; [*c.*1900] Arthur (1989) 42; *Sussex County Mag.* (1933) 801. **Devon** *Devonshire Assoc.* 11 (1879) 105; Hewett (1900) 78–9. [*c.*1915] Lakeham (1982) 45; *Devonshire Assoc.* 65 (1933) 127. **London** N&Q 4S:8 (1871) 505. **Essex** [*c.*1939] *Folk-Lore* 62 (1951) 263. **Bedfordshire** Marsom (1950) 183. **Buckinghamshire** [1911] *Folk-Lore* 43 (1932) 104. **Oxfordshire** [1920s] Harris (1969) 113; *Folk-Lore* 54 (1943) 238. **Herefordshire** Leather (1912) 80. **East Anglia** Varden (1885) 104. **Suffolk** Gurdon (1893) 22. **Norfolk** [*c.*1870] Haggard (1935) 17; [*c.*1920] Wigby (1976) 68. **Lincolnshire** Gutch & Peacock (1908) 111. **England** Addy (1895) 89. **Yorkshire** Nicholson (1890) 142–3; *Folk-Lore* 43 (1932) 255. **Lancashire** Harland & Wilkinson (1873) 226–7. **Westmorland/Lancashire** [*c.*1939] *Folk-Lore* 62 (1951) 263. **Cumberland** Penfold (1907) 56. **Wales** Trevelyan (1909) 318; Jones (1930) 143. **West Wales** Davies (1911) 283. **Denbighshire** *Bye-Gones* (29 June 1887) 334. **Ireland** *Folk-Lore* 8 (1897) 388; Hickey (1938) 269. **N.Ireland** Foster (1951) 60. **Unlocated** N&Q 4S:1 (1868) 362.
Other cures: Sussex [*c.*1900] Arthur (1989) 42. **Highland Scotland** Polson (1926) 34. **Co. Wexford** [1938] Ó Muirithe & Nuttall (1999) 97.

prams: buying

see CRADLES.

pregnancy: chairs and beds

For at least the last forty years, it has been said, if not actually believed, that a female should not sit down on a chair just vacated by a pregnant woman, or she herself will fall pregnant in the near future:

Whoopee! We're pregnant. Ten young wives who work for the gas board all became pregnant . . . after sitting on the office 'whoopee cushion'. The secretaries at North Thames Gas in Ilford, Essex, say the cushion has magical fertility powers. Now nine of the girls have had their babies – including one set of twins – and the 11th baby is due soon. New mum Sharon Jago said: 'Every time one of us sat on it, she fell pregnant soon after'.
Essex *Sun* (21 Oct. 1985)

This notion does not seem to have been noted by folklorists, and it is perhaps a relatively modern belief. Nevertheless, it has been widespread in Britain since the 1960s, and the symbolism involved is not hard to find. A similar belief in the 1930s focused on the bed in which a baby had been born:

Last week I was washing a patient in the district when a neighbour came in. I . . . hastily brought forward a chair. 'No fear of my sitting on the bed,' said she, 'or you know what happens. I'll be the next in bed!'
London [1936] *Folk-Lore* also Lincolnshire [1930s] Sutton

London [1936] *Folk-Lore* 51 (1940) 117. Essex *Sun* (21 Oct. 1985) 16. Lincolnshire [1930s] Sutton (1992) 135.

pregnancy: parsley

see PARSLEY: PREGNANCY.

pregnancy: pendulum divination

A traditional way of determining the sex of an unborn baby is to suspend a wedding ring or a needle, by a hair or thread, over the mother-to-be's stomach, and watch for oscillations. The item will move either in a circular manner, or a straight line from side to side, and this indicates a boy or a girl. Unfortunately, there is no agreement about which movement means which sex. PENDULUM DIVINATION has been practised in Britain in many other contexts since at least the

sixteenth century, but for determining sex its first recorded version only dates from the First World War, reported in A. R. Wright's *English Folk-Lore* (1928), and that refers to the sexing of hen's eggs by the same process. Nevertheless a similar process was popular in the nineteenth century in connection with wedding divination (*see* PENDULUM DIVINATION). Only occasional published references to babies have been found since, but it is certain that the procedure was known, and probably widely practised, throughout the twentieth century. In March 2002, an expectant mother posted a message to a baby discussion list on the Internet asking for details:

Does anybody know when you dangle your wedding ring on a piece of cotton over your bump, and it either goes left – right, or round in a circle, which means a boy and which means a girl. Thanks, Bev.

A few responses were posted, which showed continued confusion over whether the circles meant a girl or a boy, but the correspondence demonstrated that this method of prediction was still being regularly tried, even if only in fun, in the twenty-first century. Interestingly, one detailed response from the daughter of a pet-shop manager claimed that the procedure was still used routinely by breeders to sex young birds.

See also OD.

All the following quoted in Opie & Tatem, 302–3: Norfolk Wright (1928) 36. Yorkshire [1950] Opie & Tatem, 303. Ayrshire *Annabel* (Oct. 1973) 4. General *Weekend* (17 Dec. 1961) 18.

pregnant women: lions

see LIONS: PREGNANT WOMEN.

primroses (*Primula vulgaris*)

Primroses are one of several early-blooming flowers which should not be brought indoors for fear of bad luck:

Death-tokens – Snowdrop and primrose equally dreaded if only one is brought into the house – because it used to be much sought after to strew on graves, and to dress up corpses in the coffin.
Sussex Latham (1878)

As with DAFFODILS, when a reason for this ban is stated, it is often connected to the fate of any chicks or goslings belonging to the household:

A Suffolk farmer's wife was rather annoyed with her young daughter because on a fine day in early spring the child had brought a bunch of primroses into the house. 'If you are going to bring primroses indoors,' the mother said tartly, 'You'll have to bring in more than that. Take them out and pick a bigger bunch!' . . . [A local explained] *'Of course you had to bring in at least thirteen primroses into the house. Do you bring less, it were no use; it didn't serve. Thirteen was the number – or more. It didn't matter if you had more; but you dursn't have less.'*

Suffolk Evans (1966)

The belief in the unluckiness of primroses was widespread across England, but rarely reported elsewhere. The earliest references are from the 1850s, but it was already described as old by then and, although the connection with poultry has faded, many people still avoid bringing the flower indoors.

Compare DAFFODILS; SNOWDROPS.

Sussex Latham (1878) 52; *Folk-Lore* 25 (1914) 369; *Sussex County Mag.* 23 (1949) 383. **Dorset** [1983] Vickery (1995) 293. **Somerset** [1923] Opie & Tatem, 319. **Devon** *Devonshire Assoc.* 9 (1877) 89; Hewett (1900) 57. **Herefordshire** Leather (1912) 17. **Worcestershire** N&Q 2S:3 (1857) 343. **East Anglia** Varden (1885) 113–14. **Suffolk** N&Q 1S:7 (1853) 201; Evans (1966) 68. **Norfolk** N&Q 1S:7 (1853) 201; Fulcher Collection (*c.*1895); [*c.*1912] Randell (1966) 97. **Shropshire** Gaskell (1894) 264. **Yorkshire** Henderson (1866) 85. **Lancashire** [1983] Vickery (1985) 48. **Co. Durham** Brockie (1886) 211. **Co. Limerick** [1984] Vickery (1995) 293. **General** Baker (1996) 126.

puritan streak in superstition

Not an ideal term, but by 'puritan streak' is signified the many instances where superstitions appear to be based on a moral imperative and threaten a judgement for transgression. Even if the moral tone is not obviously present in the superstition itself, it is often found in people's explanations of their beliefs, and examples can be found at various points in the present work. It can be most clearly seen in beliefs regarding MIRRORS where young people (usually women) are cautioned against spending time looking at their own reflections, and in others such as when we are told not to SING or LAUGH before breakfast lest we cry before supper.

The moral tone may also be present in some protective actions such as SPITTING on items which come your way by chance. This is more debatable, as there is another almost intangible principle involved here that seems to be based on the fact that the very act of *receiving* something good opens one up to potential ill-wishing or bad luck.

purses: mole or weasel skin

A handful of references claim that purses made of certain animal skins were particularly lucky. For Oliver Goldsmith's *Vicar of Wakefield*, it was a weasel purse – 'My wife was usually fond of a weasel-skin purse, as being the most lucky' – which we could perhaps dismiss as a humorous invention if it were not confirmed by Speranza Wilde. In other parts it was a MOLE-skin:

Whoever carries the paw of a mole about him will never have toothache, and whoever uses a mole-skin purse will never want money to put in it. These purses are very common; they are made like a bag, terminated by the tail, tassel-wise. I have seen them at Edgmond, but the reason for using them comes from Pulverbatch and Ruyton.

Shropshire Burne (1883)

Shropshire Burne (1883) 214. **Angus** [1950] Opie & Tatem, 257. **Ireland** Wilde (1888) 204. **Literary** Oliver Goldsmith, *The Vicar of Wakefield* (1766) Ch. 12; Strickland (1861) 319–20.

purses: string

In an otherwise unreported superstition, two informants reported by Opie and Tatem stated that people kept pieces of string in their purses or handbags, for luck.

Hampshire [1969] Opie & Tatem, 320. **Dundee** [1952] Opie & Tatem, 320.

quilts

Two references link the making of patchwork quilts and women's marriage prospects, but seem to contradict each other on essential points:

Patchwork quilt – If a lady completes one of these without assistance, she will never be married.

Unlocated N&Q (1861)

Along the Berkshire border it is said that if a patchwork quilt is begun in any house, the daughters will remain unwed until it is finished, but once it is complete, one or more will marry within the year.

Oxfordshire *Oxon Folk-Lore Soc.* (1952)

The earlier could be an example of the fear of TEMPTING FATE. The fact that they are nearly a hundred years apart argues for a more widespread tradition than is apparent from the paucity of evidence.

Oxfordshire *Oxon Folk-Lore Soc.* (1952) 6. **Unlocated** N&Q 2S:12 (1861) 490.

rabbits: black/white

A few references report traditions centred on black or white rabbits, either of which could be witches:

In 1930 I was on holiday in the neighbourhood of Ottery St. Mary, Devon, where my great-aunt ... lived. [At a local field] I took a gun up there one day and saw a good many rabbits ... Several were of a noticeably darker colour than the others. They were not black, but were much nearer black than they were to the ordinary rabbit colour ... I mentioned the dark rabbits to my great-aunt ... She said, in a rather shocked voice, 'But, my dear, nobody shoots those'. I asked why, and she said, 'Don't you really know the reason? They might be witches'. She also told me that there had been a certain number of very dark rabbits in these fields as far back as she could remember.   Devon *Folk-Lore* (1957)

White rabbits were also regarded as death omens:

I have been solemnly assured, in 1856–61, that a white rabbit was occasionally seen in the village of Churston Ferrers, and it was generally believed to be a sign that a person who was very ill, was about to die.   Devon *Devonshire Assoc.* (1885)

It is not unusual for unnaturally black or white animals to be regarded with distrust.

Somerset *Folk-Lore* 68 (1957) 435. **Devon** *Devonshire Assoc.* 17 (1885) 124; *Devonshire Assoc.* 64 (1932) 155; *Folk-Lore* 68 (1957) 296. **Worcestershire** *Folk-Lore* 4 (1893) 258. **Yorkshire** Fletcher (1910) 111–13. **Lancashire** *Folk-Lore* 68 (1957) 435. **Wales** Trevelyan (1909) 282.

rabbit's foot

see HARE'S/RABBIT'S FOOT.

rain

see ASCENSION DAY: WATER; FUNERALS: RAIN; RAIN, RAIN, GO AWAY.

'rain, rain, go away'

A widespread children's rhyme, still well known today, which invites the rain to 'go away'. In some of the earlier reports, the implication is that the rhyme was expected, at least by the children, to work as a CHARM which really could influence the weather:

Little children have a custome, when it raines to sing, or charme away the raine; thus they all join in a chorus and sing thus, viz.

> *Raine, raine, goe away,*
> *Come again a Saterday.*
>   Unlocated Aubrey (1686)

The wording varies considerably in detail, but the overall structure is constant.

In the East Riding children say

> *Rain, rain, go away*
> *Come again another day*
> *Rain, rain come down and pour*
> *Then you'll only last an hour.*
>   Yorkshire Addy (1895)

Rain rain go away
Come again another day
Go to France and go to Spain
And mind you don't come back again.
            Norfolk Fulcher Collection (*c*.1895)

The earliest version so far found dates from 1659, but as it was then included in a book of proverbs, it was presumably already in reasonably wide circulation.

Norfolk Fulcher Collection (*c*.1895). **Lincolnshire** Rudkin (1936) 14. **Northern England** [1850s] *Denham Tracts* (1895) 22; Henderson (1866) 15; *Newcastle Weekly Chronicle* (11 Feb. 1899) 7. **Yorkshire** Addy (1895) 118. **Scotland** Chambers (1847) 155. **Unlocated** Aubrey (1686/1880) 180; Halliwell (1849/1970) 147. **General** J. Howell, *Proverbs* (1659) 20. **Various** Opie (1951) 360–1.

rainbows

Rainbow superstitions in Britain and Ireland reveal an ambivalence that is difficult to synthesize or explain. Modern beliefs appear to be mostly positive, including the idea that one should make a wish when you see one, and the now ubiquitous connection between the rainbow and the 'pot of gold':

Sometimes it is said one may wish upon a rainbow; and a master at Ballingry, Fife, found his class believed that the first to see a rainbow was lucky, provided the person called out to his friends, 'First to see a rainbow'. He recollected that this had also been the practice when he was a boy (at Cowdenbeath c.1944).

Fifeshire Opie (1959)

If you ever see three rainbows, you will be rich and lucky late in life. **Somerset** [1925] Tongue

Other superstitions, however, reveal a much darker side to the rainbow, at least in certain circumstances:

A rainbow with both ends on one island is a sign of death. **Orkney** N&Q (1909)

A rainbow over a house is a sign of death.

Co. Longford Béaloideas (1936)

If two ends of a rainbow be seen in the same townland, it forebodes the death of one in that townland. **Co. Wexford** Folk-Lore (1899)

This unequivocally gloomy view of the rainbow seems restricted to Scotland and Ireland.

A further strand of tradition lies in rhymes recited by children on seeing a rainbow, in a very similar way to the way in which children have long greeted ladybirds, CROWS, and other natural phenomena:

Rainbowie, rainbowie
Dinna rain o'me
Rain o'John o'Groat's house
Or far beyond the sea

Caithness Rinder (1895)

Children also had a custom of 'stepping on' the rainbow, similar to the 'crossing out' described below. Coloured patches of petrol on the road were held to be the place where the rainbow has stood, and a child could put a foot on it and declare:

Rainbow rainbow bring me luck
If you don't, I'll break you up.

Essex [1985] Opie & Tatem

Although another informant cautioned that if you step over such an oily patch 'one will get one's sums wrong' (**Suffolk** [1959] Opie & Tatem, 322). Rainbows were also widely used in weather-lore, beyond the scope of this work.

Lucky: **Somerset** Tongue (1965) 141. **Oxfordshire** Oxon Folk-Lore Soc. (1952) 9. **Fifeshire** Opie (1959) 219.
Unlucky: **Orkney** N&Q 10S:12 (1909) 483–4. **Shetland** Saxby (1932) 183. **Co. Longford** Béaloideas 6 (1936) 260. **Co. Wexford** Folk-Lore 10 (1899) 364.
Children's rhyme: **Oxfordshire** N&Q 3S:2 (1862) 485. **Berwickshire** Henderson (1856) 135; Henderson (1866) 15–16. **Caithness** Rinder (1895) 53.

rainbows: crossing out

A widespread children's belief maintained that it was possible to make a rainbow disappear by 'crossing it out':

When a schoolboy [before 1850s] I recollect that we were wont, on the appearance of a rainbow, to place a couple of straws or twigs on the ground in the form of a cross, in order to dispel the sign in the heavens, or, as we termed it, to 'cross out the rainbow'.

Northern England Denham Tracts (1895)

It is not clear why children felt they needed to get rid of the rainbow, apart from the simple fact that they could do so. As indicated above, some traditions held that the appearance of a rainbow, at least in some circumstances, was an unlucky omen, and this could explain the children's impulse. More likely, however, is the vague idea that the rainbow somehow caused the rain, and if it was removed the rain would go too.

Two children were playing in the road, when one said to the other, 'Oh, there's a rainbow! Let's cut it'. She then sought for and found two straws, which she placed crosswise on the road. One of the straws was placed in the direction of the expanded bow, and the other at right angles to it, thus cutting the bow asunder. Hearing what the child said, I turned round to observe the bow, and the process of cutting it. Asking the child what it was for, or why she did that, she was very shy; but at last I understood her to say that it was to stop the rain. **Devon** Devonshire Assoc. (1878)

Devon Devonshire Assoc. 10 (1878) 104. **England** Addy (1895) 83, 85. **Northern England** [before 1850s] Denham Tracts 2 (1895) 58. **Co. Durham** Brockie (1886) 217; Folk-Lore 20 (1909) 217; Leighton (1910) 49. **English Gypsies** Groome (1880) 12. **Lanarkshire** Folk-Lore 20 (1909) 353–4. **Ireland** [1985] Opie & Tatem, 322. **Unlocated** N&Q 7S:10 (1890) 366.

rainbows: pointing at

It was held by some to be unlucky to point at the MOON or the STARS, and rainbows came under the same protection from disrespect:

It is a well-known belief in Shropshire that it is bad luck to point to a rainbow. It was so engraved upon my young mind that half a century has not erased the impression and even now I would never raise my hand to a rainbow.

Shropshire [c.1830s] Bye-Gones

As with the moon and star beliefs, there is little sense of a coherent tradition involved here.

Informants said it was 'unlucky', or implied that it was 'disrespectful', but exactly why is never stated, and the impression is that no one really knew. None of these superstitions is reported before about the 1820s.

Herefordshire *Leather* (1912) 87. **Worcestershire** Salisbury (1893) 77. **Shropshire** *Bye-Gones* (7 Dec. 1887) 466. **Derbyshire** [1985] Opie & Tatem, 322. **Radnorshire** [1953] Opie & Tatem, 322. **General** Opie (1959) 219.

rats: expelling

Rats and mice, it seems, respond well to civility and/or legal formulae, and a time-honoured method of getting rid of them is to ask them politely to leave – either verbally, or written on a piece of paper which is put down their hole or pinned up nearby:

When these creatures become superabundant in a house of the humbler class, a writ of ejectment, in the following form, is served upon them, by being stuck up legibly written on the wall:

> *Ratton and mouse*
> *Lea' the puir woman's house*
> *Gang awa' owre by to 'e mill*
> *And there ane and a' ye'll get your fill.*
> Scotland Chambers (1870)

In other cases, set CHARMS could be used, in a similar way:

A charm for driving rats away bore the following inscription:

> R. A. T. S
> A. R. S. T
> T. S. R. A
> S. T. A. R

This was placed in the mouth of the king of the rats, although how that creature was caught is not explained. Wales Trevelyan (1909)

More direct measures were also possible:

I am sorry to say that a more cruel superstitious practice is sometimes inflicted on the little animal; for it is not many years since I accidentally entered the kitchen in time to save a poor little mouse from being hung up by the tail and roasted alive, as the means of expelling the others of its race from the house. I trust that this barbarous practice will soon be forgotten. Norfolk N&Q (1850)

The rather obscure line in Shakespeare's *As You Like It* (1600) – 'I was never so berim'd since Pythagoras time that I was an Irish rat' – is probably a reference to the practice. Although not found in British sources before the early seventeenth century, this notion is of considerable age. Opie and Tatem quote a passage from *Geoponika* from the 1st century AD, which advises one to 'Take some paper and write these words', 'adjuring' the mice to leave.

Norfolk N&Q 1S:2 (1850) 197. **Shropshire** *Folk-Lore* 49 (1938) 231. **Wales** Trevelyan (1909) 230. **Scotland** Chambers (1870) 339. **Co. Kerry** *Folk-Lore* 31 (1920) 236. **Unlocated** *Daily Express* (31 Jan. 1962) 7. **General** Brand (1810) 107. **Literary** Shakespeare, *As You Like It* (1600) 3:2.

rats: gnawing

Rats or mice gnawing one's clothes, or the furniture and fittings of one's room, has long been regarded as a sign of bad luck, or even death:

That it is a great signe of ill lucke, if rats gnaw a man's cloathes. Melton (1620)

Rats gnawing the hangings of a room is reckoned the forerunner of a death in the family. Unlocated Grose (1787)

This notion was only reported a few times in the later folklore collections, but it has a venerable history. It was presumably behind Chaucer's comment in *The Parson's Tale*, about 'hem that bileeven on divynailes, as by . . . gnawynge of rattes', and the idea was certainly prevalent in classical times. Theophrastus' *Superstitious Man* (c.319 BC) was worried by a mouse gnawing his meal-bag, and Pliny wrote of General Carbo's death being predicted by mice chewing his shoelaces (*Natural History* Bk 8, Ch. 82). Even St Augustine of Hippo (AD 396) denounced the superstition, and added the dry comment, attributed to Cato but still very relevant today:

When consulted by a man whose shoes had been gnawed by mice, observed that there was nothing strange about the fact, but that it would have been strange indeed if the shoes had gnawed the mice. De Doctrina Christiana

Wiltshire *Wilts. N&Q* 1 (1893–5) 152. **Worcestershire** *Folk-Lore* 20 (1909) 344. **Wales** Trevelyan (1909) 283. **Unlocated** J. Turner, *Memoirs* (1648) quoted Opie & Tatem, 323; Grose (1787) 48. **General** Melton (1620). **Literary** Chaucer, *Parson's Tale* (c.1395) lines 600–4. **Classical** Pliny, *Natural History* (AD 77) Bk 8, Ch. 82; St Augustine of Hippo, *De Doctrina Christiana* (AD 396) Bk 1, Ch. 20.

rats/mice: exodus

'Like rats from a sinking ship' is still a widely known proverbial saying, which has a long history. In the earliest versions, it was mice or rats leaving a house which predicted that it would soon fall down:

It is found by observation, that rats and dormice will forsake old and ruinous houses, three months before they fall, for they perceive by an instinct of nature, that the joints and fastening together of the posts and timber of the houses, by little and little will be loosed and so thereby that all will fall to the ground. Lupton (1579)

At this stage, it was clearly taken literally. In later traditional versions, however, it is not just the building which is at risk:

If rats left a dwelling-house of a sudden, some took it as a token that the death of one of the inmates was at hand. Others regarded such a thing as a sure indication that the house was to tumble down at no distant date. Sailors looked upon their departure from a ship as a forewarning of its speedy wreck.
Northeast Scotland Gregor (1881)

Superstition becomes proverb. 'Rats leaving a sinking ship' is still a much-used phrase but based on the idea that certain animals really can sense coming disaster. An illustration from Century Magazine, *1894.*

Co. Durham Brockie (1886) 122. **Northeast Scotland** Gregor (1881) 128. **Orkney/Shetland** Brand (1703) 111–12. **General** Lupton (1579) Bk 2, Para. 87; J. Harvey, *Concerning Prophesies* (1588) 81; Francis Bacon, *Essays of Wisdom for Man's Self* (1625) in Arber 7 (1871) 187. **Literary** Shakespeare, *The Tempest* (1611) 1:2; John Webster, *Duchess of Malfi* (1623) 5:2; John Gay, *Fables* 2 (1738) 'Jackal, Leopard, etc.'; Walter Scott, *St. Ronan's Well* (1824) Ch. 25; James Payn, *In Market Overt* (1895) Ch.26.

rats/mice: forbidden words

Rats and mice are occasionally mentioned in the list of many animals whose name should not be mentioned at sea, or on the way to FISHING:

In these islands the fishermen never talk of rats as such, but when these animals are spoken of the name used is 'cold iron'. They believe that rats can understand human speech, and they dislike being gossiped about, and are apt to take revenge upon anyone speaking of them by gnawing their fishing gear, sea-boots, etc., but all is safe if 'cold iron' is the name used. Galway *Spectator* (10 Aug. 1907)

East Anglia [1953] Opie & Tatem, 322. **Banffshire** Folk-Lore 4 (1886) 13. **Galway** *Spectator* (10 Aug. 1907) 190. **Isle of Man** Rhys 1 (1901) 345.

rats/mice: influx

The sudden departure of rats or mice is a long-standing proverbial warning of forthcoming disaster (*see above*), but less well known is the idea that an influx of the creatures is also a very bad omen:

The sudden appearance of rats or mice in Cornish houses is said to be a certain forerunner of sickness and death. Many curious tales are told in confirmation of this superstition; one I particularly remember was in connection with a young man who was killed on the West Cornwall Railway. After the accident, they vanished as quickly as they came. Cornwall *Folk-Lore Jnl* (1887)

This omen does not appear to be anything like the age of that of the rodent exodus, being first reported only from the mid nineteenth century. Nevertheless, it must have been reasonably well known by that time, as its first known appearance, in the *Illustrated London News*, features in an article parodying current superstitions.

Somerset [1923] Opie & Tatem, 323. **Devon** N&Q 4S:9 (1872) 134–5. **Cornwall** *Folk-Lore Jnl* 5 (1887) 217. **Wiltshire** Wilts. N&Q 1 (1893–5) 58. **Northamptonshire**

N&Q 1S:2 (1850) 164. **Neath** Phillips (1925) 597.
Northeast Scotland Gregor (1881) 128. **General**
Illustrated London News (27 Dec. 1851) 779.

ravens

The ominous nature of the raven is a standard
motif in beliefs across the British Isles:

*Another sign of death is a black raven appearing
a few nights before a person dies. At the old
church of Bannow there are plenty of ravens seen
before a death. Nearly every time a person dies
down near Bannow, the raven will be seen and
heard on one of the old walls of the church and
he will go along the top of the wall and make
some of the most awful noises that ever you
heard. That raven is there for years and years.*

Co. Wexford [1938] Ó Muirithe & Nuttall

The bird's cry is evidence enough of its meaning, and all it needs to do is fly over or settle near
someone's house, especially if accompanied by
another, and if someone is already ill:

*John Vincent said that a man was sick at Derry
Hill. Two ravens flew over the house* [crying]
'Corpse, Corpse'. The man died the next day.

Wiltshire Kilvert, *Diary* (26 May 1873)

Similarly, the raven as death omen is almost a
cliché in literature, from the sixteenth century
onwards, where its dark side was expressed in
synonyms such as 'night-crow' or 'night-raven'.
Shakespeare uses the image at least four times,
as do other playwrights of his generation, and
later writers keep to the same themes:

*The raven croak'd as she sat at her meal,
And the old woman knew what she said;
And she grew pale at the raven's tale,
And sicken'd and went to bed.*

Southey, *The Old Woman of Berkeley* (1799)

There is no need for any other explanation
than common sense to discover why the raven
had such a bad reputation. Its size, colour,
carrion-eating habits, and raucous cry are
sufficient. Its reputation was also well known in
the classical era, and both Virgil and Pliny
comment on its ominous nature.

Sussex Latham (1878) 55–6. **Somerset** Tongue (1965) 47.
Devon Hewett (1900) 57; *Devonshire Assoc.* 57 (1926)
112; *Devonshire Assoc.* 100 (1968) 366; *Devonshire Assoc.*
103 (1971) 268. **Cornwall** N&Q 1S:7 (1853) 496; N&Q
1S:12 (1855) 37; Hunt (1865) 166, 238–9; Couch (1871)
167. **Wiltshire** Francis Kilvert, *Diary* (26 May 1873).
Berkshire Lowsley (1888) 25. **Essex** *Monthly Packet* 24
(1862) 434–7. **Worcestershire** Salisbury (1893) 71. **East
Anglia** Varden (1885) 116–17. **Suffolk** Zincke (1887) 171.

Lincolnshire Gutch & Peacock (1908) 41–2.
Staffordshire Poole (1875) 80. **Shropshire** Burne (1883)
225. **England** Addy (1895) 68. **Lancashire** Harland &
Wilkinson (1882) 139. **Northumberland** *Newcastle
Weekly Chronicle* (7 Feb. 1899) 7. **Co. Durham** Leighton
(1910) 63. **Wales** Trevelyan (1909) 283; Jones (1930) 178.
Mid-Wales Davies (1911) 213, 225. **Highland Scotland**
Kearton (1922) 58–9; Polson (1926) 18. **Dumfriesshire**
Corrie (1890/91) 43. **Shetland** Saxby (1932) 123. **Ireland**
Wilde (1888) 177. **Co. Wexford** [1938] Ó Muirithe &
Nuttall (1999) 184. **Co. Mayo** *Folk-Lore* 29 (1918) 310.
Jersey *Folk-Lore* 25 (1914) 246. **General** George Gifford,
Subtill Practises of Devilles (1587) C1–2; Robert
Cawdray, *Treasure or Storehouse of Similes* (1600) 444;
A. Ross, *Arcana Microcosmi* (1652) 220; Bourne
(1725/1810) 97. **Literary** Shakespeare, *3 Henry VI* (1590)
5:7; Shakespeare, *Titus Andronicus* (1593) 2:3; Thomas
Middleton, *Father Hubbard's Tales* (1604); Shakespeare,
Othello (1604) 4:1; Shakespeare, *Macbeth* (1606) 1:5;
Thomas Deloney, *Thomas of Reading* (1623) Ch. 11;
John Gay, *The Shepherd's Week* (1714) Friday, lines
103–4; Tobias Smollett, *Roderick Random* (1748) Ch. 13;
Thomas Tickell, *Colin and Lucy* (1748); Robert Southey,
The Old Woman of Berkeley (1799); Thomas Hardy,
'Premonitions', in Hardy (1925). **Classical** Virgil,
Eclogues (c.40 BC) 9; Pliny, *Natural History* (AD 77) Bk
10, Ch. 15.

red hair

There is a long tradition of distrust of red-haired
people in Britain, which shows itself in a number
of linked superstitions. The general prejudice
holds that red-haired people are devious, cruel,
lascivious, unlucky, and generally untrust-
worthy:

*It seems to be generally supposed, by those who
harbour the doctrine, that red-haired people are
dissemblers, deceitful, and, in fact, not to be
trusted like others whose hair is of a different
colour; and I may add that I myself know persons
who, on that account alone, never admit into
their service any whose hair is thus objectionable.*

N&Q (1853)

The dislike is widely manifest in the idea that
meeting a red-haired WOMAN first thing in the
morning or on the way to work is particularly
unlucky:

*There is a great objection to meeting a woman
when going out to a fair or market, but especially
is it unlucky to meet a red-haired one – indeed,
so much so, that many people would turn back
were this to happen to them, as the luck would
certainly be against them.*

Co. Leitrim *Folk-Lore* (1894)

This superstition is particularly associated
with fishermen and miners. Red-haired people

are again singled out as particularly unwelcome as first footers at NEW YEAR:

It's not lucky for a woman or a red-haired man to come into your house first on a New Year's Day; there'll be a death in it afore the year's out (from female servant aged forty).

Shropshire N&Q (1875)

In addition to their supposed character faults, red-haired children are said to be the result of their mother's infidelity, or of intercourse during menstruation, or to be descendants of the archetypal villains of British tradition, the Danes. The prejudice is certainly not new. Opie and Tatem identify three examples earlier than the mid fifteenth century, starting with the *Proverbs of Alfred* (c.1200), and it was simply taken for granted by seventeenth-century dramatists, in such lines as George Chapman's *Bussy D'Ambois* (1607), 'Worse than the poison of a red-haired man'.

Several stock evil characters were popularly held to have had red hair (or at least a red beard), most notably Judas Iscariot, Cain, Mary Magdalene, and Shylock, and this fact is often cited as the origin of the superstitious feeling against the colour. This may be so, but it is equally possible that these characters were assigned these attributes because of an existing prejudice.

Somerset [1907] Tongue (1965) 137. Worcestershire Berkeley & Jenkins (1932) 33. Shropshire N&Q 5S:3 (1875) 465. Cheshire N&Q 12S:2 (1916) 197. England Addy (1895) 95. Northern England [1850s] Denham Tracts 2 (1895) 24. Lancashire Harland & Wilkinson (1873) 225; N&Q 12S:2 (1916) 196. Co. Durham Folk-Lore 71 (1960) 252. Wales Trevelyan (1909) 329–30. Highland Scotland Macbain (1887/88) 250. Dumbartonshire Folk-Lore 6 (1895) 395. Morayshire Folk-Lore Jnl 7 (1889) 43–4. Ireland Gent. Mag. (1865) 700; Wilde (1888) 141, 206, 211–12. N. Ireland Foster (1951) 48. Co. Dublin 4S:4 (1869) 505; Folk-Lore 4 (1893) 363. Co. Longford Béaloideas 6 (1936) 263. Co. Leitrim Folk-Lore 5 (1894) 199. Co. Tyrone Lore & Language 1:7 (1972) 7. Aran Islands Procs. Royal Irish Academy 3S:2 (1891–3) 818. Unlocated N&Q 12S:2 (1916) 196, 239. General Secreta Secretorum (1422) 229, quoted Opie & Tatem, 325; Caxton, Boke of Curtesye (c.1430); Gaule (1652) 183–4; N&Q 1S:7 (1853) 616; N&Q 1S:8 (1853) 86; N&Q 12S:2 (1916) 128, 196–7; N&Q 184 (1941) 290; Simpson & Roud (2000) 292. Literary George Chapman, Bussy D'Ambois (1601) 3:1; Thomas Middleton, A Chaste Maid in Cheapside (1630) 3:2; Philip Massinger & Nathaniel Field, Fatal Dowry (1632) 4:1; E. Gayton, Festivous Notes on Don Quixote (1654/1768) 146; Jonathan Swift, Gulliver's Travels (1726) Pt 4, Ch.8.

red thread: cures

Pieces of red thread or ribbon were used in a range of cures, usually simply tied round an appropriate part of the body. The most common cure was to tie a red thread round the neck to counter a nosebleed (*see* NOSEBLEED CURES: RED THREAD) where the symbolic similarity of red and blood seems to be the basis, but the connection with other diseases is less obvious:

A remedy for quinsy is a skein of crimson silk, or a narrow piece of crimson ribbon, worn round the neck. If the patient be a man, the ribbon or silk must be tied round the neck by the hands of a maiden. Worcestershire Salisbury (1893)

Red thread or cloth was also commonly recommended for relief from RHEUMATISM, TEETHING, SPRAINS, and less often, for easing the pains of childbirth:

In a Hampshire village until a recent date, if not at the present time, a piece of red tape was tied round one of the thighs of a woman in child-bed, as it was supposed to mitigate the labour-pains and to prevent mishap.

Hampshire Folk-Lore (1898)

In the cures which are not obviously blood-related, it is possible that the belief is simply an overspill from the equally widespread notion that a red thread protects against the evil eye and the work of other ill-wishers (*see below*). Both interpretations have a long history in the British Isles, as the Anglo-Saxon manuscripts published by Cockayne (1865) include examples in both categories, and even in more modern times the distinction between protection and cure can easily be blurred:

Sometimes a little red silk bag containing two hazel-twigs is hung from the neck by a red silk thread as a protection against illness and harm in general. The red silk is also very commonly seen round the necks of children as a preventive of the common cold, and it is never removed, even in the swimming-bath. This is accounted for by the fact that it is also supposed to preserve its owner from death by drowning.

Yorkshire Folk-Lore (1932)

Many other accounts detail the use of thread or ribbon to cure or protect, but without naming any specific colour. *See* THREAD.

Hampshire Folk-Lore 9 (1898) 79. Essex Folk-Lore 21 (1910) 223. Worcestershire Salisbury (1893) 71; Folk-Lore 20 (1909) 346. Warwickshire Bloom (c.1930) 25–6. Northern England [1850s] Denham Tracts 2 (1895) 48. Yorkshire Folk-Lore 43 (1932) 256. Westmorland/Lancashire [c.1939] Folk-Lore 62 (1951) 263. Wales Trevelyan (1909) 311. Cardiganshire Folk-Lore 37 (1926) 173. Angus [1954] Opie & Tatem, 326. Ireland N&Q 1S:1 (1850) 349; Wilde (1888) 197. General [*c*.1040] Cockayne 2 (1865) 55; John of Gaddesden, *Rosa Angelica* (1314) quoted Opie & Tatem, 326; Topsell (1607) 536. **Literary** George Eliot, *Silas Marner* (1861) Ch.2.

red thread: protective

A piece of red thread, tied round a farm animal or a person, was widely believed to be effective as a protective amulet, particularly in Scotland and Ireland, but also in the northernmost counties of England, and in Wales. The thread was particularly effective if wound round a piece of ROWAN, as summed up in a well-known couplet which existed in numerous versions on both sides of the Scottish border:

Rowan tree and red thread
mak the witches tine their speed

or

Rowan ash and red thread
Keep the devils frae their speed.
                         Scotland/Northern England N&Q (1937)

The protective thread is most commonly described as effective for cattle, but it was also useful for vulnerable humans, especially children:

It is a common practice with the housewives [in Buchan] *to tie a piece of red worsted around their cows' tails, previous to turning them out to grass for the first time in the spring. It secures their cattle, they say, from an evil eye, and from being elf-shot by fairies.*   Scotland N&Q (1851)

Many charms are still remembered, often with a kind of half belief . . . Against the evil eye: red thread tied to a cradle, or knots of red ribbon on a baby's clothes.   Wales Jones (1930) 142

Red thread could also be used in cures (*see above*) and other curing traditions also utilized thread or ribbon of various descriptions but of no stipulated colour (*see* THREAD).

The belief in red thread was already in circulation in medieval Britain, as it is mentioned in the Saxon manuscripts edited by Cockayne (1864), although the Saxon scribes copied most of their material from classical and continental sources:

For a lunatic, take this wort [clove-wort], *and wreathe it with a red thread about the man's swere (neck) when the moon is on the wane, in the month which is called April, in the early part of October, soon he will be healed.*
                         MS Cotton Vitell. [*c*.1050]

It was certainly around a long time before that, as evidenced by its inclusion in the writings of St John Chrysostom of Antioch (AD 390) where he complains of its use to protect children as being unchristian.

Co. Durham Brockie (1886) 117–19. **Wales** Jones (1930) 142. **Scotland/Northern England** N&Q 173 (1937) 232. **Scotland** Train (1814) 27; Hone, *Every-Day Book* 2 (1827) 344; N&Q 1S:4 (1851) 380–1. **Highland Scotland** Macbain (1887/88) 252, 262. **Western Scotland** Napier (1879) 80. **Berwickshire** N&Q 2S:1 (1857) 486. **Shetland** *New Stat. Acct.* (1845) 142. **Co. Longford** *Béaloideas* 6 (1936) 261–2. **Co. Tyrone** *Lore & Language* 1:7 (1972) 10. **Connemara** *Folk-Lore* 4 (1893) 358. **General** MS Cotton Vitell. [*c*.1050] in Cockayne (1864) 101. **Early Christian** St John Chrysostom, *Homilies on Corinthians* (AD 390) 12.

returning

see TURNING BACK.

rheumatism

An extremely wide variety of ways to cure or prevent rheumatism have been recorded, but few are unique and many of the recommended items or procedures are the same as those used for CRAMP and other ailments. Rheumatism remedies can be categorized as follows: those which involve carrying an item about the person, usually in the pocket; direct application of special substances to affected areas; eating or drinking specified things; wearing special things; and purely 'magical' beliefs.

A wide range of items to be carried in the pocket have been recommended, but by far the most popular remedy was to carry a small potato (*see* POTATOES). Other items included sulphur/brimstone, NUTMEG, ACORNS, HARE'S FOOT, MOLE'S FOOT, jaw of a female HEDGEHOG, hazelnuts, horse chestnuts, a MAGNET, and a piece of CAUL.

Substances which were recommended for direct application included stinging nettles, bee stings, dog grease, badger fat, horse linament, cowpats, herring skins, and paraffin. Items recommended for ingestion included raw onions, tea made with ivy leaves, and tansy-tea.

The most common item recommended for wearing was a garter made of eelskin:

Men who worked in the dykes stood in water up to their ankles day after day and were very prone to the rheumatics, but they believed that a pair o' eel-skin garters wore just under their knees kept the rheumatics from rising any further.
                         Huntingdonshire Marshall (1967)

Again, the same remedy is also recommended for cramp (*see* CRAMP/RHEUMATISM CURES: GARTERS for references). The copper bracelet still worn by many rheumatism sufferers today also has its nineteenth-century antecedents:

the notion that a 'galvanic ring', as it is called, worn on the finger, will cure rheumatism. One sometimes sees people with a clumsy-looking silver ring which has a piece of copper let into the inside, and this, though in constant contact throughout, is supposed (aided by the moisture of the hand) to keep up a gentle, but continual galvanic current, and so to alleviate or remove rheumatism.   Unlocated Chambers (1878)

Red flannel was also recommended, as in other ailments, as was a silken THREAD:

A skein of silk to be tied tightly round the loins in bad cases of rheumatism. This I had from an schoolmaster . . . who had tried it on himself, and said he thought it kept in the electricity.
Gloucestershire N&Q (1873)

The most widespread of the purely 'magical' cures was the idea that undergoing the church rite of CONFIRMATION would help:

When I was confirmed an old woman, of seventy odd, also presented herself to the bishop. She had been confirmed two or three times before, believing the bishop's blessing an infallible remedy for rheumatism, from which she suffered. It was her last chance; the vicar discovered her fraud.
Wiltshire *Wilts. N&Q* (1893–5)

Another remedy reported by a few informants:

I was told by an old sea captain that, if you wanted to prevent rheumatism, you should always put on your stockings left leg first; he said he had proved its efficacy.
Devon *Devonshire Assoc.* (1932)

while others suggested putting your SHOES in the form of a cross when you go to bed.

The natural warmth and alleged drawing power of live or newly slaughtered animals (*see* PIGEONS: CURES) is also invoked for rheumatic pains:

When a man was afflicted with pains in his joints, a black sheep was flayed alive, and the skin, while still warm, and the sheep still living, was placed over the rheumatic limbs of the patient.   Isle of Lewis [*c*.1820s] *Folk-Lore*

Kent *Folk-Lore* 25 (1914) 367. Sussex Latham (1878) 39; N&Q 7S:4 (1887) 534; [*c*.1900] Arthur (1989) 42; Allen (1995) 45, 85–6, 169. Somerset [1912] Tongue (1965) 145.

Devon *Devonshire Assoc.* 11 (1879) 105; *Folk-Lore* 12 (1901) 351; [*c*.1912] Lakeham (1982) 48; *Devonshire Assoc.* 64 (1932) 163; *Devonshire Assoc.* 65 (1933) 127; *Devonshire Assoc.* 67 (1935) 138; *Devonshire Assoc.* 83 (1951) 75; *Devonshire Assoc.* 100 (1968) 366; *Devonshire Assoc.* 104 (1972) 267. Cornwall Polwhele (1826) 607; Hunt (1865) 212, 215; *Folk-Lore Jnl* 5 (1887) 196, 207. Wiltshire Smith (1874) 325; *Wilts. N&Q* 1 (1893–5) 9. Berkshire Salmon (1902) 420. London N&Q 9S:12 (1903) 126. Essex [*c*.1939] *Folk-Lore* 62 (1951) 263; *Folk-Lore* 70 (1959) 414. Buckinghamshire [1911] *Folk-Lore* 43 (1932) 104. Oxfordshire [1920s] Harris (1969). 113. Gloucestershire N&Q 4S:11 (1873) 499; Hartland (1895) 55; *Folk-Lore* 13 (1902) 173. Herefordshire Leather (1912) 80. Worcestershire/Shropshire *Gent. Mag.* (1855) 385. Huntingdonshire Marshall (1967) 221. Warwickshire [*c*.1910] Stewart (1971) 76; Bloom (*c*.1930) 18. Midland England *Midland Garner* 1 (1884) 23. Northamptonshire N&Q 1S:2 (1850) 36–7. East Anglia Varden (1885) 104; Hatfield (1994) 45–8. Suffolk Gurdon (1893) 20. Norfolk [*c*.1870] Haggard (1935) 17; [*c*.1920] Wigby (1976) 68; *Folk-Lore* 40 (1929) 116. Lincolnshire N&Q 6S:9 (1884) 346–7; Gutch & Peacock (1908) 107, 111; Sutton (1992) 151. Shropshire Burne (1883) 193–4. Staffordshire Poole (1875) 83. Derbyshire N&Q 11S:12 (1915) 298. Northern England [1850s] *Denham Tracts* 2 (1895) 48. Lancashire N&Q 1S:3 (1851) 56; Harland & Wilkinson (1882) 75; *Folk-Lore* 14 (1903) 85–6. Westmorland/Lancashire *Folk-Lore* 62 (1951) 263. Wales Trevelyan (1909) 311; Jones (1930) 143. Welsh/English Gypsies Groome (1880) 13. Monmouthshire *Bye-Gones* (12 Jan. 1887) 221. Cardiganshire *Folk-Lore* 37 (1926) 173. Denbighshire *Bye-Gones* (29 June 1887) 334. Banffshire Gregor (1974) 271. Dundee Henderson (1866) 128–30. Isle of Lewis [*c*.1820s] *Folk-Lore* 6 (1895) 167. Ireland Wilde (1888) 202; *Folk-Lore* 8 (1897) 389; Hickey (1938) 269. N. Ireland Foster (1951) 58, 60. Co. Cork Culloty (1993) 58. Co. Cavan Maloney (1972) 77. Unlocated N&Q 3S:3 (1863) 262; N&Q 5S:1 (1874) 204; Chambers 1 (1878) 732; N&Q 7S:4 (1887) 415, 534; Igglesden (*c*.1932) 206. General Black (1883) various pages.

rice

The only way that rice seems to have featured in mainstream superstition and tradition is at weddings when it was thrown over the bride and groom as they left the church (*see* WEDDINGS: CONFETTI), but other traditions about rice as food are described in isolated reports. Each of them has the hallmarks of a rumour or CONTEMPORARY LEGEND which may have been widely known in its day, but the paucity of references probably means that they were relatively short-lived or of limited circulation.

Correspondence in *Notes & Queries* highlights a belief about raw rice current among young women in the later nineteenth century:

In connection with the death of a young woman named Mary Cadwallader, it was stated before the Birkenhead Coroner yesterday that she had an inordinate appetite for raw rice. It was explained that many girls eat raw rice to improve their complexions, and in this case, the doctor said, the eating of so much rice had a good deal to do with the girl's death (quoting the Morning Post *19 August 1910).*   Cheshire N&Q (1911)

Hazlitt (1905) reported a belief amongst sailors that eating rice caused blindness, and that they referred to it as 'strike-me-blind'. This report is repeated in later works on slang, but is not independently confirmed. The phrase 'Strike-me-blind!' was a mild expletive in general circulation at least since the late seventeenth century, along with 'strike me dead' and many other variations (*see* Partridge (1961)) and it was presumably taken over ready-made to fit the sailors' 'new' belief.

A similar background in rumour and legend seems to account for a notion reported in 1863, that rice affects human fertility:

There is a widely-spread notion among the poorer classes that rice, as an article of food, prevents the increase of the population . . . not long ago there was a great outcry against the giving of rice to poor people under the poor law, as it was said to be done with a purpose.
Suffolk [1863] Chambers 2

Suffolk [1863] Chambers 2 (1878) 39. **Cheshire** N&Q 11S:3 (1911) 189, 258. **Unlocated** Hazlitt (1905) 510.

rickets

Rickets was one of the conditions which could be cured by passing a child through a hole in a tree (*see* ASH TREES), a stone (*see* STONES: HOLED), or over and under a DONKEY. Another treatment, apparently only reported from Wales, involved snipping the child's ear:

Before the Neath magistrates an old woman was charged with cutting a baby's ear with a razor. The solicitor who appeared for the defendant admitted that his client had committed the assault, but claimed she possessed a peculiar gift for curing children of rickets by means of this operation. On her promise that she would not exercise her peculiar gift in future, the defendant was discharged on payment of the costs.
Neath *Folk-Lore* (1915)

Walter Gregor also described a complex procedure from Banffshire, which involved three blacksmiths of the same name and an apparent mimicking of the smiths reforging the child's bones (Gregor (1874)).

Cornwall Hunt (1865) 215–16; *Folk-Lore Jnl* 5 (1887) 211. **London** N&Q 1S:12 (1855) 260. **Warwickshire** Langford (1875) 20. **East Anglia** Varden (1885) 103. **Suffolk** [1812] Gurdon (1893) 23. **West Wales** Davies (1911) 286. **Neath** *Folk-Lore* 26 (1915) 213–14. **Cardiganshire** Jones (1930) 144. **Banffshire** Gregor (1874) 269–70. **Jersey** *Folk-Lore* 25 (1914) 248–9.

right

see SUNWISE.

rings

see CRAMP; ENGAGED COUPLES; EPILEPSY; LOVE DIVINATION: WEDDING CAKES; WEDDINGS: RINGS.

ringworm

Ringworm is a fungal infection of the skin or scalp, which sometimes manifests itself in rings of sores, hence the name. Ringworm also affects animals, and humans can be infected by direct contact, or by infected materials, and this was particularly problematic for farm-workers and their families. Nowadays treatable by a range of antifungal agents, in the past ringworm was the subject of numerous home-made cures and was also thought susceptible to CHARMING by those skilled in such arts, including SEVENTH SONS.

Some years ago, I myself caught ringworm from a calf. It spread alarmingly, and treatment from a doctor made it if anything worse. But after a visit to a local charmer, it began to die down, and in about a fortnight all the spots had vanished except one isolated one which had not been shown to him. I hastily visited him again, and this did the trick.   Devon *Devonshire Assoc.* (1953)

Many charmers could cure the ringworm simply by looking at the infection and saying something. Some could even work at a distance:

A farmer on an ancient Dartmoor tenement told Miss Lois Deacon about 1952 that he had got a 'charmer' who cured his bullocks of ringworm, by telephone.   Devon *Devonshire Assoc.* (1959)

Details of the verbal charm are not often recorded, but the few available are all variations of a simple rhymed request for the ringworm to go away:

The person afflicted with ringworm takes a little ashes between the forefinger and thumb, three

*successive mornings, and before having taken any
food and holding the ashes to the part affected,
says:*

> Ringworm, ringworm, red
> Never mayest thou either spread or speed
> But aye grow less and less
> And die away among the ash.

*At the same time, throwing the little ashes held
between the forefinger and thumb into the fire.*

Shetland *New Stat Acct. of Scotland* (1845)

Grease from a church bell was often recommended for application to the sores, combining a reputedly effective ointment with the benefit to be gained from holy things:

*At Oswestry, grease (called 'bletch') from the
church bell is an approved remedy for ring-worm.
'There is no doubt, sir,' said the church-cleaner,
'that it is a very good thing for the purpose', but
it appears that the ringers are not so often applied
to for this grease of late years as formerly, for
people have begun to use the 'bletch' from cart-
wheels instead. The church officials disapprove of
this, as an innovation, and aver that whereas
grease which has been in contact with bell-metal
is efficacious, that which has only touched iron is
useless for the purpose of healing.*

Shropshire Burne (1883)

There is no sharp dividing line in these cures between magical and non-magical ingredients, as the spoken words of charm or prayer would often accompany the application of herbal ointments. Ingredients vary considerably, including soda, celandine, clotted cream, ink, onion, fasting spittle, houseleek, seaweed, powdered cuttlefish, rubbing with a gold ring or silver watch, blood of a black cat, and, as in a manuscript from 1589:

*For ringworm wash the patient's head with urine
of the ox, until the blood comes, then sprinkle it
with powder made from the white droppings in
the henhouse, dried in the oven, or with fine soot
mixed with strong vinegar.*

Guernsey *Channel Islands Ann. Anth.* (1972–3)

Unofficial and homemade treatments were still in use in the late twentieth century, and probably still are. Buckley (1980) gives examples of traditional methods of cure still in use in Ulster at the time.

Cures and charms for ringworm are also often specifically linked with SHINGLES.

Kent N&Q 10S:7 (1907) 336. **Hampshire** Hampshire Fed. W. I.s (1994) 76. **Devon** Hewett (1900) 78; [1900]

Devonshire Assoc. 65 (1933) 127; *Devonshire Assoc.* 57 (1926) 121; *Devonshire Assoc.* 85 (1953) 217, 219–20; *Devonshire Assoc.* 91 (1959) 199. **Cornwall** *Old Cornwall* 2:2 (1931–6). **Surrey** N&Q 10S:7 (1907) 206. **Oxfordshire** *Oxf. FL Soc. Ann. Record* (1956) 11–13. **Warwickshire** Bloom (*c.*1930) 28. **Lincolnshire** [*c.*1680] Peacock (1877) 251. **Shropshire** Burne (1883) 191. **England** Addy (1895) 91. **Northumberland** Bigge (1860–62) 89; Henderson (1866) 110. **Wales** Trevelyan (1909) 319; Jones (1930) 143–4. **Highland Scotland** Polson (1926) 34. **Banffshire** Gregor (1874) 270–1. **Galloway** Chambers (1826) 283. **Shetland** *New Stat. Acct Scotland* (1845) 141. **Ireland** Hickey (1938) 269. **N. Ireland** Foster (1951) 57; Buckley (1980). **Co. Limerick** *Folk-Lore* 19 (1908) 317. **Co. Wexford** [1938] **Co. Longford** *Béaloideas* 6 (1936) 268. **Co. Cavan** Maloney (1972) 77. **Co. Cavan/Co. Leitrim** Logan (1965) 53. **Ó Muirithe & Nuttall** (1999) 97. **Guernsey** [1589] *Channel Islands Ann. Anth.* (1972–3) 19. **General** *Folk-Lore* 68 (1957) 415.

rising of the lights

The traditional remedy for the medical condition called 'rising of the lights' (which affected the lungs) was to take quantities of lead shot:

*The wife of a Derbyshire clergyman tells me it is
a common notion among the miners that
pulmonary consumption is caused by the
upheaving of the lungs, and that shot is swallowed to weight them down into their normal
place. The lady says she has lately been a constant
visitor to the Chesterfield hospital or infirmary
. . . when several instances of this strange folly
came to her personal knowledge.*

Derbyshire N&Q (1885)

This remedy was quite widely known and still being quoted in the 1950s.

Kent *Folk-Lore* 40 (1929) 119. **Sussex** *Country Life* (18 Sept. 1958) 603. **Hampshire** *Country Life* (3 July 1958) 28. **Dorset** N&Q 2S:6 (1858) 522; *Country Life* (3 July 1958) 28. **Huntingdonshire** [1880s] Marshall (1967) 222. **Suffolk** *Gent. Mag* (1867) 728–41. **Norfolk** *Folk-Lore* 40 (1929) 119. **Derbyshire** N&Q 6S:12 (1885) 205.

rites of passage

see LIFE-CYCLE CUSTOMS.

robins: at window

Despite the general popularity of robins, and strong traditions protecting them from harm, the bird has also been regarded in some contexts as an omen of death. Any BIRD tapping or 'crying' at a window, for example, was taken as a death sign, particularly if someone in the house was ill, but the prediction was believed to be especially potent if the bird was a robin.

The people in our neighbourhood believe that if a robin attaches himself to a house and afterwards pecks upon the window, there will certainly be a death in the house. It happened in our house; a robin pecked upon the window and a death did follow.   Cardiganshire *Folk-Lore* (1928)

Tapping at the window may be the most overt sign, but robins simply hanging around a house was also enough to unnerve some people:

There had been illness in the house, and one or more robins had been piping plaintively about the house. (Not their ordinary song but a long drawn-out wail.) My wife was speaking about the robins to D.G.A., and she said, 'Yes, they have been crying about the house. My father and mother would be in a way. I don't mind it so much myself, I have been trying to chase them away. My father says it's no good trying to persuade him that a death will not follow when they cry like that, unless you can succeed in driving them away.' My wife adds that D.G.A. seemed really distressed by the presence and cry of the bird.
                    Buckinghamshire [1914] *Folk-Lore*

It is just possible to square the protected status with the fear of the robin, if one regards the tapping and crying as a beneficent 'call' to a new life, but there is no hint that any informants believed this. This death omen was feared in the same way as all others were. It does not, however, seem to be very old, as the earliest reference so far found dates only from 1829. It is much more widely reported in the twentieth century.

See also ROBINS: IN HOUSE.

Sussex *Sussex County Mag.* (1932) 91; *Sussex County Mag* 13 (1939) 56. Hampshire [1971] Opie & Tatem, 329. Somerset Poole (1877) 40. Dorset Udal (1922) 180. Devon N&Q 4S:1 (1868) 87; Yonge (1892) 'February'; *Devonshire Assoc.* 57 (1926) 112; *Devonshire Assoc.* 91 (1959) 203. Wiltshire [1984] Opie & Tatem, 329. Buckinghamshire *Folk-Lore* 43 (1932) 107. Oxfordshire Wright (1913) 216. Gloucestershire *Folk-Lore* 66 (1955) 324. Northamptonshire N&Q 1S:2 165. Suffolk Henderson (1866) 50. Northumberland Brockett (1829) 'Robin'. Cardiganshire *Folk-Lore* 39 (1928) 174. Highland Scotland Polson (1926) 18. Caithness [1943] Opie & Tatem, 329. Guernsey MacCulloch MS (1864) 501; Carey (1903) 506. Unlocated N&Q 4S:1 (1868) 10; Igglesden (c.1932) 76.

robins: Christmas cards

In what is probably an extension of the idea that BIRDS in the house are extremely unlucky, some people go so far as to eschew Christmas cards which depict robins:

Doreen Fleet says that whenever she buys a box of assorted Christmas cards, 'any with a bird on get thrown out' – the poor robins end up in the bin.   Yorkshire Gill (1993)

A young woman told me it was a death sign to receive a Christmas card with a robin on it. This saying dashed me considerably at the time, as I had just had cards with robins printed. However, I sent them out in spite of the warning, and I am happy to say there was no undue mortality amongst my friends that year.
                    Gloucestershire *Folk-Lore* (1955)

Although only noticed occasionally in the literature, this belief was certainly quite widespread in the second half of the twentieth century and is probably still in existence.

Gloucestershire *Folk-Lore* 66 (1955) 324. Yorkshire Gill (1993) 67.

robins: in house

Any bird flying into a house was widely regarded as a sign of forthcoming misfortune or death, but for many people the omen was particularly bad if that bird was a robin.

Mrs A., a resident here, says that every time a robin comes into her house there is trouble. She cites three instances, two in which the omen was followed by a serious illness, and a third, when robins entered repeatedly, by death.
                    Buckinghamshire *Folk-Lore* (1910)

There is no evidence that this particular concern with robins is any older than late Victorian times, although it certainly existed with regard to other birds at least since the seventeenth century (*see* BIRDS: IN HOUSE). A similar tradition pertained to robins tapping at the window (*see above*).

Kent *Folk-Lore* 23 (1912) 354. Somerset [1920] Tongue (1965) 46. Devon *Devonshire Assoc.* 57 (1926) 112. Berkshire *Folk-Lore* 5 (1894) 337. Buckinghamshire *Folk-Lore* 21 (1910) 223. Norfolk Fulcher Collection (c.1894); Lincolnshire Elder (1997) 186. Argyllshire *Folk-Lore* 21 (1910) 90.

robins: protected from harm

A handful of birds were traditionally protected from molestation – SWALLOWS, HOUSE-MARTINS, and WRENS, for example – but by far the most widespread was the robin redbreast. All over Britain and Ireland it was strongly believed that the robin should be left alone, and versions of a traditional rhyme are reported in most folklore collections.

The robin red-breast and the wren
Are God Almighty's cock and hen.

East Anglia Forby (1830)

This was taken very seriously – even by bird-nesting boys – and the robin and its nest were unmolested:

Should any boy [take its eggs], his companions hoot and hiss at him, singing all the while: 'Robin takker, robbin takker, Sin, sin, sin!' until he is driven from their midst.

Yorkshire Nicholson (1890)

Those who kill a robin or a wren
Will never prosper, boy or man

I remember that a boy in Redruth killed a robin; the dead robin was tied round his neck, and he was marched by the other boys through the town, all of them singing the above lines.

Cornwall Hunt (1865)

The significance of this protection from molestation is probably lost on the modern reader, but up to the late nineteenth century, the wholesale destruction of birds' nests and eggs by village boys was a commonplace of rural life in Britain. As Flora Thompson noted, from her own experience in the 1880s and 1890s:

The birds' nesting was a cruel sport, for not only was every egg taken from every nest they found, but the nests themselves were demolished and all the soft moss and lining feathers were left torn and scattered around on the grass and bushes.

Oxfordshire Thompson (1939)

In addition to the direct action of disapproving juveniles, there were many other penalties for ignoring this interdiction. They varied from the general 'you'll have bad luck for ever', to the specific 'your cows will give bloody milk', 'your hand will shake thereafter', 'you will break an arm or leg', 'you or a loved one will die', and, more strangely, 'all the crockery in your house will break'.

A number of reasons were given for the robin's status. There were several versions of an international legend connecting the bird with the crucifixion of Christ, which explained its red breast:

it was the robin that plucked out the sharpest thorn that was piercing Christ's brow on the cross; and in so doing the breast of the bird was dyed red with the Saviour's blood, and so has remained ever since a sacred and blessed sign to preserve the robin from harm and make it beloved of all men.   Ireland Wilde (1888)

Another influential boost to the robin's reputation came in the form of a popular song, 'The Norfolk Gentleman his Last Will and Testament' or 'The Children in the Wood', first published in 1595, but printed time and again by the sixteenth-century BROADSIDE presses. The song contained the story of two lost children who died alone in the woods, and whose bodies were covered with leaves and moss by robins out of pity. This notion became something of a literary cliché, appearing in the works of numerous seventeenth-century poets and dramatists, including Shakespeare (*Cymbeline*, c.1610), Webster (*White Devil*, 1612) and Herrick ('To Robin Red-Brest', 1648). The song was rewritten, in much shortened form, by William Gardiner in the early nineteenth century as 'The Babes in the Wood' a song which became tremendously popular and which formed the basis of numerous pantomimes and plays. 'Babes in the Wood' is still sung today by traditional singers (e.g. the Copper Family from Sussex on Topic CD *Come Write Me Down*, Topic TSCD534 (2001)).

The earliest clear reference to the robin being a protected species appears in the *British Apollo* (1709), in which a correspondent points out the 'malicious and envious' nature of the bird in real life, and asks 'why many people should have so much esteem for this bird, as to account it a crime to do it any injury'. Only four years later, a writer in the *Guardian* (1713) suggests that robins 'owe their security to the old ballad of the *Children in the Wood*'.

Hampshire [1970] Opie & Tatem, 330. Somerset Poole (1877) 40. Devon Bray (1838) 289–90; Henderson (1866) 92; *Devonshire Assoc.* 57 (1926) 112–13. Cornwall N&Q 1S:12 (1855) 38; Hunt (1865) 235; Henderson (1866) 92; Couch (1871) 168; *Folk-Lore Jnl* 5 (1887) 213–14; *Old Cornwall* 1:11 (Summer 1930) 4–6. Wiltshire Smith (1874) 329; *Wilts. N&Q* 1 (1893–5) 102. Berkshire Lowsley (1888) 25; *Folk-Lore* 5 (1894) 337. Surrey N&Q 5S:3 (1875) 84–5. Essex Swainson (1886) 16; [c.1939] *Folk-Lore* 64 (1953) 293. Hertfordshire N&Q 11S:10 (1914) 139. Buckinghamshire Henderson (1866) 92; [1910] *Folk-Lore* 43 (1932) 107. Oxfordshire [1880s] Thompson (1939) 153; *Folk-Lore* 24 (1913) 89.

Herefordshire Leather (1912) 26. **Warwickshire**
Langford (1875) 22. **Northamptonshire** N&Q 1S:2
(1850) 164–5. **East Anglia** Forby (1830) 409–10; [1972]
Opie & Tatem, 329. **Norfolk** Fulcher Collection (*c.*1894);
[*c.*1912] Randell (1966) 94; [*c.*1920] Wigby (1976) 68.
Lincolnshire Thompson (1856) 732, 735; Swaby (1891)
91; *Folk-Lore* 20 (1909) 489. **Shropshire** Burne (1883)
216–17; Gaskell (1894) 267. **Staffordshire** Poole (1875) 81.
England Addy (1895) 70. **Derbyshire** N&Q 4S:9 (1872)
24–5; [*c.*1890s] Uttley (1946) 132. **Northern England**
Newcastle Weekly Chronicle (4 Feb. 1899) 7. **Yorkshire**
N&Q 1S:6 (1852) 311–12; N&Q 4S:1 (1868) 193–4; N&Q
4S:8 (1871) 505; Addy (1888) xix; Nicholson (1890)
129–30; N&Q 11S:10 (1914) 78. **Lancashire** Hardwick
(1872) 242; Harland & Wilkinson (1873) 218–19;
Harland & Wilkinson (1882) 142; [1885] Spencer (1966)
12–13; [*c.*1939] *Folk-Lore* 64 (1953) 293. **Westmorland**
[*c.*1939] *Folk-Lore* 64 (1953) 293. **Co. Durham** Brockie
(1886) 132, 134. **Wales** Howells (1831) 67; Henderson
(1866) 92; Igglesden (*c.*1932) 78. **Mid-Wales** Davies
(1911) 223. **Montgomeryshire** Hamer (1877) 260.
Western Scotland Chambers (1842) 41; Napier (1879)
111. **Northeast Scotland** Gregor (1881) 138.
Dumfriesshire Corrie (1890/91) 80. **Glasgow** [*c.*1820]
Napier (1864) 394–5. **Ireland** Wilde (1888) 177–8, 180,
211. **S.E. Ireland** N&Q 3S:5 (1864) 353. **Unlocated** Grose
(1787) 64; [1974] Opie & Tatem, 329. **General** *British
Apollo* (2 Mar 1709); *Guardian* (21 May 1713) quoted
Opie & Tatem, 329; *Gent. Mag.* (1796) 636. **Literary**
Shakespeare, *Cymbeline* (*c.*1610) 4:2; John Webster, *The
White Devil* (1612) 5:4; Robert Herrick, 'To Robin Red-
Brest', *Hesperides* (1648).

For summary of foreign analogues, *see* Swainson (1886)
13–18.

---

rooks (*Corvus frugilegus*)

Large black birds, such as CROWS and RAVENS,
have an almost invariably negative reputation in
British superstition, but the traditional view of
rooks is more mixed, and some people believed
it was actually lucky to have them around:

*Rooks building near a house are a sign of pros-
perity.*   East Anglia Forby (1830)

*Rooks are very much liked in our neighbourhood;
they are supposed to keep the crows away, and,
as the crow steals chickens, the rook is thus
regarded as a protector.*

Cardiganshire *Folk-Lore* (1928)

In the most widespread tradition about them,
rooks were closely linked with death, but this
belief was couched in a less direct way than most
death omens. The superstition in question maintained that if the head of the family on whose
land they nested died, the rooks would immediately vacate their nests. In some cases, the
sequence was reversed, and rooks vacating their
rookery was taken as a sign that a family bereavement was imminent:

*When rooks desert a rookery, it foretells the
downfall of the family on whose property it is. It
is a popular tradition that the rooks deserted the
rookery at Chipchase, when the respected family
of Reed left it.*   Northumberland Bigge (1860–62)

*A singular circumstance is reported in connexion
with the recent suicide of Mr. Graves, of Linwood
Grange. Near the house a colony of rooks had
established themselves, and on the day of the
funeral, immediately on the appearance of the
hearse, the birds left the locality in a body, desert-
ing their nests, all of which contained young. A few
only have returned.*   Lincolnshire N&Q (1879)

On the other hand, there were some people
who thought rooks were definitely unlucky.
Many people did not make any distinction
between crows and rooks, and it is likely that
some of the negative beliefs about the former
have contaminated those of the latter.

*Rooks are reckoned ominous if they appear.
People expect a famine to follow soon after.*
Orkney [1774] Low

*If a raven or rook perches and caws on or near a
house where a sick person is lying, it foretokens
the patient's death.*   Wales Trevelyan (1909)

*We believed that a crow or rook carried a plague
or brought a disease that could kill you, and that's
why they are unlucky.*

Lincolnshire [*c.*1930s] Sutton

A handful of references relate that rooks refuse
to build their nests on Sundays or on ASCEN-
SION DAY. Rooks were also the birds which were
reputed to 'drop' on anyone who failed to follow
custom by wearing new clothes at Easter (*see*
CLOTHES: NEW, EASTER), and their behaviour
was also observed closely for weather predictions.
Only one of these traditions can be traced with
any certainty before 1800, and again this is in
sharp contrast with raven and crow superti-
tions, which are considerably older.

Rooks leaving: **Southern England** Jefferies (1879) 152.
Devon N&Q 1S:2 (1850) 512; Hewett (1900) 57–8;
Devonshire Assoc. 67 (1935) 132. **Cornwall** Polwhele
(1826) 608; N&Q 5S:6 (1876) 24. **Wiltshire** *Wilts.
N&Q* 1 (1893–5) 316. **East Anglia** Forby (1830) 414.
Norfolk [1920s] Wigby (1976) 69. **Lincolnshire** N&Q
5S:11 (1879) 506. **Shropshire** Burne (1883) 217–18.
Lancashire Spencer (1966) 9. **Co. Durham** Brockie
(1886) 131; Leighton (1910) 63. **Northumberland** Bigge
(1860–62) 92; Henderson (1866) 90. **Wales** Trevelyan
(1909) 328. **Northeast Scotland** Gregor (1881) 136. **N.
Ireland** Foster (1951) 133.
Lucky to have around: **East Anglia** Varden (1885) 113.
Shropshire Burne (1883) 217–18. **Yorkshire** Nicholson

(1890) 131–2. **Co. Durham** Brockie (1886) 212.
Pembrokeshire *Folk-Lore* 39 (1928) 173. **Cardiganshire**
Folk-Lore 39 (1928) 174. **Unlocated** Igglesden (*c*.1932) 75.
Unlucky to have around: **Kent** *Folk-Lore* 23 (1912) 354.
Lincolnshire [*c*.1930s] Sutton (1992) 142. **Wales**
Trevelyan (1909) 283. **Scottish borders** [*c*.1816]
Henderson (1866) 90. **Orkney** [1774] Low (1879) 49.
Ireland Wilde (1888) 181. **Co. Kerry** *Folk-Lore* 31 (1920)
236.
Nest building: **Devon** Hewett (1900) 45. **Norfolk** Wigby
(1976) 69. **Unlocated** N&Q 6S:1 (1880) 55.

rope

The main superstitions regarding rope are
concerned with the HANGMAN'S ROPE, and are
dealt with in the appropriate place, but three
further reports indicate the existence of other
beliefs in which ropes feature. The first is fairly
clearly based on fear of hanging:

*It is unlucky to pass under a hempen rope; the
person who does so will die a violent death, or is
fated to commit an evil act in after life, so it is
decreed.* Ireland Wilde (1888)

The other two are based on the principle of
passing through in order to effect cure, although
the effect as well as the scale is quite different.

*Whooping cough – Plait a straw rope – a 'raip' –
the contrary way, and tie the ends of it. Put the
patient through the loop so formed in company
with a cat. The cat carried off the disease, and
died in a short time.* Banffshire Gregor (1874)

The same writer describes a process whereby a
boat which was believed to have been forespo-
ken (bewitched) had a circular rope passed over
and under it to remove the spell (**Northeast
Scotland** Gregor (1881)).

Northeast Scotland Gregor (1881) 199–200. **Banffshire**
Gregor (1874) 270. **Ireland** Wilde (1888) 206.

rose, the

see ERYSIPELAS.

rosemary: wife is master

It was popularly believed that rosemary grows
best in the gardens of families where the woman
is the master. Our first knowledge of this tradition is in a query published in the early eighteenth century:

*Pray tell me the reason, that where the rosemary
grows, there it is said the woman reigns.*
Unlocated *British Apollo* (8 Dec. 1708)

The same idea was reported in later years, and
was much more widely known than is indicated
by the few references listed below.

See also PARSLEY; WEDDINGS: DOMINANT
PARTNER.

Sussex Parish (1875) 73. **Hertfordshire** N&Q 1S:6 (1852)
123. **Yorkshire** *North Country Lore* (Oct. 1890) 474.
Unlocated Hone, *Year Book* (1832) 4 Jan.

roses: love divination

A well-known LOVE DIVINATION procedure
was called a Midsummer rose or Christmas rose,
as these were the two key days in the custom:

*Another plan is to gather a rose on midsummer
eve, and carry it home, walking backwards, and
not speaking a word. It must be carefully
preserved in clean white paper, till the following
Christmas Day, and then the girl must wear it; it
will be taken from her by her future husband.*
Herefordshire Leather (1912)

Essentially the same procedure was described
in the earliest references in the late eighteenth
century, but there were other traditional connections between roses and love. Herrick linked
rosebuds with divination:

*or by rosebuds divine.
who'll be her Valentine.* Herrick, *Hesperides* (1648)

and another is described from Scotland:

*In the West of Scotland if a white rose bloomed
in autumn it was a token of early death to someone, but if a red rose did the same, it was a token
of an early marriage. The red rose, it was said,
would not bloom over a grave. If a young girl had
several lovers, and wished to know which of them
would be her husband, she would take a rose leaf
for each of her sweethearts, and naming each leaf
after the name of one of her lovers, she would
watch them till one after another they sank, and
the last to sink would be her future husband.*
Western Scotland Napier (1879)

Devon Bray (1838) 287; N&Q 3S:2 (1862) 62. **Cornwall**
Western Antiquary 3 (1883) 91. **Herefordshire** Leather
(1912) 61. **Western Scotland** Napier (1879) 128–9.
Unlocated *Gent. Mag.* (1787) 719. **Literary** Robert
Herrick, *Hesperides* (1648); *Connoisseur* 56 (1755) 334.

rowan (*Sorbus aucuparia*)

Of the various recorded traditional ways of
protecting people, animals, and property from
witches, fairies, or any other form of ill-wishing,

one of the most widespread was to use a piece of the rowan tree. It was valued across the British Isles, and particularly in Scotland and Ireland.

A horse-shoe nailed over the threshold was supposed to afford perfect immunity, neither witch nor warlock being able to enter a dwelling where this mode of protection had been adopted. By some a branch of rowan tree was looked upon with equal favour, and bundles of small rowan tree twigs were constantly kept suspended over the doorway, or attached to the top of the box-bed or corner cupboard. Dumfriesshire Corrie (1890/91)

As with other protective substances, such as HORSESHOES and holed STONES, pieces of rowan were particularly useful for hanging in cow-houses and dairies, to protect vulnerable cattle and processes such as butter-making:

The rowan was in our district constantly used as a charm against witchcraft, and was believed to be a certain aid to the dairymaid when the butter refused to 'come'. Butter-churning is known to be a 'kittle' thing, but the rowan surely counteracts the evil influence that prevents the butter 'coming'. The cow was protected by a branch of the rowan tree tied to her horns.
Northumberland Neville (1909)

It could also be used in a more directly personal way:

A practice which was at one time very prevalent [consisted] of wearing a small piece of the branch of the roan-tree, wrapped round with red thread and sewed into some part of the garments, to guard against the effects of an evil eye, or witch-craft. Shetland *New Stat. Acct.* (1845)

Pieces of RED THREAD were protective in themselves, and doubly so when combined with rowan. The tree was also called by various local names, including mountain ash, wicken, wiggen, witty, quickbeam, and witch wood. Carters and horsemen made sure their whip-stocks were made of rowan:

If your whip-stock's made of rowan
You may gan through ony toon.
Yorkshire Nicholson (1890)

One of the earliest clear references is of a similar kind, describing how ox-yokes were made to serve the same protective purpose:

In Herefordshire ... they are not uncommon; and they used, when I was a boy, to make pins for the yokes of their oxen of them, believing it had the virtue to preserve them from being fore-spoken, as they call it; and they used to plant one by their

dwelling-house, believing it to preserve from witches and evil eyes.
Herefordshire Aubrey,
Natural History of Wiltshire (1685)

Almost a hundred years before, James I had written of rowan's protective uses in his *Daemonologie* (1597), and there is no shortage of sources ever since.

Somerset [1920–30] Tongue (1965) 143. **Devon** *Devonshire Assoc.* 15 (1883) 99; *Devonshire Assoc.* 57 (1926) 110; *Devonshire Assoc.* 66 (1934) 82. **Cornwall** N&Q 1S:12 (1855) 37; Couch (1871) 166; *Western Antiquary* 3 (1883) 91; *Folk-Lore Jnl* 5 (1887) 196. **Essex** Vickery (1995) 320. **Herefordshire** Aubrey, *Natural History of Wiltshire* (1685/1947) 56; Leather (1912) 18, 65–6. **Lincolnshire** *Gent. Mag.* (1832) 493; Cole (1886) 26; Gutch & Peacock (1908) 26–7, 124. **Shropshire** Burne (1883) 246. **England** Addy (1895) 72, 79. **Derbyshire** N&Q 173 (1937) 232. **Northern England** Brockett (1829) 250; [1850s] *Denham Tracts* 2 (1895) 30. **Yorkshire** Addy (1888) xxii; Nicholson (1890) 125–6; Neville (1909) 112–13; Morris (1911) 242–3; Ford (1953) 97–8. **Lancashire** Harland & Wilkinson (1882) 72; Cowper (1897) 375. **Westmorland** Hone, *Table Book* (1827) 337–8. **Co. Durham** Brockie (1886) 117–19; *Folk-Lore* 20 (1909) 73; Leighton (1910) 45–6. **Northumberland** Neville (1909) 113. **Wales** Trevelyan (1909) 102–3. **Welsh/English Gypsies** Groome (1880) 13. **Scotland** Lightfoot (1777) 257; Grose (1787) 59; N&Q 1S:4 (1851) 380–1; *Folk-Lore* 45 (1934) 344. **Scotland/England** N&Q 173 (1937) 232. **Highland Scotland** Macbain (1887/88) 252, 261–2, 267. **Kirkcudbrightshire** [c.1730] *Stat. Acct. Scotland* 9 (1793) 328. **Dumfriesshire** Corrie (1890/91) 76. **Berwickshire** N&Q 2S:1 (1857) 486. **Aberdeenshire** N&Q 3S:2 (1862) 483–4; *Folk-Lore Jnl* 7 (1889) 41. **Morayshire** *Folk-Lore Jnl* 7 (1889) 41. **Ross & Cromarty** Armstrong (1976) 36. **Glasgow** Napier (1864) 394. **Shetland** *New Stat. Acct* (1845) 142. **Ireland** Wilde (1888) 201–2. **N. Ireland** Foster (1951) 110. **Co. Wexford** *Folk-Lore Record* 5 (1882) 81. **Co. Limerick** [1984] Vickery (1995) 320. **Co. Longford** *Béaloideas* 6 (1936) 262. **Isle of Man** [c.1850] Cashen (1912) 4; Gill (1934) 69; [1985] Vickery (1995) 320. **General** Vickery (1995) 319–22.

running water:
cures/protects

A series of related beliefs focused on the curative and protective qualities of running water:

Various are the cures for hooping-cough ... crossing running water three times is said to be infallible, but is rather difficult to manage, as the water must be crossed a fourth time to get home Yorkshire *Monthly Packet* (1863)

Several WHOOPING COUGH cures used a similar approach, and treatment for children suffering from THRUSH also used such water. Some cures utilized stones from a stream, and others used rushes; south-running water was thought particularly effective. In some of the cures which take place in the stream itself, such as ones for thrush, the basic motif is that the water will take the disease away. Others, however, appear to rely on the special qualities of the water itself.

On the more magical side, it was generally believed that witches and other evil spirits could not cross running water, as readers of Burns' *Tam o' Shanter* will remember.

Evil spirits cannot follow one across a running stream, and the water from the ford, over which dead and living pass, has efficacy against the evil eye. A south running stream had virtues in its water more than any other stream.

Highland Scotland Macbain (1887/88)

This may be why such water was thought particularly effective against ailments caused by supernatural agencies such as bewitched or ELF-SHOT COWS.

These beliefs have a long history. The Harleian manuscript of about AD 1000, published by Cockayne as *Leechdoms*, refers to running water as 'the holy drink against one full of elfin tricks'.

See also WATER.

Devon *Gent. Mag.* (1746) 645; N&Q 1S:2 (1850) 512; N&Q 1S:8 (1853) 265; *Devonshire Assoc.* 83 (1951) 75. **Buckinghamshire** [1910] *Folk-Lore* 43 (1932) 105. **Yorkshire** *Monthly Packet* 25 (1863) 549–51. **Northumberland** [1850s] *Denham Tracts* (1895) 326; Henderson (1866) 110. **Wales** Trevelyan (1909) 6. **Highland Scotland** *Folk-Lore Jnl* 1 (1883) 396; Macbain (1887/88) 269. **Shetland** Reid (1869) 22, 33. **Ireland** *Gent. Mag.* (1865) 702; Wilde (1888) 94. **Co. Cavan** *Folk-Lore* 17 (1906) 206–7. **Literary** Robert Burns, *Tam o' Shanter* (1791) line 208. **General** [*c.*1000] Cockayne 3 (1866) 11–13.

sage: love divination

Sage leaves were recommended for use in a LOVE DIVINATION procedure:

There is an example told me by one who had herself made trial of it. Twelve sage leaves had to be gathered on a given day at noon, and put into a saucer; they were then kept in the saucer till the midnight following; at this hour the 'chamber' window was thrown open, and one by one the sage leaves were dropped down into the road simultaneously with each stroke of the hour on the clock. It was believed by the young maidens that the future husband would then be seen or his step heard in the street below.

Yorkshire Morris (1911)

Details vary – the number of leaves, the correct night (ST MARK'S; All Saints; Christmas Eve; MIDSUMMER), the behaviour of the lover, and most informants said that the leaves should be collected at midnight – but the basic shape is always the same. There is no sign of this particular divination before the mid nineteenth century, but an earlier, and very different, procedure was described in the chapbook *History of Mother Bunch of the Weste* (*c.*1780). In this the sage is placed in water, which is then sprinkled on to a girl's shift, in a way reminiscent of the washed shirt (*see* LOVE DIVINATION: WASHING SHIFT). Divinations using sage were only reported from a relatively restricted area of England.

Shropshire Burne (1883) 177; *Bye-Gones* (30 Nov. 1887) 463. **Northamptonshire** Sternberg (1851) 185. **Lincolnshire** Penny (1915) 76. **England** Addy (1895) 88. **Yorkshire** Morris (1911) 229. **Literary** *History of Mother Bunch of the Weste* (*c.*1780) 30–2.

sage: wife dominant

Sage shares with PARSLEY and ROSEMARY the reputation of growing best where the wife is the dominant partner:

If the sage tree thrives and grows
The master's not master, and that he knows.

Warwickshire Langford (1875)

And as a test of the same:

After a wedding the bride and bridegroom must each plant a small sage bush. The size to which the bushes grow will show which will be the ruler of the house.   Devon *Devonshire Assoc.* (1945)

See also WEDDINGS: DOMINANT PARTNER.

Devon *Devonshire Assoc.* 67 (1935) 132; *Devonshire Assoc.* 77 (1945) 94; Vickery (1995) 328. **Buckinghamshire** *Midland Garner* 1 (1884) 23. **Oxfordshire** *Folk-Lore* 34 (1923) 327. **Warwickshire** Langford (1875) 22.

sailor's collar: touching

A widespread twentieth-century belief was that touching a sailor, or more specifically his collar, was lucky:

In a Birmingham factory, on the appearance of a sailor, the hands crowd round the visitor and touch him 'for luck'.   Birmingham N&Q (1916)

Another report, from the same year, confirms that the custom was 'all the rage' at the time, and seeks to identify a point of origin, which is unlikely to be the real one:

The Lucky Touch: A Queer Custom which Puzzles Jack in Yorkshire Towns: Touch a Sailor for luck! 'Wherever we go in Yorkshire towns' said a sailor on leave, 'we encounter girls who tap us for luck! In York, Bradford, Halifax, it is just the same as in Leeds. Even kiddies will run across the street to touch us. Do we mind? Oh, no'. A first class artificer, who was on board the Triumph when she was torpedoed, said the custom, which was confined to Yorkshire, started at a Hull party, where a woman touched a sailor's collar and then said: 'just for luck'. From Hull the practice seems to have spread to all parts of Yorkshire . . . Some of our fellows who come to Yorkshire lose their tempers because of the frequency with which they are 'tapped' in the streets.
Yorkshire N&Q (1916) quoting *Yorkshire Evening Post*

Nevertheless, no reports have come to light before these in 1916, so it probably started during the First World War and lasted for some time afterwards, being given a new lease of life by the Second. It is quite possibly still alive in some areas.

Devon [1923] Opie & Tatem, 335. **Essex** [1940] Blishen (1972) 28; [1953] Opie & Tatem, 335. **Oxfordshire** [1920s] Surman (1992) 60; *Oxf. & Dist. FL Soc. Ann. Record* (1955) 16. **Birmingham** N&Q 12S:1 (1916) 430. **Lincolnshire** [1984] Opie & Tatem, 335. **Yorkshire** N&Q 12S:1 (1916) 491, quoting *Yorkshire Evening Post*. **Unlocated** Igglesden (*c.*1932) 129.

St Agnes' Eve (20/21 January)

Agnes was a young Roman Christian, martyred *c.*AD 304, who had previously, legend states, dedicated herself to Christ and eschewed any marriage. She was later accepted as the patron saint of young girls, and in Britain the eve of her feast day became one of the key nights for LOVE DIVINATION practices:

The women have several magical secrets, handed down to them by tradition, for this purpose, as, on St Agnes' night, 21st day of January, take a row of pins, and pull out every one, one after another, saying a Pater Noster (Our Father), or sticking a pin in your sleeve, and you will dream of him, or her, you shall marry . . .

> *And on sweet St Agnes night*
> *Please you with the promis'd sight*
> *Some of husbands, some of lovers*
> *Which an empty dream discovers.*
> Unlocated Aubrey, *Miscellanies* (1696)

Some examples, as here, have specific reference to the saint, but the majority are divinations which also occur on other key nights, such as making a DUMB CAKE, throwing HEMP SEED, sticking pins in ONIONS, and eating eggshells full of salt (*see* LOVE DIVINATION: EGGS EATEN).

The connection between hopeful lovers and St Agnes was already widely known in the seventeenth century, and is mentioned by many writers of the time. Its popularity was given a further boost by John Keats' popular romantic poem 'The Eve of St Agnes', first published in 1820.

Lincolnshire N&Q 11S:5 (1912) 113. **Yorkshire** Blakeborough (1898) 73. **Yorkshire/Lancashire** Wright (1913) 261–2. **Lancashire** *Lancashire Lore* (1971) 49. **Co. Durham** Leighton (1910) 53. **Northumberland** Henderson (1866) 70–71. **Unlocated** Aubrey, *Miscellanies* (1696/1857) 131; Grose (1787) 53; Halliwell (1849) 219. **General** Robert Burton, *Anatomy of Melancholy* (1651) Pt 3, sect. 2, memb. 3; *Poor Robin's Almanack* (1734); *Time's Telescope* (1832) 15. **Literary** Ben Jonson, *A Particular Entertainment* (1603); E. S. *Cupid's Whirligig* (1607); John Marston, *Insatiate Countess* 1 (1613); *Mother Bunch's Closet Newly Broke Open* (1685) 3; *History of Mother Bunch of the Weste* (*c.*1780) 30.

St Anthony's fire

see ERYSIPELAS.

St Luke's Day (18 October)

St Luke seems to have made little impression on British superstition, although the eighteenth-century chapbook of Mother Bunch describes a love divination and assigns it to St Luke's Day, including the lines:

St. Luke, St. Luke, be kind to me
In dreams let me my true love see.
> *History of Mother Bunch of the Weste* (*c.*1780) 28

This is very similar to other descriptions of procedures more commonly carried out on ST AGNES night. No other authority claims St Luke's as a night for divination, although Halliwell (1849, 217–18) reprints details from *Mother Bunch*. The few calendar customs associated with the day are described in Banks 3 (1941) 101, and Wright & Lones 3 (1940) 99–102.

St Mark's Eve/Day
(24/25 April)

St Mark's Eve was traditionally an uncanny time in England – a night when young people carried out LOVE DIVINATIONS to conjure up the WRAITHS of their future spouses and when anyone brave enough could watch in the church PORCH to see who would die in the coming year, or engage in ASH-RIDDLING for a similar effect. The night shares these supernatural attributes with several others in the year, most notably NEW YEAR, Christmas, and HALLOWE'EN, when many of the same customs took place. Despite its popularity for such matters, St Mark's had little that is unique and it is not known why the night was regarded as amenable to the supernatural in this way.

A few examples of the less common procedures can be given:

If you watch in a stable at midnight on St Mark's Eve you will see the horses, and the cattle too, go down on their knees at 12 o'clock. If you are there and can prevent a horse going down on its knees, the Devil will appear riding on a black pig. Lincolnshire Rudkin (1936)
(see also ANIMALS KNEELING)

A person born on St Mark's Eve is able to see 'things', that is, he has the power of seeing both evil and good spirits; he also can see the stars at noon-day. Lincolnshire Peacock (1877)

On St Mark's Eve a party of males and females, but never a mixed company, place on the floor a lighted pigtail, or farthing candle, which must have been stolen. They then sit in solemn silence, their eyes fixed on the taper. When it begins to burn blue, the intended lovers will appear and cross the room. The doors and cupboards must remain unlocked. Yorkshire Carr (1824)
(see also CANDLES: BLUE FLAME)

Perhaps a surer, though a bolder way, is for the adventurous youth or maid to walk round the church, at dead of night, on St Mark's Eve, looking into each window as they pass, and in the last there will appear the face of the one they are to wed. Lincolnshire Swaby (1891)

See also CHAFF RIDDLING; DUMB CAKE; HEMP SEED DIVINATION; LOVE DIVINATION: MIRRORS; LOVE DIVINATION: PREPARED MEAL; LOVE DIVINATION: WASHING SHIFT; SAGE.

Devon Hewett (1900) 33. **East Anglia** Varden (1885). **Norfolk** Fulcher Collection (c.1895). Lincolnshire

Peacock (1877) 211–12; Swaby (1891) 90; Rudkin (1936) 40. **Yorkshire** Carr (1824). **England** Addy (1895) 88. For other aspects of St Mark's Eve and Day, *see* Wright & Lones 2 (1938) 183–94.

St Martin's Day
(11 November)

Also called *Martinmas* and *Holland-tide*. In Ireland, and to a lesser extent in Scotland, a widespread superstitious custom on St Martin's Eve dictated that blood should be spilt:

In many parts of the country, on the eve of the feast of St Martin a cock or hen was killed, and a little of his blood sprinkled on the door jambs, the threshold and the hearth. The bird is eaten on the next day. Co. Laoighis *Béaloideas* (1939)

One reason for the killing of animals on St Martin's Eve is the belief that some blood must be shed on that day. Scotland Forbes (1905)

The sprinkling was reputed to bring good luck for the coming year. The custom was already well established at the beginning of the nineteenth century. It is not clear why this day was chosen, although in earlier times November was the month when cattle that would not be kept over the winter would be slaughtered – hence its Saxon name of *Blod-monath* or blood-month. In England and Scotland, Martinmas was also associated with goose-eating, but this was a pale reflection of the main goose time of MICHAELMAS (29 September).

A subsidiary belief in Ireland, also reported from 1820 onwards, prohibited the use of wheels on this day, which effectively stopped women from spinning, millers from operating, fishermen from setting out to sea, and so on.

Scotland Forbes (1905) 106. **Ireland** Wilde (1888) 141; Danaher (1972) 230–2. **N. Ireland** Foster (1951) 30. **Co. Laoighis** *Béaloideas* 9 (1939) 28. **Co. Wexford** [1938] Ó Muirithe & Nuttall (1999) 162. **Co. Leitrim** *Folk-Lore* 7 (1896) 178–9. **Co. Athlone** Mason 5 (1814–19) 75–6. For general Martinmas customs in Scotland and England, *see* Banks 3 (1941) 177–80; Wright & Lones 3 (1940) 159–66.

salt: borrowing

Less well known than many other salt superstitions, several beliefs cluster around the notion of borrowing or giving away salt:

It is held unlucky to borrow salt. It may be begged, or if a neighbour will not give it she may

salt

Many superstitions are elusive because we lack basic information about their history and development and must rely on scattered references in which key factors are absent or obscure. In the case of salt and the superstitions in which it features, however, there is plenty of information, but it has to be admitted that firm conclusions are still elusive. There is no doubt that salt has been an extremely valuable commodity throughout recorded history. Whole empires have been founded on trade in it, wars have been fought to gain control of it, everybody needed it in one way or another. It made food preservation possible, and was also used to preserve the dead. There is also no doubt that in various civilizations, including those of the British Isles, salt was used in symbolic, magical, and religious ways. But how widely known these were, when they started, and how they fitted together is extremely difficult to fathom. The most widespread British superstition – that it is unlucky to spill salt – does not obviously mesh with any of these areas, and we must avoid the usual formula 'Salt was used in religious rites, therefore it was holy, therefore it was sacrilegious to waste it'.

The main problem is that it is not always easy to separate the symbolic from the magical. Indeed, in this context they may be inseparable. Salt was burnt to counteract the power of witches, while in other reports it was simply placed in a baby's cradle. Salt brought in by a first footer or given to a baby on its first visit to one's house is apparently symbolic of the necessities of life, but any of the principals in these superstitious customs may also have contained on anti-witchcraft motif, even if only as an added extra. Context is vital:

The spilling of salt is not here always considered unlucky, nor is it yet by many; indeed, such a belief would be very awkward for those who cure fish. Highland Scotland Polson (1926)

We must exercise caution, because salt can be used in simple practical ways, with no hidden meaning:

A general relief for earache and toothache was a small flannel bag filled with common salt. The salt-filled bag would be put in the oven to get it well and truly hot, and this would be held against the pain. Oxfordshire [1920s] Harris

Similarly, the use of salt in love-divination procedures, such as eating a salt-laden egg before

going to bed, combines the difficulty of eating a quantity of salt with its thirst-producing qualities (*see* LOVE DIVINATION: EGGS EATEN).

A few stray beliefs are given here which do not quite fit the categories discussed below, followed by a short piece from *Punch* in 1881.

'I don't like to be short of salt,' a woman said to me recently. 'They say, short of salt, short of money'. The speaker is Cambridgeshire born but has lived mostly in London. London N&Q (1937)

A tradition prevails at Shields, that when the plague raged there, in the middle of the seventeenth century, the persons employed about the salt works entirely escaped the infection. Co. Durham Brockie (1886)

A plate of salt, upon which a dead man's hand has rested overnight, used to be considered good for chilblains. Yorkshire Blakeborough (1898)

In making start for the fishing for the first time, care must be taken . . . to have salt in the boat. Isle of Man [c.1850] Cashen

The folk-lore with regard to salt is conflicting. If you have spilt salt on the table, and have then thrown a handful over your left shoulder, the servant who receives this in his eyes seldom considers that ill-luck has been averted. If you help your neighbour to salt, you and she are certain to quarrel if, at the time of your uncalled-for politeness, she is eating ham, bacon, meringues, or ice-puddings. Some people when they have spilt salt on the tablecloth, immediately pour a glass of claret over it, to take out the stain. But this is invariably late in the evening, and arises rather from a confusion of ideas than from any accurate knowledge of folk-lore. Punch (1 Jan. 1881)

See also BABIES: FIRST FOOD; BABIES: FIRST VISIT; CHRISTENING; TEETH: DISPOSAL OF.

For a general historical review of salt, *see* Mark Kurlansky, *Salt: A World History* (2002).

Devon Hewett (1900) 50. London N&Q 173 (1937) 459. Oxfordshire [1920s] Harris (1969) 114. Norfolk *Norfolk Archaeology* 2 (1849) 299. Yorkshire Blakeborough (1898) 135. Co. Durham Brockie (1886) 220. Highland Scotland Polson (1926) 127. Berwickshire Anson (1930) 38. Isle of Man [c.1850] Cashen (1912) 27. General *Punch* (1 Jan. 1881) 310.

come to the borrower's house and fetch the quantity borrowed; but the borrower must not return it. Herefordshire Leather (1912)

Similarly,

No knowledgeable person will lend salt, 'No, indeed' an old crone will say, 'I will not lend you any, but I'll give you some. Let's have nyen o' yer salt back here'. If you borrow salt, it is very unlucky to return it. Co. Durham Brockie (1886)

In the same way as it was unlucky to take FIRE out of the house, for fear of diminishing a vital symbolic element for the rest of the year, it was held particularly unlucky to give out salt at NEW YEAR or May Day, particularly in Ireland.

Compare SALT: HELPING TO; OUTGOING/INCOMING.

Devon *Devonshire Assoc.* 59 (1927) 156. Herefordshire Leather (1912) 86. Worcestershire *Folk-Lore* 6 (1895) 305. Cheshire N&Q 11S:2 (1910) 150. England Addy (1895) 98. Nottinghamshire [1953] Opie & Tatem, 340. Co. Durham Brockie (1886) 207. Northumberland Bigge (1860–62) 92. Orkney N&Q 10S:12 (1909) 483–4. Ireland Wilde (1888) 106, 205. Co. Tyrone *Lore & Language* 1:7 (1972) 7.

---

salt: burning

Salt was deliberately burnt in a variety of contexts, all apparently concerned with casting spells or protecting against ill-wishing by others.

The power of a witch is supposed to be destroyed by sprinkling salt into the fire nine mornings in succession. The person who sprinkles the salt must be the one affected by the supposed witchcraft, and as the salt drops down must repeat, 'Salt! salt! I put thee into the fire, and may the person who has bewitched me neither eat, drink, nor sleep until the spell is broken'.
Lancashire Harland & Wilkinson (1873)

As with other spell-making, there was a sense that even protective actions were perilously close to witchcraft, and therefore ungodly and dangerous. A conversation reported from Gloucestershire in 1905 demonstrates this ambivalence, and at the same time reveals different uses of similar practices:

Now I had been told that Luke used to do some protective charming every year for a farmer now dead, in which the burning of salt figured. As this is in itself an evil and unlucky thing, I asked questions, but got no answer save an uncomfortable look. But the little old woman from the other side of the hearth [Luke's wife] burst out excitedly: 'Burn salt? why, yes! you can fetch a man wi' that! If a girl have been wronged by a man, or if you do want revenge, you can fetch him back at midnight. You do make a good fire, and you mustn't speak or let anyone stir it. An' as it strikes midnight you do put the salt on the fire, and wishes him back to speak to you. An' as it strikes you finishes, and him will come, aye! – through water! No poker, no tongs in the corner, or him will take 'em and stir out the trouble you be making. That'll bring un back, it will, I know, for I did try it myself'. Here old Luke broke in, 'Don't you do it, don't you listen, Missy. They as are good at charming mustn't do the devil's work, and that's devil's work, that is'. But that the charmer himself sometimes used to burn salt in his charming is certain. I do not know if it was a case of fighting evil with evil, but a farmer's widow told me how in her husband's time, old Luke used to come and charm the cattle. He would ask for half a pound of salt and go off alone to the 'folder'. After a while he would send it back to the kitchen to be burned. But he would not tell us what he did. Gloucestershire *Folk-Lore* (1905)

As indicated by Luke's wife, salt was burnt in LOVE DIVINATIONS and magic.

A handful of nineteenth-century informants indicated a custom of sprinkling salt on the doorstep after an unwelcome visitor has left, to ensure that they do not come again (*see* SALT: HOUSES). This is clearly related to the following, noted in the 1920s:

If somebody comes into the house you don't care about, you must sprinkle salt where they have been, sweep it up and burn it, and they'll never come again. Somerset [1923] Opie & Tatem

Salt was also sprinkled on a tooth before it was thrown on to the fire, and the connection with protection discussed here may provide an explanation for why that was done (*see* TEETH: DISPOSAL OF). In a few reports, salt is cast on the fire after an ill-omened action, such as putting a lantern on the table, has been carried out, to counteract the bad luck. This is similar to other remedial strategies such as spitting after walking under a LADDER.

Burning salt does not appear in the literature before the 1830s, although salt as generally protective against witchcraft is demonstrably older (*see below*).

Somerset [1923] Opie & Tatem 340–1. Devon *Devonshire Assoc.* 67 (1935) 131. Gloucestershire *Folk-Lore* 12 (1902) 172; *Folk-Lore* 16 (1905) 169. Lincolnshire

Gent. Mag. (1832) 494. **Nottinghamshire** Howitt 2
(1838) 220. **Northern England** Henderson (1879) 176.
Yorkshire [1955] Opie & Tatem, 341. **Lancashire**
Harland & Wilkinson (1873) 235. **Scotland** [*c.*1810]
Chambers (1872) 23. **Guernsey** Carey (1903) 507.
Unlocated N&Q 1S:2 (1850) 259.

salt: houses

The idea that salt can be protective or cleansing
seems to be at the root of a number of reports
which reveal customs adopted by people moving
into a new HOUSE.

*When anyone moved into a new house, or
changed houses, a child was sent into every room
with a bag of salt, which he was told to sprinkle
on the hearths and in every corner. I have myself
been told off for the job.*

> Co. Durham *Folk-Lore* (1909)

In other cases, however, where the salt was
simply carried in, it is more likely that it was a
symbol of the staples of life, along with others
such as bread, drink, and coal.

*When people remove into a new house it is
customary to take a bar of salt into the building
before taking in any of the furniture. This is
supposed to secure good luck. When this salt ceremony is forgotten or neglected, some people, especially women, are very much perturbed. I have
discovered that this curious old belief about salt
is very common at present in the towns of
Aberystwyth, Carmarthen, and Tenby, and other
parts of West Wales.* West Wales Davies (1911)

A very different use of salt was reported once
or twice in Scotland:

*If any visitors be undesirable, she should sprin-
kle salt on the floor when they leave, and it is
certain they will never trouble her again.*

> Highland Scotland Polson (1926)
> also Orkney N&Q (1909)

(See SALT: BURNING for related examples.)
There are plenty of older examples of salt being
used for protection (*see above* and *below*) but
none of these specific to moving house have been
found before the mid nineteenth century.
See also HOUSES: MOVING IN.

Herefordshire Leather (1912) 86. **Lancashire** Harland &
Wilkinson (1873) 236. **Co. Durham** *Folk-Lore* 20 (1909)
217. **Wales** N&Q 1S:6 (1852) 193. **West Wales** Davies (1911)
216. **Cardiganshire** *Folk-Lore* 37 (1926) 174. **Highland
Scotland** Macbain (1887/88) 261–2; Polson (1926) 128.
Dumfriesshire Corrie (1890/91) 41. **Orkney** N&Q 10S:12
(1909) 483–4. **Unlocated** *Folk-Lore* 45 (1934) 267.

salt: helping to

Widely reported in the second half of the nineteenth century, the idea that to help someone else
to salt at the meal-table, or elsewhere, would
bring bad luck to them gave rise to a well-known
saying – 'Help me to salt, help me to sorrow'.

*I have heard this expression many times from my
mother, a native of Norfolk, and I well remember as a lad in that county the comparatively
large number of salt-cellars in evidence at
dinners and suppers, placed upon the tables,
presumably, to enable the guests to avoid having
to ask their neighbours to pass the salt.*

> Norfolk N&Q (1910)

As indicated in the general heading on salt
(*above*), it is not clear how this could have developed in the context of other salt beliefs, but on
present evidence it is a relative latecomer on the
scene. It is likely that Addison did not know of it
when he wrote his satirical *Superstitious Man*
piece in 1711, as his hostess berates him for spilling
the salt, not for passing it to her. The first known
reference is from Grose in 1787, but it seems well
established by its second appearance in 1830:

*Who shrinks from being helped to salt as if one
were offering arsenic?* Berkshire Mitford (1830)

It was still being reported into the late twentieth
century.
Compare SALT: BORROWING.

Dorset Udal (1922) 283. **Devon** N&Q 11S:2 (1910) 198;
Devonshire Assoc. 59 (1927) 157. **Berkshire** Mitford
(1830) 299. **London** N&Q 11S:2 (1910) 198. **Middlesex**
[1984] Opie & Tatem, 340. **Essex** [*c.*1914] Mays (1969)
163–4. **Oxfordshire** [1890s] Thompson (1943) 488.
Herefordshire Leather (1912) 86.
Worcestershire/Shropshire *Gent. Mag.* (1855) 385.
Warwickshire Langford (1875) 11; N&Q 11S:2 (1910) 198.
Northamptonshire N&Q 11S:2 (1910) 198. **East Anglia**
N&Q 4S:2 (1868) 221; Varden (1885) 113. **Norfolk**
Fulcher Collection (*c.*1895); N&Q 11S:2 (1910) 198.
Lincolnshire *Grantham Jnl* (29 June 1878); N&Q 11S:2
(1910) 198. **Cheshire** N&Q 11S:2 (1910) 150.
Staffordshire Poole (1875) 79. **England** Addy (1895) 97.
Derbyshire *Folk-Lore Jnl* 2 (1884) 280. **Northern
England** Henderson (1866) 89. **Yorkshire** Nicholson
(1890) 43. **Lancashire** [*c.*1914] Corbridge (1964) 156–60.
Cumberland Gibson (1858) 106. **Co. Durham** Leighton
(1910) 61. **West Wales** Davies (1911) 216. **Scotland** N&Q
1S:12 (1855) 200; [1983] Opie & Tatem, 340. **Highland
Scotland** Macbain (1887/8) 269. **Unlocated** Grose (1787)
65–6; N&Q 1S:7 (1853) 153.

salt: placed on corpse

In times when corpses were routinely kept in the house for the interval between death and burial, various conventions and rituals were followed, on both the practical and symbolic level. A widespread practice was to place a dish of salt on the breast of the corpse, as soon as possible after death, and it remained there until the body was placed in the coffin.

I remember to have seen hanging up in the entrance of a relative's home at Clapham, many years ago, a large brass shallow dish, with a representation (cast in the metal) of Adam, Eve, the serpent, the tree, etc. Inquiring the use of so curious-looking an article, I was told that such vessels were not uncommon in the houses of old families in Hertfordshire, and it was generally placed, filled with salt, immediately after death upon the breast of the deceased member of the family.

Hertfordshire N&Q (1855)

This ornate vessel is unusual: most reports simply say a pewter or wooden plate or dish was used. Some informants also reported a turf, or a small quantity of earth, in addition to the salt, or a bowl of water on the floor underneath:

On the death of a Highlander . . . the friends lay on the breast of the deceased a wooden platter containing a small quantity of salt and earth, unmixed. The earth, an emblem of an corruptible body; the salt, an emblem of the immortal soul.

Highland Scotland Pennant (1771)

Where a reason for the practice was stated, informants gave overwhelmingly practical explanations. It would keep the body from swelling, keep the body sweet, and so on.

The custom of placing a plate of salt on the breast of a corpse is occasionally observed in Sussex. I saw it done in this village a day or two ago, and was told that it was to prevent the corpse swelling.

Sussex N&Q (1882)

Nevertheless, there were also symbolic aspects, as mentioned by Pennant: the preservative qualities of salt made it an ideal symbol of eternity, and a few informants specifically stated that the salt helped to keep away evil spirits. The latter, despite being in decided minority, have been taken up and magnified by many writers on superstition who have presumed a magical impetus to the whole proceeding, but this is not borne out by the mass of the evidence.

The connection between salt and death is not hard to explain on the practical level. All communities would have been familiar with salt as a preservative of meat and fish. It was also used in earlier times as the basic ingredient for embalming and semi-embalming processes necessary when bodies were to be kept on show, or transported some distance before burial. This type of treatment would necessarily be restricted to the rich and famous, and is unlikely to have engendered the salt-on-the-breast custom. Nevertheless, it may have contributed to a popular connection between salt and death.

The practice of placing salt on a corpse was extremely widespread, being reported from every quarter of Britain and Ireland, from its first mention by Pennant in 1771 until well into the twentieth century.

The supposed close connection between this custom and the use of salt in other contexts in the presence of the deceased assumed by some authorities has also led to unwarranted speculation on ancient magical origins. Superficial similarities with mourners eating bread and salt, which took place in some communities, and the figure of the SIN-EATER have not shed any light on the origin or development of the bowl of salt.

Sussex N&Q 6S:6 (1882) 335. **Dorset** Udal (1922) 185. **Somerset** N&Q 1S:11 (1855) 7; *Folk-Lore* 34 (1923) 165; Kettlewell (1927) 34. **Hertfordshire** N&Q 1S:11 (1855) 55; Gomme Collection: Corres., Frances Atkinson (30 Sept. 1892). **Oxfordshire** [1880s/1906] Thompson (1943) 320. Herefordshire Leather (1912) 120. **Huntingdonshire** [1880s] Marshall (1967) 248. **East Anglia** Forby (1830) 426. **Suffolk** Evans (1965) 217. **Norfolk** *Folk-Lore* 40 (1929) 123. **Leicestershire** *Gent. Mag.* (1785) 603. **England** Addy (1895) 90. **Derbyshire** Addy (1895) 123. **Northern England** [1850s] *Denham Tracts* 2 (1895) 73. **Yorkshire** [*c.*1828] Home (1915) 216; *Leeds Mercury* (4 Oct. 1879). **Lancashire** N&Q 4S:6 (1870) 211. **Cumberland** Penfold (1907) 60; *Folk-Lore* 31 (1920) 154. **Co. Durham** Brockie (1886) 200; Leighton (1910) 51. **Wales** N&Q 1S:4 (1851) 163; Trevelyan (1909) 275. **Monmouthshire** *Folk-Lore* 16 (1905) 66. **Montgomeryshire** Hamer (1877) 258. **Anglesey** [*c.*1920] *Gwerin* 2 (1959) 176. **Highland Scotland** Pennant (1771) 69; Macbain (1887/88) 254–5. **S. W. Scotland** *Folk-Lore Jnl* 3 (1885) 281; Wood (1911) 219. **Dumfriesshire** Shaw (1890) 10; Corrie (1890/91) 44. **Aberdeenshire** [*c.*1890] Milne (1987) 2. **Galloway** Mactaggart (1824) 210. **Orkney** Firth (1920) 84. **Ireland** N&Q 1S:10 (1854) 395. **N. Ireland** Foster (1951) 22.

salt: protective

Salt had a symbolic protective role in a range of contexts (*see also* SALT: BURNING). Some writers, such as Scot (1584) and Aubrey (1686), stated that it was specifically consecrated salt, like Holy water, which was useful against witchcraft, but later sources speak of salt as effective in its own right. Two everyday things which needed protection were newborn babies and calves:

It was customary to place a small; bag of salt in the cradle until the babe was baptised, to protect the babe from witches.   Wales Trevelyan (1909)

Only five years ago I had a cow that took milk-fever after calving. An elderly woman immediately asked if we had been careful to rub a pinch of salt along her back at the moment she calved.   Northumberland [c.1850] *Denham Tracts*

The use of salt in religious and magical rites is amply recorded in early history, and there are numerous examples in classical and biblical sources. For example, the protection of babies mentioned above, and the use of salt in baptism, may be based on a literal reading of Ezekiel 15:8:

And as for thy nativity, in the day thou wast born thy navel was not cut, neither wast thou washed in water to supple thee; thou wast not salted at all nor swaddled at all.

Norfolk *Norfolk Archaeology* 2 (1849) 299. **Northumberland** [c.1850] *Denham Tracts* (1895) 365; Bigge (1860–62) 93; Neville (1909) 113. **Wales** Trevelyan (1909) 267; *Sunday Times* (19 Feb. 1950) 5. **Western Scotland** *Athenaeum* (1846) 988; Napier (1879) 30, 36–7. **Stirlingshire** *Stat. Acct Scotland* 16 (1795) 121–2. **Ireland** William Camden, *Britannia* (1586); Wilde (1888) 204. **Isle of Man** Waldron (1744) 143. **General** Hamilton, *Catechisme* (1551) 131, quoted Opie & Tatem, 341; Scot (1584) Bk 12, Ch. 20; Aubrey, *Remaines* (1686/1880) 121.

salt: spilling

The bad luck consequent on spilling salt is one of the best-known superstitions in the British Isles today. It is likely that every adult knows it, even if they do not believe it.

If salt be accidentally overturned, it is unlucky for the person towards whom it falls. But if that person, without hesitation or remark, take up a single pinch of salt between the finger and thumb of his right hand, and cast it over his left shoulder, the threatened misfortune will be averted.   Lincolnshire *Gent. Mag.* (1833)

The belief has remained basically the same for over 400 years, but there have been some changes in that time.

According to the available evidence – and we have more for this superstition than for most others – the history and development of the belief is interesting, but inconclusive. The earliest recorded example is from Reginald Scot's *Discoverie of Witchcraft* of 1584:

Amongst us there be manie women, and effinat men (marie papists alwaies, as by their superstition may appeere) that make great divinations upon the shedding of salt, wine, etc.   Scot (1584)

The next two references – Gifford (1587) and Nashe (1594) – follow soon afterwards, and we can take this as evidence that it was already well known at the time, or even that it was new and 'in fashion'. From then on it is reported regularly up to the present day.

One feature of the earlier references (as shown in the first quotation above) that has now been forgotten is that it was only unlucky for the person *towards* whom the salt fell. This motif is mentioned regularly from 1587 to 1833, but then seems to disappear. Another change is that earlier references often threatened an argument or quarrel as the result of the spillage, whereas it is now universally simply bad luck. Occasional references in the late nineteenth century said that every grain of spilt salt represents a tear to be cried later.

The modern way to avoid the promised ill-luck is to throw a pinch over your shoulder (most people stipulate the left shoulder). An alternative method was to throw a pinch into the fire. This is first mentioned in 1711 but a later reference (1771) combines the two and instructs the salt spiller to throw it *over their shoulder into the fire.* The fire motif continued to be cited occasionally into the 1880s, but the shoulder motif is quoted far more often (*compare* SALT: BURNING).

One modern explanation of the shoulder action is that the Devil sits on your left shoulder, and the salt will blind him. The notion that the thrown salt blinds the Devil goes back to at least the 1920s, but the motif of the Devil sitting on the left shoulder is much more recent and was probably invented simply to explain the throwing. Many writers confidently state that the salt-spilling superstition originated at the Last Supper, at which, we are told, Judas Iscariot upset the salt, and it was henceforth deemed unlucky. It is repeatedly claimed that Leonardo da Vinci's painting of the Last Supper shows this, but it does not. This origin explanation was already current in 1865, when *Notes & Queries* contributors discussed the matter, but it has nothing in its favour and, as usual, does not explain the 1,500-year gap between the supposed origin and the first verifiable reference. There appears to be no precedent for this superstition in the classical era. The real origin therefore remains unknown.

The ban on spilling salt only seems to have applied to *accidental* spillages. There are several other traditions in which salt was thrown (e.g. as a welcome, like confetti, or into the fire to cast spells or protect) or scattered (*see* SALT: HOUSES).

Sussex Latham (1878) 12. **Somerset** Poole (1877) 41; [1923] Opie & Tatem, 343; Tongue (1965) 143. **Dorset** Udal (1922) 283; *Dorset Year Book* (1961–2) 73. **Devon** N&Q 1S:6 (1852) 193; Hewett (1900) 53; N&Q 10S:12 (1909) 66. **Cornwall** Hunt (1865) 241; *Old Cornwall* 2 (1931–6) 38. **Wiltshire** Smith (1874) 329; *Wilts. N&Q* 1 (1893–5) 103. **Berkshire** Mitford (1830) 301. **London** *Observer Supp.* (24 Nov. 1968) 12. **Essex** [*c*.1920] Ketteridge & Mays (1972) 142. **Oxfordshire** [*c*.1850s] Plowman (1919) 117; [pre-1900] *Folk-Lore* 24 (1913) 90; [1920s] Surman (1992) 61–2; Harris (1969) 125. **Herefordshire** Leather (1912) 86. **Worcestershire** Salisbury (1893) 71; Berkeley & Jenkins (1932) 35. **Warwickshire** Langford (1875) 11; [*c*.1924] Hewins (1985) 93. **Bedfordshire** *Folk-Lore* 37 (1926) 77. **Cambridgeshire** *Folk-Lore* 25 (1914) 365. **East Anglia** N&Q 4S:2 (1868) 554; Varden (1885) 113. **Suffolk** *Moor* (1823) 384; *Folk-Lore* 35 (1924) 350. **Norfolk** *Norfolk Archaeology* 2 (1849) 296. **Lincolnshire** *Gent. Mag.* (1833) 590–3; Swaby (1891) 91; Good (1900) 108; Rudkin (1936) 17; [1940s] Sutton (1992) 127–8. **Shropshire** Burne (1883) 278. **Staffordshire** Hackwood (1924) 149. **England** Addy (1895) 96–7, 143. **Derbyshire** *Folk-Lore Jnl* 2 (1884) 280. **Nottinghamshire** [1987] Opie & Tatem, 343. **Northern England** Brockett (1829) 285; Henderson (1866) 89; N&Q 12S:10 (1922) 477. **Yorkshire** N&Q 1S:6 (1852) 311–12; *Leeds Mercury* (4 Oct. 1879); Nicholson (1890) 43; N&Q 12S:10 (1922) 431; *Folk-Lore* 43 (1932) 253. **Yorkshire/Lancashire** [*c*.1915] Corbridge (1964) 156–60. **Co. Durham** Brockie (1886) 212; Leighton (1910) 61. **Northumberland** Neville (1909) 110–11; Bosanquet (1929) 76. **Wales** Trevelyan (1909) 328–9. **West Wales** Davies (1911) 216. **Western Scotland** Napier (1879) 139–40. **Highland Scotland** Macbain (1887/88) 262, 269; Polson (1926) 127. **Dumfriesshire** Shaw (1890) 13. **Orkney** N&Q 10S:12 (1909) 483–4. **Ireland** N&Q 3S:7 (1865) 385; Wilde (1888) 205. **Co. Longford** *Béaloideas* 6 (1936) 264. **Co. Tyrone** *Lore & Language* 1:7 (1972) 12. **Jersey** *Folk-Lore* 25 (1914) 246. **Unlocated** N&Q 1S:2 (1850) 150; N&Q 12S:11 (1922) 94, 196; Igglesden (*c*.1932) 53. **General** Scot (1584) Bk 11, Ch. 15; George Gifford, *Subtill Practises of Devilles* (1587) C2; Thomas Nashe, *Terrors on the Night* (1594); Joseph Hall, *Characters of Vertues and Vices* (1608) 'Superstitious Man'; Thomas Cooper, *Mystery of Witchcraft* (1617) 137, quoted Sternberg (1851); Melton (1620); Nathaniel Home, *Daemonologie and Theologie* (1650) 58–60; Gaule, *Mag-astro-mances* (1652) 320; *British Apollo* (1708); Bourne (1725); Brand (1810) 97; Thomas Pennant, *Journey from Chester to London* (1771) 31; *Gent. Mag.* (1796) 636; Brand 3 (1849) 160–9; *Punch* (1 Jan. 1881) 310; Foli (1902) 107; N&Q 12S:10 (1922) 477; Hoggart (1957) Ch. 2; Literary George Wither, *Abuses Stript an Whipt* (1613) 2:1; John Webster, *Duchess of Malfi* (1623) 2:3; William Congreve, *Love for Love* (1695) 3:1; Addison, *Spectator* (8 Mar. 1711); John Gay, 'The Farmer's Wife and the Raven', *Fables* (1727); Swift (1738); *Connoisseur* 59 (1755) 353; *Old Women's Sayings* (*c*.1835). **Italy** N&Q 2S:12 (1861) 490.

saucepans

A number of household items, such as SHOES, UMBRELLAS, and BELLOWS should not be placed on a TABLE, for fear of ill luck, but one informant claimed this even extended to saucepans:

In December 1936 I took to a Torquay house a milk-saucepan as a small gift, and the recipient exclaimed: 'Don't put it on the table or there'll be a quarrel!' The same result, they said, follows a crossed knife and fork.

Devon *Devonshire Assoc.* 70 (1938) 116

Saviour's Letters

A Copy of a Letter by our Saviour Jesus Christ was an extremely popular BROADSIDE, first issued in the late eighteenth century but kept in print throughout the nineteenth century by many of the leading printers. The sheet was elevated to the status of a charm and was hung above the bed in many cottages:

Amongst her treasures she has two old broadsides which she calls 'Saviour's Letters'. They are the well-known apocryphal Letter of Agbarus of Edessa, and they were used by her mother and grand-mother as charms against illness, and were pinned inside their dresses to ensure safety in childbirth. I have heard of instances of these particular broad-sides being used as charms in other cottages in South Berkshire, but this is the only case in which I have found them still in existence. Even the oldest inhabitants can generally only remember their parents or grandparents having them. The old woman in question keeps hers carefully in the family Bible. **Berkshire** Salmon (1902)

Wiltshire N&Q 2S:1 (1856) 331. **Berkshire** Salmon (1902) 423–4. **Herefordshire** Leather (1912) 112, 259 (includes facsimile of the broadside). **Wales** *Bye-Gones* (30 Nov., June 1887) 461–2.

scalds

see BURNS/SCALDS.

scarlet fever

Scarlet fever is not mentioned specifically in many folk cures, and where it is named the remedy is usually one that is also prescribed for other fevers, such as peeled ONIONS to draw away the germs, and passing the sufferer over and under a DONKEY as in WHOOPING COUGH cures. The disease bought out an interesting attempt at a homemade charm in one case:

When I was a child there was an outbreak of scarlet fever in the district. I well remember my nurse writing texts – or as she called them 'textses' – from the Bible, and making a little bag to hold them and hanging it round my neck. When I say texts, they were really extracts from the Old Testament, genealogies containing strange names, perhaps a suggestion of the 'abracadabra' plague charms. My mother, considering this superstitious, removed them, but they were soon replaced with fresh texts, by my nurse.
Shropshire *Folk-Lore* (1938)

The principle of LIKE CURES LIKE dictated that the colour red should feature strongly in any cure for scarlet fever:

In 1859 a doctor of the old school ordered a patient suffering from scarlet fever to be dressed in red night and day clothing. Red curtains were suspended from the window-pole, and the old-fashioned four-posted bedstead was draped with red material. Smallpox patients were also enveloped in red, and red blinds or curtains were drawn across the windows. At the first approach of scarlet fever or smallpox, the person was subjected to red treatment. There was an old superstition that if scarlet fever or small-pox were epidemic, red flannel worn around the neck, or next to the skin on any part of the body, warded away the disease. Even in the present day the peasantry of Wales cling very closely to the old superstition about a bit of red flannel as a preventive against fever, smallpox, and rheumatism
Wales Trevelyan (1909)

Devon *Devonshire Assoc.* 91 (1959) 199. **Warwickshire** Bloom (*c*.1930) 29–30. **Shropshire** *Folk-Lore* 49 (1938) 228. **Yorkshire** *Folk-Lore* 8 (1897) 386. **Wales** Trevelyan (1909) 311. **Ireland** N&Q 1S:6 (1852) 600.

schoolchildren: caning

Schoolchildren had strategies for coping with their particular occupational hazard: being caned. They firmly believed that placing a hair across their palm would not only alleviate the pain but also split the teacher's cane:

In the Victorian era the cane . . . was in the hands of almost every pedagogue, and the myth that a few hairs from the head – not necessarily from one's own head – laid upon the palm of the hand before receiving the chastisement, would be effectual in mitigating the punishment, was almost universal . . . It was supposed that the hairs had

the effect of splitting the cane, and thus making the punishment ineffective.   Unlocated N&Q (1915)

One variation on the same theme held that the hair had to be inserted into the cane somehow. Other children believed that rubbing the palm, or the cane, with a raw onion, or simply spitting on the hand had a similar effect.

These beliefs were widely known in late nineteenth and early twentieth centuries, but there is no evidence that they existed before the 1870s. A report on *Notes and Queries* (1915) showed that the hair belief was also known in New Hampshire.

Cornwall *Folk-Lore Jnl* 5 (1887) 214. **England** Addy (1895) 78. **Derbyshire** [1890s] Uttley (1946) 126. **Derbyshire:** N&Q 11S:11 (1915) 409–10. **Yorkshire** Nicholson (1890) 42–3. **Lancashire** Harland & Wilkinson (1873) 224. **Co. Tyrone** *Lore & Language* 1:7 (1972) 12. **Co. Antrim** N&Q 11S:11 (1915) 277. **Unlocated** N&Q 11S:11 (1915) 347. **General** Opie (1959) 375. Literary, Jones (1954) 15–17. **USA** N&Q 11S:11 (1915) 277–8.

scissors: dropped

Dropping a pair of scissors has been deemed significant by many people since the late nineteenth century – especially by dressmakers and others for whom they are basic tools of the trade. There is little agreement, however, on the exact meaning:

If you drop a pair of scissors and they stand up on their double point, you will hear of a wedding, but, if only on one point, it is a sign of death.
Worcestershire *Folk-Lore* (1909)

If a pair of scissors, a knife, or a needle falls to the floor and sticks in an upright position, an unexpected guest will arrive ere long.
Argyllshire *Folk-Lore* (1910)

[Milliner's workshop, interwar years] . . . *but when your scissors came apart it foretold a death. The girl who drops her scissors must never pick them up. She must ask a companion to do so. Then too the exact way in which they fell must be noted. If the points stick into the floor, somebody is going to leave.*   London Henrey (1955)

The notion that it is unlucky to pick up dropped items yourself also applies to other domestic items such as UMBRELLAS and CUTLERY.
Compare KNIVES; DROPPING THINGS.

Somerset [1923] Opie & Tatem, 345. **Devon** *Devonshire Assoc.* 60 (1928) 120. **Wiltshire** Wiltshire (1975) 89. **London** Henrey (1955) 97–8. **Herefordshire** Leather (1912) 87. **Worcestershire** *Folk-Lore* 20 (1909) 344.

Shropshire Burne (1883) 280. **Argyllshire** *Folk-Lore* 21 (1910) 89. **Co. Wexford** *Folk-Lore Record* 5 (1882) 83. Unlocated Igglesden (*c.*1932) 209.

scissors: gift

Scissors are included in the general superstition that one must never give a gift of a sharp object to a friend unless s/he gives something back in exchange, such as a small coin. Otherwise, the transaction will 'cut the love' between you:

Mustn't give knife or anything sharp-edged or 'will cut your love asunder' – I once presented a servant with a pair of scissors, who at first seemed pleased, then coloured deeply, and producing a penny from her pocket begged me to take it, observing it was so unlucky to accept any sharp instrument without making some return for it.
Sussex Latham (1878) 12

See KNIVES: GIFT for full discussion and references.

screaming skulls

see SKULL LEGENDS.

scrofula (King's Evil)

Tuberculosis of the lymph nodes, usually in the neck, which was characterized by abscesses and running sores; now rare, but formerly widespread. It was universally known as the 'King's Evil', because British and French sovereigns claimed the power to heal it by touch. Special gold coins struck for the occasion were given to sufferers and worn around the neck as amulets to keep the disease at bay. This system was clearly wide open to abuse, and there were numerous attempts to keep control of the situation and ensure that only deserving cases (i.e. those who could be trusted not to sell the gold) were admitted to the sovereign's presence. Applications for treatment were thus filtered through local parish officials. Edward the Confessor (1042–66) was the first English king known to 'touch' for the disease, and the Plantagenets, Tudors, and Stuarts continued the tradition, with Charles II being particularly active. There is no doubt that the belief bolstered the royal families' claims to God-given powers and was continued for that reason, and there was some jealousy between the French and English to prove who had the gift first, to demonstrate which dynasty had strongest historical claims to royalty. The tradition died out when the Hanoverians came to the throne with George I in 1714.

Not everyone had ready access to the king, but fortunately there were other strategies available at local level. Scrofula was one of the diseases in which SEVENTH SONS and daughters specialized; they were said to cure it simply by touching, which was presumably in imitation of the royal touch. They also used other methods, such as the widespread cure which called for dismembered FROGS or TOADS:

A seventh son . . . is a very potent personage, and to him, far rather than to any regular practitioner, will the simple people of Devonshire have recourse in every case of any commonly prevalent disease, such as king's evil. A girl thus afflicted, having gone for advice to a seventh son, he proceeded to borrow a penknife from a young woman, without telling her to what purpose he meant to apply it, and therewith cut off and skinned the hind leg of a living toad. The skin was then sewn up in a bag, and the toad buried. The girl wore the charm around her neck, and as the buried animal decayed, so did her disease vanish away.
Devon *Monthly Packet* (1864)

Along with other major skin problems, swellings and goitres, scrofula could be tackled by rubbing the affected area with a DEAD MAN'S HAND:

Remedies to cure the King's or Queen's evil, is first to touch the place with the hand of one that died an untimely death. Otherwise: let a virgin fasting lay her hand on the sore, and say: 'Apollo denieth that the heat of the plague can increase, where a naked virgin quencheth it'; and spit three times upon it.
Scot (1584)

The dead-hand cure was still being resorted to in the late nineteenth century, as evidenced by the report of a woman bringing a child to a coroner's inquest to request access to a dead body, published in the *Western Morning News* on 8 July 1879 (*see Devonshire Assoc.* 12 (1880)).

Other variations on this theme were, if anything, even more trying for the sufferer:

If a woman have the king's evil, put a piece of bread and butter in the hand of a man that has been killed, and make her eat it out of the hand. If a man [be thus afflicted] *it must be a woman's hand.*
Shropshire Burne (1883)

Another way of involving the dead in the cure was to rub the sores with a HANDKERCHIEF, and then throw the latter into the open grave at a funeral.

Sussex Latham (1878) 45. **Dorset** N&Q 5S:4 (1875) 83; *Procs. Dorset Nat. Hist. & Ant. Field Club* 35 (1914) 85. **Somerset** Poole (1877) 53; *Folk-Lore* 6 (1895) 205; *Folk-Lore* 7 (1896) 295–6; Burgess & Rann (1897) 118; *Folk-Lore* 66 (1955) 327; Tongue (1965) 136. **Devon** *The Times* (16 Jan. 1851) 7; *Monthly Packet* 28 (1864) 443–7; N&Q 5S:2 (1874) 184; *Devonshire Assoc.* 9 (1877) 92–3; *Devonshire Assoc.* 11 (1879) 105; *Devonshire Assoc.* 12 (1880) 102–3; Hewett (1900) 45, 72, 76; *Devonshire Assoc.* 63 (1931) 130; *Devonshire Assoc.* 66 (1934) 83; *Devonshire Assoc.* 85 (1953) 218; *Devonshire Assoc.* 87 (1955) 353–4. **Cornwall** N&Q 1S:5 (1852) 412–3; *Jnl Royal Inst. Cornwall* 20 (1915) 126. **Wiltshire** Aubrey, *Remaines* (1686/1972) 238; Aubrey, *Miscellanies* (1696/1857) 124. **London** Samuel Pepys, *Diary* (23 June 1660). **Hertfordshire** N&Q 1S:2 (1850) 68. **Worcestershire/Shropshire** *Gent. Mag.* (1855) 384–6. **Staffordshire** Hackwood (1924) 151–2. **Shropshire** Burne (1883) 194, 202. **Northern England** [1850s] *Denham Tracts* 2 (1895) 39. **Yorkshire** [*c*.1730] Dawson (1882) 200. **Lancashire** [1682] Harland & Wilkinson (1882) 77–8. **Highland Scotland** Macbain (1887/88) 258. **Highland Scotland** Polson (1926) 31. **Ross-shire** *Folk-Lore* 11 (1900) 448. **Caithness** Sutherland (1937) 104. **Hebrides** *Folk-Lore* 11 (1900) 448. **Shetland** *New Stat. Acct* Scotland (1845) 85. **Ireland** Hickey (1938) 269. **Co. Cavan** *Folk-Lore* 19 (1908) 316. **Co. Leitrim** *Folk-Lore* 5 (1894) 199. **Co. Galway** *Spectator* (10 Aug. 1907) 190. **Guernsey** MacCulloch (1864) 425–6. **Jersey** L'Amy (1927) 100. **Isle of Man** Harrison (1869) 183. **General** Scot (1584) Bk 12, Ch. 14; Barnes (1895); Crawfurd (1911); N&Q 160 (1931) 206, 248–9, 268, 284; *Folk-Lore* 61 (1950) 1–14; Thomas (1971) 192–8. **Literary** Shakespeare, *Macbeth* (1606) 4:3; *The Tatler* 11 (1709) 104.

sea-beans

see LUCKY BEANS.

seagulls

In coastal areas, seagulls were viewed with suspicion, or at least caution. They were usually left unmolested, but the reason varied. The strongest tradition was that they were the souls of seamen who had died at sea, but their behaviour could also be interpreted as a death omen:

When they mew incessantly around a seafarer's home it is said to presage a death. When a very well-known Haut pas *boatowner died immediately before the 1939–45 war it was noticed by all the neighbours how restless and noisy flocks of gulls were around the house all day as he lay dying. They were said to have been agitated in the same fashion around the places inland where members of his family were working.*

Guernsey De Garis (1975)

But they could also be vindictive:

Round the Somerset seaboard there are strong traditions about seagulls, which are believed to

be the souls of drowned sailors. Round the Porlock to Lynmouth coast they warn you not to feed a seagull, and above all not to look it in the eyes. If you do, one day when you are clinging to a wreck, or perhaps only swimming, it will find you and peck out your eyes, and leave you to drown.

Somerset Tongue (1965)

Given the nature, look, and cry of the seagull, one would expect there to have been beliefs about them in the distant past, but at present none has been found before late Victorian times.

Sussex Woodford (1968) 60. **Somerset** Tongue (1965) 48. **Cornwall** *Old Cornwall* 2 (1931–6) 40. **London** [1987] Opie & Tatem, 346. **Norfolk** Randell (1966) 101. **Yorkshire** *Folk-Lore* 21 (1910) 227. **Highland Scotland** Macgregor (1878) 31. **Banffshire** *Folk-Lore Jnl* 4 (1886) 14. **Aberdeenshire** *Folk-Lore Jnl* 3 (1885) 306. **Shetland** Saxby (1932) 182. **Guernsey** De Garis (1975) 136. **Unlocated** Igglesden (*c*.1932) 79–80.

second sight

Second sight is the usual English name for a power of seeing into the future, possessed typically by certain people in the Gaelic Highlands and Islands of Scotland but also by others elsewhere. It was first noticed by the outside world in the late seventeenth century, and has since attracted a great deal of scholarly attention. Much material on the subject already exists. Some still claim to have the power.

The second sight is a singular faculty of seeing an otherwise invisible object, without any previous means used by the person that sees it for that end; the vision makes such a lively impression upon the seers, that they neither see nor think of anything else, except the vision, as long as it continues; and then they appear pensive or jovial, according to the object which was represented to them.

Western Isles Martin (1703)

This is one of the earliest published descriptions, written by Martin Martin after a trip to the Western Isles about 1695. The matter was clearly in the air at that time, as George Sinclair had mentioned it in 1685, Robert Kirk had published his thoughts on the matter in 1691, and John Aubrey in 1696. Samuel Pepys corresponded with Lord Reay on the subject in 1699, and Royal Society member Robert Boyle had been interested in it from 1678 to his death in 1691.

Second sight quickly developed into a battleground of belief. Investigators such as Kirk and Boyle were concerned to prove its existence, to help counter what they saw as dangerous new ideas which denied the reality of the supernatural and spiritual world completely. They foresaw that such a sceptical view tended to the conclusion that even religion itself was false. For others, such as Boswell and Johnson, who visited the Hebrides in 1773, the area was one of the last unspoilt places where the inhabitants were wild, but free of the cant and enervating artifice of contemporary 'civilization', and the possible existence of such supernatural powers was terribly romantic. Novelists were happy to use the motif in their tales, but some, like Thomas Pennant, thought the whole notion was 'founded on impudence and nurtured by folly' (Pennant (1774)).

Many Scottish writers accepted the reality of second sight in their nationalistic quest to identify and preserve true Scottish or Gaelic customs and values against the colonizing onslaught of the dominant English language and culture. Second sight was something special which demarcated the Highlanders from their neighbours, and acceptance became necessary for any true patriot, even if their otherwise sceptical view of the world would direct them towards disbelief. Hence Alistair Macgregor, addressing the Caledonian Medical Society in 1899, could say:

It is fortunate that this article, dealing with the subject of Second Sight appears in the journal of a society, the majority of whose members are Scottish-born – otherwise I fear it would meet with scant courtesy . . . Hence my fellow-Caledonians – partly from national sentiment, and partly perhaps from having had themselves some experience of second sight, personally or from hearsay – may be expected to have more sympathy with a dissertation on a supernatural belief indigenous to their native country than they would have had it been an alien.

Macgregor (1899)

Even within the nationalistic camp there have been factions and fashions and differing viewpoints. It comes as something of a surprise these days, when the word 'Celtic' is regularly used as an honorific title, to learn that less than a hundred years ago some Scottish writers approached the matter from the opposite direction:

In any enquiry into the natural history of Second-Sight the natural genius of the Highland people cannot be overlooked. It will not be out of place to note that it is historically true that the Highlanders, in the North and West of Scotland, have a strong strain of Norse blood, and that where the Celtic blood predominates, as in Ireland and France, the temperament is characterised by a

hilariousness and fickleness which is markedly absent in the Highlands.   Macrae (1908)

Debate on the second sight phenomenon has been particularly vulnerable to these religious and politico-social pressures and it is even now difficult to avoid them.

From the earliest accounts onwards, there has been disagreement over whether or not the faculty of second sight was hereditary. Believers found themselves in a dilemma. The power was clearly not possessed by every child of every acknowledged seer, but the hereditary principle was vital to the view that second sight contributes strongly to the 'specialness' of Highland society. The consensus has therefore been that the faculty must be hereditary, but does not manifest itself in every generation. The non-believer would argue that this very convenient answer means that any random person who claims to have the power can be slotted into the hereditary scheme by saying that one of his/her ancestors must have had it, and even outsiders can assume a Gaelic connection in their family history.

There has also been debate about the fundamental nature of the second sight gift. Some, like George Sinclair, a professor of philosophy in the College of Glasgow, assumed it was the Devil's work:

I am undoubtedly informed, that men and women in the Highlands can discern fatality approaching others, by seeing them in waters, or with winding sheets about them . . . It is not improbable, but that such preternatural knowledge comes first by a compact with the devil, and is derived downward by succession to their posterity, many of such I suppose are innocent, and have this sight against their will and inclination.   Sinclair (1685)

But the majority of writers stressed the anguish that many seers felt, and claimed that most of them would be free of the gift if they could achieve release.

Descriptions of what the seers actually experience vary considerably. Most accounts focus on sight, but smell and sound can also play a part. Earlier accounts focused on 'sad and dismal' events, although the occasional vision foresees a wedding or other happy event. Some visions are symbolic (*see below*), while others are more literal:

of a Highland gentleman of the Macdonalds, who having a brother that came to visit him, saw him coming in, wanting a head; yet told not his brother he saw any such thing; but within twenty-four hours thereafter, his brother was taken (being a murderer), and his head cut off, and sent to Edinburgh.   Aubrey, *Miscellanies* (1696)

It is not altogether clear what should properly be included in a definition of second sight. Some of the descriptions include standard omens found all over the British Isles such as DEATH KNOCKS, CORPSE CANDLES, WRAITHS, and phantom funerals, and some even state that those born at midnight, born with a CAUL, or who are SEVENTH SONS will have the gift. These are also reported all over Britain as explaining why some people see fairies and ghosts more than others.

The most important way in which second sight appears to be different from other visions and portents is that it is a personal gift which the seer experiences regularly, rather than being a random or one-off phenomenon. Another key difference lies in the structured symbolism which appears in the earlier descriptions. So, for example, a death was forecast by the seer having a vision of the doomed person wrapped in a shroud, and the higher up the body the shroud appeared, the sooner the death would occur. The 'sight' of an empty chair could symbolize the death of its usual occupant. There were even rules governing the time of day that the vision occurred and the elapse of time before fulfilment:

If an object is seen early in the morning (which is not frequent) it will be accomplished in a few hours afterwards. If at noon, it will commonly be accomplished that very day. If in the evening, perhaps that night; if after candles is lighted, it will be accomplished that night: the latter always in accomplishment by weeks, months, and sometimes years, according to the time of night the vision is seen.   Martin (1703)

Other aspects also varied. The earlier accounts stressed the trance-like state into which the seers fell while they saw their vision, but in later descriptions the vision often seems so 'normal' that the seer expects companions to have seen the same thing.

Non-seers could join in a vision by touching the seer – sometimes a mere touch is enough; others maintain that the best way is to stand on the seer's foot and look over his/her shoulder. According to most accounts, this is only a temporary sharing of powers that ceases as soon as the physical contact is broken, but those who believe that the power can be communicated deliberately usually include something like this in their description of the method involved.

Several seers have achieved lasting fame in Scotland and still have their supporters, as do all seers from Nostradamus to Old Mother Shipton. The best known is *Coinneach Odhar* (Kenneth Mackenzie), known as the Brahan Seer since 1896 when his prophecies were first published. He probably lived in the 1570s, if at all, and books of his prophecies were reprinted throughout the twentieth century, and still remain in print today.

Yorkshire *Observer Supp.* (24 Nov. 1968) 10. **Lancashire** Harland & Wilkinson (1882) 105. **Scotland** Henderson (1866) 294–8. **Highland Scotland** Sinclair (1685) 142; Kirk (1691); Aubrey, *Miscellanies* (1696/1857) 174–95; Macbain (1887/88) 252; *Celtic Mag.* 12 (1887) 324–32; Campbell (1900); Campbell (1902). **Argyllshire** *Folk-Lore* 21 (1910) 90. **Western Isles** Martin (1703) 180. **Hebrides** Pennant (1774) 280; Samuel Johnson, *Journey to the Western Islands of Scotland* (1785) 156; Boswell 1 (1791) 529–30. **Isle of Skye** *Celtic Monthly* 9 (1901) 145–7; Bennett (1992) 180–2. **Inverness-shire** Bennett (1992) 183–6. **General** Brand (1810) 103. **Literary** [in Walter Scott's novels] Parsons (1964) 151–8.
Major accounts: Norman Macrae, *Highland Second-Sight* (Dingwall: Souter, 1908); Alastair Macgregor, 'Second Sight', *Caledonian Medical Jnl* 3 (1899) 42–56, 141–56; John MacInnes, 'The Seer in Gaelic Tradition', in Davidson (1989) 10–24; Eilidh Watt, 'Some Personal Experiences of the Second Sight', in Davidson (1989) 25–36; Shari A. Cohn, 'A Survey on Scottish Second Sight', *Jnl Soc. for Psychical Research* 59 (1994) 385–400; Shari A. Cohn, 'A Historical Review of Second Sight: The Collectors, their Accounts and Ideas', *Scottish Studies* 33 (1999) 146–85; Michael Hunter, 'The Discovery of Second Sight in Late 17th-Century Scotland', *History Today* (June 2001) 48–53.

sengreen

see HOUSELEEK.

seventh sons/daughters

A seventh son was widely believed to have certain gifts by virtue of his birth, both in the direction of healing and in psychic powers. The usual rule was that he had to be the seventh in an unbroken line of males, from the same parents, and the seventh son of a seventh son had even more pronounced powers. There is some disagreement about whether seventh daughters were also gifted. Many authorities flatly deny it, while others argue that in the case of females it was the *ninth* child which mattered. A significant number, however, accepted that seventh daughters were just as good as seventh sons:

I had an intimate knowledge of a seventh child, a relative, who was said to possess the power of healing by touch, and also the gift of clairvoyance, because she was born at midnight in All-Hallows – so her Derbyshire friends asserted. She certainly had clairvoyance to some degree, and had a curious way with young girls, after a quiet look at their faces telling them things concerning their future lives, some of which came about afterwards. Her touch was singularly soothing, and gave relief to pain. Derbyshire N&Q (1914)

The most widely known attribute of the seventh child was that s/he could cure the King's Evil (SCROFULA), simply by touch, in the same way as the ruling monarch used to do, but all other diseases and complaints also came under their remit, especially skin diseases and children's complaints such as WHOOPING COUGH.

A notion much prevails here, that the seventh son of a seventh son has the gift of healing. This very day, July 7, 1823, a man so designated is perambulating the parish of Newlyn. He has been applied to for the cure of rheumatism; but he professes to cure wounds only. Cornwall Polwhele (1826)

Many simply touched or rubbed the patient, while others also used charms, herbs, medicines, and so on, to increase their efficacy. Some made a living at this, but many reports stress the belief that they would lose their gifts if paid for their services, or even if they were thanked.

In Ulster it is truly no joke to be a seventh son, for I knew in my childhood of small traders in country towns who were pestered by patients, to the great hurt of their business. They could not refuse their aid to those who had been brought in springless carts some thirty miles of mountain road, but they detested their own celebrity. My impression is that they chiefly dealt with erysipelas and such diseases, and that they professed to cure by prayers and in the name of God. In Norfolk the superstition is so strong that the seventh son was – till recent days – fated to be a doctor from his cradle. N. Ireland N&Q (1914)

Seventh sons were often nicknamed 'doctor' in their communities, and a regular motif in descriptions is that they would have followed the medical profession if their parents could have afforded it:

When Doctor Stanley Rayner was called to court at Church (Lancs.) yesterday, police explained, 'Doctor is his Christian name. He has no professional qualifications. Magistrate's Clerk Mr C.N. Dixon added: 'It is the custom in these parts to call the seventh son of a seventh son Doctor'. Lancashire *Daily Express* (16 May 1958)

A strange tradition, found most strongly in Ireland but also elsewhere, was that seventh sons have particular power over worms. It seems that the child's power is released or enhanced if, soon after birth, worms are placed in their hands and allowed to die:

When the child is born the nurse puts a worm in a piece of muslin into each hand, and ties the hand up till the worm dies. One worm must be male, the other female. When the worms die they are thrown away and nothing more is done. When the boy grows up you may get him to draw a line or a circle or any mark in the road, put a worm near that mark, it will crawl towards the mark and then draw back as if terrified, repeating this action again and again and again, till it really crosses the line and remains motionless. If you examine it you will find it is dead. The actions of the worm are described as giving you the impression that it is mesmerised. If that same boy puts his finger into a pail of worms, every single one will die almost at once. My cousin says that having got a pail of worms for fishing with, he will avoid meeting the seventh son of a seventh son (who are sure to be well known) lest their trouble should go for nothing and the worms should die. Co. Meath *Folk-Lore* (1893)

This power over worms is not explained further, but it is given as proof of the seventh son's powers. There is a faint echo in other beliefs, for example that children born at Whitsun are fated to kill or be killed. One way to fulfil this destiny was to kill an insect or small animal in the baby's hand as soon as possible after birth.

The basic seventh son belief was extremely widespread, and was found in every quarter of Britain and Ireland. It has been documented regularly since at least the sixteenth century, with Thomas Lupton's *A Thousand Notable Things* (1579) providing the earliest clear description:

It is manifest by experience that the seventh male child by just order (never a girl or wench being born between) doth heal only with touching through a natural gift, the King's Evil. Lupton (1579)

A probable predecessor is found 300 years earlier, in the medieval Welsh manuscript published as the *Physicians of Myddvai*, which shows that the seventh son was already regarded as special:

Wash the warts with the water from a font in which the seventh son of the same man and wife is baptised. Wales *Physicians of Myddvai* (c.1250)

The origins of the belief remain obscure. The usual assumption that it is simply a manifestation of the presumed 'mystical power' of the number seven is little more than guesswork. There is little evidence that seven was prized any more than any other odd number between one and ten in British tradition. Virtually the same belief was found in France and, to a lesser degree, other European countries, and it is probable that an origin should be sought there. It is probably no accident that France also had a strong tradition of kings healing by touch, which developed at roughly the same time as in Britain.

It is also just possible that the belief has biblical roots. In Acts 19 – which is concerned with healing miracles, magic and exorcism, and the 'riot at Ephesus' – 'seven sons of one Sceva, a Jew, and chief of the priests' are introduced. Other than their number, however, they have no attributes to make them candidates for the originals of our traditional seventh sons.

Somerset N&Q 5S:12 (1879) 466; Folk-Lore 6 (1895) 205; Folk-Lore 7 (1896) 295–6; Folk-Lore 66 (1955) 327; Tongue (1965) 136. New Forest Wise (1867) 177. Devon N&Q 1S:5 (1852) 572; The Monthly Packet 28 (1864) 443–7; Devonshire Assoc. 8 (1876) 54–5; Hewett (1900) 45, 52; N&Q 11S:10 (1914) 135, 174; Devonshire Assoc. 57 (1926) 120–1; Devonshire Assoc. 63 (1931) 130–1; [1986] Opie & Tatem, 347. Cornwall Polwhele (1826) 607; N&Q 1S:5 (1852) 412–13; Folk-Lore Jnl 5 (1887) 198. London The Times (28 May 1988) 2. Wiltshire Aubrey, Miscellanies (1696/1857) 124. Oxfordshire [pre-1900] Folk-Lore 24 (1913) 91. Gloucestershire Folk-Lore 13 (1902) 172. Herefordshire Leather (1912) 70. Norfolk N&Q 11S:10 (1914) 135. Lincolnshire Peacock (1877) 55. Shropshire Burne (1883) 186. England Addy (1895) 91, 98. Derbyshire N&Q 11S:10 (1914) 174. Northern England [1850s] Denham Tracts 2 (1895) 39, 273–4; Henderson (1866) 177–8. Yorkshire [1663] Depositions from York Castle (1861) 101; N&Q 1S:5 (1852) 617; Blakeborough (1898) 137. Lancashire Cowper (1897) 373; Daily Express (16 May 1958). Co. Durham Brockie (1889) 209; Leighton (1910) 49. Northumberland [1760] N&Q 11S:10 (1914) 216. Wales Physicians of Myddvai (c.1250) 456; Trevelyan (1909) 265. Scotland Kirk (1691); N&Q 170 (1936) 266. Highland Scotland Macbain (1887/88) 252; Polson (1926) 31. Western Scotland Napier (1879) 90–1. Banffshire Gregor (1874) 270–1. Ross-shire Folk-Lore 11 (1900) 448. Caithness Sutherland (1937) 104. Hebrides Folk-Lore 11 (1900) 448. Ireland Wilde (1888) 201–5; Hickey (1938) 269. N. Ireland N&Q 11S:10 (1914) 135; Foster (1951) 64. Co. Meath N&Q 4S:9 (1872) 257; Folk-Lore 4 (1893) 363–4. Co. Tipperary Folk-Lore 4 (1893) 360. Co. Wicklow Folk-Lore 4 (1893) 360. Co. Longford Béaloideas 6 (1936) 259. Co. Cavan Folk-Lore 19 (1908) 316. Co. Leitrim Folk-Lore 5 (1894) 199; Logan (1981) 63. Connaught N&Q 1S:12 (1855) 260. Connemara Folk-Lore 4 (1893) 357. Isle of Man Moore (1891) 157. Guernsey De Garis (1975) 6. Unlocated Grose (1787) 73; N&Q 11S:10 (1914) 88; N&Q 183 (1942) 82. General Lupton (1579) Bk 2, Para. 2; Gent. Mag. (1796) 636;

Brand 3 (1849) 333; Keightley (1850) 411. Literary R. Brome, The Antipodes (1640), quoted N&Q 6S:12 (1885) 204–5; The Tatler 11 (1709) 104.

shaking hands

It was considered unlucky to shake hands across a TABLE. An entry in London servant Hannah Cullwick's Diary for November 1872 reads:

I open'd the door and curtsied. She held her hand out over the table, but as I'd heard that's bad luck I said, 'I won't shake hands over a table, ma'am' and run round to her.   London Cullwick (1984)

Others reported that it was unlucky for four people to shake hands across each other. Still others said that the latter was the sign of a wedding:

But others, on the contrary and in some cases from the very same villages as the first party – aver that shaking hands across is a sign of a wedding, and A— R— declares, in confirmation of this, that not long ago she saw four persons do so, and the banns of one of them were put up the next Sunday. But there is no disagreement as to the ill omen of two persons shaking hands across a table – that is very unlucky, but who shall say why?   Shropshire Burne (1883)

In either form, the belief has not often been reported, and, as with other TABLE beliefs, the first references only date from the late nineteenth century.

Cornwall Jnl Royal Inst. Cornwall 20 (1915) 133. London [1872] Cullwick (1984) 249. Worcestershire Folk-Lore 6 (1895) 305. Shropshire N&Q 5S:3 (1875) 465; Burne (1883) 286. West Wales Davies (1911) 216.

shamrocks

The shamrock is one of the most widely recognized symbols in the English-speaking world, effectively connoting 'Irishness', and easily eclipsing Ireland's official symbol, the harp. The word 'shamrock' cannot be found earlier than the sixteenth century, when several writers refer to the Irish being fond of eating it. In these early references, the spelling varies considerably and is often given as 'sham-root', and even in later times it is not always clear which plant is being referred to. So, for example, Stanyhurst's Description of Ireland (1577) refers to 'water cresses, which they term shamrocks'. This connection with food is the only context in which the shamrock appears until about the 1680s, but from that time it also begins to be described as a national symbol worn on St Patrick's Day:

The 17th of March yearly is St Patricks, an immoveable feast . . . when . . . the vulgar superstitiously wear shamroges, 3-leav'd grass.
[1681] *Jnl Kilkenny Arch. Soc.* (1858)

By the early eighteenth century, the symbol had become widely known, so that Richard Steele could simply refer to 'The English oak, the Scotch thistle, the Irish shambrogue' in the *Spectator* (1712) and expect to be understood.

The intimate connection between the Irish and the shamrock appears to originate with a story about St Patrick, which also appeared around the turn of the eighteenth century:

When St Patrick landed near Wicklow the inhabitants were ready to stone him for attempting an innovation in the religion of their ancestors. He requested to be heard, and explained unto them that God is an omnipotent, sacred spirit, who created heaven and earth, and that the Trinity is contained in the Unity; but they were reluctant to give credit to his words. St Patrick, therefore, plucked a trefoil from the ground and expostulated with the Hibernians: 'Is it not as feasible for the Father, Son, and Holy Ghost, as for these three leaves thus to grow upon a single stalk?' Then the Irish were immediately convinced of their error, and were solemnly baptised by St Patrick.
Jones (1794)

This story does not appear in earlier biographies of St Patrick, nor in the various Lives of Saints, so it appears to be newly coined at about the same time that writers begin referring to the shamrock as a national symbol. It is not clear which came first, but it is likely that the story gave rise to the custom.

Despite this intimate connection with the Trinity, Irish people have shared in the general affection for the four-leafed CLOVER:

The fortunate possessor of the four-leaved shamrock will have luck in gambling, luck in racing, and witchcraft will have no power over him. But he must always carry it about his person, and never give it away, or even show it to another.
Ireland Wilde (1888)

[1681] *Jnl Kilkenny Arch. Soc.* 1 (1858) 183; *Spectator* (12 Aug. 1712); Edward Jones, *Musical and Poetical Relicks of the Welsh Bards* (2nd edn, 1794) 13, quoted Colgan (1896) 212. **Ireland** Wilde (1888) 204; Nathaniel Colgan, 'The Shamrock in Literature: A Critical Chronology', *Jnl Royal Soc. Antiquaries Ireland* 5S:6 (1896) 211–226; Vickery (1995) 344–51. Also see *OED* for early examples of the word.

shaving

Shaving is sometimes included in beliefs governing the cutting of HAIR and FINGERNAILS. Fridays and Sundays are usually the days on which these actions are unwise, but occasionally other days are singled out:

If you wish to have luck, never shave on a Monday.   Unlocated N&Q 1S:7 (1853) 81

sheep: first lamb seen

One of the simple prognostications of good or bad luck in springtime, thus one of the important symbolic BEGINNING points in the year, focuses on the first new lamb that you see:

A friend familiar with rustic affairs told me the other day, that in seeing young lambs for the first time in the fields, they should be looked at in front, as it was most unlucky to take sight of them behind, as something would go wrong in consequence.   Unlocated N&Q (1880)

Exactly the same was said of foals (*see* HORSES: FIRST FOAL SEEN) and other animals. The symbolism is reasonably obvious and is rarely commented on, but informants occasionally said something on the lines of 'if you see the tail first you'll go backwards all year'. The belief was very widely noted across England, Scotland, and Wales, but not, it seems, in Ireland. Nevertheless, it cannot be shown to be very old, as the earliest known reference is only in Chambers' book of Scottish rhymes published in 1826.

A few other interpretations of the 'first lamb' have also been noted, but much more rarely than that given above. It was lucky if the lambs were moving around, but unlucky if lying down. It was also unlucky to see a black lamb before a white one. A different interpretation on the way the first lamb was facing:

'You notice which way the first lamb you see looks and that-a-way you'll go to live'; said to farmservants, with reference to their yearly change of service at May-day.   Lincolnshire Cole (1886)

Heads or tails: Sussex *Sussex County Mag.* 18 (1944) 261. **Somerset** [1923] Opie & Tatem, 157. **Devon** *Devonshire Assoc.* 61 (1929) 126. **Oxfordshire** *Midland Garner* 1 (1884) 19. **Gloucestershire** *Folk-Lore* 12 (1902) 171. **Herefordshire** Leather (1912) 23. **Worcestershire/Shropshire** *Gent. Mag.* (1855) 385. **Worcestershire** Salisbury (1893) 71; Berkeley & Jenkins (1932) 34. **Lincolnshire** *Gent. Mag.* (1832) 493; Thompson (1856) 735; N&Q 6S:2 (1880) 35. **Shropshire** Burne (1883) 212; *Byegones* (1888) 126–6; [1981] Opie & Tatem, 157.

England Addy (1895) 67, 93. **Derbyshire** *Folk-Lore Jnl* 2 (1884) 280. **Northern England** Henderson (1866) 88–9. **Lancashire** Henderson (1866) 88–9; Harland & Wilkinson (1882) 139, 142. **Co. Durham** Leighton (1910) 62. **Northumberland** Neville (1909) 110. **Wales** *Folk-Lore* 30 (1919) 156–7. **Mid-Wales** Davies (1911) 215. **Montgomeryshire** Hamer (1877) 261. **Anglesey** N&Q 6S:2 (1880) 258. **Highland Scotland** Chambers (1826) 284; Macbain (1887/88) 250, 265. **Caithness** Sutherland (1937) 104. **Unlocated** N&Q 1S:5 (1852) 293; N&Q 6S:1 (1880) 393; Igglesden (*c.*1932) 105. *Other interpretations*: **Lincolnshire** Cole (1886) 47; Rudkin (1936) 22. **England** Addy (1895) 93. **Dumfriesshire** Corrie (1890/91) 80. **Orkney** *New Stat. Acct* (1845) 143; N&Q 10S:12 (1909) 483–4.

sheets

see TABLECLOTHS.

shingles (*Herpes zoster*)

The viral infection shingles, characterized by a painful red skin rash, attracted a number of traditional cures, but two were relatively widespread. One involved the application of grease from a church bell:

When William Partlett was getting old he had shingles, and appears not to have been satisfied with the way he was getting on. So he got Charles Webb, the sexton, to go to the belfry and get him some grease from the bells. The next time the doctor came he found the old man smothered in black grease.
                                    Oxfordshire *Folk-Lore* (1929)

This grease was variously called 'dowment', 'comb', or 'coomb'. The same procedure was also regularly recommended for RINGWORM, and the fact that the grease came from a *church* bell gave it extra potency in many sufferers' eyes.

The second widespread treatment was to apply cat's blood – some specified a black CAT, but most were not so particular:

It is generally believed that shingles could be cured by the application of cat's blood to the affected part. The blood could be obtained from the ear or tail of the animal.   Wales Trevelyan (1909)

Cat's blood was also used in other cures, and this procedure was already in circulation in the late seventeenth century.

Other cures for shingles were reported less regularly, including the following unusual use for eagle's flesh.

In a recent number of the **British Medical Journal** *it was stated that in parts of Wales it was believed that the saliva of a person who had eaten*

eagle's flesh smeared on the eruption of herpes zoster (shingles) would cure the painful eruption; and that certain persons made quite a small living out of the superstition, having eaten eagle's flesh and curing herpes for a consideration.
                                    Wales N&Q (1886)

A surprising number of informants also voiced a belief that was clearly widespread: if the rash spread around the waist to form a continuous ring, the patient was bound to die.

Bells: **Dorset** *Procs. Dorset Nat. Hist & Ant. Field Club* 35 (1914) 83. **Surrey** N&Q 6S:5 (1882) 345–6; N&Q 10S:7 (1907) 206. **Oxfordshire** N&Q 6S:6 (1882) 375; *Folk-Lore* 40 (1929) 383; *Oxf. FL Soc. Ann. Record* (1956) 11–12. **Gloucestershire** [1917] *Trans. Bristol & Glos. Arch. Soc.* 53 (1931) 264. **Herefordshire** *Folk-Lore* 44 (1933) 309. **Worcestershire** Salisbury (1893) 70. **Warwickshire** Bloom (*c.*1930) 28. **General** N&Q 6S:6 (1882) 375. ***Cats:*** **Devon** *Devonshire Assoc.* 12 (1880) 102; *Devonshire Assoc.* 17 (1885) 119. **Wales** Trevelyan (1909) 316. N. **Ireland** Foster (1951) 62. **General** H. Woolley, *Queen-Like Closet* (1684) Supp. 35; D. Turner, *Diseases of the Skin* (1712). ***Other cures:*** **Devon** *Devonshire Assoc.* 10 (1878) 101; *Devonshire Assoc.* 59 (1927) 167. **Cornwall** *Folk-Lore Jnl* 5 (1887) 205–6. **Shropshire** Burne (1883) 189. **Wales** N&Q (1886) 145. **Aberdeenshire** *Folk-Lore* 25 (1914) 350. **Ireland** Logan (1981) 71–2.

shoelaces

Even something as trivial as a shoelace can have its significance to the believer, and it is usually ominous of bad luck if it breaks or comes untied.

When you discover your shoe-lace is loose, walk nine paces before tying it, otherwise you will tie ill-luck to you for that day
                                    Yorkshire Blakeborough (1898)

Trivial as it may seem, the broken shoelace can be shown to be one of our oldest superstitions in Britain – John of Salisbury (1159) quotes a story about the apostle Mark 'bursting the latchet of his shoe', and to bridge the long gap between then and the twentieth-century examples quoted below, Gaule (1652) includes the bursting latchet in his list of 'superstitious ominations'. Opie and Tatem also quote Cicero (*De Divinatione* II, 40, 45 BC) for good measure.

Surrey Igglesden (*c.*1932) 221. **Essex** [1917] Mays (1969) 164. **Yorkshire** Blakeborough (1898) 150. **Monmouthshire** [1954] Opie & Tatem, 350. **Orkney** N&Q 10S:12 (1909) 483–4. **General** John of Salisbury, *Policraticus* (1159) Bk 2; Gaule (1652) 181.

shoes

Shoes are the central item in a number of widespread beliefs, reported below, but they also play a smaller part in others. They feature often in LOVE DIVINATION procedures. Lovers place their shoes in a certain pattern on retiring to bed, or when they hear the CUCKOO they look for a hair in their shoe which will be the same as their future spouse:

When a four-leaf clover is found, place it in the heel of your left boot, first person you meet of the opposite sex will be your life partner.
Yorkshire Nicholson (1890)

Placing items in the shoe is also recommended in various cures:

Cure for ague: Leaf of tansey in shoe.
Sussex Latham (1878)

For ordinary colds a few bulbs of the Crow-onion (allium viniale) were taken, dried and powdered and enclosed in pieces of flannel to form a sock, which was placed in the patient's shoe.
Warwickshire Bloom (c.1930)

Various prescriptions call for a cross to be made of the shoe – to avoid CRAMP, or in response to certain stimuli:

Lucky to make a cross with spittle on your boot when you see a white horse. Orkney N&Q (1909)

A number of other beliefs, reported rarely, warn that shoes must be handled carefully:

To dream of shoes is unlucky.
Gloucestershire *Folk-Lore* (1923)

Left on the stairs, boots or shoes foretell illness, generally of their owner. Wales *Folk-Lore* (1920)

She also stipulated that shoes must never be stored higher than one's own height. It is bad luck to place them on a high shelf. Yorkshire Gill (1993)

But there is disagreement over their role in the WEDDING outfit:

Some people say it is very unlucky to wear new shoes at a wedding, while others believe it is lucky to do so. These contradictory beliefs I found at Orcop, and other parts of the Ross district, side by side. Herefordshire Leather (1912)

Sussex Latham (1878) 39. Berkshire *Folk-Lore* 5 (1894) 337. Gloucestershire *Folk-Lore* 34 (1923) 157. Herefordshire Leather (1912) 114. Warwickshire Bloom (c.1930) 29. Yorkshire Nicholson (1890) 124; Gill (1993) 90–1. Wales *Folk-Lore* 31 (1920) 320. Orkney N&Q 10S:12 (1909) 483–4.

shoes: burning

Burning leather is universally acknowledged as producing an unpleasant smell, but some recommended it for various reasons, while others thought it unlucky.

If you burn a boot on Christmas Eve, it will keep you in shoe leather all next year.
Devon *Devonshire Assoc.* (1958)

It is lucky to burn any old boots available, before starting on a journey. A Herefordshire servant told her mistress that she had seen the hop-pickers, who were to leave the next day, with such funny old boots laid out all round the fire. 'They [are] sure to burn them,' she said, 'Mother always does before going away anywhere; she says it's such a lucky thing to do'.
Herefordshire Leather (1912)

A woman residing at Hamble, Hants., who was lately taken ill very suddenly, said to a person who called to inquire after her, 'Ah! I be ill all over; and no wonder; it as good as serves me right, for I burnt a pair of old shoes yesterday'.
Hampshire N&Q (1884)

Burning leather was also believed to have another effect – 'Burn some leather – change the weather' (*Devonshire Assoc.* (1959)), and in a sixteenth-century manuscript from Guernsey, it was recommended as a way of enticing out a serpent which had crept into someone's mouth and taken up residence inside them (*see* ANIMAL INFESTATION).

Devon *Devonshire Assoc.* 88 (1956) 253; *Devonshire Assoc.* 90 (1958) 246; *Devonshire Assoc.* 91 (1959) 201. Hampshire N&Q 6S:9 (1884) 49. Herefordshire Leather (1912) 258. England Addy (1895) 92. Guernsey [1589] *Channel Islands Ann. Anth.* (1972–3) 19.

shoes: Christmas

Three references indicate a belief that it is unlucky to receive new shoes or anything made of leather at Christmas:

[A farmer's daughter], *who from her country connexions is well versed in rural lore, also informed me that it is considered very unlucky for new shoes or tanned leather to be received into the house during the Christmas week or on New*

Year's day. A small Herefordshire farmer some-time since made lamentation to her, that a pair of new shoes had been unwittingly received into his house on Christmas morning, and said it was 'a bad job' for he 'lost a sight of cattle that year'.
Worcestershire/Herefordshire N&Q (1875)

Ella M. Leather included the belief in her collection of Herefordshire folklore (1912) and commented that it still survived in her time, and it was again mentioned by Crippen in the 1920s. Its independent existence is thus confirmed, but the restricted geographical area of these reports may indicate either a purely local superstition or an accident of the record. Further examples are needed before anything concrete can be said.

Worcestershire/Herefordshire N&Q 5S:3 (1875) 6–7. Herefordshire Leather (1912) 109. Unlocated Crippen (1923) 168.

shoes: on table

There are several items which superstition dictates must not be placed on a TABLE, but far and away the commonest is shoes.

It is unlucky to put boots on the table, but the ill-luck may be counteracted by spitting on the soles. Some years ago, after examining and condemning a pair of narrow-toed boots in a ploughman's house, I placed them on the table and the ploughman's wife immediately removed them, saying: 'Would ye hae strife in the hoose afore nicht?' She was consoled when I told her, what she did not know, how the evil might be averted.
Aberdeenshire Folk-Lore (1914)

Most references stipulate *new* shoes, and the penalty varies. Simple ill luck or a quarrel are the most often quoted, but some versions predict 'you'll never marry', or even imminent death.

A few only provide antidotes. SPITTING on the shoes is prescribed by one or two informants, while others insist that the person who was unwise enough to put the shoes on the table must be the one to remove them. A more elaborate ceremony was also possible:

a man who absent-mindedly placed a pair of new shoes on the table after his return from the shops. When he realised, he quickly placed them on the floor, stood in front of them and jumped over them backwards to avert the ill luck which would follow this serious mistake.   Yorkshire Gill (1993)

No plausible explanation has been offered for this superstition. It has been suggested that shoes on the table suggest a corpse lying there. Charles Igglesden, always ready with an explanation, takes a further flight of fancy and declares:

The dread of placing boots on a table or chair probably started in the days when the hanging of criminals was so common that a small theft was considered a crime sufficiently bad to merit death. Boots placed where they could not reach the ground suggested the dangling of the body – and the gallows.   Unlocated Igglesden (c.1932)

There is not the slightest evidence to support this idea and it thus bears as much weight as any other pure guesses might, but it has gained some currency in general circulation.

This is by no means an ancient belief, as the first known reference only dates from 1869, but it is still widely known and followed:

[Oxfam shop worker, November 2001] A customer came up to me with a pair of slippers, hesitated, and said 'I suppose a counter isn't really a table'. I was puzzled and she explained that her mother had trained her never to put shoes on a table. So then I understood and reassured her – but even so I noticed that she passed the slippers to me hand-to-hand for me to bag up, so that it was I, not her, who put them down on the counter in order to take her money.   Sussex Nov. 2001

Other items which must not be placed on a table are BELLOWS and UMBRELLAS.

Kent N&Q 4S:4 (1869) 507; *Folk-Lore* 23 (1912) 354. Sussex Steve Roud Collection, Nov. 2001. Somerset Tongue (1965) 143. Devon *Devonshire Assoc.* 10 (1878) 106; *Devonshire Assoc.* 15 (1883) 107; Hewett (1900) 54; N&Q 10S:12 (1909) 66; *Devonshire Assoc.* 60 (1928) 119; *Devonshire Assoc.* 65 (1933) 125; *Devonshire Assoc.* 67 (1935) 134; *Devonshire Assoc.* 71 (1939) 127. Cornwall *Old Cornwall* 2 (1931–6) 38. London N&Q 6S:9 (1884) 66; N&Q 6S:9 (1884) 137. Essex [c.1917] Mays (1969) 164; *Folk-Lore* 31 (1920) 320. Oxfordshire [1920s] Surman (1992) 60–1. Gloucestershire [1984] Opie & Tatem, 350. Herefordshire Leather (1912) 87, 118. Cambridgeshire *Folk-Lore* 25 (1914) 364. Suffolk *Folk-Lore* 35 (1924) 350. Norfolk Fulcher Collection (c.1895). Lincolnshire Gutch & Peacock (1908) 165; Rudkin (1936) 17. Shropshire N&Q 4S:4 (1869) 307; Burne (1883) 280. Shropshire/Staffordshire N&Q 6S:9 (1884) 137. Midland England N&Q 6S:9 (1884) 137. England Addy (1895) 101. Derbyshire [1890s] Uttley (1946) 127. Yorkshire *Folk-Lore* 21 (1910) 225–6; Gill (1993) 90–1. Lancashire *Lancashire Lore* (1971) 6. Northumberland Bosanquet (1929) 76. West Wales Davies (1911) 216. Scotland *Folk-Lore* 45 (1934) 162. Highland Scotland Polson (1926) 128. Argyllshire *Folk-Lore* 21 (1910) 89. Aberdeenshire *Folk-Lore* 25 (1914) 349. Orkney N&Q 10S:12 (1909) 483–4. Co. Tyrone *Lore & Language* 1:7 (1972) 11. Unlocated Igglesden (c.1932) 225. General Hoggart (1957) Ch. 2.

shoes: placed in position

A straightforward variation on the common LOVE DIVINATION principle that ritualistic action and spoken charm lead to dreams of the future spouse or true love. The key variable in this version is the placing of the shoes:

An inmate of St Katharine's Hospital, Ledbury, had yet another method. She used to place her shoes in the form of a 'T' on going to bed, saying: –

> *I put my shoes in the form of a T*
> *That I in my dream my true love may see*
> *The shape of his body, the colour of his hair*
> *And the holiday clothes my true love doth wear*

But she did not remember that this was successful.
Herefordshire Leather (1912)

In some instances, the shoes are also placed under the pillow. Placing the shoes in a T or cross shape is also a regular element in CRAMP cures.

Dorset Halliwell (1849) 217. **Devon** N&Q 3S:2 (1862) 62; Crossing (1911) 148–9. **Cornwall** *Old Cornwall* 1:2 (Oct. 1925) 35–6. **Oxfordshire** *Folk-Lore* 24 (1913) 79–80; *Oxon Folk-Lore Soc.* (1952) 7–8. **Herefordshire** Leather (1912) 62–3. **England** Addy (1895) 85. **Radnorshire** *Folk-Lore* 6 (1895) 202–4. **Pembrokeshire** Sikes (1880) 303. **Jersey** *Folk-Lore* 25 (1914) 247–8.

shoes: putting on

The desire for a good BEGINNING is a very powerful force in superstition, and is manifest in numerous beliefs which govern how one behaves at the start of any project, journey, or period of time. Thus, to ensure good luck during the day, it is essential that you start the day right, by getting out of BED on the right side, and:

Before anyone sets out, care should be taken that the right shoe be put on first, but if inadvertently the left shoe be tried on the right foot, that person will have some accident before the end of the day. It is also best that the right shoe be taken off before the left. **Highland Scotland** Polson (1926)

The general rule of right means good and left means bad applies here, as elsewhere, but is far from universal. Indeed, some informants specifically state the opposite:

To put the right boot on first is unlucky. Huntsmen in the district believe that to do this, or to put a riding boot on the wrong foot, foretells a mishap in the hunting field.
Yorkshire *Folk-Lore* (1910)

Occasionally, too, putting the left shoe on first is a prescription to prevent TOOTHACHE.

The care taken over shoes (and often stockings) appears to be at variance with a widespread belief about clothes which maintains that putting a garment on wrongly, by accident, is lucky (*see* CLOTHES: INSIDE OUT).

Sussex Latham (1878) 12. **Essex** [1983] Opie & Tatem, 353. **Lincolnshire** Thompson (1856) 374. **Shropshire** N&Q 5S:3 (1875) 465. **Yorkshire** *Folk-Lore* 21 (1910) 226. **Highland Scotland** Polson (1926) 128. **Orkney** N&Q 10S:12 (1909) 483–4. **Unlocated** *Radio Times* (27 May 1960) 25.

shoes: squeaking

A minor superstition, only recorded a handful of times, but clearly more widespread than the evidence suggests – and still being said:

Somebody walked past and their shoes squeaked. My colleague commented 'My grandma used to say that if you have squeaky shoes it means you haven't paid for them'.
London law firm, 3 July 2002

The earliest known example dates from Norfolk in the 1840s, and all the references found give exactly the same meaning. It can be compared to beliefs that a thread or pin left in CLOTHES means that the tailor has not been paid.

Sussex [c.1910] Opie & Tatem, 350. **Dorset** Udal (1922) 274. **London** Steve Roud Collection (3 July 2002). **Norfolk** *Norfolk Archaeology* 2 (1849) 45. **Lincolnshire** *Grantham Jnl* (29 June 1878). **Yorkshire** Nicholson (1890) 45; [c.1930] Opie & Tatem, 350; [1987] Opie & Tatem, 350. **Aberdeenshire** [1952] Opie & Tatem, 350.

shoes: throwing

From at least the sixteenth century to the middle of the twentieth, a standard way of wishing somebody good luck on a journey or for a new undertaking was to throw an old shoe after them:

To throw an old shoe after a person who is leaving home and intends to be some time absent, will be the means of bringing him or her good luck. The person who told her neighbour of this said that, when she left home for the first time, her mother threw an old shoe after her, and that was the cause of the happiness and prosperity which attended her as long as she was absent.
Jersey *Folk-Lore* (1914)

This notion was already proverbial in the first known mention by John Heywood in 1546 and was probably old even by his time:

And home agayne hytherward quicke as a bee
Nowe for good lucke, caste an olde shoe after
mee.

Heywood, *Proverbs* (1546)

From the 1820s, shoe-throwing was increasingly described as primarily a wedding custom:

The bride went straight away to her carriage.
Someone thrust an old white pair of satin shoes
into my hand with which I made an ineffectual
shot at the post boy, and someone else behind me
missed the carriage altogether and gave me with
an old shoe a terrific blow on the back of the head.

Wiltshire Kilvert, *Diary* (1 Jan. 1873)

In this context, the connection survived for a while in the custom of tying old shoes to the back of the newlyweds' car. Nevertheless, the general 'good luck' meaning also continued to be current at least until the mid twentieth century: 'About 1939, my father was going for a job interview, and my mother said "Throw a shoe after him for luck", so I did' (**Surrey** Steve Roud Collection, Feb. 2001).

An ingenious theory as to the origin of the custom was proposed by John Thrupp in 1853 (N&Q 1S:7), which has since been quoted by a sufficient number of writers to take on a certain air of orthodoxy. Thrupp quotes several biblical passages, in which the giving of shoes symbolized the surrendering or rejecting of rights of property, ownership, and/or dominance. In Psalms 60 and 119, for example, casting a shoe is used in the sense of the 'casting off' of a people, but in Deuteronomy 25, it was specifically concerned with marriage. Thrupp therefore argued that the modern throwing of the shoe at a wedding is a relic of this symbolism – the acknowledgement from the bride (or her family) that henceforth she is under a new master to whom she owes her allegiance. Unfortuately, this theory holds little water.

The main problem is that it assumes that the shoe-throwing was originally a wedding custom, but this is not borne out by the evidence to hand. The first mention of the custom in reference to a wedding is 1823, whereas the general 'good luck' context is well recorded right back to 1546, nearly 300 years earlier. It therefore seems clear that the use of shoes in weddings is an outgrowth of the 'good luck' meaning, and the question of dominance and ownership is not relevant. In addition, the whole shape of the custom is wrong for such an origin. The shoes are thrown, not given;

it is the onlookers who throw the shoes, not the bride's father or any other of the principals, and it is usually done after the ceremony, on the going away of the bride and groom. Some other far-fetched theories are summarized in *Folk-Lore* 6 (1895) 258–81.

Also in the wedding sphere, confusion can be generated for origin theorists by the existence of other customs with 'throwing' motifs. Some writers attempt, unsuccessfully, to draw parallels with throwing rice or confetti, for example, or throwing the stocking or the bouquet (*see* WEDDINGS). A synthesis of two customs was possible, of course, as shown in a unique report from Kent (which is also often quoted to imply general currency):

Throwing the old shoe – This is a well-known
custom, but in Kent it is done thus: one of the
bridesmen throws the shoe, the bridesmaids run
after it, believing that the one who gets it will be
married first. She then throws it among the men,
and it is supposed the one who is hit will also be
married before the others. The lady probably
aims at him she likes best, which is one step
towards the fulfilment of the omen at least.

Kent N&Q (1861)

Several reports describe wives throwing shoes to wish departing fishermen luck and a safe return, and a divinatory element is sometimes included:

When a fisherman was leaving home to go to fish
on Monday, his wife threw an old shoe after him.
If it stopped mouth up, with the point of the shoe
pointing the way he was going, it was very lucky;
but if the point showed back towards the house,
he might as well go back himself, as it would be
a poor week's fishing. This throwing of the shoe
was also a sure indication whenever a person had
any venture such as a law-suit, going to sell a cow
or horse at a fair, or getting married.

Isle of Man [*c.*1850] Cashen

A shoe could also be thrown over the shoulder to decide which way to go.

Kent N&Q 2S:12 (1861) 490. **Dorset** Udal (1922) 286. **Devon** Hewett (1900) 23. **Wiltshire** Francis Kilvert, *Diary* (1 Jan. 1873); *Wilts. N&Q* 1 (1893–5) 316. **Surrey** [1939] Steve Roud Collection 2001. **Oxfordshire** [1920s] Surman (1992) 60–1. **Norfolk** N&Q 1S:2 (1850) 197. **Lincolnshire** *Gent. Mag.* (1833) 590–3; Thompson (1856) 735; Swaby (1891) 91. **Midland England** *Midland Garner* 1 (1884) 23. **Shropshire** Burne (1883) 274. **England** Addy (1895) 121. **Yorkshire** Yorkshire Hone, *Table Book* (1827) 588; N&Q 1S:2 (1850) 197; Timbs (1860) 120; Jeffrey (1923) 191. **Lancashire** Harland & Wilkinson (1882) 264. **Northern England** Brockett (1829) 221. **Co. Durham** Brockie (1886) 194–5. **Northumberland** Bosanquet (1929) 37. **Wales** Trevelyan (1909) 325. **Mid-Wales**

Davies (1911) 215. **Flint** [1823] Lucy (1983) 31. **Scotland** N&Q 5S:12 (1879). **Dumfriesshire** Corrie (1890/91) 41. **Orkney** Laing (1885) 73. **Ireland** Wilde (1888) 212. **Jersey** *Folk-Lore* 25 (1914) 246–7; L'Amy (1927) 98. **Isle of Man** [*c*.1850] Cashen (1912) 28–9. **Unlocated** N&Q 1S:1 (1850) 468; N&Q 4S:12 (1873) 327. **General** Brand (1777) 94; Grose (1787) 63; *Gent. Mag.* (1796) 636; N&Q 1S:7 (1853) 411–12; *Chambers's Jnl* (1873) 810; *Midland Garner* 2 (1884) 23; *Everybody's Book of Correct Conduct* (1893) 95–6; *Folk-Lore* 6 (1895) 258–81. **Literary** John Heywood, *Proverbs* (1546) Pt 1, Ch. 9; Charles Dickens, *David Copperfield* (1850) Ch. 10.

shoes: wear

A handful of references prognosticate one's general future prospects by the way that one's shoes wear. The divination is usually given in a short verse:

If you trip at the toe, You'll live to see woe
If you trip at the heel, You'll live to see a deal
Trip at the ball (sole), Live and spend all
Trip at the side, Live to be a bride.

Norfolk Fulcher Collection (*c*.1895)

Although the same key words usually appear (as dictated by the needs of rhyme), the meaning is often very different. Thus, to rhyme with 'heel', we are offered, in addition to the one given above, 'live to spend a deal' and 'live to save a deal'. There is no evidence that this notion is any older than the earliest known reference, in 1885, although it was probably more widely known than is suggested by the relatively few recorded versions, and it was still being quoted in the 1980s.

Somerset [1923] Opie & Tatem, 354. **Cornwall** *Folk-Lore Jnl* 5 (1887) 220. **London** [1956] Opie & Tatem, 354. **Cambridgeshire** [1937] Porter (1969) 390. **Norfolk** Fulcher Collection (*c*.1895). **Suffolk** Varden (1885) 114. **Co. Durham** Brockie (1886) 207. **Wales** Trevelyan (1909) 329. **Breconshire** *Folk-Lore* 24 (1913) 509. **Unlocated** *Household Words* (29 Sept. 1888) 435; Lean 2 (1903) 43; *Mirror* (7 July 1986) 20.

shooting stars: baby born

A belief, or more likely just a cute story told to children, maintains that a shooting star is a sign that a new baby (sometimes specifically a boy) has been born:

Children were told that a baby boy was born every time a shooting star fell.

Dorset [1950s] *Folk-Lore*

In some cases, the star is said to be the new soul of the baby itself; in others, shooting stars

are said to be the souls of those who have recently died. It is conceivable that the star-and-baby version is linked to the Christian nativity story. But even if that is its root, there is no evidence that it is anything more than a Victorian literary invention on the subject.

Compare SHOOTING STARS: DEATH.

Kent [1930s] Kent (1976) 101. **Somerset** [1923] Opie & Tatem, 376. **Dorset** [1950s] *Folk-Lore* 89 (1978) 158; **Surrey** [1955] Opie & Tatem, 376. **Norfolk** Fulcher Collection (*c*.1895). **Essex** *Folk-Lore* 64 (1953) 295. **Westmorland/Lancashire** *Folk-Lore* 64 (1953) 295. **Yorkshire** N&Q 5S:6 (1876) 506.

shooting stars: death

In direct opposition to beliefs which maintain that shooting stars signify babies being born (*see above*) a commoner superstition holds that a shooting star bodes great ill-luck or even death. In some cases, the belief is clearly an extension of that which links the coming of a COMET with the approaching death of famous or great people – 'No less an ominous fate than blazing stars to princes' (Webster, *White Devil* (1612)) – but in others, the unfortunate one is of more humble estate:

A Huntingdonshire woman was telling me of the death of her baby, on June 5, after five days' illness. She said: 'I had a warning that it was to go. The night before it was took I was passing your gate, Sir, and a great star fell down from the sky plump before me. It did not go into the ground, but burst about a foot above the road. As soon as I got home I told mother about it, and said it was a warning for someone. She said, "Perhaps it's for grandfather". I said, "May be, mother; but I fear it's for someone nigher". The next day my poor babe was took'.

Huntingdonshire N&Q (1866)

Early references all refer to great happenings, but by the early eighteenth century, ordinary people felt threatened by the phenomenon – 'I have known the shooting of a star spoil a night's rest' (*Spectator* (1711)). The idea was reported sporadically well into the twentieth century.

Somerset [*c*.1912] Tongue (1965) 140. **Essex** [*c*.1920] Ketteridge & Mays (1972); [*c*.1939] *Folk-Lore* 64 (1953) 295. **Huntingdonshire** N&Q 3S:10 (1866) 25. **England** Addy (1895) 60. **Westmorland/Lancashire** [*c*.1939] *Folk-Lore* 64 (1953) 295. **Cumberland** Penfold (1907) 58. **Radnorshire** [1953] Opie & Tatem, 376. **Unlocated** N&Q 10S:7 (1907) 197. **Literary** William Horman, *Vulgaria* (1519) 94; John Webster, *White Devil* (1612) 3:2; Thomas Draxe, *Bibliotheca Scholastica Instructissima* (1633); Cyril Tourneur, *The Revenger's Tragedy* (1607) 5:3; Addison, *Spectator* (8 Mar. 1711).

shrews

Shrews enjoyed a baneful reputation (*see below*) which resulted in a reluctance to meet or see one, and a belief that it was unlucky to do so:

An old man of Ruyton-of-the-Eleven-Towns avers that if you see a shrew-mouse . . . you must cross your foot or you will suffer for it. 'I did once [suffer for it]. I was with another boy, looking for wimberries, and I fell and hurt myself after seeing one'.   Shropshire Burne (1883)

Other shrew beliefs were more commonly said of other rodents. They could, for example, be treated like other RATS and MICE, and asked to leave:

During the winter of 1962, the Three Fords inn at Clyst St Mary was infested with shrews. They were regarded almost as pests, but at the beginning of February the licensee's wife very politely asked them to leave – and they did.
                    Devon *Devonshire Assoc.* (1963)

Or they could take the place of MOLES in helping with RHEUMATISM:

He believed that to prevent the onset of rheumatism all one had to do was to carry a dead shrew in one's pocket.   Sussex [1936] Summers

Sussex [1936] Summers (1972) 48. Devon *Devonshire Assoc.* 95 (1963) 98. Northamptonshire N&Q 1S:2 (1850) 164. Shropshire Burne (1883) 214. Co. Durham Brockie (1886) 221.

---

shrews: cannot cross paths

A widespread misconception about shrews and other small creatures such as field-mice was that they were unable to cross paths or cart ruts:

Strolling in the garden of another villager, I saw a mouse, not one of the little devouring animals so abhorred by clean and careful housewives, but a pretty taper-snouted out-door resident, quite as destructive in his habits, lying dead upon one of the paths. No marks of violence were visible upon it, and I was earnestly assured that these mice, whenever they attempt to cross a footpath, always die in the effort. Putting a credulous face upon this piece of information, I was met by the reply, 'Ah! you Lunnuners doant know everything; why I've found 'em dead upon the paths scores o' times, and I know they can't get across alive.   Hertfordshire N&Q (1852)

The first reference to this notion in English is in Edward Topsell's *History of Four-Footed Beasts*

(1686), and, as with other shrew beliefs, it is likely that his generation gleaned this idea from Pliny's *Natural History* (AD 77), which states that a shrew will 'die immediately if it goes across the rut made by a wheel', and thus introduced it to British tradition (*see also* SHREWS: HARMFUL).

Sussex Latham (1878) 42. Somerset [1923] Opie & Tatem, 355. Hertfordshire N&Q 1S:6 (1852) 123. Shropshire Burne (1883) 214. General Topsell (1607) 536. Classical Pliny, *Natural History* (AD 77) Bk 8, Para. 83.

---

shrews: harmful

It was formerly believed that shrews were poisonous, and had the power to lame humans and cattle simply by crawling over them:

A vulgar superstition once prevailed that this poor creature was of so baneful and venomous a nature that whenever it crept over a horse, cow or sheep, the animal so touched became afflicted with cruel anguish, and threatened with the loss of the use of its limbs. To repel this imaginary evil, it was customary to close up the shrew alive in a hole bored in an ash, elm or willow-tree; and afterwards to whip the cattle thus tormented, with one of the boughs, which was considered an efficacious cure.   Northern England Brockett (1829)

Some of the earlier references, as here, state that various trees could be used in this procedure, but most authorities specify the ASH, and a tree thus treated was locally prized for its curative properties, and was termed a 'shrew-ash'.

A less widespread way of preparing an ash tree to counter the shrew menace, was to use a HORSESHOE:

In grubbing up old stumps of ash trees, from which many successive trees have sprung, in the parish of Scotton, there was found, in many instances, an iron horse-shoe. The one shown to me measured 4 1/2 in. by 4 1/4 in. The workmen seemed to be familiar with this fact, and gave the following account – The shoe is so placed to 'charm' the tree, so that a twig of it might be used in curing cattle over which a shrewmouse had run, or which had been 'overlooked'. If they were stroked by one of these twigs, the ease would be charmed away.   Yorkshire? N&Q (1878)

A third remedy utilized a well-known principle of folk medicine – wearing a creature, or its remains, around the neck:

To keep beasts safe that the blind mouse, called a shrew, do not bite them, enclose the same mouse

quick [alive] in chalk [clay], which when it is hard, hang the same about the neck of the beast.
General Lupton (1579)

This mistaken notion about the innocuous shrew was extremely well known, and although naturalists had been pointing out its fallacy since at least the eighteenth century, it was widely believed in rural areas into the twentieth century. Elements of the belief were already in place in Britain in the mid sixteenth century, and there is no doubt that it was derived directly from the writings of Pliny. The relevant points of Pliny's *Natural History* (AD 77) include several of the elements of the British superstition:

The bite of a shrew-mouse in Italy is venomous, but the venomous species is not found in the district beyond the Apennines. Also wherever it occurs it dies if it crosses the track of a wheel . . . (Bk 8 Para 83). If it has bitten draught animals, a freshly killed mouse is applied with salt, or a bat's gall, in vinegar. The shrew-mouse itself, torn asunder and applied, is a remedy for its own bite. It is best if the mouse applied is the one which gave the bite, but they preserve them for this purpose in oil, or enclosed in clay. Another remedy for its bite is earth from a wheel rut. Pliny, *Natural History* (AD 77)

For the wheel-rut element, *see above*. The most interesting fact here is that although Pliny states that shrews are dangerous, he does not mention the notion of the shrew-ash, which was the most common of the British remedies, and the earliest reference we have to that particular motif is in Robert Plot's book on Staffordshire natural history (1686). It should also be noted that all the available references are from England.

NB: Judging by the wording used, several of the writers listed below are quoting the well-known piece by Gilbert White about Hampshire in 1776. It is not clear whether they are simply adopting his wording and applying it to traditions in their own locality, or simply copying his work and implying the existence of local beliefs.

Sussex Latham (1878) 42; *Sussex Notes & Queries* 2 (1929) 178–9. **Hampshire** [1776] White (1788) 185–6; Yonge (1898) Ch. 16. **Somerset** [*c*.1905] Tongue (1965) 221. **Devon** *Devonshire Assoc.* 65 (1933) 123 [corrected 66 (1934) 74]; *Devonshire Assoc.* 66 (1934) 74; *Devonshire Assoc.* 103 (1971) 268. **Wiltshire** Akerman (1842) 25–6; Smith (1874) 323–4. **Surrey** *Folk-Lore* 9 (1898) 330–6. **Lincolnshire** Peacock (1877) 134; Watkins 10–11. **Staffordshire** Plot (1686) 222. **Northern England** Brockett (1829) 267; *Newcastle Weekly Chronicle* (11 Feb. 1899) 7. **Yorkshire?** N&Q 5S:9 (1878) 65. **Co. Durham** Brockie (1886) 127–8. **General** T. Elyot, *Dictionary* (1545) quoted Opie & Tatem, 354; Lupton (1579) Bk 7,

Para. 52; Bk 10, Para. 11; Topsell (1607) 536, 541; W. Gibson, *Farrier's New Guide* (1721) 61; Samuel Johnson, *Dictionary of the English Language* (1755); *The Mirror* (17 Mar. 1832) 179–80. **Literary** George Eliot, *Mill on the Floss* (1860) Pt 1, Ch. 1. **Classical** Pliny, *Natural History* (AD 77) Bk 8, Para. 83; Bk 29, Para. 27.

shudder

A sudden shiver will often elicit the comment that 'someone is walking over my grave', and this has been the case for at least the last 250 years. It is not clear whether this has ever been a genuine belief, or simply a proverbial metaphor, but it has remained remarkably stable since its first recorded reference in Swift's *Polite Conversations* of 1738, and to be included in that work it must have been a well-known phrase of the time. Fifty years later, Grose could poke gentle fun at the idea:

A person being suddenly taken with a shivering, is a sign that some one has just then walked over the spot of their future grave. Probably all persons are not subject to this sensation; otherwise the inhabitants of those parishes whose burial-grounds lie in the common foot-path, would live in one continual fit of shaking. Unlocated Grose (1787)

A similar objection could be made that those destined to be buried or lost at sea would never experience the sensation – although the clever answer is that people in ships 'walk' over the site of the drowning.

A few variations have been recorded:

When people experience a cold shiver they say, 'A donkey is walking over my grave', or, 'Death is picking my grave' . . . If a person shivers before a roaring fire or in the heat of summer, the people say 'The spirits are searching for your grave'.
Wales Trevelyan (1909)

If a sudden shivering comes upon you death is running over your house. England Addy (1895)

Dorset Udal (1922) 285. **Cornwall** N&Q 1S:12 (1855) 38; Hunt (1865) 239–40; Couch (1871) 169. **London** [1987] Opie & Tatem, 356. **Oxfordshire** [pre-1900] *Folk-Lore* 24 (1913) 91. **Worcestershire/Shropshire** *Gent. Mag.* (1855) 385. **East Anglia** Varden (1885) 113. **Norfolk** Fulcher Collection (*c*.1895). **Lincolnshire** *Grantham Jnl* (29 June 1878); Swaby (1891) 93. **Shropshire** Burne (1883) 269. **Staffordshire** Poole (1875) 79. **England** Addy (1895) 90. **Yorkshire** Nicholson (1890) 44. **Co. Durham** Henderson (1866) 85; Brockie (1886) 211; Leighton (1910) 60. **Wales** Trevelyan (1909) 281, 283. **Western Scotland** Napier (1879) 138. **Unlocated** Grose (1787) 59; N&Q 11S:9 (1914) 150; Gales (1914) 229. **Literary** Swift (1738); *Connoisseur* 59 (1755) 354; *Old Women's Sayings* (*c*.1835); Charles Dickens, *Dombey* and Son (1848) Ch. 24. *Illustrated London News* (27 Dec. 1851) 779.

sieve and shears

A relatively complex divinatory procedure involving a sieve and a pair of shears, used to discover thieves or lost items and occasionally for LOVE DIVINATION. As with the related BIBLE AND KEY, the process relies on the power of inanimate objects to react to the naming of the culprit:

Sticke a paire of sheeres in the rind of a sive, and let two persons set the top of each of their forefingers upon the upper part of the sheeres, holding it with the sive up from the ground steddilie, and ask Peter and Paule whether B or C hath stolne the thing lost, and at the nomination of the guiltie person, the sive will turne round.

Scot (1584)

Essentially the same procedure was still being used in the 1840s:

An old farmer told me recently of an incident of his youth. In his particular village in Yorkshire there had been some thefts at the hall. Who had committed them they could not find out. He says, as a lad he remembers the household of the hall being gathered together, and someone (I forget who it was) taking a sieve in which a pair of

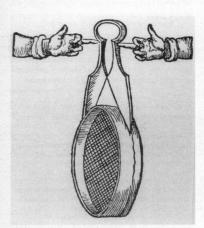

Many descriptions of sieve and shears divination exist, but it is unusual to find the subject illustrated. This comes from Reginald Scot's Discoverie of Witchcraft, 1584.

shears had been stuck upright, and going round to each person, and repeating the following words:

'Bless St Peter
Bless St Paul
Bless the God that made us all'

If so-and-so (naming the person that he turned the sieve before each one in the room) stole the money, turn sieve'. When opposite one woman the sieve did turn nearly round in the hands of the person who held it. The woman taught the village school . . . such was the prejudice against her after this, that she left the village, and, dying about four months later, confessed to stealing the money.   Yorkshire [1840s] N&Q

One of the obvious disadvantages of this type of divination is that it relies on the operators saying the name of the culprit, so it is presumably of little use if a stranger carried out the deed. One or two references additionally mention keys, which Lady Wilde explains:

To find stolen goods – Place two keys on a sieve, in the form of a cross. Two men hold the sieve, while a third makes the sign of the cross on the forehead of the suspected party, and calls out his name loudly, three times over. If innocent, the keys remain stationary; but if guilty, the keys revolve slowly round the sieve, and then there is no doubt as to who is the thief.   Ireland Wilde (1888)

Scot's description in 1584 is the earliest known in Britain, but other references come thick and fast soon afterwards and throughout the seventeenth century. It was sufficiently well known at the time for writers such as Jonson (1612) and Melton (1620) to refer to it in passing, and a technical term for the process, *coscinomancy*, was current by at least 1603 (Christopher Heydon, *A Defence of Judiciall Astrologie*). Indeed, it was already in apparent everyday use in 1602 when two Shetlanders were accused of witchcraft (*see* Goudie (1889)). Unusually for such a complex procedure, these British examples are very close to those reported from classical times. The Greek pastoral poet Theocritus provides the first reference:

To Agrio, too, I made the same demand
A cunning woman she, I cross'd her hand
She turn'd the sieve and shears, and told me true
That I should love, but not be lov'd by you.

Idylls (c.275 BC)

Scot was already aware that 'This is a great practise in all countries', and it is probable that the procedure was introduced into Britain by writers such as Scot quoting Continental European sources, which were in turn based on Classical writings. But further research in those foreign sources is necessary before this likely chain of events can be verified. Despite these respectable historical antecedents, however, the sieve and shears is not reported often after the turn of the nineteenth century, and is certainly far less common in later years than the Bible and key.

Sieves also feature in other divination procedures; see ASH-RIDDLING and CHAFF-RIDDLING.

Yorkshire [1840s] N&Q 8S:2 (1892) 305. Northumberland Brockett (1829) 246. Shetland [1602] Goudie (1889) 185–7; [1893] Black (1903) 160. Ireland Wilde (1888) 207. Unlocated Grose (1787) 54–5. General Scot (1584) Bk 12, Ch. 17; Melton (1620); Aubrey *Remaines* (1686/1880) 25; N&Q 8S:2 (1892) 416. Literary Ben Jonson, *The Alchemist* (1612) 1:1; Samuel Butler, *Hudibras* (1664) Pt 2, Canto 3; William Congreve, *Love for Love* (1695) 2:1. Classical Theocritus, *Idylls* (*c.*275 BC) 3:31.

silver

Silver features in many beliefs and traditions, and although it is generally regarded in a positive light, some traditions held it to be unlucky in certain circumstances. It also had an important role in a number of well-known cures, the most widely reported of which was for EPILEPSY. The sufferer had to gather small sums from people at church and change these for silver coins which had formed part of the collection and were thus regarded as blessed. These silver coins were then melted down to make a ring which was worn to ward off fits. A regular remedy for cattle which had been ELF-SHOT, or anyone suffering the effects of an EVIL EYE, consisted of placing silver in water and using this 'silver water' to effect the cure:

A charm for the evil eye. An old woman living on Loch Rannoch gave me the following particulars as to the cure of human beings or cattle 'over-looked' by the evil eye. Draw water between sunset and sunrise from a stream crossing a public road which has been passed over by the living and the dead. Put a piece of silver in the water and pour it over the person or animal you desire to cure in the name of the Trinity. If the sickness has been caused by the evil eye the silver will stick to the bottom of the vessel. My inform-ant said she had frequently used the charm herself, and that in her younger days some people possessed magic stones which were employed instead of the silver piece.

Perthshire *Folk-Lore* (1897)

Rings made of silver were also worn for CRAMP.

Coins, especially sixpences, which were bent ('crooked') or which had holes in, were regarded as particularly lucky to own, or to give as a gift (*see* MONEY: CROOKED/HOLED COINS), and silver in general was believed to have protective power:

The fairies do not like a bridegroom, and he must also beware of the machinations of a jilted sweet-heart. Let him on the day of marriage put silver in the sole of the stocking of his right foot as he puts it on, and evil power will not affect him.

Highland Scotland Macbain (1887/88)

Another way in which the protective power of silver was used was in the dairy:

A goodwife at Moreton Say is accustomed to put a silver coin into the churn when the cream swells instead of turning into butter.

Shropshire Burne (1883)

This notion that evil powers disliked silver was also at the root of the widespread idea that witches, when in the form of HARES or other animals, could only be harmed by a silver bullet.

But silver was regarded less positively when contrasted with gold, and sometimes had an unlucky edge: 'to dreame of gold good lucke, but of silver ill' (Melton (1620)). A belief that it was actually unlucky to find silver money lasted at least from the seventeenth to the nineteenth centuries:

Whereas it is ordinarie to divine of future things by some such like, as by finding a piece of iron, signifying good lucke – but if silver be found then it is evill.

Thomas Cooper, *Mystery of Witchcraft* (1617)

To find silver, however acceptable it may be at the time, is sure to prove unlucky to the finder.

Northamptonshire Sternberg (1851)

Northamptonshire Sternberg (1851) 169. Shropshire Burne (1883) 165. Cambridgeshire Porter (1969) 15. Yorkshire Blakeborough (1898) 203; *Observer Supp.* (10 Nov. 1968) 24. Lancashire Harland & Wilkinson (1882) 75. Northumberland Bigge (1860/62) 94. Cardiganshire [1953] *Folk-Lore* 63 (1952) 49. Skye *Folk-Lore* 34 (1923) 92. Shetland Reid (1869) 24; Black (1903) 160. General Thomas Cooper, *Mystery of Witchcraft* (1617) 137; Melton (1620). Literary Walter Scott, *Old Mortality* (1816) Ch. 16; Walter Scott, *The Pirate* (1822) Pt 1, 142.

silver water

'Silver water' was water in which a silver coin, preferably one with a cross on it, was placed for use in cures for ailments with supernatural cause, such as the ELF-SHOT.

Caithness *Folk-Lore* 16 (1905) 336. Northwest Ireland *Folk-Lore* 17 (1906) 202–3.

sin-eater

Our knowledge of the sin-eater, who was employed at funerals to eat food and thereby take on the sins of the deceased, commences with a description by antiquarian John Aubrey:

In the Country of Hereford was an old custom at funerals to hire poor people, who were to take upon them all the sins of the party deceased. One of them I remember lived in a cottage on Ross-high way. (He was a long, lean, ugly, lamentable poor rascal.) The manner was that when the corpse was brought out of the house and laid on the bier, a loaf of bread was brought out, and delivered to the sin-eater over the corpse, as also a mazer-bowl of maple (Gossips bowl) full of beer, which he was to drink up, and sixpence in money, in consideration whereof he took upon him (ipso facto) all the sins of the defunct, and freed him (or her) from walking after they were dead. Herefordshire Aubrey, *Remaines* (1686)

Aubrey continues by quoting the 'scape-goat' of ancient law in Leviticus 16:21–2, and then quotes further recent examples from Herefordshire and Wales. Aubrey's manuscript was not fully published until 1880, but his writings were recycled in a number of other nineteenth-century publications. Further material from Aubrey was included in John Bagford's letter on the antiquities of London, dated 1714/15, which refers to the custom existing in Shropshire (*see* Hone (1832) and Brand 2 (1849)).

Thomas Pennant also provided a description of a funeral custom from the 1770s, in which food, drink, and money were given to poor people, across the coffin. He does not mention anything about sins (**Wales** Pennant (1784)).

The later history of scholarship on the sin-eater is a tangled web of misinformation and misunderstanding, which engendered two major published controversies. In 1852 a Mr Moggridge gave some observations on the custom of the sin-eater to the Cambrian Archaeological Association, in which he claimed that it was 'said to have prevailed to a recent period' not far from Llandebie, Carmarthenshire. His statement was published in the Association's journal and went unchallenged until the 1870s, when many who knew the area and its customs well stated categorically that no such practice had prevailed there in the nineteenth century, if ever. Their evidence included statements given by inhabitants of Llandebie who had been resident even before Moggridge's account was given. Other Welsh researchers joined in, and found no trace of the custom. Wirt Sikes (United States Consul for Wales), for example, reserved judgement, but expressed some considerable doubt:

as regards the sin-eater, and I have searched diligently for it. The subject has engaged my attention from the first moment I set foot on Cambrian soil, and I have not only seen no reference to it in Welsh writings, but I have never met any unlettered Welshman who had ever heard of it. Sikes (1880)

A second controversy raged in the 1890s. Apparently unaware of the doubt cast upon Moggridge's account, leading folklorist E. Sidney Hartland published an article in the 1892 volume of *Folk-Lore*, where he used it as evidence to support his view that sin-eating was 'a relic of a savage feast where the meat consumed was the very body of the deceased kinsman' (Hartland, 155). A long-running argument then broke out in the pages of *The Times, Notes & Queries*, and, particularly, *The Academy*, in which Hartland was taken to task by J. P. Owen, N. W. Thomas, and others, for perpetuating the notion of the sin-eater's recent existence in Wales, and also for his general conclusions. It would be useful if a reliable modern scholar would undertake a study of the evidence and present a reasoned account of the matter.

To summarize: Aubrey, though a gullible collector, can hardly have invented the descriptions he noted down, and though he often took too literally stories or legends, in this case he claims to be writing from his own experience. On balance, his account must stand as at least mostly accurate. Moggridge's comments have been effectively discredited, and the existence of the custom in Wales in the nineteenth century is in serious doubt. We can safely dismiss Hartland's theories on cannibalism as both unlikely and unnecessary. There are plenty of strands in the history of Christian funeral practices which could have resulted in such a custom, and biblical references such as Hosea 4:8, 'They eat up the sin of my people' could have contributed. Discussion is often confused by reference to other funeral customs, such as placing a plate of salt on the breast of the corpse (*see*

SALT: PLACED ON CORPSE), and the general provision of food and drink to mourners, which was often surrounded by customary rules and ceremonies. The most reasonable conclusion is provided by Jacqueline Simpson:

These customs are best understood as echoes of medieval Requiems, and of the custom of giving alms to the poor (including food) in exchange for their prayers, normally distributed beside the grave or coffin.   Simpson & Roud (2000)

The key point in Aubrey's account, which later writers have questioned, is that the custom seems to have been formalized to include a 'professional' sin-eater. There are reliable, though not common, later accounts of the food and drink given to the mourners being regarded as necessary to help the deceased's soul on its way:

When you drink wine at a funeral every drop that you drink is a sin which the deceased has committed. You thereby take away the dead man's sins and bear them yourself.   England Addy (1895)

See also Leather (1912) 121 and *Folk-Lore* 51 (1940) 295 for Herefordshire examples.

Somerset Tongue (1965) 137. Herefordshire/Wales Aubrey, *Remaines* (1686/1880) 35–6. Herefordshire Leather (1912) 121; [1925] *Folk-Lore* 51 (1940) 295. Lincolnshire Sutton (1992) 161–2. Shropshire Hone, *Year Book* (1832) 429–30; Brand 2 (1849) 246–7. England Addy (1895) 124. Wales Thomas Pennant, *A Tour in Wales 1770* 2 (1784) 338; Sikes (1880) 326–7. Carmarthenshire *Archaeologia Cambrensis* NS 3 (1852) 330–2. General N&Q 1S:4 (1851) 211; N&Q 1S:6 (1852) 390, 541; N&Q 5S:6 (1876) 505; N&Q 5S:7 (1877) 14; N&Q 8S:8 (1895) 288, 332; N&Q 8S:9 (1896) 109–11, 169–70, 236–7, 296; Simpson & Roud (2000) 327–8. For the Hartland controversy: E. Sidney Hartland, *Folk-Lore* 3 (1892) 145–57; Gertrude Hope, *Folk-Lore* 4 (1893) 392–3; G. M. Godden *Folk-Lore* 3 (1892) 546–9; N. W. Thomas *The Times* (18 Sept. 1895), N&Q 8S:9 (1896) 169–70; Hartland, *The Academy* (9 Nov. 1895) 387–8; (16 Nov. 1895) 413–14; (23 Nov. 1895) 435; J. P. Owen, *The Academy* (7 Dec. 1895) 484; (21 Dec. 1895) 545–7; (4 Jan. 1896) 14–15; Continuing correspondence by Hartland, Thomas, Owen, and others in *The Academy* (11 Jan. 1896) 37; (18 Jan. 1896) 56–7; (25 Jan. 1896) 78–9; (29 Feb. 1896) 178–9; (7 Mar. 1896) 200–1; (14 Mar. 1896) 222–3; (21 Mar. 1896) 241–2; (28 Mar. 1896) 265; (25 Apr. 1896) 346; (2 May 1896) 366; (9 May 1896) 385; (16 May 1896) 407; (23 May 1896) 428–9.

singing

A widely known proverbial expression dictates that if you 'sing before breakfast, you'll cry before night':

[Remembering a childhood in Lancashire (born 1906)] *To this day . . . I never sing before breakfast in case I cry before the day is out.*
    Lancashire Corbridge (1964)

While the central meaning remains consistent, numerous variations in the wording have been reported, for example:

Sing before breakfast
Greet after 't.
    Northeast Scotland Gregor (1881)

If you sing before bite,
You'll cry before night.
    Cornwall Folk-Lore Jnl (1887)

The basis of the belief can be seen as an example of the PURITAN streak which runs through much superstition, whereby undue levity is threatened with retribution, or more convincingly that it is TEMPTING FATE to be too cheerful and that unusually high spirits portend coming misfortune. Either way, it makes for a somewhat gloomy disposition. The earliest version, in the form of 'Laugh before breakfast you'll cry before supper', is included in Kelly's volume of Scottish proverbs (1721), but the sentiment, if not the exact wording, is evident a long while before that as 'You wax merry this morning, God give grace you weep not [before] night' (John Palsgrave, *Lesclarissement de la Langue Francoyse* (1530) 776).

Singing is also proscribed in other contexts, although these are more rarely reported:

One should not sing when making a bed, else sleep will not be theirs . . . [and] Never sing while you are baking.
    Highland Scotland Macbain (1887/88)

If you sing at the table (after partaking of a meal) you will die in the workhouse.
    Norfolk Fulcher Collection (c.1895)

Sussex Latham (1878) 11. Somerset [1923] Opie & Tatem, 359. Cornwall *Folk-Lore Jnl* 5 (1887) 220. Wiltshire Wilts. N&Q 1 (1893–5) 61, 103. Essex [1998] Rees (2001a) 172. Oxfordshire [pre-1900] *Folk-Lore* 24 (1913) 90. Norfolk Fulcher Collection (c.1895). Lancashire Harland & Wilkinson (1873) 229. [c.1912] Corbridge (1964) 156–60. Yorkshire Addy (1895) 95. Co. Durham Henderson (1866) 85. Brockie (1886) 211; Leighton (1910) 59. Wales Trevelyan (1909) 325. Scotland Kelly (1721) 332. Highland Scotland Macbain (1887/88) 256, 262; Polson (1926) 128. Northeast Scotland Gregor (1881) 31. Angus [1950] Opie & Tatem, 359. Unlocated N&Q 1S:7 (1853) 81; N&Q 1S:11 (1855) 416; Igglesden (c.1932) 177. General Foli (1902) 108.

six six six

see NUMBER 666.

skirt hem

see CLOTHES: SKIRT HEM.

skull legends

A number of old houses in England and Wales possess a human skull – or part of one – which local tradition maintains must never be taken away:

> There are the remains of a skull, in three parts, at Tunstead, a farmhouse about a mile and a half from Chapel-en-le-frith. It is said that if this skull is removed everything on the farm will go wrong. The cows will be dry and barren, the sheep have the rot, and horses fall down, breaking knees and otherwise injuring themselves. I saw this skull about six weeks ago, and many of the country people still believe that it has these magic powers.
>
> Derbyshire N&Q (1873)

The defining motif is that the skull must not be removed from the premises, and although the penalty for removal varies, unpleasant poltergeist-type phenomena is the norm, and the threatened death of one of the family or general bad luck is common. Most of the skulls have relatively well-developed 'historical' stories to explain their nature, and the skull often remains unburied at the request of its former owner, or as the result of a murder, suicide or execution. As is the usual nature of such legends, they are internally satisfying as stories but do not bear close examination as historical fact.

The most comprehensive study of such skulls is Andy Roberts and David Clarke, 'Heads and Tales: the Screaming Skull Legends of Britain', *Fortean Studies* 3 (1996). They identify twenty-seven known examples, from Sussex, Somerset, Cornwall, Dorset, Wiltshire, Derbyshire, Lancashire, Yorkshire, Cumberland, and Clwyd. Two of the best known are Bettiscombe (Dorset) and Tunstead Farm (Derbyshire). Roberts and Clarke provide an excellent synopsis of the available material, and they argue strongly for a continuous thread linking prehistoric cults of severed heads and skulls to the extant skull legends. Unfortunately, the very existence of such cults is now under question (*see*, for example, Hutton (1991) 194–5) and Roberts's and Clarke's conclusions are necessarily based on the assumption,

for which there is no evidence, that such beliefs have remained in existence but unrecorded for hundreds, even thousands, of years.

The term 'screaming skulls' has been widely applied to the genre, on the assumption that the skulls object to being removed by emitting an ear-piercing scream. The traditional stories do not include this element, which has clearly been grafted on to the tradition by 'improving' writers, and it should be dropped and an alternative generic name found, if it is not too late.

Derbyshire N&Q 4S:11 (1873) 64–5. **General** Roberts & Clarke (1996); Westwood (1985) 13–14, 134, 327–8.

skulls

Human skulls, or parts of them, have long been used in various ways in a number of traditional cures, the most common being EPILEPSY and TOOTHACHE. Other isolated examples have been listed, for example:

> Against the biting of a mad dog – Take pills made of the skull of one that is hanged.   Scot (1584)

> Moss growing on a human skull, if dried, powdered, and taken as snuff, will cure the headache.   Grose (1787)

Another reference indicates a tradition of 'swearing on a skull':

> In April 1851 a man was committed to Mayo prison for cutting off the head of a corpse but a few days interred. His object in severing the head was that of clearing himself of some imputed crime by swearing on a skull, a superstition said to be very common in that part of Ireland.
>
> Co. Mayo N&Q (1852)

Co. Mayo N&Q 1S:5 (1852) 485. **General** Scot (1584) Bk 12, Ch. 14; Grose (1787) 56.

skulls: moss growing on

The commonest medical use for human skulls was in curing EPILEPSY and TOOTHACHE, but the moss which grew on them was thought valuable for a number of other cures. These included staunching blood from a wound or nosebleed, alleviating a headache, and as a protection against the plague.

> It is approved, that the moss which groweth upon the skull of a dead man, unburied, will staunch blood potently.   Bacon, *Sylva Sylvarum* (1627)

> Moss growing on a human skull, if dried,

*powdered, and taken as snuff, will cure the
headache.*   Grose (1787)

Cures like these are mentioned regularly in
seventeenth- and eighteenth-century sources,
but do not seem to have lasted well, whereas the
epilepsy and toothache cures were abundantly
reported in the nineteenth and twentieth
centuries. Nevertheless, an inconclusive report
from Co. Clare in 1911 indicates the existence of
some such moss tradition:

*There is some belief relating to moss upon skulls
which I could not get explained, but I was asked
not to pull it off.*   **Co. Clare** *Folk-Lore* (1911)

London [*c.*1665] *Archaeologia* 37 (1857) 4. **Co. Clare**
Folk-Lore 22 (1911) 56. **General** *Arcana Fairfax* (*c.*1620);
Francis Bacon, *Sylva Sylvarum* (1627) 980; J. Gregory,
Posthuma (1649) 63; R. Boyle, *Works* 4 (1744) 212; Grose
(1787) 56.

skylarks *(Alauda arvensis)*

The lark is protected by tradition in Orkney,
Shetland, and other parts of Scotland, where its
nickname is 'Our Lady's Hen':

*Throughout the whole of Shetland, the skylark is
held almost as sacred as the red-breast is with us;
therefore it is but seldom that either the birds or
their eggs are disturbed. In some parts of the
north isles, when the reason of this forbearance
is sought, the usual reply is, 'weel, if ye look under
a laverock's tongue, ye'll see three spots, and they
say that every one is a curse upo' him that inter-
feres wi' it.'*   **Shetland** Saxby (1874)

Scotland Chambers (1842) 41. **Galloway** Mactaggart
(1824) 212. **Argyllshire** Maclagan (1901) 206. **Shetland**
Saxby (1874) 88; N&Q 6S:9 (1884) 26. **Orkney** Brand
(1703) 61; Buckley & Brown (1891) 122. **General and
foreign** Swainson (1886) 92–5.

sleep

Most of the material on sleep is concerned with
BEDS – their orientation, position within the
room, the FEATHERS in the mattress, and so on.
Another belief focused on the danger of sleeping in the light of the MOON.

There were many adages about sleep, not
exactly superstitions, but they could become so
if followed obsessively:

*The 'beauty sleep' is sleep before midnight . . . The
number of hours one should sleep –*

*Nature requires five (or six)
Custom takes seven*

*Idleness takes nine
And wickedness eleven*

                            Unlocated N&Q (1938)

*Hours of sleep – 'Six for a man, seven for a
woman, eight for a fool'. Another adage I learnt
was:*

*Early to bed and early to rise
Makes a man healthy, wealthy and wise
Pleasant dreams, sweet repose
Shut the door on the doctor's nose
Pleasant dreams and sweet repose
All the bed and all the clothes.*
                            Wiltshire *Wilts. N&Q* (1893–5)

On a more serious level, a handful of references detail a belief that one must be careful not
to wake a sleeper, as his/her 'soul' or 'spirit' might
be abroad and not get back in time:

*There is a belief that a sleeping person should not
be wakened too suddenly; his soul may not have
time to return to his body. The soul in such cases is
fancied to be an insect – a bee usually, and hence
comes the idea of the bee-soul, which appears in
some Highland superstitions. A young lad was
sleeping outside on a sunny slope one day, and
somebody came upon him and roughly wakened
him. The lad was practically insane thereafter, but
a skilled person was consulted. He directed that the
lad should a year exactly from the first time
again sleep where he was before, and be allowed to
waken of his own accord. This was done, and, as
he slept, the wondering onlookers saw a beautiful
bee coming along and enter the lad's mouth. When
he awoke he was perfectly sane and sound.*
                            Highland Scotland Macbain (1887/88)

See also BEES: SOULS.

Wiltshire *Wilts. N&Q* 1 (1893–5) 102–3. **Wales** Trevelyan
(1909) 325–6. **Highland Scotland** Macbain (1887/88) 260.
Banffshire Gregor (1874) 268–9. **N. Ireland** Foster (1951)
15. **Co. Tyrone** *Lore & Language* 1:7 (1972) 8. **Unlocated**
N&Q 175 (1938) 476.

snails: cures

Snails have been used in cures for numerous
ailments, including WHOOPING COUGH,
consumption, AGUE, JAUNDICE, gout, SPRAINS,
EARACHE, and general 'weakness'. Methods of
application are similarly various: they can be
eaten raw, boiled in milk, made into a broth,
roasted and powdered, rubbed on the skin, or
encased in a bag and worn round the neck.

snails

Snails were used extensively in cures and they also featured in minor divination procedures (*see below* and WART CURES: SNAILS). They were also commonly eaten, sometimes for medicinal purposes – snail broth was reputedly good for consumption – but also simply as food:

I was just now interrogating a village child in reference to the addresses to snails . . . when she acquainted me with the not very appetising fact that she and her brothers and sisters had been in the constant habit of indulging in this horrible 'Limacotrophy'. 'We hooks them out of the wall (she says) with a stick, in winter time, and not in summer time (so it seems they have their seasons); and we roasts them, when they've done spitting, they be a-done; and we takes them out with a fork, and eats them. Sometimes we has a jug heaped up, pretty near my pinafore-full. I loves them dearly'.   Unlocated N&Q (1851)

Occasional references indicate that snails were useful in the cream-making process:

Deep in the country is a belief that snails found in damp ditches are infallible for converting milk into cream . . . To make the cream rise . . . you must search the water-side and runnels for snails in the rise of the sun; you must pick the fattest and juicyest, and, crushing them in a linen bag or piece of muslin, squeeze the juice into the milk.
    Unlocated *Observer* (20 Jan. 1924)

Oxfordshire N&Q 1S:3 (1851) 221–2. Co. Laoighis *Béaloideas* 9 (1939) 33. Unlocated N&Q 1S:3 (1851) 207, 221, 336; *Observer* (20 Jan. 1924).

Cure for earache – Get snail, let the froth, when pricked, drop into the ear.
    Gloucestershire Hartland (1895)

It was reported that the tinkers in the Scottish Highlands use snail oil to rub on sprained muscles. The writer also mentioned a 'spry old woman in her nineties' who attributed her agility to regular massage with snail oil.
    Highland Scotland *Folk-Lore* (1962)

Thus the colliers and forgemen who indulged too heavily in malt beverages were wont to seek the rectification of a disordered system by doses of a concoction made from powdered snails.
    Staffordshire Hackwood (1924)

Baked snails made into jelly rubbed into the legs or back of a weakly child was a local cure.
    Worcestershire Berkeley & Jenkins (1932)

Snail soup is drunk even today for the cure of consumption.   Yorkshire Blakeborough (1898)

Isle of Wight IOW Fed. W. I.s (1994) 95–6. Wiltshire *Wilts. N&Q* 1 (1893–5) 370. Berkshire *Folk-Lore* 72 (1961) 352. Oxfordshire N&Q 1S:3 (1851) 221–2; *Oxf. FL Soc. Ann. Record* (1956) 13. Gloucestershire N&Q 4S:4 (1873) 500; *Glos. N&Q* 1 (1881) 43; Hartland (1895) 51. Worcestershire Berkeley & Jenkins (1932) 33. Cambridgeshire Porter (1969) 74. East Anglia Varden (1885) 105. Suffolk *Gent. Mag.* (1867) 728–41. Norfolk N&Q 3S:5 (1864) 237. Norfolk/Lincolnshire *Folk-Lore* 40 (1929) 116–17. Staffordshire Hackwood (1924) 151. England Addy (1895) 91. Yorkshire Nicholson (1890) 142; Blakeborough (1898) 138. Wales Trevelyan (1909) 317–19; Jones (1930) 143. Highland Scotland Polson (1926) 31; *Folk-Lore* 73 (1962) 134. Shetland Brand (1703) 108. N. Ireland Foster (1951) 61. Co. Longford *Béaloideas* 6 (1936) 265–6. Unlocated Igglesden (*c.*1932) 204.

---

snails: divination

A regular method of LOVE DIVINATION which relied on the random movements of a snail to reveal the letters of the future spouse's name:

To know the name of the person you are destined to marry, put a snail on a plate of flour – cover it over and leave it all night; in the morning the initial letter of the name will be found traced on the flour by the snail.   Ireland Wilde (1888)

Variations include throwing the snail over your shoulder, and even baking the poor thing:

I myself know of a comparatively recent case in Co. Cork, where the little slug was hunted for and found early on may morning, placed on a plate sprinkled with flour, and baked alive in the oven that its writhings might trace in the flour the initials of the future lucky man.
    Ireland *Folk-Lore* (1916)

The procedure is reported most often from Ireland, where May Day was a favourite time for its operation, but the earliest reference is from John Gay's evocation of English milkmaids and shepherds:

Last May-day fair I searched for to find a snail
That might my secret lover's name reveal
I seiz'd the vermin, home I quickly sped
And on the hearth the milk-white embers spread
Slow crawled the snail, and if I right can spell

In the soft ashes mark'd a curious L.
Gay, The Shepherd's Week (1714)

The belief was still being reported in the 1950s.

Somerset [1923] Opie & Tatem, 361. **Shropshire** Burne (1883) 179. **Glamorganshire** [1957] Opie & Tatem, 362. **Breconshire** [1954] Opie & Tatem, 361. **Stirlingshire** Hone, *Every-Day Book* (1827) 343. **Ireland** *Folk-Lore Record* 5 (1882) 82; Wilde (1888) 104–5, 206; *Folk-Lore* 27 (1916) 262. **Literary** John Gay, *The Shepherd's Week* (1714) Thursday, lines 49–54.

---

snails: meeting and throwing

Superstitions regarding meeting or seeing a snail vary considerably in meaning. Some references report decidedly negative reactions:

The following is a translation of a well-known Gaelic rhyme:

> *I heard the cuckoo while fasting*
> *I saw the foal with its back to me*
> *I saw the snail on the flagstone bare*
> *And I knew the year would not go well with*
> *   me.*   Highland Scotland Macbain (1887/88)

It is unlucky for a miner to meet a snail when entering a mine, as it betokens calamity, or probably the exhaustion of the lode on which he is then at work.   Devon Hewett (1900)

Others are positive:

If, on leaving your house, you see a black snail, seize it boldly by one of its horns and throw it over your left shoulder; you may then go on your way prosperously, but if you fling it over your right shoulder, you will draw down ill luck. This practice extends as far south as Lancashire.
Lancashire Henderson (1866)

These beliefs have not been recorded before the early nineteenth century, but the few examples are widely spread.

Devon Hewett (1900) 55. **Cornwall** *Folk-Lore Jnl* 5 (1887) 186. **Yorkshire** Blakeborough (1898) 133. **Lancashire** N&Q 1S:3 (1851) 56; Henderson (1866) 86; Harland & Wilkinson (1882) 154. **Highland Scotland** Macbain (1887/88) 265; Polson (1926) 129. **Stirlingshire** Hone, *Every-Day Book* 2 (1827) 343.

snails: rhyme

A widespread rhyme, chanted by children all over Britain as they picked up a snail, in the apparent belief that it will do as instructed:

Snail, snail, put out your horns
I'll give you bread and barleycorns.
Lancashire Halliwell (1849)

Snail, snail come out of your hole
Or else I'll beat you black as a coal.
Wiltshire Wilts. N&Q (1893–5)

The wording varies considerably from version to version, but the mixture of threat and promise is often present. Many hint at a story or further tradition behind the rhyme, but without giving any clue as to what it is:

Shell a muddy, shell a muddy
Put out your horns
For the king's daughter is
Coming to town
With a red petticoat and a green gown.
Southern Ireland N&Q (1851)

Saying the rhyme, some children then tossed the snail over their shoulder, for luck (*see also* SNAILS: MEETING AND THROWING).

Even Iona and Peter Opie (1951) can offer no explanation for the words of the rhyme. They show the earliest printed version in English as appearing in *Tom Thumb's Pretty Song Book* of *c.*1744, where it is already a children's rhyme, although there is a possible reference in Shakespeare, where a man refers to the traditional horns of the cuckold and so buffets himself on the forehead, crying 'peer out, peer out!' (*Merry Wives of Windsor* (1602) 4:2). The fact that analogous verses, some very similar to the British examples, have been reported from all over Europe, and even as far away as China, has led to an assumption that the rhyme has ancient roots, but this is at best unproven. Other widespread children's verses have a similar feeling of being CHARMS or cut-down legends in disguise – the 'crow, crow, get out of my sight' verse (*see* CROWS), for example – but there is no evidence that any of them are any more than simple children's rhymes.

Devon N&Q 1S:3 (1851) 179; Henderson (1866) 16–17. **Cornwall** *Folk-Lore Jnl* 5 (1887) 193; [1890s] *Old Cornwall* 1:12 (1930) 3–4. **Wiltshire** *Wilts. N&Q* 1 (1893–5) 315. **Surrey** N&Q 1S:3 (1851) 132–3. **Gloucestershire** *Glos. N&Q* 1 (1881) 43. **Suffolk** Gurdon (1893) 143. **Northern England** Henderson (1866) 16–17. **Yorkshire** Nicholson (1890) 133. **Lancashire** Halliwell (1849) 175–7. **Co. Durham** Leighton (1910) 49. **Southern**

Ireland N&Q 1S:3 (1851) 179. **General** Opie (1951) 390–2. For foreign analogues, *see:* Halliwell (1849) 175–7; N&Q 1S:3 (1851) 132–3; Opie (1951) 390–2.

snails: wart cures

One of the regularly reported cures for WARTS is to rub them with a snail or slug (sometimes piercing it first). In most cases, the added instruction is to place the snail upon a thorn on the premise that as the snail wastes away so do the warts.

A young lady of our acquaintance informs us that her uncle, who was a farmer at a small village just outside Leeds, cured her of a stubborn wart on one of her hands by means of a black snail. He rubbed the wart with the under-side of the snail and afterwards transfixed the poor little thing on a thorn of the garden-hedge. Strange as it may seem, the wart soon disappeared.

Yorkshire *Leeds Mercury* (4 Oct. 1879)

For full discussion and references, *see* WART CURES: SNAILS.

snakes: ash trees

A belief which was apparently restricted to the West Country and Wales was that snakes had a particular antipathy to the ash tree:

The leaves of the ash-tree are looked upon as a sure charm against the bites of snakes and vipers. In Devonshire they say that to trace a circle with an ash-stick round a sleeping viper will kill it.

Devon *Devonshire Assoc.* (1927)

Robert Hunt relates a Cornish story to demonstrate the belief:

Snakes avoid the ash-tree – It is said that no kind of snake is ever found near the 'ashen-tree' and that a branch of the ash-tree will prevent a snake coming near a person. A child, who was in the habit of receiving its portion of bread and milk at the cottage door, was found to be in the habit of sharing its food with one of the poisonous adders. The reptile came regularly every morning, and the child, pleased with the beauty of his companion, encouraged the visits. The babe and the adder were close friends, eventually this became known to the mother, and, finding it to be a matter of difficulty to keep the snake from the child whenever it was left alone – and she was frequently, being a labourer in the fields, compelled to leave her child to shift for itself – she adopted the precaution of binding an 'ashen-

twig' about its body. The adder no longer comes near the child, but from that day forward the child pined, and eventually died, as all around said, through grief at having lost the companion by whom it had been fascinated.

Cornwall Hunt (1865)

Cornwall Hunt (1865) 223; Couch (1871) 166; *Folk-Lore Jnl* 5 (1887) 207; [1890s] *Old Cornwall* 1:12 (1930) 5. **Devon** Hewett (1892) 28; *Devonshire Assoc.* 59 (1927) 156. **Wales** Trevelyan (1909) 171.

snakes: deaf and blind

There has long been a superstition that the adder has no power of hearing:

'Deaf as an adder' is a common saying in the fen, and

> *If I could hear as well as see*
> *No man would be the death o' me,*

Huntingdonshire [1880s] Marshall

and many believed that the markings on the belly of the snake actually depicted these words. The notion that the adder is deaf has biblical precedent, as Psalms 58:4 states, 'Their poison is like the poison of a serpent; they are like the deaf adder that stoppeth her ear'. The belief probably entered British tradition after the publication of the King James Bible made such literal borrowings possible.

In a similar way, the slowworm was believed to be blind, and features in some versions of the rhyme:

> *If the adder could hear, and the blindworm could see*
> *Neither man nor beast would ever go free.*

London Burne (1883)

Kent N&Q 2S:1 (1856) 331; N&Q 4S:1 (1868) 361. **Sussex** N&Q 1S:7 (1853) 152; Latham (1878) 15. **London** Burne (1883) 239. **Suffolk** Fitzgerald (1887) 515; Gurdon (1893) 10. **Huntingdonshire** [1880s] Marshall (1967) 123–4. **Shropshire** Burne (1883) 239.

snakes: die at sunset

It was widely believed that snakes, however badly injured, would not die until sunset:

A snake, 3ft long, was killed at noon by a school-boy in a Dorsetshire village and brought to me at once. On my offering to handle it, I was warned by one of the children that it was not dead, and when I pointed out that its battered condition was incompatible with it being alive, I was at once told that 'this was not real death, as neither snakes nor slow-worms can ever really die till after sunset'.   Dorset N&Q (1904)

Although not exclusive to the south of England, the majority of reports have come from there; however, the number may be inflated a little by duplication. The earliest dates from only 1850, but it was clearly already widespread at that date. Thomas Hardy used the motif in his Wessex novel *Return of the Native* (1878), and, according to *Notes & Queries* in 1904, the belief was also well known in the southern United States.

In the absence of any other explanation, it must be assumed that the belief simply arose through mistaken observation of nature.

Sussex Latham (1878) 15. Somerset *N&Q for Somerset & Dorset* 9 (1904–5) 113. Dorset N&Q 10S:1 (1904) 168; *N&Q for Somerset & Dorset* 9 (1904–5) 113. Somerset/Devon/Cornwall N&Q 1S:2 (1850) 510. Devon *Devonshire Assoc.* 39 (1907) 107; *Devonshire Assoc.* 100 (1968) 366. Cornwall *Folk-Lore Jnl* 5 (1887) 207. Berkshire N&Q 13S:1 (1923) 299. Surrey N&Q 13S:1 (1923) 172. Gloucestershire [1896] *Trans. Bristol & Glos. Arch. Soc.* 53 (1931) 263. Northamptonshire N&Q 1S:2 (1850) 164. East Anglia Varden (1885) 114. Shropshire Burne (1883) 239. Unlocated N&Q 1S:8 (1853) 146. Literary Thomas Hardy, *Return of the Native* (1878) Bk 4, Ch. 7. USA N&Q 10S:1 (1904) 333.

snakes: eating to stay young

An assured method of staying young, or even growing younger, was to eat a snake:

Physyke doth appprobat adders flesshe good to be eaten, saying it doth make an old man yonge, as it apperreth by a harte eating an adder maketh him yonge again.
                Borde, *Regimente or Dyetary of Health* (1562)

Judging by the number of writers who refer to the practice, it was clearly well known in sixteenth- and seventeenth-century Britain, but it does not seem to have lasted in the tradition. Victorian folklorists did not report its existence, and it seems to have fallen into oblivion by their time. The basis of the belief is probably that as a snake apparently 'rejuvenates' itself by casting its old skin each year, its flesh will have a similar effect on humans.

A possibly related belief was current in Wales:

In stories told by aged people, men and women, it was said that the person who could muster up courage to eat the flesh of the white snake would soon be able to understand the language of 'beasts, birds, reptiles, and fish'.
                Wales Trevelyan (1909)

Wales Trevelyan (1909) 172. General & Literary William Horman, *Vulgaria* (1519) 29, 40; Topsell (1607) 616; Andrew Borde, *Regimente or Dyetary of Health* (1562) 16; John Lyly, *Euphues and His England* (1581) 368; Thomas Dekker, *The Honest Whore Part 2* (1604) 1:2; Peter Hausted, *The Rival Friends* (1632) 5:2; Beaumont & Fletcher, *The Elder Brother* (1637) 4:4; Thomas Fuller, *The Holy State and the Profane State* (1642) 12:3; Philip Massinger, *The Old Law* (1656) 6:1.

snakes: in house

A handful of reports indicate a belief that a snake coming to your doorstep, or into your house, foretold a death in the family:

I was told in Orcop that an adder coming to the door was a sign of death. A doorstep seemed an unlikely place for an adder, but my informant assured me she had known this 'come true'.
                Herefordshire Leather (1912)

This does not seem to have been a well-known belief, although the three reported instances reveal a reasonably wide geographical spread. Nor can it be shown to be long-lasting, as they span less than three decades.

Herefordshire Leather (1912) 119. East Anglia Varden (1885) 117. Wales Trevelyan (1909) 172.

snakes: kill the first you meet

On seeing the first snake of the year, whether dangerous adder or harmless slowworm, one should kill it immediately:

The mother of a member met an old woman who stopped and beat a 'sleu' (slow) worm to death, breaking her umbrella over it. Asked why she did this she replied, 'Ah! Now I have killed all my enemies'.
                Suffolk *Folk-Lore* (1924)

This is only reported from the late nineteenth century, and not very widely. The motif of killing the first of a particular species that you see is also featured in beliefs about other creatures, notably BUTTERFLIES and WASPS, and in the latter case it was also said that this action ensured that you would triumph over your enemies.

Sussex Latham (1878) 9; *Sussex County Mag.* 5 (1931) 122. Somerset [1923] Opie & Tatem, 362. Cornwall Couch (1871) 168. Suffolk *Folk-Lore* 35 (1924) 352.

snakes: skins

A range of disparate traditions indicate faith in the curative and magical properties of snakeskins. The most common is the use of a snakeskin to cure or ward off HEADACHES:

The cure for headache was to get the skin of the viper and sew it in to the lining of the hat – people would hunt many miles for these skins in the month of April when the vipers shot their skin, and anyone finding one could make a good price for it for that purpose.   Norfolk [1870s] Haggard

Oddly enough, the instruction to wear the skin around the head also features in some reports for the extraction of thorns and even 'griping of the guts' (Aubrey, *Remaines* (1686)).

The second common medical use of a snakeskin is in the extraction of thorns or splinters, although care must be taken to use it the right way:

The skin cast by a snake is very useful in extracting thorns, &c. from the body, but, unlike other remedies, it is repellent, not attractive; hence it must always be applied on the opposite side to that on which the thorn entered. In some cases where the skin has been applied on the same side, it has forced the thorn completely through the hand.   Devon/Cornwall N&Q (1851)

This, too, was mentioned by Aubrey as current in the 1680s.

On the magical side, two reports from Cornwall claim an efficacy against fire:

The skin of an adder suspended from the ceiling is considered (as an amulet) a preventive from fire. I have often in the west of Cornwall, observed the skins of adders in cottages. To render the skin efficacious, I think there are some that hold that it must be taken up recent, just as the adder has disengaged herself from it.   Cornwall Polwhele (1826); Couch (1871)

which is possibly related to another:

It'll bring you good luck to hang an ether-skin o'er the chimbly.   Leicestershire N&Q (1853)

One last isolated reference, which may indicate a wider tradition:

It is said in Wales that a snake-skin plaited into a whip and used by a waggoner or carrier of any kind, would enable his horses to draw the heaviest load.   Wales Trevelyan (1909)

Headaches: Sussex Aubrey, *Remaines* (1686/1880) 18. **Wiltshire** Jefferies (1878) Ch. 2. **Oxfordshire** *Oxf. FL*

Soc. Ann. Record (1956) 13. **Worcestershire** Salisbury (1893) 70. **Cambridgeshire** N&Q 2S:1 (1856) 386. **Suffolk** Gurdon (1893) 23–4. **Norfolk** [c.1870s] Haggard (1935) 15–16; **Lincolnshire** [1850] Peacock (1877) 131; N&Q 1S:8 (1853) 382.
Extraction of thorns: **Devon** [1797] *Swete MS* (Devon Record Office) quoted Opie & Tatem. 363; *Devonshire Assoc.* 92 (1960) 372. **Devon/Cornwall** N&Q 1S:3 (1851) 259. **Herefordshire** Leather (1912) 81. **Unlocated** Aubrey, *Remaines* (1686/1880) 224. **General** *The Times* (2 Sept. 1972) 14.
Miscellaneous: **Sussex** Aubrey, *Remaines* (1686/1880) 38. **Devon** [1936] *Devonshire Assoc.* 83 (1951) 74. **Essex** N&Q 12S:1 (1916) 346. **Oxfordshire** *Oxf. FL Soc. Ann. Record* (1956) 13. **Leicestershire** N&Q (1853) 152. **Wales** Trevelyan (1909) 172, 312. **Welsh Gypsies** Jarman (1991) 186. **Morayshire** *Folk-Lore Jnl* 7 (1889) 43.

snakestones

Several different items are commonly called 'snakestones': stones which look like snakes; stones with snake-like markings; stones which are purportedly found within a snake's body; stones which are purportedly manufactured by snakes. In each case the 'stone' is valued, usually as an amulet or to cure certain ailments including, typically, snakebite, and eye ailments.

Stones which look like snakes usually turn out to be fossil ammonites, and there is a legend as to how these were formed – snakes were so numerous around Whitby Abbey that the abbess, St Hilda, beheaded them and turned them all to stone. The same tale is told about other holy people in various parts of the country, particularly St Keyna, of Keynsham in Somerset.

'Stones' which have been created by snakes vary considerably, but are usually glass beads or rings believed to be the result of snakes getting together and breathing or secreting bubbles which solidify:

The country people retain a conceit, that the snakes by their breathing about a hazel wand, and make a stone ring of blue colour, in which there appeareth the yellow figure of a snake; and that beasts that are stung being given to drink of the water wherein this stone has been soaked, will therethrough recover.   Cornwall Carew (1602)

These traditions were widespread in Wales, with local names such as *Maen Magl* and *Glain y Neidr*, and also in parts of Cornwall. Once noticed by antiquarians such as Edward Lhuyd, they were naturally associated with Pliny's famous description of *Ovum anguinum* (serpent's egg) which was, he stated, 'famous in the Gauls', and was formed by snake saliva but was the size of a medium apple and thus not directly comparable to the small glass beads found in Britain. On the principle that anything old must be connected with the Druids, antiquarians dubbed Pliny's object the 'Druid's egg'.

Elsewhere in Britain, glass rings or beads with holes were believed to have been created by the sting of an adder, and one of their local names was therefore 'adder-stones'. They were prized in the same way as other holed stones (*see* STONES: HOLED).

Adder-stone – A perforated stone, imagined by the vulgar to be made by the sting of an adder. Stones of this kind are suspended in stables as a charm to secure the horses from being hag-ridden; and are also hung up at the bed's head, to prevent the night-mare.

Northern England Brockett (1829)

Other stones, either natural or used by previous inhabitants as spindle-whorls, were also called snakestones, or adder-stones. There was also a tradition that snakes had a precious stone in their heads, similar to the more famous TOAD-STONE:

In the heads of toads and adders stones of varied power were said to be engendered, and they were always associated with witchcraft and magic.

Wales Trevelyan (1909)

Ammonites: **Somerset** Alban Butler, *Lives of the Saints* (1812) Oct. (St Keyna). **Oxfordshire** Plot, *Nat. Hist. Of Oxfordshire* (1677). **Northern England** Brockett (1829) 278. **Yorkshire** Alban Butler, *Lives of the Saints* (1812) Nov. (St Hilda); Robinson (1876) 'Snakes'. **Literary** Michael Drayton, *Polyolbion* (1622) song 28. Walter Scott, *Marmion* (1808) 2:13 and note 26. **Various** Skeat 49–57.
Snakes creating stones: **Cornwall** Carew (1602) 21; Hunt (1865) 220; N&Q 6S:1 (1880) 23; Lincolnshire Peacock (1877) 134. **Wales** Edward Lhuyd's additions to Camden, *Britannia* (1695) 419; Trevelyan (1909) 171; Jones (1930) 143. **Welsh Gypsies** Jarman (1991) 185. **Glamorganshire** Folklore 94 (1983) 184–91; **Galloway** Mactaggart (1824) 5. **General** N&Q 1S:11 (1855) 345. **Classical** Pliny, *Natural History* (AD 77) Bk 29, Ch. 12; Brand 3 (1849) 369–71.
Others: **Northern England** Brockett (1829) 3–4. **Wales** Trevelyan (1909) 171. **Hebrides** Martin (1703) 134. **Ireland** *Gent. Mag.* (1865) 699.
Major studies: Walter W. Skeat, 'Snakestones and Stone Thunderbolts as Subjects for Systematic Investigation', *Folk-Lore* 23 (1912) 45–80; W. R. Halliday, 'Snake Stones', *Folk-Lore* 32 (1921) 262–71; 33 (1922) 118–19; Prys Morgan, 'A Welsh Snakestone, its Tradition and Folklore', *Folk-Lore* 94 (1983) 184–91.

sneezing: babies

Considering the general concern for interpreting sneezes, it is no surprise that a few sources include beliefs about babies sneezing, but they do not quite agree on meaning. For example:

Douce nurses are full of strange ideas concerning the 'bit girlies and laddies' under their charge. According to some, a child does not break the fairy spell until it has sneezed once, and the greatest concern is evinced until this sign of good omen takes place. **Caithness** Rinder (1895)

If a child just born sneezes it will live.

Connemara *Folk-Lore Jnl* (1884)

For a child to sneeze during the [christening] *ceremony is unlucky.* **Lincolnshire** Swaby (1891)

Lincolnshire Swaby (1891) 89. **Scotland** N&Q 1S:12 (1855) 200. **Caithness** Rinder (1895) 52. **Connemara** *Folk-Lore Jnl* 2 (1884) 257.

sneezing: 'bless you'

The idea that a sneeze must be answered with a salutation from bystanders appears to be known across the whole of Europe, and may well be found all over the world. In modern Britain 'bless you' is the universal wording, but in earlier times there was more variation, and raising of hats and bowing were also required:

We have a custom (yet in mode) that when one sneezes every one else puts off his hat and bows, and cries 'God bless ye Sir'. I have heard, or read a story that many years since, that sneezing was an epidemical disease, and very mortal, which caused this yet received custom, quaere de hoc.

Aubrey, *Remaines* (1686)

Nearly everyone in Britain knows the supposed origin – that sneezing was a major symptom of the plague, and therefore the blessing was necessary. If the Great Plague of London (1665) is the one referred to, which is likely, the theory is completely wrong – sneezing was not a symptom, and the custom was known centuries earlier. But the tradition that the custom started with a specific epidemic has been in circulation for a very long time. The earliest English reference to saluting a sneeze, Caxton's *Golden Legend* (1483) relates how a great pestilence was sent among the early Christians, which caused 'cruel and sudden' death, often with a sneeze. So 'God help you' or 'Christ help' became the custom when anyone sneezed. Five hundred years later, something very similar was still being passed on:

Among the many other things 'my grandmother taught me', was the fabled significance of sneezing. 'Bless you!' she said whenever we sneezed, and no one else in our family, or, as I remember, in all our acquaintance – ever in those days said this, or knew any reason for saying it. I think it was she who told me that the priests used to say it during the Black Death, because a sneeze was the mortal symptom and the 'Bless you' a pious valediction to those about to die.

London [*c.*1910] Rolph

An alternative explanation, seldom heard nowadays, was sometimes offered by Victorian writers, who vaguely attribute it to 'the ancients', that people only sneezed once in their lives, and then immediately died. Hence the urgent need for a blessing. A memory of this story may be at the root of a Welsh story:

People in Wales formerly would instantly use every endeavour to suppress sneezing, for there was an old story prevalent in some counties that a man was once killed by a single sneeze.

Wales Trevelyan (1909)

There are also antecedents to the blessing of sneezes from the classical period. Pliny, for example, asked 'Why do we say "good health" to those who sneeze?' in his *Natural History* of AD 77.

Hampshire N&Q 167 (1934) 230. Somerset [1905–12] Tongue (1965) 137. Cornwall *Jnl Royal Inst. Cornwall* 20 (1915) 131. Wiltshire *Wilts. N&Q* 1 (1893–5) 152. Berkshire Mitford (1830) 229. Surrey N&Q 8S:1 (1892) 106. London [*c.*1910] Rolph (1980) 86. Warwickshire Bloom (*c.*1930) 28–9. Lincolnshire *Grantham Jnl* (29 June 1878). England [1870–93] N&Q 167 (1934) 304. Derbyshire *Folk-Lore Jnl* 2 (1884) 280. Yorkshire Nicholson (1890) 87. Lancashire Harland & Wilkinson (1882) 68. Co. Durham Henderson (1866) 106; Brockie (1886) 216. Wales Trevelyan (1909) 326. Highland Scotland Macbain (1887/88) 256; Campbell (1900) 238. Ireland N&Q 167 (1934) 267. Unlocated [1880s] N&Q 167 (1934) 215; N&Q 167 (1934) 158. General Aubrey, *Remaines* (1686/1972) 218; [1688] N&Q 167 (1934) 117. Classical Pliny, *Natural History* (AD 77) Bk 28, Ch. 5.

sneezing: cats

see CATS: HAVING A COLD.

sneezing: days rhyme

A rhyme which purported to give meanings for sneezes on certain days was noted a number of times in the nineteenth and twentieth centuries. The earliest version is very similar to the one which is still most often quoted today, although with minor variations:

If you sneeze on a Monday, you sneeze for danger
Sneeze on a Tuesday, kiss a stranger
Sneeze on a Wednesday, sneeze for a letter
Sneeze on a Thursday, something better
Sneeze on a Friday, sneeze for sorrow
Sneeze on a Saturday, see your sweetheart tomorrow
Sneeze on a Sunday, and the devil will have dominion over you all the week.

If you sneeze any morning before breakfast, you will have a present before the week is out. Of course, the above rhymes are not intended to apply to sneezing produced by cold or snuff-taking, etc.   Hertfordshire *Athenaeum* (1848)

It is not clear whether this rhyme was genuinely popular. Several similar day-of-the-week rhymes existed, concerning things as diverse as cutting FINGERNAILS to WASHING clothes. They all appear first in the 1830s or 1840s, and they all have a suspiciously literary flavour about them.

Dorset [1888] Udal (1922) 286. Devon N&Q 1:4 (1851) 98–9; *Devonshire Assoc.* 10 (1878) 105–6; Crossing (1911) 134; *Devonshire Assoc.* 66 (1934) 78. Hertfordshire *Athenaeum* (1848) 142. Buckinghamshire Henderson (1866) 1. Warwickshire Langford (1875) 15; Bloom (*c.*1930) 28–9. Norfolk Fulcher Collection (*c.*1895). Yorkshire [1950] Opie & Tatem, 365. Lancashire Harland & Wilkinson (1882) 68.

sneezing: left or right

A few sources distinguish the luck of sneezes to left or right, with the fairly obvious conclusion:

Sneezing may be lucky or unlucky as the case may be; if a sneeze is given to the right, it falls in the former category; if to the left, contrariwise.

Warwickshire Bloom (*c.*1930)

Should a sailor sneeze on the right side when embarking on ship it means a lucky voyage ahead, but a sneeze on the left means foul weather.   Unlocated Igglesden (*c.*1932)

The Welsh say . . . To sneeze to the right is lucky, to the left unfortunate; right in front of you, good news is coming.   Wales Trevelyan (1909)

Although there is no evidence that this belief goes back before the twentieth century in Britain, it was well known in classical literature. Opie & Tatem quote pieces by Catullus (*c.*50 BC) and Plutarch (AD 110).

Warwickshire Bloom (*c.*1930) 28–9. **Wales** Trevelyan (1909) 326. **Unlocated** Igglesden (*c.*1932) 123. **Classical** Opie & Tatem, 366.

sneezing: number

People in Britain have tried to read meaning in the number of sneezes since at least the sixteenth century. The earliest description is by a sceptical Reginald Scot in 1584:

whereupon they prognosticate good or bad luck. And a great matter is made of neezing, wherein the number of neezings and the time thereof is greatly noted. The physician may argue a strength towards in his patient, when he heareth him neeze twice, which is a natural cause to judge by, and conjecture upon. But sure it is mere casual, and also very foolish and incredible, that by two neezings, a man should be sure of good luck or success in his business.   Scot (1584)

Most early sources give once lucky, twice unlucky, three times lucky, but more modern versions, expressed in a rhyme first noted in the late nineteenth century, have no bad numbers:

One for a kiss
Two for a wish
Three for a letter
Four something better.
          Norfolk Fulcher Collection (*c.*1895)

A list of sneeze meanings appears in the Burghley Papers, of the time of Elizabeth I (1558–1603), and is reprinted in *Notes & Queries* (1886). It gives twenty-two interpretations of the number of sneezes, combined with time and situation in which they occur. So, for example:

If a man after he have made a bargain with another for any thing then sneeze one time it signifieth that his bargain shall stand firm. But if he sneeze three times the bargain will not continue.   Unlocated N&Q (1886)

See also SNEEZING: TIME/SITUATION.

Hampshire [1923] Opie & Tatem, 366. **Somerset** Tongue (1965) 137. **Wiltshire** *Wilts. N&Q* 1 (1893–5) 152. **Middlesex** [1984] Opie & Tatem, 366. **Oxfordshire** [pre-1900] *Folk-Lore* 24 (1913) 91. **Warwickshire** Bloom (*c.*1930) 28–9. **Suffolk** N&Q 8S:11 (1897) 472. **Norfolk** Fulcher Collection (*c.*1895). **Lincolnshire** Rudkin (1936) 20. **Wales** Trevelyan (1909) 326. **Scotland** N&Q 1S:11 (1855) 17. **Unlocated** N&Q 6S:1 (1880) 42; N&Q 7S:2 (1886) 165–6, quoting Burghley Papers (Lansdown MS 121). **General** Scot (1584) Bk 11, Ch. 13; Bk 11, Ch. 19.

sneezing: time/situation

A number of sources include short pieces detailing the good or bad luck consequent on sneezing at a particular time of day or in a particular situation or place, but they are too various to be easily summed up, especially as they often include a further element of how many sneezes occur.

If you sneeze three times on Monday morning you are sure to have a present before the week is out.   East Anglia N&Q (1871)

If you sneeze on a Saturday night after the candle is lighted, you will next week see a stranger you never saw before.   Devon N&Q (1851)

One or two times of day appear more regularly than others. Sneezing before breakfast, or early in the morning, is often mentioned, but the result varies from informant to informant. Another regular time is when one is putting on one's shoes. Sources generally agree that three sneezes early in the morning are a sign that the sneezer should go back to bed.

The piece on sneezing from Elizabeth I's reign (quoted above) includes the following rule:

If a man lie awake in his bed, and sneeze one time it is a sign of some great sickness or hindrance. If two men do sneeze both at one instant it is a good sign, and then let them go about their purpose if that it be either by water or land, and they shall prosper.   Unlocated N&Q (1886)

See also SNEEZING: NUMBER OF SNEEZES.

Somerset [1923] Opie & Tatem, 366. **Devon** N&Q 1:4 (1851) 99; Hewett (1900) 54. **East Anglia** N&Q 4S:7 (1871) 361. **Yorkshire** N&Q 8S:11 (1897) 314. **Wales** Trevelyan (1909) 326. **Unlocated** Scot (1584) Bk 11, Ch. 13; N&Q 7S:2 (1886) 165–6, quoting Burghley Papers (Lansdown MS 121); *Athenaeum* (1848) 142; N&Q 4S:1 (1880) 42.

snowdrops (*Galanthus nivalis*)

One of several white flowers which it was thought unlucky to bring into the house, as they brought sickness and death.

Last year we picked one from the woods when there were thousands out. When George [neighbour and gardener] came to tie up the raspberry canes he must have seen it on the window-sill for he was full of gloom. He said it foretold a death . . . It is entirely our fault that one of his chickens died and that their egg yield went down . . .

So this year we must be more careful. George has told us all the unpleasant things he knows about snowdrops. 'We called them "corpses in shrouds" when we were little, and we never took them indoors at all. All white flowers is unlucky'.

Unlocated *The Times* (15 Feb. 1966)

The phrase 'corpses in shrouds' was used by several informants. It is surprising how seriously these fears could be taken:

When a schoolfellow of mine died of typhoid fever, the lady Principal of the boarding-school wrote to my parents, charging them with being the authors of the calamity, in that they had a short time before sent me a box of snowdrops.

Unlocated [1870s] Wright

There is some crossover with PRIMROSES and DAFFODILS in the snowdrop's traditional connection with chickens. In this context, the number of flowers brought into the house in spring determines the number of chicks that would hatch. Hen-keepers thus insisted on at least thirteen blooms in a bunch; any fewer would bring disaster to the brood. Most informants had no problem with snowdrops outdoors, and many were even pleased to see them:

Many things discovered for the first time in the year had the property of bestowing a wish, we said. So off we started, wishing with the first snowdrop we saw, with the first primrose we found, with the first strawberry we ate.

Derbyshire [1890s] Uttley

Sussex Latham (1878) 52; *Sussex County Mag.* 23 (1949) 383. **Devon/Sussex** N&Q 160 (1931) 138. **Devon** *Devonshire Assoc.* 105 (1973) 214. **Somerset** N&Q 8S:7 (1895) 258; N&Q 160 (1931) 138. **London** N&Q 160 (1931) 100, 195. **Essex** [*c.*1915] Mays (1969) 163. **Oxfordshire** N&Q 8S:7 (1895) 167; [1920s] Harris (1969) 125. **Norfolk** [1984] Vickery (1995) 355. **Cambridgeshire** [1993] Vickery (1995) 355. **Warwickshire** Bloom (*c.*1930) 44. **Herefordshire** Leather (1912) 17. **Worcestershire** [1900] *Folk-Lore* 20 (1909) 343; Berkeley & Jenkins (1932) 37; *The Times* (12 Feb. 1960) 15. **Shropshire** N&Q 5S:3 (1875) 465; Burne (1883) 248. **Derbyshire** [1890s] Uttley (1946) 135. **Lancashire** [1982] Vickery (1995) 354–5. **Dyfed** [1983] Vickery (1995) 355. **Mull** Bennett (1992) 182. **N. Ireland** Foster (1951) 110. **Co. Tipperary?** *The Times* (15 Feb. 1960) 14. **Unlocated** [1870s] Wright (1913) 217; N&Q 160 (1931) 160; *The Times* (15 Feb. 1966) 12.

soap

Three different beliefs regarding soap have been noted, although none very often. It may perhaps be thought that soap slipping out of one's hand

would be too common an occurrence to be noteworthy, but there is more than one report from the nineteenth century of a superstition that it is at best unlucky, and at worst means a forthcoming death:

A woman in the Highlands, named Kate Elshender . . . went to a quarry hole to wash her clothes. As she passed the village shop she went in and bought half a pound of soap, and proceeded to wash; the soap slipped out of her hands, and she went back and bought another half pound. The shopkeeper warned her to be careful, remembering the old superstition, but she laughed and went off again. It again slipped from her hands, and she returned for a third half pound of soap. This time the old woman in the shop was thoroughly frightened, and begged and prayed her not to go back again; but she would go, in spite of everything that could be said to her. Shortly after the old woman, being quite unable to rest in her shop, went away to the quarry, she found no one there, and the clothes lying on the side of the hole. She gave the alarm, and, on search being made, the said Kate Elshender was discovered, drowned, at the bottom of the quarry hole.

Highland Scotland N&Q (1876)

Other reports focus on passing soap:

Two persons, more especially if they are sisters, must not pass soap from hand to hand; it should be put down first, so that the other can take it up.

Herefordshire Leather (1912)

This could simply be to avoid the danger of dropping it. A superstition in the theatre world maintains that if you leave soap behind you at a venue, you will never return there. Several informants implied that these beliefs were much more widely known than is shown by the relative paucity of references.

See also WASHING.

Dropping or passing: **Devon** *Devonshire Assoc.* 57 (1926) 130. **Herefordshire** Leather (1912) 87. **Wales** Trevelyan (1909) 7, 210. **Highland Scotland** N&Q 5S:6 (1876) 323. **Unlocated** N&Q 5S:4 (1875) 9. ***Theatre:*** **Middlesex** [1984] Opie & Tatem, 367. **Unlocated** Igglesden (*c.*1932) 233–4; Granville (1952) 179; *Observer Supp.* (24 Nov. 1968) 13.

southernwood (*Artemisia abrotanum*)

According to two reports, lads in Cambridgeshire wore sprigs of southernwood to attract young women or to signal their desire for marriage –

hence the local names for the plant, 'Lad's love' and 'Boy's love'. A very different tradition was recorded in Devon:

Boy's Love, *a herb, is unlucky. A woman was sick in her lonely cottage. A neighbour, visiting her, went into the garden. She found a considerable quantity of the herb growing, pulled it all up – and the patient recovered.*

Devon *Devonshire Assoc.* (1971)

Devon *Devonshire Assoc.* 103 (1971) 268.
Cambridgeshire Porter (1969) 2; [1989] Vickery (1995).

spades

A spade may be a perfectly innocent tool to most people, but for the superstitious mind its overwhelming characteristic is its connection with the grave:

If in your house a man shoulders a spade
For you or your kinsfolk a grave is half made.

Warwickshire Langford (1875)

In almost all the reported cases, the carrying 'on the shoulder' is the particularly ominous detail. This omen was only reported from a relatively restricted area of England, and only since the mid nineteenth century. Sensitivity to the spade continued well into the twentieth century:

Should anyone at a distance hail, or try to attract your attention, by waving a shovel, grab a handful of earth and immediately fling it in their direction, or soon you will be buried.

Lincolnshire Rudkin (1936)

See also HOUSES.

Dorset Udal (1922) 286. Wiltshire Wiltshire (1975) 84. Herefordshire [*c.*1895] *Folk-Lore* 39 (1928) 386; Leather (1912) 119. Worcestershire [1930s] Archer (1969) 104. Warwickshire Langford (1875) 15. Suffolk *Folk-Lore* 35 (1924) 351. Lincolnshire Rudkin (1936) 15. Shropshire Burne (1883) 280. Unlocated N&Q 1S:12 (1855) 488.

sparrows
(*Passer domesticus*)

Considering its ubiquity, the sparrow does not feature strongly in British superstition. The few beliefs reported occur only in scattered instances and do not reveal any coherent or widespread traditions. The sparrow shares with other birds the gift of prophecy of coming death if it flies against a window:

A few minutes afterwards a sparrow came, dashed its bill against the window and flew away again. 'Oh!' said Mrs S., 'something is the matter with poor Edward' (her brother). She had hardly said the word when a man on horseback rode up and said, when S. opened the door to him, 'Don't frighten poor Mary, but master has just expired.'

London Kelly (1863)

John Aubrey also relates a curious story of a sparrow persistently pecking at the window of the room where Major John Morgan lay sick in 1643, but in this case the man recovered and the bird went away (*Miscellanies* (1696)).

Two more sparrow traditions are mentioned but not confirmed from elsewhere:

In Papa Stour the sparrows are very destructive to the corn, and the Papa Stourians believed that the beadle of the kirk had the power of 'telling' the sparrows away so as never to return, for which they paid him a fee. Shetland Reid (1869)

A Kentish boy, speaking of his exploits in bird-catching, said that he had caught a sparrow, but did not keep it, as if he had his father and mother would die. Kent N&Q 2S:5 (1858)

In the latter example, the boy may have been drawing upon one of the regular ROBIN traditions.

See also BIRDS: AT WINDOW.

Kent N&Q 2S:5 (1858) 218. Wiltshire Aubrey, *Miscellanies* (1696/1857) 45–6. London Kelly (1863) 104–5. Shetland Reid (1869) 25. General Swainson (1886) 61–2.

spectacles

An apparently unique description of a street custom obviously disguises a more widespread custom:

When I first came to London, I was constantly annoyed by a certain class of persons 'spitting aside' when they passed me. I one day asked a servant girl, who by accident spat upon my foot, what she meant by it, and the reply was, 'I should have bad luck if I didn't spit at a gentleman in spectacles'. London N&Q (1868) 202

This is probably related to other games whereby children had to say something or carry out some action when they saw someone with a beard, or wearing the first STRAW BOATER in spring, and so on. It is impossible to say more, until other examples are found. Opie and Tatem identified an article in the

Daily Sketch (22 Sept. 1954) which may indicate a wider antipathy to spectacles, as it demonstrated that at least one family of Gypsies had a strong aversion to their daughter marrying a man who wore glasses. This, however, was nearly one hundred years later, and the two are probably not connected.

speedwell

A widespread belief about the speedwell flower explains why it is often called 'bird's eyes':

Speedwell is called 'birds-eyes' . . . If you pluck birds-eyes, the birds will come and pluck out your eyes when you are asleep. Even if the windows are shut? Oh yes, they'd break the glass and get in.   **Essex** *Monthly Packet* (1862)

Essex *Monthly Packet* 24 (1862) 434–7. **Leicestershire** [1983] Vickery (1995) 358. **Cheshire** Hole (1937) 47. **Yorkshire** Vickery (1995) 358. **Humberside** [1985] Vickery (1995) 358.

spiders: cure ague

Spiders were routinely used in cures for various ailments, but particularly for AGUE and WHOOPING COUGH, and cobwebs were, and still are, used to treat BLEEDING. The remedies for ague and whooping cough overlap, but are in separate entries for ease of reference.

Three principal methods were employed in ague cures: in the first the spider was taken as medicine, swallowed (usually alive); in the second, a pill was made of cobwebs (sometimes with a live spider inside) and swallowed; while in the third, which was also the favoured method for whooping cough, the spider was used externally, enclosed in a nutshell or bag and allowed to die of its own accord.

A few years since, a lady in the south of Ireland was celebrated far and near, amongst her poorer neighbours for the cure of [the ague]. *Her universal remedy was a large house-spider alive and enveloped in treacle or preserve. Of course, the parties were carefully kept in ignorance of what the wonderful remedy was.*
Southern Ireland N&Q (1850)

The spider could be served in various ways – covered in jam or treacle, surrounded by dough or bread, in an apple, placed in water and drunk 'when it do curly up', and so on. The idea of the patient being kept in ignorance of the real nature of the medicine is mentioned regularly and may be more than simple sparing of the sensibilities,

as in several cases it was clearly considered a necessary part of the cure.

'Cobweb pills' could simply be cobwebs rolled into a ball and swallowed, or mixed with more palatable ingredients such as jam. Some recommended the spider should also be taken, rolled in the web.

In the spring of 1871 I was staying at Wakefield. I was making merry over Wesley's Primitive Physic, and particularly over cobweb pills as a cure for ague, or for anything. Mrs Pearson quietly observed, 'you may laugh, but I have many times cured Mr Pearson of ague with cobweb pills, when we were abroad'.
Yorkshire [1871] N&Q

The third procedure involved capturing a live spider, enclosing it in some suitable receptacle and wearing it around the neck or elsewhere on the body. In principle very widespread in folk medicine, it was thought that as the spider wasted away, so would the complaint.

Ague, it was believed, could be cured by putting a spider into a goose quill, sealing it up, and hanging it about the neck, so that it would be near the stomach. This disease might also be cured by swallowing pills made of spider's web. One pill a morning for three successive mornings before breakfast.
Western Scotland Napier (1879)

The only unusual feature here is the use of a goose quill to hold the spider – in most cases a walnut shell or linen bag is specified. A well-known piece from Robert Burton's *Anatomy of Melancholy* shows that the walnut-shell cure was well known in the early seventeenth century and also indicates the power which the ancient writers exerted over educated readers of the time. Burton scoffs at his mother's ague cure, until he finds it has classical antecedents:

Being in the country in the vacation time not many years since, at Lindly in Leicestershire, my father's house, I first observed this amulet of a spider in a nut-shell lapped in silk, etc. so applied for an ague by my mother: whom although I knew to have excellent skill in chirurgery, sore eyes, aches, etc. and such experimental medicines, as all the country where she dwelt can witness, to have done many famous and good cures upon divers poor folks, that were otherwise destitute of help – yet, among all other experiments, this, methought, was most absurd and ridiculous: I could see no warrant for it. Why a spider for a fever? For what antipathy? Till at length, rambling amongst authors (as I often do)

spiders

Spiders enjoy a surprisingly positive reputation in British superstition, as elsewhere in Europe. Apart from their use in cures, which invariably ends in their death (*see below*) they are widely protected from harm by closely linked beliefs which hold that they are lucky to have around, and that it is very unlucky to harm them. Specific beliefs are given separate treatment below, but a few stray beliefs which do not fit the general pattern have been reported but rarely:

If you see a spider at night it's a sure sign you'll have a letter in the morning.

Norfolk Fulcher Collection (*c.*1895)

It is a current belief that 'if you kill a spider there will surely be rain the next day' [Normally said of BEETLES].   Isle of Wight N&Q (1917)

A spider running towards you in the morning is a token of misfortune.   Wales Trevelyan (1909)

Opie and Tatem also include three twentieth-century informants who maintained that seeing a big spider presages a death. This is otherwise unreported, apart from one reference from the Derbyshire area in Addy (1895).

Cobwebs are widely recommended for wounds (*see* BLEEDING), but Lupton suggests another use for spiders in this context:

If a spider be put in a linen cloth a little bruised and holden to the nose that bleeds (but touch not the nose therewith, but smell to the same) by and by the blood will stay, and the nose will leave bleeding. This is very true for the venomous spider is to the contrary, and such an enemy to man's blood, that the blood draws back, and shuns the spider presently. A marvellous thing.   Lupton (1631)

Isle of Wight N&Q 12S:3 (1917) 395. **Norfolk** Fulcher Collection (*c.*1895). **Derbyshire** Addy (1895) 68. **Wales** Trevelyan (1909) 328. **General** Lupton (1631) Bk 8, Para. 88.

I found this very medicine in Dioscorides, approved by Matthiolus, repeated by Aldrovandus, cap. de Aranea, lib. de insectis, I began to have a better opinion of it, and to give more credit to amulets, when I saw it in some parties answer to experience.

Burton, *Anatomy of Melancholy* (1621)

The cure certainly has a long history. Pliny, for example, in a detailed section on ague cures, includes both 'hairy grubs found on thornbushes ... shut up four of these grubs in a walnut shell and attach as an amulet', and 'the spider itself attached as an amulet in a reed, in which form it is also said to be beneficial for other fevers' (Pliny, *Natural History* (AD 77) Bk 30, Sect. 30). Nevertheless, it is most unlikely that the marked similarities between classical and seventeenth-century British cures are the result of an unbroken tradition bridging the intervening millennia. These cures, and other traditions, have entered British culture by way of doctors, herbalists, and other educated practitioners reading, and valuing, classical sources. By including them in their own publications they have recycled ideas from over a thousand years before. Although clearly in the sphere of folk medicine by the nineteenth century, each of these three treatments had earlier been included in what passed for orthodox medicine of the time. Numerous publications, from John Gerard's *Herball* (1597) to William Salmon's *London*

Dispensatory (1678), and John Wesley's *Primitive Physick* (1747) attest to a serious faith in these spider cures.

It also seems certain that the choice of the spider here is an example of LIKE CURES LIKE – a 'shivery shakery' insect for a shivery disease.

Spider taken internally: Kent [*c.*1897] *Folk-Lore* 23 (1912) 353. **Sussex** [1624 and 1745] Allen (1995) 22–3; *Sussex Life* (Jan. 1973) 34. **Somerset** N&Q 10S:1 (1904) 273–4. **Wiltshire** [1922] Opie & Tatem, 370. **East Anglia** Varden (1885) 102. **Suffolk** *Gent. Mag.* (1867) 728–41. **Yorkshire** [1820] N&Q 151 (1926) 404. **Southern Ireland** N&Q 1S:2 (1850) 259. **Unlocated** [1743–4] Chambers 1 (1878) 732.:
Cobweb pills: Devon [1781] N&Q 10S:1 (1904) 205. **Lincolnshire** Gutch & Peacock (1908) 116. **Yorkshire** [1871] N&Q 10S:1 (1904) 317–18. **Western Scotland** Napier (1879) 95. **General** Wesley, *Primitive Physick* (1747) 26.
Worn as amulet: Somerset N&Q 1S:2 (1850) 130; Henderson (1866) 118; Poole (1877) 52; [1923] Opie & Tatem, 370. **Leicestershire** Robert Burton, *Anatomy of Melancholy* (1621) Pt 2, Sect. 5, Mem. 1, Subs. 5. **Derbyshire** N&Q 11S:2 (1910) 109. **Lancashire** Harland & Wilkinson (1882) 75. **Western Scotland** Napier (1879) 95. **Unlocated** *Diary* of Elias Ashmole, (11 June 1681). **General** Paracelsus, *Dispensatory* (1656 edn) quoted N&Q 11S:3 (1911) 174; [1743–4] Chambers 1 (1878) 732. **Literary** Henry Wadsworth Longfellow, *Evangeline* (1849). **Classical** Pliny, *Natural History* (AD 77) Bk 30, Para. 30.

spiders: cure whooping cough

One of the numerous widely practised folk cures for WHOOPING COUGH required a live spider. As with one of the regular AGUE cures (*see above*), the process involved catching a spider, imprisoning it in a bag (or other receptacle) and placing it round the neck of the sufferer, or elsewhere in the house. As the spider wasted away so did the disease.

A farmer, from the neighbourhood of Reepham, in Norfolk, gravely told me the following certain cure for the hooping-cough. Whenever any of his children were attacked with it he caught a common house-spider, which he tied up in muslin and pinned over the mantel-piece. So long as the spider lived, the cough remained; but when it died, the cough went away. He assured me he had cured all his children in this way; and that when two were affected at the same time, they recovered when their respective spiders died, which was not in the order in which they were attacked. My informant, though illiterate, was a wealthy man; farming several hundred acres and bringing his sons up for professions.

Norfolk N&Q (1856)

The idea that the disease wanes as the active agent of the cure wastes away is a commonplace motif of folk medicine, used extensively, for example, in WART cures. Several reports include a spoken charm as part of the process, as well as certain other small rituals:

The parent of the child finds a dark spider in her own house, holds it over the head of the child, and repeats the following:

> *Spider as you waste away,*
> *Whooping-cough no longer stay*

The insect must then be placed in a bag and hung up over the fireplace; when the spider has wasted away the cough will be gone.

East Anglia Varden (1885)

Spiders were clearly chosen as agents in ague cures on the principle of LIKE CURES LIKE, but the basis of their application in the case of whooping cough is not so obvious. It is noticeable, however, that whereas the ague cure is well reported in Britain from the sixteenth century onwards, the earliest reference to its use for whooping cough is from the mid nineteenth. On the present evidence, it is possible that the procedure was simply transferred from one disease to the other, for no other reason than that it was widely reputed to work well. Alternatively, those versions which include the spider being waved around the patient's head or, in some cases held to his/her mouth, may suggest that the principle involved was simply attempted TRANSFERENCE of the disease to the creature.

Compare CATERPILLARS: CURES.

Isle of Wight IOW Fed. W. I.s (1994) 94. **West Country** N&Q 5S:6 (1876) 144–5. **Devon** *Daily Chronicle* (3 June 1911); *Devonshire Assoc.* 83 (1951) 75. **Cornwall** *Old Cornwall* 1:3 (Apr. 1926) 8; *Old Cornwall* 2:1 (1931) 20. **Herefordshire** Leather (1912) 83. **East Anglia** Varden (1885) 101. **Suffolk** *Gent. Mag.* (1867) 728–41; *Folk-Lore* 35 (1924) 356. **Norfolk** N&Q 2S:1 (1856) 386; Dyer (1880) 154; Dew (1898) 77–81; *Folk-Lore* 40 (1929) 117. **Lincolnshire** N&Q 3S:9 (1866) 319; Peacock (1877) 234. **Shropshire** Burne (1883) 194, 204–5. **Wales** Trevelyan (1909) 320.

spiders: kissing

A curious connection between cobwebs and kissing has been reported, in the form of a popular saying:

In Cornwall it is a common saying that, in a house where cobwebs are plentiful, kissing is scarce.

Cornwall N&Q (1870)

As with all such sayings, the reason is rarely stated, but a satisfactory explanation is occasionally given:

In Hampshire, if a cobweb is seen, 'it is a sign that the housemaid wants kissing'. On inquiring the meaning of this expression, I was told that when the housemaid is saluted she naturally holds up her head and thus becomes aware of the neglect.

Hampshire N&Q (1863)

Two reports from the Channel Isles, however, provide a contrasting belief:

Another peculiar custom was the apparently slovenly manner that some girls had of dusting their bedrooms, for although they attacked the dust remorselessly, they invariably left the cobwebs, and some have even been known to introduce spiders in to the room. For, if they were engaged, every cobweb that caught their eye on awakening in the morning, presaged a kiss from their fiancé.

Jersey L'Amy (1927)

Dorset Udal (1922) 275. **Devon** *Devonshire Assoc.* 91 (1959) 201. **Cornwall** N&Q 4S:6 (1870) 212. **Hampshire** N&Q 3S:3 (1863) 262. **Oxfordshire** *Midland Garner* 1 (1884) 22. **Guernsey** De Garis (1975) 140. **Jersey** L'Amy (1927) 96–7.

spiders: lucky/protected

Spiders are widely believed to be lucky to have around the house or to find on your person. They are also protected by the idea that it is very unlucky to harm them, a warning which was taken very seriously by believers:

My grannie was a Calbourne woman, and when I was setting up house she warned me thus: 'Now my child, you are young, but whatever you do in your life never kill a spider. If you are sweeping, and come on a web, don't destroy it till the spider is safe, then you may sweep away the web; but if you kill the spider it will surely bring poverty to your house'.   Isle of Wight N&Q (1917)

This advice is summed up in a widely reported rhyme:

If you wish to thrive
Let the spider go alive.   Orkney N&Q (1909)

or, less poetically:

Who kills a spider
Bad luck betides her.   Devon Hewett (1900)

A reason for this prohibition is rarely given, but where it is, it is invariably a reference to one of the legends which claim that the spider acted to help or protect Jesus in some way:

A minister visiting an old Border woman in her last illness, observed a spider near her bed, and attempted to remove it, when the invalid desired him to let it be, and reminded him that when our Blessed Lord lay in the manger at Bethlehem, a spider came and spun a beautiful web which protected the Babe from all the dangers which surrounded Him – cold and frost and the searchers and soldiers of King Herod.

England/Scotland Borders N&Q (1935)

A more developed story has Mary and her baby taking refuge in a cave, and a spider quickly weaving a complicated web across the entrance to fool the pursuers into believing that no one had recently entered. The is a widespread international folk-tale motif (Aarne-Thompson B523.1), reported across Europe and also in Asia and Africa, told of various heroes and religious figures.

Despite its widespread nature, this general belief in the luckiness, and resultant protection, of spiders can only be traced to the eighteenth century, although in the specialized version of the money-spider it can be shown to be older (*see below*). One other minor variation, reported a few times, is that the spider betokened new clothes:

A spider running over any part of the body-clothes indicated a piece of new dress corresponding to the piece over which the spider was making its way.   Northeast Scotland Gregor (1881)

Isle of Wight N&Q 12S:3 (1917) 395. Kent N&Q 3S:3 (1863) 262. **Dorset** *Dorset Year Book* (1961–2) 74; [1982] Opie & Tatem, 372. **Somerset** [1923] Opie & Tatem, 371. **Devon** *Devonshire Assoc.* 121 (1989) 244; Hewett (1900) 54, 58; *Devonshire Assoc.* 67 (1935) 132; *Devonshire Assoc.* 121 (1989) 244. **Cornwall** *Old Cornwall* 2 (1931–6) 40. Herefordshire Leather (1912) 28. **Cambridgeshire** Porter (1969) 50. **Suffolk** *Folk-Lore* 25 (1914) 366. Norfolk Fulcher Collection (*c.*1895); *Norfolk Chronicle* (20 Dec. 1902). Lincolnshire Rudkin (1936) 17. Shropshire Burne (1883) 239. **Derbyshire** [*c.*1890s] Uttley (1946) 133; N&Q 12S:4 (1918) 29. **England** Addy (1895) 66. **Yorkshire** Henderson (1866) 267; Nicholson (1890) 136; Addy (1895) 66; [1965] Opie & Tatem, 371–2. **Westmorland/Lancashire** [*c.*1939] *Folk-Lore* 64 (1953) 294. **Co. Durham** Brockie (1886) 139; *Folk-Lore* 20 (1909) 217. **Northumberland** Bigge (1860–62) 91. Pembrokeshire *Folk-Lore* 39 (1928) 173. Monmouthshire *Folk-Lore* 49 (1938) 290. **England/Scotland Borders** N&Q 169 (1935) 460. **Highland Scotland** Macbain (1887/88) 262. **Western Scotland** Napier (1879) 115. **Northeast Scotland** Gregor (1881) 147. Glasgow [*c.*1820] Napier (1864) 397. **Orkney** N&Q 10S:12 (1909) 483–4. **General** Brand (1777) 93; Brand (1810) 102. **Unlocated** *Watford Observer* (11 Feb. 1994) 20.

spiders: money-spinners

A widespread belief in the general luckiness of spiders has given them protection in everyday encounters (*see above*). A specialized version of this is the belief that if a tiny spider settles on your person you will receive wealth or some other desirable gift, but, conversely, if you kill one you court poverty:

There is a small black spider that often gets on our clothes or hats; this is called a 'money spider', and if you kill it you will be sure to suffer for it by lack of the needful.   Yorkshire N&Q (1852)

These tiny spiders are thus generally called 'money spiders' or 'money spinners'. In many cases it was simply enough for the spider to land on you, but others advised particular rituals to ensure the good fortune; including putting the spider in your pocket, eating it, and throwing it over your shoulder.

The Berkshire children observe a somewhat different rite with the money spider. The insect is raised by the filament on which it often descends upon the clothes, and passed three times slowly round the child's head, either by the person on whom it descended or by a companion. Then it is carefully deposited once more upon the apparel near the spot of its original descent. On no account must it be brushed off. Careful performance of the above ceremonial is sure to bring the money which the spider's visit portends.

Berkshire N&Q (1879)

The superstition can confidently be traced at least to the late sixteenth century – in Nashe's *Terrors of the Night* (1594), where the creature is already termed a 'spinner' ('If a spinner creep upon him he shall have gold rain down from heaven') – and it is reported regularly ever since, although the vast majority of published references are from England. Many people still call tiny spiders 'money spiders'.

Dorset *Dorset Year Book* (1961–2) 74. **Somerset** Tongue (1965) 138. **Cornwall** [1921] Rowse (1942) 258. **Devon** Hewett (1900) 54. **Wiltshire** *Wilts. N&Q* 1 (1893–5) 316; [1922] Opie & Tatem, 369. **Berkshire** N&Q 5S:12 (1879) 295. **Essex** [1983] Opie & Tatem, 369. **Worcestershire** Salisbury (1893) 77. **Warwickshire** Langford (1875) 11. **Northamptonshire** N&Q 1S:2 (1850) 165; N&Q 1S:3 (1851) 3–4; N&Q 5S:12 (1879) 254. **Cambridgeshire** *Folk-Lore* 25 (1914) 365; Porter (1969) 50. **East Anglia** Varden (1885) 112. **Norfolk** *Norfolk Chronicle* (20 Dec. 1902); [1961] Opie & Tatem, 369. **Staffordshire** Hackwood (1924) 149. **Yorkshire** N&Q 1S:6 (1852) 311–12; Nicholson (1890) 136; [1983] Opie & Tatem, 369. **Derbyshire** [c.1890s] Uttley (1946) 133; N&Q 12S:4 (1918) 29. **Co. Durham** Leighton (1910) 60. **England/Scotland Borders** [c.1816] Henderson (1866) 83. **Orkney** N&Q 10S:12 (1909) 483–4. **Guernsey** De Garis (1975) 140. **Unlocated** *Chambers's Jnl* (1873) 810; N&Q 6S:1 (1880) 225; Hone, *Year Book* (1832) 126–8. **Literary** Thomas Nashe, *Terrors of the Night* (1594) D1.

spilling

The accidental spilling of any everyday item can be interpreted as ominous, but certain things are singled out in specific superstitions. Spilling can also be compared to DROPPING THINGS and FALLING.

See SALT.

spitting: hands

Spitting on the palm of the hand is reported in several contexts, but it is difficult to see to what extent they are different aspects of the same belief, or only related at superficial level. The motif of spitting on coins received in buying and selling is widely recorded (*see below*), but in some cases, it was the hands on the receiving end:

Fisherwomen not unfrequently spit upon their hands on taking their first piece of money for the day. Jersey *Folk-Lore* (1914)

and another aspect within the same context of striking a bargain:

When selling animals the bargain is not finally sealed until both parties spit on the palms and shake hands and the buyer gives the seller back a luck-penny. Co. Tyrone *Lore & Language* (1972)

An apparently different notion is represented by people spitting on their hands when facing a task needing strength or skill. People still do this, at least in pretence, in a gesture which means something like 'well, let's get stuck in'.

Men spat on their hands before they attempted work needing great strength, and it was not only to get a good grip on the tool.

Derbyshire [1890s] Uttley

Nevertheless, as Alison Uttley here implies, the gesture is not simply pragmatic, it also implies an attempt at ensuring good luck and staying-power.

Country boys and fellows (I believe all England over) when they prepare themselves to go to cuffs [boxes]; before they strike, they do spit in their hands, for good luck to their endeavours.

England Aubrey, *Remaines* (1686)

It seems that the oldest versions are more concerned with grip and strength than luck. Opie and Tatem identified some earlier British references, such as one from 1577 which says 'spit on your hands and take good hold', and another of 1613 describing a blacksmith spitting on his hands before shoeing a horse. We also have evidence from classical times, in the shape of Pliny, who wrote, 'before making an effort, spit into the hand . . . to make the blow more heavy' (*Natural History*, AD 77).

Essex [1957] Opie & Tatem, 373; Mays (1969) 20. **Suffolk** Fitzgerald (1887) 510; Claxton (1954) 89. **England** Aubrey, *Remaines* (1686/1972) 247. **Derbyshire** [1890s] Uttley (1946) 126. **Yorkshire** Nicholson (1890) 42. **Co. Tyrone** *Lore & Language* 1:7 (1972) 12. **Jersey** *Folk-Lore* 25 (1914) 247. **Unlocated** Grose (1787) 64. **General** J. Grange, *Golden Aphroditis* (1577) quoted Opie & Tatem, 372; W. Browne, *Britannia's Pastorals* (1613) Bk 1, 5:98, quoted Opie & Tatem, 372. **Literary** Swift (1738). **Classical** Pliny, *Natural History* (AD 77) Bk 28, Para. 7.

spitting: oaths and fights

Spitting was formerly an integral part of boys' traditional codes of behaviour, when swearing an oath or preparing to fight:

In this parish there is a traditional custom amongst the boys of 'spitting their death' to

spitting

Spitting occurs in a number of superstitious contexts – for luck, for protection, to counteract bad luck, to express contempt, to underline an oath, seal a bargain, effect a cure, and more.

Spitting for luck is still practised in countless ways; for instance, on money received or found; on a piece of coal; through a ladder; on a horse-shoe; for a bad smell; on a finger, and touching the toes of the boots when a black-and-white horse is espied; on marbles or buttons whilst playing games with them, etc.

Unlocated N&Q (1911)

We may understand the contexts, but we still do not know why this particular action is required. The main spitting customs are treated separately, and the motif also forms part of numerous other beliefs. A few further examples can also be given:

A few weeks ago I noticed one of my schoolboys taking up a white stone from the road, spitting upon it, and then throwing it over his head. In doing so he repeated the following distich:

Lucky, lucky stone
Bring me luck, when I go home

Upon enquiry I found that it would afterwards be unlucky for him to look back when turning round a corner. North Wales [c.1893] Folk-Lore

The influence of the 'evil eye' is felt as strongly in this county as in any other part of the world, and various means are resorted to in order to prevent its effects . . . Spitting three times in the person's face; turning a live coal on the fire; and exclaiming 'The Lord be with us' are other means of averting its influence.
Lancashire/Yorkshire Harland & Wilkinson (1882)

Within the last few years I saw a gentleman, walking earnestly through the streets of Carlisle, spit over his left shoulder to avert misfortune, he having inadvertently passed under a ladder.
Cumberland N&Q (1882)

I remember reading of an Englishman who went into a church in Wales, where, during the sermon, whenever the devil was named the people spat, as expressing abhorrence. Wales N&Q (1882)

London N&Q 4S:2 (1868) 202. Lancashire/Yorkshire Harland & Wilkinson (1882) 69. Cumberland N&Q 6S:6 (1882) 357. Wales N&Q 6S:6 (1882) 356. North Wales [c.1893] Folk-Lore 25 (1914) 372. Unlocated N&Q 11S:3 (1911) 217–18.

---

confirm a promise. *This is done by crossing the forefingers, looking earnestly at them while repeating the promise, and then spitting upon the ground. A boy who breaks this solemn asseveration is regarded as unworthy of any confidence.*
Devon N&Q (1911)

In Lancashire boys spit over their fingers in order to screw up their courage to fighting point, or to give them luck in battle. Sometimes they do this as a sort of asseveration, to attest their innocence of some petty crime laid to their charge.
Lancashire Harland & Wilkinson (1882)

Another version, which also includes spit and fingers, will be more familiar to today's readers:

Boys spat on a finger and drew it across the throat before taking the great oath of innocence

See this wet
See this dry
I'll cut my throat before I lie.
Derbyshire [1890s] Uttley

Devon N&Q 11S:3 (1911) 217. England Addy (1895) 131–2. Derbyshire [1890] Uttley (1946) 126. Yorkshire

Nicholson (1890) 27–8. Lancashire Harland & Wilkinson (1882) 69–70. Co. Durham Brockie (1886) 185–6; Leighton (1910) 61. Ireland N&Q 11S:3 (1911) 396. Unlocated N&Q 11S:3 (1911) 295. Various Opie (1959) 124–7.

---

spitting: white horses

A widespread children's custom was to spit on the ground whenever they saw a white or grey horse, to avoid bad luck. In most cases, simply spitting was sufficient, others had to spit on their shoe or over their shoulder, while some had an even more complicated procedure to perform:

During my boyhood it was a common practice with children, when they saw a grey horse, to 'spit three times' and 'go where the spit goes' (as the initiating phrase expressed it) in order to be lucky. The modus operandi was to eject spittle as far from the operator as possible, and for him to take his stand for the second ejection upon the spot where the first emission fell; and so for the third. The practice, notwithstanding the progress of education, has not entirely died out, as I find my own children have been taught the charm, or whatever it might be called.

Devon? N&Q 1S:6 (1852) 193

See HORSES: WHITE/GREY for further references.

spittle

Across the gamut of folk medicine, spittle is thought to have curative or restorative powers, and in most cases it is specifically 'fasting spittle' which is called for, i.e. spittle that is produced first thing in the morning, before eating.

The fasting spittle of a whole and sound person doth quite take away all scurviness . . . or redness of the face, ringworms, tetters, and all kinds of pustules or wheals by smearing or rubbing the place therewith. Lupton (1579)

It was particularly recommended for bad eyes and skin problems, especially of children, and was a standard cure for WARTS.

The fasting spittle of the mother heals all birthmarks and colds in the eyes of young babies.

Devon *Devonshire Assoc.* (1935)

One of my children being badly cut on his forehead, a Huntingdonshire woman told his nurse that if she wished the wound not to leave a scar, she must wet it every morning with her spittle before she had eaten or drunk.

Huntingdonshire N&Q (1865)

The fact that animals, and humans in certain circumstances, lick their wounds, presumably suggested this idea. It certainly has deep roots. Pliny (AD 77) recommended it for sore eyes, and the Saxon manuscript of *c.*1000 published as *Leechdoms* by Cockayne, advises those suffering from the 'penetrating worm' (sharp pains) to sing a charm on the wound and to 'smear it with thy spittle'.

Devon *Devonshire Assoc.* 67 (1935) 139. Huntingdonshire N&Q 3S:7 (1865) 275. **General** [*c.*1000] Cockayne 3 (1866) 11; Lupton (1579) Bk 1, Para. 57. **Classical** Pliny, *Natural History* (AD 77) Bk 28, Paras 7, 22.

splinters

see THORNS.

spoons: dropping

A wide range of domestic items were believed to take on significance if they were DROPPED. A dropped KNIFE or fork meant that a visitor would be arriving soon. A spoon is also sometimes included in this meaning, but it could also mean bad news or a disappointment:

If you drop a spoon the hollow side uppermost it means a surprise for you. If you drop it hollow side down it means a disappointment.

Lincolnshire Rudkin (1936)

Again, in common with other dropping beliefs, the item must be picked up by someone else:

A servant dropped a spoon, and as she made no attempt to pick it up, her mistress told her to do it. Without speaking, the girl left the kitchen, but soon returned with another maid who performed the duty. The one who dropped the spoon explained her subsequent procedure by saying that if she herself had picked it up she would have met with some dire misfortune. Unlocated N&Q (1914)

None of these cutlery superstitions seems to be older than the late nineteenth century.

London [*c.*1920s] Gamble (1979) 89. **Essex** [*c.*1917] Mays (1969) 164. **Bedfordshire** *Folk-Lore* 37 (1926) 77. **Worcestershire** *Folk-Lore* 20 (1909) 345. **Lincolnshire** [*c.*1940s] Sutton (1992) 139. **England** Addy (1895) 101. **Lincolnshire** Rudkin (1936) 19. **Yorkshire** *Folk-Lore* 21 (1910) 226. **Unlocated** N&Q 11S:10 (1914) 146, 196.

spoons: two in a saucer

A widespread domestic superstition holds that two spoons in somebody's saucer presages a wedding. This meaning is the most commonly reported, but considering the simple nature of the belief, a surprising number of variants have been recorded. For example:

Two spoons in a saucer means a wedding. One spoon in the saucer and one in the cup means a disappointment.

Norfolk Fulcher Collection (*c.*1895)

If by chance a girl have two teaspoons in her saucer, it is said to be a sign that she will have two husbands. Herefordshire Leather (1912)

Two spoons in a cup: one woman'll become pregnant
Two spoons in a saucer means a wedding.

Lincolnshire Sutton (1992)

Two spoons in a cup, you'll be kissed by a fool.

Suffolk *Folk-Lore* (1924)

In common with many domestic superstitions, this one seems to be a Victorian invention. There is no sign of it before 1872, and it is most commonly reported in the twentieth century. It has lasted well, however, and is still regularly quoted in appropriate circumstances.

Somerset [1923] Opie & Tatem, 374–5. **Wiltshire** Wiltshire (1975) 85; [1981] Opie & Tatem, 374–5. **Berkshire** Folk-Lore 5 (1894) 338. **Herefordshire** Leather (1912) 114. **Oxfordshire** Folk-Lore 20 (1909) 219; *Oxon Folklore Soc.* (1952) 6. **Suffolk** Folk-Lore 35 (1924) 350. **Norfolk** Fulcher Collection (c.1895). **Lincolnshire** Sutton (1992) 140. **Shropshire** Burne (1883) 279. **Derbyshire** N&Q 4S:10 (1872) 495. **Nottinghamshire** N&Q 9S:9 (1902) 357. **Yorkshire** Folk-Lore 21 (1910) 226; [1982] Opie & Tatem, 374–5; Gill (1993) 94. **Lancashire** Corbridge (1964) 156–60. *Lancashire Lore* (1971) 6. **Mid-Wales** Davies (1911) 217. **Monmouthshire** [1954] Opie & Tatem, 374–5. **Aberdeen** [1952] Opie & Tatem, 374–5. **Orkney** N&Q 10S:12 (1909) 483–4. **Co. Longford** *Béaloideas* 6 (1936) 260. **Co. Tyrone** *Lore & Language* 1:7 (1972) 9.

---

sprains

Sprains have always been thought amenable to unofficial methods of healing, and a range of different approaches have been recorded. Numerous substances were recommended for direct application – elm bark juice, bog moss, marsh mallow, comfrey, chickweed, eel skins, toad oil, and snail oil:

In May 1962 it was reported that the tinkers in the Scottish Highlands use snail oil to rub on sprained muscles. The writer also mentioned a spry old woman in her nineties who attributed her agility to regular massage with snail oil.
                    Highland Scotland *Folklore* (1962)

But many put their faith in more magical methods, involving a verbal CHARM, or a knotted THREAD, or both:

When a person has received a sprain, it is customary to apply to an individual practised in casting the 'wresting thread'. This is a thread spun from black wool, on which are cast nine knots, and tied round a sprained leg or arm. During the time the operator is putting the thread round the affected limb, he says, but in such a tone of voice as not to be heard by the bystanders, nor even by the person operated upon:

> *The Lord rade, And the foal slade*
> *He lighted, And he righted*
> *Set joint to joint, Bone to bone*
> *And sinew to sinew*
> *Heal in the Holy Ghost's name fire.*
>   Shetland *New Stat. Acct Scotland* (1845)

These methods were surprisingly widespread in the nineteenth and well into the twentieth century and, although particularly popular in Scotland and Ireland, were also recorded elsewhere in the British Isles.

A range of people were thought particularly skilled in sprain curing. Gregor (**Banffshire** (1974)) claimed that those who were 'born feet first' had a natural ability in this direction, and others put their faith in the local 'stamper':

The Stramp Streemer or Strainer – A person skilled in this art, stamps with the foot on the part affected, and after the first pang, it is said to be painless. W.R. of Belsay Lake House, stamped, for sprain, the arm of J.T. and cured her. The limb ought afterwards to be bound up with an eel's skin.   Northumberland Bigge (1860–62)

Direct application: **Lincolnshire** Gutch & Peacock (1908) 118. **Shropshire** Folk-Lore 49 (1938) 230. **Co. Durham** Neasham (1893) 252. **Scotland** N&Q 2S:4 (1857) 486. **Highland Scotland** Folklore 73 (1962) 134. **Galloway** Mactaggart (1824) 18. **Co. Antrim** Patterson (1880) 35. **Co. Leitrim** Logan (1981) 125. **Co. Cavan** Maloney (1972) 77. **Co. Cork** [1937] Culloty (1993) 62. *Charm and/or thread*: **Devon** *Devonshire Assoc.* 27 (1895) 65; Crossing (1911) 144. **Devon/Cornwall** N&Q 1S:3 (1851) 258. **Cornwall** Couch (1871) 148; *Folk-Lore Jnl* 5 (1887) 202; *Old Cornwall* 2:1 (1931) 20. **Herefordshire** [1804] Leather (1912) 74. **Worcestershire** *Folk-Lore* 20 (1909) 346. **Shropshire** Folk-Lore 6 (1895) 202–4. **Northumberland** Bigge (1860–62) 90; Henderson (1866) 123. **Breconshire** Folk-Lore 24 (1913) 507. **Scotland** [1933] Maclean (1959) 194. **Highland Scotland** Macbain (1887/88) 258. **Banffshire** Gregor (1874) 271. **Ross-shire** [1890s] MacDonald (1936) 58, 152–4. **Shetland** New Stat. Acct Scotland (1845) 141. **Orkney** N&Q 1S:10 (1854) 220–1; Mackenzie (1895) 73. **Ireland** Wilde (1888) 195. **N. Ireland** Foster (1951) 57; Ulster Folklife 26 (1980) 15–34. **Ross-shire** Folk-Lore 11 (1900) 448–9. **Co. Longford** Béaloideas 6 (1936) 267. **Co. Cavan** Logan (1963) 89. **Co. Leitrim** Logan (1981) 125. Unlocated *Folk-Lore* 53 (1942) 126.

---

spurge

see WART CURES: SPURGE.

staff divination

A traditional way of deciding which way to go was to stand a stick upright and let it fall where it will.

When a pilgrim at any time gets bewildered, he poises his staff perpendicular on the way, then leaves it to itself, and on whatever direction it falls, that he pursues; and this little trait of superstition is termed the 'Airt o' the Clicky' – the direction of the staff. And townsmen, when they mean to take a trip into the country for pleasure, and are quite careless to what part of it they wend their way, this they decide sometimes in the same way – the fallen stick determines the course to be pursued. Galloway Mactaggart (1824)

This can be extended into a more complex operation:

When one is setting out on any undertaking the staff was thrown to find out whether there would be success or not. The staff was taken by the end and thrown as high as possible, and in such a way as to turn over and over lengthwise. If the head of the staff fell in the direction in which the journey was to be undertaken, there would be success. Servants, on setting out to a feeing market, threw the staff to divine in what direction they were to go for the next half-year. They were to go in the direction in which the head of the staff lay when it fell. Northeast Scotland Gregor (1881)

Another variation on the stick theme was used by children:

Boys resorted to it in their games in order to determine between two parties, to settle for example which side should take a certain part in a game, or which of two lads, leaders in a game, should have the first choice of associates. A long stick was thrown into the air and caught by one of the parties, then each alternately grasped it hand over hand, and he who got the last hold was the successful party. He might not have sufficient length of stick to fill his whole hand, but if by closing his hand upon the end projecting from his opponent's hand, he could support the stick, this was enough. Western Scotland Napier (1879)

Lincolnshire *Gent. Mag.* (1832) 493. **Northeast Scotland** Gregor (1881) 29–30. **Western Scotland** Napier (1879) 107–10. **Galloway** Mactaggart (1824) 11.

stairs: passing on

A widespread belief, still often quoted, that it is unlucky to pass someone on the stairs:

A lady from the country ascending the stairs of a house in the neighbourhood of Bedford Square, saw another lady, occupying apartments in the house, in the act of descending the same flight. The first-named lady, a visitor, stood on one side to allow the lodger to pass her. 'No thank you,' said the latter; 'I never pass anyone on the stairs; it would be unlucky'. On this, the speaker retreated to her own rooms until the visitor had passed. London N&Q (1890).

The majority of references simply give 'bad luck' as the result, but one or two suggest that it means a quarrel or a parting, and one source claims that 'you would not meet in heaven' (Wiltshire (1975)). Only occasionally is a way of averting misfortune given:

When two people meet on the stairs, they should touch each other and speak, to avert misfortune. It is possible that the polite custom of waiting at the stair-foot or stair-head until someone already on the stairs has ascended or descended may be due as much to superstition as to good manners. Oxfordshire *Oxf. & Dist. FL Soc. Ann. Record* (1955)

On the available evidence, this notion is surprisingly recent and is certainly not so old as those concerning STUMBLING on the stairs (*see below*). The first known reference is only from 1865, but it is regularly mentioned ever since and is still widely reported at the present day. It was listed by over 20 per cent of the respondents in the 1998 Superstitions Survey (*see* Introduction). Oddly enough, all the references listed below are from England. This is unlikely to be a true reflection of the geographical spread of the superstition, and should be further researched. It is one of those beliefs which have at least a tenuous practical application, and followers often rationalize it as sensible advice to prevent accidents, or as mere courtesy.

Kent *Folk-Lore* 23 (1912) 354. **Dorset** Udal (1922) 286; *Dorset Year Book* (1961–2) 74. **Devon** N&Q 7S:9 (1890) 397, 511–12; Hewett (1900) 54; N&Q 10S:12 (1909) 66. **Cornwall** Hunt (1865) 239; *Jnl Royal Inst. Cornwall* 20 (1915) 133; *Old Cornwall* 2 (1931–6) 39. **Wiltshire** *Wilts. N&Q* 1 (1893–5) 102; Wiltshire (1975) 87. **Hampshire** [1960] Opie & Tatem, 375. **Berkshire** *Folk-Lore* 5 (1894) 338. **London** N&Q 7S:9 (1890) 325–6; *Folk-Lore* 37 (1926) 366; *Folk-Lore* 39 (1928) 95; [1985] Opie & Tatem, 375. **Essex** [*c*.1915] Mays (1969) 163. **Oxfordshire** [pre-1900] *Folk-Lore* 24 (1913) 90; *Oxf. & Dist. FL Soc. Ann. Record* (1955) 16–17. **Herefordshire** Leather (1912) 87. **Worcestershire** Berkley & Jenkins (1932) 34. **Warwickshire** [*c*.1925] Hewins (1985) 93. **Norfolk** Fulcher Collection (*c*.1895). **Shropshire** Burne (1883) 283. **England** Addy (1895) 99. **Yorkshire** N&Q 7S:9 (1890) 397; [1987] Opie & Tatem, 375; *Folk-Lore* 21 (1910) 226; Gill (1993) 90. **Northumberland** *Folk-Lore* 35 (1924) 351; Bosanquet (1929) 76. **Unlocated** N&Q 146 (1924) 397.

stairs: stumbling

A widely reported pair of superstitions are concerned with stumbling or tripping on the stairs, but with two very different meanings for the two directions of travel.

But then I stumbled coming down stairs, and met a weasel; bad omens those.

Congreve, *Love for Love* (1695)

If a girl stumbles when going upstairs, it is a sign that she will marry shortly, but she must not look back after stumbling or the omen will not be fulfilled. According to another version, it is the next person to come upstairs who will marry.

Oxfordshire *Oxf. & Dist. FL Soc. Ann. Record* (1952)

Stumbling down is reported less often, perhaps because it is so obviously unfortunate that many people do not regard it as a superstition at all. The earliest reference, from Congreve's play, makes it clear that it was already a bad omen in the late seventeenth century, and it is similarly reported over the following years. Opie and Tatem report a Swansea girl saying, in 1952, 'If you trip coming downstairs a funeral is imminent'. One informant offered a way to avoid the coming misfortune:

It was accounted unlucky to tumble down stairs; hence when a misfortune of that sort occurred within the hearing of another person, it was usual for the latter to divert the omen by calling out loudly 'Tumble up!'   Lancashire N&Q (1870)

Tripping up the stairs – by accident, of course – has been reported far more often, with a remarkably consistent meaning of a coming wedding. The only variable detail is who the wedding is to include – some say the tripper will get married, or be invited to a wedding, while for others it is the next person to ascend the stairs. Many do not specify. The wedding prognostication is first reported a few years after the downstairs omen, in the humorous survey of superstitions published in the *Connoisseur*:

and if she stumbles as she is running up stairs, imagines she shall go to church with her sweetheart before the week is at an end.

Connoisseur (1755)

and is regularly reported until the mid twentieth century. Despite its previous popularity, it is now probably only known to a few people who quote their parents' or grandparents' beliefs.

Tripping downstairs: Cornwall *Old Cornwall* 2 (1931–6) 39. Lancashire N&Q 4S:6 (1870) 211. Glamorganshire [1952] Opie & Tatem, 375. General Brand (1777) 95. Literary William Congreve, *Love for Love* (1695) 2:1. *Tripping upstairs*: Sussex [*c*.1914] Opie & Tatem, 375. Somerset [1923] Opie & Tatem, 375. Devon Hewett (1900) 49. Wiltshire *Wilts. N&Q* 1 (1893–5) 102;

Wiltshire (1975) 87. Berkshire *Folk-Lore* 5 (1894) 338. Essex [*c*.1920] Ketteridge & Mays (1972) 142. Oxfordshire [pre-1900] *Folk-Lore* 24 (1913) 90; *Oxf. & Dist. FL Soc. Ann. Record* (1952) 6. Warwickshire Langford (1875) 11. East Anglia Varden (1885) 110. Suffolk *Folk-Lore* 25 (1914) 366. Lincolnshire Sutton (1992) 142. Shropshire Burne (1883) 283. England Addy (1895) 99. Yorkshire Nicholson (1890) 45; *Folk-Lore* 43 (1932) 252. Co. Durham Henderson (1866) 85; Brockie (1886) 211; Leighton (1910) 60. Northumberland *Folk-Lore* 36 (1925) 253. Wales Trevelyan (1909) 270; [1923] *Folk-Lore* 45 (1934) 161. Orkney N&Q 10S:12 (1909) 483–4. Unlocated Grose (1787) 63; N&Q 2S:12 (1861) 491; *Chambers's Jnl* (1873) 810. Literary *Connoisseur* 56 (1755) 332; *Old Women's Sayings* (*c*.1835).

stairs: turning on

The least commonly reported superstition about stairs maintains that it is unlucky to turn round on the stairs. Only reported a handful of times, this could be an extension of the other stair superstitions, especially that which forbids passing on the stairs, or it could be seen as a specialist example of the widespread rule against TURNING BACK in general:

If you forget anything, never turn back or misfortune will overtake you. If on the stairs, do not stop but continue to the top, sit down and consider before you return or bad luck will follow.

Hampshire N&Q (1890)

As with the passing-on-the-stairs belief, this is reported from only the late nineteenth century onwards, and from only England and Wales.

Devon *Devonshire Assoc.* 71 (1939) 127. Somerset [1923] Opie & Tatem, 375. Hampshire N&Q 7S:9 (1890) 486. Essex [1964] Opie & Tatem, 375. Leicestershire *Daily Express* (17 July 1962) 11. Radnorshire [1953] Opie & Tatem, 375.

standing stones

see COUNTING: STANDING STONES.

stars

see also SHOOTING STARS.

stars: pointing at

A widespread superstition held that it was unlucky to point at, or try to count, the stars, in the same way as it was unwise to point at the MOON. In many cases the prohibition was couched in terms of 'sin' and 'irreverence' rather than 'luck':

I remember being rebuked more than once for pointing at the stars when a child . . . I do not think any definite reason was given, but I was made to feel that I had been guilty of shocking irreverence.

Nottinghamshire/Warwickshire N&Q (1902)

Some children believed that if you counted the stars, retribution would be swift and sure:

It is wrong to point at the stars, or even to count them; you may be struck dead for doing so.

Co. Durham Leighton (1910)

It comes as no surprise that some popular writers have assumed that these superstitions are remnants of moon- or star-worship, but there is no evidence whatsoever that this is so, and it is extremely unlikely that any such beliefs could have lasted so long. A notion that the moon and stars are special is easily fitted into a Christian context, and Victorian ideas about the rudeness of pointing supply the other element. There is no sign of these beliefs before the mid nineteenth century.

See also MOON: POINTING AT; COUNTING.

Sussex N&Q 6S:5 (1882) 14–15. **Worcestershire** Salisbury (1893) 77. **Suffolk** [1953] Opie & Tatem, 377. **Northamptonshire** Sternberg (1851) 170. **Nottinghamshire/Warwickshire** N&Q 9S:9 (1902) 358. **England** Addy (1895) 56. **Derbyshire** [*c*.1852] N&Q 9S:9 (1902) 357–8. **Lincolnshire** N&Q 6S:5 (1882) 15. **Yorkshire** Henderson (1866) 88. **Co. Durham** Leighton (1910) 61. **Unlocated** N&Q 9S:9 (1902) 227.

stepping over

Stepping or jumping over a child's head was a sure way of stunting any further growth:

The mother should be careful to see that no child is allowed to jump over the head of another, as in that case the overleapt infant would never grow.   Co. Durham Leighton (1910)

This belief was reported almost exclusively from northern England and Scotland, where 'crile' or 'creel' were dialect terms for a dwarf or stunted person, and as a verb signified to deliberately throw your leg over someone to tease them. The superstition was reported a number of times in the nineteenth century, and would not seem to be any older, apart from a very early version in the *Gospelles of Dystaves* (1507), a translation of a Low Country text, which is so close in meaning that there must be a connection somehow:

If it happen that some body stride over a little child, know ye for certain that he shall never grow more but if they stride backwards over it again . . . of such thing cometh dwarves and little women.

Herefordshire [1880] Opie & Tatem, 377. **Northern England** Brockett (1846) 'crile'; *Newcastle Weekly Chronicle* (4 Feb. 1899) 7; N&Q 10S:9 (1908) 494. **Yorkshire** [*c*.1829] N&Q 10S:9 (1908) 494. **Co. Durham** N&Q 10S:9 (1908) 494; Leighton (1910) 49. **Northumberland** Heslop (1892) 'creel'. **Fife** N&Q 10S:10 (1908) 36.

sticks

see STAFF DIVINATION; WALKING STICKS.

stiles

see GATES/STILES.

stoats

see WEASELS/STOATS.

stockings

see SHOES; THROAT CURES: STOCKINGS; TOOTHACHE: SHOES/STOCKINGS.

stolen goods

Included in the standard fare of local CUNNING MEN and white witches throughout the country was the professed ability to locate stolen or lost items:

Miss Hales's diamond ring, which had been lost, has been found in a box in a cupboard where it was not usually kept. What makes the case the more singular, a 'wise man' living at Shipdham (whom her maids had consulted) predicted that it would be found 'before Saturday'. Query: Was he in connivance with the thief? It is said that these 'wise men' are often thus useful in the recovery of stolen property, and it was only in this sense that Miss Hales allowed her servants to consult the fellow.   Norfolk [1860] Armstrong

Such people had various ways of obtaining knowledge, often including reflections in mirrors or pails of water (early versions of the modern crystal ball) in which the victims were invited to peer (Kittredge (1929)).

For those who did not wish to call in a profes-sional, there were two well-known procedures which could be carried out in their own home – the BIBLE AND KEY and the SIEVE AND SHEARS.

To detect a thief: As soon as the theft is discov-ered, suspicion immediately falls on some unfor-tunate person in the parish whose reputation is perhaps a little shady. The suspected person is at once brought to trial, not in person, but in secret, by means of his or her name being written on a slip of paper which is placed within the leaves of a Bible. The key of the front door is placed beside it, with the wards resting on the eighteenth verse of the fiftieth psalm. Both are kept in position by tying the left leg garters of two persons around the Bible. These two place their right hand fore-fingers under the bow of the key, and repeat in monotone the verse above named. If the Bible moves to the right or left the suspected person is condemned; if it remains stationary, he is acquit-ted. Devon Hewett (1892)

This preoccupation with stolen goods has a long history: both the 1563 and 1604 WITCH-CRAFT ACTS specifically forbid using any witch-craft, enchantment, charm, or sorcery to locate 'goods or things lost or stolen', and long before that the Anglo-Saxons had a number of charms to assist them (*see Folk-Lore* (1946) and Storms (1948)).

A strange superstition was reported from Highland Scotland a few times in the late nine-teenth century. It appears that it was thought unlucky to retrieve items which had been stolen:

There was among many a strong reluctance to report a theft to the magistrate, or to give any clue to the detection of a thief. To do so was accounted unlucky. It was also looked upon as a source of mishap that a friend of the woman paid back part of the money. This caused so much annoyance to the owner, that he could not rest in peace till he had given away in charity the whole sum that had been paid back. 'I'll have nae stoun fangs i' the hoose' said the man.
Northeast Scotland Gregor (1881)

England *Folk-Lore* 45 (1934) 162. Devon Hewett (1892) 72. Norfolk [1860] Armstrong (1949) 72. England Addy (1895) 80. Highland Scotland Polson (1926) 129.

Northeast Scotland Gregor (1881) 32–3. Co. Leitrim *Folk-Lore* 5 (1894) 198. Unlocated [1693] *Folk-Lore* 21 (1910) 375–7. General Kittredge (1929) 185–203; *Folk-Lore* 57 (1946) 7–11; Storms (1948) 202–17, 302, 311.

stones

see also CURSING.

stones: holed

By far the most widespread superstition about a mineral concerned stones with a natural hole in them, which were prized as lucky and protective. They could be hung up to protect a building against witchcraft, or carried on the person to ward off an EVIL EYE, but the two most widely reported uses were to hang them in a stable to protect the horses against being ridden in the night by witches (HAG-RIDDEN), or on the bedstead to protect humans against the NIGHT-MARE. The latter was not simply a bad dream but a terrible affliction in the night in which the victim feels a huge weight on his/her chest:

A stone with a hole in it, hung at the bed's head, will prevent the night-mare; it is therefore called a hag-stone, from that disorder, which is occasioned by a hag, or witch, sitting on the stomach of the party afflicted. It also prevents witches riding horses; for which purpose it is often tied to a stable key. Unlocated Grose (1787)

It was not an uncommon thing on going into the stable in the morning to find the horses, which had been left all right overnight, all in a sweat and reeking – like horses that had been over-ridden – and in a state of fear and trembling. This was supposed to be caused by their having been ridden by the witches during the night. This sort of thing never happened after the horses were protected by the suspended stones.
Lancashire Weeks (1910)

A Yorkshire stable is rarely seen without a horse shoe; perhaps three, nailed on the door to keep the witches off, and some years ago, the small round pebbles on the Bridlington coast, with holes washed in them by the tide, were hung round children's necks for the same purpose.
Yorkshire *Monthly Packet* (1863)

The specific evils that the stone could counter varied from place to place, but were nearly always on the theme of what harm others (witches, fairies, malignant neighbours) could do to your home, family, trade, or stock. As indi-cated, the stones were particularly common on farms, protecting livestock, but workers in other trades relied on holed stones for luck and protection, in particular those in mining and fishing:

rolled flints with a natural bore, tied as charms inside the bows of Weymouth boats. I have watched a boatman in the act of fastening one in his craft.   Dorset N&Q (1895)

A holed stone was valued for its intrinsic power, and there is no evidence that it needed any special treatment or preparation before use, although some clearly believed that it only began to work once the string had been threaded through the hole for it to hang on. A number of sources indicate that the stone was most powerful if it was found by chance, or presented as a gift.

In Britain, the documentary record commences in the seventeenth century, but the belief was clearly already well known by then. Thomas Browne asked:

what natural effects can reasonably be expected, when to prevent the ephialtes or night-mare we hang up an hollow stone in our stables.
                      Browne, *Pseudodoxia Epidemica* (1646)

Holed-stone traditions were extremely common in much of the British Isles – particularly in England, Southern and Eastern Scotland, Northern Ireland, and the Isle of Man, but less so in the rest of Ireland and Wales. According to T. D. Davidson (1965) the holed stone is known as an amulet, or curing stone, across most of Europe, with examples particularly close to the British usage common in Scandinavia. Beliefs such as these, which include a tangible artefact, are particularly conducive to distribution studies, and further comparative research on these lines would be informative.

Some holed stones were believed to have been formed by snakes, either by their bite causing the hole, or the stone itself being fashioned by the secretion of numerous adders forming rings (*see* SNAKE STONES).

England Aubrey, *Remaines* (1686/1972) 231. Dorset N&Q 8S:8 (1895) 52; *Folk-Lore* 89 (1978) 158. Hertfordshire *Folk-Lore* 66 (1955) 416–17. Northamptonshire [1823] Clare (1993) 140. Bedfordshire N&Q 10S 7 (1907) 26. East Anglia Varden (1885) 103. Suffolk N&Q 1S:4 (1851) 53; Glyde (1866) 175; *Gent. Mag.* (1867) 307–22, 728–41; *Folk-Lore* 56 (1945) 270. Norfolk [*c.*1870] Haggard (1935) 16; *Folk-Lore* 40 (1929) 124. Lincolnshire Peacock (1877) 134; Heanley (1902) 17–18. Northern England Brockett (1829) 3–4, 157–8. Yorkshire N&Q 1S:1 (1850) 429; Nicholson (1890) 87; *Observer Supp.* (24 Nov. 1968) 10. Westmorland/Lancashire [*c.*1939] *Folk-Lore* 62 (1951) 262. Lancashire N&Q 1S:3 (1851) 56; *Monthly Packet* 25 (1863) 549–51; Harland & Wilkinson (1882) 72, 154; Weeks (1910) 107–9. Co. Durham Brockie (1886) 32; *Folk-Lore* 20 (1909) 74; Leighton (1910) 46. Northumberland Neasham (1893) 250; Neville (1909) 111–12; N&Q 146 (1924) 96. Wales Trevelyan (1909) 324; Jones (1930) 142. Berwickshire N&Q 2S:1 (1857) 486. Caithness *Folk-Lore* 16 (1905) 335–6. N. Ireland Dent (1964) 46–8. Guernsey Carey (1903) 507; De Garis (1975) 125. Unlocated Grose (1787) 57–8; N&Q 8S:6 (1894) 433. General Browne, *Pseudodoxia Epidemica* (1646) Bk 5, Ch. 21; Aubrey, *Miscellanies* (1696/1857) 140; *Gent. Mag.* (1796) 636; Dent (1964) 46–8. Major studies: Dent (1964); Dent (1965).

stones: holed, passing through

A number of large holed stones around the country have local traditions which claimed that they were useful for healing various ailments. Where the hole is large enough to crawl through, or pass a child through, this action was reputed to effect the cure:

Beyond the village of Lanyon, on a furzy down, stands the Mên-an-tol, or the 'holed stone'. If scrofulous children are passed naked through the Mên-an-tol three times, and then drawn on the grass three times against the sun, it is felt by the faithful that much has been done towards insuring a speedy cure. Even men and women who have been afflicted with spinal diseases, or who have suffered from scrofulous taint, have been drawn through this magic stone, which all declare still retains its ancient virtues.
                                      Cornwall Hunt (1865)

The Mên-an-tol, first described by Borlase in 1754, is probably the best known of these stones, but Leslie Grinsell (1976) lists many others in his survey of the folklore of prehistoric sites. It is ironic that one of the ailments regularly quoted as cured by the process of 'passing through' is back problems, but others were many and various, including scrofula, rickets, whooping cough, and epilepsy.

It has been suggested that the motif of drawing somebody through a hole is symbolic of 'rebirth'. However, there does not seem to be any basis for this interpretation, and the more careful authorities regard the procedure as a means of TRANSFERENCE of the disease to the stone. The motif of passing invalids through apertures is extremely widespread, and not restricted to holed stones. Children, especially, were passed under BRAMBLES, through split ASH TREES, and holes in the ground. Our Anglo-Saxon ancestors held several beliefs in the curative properties of stones, and also faith in the 'passing through' motif. The authorities attempted repeatedly to put a stop to such activities, as in the following from the eleventh century:

If anyone passed his child for the sake of its health through a hole in the earth, and then fills the hole behind him with thorns, he shall do penance for forty days on bread and water.
      First Pentitential (Corpus Christi MS C.C.C.C. 190, 11th cent.) quoted in Bonser (1963)

Other traditions clustered around holed stones, and even if the hole was too small to pass through, it could be used in other ways.

Barren women in Ireland once believed if they slept a night on one of the megaliths known as Diarmuid and Grania's Beds, they would be cured. The holed stone at Glencolmcille was much resorted to for this purpose, and a Tyrone clergyman told me recently that some women in his district believe in the power of certain stones and wells to cure barrenness. The Hole-Stone at Doagh used to be a favourite place for lovers to plight their troth by holding hands through the hole.   N. Ireland Foster (1951)

Cornwall Borlase (1754) 169; Hunt (1865) 191, 215–16; Hillaby (1970) 27. Scotland Folk-Lore 29 (1918) 86. Aberdeen Graham (1950) 12. N. Ireland Foster (1951) 118. General Bonser (1963) 240, 342–4; Grinsell (1976) numerous pages.

stones: standing

see COUNTING: STANDING STONES.

stones: white

Naturally white stones were also prized, for luck or for their curative powers:

A few weeks ago I noticed one of my schoolboys taking up a white stone from the road, spitting upon it, and then throwing it over his head. In doing so he repeated the following distich:

   Lucky, lucky stone
   Bring me luck, when I go home

Upon enquiry I found that it would afterwards be unlucky for him to look back when turning round a corner.   North Wales Folk-Lore (1914)

White stones seem to have had some significance in Ulster . . . Witches who practised white magic often used a white stone. Joe Tate of Magilligan placed a white stone in clear water when he wished to discover who was blinking cattle or

doing other mischief. When he gazed into the water the face of the witch appeared.
      N. Ireland Foster (1951)

Lincolnshire Rudkin (1936) 16. North Wales Folk-Lore 25 (1914) 372. West Wales Davies (1911) 216. N. Ireland Foster (1951) 120.

storms

In the same way that the appearance of a COMET was believed to presage major changes in the fate of nations, the idea that storms and wild weather accompanied the death of great persons was formerly widely believed:

Waked with a very high wind, and said to my wife, 'I pray God I hear not of the death of any great person, this wind is so high'; fearing that the Queen might be dead.
      London Pepys, Diary (19 Oct. 1663)

This connection between storms and the rich and famous was widely reported, but there are also indications that a similar belief held good further down the social scale:

The weather on the day of the funeral was most carefully observed. A shower on the mould of an open grave – the 'meels' – was taken as an indication that the soul of the departed was enjoying happiness. A hurricane told of some foul deed done, but never brought to light, or of a bad life, however fair to the eye, or of a compact with Satan.
      Northeast Scotland Gregor (1874)

Storms, like WINDS, could also be raised deliberately, and if local stories are to be believed, witches and conjurors could call them up at will. For example, a Shetland story told of the regular depredations by the crew of a ship which moored off the island, and which the locals were powerless to resist by conventional means. The community leaders therefore approached an old woman of certain reputation:

They told their tale and she replied: 'Abonjinit, abonjinit! I canna du ony gud, an I canna du muckle herm; bit ye gang an tell da folk ta mak fast dir boats and tak weel aboot dir grains o corn.' The men departed and secured their boats, stacks of corn, and all loose property about the island. That night a wild storm burst on the Atlantic, and in the morning the isles-men saw the dreaded vessel founder in the offing.
      Shetland Black (1903)

London Samuel Pepys, Diary (19 Oct. 1963). Worcestershire N&Q 1S:6 (1852) 531. Warwickshire

N&Q 11S:3 (1911) 207. **Lincolnshire** N&Q 1S:9 (1854) 494. **Northern England** *Denham Tracts* 2 (1895) 29–30. **Northeast Scotland** Gregor (1874) 147. **Shetland** Black (1903) 154. **Unlocated** N&Q 6S:1 (1880) 212. *See also* Opie & Tatem, 452–3, for references from the twelfth century onwards.

straw boaters

British children and young people had various games based on the need to say some special words and/or carry out special actions when they saw certain specified items in the street. A sure sign of summer from Edwardian times onwards was the appearance of people wearing straw boaters in the street, and there was intense competition between friends as to who could react fastest to seeing someone sporting such a hat:

It was good luck to see someone wearing a straw boater, referred to by us as 'bashers'. Immediately one was sighted there was a cry of 'basher' accompanied by a lick of the right thumb, a quick touch of the left palm with the moistened digit, then the right fist was slammed into the left palm, and the first one to achieve the satisfying smack scored a point against her slower companion.

Oxfordshire [1920s] Surman

These traditions straddled the boundary between custom and superstition, but the mention of 'luck' makes them relevant to the latter field. The required response differed quite widely, as seen by comparing the above with another report from the same county:

A curious custom is said to have persisted in Tackley until just before the outbreak of the 1939–45 war. Children there, on meeting a man in a straw hat touched their own elbows and hands alternately, and sang:

> *Strawberry man, strawberry man, bring me*
> *   good luck*
> *Today or tomorrow, to pick something up*

They then threw a stone or some other small object over their left shoulders.

Oxfordshire *Oxf. & Dist. FL Soc. Ann. Record* (1955)

Other children had to SPIT or CROSS their FINGERS. Iona and Peter Opie also collected many versions of the custom, from Norfolk, Hampshire, Bedfordshire, Cheshire, Nottinghamshire, and Forfarshire.
Compare SPECTACLES.

Oxfordshire [1920s] Surman (1992) 60; [Before 1939] *Oxf. & Dist. FL Soc. Ann. Record* (1955) 17. **Various** Opie (1959) 215.

string

see THREAD/STRING.

stumbling

Abundant evidence exists to show that stumbling has been regarded as a bad omen in various contexts since classical times, and in Britain since at least the medieval era. Given the almost obsessive concern for good BEGINNINGS in many minds, it is hardly surprising that to stumble at the beginning of a journey, or at the start of the day, is counted as very ominous indeed:

That if a man stumbles in a morning as soon as he comes out of doors, it is a sign of ill luck.

Melton (1620)

and 'to stumble on the threshold', meaning to make a bad start at anything, was already an old saying when recorded by John Aubrey in 1686. But the threshold could be approached from two directions, and many would also worry about stumbling on the way in:

For many men that stumble at the threshold
Are well foretold that that danger lurks within,

Shakespeare, *Henry VI Pt 3* (1593)

This notion was still current in 1923:

Should a stranger fall down on entering your house for the first time, ill luck will be on your dwelling connected with that visitor.

Wiltshire [1923] Opie & Tatem

Beginnings are concerned with metaphorical as well as physical journeys, and a wedding was a particularly important time for steady feet:

Omens of misfortune are many and varied. It is unlucky . . . if the bride or groom stumble when going up to the altar.   Unlocated *Folk-Lore* (1957)

Similarly, at the other end of life's span, 'stumbling over a grave' or while attending a funeral are other special cases, which neatly combine the general superstition with the specific omen of death. Again, Shakespeare supplies an early example, 'How oft to night have these aged feet stumbled at graves' (*Romeo and Juliet* (1592)) and Speranza Wilde spells out its meaning 300 years later:

If anyone stumbles at a grave it is a bad omen; but if he falls and touches the clay he will assuredly die before the year is out.

Ireland Wilde (1888)

One more regularly reported aspect of the belief maintains that it is a bad omen if your HORSE stumbles while you are riding it.

How superstitiously we mind our evils!
The throwing down salt, or crossing of a hare,
Bleeding at nose, the stumbling of a horse,
Or singing of a cricket, are of power
To daunt whole man in us.

Webster, *Duchess of Malfi* (1623)

Nevertheless, one of the apparent perversities of British superstition holds that stumbling on the stairs is not necessarily a bad thing. Stumbling down is indicative of bad luck, but tripping while going up is usually said to be the sign of a wedding (*see* STAIRS: STUMBLING). Similarly, to trip over on stage is not so bad as it might be:

To fall on the stage augurs a long engagement for the faller, and this was 'proved' to the compiler's knowledge, for, on the first night of Bram Stoker's vampire play Dracula, a player tripped over the doorsill and fell heavily on the stage. The play ran for two years in London, and had a New York run.

Unlocated Granville (1952)

In Britain, the twelfth-century Kentish monk Nigel de Longchamps provided proof that the basic stumbling belief was already in force in his time, and it was still occurring frequently in writings of the later seventeenth century. Nevertheless, it seems to lose its force as a major omen from that time, and although reported into recent times, it is clear that it had gradually gone out of fashion. Stumbling in a particular context (e.g. walking up the aisle at a wedding) may still excite comment, but it is unlikely that many would be overcome with fear if they simply tripped on the way out to work in the morning, or when off on holiday.

See also STAIRS.

Sussex Woodford (1968) 59–60. Wiltshire [1923] Opie & Tatem, 380. Wales Trevelyan (1909) 329. Elgin *Folk-Lore Jnl* 7 (1889) 46. Galloway Mactaggart (1824) 380. Ireland Wilde (1888) 154. Unlocated Granville (1952) 179; *Folk-Lore* 68 (1957) 418. General Nigel de Longchamps, *Mirror for Fools* (1180); Scot (1584) Bk 11, Ch. 15; Bishop Hall, *Characters* (1608) 'Superstitious Man'; Melton (1620); Aubrey, *Remaines* (1686/1972) 217; *Poor Robin's Almanack* (1695). Literary Edmund Spenser, *Shepheardes Calender* (1579) May; Shakespeare, *Romeo and Juliet* (1592) 5:3; Shakespeare, *Henry VI Pt 3* (1593) 4:7; John Webster, *Duchess of Malfi* (1623) 2:3.

stye cures

Three main folk cures for a stye in the eye have been widely recorded, along with numerous miscellaneous herbal and a few magical remedies. By far the most commonly reported remedy was to stroke the eye with a piece of gold – a wedding ring was usually recommended, presumably because that would be the only gold an average family would have to hand. The stroking was usually subject to certain rules covering at least the number of times and sometimes the manner in which it was done as well:

Sore eyes and craobhour *could be treated . . . rub a gold ring to it in the form of the cross nine times each morning for three consecutive days.*

Co. Cork [1937/8] Culloty

Nine strokes with a wedding-ring would, it was said, cure a stye, or 'styne' as we were wont to call it, in the eye. In order to have its due effect, the ring must be taken off the finger of its owner, and as our good mother could not be persuaded to part with the precious token in such a cause, our relief had to be wrought in some more legitimated manner. Lincolnshire *Grantham Jnl* (22 June 1878)

Nine times is the commonest number cited. The association between gold and eye cures has a long history in Britain. In the Saxon medical manuscript (*c*.1050) reprinted in Cockayne's *Saxon Leechdoms*, knotgrass is scratched around with a gold ring, and then used for 'leechdom of sore eyes'. It was sufficiently commonplace to be mentioned in passing by seventeenth-century dramatists such as John Webster in his *Duchess of Malfi* (1623), and Beaumont and Fletcher's *The Mad Lover* (*c*.1618). The remedy was still being mentioned in the early twenty-first century:

My mother's sovereign remedy for a pouk on the eye was to roll a wedding ring across it a few times. It always worked.

Unlocated *BBC Radio 4* (31 July 2002)

The second most popular cure was to use the hair of a cat's tail:

Here is a remedy for curing a stye in the eye, or what is locally known as a 'quillaway'. You stroke the eyelid with a Tom-cat's tail three times, three mornings running, and it must be done very early, before the dew is off the ground. Another informant who knew of this practice said a single hair was equally efficacious, but it must be from a cat. Cornwall *Old Cornwall* (1931)

Some specify a black cat, while others distinguish between the sufferers:

A cure for a stye in the eye, given to me by my father – Take a cat (if for a man a male, and if for a woman a female) and strike the eye with its tail.   **Devon** *Devonshire Assoc.* (1883)

CATS were used in cures for various ailments, including eye complaints, at least from the early eighteenth century. Some remedies utilized cats' blood, while others involved slaughtering the animal, as in Topsell's *Four-Footed Beastes* (1607): 'for the pain and blindness in the eye . . . Take the head of a black cat . . . and burn it to a powder'. Rubbing a sore eye with a cat's tail is recommended in the *Yea and Nay Almanack* of 1678 (quoted in Opie and Tatem, 59), and was clearly well known a century later, when Parson Woodforde of Norfolk was suffering from a sore eye:

The stiony on my right eye-lid still swelled and inflamed very much. As it is commonly said that the eye-lid being rubbed by the tail of a black cat would do it much good if not entirely cure it, a little before dinner I made a trial of it, and very soon after dinner I found my eye-lid much abated of the swelling and almost free from pain. Any other cat's tail may have the above effect in all probability – but I did my eye-lid with my own black Tom cat's tail.
Norfolk Woodforde, *Diary* (11 Mar. 1791)

However, five days later he was still trying various ways to get rid of the stye.

The third method of cure, reported exclusively from Ireland, involves gooseberry thorns. In contrast to the gold rings and cats' tails, the thorns are not used directly on the stye:

A treatment which is practised in many parts of Ireland is the use of a twig of a gooseberry bush with nine thorns. All the other thorns are broken off the twig until only nine remain and care is taken to ensure that each thorn points in the direction opposite to the thorn next to it. Each thorn is pointed at the sty and an Our Father, a Hail Mary and a Gloria are said each time. The ritual is repeated daily for nine days to complete the cure. In any case, the sty would be well on the way to being healed at the end of nine days, if treated by fasting spit or with nine gooseberry thorns, or by any other method.   **Ireland** Logan (1981)

Other versions are less complex, but the principle is always similar.

Numerous other cures have been recorded, with the most straightforward suggesting bathing the stye with fasting SPITTLE, MAY DEW, cold tea, and DANDELION juice. One or two simply involve pointing at the stye (in a similar way as the gooseberry thorns were used

above) and telling it to go, but the nature of the pointing object varies:

In another cure for the same trouble, the charmer stands with a rolling-pin and points it at the sufferer, who must say, 'What are you pointing at?' 'At your eye,' answers the charmer, 'I drive the stye away', and away it goes.
Cornwall *Old Cornwall* (1931)

A single reference reports a tradition which explains how a stye is formed in the first place:

It was believed that if a present were given, especially if it were given to a sweetheart, and then asked back again, the giver would have a stye on the eye.   **Western Scotland** Napier (1879)

Gold ring: **Sussex** Latham (1878) 45. **Devon** N&Q 5S:2 (1874) 184; *Devonshire Assoc.* 10 (1878) 106; *Devonshire Assoc.* 59 (1927) 167. **Cornwall** *Folk-Lore Jnl* 5 (1887) 203–4. **Gloucestershire** *Folk-Lore* 34 (1923) 157. **Herefordshire** Leather (1912) 81. **Warwickshire** Bloom (c.1930) 31. **Bedfordshire** Marsom (1950) 183. **Cambridgeshire** Porter (1969) 81. **Suffolk** Moor (1823) 408; Claxton (1954) 90. **Lincolnshire** *Grantham Jnl* (22 June 1878); Swaby (1891) 91; [1940s] Sutton (1992) 151. **Staffordshire** Hackwood (1924) 152. **Derbyshire** Uttley (1946) 113–14. **Northern England** Brockett (1829) 294–5. **Yorkshire** Nicholson (1890) 88. **Co. Durham** *Folk-Lore Jnl* 2 (1883) 120; Brockie (1886) 222. **Wales** Jones (1930) 142–3. **Western Scotland** Napier (1879) 96–7. **Glasgow** [1940s] MacLeay (1990) 48. **Ireland** Logan (1981) 58. **Co. Cork** [1937/8] Culloty (1993) 58. **Co. Tipperary** *Folk-Lore* 8 (1897) 387. **Unlocated** N&Q 160 (1931) 304; BBC *Radio 4 – Home Truths* website (31 July 2002). **General** [c.1050] Cockayne 1 (1864) 113; N&Q 5S:8 (1877). **Literary** Beaumont & Fletcher, *The Mad Lover* (c.1618) 5:4; Beaumont & Fletcher, *The Elder Brother* (1637) 2:4; John Webster, *Duchess of Malfi* (1623) 1:2. **Cat's tail:** **Kent** [1930s] Kent (1977) 99. **Devon** N&Q 5S:2 (1874) 184; *Devonshire Assoc.* 10 (1878) 106; *Devonshire Assoc.* 15 (1883) 100; *Devonshire Assoc.* 59 (1927) 167; *Devonshire Assoc.* 77 (1945) 94. **Cornwall** Hunt (1865) 240; *Folk-Lore Jnl* 5 (1887) 203–4; *Old Cornwall* 2:1 (1931) 19; *Bath Folk-Lore Jnl* 1 (1883) 331. **Herefordshire** Leather (1912) 81. **Warwickshire** Bloom (c.1930) 31. **Northamptonshire** N&Q 1S:2 (1850) 36–7. **Cambridgeshire** *Folk-Lore* 25 (1914) 365. **Norfolk** James Woodforde, *Diary* (11 Mar. 1791). **General** *Yea and Nay Almanack* (1678). **Gooseberry thorn:** **Ireland** Wilde (1888) 198; Logan (1981) 58. **Co. Wexford** N&Q 3S:1 (1862) 446–7; [1938] Ó Muirithe & Nuttall (1999) 97, 100. **Co. Longford** *Béaloideas* 6 (1936) 267. **Co. Cavan** Logan (1963) 89. **Co. Londonderry** *Folk-Lore* 4 (1893) 356. **Miscellaneous cures:** **Devon** *Devonshire Assoc.* 12 (1880) 105–6; *Devonshire Assoc.* 59 (1927) 167. **Cornwall** *Old Cornwall* 2:1 (1931) 19–20. **Wiltshire** *Wilts. N&Q* 1 (1893–5) 316. **Oxfordshire** [1920s] Harris (1969) 114. **Welsh Gypsies** Jarman (1991) 187. **Highland Scotland** Macbain (1887/88) 257. **Western Scotland** Napier (1879) 96–7. **Caithness** Rinder (1895) 62. **Ireland** Logan (1981) 59. **Co. Cork** [1937/8] Culloty (1993) 58–9. **Guernsey** MacCulloch (1864) 505.

suicides

Until the 1820s, those found guilty of suicide were denied burial in consecrated ground and were interred by the public roadway (but not necessarily at a crossroads) with a wooden stake driven through their body. Thus the Parish Register of Pleasley, Derbyshire, simply states:

Thomas Maule found hanging on a tree by the wayside after a drunken fit . . . Same night at midnight buried at the highest crossroads with a stake in him.   Derbyshire [1573] Jupp & Gittings

This treatment of suicides was clearly officially sanctioned and widely followed, but it is unclear on what legal basis it rested. Sir James Fitzjames Stephen (*History of the Criminal Law of England*, 1883) could find no legal authority for the custom or any earlier comment by legal historians. Stray references show that it was already in existence in the sixteenth century, and it is mentioned frequently from that time in a variety of sources, usually with no comment – simply as a matter of course.

The custom is clearly in line with the popular horror of suicide engendered by the Christian churches, who regarded self-murder as one of the worst of crimes, and it is likely that the stake and the unconsecrated burial were designed to enhance the deterrent rather than arising from fears of the dead walking. The latter remains a possibility, of course, and it is quite feasible that at local level this is how it was viewed. Careless writers on the topic have assumed that the stake was to prevent the body becoming a vampire, but there was no vampire tradition in Britain until it was imported from eastern Europe in the eighteenth and nineteenth centuries. (The latter must be qualified by mention of some stories collected by William of Newburgh in the twelfth century (*Historia Rerum Anglicarum*) which refer to vampire-like creatures – see summary in Simpson & Roud (2000) 374.)

At local level, where the unfortunate person would have been known to many of the coroner's jury, feelings could run very high, and pulled in different directions. Any attempt to circumvent custom and bury the body in the churchyard could be met with violent opposition, while the friends and family of the deceased would sometimes disinter the body from beside the highway and, under cover of night, sneak it into a quiet part of the churchyard. By the early nineteenth century, public opinion was clearly moving towards a more compassionate and tolerant attitude to suicides, but until the law could be altered, little could be done to change the way things were done. The following piece, giving a rare firsthand account, is worth quoting in full:

John and Lancelot Younghusband committed suicide 10th November 1818. They were two respectable and wealthy farmers just adjoining the town of Alnwick. The sensation must be imagined that pervaded the little town of Alnwick, when it was discovered that the brothers had committed suicide at the same time; consequently must have consulted and agreed to each other's self murder, if not assisted in it. This was the great difficulty with the jury, or they would have returned the usual verdict of temporary insanity . . . I found the jury had returned a verdict of felo de se, *and that I was called, upon the Coroner's warrant, along with my brother churchwardens and the constables of the parish, to inter the bodies in the public highway. I distinctly recollect that the coroner, Mr T. A. Russell, told us the law did not require the burial to be at cross-roads. As we wished to spare the feelings of friends, and as a public footpath led through Alnwick churchyard, we thought we fulfilled the requirements of the law by interring the bodies along it, so as not to interfere with consecrated ground – which was done by making the graves in a direction opposite to the usual method. There they would have remained had not the late Sir David W. Smith sent for the parish officers, and threatened them with a prosecution at the suit of the Crown, if the bodies were not interred according to the law in a public road. It was not till the evening that the parish officers resolved to disinter and re-bury the bodies of the unfortunate men, and this was carried out, though not exactly at midnight, nor were the graves made at cross-roads. The wish was to have the graves dug at the March between the Duke of Northumberland and Mr Hewitson's estate at Heckley in a lane, called Hindly Lane, leading from Heckley to Eglingham, where the Younghusbands farmed, and perhaps within a quarter of a mile from where the double suicidal act was committed, but the ground was so full of rocks, the gravediggers not being able speedily to accomplish their work, so that we gave directions for them to come further down the lane, which might be four or five hundred yards from the March, but not at a crossing; there the graves were dug at the side of the road, not where carts and horses travelled. I do not think it was ten o'clock when we returned from the melancholy duty with most distressed minds and harassed feelings. The burial was witnessed by a vast concourse of people from Alnwick and the surrounding neighbourhood. I really think that this painful circumstance had some influence on our legislators . . .*

It is however said that the bodies did not rest long at the wayside, being removed under the cloud of night, and that they found a third final resting place in the graveyard of Alnwick Church. Anciently a stake was driven through the body of a suicide, but in the above instance this act was dispensed with.

Northumberland [1818] *Denham Tracts*

The custom was finally abolished five years later by Act of Parliament (4 Geo. 4, c.52, 1823), which made it unlawful for any coroner to order interment of a suicide in 'any public highway', and specifically banned the customary stake through the body. Suicides were henceforth to be buried in the churchyard or other burial-ground between nine and twelve at night, and without religious rites. The time limitation and the refusal of religious rites were both repealed in 1882 (45 & 46 Vic., c.19).

Many superstitions clustered around suicides and the peculiar nature of the burials. The presence of a buried body by the road predictably led to local ghost stories, but less obvious were tales which focused on the stake, which could grow into an eerie misshapen tree (**Sussex** N&Q (1851)), or even became the focus of a children's game:

In the Mile End Road, South Shields, at the corner of a garden wall, on the left hand side going northward, just adjoining Fairless's old ballast way, lies the body of a suicide, with a stake driven through it. It is, I believe, that of a poor baker, who put an end to his existence sixty or seventy years ago, and who was buried in this frightful manner, at midnight, in unconsecrated ground. The top of the stake used to rise a foot or two above the ground within the last thirty years, and boys used to amuse themselves by standing with one foot upon it.   Co. Durham Brockie (1886)

There was a strong tradition that a suicide's body would not decompose until the time came when s/he would have died in the natural course of things, and there was also a widespread reluctance to touch a suicide's body – even to help retrieve a drowned body from the water, or to cut one down:

Never touch a suicide – it's bad luck – so a person that has hung himself is allowed to hang until the police come.   Norfolk Folk-Lore (1929)

Fishermen in the Highlands were determined not to allow a suicide to be buried too near the coast:

It was believed in the north, as in Skye and about Applecross in Ross-shire, no herring would be

caught in any part of the sea which could be seen from the grave of a suicide.

Highland Scotland Campbell (1900)

Nevertheless, a number of cures, especially for EPILEPSY, called for the sufferer to touch a suicide's corpse, or even to drink water from a suicide's SKULL.

See also CHURCHYARDS: NORTH SIDE.

Sussex N&Q 1S:4 (1851) 329–30; Jefferies (1889) 92. Somerset N&Q 8S:4 (1893) 189. Devon N&Q 5S:1 (1874) 204; N&Q 7S:3 (1887) 106; *Devonshire Assoc.* 66 (1934) 87. London [1687] N&Q 7S:3 (1887) 359; N&Q 1S:7 (1853) 617; N&Q 7S:3 (1887) 106, 237–8, 359. Essex [*c.*1939] *Folk-Lore* 62 (1951) 262. East Anglia Forby (1830) 407. Norfolk *Folk-Lore* 40 (1929) 123. Derbyshire [1573] Jupp & Gittings (1999) 150. Lincolnshire N&Q 1S:4 (1851) 212–13. Co. Durham Brockie (1886) 151–2. Northumberland [1818] *Denham Tracts* 2 (1895) 63–4. Highland Scotland Macbain (1887/88) 255, 258–9; Campbell (1900) 242–3. Northeast Scotland Gregor (1874) 148–50. Southwest Scotland Wood (1911) 239. Ross & Cromarty *Scotsman* (31 Jan. 1884) quoted *Folk-Lore Jnl* 2 (1883) 121; *Scotsman* (20 Jan. 1887) quoted *Folk-Lore Jnl* 5 (1887) 159–61. Glasgow [*c.*1820] Napier (1864) 398; Napier (1879) 86–7. Caithness Rinder (1895) 56, 63. General Andrews (1897) 105–14. Literary John Clare, *The Cross Roads or Haymakers Story* (1820) in Clare (1993) 23; Thomas Hood, *Faithless Nelly Gray* (1825).

sunwise

When an action had to follow a direction, either to the left or right, many people felt more comfortable if it followed the direction of the sun – 'sunwise', to the right or clockwise:

For luck, every thing and every person must, at the start, turn sunwise – Cardeiseil air gach ni – Sunwise turn for everything.

Highland Scotland Macbain (1887/88)

The two commonest contexts were funerals, where it was ensured that the procession approached the churchyard the right way, and sometimes even circled it, and in the fishing industry where boats, whenever possible, were turned to the right. (*See* FUNERALS: SUNWISE; FISHING: TURNING SUNWISE.) A similar concern was shown at some weddings:

The bride is conducted to her future spouse . . . in the course of the sun. This is called, in the Gaelic, going round the right, or lucky way.

Perthshire *Stat. Acct Scotland* (1794)

But many other actions, even seemingly trivial ones, such as laying the table, passing the port, and stirring things were habitually done in the same way:

Even in the middle of the twentieth century girls in Portnahaven were urged to stir food in a clockwise direction only; otherwise the mixture would go wrong, or, worse, some unrelated evil might occur.   Argyllshire *Folk-Lore* (1965)

The opposite, or leftwards way was called *withershins* or *widdershins*, a word with Germanic roots, and for those who cared about direction this was obviously unlucky. Witches were believed to turn this way deliberately in their dancing and when casting spells.

It is not easy to achieve an adequate understanding of this belief, or set of beliefs. The popular view is that it was universally known and followed, and was a survival from ancient sun worship, but the evidence does not bear this out at all. Although there are isolated reports from England, the majority of the known references are from Scotland, and not as many as one would expect if the custom was universally followed. There are no known references before the 1770s (apart from in the context of passing the drink round the table), although complaints about witches doing things the contrary way are found from the 1580s onwards. There seems to have been a large element of sunwise being the norm, as clockwise is for us today in many contexts, for the right-handed majority. 'Sunwise' is sometimes merely a description rather than a prescription. But there is no denying the fact that in certain contexts, where ritual plays an important part – funerals and weddings, for example – the concept of luck or ill luck is to the fore in many minds, and every detail counts.

Hampshire Eggar (1924) 149. **Worcestershire** Berkeley & Jenkins (1932) 34. **Gloucestershire** [1988] Opie & Tatem, 385. **Suffolk** [1988] Opie & Tatem, 385. **Yorkshire** [1982] Opie & Tatem, 386. **Western Scotland** Napier (1879) 133. **Banffshire** *Folk-Lore Jnl* 3 (1885) 310. **Perthshire** *Stat. Acct Scotland* 11 (1794) 621. **Highland Scotland** Macgregor (1878) 129; Macbain (1887/88) 271. **Morayshire** Shaw (1775) 230. **Argyllshire** *Folk-Lore* 76 (1965) 46. **Hebrides** McPhee (1970) 150. **Ireland** Wilde (1888) 141. **Connemara** *Folk-Lore* 4 (1893) 358. **Isle of Man** *Folk-Lore* 5 (1894) 224. **Literary** Walter Scott, *Waverley* (1814) Ch. 24.

---

swallows/housemartins

The swallow and the housemartin mostly share the same positive characteristics in British tradition, although the former features much more often. In general, it is lucky to see both of them and to have them around the house, and they are thus protected from harm:

If swallows or martins begin to build their nests about a house or barn, it is looked upon as predicating good luck to the occupier. 'The more birds the better luck'. On the contrary, when they forsake a haunt, the occupiers become apprehensive of misfortune. Hence farmers will always protect such birds, and often ill-use boys who may be stoning them, or attempting to rob their nests.
Lancashire Harland & Wilkinson (1882)

Their specially protected status, which they share with ROBINS and WRENS, is summed up in the widespread quatrain:

The robin and the wren
Are God Almighty's cock and hen
The martin and the swallow
Are God Almighty's bow and arrow.
Warwickshire Halliwell (1842)

The first two lines of this verse are remarkably stable throughout the British Isles, but the final two vary considerably, presumably because of the difficulty in finding a decent rhyme for 'swallow'. This wide variance in meaning also suggests that, in contrast to robins and wrens, there was no widespread belief or legend to support that part of the rhyme. Some examples are:

. . . Are the next to birds that follow.
. . . Are God's best scholars.
. . . Are God Almighty's shirt and collar.

Penalties for harming the birds range from the common 'bad luck' to specific misfortunes such as death, broken limbs, and the cows giving bloody milk. These are also said of those who hurt robins. In a few cases the 'death' penalty is supported by the notion that:

when the birds gather, as they do in thousands, before they leave us for the year, and sit in long rows along the leads of the church, they are settling who is to die before they come again.
Norfolk N&Q (1864)

and, naturally, those who have harmed them or their nests would receive short shrift.

As harbingers of spring, swallows are generally welcomed, although in Scotland it was only fortunate if you were sitting down when you first saw one:

Sit and see, the swallow flee
Gang and hear the gowk yell
See the foal afore its minnies e'e
And luck that year will fa'thysell

Which means, when we are sitting, the first time

superstition in 1620

Sir John Melton came from a Yorkshire family, was knighted in 1632 and was elected to Parliament, but died in 1640 before he could take his seat. He was a merchant, civil servant, author and politician, and he provided us with the first systematic list of superstitions in *Astrologaster, or the Figure-Caster*. We do not know what prompted Melton to choose these particular superstitions from the 'thousand more' available to him, but we can hazard that it would go against his argument if he chose obscure or little-known beliefs. If we therefore assume that these represent at least the reasonably well-known ones of the age, it gives us the opportunity for comparison over time. Words in square brackets indicate the relevant entries in this Guide.

A Catalogue of Many Superstitious Ceremonies, especially old men and women hold, which were first found out and invented by Figure-Casters, Cunning Men and Women in former ages, yet to this day are held for certaine and true observations

1. *That if any thing be lost amongst a company of servants, with the tricke of the Sive and the Sheeres, it may be found out againe, and who stole it.* [SIEVE AND SHEARS]
2. *That Toothaches, Agues, Cramps, and Fevers, and many other diseases may be healed by mumbling a few strange words over the head of the diseased.* [CHARMS]
3. *That by a certaine tuft of haire growing on the foremost part of a mans forehead, it may be knowne whether he shall bee a widdower or no.* [WIDOW'S PEAK]
4. *That a man may know whats a clocke, onely by a Ring and a silver Beaker.* [PENDULUM DIVINATION]
5. *That it is very ill lucke to have a Hare crosse one in the high way.* [HARES]
6. *That to have yellow speckles on the nailes of ones hand is a great signe of death.* [FINGER-NAILS]
7. *That when the left cheeke burnes, it is a signe*

ASTROLOGASTER,
OR,
THE FIGVRE-CASTER.

Rather the Arraignment of Artlesse Astrologers, and Fortune-tellers that cheat many ignorant people vnder the pretence of foretelling things to come, of telling things that are past, finding out things that are lost & expounding Dreames, calculating Deaths and Natiuities, one againe brought to the Barre.

By Iohn Melton.

Cicero. *Stultorum plena sunt omnia.*

Imprinted at London by *Barnard Alsop,* for *Edward Blackmore,* and are to be sold in *Paules* Churchyard, at the Signe of the *Blazing-Starre.* 1620.

The frontispiece to John Melton's Astrologaster (1620).

some bodie talkes well of you, but if the right cheeke burnes it is a signe of ill. [EARS/ CHEEKS: BURNING]
8. *That when a mans nose bleeds but a drop or two, that it is a signe of ill lucke.* [NOSE-BLEED CURES]
9. *That when a mans nose bleeds but one drop, and at the left nostrill, it is a signe of good lucke, but on the right ill.* [NOSEBLEED CURES]
10. *That if a man stumbles in a morning as soone as he comes out of dores, it is a signe of ill lucke.* [STUMBLING]

we see the swallow flying; walking, when we first hear the cuckoo; and the first foal we meet with, if it be before the eyes of its mother, that will be a fortunate year. Galloway Mactaggart (1824)

Despite the almost universal positive reputation of the swallow across most of the British Isles, for some communities in Scotland and Ireland it was 'the devil's bird', and its protection based more on fear than admiration:

The swallow was looked upon as belonging to evil; at the same time a swallow's nest upon a house was held as an omen of good fortune to the house. The common expression about the robin and the swallow was that the robin had a drop of God's blood in it, and the swallow had a drop of the devil's blood. Glasgow [*c.*1820] Napier

Archbishop Whatley tells us, however, that in Ireland the swallow is called the 'devil's bird' by the vulgar, who hold that there is a certain hair

11. *That if a man walking in the fields, finde any foure-leaved grasse, he shall in a small while after finde some good thing.* [CLOVER]

12. *That it is not good to put on a new sute, pare ones nailes, or begin any thing on a Childermas day.* [CLOTHES; FINGERNAILS; HOLY INNOCENTS' DAY]

13. *That if a man be drowsie, it is a signe of ill lucke.*

14. *That it is a signe of ill lucke to finde money.* [MONEY]

15. *That it is naught for a man or woman to lose their hose Garter.* [CLOTHES: GARTERS]

16. *That it is a very unfortunate thing for a man to meete early in a morning an ilfavoured man or woman, a rough-footed Hen, a shag-haird Dogge, or a blacke Cat.* [MEETING]

17. *That it is a signe of death to some in that house, where Crickets have bin many yeeres, if on a sudden they forsake the Chimney Corner.* [CRICKETS]

18. *That if a man dream of egs or fire, he shall heare of anger.*

19. *That to dreame of the devill is good lucke.*

20. *That to dreame of gold good lucke, but of silver ill.*

21. *That if a man be born in the day time, he shal be unfortunate.* [BABIES: WHEN BORN]

22. *That if a child be borne with a Caule on his head, he shall be very fortunate.* [CAULS]

23. *That when the palme of the right hand itcheth, it is a shrewd signe he shall receive money.* [HANDS]

24. *That it is a great signe of ill lucke, if Rats gnaw a mans cloathes.* [RATS: GNAWING]

25. *That it is naught for any man to give a paire of knives to his sweet heart, for feare it cuts away all love that is betweene them.* [KNIVES: GIFT]

26. *That it is ill lucke to have the Saltseller fall towards you.* [SALT]

27. *That if the Beere fall next a man, it is a signe of good luck.*

28. *That if a Candle burne blew, it is a signe there is a spirit in the house, or not farre from it.* [CANDLES]

29. *That when the Cat washeth her face over her eare, wee shall have great store of raine.* [CATS]

30. *That if a horse stumble on the high way, it is a signe of ill lucke.* [STUMBLING]

31. *That when a mans nose itcheth, it is a signe he shall drinke wine.* [NOSE]

32. *That if your lips itch, you shall kisse some body.*

33. *That it is a very ill signe to be Melancholy.*

These, and a thousand more as vaine as these, I could reckon up, were it not that I should make too long a digression from my matter; with which so many people as so deepely besotted, that a whole Universitie of Doctors cannot roote these superstitious observations out of their minde for what an idlenes is it in them to thinke that there is either Bonum or Malum omen in these things? what ill lucke can there be in it, when a Hare crosseth you, except it is your ill lucke not to catch her, or when you have caught her to let her go againe? (as the Welchman did), what ill lucke can it be to a man to stumble, except he fall down & breake his nose? what ill lucke can there be in finding mony, except it be counterfet? but if it be currant I cannot be perswaded if he that takes it up be not as very a foole as Iohn of the Hospitall (that could not abide money) will take it for ill lucke, but if it be ill lucke, God send me ill lucke every day. What ill lucke is there in losing a Hose garter, except it be to put a man to the charge to buy a new payre? So that I cannot picke out any thing in these observations why they should bee signes of good or badde lucke. Therefore I cannot perswade my selfe, but you and such Figure-flingers as you, that sowe the superstitious seeds in the hearts of credulous people, is onely to get to your selves praise, but especiall money.

---

on every one's head, which if a swallow can pick off, the man is doomed to eternal perdition.
Ireland Henderson (1866)

It could also be most unlucky in particular circumstances:

[A lady] *was visiting the sick child of a poor woman – a girl about twelve years old – and the child had said something about a hope of soon being able to get out again, when the mother* replied, 'You know you never will get well again!', *and, turning to my informant, said – 'A swallow lit upon her shoulder, ma'am, a short time since, as she was walking home from church, and that is a sure sign of death.'* Unlocated N&Q (1867)

The protected nature of the swallow was already established in the early sixteenth century, when Martin Parker mentioned it in his poem on the nightingale (1632), and over a century earlier it was included in the Low Countries text trans-

superstition in 1711

Addison, from *The Spectator* (8 Mar. 1711)

Going yesterday to Dine with an old Acquaintance, I had the Misfortune to find his whole Family very much objected. Upon asking him the Occasion of it, he told me that his Wife had dreamt a strange Dream the Night before, which they were afraid portended some Misfortune to themselves or to their Children. At her coming into the Room, I observed a settled Melancholy in her Countenance, which I should have been troubled for, had I not heard from whence it proceeded. We were no sooner sat down, but, after, having looked upon me a little while, My dear, says she, turning to her husband, you may now see the Stranger that was in the Candle last Night. Soon after this, as they began to talk of Family Affairs, a little Boy at the lower end of the Table told her, that he was to go into Join-hand on Thursday: Thursday, says she, no, Child, if it please God, you shall not begin upon Childermas-day; tell your Writing-Master that Friday will be soon enough. I was reflecting. I was reflecting with myself on the Odness of her Fancy, and wondering that any body would establish it as a Rule to lose a Day in every Week. In the midst of these my Musings she desired me to reach her a little Salt upon the Point of my Knife, which I did in such a Trepidation and hurry of Obedience, that I let it drop by the way; at which she immediately startled, and said it fell towards her. Upon this I looked very blank; and, observing the Concern of the whole Table, began to consider my self, with some Confusion, as a Person that had brought a Disaster upon the Family. The Lady however recovering her self, after a little space, said to her Husband with a Sigh, My Dear, Misfortunes never come Single. My friend, I found, acted but an under Part at his Table, and being a Man of more Good-nature than Understanding, thinks himself obliged to fall in with the Passions and Humours of his Yoke-fellow; Do not you remember, Child, says she, that the Pidgeon-House fell the very Afternoon that our careless Wench spilt the salt upon the Table? Yes, says he, my Dear, and the next Post brought us an Account of the Battel of Almanza. The Reader may guess at the figure I made, after having done all this Mischief. I dispatched my Dinner as soon as I could, with my usual Taciturnity; when, to my utter Confusion, the Lady seeing me [quitting] my Knife and Fork, and laying them across one another upon my Plate, desired me that I would humour her so far as to take them out of that Figure, and place them side by side. What the Absurdity was which I had committed I did not know, but I suppose there was some traditionary Superstition in it; and therefore, in obedience to the Lady of the House, I disposed of my Knife and Fork in two parallel Lines, which is the figure I shall always lay them in for the future, though I do not know any Reason for it.

It is not difficult for a Man to see that a Person has conceived an Aversion to him. For my own part, I quickly found, by the Lady's Looks, that she regarded me as a very odd kind of Fellow, with

lated into English as the *Gospelles of Dystaves* (1507) Pt 2, Para. 7.

Southern England Jefferies (1879) 152. **Kent** N&Q 3S:12 (1867) 203, 477. **Sussex** Latham (1878) 13; Lovett (1928) 16; *Sussex County Mag.* 23 (1949) 383. **Somerset** [1908/1920] Tongue (1965) 46; [1923] Opie & Tatem, 386–8. **Devon** *Devonshire Assoc.* 18 (1886) 105; Hewett (1900) 59. **Wiltshire** Smith (1874) 329; *Wilts. N&Q* 1 (1893–5) 155. **Berkshire** Lowsley (1888) 23. **Surrey** Lovett (1928) 16. **Essex** Halliwell (1842) 154. **Oxfordshire** [1880s] Thompson (1939) 153; *Folk-Lore* 24 (1913) 89; [1968] Opie & Tatem, 386–8. **Herefordshire** Leather (1912) 26. **Midland England** *Midland Garner* 1 (1884) 23. **Warwickshire** Halliwell (1842) 154. **Cambridgeshire** Porter (1969) 39. **East Anglia** Forby (1830) 409–10. **Suffolk** Chambers 2 (1878) 678; *Folk-Lore* 35 (1924) 350. **Norfolk** N&Q 3S:5 (1864) 237; *Folk-Lore* 49 (1938) 91. **Huntingdonshire** [c.1940] Opie & Tatem, 386–8. **Shropshire** Burne (1883) 217. **Cheshire** N&Q 5S:10 (1878) 65. **England** Addy (1895) 67. **Derbyshire** N&Q 4S:9 (1872) 24–5. **Yorkshire** Hone, *Every-Day Book* 2 (1827) 781; Henderson (1866) 91; Addy (1888) xix; [1954]

Opie & Tatem, 386–8. **Lancashire** Harland & Wilkinson (1882) 143; Spencer (1966) 7–8. **Co. Durham** Brockie (1886) 131–2; Leighton (1910) 63. **Wales** Trevelyan (1909) 107, 325–6; Jones (1930) 178. **Mid-Wales** Davies (1911) 223. **Scotland** Chambers (1826) 284. **Scotland/England borders** [c.1816] Henderson (1866) 90. **Western Scotland** Napier (1879) 112–13. **Dumfriesshire** Shaw (1890) 13. **Angus** (1954) Opie & Tatem, 386–8. **Glasgow** [c.1820] Napier (1864) 394–5. **Galloway** Mactaggart (1824) 211. **Aberdeenshire** *Folk-Lore* 25 (1914) 349. **Ireland** Henderson (1866) 91. **Co. Wexford** *Folk-Lore Record* 5 (1882) 83. **Co. Antrim** [c.1905] McDowell (1972) 131. **Guernsey** De Garis (1975) 134. **Unlocated** Grose (1787) 64–5; N&Q 2S:6 (1858) 522; N&Q (1867) 477. **General** Browne, *Pseudodoxia Epidemica* (1650) Bk 5, Ch. 23; *Guardian* (21 May 1713) quoted Opie & Tatem, 387; *Gent. Mag.* (1796) 636; Brand (1810) 101. **Literary** Martin Parker, *The Nightingale Warbling Forth her Owne Disaster* (1632).

an unfortunate Aspect; For which Reason I took my leave immediately after Dinner, and withdrew to my own Lodgings. Upon my Return home, I fell into a profound Contemplation on the Evils that attend these superstitious Follies of Mankind; how they subject us to imaginary Afflictions, and additional Sorrows that do not properly come within our Lot. As if the natural Calamities of Life were not sufficient for it, we turn the most indifferent Circumstances into Misfortunes, and suffer as much from trifling Accidents, as from real Evils. I have know the shooting of a Star spoil a Night's Rest; and have seen a Man in Love grow pale and lose his Appetite upon the plucking of a Merry-thought. A Screech-owl at Midnight has alarmed a Family, more than a Band of Robbers; nay, the Voice of a Cricket hath struck more Terrour, than the Roaring of a Lion. There is nothing so inconsiderable [which] may not appear dreadful to an Imagination that is filled with Omens and Prognosticks. A Rusty Nail, or a Crooked Pin, shoot up into Prodigies.

I remember I was once in a mixt Assembly, that it was full of Noise and Mirth, when on a sudden an old Woman unluckily observed there were thirteen of us in Company. This remark struck a panick Terror into several [who] were present, insomuch that one or two of the Ladies were going to leave the Room; but a Friend of mine, taking notice that one of our female Companions was big with Child, affirm'd there were fourteen in the Room, and that, instead of

portending one of the Company should die, it plainly foretold that one of them should be born. Had not my Friend found this Expedient to break the Omen, I question not but half the Women in the Company would have fallen sick that very Night.

An old Maid, that is troubled with the Vapours, produces infinite Disturbances of this kind among her Friends and Neighbours. I know a Maiden Aunt, of a great Family, who is one of those antiquated Sybils, that forebodes and prophesies from one end of the Year to the other. She is always seeing Apparitions, and hearing Death-Watches; and was the other Day almost frighted out of her Wits, by the great House-Dog, that howled in the Stable at a time when she lay ill of the Tooth-ach. Such as extravagant Cast of Mind engages Multitudes of People, not only in impertinent Terrors, but in supernumerary Duties of Life, and arises from that Fear and Ignorance which are natural to the Soul of Man. The Horrour with which we entertain the Thoughts of Death (or indeed of any future Evil), and the Uncertainty of its Approach, fill a melancholy Mind with innumerable Apprehensions and Suspicions, and consequently dispose it to the Observation of such groundless Prodigies and Predictions. For as it is the chief Concern of Wise-Men, to retrench the Evils of Life by the Reasonings of Philosophy; it is the Employment of Fools, to multiply them by the Sentiments of Superstition.

sweeps

see CHIMNEY SWEEPS.

---

sympathy

One of the basic principles of superstition, and also one of the key factors in both folk medicine and witchcraft, is that items which are in close contact with each other are connected by an invisible sympathetic force, and remain so, even when they are physically separated. Actions carried out on one will thus affect the other. The classic example is the notion that if someone is wounded by a sword, the wound will not heal if the sword is allowed to get dirty or rusty. The weapon must be kept clean and bright, and the wound will follow suit.

One effect of this belief is to negate the

temporal sequence of cause and effect. If a man is bitten by a dog, and the dog later develops rabies, the man will also be affected. The only safe action is to kill the dog immediately, to make sure it does not get sick.

In witchcraft, the use of fingernails, hair, or a piece of clothing of an intended victim is commonplace. These items were once intimately connected with the person and are thus assumed to have a continued connection, and they can be incorporated into EFFIGIES or other aids to spell-making. In the absence of, or in addition to, such physical items, sympathy can also be created by naming the effigy after the victim. But another side of the same principle provides the victim with a remedy. When a witch casts an evil spell s/he remains in sympathetic connection with the victim as long as the spell is in operation, but this connection is seen as a two-way conduit. Provided the victim or his/her agent can

find the appropriate words, items, and procedures, this channel can be used to transmit a
counter-charm, even if the identity of the original ill-wisher is unknown. This scenario
provides the central motif in many stories of
local witchcraft:

*In the year 1888 a cousin of my father's, called
Reed, lost four of his best cows; each one died with
one horn stuck in the ground tight to its poll. My
father saw some of the cows, and everyone said
they had been 'witched' and advised Reed to see
the white witch. This he did, and to his surprise
found that the white witch was able to describe
his case and told him what to do if he lost another.
He was to take out the heart and fill it with glass,
nails, pins, and any other sharp thing, and roast
it three nights in succession after the rest of the
household had retired. The white witch told him
that probably the second or third night someone
would call at the house, but in no case was he to
answer or to speak. To Mr Reed's surprise, the
next morning he heard that one of his own workmen had lost his life.*

Devon *Devonshire Assoc.* 65 (1933) 126

For further discussion and examples in folk
medicine, *see* Black (1883) 49–64.

tablecloths

The dominant superstition regarding tablecloths
is the fear of finding a 'coffin' shape created in
the centre when folded up (*see below*). A few
other beliefs have been reported occasionally:

*A visitor at a north Devon home expressed horror
at seeing the table laid with a green cloth – and a
white cat in the room as well* [compare GREEN].

Devon *Devonshire Assoc.* (1971)

*Fruit stains on table linen will not disappear
until the fruit is finished for the season.*

Devon *Devonshire Assoc.* (1935)

*It is unlucky to leave a white tablecloth on the
table all night.*   Yorkshire *Folk-Lore* (1909)

*Anyone who, in folding a tablecloth or the like,
hits on the middle of it at once, will marry within
the year.*   Ireland? *Folk-Lore* (1923)

*If you are wrapping up table-cloths, or other
linen, or carpets, and the ends do not meet evenly,
you will not be married that year.*

England Addy (1895)

*Mice eating holes in the tablecloth was consid-
ered a sure sign of death* [see also RATS: GNAW-
ING].   Wiltshire *Wilts. N&Q* (1893–5)

Devon *Devonshire Assoc.* 67 (1935) 134; *Devonshire
Assoc.* 103 (1971) 269. **Wiltshire** *Wilts. N&Q* 1 (1893–5)
152. **England** Addy (1895) 96. **Yorkshire** *Folk-Lore* 20
(1909) 348. **Ireland?** *Folk-Lore* 34 (1923) 157

tablecloths: coffin

A widespread recent superstition cautions those
folding linen items such as tablecloths and sheets
to avoid creating a diamond-shaped crease in the
middle, as this is usually interpreted as a 'coffin':

*Recently, a Stratford lady of considerable mental
attainment assured the writer that, before her
husband died, for some weeks the newly-washed
table linen showed a 'diamond' in the centre, and
however carefully the cloth was folded it could
not be avoided. The trouble ceased with his
death.*   Warwickshire Bloom (c.1930)

As with other beliefs, there can be a refinement
according to size:

*A diamond-shaped fold left in a linen tablecloth
is a sign of death. A large one indicates an adult,
a small one a child. My husband's sister saw a
diamond on the day before her father's death,
and another sister saw one several days before.*

Devon *Devonshire Assoc.* (1927)

The belief has a relatively short recorded history
– starting only in 1868 – but it was still well known
in the late twentieth century, although clearly
losing its power to cause real concern:

*Many elderly people still look for 'coffin marks'
or 'coffin folds' in newly laundered linen, even if
they do not now seriously believe, as their grandmothers did, that such creases are omens of
death.*   Cambridgeshire Porter (1969)

All the known references are from England.

Dorset Udal (1922) 181–2. **Devon** Hewett (1900) 22;
Devonshire Assoc. 59 (1927) 162. **Berkshire** Lowsley
(1888) 23. **Herefordshire** Leather (1912) 118.
Warwickshire Bloom (c.1930) 44. **Huntingdonshire**
[1880s] Marshall (1967) 246. **Cambridgeshire** Porter
(1969) 24. **Lincolnshire** Gutch & Peacock (1908) 152;
Rudkin (1936) 17. **Yorkshire** [1956] Opie & Tatem, 390;
[1982] Opie & Tatem, 390. **Unlocated** N&Q 4S:1 (1868)
193.

tables: items placed on

The major superstitions which advise against
placing SHOES, BELLOWS, or UMBRELLAS on
tables are considered elsewhere (*see* SHOES: ON
TABLE; UMBRELLAS: ON TABLE; BELLOWS: ON

TABLE), but there are a few other items which are similarly treated. Each is only reported once or twice and, as with other table beliefs, none is apparently older than the 1890s. Taken together, they indicate a general worry about inappropriate items on tables, but further explanation is lacking.

Formerly, no farmer put his lantern on the table, on account of the unfortunate effect on his cows; the lantern must always be placed underneath the table. The reason our cows calved a month too soon was because the master put his lantern always on the table. The old-fashioned tin lanterns, for candles, with horn plates for the side, are now little used, paraffin safety lamps having superseded them. Herefordshire Leather (1912)

It is unlucky to put a lantern on the table, and people say:

A lantern on the table
Is death in the stable.

England Addy (1895)

Placing shoes or a dustpan and brush on a table is a sign of a quarrel. Norfolk Fulcher Collection (c.1895)

In December 1936 I took to a Torquay house a milk-saucepan as a small gift, and the recipient exclaimed: 'Don't put it on the table or there'll be a quarrel!' The same result, they said, follows a crossed knife and fork. Devon *Devonshire Assoc.* (1938)

Never put your feet on a table, or there will be quarrels. Somerset Tongue (1965)

[Milliner's workshop, interwar years] *When a chair was passed over a table it foretold a row.* London Henrey (1955)

Somerset Tongue (1965) 143. Devon *Devonshire Assoc.* 70 (1938) 116. London Henrey (1955) 97–8. Herefordshire Leather (1912) 23. Norfolk Fulcher Collection (c.1895). England Addy (1895) 100.

tables: shaking hands over

see SHAKING HANDS.

tables: sitting on

Although not as widespread as the prohibition against putting shoes on a table, a handful of references warn unmarried women against sitting on tables. The precise meaning of the action varies between wanting a husband and never getting one:

Spinsters ran grave risks in sitting on a table, thereby forfeiting all chances of matrimony.
Cornwall [1890s] *Old Cornwall*

If you sit on a table it is a sign that you want to get married. Lincolnshire Rudkin (1936)

The belief seems to be of recent vintage, not reported before the 1890s, but lasting well into the twentieth century, as is shown by the references in Opie and Tatem. Two other meanings for table-sitting have also been reported, but once only each:

Fishing community . . . Sitting on a cabin table will bring on a gale. Norfolk *Folk-Lore* (1929)

If two people sat on a table it meant a quarrel.
Yorkshire [1982] Opie & Tatem

Somerset [c.1905] Tongue (1965) 143; [1923] Opie & Tatem, 390. Cornwall [1890s] *Old Cornwall* 1:12 (1930) 4. Surrey [1955] Opie & Tatem, 390. Buckinghamshire [1912] *Folk-Lore* 43 (1932) 110. Cambridgeshire *Folk-Lore* 25 (1914) 364. Suffolk [1953] Opie & Tatem, 390. Norfolk Fulcher Collection (c.1895). *Folk-Lore* 40 (1929) 121–2. Lincolnshire Rudkin (1936) 21. England Addy (1895) 97. Yorkshire [1982] Opie & Tatem, 390. Argyllshire *Folk-Lore* 21 (1910) 89. Unlocated Igglesden (c.1932) 154.

talking

Two regularly reported beliefs about talking – saying things at the same time, and a sudden silence occurring in the conversation – are treated below. A number of other traditions have been recorded less frequently, but each may have been more widely known. A slip of the tongue, for example, predicted a stranger.

'If you chance to say your words backwards,' said [a maid] *'you'll sure to see a stranger afore night. Only yesterday I says, "I'll bread the toast" instead o' saying "I'll toast the bread", what I meant to, and it was yesterday afternoon I seed Mr Robert'.* Shropshire/Staffordshire N&Q (1884)

Talking to yourself is not necessarily the 'first sign of madness' as said in modern times:

The other day a woman told me what I had never heard before, that a person who talks to himself is thought to be talking to the devil – 'Hark at him, you know who he's got with him', people will say. Unlocated N&Q (1928)

If a person spoke aloud to himself, it was a sign that he would meet with a violent death.
Western Scotland Napier (1879)

More seriously, one's future prosperity might depend on following certain rules when speaking to ill-wishers in Scotland:

Another mode of counteracting the evil of an 'ill fit' is to have 'the first word o' the one that has the evil power', that is, to be the first to speak.
Aberdeenshire *Folk-Lore Jnl* (1886)

When a boy in Deeside, forty years ago, I knew an old woman who was reputed to be 'uncanny' and come of 'uncanny' folk. I was told, when I met her, always to speak to her before she could speak to me, as that would counteract her 'ill ee'.
Aberdeenshire N&Q (1903)

It is . . . unlucky to be praised by a witch, or indeed to hold any conversation with her, and our only safety against sudden death soon after consists in having the last word. Hence the old phrase, 'Some witch or other has shaken hands wi' him, and gotten the last word'. Scotland [*c*.1816] Henderson

Shropshire/Staffordshire N&Q 6S:9 (1884) 137. Scotland [*c*.1816] Henderson (1866) 143. Western Scotland Napier (1879) 138. Aberdeenshire *Folk-Lore Jnl* 4 (1886) 13; N&Q 9S:11 (1903) 208. Unlocated N&Q 155 (1928) 459.

---

talking: at the same time

It has been widely believed that it is significant when two people say the same thing at the same time, although the exact nature of that significance is a matter of debate. The most commonly reported meaning, at least in the twentieth century, is that the two people should make a wish. In many cases, especially where collected from children, an interesting ritual is prescribed:

[Girls school, 1876] *If two girls speak at the same time, they hook the little fingers of their right hands together, and wish a wish, and then loose. They must not speak again till some one asks them a question, or the charm is broken.*
Co. Durham [1876] *Folk-Lore*

A further elaboration, as reported by Opie and Tatem, is that the two must name a poet, but not Shakespeare or Burns, as they spear or burn the wish. A similar custom was enacted when speakers accidentally spoke in rhyme:

Schoolgirls . . . If, when talking together, one accidentally makes a rhyme, she wishes; and, should she be asked a question before she speaks again, to which she can answer Yes, she thinks she is sure to get it. Cornwall *Folk-Lore Jnl* (1887)

The 'wish' meaning was reported regularly from the 1870s to the later twentieth century, but during the same period, others believed that one of them would soon receive a letter, or that someone was thinking of them. The only significance noted before the nineteenth century is a connection with marriage:

Colonel, you shall be married first; I was going to say that. Swift (1738)

If she happens to bring out anything in conversation which another person was about to say, she comforts herself that she shall be married before them. Connoisseur (1755)

and a similar meaning was given in Cornwall in the 1860s and 1880s. These generally positive meanings, however, are not universal:

If two people express the same thought at the same moment, one of them will die before the year is out. Wales Trevelyan (1909)

If two persons unintentionally begin to say the same thing at once they will die together.
Argyllshire *Folk-Lore* (1910)

Wish: Somerset [1935] Opie & Tatem, 368. England Addy (1895) 78, 95. Derbyshire [1890s] Uttley (1946) 155. Yorkshire Blakeborough (1898) 131. Co. Durham [1876] *Folk-Lore* 20 (1909) 77. Glamorgan [*c*.1914] Opie & Tatem, 368. Glasgow [1952] Opie & Tatem, 368. **Rhyme:** Cornwall *Folk-Lore Jnl* 5 (1887) 214. Herefordshire Leather (1912) 86. England Addy (1895) 100. **Letter:** Kent [1923] Opie & Tatem, 368. Gloucestershire *Folk-Lore* 34 (1923) 156. Cambridgeshire *Folk-Lore* 25 (1914) 365. Suffolk *Folk-Lore* 35 (1924) 351; [1953] Opie & Tatem, 368. Unlocated Igglesden (*c*.1932) 232. **Marriage:** Cornwall Hunt (1865) 241; *Folk-Lore Jnl* 5 (1887) 215. Literary Swift (1738); *Connoisseur* 56 (1755) 332. **Die:** Wales Trevelyan (1909) 282. Argyllshire *Folk-Lore* 21 (1910) 90.

---

talking: silence

A sudden lull, or unexplained silence in the conversation, is often said to be caused by an angel passing by (*see* ANGELS), although occasionally it is by some other agency:

When people talking became suddenly silent, they said, 'The parson is passing; no luck today'.
Wales Trevelyan (1909)

If a silence falls on a group of people who have previously been talking it's because a spirit has passed by. Co. Tyrone *Lore & Language* (1972)

The sudden silence was also ominous in classical times, although, as described by Pliny, the

tea

Superstition looms large in the business of making the tea, which was a far more complex and demanding process in the past than it is today. Nevertheless, the bulk of the beliefs surrounding tea are relatively non-threatening. There is certainly generic bad luck awaiting the unwary, but little promised death and destruction, and mostly it is a matter of weddings, strangers, letters, and, at worst a family quarrel or 'ginger-headed twins'. In addition to the widespread beliefs given separate treatment below, a number of others have been recorded occasionally, including the following:

It is unlucky to throw away tea leaves; they should always be laid on the back of the fire; this keeps away poverty.   Co. Durham Brockie (1886)

If you burn your tea-leaves and dust you'll be sure to get rich (from female servant aged forty).
      Shropshire N&Q (1875)

I have frequently noticed in the harvest field, where tea is usually provided that the men will take a drink of cider after tea, before commencing work. I once remarked the fact to a Lustleigh farmer, who informed me that tea was considered injurious if not washed down, hence the saying:

If you want to live for ever
You must wash the tea off your liver.
      Devon *Devonshire Assoc.* (1880)

In some parts of Oxfordshire it is believed that the last nine drops of tea poured from the teapot, after the guests are served, will cure the heartache.   Oxfordshire Brand (1849)

Strew tea leaves across the road in front of the house and evil spirits will be kept away.
      Worcestershire Berkeley & Jenkins (1932)

A woman in a Rutland village on returning from a visit brought with her a teapot, which she gave as a present to a young woman friend. She explained that she did so 'because no one had good luck until she had made tea out of her own teapot'. She told me that this was 'an old saying'.
      Rutland N&Q (1883)

Two sources record that it is unlucky to stir the tea in the pot – these are probably versions of the better-known 'stir with a knife, stir up strife' belief, *see* KNIVES: STIRRING WITH. Cold tea was also effective for bathing sore eyes (Worcestershire [*c.*1900] Knight; Ireland Logan (1981)). *See also* SPOONS: TWO IN A SAUCER.

Devon *Devonshire Assoc.* 12 (1880) 111; Hewett (1900) 54. Oxfordshire Brand 3 (1849) 317; [pre-1900] *Folk-Lore* 24 (1913) 91. Worcestershire [*c.*1900] Knight (1960) 180–1; Berkeley & Jenkins (1932) 35. Shropshire N&Q 5S:3 (1875) 465. Rutland N&Q 6S:8 (1883) 226. Co. Durham Brockie (1886) 207. Ireland Logan (1981) 59.

meaning was different to any of those reported in Britain. His belief was that the silence only occurred when there was an even number present and that it was 'a sign that the good name and repute of every individual present is in peril'.

Wales Trevelyan (1909) 328. Co. Tyrone *Lore & Language* 1:7 (1972) 10. Classical Pliny, *Natural History* (AD 77) Bk 28, Para. 5.

tea: bubbles

One of the apparently meaningless superstitions with respect to tea is that bubbles on the surface of your teacup are significant in some way. The most common prediction, which is still heard today, is that it means money coming to you:

Young persons may occasionally be detected in the act of stirring a cup of tea, or other liquid, so as to cause it to rotate rapidly, and produce a circle of foam in the centre. The quantity of foam indicates the amount of money which will ultimately be bequeathed to the person who thus try their fortunes.   Lancashire Harland & Wilkinson (1873)

There is little agreement overall as to precise meaning, especially considering the relatively few times the belief has been noted. The earliest known version, from 1832, claims that bubbles denote 'kisses', while another maintains that bubbles in the centre mean money, and those at the side, kisses. Two other informants give totally different meanings:

If you get bubbles on your tea it means you'll soon cross water.   Co. Tyrone *Lore & Language* (1972)

Bubbles in the tea-cup [mean] *the visit of a stranger.*   Essex [*c.*1915] Mays

Somerset [1923] Opie & Tatem, 391. Essex [*c.*1915] Mays (1969) 164–5. Derbyshire N&Q 4S:10 (1872) 495. Lancashire Harland & Wilkinson (1873) 228. Co. Durham [1984] Opie & Tatem, 391. Glamorganshire [1970] Opie & Tatem, 391. Dumfriesshire Corrie (1890/91) 83. Co. Tyrone *Lore & Language* 1:7 (1972) 12. Unlocated Hone, *Year Book* (1832) 126–8.

Reading the tea-leaves was a very popular pastime and was often treated seriously and sympathetically by artists. This engraving dates from c.1850.

tea: leaf reading

Reading the tea-leaves is nowadays a cliché of popular fortune-telling, but there is evidence that it was taken quite seriously in the past, and was widely popular for nearly 200 years. The earliest three references come so close together, 1726 to 1731, that the obvious conclusion is that it was fashionably new at that time. The first is an advertisement in the *Dublin Weekly Journal* (1726) for the 'famous Mrs Cherry' who professed to be expert at the 'occult science of tossing of coffee grounds', and five years later a contributor to the *Gentleman's Magazine* described seeing it in practice:

a lady and her company in close cabal over their coffee; the rest very intent upon one, who by her dress and intelligence he guessed was a tire-woman; to which she added the secret of divining by coffee-grounds; she was then in full inspiration, and with much solemnity observing the atoms round the cup; on one hand sat a widow, on the other a married lady, both attentive to the predictions given of their future fate. The lady (his acquaintance), though married, was no less earnest in contemplating her cup than the other two. They assured him that every cast of the cup

is a picture of all one's life to come; and every transaction and circumstance is delineated with the exactest certainty. Gent. Mag. (1731)

Most of these early references refer to coffee grounds, but tea-leaf reading gradually became the norm. Nearly all the available descriptions stress that the natural audience for tea-leaf readings was overwhelmingly female, and primarily concerned with love and matrimonial prospects.

the apparitions which, in my childish days, the nurses used to discover in their tea-cups when they had, by a dextrous sort of circular jerk, emptied the last remains of the tea in such a manner as to leave the dregs scattered well over the bottom and sides of the cup. Some were more skilful (or more imaginative) in their interpretations than others. A church, a carriage-and-pair, or a coach-and-four, was often discovered; a gravestone or a coffin occasionally occurred, but never, I think, in the seer's own tea-cup!

Shropshire Burne (1883)

Instructions for reading the leaves were published regularly throughout the nineteenth and twentieth centuries, in small books devoted to the subject and also in others on fortune-telling, DREAM BOOKS, and so on. Modern examples of the genre still sell in sufficient numbers to keep them in print even in the present day.

Sussex Latham (1878) 32. **Wiltshire** *Wilts. N&Q* 1 (1893–5) 151. **Worcestershire** *Folk-Lore* 36 (1925) 87–8; **Worcestershire/Shropshire** *Gent. Mag.* (1855) 385. **Norfolk** [*c.*1870s] Haggard (1935) 7. **Shropshire** Burne (1883) 277–8. **Derbyshire** N&Q 9S:11 (1903) 355–6. **Yorkshire** *Folk-Lore* 21 (1910) 227. **Lancashire** Harland & Wilkinson (1882) 140. **Wales** Davies (1911) 14–15. **Scotland** N&Q 1S:10 (1854) 534–5. **Western Scotland** Napier (1879) 110. **Dumfriesshire** Corrie (1890/91) 83. **Highland Scotland** Campbell (1900) 266–7. **Orkney** N&Q 10S:12 (1909) 483–4. **Dublin** *Dublin Weekly Jnl* (11 June 1726) quoted N&Q 1S:10 (1854) 420–1. **Jersey** *Folk-Lore* 25 (1914) 248. **Guernsey** De Garis (1975) 22. **Unlocated** *Gent. Mag.* (1731) 110. **Literary** *Connoisseur* 56 (1755) 333. **General** *Round about our Coal-Fire* (1731) 21; *Illustrated London News* (27 Dec. 1851) 779. **Literary** Oliver Goldsmith, *The Vicar of Wakefield* (1766) Ch. 10.

tea: milk and sugar

There used to be a well-known division between those who insisted upon putting their milk in the cup before the tea, or vice versa, but there is also another side to the problem, as you run the risk of losing your loved one.

If you put cream in your tea before the sugar it will 'cross your love'.   Derbyshire N&Q (1872)

None of the tea superstitions make much logical sense. This one only appears in the late nineteenth century, and all the known references are from the same part of England.

England Addy (1895) 93. **Derbyshire** N&Q 4S:10 (1872) 495. **Northern England** N&Q 4S:2 (1868) 553. **Yorkshire** Nicholson (1890) 46; *Folk-Lore* 43 (1932) 253–4.

tea: pot lids

If you accidentally leave the lid off the pot when making tea, it means a stranger will call soon:

David Evans, a millwright, of Llandilo, informed me a short time ago, that one evening when he was staying in Lampeter, the woman of the house who was preparing tea for supper at a late hour, forgot to replace the lid on the pot. When she found it out, she exclaimed, 'A stranger is sure to come here tonight'. The husband and wife, and the millwright sat down by the fire till a late hour, but there was no sign of a stranger, just as they were going to bed, however, there was a knock at the door, and a stranger came in!

West Wales Davies (1911)

The meaning is quite stable across most versions, spanning the years between the 1850s and the 1980s, although two informants reported different meanings:

If you leave the teapot lid off, you will be sent for.
Suffolk *Folk-Lore* (1924)

If you leave the teapot lid off, you will have to call the doctor before the day is out.
Somerset Tongue (1965)

No rational suggestion has been made as to the origin of this belief, and nor is there any identifiable motif at play beyond petty accidental happenings. One homely suggestion is that the lid left off the pot somehow constitutes an 'invitation' to the caller, but it is not clear why. The superstition was more widely known in the late twentieth century than is shown by the number of references listed, and is probably still said in some households.

Somerset Tongue (1965) 143. **Wiltshire** Wiltshire (1975) 85. **Essex** [1983] Opie & Tatem, 393. **Herefordshire** Leather (1912) 86–7. **Worcestershire/Shropshire** *Gent. Mag.* (1855) 385. **Suffolk** *Folk-Lore* 35 (1924) 351. **Lincolnshire** Rudkin (1936) 18. **Shropshire** N&Q 5S:3 (1875) 465; Burne (1883) 277–8. **Derbyshire** N&Q 4S:10 (1872) 495. **Co. Durham** N&Q 5S:6 (1876) 397. **Wales** Davies (1911) 217; *Folk-Lore* 30 (1919) 156.

tea: pouring

It is bad luck for two people (usually specifically women) to pour tea from the same pot:

This evening as I was about to take the teapot from 'the neat-handed Phyllis' who looks after my wants, she – then pouring the hot water from it – said, 'It's bad luck for two to pour out of a pot, isn't it, sir?'   Worcestershire N&Q (1885)

This is the earliest version. Later informants claim that it will result in a pregnancy, or even that one of the women will have 'ginger-haired twins'. The latter meaning is still heard. Other domestic beliefs warn against two people doing the same thing, such as WASHING HANDS in the same bowl, or drying on the same TOWEL, but it is difficult to see any reason behind these ideas. This is not a particularly old or widespread belief, but it provides a useful case study in development. It may be expecting too much of what is a minor superstition, but plotting the given meaning in all versions in chronological order appears to show a developmental model which might be applied to other beliefs, given sufficient evidence:

1885 – bad luck
1909 – bad luck
1914 – increase in the family
1924 – bad luck
1926 – wedding
1932 – pregnant
1939 – pregnant
1940 – ginger twins
1959 – red-headed twins
1972 – ginger-headed twins
1973 – red-headed twins
1975 – pregnant
1983 – twins
1994 – ginger twins

The first versions simply state 'bad luck', but by 1914, the specific idea of getting pregnant has crept in, and by 1940 this is further embellished to 'ginger-headed twins'. If this is a true picture of this belief's development, it shows two very important things. First, it demonstrates how much change can take place in a hundred years; and secondly, it shows how futile it is to take a modern example and extrapolate backwards in time to invent a supposed origin to fit it. The earliest and latest examples have nothing in common.

Kent Igglesden (c.1932) 155–6; [1983] Opie & Tatem, 391. Devon Devonshire Assoc. 91 (1959) 201; Devonshire Assoc. 104 (1972) 267; Devonshire Assoc. 105 (1973) 214. Wiltshire Wiltshire (1975) 85. London Folk-Lore 37 (1926) 365; Folk-Lore 51 (1940) 117. Oxfordshire [1920s] Surman (1992) 61. Worcestershire N&Q 6S:12 (1885) 466; Folk-Lore 20 (1909) 345; Folk-Lore 25 (1914) 370. Cambridgeshire Folk-Lore 50 (1939) 185. Suffolk Folk-Lore 35 (1924) 351; Rees (2001b) 17–18.

tea: stalk

Like so many other trivial domestic happenings, a stalk or leaf of tea floating in your cup indicates the coming of a stranger, or at least a visitor, and there is a set routine to learn more about him/her:

A stalk swimming in your tea shows that a stranger is coming, it is placed on the back of the hand and the wrist patted. If it should fall at the first pat the stranger will arrive that day, if, at the second pat, on the second day and so on. You then repeat the operation to ascertain the hour . . . If the stalk be a hard one the stranger will be a man, if soft a woman. If the stranger be not welcome to come, the tea stalk must not be placed on the hand, but should be taken out of the teacup and thrown under the table. Berkshire Lowsley (1888)

Details vary remarkably little, although there are minor refinements and some special cases:

If a tea-stalk floats in the cup, it is called 'a beau'. Unmarried ladies, when this happens, should stir their tea round briskly, and then plant the spoon uprightly in the middle of the cup, holding it quite still with the fingers. If the 'beau' in its gyrations is attracted to the spoon and clings to it, the 'beau' will be certain to come that evening. If the sides of the cup attract, the 'beau' will not come. I may observe that it depends on the state of the atmosphere whether the tea-stalk is attracted to the middle or the sides of the cup.
Derbyshire N&Q (1872)

The belief was extremely well known, and the 'stalk in the cup' was almost as proverbial as the 'stranger on the bar' (see FIRE) and the 'stranger in the candle' (see CANDLES). Only one informant has given a different meaning. Remembering a childhood in Essex around 1915, he claimed that two tea-leaves afloat in the cup meant travel (Mays (1969)).

This superstition appears a little earlier than other tea traditions (apart from tea-leaf reading), and is first found in Glasgow about 1820. It was probably not brand new then, as only ten years later, Mary Mitford could mention it in passing, as if everyone would understand, 'Who . . . searches the tea-cups for coming visitors?' (Berkshire Mitford (1830)).

Somerset [1923] Opie & Tatem, 392. Cornwall Hunt (1865) 235; N&Q 5S:8 (1877) 126. Berkshire Mitford (1830) 299; Lowsley (1888) 23. Essex [c.1915] Mays (1969) 164–5. Oxfordshire [pre-1900] Folk-Lore 24 (1913) 91; [1920s] Surman (1992) 61. East Anglia N&Q 4S:2 (1868) 221, 554. Suffolk Folk-Lore 35 (1924) 352. Lincolnshire Peacock (1877) 241. Shropshire Burne (1883) 277. Derbyshire N&Q 4S:10 (1872) 495; [1890s] Uttley (1946) 127. Yorkshire [1983] Opie & Tatem, 392. Lancashire Harland & Wilkinson (1882) 139. Scotland N&Q 1S:10 (1854) 534. Northeast Scotland Gregor (1881) 31–2. Glasgow [c.1820] Napier (1864) 397. Co. Tyrone Lore & Language 1:7 (1972) 12. Unlocated Igglesden (c.1932) 176.

teeth: babies' first

Another belief regarding children's teeth, reported only from Midland and Northern England and Scotland since the mid nineteenth century, held that if a child's first tooth was in its upper jaw it was at best unlucky, and at worst a sign that it would not live long:

A Rutland woman was telling me that her baby had just cut his first tooth, but that she was sorry to say that it was in his upper jaw. I said that I supposed it did not make much difference

teeth

Teeth are the focus of several widespread superstitions (*see below*), but there are a number which do not fit the general pattern. Examples are as follows:

At the sight of a toad, children would keep their mouths shut, lest the toad count their teeth, causing them to fall. Wales Jones (1930)

If you pull a tooth out in the dark, it will not hurt you. Yorkshire *Folk-Lore* (1909)

It is unlucky to count your teeth.
England Addy (1895)

See also TOOTHACHE.

England Addy (1895) 101. Yorkshire *Folk-Lore* 20 (1909) 348. Wales Jones (1930) 198.

---

whether it was in the upper or lower jaw. She replied that it made all the difference in the world, as if it was in the upper jaw it was a sign that the child would not live. Rutland N&Q (1878)

or, as a Scottish rhyme expressed it:

If ye cut yir first teeth abeen
Ye winna dance i' yir mairraige sheen.
Scotland *Folk-Lore* (1895)

The earliest known reference dates back to only 1849, but a version in the Opie collection shows it was still current into the 1950s.

Rutland N&Q 5S:10 (1878) 165. **England** Addy (1895) 94. **Northern England** [1850s] *Denham Tracts* 2 (1895) 24, 75. **Nottinghamshire** N&Q 7S:11 (1891) 305. **Yorkshire** [1957] Opie & Tatem, 393. **Co. Durham** Leighton (1910) 47–8. **Scotland** *Folk-Lore* 6 (1895) 394–5. **Western Scotland** Napier (1879) 137. **Unlocated** Brand 2 (1849) 87.

---

teeth: disposal of

The idea that teeth which are lost, either as milk-teeth or by extraction or accident, should be disposed of in traditionally sanctioned ways is found in most, if not all, European cultures and, probably, throughout most of the world. In Britain, the standard ceremony for shed teeth, which lasted from at least the late seventeenth to the late twentieth century, was for the tooth to be burnt, usually after covering it with salt, and often with an accompanying rhyme:

Milk teeth were burned, with a pinch of salt sprinkled on them, and the following rune was repeated by mother and child as the tiny tooth was tossed into the heart of a blazing fire:

Old tooth, new tooth
Pray God send me a new tooth

We said this with the air of performing a serious rite. It was a tradition, and we followed it.
Derbyshire [c.1890] Uttley

Reasons for this procedure varied, and non-compliance was sometimes simply given as 'being unlucky', but two specific themes are commonly cited. The first was particularly apposite for children's milk-teeth, for, if the tooth were lost and a dog (or other animal) got hold of it, the replacement would grow like an animal's tooth.

The second also applied to adults – on the Day of Judgement we will all have to account for any missing body parts. Extracted teeth should therefore either be ceremoniously burnt, or kept safely somewhere in the house, while AMPUTATED limbs and so on should be given a decent burial.

It was the custom in Derbyshire for people to preserve their teeth in jars until their deaths, after which the teeth were put into their coffins and buried with them. Mothers would also preserve the teeth of their infant children and keep them in jars. It is said that when you go to heaven you will have to account for all the teeth that you have had upon earth. A man said that his grandmother used to call out at a funeral, 'Have you got his teeth in the coffin?' or 'Don't bury him without his teeth'.
Derbyshire Addy (1895)

When a boy I remember being told, both in Lancashire and in Yorkshire, that the penalty for not burning an extracted tooth is to search for it in a pail of blood in hell after death.
Lancashire/Yorkshire N&Q (1870)

The earliest reference to the salt and fire ceremony occurs in 1686, in John Aubrey's manuscript collection of customs and beliefs. Considering the deluge of references from the nineteenth and twentieth centuries, listed below, it is distinctly odd that none has been noted between Aubrey and 1830. This may be an accident in the record, or may indicate that the belief underwent a revival in the early nineteenth century.

teeth: charms for cutting

From Edward Lovett, *Magic in Modern London* (1925)

One Saturday night, about 1905, I was in a poor man's market in South London, when I saw upon a hawker's barrow a small card box containing a couple of calf's teeth. I asked the man in charge what they were for, and his answer was: 'You wouldn't believe me if I told you'. To this I replied that I knew already what he would tell me, and that I would give him sixpence for them. He was quite pleased with this, and, having completed the deal, he said, 'And what do you think you are going to do with 'em?' I told him that they would be put into a little bag and tied round the neck of a baby that was cutting its Wrst teeth with diYculty. He

seemed very surprised that I should have heard of this.

I have made many records of a somewhat similar nature, except in the large majority of cases the teeth so used are not only human, but actually those of the child's mother. Upon further investigation I found that in many cases, if a young girl 'lost' a tooth (i.e. came out), she put it away very carefully so that in the event of her marrying and having children she would hang the tooth round the neck of the child during the period of cutting its teeth. Again, when children shed their milk teeth these teeth should be at once thrown into the Wre and burned. If this be not done at once it is thought that a dog's tooth will grow in the place of the old one.

In marked contrast to the above, the occasional reference advises that the tooth should be thrown over the shoulder or head. In Renfrewshire, the promise was that treasure would be found the next day at the spot where the tooth had fallen (N&Q (1869)), while in Wales a rhyme similar to the one which accompanied the burning was recited as the tooth was thrown:

A sweet tooth for the cat
A bitter tooth for the dog
A yellow tooth for the hog
A white tooth for me.   Wales Jones (1930)

The twentieth century saw a marked change in the way children's milk-teeth were treated. From at least the 1920s, the idea existed that the fairies were interested in taking the teeth in exchange for money, at least in some families. For much of that time it was simply 'the fairies' who would take the tooth, if left under the child's pillow (or occasionally elsewhere), but at some point after the Second World War the 'Tooth Fairy' became the staple character in the deal. As the fire-and-salt method was still being cited into the 1950s and 1960s, it overlapped for some decades with the fairies, and correspondence in FLS *News* 14 and 15 (1992) shows that some children were well aware that different methods existed and endeavoured to use those which promised money in return, which must have given the fairies a distinct edge over older methods. It is usually assumed that the Tooth Fairy character was introduced from America, and this may well be so, but Tuleja (1991) and Wells (1991) show that the fairy connection has no longer history in the USA than in Britain – arising and gaining popularity at roughly the same time in both countries.

Nowadays, the Tooth Fairy is ubiquitous on both sides of the Atlantic, and crops up in children's books, board games, advertisements, dental health campaigns, and political cartoons, without explanation. For example, in 1992, when the Thatcher government adopted a payment policy which led to dentists leaving the National Health Service in droves, at least two political cartoonists (*Independent on Sunday*, 28 June 1992; *Guardian*, 7 July 1992) used the tooth fairy motif to comment on the situation. Newspaper columnists regularly lament how the silver sixpence given by the fairies of yesteryear became, by stages, a shilling, a half-crown, a pound coin, and so on. As with all emerging folklore, there is plenty of scope for elaboration:

Has anyone ever discovered why the fairies are willing to part with their silver in exchange for milk teeth? Our children asked this question from the start. They were told that fairies used them as bricks with which to build their houses.
London *Guardian* (14 Oct. 1988)

At bedtime one night my son, then aged about seven, asked what the fairies would do with the milk tooth under his pillow. I thought fast and told him that it would be made into tiny ornaments to decorate fairyland.
Yorkshire *Guardian* (20 Oct. 1988)

The relative dating of the different tooth superstitions, as detailed above, seems reasonably clear, but two references indicate a potentially more complex picture which needs further study. The first, from the autobiography of author Kenneth Grahame, shows that at least as early as the 1870s, some children expected a financial reward for lost teeth:

Edward was standing ginger-beer like a gentle-
man, happening, as the one that had last passed
under the dentist's hands, to be the capitalist of
the flying hour. As in all well-regulated families,
the usual tariff obtained in ours; half-a-crown a
tooth; a shilling only if the molar were a loose
one. This one, unfortunately – in spite of
Edward's interested affectation of agony – had
been shakiness undisguised; but the event was
good enough to run to ginger-beer.

Berkshire [*c.*1870] Grahame

The second is even more difficult to account for.
In one of Robert Herrick's poems, published in
1648, in which he describes the palace of the fairy
king Oberon, he clearly establishes a link
between fairies and children's teeth – perhaps
merely by coincidence:

Many a counter, many a die,
Half rotten, and without an eye
Lies here abouts; and for to pave
The excellency of this cave,
Squirrils and childrens teeth late shed,
Are neatly here enchequered
With brownest toadstones.

Herrick, *Hesperides* (1648)

Fire and/or salt: Sussex Latham (1878) 44. **Devon**
Elworthy (1895) 437. **Cornwall** *Folk-Lore Jnl* 5 (1887)
208; [1890s] *Old Cornwall* 1:12 (1930) 4; *Old Cornwall*
1:9 (1929) 41; *Old Cornwall* 2 (1931–6) 39. **Wiltshire**
Wilts. N&Q 1 (1893–5) 103. **Berkshire** [*c.*1890] Grahame
(1898) 133. **Buckinghamshire** [1912] *Folk-Lore* 43 (1932)
110. **Oxfordshire** *Folk-Lore* 68 (1957) 414. **Warwickshire**
Bloom (*c.*1930) 26–7. **Northamptonshire** Sternberg
(1851) 166. **East Anglia** Forby (1830) 414; Varden (1885)
114. **Suffolk** *Gent. Mag.* (1867) 728–41; Claxton (1954)
89; Evans (1965) 217. **Norfolk** N&Q 4S:6 (1870) 131.
Lincolnshire *Grantham Jnl* (22 June 1878). **Shropshire**
Burne (1883) 268. **Staffordshire** [1954] Opie & Tatem,
393–4. **Derbyshire** *Folk-Lore Jnl* 2 (1884) 280; [*c.*1890]
Uttley (1946) 125; Addy (1895) 125. **Northern England**
Denham Tracts 2 (1895). **Yorkshire** Nicholson (1890) 87;
Folk-Lore 6 (1895) 301; Addy (1895) 91; Blakeborough
(1898) 131; [1920s] *Guardian* (20 Oct. 1988) 22; Opie
(1959) 304. **Yorkshire/Lancashire** N&Q 4S:6 (1870) 131.
Lancashire N&Q 4S:6 (1870) 68–9; Harland &
Wilkinson (1882) 141. **Co. Durham** Brockie (1886) 220;
Leighton (1910) 48; N&Q 173 (1937) 83.
Northumberland Bigge (1860–62) 93. **Wales** [1953] Opie
& Tatem, 393–4. **Western Scotland** N&Q 1S:10 (1854)
232–3. **Jersey** *Folk-Lore* 38 (1927) 179. **Unlocated** Aubrey,
Remaines (1686) 11; N&Q 1S:9 (1854) 345; N&Q 2S:12
(1861) 492; N&Q 3S:2 (1862) 342; N&Q 4S:6 (1870) 340.
General N&Q 4S:6 (1870) 340.
Thrown over shoulder: Wales Jones (1930) 198; Opie
(1959) 304–5. **Highland Scotland** Macbain (1887/88)
256. **Renfrewshire** N&Q 4S:4 (1869) 212. **Co. Longford**
Béaloideas 6 (1936) 263.
Fairies: Somerset Tongue (1965) 137. **Oxfordshire**
[1920s] Surman (1992) 61. **Staffordshire** [1954] Opie &
Tatem 393–4. **Manchester** [1987] Opie & Tatem 393–4.

Glasgow [1940s] MacLeay (1990) 48. **Unlocated** Opie
(1959) 305. **Various** *Guardian* (14 & 20 Oct. 1988).
Historical Wells (1991); Tuleja (1991).
European analogues: Germany Aubrey, *Remaines*
(1686) 11. **Anatolia** N&Q 4S:8 (1871) 322.
Switzerland/Sweden N&Q 4S:6 (1870) 131. **France**
N&Q 173 (1937) 300. **Various** Tuleja (1991).

teeth: dreaming of

Despite the demonstrably widespread long-
standing popular interest in DREAMS and their
meanings, few dream interpretations seem to
have entered the public consciousness sufficiently
strongly to be noted in any numbers by folklorists and other collectors. One of the few which
has done so is that to dream of losing one's teeth
means that you will soon lose a friend or relative:

A Warwickshire lady, writing to inform me of the
illness of her mother, said, 'I dreamed last night
that one of my teeth came out – a very bad dream
indeed; but the candles are all right yet' To dream
of losing a tooth, or to see a winding-sheet in the
candle, are taken to be prophetic of an immediate
death in the family. Warwickshire Langford (1875)

The meaning has remained remarkably constant
for 900 years, being given the same interpretation
in a medieval manuscript reprinted by Cockayne
as by a South Shields woman in 1985, reported by
Opie and Tatem. This meaning was also included
in many nineteenth-century DREAM BOOKS,
which will have helped to stabilize it.

Sussex Latham (1878) 14. **Cornwall** *Old Cornwall* 2
(1931–6) 40. **Herefordshire** [*c.*1895] *Folk-Lore* 39 (1928)
391. **Warwickshire** Langford (1875) 19. **Lincolnshire**
Grantham Jnl (22 June 1878); Gutch & Peacock (1908)
165. **England** Addy (1895) 93. **Yorkshire** Nicholson
(1890) 44. **Northern England** Denham (1895) 272.
Cumberland Penfold (1907) 58. **Co. Durham** [1985]
Opie & Tatem 394. **England/Scotland border** [*c.*1816]
Henderson (1866) 84. **Co. Longford** *Béaloideas* 6 (1936)
260. **General** [*c.*1050] Cockayne 3 (1866) 203; Browne,
Pseudodoxia Epidemica (1641) Bk 4, Ch. 5. **Literary**
Thomas Killigrew, *The Parson's Wedding* (1663) 2:5.

teeth: early

There is a range of traditional interpretations
concerning a baby who is born with teeth, or
who teethes early. In many cases, it means that
the mother will soon fall pregnant again:

Soon teeth soon toes – This means that if your
baby's teeth begin to sprout early, you will soon
have toes, i.e. another baby.

Northern England [1850s] *Denham Tracts*

However, a similar saying – 'Soon toothed, soon with God' – was included in seventeenth-century proverb collections, indicating an early death, and 'soon toothed, soon turfed' was still being quoted in late nineteenth-century Worcestershire. Even worse:

To be born with teeth is an extremely bad sign. The usual theory is that it foretells death by violence, but one midwife informed me a few years ago that the true meaning is even worse. 'I never speak of it,' she said, 'and if anyone asks me I deny it, for the sake of the mother; but it means that the child will grow up to be a murderer'. It is possible that this is the older form of the superstition. A milder version gives it as a sign of a very bad temper; and in some districts it has been watered down to a vague prophecy of simple ill-luck.   Unlocated *Folk-Lore* (1957)

The early-baby interpretation first appears in the mid nineteenth century, while the early death was already proverbial 200 years earlier. But the confusion still exists:

I have heard of two superstitions about babies born with a tooth or teeth and am puzzled because they seem to be contradictory. One is that the child will be extremely clever, the other, which is quite horrendous, is that the child is born to be hanged.   London *The Mirror* (28 Aug. 1987)

London *The Mirror* (28 Aug. 1987) 20. **Worcestershire** N&Q 7S:5 (1888) 285. **Lancashire** Harland & Wilkinson (1873) 221. **Northern England** [1850s] *Denham Tracts* 2 (1895) 48. **Co. Durham** Leighton (1910) 47–8. **Montgomeryshire** Hamer (1877) 259. **Denbighshire** Jones (1930) 198. **Dumfriesshire** Corrie (1890/91) 37. Unlocated *Folk-Lore* 68 (1957) 413. **General** James Howell, *Proverbs* (1659) 4a; John Ray, *Proverbs* (1670) 52. **Literary** Shakespeare, *Henry VI Part III* (1593) 5:6.

teeth: gap between

There is general agreement that having a gap between your two front teeth is significant and predicts the possessor's future or character, but unfortunately there is no consensus as to its exact meaning. Most say it is fortunate in some way – you will be lucky, rich, or will travel far, and in the author's teenage years (1960s) it was reputed to be sexy.

The old women say, watch well when the child has finished cutting its first teeth, for if there is a parting between the two front teeth to admit the passing of a sixpenny-piece, that individual will have riches and prosperity all through life.
          Wales Trevelyan (1909)

Nevertheless, two Scottish informants viewed the matter very differently:

If the two front teeth are apart it shows that there is a fondness for the opposite sex, or, as an old woman expressed it, indicates a 'lichtsome character' ... If the teeth are far apart from each other the person will be short-lived.
          Aberdeenshire *Folk-Lore* (1895)

Reports appear fairly regularly from the mid Victorian times, and it would seem to be yet another minor belief which emerged in the nineteenth century if it were not for two lines in the *Canterbury Tales* nearly 500 years earlier:

She koude muchel of wandrynge by the weye Gat-tothed was she, soothly for to seye.
          Chaucer *Canterbury Tales* (c.1387).

Northamptonshire Sternberg (1851) 171–2. **Norfolk** Fulcher Collection (c.1895). **Lincolnshire** Rudkin (1936) 16. **Shropshire** Burne (1883) 268. **Cheshire** [1964] Opie & Tatem, 394. **England** Addy (1895) 94. **Wales** Trevelyan (1909) 268. **Radnorshire** [1953] Opie & Tatem, 394. **Denbighshire** Jones (1930) 198. **Aberdeenshire** *Folk-Lore* 6 (1895) 396. **Guernsey** De Garis (1975) 8. Unlocated N&Q 1S:6 (1852) 601; *Chambers's Jnl* (1873) 810. **Literary** Chaucer, *Canterbury Tales* (c.1387) Gen. Prologue, lines 467–8.

teething

Various remedies have been tried by parents and nurses to help babies who have trouble cutting their first teeth. Three main approaches have traditionally been recommended: placing items in bags to be worn around the baby's neck; rubbing the gums with particular materials; and necklaces made of minerals or plants.

Items placed in bags include WOODLICE and DONKEY's hairs – both of which are more often recommended for other ailments:

A woman at Ledgemoor (King's Pyon) used to catch seven or nine woodlice, and place them, while still alive, in a little bag round her babies' necks to help them cut their teeth. At Kingstone, a woman used twenty-one woodlice, sewn up alive in black ribbon, for the same purpose. The Rev. Hyett Warner found that one of his parishioners believed in the efficacy of hairs from the cross on a donkey's back; she hung them round the child's neck, sewn up in a little silk bag. At Staunton-on-Wye a necklace of hair from the donkey's cross was worn during the whole period of teething. The mother explained that 'It must be someone else's donkey'.
          Herefordshire Leather (1912)

Others used teeth, of humans or animals, and young women often kept any teeth they lost to use for their future babies (*see* Lovett (1925)). John Aubrey commented that the Irish 'do use a wolves fang-tooth [holder] set in silver and gold for this purpose' (*Remaines* (1686)).

Necklaces could be made of various materials – glass beads, deadly nightshade berries, myrtle stems, henbane roots, elder, orris root, and so on, but the most widespread and oldest amulet was CORAL:

Though coral doth properly preserve and fasten the teeth on men, yet it is used in children to make an easier passage for them; and for that intent is worn about their necks. But whether this custom were not superstitiously founded, as presumed an amulet or defensative against fascination, is not beyond all doubt.

Browne, *Pseudodoxia Epidemica* (1672)

As Browne was aware, coral was also believed to be an effective protection against witchcraft, and it is not clear whether this aspect of its magical power, or its reputed practical effect directly upon the teeth and gums, contributed most to its widespread use, even to the present day. Several other sixteenth- and seventeenth-century writers also link coral and teething, and it was clearly well known at the time. They presumably got the idea direct from classical writers such as Pliny.

A different approach to teething was to rub the gums with particular plants or with the mother's wedding ring.

Devon Hewett (1900) 76. Cornwall *Old Cornwall* 1:9 (1929) 41. London [*c.*1905] Lovett (1925) 25–6. Buckinghamshire *Midland Garner* 1 (1884) 22. Herefordshire Leather (1912) 70, 81. Warwickshire Bloom (*c.*1930) 25–6. Suffolk *Suffolk N&Q* (1877). Norfolk [*c.*1920] Wigby (1976) 65; *Folk-Lore* 40 (1929) 123. England Addy (1895) 90. Welsh/English Gypsies Groome (1880) 13. Ireland Aubrey, *Remaines* (1686/1972) 233; *Folk-Lore* 8 (1897) 388. Guernsey De Garis (1975) 8. General Scot (1584) Bk 13, Ch. 6; Hugh Plat, *The Jewell-House of Art and Nature* (1594); Pierre Erondelle & John Fabre, *A French Garden for English Ladyes and Gentlewomen to Walk in* (1621) quoted Brand 2 (1849) 86; William Coles, *Adam in Eden* (1657); Browne, *Pseudodoxia Epidemica* (1672) Bk 5, Ch. 22; Aubrey, *Remaines* (1686/1972) 233; Brand 2 (1849) 85–6; Wright (1913) 248; *Dental Mag.* (Feb. 1948) 3, quoted Opie & Tatem, 96. Literary John Webster, *Cure for a Cuckold* (1661) 1:1. Classical Pliny, *Natural History* (AD 77) Bk 32, Ch. 11.

tempting fate

The fear of tempting fate is one of the fundamental motifs of British superstition, and it runs

like a thread through many recent and current beliefs. Indeed, it is arguably the one superstitious motif which still retains a general influence over behaviour in the modern world. It is most clearly manifest in the habit of saying TOUCH WOOD, or 'God willing' whenever we boast or seem too sure of ourselves and our fortune, but the same principle is involved in a number of other beliefs and customs. Every prospective parent who is reluctant to buy a pram or CRADLE before the baby is born is worried what fate will do, as are those who will not put up a new CALENDAR before the New Year, or even display a new month before it starts. Past beliefs, clearly based on the same fear, included a reluctance to COUNT things, to announce the exact number of lambs born or fish caught, and to WEIGH or MEASURE babies.

In Britain, many of us are none too sure who or what is 'fate'. Admittedly, some believe that the Devil and his helpers are determined to thwart our plans and dash our hopes, but for those who do not have such religious faith, it is difficult to put into words exactly how 'fate' works. It seems to have little in common with the Fates of the ancient world who were believed to personally govern the destiny of every human being and to weave the course of our lives.

theatre

Actors comprise one of the occupational groups which seem to take an affectionate pride in their superstitions and to regard them almost as a badge of office. Many actors, both professional and amateur, will freely agree that they are superstitious in the way they approach their craft, and will even admit to behaviour which, in any other context, would be labelled 'obsessive' and cause concern for their mental health. On the surface, there seems to be no end to the variety of actors' superstitions, with many having highly individual personal beliefs which are apparently unique to them, but as with other superstitious practices, most of them fit into one of two main categories – the wearing, carrying, or owning of 'lucky' items, and the insistence on following or avoiding certain patterns of behaviour before a performance. All these beliefs are focused on luck within the theatre – how the actor's performance will be received, how long the play will run, whether the actor will get another part, and so on, rather than with any aspect of life in the world outside.

Lucky items are extremely common. The individual pieces vary considerably, but they usually have some significant history or past association for which they are prized, for example, gifts from family or fellow actors (especially already successful ones), items associated with the actor's first or most successful role, or something found on the way to a first audition. Some have a few choice pieces, while others collect roomfuls.

Continuity is important. Many actors, like John Moore, will always keep a prop from the previous play, an ash-tray, a pencil, a pair of spectacles, a scarf. Some actors will always use an old set of make-up sticks on a first night and will never break into a new stick, bottle or tube until the play has been running at least a week.   Huggett (1981)

A second important category is the wearing of a particular piece of clothing – a lucky tie, dressing gown, pair of socks – while another is to take the same route to the venue. Other actors have private rituals of saying or doing certain things – on the lines of 'turn round three times':

I heard lately that when a celebrated actress was playing she never went on to the stage at the Opera without going through a curious performance with each person she met, as soon as she came out of her dressing-room. If she met one of the actors, or even a super, she made him hold up his thumb in front of her; then, placing her thumb on his, she turned her hand round, at the same time pressing downwards. If the thumb on which she pressed held firm she was satisfied, but if it gave way she imagined that she would break down during the performance.   N&Q (1878)

Actors share both of these types of superstition – wearing particular items of clothing, and careful control of behaviour immediately before performance – with professional sportsmen and -women. Similarly, many actors' superstitions are simply versions of those known in the wider world – RABBIT's foot is lucky, dislike of THIRTEEN, avoidance of PEACOCK feathers and open UMBRELLAS on the stage and WHISTLING anywhere in the building, and the idea that if a WOMAN is the first audience-member to enter on first night the play will fail. Others are more specialist: tripping up on stage is lucky (whereas in other contexts STUMBLING is usually bad); real flowers and knitting on stage are very unlucky. Another strong belief is that one must never speak the last lines of a play in rehearsal. It is notable that none of these superstitions can yet be traced before the early twentieth century.

Certain tunes were regarded as unlucky to play, although again there is no mention of this notion before the 1930s. Those most commonly mentioned in this context are 'Three Blind Mice' and 'I Dreamt I Dwelt in Marble Halls',

from Balfe's *Bohemian Girl* (1843):

Under the heading of 'Sing a Song with your Fingers Crossed', the Daily Express *of 26 Jan 1955 prints what it calls a 'musicians' superstition' against this song from* The Bohemian Girl. *'Bad luck, even death, may follow. It is considered a bad omen even if it is just whistled or hummed on a first night.'*   Folk-Lore (1955)

One of the best-known theatrical superstitions is that Shakespeare's play *Macbeth* is extremely unlucky to stage, and that productions are always bedevilled by misfortune. The name of the play is therefore never spoken (euphemisms such as 'the Scottish play' being used instead), and quotations from its text scrupulously avoided. Various theories have been put forward to explain this belief, ranging from the fanciful to the prosaic. In the latter category, actress Sybil Thorndike commented:

I have always heard that the superstition about quoting Macbeth *arose from the old days of stock companies, when this play was always put on when business was bad (being a favourite), so that it often presaged the end of a season. This is the only explanation I have heard.*   Folk-Lore (1936)

At the other extreme are notions of real curses. Actor and author Richard Huggett, for example, devoted a whole chapter of his 1981 book on theatrical superstitions to 'the "Curse of Macbeth"'. He is clearly a firm believer in the reality of the curse, and claims that it started as soon as the play was first performed and has continued ever since, suggesting that it was Shakespeare's fault for including a real witch's curse in the first Act. Unfortunately, despite his claim of a four-hundred-year history for the curse, all his detailed examples of dire misfortunes are drawn from twentieth-century productions, and he offers no evidence that there was any concept of the play being regarded as unlucky before that time. Nor has any other pre-twentieth-century source been located anywhere else. The earliest to come to light is in Sharper Knowlson's book on superstition in 1910, although his phrase 'old actors' implies a longer standing tradition:

Old actors believe the witches' song in Macbeth *to possess the uncanny power of casting evil spells, and the majority of them strongly dislike to play in the piece. Hum the tune in the hearing of an old actor and the chances are you will lose his friendship.*   Knowlson (1910)

Most of the other reports from the first half of the century also focus on the tunes, and the fact that bad luck will follow if they are whistled or hummed, which is in line with other beliefs about unlucky tunes, already mentioned.

N&Q 5S:10 (1878) 147; Folk-Lore Record 2 (1879) 203–5; Knowlson (1910) 225–9; Thompson (1932) 281–4; Igglesden (c.1932) 233–4; Booth (1933) 95–116; Granville (1952) 179; Folk-Lore 66 (1955) 365; Observer Supp. (24 Nov. 1968) 12–13; Huggett (1981) passim; Opie & Tatem, 228, 395–7.

thirteen

One of the most widely distributed superstitions of modern times is that the number thirteen is unlucky. This notion occurs in numerous guises, but in particular in the belief that FRIDAY 13th is an unlucky day, that thirteen people at a gathering or meal is so unlucky that one of them will die within a year, and that houses, flats, ocean liner cabins, hotel rooms, and so on, numbered thirteen are so unpopular that they are invariably changed to 12A or 14.

To meet the views of superstitious people, the Harrow Council have decided in future to substitute 12a for 13 in the numbering of houses (Morning Post 6 Oct 1913). It is rather astonishing that the present year is not referred to as 1912a. London N&Q (1913)

Despite the modern popular opinion that fear of the number thirteen is an ancient belief, the idea of thirteen as an unlucky number, or Friday 13th as an unlucky day, cannot be traced back further than the mid nineteenth century, and appears to be a Victorian invention. Only in the sense of thirteen at table, or thirteen in a company, can we find any earlier references, and these indicate that that belief first took shape around the turn of the eighteenth century.

A number of questionable origin-theories have been put forward to explain the dislike of the number. Some, for example, claim that sixteenth- and seventeenth-century witches organized themselves in covens of thirteen, thus giving the number a bad name for the godly. The evidence for covens is scant, as they mainly existed in the imaginations of the prosecutors, and even where witches' confessions speak of groups and gatherings, thirteen is hardly ever mentioned. The whole notion of covens of thirteen was floated by Margaret Murray in her attempts to prove that witchcraft was the survival of an old pagan religion, which it was not, but her theories have been enthusiastically perpetuated by inXuential writers such as Robert Graves and Gerald Gardner, and many modern

devotees who appreciate the value of a good conspiracy theory to underpin belief.

The other main theory is that the number is unlucky because there were thirteen people at the Last Supper, and Jesus was killed soon after. This explanation probably has a grain of truth, but not in the way it is generally presented. Put simply, before the Reformation, it was standard Christian practice to replicate the way that Jesus did things whenever possible, and this included the organization of personnel into groups of thirteen. The Oxford English Dictionary thus gives one of the early uses of 'convent' as meaning 'a company of twelve (or, including the superior, thirteen) "religious" persons whether constituting a separate community or a section of a larger one'. After the Reformation, however, such activities were rebranded as 'superstitious' by the new Protestant churches, and forbidden. Almost overnight they were changed from 'good' to 'bad'. The negative aspects of the number thirteen can thus only date from after the late sixteenth century.

In fact, the earliest reference we can find for thirteen being generally unlucky was published in 1852:

Odd numbers. They are lucky, except the number thirteen, which is the unluckiest of numbers. Yorkshire N&Q (1852)

This notion is repeated occasionally in the literature from then until the end of the century, but after that it soon became widely known and, it must be said, fashionable.

One regular context in which thirteen was actually stipulated was the setting of hens, when that number of eggs was insisted upon; see EGGS: SETTING AN ODD NUMBER.

See also FRIDAY 13TH; THIRTEEN: AT TABLE.

Dorset N&Q 11S:8 (1913) 393; Devonshire Assoc. 60 (1928) 126. London N&Q 11S:8 (1913) 347; Folk-Lore 38 (1927) 306–8; Folk-Lore 39 (1928) 95; Folk-Lore 68 (1957) 366; [1985] Opie & Tatem, 399. Essex [1983] Opie & Tatem, 399. Somerset [1923] Opie & Tatem, 398. Oxfordshire [1920s] Surman (1992) 60. Warwickshire Folk-Lore 26 (1915) 97. England Folk-Lore 38 (1927) 306. Derbyshire The Times (10 May 1954) 4. Yorkshire N&Q 1S:6 (1852) 311–12; Folk-Lore 43 (1932) 255. Northumberland Scotsman (4 Aug. 1924) quoted N&Q 147 (1924) 94. Scotland [1922] Maclean (1959) 198. N. Ireland Foster (1951) 131. Unlocated Chambers's Jnl (1873) 809; Westminster Gazette (3 Nov. 1893) 1; N&Q 11S:8 (1913) 434. General N&Q 4S:1 (1868) 575; N&Q 4S:11 (1873) 330; Folk-Lore 38 (1927) 307; N&Q 192 (1947) 193.

thirteen at table/in company

The only one of the superstitions regarding THIRTEEN which can be traced back beyond the Victorian era is that thirteen people at a table, or in a company, is unlucky.

Dining lately with a friend, our conviviality was suddenly interrupted by the discovery of a maiden lady, who observed that our party consisted of thirteen. Her fears, however, were not without hope, till she found, after a very particular enquiry, that none of her married friends were likely to make any addition to the number. She was then fully assured that one of the party would die within the twelvemonth.

Gent. Mag. (1796)

The one who will die soon is usually specified as the first one to rise from the table.

Thirteen at table is unlucky – he who rises first runs most risk; better, in such a dilemma to all rise at once.   Dumfriesshire Shaw (1890)

Several of the published accounts detail tricks to avoid the fate once the number of guests has been realized, in addition to everyone standing up at the same time: the hostess quietly leaves the room and eats in the kitchen, one person sits at another table, the house cat joins the company, or they discover that one of the women present is pregnant and therefore counts as two.

The earliest intimation that we have of this danger of thirteen in a company is found in a story which appears in a letter written in 1697 by John Aubrey to Awsham Churchill, the London bookseller, published in the fourth edition (1857) of Aubrey's *Miscellanies*. Aubrey there refers to 'a very pretty remark' in the *Athenian Mercury* of June 1695, which tells the story of two women who were close friends, but one became very ill with smallpox. She sent for her friend, but the latter failed to come as she was worried about catching the disease. The sufferer died, and her ghost later appeared to her friend, warning her, 'you have not long to live, therefore prepare to die; and when you are at a feast, and make the thirteenth person in number, then remember my words'. The piece ends with the key words: 'The gentleman that told this story, says that there is hardly any person of quality but what knows it to be true'. In other words, it was a CONTEMPORARY LEGEND of the time.

By the second known reference, the superstition has taken on all the details we recognize:

I remember I was once in a mixt assembly that was full of noise and mirth, when on a sudden an old woman unluckily observed there were thirteen of us in company. This remark struck a pannick terror into several who were present, insomuch that one or two of the ladies were going to leave the room; but a friend of mine, taking notice that one of our female companions was big with child, affirm'd there were fourteen in the room, and that, instead of portending one of the company should die, it plainly foretold one of them should be born. Had not my friend found this expedient to break the omen, I question not but half the women in the company would have fallen sick that very night.

Addison, *Spectator* (8 Mar. 1711)

In the absence of other evidence to the contrary, it is suggested that the point of origin of this particular superstition comes between these dates, 1695 and 1711, and is based on a popular ghost legend of the time.

In common with the other 'thirteen' beliefs, this one has attracted its fair share of invented origins based on guesswork. Most people are satisfied with the simple explanation that there were thirteen at the Last Supper, and this explanation has been widely accepted since the mid nineteenth century at least, but it has never been intellectually satisfying. Certainly, the Last Supper was soon followed by death (of two of the principals, in fact – Judas and Jesus), but there must have been many other gatherings, including meals, at which the thirteen were present which were not at all unlucky. One must also face the sleight of hand of popular writing on superstition. When a writer states that the superstition of thirteen at the table is based on the Last Supper, the implication is that it dates from that time, but as we have seen, this rests on the assumption that it existed, but went unrecorded, for some 1,600 years.

A different explanation, however, claims roots for the belief in Norse mythology. It cites a banquet which Odin held at Valhalla for twelve guests, which Loki gatecrashed and murdered Balder (e.g. Haining (1979); Potter (1990); *Daily Mail* (13 July 2001) 13). Unsurprisingly, nothing here is correct. Folklorist Jacqueline Simpson demolishes the whole idea, with reference to the original poem called 'Lokasenna':

The feast in question was held by Aegir, god of the sea, at his hall; 18 gods and goddesses are named as present (that includes Aegir, the host, Loki, the gatecrasher, and Thor, who arrived late); and the murder of Balder took place on an entirely different occasion.   *FLS News* 35 (Nov. 2001)

A scene of consternation as a group of diners from 1851 realize that their party consists of thirteen people.

A further explanation is the equally erroneous notion that because witches gathered in covens of thirteen it became unlucky for ordinary people to do so. As detailed above (THIRTEEN) this 'misrepresentation' was put forward by Margaret Murray, but is not borne out by the evidence. Even if witch covens and sabbaths had not existed almost exclusively in the minds of the witchcraft prosecutors, those accused of being witches rarely mentioned the number thirteen in their confessions. Indeed, as also discussed above, before the Reformation thirteen was a normal number for organizing people in places such as a monastery or almshouse. It was a godly way of doing things because it directly copied what Jesus himself had done. It was only after the Reformation that thirteen persons could possibly be thought unlucky.

Dorset *Folk-Lore* 89 (1978) 158. Devon *Devonshire Assoc.* 10 (1878) 104; Hewett (1900) 57. Cornwall *Old Cornwall* 2 (1931–6). 38. Berkshire Lowsley (1888) 22. Oxfordshire [1850s?] Plowman (1919) 117; [1920s] Surman (1992) 62. Worcestershire/Shropshire *Gent. Mag.* (1855) 385. Warwickshire Bloom (*c.*1930) 42. Suffolk Moor (1823)

427–8; Fitzgerald (1887) 384. Lincolnshire Swaby (1891) 92; Good (1900) 108; Sutton (1992) 128–9. Shropshire Burne (1883) 262–3. England Addy (1895) 96. Northern England Henderson (1866) 33. Yorkshire Nicholson (1890) 43. Lancashire [*c.*1915] Corbridge (1964) 156–60. Co. Durham Leighton (1910) 51. Northumberland Bosanquet (1929) 76. West Wales Davies (1911) 216. Scotland Jamieson, *Scottish Dict.* (1808) 'De'il's dozen'. Highland Scotland Macbain (1887/88) 270; Polson (1926) 127. Glasgow [1985] Opie & Tatem, 398. Banffshire *Folk-Lore Jnl* 1 (1883) 363–4. Dumfriesshire Shaw (1890) 13. Jersey *Folk-Lore* 25 (1914) 247. New South Wales (Scottish) [1844] Boswell (1965) 97. Unlocated *Athenian Mercury* (June 1695) quoted John Aubrey, *Miscellanies* (1857 edn) 207–8. General *Gent. Mag.* (1796) 573; N&Q 4S:11 (1873) 330; *Folk-Lore* 38 (1927) 307; *FLS News* 35 (Nov. 2001) 14–15. Literary Addison, *Spectator* (8 Mar. 1711); Grose (1787) 69; *Illustrated London News* (27 Dec. 1851) 779; Igglesden (*c.*1932) 58. France N&Q 4S:11 (1873) 330.

thorns

As with many everyday ailments and problems, anyone with a thorn or splinter in their flesh has a choice of traditional methods to deal with it, ranging from the magical to the herbal. In the former sphere, it was common to recite a CHARM while attempting the extraction, and in common with most verbal charms designed for healing, thorn charms do little more than evoke an appropriate image from Christ's life – in this case the crown of thorns:

I send you a charm which the old women in Wiltshire vow to be very efficacious. When I came home from birds'-nesting, with my hands, and sometimes my face, well studded with thorns, they were extracted with a needle, and the finger passed over the wound, with these words:

> *Unto the Virgin Mary our Saviour he was born*
> *And on his head he wore the crown of thorn*
> *If you believe this true, and mind it well*
> *This hurt will never fester, nor yet swell.*
> Wiltshire *Athenaeum* (1846)

The briar that spreads, the thorn that grows, the sharp spike that pierced the brow of Christ, give you power to draw this thorn from the flesh, or let it perish inside; in the name of the Trinity, Amen. Ireland Wilde (1888)

These charms were widely used over Britain and Ireland, although Scotland is strangely absent from the recorded versions listed below. The actual words vary considerably, but the core symbolism is always the same, and has been since the first known versions in Howard's *Defensative Against Supposed Prophesies* (1583), and in those noted by Samuel Pepys:

Jesus that was of virgin born, was pricked both with nail and thorn;
It neither wealed, nor belled, rankled, nor boned;
In the name of Jesus no more shall this.

Christ was of a virgin born,
And he was pricked with a thorn;
And it did neither bell, nor swell;
And I trust in Jesus this never will.
London Pepys, *Diary* (31 Dec. 1664)

More direct methods of dealing with a thorn involved the application of certain substances reputed to be effective in 'drawing out' or 'expelling' poisons or foreign bodies from a wound. A FOX's tongue was often recommended here:

In County Louth about twenty years ago a girl drove a needle into her hand, and as the local dispensary doctor could do nothing for her, her parents had recourse to a wise man then living near Castlebellingham. He prescribed the

making of a hole in the patient near where the needle was supposed to be, and the insertion of a fox's tongue and a magnet, asserting that this combination was strong enough to 'draw a needle out of the Devil'. I believe that this treatment was tried, but I never heard the result.
Co. Louth *Folk-Lore* (1908)

This cure seems particularly well known in Ireland, but is also reported from late Victorian Yorkshire. An alternative remedy was an adderskin, which had to be used with care as it would repel rather than draw the thorn:

The skin cast by a snake is very useful in extracting thorns, &c. from the body, but, unlike other remedies, it is repellent, not attractive; hence it must always be applied on the opposite side top that on which the thorn entered. In some cases where the skin has been applied on the same side, it has forced the thorn completely through the hand. Devon/Cornwall N&Q (1851)

Other cures recommended were the application of heated cobbler's wax, a piece of fat bacon, or, in a sixteenth-century manuscript from Guernsey, the plant clary, or wild sage. A handful of references indicate a belief that if you bite or eat the thorn once it has been extracted, the wound will not fester.

See also SNAKES.

Charms: Sussex Henderson (1879) 171. Somerset [1946] Tongue (1965) 223. **Devon** *Devonshire Assoc.* 18 (1886) 104; *Devonshire Assoc.* 27 (1895) 65–6; Hewett (1900) 71; *Folk-Lore* 11 (1900) 217; *Devonshire Assoc.* 63 (1931) 130; *Devonshire Assoc.* 88 (1956) 256–7. **Cornwall** N&Q 2S:4 (1857) 25; Hunt (1865) 213–14; Couch (1871) 149; Dyer (1880) 173; *Folk-Lore Jnl* 5 (1887) 200–1. **Western England** *Athenaeum* (1846) 1018. **Wiltshire** *Athenaeum* (1846) 956. **London** Samuel Pepys, *Diary* (31 Dec. 1664). **Gloucestershire** *Folk-Lore* 13 (1902) 173. **Herefordshire** [1804] Leather (1912) 73. **Northamptonshire** N&Q 1S:2 (1850) 36–7. **East Anglia** Varden (1885) 100–1. **Suffolk** Glyde (1866) 173. **Shropshire** Burne (1883) 185; *Folk-Lore* 6 (1895) 202–4. **Yorkshire** Halliwell (1849) 211. **Pembrokeshire** *Archaeologia Cambrensis* 89 (1934) 183–4. **Ireland** Wilde (1888) 190–1; Logan (1981) 112–14. **Unlocated** *Folk-Lore* 53 (1942) 125–6. **General** N. Howard, *Defensative Against Supposed Prophecies* (1583).
Fox tongue: Yorkshire *Folk-Lore* 8 (1897) 387. **Co. Cork** [1937] Culloty (1993) 62. **Co. Louth** *Folk-Lore* 19 (1908) 317. **Co. Donegal** *Folk-Lore* 4 (1893) 351. **Co. Leitrim** *Folk-Lore* 5 (1894) 199.
Snakeskin: Devon/Cornwall N&Q 1S:3 (1851) 259. **Devon** *Devonshire Assoc.* 92 (1960) 372. **Herefordshire** Leather (1912) 81.
Miscellaneous: Devon *Devonshire Assoc.* 88 (1956) 256–7. **Ireland** Logan (1981) 114. **N. Ireland** Foster (1951) 60. **Guernsey** [1589] *Channel Islands Ann. Anth.* (1972–3) 24.

Biting: Devon *Devonshire Assoc.* 17 (1885) 122. **East Anglia** Forby (1830) 415. **Co. Longford** *Béaloideas* 6 (1936) 267.

thread/string

There are strong traditions that a piece of RED THREAD tied around a person or farm animal protects it from witchcraft and/or cures or prevents a range of ailments – especially NOSE-BLEED and RHEUMATISM. Many other sources simply describe a thread being used, but without mentioning any colour, and while it is likely that some of these belong to the same tradition, there were apparently many different beliefs with this basic feature.

Thread cures were reported from most parts of the British Isles, but a particularly strong tradition existed in Scotland, where it was combined with a verbal CHARM to alleviate a SPRAIN:

The following charm is applied for the cure of sprains. A linen thread is tied about the injured part after the solemn repetition of the charm. The thread is called the 'wristing thread', from the wrist or ankle being the part to which it is most commonly applied:

> *Our Saviour rade*
> *His fore foot slade*
> *Our Saviour lighted down*
> *Sinew to sinew, joint to joint*
> *Blood to blood and bone to bone*
> *Mend thou in God's name.*

Orkney N&Q (1854)

A thread having on it nine knots, was tied round the sprained part. As the thread was being tied the following incantation was muttered:

> *Nine knots upo' this thread*
> *Nine blessings on thy head*
> *Blessings to take away thy pain*
> *And ilka tinter of thy strain fire.*

Orkney Mackenzie (1895)

Again, knots are a regular feature of thread cures, presumably, in the case of the sprain, symbolizing the pain of the damaged muscles. Elsewhere, threads and ribbons were used to cure a range of ailments, and silk or velvet was often specified:

I know of more than one person in a good social position who profess to have been cured of a rheumatic affection by wearing a skein of silk round the affected part – who still wear it, and who say that since they have done so, they have had no return of the rheumatism.

Unlocated N&Q (1874)

I knew a baby that always wore a mysterious black velvet band round its neck, which the mother said was a certain preventive against teething troubles for all her children had worn a like talisman in infancy and no one of them had ever had any difficulty in cutting its teeth.

Unlocated Wright (1913)

The latter is at a halfway point between protection and cure. A statement made in the 1893 volume of *Folk-Lore*, on customs in Dublin, simply states, 'A thread is sometimes tied round the toe of a corpse', and unfortunately gives no further information. Nevertheless, a participant in a BBC radio programme in 1966 commented that sailors would 'put twine round their toe to ward off the Devil' (*see* Opie & Tatem, 402).

See also CLOTHES: THREAD/PIN LEFT IN.

Devon *Devonshire Assoc.* 21 (1889) 114–15. **Cornwall** *Devonshire Assoc.* 9 (1877) 96. **Gloucestershire** N&Q 4S:11 (1873) 499. **Lancashire** Harland & Wilkinson (1882) 75. **Highland Scotland** Macbain (1887/88) 258. **Banffshire** Gregor (1874) 269. **Orkney/Shetland** Brand (1703) 117. **Orkney** N&Q 1S:10 (1854) 221; Mackenzie (1895) 73. **Shetland** *New Stat. Acct Scotland* (1845) 141. **Dublin** *Folk-Lore* 4 (1893) 363. **Co. Longford** *Béaloideas* 6 (1936) 266. **Unlocated** N&Q 2S:12 (1861) 492; N&Q 5S:1 (1874) 204; Wright (1913) 248; [1966] Opie & Tatem, 402.

three breakages

A specialized version of the general idea that bad luck comes in THREES holds that if you break something, it will be the first of three:

One of my servants having accidentally broken a glass shade, asked for two other articles of little value, a wine bottle and a jam crock, that she might break them, and so prevent the two other accidents, perhaps to valuable articles, which would otherwise follow the accident to the glass shade.

Unlocated N&Q (1891)

The idea was reasonably widespread in the late nineteenth century, but has so far only been traced back to the 1860s.

Devon *Devonshire Assoc.* 8 (1876) 57. **Herefordshire** Leather (1912) 87–8. **East Anglia** Varden (1885) 114. **Suffolk** Chambers 2 (1864) 105. **Lincolnshire** Sutton (1992) 140. **Shropshire** Burne (1883) 281. **England** Addy (1895) 94. **Yorkshire** Blakeborough (1898) 127. **Lancashire** *Lancashire Lore* (1971) 66. **Co. Durham** Leighton (1910) 62. **Unlocated** N&Q 7S:12 (1891) 489.

three

In general in British superstition, odd NUMBERS are held to be preferable to even ones, and three is often included in that positive light. But in other contexts, three is definitely unlucky – a death in a community will always be followed by two others; break one thing, break three; lighting THREE CIGARETTES from one match is fatal; and it is usually three DEATH KNOCKS that are heard. In addition, there is the general 'rule' that bad things come in threes, which can be interpreted broadly:

Bad luck and tragedy had to be tidied up for our Mum by running in threes, whether it was another dreaded conception by one of her neighbours, the death of a public figure, a whitlow, or a broken tea cup, the fates combined to keep her on tenterhooks until she had heard of a second and third occurrence.   London [1920s] Gamble

or more narrowly defined:

[Grammar school boy at the site of a crashed British plane] *Two plane crashes in two days, if there's two there's bound to be three.*
Norfolk [1940] *Mass Observation Diary* of Muriel Green

'Bad things come in threes' is still heard regularly, but so is 'third time lucky'.

Dorset Udal (1922) 283. **London** [1920s] Gamble (1979) 89. **Northamptonshire** Sternberg (1851) 171. **Suffolk** *Gent. Mag.* (1867) 307–22. **Norfolk** *Mass Observation Diary* of Muriel Green, quoted in Sheridan (1990) 85. **Yorkshire** Nicholson (1890) 47–8. **Lancashire** *Lancashire Lore* (1971) 6. **Galloway** Mactaggart (1824) 211. **Literary** Addison, *Spectator* (8 Mar. 1711).

three candles

see CANDLES: THREE

three cigarettes

A relatively well-known, but under-documented, belief holds that it is unlucky to light three cigarettes with the same match. The earliest known reference is a letter from a Private Bradstow, published in *Notes & Queries* in March 1916:

A smokers' superstition – What is the origin of the extremely common superstition against lighting three cigarettes with one match? Hundreds of times I have seen two cigarettes lit up, and then the match solemnly blown out lest it should light the third; but if there are four cigarettes to light there is no objection!
Unlocated N&Q (1916)

It is clear from this that the superstition was already widely known, and within three weeks of publication two other correspondents had provided slightly different versions of what is now the standard origin-story:

Some soldiers, during a war, were in a supposed place of safety, and thought they would smoke. One of these, after lighting the cigarettes of two men, was in the act of lighting his own (with the same match) when he was shot dead by the enemy. The idea was that if the match had been

extinguished after the second man had 'lighted up' the third man would not have been seen and shot. The light lasted just that fraction of a second too long. Hence the superstition that it is unlucky to light three cigarettes with one match.
Unlocated N&Q (1916)

The second writer sets the scene in the Boer War. Another informant, George Coppard, who published his war diaries in 1968, includes a description of the superstition, mentioning the Boer War origin, under the section for June 1915, but does not actually state that he knew the belief at that time. The fact that the belief, and the soldier-related story, first appears during the Great War gives us confidence to assume that it was then a relatively new superstition, although one of A. R. Wright's informants claimed to have known it in the Boer War. As such, the three-cigarettes belief could simply have been invented sometime in the Boer War, and become widely disseminated in the trenches between 1914 and 1916. Once there, we know from the Angel of Mons episode the speed with which such beliefs could spread in an army at the front. Nevertheless, published Boer War diaries do not seem to mention the superstition.

So the matter would rest, were it not for Private Bradstow's last sentence, where he states that there was no objection to *four* cigarettes. We have no confirmation that his interpretation was correct, but if he was not mistaken, the story about the enemy sniper collapses, as in that case a *fourth* light would certainly be more unlucky than a *third*. In the private's version, the focus is apparently on the number three, rather than the time-lag between first and last cigarette. There were other superstitions in which THREE LIGHTS or candles were considered unlucky, or sometimes as lucky. It has been suggested that the cigarette belief was descended from them, but at the present state of knowledge this is far from proven and must remain so until further examples are brought to light.

Oxfordshire [1920s] Surman (1992) 62. Warwickshire [1970s] FLS News 39 (Feb. 2003) 8. Australia Folk-Lore 42 (1931) 197. Unlocated N&Q 12S:1 (1916) 208; N&Q 12S:1 (1916) 276. General [1915?] Coppard (1968) 20; Folk-Lore 37 (1926) 299; Folk-Lore 38 (1927) 205–6.

three deaths

The worst example of the negative sides of the number THREE maintains that once death has visited a community, it will come three times:

One funeral makes three, that is, should there have been an interval of some duration without any burial taking place, and then death occurs, two more will speedily follow.
Lincolnshire Gutch & Peacock (1908)

As with the other superstitions based on the number three, this one has not been traced before the 1850s, but it was widely known right into the late twentieth century – and may be believed still.

Sussex Sussex County Mag. (1943) 288; [1984] Opie & Tatem, 403. Dorset Folklore 89 (1978) 158. Herefordshire Francis Kilvert, Diary (26 Dec. 1878). Lincolnshire Gutch & Peacock (1908) 237; [c.1940s] Sutton (1992) 163. Northern England Henderson (1866) 46. Yorkshire N&Q 2S:5 (1858) 209; Blakeborough (1898) 127. Lancashire Harland & Wilkinson (1873) 228; Lancashire Lore (1971) 54. Northumberland [1850s] Denham Tracts 2 (1895) 271–2. Radnorshire [1953] Opie & Tatem, 403. Hebrides Beckwith (1964) 172–3.

three dishes divination

A well-known divinatory custom, known all over Britain and Ireland, but most often reported from Scotland. The process involves a blindfolded person choosing one of three (occasionally more) dishes or objects which symbolize that person's future. The classic description appears in a note to Robert Burns' poem 'Hallowe'en':

Take three dishes, put clean water in one, foul water in another, and leave the third empty; blindfold a person, and lead him to the hearth where the dishes are ranged; he (or she) dips the left hand; if by chance in the clean water, the future husband or wife will come to the bar of matrimony, a maid; if in the foul, a widow; if in the empty dish, it foretells, with equal certainty, no marriage at all. It is repeated three times, and every time the arrangement of the dishes is altered.
Scotland Robert Burns (1786)

The symbolic items can vary: gold ring, another ring, thimble; earth, water, meal; and in an Isle of Man version, other items, such as a piece of net, were added to symbolize different trades. The procedure could also take place out of doors, for example in the harvest field (Berkshire Salmon (1902)).

The majority of instances took place at the key points in the year known for divination – HALLOWE'EN, NEW YEAR, MIDSUMMER.

Devon N&Q 3S:2 (1862) 62. Berkshire Salmon (1902) 422. Gloucestershire [c.1890s] Folk-Lore 34 (1923) 155. Wales Davies (1911) 12. Scotland Robert Burns, fn. to 'Hallowe'en' (1786). Northeast Scotland Gregor (1874) 105–6. Ireland Gent. Mag. (1865) 702. Isle of Man Folk-Lore 2 (1891) 311.

three drains

see PAVEMENTS.

three: third time lucky

Although a well-known proverbial phrase, the idea that a third attempt is likely to be successful does not appear in many folklore collections, perhaps because it was too common to be regarded as worth noting:

This is the third Thursday we have retired to rest hoping that the next morning we should welcome home my aunt and cousins – may the third bring its reputed good fortune.
New South Wales (Scottish) [1848] Boswell

If you fail twice in trying to do a thing, you will probably succeed in the third trial. 'The third time's catchy time'.   Co. Durham Leighton (1910)

The notion has been proverbial since at least the fourteenth century, but the wording varies considerably – 'The third is a charm', 'The third pays for all', 'The third time pays home', or, as in *Sir Gawain and the Green Knight*, 'Third time prove best'.

Birmingham [1987] Opie & Tatem, 403–4. Co. Durham Leighton (1910) 62. Wales Trevelyan (1909) 326. Scotland Kelly (1721) 26. New South Wales (Scottish) [1848] Boswell (1965) 161. Literary Sir Gawain and the

Green Knight (c.1380) line 1680; Shakespeare, *Twelfth Night* (1601) 5:1. **General** J. Higgins, *First Parte of Mirror for Magistrates* 1 (1574) 24; *Warning for Fair Women* (1599) E3.

---

throat cures: stocking

A widespread cure for a sore throat was to tie a stocking around it, in most cases one which had been worn that day:

If you have a sore throat put a stocking round it and keep it there overnight. It has to be the stocking you've worn that day, and put the foot part round the painful part of your throat. It's probably a sock for a man and a stocking for a woman. I learnt this from my mother in the 1920s.

South London [Dec. 2001] Steve Roud Collection

A number of informants insisted on the *left* stocking, while others maintained, more logically, that the stocking should be filled with heated salt or sand:

We had a salt cure for sore throats. You put a packet of salt in a saucepan and make it very hot. Then you empty it into a woman's nylon stocking and let it cool a little but not too much. Then you tie it round your throat and there's something in the salt that cure tonsillitis.

Irish Travellers [1940s] Joyce

On present evidence, this is a mainly English and Irish, late nineteenth- and twentieth-century belief only, but it was still being quoted (at least by old people) at the time of writing.

References marked * specify the *left* stocking: **Sussex** [c.1900] Arthur (1989) 42. **Somerset** [1923] Opie & Tatem, 377 **Devon** * *Devonshire Assoc.* 67 (1935) 138. **Surrey** [1965] *Opie & Tatem, 377–8. **South London** [Dec. 2001] Steve Roud Collection. **Essex** [c.1917] Mays (1969) 165. **Herefordshire** * Leather (1912) 81. **Bedfordshire** Marsom (1950) 183. **Norfolk** [c.1920] Wigby (1976) 66. **Suffolk** Claxton (1954) 90. **Lincolnshire** Sutton (1992) 151. **Northumberland** *Bigge (1860–62) 93; [c.1905] Peacock (1986) 73. **N. Ireland** Foster (1951) 60. **Irish Travellers** [1940s] Joyce (1985) 16.

---

thrush (*Candidosis*)

The yeast infection commonly called 'thrush' was previously common in children, where it was characterized by white patches in the mouth, and thus often locally called 'white mouth'. It was thought particularly susceptible to semi-magical cures, and a range of remedies have been reported. Cures for mouth and throat ailments often included blowing or breathing into the

mouth of the patient, and this approach predominated in thrush remedies. The person doing the breathing was usually somebody with special gifts – a POSTHUMOUS CHILD, a LEFT TWIN, or someone with a reputation for charming – or it could be an animal, such as a gander, duck or FROG.

It is believed that everyone has 'thrush' once in his life, either soon after birth, or shortly before death; if an adult has it during illness, recovery is thought impossible. A Pembridge woman used to think that she cured her baby of thrush by holding the head of a live frog in its mouth. 'Not to touch, mind,' she said, 'but to get the breath. I mind one time as I done it, the frog drawed a breath and puffed hisself out ever so, and the youngster was well the day after'.

Herefordshire Leather (1912)

It is not altogether clear whether people believed that the breath had curative power, or the disease was being TRANSFERRED to the breather. In the case of an animal, presumably the latter, but in the case of a human charmer this would seem unlikely.

A different approach was more explicit in the way it worked:

Take three rushes from any running stream, and pass them separately through the mouth of the infant; then plunge the rushes again into the stream and as the current bears them away, so will the thrush depart from the child.

Devon N&Q (1853)

RUNNING WATER also features in cures for other diseases. Some informants suggested that reciting the second verse of the eighth Psalm added to the cure's power: 'Out of the mouth of babes and sucklings hast thou ordained strength because of thine enemies, that thou mightest still the enemy and the avenger'.

Sussex Latham (1878) 47; *Sussex County Mag.* 5 (1931) 122; Allen (1995) 154–5. **Devon** Bray (1838) 293; N&Q 1S:2 (1850) 512; N&Q 1S:8 (1853) 146; *Devonshire Assoc.* 21 (1889) 114–15; Baring-Gould (1901) 126; N&Q 9S:12 (1903) 47; *Devonshire Assoc.* 60 (1928) 123–4; *Devonshire Assoc.* 85 (1953) 218. **Cornwall** N&Q 1S:12 (1855) 37; Couch (1871) 165; *Devonshire Assoc.* 9 (1877) 96; *Folk-Lore Jnl* 5 (1887) 210; *Jnl Royal Inst. Cornwall* 20 (1915) 130. **Essex** *Folklore* 70 (1959) 414. **Warwickshire** *Folk-Lore* 24 (1913) 241; Bloom (c.1930) 25. **Worcestershire** *Folk-Lore* 28 (1917) 311. **Worcestershire/Shropshire** *Gent. Mag.* (Oct. 1855) 386. **Herefordshire** Leather (1912) 82. **Norfolk** Dew (1898) 77–81. **Lincolnshire** N&Q 3S:9 (1866) 319. **Cheshire?** N&Q 1S:8 (1853) 265; *Folk-Lore* 66 (1955) 326–7. **Shropshire** Burne (1883) 200–1; *Folk-Lore* 49 (1938) 229. **England** Addy (1895) 92. **Yorkshire** Nicholson (1890) 141; Morris (1911) 247. **Ireland** N&Q

6S:3 (1881) 163; Hickey (1938) 269; Logan (1981) 53. **Co. Kerry** *Folk-Lore* 19 (1908) 316. **Co. Cork** *Folk-Lore* 8 (1897) 180; [1937] Culloty (1993) 58–9. **Co. Longford** *Béaloideas* 6 (1936) 266. **Unlocated** Aubrey, *Miscellanies* (1696/1857) 137–8; Chambers 1 (1878) 733.

thumbs

Thumbs have featured in a number of non-superstitious gestures for centuries, to signal, for example, a greeting, to seal a bargain, and as a symbol of approval or affirmation. However, the thumb also featured in a widespread protective and good-luck gesture, long before CROSSED FINGERS were even heard of:

Children, to avoid approaching danger, are taught to double the thumb within the hand. This was much practised whilst the terrors of witchcraft remained. It was a custom to fold the thumbs of dead persons within the hand, to prevent the power of evil spirits over the deceased. Northumberland Hutchinson (1778)

Several other reports speak of children adopting the gesture when passing the house of a suspected witch. To illustrate the longevity of the custom, Opie and Tatem print an example from Ovid's *Fasti*, from the first century AD, in which it was used against ghosts, and also a quotation from the 1980s in which an actress described an effect very similar to the modern fingers-crossing:

My mother always used to say that she'd hold her thumbs for me, on a first night. Gloucestershire [1987] Opie & Tatem

London [1984] Opie & Tatem, 404–5. **Gloucestershire** [1987] Opie & Tatem, 405. **Shropshire** Burne (1883) 273–4. **Northern England** Brockett (1829) 85. **Yorkshire** Hone, *Table Book* 2 (1827) 583; Ford (1953) 97. **Co. Durham** *Folk-Lore Record* (1879) 205. **Northumberland** Hutchinson 2 (1778) App. 4. **Scotland** Chambers (1826) 278. **General** Grose (1787) 29–30. **Classical** Ovid, *Fasti* 5 (*c.*AD 17) lines 433–6.

thunder and lightning: doors open

A widespread strategy for dealing with the perceived danger of thunder and lightning was to ensure that if it hit the house, it could escape without causing damage. Doors and windows were therefore opened as soon as the storm appeared:

There were lights in the houses all over the village and the cottage doors and windows were opened wide to let the lightning out easily if it should come in. Wiltshire Kilvert, *Diary* (23 July 1874)

As with the related belief that mirrors and other shiny objects should be covered in a thunderstorm, there is no sign of this belief before the mid nineteenth century, but it was still widespread in the twentieth.

Kent [1930s] Kent (1977) 93. **Wiltshire** Francis Kilvert, *Diary* (23 July 1874). **Suffolk** Gurdon (1893) 135. **Lincolnshire** Watkins (1886) 12. **Derbyshire** [1890s] Uttley (1946) 132. **Lancashire** *Lancashire Lore* (1971) 66.

thunder and lightning: pointing/counting

A few references deal with apparently linked beliefs warning against drawing attention to thunder and lightning, by pointing, counting, or even speaking of it:

It is wicked to point towards the part of the heavens from which lightning is expected. I have seen a little boy, for this offence, made to kneel blindfold on the floor, to teach him how he would feel if the lightning came and blinded him. Unlocated N&Q (1862)

the boys of the place believed that if they made any mention of the lightning immediately after the flash 'the seat of their trousers would be torn out' as one graphically described it to me. This was some years ago, and I well remember the attempts that were made at different times to induce some one to speak of the lightning to see if the accident really would take place. Yorkshire N&Q (1890)

These can be compared with the more common notions about the impropriety of POINTING at the MOON, STARS and RAINBOWS. It was also reported, from Essex about 1917, that it was unlucky to count the interval between the lightning flash and the thunder clap. This is surprising, as many people do this in modern times to 'work out how far away the storm is'.

Devon N&Q 11S:12 (1915) 257. **Essex** [*c.*1917] Mays (1969) 164. **Yorkshire** N&Q 7S:9 (1890) 244. **Unlocated** N&Q 3S:2 (1862) 342.

thunder and lightning: reflective surfaces

It was believed important to protect the household in a thunderstorm by covering all mirrors and other reflective surfaces. This included items made of metal, such as knives and forks, scissors and needles, and even jugs of water.

She put all the cutlery away because she said if you touched knives and forks during a storm you would get a shock. Then she turned all the mirrors to the wall in case the house caught fire. She believed you would get bad luck if you didn't turn the mirrors round. Lincolnshire Sutton (1992)

The perception of the danger of light-reflecting objects when lightning was threatened hardly needs explanation, but all the recorded examples are from England, and the majority from the twentieth century. However, two of the correspondents to N&Q in 1900 write of knowing the belief for 'fifty years', so it must be mid Victorian at least. A different belief, reported from Scotland and Ireland, recommended putting metal (e.g. the tongs) into the fire (*see* THUNDER AND LIGHTNING: TONGS).

See also MIRRORS: THUNDER AND LIGHTNING.

Kent [1930s] Kent (1977) 93. Wiltshire *Wilts. N&Q* 1 (1893–5) 316. London N&Q 9S:6 (1900) 131; [1920s] Gamble (1979) 89; [1985] Opie & Tatem, 251. Essex [*c*.1917] Mays (1969) 163. Hertfordshire N&Q 9S:6 (1900) 7. Cambridgeshire Porter (1969) 69. Suffolk Evans (1965) 218. Lincolnshire Sutton (1992) 139. Staffordshire [1850s] N&Q 9S:6 (1900) 131. Derbyshire [1890s] Uttley (1946) 132. Derbyshire *Daily Express* (10 Aug. 1954). Yorkshire Gill (1993) 94. Lancashire [*c*.1915] Corbridge (1964) 156–60; *Lancashire Lore* (1971) 66. Unlocated [1850s] N&Q 9S:6 (1900) 131. Literary Charles Dickens, *Martin Chuzzlewit* (1843–4) Ch. 43.

thunder and lightning: ripens corn

Sheet lightning had its uses:

An old lady living near to me was conversing with a neighbour during one of these displays and remarked that there was nothing to cause alarm, as sheet-lightning was just sent to ripen the corn. This belief, I have since heard, is current in Wiltshire among the farm-folk.

Wiltshire N&Q (1938)

This was certainly more widespread than the following few twentieth-century references indicate, but until more examples are found we cannot assess just how widely known it was.

Wiltshire N&Q 175 (1938) 172. Lincolnshire N&Q 175 (1938) 214. Lancashire [*c*.1915] Corbridge (1964) 156–60.

thunder and lightning: sours drink

It is still common knowledge that milk will go sour if left out of the fridge in thundery weather, but in the past this was also said of other liquids, particularly beer. The remedy was to place a heavy weight, such as an iron bar, on the receptacle which held the liquor:

In Herefordshire, and other parts, they do put a cold iron bar upon their barrels, to preserve their beer from being soured by thunder. This is common practice in Kent.

Herefordshire/Kent Aubrey, *Miscellanies* (1696)

This precaution shows that whereas the modern believer would explain that the atmosphere in a thunderstorm turns sultry, so affecting the milk, our ancestors believed that it was the vibrations of the thunder which did the damage. This reasonable picture is complicated, however, by an allied belief, still reported well into the twentieth century:

A Fen mother would never suckle her child during a thunderstorm; she would draw off the milk, which was thought to be tainted with brimstone and sulphur, and throw it away.

Cambridgeshire Porter (1969)

Kent Aubrey, *Miscellanies* (1696/1857) 140, and *Remaines* (1686/1880) 22. Devon Hewett (1900) 50. Herefordshire Aubrey, *Miscellanies* (1696/1857) 140, and *Remaines* (1686/1880) 22. Cambridgeshire Porter (1969) 17. England Addy (1895) 87. Co. Tyrone *Lore & Language* 1:7 (1972) 9. Literary John Gay, *The Shepherd's Week* (1714) Wednesday, lines 43–4; Tobias Smollett, *The Expedition of Humphry Clinker* (1771). General *The Agreeable Companion* (1742) 42.

thunder and lightning: tongs

In one of the main English thunder beliefs, people are warned not to touch bright metal items such as scissors and knives (*see* THUNDER AND LIGHTNING: REFLECTIVE SURFACES); but in a different approach reported more rarely from Scotland and Ireland, we are advised to place iron in the fire to avert danger:

In a storm of thunder and lightning iron, for instance the poker and tongs, put in the fire, averts all danger from the house. This curious belief seems to have been widespread at one time throughout the western Highlands, though now its memory barely survives.

Highland Scotland Campbell (1900)

Highland Scotland Macbain (1887/88) 270; Campbell (1900) 135. Co. Longford *Béaloideas* 6 (1936) 263.

tide

Considering the ubiquity of notions that the MOON's phases affect many aspects of human life and health, it is not surprising that the tide was believed to have a somewhat similar effect, at least in coastal areas. The basic idea was that births took place at the flowing of the tide, and deaths at its ebb. This was the natural state of things, for animals as well as humans, and any deviation from the pattern was unlucky.

A very widely-spread belief exists all along the sea-coast of Wales as to the effect the tide has on human life. It is believed that children are born as the tide comes in, and people die as the tide goes out. The late Mr Noott, of Cardigan, a doctor with a large practice, was firmly persuaded that this was the case, and he ushered hundreds of children into the world in his time and stood beside very many death-beds.
                                        Wales Folk-Lore (1898)

The state of the tide was anxiously watched when anyone lay ill in the house, as they would be in particular danger every time the tide turned. This idea was expressed in the earliest British reference, by the East Anglian agricultural writer Thomas Tusser:

*Tyde flowing is feared, for many a thing
Great danger to such as be sick it doth bring,*
                                        Suffolk Tusser (1557)

and it was clearly known to Shakespeare when he described Falstaff dying at the turn of the tide (*Henry V* (1600)). Dickens also used the idea in *David Copperfield* (1850). Surprisingly, the notion still seems current at the end of the twentieth century:

Question: Does anyone have evidence suggesting that sheep tend to give birth when the tide is high in coastal regions? **Guardian** (1 Dec. 1989)

The basic belief was well known all over Europe, and was also well documented in classical times. See, for example, Pliny's *Natural History* (AD 77) where he quotes Aristotle to the effect that 'no animal dies except when the tide is ebbing', and comments that this has been found true of humans as well.

In some Scottish fishing communities, the state of the tide, like the phase of the moon, was taken even more seriously, regulating when people got married, when important tasks were commenced, when eggs were set under hens, and even when to pull up weeds in the garden.

Somerset [1939] Tongue (1965) 136. **Cornwall** N&Q 1S:12 (1855) 38; Couch (1871) 168; Folk-Lore Jnl 5 (1887) 217. **Suffolk** Thomas Tusser, *Five Hundred Points of Good Husbandrie* (1557) Ch. 14. **Norfolk** Varden (1885) 117. **Yorkshire** N&Q 1S:6 (1852) 311–12; Henderson (1866) 41–2. **Lancashire** *Lancashire Lore* (1971) 49–50. **Co. Durham** Leighton (1910) 51. **England** Folk-Lore 68 (1957) 413. **Wales** Folk-lore 9 (1898) 189. **Northeast Scotland** Gregor (1881) 141. **Banffshire** Folk-Lore Jnl 4 (1886) 9. **Shetland** Gent. Mag. (1882) 362; Vickery (1995) 372. **Orkney** Old Stat. Acct Scotland 15 (1791–99) 311. **Isle of Man** [c.1850] Cashen (1912) 6. **General** Guardian (1 Dec. 1989). **Literary** Shakespeare, *Henry V* (1600) 2:3; Charles Dickens, *David Copperfield* (1850) Ch. 30. **Classical** Pliny, *Natural History* (AD 77) Bk 2, Ch. 101; N&Q 9S:8 (1901) 232. For some continental references, *see* Lean 2 (1903) 576.

tide: cures

The well-known idea that the tide 'takes things away' (*see above*) is at the root of a cure recommended for a range of ailments, particularly WHOOPING COUGH and fever:

To cure fever, place the patient on the sandy shore when the tide is coming in, and the retreating waves will carry away the disease and leave him well. **Ireland** Wilde (1888)

In the case of whooping cough, the effectiveness of the tide is combined with the notion that breathing particular 'airs' can help cure it, and the fresh air of the seaside was regularly recommended (*see* AIR CURES). In addition, in cases where sea-water itself was believed to have curative properties, it had extra efficacy if it was gathered at the time of the incoming tide. Tide-cure beliefs were far more widespread than is indicated by the few references listed here.

Lincolnshire Sutton (1992) 152. **Yorkshire** Wright (1978) 18. **Lancashire** *Manchester Guardian* (13 Oct. 1956) 5. **Wales** Trevelyan (1909) 320. **Aberdeenshire** Folk-Lore Jnl 2 (1884) 356. **Ireland** Wilde (1888) 206.

'tinker, tailor'

The extremely well-known fortune-telling rhyme, used mainly by children while counting fruit stones, buttons, beads on a necklace, spikelets on rye grass, or anything else close to hand, and thereby foretelling their own destiny, or that of their future husband:

Tinker, tailor, soldier, sailor,
Rich man, poor man, beggarman, thief.

Oxfordshire [1920s] Harris

This is quite a standard version, but the exact words have varied considerably over the years:

Rich man, poor man, beggar man, farmer, tinker,
tailor, plough-boy, thief.

Herefordshire Leather (1912)

A lord, a laird, a couper [horse thief], a caird, a
rich man, a poor man, a hangman, a thief.

Scotland N&Q (1875)

Soldier, sailor, tinker, tailor, gentleman, apothec-
ary, ploughboy, thief.   England N&Q (1875)

For matrimonial prospects, the items can be counted again to ascertain the wedding vehicle, clothes, and, most importantly, when:

Coach, carriage, wheelbarrow; Silk, satin, cotton,
rags; This year, next year, sometime, or now,
never.   Wiltshire *Wilts. N&Q* (1893–5)

The earliest clear version is published in Moor's dictionary of *Suffolk Words and Phrases* in 1823, although if he was reporting his own childhood, that would set it back to the 1770s. In another context, however, the line 'A soldier and a sailor, a tinker and a taylor' had already appeared in Congreve's play *Love for Love* in 1695. Further back still, Caxton's book on *The Game and Playe of the Chesse* (*c.*1475) gave names indicative of trades to the pawns: Labourer, Smith, Clerk, Merchant, Physician, Taverner, Guard, and Ribald. No clear line of descent has yet been shown from this to our 'Tinker, Tailor' rhyme, but the chessmen remain possible antecedents.

England N&Q 5S:4 (1875) 35. **Somerset** [1923] Opie & Tatem, 52. **Dorset** [1930s] *Folk-Lore* 89 (1978) 155. **Wiltshire** *Wilts. N&Q* 1 (1893–5) 151. **Hampshire** N&Q 9S:6 (1900) 457; [1988] Opie & Tatem, 52. **Oxfordshire** [1920s] Harris (1969) 142. **Huntingdonshire** [1880s] Marshall (1967) 188. **Herefordshire** N&Q 9S:6 (1900) 456–7; Leather (1912) 63. **Northamptonshire** Sternberg (1851) 162. **Suffolk** Moor (1823) 377–8. **Yorkshire** Nicholson (1890) 126. **Manchester** [1953] Opie & Tatem, 52. **Westmorland** *Denham Tracts* 2 (1895) 46. **Wales** Trevelyan (1909) 238. **Scotland** N&Q 5S:3 (1875) 465. **Perthshire** [1954] Opie & Tatem, 52. **Aberdeenshire** N&Q 9S:6 (1900) 273. **Forfarshire** Opie (1959) 338–9. **Unlocated** Halliwell (1849) 222; N&Q 9S:6 (1900) 30, 371. **General** Opie (1951) 404–5 (also lists European analogues).

toad-eaters

At every fair, market, and public gathering until the late nineteenth century, the crowd would expect a mountebank or two, flamboyantly selling wonder cures of his own design and mixing, in addition to more usual herbs and conventional ointments. Mountebanks specialized in crowd-pulling antics and entertainments, and their shows were popular. The widespread notion that toads were poisonous (*see below*) gave rise to a regular section of the show which featured an accomplice who would eat toads, in full view of the crowd, who expected him to die at their feet, and he appeared to do so. But a dose of the wonder cure brought him back to rude health before their very eyes.

See description in Allen (1995) 155–60, relating to Sussex but relevant for the rest of the country.

toadmen

see HORSEMAN'S WORD.

toads: cure King's Evil

One of the main diseases that toads were thought to be particularly effective in curing was SCROF-ULA or the King's Evil. As in other toad cures, part of the toad – or the whole thing baked and powdered – is worn about the person of the sufferer. In the hands of a SEVENTH SON, the cure is even more powerful:

A seventh son . . . is a very potent personage, and
to him, far rather than to any regular practi-
tioner, will the simple people of Devonshire have
recourse in every case of any commonly preva-
lent disease, such as king's evil. A girl thus
afflicted, having gone for advice to a seventh son,
he proceeded to borrow a penknife from a young
woman, without telling her to what purpose he
meant to apply it, and therewith cut off and
skinned the hind leg of a living toad. The skin was
then sewn up in a bag, and the toad buried. The
girl wore the charm around her neck, and as the
buried animal decayed, so did her disease vanish
away.   Devon *Monthly Packet* (1864)

Sussex Latham (1878) 45. **Somerset** Burgess & Rann (1897) 118. **Devon** *Monthly Packet* 28 (1864) 443–7; *Devonshire Assoc.* 11 (1879) 105; Hewett (1900) 76. **Hertfordshire** N&Q 1S:2 (1850) 68. **Shropshire** Burne (1883) 194. **Yorkshire** [*c.*1730] Dawson (1882) 200.

toads: cure nosebleeds

see NOSEBLEED CURES: TOADS.

toads/frogs: in house

Wild animals coming into the house are usually believed to have predictive meaning, and they tend to be either death omens or to mean the arrival of strangers. There is a sharp division in beliefs concerning the meaning of toads or frogs entering the house. In some cases, it is unreservedly positive:

A frog coming in at the door is a sign of marriage in the family.   Co. Longford *Béaloideas* (1936)

But more often the meaning is bad:

If snakes, toads, or frogs enter a house in May, they bring sickness or misfortune.
                    Wales Trevelyan (1909)

and this is often attributed to their traditional connection with witches:

The toad and the black cat are the most usual attendants of the witch, or rather the forms her imps most commonly assume. The appearance of a toad on the doorstep is taken for a certain sign that the house is under evil influence, and the poor reptile is put to some frightfully barbarous death.   Cornwall Couch (1871)

The 'barbarous death' was usually being thrown on the fire. Nevertheless, in some places, the toads were treated more carefully, precisely because they might be connected with witchcraft, and therefore should not be offended. Despite the long-lasting nature of other toad and frog beliefs, concern about them coming into the house is only reported from the 1830s onwards. It is likely that earlier references will be found.

Dorset Roberts (1834) 262. **Somerset** [1922/1923] Opie & Tatem, 408. **Devon** *Devonshire Assoc.* 8 (1876) 52. **Cornwall** Couch (1871) 146. **Herefordshire** [c.1895] *Folk-Lore* 39 (1928) 391. **Wiltshire** [1922] Opie & Tatem, 408. **Norfolk** [c.1870s] Haggard (1935) 18; [1920s] Wigby (1976) 69. **Wales** Trevelyan (1909) 172. **Co. Longford** *Béaloideas* 6 (1936) 260. **Unlocated** Igglesden (c.1932) 97.

toads/frogs: magic bone

A number of traditions relate that there is a particular bone in a toad's body which, if located and removed in the right way, will confer important power on its owner. This bone was regularly cited as the key to the HORSEMAN'S WORD, which involved uncanny mastery over horses.

There are several ways of obtaining this bone. The simplest part was to place the toad on an ant hill and wait for the flesh to be consumed.

Then the 'magical' procedure commenced by throwing the bones into running water:

Toad charm for witching – You take a black toad an' put it in an ant-'ill, an' leave it there while bones is all cleaned. Then take the bones and go down to a good stream of runnin' water an' throw the bones i' the stream. All the bones but one will go down stream an' that one as won't go downstream is the breast-bone. Now, you must get 'old of this 'ere bone afore the Devil gets it, an' if you get it and keep it allus by you – in your pocket, or wear it – then you can witch; as well as that you'll be safe from bein' witched yourself.
                    Lincolnshire Rudkin (1936)

Some versions add various other details, of things happening to test the resolve of the operator. Loud and dreadful noises will occur just behind him, but he will be lost if he looks back or takes his eye off the bone.

The same bone was said to give its owner mastery over women, but women could also use it for their own advantage in 'love magic'. Nevertheless, the element of female coercion means that reported cases nearly always result in an unhappy ending:

In another instance related in East Yorkshire, the girl took a live frog, stuck it all over with pins, put it in a box, kept it shut up for a week, after which she looked in and found that the frog was dead. She kept it until it was consumed away to bones. Then she took out of the frog a small key-shaped bone, got into the company of the young man she wanted, fastened the bone to his coat, and said:

> *I do not want to hurt this frog*
> *But my true lover's heart to turn*
> *Wishing that he no rest may find*
> *Till he come to me and speak his mind*

After this he had a week's torture, as the frog had, and then he went to her and said he had had a queer sensation for a week, but he didn't know what it meant. 'However,' he said, 'I will marry thee, but I know we shall never be happy'. They were married, and lived very uncomfortably together.   Yorkshire Addy (1895)

The belief in the power of this bone has been around in Britain for a long time. Reginald Scot mentions it in his *Discoverie of Witchcraft* (1584), where he describes it as engendering love. The whole idea was probably imported by writers of Scot's generation from the writings of the Roman writer Pliny, who was a great favourite with them. Pliny's account describes letting ants clean the bones of a frog, throwing a special bone into boiling water, and using the bone to gain

Toads and frogs were often included in the list of potential witches' familiars. This woodcut dates from c.1630.

mastery over dogs and, if it is worn as an amulet, it acts as an aphrodisiac.

Cornwall *Old Cornwall* 1:3 (Apr. 1926) 8. **Cambridgeshire** *Folk-Lore* 25 (1914) 363–4. **Norfolk** Haggard (1935) 13–14. **Suffolk** Evans (1960) 260–71. **Lincolnshire** *Folk-Lore* 12 (1901) 168–9; Rudkin (1936) 23. **Yorkshire** Addy (1895) 79. **Western Scotland** Napier (1879) 89–90. **Aberdeenshire** *Folk-Lore* 25 (1914) 363–4. **Northeast Scotland** Gregor (1881) 144. **General** Scot (1584) Bk 6, Ch. 7. **Classical** Pliny, *Natural History* (AD 77) Bk 32, Para. 18.

toads/frogs: meeting

Toads do not have an overly positive reputation in British traditions, being regarded as poisonous, vindictive, and likely to be a witch's familiar, but the main meaning attributed to MEETING one is surprisingly good. In early references, it is clearly a lucky sign:

Meeting with a toad announces success to come, though for myself I can scarcely bear the sight of one.   John of Salisbury, *Policraticus* (1159)

or by meeting of a toad a man should escape a danger, or achieve an enterprise.   Scot (1584)

and similar meanings were still being reported in the twentieth century. Nevertheless, a few reports disagree:

If on your way to market you see a snake, a toad, or a frog, crossing your path, you will not have luck in buying or selling. If the first frog you see in spring leaps in water, and not on land, you will have more loss than gain during that year.
    Wales Trevelyan (1909)

Somerset [1922] Opie & Tatem, 409. **Devon** Hewett (1900) 23. **Wales** Trevelyan (1909) 172. **Edinburgh** *Edinburgh Mag.* (Nov. 1818) 412. **Highland Scotland** Polson (1926) 30. **General** Nigel de Longchamps, *Mirror for Fools* (1180) 97; John of Salisbury, *Policraticus* (1159) 50; Scot (1584) Bk 11, Ch. 19.

toads/frogs: used in spells

The reputation of toads and frogs as connected with witches and having magical curative powers led to them being used in various ways to cast or counter spells. One includes the common motif of sticking pins into something in the course of 'love magic':

To regain your lover – Supposin' a lass' young man 'as done some' ats she doesn't like, an' she's mad wi' 'im an' wants to get 'er own back, she must tak' a frog (or a toad) an' put it in a jar an' tie paper over the top o' the jar same as you would do jam; then she must stick pins into this 'ere paper, sayin':

    It's not this frog (or toad) I wish to prick
    By my true lover's heart I want to stick

Then she must set the jar upside down so as the frog (or toad) falls on the pins, an' leave it. She must do this nine times in succession.
    Lincolnshire Rudkin (1936)

A toad could sometimes be used instead of a wax image to bring harm to a victim (*see* EFFI-GIES), and other parts of the toad could have powers if treated correctly:

It was, and perhaps still is, believed that a person wearing a toad's heart concealed about the body can steal with impunity, as he cannot be found out. A farmer watched one of his men, suspected of petty pilfering, and overheard him boasting to his fellow-workmen thus – 'They never catches me – and they never ooll neither. I allus wears a toad's heart round my neck, I does'.

Herefordshire *Folk-Lore* (1913)

Devon *Devonshire Assoc.* 65 (1933) 126. Herefordshire *Folk-Lore* 24 (1913) 238. Lincolnshire Rudkin (1936) 23. Derbyshire Addy (1895) 79; N&Q 10S:2 (1904) 205–6. Yorkshire Addy (1895) 79. Welsh/English Gypsies Groome (1880) 14–15.

toads: poisonous

Toads have traditionally been regarded as poisonous to both animals and humans:

When cattle exhibit certain symptoms of illness, they are vulgarly supposed to have been smitten by a toad – that harmless and really useful creature, which suffers so dreadfully in common estimation, on account of its dirty-looking, rough, warty-skin, and slovenly crawling gait, and in spite of its bright and beautiful eyes. The idea may be said to be universal that the toad is very 'smittle', in plain English, venomous. The beast that a toad is falsely accused of having bitten or smitten, must be passed in due form through the need-fire, in order to expel the poison.

Co. Durham Brockie (1886)

Some species do in fact have sacs of toxins on their skin, but traditional belief goes one better and maintains that they can actually spit their venom:

It is said that toads spit fire, and that they will fly at you if driven into a corner.

England Addy (1895)

The venomous nature of toads was already widely believed in the sixteenth century, and is mentioned by Shakespeare in *As You Like it* (1600). It was still being taken for granted by many right into the twentieth century.

See also TOAD-EATERS.

Northamptonshire N&Q 1S:3 (1851) 3. Lincolnshire Watkins (1886) 11. England Addy (1895) 67. Yorkshire Nicholson (1890) 127. Co. Durham *Folk-Lore Jnl* 2 (1883) 120; Brockie (1886) 141–2; Leighton (1910) 62.

Scotland N&Q 2S:4 (1857) 486. General Lupton (1579) Bk 1, Para. 1; John Withals, *Dictionary in English and Latin* (1586); White (1788) 46; *The Mirror* (17 Mar. 1832) 180; N&Q 6S:4 (1881) 429; N&Q 6S:5 (1882) 32, 173, 375–6. Literary Shakespeare, *As You Like it* (1600) 2:1.

toadstones

It was firmly believed, at least from the fifteenth century, that certain toads had a jewel-like stone in their heads, which could be extracted and worn as an amulet:

The editor is possessed of a small relique, termed by tradition a toad-stone, the influence of which was supposed to preserve pregnant women from the power of daemons, and other dangers incidental to their situation. It has been carefully preserved for several generations, was often pledged for considerable sums of money, and uniformly redeemed from a belief in its efficacy.

Scotland Scott, *Minstrelsy* (1802)

Shakespeare was aware of it:

Sweet are the uses of adversity
Which, like the toad, ugly and venomous
Wears yet a precious jewel in his head.

Shakespeare *As You Like It* (1600)

Other useful attributes were that the stone was believed to change colour when poison was near, and it cured bites and stings at a touch. A traditional way of obtaining the stone was to place a dead toad in an anthill; the same method was employed to find the magic bone used to control horses (*see* TOADS/FROGS: MAGIC BONE). When surviving toadstones have been examined, they usually turned out to be fossilized teeth of fish or sharks. Opie and Tatem list two late fifteenth-century references, and the notion was clearly widespread at least until the late eighteenth. For another amulet useful in childbirth, *see* EAGLE-STONE.

Edward Fenton, *Certaine Secrete Wonders of Nature* (1569) 42; Lupton (1579) Bk 1, Para. 52; Bk 7, Para. 18. Thomas Nashe, *Anatomie of Absurditie* (1589) 40; Shakespeare, *As You Like It* (1600) 2:1; Edward Topsell, *History of Serpents* (1608) 188; Francis Bacon, *Sylva Sylvarum* (1627) Para. 968; Thomas Pennant, *British Zoology* 3 (1776) 15; Grose (1787) 67; Walter Scott, *Minstrelsy of the Scottish Border* 2 (1802) 219; *Devonshire Assoc.* (1873) 200–1.

tobacco

Tobacco appears to have escaped inclusion in British superstitions (apart from the THREE

CIGARETTES belief), but it was regularly recommended in cures for a range of problems – notably to stop BLEEDING, TOOTHACHE, and EARACHE:

The whole families used to turn out together, to reap and bind, and it was considered 'lucky' if the child, just promoted to reaping, cut herself with the sickle. Even if the top of a finger was cut off, it was speedily joined on with a quid of tobacco, after the remarkable practice of surgery which prevailed before the days of Union doctors.

Hampshire Yonge (1892)

Hampshire Yonge (1892) 177. Gloucestershire *Trans. Bristol & Glos. Arch. Soc.* 53 (1931) 264. Worcestershire Berkeley & Jenkins (1932) 33. Lincolnshire Rudkin (1936) 27. Yorkshire Nicholson (1890) 140. Westmorland/Lancashire/Essex [*c.*1939] *Folk-Lore* 62 (1951) 262. Galloway Mactaggart (1824) 11. Co. Cork [1937] Culloty (1993) 58; Vickery (1995) 372.

---

tongues: lucky bit

Among the many items which Victorians could carry 'for luck', perhaps the oddest was the tip of a calf or ox's tongue, generally called a 'lucky bit':

There was a cold tongue on the breakfast table. An elderly clergyman, who was a guest, said, 'Will you allow me to cut off the tip?' 'Certainly,' was the reply, 'but you will find it very hard'. 'So much the better,' observed the clergyman, as he cut off the piece and then put it into his pocket, saying, 'If you carry about with you the tip of a cow's tongue it will bring you good luck'. It appeared that he had amassed a goodly collection of tips of tongues.

Unlocated N&Q (1884)

Why this piece of tongue was so valued is never explained, but from at least 1851, when the first known reference appeared, it was a widespread fashion, affecting most levels of society:

Not long since an old lady was observed to turn out the contents of her capacious pocket, and among the strange assortment of articles exposed to view was not only a knuckle-bone for cramp, but also the tip of an ox tongue, which was considered an unfailing guarantee of good luck.

Cornwall *Cassell's Saturday Jnl* (1893)

According to Igglesden, the notion lasted well into the twentieth century, but it seems to have faded mid century and is now seemingly forgotten. All the recorded examples are from England.

Somerset [*c.*1865] *Folk-Lore* 28 (1917) 315. Cornwall *Folk-Lore Jnl* 5 (1887) 201–2; *Cassell's Saturday Jnl* (1893). London Igglesden (*c.*1932) 146. Lincolnshire

Grantham Jnl (22 June 1878). Northamptonshire Sternberg (1851) 172–3. England Addy (1895) 97. Unlocated N&Q 6S:9 (1884) 185.

tongues: lying

If you have a pimple or sore spot on your tongue, the general opinion is that you have been telling lies:

It was bad enough to have a sore spot at the end of one's tongue without suffering the moral pain of being told that it was a proof that one had been telling 'stories'.

Lincolnshire *Grantham Jnl* (29 June 1878)

This idea was widely known in the early seventeenth century, as evidenced by Shakespeare's 'If I prove honey-mouth'd, let my tongue blister' (*Winter's Tale*) and John Aubrey's comment that it was known when he was a little boy. It has been regularly reported ever since – and can still be heard. Much the same was said in classical times (e.g. Theocritus, *Idylls* (*c.*275 BC) 12), which raises the possibility that it entered British tradition through translation direct from ancient Greek writings.

Somerset [1907] Tongue (1965) 137. Devon *Devonshire Assoc.* 61 (1929) 127. Cornwall *Jnl Royal Inst.* Cornwall 20 (1915) 131. Lincolnshire *Grantham Jnl* (29 June 1878). Staffordshire Hackwood (1924) 149. Yorkshire Nicholson (1890) 45. Lancashire Harland & Wilkinson (1873) 236. Teesside [1947] Opie & Tatem, 410. Unlocated Aubrey, *Remaines* (1686/1972) 221. Literary Shakespeare, *Winter's Tale* (*c.*1611) 2:2; Swift (1738).

---

tooth fairy

see TEETH: DISPOSAL OF.

---

toothache: charm for

An extraordinarily widespread and long-lived CHARM, reputed to counter toothache, relates how Christ cured one of his disciples of the problem and promised that anyone who cited His words thereafter would be similarly protected. Although the charm exists in numerous versions, with many differences in detail, it remains recognizably the same piece. A fairly standard version is as follows, but because the verse was often written down by at best semi-literate local charmers, versions actually noted from primary sources are rarely so coherent:

toothache

Toothache is one of the prime candidates for folk medicine, and a bewildering variety of cures have been recorded. As with many other areas of folk medicine, cures can be assigned to one of several categories: (1) the pain can be sent away by the recitation of special CHARMS, or prevented by writing the charms down and keeping them about the person; (2) it can be cured or prevented by carrying certain items, such as nuts or animal teeth, in the pocket or elsewhere; (3) it can be alleviated by placing items in the mouth, such as TOBACCO, or against the face; (4) a variety of other actions are recommended, which seem to have no logical connection with the toothache, such as putting the left stocking on first, cutting the FINGERNAILS on GOOD FRIDAY, and so on.

The toothache cure is also one of the few areas of folklore which seem to include significant genuine survivals from medieval, and probably earlier, tradition. The notion that the pain is caused by a worm in the tooth and that of the 'St Peter' charm (*see below*) are both found in Anglo-Saxon manuscripts and were collected widely in the nineteenth century. There is every likelihood that these had survived in use over the intervening centuries rather than being reintroduced by literary intervention.

The most common cures are treated separately, but the following is a sample of other remedies – some purely magical, others herbal:

Cure for toothache – A boy who was crazed with toothache was given 'some of his own physic' i.e. his gums were rubbed with his own water while still warm, with good results. Lincolnshire Rudkin (1936)

For toothache people were told to take a sharp twig of willow and therewith pick their decayed teeth until they bled. After that the twig was to be thrown into a running stream. This was a perfect cure. It was customary to peel the bark of the elder-tree upward, and make a decoction with it, which was administered three times a day for toothache. Wales Trevelyan (1909)

Against toothache: a verse of Scripture written on a piece of paper and held before the fire; a stocking off the left foot folded crosswise and placed under the pillow at night; a red woollen stocking or cloth tied round the face. Wales Jones (1930)

Within the recollection of the present vicar of the parish of Churcham, Gloucestershire, after public baptism, the then parish nurse invariably washed out the mouth of the recently regenerated infant with the remaining sacrificial water. She assured the vicar it was a safeguard against toothache. Gloucestershire N&Q (1874)

Carry in your pocket the two jaw-bones of a haddock; for ever since the miracle of the loaves and fishes these bones are an infallible remedy against toothache, and the older they are the better, as nearer the time of the miracle. Ireland Wilde (1888)

A cat's skin is a good remedy for toothache. You should keep a dried cat's skin and hold it to your cheek when your tooth aches. England Addy (1895)

Cure for toothache – Put your finger on the fifth nail from the handle of the church door and say the creed three times. Cornwall *Jnl Royal Inst. Cornwall* (1915)

A general relief for earache and toothache was a small flannel bag filled with common salt. The salt-filled bag would be put in the oven to get it well and truly hot, and this would be held against the pain. Oxfordshire [1920s] Harris

Miscellaneous cures: Dorset *Procs. Dorset Nat. Hist & Ant. Field Club* 35 (1914) 83–4. Devon *Devonshire Assoc.* 11 (1879) 105; Hewett (1900) 67; [c.1920] Lakerham (1982) 48. Cornwall *Jnl Royal Inst. Cornwall* 20 (1915) 129. Essex [c.1939] *Folk-Lore* 62 (1951) 263. Oxfordshire [1920s] Harris (1969) 114. Gloucestershire N&Q 5S:1 (1874) 383; *Folk-Lore* 13 (1902) 173. Worcestershire Salisbury (1893) 70. Cambridgeshire Porter (1969) 88. Suffolk [1779] Gurdon (1893) 28. Norfolk [c.1920] Wigby (1976) 65–6. Lincolnshire [1865] N&Q 10S:2 (1904) 447; Rudkin (1936) 27. West Midlands W. Midlands Fed. W. I.s (1996) 73. Shropshire Burne (1883) 194. England Addy (1895) 89. Derbyshire Uttley (1946) 112. Westmorland/Lancashire [c.1939] *Folk-Lore* 62 (1951) 262. Co. Durham Brockie (1886) 117–19, 220. Wales Trevelyan (1909) 316, 320; Jones (1930) 142. Highland Scotland Polson (1926) 33. Hebrides *Folk-Lore* 11 (1900) 445–6. Wigtonshire *Folk-Lore* 26 (1915) 208–9. Banffshire Gregor (1874) 271–2. Ireland Wilde (1888) 196; Hickey (1938) 269. Co. Cork [1937] Culloty (1993) 62. Co. Kerry *Folk-Lore* 31 (1920) 236. Co. Wexford Ó Muirithe & Nuttall (1999) 100. Co. Dublin Logan (1981) 129. Co. Cavan Maloney (1972) 78. Guernsey [1589] *Channel Islands Ann. Anth.* (1972–3) 22–4. Unlocated Igglesden [c.1932] 206. General [1661] N&Q 1S:4 (1851) 52–3.

As Peter sat on a marble stone
The Lord came to him all alone
Peter, what makes thee sit there
My Lord, I am troubled with the toothache
Peter arise, and go home

And you, and whosoever for my sake
Shall keep these words in memory
Shall never be troubled with the
    toothache.

Ireland N&Q (1850)

The majority of versions feature St Peter, but occasionally it is St John or even the Virgin Mary, and the sufferer is usually sitting on a stone, but is sometimes 'by a gate'. The charm is unusual in British tradition in that it can be shown to have genuine medieval roots. A Latin version appears in the collection of Saxon cures (MS Harl. 585) written down about AD 1000, and published by Cockayne, and a later one in the Welsh manuscript of c.1250 published as *Physicians of Myddvai*. The record is then silent until the late seventeenth century, and from then it appears regularly into the twentieth. At present, it is not possible to say whether the charm had existed in traditional form between the thirteenth and sixteenth centuries, or whether it was reintroduced at the later date from a literary source. Only further research will shed such light.

Charms for other ailments, such as BLEED-ING, were usually recited, or rather mumbled to preserve secrecy, over the sufferer, but a characteristic of the toothache charms is that they were more likely to be written down, and this may have contributed to the longevity of the St Peter version. Indeed, their efficacy in keeping the toothache at bay relied on their being kept on the person at all times – often simply in the pocket, or suspended in a bag around the neck, but sometimes more elaborately:

> *Dinah, she were just mad with the toothache, and she says, 'I don't care what I do so as it'll do me some good' and down she goes to Wood Ford, and John he gives her the charm; a bit of paper folded small and sealed with three blobs of sealing-wax so as you could not look inside of it no way, and she were to sew this in the middle of her stays.*
>
> Pembrokeshire *Folk-Lore* (1904)

Many other accounts of charming for toothache are available, showing all the usual characteristics of the genre. Many of them hint at a verbal charm but do not give enough detail to identify it, and most of these are likely to be further examples of the St Peter text already quoted. A few, however, give a completely different charm, and demonstrate a wider repertoire available to the charmer. They do not always make total sense:

> *To cure the tooth-ache – Mars, hur, abursa, aburse/Jesus Christ for Mary's sake/Take away this tooth-ache. Write these words three times; and as you say the words, let the party burn one paper, then another, and then the last. He says he saw it experimented, and the party immediately cured.*
>
> Unlocated Aubrey, *Miscellanies* (1696)

'*St Peter*' *Charm*: **Southeast England** N&Q 1S:1 (1850) 293. **Sussex** Latham (1878) 40. **Devon** Hewett (1900) 67; *Procs. Dorset Nat. Hist & Ant. Field Club* 35 (1914) 82. **Devon/Cornwall** N&Q 1S:3 (1851) 259. **Cornwall** Hunt (1865) 215; Couch (1871) 148; *Folk-Lore Jnl* 5 (1887) 201. **Gloucestershire** [1811] *Folk-Lore* 109 (1998) 111. **Herefordshire** Havergal (1887) 46; Leather (1912) 74–5. **Worcestershire** N&Q 2S:12 (1861) 501. **Shropshire** [early 19th cent.] *Folk-Lore* 6 (1895) 202–4; N&Q 2S:12 (1861) 501. **Northern England** [1850s] *Denham Tracts* 2 (1895) 9–10. **Lancashire** N&Q 4S:8 (1871) 506; Harland & Wilkinson (1873) 226; Harland & Wilkinson (1882) 75–6. **Wales** Trevelyan (1909) 227. **Pembrokeshire** *Folk-Lore* 15 (1904) 196–7. **Radnorshire** *Folk-Lore* 6 (1895) 304. **Breconshire** *Folk-Lore* 24 (1913) 507. **Scotland** Maclean (1959) 192–3. **Highland Scotland** Polson (1926) 32–3. **Caithness** Sutherland (1937) 108. **Sutherland** Rinder (1895) 63. **Aberdeenshire** N&Q 1S:1 (1850) 397. **Orkney** N&Q 1S:10 (1854) 220–1. **Ireland** N&Q 1S:1 (1850) 349, 429; Wilde (1888) 196; Logan (1981) 127–8. **Co. Leitrim** *Folk-Lore* 5 (1894) 198. **Unlocated** *Athenian Mercury* 3 (1691) No. 22; Halliwell (1849) 212; N&Q 1S:3 (1851) 20.

Other accounts: **Devon** [1616] *Devonshire Assoc.* 64 (1932) 163–4; *Devonshire Assoc.* 91 (1959) 200. **Cornwall** Polwhele (1826) 610. **Bristol** *Folk-Lore* 5 (1894) 338. **Herefordshire** [1804] Leather (1912) 71–3. **Shropshire** Burne (1883) 193. **Cumberland** Penfold (1907) 55. **Wales** Jones (1930) 142. **Highland Scotland** Macbain (1887/88) 270. **Orkney** [c.1865] N&Q 7S:5 (1888) 262; Mackenzie (1895) 59. **Unlocated** John Aubrey, *Miscellanies* (1696/1857) 135; N&Q 4S:7 (1871) 483. **General** Melton (1620).

toothache: cures on wrist

An odd set of cures for toothache calls for HORSERADISH, or other substance, to be fixed to the wrist of the sufferer:

> *Once when I had toothache very bad, a woman told me to get some scraped horse-radish and put it on my wrist below my thumb here. She said it was to go on the left-side wrist for a left-side tooth and on the right-side wrist for a right-side tooth, then it would draw the pain. My word! I had an arm with it! But it did not do the tooth any good at all.*
>
> Lincolnshire N&Q (1904)

The reference from Shropshire recommends a mustard plaster in the same way, while an earlier publication called for:

> *Allom as big as a walnut, garlic a handful, twenty beans, a handful of bay-salt, pepper; beat it together; lay it to the wrists four and twenty hours or more.*
>
> A Closet for Ladies and Gentlewomen (1636)

Some physical connection between the wrist and the teeth was presumably thought to exist, but this is not explained in the sources here listed.

Surrey Bourne (1901) 220–1. **Lincolnshire** N&Q 4S:1 (1868) 550; N&Q 10S:2 (1904) 446–7. **Shropshire** Burne (1883) 189. **General** *A Closet for Ladies and Gentlewomen* (1636) quoted *Bye-Gones* (20 Apr. 1887) 294.

toothache: fingernails

Several toothache cures seem to have no logical basis, even in the context of folk cures which operate by less than obvious rules. A number of reports claim that cutting your FINGERNAILS and toenails on GOOD FRIDAY will protect you from toothache for the rest of the year:

Cut all your nails before twelve o'clock on Good Friday, but never cut them on any other Friday in the year, and you will not have toothache.
                              Worcestershire *Folk-Lore* (1909)

In one version the procedure includes at least a clear TRANSFERENCE of the ailment to a tree, which is a well-attested motif in folk cures:

Cut your toe and finger nails, take these parings, wrap in tissue paper, and insert the packet into a slit made in the bark of an ash tree before sunrise. You will never have toothache again as long as you live.   **Devon** Hewett (1900)

See TOOTHACHE: NAILS for another way of transferring toothache to a tree.

Devon Hewett (1900) 75; *Devonshire Assoc.* 63 (1931) 131. **Gloucestershire** N&Q 3S:11 (1867) 233–4. **Worcestershire** *Folk-Lore* 20 (1909) 346. **Shropshire** Burne (1883) 260–1.

toothache: love pain

A handful of references indicate a tradition that links toothache with love, dating from at least the mid eighteenth century:

If you have the tooth-ache you don't love true.
                              Connoisseur (1755)

If a girl about to be married has toothache, she will sometimes be told 'Ah, it's a sign you don't love true'.   **Herefordshire** Leather (1912)

The toothache is commonly called the 'love pain' and therefore the sufferer does not receive much commiseration.   **Norfolk** N&Q (1860)

Herefordshire Leather (1912) 88, 114. **Norfolk** N&Q 2S:9 (1860) 381. **Literary** *Connoisseur* 59 (1755) 353.

toothache: moles

It was unfortunate for the MOLE that it was thought to have curative properties for various human ailments, including RHEUMATISM and toothache:

A lady noticing a little bunch of something tied up with string and hung to the mantelpiece of a cottage at Burford (South Salop), asked what it was, and was told, 'They are oonts' feet for the toothache' – namely the feet of unfortunate moles, cut off while the animal is alive, and carried about as a talisman.   **Shropshire** Burne (1883)

While it could possibly be argued that animal feet could have some effect on human ailments such as cramp and rheumatism, concentrated as they often are in the limbs, it is difficult to think of any reason why carrying a mole's foot could be connected with toothache, and no explanation is ever given. Recorded examples only start in the 1850s, and the belief seems to be restricted to the southern half of England.

See also MOLES; TOOTHACHE: FINGERNAILS.

Sussex Latham (1878) 40. **Wiltshire** N&Q 3S:5 (1864) 393. **Herefordshire** Leather (1912) 82. **Lincolnshire** Rudkin (1936) 27. **Shropshire** Burne (1883) 193. **Staffordshire** Poole (1875) 83–4. **Staffordshire/Shropshire** N&Q 1S:10 (1854) 6.

toothache: nails

The transfer of a disease or other ailment to a tree is a well-known motif in folk medicine, and a group of references attest to this method of curing the toothache:

To cure the tooth-ache – Take a new nail and make the gum bleed with it, and then drive it into an oak. This did cure William Neal's son, a very stout gentleman, when he was almost mad with the pain, and had a mind to have pistolled himself.   **Unlocated** Aubrey, *Miscellanies* (1696)

Although only sporadically recorded, this belief was clearly widespread and has long roots in Britain. Both John Aubrey and Kenelm Digby described it in the seventeenth century, and essentially the same procedure was noted in the thirteenth-century Welsh manuscript later published as the *Physicians of Myddvai*.

See also TOOTHACHE: FINGERNAILS for another method of transferring toothache to a tree.

Wiltshire N&Q 1S:10 (1854) 505. **Suffolk** *Folk-Lore* 25 (1914) 365. **Cumberland** Bulkeley (1886) 226. **Wales**

Physicians of Myddvai (c.1250) 454. **Scotland** Grose (1787) 55. **Western Scotland** Napier (1879) 131. **Dublin** Logan (1981) 129. **Unlocated** Aubrey, *Miscellanies* (1696/1857) 138. **General** Kenelm Digby, *Choice and Experimental Receipts in Physick and Chirurgery* (1668) 45.

toothache: nuts

A handful of late nineteenth-century references claim that a way to avoid toothache is to carry a 'double nut' in your pocket:

A country woman a short time ago came into one of the Exeter shops for some goods, and while waiting she observed a large bag of Barcelona nuts. She began turning them over. This attracted the person in attendance, and he enquired if she was looking for anything, whereupon the woman said she was looking for a double nut. 'Well, and what would that be for?' asked the attendant. The woman replied, 'Oh it's a sure cure for the toothache, or if you carry it in your pocket you will never have it'. **Devon** *Devonshire Assoc.* (1879)

Sussex Latham (1878) 40. **Devon** *Devonshire Assoc.* 11 (1879) 105. **Lincolnshire** *Grantham Jnl* (22 June 1878). **Shropshire** Burne (1883) 243.

toothache: shoes/stockings

A surprisingly well-known superstition maintains that you can keep toothache at bay simply by controlling how you put on your stockings or shoes:

Another remedy against toothache is, always in the morning to begin dressing by putting the stocking on the left foot. **Cornwall** *Folk-Lore Jnl* (1887)

A somewhat different slant is provided in a related Welsh belief:

There is also a charm for toothache. Take your left stocking, fold it in the form of a cross, put it under your pillow and sleep on it. **Cardiganshire** *Folk-Lore* (1928)

In all the recorded versions it is the left stocking or shoe that is recommended.

See also SHOES: PUTTING ON.

Devon *Devonshire Assoc.* 63 (1931) 131. **Cornwall** *Folk-Lore Jnl* 5 (1887) 201. **Worcestershire** *Folk-Lore* 20 (1909) 346. **East Anglia** Varden (1885) 104. **Suffolk** Glyde (1966) 174. **Shropshire** *N&Q* 5S:3 (1875) 465; Burne (1883) 270. **Wales** Jones (1930) 142; Igglesden (c.1932) 206. **Cardiganshire** *Folk-Lore* 39 (1928) 175. **General** *Radio Times* (27 May 1960) 25.

toothache: skulls/dead fingers

Items connected with the dead are recommended in a number of cures, including human SKULLS for EPILEPSY, a DEAD MAN'S HAND for goitre, CRAMP rings made of coffin handles, and so on, and a range of remedies for toothache are on similar lines. The most direct, and most common, is to carry a tooth taken from a skull. Mrs Bray reported such a cure in her native Devon, and commented that it was still in regular use:

We have another practice, which I am assured is frequently observed as a cure for the tooth-ache; a very general complaint in this neighbourhood . . . if the sufferer have a tooth left sufficiently whole to enable him to use it. Take an old skull found in the churchyard, bite a tooth out of it, and keep it in your pocket all the year round, and never more will you have pain in your teeth or gums. **Devon** Bray (1838)

The detail about the sufferer biting the tooth from the skull is a regular feature in these cures. Some informants maintained that the aching tooth had to be rubbed with the skull's tooth to be effective. John Aubrey, who was born in 1626, remembered the cure from his childhood:

I remember at Bristow (when I was a boy) it was common fashion for the women, to get a Tooth out of a skull in ye churchyard, which they wore as a preservative against the Tooth-ach. **Bristol** Aubrey, *Remaines* (1686)

And it was also included in Thomas Lupton's *A Thousand Notable Things* (1579) and Scot's *Discoverie of Witchcraft* (1584). The ultimate source for the British examples is probably Pliny's *Natural History* (AD 77, Bk 28, Para. 2) whose works were extremely popular with English writers of the period.

A more rarely reported cure was to rub the tooth with the finger of a dead hand, and other variations on the 'dead' theme are as follows:

To bury an old tooth in the churchyard will relieve the owner of toothache. **Wales** Trevelyan (1909)

Go to a graveyard; kneel upon any grave; say three paters and three aves for the soul of the dead lying beneath. Then take a handful of grass from the grave, chew it well, casting forth each bite without swallowing any portion. After this process the sufferer, were he to live a hundred years, will never have toothache any more. **Ireland** Wilde (1888)

See also GALLOWS.

Tooth from skull: **Devon** Bray (1838) 291–2; Henderson (1866) 113; Varden (1885) 104; Hewett (1900) 67; *Devonshire Assoc.* 66 (1934) 83. **Bristol** Aubrey, *Remaines* (1686/1880) 164–5. **Northamptonshire** N&Q 1S:2 (1850) 36–7. **Staffordshire** Poole (1875) 83–4. **Yorkshire** Blakeborough (1898) 131; *Folk-Lore* 21 (1910) 227. **Westmorland/Lancashire** [*c.*1939] *Folk-Lore* 62 (1951) 262. **Co. Durham** N&Q 4S:9 (1872) 257. **Banffshire** Gregor (1874) 271. **Co. Dublin** N&Q 1S:4 (1851) 227–8. **Co. Longford** *Béaloideas* 6 (1936) 267. **General** Lupton (1579) Bk 10, Para. 15; Scot (1584) Bk 12, Ch. 14. *Other cures*: **Essex** [*c.*1939] *Folk-Lore* 62 (1951) 263. **Wales** Trevelyan (1909) 321. **Ireland** Wilde (1888) 196; Hickey (1938) 269.

toothache: the worm

Toothache was generally thought to be caused by a worm, gnawing at the tooth:

I remember about twenty years ago, a Lancashire servant who not merely believed that her toothache was caused by a worm, but, after fumigating the tooth with tobacco, affirmed that a small worm or grub had dropped out, that it was grey-coloured, and much resembled a very small nut-maggot. We were all highly dubious as to the truth of the story, but the servant insisted that she could not be mistaken.

Lancashire N&Q (1876)

The notion was so generally accepted that many people, particularly in Scotland, referred to toothache simply as 'the worm'. This naturally led to cures directly aimed at killing or removing the worm, and the use of herbs or fumigation techniques to this purpose was widespread. It also led to cures which acted more symbolically on the worm idea, by introducing similar objects into the equation. One cure involved rolling a caterpillar in a piece of cloth and placing it on the tooth, while another used a real worm:

In one case, known to the writer, a woman, in the hope of getting rid of the pain, carried in her mouth an earthworm, in the early morning into a neighbouring parish, a distance of about two miles, and there spat it out. On her return she reported the pain gone.

Highland Scotland Polson (1926)

The theory that diseases and complaints such as toothache were caused by worms was a major feature of Anglo-Saxon medicine, and has been identified as one of the few areas in which the medical theories of medieval England followed Teutonic tradition rather than drawing upon classical sources. The Saxon *Leech Book* (6:1–8) of the first half of the tenth century (published by Cockayne (1865)) includes, for example, several herbal remedies for toothache, with such phrases as 'for tooth work, if a worm eat the tooth' and 'leechdoms for sharp pain in the tooth and for worms'.

Sussex *The News* (7 Jan. 1810). **Middlesex** N&Q 5S:5 (1876) 476. **Shropshire** *Folk-Lore* 49 (1938) 229. **Derbyshire/Nottinghamshire** N&Q 5S:5 (1876) 476. **Lancashire** N&Q 5S:5 (1876) 476. **West Wales** Davies (1911) 282–3. **Highland Scotland** Macbain (1887/88) 257; Polson (1926) 33. **Aberdeenshire** N&Q 5S:5 (1876) 155. **Caithness** Rinder (1895) 58. **Orkney** Brand (1703) 62. **Literary** Shakespeare, *Much Ado About Nothing* (1598) 3:2. *Anglo-Saxon material*: Cockayne 2 (1865) 50–3; Bonser (1963) 277–81.

touching iron

Touching iron and TOUCHING WOOD are often regarded as two aspects of the same superstitious impulse, but whereas the 'touching' part is similar, they are used in very different contexts. The most common use for touching iron was when someone had uttered a forbidden word, such as 'pig' while at sea, or when confronted by a potentially dangerous or unlucky person, such as a witch:

A custom . . . prevailed till recently among the fishermen of the east coast of Scotland . . . the practice was to touch iron – 'cauld iron' as they called it. It was apparently derived from the belief in witchcraft and always was occasioned by some person or object present, or by an expression used by a person present. I have, for example, been told by a venerable housekeeper that once, when speaking to one of these men in her kitchen, she was interrupted by the entrance of an old woman, reputed to be a witch. The fisherman's consternation was great, and he made it exceedingly emphatic by uttering the words 'Cauld iron!' and affecting at the same time a successful dash towards an iron hook fixed in the ceiling.

Eastern Scotland N&Q (1906)

Touching iron is not recorded nearly so often as the ubiquitous touching wood, and only seems to have been widely used in Scottish fishing communities in the nineteenth and twentieth centuries. The earliest reference so far found, as quoted by Opie and Tatem, is from the 1730s:

In Queen Mary's reign 'tag' was all the play; where a lad saves himself by touching cold iron.

The Craftsman (4 Feb. 1738)

The earliest references to 'touch wood' also refer to a children's game, and it seems, on present evidence, that both superstitions developed from there. Nevertheless, iron was seen as protective long before this (*see* IRON: PROTECTS), so what may have developed is simply the touching action, grafted on to a much older belief.

Staffordshire *Folk-Lore* 52 (1941) 237. **Glamorganshire** [1952] Opie & Tatem, 213. **Scotland** Guthrie (1885) 149. **Eastern Scotland** N&Q 10S:6 (1906) 230. **General** *The Craftsman* (4 Feb. 1738) quoted Opie & Tatem, 213. **Literary** J. M. Barrie, *Sentimental Tommy* (1896) 175.

touching wood

One of the best-known superstitions in the British Isles today. We touch wood and/or we say 'touch wood' whenever we have boasted, or tempted fate in some way.

We 'tap wood', for instance, after saying I've never had a fall from my bicycle (some of us do this instinctively almost before the sentence is out of our mouths). Northumberland Bosanquet (1929)

As indicated here, for many people the action is almost involuntary. If superstitions were subject to the laws of evolution, the ultimate evolutionary goal for a belief would be that it becomes so much part of everyday life and speech that it ceases to be regarded as a belief at all. This is what has happened to 'touch wood'. Even for those who do not believe the notion of tempting fate, boasting is still seen as mildly unacceptable social behaviour, and many say 'touch wood' as a way of signalling to listeners that we are aware of the social niceties and to add a touch of humility to balance our transgression.

As usual with well-known superstitions, this one is not nearly as old as it is often claimed to be, and can only be traced to the early nineteenth century, and even then not in the form we know it. It is instructive to examine some of the reports of its existence, from relatively recent times:

Sitting by a school-fellow in form the other day, he remarked that he had not been put to construe for some days; immediately after saying this he rapped underneath the form on which he was sitting. On my expressing my surprise, he said it was an old superstition, possibly in Kent or Lincolnshire, that when anybody said that something – invariably something not wished for – had not happened to him lately, rapping underneath anything near would prevent its fulfilment. Rutland N&Q (1877)

Two points arise from this extract. The first is that the boy seems to be following what would now be the German or American version by knocking underneath rather than touching wood. But perhaps more importantly, the writer seems to be unfamiliar with the custom.

'touch wood' used as a superstitious expression to avert ill-luck. We had in common use before the World War the German form 'unberufen', but it is not now fashionable; the Latin 'absit omen' is too pedantic, and too little known to be of popular use. A French form, easily said and remembered, might be an addition to our parlance. N&Q (1930)

This description also implies a wider range of words and actions than is available at present, and this comes from within the reach of living memory. Another variation from the past:

Rub your hand on wood . . . after a boastful speech or speaking too confidently of the future; in east Clare you touch wood twice, with the phrase 'Good word (or time) be it spoken', after an impudent expression. Co. Clare *Folk-Lore* (1911)

The two most popular explanations of origin are that the belief goes back to pagan times when we believed in tree spirits, or that we are invoking Christ's protection by referring to the wood of the Cross. The former is nothing but guesswork, based on the conviction that all superstitions must be ancient, and it has the usual problem of spanning thousands of years with no evidence at all of its existence, or, for that matter, any evidence that 'we' ever believed in tree spirits. The second may have some truth in it, in that devout Christians often found religious connotations for everyday actions, and although it is unlikely to be the origin of the custom, it may well have been a significant factor in its history.

The real origin appears to be much more prosaic. The two earliest references, as identified by the indefatigable Opie and Tatem, are as late as 1805 and 1828, and both refer to a children's game, Tig-touch-wood, or similar. In this chasing game, one is safe when touching wood, and there were spoken elements, such as 'Tiggy, tiggy, touch wood, I've got no wood', chanted to tease the chaser. Tiggy-touch-wood was an extremely well-known game, and it is quite feasible that the words passed into everyday language. This is not a new origin theory. When the custom was discussed by contributors to *Notes & Queries* in 1906, many of the writers assumed that the phrase and the action were simply extended from the game. Before this theory can be finally accepted, however, an examination of the history of European forms of the custom would be advisable.

Dorset *Dorset Year Book* (1961–2) 73. **Bristol** N&Q 10S:6 (1906) 174. **London** [1987] Opie & Tatem, 450. **Oxfordshire** Surman (1992) 60. **Shropshire/Cheshire** N&Q 10S:6 (1906) 130. **Rutland** N&Q 5S:7 (1877) 164. **Derbyshire** Uttley (1946) 124. **Nottinghamshire** N&Q 10S:6 (1906) 231–2. **Lancashire** [*c.*1915] Corbridge (1964) 156–60. **Cumberland** Anderson (1805) 35. **Northumberland** Bosanquet (1929) 79. **Wales** Trevelyan (1909) 325. **Scotland** *Scottish Studies* 3 (1959) 199. **Co. Clare** *Folk-Lore* 22 (1911) 203. **Unlocated** N&Q 10S:6 (1906) 174, 231; *Folk-Lore* 25 (1914) 380–1. **General** *Boy's Own Book* (1828) 24; N&Q 10S:6 (1906) 230–1; Wright (1913) 230; N&Q 159 (1930) 213; Hoggart (1957) Ch. 2. **Literary** Dorothy L. Sayers, *Nine Tailors* (1934) 69. **Germany** N&Q 10S:6 (1906) 174, 231.

towels: sharing

A handful of authorities report a superstition that it is unlucky for two people to share the same towel to dry their hands:

and don't dry your hands with another person on the same towel. If you do you will quarrel. This is a superstition which still lingers
                    Dorset *Dorset Year Book* (1961–2)

People who wipe on the same towel will go a-begging together.   England Addy (1895)

The latter report comes from the Derbyshire area, and is the earliest known, but all the others are from the West Country. This is most likely a late offshoot of the more widespread and older belief that two people using the same washing water will quarrel, or be generally unlucky.
    See also WASHING HANDS TOGETHER.

Dorset Udal (1922) 287; *Dorset Year Book* (1961–2) 74. **Somerset** [1940] Tongue (1965) 143. **Devon** N&Q 10S:12 (1909) 66. **Wiltshire** Wiltshire (1975) 85–6. **England** Addy (1895) 99.

transference

One of the basic principles of folk medicine, everywhere in the world, is that diseases and other medical problems can be transferred to other people, animals, or even inanimate objects. This is not simply a matter of contagion, as spreading a contagious disease does not improve the original sufferer's position: in transference the sufferer is supposed to be actually cured by its operation. Nevertheless, most authorities assume that the transference principle was first articulated when primitive humans noticed that diseases were contagious. This is unprovable, but

that matters little in this case, as it is the operation of the principle rather than its origin which is interesting.

Many superstitious cures appear to be relatively straightforward examples of transference in action, such as when some hair of a WHOOPING COUGH sufferer is fed to a dog, or when WARTS are touched with stones which are then thrown away for someone else to pick up. Indeed, most wart cures seem to be based on the idea of transference. In other cures, however, the principles involved are not so clear-cut. When a child was passed through a split ASH tree to cure its rupture, for example, the cure is effected later, when the tree is bound up and begins to heal itself. The principle here seems to be more one of SYMPATHY than transference, or perhaps of both at once. But if the same cure is attempted by passing the patient through a holed stone, which in itself cannot heal, transference seems the best explanation.

For further discussion and examples, see Black (1883) 34–48.

turning back

One of the most widespread superstitions in Britain, at least in the nineteenth and twentieth centuries, has been that it is very unlucky to turn back when you have started on a journey, however mundane or trivial the trip may be:

It is unlucky, after one has started on a journey to be recalled and told of something previously forgotten. A clergyman from Yorkshire tells me that his grandfather, though anything but a weak man, would never turn back when he had once started on an expedition: he has been known to stand on horseback at the end of his grounds, shouting to the house for something that he had forgotten, rather than turn back for it.
                    Yorkshire Henderson (1866)

The prohibition is strongest for people setting out from their own home, but is also relevant for those leaving houses they have visited:

In the event of a visitor forgetting his or her gloves, on departure from the house of a friend or relation the forgetful one must – if returning for them – sit down, and then put on the gloves, standing whilst donning them; otherwise that person will never return again.
                    Lincolnshire Rudkin (1936)

There are numerous stories of people sending others back to collect forgotten items, or shouting instructions from the garden gate, to avoid returning at all costs. But for those who could not avoid it, there were traditionally sanctioned ways of cheating fate, based on the principle that if one did something else before setting out again, you could pretend the first journey had been completed and you were starting a *new* journey now. Such ruses include the advice to sit down, count to ten, eat or drink something, and so on, to break the bad luck:

If I turned back on my way to school to pick up a forgotten book, I would sit down on a chair for a second to 'break the spell' before I rushed out again. Lancashire [*c.*1915] Corbridge

FISHERMEN and miners on their way to work were particularly affected by this superstition, but the belief was also strong in other key contexts, especially WEDDINGS:

At a hotel fire in Edinburgh some few years ago, three persons were fatally burned, and a honeymoon couple were amongst the injured. It was noted in the local press at the time that this couple, on leaving the house after the marriage ceremony and finding they had forgotten something, had returned to it in spite of the guests warning them that this was a most unlucky thing to do. Edinburgh *Folk-Lore* (1938)

It is not easy to fit this superstition into a general scheme of beliefs. It appears to be based on the common BEGINNINGS principle – that a journey or project which begins well will continue well. As the reported instances rarely stipulate any *reason* for the turning back, it must be concluded that such an interruption to the journey was simply bad in itself, which, unfortunately, moves us no further forward. A probable red herring has been introduced by writers who quote the biblical precedents of Lot's wife, and others who are forbidden to look back. Despite the ambiguity in the phrase 'turning back', it is clear from the contexts involved there that the prohibition concerns looking rather than physically returning.

The fear of turning back is one of the few superstitions which can definitely be traced back to the medieval era in Britain. The English cleric/philosopher John of Salisbury (*c.*1110–80) wrote:

If one is called back as he starts on a journey he should not on that account, if he has set out with the blessing of the Lord, give it up. John of Salisbury, *Policraticus* (1159)

Nevertheless, when faced with another belief – the ill omen of a STUMBLE, for example – considered advice might be to turn back after all:

Hurrying away, he stumbled at the gate. Some laughed, and neighbours said 'Unfortunate! This shows you'd best turn back'. Nigel de Longchamps, *Mirror for Fools* (1180)

The prohibition on turning back has been noted all over the British Isles, and was still being recorded in the 1980s.

Dorset Udal (1922) 280. Devon Hewett (1900) 54; *Devonshire Assoc.* 57 (1926) 130; *Devonshire Assoc.* 74 (1942) 103. Cornwall Hunt (1865) 241; [1890s] *Old Cornwall* 1:12 (1930) 4–5; [1922] Rowse (1942) 264; *Old Cornwall* 2 (1931–6) 39. Wiltshire *Wilts. N&Q* 1 (1893–5) 103–4. Hampshire *N&Q* 7S:9 (1890) 486; [1984] Opie & Tatem, 414. London *Observer Supp.* (24 Nov. 1968) 8. Herefordshire Leather (1912) 87. Worcestershire *Folk-Lore* 20 (1909) 346; Berkeley & Jenkins (1932) 34. East Anglia Varden (1885) 113. Suffolk *Folk-Lore* 35 (1924) 351. Lincolnshire Swaby (1891) 92; Gutch & Peacock (1908) 164; Rudkin (1936) 18. Shropshire/Staffordshire Burne (1883) 274. England Addy (1895) 97. Northern England/Yorkshire Henderson (1866) 87; Nicholson (1890) 43; [1978] Opie & Tatem, [1984] Gill (1993) 90. Lancashire [*c.*1905] Corbridge (1964) 156–60. Co. Durham Brockie (1886) 212. Wales Trevelyan (1909) 329. Mid-Wales Davies (1911) 215. Northeast Scotland Gregor (1881) 30. Highland Scotland Polson (1926) 129. Galloway Mactaggart (1824) 210. Dumfriesshire Shaw (1890) 11. Glasgow [*c.*1820] Napier [1864] 396. Edinburgh *Folk-Lore* 49 (1938) 91. Orkney Laing (1885) 73; *N&Q* 10S:12 (1909) 483–4. Co. Meath/Co. Tipperary *Folk-Lore* 15 (1904) 462. Co. Longford *Béaloideas* 6 (1936) 263. Co. Tyrone *Lore & Language* 1:7 (1972) 10. Isle of Man [1850] Cashen (1912) 27. Unlocated *N&Q* 155 (1928) 459; Igglesden (*c.*1932) 216. General John of Salisbury, *Policraticus* (1169). Literary Nigel de Longchamps, *Mirror for Fools* (1180); John Bunyan, *Pilgrim's Progress* (1678) 3–4.

turnips: love divination

A LOVE DIVINATION procedure more usually associated with apple peel is occasionally reported using a turnip:

Another popular method of love-divination was to pare a turnip round and round without breaking, and then to hang the long spiral peeling over the doorway; the name of the first person who afterwards entered being supposed to correspond with that of the future partner in life. Dumfriesshire Corrie (1890/91)

A different slant is provided in a version from Wales:

If a girl wishes to know the name of her future husband, she steals a turnip from her neighbour's field (it must be stolen and not given); she peels it in one continuous strip, not breaking the peel, and then buries this peel in the garden; the turnip

itself she hangs up behind the door; then she goes and sits beside the fire, and the first man who enters after that will bear the name of her future husband.   Pembrokeshire *Folk-Lore* (1928)

See APPLES: PEEL DIVINATION for more examples and references.

Cumberland Gibson (1858) 105. Pembrokeshire *Folk-Lore* 39 (1928) 173. Dumfriesshire Corrie (1890/91) 39–40.

twins

see LEFT TWIN.

two together

A number of superstitions warn against two people doing certain domestic tasks together.

The most widespread version is concerned with WASHING hands in the same water, while others involve drying hands on the same TOWEL, pouring tea from the same TEAPOT, making up a FIRE, and approaching the oven when baking BREAD. There may well be more.

The result of such ill-advised action is sometimes simply described as bad luck, but where a reason is given it is usually that they will quarrel.

The hand-washing belief is not only the most widespread of these but is also the only one which has a documented history back before the nineteenth century. It seems that strong superstitions both beget offspring and influence weaker ones, and it is proposed that these minor beliefs have all been formulated simply by direct extension from the hand-washing belief.

umbrellas: on bed

Occasionally, it has been reported unlucky to place an umbrella on a bed – it is either unlucky or portends a long illness. This is probably an extension of the much more widely known belief about placing umbrellas on tables (*see below*).

Somerset [1923] Opie & Tatem, 415. Yorkshire [1982] Opie & Tatem, 415. Scotland *Folk-Lore* 45 (1934) 162.

umbrellas: on table

A number of items must not be placed on a TABLE, for fear of bad luck or a quarrel, including SHOES, BELLOWS, and umbrellas:

upon his entering a house, someone took his umbrella and coat, and was about to deposit them, for the moment, on a table, and then remarked: 'Oh but I mustn't put your umbrella on the table'.
Yorkshire *Newcastle Weekly Chronicle* (8 May 1937)

A different, but probably related, belief has been reported only rarely:

To lay an umbrella on a bed portends a long illness.   Scotland *Folk-Lore* (1934)

As with other umbrella and table beliefs, these only appear in late Victorian times.

Hampshire N&Q 7S:9 (1890) 486. Devon Hewett (1900) 55. Shropshire Burne (1883) 280. Yorkshire *Folk-Lore* 21 (1910) 225. Scotland *Folk-Lore* 45 (1934) 162. Guernsey Carey (1903) 507.

umbrellas: opening indoors

One of the best-known superstitions of modern times holds that it is unlucky to open an umbrella in the house:

If you open an umbrella in the house and hold it over your head, there will be a death in the house before the year is out.
Worcestershire *Folk-Lore* (1909)

Most present-day informants simply claim it leads to bad luck, but earlier authorities, as here, were more likely to maintain that it meant death:

It is unlucky to open an umbrella in the house, especially if it is held over the head, when it becomes a sign of death.   Shropshire Burne (1883)

This is an excellent example of the simple and limited nature of most modern beliefs, which help to ensure a remarkably stable content and meaning. In the Superstitions Survey carried out through the Folk-Lore Society in 1998 (*see* Introduction), the umbrella-indoors belief was the sixth most often reported superstition, being listed by 39 per cent of respondents, and informal polling since that time indicates that it should perhaps be in the top five.

No remotely sensible suggestion has been made as to why an umbrella indoors is considered so bad, although it could be argued that the belief is simply an example of the basic principle of 'appropriate categories' – outdoor items should not be brought indoors. The belief is essentially a twentieth-century phenomenon, with no sign of it yet before the

1880s. Umbrellas only became widely used in the early nineteenth century, which would seem to preclude any ancient origin, but this does not stop the origin-theorists from having a go. An etiological explanation is in circulation at the time of writing [Aug. 2002], which must take the prize, against stiff opposition, for the most far-fetched theory of origin yet proposed for a current superstition. It explains that, originally, umbrellas were not designed to keep the rain off, but were to provide shade from the sun. As the sun was worshipped at that time, putting an umbrella up indoors was an insult to the sun-god and thus invited retribution. A less ambitious explanation at least has the virtue of simplicity, and has the hallmarks of an evocative explanation given to children:

We believed that goblins hid inside the umbrella and when it was opened the goblins would fly out.
Lincolnshire Sutton (1992)

Hampshire N&Q 172 (1937) 304. **Somerset** Tongue (1965) 141. **Devon** [*c*.1915] Lakeham (1982) 47. *Devonshire Assoc.*. 65 (1933) 125. **Cornwall** [1890s] *Old Cornwall* 1:12 (1930) 4. **Surrey** [*c*.1880] N&Q 172 (1937) 304; [1961] Opie & Tatem, 415. **London** [1985] Opie & Tatem, 415. **Essex** [*c*.1920] Ketteridge & Mays (1972) 143; [1983] Opie & Tatem, 415; Sutton (1992) 141. **Buckinghamshire** [1911] *Folk-Lore* 43 (1932) 109. **Oxfordshire** [1920s] Surman (1992) 60. **Worcestershire** *Folk-Lore* 20 (1909) 345; Berkeley & Jenkins (1932) 37. **Suffolk** *Folk-Lore* 35 (1924) 351. **Lincolnshire** Gutch & Peacock (1908) 165; Sutton (1992) 141. **Shropshire** Burne (1883) 280. **Yorkshire** *Folk-Lore* 21 (1910) 225–6. **Lancashire** [*c*.1915] Corbridge (1964) 156–60; *Lancashire Lore* (1971) 6, 66. **Wales** Trevelyan (1909) 327. **Aberdeenshire** *Folk-Lore* 25 (1914) 349. **Argyllshire** *Folk-Lore* 21 (1910) 89. **Orkney** N&Q 10S:12 (1909) 483–4. **Co. Longford** *Béaloideas* 6 (1936) 263. **Co. Tyrone** *Lore & Language* 1:7 (1972) 11. **Guernsey** Carey (1903) 507. **Unlocated** N&Q 160 (1931) 44; Igglesden (*c*.1932) 210.

umbrellas/walking sticks: dropping

Umbrellas and walking sticks share certain characteristics with other everyday items such as GLOVES and CUTLERY, in the event of their being accidentally dropped. Not only was it unlucky to drop the item, but it was particularly bad to pick it up oneself, so someone else had to do it:

In 1930 I dropped my umbrella in a train and was told by a country-woman in the compartment that I must not pick it up myself or I should have bad luck. In 1932 I dropped a parcel and was told by another country-woman the same thing.
Devon *Devonshire Assoc.* (1933)

Some took the interdiction quite seriously:

Not long since, in one of the principal streets [of Bury] *I heard a young shop-woman exclaim to a sceptical female friend who was standing smilingly by a fallen umbrella, 'Oh, do pick it up please! I am so superstitious, I am frightened something will happen if I pick it up'.*
Lancashire N&Q (1914)

As with other 'dropping' superstitions, this one varies a little in detail. For some, it was important that the umbrella owner did not thank the picker-up, others believed that the latter would get good luck, or a surprise, for their timely intervention.

The belief cannot be shown to be any earlier than the first decade of the twentieth century, and the basic superstition remained very stable in form and meaning from that time. Two earlier references go against the trend, however. Addy suggests that dropping your walking stick means you will soon meet a friend (**England** Addy (1895) 102), and an odd meaning was reported from Scotland – 'To drop your umbrella or walking-stick shows that your mind is likely to give way' (**Dumfriesshire** Shaw (1890) 13).

Devon *Devonshire Assoc.* 65 (1933) 124. **Surrey** [1959] Opie & Tatem, 126. **London** *Folk-Lore* 37 (1926) 366. **Worcestershire** *Folk-Lore* 20 (1909) 345. **Northamptonshire** *Folk-Lore* 25 (1914) 366. **Lincolnshire** Rudkin (1936) 17. **Staffordshire** *Folk-Lore* 28 (1917) 452. **Yorkshire** *Folk-Lore* 21 (1910) 226. **Lancashire** N&Q 11S:10 (1914) 196. **Northumberland** Bosanquet (1929) 77. **Wales** Trevelyan (1909) 327. **Mid-Wales** Davies (1911) 215. **Glamorganshire** [1954] Opie & Tatem, 126. **Neath** Phillips (1925) 597. **Aberdeenshire** *Folk-Lore* 25 (1914) 349. **Sutherland** [1952] Opie & Tatem, 414. **Orkney** N&Q 10S:12 (1909) 483–4. **Unlocated** N&Q 155 (1928) 459; Igglesden (*c*.1932) 210.

urban myths

see CONTEMPORARY LEGEND.

Virgin Mary's nuts

see LUCKY BEANS.

walking sticks

One of the items which, if dropped, should be picked up by someone else, or bad luck will follow (*see* UMBRELLAS). Nevertheless, one authority offers a different meaning: 'If you let your stick fall you will be sure to meet a friend immediately afterwards' (**England** Addy (1895) 102).

See STAFF DIVINATION.

wart cures: animal blood

Washing warts with pig's blood was recommended in several Scottish sources. The blood of other animals – MOLES, MICE, CATS – was also reported a few times in the *English Folk-Lore Survey* in the 1960s (see Hatfield (1998)), and bullock's blood in Northern Ireland.

Wiltshire Whitlock (1976) 166. **Highland Scotland** Macbain (1887/88) 257; Polson (1926) 34–5. **Western Scotland** Napier (1879) 97. **Galloway** Mactaggart (1824) 463. **N. Ireland** Foster (1951) 62.

wart cures: apple

One of numerous plant remedies which were reported fairly often:

Cut an apple in two, and rub each half over the warts; then tie the apple together again with a piece of string and bury it. As the apple decays, so will the warts disappear.

Devon *Devonshire Assoc.* (1926)

The detail about tying the two halves together occurs regularly. Reported by three correspondents in the *English Folk-Lore Survey* in the 1960s, but not in the *Folk-Lore Society Survey* of 1998; *see* Hatfield (1998).

Devon [1900] *Devonshire Assoc.* 57 (1926) 121. **Shropshire** Burne (1883) 200. **England** Addy (1895) 89. **Northern England** Henderson (1866) 108–10. **Co. Durham** Brockie (1886) 223. **N. Ireland** Buckley (1980) 25.

wart cures: beans

One of the most commonly reported vegetable substances for wart cures is the humble broad bean:

Rachel, the servant who is a dressmaker now, she had her hands nearly covered wi warts, and her missis wish'd she would go to the chemist's; so they give her vitril and agafortis to touch em with, and after all the warts come on again; but at last she charm'd hern off with a broadbean shell – that is, to rub the warts well wi the inside (9 times I think), and then bury the shell, and tell no one where, and as it rots so the warts die.

Unlocated N&Q (1870)

The secrecy and the burying are standard motifs, but are not always included, and many informants seemed to have faith simply in some property of the bean pod itself. Broad beans were top of the list of plants recorded in the *English Folk-Lore Survey* of the 1960s, just beating DANDELIONS, and well ahead of any other species. They were also included in the Folk-Lore Society's *Wart Cure Survey* in 1998, and are still regularly recommended.

Isle of Wight [1988] Vickery (1995) 50. **Kent** *Folk-Lore* 62 (1951) 328. **Sussex** [1991] Vickery (1995) 50. **Somerset** [1991] Vickery (1995) 50. **Devon** *Devonshire Assoc.* 57 (1926) 121. **Wiltshire** Whitlock (1976) 165. **Oxfordshire** [1920s] Harris (1969) 114. **Worcestershire** Salisbury (1893) 70. **Warwickshire** Bloom (*c*.1930) 30–1. **East Anglia** [1920s] Hatfield (1994) 56–9. **Suffolk** *Gent. Mag.* (1867) 728–41; *Folk-Lore* 35 (1924) 356–7. **Norfolk** N&Q 4S:6 (1870) 130; *Folk-Lore* 35 (1924) 356–7; *Folk-Lore* 40 (1929) 116–17; Randell (1966) 85–6; *Folk-Lore* 102:2 (1991) 240. **Lincolnshire** Peacock (1877) 268–9; Sutton (1992) 152. **Shropshire** Burne (1883) 200; *Folk-Lore* 49 (1938) 226–8. **England** Addy (1895) 88. **Yorkshire** N&Q 1S:6 (1852) 311–12. **Glamorgan** [1954] Opie & Tatem, 422. **Unlocated** Halliwell (1849) 208; N&Q 1S:6 (1852) 519–20; N&Q 4S:6 (1870) 69; *Bye-Gones* (28 Dec. 1887) 478.

wart cures: blacksmith's water

A number of wart cures recommend the use of water collected from specific places (*see* WART CURES: WATER), and a few people placed particular faith in the water found at the local BLACKSMITH'S forge:

Another one for warts used forge water. When the blacksmith was shoeing horses he'd take the red-hot horseshoe out of the fire with pincers and he'd dip it into a barrel of water to cool it. The barrel would be there for maybe a year with the blacksmith using it every day. If you had warts on your hand you dipped it into the forge water.

Irish Travellers [1940s] Joyce

Such water was also recommended for other ailments, such as CHILBLAINS and consumption. Also listed from three respondents in the *English Folk-Lore Survey* of the 1960s; *see* Hatfield (1998).

See also WART CURES: WATER.

West Wales Davies (1911) 282. **Irish Travellers** [1940s] Joyce (1985) 16. **Co. Longford** *Béaloideas* 6 (1936) 266.

wart cures

It is clear from the number of cures which have been reported over the years that the incidence of warts in the past was very much higher than in the present day. While people nowadays still get warts, it is very unusual to find anyone with their hands 'covered in warts' as is often described in previous generations. Warts are far and away the favourite things for folk medicine to cure, and recipes come in a bewildering variety of forms. Closer analysis, however, reveals a relatively restricted number of formulas that form the core of the cures, around which variant details cluster. A certain degree of confusion is inevitable because these formulas can exist in isolation from each other, or can be found in any combination.

On another level, wart cures can also combine procedures that are possibly genuinely therapeutic (such as the use of certain plants) and which thus belong to the physical world of at least alternative medicine, with others which are frankly magical (such as the reciting of charms or counting the warts). Again, it is not always clear which category some elements belong to, as individual variations blur the boundaries.

Wart cures can be classified by the physical items used – plants, sticks, stones, snails, and so on – or by the processes involved – touching, rubbing, counting, etc. It is in the sphere of physical items that the widest variety occurs, but there are a few items which are commonplace and dozens of others which are reported only once or twice. The commonest are particular plants: broad beans, celandine, dandelions, apples, cereals, elder, potatoes; animals or animal products: snails, meat, hair, blood; and inorganic materials or objects – stones, cinders, pins, and string.

Regular processes include rubbing, anointing, touching, counting, looking at, reciting verbal charms, buying or selling, wishing, and those designed to dispose of the item used, by burying, throwing over the shoulder, and so on.

burying
The motif of burying the item used to touch the warts is extremely common, especially with immediately perishable materials such as meat and fleshy plants. The explanation for the burial is that 'as the item rots, so the warts will waste away'. This presumes a lasting connection or SYMPATHY between the item and the wart, which is presumably set up by contact at the rubbing stage. In the very commonly reported SNAIL cures, however, the animal is not buried but placed upon a thorn, yet the principle of 'wasting away' is exactly the same. The picture is clouded, however, by the possibility that the rubric 'as the – rots' is simply a metaphor for time passing – i.e. 'by the time the – rots, your warts will be gone'. It is clear from the wording of some reports that this is how it was interpreted by some practitioners, but they are in a distinct minority.

charming
The generic term for curing warts is 'charming', but a distinction can be made between those methods described above, and those which rely solely or mainly on charms or the innate power of the curer. Many descriptions of cures stress that the charmer simply 'looked at' the warts, and did not touch them at all. Where the warts duly disappeared, this is taken as definite proof of that innate power. Similarly, other descriptions relate how the charmer could work over the telephone or 'at a distance'.

wart cures: bread

In a handful of reports only, bread is used in a similar way to the more well-known raw meat – it has to be stolen, rubbed on the wart, and buried:

The person who has warts must, in profound secrecy, pinch as many pieces from a freshly-baked loaf, and then bury them, the warts disappearing as the pieces decay.
Herefordshire [c.1895] *Folk-Lore*

Also reported by one respondent in the *English Folk-Lore Survey* of the 1960s; *see* Hatfield (1998).

Devon *Devonshire Assoc.* 63 (1931) 131. Herefordshire [c.1895] *Folk-Lore* 39 (1928) 389; Leather (1912) 84. Norfolk *Folk-Lore* 40 (1929) 116–17. Lincolnshire Peacock (1877) 268–9.

wart cures: buying and selling

From the folklorist's point of view, the buying and selling of warts is one of the most interesting motifs involved in wart cures. Whereas many other cures combine varying degrees of physical and the magical elements, the idea that warts can be cured simply by being bought falls squarely in the magical camp. Although sometimes

Oddly enough, verbal charms take a much smaller part in wart cures than in other medicinal spheres. Although many informants who recount contact with wart-charmers mention a muttering or mumbling of words, wart charms are not recorded in anything like the numbers that they are for, say, BLEEDING or TOOTHACHE.

counting

In many other areas of belief, COUNTING is unwise because it TEMPTS FATE and therefore courts disaster, but in wart cures an accurate count of the warts is often an essential element. This is especially so in those cures which use any form of magical intervention, and it is only those with a gift for such things that can succeed solely by counting the warts.

rubbing/anointing

Many cures call for the warts to be rubbed or anointed with some substance, normally organic – a snail, the sap from dandelion, celandine or other plant, fasting spittle, and so on. In most cases, this action implies a belief in the therapeutic properties of the substance itself, and the cure therefore resides in the world of the physical rather than the magical. But if the recommended procedure then goes on to dictate how the substance is to be disposed of, we usually step over the line into the magical sphere of sympathy or transference.

sympathy

Another general principle is that of a continued sympathetic connection between items which have previously been in contact with each other. Thus, in the case of a wound caused by a knife, keeping the knife clean will help the wound to recover, or the belief that if you get bitten by a dog, and that dog later contracts rabies, you too will suffer. The key point here is that this principle sidesteps the usual rules covering cause and effect, by removing the regular time sequence – A causes B, therefore A must come before B. The sympathetic principle is best seen in cures where an item is buried.

touching

In contrast to the rubbing with organic materials, some cures recommend touching each wart, usually with inorganic substances such as stones, cinders, and so on, but also with some of the harder organic materials such as sticks of elder. There is much less likelihood here that the substance itself is thought to be curative, but it seems likely that this operation is either simply an adjunct to the counting operation, or that by this contact the wart is transferred to the item used.

transference

One of the general principles of folk medicine is that ailments and conditions can be cured by passing them on to other people, animals, or even to inanimate objects. In some wart cures this is quite explicit, for example when the sufferer throws a bag of pebbles into the road and whoever picks it up gets the warts.

Material on wart cures is scattered throughout the folk-lore and folk medicine literature, and we are still awaiting the definitive study of wart cures in all forms. The following all include significant information and material: James Hardy, 'Wart and Wen Cures', Folk-Lore Record 1 (1878) 216–28; W. G. Black, Folk Medicine (1883); Susan Drury, 'Plants and Wart Cures in England from the Seventeenth to the Nineteenth Century: Some Examples', Folk-Lore 102:1 (1991) 97–100; Gabrielle Hatfield, Country Remedies (1994); Gabrielle Hatfield, Warts: Summary of Wart-Cure Survey for the Folk-Lore Society (1998). A list of plant and other wart cures gathered from readers of the Western Gazette in the early 1970s can be found in Whitlock (1976) 164–6.

combined with other motifs, the act of selling your warts often constitutes the whole cure:

In this village we had two people of whom it was said that they had the power to charm away warts. I visited the lady one day and she noticed a particularly nasty wart on my left hand. She said, 'I'll buy that wart from you'. She gave me a penny and to this day I can only say that the wart fell off during the following weeks.   Lincolnshire [1940s] Sutton

The idea that warts can be sold has a long history. In 1579, for example, Thomas Lupton started the description of a wart cure with the words, 'If one doth buy warts of them that have them, and give them a pin therefore' [see WART CURES: PINS

for full quote], and in 1648 Robert Herrick included the line 'Those warts, which we to others, from ourselves, sell' in one of his poems. People are still having their warts bought in the present day.

The procedure is, as far as is known, unique in folk medicine. No other ailment is thought susceptible to financial transaction in this way. One odd thing about the process is that, according to the usual rules of TRANSFERENCE, an ailment removed from a sufferer goes to someone, or something else. There are one or two descriptions in which the purchaser inadvertently ends up with the warts on his/her own hands, but usually they simply disappear. One cannot help wondering where they go.

Kent [1930s] Kent (1976) 20–1. Devon *Devonshire Assoc.* 110 (1978) 217–18. Wiltshire Whitlock (1976) 165. London [mid 1980s] Steve Roud Collection. Essex [*c*.1915] Mays (1969) 165. Lincolnshire Peacock (1877) 268–9; Gutch & Peacock (1908) 109; Rudkin (1936) 26; [1940s] Sutton (1992) 151. Norfolk Randell (1966) 85–6. England Addy (1895) 89. N. Ireland Foster (1951) 62; Buckley (1980) 21. Co. Meath/Co. Tipperary *Folk-Lore* 15 (1904) 460. General Lupton (1579) Bk 6, Para. 59; Hatfield (1998) 6–8. Literary Robert Herrick, *Hesperides* (1648) 'Oberon's Palace'.

wart cures: celandine

The greater CELANDINE (*Chelidonium majus*) is one of the plants which are reputed to be effective on warts simply by application of its juice.

Get up a plant of golden celandine at midnight under the moon. Bury it for three days – dig it up and squeeze the juice over the wart – the juice of the greater celandine, without the ceremonies, is a common country cure for warts.

Shropshire [*c*.1905] *Folk-Lore*

The operation described here is more complex than usual: most informants simply apply the juice of the fresh plant. Celandine was third in the list of plants in the *English Folk-Lore Survey* in the 1960s (after broad BEANS and DAN-DELIONS) and was also included in the Folk-Lore Society's *Wart Cure Survey* in 1998. Celandine's popularity in this context in previous times is confirmed by a number of local names for it, such as wart flower, wart wort, and wart plant. It is also claimed to be one of the cures for which science offers some confirmation. Vickery points out that the sap of the greater celandine contains alkaloids such as chelidonin and chelerythrin which may be effective in skin treatment.

Kent [1991] Vickery (1995) 161. Devon *Devonshire Assoc.* 81 (1949) 91. Cornwall Davey (1909) 23. London [1956] Vickery (1995) 160–1. East Anglia [1920s & 1990s] Hatfield (1994) 56–9. Norfolk *Folk-Lore* 40 (1929) 116–17. Shropshire [*c*.1905] *Folk-Lore* 49 (1938) 226–8.

wart cures: cereals

The use of ears or grains of cereal (usually wheat or barley) is regularly reported, although the method is not always the same in each case. The process included the familiar motifs of COUNT-ING the warts and matching the number, but while some advised leaving them in the road for others to find, some buried the grains and waited for them to rot.

[An old man of seventy] *When I was a boy, if anyone had warts on his hands, we used to get as many grains of wheat as there were, and put one on each, and then the grains were tied up in paper, and the person who had the warts went to the nearest cross-roads and threw the wheat over his shoulder; and it was thought that whoever picked the parcel up would have the warts – at any rate they disappeared.*

Shropshire Burne (1883)

Oxfordshire [1920s] Surman (1992) 62. Herefordshire Havergal (1887) 45; [*c*.1895] *Folk-Lore* 39 (1928) 389; Leather (1912) 83. Shropshire Burne (1883) 200. Scotland N&Q 1S:2 (1850) 19–20. Highland Scotland Polson (1926) 34–5. Banffshire Gregor (1874) 271. Co. Donegal Vickery (1995) 80. Unlocated *Bye-Gones* (28 Dec. 1887) 478.

wart cures: charming

Countless wart cures involve the use of organic or inorganic materials with which the warts are touched in one way or another. Another group of cures, however, relies solely, or mainly, on the power of the charmer him/herself – the act of buying the wart (*see above*) is an example, as is the recitation of a verbal charm, or simply 'looking at' the warts to make them disappear.

A boy had his hands covered with warts, which disfigured them most unpleasantly. As the lad passed the window of an old woman in the town who dabbled a little in charms and spells, she looked out and called to him to count his warts. He did so, and told her the exact number. 'By such a day,' she said, naming a day within a fortnight, 'they shall all be gone'. She shut the window and the boy passed on, but by the day indicated every one of the warts, which had troubled him for years, was gone.

Wiltshire Henderson (1866)

A number of informants related stories of 'distance curing', in which some charmers apparently specialized:

I have recently heard of a Yealmpton soldier who, when he was serving in France in the First World War, had the warts (very bad ones) charmed off his hands by an old woman at home, who had never met him, but had simply looked at his photograph shown her by his mother.

Devon *Devonshire Assoc.* (1957)

Some charmers were apparently born with the gift of curing – SEVENTH SONS, for example – but in common with other charming and healing abilities, the ability to treat warts could be passed on from generation to generation. The usual proviso was that the secret must be passed to someone of the opposite sex, and thus alternate between males and females.

A lady in West Norfolk wrote to me that, when she was a girl, an old man in the village, a noted wart charmer, was dying. Having no one of his own folk to pass over his power, he sent for the parson's daughter (my informant's sister) and told her the secret. This she could never divulge, or the power would be lost. She kept the secret and performed very many successful cures.
                         Norfolk *Folk-Lore* (1929)

Again, in accordance with general feeling about such healing powers, wart-charmers usually refused payment, although a subsequent gift was quite acceptable. Many even insisted that they must not even be thanked. The wart sufferer must also not tell anyone what had been done:

In 1937 I was told of a child near Pontesbury who refused to go to a doctor for her warts. She told my informant, rather shamefacedly, 'It's being done'. Afterwards it transpired that she had been to a wart charmer, who had taken her into a dark room and 'spoke over her'. The warts were not cured but the child said that this was because she had talked about it, which the charmer had said she was on no account to do.
                      Shropshire *Folk-Lore* (1938)

Devon [c.1920s] Lakeham (1982) 43–5; *Devonshire Assoc.* 57 (1926) 121; *Devonshire Assoc.* 65 (1933) 127–8; *Devonshire Assoc.* 86 (1954) 300; *Devonshire Assoc.* (1957) 285–6; *Devonshire Assoc.* 92 (1960) 371–2; *Devonshire Assoc.* 102 (1970) 271; *Devonshire Assoc.* 110 (1978) 217. **Cornwall** *Folk-Lore Jnl* 5 (1887) 199–200. **Wiltshire** Henderson (1866) 108–10. **Oxfordshire** *Folk-Lore* 66 (1955) 326. **Worcestershire** *Folk-Lore* 71 (1960) 256. **Warwickshire** Bloom (c.1930) 30–1. **Bedfordshire** Marsom (1950) 182. **Norfolk** *Folk-Lore* 40 (1929) 116–17. **Shropshire** *Folk-Lore* 49 (1938) 226–8. **Staffordshire** *Folk-Lore* 66 (1955) 326. **Yorkshire** Blakeborough (1898) 138–9. **N. Ireland** Buckley (1980) 25. **Guernsey** MacCulloch MS (1864) 400–1. **Unlocated** N&Q 4S:12 (1873) 469.

---

wart cures: cinders

Rubbing warts with cinders from the domestic fire is reported fairly regularly as a cure, but in almost exactly the same terms as the very common cure using stones (*see below*), of which it is probably an offshoot:

There is a charm for warts in our neighbourhood; get up early in the morning, choose from the fireplace one piece of ash or cinder for each wart you have, sew the ashes up in a bag, wear the bag for a day, and then throw it away; you will get rid of your warts, but if any unfortunate person

finds the bag he will get them instead. I know someone who tried this cure, and it was quite successful.   **Cardiganshire** *Folk-Lore* (1928)

Northern England Henderson (1866) 108–10. **Lancashire** N&Q 1S:3 (1851) 516. **England** Addy (1895) 89. **Wales** Jones (1930) 142. **Cardiganshire** *Folk-Lore* 39 (1928) 174–5.

wart cures: counting

COUNTING is one of the standard magical elements in the battery of wart-cure motifs. It often appears in conjunction with other elements, but in the cases listed below it appears to be the sole activity involved:

I had a large number of warts on my hands and arms; I counted them carefully and told the number to an old man who charms for warts, as his father and grandfather had done, and they soon disappeared. It is not necessary to tell the man personally; all he requires is the name of the person and the exact number of warts. No charge is made.   **Devon** *Devonshire Assoc.* (1926)

A marked characteristic of these reports in which counting takes the central role is that they are all concerned with cures carried out by others, rather than being self-administered as most other wart cures are. The people involved are usually those with a reputation for being curers, which suggests that counting is thought to be effective only in combination with other elements or in the hands of someone with a gift.

A variation recorded in the Channel Islands, involved 'uncounting':

Perhaps the standard method, and one which is also common in Guernsey, is that known as 'décompter' – to uncount, or to count backwards. In this case, the practitioner makes the sign of the cross upon the part affected, then he or she begins counting from the number nine backwards to zero, on the second day from eight; on the third from seven, and so on. This is supposed to be an infallible remedy.   **Jersey** L'Amy (1927)

Devon *Devonshire Assoc.* 57 (1926) 121. **Cornwall** N&Q 1S:12 (1855) 37. **Essex** *Folk-Lore* 70 (1959) 414–15. **Buckinghamshire** N&Q 4S:6 (1870) 340. **Worcestershire** Salisbury (1893) 70. **Warwickshire** Langford (1875) 12. **East Anglia** Varden (1885) 104; Hatfield (1994) 10. **Suffolk** *Gent. Mag.* (1867) 728–41. **Norfolk** N&Q 4S:6 (1870) 130. **England** Addy (1895) 89. **Guernsey** MacCulloch MS (1864) 400–1. **Jersey** L'Amy (1927) 91–2.

wart cures: dandelions

The DANDELION is one of the plants which is regularly claimed to have a direct curative effect on warts, simply by rubbing on the juice. It was only mentioned in a handful of folklore works, but its popularity in recent years is demonstrated by a strong showing in two surveys: it was the second most-recommended plant in the *English Folk-Lore Survey* in the 1960s (with 21 respondents, compared to 26 for broad BEANS) and was the most often listed in the Folk-Lore Society's *Wart Cure Survey* in 1998 (for both, *see* Hatfield, (1998)). On this, admittedly slim, evidence, it seems to have grown in popularity over the twentieth century.

Worcestershire Berkeley & Jenkins (1932) 36. **East Anglia** Hatfield (1994) 56–9. **Lincolnshire** Gutch & Peacock (1908) 109; Rudkin (1936) 26. **Highland Scotland** Polson (1926) 34–5. **Co. Cavan** Maloney (1972) 78.

wart cures: eels

Take an eel and cut off the head. Rub the warts with the blood of the head. Then bury the head in the ground. When the head is rotten the warts fall off.　　　　　　　　　　Devon Hewett (1900)

Despite the fact that EELS' blood as a cure for warts has only been noted a handful of times since the mid nineteenth century, it turns out to be one of the oldest of all known wart remedies. The following passage from the Welsh medieval manuscript *Physicians of Myddvai* is uncannily similar to the Devon example quoted above, 650 years later:

Take an eel and cut its head off, anoint the parts, where the warts are situated, with the blood, and bury the head deep in the earth; as the head rottens, so will the warts disappear.

One respondent to the *English Folk-Lore Survey* of the 1960s also mentioned eels' blood.

Devon Hewett (1900) 66. **Northern England** Henderson (1866) 108–10. **Co. Durham** Brockie (1886) 223. **Northumberland** Bigge (1860–62) 89. **Wales** *Physicians of Myddvai* (c.1250).

wart cures: elder

Cutting notches in a stick – one notch for each wart – is a widespread motif in wart cures, and while many informants do not specify the type of stick, a significant number name the ELDER as the proper species to use for the purpose. This is certainly consistent with numerous other beliefs on the healing properties of the elder tree (*see* ELDER: CURES):

A year or two ago I was staying in Somersetshire, and a having a wart myself, was persuaded to have it 'charmed'. The village charmer was summoned; he first cut off a slip of elder-tree and made a notch in it for every wart. He then rubbed the elder against each, strictly enjoining me to think no more about it, as if I looked often at the warts the charm would fail. In about a week the warts had altogether disappeared, to the delight of the operator.　　　　　Somerset N&Q (1850)

What should be done with the stick after the notching and rubbing varies from informant to informant, although most of them specify one of the two standard wart motifs – either bury the stick and let it rot, or throw it on to the road so that whoever finds it gets the warts.

Wart cures using notched sticks appear to combine both magical and physical elements. For many users, and especially the semi-professional wart-charmer, the elder would have connotations of physical medicine overspilling from other cures involving the tree, but in this case the warts are simply touched with the stick, which can hardly have been believed to have much direct therapeutic value. The notches can simply be seen as a method of keeping tally of the important COUNTING, or they can be viewed as the essential process that sets up a lasting sympathetic connection between wart and stick, which must exist if the warts are to fade as the stick rots away. Several versions of the cure call for a cross to be cut in the wood, in addition to the notches, thus bringing a pious aspect to the cure.

This cure was already in circulation, in essentially the same form, in the early seventeenth century:

the like is done by rubbing of warts with a green elder stick, and burying the stick to rot in the muck.　　　　　Bacon, *Sylva Sylvarum* (1627)

Elder was still being regularly reported in the 1960s, as shown in the *English Folk-Lore Survey* (*see* Hatfield (1998)).

Other parts of the elder could also be utilized, as in this seventeenth-century reference:

Wartes – wash them with the juice of the [elder] berries when the berries be black and doe so every night and so binde them to in the nights.
　　　　　Langham, *The Garden of Health* (1633)

See also WART CURES: STICKS/TREES.

Somerset N&Q 1S:2 (1850) 150; Poole (1877) 52–3. **Berkshire** Salmon (1902) 420. **London** N&Q 1S:11 (1855) 7–8. **Herefordshire** Leather (1912) 83. **Northamptonshire** N&Q 1S:2 (1850) 36–7. **Suffolk** *Folk-Lore* 35 (1924) 356–7. **Shropshire** Burne (1883) 199. **Derbyshire** [1890s] Uttley (1946) 114–15. **England** Addy (1895) 88. **West Wales** Davies (1911) 282. **Monmouth** [1954] Opie & Tatem, 422. **Co. Longford** *Béaloideas* 6 (1936) 266. **Unlocated** Opie (1959) 315. **General** Francis Bacon, *Sylva Sylvarum* (1627) 264; W. Langham, *The Garden of Health* (1633).

wart cures: fasting spittle

SPITTLE is a powerful agent in a range of cures, including warts, and 'fasting' spittle is the most effective of all. Technically, 'fasting' simply means not having eaten for a long time, but in this context most people used it to signify first thing in the morning, before breakfast:

One of the best known remedies for many ills, and one still very much in use, is fasting spittle. This was used for scurvy, skin blemishes, warts, bites, and sore eyes. A girl in my class at school [c.1910–15] who had weak ailing eyes, under the doctor's orders, wetted her eyes each morning with fasting spittle . . . I have used fasting spittle for warts and last year a man told me that he had cured himself of what a surgeon had described as a skin cancer by wetting it each morning with fasting spittle.
Sussex *Sussex Life* (Jan. 1973)

The use of saliva also featured as the fifth most popular wart cure reported in the *English Folk-Lore Survey* in the 1960s (*see* Hatfield (1998)).

Sussex *Sussex Life* (Jan. 1973) 34. **Devon** *Devonshire Assoc.* 57 (1926) 121. **Wiltshire** Whitlock (1976) 166. **Bedfordshire** Marsom (1950) 182. **Suffolk** *Folk-Lore* 35 (1924) 356–7. **Staffordshire** Hackwood (1924) 150. **England** Addy (1895) 88, 89. **Montgomeryshire** Hamer (1877) 261–2. **Cardiganshire** Davies (1911) 282. **Highland Scotland** Macbain (1887/88) 257; Polson (1926) 34–5. **Western Scotland** Napier (1879) 98–9. **Dumfriesshire** Shaw (1890) 13. **Ireland** Hickey (1938) 269. **N. Ireland** Foster (1951) 62. **Co. Longford** *Béaloideas* 6 (1936) 266. **Co. Wexford** [1938] Ó Muirithe & Nuttall (1999) 97. **Co. Cork** Culloty (1993) 59.

wart cures: funerals

A number of informants described procedures which were designed to pass their warts on to a corpse on its way to be buried:

In some parts of Ireland, especially towards the south, they place great faith in the following charm – When a funeral is passing by, they rub the warts and say three times 'May these warts and this corpse pass away and never more return'; sometimes adding 'in the name of the Father, Son, and Holy Ghost'.
Southern Ireland N&Q (1850)

Most versions are very similar to this, but in some it was necessary to pick up a stone or handful of dust and throw if after the passing funeral.

At first glance, these funeral-based cures seem quite different from more mainstream procedures, but the difference is only superficial. There is little evidence that there were magical beliefs connecting death and warts at the core of the belief, and the cures appear to be simply another combination of the well-known motifs of 'as the item rots' and the belief that warts can be passed on by wishing or 'charming' without the need for physical contact between curer, curing agent, and wart.

Unusually for wart cures the central motif of sending the warts away with a corpse seems genuinely regional. Apart from a solitary report from London (as late as 1960), all known versions come from Ireland. The solitary Devon example is based on a different principle. Here, stolen bread and cheese is rubbed on the warts and crumbled into an open grave as the words 'dust to dust' are spoken, and this is closer to the widespread raw meat and bread cures.

One or two of the wart cures that involve placing pins in a bottle prescribe placing it in a grave rather than simply burying it. In a few sources, warts are included in the list of skin ailments which can be cured by stroking with a DEAD MAN'S HAND, a procedure which is normally reserved for much more serious medical conditions. It seems unlikely that anyone would be sufficiently desperate about their warts to undergo such a horrifying ordeal (*see*, for example: **Suffolk** *Folk-Lore* 56 (1945) 270; **Galloway** Mactaggart (1824) 463)).

Devon *Devonshire Assoc.* 63 (1931) 131. **London** [1960] Opie & Tatem, 423. **Ireland** Wilde (1888) 198. **Southern Ireland** N&Q 1S:2 (1850) 226. **N. Ireland** Foster (1951) 62. **Co. Londonderry** *Folk-Lore* 4 (1893) 356. **Co. Donegal** *Folk-Lore Record* 1 (1878) 223; *Folk-Lore* 4 (1893) 355–6. **Literary** N&Q 11S:4 (1911) 446.

wart cures: hair

An operation which appears to take a different approach to warts, by acting directly on the wart but without the aid of any other substance. The

plan simply is to strangle the wart by tying a
HAIR around it:

*For warts the cures are many and various. If you
tie a horsehair round the neck of a wart, according to some, the wart will quickly go away of its
own accord.*   Cumberland Penfold (1907)

Some informants stipulate a horse hair, others a
human hair. Another use of hair in this context
involves tying knots in the hair and throwing it
away (*see* WART CURES: STRING).

As if to demonstrate the way in which wart
cures can be merged, Richard Hoggart reported
a strange hybrid cure, which makes one wonder
whether variants might sometimes be created by
people's misunderstanding:

*I know of two recent urban experiments with
horsehair and steak to remove warts; the steak is
buried in the ground with the hair tied round it,
and the wart thereafter withers and finally drops
off.*   Unlocated Hoggart (1957)

Bedfordshire Marsom (1950) 182. Norfolk [1952] *Folk-
Lore* 105 (1994) 101; *Folk-Lore* 102:2 (1991) 240.
Lincolnshire Sutton (1992) 151. England Addy (1895) 88.
Northern England Henderson (1866) 108–10.
Cumberland Penfold (1907) 56. Co. Durham Brockie
(1886) 223. Northumberland Bigge (1860–62) 89. Co.
Cork Culloty (1993) 59. Unlocated Hoggart (1957) 30.

wart cures: matches

Six respondents to the *English Folk-Lore Survey*
in the 1960s (*see* Hatfield (1998)), recommended
the use of matches on warts, as also used by Irish
tinkers:

*There were loads of cures for warts and they
really worked. One used red matches, you wet a
match and rub it on the wart three times a day
for a week, and then the wart suddenly disappears, the sulphur eats it away.*
          Irish Travellers [1940s] Joyce (1985) 16

wart cures: meat

One of the most commonly reported traditional
methods of curing warts involved raw meat:

[From servant girl about 22 years old] *Warts
may also be removed, she says, by stealing a piece
of meat – no matter from whom, or whether it
be fresh or salt – and burying it in the ground.
As the flesh rots, the warts will disappear. Her
grandfather told her that he, to get rid of his
warts, had stolen a bit of bacon from his aunt and
buried it, and that he soon lost his warts.*
          Devon *Devonshire Assoc.* (1878)

The insistence on stolen meat is an almost
universal feature, at least from the eighteenth
century onwards, but the essential detail missing
in the quoted example is that the meat must be
rubbed on the warts before it is buried. Another
regular element is that the whole operation must
take place in complete secret or it will not work.
In many cases, the type of meat is not specified,
but where it is, bacon and beef are named in
about equal numbers. As the wasting of the meat
relies entirely on the rotting of the meat, some
informants advised shortening the process by
burying it in an anthill or dung-heap. Apart from
such variant details, the cure is remarkably stable
across the whole of the British Isles, from its
earliest mention to the present day. The meat
cure is no modern invention, dating at least from
Thomas Lupton's *A Thousand Notable Things of
Sundry Sorts:*

*Wartes rubbed with a peece of raw beefe and the
same beefe being buried within the grounde: the
wartes will weare and consume, as the beefe doth
rot in the ground. Proved.*   Lupton (1579)

It was also recommended in a number of herbals
and other works of medicine, including Culpeper's
Complete Herbal and English Physician (1653). It
has also lasted well into the recent past. It was far
and away the most reported method in the *English
Folk-Lore Survey* of the 1960s, being mentioned by
nearly three times as many respondents as the next
most popular method. It was also recorded
several times in the Folk-Lore Society's smaller
Wart Cure Survey of 1998.

The motifs involved in the meat cure –
rubbing with an organic substance, burial as the
method of disposal, and the idea that as the item
wastes away, so will the warts – are common ones
in wart cures. As discussed in the general WART
CURES entry, and in that on the similar SNAIL
cures, the principles involved are a combination
of TRANSFERENCE and SYMPATHY. Leaving
aside any potential direct benefit from contact
with the meat, the essence appears to be that the
rubbing transfers the 'illness' to the meat. But as
the supposed operation continues *after* the
contact has finished, there must be some sort of
sympathetic connection between meat and wart
to ensure mutual wasting away.

Isle of Wight IOW Fed. W. I.s (1994) 95. Sussex
Latham (1878) 41. Devon N&Q 1S:11 (1855) 8;
Devonshire Assoc. 10 (1878) 102; Hewett (1892) 28;
Devonshire Assoc. 59 (1927) 168. Cornwall N&Q 1S:12
(1855) 37; Hunt (1865) 211; Couch (1871) 167; *Folk-Lore
Jnl* 5 (1887) 200; [1890s] *Old Cornwall* 1:12 (1930) 4.
Wiltshire *Wilts. N&Q* 1 (1893–5) 156; Whitlock (1976)
165. Essex [1983] Opie & Tatem, 423. Oxfordshire

[1920s] Surman (1992) 62; *Oxf. FL Soc. Ann. Record* (1956) 12. **Herefordshire** Leather (1912) 84. **Worcestershire** Berkeley & Jenkins (1932) 36. **Warwickshire** Bloom (*c.*1930) 30–1. **Northamptonshire** Sternberg (1851) 166. **Bedfordshire** Marsom (1950) 182. **East Anglia** Varden (1885) 104. **Suffolk** *Gent. Mag.* (1867) 728–41; *Folk-Lore* 35 (1924) 356–7. **Norfolk** *Folk-Lore* 40 (1929) 116–17; *East Anglian Mag.* (Aug. 1935) 94. **Lincolnshire** *Grantham Jnl* (22 June 1878). **Shropshire** Burne (1883) 199; *Folk-Lore* 49 (1938) 226–8. **Staffordshire** Poole (1875) 84. **Buckinghamshire** *Folk-Lore* 43 (1932) 104. **West Midlands** W. Midlands Fed. W. I.s. (1996) 73. **Northern England** Henderson (1866) 108–10. **Yorkshire** N&Q 1S:6 (1852) 311–12; Nicholson (1890) 141. **Yorkshire/Lancashire** N&Q 1S:2 (1850) 68. **Lancashire** *Lancashire Lore* (1971) 51. **Cumberland** Penfold (1907) 56. **Co. Durham** Brockie (1886) 223; Leighton (1910) 53. **Northumberland** Bigge (1860–62) 89. **Wales** Trevelyan (1909) 320; Jones (1930) 142. **West Wales** Davies (1911) 281–2. **Montgomeryshire** Hamer (1877) 261–2; *Bye-Gones* (7 Dec. 1887) 465. **Monmouthshire** [1954] Opie & Tatem, 423. **Scotland** *People's Friend* (8 Nov. 1882) 711. **Highland Scotland** Macbain (1887/88) 257. **Western Scotland** Napier (1879) 97. **Banffshire** Gregor (1874) 271. **Caithness** Rinder (1895) 63. **Co. Cork** [1937] Culloty (1993) 59. **Co. Tipperary** *Folk-Lore* 8 (1897) 387. **Co. Galway** *Béaloideas* 1 (1928) 328. **Co. Longford** *Béaloideas* 6 (1936) 266. **Co. Londonderry** *Folk-Lore* 4 (1893) 356. **Jersey** L'Amy (1927) 91–2. **Unlocated** Grose (1787) 517; Chambers 1 (1878) 733; Igglesden (*c.*1932) 206; Hoggart (1957) 30. **General** Lupton (1579) Bk 6, Para. 59; Nicholas Culpeper, *Complete Herbal and English Physician* (1653) 221.

---

wart cures: moon

The MOON features in a variety of ways of removing warts, although none of them has been reported widely enough to count as major cures.

In a handful of instances, it is the moonlight which is the effective agent.

Yet another is to wash the hands in the moon's rays focussed in a dry metal basin, saying:

I wash my hands in this dry dish
Oh man in the moon, do grant my wish
And come and take away this.
                    Cornwall *Folk-Lore Jnl* (1887)

This procedure was reported by folklorists a few times in the late nineteenth century, and was previously mentioned by both Sir Thomas Browne (1650) and Sir Kenelm Digby (1658) as current practice in their time. What happened to it between the mid seventeenth and the late nineteenth century is at present unclear.

Another set of cures calls for action at a particular phase of the moon:

When the person troubled with warts first sees a new moon, he is to take a small portion of earth

from under the right foot and make a paste of it, and lay it upon the wart, and tie a cloth over it, which is not to be removed till the change of the moon, when the wart will be completely removed.
                    Glasgow [*c.*1820] Napier

This may be related to a cure current in classical times, as recorded by Pliny:

Warts are removed by those who, after the twentieth day of the month, lie face upwards on a path, gaze at the moon with hands stretched over their head, and rub the wart with whatever they have grasped.   Pliny, *Natural History* (AD 77)

Alternatively, the principle of 'wishing when you see a new moon' can be brought to bear on the wart problem: Blow them away to the new moon the first time you see it (**Devon** *Devonshire Assoc.* (1926)).

See also MOON: WART CURES.

Washing in moonlight: **Cornwall** *Folk-Lore Jnl* 5 (1887) 200. **England** Addy (1895) 89. **General** Browne, *Pseudodoxia Epidemica* (1672 edn) Bk 5, Ch. 23, Para. 9; K. Digby, *Late Discourse* (1658) 43.
Earth under foot: **Yorkshire** Morris (1911) 248. **Western Scotland** Napier (1879) 97. **Glasgow** [*c.*1820] Napier [1864] 397. **Co. Londonderry** *Folk-Lore* 4 (1893) 355.
Miscellaneous: **Devon** *Devonshire Assoc.* 57 (1926) 121. **Wiltshire** Whitlock (1976) 166. **Classical** Pliny, *Natural History* (AD 77) Bk 28, Para. 12.

---

wart cures: pins

PINS are used in a variety of wart cures, sometimes as an apparently essential element, but more often in a peripheral role. In most cases the pin is the item which is used to touch the warts, either one pin for all, or one each:

The Vicar of Bodmin found, not long since, a bottle full of pins in a newly-made grave. I have heard of this as an unfailing remedy; each wart was touched with a new pin, and the pin then dropped into the bottle. I am not quite certain that it was necessary that the bottle should be placed in a new-made grave; in many cases burying it in the earth, and especially at a 'four crossroads' was quite sufficient. As the pins rust, the warts decay.   Cornwall Hunt (1865)

There was also a simpler method:

Boys take a new pin, cross the warts with it nine times, and fling it over the left shoulder.
                    Northern England Henderson (1866)

The burying motif is a commonplace in wart cures, and even the crossroads and new-made graves are regularly found in other contexts. Similarly, throwing over the shoulder is much better known using stones. As none of the procedures are unique to pins, any claim to there being a separate sub-genre defined by the use of the pin is very weak. Nevertheless, an interesting combination of the 'buying' motif and the pin is provided in an early reference:

If one doth buy warts of them that have them, and give them a pin therefore; if the party that hath the warts, pricke the same pin upon some garment that he weares daily, or commonly, the wart or warts without doubt will diminish and weare away privily, and bee cleane gone in a short time. This was told mee for an often tryed and proved thing; yea, and by such a one as had seene the experience thereof.   Lupton (1579)

Another way in which pins were disposed of, after touching the warts, was by sticking them into a tree, usually specifically an ash (*see* WART CURES: STICKS AND TREES).

Burying pins until they rust was also reported by one respondent in the *English Folk-Lore Survey* in the 1960s.

Cornwall Hunt (1865) 210; *Folk-Lore Jnl* 5 (1887) 200. Essex N&Q 4S:6 (1870) 340. East Anglia Varden (1885) 104. Shropshire Burne (1883) 201; *Folk-Lore* 49 (1938) 226–8. Northern England Henderson (1866) 108–10. General Lupton (1579) Bk 6, Para. 59.

wart cures: potato

Rubbing with a raw potato was reported a few times only, with the usual burying motif:

When I was a girl there was a man called Georgie Moses and he was a charmer in the village. He sat on the bridge by the pub and if you had warts he told you to cut a potato in half and rub it on the warts, and then bury it in the garden. They said that as the potato rotted so did the wart.
Devon Lakeham (1982)

Also reported by five respondents in the *English Folk-Lore Survey* of the 1960s; *see* Hatfield (1998).

Devon Lakeham (1982) 43–5. Co. Durham Brockie (1886) 223. N. Ireland [1940s] *Folk-Lore* 103:1 (1992) 114; Foster (1951) 62. Co. Londonderry *Folk-Lore* 4 (1893) 355.

wart cures: snails

One of the two most common traditional wart cures involves the application of a snail, or sometimes a slug, directly to the wart, followed by a set method of disposal:

Warts – for these the snail is also in request. Proceed in this wise. Pierce the mollusc with a pin as many times as you have warts in number, then stick the snail on a blackthorn on the hedgerow; as the creature dies, so will the warts wane and disappear.   Gloucestershire N&Q (1873)

A few minor variations occur in the details, but for the vast majority the main shape is the same. It is debatable whether the snail slime has any direct effect on the wart, and thus whether that part of the cure is science or superstition, but the second part of the cure is definitely in the realm of the latter. The principle that the item used to touch or rub the warts must be allowed to decay is one of the main commonplaces of wart cures, and occurs in numerous guises. Taken all together, they seem to combine elements of both TRANSFERENCE and SYMPATHY, in that for the warts to fade as the snail does implies a continued connection between them. An alternative, more prosaic, explanation is that the snail rotting is simply a metaphor for the lapse of time necessary for the cure to take effect.

Unusually for the snail cures, Flora Thompson describes a throwing motif commoner with non-perishables (*see* WART CURES: STONES):

A few innocent charms and superstitious practices were all that remained of magic. Warts were still charmed away by binding a large black slug upon the wart for a night and a day. Then the sufferer would go by night to the nearest crossroads and, by flinging the slug over the left shoulder, hope to get rid of the wart.
Oxfordshire [1890s] Thompson

The snail cure has lasted well in the tradition, being regularly reported in the late twentieth century and featuring strongly in both the *English Folk-Lore Survey* in the 1960s and the Folk-Lore Society's *Wart Cure Survey* of 1998 (*see* Hatfield (1998)). It has been around for at least 350 years, in essentially the same form:

How to cure warts: Go into the field and take a black snail, and rub them with the same nine times one way, and then nine times another, and then stick that said snail upon a black-thorn, and the warts will waste.
Culpeper, *Complete Herbal and English Physician* (1653)

Devon *Devonshire Assoc.* 10 (1878) 102; *Devonshire Assoc.* 84 (1952) 297; *Devonshire Assoc.* 89 (1957) 285; *Devonshire Assoc.* 96 (1964) 98. Cornwall *Jnl Royal Inst. Cornwall* 20 (1915) 124. Wiltshire [1922] Opie & Tatem, 423. Oxfordshire [1890s] Thompson (1945) 487–8; [1920s] Harris (1969) 114. Gloucestershire N&Q 4S:4 (1873) 500; *Glos. N&Q* 1 (1881) 43; Hartland (1895) 51. Herefordshire [c.1895] *Folk-Lore* 39 (1928) 389; Leather

(1912) 84. **Worcestershire** Salisbury (1893) 70. **Warwickshire** Bloom (*c.*1930) 30–1. **Northamptonshire** N&Q 1S:2 (1850) 36–37. **Cambridgeshire** *Folk-Lore* 64 (1953) 425. **East Anglia** Varden (1885) 104. **Suffolk** *Gent. Mag.* (1867) 728–41; *Folk-Lore* 35 (1924) 356–7; *East Anglian Mag.* 13 (1953/4) 395. **Norfolk** *Folk-Lore* 40 (1929) 116–17; Haggard (1935) 17; Randell (1966) 85–6. **Lincolnshire** Peacock (1877) 268–9; Gutch & Peacock (1908) 109; Rudkin (1936) 26. **Shropshire** Burne (1883) 201. **Staffordshire** Poole (1875) 84. **England** Addy (1895) 89. **Yorkshire** *Leeds Mercury* (4 Oct. 1879); Nicholson (1890) 141; Morris (1911) 248. **Lancashire** N&Q 1S:3 (1851) 56; Harland & Wilkinson (1882) 78–9, 154; *Folk-Lore* 24 (1913) 89. **Cumberland** Penfold (1907) 56. **Co. Durham** Brockie (1886) 223. **Northumberland** Bigge (1860–62) 89; Henderson (1866) 108–10. **Wales** Jones (1930) 142. **Radnorshire** [1954] Opie & Tatem, 423. **Montgomeryshire** Hamer (1877) 261–2; *Bye-Gones* (7 Dec. 1887) 465. **Highland Scotland** Polson (1926) 34–5. **Western Scotland** Napier (1879) 97. **Dumfriesshire** Corrie (1890/91) 80. **Ireland** Hickey (1938) 269. **Co. Longford** *Béaloideas* 6 (1936) 266. **Co. Leitrim** *Folk-Lore* 5 (1894) 199. **Co. Cavan/Co. Leitrim** Logan (1965) 52. **Co. Antrim** *Folk-Lore* 4 (1893) 356. **Isle of Man** *Folk-Lore* 2 (1891) 294–5. **Unlocated** N&Q 4S:6 (1870) 69; *Bye-Gones* (28 Dec. 1887) 478. **General** Nicholas Culpeper, *Complete Herbal and English Physician* (1653) 221; Hatfield (1998).

wart cures: soda

Rubbing the warts with washing soda is only occasionally recommended in folklore works, but was the third most popular substance in the *English Folk-Lore Survey* of the 1960s; *see* Hatfield (1998).

Wiltshire Whitlock (1976) 164–5. **Bedfordshire** Marsom (1950) 182. **Co. Cavan** *Folk-Lore* 19 (1908) 315.

wart cures: spurge

One of the many plants whose juice was considered directly effective when squeezed on warts was the spurge, but it is not always clear which variety was used. Some informants specifically identified sun spurge, petty spurge, or wood spurge, while others simply called it 'spurge'.

The milky juice of a weed – the petty spurge – was rubbed on a wart. It healed one of mine, but it had to be this particular weed with a tiny yellow flower. It was very common, but you have to hunt for it today. **Devon** [*c.*1912] Lakeham

It is also one of those cures which lasted well into the recent past and, presumably, the present. Nine respondents in the *English Folk-Lore Survey* of the 1960s, and one in the Folk-Lore Society's *Wart Cure Survey* of 1998 named spurge as a

known cure, although the informant in the latter sample labelled it 'unsuccessful'.

Devon [*c.*1912] Lakeham (1982) 48; *Devonshire Assoc.* 102 (1970) 272. **Berkshire** [1986] Vickery (1995) 359. **Oxfordshire** [1976] Vickery (1995) 359. **Warwickshire** Bloom (*c.*1930) 30–1. **Bedfordshire** Marsom (1950) 182. **East Anglia** [1920s & 1990s] Hatfield (1994) 56–9. **Derbyshire** [1890s] Uttley (1946) 114–15. **Co. Cork** Culloty (1993) 59.

wart cures: sticks/trees

The commonest species of tree used in wart cures is the ELDER (*see above*). Various other species are mentioned a few times in this context, including HAZEL, ASH, ELM, and OAK, but very often the cure simply calls for 'a stick':

Another mode is to cut as many notches in a piece of stick as you have warts. The stick is then buried, and as it decays the warts vanish.
    Yorkshire *Leeds Mercury* (4 Oct. 1879)

The cutting of the notches seems to be simply part of the usual process of counting the warts, on a par with having one stone or grain of cereal for each wart, and to have no other significance. Similarly, burying the item is a commonplace element in wart cures, although in this case it seems singularly inappropriate. A buried stick would surely take too long to rot (unless chosen very carefully) to satisfy an impatient sufferer. In some versions, the stick should be thrown into the road, and whoever picks it up gets the warts. Again this is similar to the way stones were used in cures and is more logical than burying the stick.

Some other cures involving wood are more complex, but are still based on familiar wart-curing principles. One group involves sticking PINS into a tree, usually an ASH.

Whoever will charm away a wart must take a pin and go to an ash-tree. He then crosses the wart with the pin three times, and, after each crossing, repeats:

    Ash-tree, ashen-tree
    Pray buy this wart of me

after which he sticks the pin in the tree, and the wart soon disappears, and grows on the live tree instead. This must be done secretly.
    Unlocated Halliwell (1849)

Both notches in sticks and pins in an ash tree were listed by respondents in the *English Folk-Lore Survey* in the 1960s. Other miscellaneous cures include using charred sticks from the fire, and 'counting the boles' on an elm tree.

Notches in stick: Devon [1900] *Devonshire Assoc.* 57 (1926) 121. Berkshire L. S. (1909) 152. Buckinghamshire *Folk-Lore* 43 (1932) 104. Herefordshire [*c.*1895] *Folk-Lore* 39 (1928) 389. Worcestershire Berkeley & Jenkins (1932) 35. Warwickshire Bloom (*c.*1930) 30–1. Bedfordshire Marsom (1950) 182. Suffolk *Folk-Lore* 35 (1924) 356–7. Lincolnshire Swaby (1891) 91. Shropshire *Folk-Lore* 49 (1938) 226–8. Yorkshire *Leeds Mercury* (4 Oct. 1879). Montgomeryshire Hamer (1877) 261–2.
Pins in ash trees: Sussex Latham (1878) 41. Somerset Tongue (1965) 220. Suffolk *Gent. Mag.* (1867) 728–41. Leicestershire N&Q 1S:7 (1853) 81. Unlocated Halliwell (1849) 208.
Miscellaneous: Sussex Latham (1878) 41. Cornwall Hunt (1865) 211. Suffolk *Folk-Lore* 35 (1924) 356–7.

wart cures: stones

A number of traditional wart cures involved touching the warts with an object which is then disposed of in a set manner. A widespread example of this motif used pebbles as the main agent:

Another way of charming away warts is to pick up small white stones from a brook – one stone for each wart – and rub the warts with them. Then the stones are to be tied up in paper, and the person who has the warts is to go to the nearest crossroads and throw the stones over his shoulders, and whoever picks up the parcel gets the warts. A young woman in the parish of Llanarth in Cardiganshire, did this, and got rid of her warts. Soon after this a woman who lives in the neighbourhood passed by, and picked up the parcel of stones, thinking it contained some biscuits or sweets which one of the school children had lost on the way home from school. But to her great surprise, when she opened the paper, she only found small white stones! After this the old woman found her hands covered with warts, but she in her turn charmed them away by washing them with spittle from the mouth. My informant was the old woman herself.

Cardiganshire Davies (1911)

Details vary somewhat from version to version, but the overall pattern is remarkably similar. The stones are not always described, but when they are they are usually white; the shoulder is not always identified, but is usually the left; the place is not always specified, but is often a crossroads. A further detail is that the thrower must not look to see where the stones have landed.

The motifs involved here are all classic elements of wart cures – touching, counting, throwing away, and most notably, the principle of TRANSFERENCE. Wart cures that involve the use of inorganic items such as stones are more easily categorized than those which use plant or animal matter. Whereas a snail's slime or a dandelion's sap, for example, may perhaps have some curative value in themselves, touching the warts with a stone clearly operates on the purely magical level. The element of transference, in this case, is also more explicit than in other cures. It is not entirely clear, however, what happens to the warts if nobody picks up the stones to complete the chain of transference. Presumably, the warts continue to reside in the stones, otherwise they would not disappear from the sufferer's hands.

The earliest example of this wart cure using stones dates from Lancashire in 1851, but Robert Southey (*Letters from England*) described exactly the same process in 1807 using dried peas or beans, and centuries before, the Latin author Pliny wrote the same thing:

On the first day of the moon, each wart must be touched with a single chickpea, after which the party must tie up the peas in a linen cloth and throw it behind them.

Pliny, *Natural History* (AD 77)

This must not be taken to mean that the belief is as old in Britain. Given the popularity of Pliny's works with British writers, physicians, and herbalists from the sixteenth century onwards, it seems certain that the cure was introduced to British tradition by way of direct translation from Pliny, and it thus has a relatively recent literary origin.

Despite its widespread nature in the nineteenth and early twentieth centuries, the cure has not lasted as well as many others. Twelve respondents to the *English Folk-Lore Survey* in the 1960s reported cures involving stones thrown away, but none was included in the Folk-Lore Society's *Wart Cure Survey* of 1998. It is still mentioned on occasion but usually in terms of a piece of romantic past rather than current practice.

See also WART CURES: CINDERS.

Devon Hewett (1900) 82; *Devonshire Assoc.* 57 (1926) 121; *Devonshire Assoc.* 85 (1953) 220; *Devonshire Assoc.* 89 (1957) 285. Cornwall Hunt (1865) 211; *Folk-Lore Jnl* 5 (1887) 200. London [1960] Opie & Tatem, 424. Herefordshire Leather (1912) 84. East Anglia Varden (1885) 104. Norfolk *Folk-Lore* 40 (1929) 116–17. Lincolnshire Peacock (1877) 268–9; *Grantham Jnl* (22 June 1878); Rudkin (1936) 26. Shropshire Burne (1883) 201. Northern England Henderson (1866) 108–10. Yorkshire Nicholson (1890) 88; Blakeborough (1898) 146; [1953] Opie & Tatem, 424. Lancashire N&Q 1S:3 (1851) 56; Harland & Wilkinson (1882) 78–9, 154. Cumberland Gibson (1858) 107; Penfold (1907) 56. Co. Durham Brockie (1886) 223. Northumberland Bigge (1860–62) 89. Wales Jones (1930) 142. Cardiganshire Davies (1911) 282. Montgomeryshire *Bye-Gones* (7 Dec.

1887) 465. **Wigtonshire** *Folk-Lore* 26 (1915) 209. **Ireland**
N&Q 3S:8 (1865) 146. **Co. Cork** [1937] Culloty (1993)
59. **Co. Wexford** [1938] Ó Muirithe & Nuttall (1999) 97.
General Southey (1807) 50. **Classical** Pliny, *Natural
History* (A D 77) Bk 22, Para. 72.

wart cures: straw

In a number of reports, straw, rushes, reeds, or
their equivalent were the active ingredients in the
cure, but there was far more variation between
versions than is usual with other wart cures. In
some cases, the straw was simply rubbed on the
warts and then disposed of, while in others it was
the knots or 'knees' in the stalks which mattered
and were counted to match the number of warts.

*Rub one of the joints of a barley stalk (glùn an
eòrna) to the wart – one joint for each wart – and
go unknown to anyone and bury the stalks. As
they rot, the warts decay.*
                       Highland Scotland Macbain (1887/88)

*To remove warts take a straw having nine knots
or joints in it, and rub the warts three times with
each of the nine knots on three successive mornings.*   Co. Cavan *Folk-Lore* (1908)

Similarly, the straw could be buried or thrown
away – both commonplace motifs in wart cures:

*Pick three rushes and rub them over the warts;
then tie them together and throw them away.
'The person who picks them up will get the warts'.*
                       Devon *Devonshire Assoc.* (1926)

Like several other items which are buried in
wart cures, straw seems an odd choice because
it does not rot quickly enough to satisfy an impatient wart sufferer. This was acknowledged by
one Cornish informant:

*I was then told to bury the bundle, and that when
the straw was rotted the warts would disappear.
I buried the bundle under a turf on the lawn.
Nothing happened to the warts for two months
or more, so I lifted the turf, as the weather had
been dry, the straw was still in good condition. I
then took the bundle to a ripe spot in a cow yard,
and buried it in the dung. In about two or three
weeks every wart was gone, and I have never had
one since.*   Cornwall *Devonshire Assoc.* (1932)

Devon Henderson (1866) 108–10; *Devonshire Assoc.* 57
(1926) 121. **Cornwall** N&Q 2S:4 (1857) 25; Couch (1871)
149; *Devonshire Assoc.* 64 (1932) 164. **Cumberland**
Gibson (1858) 107. **Highland Scotland** Macbain
(1887/88) 257. **Co. Cork** Culloty (1993) 59. **Co.
Tipperary** *Folk-Lore* 8 (1897) 386–7. **Co. Londonderry**
Folk-Lore 4 (1893) 315. **Co. Cavan** *Folk-Lore* 19 (1908)
315.

wart cures: string

A regular way of marking the number of warts
once counted was to tie a KNOT in a piece of
string, thread, or occasionally HAIR – one knot
for each wart.

*Take a piece of twine, tie in it as many knots as
you have warts, touch each wart with a knot, and
then throw the twine behind your back into some
place where it may soon decay – a pond, or a hole
in the earth. But tell no one what you have done.
When the twine is decayed, your warts will
disappear; without any pain or trouble – being,
in fact, charmed away.*   Devon *Athenaeum* (1846)

The knotted string cure was listed by four
respondents in the *English Folk-Lore Survey* in
the 1960s.

Devon *Athenaeum* (1846) 1069; [1900] *Devonshire
Assoc.* 57 (1926) 121. **Cornwall** Hunt (1865) 210–11; *Folk-
Lore Jnl* 5 (1887) 200. **Herefordshire** Leather (1912) 84.
Shropshire *Folk-Lore* 49 (1938) 226–8. **Lincolnshire**
Rudkin (1936) 26. **Yorkshire** *Leeds Mercury* (4 Oct.
1879). **Lancashire** N&Q 1S:2 (1850) 68. **Caithness**
Rinder (1895) 63. **Isle of Man** *Folk-Lore* 2 (1891) 294–5.

wart cures: toads

Considering the general belief that handling
TOADS will give you warts, it is surprising to find
a few informants recommending their use as a
cure.

*Wart cure – Take a toad and rub it on the wart,
then pass the toad to someone else, who must take
and hang the toad on a thorn bush. As the toad
dies and withers so will the warts die and wither
away.*   Lincolnshire Rudkin (1936)

Even more surprising, it was mentioned to the
author in an East Sussex village as a cure in 2002,
although perhaps not seriously.

Sussex [2002] Steve Roud Collection. **Suffolk** *Folk-Lore*
35 (1924) 356–7. **Lincolnshire** Rudkin (1936) 25.

wart cures: water

A number of cures call for warts to be bathed in
water collected in a certain way, or, more
commonly, from a particular place:

*If you were goin' along the road an' happen on a
wee drap o' water in the hollow of a stone, where
you would not expect to find it, take an' wash the
wart with it three times, an' the wart will wear
away.*   Co. Londonderry *Folk-Lore* (1893)

There is some indication that it is not the stone that matters so much as the fact that it must be water that has 'not touched the ground'. This type of cure seems to be almost exclusively from Ireland and Scotland, although Wales has a similar one:

warts to be washed in rainwater collected in an oak stump and left to dry of themselves – all of these processes to be carried out secretly.
                                    Wales Jones (1930)

The water from particular local healing wells is also sometimes recommended for warts. Similarly, water from other sources can achieve at least a localized reputation:

Water which seeps through the roof of a mine-gallery at Cowdenbeath in West Fife has got a widespread reputation as a cure for warts, and requests for bottles of it are continually reaching the miner who first drew attention to its supposed properties.   Fifeshire *Folk-Lore* (1952)

See also WARTS: BLACKSMITH'S WATER.

Wales Jones (1930) 142. **Cardiganshire** Davies (1911) 282. **Highland Scotland** Macbain (1887/88) 257; Polson (1926) 34–5. **Fifeshire** *Folk-Lore* 63 (1952) 177. **Banffshire** Gregor (1874) 271. **Co. Galway** *Béaloideas* 1 (1928) 328. **Co. Cavan/Co. Leitrim** Logan (1965) 52. **Co. Leitrim** *Folk-Lore* 5 (1894) 199. **Co. Londonderry** *Folk-Lore* 4 (1893) 356.

warts: causes

By far the most commonly quoted cause for warts on the hands is washing them in water that had been used to boil eggs.

Not long ago two young and intelligent ladies stated that they had inadvertently washed their hands and arms in egg water, and in each case this had been followed by large numbers of warts.
                        Lancashire Harland & Wilkinson (1882)

But there were other causes. Warts could be spread by blood:

Beware not to let blood from a wart fall upon the hand . . . in the north of Ireland they say a wart will rise for every drop of blood.
                        N. Ireland *Folk-Lore Record* (1878)

Children in particular were convinced that warts could be passed on by touch:

[Remembering childhood, late 1940s] She turned back to me and jabbed me with the wart on the end of her forefinger. It was full of little holes on the top, like a salt shaker, and was seething with germs, little warts really. When you touched

anyone with a wart you made him get them. And she'd touched me with hers. I couldn't take my eyes off the horrible ugly thing, as big as sixpence it was and she saw me looking at it. 'What's wrong wi' your kipper?' 'You shouldn't have touched me with your wart,' I said, sick in my stomach, 'You could make me get one'.
                                    Glasgow Liverani (1975)

Three plants which were reputed to cause warts are reported in Vickery (1995): in Cornwall, the picking of the flowers of the sheep's bit (*Jasione montana*), and the handling of corn poppies, and in Kent the juice of the snowberry (*Symphoricarpos albus*) were all carefully avoided.

Kent [1930s] Vickery (1995) 354. **Devon** *Devonshire Assoc.* 64 (1932) 164. **Cornwall** Davey (1909) 19; Vickery (1995) 351. **Warwickshire** Bloom (*c.*1930) 30–1. **Yorkshire** Nicholson (1890) 46; Morris (1911) 249. **Lancashire** Harland & Wilkinson (1882) 121. **Co. Durham** Brockie (1886) 223. **Highland Scotland** Campbell (1900) 230. **Glasgow** [1940s] Liverani (1975) 143–4. **N. Ireland** *Folk-Lore Record* 1 (1878) 224. **Co. Tyrone** *Lore & Language* 1:7 (1972) 13.

washing blankets: May

A handful of twentieth-century references specifically prohibit washing blankets in May, either because they will shrink or, more ominously:

Wash blankets in May
Wash (or drive) the family away.
                        Buckinghamshire *Folk-Lore* (1932)

More or less the same rhyme is reported for WASHING CLOTHES on NEW YEAR's Day and GOOD FRIDAY. As with several other washing beliefs, this one seems particularly strong in the English West Country.

Somerset [1923] Opie & Tatem, 242. **Devon** *Devonshire Assoc.* 102 (1970) 271; [1987] Opie & Tatem, 242. **Buckinghamshire** [1913] *Folk-Lore* 43 (1932) 110. **Unlocated** Igglesden (*c.*1932) 99.

washing clothes: day of the year

The domestic wash-day has had its share of superstition, although the most widespread beliefs are simply concerned with when, rather than how, the washing is carried out. There were a number of days in the year when washing was forbidden, most commonly NEW YEAR's Day and GOOD FRIDAY, but HOLY INNOCENTS' DAY and ASCENSION DAY are sometimes mentioned.

The ban on Good Friday washing is supported by a story about Jesus Christ:

Blessed is the woman who bakes on Good Friday, and five Fridays afterwards, but cursed is the woman who washes on Good Friday and five Fridays afterwards. The reason given for this is: When our Lord was going to be crucified He went to a woman's house to ask for succour. She was washing, and threw soap-suds at Him; then He went to another woman's house, she was baking, and gave Him a cake. He cursed in the one case and blessed in the other. Berkshire Salmon (1902)

In a number of versions, clothes put out to dry on Good Friday will be found spotted with blood, or worse, the very soap-suds will turn red. As with all these washing prohibitions, the risk is also that you will 'wash one of the family away'.

New Year's Day is the other major day on which washing was forbidden:

In South Worcestershire there is a saying that if you wash on New Year's Day you wash for the dead – i.e. that the person whose clothes are washed will die before the year is out. And also near Singleton in Sussex, a belief that anyone who washes clothes on that day washes away the life of a member of the family – whether their clothes are washed or not – a slight variation.
Worcestershire/Sussex *The Times* (22 May 1934)

There are other beliefs prohibiting any work on NEW YEAR'S Day, and it is likely that the ban on washing was simply a specific example of this.

In many households, HOLY INNOCENTS' DAY, or Childermas Day, was the most ominous day of the year, with bad luck that even tainted the day of the week on which it occurred, for the rest of the year. Washing was again one of the domestic activities specifically prohibited:

Innocents' Day – that's another day you shouldn't do the washing. It wouldn't matter on St Stephen's Day, but Innocents' Day, the day after . . . If Mam found herself ready to wash on Innocents' Day, it had to be put off.
Devon [*c*.1912] Lakeham (1982)

In some quarters, Ascension Day or Holy Thursday is similar to New Year's Day in that no work should be done, and washing carries the usual penalty:

There is a curious superstition in these parts among some of the older people that if you hang out sheets on Ascension Day, whether to dry or merely to air them, there will be a death in the family before the year is out.
Lincolnshire *The Times* (8 May 1934)

Only one reference names Ash Wednesday as the day you must not wash (Berkshire Salmon (1902)).

Two aspects of these traditions emerge from the references listed below. Firstly, they are surprisingly recent – no report before 1836, and the majority from the twentieth century. Secondly, they are all from England (apart from one reference from Guernsey). The New Year and Holy Innocents versions are particularly restricted, all coming from the West Country.

A specialized version of the no-washing rule is found in fishing communities. Not only are such families more likely to abide by the interdiction against washing on particular days, but many also have the added ban on washing on the day their men set sail, as the symbolic connection between washing and being 'washed away' is too close for comfort:

Fishermen's womenfolk say: 'Never wash on the day your man goes away, or you wash him away'.
Suffolk *Folk-Lore* 35 (1924)

See also MAY: WASHING BLANKETS; NEW YEAR: WASHING CLOTHES.

Good Friday: Somerset/Dorset *Folk-Lore* 31 (1920) 244–5. **Devon** Bray (1836) 286; Hewett (1900) 54; Crossing (1911) 134–5. **Berkshire** *Folk-Lore* 5 (1894) 337; Salmon (1902) 423. **Gloucestershire** *Folk-Lore* 13 (1902) 175. **Worcestershire** Berkeley & Jenkins (1932) 34. **Worcestershire/Shropshire** *Gent. Mag.* (1855) 384–6. **Warwickshire** Bloom (*c*.1930) 40. **England** Addy (1895) 114. **Yorkshire** Henderson (1866) 62–3.
New Year: Sussex *The Times* (22 May 1934) 15. **Hampshire** [1969] Opie & Tatem, 286. **Dorset** Udal (1922) 287. **Somerset** [1923] Opie & Tatem, 286. **Devon** N&Q 5S:7 (1877) 26; N&Q 8S:9 (1896) 46; *Devonshire Assoc.* 33 (1901) 128; Crossing (1911) 134–5; *Devonshire Assoc.* 72 (1940) 115–16; *Devonshire Assoc.* 98 (1966) 88; *Devonshire Assoc.* 105 (1973) 213; *Devonshire Assoc.* 118 (1986) 246. **Cornwall** *Old Cornwall* 2 (1931–6) 39. **Worcestershire/Sussex** *The Times* (22 May 1934) 15. **Yorkshire** Gill (1993) 105–6. **Guernsey** De Garis (1975) 69.
Holy Innocents: **Devon** [*c*.1912] Lakeham (1982) 46; *Devonshire Assoc.* 67 (1935) 142. **Cornwall** *Old Cornwall* 10 (1929) 42; *Old Cornwall* 2 (1931–6) 39; [1985] Opie & Tatem, 70.
Ascension Day: Oxfordshire *Midland Garner* 2 (1884) 19. **Worcestershire** *Folk-Lore* 20 (1909) 345. **Lincolnshire** *The Times* (8 May 1934) 10. **Yorkshire** Addy (1895) 116; *Folk-Lore* 20 (1909) 349.

washing clothes: days rhyme

In addition to the restrictions on washing on certain days in the year (*see above*), there was also a rhyme which dictated which days were suitable for the job:

They who wash on Monday, have all the week to dry
They who wash on Tuesday, are not so much awry
They who wash on Wednesday, are not so bad as the morrow
They who wash on Thursday, wash for sorrow
They who wash on Friday, wash in haste and need
They who wash on Saturday, Oh they are sluts indeed.

Bedfordshire *Bedfordshire Mag.* (1954)

Versions vary little, and it is not clear how well known this was. The earliest known version only dates from the 1840s – about the same time that similar day-by-day rhymes about FINGERNAIL cutting and SNEEZING appeared.

Cornwall Hunt (1865) 237. Bedfordshire *Bedfordshire Mag.* 4 (Spr. 1954) 172. Norfolk Fulcher Collection (*c.*1895). Lancashire Halliwell (1849) 187.

washing clothes: splashing

The perils of the domestic wash-day are not solely confined to when the work is done. A handful of references agree that:

The woman who wets her apron very much, or splashes the water much about, will have a drunken husband.   Wales Trevelyan (1909)

The symbolism is fairly obvious, but the main surprise here is that this was still being said (by a young student) in the 1980s.

Suffolk Claxton (1954) 89. England Addy (1895) 100. Yorkshire [1982] Opie & Tatem, 425. Wales Trevelyan (1909) 6.

washing hands: egg water

A cautionary belief warns against washing hands in egg water:

Water in which eggs have been boiled or washed should not be used for washing the hands or face. It is also a common saying when mischance

befalls a person through his own stupidity, 'I believe egg water was put over me'.
Highland Scotland Campbell (1900)

This extract indicates that the belief was more widely known in Scotland than the single reference reported here. The commoner direct result of such careless washing is that you will get WARTS, although there was a ready cure:

Wash your hands with water in which eggs have been boiled and it will cause warts. Wash them nine times with water in which potatoes have been boiled and it will cure them.
Co. Durham Brockie (1886)

On the other hand, another connection between warts and eggs is more beneficial:

Warts could also be cured by the application of the white of a duck egg.   Essex Mays (1969)

See also WARTS: CAUSES.

Devon *Devonshire Assoc.* 64 (1932) 164. Warwickshire Bloom (*c.*1930) 30–1. Yorkshire Nicholson (1890) 46; Morris (1911) 249. Lancashire Harland & Wilkinson (1882) 121. Co. Durham Brockie (1886) 223. Highland Scotland Campbell (1900) 230. Co. Tyrone *Lore & Language* 1:7 (1972) 13.

washing hands together

A widespread belief holds that it is unlucky for two people to use the same water to wash their hands, either at the same time or, more rarely, in succession. Where a specific result is prophesied, it is that they will quarrel:

If a person wash in the water which another person has washed in, he and that person will quarrel before the day is out, unless the latter, before commencing his ablutions, takes the precaution of making the form of the cross with his finger on the water. Some, however, contend that the safest course is . . . [to] spit in the bowl, and some do both.

Northamptonshire Sternberg (1851)

Sternberg here gives the two traditional remedies – making a cross on the water, or spitting in it. The belief was a popular one: it was collected from most parts of Britain and Ireland, particularly from the nineteenth century onwards. It was clearly in circulation in its current form in the seventeenth century; John Aubrey, for example, notes:

'Tis an old received opinion that if two doe pisse together, they shall quarrel; or if two doe wash their hands together, they will quarrel.

Aubrey, *Remaines* (1686)

It is difficult to see how such a superstition came about. In the days before indoor plumbing, it must have been extremely common to share water for washing hands. If making the sign of the cross could be shown to be an early element in the belief, it would be possible to argue that in pre-Reformation times it would have been normal practice to 'bless' the water before use, and it was the failure to do so which occasioned the bad luck. Unfortunately for this interpretation, the earliest mention of 'crossing' as part of this belief occurs in 1851 (and the 'spitting' also appears at the same time).

Another possibility is offered by reference to Reginald Scot in 1584. He gives a cure for the AGUE which specifically calls for two people to wash their hands together:

More charmes for agues . . . Wash with the partie, and privilie saie this psalme 'Exaltabo te deus meus, rex, etc.'

Scot (1584)

If this was a common motif in cures, it is possible that it became thought of as unlucky simply because it implied that the 'disease' would be transferred from the sufferer to the other handwasher. Again, if this cure stretched back only a few more years before Scot, it is likely to have involved 'crossing'. However, in the absence of more evidence, this is simply speculation.

A few informants have reported a similar belief that it was unlucky for two people to dry their hands on the same TOWEL.

See also TWO TOGETHER.

Kent N&Q 3S:12 (1867) 477. **Hampshire** [1983] Opie & Tatem, 425. **Devon** N&Q 1S:6 (1852) 193; *Devonshire Assoc.* 9 (1877) 91–2; *Devonshire Assoc.* 17 (1885) 126. **Cornwall** *Jnl Royal Inst. Cornwall* 20 (1915) 132. **Wiltshire** Wiltshire (1975) 85–6. **Oxfordshire** *Folk-Lore* 34 (1923) 325–6. **Gloucestershire** *Folk-Lore* 34 (1923) 157. **Herefordshire** Leather (1912) 87. **Worcestershire** Salisbury (1893) 72; *Folk-Lore* 20 (1909) 346. **Northamptonshire** Sternberg (1851) 168–9. **Suffolk** *Folk-Lore* 35 (1924) 350. **Lincolnshire** *Grantham Jnl* (22 June 1878). **Rutland** N&Q 4S:8 (1871) 50, 505. **Shropshire** Burne (1883) 275–6. **England** Addy (1895) 99. **Yorkshire** N&Q 1S:6 (1852) 311–12; N&Q 4S:9 (1872) 45; Nicholson (1890) 45. Co. **Durham** Henderson (1866) 84; Brockie (1886) 210–11; Leighton (1910) 60–1. **Wales** N&Q 8S:9 (1896) 425; Jones (1930) 180. **West Wales** Davies (1911) 216. **Highland Scotland** Campbell (1900) 231; Polson (1926) 128. Co. **Longford** *Béaloideas* 6 (1936) 263. **Unlocated** Grose (1787) 65; Igglesden (*c.*1932) 213. **General** Scot (1584) Bk 12, Ch. 18; Gaule, *Mag-Astro-Mances* (1652) 181; Aubrey, *Remaines* (1686/1972) 245;

Gent. Mag. (1796) 636; *Punch* (1 Jan. 1881) 310; Foli (1902) 107.

wasps

In common with butterflies and snakes, it used to be said that the first wasp you see in the year should be killed at once:

The first wasp seen in the season should always be killed. By so doing you secure to yourself good luck and freedom from enemies throughout the year.

Northamptonshire N&Q (1850)

The 'freedom from enemies' motif is often claimed, although not explained. Only a handful of examples of this belief have been noted, dating from 1850 to the 1920s, and it is therefore difficult to gauge its relative popularity. The writings of Pliny are sometimes cited to account for the belief, but they are unlikely to be relevant here. He wrote that certain fevers could be cured by capturing a wasp and wearing it round the neck – a well-known motif in later folk medicine (*see*, for example, WHOOPING COUGH and AGUE). Pliny stipulates the first wasp seen in the year for this purpose, but his remedy has nothing else in common with our modern superstition.

Somerset [1922] Opie & Tatem, 426. **Herefordshire** Leather (1912) 28. **Northamptonshire** N&Q 1S:2 (1850) 164–5. **England** Addy (1895) 66. **Classical** Pliny, *Natural History* (AD 77) Bk 30, Para. 30.

watching the porch

see PORCH WATCHING.

watching the supper

see LOVE DIVINATION: PREPARED MEAL.

water: boiling

One of the many beliefs included in the *CONNOIS-SEUR* article in the 1750s claims a meaning for water boiling over:

I heard one of my cousins tell the cookmaid that she boiled away all her sweethearts, because she had let her dishwater boil over.

Connoisseur (1755)

This is not found anywhere else, and might simply have been invented by the author for comic effect, although most of the other items included there are genuine. Another single reference may, however, be relevant:

If you let boiling water fall on the carpet it is a sign of a quarrel.   Somerset [1923] Opie & Tatem

Somerset [1923] Opie & Tatem, 35. Literary *Connoisseur* 59 (1755) 353.

water: cures/protects

see RUNNING WATER: CURES/PROTECTS.

weasels/stoats

Stoats and weasels are not always clearly distinguished in reports of superstitions, and seem to have been more or less interchangeable in many people's minds. They feature in a number of traditions, but only the first is reported with any regularity. Along with other animals (most notably HARES, but sometimes PIGS and other species) they were both regarded as unlucky to meet when setting out from home:

It is a bad omen to meet a hare or a stoat when setting out on a journey. An old farmer who lived near Longtown was once taking his cattle to market. They had travelled some miles of the road when a stoat crossed in front of them. 'Turn 'em back, boys,' he shouted to the drovers; 'Turn 'em back, no luck today', and back they all had to go.   Herefordshire Leather (1912)

The belief has a long history in Britain – Congreve gives a clear example when his superstitious character Foresight exclaims, 'I stumbled coming down stairs, and met a weasel; bad omens those' (*Love for Love* (1695)). A hundred years before, George Gifford had made the connection between weasels and witches' familiars in his *Subtill Practices of Devilles* (1597), and this may be the basis for the ill-fortune of meeting one. A very long time before that, however, Theophrastus' 'Superstitious Man' was nonplussed by a weasel crossing his path. It is most unlikely that there is any lineal descent from ancient Greece to sixteenth-century Britain, and the coincidence must be put down either to unconnected spontaneous creation or to the fact that early British writers were obsessed with finding classical parallels for everything.

Two accounts from Ireland indicate a particular, but unfounded, fear of these animals:

Weasels in Tipperary and Wicklow are hunted down and dreaded, and they are supposed to be able to spit fire and injure men and beasts. They are supposed to steal the milk from cows.
Co. Wicklow/Co. Tipperary *Folk-Lore* (1893)

Most country people have an inherent dislike of stoats or whitterats as they are known in most parts of Ulster, for we thought that they would leap at our throats and suck our blood . . . a Scottish woman from Caithness tells me that the same belief is common there.
N. Ireland/Caithness Foster (1951)

This could explain why some people were particularly polite to them, or again this could be because of the witch connection:

Weasels, so-called (properly stoats) are greatly respected, and addressed as 'Pretty lady' in Irish, with raised hat.   Connemara *Folk-Lore* (1893)

In Welsh folk medicine, a weasel's tooth could be carried to counter RHEUMATISM or WHOOPING COUGH. Purses made of weasel skin are occasionally reported as lucky. *See* PURSES: MOLE OR WEASEL SKIN.

Unlucky to meet: Herefordshire Leather (1912) 23. **East Anglia** Varden (1885) 113. **Yorkshire** Blakeborough (1898) 150. **Wales** Trevelyan (1909) 281, 327. **Perthshire** [1954] Opie & Tatem, 431. **Co. Clare** *Folk-Lore* 22 (1911) 456. **Co. Longford** *Béaloideas* 6 (1936) 263. **General** G. Gifford, *Discourse of the Subtill Practices of Devilles* (1587) quoted Opie & Tatem, 431; *British Apollo* (9 Jan. 1710); Brand (1777) 95. **Literary** William Congreve, *Love for Love* (1695) 2:1. **Classical** Theophrastus, *Characters* (*c.*319 BC).
Other beliefs: Wales Trevelyan (1909) 318, 320. **Caithness** Foster (1951) 129. **N. Ireland** Foster (1951) 129. **Connemara** *Folk-Lore* 4 (1893) 358. **Co. Wicklow/Co. Tipperary** *Folk-Lore* 4 (1893) 361.

wedding cakes

see LOVE DIVINATION: WEDDING CAKES.

wedding dress: pins

see PINS: WEDDING.

weddings: banns

In church weddings, the 'banns of marriage' constituted the published intention to marry, and were read out in the parish churches of the intended couple on the three Sundays preceding the ceremony. Banns, in one form or another, had been in operation since the thirteenth century, but were regularized and made compulsory in England and Wales (unless a special licence were obtained) by Hardwicke's Marriage Act of 1754. In small communities they ensured that everyone knew who was planning to marry whom, and made clandestine marriages more difficult. The reading of the banns became another point in the marriage process around which beliefs could form. A superstition which has hopefully been forgotten held that an engaged couple should not be in church when they were 'called':

A Worcestershire woman was asked the other day why she did not attend church on the three Sundays on which her banns of marriage were proclaimed. She replied, that she should never dream of doing so unlucky a thing; and, on being questioned as to the kind of ill-luck that would have been expected to have followed upon her attendance at church, she said that all the offspring of such a marriage would be born deaf and dumb, and that she knew a young woman who would persist in going to church to hear her banns 'asked out' and whose six children were in consequence all deaf and dumb.

Worcestershire N&Q (1856)

In other versions it is only the first child which will be so afflicted. This is a good example of the way in which superstitions have been sanitized in modern society. While many things are still said to be bad luck, it is almost unthinkable that anyone would approach a young bride-to-be and tell her that her babies will be deaf and dumb because of her failure to abide by some arcane rule. Recorded examples cover only a brief time-span, but are widely spread geographically.

The other superstition regarding banns was that it was unlucky to break the sequence of announcements, or to 'mock the church' by cancelling the wedding after the third reading:

Five years ago a relative of ours had her banns called in a little village in the Clun Valley, in Shropshire. There being no incumbent at the time, the visiting clergyman only came on altern-ate Sundays. On the intervening Sunday, the sexton-cum-verger insisted on calling the banns outside the church door 'to the four winds', as it was unlucky to break the sequence. As he did so he turned to each point of the compass.

Shropshire *Folk-Lore* (1957)

Hearing own banns: **Sussex** Parish (1875) 'Church-cried'; *Sussex County Mag.* (1942) 364. **Wiltshire** Wiltshire (1975) 96. **Herefordshire** Leather (1912) 114. **Worcestershire** N&Q 2S:1 (1856) 202. **Northern England** Henderson (1866) 27. **Yorkshire** Blakeborough (1898) 95. **Lancashire** Harland & Wilkinson (1873) 222. **Co. Durham** Brockie (1886) 194–5; Leighton (1910) 50. **Dumfriesshire** Corrie (1890/91) 40.

Sequence broken: **Wiltshire** Wiltshire (1975) 96. **Shropshire** *Folk-Lore* 68 (1957) 503. **Wales** Trevelyan (1909) 271. **Perthshire** *Stat. Acct Scotland* 15 (1795) 258. **Orkney** N&Q 10S:12 (1909) 483–4.

weddings: bride and groom, dominant partner

Certain trivial occurrences in the wedding day, and after, were taken as indications of which of the newly-weds would be the dominant partner in years to come.

As the married couple leave the church, if the woman puts her foot out of the door before the man, she will be master.

Devon *Devonshire Assoc.* (1928)

The bride should always buy something as soon as she is married, and before the bridegroom can make a purchase. 'Then she'll be master for life' say the old women. It is customary for brides to buy a pin from their bridesmaids in order to retain their privilege in the mastery of their husbands.

Wales Trevelyan (1909)

A completely different slant on the same theme is provided by an old tradition recorded by Thomas Fuller in his *Worthies of England* (1662). He reported that the first to drink the waters of St Kenelm's well, near St Neot's, Cornwall, would gain the mastery. The idea was worked into a poem by Robert Southey in 1798, which ends with the defeat of the bridegroom:

I hasten'd as soon as the wedding was done
And left my Wife in the porch:
But I' faith she had been wiser than me,
For she took a bottle to church.

Southey, *The Well of St Keyne* (1798)

Another manifestation of the same prediction was for the bride and groom, or their friends, to plant SAGE or ROSEMARY in their garden to see whose plant flourished best.

Similar trivial occurrences were used to predict which of the bride and groom would be the first to die (*see below*).

Somerset [1923] Opie & Tatem, 238. **Devon** *Devonshire Assoc.* 60 (1928) 126; *Devonshire Assoc.* 77 (1945) 94. **Cornwall** *Old Cornwall* 1:12 (1930) 24. **Yorkshire** *Sussex Express* (30 June 1978) 4. **Wales** Trevelyan (1909) 274. **Literary** Robert Southey, *The Well of St Keyne* (1798).

weddings: bride or groom, first to die

A number of trivial occurrences during the marriage service, or later on the wedding day, were taken to indicate which of the newly-weds would be the first to die, but there is little agreement what to watch for.

Different informants reported the first to kneel down, the first to stand up, the first to turn away from the altar, or even:

When the bride was being decked for the cere-mony her maid bid her remember not to speak too loud in church, and, on being asked why, answered, 'Why, m'm, you know that them 'at speaks loudest dies first'. Yorkshire N&Q (1880)

Even when all the festivities were over, the bride and groom must take care:

In some districts it is believed that the one of the married couple who first falls asleep will be the first to pass. An old wife thus expressed herself on the subject – 'Weel a myne, he was the first to fa' asleep; a speer't at widow Macpherson's gehn she mynt filk o' them fa'd asleep first, but she didna' myne'. Caithness Rinder (1895)

Despite this lack of agreement, the belief was widely reported from the 1850s, almost to the present day. Similar trivial items were used as prognostications as to who would be the dominant partner (*see above*).

Herefordshire Leather (1912) 114. Lincolnshire Henderson (1879) 42; Watkins (1886) 11. Shropshire Burne (1883) 294–5. Northern England Henderson (1866) 27. Yorkshire N&Q 1S:6 (1852) 311–12; N&Q 6S:1 (1880) 75; [1982] Opie & Tatem, 240. Wales Trevelyan (1909) 270. Caithness Rinder (1895) 55. Angus Laing (1885) 22. Connemara Folk-Lore 4 (1893) 359. Connaught Folk-Lore (1923) 236.

---

weddings: bride's bouquet

The bride throwing her bouquet to the assembled unmarrieds is so much a part of the current traditional wedding that it is difficult to remember that it was probably introduced into Britain, from America, within living memory.

There have been a number of wedding customs designed to predict the next person – usually the next female – to get married. Throwing the stocking (*see below*) is probably the oldest and best documented, but another desired object was a pin from the bride's dress:

If a North Oxfordshire bride throws her bouquet out of a window after the ceremony, the brides-maid who catches it, or is the first to reach it, will be the first to marry; and similarly, the girl who secures the first pin from the bride's dress when the latter is changing to go on her honeymoon will either be the next bride or will be lucky in some other way.
Oxfordshire *Oxon Folk-Lore Soc.* (1952)

In earlier times, pieces of the bride's bouquet were also treasured:

A flower from the bride's bouquet, secured before she is married, brings luck; I have seen more than one beautiful bouquet torn to pieces before the service began, through people snatching blossoms from it as the bride came into church and up the aisle. Devon *Devonshire Assoc.* (1928)

Earlier still, they were simply given away:

The bride should never keep her flowers; they are given to her dearest friend.
Wiltshire *Wilts. N&Q* (1893–5)

Throwing is also a recurrent motif – throwing old shoes, stockings, and so on. The modern custom thus very neatly combines three older elements – the next-to-be-married divination, the motif of throwing, and the luck of the bride's bouquet.

It is not easy to pin down the date of the introduction of bouquet-throwing, but the key time seems to be the early 1950s. The Oxfordshire piece quoted above shows that it had arrived by that time, while Ann Page's *Complete Guide to Wedding Etiquette* (1954 edn) says, 'The custom of throwing the bouquet to the bridesmaids is a very old one'. She is completely wrong in her assessment of its age, but shows that it was already around at the time. What seems to be a transitional stage is described in another book of wedding etiquette, combining the breaking up with the throwing:

After the wedding the bridal bouquet should be broken up and tossed among the bridesmaids and girl friends. Whoever catches these fragments is expected to enter upon the marriage state at no very distant date.
Mary Woodman, *Wedding Etiquette* (1950?)

Nevertheless, Margot Lawrence's *Guide to Wedding Etiquette* of 1963 refers to the practice as

a rather charming American tradition that is not very widely adopted here as yet, probably because English brides usually slip away quietly away from the reception without any fuss.

Further research should be able to pin it down more closely.

Devon *Devonshire Assoc.* 60 (1928) 126. **Wiltshire** *Wilts. N&Q* 1 (1893–5) 105. **Essex** [1983] Opie & Tatem, 41. **Oxfordshire** *Oxon Folk-Lore Soc.* (1952) 6. **Co. Durham** Brockie (1886) 194–5. **General** Miall (1951) 285–6; Monsarrat (1973) 210; Baker (1977) 80.

weddings: carriage

A handful of references report a belief that it was unlucky if the wedding carriage turned round at the church door after depositing the bride.

When horse-drawn transport was used, it was lucky to use grey horses, and it is still lucky to see one. Also, when the bride had been set down by the church door, the coachman was expected to drive on a little way before turning, since to turn immediately was to bring bad luck.

Wiltshire Wiltshire (1975)

Some informants even insisted on a circular route, stating that it was unlucky to go back the way you came. It is possible that this is simply a specialist example of the widespread fear of RETURNING or even looking back when setting out for work or on a journey, but this explanation is not supported by the evidence. The misfortune brought about by returning can always be avoided by sitting down and then starting a *new* journey. In all other contexts, the journey to and from the church would be classed as two journeys.

Not very often recorded, nor any older than the 1880s, but its reasonably wide geographical spread would suggest a more common belief than the few references suggest.

Wiltshire Wiltshire (1975) 97. **Shropshire** Burne (1883) 294. **Yorkshire** *Yorkshire Post* (20 Nov. 1959) 12. **Orkney** *N&Q* 10S:12 (1909) 483–4. **Unlocated** *Folk-Lore* 68 (1957) 417.

weddings: 'change the name'

Superstitions concerning weddings and marriage tend to be expressed in rhyme, and this has helped them to be remembered, even after they are no longer believed in. Many people know the following rhyme, but it is unlikely that anyone still acts on it:

[From a servant girl, about nineteen years old] *If a lady's surname after marriage begin with the same letter as her maiden surname she will be very unlucky, for:*

Change the name, but not the letter
Change for the worse, and not the better.

Devon *Devonshire Assoc.* (1878)

The first known appearance of the belief is from the USA in 1853, when a correspondent to *Notes & Queries* wrote to say that he had found it in an American book and asked if it was known in Britain. No one answered that query, but the belief was being recorded as indigenous to Britain by the mid 1860s, and without knowing the book referred to it is impossible to rule on the country of origin. It may be one of the many Victorian inventions, but earlier versions may turn up with further research.

Dorset *Folk-Lore* 89 (1978) 158. **Somerset** [*c.*1914] Opie & Tatem, 238. **Devon** *Devonshire Assoc.* 10 (1878) 106. **Cornwall** *Folk-Lore Jnl* 5 (1887) 215. **Wiltshire** *Wilts. N&Q* 1 (1893–5) 105; Wiltshire (1975) 96. **Oxfordshire** *Oxon Folk-Lore Soc.* (1952) 9. **East Anglia** Varden (1885) 112. **Suffolk** Chambers 1 (1878) 723. **England** Addy (1895) 121. **Northern England** Henderson (1866) 26. **Co. Durham** Brockie (1886) 194–5. **Angus** [1950] Opie & Tatem, 238. **USA** *N&Q* 1S:8 (1853) 150.

weddings: clocks/bells

Many people had a horror of the church clock striking while the marriage ceremony was being conducted:

A bride is fortunate in her choice if the clock chimes just before she enters the church, but will be unhappy if it strikes while she is inside. Local brides will wait outside the church until the chimes have sounded.   Yorkshire *Folk-Lore* (1910)

Most informants simply explained that it was 'bad luck', but in some versions, the death of the bride or groom is predicted.

Other aspects of bells were similarly imbued with ominous meaning:

In a South Lincolnshire village, the Banns of Marriage were 'asked up' on a Sunday in October, 1887, and on the same day, the death-bell went out for a married woman in the same parish, thereupon the superstitious people said that the bride of that week would not live through a twelve-month.   Lincolnshire Gutch & Peacock (1908)

It is an extremely bad omen if a ringer 'throws' a bell when ringing a wedding peel, or if a bell rope breaks.   Worcestershire *Folk-Lore* (1909)

On present evidence, these beliefs are no earlier than mid nineteenth century, and were only found in a relatively restricted part of England. Similar beliefs focused on clocks striking while hymns were being sung; *see* CLOCKS: STRIKING DURING CHURCH SERVICE.

Worcestershire *Folk-Lore* 20 (1909) 344; N&Q 13S:1 (1923) 172. Lincolnshire Gutch & Peacock (1908) 147. Northern England [1850s] *Denham Tracts* 2 (1895) 51. Yorkshire N&Q 7S:10 (1890) 465; *Folk-Lore* 21 (1910) 226. Cumberland Bulkeley (1886) 231. Unlocated *Folk-Lore* 68 (1957) 418.

weddings: colours

For most people currently alive, the stereotypical bridal attire is a white dress, even if increasing numbers of brides choose not to follow this tradition. Nowadays, the term 'white wedding' does not simply describe the bride's dress but the whole style of the event. Although there are records of brides wearing white in early times, it was only one of many colours which could be chosen, and it only became an expected bridal colour in the second half of the eighteenth century. It rapidly became the ideal to which many brides aspired, and has retained that reputation ever since. White also quickly took on the reputation as 'lucky', as well as fashionable, as is clear from a comment in Oliver Goldsmith's first comedy, produced in 1768:

I wish you could take the white and silver to be married in. It's the worst luck in the world in anything but white.

Goldsmith, *The Good Natured Man* (1768)

Increasing availability of cheap illustrated publications in the Victorian era brought high fashion into the homes of even the humblest of families, and raised expectations in brides' minds, even if economic reality kept them in check. Many of the key elements of what is now seen as the 'traditional' wedding were forged in that period. Throughout the nineteenth, and well into the twentieth century, the ideal of the white wedding was not readily attainable for much of the population, and most brides simply wore their best clothes, or if they bought a new dress made sure to buy something more practical than something they could wear only once.

Apart from white, there is little evidence that colour was an important factor, and the strong impression is that fashion counted much more than tradition in this sphere. There were two exceptions. GREEN was the only colour consistently branded as unlucky – for everyday wear but particularly for weddings, and that only from the later eighteenth century. Black is not often mentioned specifically, but it is clear that as the colour of mourning it was usually avoided without comment. The ban on both these colours did not simply apply to the bride's dress, but to everyone at the wedding:

No woman at a wedding ought to have a bit of black about her.   Lincolnshire Watkins (1886)

On hearing of a friend's wedding dress being completely spoilt by an accident, [a woman] said, 'Ah, she got a green dress in her trousseau, it was sure not to be lucky.'   Shropshire Burne (1883)

The widespread rhyme which covers most of the likely colours is a relatively modern invention:

Married in white, you have chosen all right
Married in grey, you will go far away
Married in black, you will wish yourself back
Married in red, you'd better be dead
Married in green, ashamed to be seen
Married in blue, you'll always be true
Married in pearl, you'll live in a whirl
Married in yellow, ashamed of the fellow
Married in brown, you'll live out of town
Married in pink, your spirits will sink.

Highland Scotland Polson (1926)

This is slightly longer than many, but there is remarkable stability across versions. Several versions were published in the 1920s and 1930s, but none has been found before that time.

Devon *Devonshire Assoc.* 65 (1933) 130; *Devonshire Assoc.* 67 (1935) 140. Wiltshire *Wiltshire* (1975) 96. Essex [c.1915] Mays (1969) 164. Oxfordshire *Oxon Folk-Lore Soc.* (1952) 8; [pre-1900] *Folk-Lore* 24 (1913) 90; Warwickshire [1982] Opie & Tatem, 44. Lincolnshire Watkins (1886) 12; Swaby (1891) 91. England Addy (1895) 121. Shropshire Burne (1883) 289–90. Northern England Henderson (1866) 21. Yorkshire Nicholson (1890) 3–5; Morris (1911) 227–8; Northumberland *Folk-Lore* 36 (1925) 253; Bosanquet (1929) 75. Highland Scotland Polson (1926) 13. Ireland Ballard (1998) 77–104. N. Ireland Foster (1951) 12. Co. Tyrone *Lore & Language* 1:7 (1972) 8. General *Folk-Lore* 68 (1957) 416; Monsarrat (1973) 179; Baker (1977) 64–72. Literary Oliver Goldsmith, *The Good Natured Man* (1768) Ch. 4; George Eliot, *Adam Bede* (1859) Ch. 55.

weddings: confetti/rice, etc.

The scattering of things over the bride and groom 'for luck' has a long history, and although the items have changed, the principle has remained the same. The earliest reference is in 1486, when Henry VII was showered with wheat by a baker's wife, who cried 'welcome and good luck', and the throwing of wheat at weddings is regularly reported from the sixteenth century onwards.

In the early 1870s, however, an apparently abrupt change takes place. Reference is suddenly made to rice, and this quickly becomes the norm:

In Sussex I have seen wheat ... scattered over the bride and bridegroom as they left the church. No doubt rice, which seems to be becoming fashionable, is used with the same meaning as that attached to wheat. Its substitution for wheat is, probably, due to the fact that it is more easily obtained in an ordinary household.

Sussex N&Q (1873)

I never, in Ireland, saw rice sprinkled on the bride at parting, until the 23rd of last October.

Ireland N&Q (1873)

Not everybody was pleased with the idea of throwing things at weddings, and etiquette writers regularly advised against it:

It is not the correct thing to throw rice or old shoes after the married couple when they go away. There is nearly always some boisterous spirit or some old-fashioned person in the company who wishes to do these things. But now that it is not the correct thing for a bride and bridegroom to wear the appearance of being newly married, it is very embarrassing for them to arrive at the station with an old shoe on the top of the carriage, and for the bridegroom to be miserably aware of rice in his pockets.

Everybody's Book of Correct Conduct (1893)

Despite this disapproval, rice continued to be thrown until well into the twentieth century, but its popularity was challenged and finally surpassed by the invention of paper good-luck symbols. By the turn of the new century, the word 'confetti', named after the bonbons, real or imitation, thrown at Italian carnivals, was being used at weddings in Britain. The paper symbols gradually took over from rice, although again there was opposition:

Over and over again I have seen both bride and bridegroom obliged to stand at the chancel steps literally covered, and the aisle littered, with the variegated bits of confetti. It is not seemly or kind that the bridal costume should be thus marred. Persons who have not the slightest intention of joining in the marriage service remain outside the church just to indulge in a refined kind of horseplay. Warwickshire *Surrey Gazette* (13 Sept. 1904)

Until the Second World War confetti and rice could both be found, separately or together:

When Princess Mary married in 1922, her mother wrote of 'throwing rice and little paper horse shoes and rose leaves after them'. Monsarrat (1973)

but in the postwar period confetti continued to be the norm.

Many writers assume that the throwing of wheat or rice was a fertility gesture, but this interpretation was not made before the Victorian folklorists started labelling everything in sight in this way. Obviously, any wedding custom or tradition is open to a fertility interpretation, but there is no evidence to support this as a general rule. It is best to simply regard it as a good-luck gesture, and the items thrown wish the couple plenty in terms of happiness and prosperity rather than children.

See also SHOES: THROWING.

Kent [1930s] Kent (1977) 42. **Sussex** N&Q 4S:12 (1873) 396. **Devon** Hewitt (1900) 23. **Bristol** *Folk-Lore Record* 3 (1880) 133; [1987] Opie & Tatem, 440. **Herefordshire** Leather (1912) 114. **Warwickshire** Langford (1875) 23; *Surrey Gazette* (13 Sept. 1904) 3. **Norfolk** [1873] Hope-Nicholson (1966) 66. **Shropshire** Burne (1883) 293. **England** Addy (1895) 121. **Derbyshire** *Folk-Lore* 69 (1958) 267. **Nottinghamshire** N&Q 4S:12 (1873) 396. **Northumberland** Bosanquet (1929) 37. **Wales** Davies (1911) 36. **Radnorshire** Francis Kilvert, *Diary* (11 Aug. 1874). **Northeast Scotland** Gregor (1881) 197. **Dumfriesshire** Corrie (1890/91) 41. **Ireland** N&Q 4S:12 (1873) 396. **Co. Limerick** Camden, *Britannia* (1586). **General** *Everybody's Book of Correct Conduct* (1893) 95–6; Monsarrat (1973) 230. **Literary** Robert Herrick, *Hesperides* (1648) 'Nuptiall Song'. **USA** N&Q 4S:12 (1873) 396.

weddings: curses

Not everyone wishes the bride and groom well on their wedding day, and rival lovers had traditional ways of venting their anger or jealousy.

Psalm 109 to this day is looked upon as a means of destroying for ever the fortunes of a young couple if read by a rival during the marriage service. Shropshire Gaskell (1894)

This Psalm is pretty powerful stuff when read with a vengeful eye. It starts with 'Hold thy peace, O God of my praise', and includes lines such as, 'For my love they are my adversaries. And they have rewarded me evil for good, and hatred for my love. Set thou a wicked man over him: and let Satan stand at his right hand'.

Other magical rites were possible:

If anyone at a marriage repeats the benediction after the priest, and ties a knot at the mention of each of the three sacred names on a handkerchief, or a piece of string, the marriage will be childless for fifteen years, unless the knotted string is burnt in the meantime.

Aran Islands *Procs. Royal Irish Academy* (1891–3)

Or a jilted girl could take direct and open action:

It is only a few years ago since a young girl went to Cusop, to the wedding of a young man who had jilted her; waiting in the church porch till the bridegroom came out, she threw a handful of rue at him, saying 'May you rue this day as long as you live'. My informant said this caused a good deal of talk at the time, and he was told that the curse would come true, because the rue was taken direct from the plant to the churchyard and thrown 'between holy and unholy ground', that is between the church and churchyard.

Herefordshire Leather (1912)

Such practices are not mentioned often in the folklore literature, but they clearly existed, for use when necessary.

Herefordshire Leather (1912) 115. Shropshire Gaskell (1894) 264. Aran Islands *Procs. Royal Irish Academy* 3S:2 (1891–3) 818.

weddings: doors

Several superstitions warned that the bride and groom must be careful about doors. They should always leave the house by the front door, and both at home and at the church they must be careful not to enter by one door and leave by another:

In Yorkshire it is a common saying – 'Be sure when you go to get married that you don't go in at one door and out at another, or you will always be unlucky.   Yorkshire N&Q (1852)

At a wedding in a Worcestershire village last October, the bride and bridegroom, at the conclusion of the ceremony, left the church by the chancel door instead of following the usual custom of walking down the church and through the nave door. One of the oldest inhabitants, in mentioning this to me, said that it 'betokened bad luck', and that she had never known a like instance but once in her life, when the married couple went out of the church through the chancel door, and the bride was a widow before the twelvemonth was over.   Worcestershire N&Q (1878)

This is a specialized version of a general superstition about DOORS. Similarly, there was a reluctance to use anything but the front for something as important as a wedding, and again there would be adverse comment:

It is very unlucky for the bride and bridegroom to leave the bride's home by the back door after the wedding. This was done near Hereford recently by a couple wishing to escape showers of rice; the old people present shook their heads, and thought it a very bad omen.

Herefordshire Leather (1912)

None of these door superstitions is reported before the mid nineteenth century.

See also DOORS: ENTER AND LEAVE BY SAME.

Oxfordshire *Oxon Folk-Lore Soc.* (1952) 9. Herefordshire Leather (1912) 114. Worcestershire N&Q 5S:10 (1878) 23. Yorkshire N&Q 1S:6 (1852) 311. Angus Laing (1885) 22. Unlocated *Folk-Lore* 68 (1957) 417.

weddings: elder sister

If a younger daughter married before her elder sister, the latter was traditionally expected to acknowledge her spinsterhood by certain prescribed actions. These varied from place to place, but were normally concerned with footwear and dancing. She was variously expected to dance in her stockinged or bare feet, wear green stockings or garters, dance in the hog-trough, or dance on the branches of furze:

as soon as we returned from church Miss M'Leod put on green stockings. I do not know the origin of the custom that when a younger sister marries the elder wears green stockings!

New South Wales (Scottish) [1844] Boswell

In some areas, a similar forfeit was expected of an elder son whose brother married before him. The custom is usually described in terms of a mild punishment or humiliation for not following the normal social conventions, but sometimes a different, more superstitious, interpretation is offered. Some say, for example, that if the elder sister neglects her duty she will never marry at all, and in at least one instance the procedure was a way of helping:

when a younger sister marries before the elder, the latter is forcibly made to wear green garters at the wedding, and any young man who takes them off is destined to be her future husband . . . and the 'best man' whom she had never seen before, took off her garters and is now her husband.   Aberdeenshire *Folk-Lore* (1908)

Regular references to this custom appear from the late eighteenth century and well into the twentieth, but it is clearly much older. Shakespeare knew of it:

[Katherine to her father] *She is your treasure, she must have a husband; I must dance bare-foot on her wedding day.*

Shakespeare, *The Taming of the Shrew* (1623)

In one form or other, the custom is reported from most parts of England and Wales, but seems to have been particularly widespread in Scotland.

Somerset *Folk-Lore* 28 (1917) 315. Cornwall *Folk-Lore Jnl* 5 (1887) 215–16; *Old Cornwall* 1:12 (1930) 4. Worcestershire Berkeley & Jenkins (1932) 35. East Anglia Varden (1885) 112. Suffolk Glyde (1866) 177. Shropshire Burne (1883) 290–1. England Addy (1895) 121. Yorkshire Jeffrey (1923) 191. Northumberland Bosanquet (1929) 38. Wales Trevelyan (1909) 274. Scotland Chambers (1826) 286; [1889] N&Q 9S:4 (1899) 112. Northeast Scotland Gregor (1881) 90. Western Scotland Napier (1879) 52. Dumfriesshire Corrie (1890/91) 41; Shaw (1890) 12. Aberdeenshire *Folk-Lore* 19 (1908) 339–40. Galloway Mactaggart (1824) 447–8. New South Wales (Scottish) [1844] Boswell (1965) 96. Unlocated Grose (1787) 62; N&Q 182 (1942) 125; 183 (1942) 22. Literary Shakespeare, *The Taming of the Shrew* (1623) 2:1.

weddings: groom must not see bride

One of the best-known wedding superstitions in the present day is that the groom must not see the bride on the morning of the wedding until she arrives at the church or wedding venue. Even many couples who have been living together for years contrive to follow the rule.

The earliest references are Scottish, starting with a mention in a Walter Scott novel which implies that it was already customary in the early nineteenth century:

It had been settled that, according to the custom of the country, the bride and bridegroom should not again meet until they were before the altar.

Scott, *A Legend of Montrose* (1819)

By the 1890s it was also being reported in England. Nevertheless, it cannot have been universal, for the pattern of many, if not most, of ordinary weddings militated against it:

It is unlucky, as well as incorrect, for the bride-groom to see the bride before he meets her at the church. This is now a general belief in all sections, but it was not always so. Until the last two or three decades of the nineteenth century, walking weddings were common amongst simple folk, 'carriage weddings' being only for the gentry. The groom and bride walked to church together, the man going first with the bridesmaid and the bride following immediately after with the best man. On the return journey, husband-and-wife led the way arm-in-arm, followed by their two attendants.

Unlocated *Folk-Lore* (1957)

Modern ideas on how weddings should be conducted have invaded the countryside in recent years. Country folk a generation ago did not know that it was unlucky for the bride to be seen by the bridegroom before they met in the church on the wedding-day. N. Ireland Foster (1951)

Wiltshire *Wilts. N&Q* 1 (1893–5) 105. Essex [1983] Opie & Tatem, 40. Lincolnshire N&Q 8S:9 (1896) 5. Yorkshire Nicholson (1890) 3–5. Co. Durham [1982] Opie & Tatem, 40. Scotland Morton (1929) Ch. 6. Western Scotland Napier (1879) 46–7. Aberdeenshire [1952] Opie & Tatem, 40. N. Ireland Foster (1951) 12. Co. Tyrone *Lore & Language* 1:7 (1972) 8. Unlocated *Folk-Lore* 68 (1957) 417. General Hoggart (1957) Ch. 2; Monsarrat (1973) 178–9. Literary Walter Scott, *A Legend of Montrose* (1819) Ch. 23.

weddings: meets funeral

For obvious reasons, it was accounted very unlucky for a wedding party to meet a funeral, and the fact that the same building usually catered for both events made this coincidence quite feasible:

In March 1952, a burial at Caversham was preceded by a wedding. One of the mourners, arriving early, found the wedding-party still in the churchyard, taking photographs. The sexton was extremely agitated by this delay because, he said, it would be most unlucky if the bride saw the funeral. Eventually, he spoke to the best man who at once realised the urgency of the matter and hurried his party away.

Oxfordshire *Oxon Folk-Lore Soc.* (1952)

For most, it was simply 'unlucky', but some said that it presaged a death of one of the wedding party – usually the bride or groom:

To meet a funeral either in going to or coming from marriage was very unlucky. If the funeral was that of a female, the young wife would not live long; if a male the bridegroom would die soon. Western Scotland Napier (1879)

It is surprising that such an obvious supersti-tion does not seem to have a long history. The earliest reference so far located, as quoted by Opie and Tatem, dates only from 1855, and although clearly quite widespread it only makes a moderate appearance in the documentary record.

Oxfordshire [1920s] Surman (1992) 60–1; *Oxon Folk-Lore Soc.* (1952) 9; *Oxf. & Dist. FL Soc. Ann. Record* (1955) 16. Warwickshire Bloom (*c.*1930) 43. Shropshire Burne (1883) 296. Staffordshire [1892] *Folk-Lore* 20 (1909) 220–1. Yorkshire Blakeborough (1898) 102. Wales

Trevelyan (1909) 271. **Western Scotland** Napier (1879) 51. **Forfarshire** [1954] Opie & Tatem, 171. **Angus** Laing (1885) 21. **Co. Longford** *Béaloideas* 6 (1936) 260. **Unlocated** *Folk-Lore* 68 (1957) 418. **General** *Fortune-Teller* (*c*.1855) 17, quoted Opie & Tatem, 171.

weddings: moon's phases

In some communities, it was considered vital that important projects and events were timed to coincide with the moon's cycle. An example of this was that weddings should always take place when the new moon was waxing, and not when it was waning. This belief was particularly strong in Orkney and Shetland.

See MOON: MARRIAGE.

weddings: rings

The wedding ring has long been one of the central symbols of both the act of marriage and, by the type of extension common in superstition, of future married life. Beliefs about the ring thus have resonance for both the wedding ceremony and later points in the married life of the couple in question.

Even before the ceremony, there were rules which must be followed:

Another difficulty in the wedding arrangements was started by the bride herself. 'It's so unlucky to try a wedding ring on', but this having been overcome by trying another ring and matching the size.   Staffordshire *Folk-Lore* (1897)

If the ring is dropped during the ceremony, the marriage will be unhappy – on the usual superstitious principle that anything which starts badly is doomed to continue that way. Some say that if the bride drops the ring she will die before the groom, and vice versa.

[17 Feb 1698] An unlucky accident the day of his marriage. He drowned a horse at Rumsey as he was bringing his wife away to Salisbury to be married; he let fall the ring after I had given it to him to put on his wife's finger.
Wiltshire *Diary of Thomas Naish* (1965)

Once married, it was very unlucky for a woman to take her ring off, for any reason, and even worse for her to lose it:

Some thought the wedding ring must never be removed and if it accidentally happened, the husband should put the ring on again; other people said it was all right to remove the wedding ring after the birth of the first child.
Wiltshire Wiltshire (1975)

If a woman loses her marriage-ring 'she will lose her man'.   Aberdeenshire *Folk-Lore* 25 (1914)

But if the ring breaks, it is a sign that the husband will soon die.

To balance these mostly negative attributes, wedding rings also feature in LOVE DIVINATION processes involving wedding cake, and are an essential part of a widespread cure for a STYE in the eye. And although the fate of the marriage seems to have been literally in the wife's hand, at least some believed there was a way out:

There was formerly a belief (which perhaps still exists) among the poorer folk at Oswestry, that if a husband failed to maintain his wife, she might give him back the wedding-ring, and then she would be free to marry again.
Shropshire Burne (1883)

Southern England [1981] Opie & Tatem, 437. **Devon** *Devonshire Assoc.* 60 (1928) 126. **Cornwall** *Folk-Lore Jnl* 5 (1887) 216; *Old Cornwall* 2 (1931–6) 40. **Wiltshire** *Diary of Thomas Naish* [17 Feb. 1698] (1965) 39–40; Wiltshire (1975) 98. **London** *Observer Supp.* (24 Nov. 1968) 8. **Essex** N&Q 3S:10 (1866) 469. **Midland England** *Midland Garner* 1 (1884) 23. **Lincolnshire** Swaby (1891) 91; Rudkin (1936) 17. **England** Addy (1895) 98, 101, 121. **Derbyshire** Uttley (1946) 113–14. **Shropshire** Burne (1883) 294–5. **Staffordshire** *Folk-Lore* 8 (1897) 91. **Yorkshire** Robinson (1861) 301; N&Q 6S:6 (1882) 9; Blakeborough (1898) 103. **Lancashire** N&Q 4S:6 (1870) 211. **Co. Durham** Brockie (1886) 194–5; Leighton (1910) 51. **Wales** Trevelyan (1909) 271. **Aberdeenshire** *Folk-Lore* 25 (1914) 349. **Orkney** N&Q 10S:12 (1909) 483–4. **Irish Travellers** [*c*.1960] Joyce (1985) 62. **Unlocated** Hone, *Year Book* (1832) 127; *Folk-Lore* 68 (1957) 418. **General** Brand 1 (1813) 35; *Sunlight Almanac* (1896) 335; Miall (1951) 285–6. **Literary** *Weekly Amusement* (8 June 1763) quoted Lean 2 (1905) 553.

weddings: 'something old, something new'

A bride's dress on her wedding day should include 'Something old, something new, something borrowed, something blue'. This is one of the strongest wedding superstitions in modern times: there can be hardly an adult in Britain who does not know the rhyme, and a great many women abide by it even though many do not believe it makes any real difference. The rhyme has become a cliché in its own right, and if the *belief* is removed from the equation, the action becomes a *custom* rather than a superstition.

It is generally true to say that the overriding instinct in most bride's plans for their wedding clothes is newness – every item of clothing should be brand new, bought specially for the occasion:

A peasant bride about to dress for her wedding, first strips herself of every article of clothing, and begins absolutely de novo to attire herself in new and unwashed garments, rejecting even pins that have been used before. But, nevertheless, it is widely accounted lucky to wear something on the wedding day which has already been worn by a happy bride at her wedding, and ladies consider it quite a compliment to be asked to lend their wedding veils to their friends for this purpose. Sometimes a lace veil has been worn in this way by successive generations. Shropshire Burne (1883)

Some references do not give the full rhyme, but simply focus on one aspect: 'A bride should wear something borrowed at her wedding' (**Wiltshire** *Wilts. N&Q* (1893–5)) and it is possible that the rhyme was composed to incorporate existing but separate elements; so far it is only the 'blue' element which can be shown to have a long history. The rhyme itself cannot be shown to be older than 1876, when a correspondent to *Notes & Queries* wrote to ask about its origin, and it did not become widely known until the twentieth century.

The rhyme does not dictate what items should be chosen in each category, but certain traditions developed, which have largely been overtaken by fashion. As mentioned above, it was common that the veil be the borrowed item, specifically from a woman who was already happily married. Oddly enough, by modern standards, the bride's shoes were usually the old item. The 'blue' was commonly a garter. Also of likely Victorian or later origin is an extra line which some add to the rhyme: 'and a silver sixpence in your shoe'.

The juxtaposition of old and new is also apparent in the following description, although this has apparently not been reported elsewhere:

The night before the wedding, the bride was dressed by the bridesmaids in her very oldest night attire. This is known to have been done at the wedding of a doctor's daughter c. 1872. Gloucestershire *Folk-Lore* 28 (1917)

England *Folk-Lore* 68 (1957) 416. Sussex [1987] Opie & Tatem, 43. Devon *Devonshire Assoc.* 60 (1928) 126. Wiltshire *Wilts. N&Q* 1 (1893–5) 316; Wiltshire (1975) 97. Hertfordshire [1988] Opie & Tatem, 42. Gloucestershire *Folk-Lore* 28 (1917) 314. Herefordshire Leather (1912) 114–15. Suffolk Gurdon (1893) 135. Norfolk? N&Q 8S:7 (1895) 145. Lincolnshire Rudkin (1936) 21; Sutton (1992) 134. Shropshire Burne (1883) 289. England Addy (1895) 121. Derbyshire Uttley (1946) 126. Lancashire Burne (1883) 290. Northumberland Bosanquet (1929) 37. Co. Durham Leighton (1910) 50. Monmouthshire *Folk-Lore* 16 (1905) 66. Co. Longford *Béaloideas* 6 (1936) 259. Royal Family *The Lady* (23 July

1981) 175. Unlocated N&Q 5S:5 (1876) 408; N&Q 182 (1942) 125. General Miall (1951) 285–6; Hoggart (1957) Ch. 2; Monsarrat (1973) 179, 231.

weddings: sun shines on

The proverbial phrase 'Happy [or Blessed] is the bride the sun shines on' is still regularly quoted in appropriate circumstances at weddings, but few modern participants would argue that the weather on the day was genuinely predictive of future happiness for the couple. The saying has been proverbial since at least the seventeenth century, and there is plenty of evidence to show that in the past many believed quite literally in the sunshine as a positive omen. More rarely heard nowadays is the companion line about rain:

Happy is the bride that the sun shines on
Happy is the corpse that the rain rains on.
Ireland *Gent. Mag.* (1865)

It was also believed that bad weather for the wedding had a lasting negative effect:

If it rains while a wedding party are on their way to church, or on returning from it, it betokens a life of bickering and unhappiness.
Cornwall Hunt (1865)

The earliest clear version of the phrase is in one of Robert Herrick's poems (1648), and it is included in the second edition of John Ray's *Collection of English Proverbs* (1678), so it was presumably already well known by that time. It has been reported regularly ever since.

See also FUNERALS: RAIN.

Sussex [1987] Opie & Tatem, 41. Somerset [1923] Opie & Tatem, 41. Devon Bray (1838) 294; Hewett (1900) 23. Cornwall Hunt (1865) 235–6. Wiltshire Francis Kilvert, *Diary* (1 Jan. 1873); *Wilts. N&Q* 1 (1893–5) 316; Wiltshire (1975) 97. Norfolk N&Q 2S:8 (1859) 300. Lincolnshire Thompson (1856) 735. Shropshire Burne (1883) 296. Northern England Henderson (1866) 21. Yorkshire N&Q 1S:6 (1852) 311–312. Co. Durham Brockie (1886) 194–5; Leighton (1910) 50. Wales Trevelyan (1909) 270; Davies (1911) 36. Glamorgan Phillips (1925) 598. Scotland Chambers (1847) 123. Highland Scotland Macbain (1887/88) 254. Dumfriesshire Shaw (1890) 12; Corrie (1890/91) 40. Angus *Edinburgh Mag.* (Nov. 1818) 412; Laing (1885) 21. Caithness Sutherland (1937) 104. Orkney N&Q 10S:12 (1909) 483–4. Ireland *Gent. Mag.* (1865) 699. Unlocated Brand (1777) 53; Grose (1787) 62; *Chambers's Jnl* (1873) 810; *Folk-Lore* 68 (1957) 417. General John Ray, *A Collection of English Proverbs* (1678) 348. Literary Robert Herrick, *Hesperides* (1648) 'A Nuptial Song'.

weddings: thresholds

One of the wedding customs which has offended many post-feminist sensibilities, carrying the bride over the threshold is often assumed to be ancient in Britain, and rooted in male domination, but neither of these assumptions is supported by the evidence.

It was considered very unlucky for a bride to place her feet on or near the threshold, and the lady, on her return from the marriage ceremony, was always carefully lifted over the threshold and into the house. The brides who were lifted were generally fortunate, but trouble was in store for the maiden who preferred walking into the house.

Wales Trevelyan (1909)

The history and development is unclear. The custom can be definitely traced in Britain in the early nineteenth century, when Walter Scott described it in a note to his novel *Guy Mannering* (1815), and from that time on it is mentioned sporadically. Various unfounded guesses at meaning have been put forward, including the idea that it is a relic of bride capture or that the threshold was a holy place which must not be defiled.

Several other threshold beliefs and customs existed, which may be relevant to an investigation of the origin of the carrying tradition. Some earlier sources mention a show of modest bridal reluctance to enter the house, as in Robert Herrick's *Hesperides* (1648), 'Now o'er the threshold force her in', but he does not mention lifting the bride. There was also the idea that whoever entered the house first would be master in the marriage:

Another prognostication determined by the bride and groom's behaviour was the question of who was going to be 'master' in the new home; whichever stepped out of the church first, or left the bride's home first after the meal, or who first crossed the threshold of their new house, and so on.

Wright (1913)

Another possibly analogous belief is the fear of bad luck for the marriage should the bride STUMBLE on entering the new home. None of these is really convincing, however, and they cannot be shown to predate references to bride-lifting.

Nevertheless, we have unusually close analogues from classical times. Plutarch (c.AD 46–c.AD 120), for example, indicates not only that a similar custom existed in his time, but that its reason was already unclear:

What should be the reason that they would not permit the new-wedded bride to pass herself over the door-sill or threshold when she is brought home to her husband's house, but they that accompany her lift her from the ground, and so convey her in?   Plutarch, *Roman Questions*

Opie and Tatem also quote Catullus' *Poems* (before 50 BC) to show that it was lucky to step high over a new threshold.

It is hardly possible that the custom has survived uninterrupted in Britain since the first century, and what is most likely – but at present unproven – that it was introduced to this country by someone, or some group, familiar with classical sources. This could have happened at any time since the Middle Ages, but more evidence is needed before any more can be said on the matter.

Wiltshire *Wilts. N&Q* 1 (1893–5) 105. **Lincolnshire** Gutch & Peacock (1908) 233–4; [c.1940s] Sutton (1992) 134. **Staffordshire** [1954] Opie & Tatem, 40. **Yorkshire** *Folk-Lore* 31 (1920) 320. **Northumberland** *Folk-Lore* 36 (1925) 251–2. **Wales** Trevelyan (1909) 273. **Scotland** Dalyell (1834) 292. **Western Scotland** Napier (1879) 51. **Angus** Laing (1885) 21. **General** Brand 2 (1849) 169; *Folk-Lore* 13 (1902) 226–51; Wright (1913) 273; Miall (1951) 285–6. **Literary** Walter Scott, *Guy Mannering* (1815) note 5. **Classical** Plutarch, *Roman Questions* Ch. 29.

weddings: throwing the stocking

In days before honeymoons, a high point of the wedding day was 'putting the bride and groom to bed', which was the excuse for a great deal of horseplay and engagement in traditional customs. The degree of refinement, or otherwise, depended on the company, but there was plenty of scope for, and tolerance of, rough play and ribaldry at all levels of society. One of the set-piece activities was 'throwing the stocking' – an example of one of the many customs at weddings which result in the selection of who is to be married next, and therefore a precursor to the modern throwing of the bride's bouquet (*see above*).

There were many variations on the basic theme. One was for the bride to do the throwing:

About the 'noon of night' the bride is put to bed by her maids, in the presence of as many spectators as the bed-room will contain, pressing, squeezing, standing upon tip-toe, and peeping over each other's heads for a glance of the blushing fair, who throws the stocking from her left leg over the right shoulder, and the person on whom it falls is to be first married.

Scotland *Edinburgh Mag.* (Nov. 1818)

In another version, the guests did the throwing, and the idea was to hit the bride or groom:

Throwing the stocking . . . the invited guests repair to the bridal chamber, where the happy pair received them sitting up in bed, in full dress, except only that they had taken off their shoes and stockings. One of the bridesmaids then took the bridegroom's stocking, and standing at the foot of the bed with her back towards it, threw the stocking with the left hand over the right shoulder, aiming at the bridegroom's face. This was done by all the unmarried females in rotation. When any of them was so fortunate as to hit the object, it was a sign that she was soon to be married. The bride's stocking was thrown by the young men at the bride's face in like manner, a like prognostic being drawn from it.

Co. Durham Brockie (1886)

This custom was very widely known all over the British Isles, although the majority of references come from Scotland and northern England, which is presumably because it continued later in these areas. It was clearly well established by the seventeenth century, and the earliest reference dates from 1604. In a letter from Sir Dudley Carleton referring to the marriage of Sir Philip Herbert and Lady Susan Vere at Whitehall, the casual way he mentions 'casting off the bride's left hose' in a list of traditional ceremonies confirms that it must date back to the previous century at least (see Monsarrat (1973) 39). Nevertheless, the custom had faded out by the mid nineteenth century, falling victim to Victorian reforms and notions of decorum which laid the foundations for the modern wedding.

England [1698] Henri Misson, *Voyageur en Angleterre* (1719) 352–3. **Cornwall** *Folk-Lore Jnl* 5 (1887) 216; *Old Cornwall* 1:12 (1930) 23. **Northern England** Brockett (1829) 305. **Lancashire** Harland & Wilkinson (1882) 264; *Lancashire Lore* (1971) 50. **Cumberland** [1863] *Folk-Lore* 40 (1929) 281. **Co. Durham** Brockie (1886) 197–8. **Scotland** *Edinburgh Mag.* (Nov. 1818) 414. **Western Scotland** Napier (1879) 52–3. **Galloway** Mactaggart (1824) 447. **Shetland** Hibbert (1822) 554. **Ireland** Ballard (1998) 123–4. **General** Monsarrat (1973) 36, 39, 51, 74, 102. **Literary** R. Fletcher, *Poems and Fancies* (1656) 230; Edward Chicken, *The Collier's Wedding* (1764) quoted Monsarrat (1973) 102; Tobias Smollett, *Humphry Clinker* (1771) 320.

weddings: touching bride/groom

Touching or rubbing against the bride or groom at a wedding was generally thought to be lucky, or in the case of a young woman, conducive to her marriage prospects:

At a wedding at Whippingham church a few years ago, I saw the cottagers' children press forward as the bride passed down the church-yard, and heard the cry: 'I touched her. That's luck for me!' I made enquiries in the parish after-wards, and learnt that faith in this old supersti-tion was still general there.

Isle of Wight N&Q (1916)

'Mind you rub against the bride' was the parting instruction of solicitous relatives to a young lady lately setting out to act as bridesmaid to a friend; the object being that she might catch the infec-tion of matrimony. Shropshire Burne (1883)

So far only recorded from the 1860s onwards.

Isle of Wight N&Q 12S:2 (1916) 112–13. **Somerset** [1923] Opie & Tatem, 240. **Shropshire** Burne (1883) 290. **Northern England** Henderson (1866) 21. **Lancashire** Harland & Wilkinson (1873) 222. **Dumfriesshire** Shaw (1890) 12. **Ireland** N&Q 12S:2 (1916) 112–13.

weighing

A number of superstitions exist which warn that it is unwise to be too precise in COUNTING or MEASURING, as it TEMPTS FATE to do so. Another example warns against weighing:

The prejudice against weighing babies before they are twelve months old is dying out fast under the influence of health visitors and clinics. It was formerly very strong, however, and there are still women who dislike the practice. A member of the Oxfordshire Folk-Lore Society was told by a district nurse in 1935 that a certain woman known to them both had refused to have her last baby weighed because an older child had 'gone funny', and she attributed this to his having been weighed too soon. Oxfordshire Folk-Lore (1957)

Where specified, the predicted result is usually that the child will die before the twelve months is over, or at best will be sickly or weak.

The superstition is nearly always voiced with regard to children, but the earliest reference, in 1709, refers to adults. Otherwise, the belief is only reported from the 1870s onwards, presumably because it was not common practice to weigh newborn babies before that time anyway. As indicated in the above quotation, the belief was still strong in the mid twentieth century, but was effectively killed by improvements in public healthcare which insisted on scientific measuring and recording of infants' details.

Dorset Udal (1922) 178. **Cornwall** *Jnl Royal Inst. Cornwall* 20 (1915) 130; *Old Cornwall* 1:9 (1929). **Oxfordshire** *Folk-Lore* 68 (1957) 414. **Herefordshire** Leather (1912) 113. **Warwickshire** Bloom (*c.*1930) 27. **East Anglia** Varden (1885) 107. **Suffolk** Chambers 2 (1878) 39. **Norfolk** Dew (1898) 77–81. **Shropshire** Burne (1883) 285. **Staffordshire** Hackwood (1924) 57. **England** Addy (1895) 96. **Lancashire** Harland & Wilkinson (1873) 221. **Western Scotland** Napier (1879) 137. **Dumfriesshire** Corrie (1890/91) 37. **Co. Longford** *Béaloideas* 6 (1936) 259. **Unlocated** *British Apollo* (7 Sept. 1709).

wheatears (*Oenanthe oenanthe*)

One of several seemingly harmless birds which were persecuted in Scotland:

This bird, for what reason I cannot say, seems to be proscribed in Orkney. Young and old destroy both nests and birds of it and this not for any other end but the seeming effects of wanton cruelty, as it seems quite a harmless creature.
                                    Orkney Low (1813)

Like the YELLOWHAMMER, the wheatear was believed to have an affinity with the TOAD and also to frequent old ruins and burial mounds. Buckley and Brown (1891) reported that by their time the prejudice against the bird seemed to have died out.

Scotland Swainson (1886) 9–11. **Orkney** Low (1813) 73; Buckley & Brown (1891) 96.

whistling: at sea

It is a well-known belief that whistling at sea conjures up a wind, and in the days of sail, seamen would only whistle under certain circumstances:

Sailors will not whistle during a voyage, nor will those who steer the pleasure boats allow any passengers to do so. One old man said, 'we only whistle when the wind is asleep, and then the breeze comes'.
                                    Yorkshire N&Q (1869)

The connection between wind and whistling was probably too obvious to need explanation, but one writer suggested a supernatural intermediary:

Fishermen – No person was allowed to whistle on board the boat; as it would attract the attention of the 'dooinney marrey' (merman), who would be sure to send more wind than was required.
                                    Isle of Man [1850] Cashen

See also WIND: OBTAINING.

Cornwall Hunt (1865) 239; *Old Cornwall* 10 (1929) 41; **Devon** *Devonshire Assoc.* 11 (1879) 110. **Suffolk** *Gent. Mag.* (1823) 16–17. **Lincolnshire** *Gent. Mag.* (1833) 590–3; Rudkin (1936) 22. **Yorkshire** Henderson (1866) 28; N&Q 4S:4 (1869) 131–2. **Co. Durham** Brockie (1886) 209. **Highland Scotland** Polson (1926) 121–2. **Northeast Scotland** *Folk-Lore Jnl* 3 (1885) 54. **Eastern Scotland** Anson (1930) 42. **Ross & Cromarty** Miller (1835) 109. **Orkney** Teignmouth 1 (1836) 286; Laing (1885) 73; N&Q 10S:12 (1909) 483–4. **Isle of Man** [1850] Cashen (1912) 27. **Unlocated** Grose (1787) 66; [1955] *Daily Mirror* (7 Nov. 1977) 22. **General** Aubrey, *Remaines* (1686/1880) 21; *Gent. Mag.* (1763) 114–15; Brand (1777) 98; Bullen (1899) 120; Campbell (1956) 159–60. **Literary** *Cock Lorel's Boat* (*c.*1510) 344.

whistling: in a mine

Whistling while underground in a mine was banned:

Miners' beliefs – No whistling is allowed while going down the skip or cage, nor even while underground; singing is allowed, but not whistling. My son was given 'a tuck in the head' by one of our miners for so doing some years ago, and he tells me this superstition is also recognized in S. Brazil and in W. Africa by our English miners there.   Devon *Devonshire Assoc.* (1936)

Most informants simply said it was unlucky, but occasionally it is implied that to whistle attracts the attention of supernatural forces which are best left alone. One writer attempted a rational explanation:

No miner will allow of whistling underground. I could never learn from the miners whether they regarded it as unlucky or not. I rather think they feel that whistling indicates thoughtlessness, and they know their labour is one of danger, requiring special attention.   Cornwall Hunt (1865)

The earliest reference to this prohibition so far found is from 1814.

Devon Bray (1838) 255; Hewett (1900) 55; *Devonshire Assoc.* 68 (1936) 93–4. **Cornwall** N&Q 1S:6 (1852) 601; Hunt (1865) 239. **Derbyshire** J. Varey, *Agriculture and Minerals of Derbyshire* 1 (1815) 316–17, quoted Opie & Tatem, 441. **Lancashire** Harland & Wilkinson (1873) 239. **Northumberland** N&Q 1S:12 (1855) 201. **Unlocated** [1984] Opie & Tatem, 441.

whistling: in the theatre

The ban on whistling in a theatre is one of the best-known theatrical superstitions:

To whistle in a theatre is a sign of the worst luck in the world, and there is no offence for which the manager will scold an employee more quickly.

Knowlson (1910)

Various reasons are given, usually practical ones such as the fact that the sound carries in old theatres and whistling would be heard by the audience, or:

before there was a Tannoy system, whistling was the signal to change the scenery.

[1985] Opie & Tatem

It was also said that whistling in the dressing room 'whistled away' the actor nearest the door. The miscreant had to leave the room, turn around three times, and wait to be told to re-enter.

No reference has been found to this superstition before Sharper Knowlson's comment in 1910, quoted above.

London *Observer Supp.* (24 Nov. 1968) 12–13. **Middlesex** [1984] Opie & Tatem, 442. **General** Knowlson (1910) 225; Thompson (1932) 282; Booth (1933) 97; Granville (1952) 179; [1985] Opie & Tatem, 442; [1987] Opie & Tatem, 442.

whistling woman/crowing hen

A crowing hen was held to be so unlucky as to warrant being killed immediately to avoid the disaster it predicted. Most often it presaged a death in the family, but in some cases it was three pieces of ill luck, or simply major, but unspecified, misfortune.

To possess a hen which took to crowing like a cock boded ill to the possessor or his family if it were not disposed of either by killing or selling. They were generally sold to be killed. Only a few years ago I had such a prodigy among a flock of hens which I kept about my works, and one day it was overheard crowing, when one of the workmen came to me, and, with a solemn face, told the circumstance, and advised me strongly to have it destroyed or put away, as some evil would surely follow, relating instances he had known in Ireland.

Western Scotland Napier (1879)

I heard a woman say that, some years ago, her hen crowed three times, and within an hour her son fell from a ladder and was injured for life.

Devon [1900] *Devonshire Assoc.*

In the real world, a crowing hen is not particularly uncommon and far from supernatural. In female birds in which the ovary is damaged either by age or disease, male hormones are released which can affect both plumage and behaviour (Forbes (1966) 1–22). The phenomenon has been noted regularly since at least Aristotle's time (384–322 BC), usually as a strange omen or portent, but later as a metaphor for undesirable traits in women and girls who try to step out of traditional gender roles and to think or behave like men. In this context, an extremely widespread proverb was quoted to express disapproval when women whistle:

*A whistling woman and a crowing hen
Are neither fit for God nor men.*

Somerset Poole (1877)

The second line varies somewhat, but the meaning is always perfectly clear. The crowing hen belief is first found in British sources in 1708, with a letter published in the *British Apollo*, and the 'whistling woman' part is found in Kelly's *Scottish Proverbs* soon afterwards, in 1721. Both the belief and the proverb were found in most parts of the British Isles ever since, even up to the present day (e.g. *Guardian* (25 Jan. 2003)).

Somerset Poole (1877) 39; [1923] Opie & Tatem, 198. **Devon** [1900] *Devonshire Assoc.* 57 (1926) 111; Crossing (1911) 137. **Oxfordshire** [1890s] Thompson (1943) 119; [pre-1900] *Folk-Lore* 24 (1913) 90. **Herefordshire** Leather (1912) 26. **Northamptonshire** N&Q 1S:2 (1850) 164. **Cambridgeshire** *Folk-Lore* 25 (1914) 366. **Lincolnshire** Swaby (1891) 93. **Shropshire** Burne (1883) 229. **Shropshire** *Folk-Lore* 49 (1938) 232. **Derbyshire** [1988] Opie & Tatem, 442. **Yorkshire** Morris (1911) 249. **Cumberland** Gibson (1858) 106. **Co. Durham** Brockie (1886) 134. **West Wales** Davies (1911) 213. **Montgomeryshire** Hamer (1877) 257. **England/Scotland borders** [c.1816] Henderson (1866) 28. **Scotland** Kelly (1721) 33. **Western Scotland** Napier (1879) 113. **Glasgow** [c.1820] Napier (1864) 396. **Ireland** Wilde (1888) 180. **Co. Monaghan** [1909] Sieveking (1988) 113. **Jersey** *Folk-Lore* 25 (1914) 246; L'Amy (1927) 98. **Unlocated** *British Apollo* (17 Sept. 1708); N&Q 4S:11 (1873) 353. **Literary** *Connoisseur* (13 Mar. 1755). **New Zealand** *Guardian* (25 Jan. 2003) 23. **France** N&Q 4S:11 (1873) 353.

white rabbits

see MONTHS: SAYING 'RABBITS'.

Whitsun: new clothes

The tradition that everybody must have new clothes at Easter was widely known from at least the sixteenth century onwards, but a handful of later references say the same thing about Whitsun. As at Easter, the local birds police the area to make sure everyone follows tradition:

New clothes on Whit Sunday or the crows will 'dirty you'.   Lancashire *Lancashire Lore* (1971)

In the nineteenth and earlier twentieth centuries, new clothes at Whitsun would have been far more common than is suggested by these few references, as they would have been an integral part of the customs of keeping Whit week festivities, and particularly Whit walks.

See CLOTHES: NEW, EASTER.

Worcestershire *Folk-Lore* 25 (1914) 370. **East Anglia** Varden (1885) 112. Yorkshire N&Q 5S:10 (1878) 287. Lancashire *Lancashire Lore* (1971) 71.

Whitsun: person born at

An Irish tradition held that a child born on Whit Sunday had an evil destiny ahead of them. They would either kill or be killed, or they would be hanged, or die some other violent death. One of the ways to avoid such a fate was to stage a symbolic 'death' for the child:

On a Whit Sunday (1821) a child was born to Pat Mitchell, a labourer. It is said that the child born on that day is fated to kill or be killed. To avert this doom, a little grave was made, and the infant laid therein, with clay lightly sprinkled on it, sod supported by twigs, covering the whole. Thus was the child buried, and at its resurrection deemed to be freed from the malediction.

Co. Kildare N&Q (1876)

Co. Kildare [1821] N&Q 5S:6 (1876) 463. Co. Longford *Béaloideas* 6 (1936) 259. Co. Laoighis *Béaloideas* 9 (1939) 31.

---

whooping cough
(*Pertussis*)

Highly infectious disease caused by bacterial infection of the respiratory tract, previously very common in children, and sometimes fatal, but now relatively uncommon and only dangerous in small babies. One of the most noticeable symptoms of the disease is bouts of violent coughing, which leave the sufferer so breathless that s/he draws breath with a palpable 'whoop'. It was extremely distressing to both child and parent, and local incidence could often reach epidemic proportions.

Of all the common diseases of the past, whooping cough attracted the widest range of folk cures, and a bewildering variety of procedures were recommended.

Sometimes the little patient is enticed to partake of a dish of roast mice, or to drink some milk which a ferret has lapped, or it is dragged through a gooseberry bush three times, under the arch formed by a bent bough which has struck root in the ground. A hair plucked from the cross on a donkey's back is placed in a bag and placed next the skin round the sufferer's neck. Among many others is the spider cure. The mother catches a house spider, holds it over the child's head, repeating three times: Spider as you waste away/Whooping cough no longer stay. The spider is then placed in a muslin bag, hung over the mantelpiece, and as it dries up, so the cough goes away. A live frog is sometimes held in the child's mouth, and afterwards hung up in the chimney. When the frog dies the cough disappears.

Norfolk Dew (1898)

Most of the general principles of folk medicine are represented in these cures, particularly TRANSFERENCE, and because the disease was clearly respiratory, many procedures involved placing an animal – the species varied, but included frog, sheep, and fish – at the child's mouth:

An old fisherman, formerly well known at the Forge, Keswick, once caught a fish, which he put into the mouth of a child suffering from whooping cough. He then replaced the fish in the Greta. He affirmed that the fish, after being placed in the mouth of the child and returned to the river, gave the complaint to the rest of its kind, as was evident from the fact that they came to the top to cough.   Cumberland N&Q (1878)

Other cures that focused on the act of breathing involved taking the child to benefit from the fresh air of mountain-tops or the seaside, or the pungent fumes of GASWORKS and other industrial processes:

Another landmark was the coming of the tar barrels. Once a year the road was would be resurfaced, and the children hung around watching the hot tar being put down, covered in gravel and rolled flat. Any child suffering from a cough, particularly whooping cough, was brought to inhale the hot tarry steam.

Surrey [1920s] Surrey Fed. of W. I.s (1992)

Other widespread cures included passing the child under and over a DONKEY, giving a HAIR of the child to a DOG to eat, feeding the child cooked MICE, asking the rider of a piebald HORSE what one should do to cure it, wearing

SPIDERS, CATERPILLARS or WOODLICE around the neck.

See also AIR CURES, ASH TREES, BEARS, BLACKBERRIES, BRIDGES, CATS, FERRETS, FOXES, GOOD FRIDAY: FOOD, GOOSEBERRIES, HEDGEHOGS, LIMEKILNS, OAKS, ROPE, SEVENTH SONS, SNAILS, STONES, TIDE, and WEASELS for further details and references.

Surrey Surrey Fed. of W. I.s (1992) 123. Sussex Allen (1995) numerous pages. Norfolk Dew (1898) 77–81. Cumberland N&Q 5S:9 (1878) 64–5. Ireland Logan (1981) 41–4. General Black (1883) numerous pages.

widdershins

see SUNWISE.

widow's peak

A widow's peak was a particular formation in the hair of a woman (or occasionally a man) which, appearing suddenly, was thought to prognosticate impending widowhood or that a future husband would not live long:

Mrs—of Scawby was tidying up her bedroom, and as she dusted the mirror she caught sight of herself; she seemed 'somehow different' and paused to look at herself more closely. She saw that she had a curl over each temple, which she had never had before. She knew quite well what this omen meant. Within the fortnight her husband was brought home ill, and died soon after.   Lincolnshire Rudkin (1936)

Others describe it as a lock or point of hair on the forehead. The term 'widow's peak' or earlier, 'widow's lock', has been in general currency since at least the mid sixteenth century (see OED), and the belief was presumably already present at that time. Certainly, by 1620 Melton could include it in his list of prevalent misconceptions:

That by a certain tuft of hair growing on the foremost part of a man's forehead, it may be known whether he shall bee a widower or no.
Unlocated Melton (1620)

It is presumably because the phrase was so common that many of the compilers of standard folklore collections failed to notice the superstition behind it. Brewer's Dictionary of Phrase and Fable (1981 edn) suggests that the V-shaped point of hair over the forehead is 'reminiscent of the front cusp of the cap formerly worn by widows'.

Cornwall Folk-Lore Jnl 5 (1887) 217. Lincolnshire Rudkin (1936) 20. Northern England Henderson (1879) 42. Co. Durham [1964] Opie & Tatem, 446. Unlocated Melton (1620); N&Q 2S:12 (1861) 492.

wild fire

see ERYSIPELAS.

wills

Many people put off making a will, despite knowing how sensible it is to make one, as the thought makes them vaguely uneasy. This may simply be because they do not wish to be reminded of their own mortality, but there is plenty of evidence that many believed the act would in fact TEMPT FATE and hasten their death, and it is likely that some still feel the same way. This notion has been around at least since the early seventeenth century, and is probably a lot older.

Why, master Cole, what have you written here? You said you would write a letter, but methinks you have made a will . . . Tis true (quoth Cole) if it please God, and I trust this writing cannot shorten my daies.
Deloney, Thomas of Reading (1623)

It is recorded sporadically ever since. We have it on Boswell's authority that Samuel Johnson (died 1784) was extremely reluctant to make his will, and only succumbed a few days before his death. A twentieth-century solicitor reported the stratagem to which he had resorted to counter this reluctance on the part of some clients:

When in practice as a solicitor, I encountered this superstition on more than one occasion. I could always summon a clerk by a stamp on the floor at my office. My practice was to take 'notes' for a superstitious client's will, 'with a view to the document'. When they were complete, I 'stamped', and a clerk brought in a letter. In his presence I asked my client to sign my 'notes' provisionally, and casually signed the notes with my clerk, in the testator's presence. They never objected to this, and the 'notes' were put away. Usually the testator never signed a complete document, but my 'notes' were perfectly valid as a will.   Unlocated N&Q (1940)

Unlocated N&Q 179 (1940) 67. General Werenfels (1748) 7; William Hazlitt, 'On Will-Making', Table Talk 1 (1821) Essay 12; Matthew Henry, Commentary on the Psalms (1853) 27. Literary Thomas Deloney, Thomas of Reading (1623) Ch. 11; John Webster, Duchess of Malfi

(1623) 2:1; Dorothy L. Sayers, *Busman's Honeymoon* (1937) Ch. 8.

wind: obtaining

Apart from the standard method of WHISTLING for a wind, there were other ways of producing the necessary breeze while at sea. Throwing a CAT overboard, or drawing it through the fire, were means; or buying a wind by throwing a coin into the sea:

At length I tried the experiment which sailors consider the last resource . . . but in which they have great faith, of throwing a sixpence overboard; and, strange to say, the enchantment seemed to work.   Scotland [1804] Philo Scotius

These coins often ended up inside fish, and were apparently nailed to the mast 'for luck' when found by fishermen (**London** Lovett (1925)). A widespread international folk-tale motif was to buy a knotted string from a witch or other person with the requisite power:

[In the Isle of Man] Witchcraft is exercised much, for women there be wont to sell wind to the shipmen coming to that country, as included under three knots of thread, so that they will unloose the knots like as they will have the wind to blow

Isle of Man Higden, *Polychronicon* (c.1350)

Traditional stories which relate how sailors bought wind in this way are relatively stereotypical. It is nearly always *three* knots, and the sailors usually undo the third one, against the advice of the seller, thus causing a storm or hurricane (e.g. Murphy (1975)).

High winds and storms were often attributed to evil spirits or the malevolent actions of witches or sorcerers, especially when kings or other notables were put in danger. An early example is provided by Bede, who recorded that when bishops Germanus and Lupus were sailing to Britain to save the faithful from the 'Pelagian' heresy [in AD 429]:

They had safely sailed half-way on their voyage from Gaul with a favourable wind when they were suddenly subjected to the hostile power of devils who were furious that such men should dare to recall the Britons to the way of salvation. The sails were torn to shreds by the gale, the skill of the sailors was defeated, and the safety of the ship depended on prayer rather than on seamanship.

Bede, *History of the English Church and People* (AD 731)

Kittredge (1929) provides numerous other examples of storms raised by witches and devils. Although we had plenty of our own homegrown witches, it was generally agreed that the people who could really control the weather were Finns and Laplanders.

Less common ways of summoning a wind were to stick a KNIFE into the mast, and in the Hebrides, according to Martin Martin in 1704, to hang a he-goat to the mast. Fishermen's wives also had to be careful not to do too much blowing, for example on the cakes they were baking, as this might 'blow up' a storm for their husbands' boats.

England Bede, *History of the English Church and People* (AD 731) Bk 1, Ch. 17. **London** Lovett (1925) 40. **River Thames** *The Times* (18 Jan. 1961) 12. **Lancashire** N&Q 4S:6 (1870) 211. **Northern England** [c.1810] *Denham Tracts* 2 (1895) 29. **Scotland** [1804] Philo Scotius, *Reminiscences of a Scottish Gentleman* (1861) 15, quoted Opie & Tatem, 446. **Highland Scotland** Polson (1926) 73, 121–2. **Kintyre** Jones (1880) 71. **Hebrides** Martin (1704) 109. **Orkney** [1814] Walter Scott, *The Pirate* (1821) n. **G. Ireland** *Sinsear* 8 (1995) 55–70. **N. Ireland** Murphy (1973) 113. **Isle of Man** Ranulph Higden, *Polychronicon* (c.1350). **General** Thomas Nashe, *Terrors of the Night* (1594) D2. **Major studies** Kittredge (1929) 152–62; *Sinsear* 8 (1995) 55–70.

windows

see BIRDS: AT WINDOW; DEATH: DOORS OPEN; GLASS: SEEN THROUGH; MOON: SEEN THROUGH GLASS; THUNDER AND LIGHTNING: DOORS OPEN.

wise women/men

One of the many regular names for local practitioners of witchcraft, charming, and other occult arts was 'wise man' or 'wise woman'. The term included the amateur and those who made a living by such activities:

When the cattle were ill in Peterchurch (1875–87), the wise woman was sent for to charm them. Whoever fetched her must speak to no one going or returning, nor must he say 'Will you come to our cow?' &c., as that would prevent the charm working. He must casually mention the cow's ailment in the course of talk, as if it were of no importance. The wise woman would understand, and go and do what was required. No thanks and no reward must be offered; by and by a present would find its way to her and nothing said.

Herefordshire Leather (1912) 71

See CUNNING MEN/WOMEN for more details and references.

wishbones (also merry-thought or marriage bones)

When modern people take the furcula or forked breastbone of a bird they have just eaten and break it between them for a wish, they are indulging in an abbreviated version of a custom which dates back at least to the seventeenth century. In earlier versions, the breaking was only part of the procedure:

When pulling a wishbone with a friend in February 1936, the housekeeper exclaimed: 'You must both put your arms round the leg of the table when you pull the wishbone'. That done, the ownership of the wish has to be decided in the following manner: the holder of the lucky portion puts both hands behind his back and asks his rival which hand he will choose. The lucky piece, with the accompanying wish, falls to one or the other according to the answer given. At Hartland the ritual is somewhat different. The two persons, male or female, clip the limbs of the wishbone with a bent little finger and pull until the wishbone is broken. The one having the longer portion then breaks this into two pieces, and holds them the shorter portion side by side, concealed in his (or her) hand, with only the three ends protruding. The other person then selects one of
these; *if he (or she) selects the longest piece, that is the piece with the 'wishing' projection, he will have his wish gratified but, if not, the right of obtaining his wish remains with the other.*

Devon *Devonshire Assoc.* (1936)

A similar procedure was described by John Aubrey in 1686, although in his version the bone was first placed on the nose while thinking a 'merry thought', and the breaking decided who would have the thought, or wish, come true. In other versions, the game was to decide who would marry first. At a wedding in Islay, presumably in the 1890s, a 'lady' reported:

M got me to break a cnamh posaidh *(marriage-bone) with him. I got the longest piece. I was then instructed to break it in two and offer both pieces as in drawing lots. I did this, and M. got the longest piece. This he broke and offered me my choice, which resulted in my getting the longer piece and so I am to be first married, as it falls to the one who gets the best in three chances. So it is always done here, as I understand.*

Argyllshire Maclagan (1901)

Devon *Devonshire Assoc.* 68 (1936) 89–90. **Warwickshire** Stewart (1971) 34. **Lincolnshire** Rudkin (1936) 21; [1940s] Sutton (1992) 130. **England** Addy (1895) 81–3. **Lancashire** Harland & Wilkinson (1873) 223. **Northumberland** Bosanquet (1929) 78. **Wales** Trevelyan (1909) 269–70. **Argyllshire** Maclagan (1901) 6.

The wishbone joined other designs, such as the horseshoe and black cat, as recognizable good-luck symbols for such commercial productions as greetings cards. This example dates from c.1914.

Galloway Mactaggart (1824) 91–2. **General** Aubrey, *Remaines* (1686/1880) 92–3. **Literary** Thomas Dekker, *Northward Ho* (1607) 3:2; Addison, *Spectator* (8 Mar. 1711)

witch bottles

When a witch or other ill-wisher casts a spell, they create an invisible connection between themselves and the object of their spite, which lasts as long as the spell remains in operation. The victim thus has a ready channel for counter-attack, even if s/he does not know the identity of the witch. While other procedures against witchcraft are mainly passive protections, the use of this connection has the added attraction of being an active counter-offensive.

The key elements in these countermeasures are the use of items closely associated with the victim, and sharp objects or heat to injure the witch. Thus, the heart of a bewitched animal, if pierced with pins or thorns and then roasted, will cause the witch excruciating pain. In cases of bewitched humans, a similar effect was achieved by placing items in a bottle which was then buried or heated – depending on whether slow or rapid torture of the witch was required. The contents of these 'witch bottles' varied, but almost always included nails or thorns to cause the pain, plus pieces of the original victim's hair, fingernails, or urine. The urine symbolized the fact that the pains caused to the witch would be concentrated in the stomach, bowels, or bladder.

The whole procedure of making witch bottles, as carried out or recommended by the CUNNING MAN, often included other magic elements, such as the need for complete silence during the operation, or the recitation of particular words. The predicted immediate effect, at least of the *heating* variety, was that the witch would immediately appear at the door and desperately try to enter to stop the torture. Strict instructions were therefore given to lock and bar all doors and windows, and even to block up any holes or other places the witch might get in. The witch, trapped outside, would be in such agony that s/he could be forced to remove the original spell.

Examples of the bottles that were hidden are still regularly found, secreted in old houses, buried under thresholds or in stables, cow-houses and gardens, and although their purpose is usually clear, it is usually difficult to date them. From literary evidence, however, it is clear that the practice was widely known in the later seventeenth century, with one key description reporting an occurrence from about the 1620s. Many of the surviving examples are of bellarmine stoneware, which was imported in large quantities from Germany in the seventeenth century. The necks of these bottles were decorated with a bearded face, and were often called 'grey beards' in consequence. Merrifield argues that the shape and decoration of these bottles suggested a new way in which existing ideas of the protective and counter-offensive qualities of pins and urine could be used.

The bottle idea could also be used in other protective ways, as, for example, when a written charm was buried to protect farm animals, or when personal items were hidden in holes in trees to effect cures.

Sussex *Sussex Arch. Colls.* 60 (1919) 147. **Somerset** Davies (1999b) 58–9. **Devon** [1889] *Devonshire Assoc.* 64 (1932) 154; Hewett (1900) 74; *Devonshire Assoc.* 103 (1971) 270–1. **London** *Folk-Lore* 65 (1954) 113; *Trans. London & Middx Arch. Soc.* 31 (1980) 157–8. **Buckinghamshire** *Records of Buckinghamshire* 20 (1978) 635–6. **East Anglia** Forby 2 (1830) 394. **Norfolk** *Norfolk Archaeology* 40 (1987) 113–4. **Lincolnshire** N&Q 2S:1 (1856) 415; *Folk-Lore* 12 (1901) 176; Sutton (1992) 138. **Unlocated** Aubrey, *Miscellanies* (1696) 140. **General** Kittredge (1929) 102–3. **Major studies:** *Folk-Lore* 66 (1955) 195–207; Merrifield (1987); the latter has illustrations.

witch-riding

see NIGHTMARES.

women in superstition

Most superstitions appear relatively sexless in themselves, applying equally to all, but there is often a subtext which reflects the general male-centred nature of society.

Folklore knows nothing of women's rights, of women as the 'superior sex' nor even of chivalrous courtesy giving honour unto the weaker vessel. With folklorists woman is the lesser man – 'as moonlight unto sunlight, and as water unto wine'. The strength and glory of manhood are the emblems of success and good fortune; the weakness of woman is the token of failure and ill-luck.
                                                    Burne (1883)

Throughout the literature it is assumed, and often stated, that women are far more superstitious than men. It is old women who perpetuate 'old wives' tales', it is young women who visit fortune-tellers, read tea leaves, and are obsessed with divinations to reveal their matrimonial prospects or find their 'tall dark stranger'. It is

Gypsy women who swindle silly servant-girls, and most witches were assumed to be women. There are indeed reports of men being 'swum' for witchcraft, but these are few and far between, and in the vast majority of reports of direct action against such people it is a woman on the receiving end:

A man from Portmahomack was tried at Tain for inflicting a wound with a knife on the forehead of an old woman, and was sentenced to three months imprisonment. He believed that the woman had bewitched him and his nets, and the rest of the crew were not willing to go out with him while he was under the curse. Accordingly, he took an opportunity to cut her 'above the breath' believing that with the first drop of blood the woman would lose the power of harming him.

Ross & Cromarty *Inverness Courier* (8 Oct. 1845)

Various people and animals were widely believed to be unlucky to MEET first thing in the morning or at the BEGINNING of a journey. HARES, MAGPIES, PIGS, and CLERGYMEN are among those which the superstitious would prefer not to see, and although the list varies from place to place, it usually includes women. Sometimes red-haired, cross-eyed, or bare-foot women are even worse, but in most cases any woman is unlucky.

On the other hand, no superstitions have been recorded where men, *per se*, were regarded as unlucky or unwelcome. Certain types of men, in certain contexts, may be unwelcome – CLERGY-MEN on fishing boats, fair-haired men at FIRST FOOTING, and so on, but never every man.

When the needs of men and women conflict, it is always women's behaviour that is controlled, not the men's. If they must not meet, it is the woman who hides, not the miner:

Miners consider it extremely unlucky to meet a barefooted woman while on the way to their work. Women are often to be seen rushing frantically out of their sight; but if one is actually met, the miners must either return home, or they must draw blood from her, which is usually done by scratching her forehead with a pin.

Ayrshire N&Q (1870)

In another widespread belief, women are forbidden to whistle, and are likened to hens which crow. The latter were always killed, as grossly unlucky; the women were simply censured (*see* WHISTLING WOMAN).

Distrust of the female goes even deeper:

The question of sex is of immense importance in superstition, for the female has an ill reputation when supernatural danger is at hand. If one were travelling by night and encountered an evil spirit, the dog would help his master, but the bitch would help the evil spirit. Hence the rule was not to take the bitch with one when travelling by night, or, if a person did so, he must tie his garter round the bitch's neck, or, as some recommend, draw blood from her tail, and then she would defend her master against the evil power. A shepherd in a lonely hill bothy had two dogs, male and female. One wet evening a bird came down the chimney, perched itself by the fire, and began to dry itself. As it grew warmer it grew larger, and finally became a woman towering high. She attacked the shepherd, and was helped by the bitch, but the dog helped the master, and with such effort that the witch fled for her life, with the dog clinging to her breasts. When the shepherd returned next day to his home in the valley below he found that a young woman, a neighbour's wife, was nigh death's door, having been mysteriously torn in face and breast the night before. Highland Scotland Macbain (1887/88)

Many of these gender-based beliefs were sufficiently ingrained that women themselves perpetuated them:

Mrs N. . . . has a strong objection to meeting a woman when setting out on a journey. When C.N. set out to enter service (in 1891), her mother went out of the house first to look if any woman was coming up the road, and, seeing one, made C. wait till she had gone by. 'There now! If I hadn't gone out, you'd have met that woman'.

Staffordshire *Folk-Lore* (1909)

There were, of course, areas which were primarily the province of women – dealing with childbirth, CHURCHING, menstruation, for example. Nevertheless, even here men's expectations intruded. Rules about churching were necessarily man-made, even if followed willingly by women. We can also assume, but we cannot prove, that it was a man who first laid down that menstruating women should not handle meat as it would spoil at their touch.

Somerset [1948] Tongue (1965) 150. Forest of Dean *Folk-Lore* 10 (1899) 365. East Anglia Varden (1885) 113. Suffolk *Folk-Lore* 56 (1945) 269. Lincolnshire Swaby (1891) 92–3. Staffordshire *Folk-Lore* 20 (1909) 222. England Addy (1895) 95. Yorkshire N&Q 5S:3 (1875) 204; Blakeborough (1898) 146–7; *Folk-Lore* 21 (1910) 225; *Observer Supp.* (24 Nov. 1968) 10. Lancashire Harland & Wilkinson (1873) 237. Westmorland *London Saturday Jnl* (13 Mar. 1841) 130. Co. Durham *Folk-Lore* 68 (1957) 424. Northumberland *Folk-Lore* 36 (1925) 252. Wales Trevelyan (1909) 327. Monmouthshire N&Q 5S:1 (1874) 384, quoting *Oswestry Advertiser* (May 1874). Northeast

Witchcraft Act of 1604

When James I (VI of Scotland) attained the English throne in 1603, he was already a confirmed believer in witchcraft and had taken a keen and personal interest in the North Berwick trials of 1591. He had published his views in his book *Daemonology* (1597), to refute the idea of sceptics like Reginald Scot (*Discoverie of Witchcraft* (1584)) and he issued a second edition in 1604. The speed with which he moved to pass a new witchcraft law is often taken as proof of his obsession, and he is portrayed as being the main begetter of the witch hunts of the seventeenth century. There is certainly some truth in this view – the opinions of the King, after all, carried a great deal of weight – but it is easy to use James I as a scapegoat, and especially for the English to abdicate responsibility for their own guilt by propagating the idea that it was the arrival of this crazed and superstitious Scottish king that perpetrated the witch mania. There were witch hunts and trials in both countries before James was even born, and the worst atrocities took place in other reigns. By the time he came to the English throne there was a general clamour from the religious and political hierarchy for tougher laws on witchcraft, and how much he simply went willingly with the tide is still debatable. It is certain that by the time of his death in 1628 he had begun to take a far more sceptical view of the whole issue.

The Witchcraft Act of 1604 repealed the existing statute passed in the reign of Elizabeth I (1563), and replaced it with a new law which followed the previous wording closely but introduced some tougher penalties and extended the remit to cover specific crimes such as digging up the dead, or using human body-parts in the course of witchcraft or sorcery. The most important change was that occult acts aimed at harming or killing another person became punishable by death, on the first offence, even if the victim did not die. Under the 1563 Act, the penalty for a first offence in this context had been a year's imprisonment.

The 1604 Act remained in force until the passing of George II's WITCHCRAFT ACT OF 1736.

[I] Be it enacted by the King our sovereign Lord the Lords spiritual and temporal and the Commons in this present Parliament assembled, and by the authority of the same, That the statute made in the fifth year of the reign of our late sovereign Lady of the most famous and happy memory Queen Elizabeth, intituled 'An act against conjurations enchantments and witchcrafts', be from the feast of St Michael the Archangel next coming, for and concerning all offenses to be committed after the same feast, utterly repealed.
[II] And for the better restraining of the said offenses, and more severe punishing the same, be it further enacted by the authority aforesaid, that if any person or persons after the said feast of Saint Michael the Archangel next coming, shall use practise or exercise any invocation, or conjuration, of any evil and wicked spirit, or shall consult, covenant with, entertain, employ, feed, or reward any evil and wicked spirit to or

---

Scotland N&Q 4S:11 (1873) 10. **Highland Scotland** Macbain (1887/88) 266–7; Campbell (1900) 231. **Ayrshire** N&Q 4S: 6 (1870) 339. **Aberdeenshire** *Folk-Lore Jnl* 6 (1888) 264. **Ross & Cromarty** *Inverness Courier* (8 Oct. 1845) quoted *Aberdeen N&Q* 7 (1914) 50. **Ireland** *Gent. Mag.* (1865) 700; Wilde (1888) 180. **Dublin** N&Q 4S:4 (1869) 505. **Aran Islands** *Procs. Royal Irish Academy* 3S:2 (1891–3) 818. **Co. Leitrim** *Folk-Lore* 5 (1894) 199. **Co. Donegal/Co. Galway** *Spectator* (10 Aug. 1907) 190. **Guernsey** Carey (1903) 507. **Unlocated** Igglesden (*c.*1932) 211–12, 216. **General** Burne (1883) 265.

---

wood

see TOUCHING WOOD.

---

woodlice

A widespread and long-lasting motif in folk medicine was to catch an insect, imprison it alive in a bag or other receptacle, and wear it on a string around the neck. Woodlice were sometimes used in this way, usually to help with babies' teething, but in one report for something far more serious:

Ninety-four years ago my mother then aged 3 had small-pox. The doctors said she would never recover, but my grandmother was told by an old lady to go and gather some wood-lice, put them in a flannel bag tied round the child's neck, and when the lice died the small-pox would die away. My mother lived to be to be 89 years old.

Unlocated N&Q (1951)

However unpleasant this may have been, it was easily surpassed by a recipe for curing various ailments, which was to swallow live woodlice:

For constipation: Live woodlice curled up in a ball. Sheep's droppings. Norfolk *Folk-Lore* (1929) *for any intent or purpose; or take up any dead man, woman, or child out of his, her, or their grave, or any other place where the dead body resteth, or the skin, bone, or any other part of any dead person, to be employed or used in any manner of witchcraft, sorcery, charm or enchantment; or shall use, practise, or exercise any witchcraft, enchantment, charm or sorcery whereby any person shall be killed, destroyed, wasted, consumed, pined, or lamed in his or her body, or any part thereof; that then every such offender or offenders, their aiders, abettors and counselors, being of any of the said offences duly and lawfully convicted and attainted, shall suffer pains of death as a felon or felons, and shall lose the privilege and benefit of clergy and sanctuary.*

[III] And further, to the intent that all manner of practise, use, or exercise of witchcraft, enchantment, charm, or sorcery should be from henceforth utterly avoided, abolished and taken away, be it enacted by the authority of this present Parliament, that if any person or persons shall from and after the said feast of Saint Michael the Archangel next coming, take upon him or them by witchcraft, enchantment, charm, or sorcery to tell or declare in what place any treasure of gold or silver should or might be found or had in the earth or other secret places, or where goods or things lost or stolen should be found or become; or to the intent to provoke any person to unlawful love; or whereby any chattel or goods of any person shall be destroyed, wasted, or impaired, or to hurt or destroy any person in his

body, although the same be not effected and done; that then all and every such person or persons so offending, and being thereof lawfully convicted, shall for the said offense suffer imprisonment by the space of one whole year, without bail or maineprize, and once in every quarter of the said year, shall in some market town, upon the market day or at such time as any fair shall be kept there, stand openly upon the pillory by the space of six hours, and there shall openly confess his or her error and offense.

[IV] And if any person or persons being once convicted of the same offenses as is aforesaid, do eftsoons perpetrate and commit the like offense, that then every such offender, being of any the said offenses of the second time lawfully and duly convicted and attainted as is aforesaid, shall suffer pains of death as a felon or felons, and shall loose the benefit and privilege of clergy and sanctuary. Saving to the wife of such person as shall offend in any thing contrary to this Act her title of dower; and also to the heir and successor of every such person his or their titles of inheritance succession and other rights, as though no such attainder or the ancestor or predecessor had been made.

[V] Provided always that if the offender in any of the cases aforesaid shall happen to be a peer of this realm, then his trial therein to be had by his peers, as is used in cases of felony or treason and not otherwise.

Kittredge (1929) 276–328; Robbins (1959) 277–81; Durston (2000).

Sow-beetle, armadillo wood-louse: when the author's father was a little boy, he had these creatures alive, administered to him as pills for whooping-cough. They are still taken for the same purpose. Lincolnshire Peacock (1877)

Compare SPIDERS; CATERPILLARS.

Worn round neck: Herefordshire Leather (1912) 70, 81. Norfolk *Folk-Lore* 40 (1929) 117. Unlocated N&Q 196 (1951) 272.
Swallowed: Devon *Devonshire Assoc.* 15 (1883) 101; *Devonshire Assoc.* 59 (1927) 166; *Devonshire Assoc.* 60 (1928) 123. Worcestershire Berkeley & Jenkins (1932) 33. Suffolk *Gent. Mag.* (1867) 728–41. Norfolk *Folk-Lore* 40 (1929) 119. Norfolk/Lincolnshire *Folk-Lore* 40 (1929) 116–17. Lincolnshire Peacock (1877) 233.

---

work

see GOOD FRIDAY: WORK; GOOD FRIDAY: WORK ON THE LAND.

---

wraiths

A wraith is the spectral double of a person, which appears to others at a distance, while s/he is still alive. Although sometimes used as a synonym for 'ghost', it is useful to preserve the distinction between the ghost as spectre of the dead and the wraith as spectre of the still living. Wraiths can appear for various reasons and purposes, and can be summoned by others or appear of their own volition, depending on the context. The four most pertinent to the present study are those summoned by particular LOVE DIVINA-TION procedures; those summoned in porch

Witchcraft Act of 1736

The Witchcraft Act of George II (c. 5) was a major watershed in the legal treatment of witchcraft and other occult and supernatural practices in Britain. Under the previous Act of James I (1604) occult practices designed to kill or harm their victims had been punishable by death, even on the first offence, and even if they did not succeed. For divination, attempts to find lost or stolen goods, or to provoke 'unlawful love' by magical means, the penalty for the first offence was one year in prison, but on the second offence death. The 1736 Act repealed the 1604 Act (apart from the clause which repealed the previous Act of Elizabeth I) and from then on it was no longer illegal to practise witchcraft because, by implication, witchcraft did not exist. Clause IV of the new Act, however, created a new offence of pretending to practise witchcraft, or fortune-telling, or locating lost or stolen goods, and threatened perpetrators with a year in prison and four sessions in the public pillory. The government thereby announced that witches and fortune-tellers were simply frauds and should only be punished as such.

The Act had been a long time coming. The last execution for witchcraft in England had been of Alicia Molland in 1684 at Exeter, although in Scotland the last was as late as 1727. An increasing majority of the educated classes in both countries had long questioned the reality of witchcraft, and the new Act merely brought the law into line with the ruling opinion of the lawmakers. This is not to argue, however, that every member of the ruling classes held this enlightened view, and as late as the 1770s religious leaders of various persuasions were still lamenting their inability to combat what they saw as a real threat to society. And whole swathes of the population – probably the majority of the ordinary people – continued to believe in witches and the full panoply of supernatural and occult practices well into the nineteenth century.

Clause IV was also used to prosecute a whole range of astrologers, fortune-tellers and the like, right into the mid twentieth century. The last to be charged under the 1736 Act was professed medium HELEN DUNCAN in 1944, and she was imprisoned for nine months. It was finally repealed by the FRAUDULENT MEDIUMS ACT of 1951.

[I] Be it enacted by the King's most excellent Majesty, by and with the advice and consent of the Lords spiritual and temporal, and Commons, in this present Parliament assembled, and by the authority of the same, that the statute made in the first year of the reign of King James I, intituled, 'An act against conjuration, witchcraft, and dealing with evil and wicked spirits, shall, from the twenty-fourth day of June next, be repealed and utterly void and of none effect (except so much thereof as repeals the statute made in the fifth year of the reign of Queen Elizabeth intituled, 'An act against conjurations, enchantments, and witchcrafts').

[II] And be it further enacted by the authority aforesaid, that from and after the said twenty-fourth day of June, the act passed in the Parliament of Scotland, in the ninth parliament of Queen Mary [1562], intituled, 'Anentis Witchcraft', shall be and is hereby repealed.

[III] And be it further enacted, that from and after the said twenty-fourth day of June, no prosecution, suit, or proceeding, shall be commenced or carried on against any person or persons for witchcraft, sorcery, enchantment, or conjuration, or for charging another with any such offense, in any court whatsoever in Great Britain.

[IV] And for the more effectual preventing and punishing any pretenses to such arts or powers as are before mentioned, whereby ignorant persons are frequently deluded and defrauded, be it further enacted by the authority aforesaid, that if any person shall, from and after the said twenty-fourth day of June, pretend to exercise or use any kind of witchcraft, sorcery, enchantment, or conjuration, or undertake to tell fortunes, or pretend, from his or her skill or knowledge in any occult or crafty science, to discover where or in what manner any goods or chattels, supposed to have been stolen or lost, may be found, every person, so offending, being thereof lawfully convicted on indictment or information in that part of Great Britain called England, or on indictment or libel in that part of Great Britain called Scotland, shall, for every such offense, suffer imprisonment by the space of one whole year without bail or mainprize, and once in every quarter of the said year in some market town of the proper county, upon the market day, there stand openly on the pillory by the space of one hour, and also shall (if the court by which said judgement shall be given shall think fit) be obliged to give sureties for his or her good behaviour, in such sum, and for such time, as the said court shall judge proper according to the circumstances of the offense, and in such case shall be further imprisoned until such sureties be given.

Davies (1999a, b) *passim*; Robbins (1959) 214–5.
For the Helen Duncan case, see *History Today* (May 2001) 6–7, and Gaskill (2001a, b)

watching; those who are seen in SECOND SIGHT visions, and those who appear to distant family and friends, usually at the point of death of the real person.

The spirits of persons about to die, especially if the persons be in distant lands, are supposed to return to their friends, and thus predict the calamity. While the spirit is thus away, the person is supposed to be in a swoon, and unaware of what is passing. His desire to see his friends is also necessary; he must have been thinking of them. I am not aware that these spirits ever speak. If no one in a family can see a spirit, most can hear them, and hence strange noises are supposed to indicate death or misfortune to distant friends.

Lancashire Harland & Wilkinson (1882)

Several of the more complex love-divination ceremonies seek to conjure up the future lover or spouse. The following example has a happy ending, but many of these 'conjuring' procedures did not:

A rite rarely neglected [at All Hallow's Eve] was the dipping of the sark sleeve in water where three laird's lands met. The garment was then taken home and hung over the back of a chair to dry, due care being exercised to place it in such a position that the maiden could have it constantly under view during the night; for should marriage be her lot in life the husband she was to get would enter the apartment and turn the garment. A story still lingers in the district of a much-respected doctor's wife who successfully practised the rite when a young and unasked maiden. She had retired to rest at the usual hour, but was too anxious as to the result of her experiment to sleep. Close upon the stroke of twelve a man she had never seen before silently entered the room, turned the sark and then, as if to leave some tangible proof of his visit, deliberately stuck a pen-knife through the sleeve of the garment. The man she saw on that Hallowe'en night was the man she afterwards married, and to her dying day she possessed an unwavering faith in the genuineness of the visit.

Dumfriesshire Corrie (1890/91)

For further examples, see HEMP SEED DIVINATION; LOVE DIVINATION: PREPARED MEAL; LOVE DIVINATION: WASHING SHIFT OR SHIRT.

An early description of porch watching:

Any person fasting on Midsummer eve, and sitting in the church porch, will at midnight see the spirits of the persons of that parish, who will die that year, come and knock at the church door,

in the order and succession in which they will die. One of these watchers, there being several in company, fell into a sound sleep, so that he could not be waked; whilst in this state, his ghost or spirit was seen by the rest of his companions, knocking at the church door.

Unlocated Grose (1787)

For further examples see PORCH WATCHING.

Accounts of encounters with wraiths of those about to die are common in the folklore literature, and are often characterized by the matter-of-fact and underplayed tone in which they are related:

Esther Morton, of Black Heddon, was gathering sticks, and made out of the way of the farmer, on whose land she was, and whom she was on the point of meeting; suddenly she remembered that he was very ill, and could not be there. She returned home alarmed, and found that her neighbour had just died. William Elliott, of Black Heddon, saw an apparition of Mary Brown pop across the fold yard, and disappear in a straw house. Remembering she was very ill, he made inquiries, being alarmed, and found that she had died at the very moment he had seen her.

Northumberland Bigge (1860–62)

For numerous examples, see Briggs (1970–1) Pt B.

Selected references: Sussex *Sussex Arch. Collections* 14 (1862) 25–34. Berkshire Salmon (1902) 423. Wiltshire Francis Kilvert, *Diary* (26 May 1873). Herefordshire Leather (1912) 29. Lincolnshire *Folk-Lore* 28 (1917) 326. England Addy (1895) 123. Derbyshire [1702] Clegg (1981) 915. Lancashire Harland & Wilkinson (1882) 105–6. Northumberland Bigge (1860–62) 93. Northeast Scotland Gregor (1874) 134–5. Dumfriesshire Corrie (1890/91) 39. Fife *Folk-Lore* 43 (1932) 337. Glasgow [*c*.1820] Napier (1864) 395. Co. Wexford [1938] Ó Muirithe & Nuttall (1999) 183–4. Isle of Man Moore (1891) 159–60. Unlocated Grose (1787) 52. General Briggs (1970–1) Pt B; Bennett (1987). Literary *Connoisseur* 59 (1755) 351.

wrens

A handful of birds were believed to be lucky to have around and generally protected from molestation, even by bird's-nesting village boys. SWALLOWS and housemartins were often afforded this honour, but the most widespread in this category was the ROBIN, and second was the wren. The latter was traditionally regarded as female, and wife of the robin, and it seems that most of the protection it received was because of the close association of the two. An extremely widespread couplet summed it up: 'The robin and the wren/Are God almighty's cock and hen', while other rhymes threatened retribution if they were harmed:

He that hurts a robin or a wren
Will never prosper sea or land.

Cornwall Couch (1871)

Nevertheless, the wren did have a few traditions in its own right:

If a wren's feather fall on you it's very lucky.

Norfolk Fulcher Collection (c.1895)

To hear a wren singing in a hedge was, to old Fenmen of the last century, a sign of coming good fortune. It was particularly lucky for a bride to hear the same sound on her way to a wedding.

Cambridgeshire Porter (1969)

The wren was also allowed a part in one of the regular robin myths, in which the robin's red breast cast it as a fire-bringer:

As the robin redbreast brought fire to the island, so the wren is supposed to have brought water. Like the robin it is therefore sacred and ought to be protected. Boys also leave its nest and eggs alone.

Guernsey De Garis (1975)

But all was not sweetness and light for the wren. It also featured in a St Stephen's Day CALENDAR CUSTOM called 'Hunting the Wren', in which it was mercilessly hunted, killed, decorated, and paraded round the village accompanied by music and song. The custom was most widespread in Ireland, but also took place in Wales, the Isle of Man, and some parts of England:

The wren is mortally hated by the Irish; for on one occasion when the Irish troops were approaching to attack a portion of Cromwell's army, the wrens came and perched on the Irish drums, and by their tapping and noise aroused the English soldiers, who fell on the Irish troops and killed them all. So ever since the Irish hunt the wren on St Stephen's Day, and teach their children to run it through with thorns and kill it whenever it can be caught.   Ireland Wilde (1888)

Devon Hewett (1900) 57, 59. Cornwall N&Q 1S:12 (1855) 38; Couch (1871) 168; *Folk-Lore Jnl* 5 (1887) 213–14. Surrey N&Q 5S:3 (1875) 84–5. Oxfordshire [1880] Thompson (1939) 153; *Folk-Lore* 24 (1913) 89. Herefordshire Leather (1912) 26. Northamptonshire N&Q 1S:2 (1850) 164–5. Cambridgeshire Porter (1969) 41. East Anglia Forby (1830) 409–10. Norfolk Fulcher Collection (c.1895). Lincolnshire Thompson (1856) 735. Derbyshire N&Q 4S:9 (1872) 24–5. Lancashire Harland & Wilkinson (1882) 142; Spencer (1966) 11. Co. Durham

Brockie (1886) 132. Wales N&Q 5S:3 (1875) 134; Trevelyan (1909) 113. Mid-Wales Davies (1911) 224. Montgomeryshire Hamer (1877) 260. Shetland [1874] Black (1903) 15. Ireland Wilde (1888) 177; Hickey (1938) 269. Guernsey De Garis (1975) 134. General *Gent. Mag.* (1796) 636; Grose (1787) 64.
For wren-hunting customs, *see*: England Wright & Lones 3 (1940) 276–7. Isle of Man Moore (1891) 133–40. Wales Owen (1987) 63–9; Ireland Danaher (1972) 243–50.

writing

A few superstitions formerly clustered around writing, all of which are now presumably defunct, as successive changes in fashion and the technology of writing have blotted them out. The commonest is the prohibition against keeping MOURNING PAPER in the house, where the focus is on the death symbolism rather than the act of writing, and it thus has its own entry. The others have only been reported infrequently.

Two twentieth-century sources report that it was regarded as unlucky to spill ink. In one the result is simply 'bad luck', but in the other, reported from a milliner's workshop between the wars, worse consequences were predicted: 'Spill ink and somebody will die'.

The apparently obscure notion that drying ink before the fire is unlucky proved surprisingly tenacious. Defoe appears to refer to it:

Others have seemed . . . impatient and exclaiming against their own want of thought if, through haste or forgetfulness, they have chanced to hold [a letter] *before the fire to dry.*   Defoe (1732)

And it was still being quoted in the 1960s:

If she holds a love letter in front of the fire to dry the ink her love will burn itself out.

Unlocated *Daily Sketch* (1 June 1964)

The neat explanation about 'burning love' is strongly reminiscent of the gift of a KNIFE, which will 'cut love'. A further belief, reported only once, from the Opies' own experience, is that it is unlucky to use blotting paper – the writing should be left to dry of its own accord.

Spilling ink: London [Interwar years] Henrey (1955) 97–8. Lincolnshire Rudkin (1936) 17.
Drying ink: Warwickshire Langford (1875) 12. Unlocated N&Q 2S:12 (1861) 491; *Daily Sketch* (1 June 1964) 6. Literary Defoe (1732) 62.
Blotting paper: London [1951] Opie & Tatem, 208.

yarrow (*Achillea mille-folium*)

Two widespread uses of yarrow are discussed under LOVE DIVINATION and NOSEBLEEDS. The plant was also seen as generally protective against bad luck and witchcraft:

A bunch of yarrow tied to Fen babies' cradles was said to make the occupants grow up to be happy and even-tempered. Cambridgeshire Porter (1969)

The plant earr-thalmhainn *or yarrow was kept in the churn as a charm against evil influences.*
Highland Scotland Macbain (1887/88)

Nevertheless, descriptions from Wales flatly contradict this assessment of the yarrow:

In Glamorgan and several other parts of Wales the yarrow is called 'the death flower'. People will not allow it to be brought into their houses, for it is said that if it is taken in, one, two, or three funerals will soon come out of the same house, or will happen in the same family. Wales Trevelyan (1909)

Further research is obviously necessary to square this particular circle.

See also Vickery (1995) 406–8 and Hatfield (1994) for various other uses of yarrow.

Cambridgeshire Porter (1969) 17, 49. Wales Trevelyan (1909) 284. West Wales Davies (1911) 214. Highland Scotland Macbain (1887/88) 267. Ireland N&Q 4S:10 (1872) 24–5.

yellowhammers (*Emberiza citrinella*)

This innocuous little bird of the bunting family formerly enjoyed an extremely sinister reputation and consequently received savage treatment from country boys across Scotland and Northern England. It was reputed to be in league with the Devil, and to receive a drop of his blood every May (sometimes every Monday) morning, and it was believed that its eggs were hatched by a TOAD sitting on them. The yellowhammer's persecutors had a rhyme to accompany their habitual destruction of both bird and nest:

Half a paddock, half a toad   [Paddock = frog]
Horrid yellow yorling
Drinks a drop of the devil's blood
Every Monday morning.
Co. Durham Brockie (1886)

They also had a traditional 'game', called

'spanghewing', in which the young birds were hung by the neck on a thread before being launched violently into the air; again, toads were treated in a similar way (Swainson (1886); Brockett (1829)). No convincing reason has been put forward for this antipathy. Writers have claimed that yellow is the Devil's colour, that the red-brown speckles on the bird's chest brought about the 'blood' story, and that the yellowhammer's eggs have markings which can be taken as diabolical writings. Swainson reports that the same Devil's blood story is told of yellowhammers in Prague. Radford and Hole (1971) report that in Wales the bird was called *Gwas y Neidr*, 'the servant of the snake', because it warned snakes of approaching enemies.

The documentary record starts in the 1820s, but the belief has the appearance of a much older superstition, and earlier references are likely to be found. The geographical spread, restricted to Scotland, Northern England, and Wales seems quite fixed, and the recorded references suggest that the belief – or at least the systematic persecution – faded away in the early twentieth century. The yellowhammer does not seem to feature otherwise in British superstition, although one more positive reference to the bird is that its colour might make it suitable to help in the cure of jaundice:

If a yellow-hammer could be caught and held before the face of a person afflicted by jaundice, a cure might be expected. Wales Trevelyan (1909)

Warwickshire Langford (1875) 13. Co. Durham Brockie (1886) 129. Northumberland Bigge (1860–62) 91; Henderson (1866) 91–2. Wales Trevelyan (1909) 114; Radford (1971) 369. Welsh Gypsies Jarman (1991) 185. Scotland Chambers (1826) 292; Chambers (1870) 191–2; Henderson (1866) 91–2; N&Q 10S:11 (1909) 386. Western Scotland Napier (1879) 112. Dumfriesshire Corrie (1890/91) 80. General Swainson (1886) 69–71.

yew (*Taxus baccata*)

The yew appears in a number of minor superstitions, but the overwhelming question about the tree is how to explain its regular, and noticeable, presence in older churchyards. Yews appear so often in this context that accident can be ruled out, and a deliberate policy presumed. There are numerous stories that are told to explain this. The commonest in the present day is that the wood of yew trees was used to make bows, and as the security of the realm depended on a ready supply of bows and bowmen, it was ordered that yews be planted in every churchyard in the land. Another is that because yews are poisonous to cattle, they were planted in churchyards to ensure that neighbouring farmers kept their fences in order, to keep their stock out of danger. A third combines the two – the yews were planted to make into bows, but they were placed in the churchyard to keep them safe because no one would dream of interfering with a church-yard tree. None of these has any evidence to support them, and nor do they hold together internally – why, for example, if bows were so important, did they only plant one or two trees in each churchyard? Who made the rule, and why can we find no record of it? These explanations are no more likely to be true than any other guesses, but they are still widely known and believed. Less well-known explanations main-tain that yews grow particularly well in corpse-laden ground (but the same question applies: why so few?), that they were planted as wind-breaks (why choose such a slow-growing species?), or that they are remnants of Druid reverence for the tree (can be dismissed as sheer nonsense).

The significant presence of ancient yews in so many churchyards, and their obvious age, has resulted in numerous local legends, on the lines of the following:

Your wish will be granted if you walk backwards round the yew tree [at Stoke Gabriel] *seven times.*

Devon *Devonshire Assoc.* (1970)

and a general feeling that the tree is connected with death and mourning. The latter may well have been formed because of their presence, or it could have been a pre-existing symbolic connection in the mind of early Christians which found expression in the deliberate planting of trees. We have no direct evidence either way, but the latter is a more satisfying, but less romantic, hypothesis than those quoted above.

The yew was regarded as the gentle guardian of the dead, and was formerly revered so much in Wales that to cut it down was considered an act of desecration, while to burn any part of it was looked upon as sacrilege. Wales Trevelyan (1909)

Somerset N&Q 1S:1 (1850) 294. Devon Bulkeley (1886) 230; *Devonshire Assoc.* 102 (1970) 272. Herefordshire Leather (1912) 64–6. Northamptonshire Sternberg (1851) 162. Cambridgeshire Porter (1969) 64. East Anglia Forby (1830) 413. England Addy (1895) 80. Yorkshire Addy (1895) 62. Wales Trevelyan (1909) 105. Carmarthenshire/Cardiganshire Davies (1911) 55–6. Ireland Wilde (1888) 212. N. Ireland Foster (1951) 111. General Hazlitt (1905) 668–70; *FLS News* 15 (1992) 3–6.

Bibliography

Abbreviations used in the Guide:

N&Q   Notes and Queries
DNB   Dictionary of National Biography
EDD   English Dialect Dictionary
OED   Oxford English Dictionary

Aarne, Antti, and Stith Thompson, *Motif-Index of Folk-Literature* (revised edn; Bloomington: Indiana University Press, 1955).

Abarbanell, J. R., 'The Thirteen Superstition Among the Fair Sex', *Belford's Magazine* 6 (May 1891) 801–16 [refers to USA].

Ackerley, R., 'Charms and Superstitions Encountered in a Country Practice', *St. Thomas's Hospital Gazette* 4 (1898) 119–24.

Addy, Sidney Oldall, *A Glossary of Words Used in the Neighbourhood of Sheffield* (London: English Dialect Society, 1888).

———, *Folk Tales and Superstitions* (Wakefield: EP, 1973) [previously published as *Household Tales with Other Traditional Remains*, 1895].

Akerman, John Yonge, *A Glossary of Provincial Words and Phrases in Use in Wiltshire* (London: John Russell Smith, 1842).

Allen, Andrew, *A Dictionary of Sussex Folk Medicine* (Newbury: Countryside Books, 1995).

Anderson, Robert, *Ballads in the Cumberland Dialect* (Carlisle: Hodgson, 1805).

Andrews, William, *Bygone Lincolnshire* (Hull: A. Brown, 1891).

———, *Bygone Leicestershire* (Leicester: Frank Murray, 1892).

———, *England in the Days of Old* (London: Wm. Andrews, 1897).

Anson, Peter F., *Fishing Boats and Fisher Folk on the East Coast of Scotland* (London: Dent, 1930).

———, *Fisher Folk-Lore* (London: Faith Press, 1965).

Appleby, Mrs Newton W., 'Folk-Lore of the County of Durham', in Leighton (1910) 44–64.

Arber, Edward, *English Reprints* (London: Arber, 1869–71).

Archer, Fred, *The Distant Scene* (London: Hodder & Stoughton, 1967).

———, *Under the Parish Lantern* (London: Hodder & Stoughton, 1969).

———, *A Lad of Evesham Vale* (London: Hodder & Stoughton, 1972).

Armstrong, Edward M., *The Folklore of Birds* (London: Collins, 1958).

Armstrong, Herbert B. J. (ed.), *A Norfolk Diary* (London: Harrap, 1949).

Armstrong, Sybil, *A Croft in Clachan* (London: Hutchinson, 1976).

Arthur, Dave, *A Sussex Life: The Memories of Gilbert Sargent* (London: Barrie & Jenkins, 1989).

Ashmole, Elias, *The Diary and Will of Elias Ashmole* (Oxford: Old Ashmolian Reprints, 1927).

Atkinson, J. C., *Forty Years in a Moorland Parish: Reminiscences and Researches at Danby in Cleveland* (London: Macmillan, 1891).

Aubrey, John, *Natural History of Wiltshire* (1685; London: Wilts. Top. Soc., 1847).

———, *Miscellanies Upon Various Subjects* (1696; 4th edn, London: Russell Smith, 1857).

———, *Remaines of Gentilisme and Judaisme* (ed. James Britten, London: Folklore Society, 1880).

———, *Three Prose Works* (ed. John Buchanan-Brown, Carbondale: Southern Illinois University Press, 1972). [includes: *Miscellanies, Remaines of Judaisme and Gentilisme, Observations*].

Aytoun, William E., *Lays of the Scottish Cavaliers* (Edinburgh: Blackwood, 1849).

Axon, William E. A., 'Divination by Books', *Manchester Quarterly* 26 (1907) 26–35.

Baker, Anne Elizabeth, *Glossary of Northamptonshire Words and Phrases* (London: Russell Smith, 1854).

Baker, Margaret, *Wedding Customs and Folklore* (Newton Abbot: David & Charles, 1977).

———, *The Folklore of the Sea* (Newton Abbot: David & Charles, 1979).

———, *Discovering the Folklore of Plants* (3rd edn, Princes Risborough: Shire, 1996).

Balfour, M. C., *County Folklore: Northumberland* (London: Folklore Society, 1904).

Ballard, Linda-May, 'Traditional Treatment of Hydrophobia', *Ulster Folklife* 32 (1986) 83–6.

———, *Forgetting Frolic: Marriage Traditions in Ireland* (Belfast: Inst. of Irish Studies, 1998).

Balleine, Revd G. R., *What is Superstition? A Trail of Unhappiness* (London: Press and Publications Board of the Church Assembly, 1939).

Banks, Mrs M. Macleod, *British Calendar Customs: Scotland* (London: Folklore Society, Vol. 1, 1937; Vol. 2, 1939; Vol. 3, 1941).

———, *British Calendar Customs: Orkney and Shetland* (London: Folklore Society, 1946).

Barb, A. A., 'Birds and Medical Magic', *Journal of the Warburg Institute* 13 (1950) 316–22.

Baring-Gould, Sabine, *Yorkshire Oddities* (London: John Hodges, 1874).

———, *Strange Survivals: Some Chapters in the History of Man* (London: Methuen, 1892).

———, *A Book of Dartmoor* (London: Methuen, 1900).

———, *Devonshire Characters* (London: John Lane, 1908).

Barker, Henry J., *Very Original English* (London: Jarrold, 1889).

Barker, W. G. M. Jones, *Historical and Topographical Account of Wensleydale* (2nd edn, London: J. R. Smith, 1856).

Barnes, Henry, 'On Touching for the King's Evil', *Transactions of the Cumberland and Westmorland Antiquarian and Archaeological Society* 13 (1895) 343–63).

Baron-Wilson, Mrs Cornwell, *Memoirs of Miss Mellon, afterwards Duchess of St Albans* (new edn, London: Remington, 1886).

Barrett, W. H., and R. P., Garrod, *East Anglian Folklore and Other Tales* (London: Routledge & Kegan Paul, 1976).

Barry, George, *History of the Orkney Islands* (2nd edn, London: Longman, 1808).

Beall, Otho T., 'Aristotle's Master Piece in America: A Landmark in the Folklore of Medicine', *William and Mary Quarterly* 3S:20 (1963) 207–22.

Beckwith, Lillian, *A Rope – In Case* (London: Hutchinson, 1968).

Beddington, Winifred G., and Elsa B. Christy, *It Happened in Hampshire* (Winchester: Hampshire Fed. of Women's Institutes, 1977).

Benham, Charles, 'Omens at Coronations', *Nineteenth Century* 50 (1901) 799–805.

Bennett, Gillian, *Traditions of Belief* (London: Penguin, 1987).

Bennett, Gillian, and Paul Smith, *Contemporary Legend: A Folklore Bibliography* (New York: Garland, 1993).

Bennett, Margaret, *Scottish Customs: from the Cradle to the Grave* (Edinburgh: Polygon, 1992).

Benwell, Gwen, and Arthur Waugh, *Sea Enchantress: The Tale of the Mermaid and her Kin* (London: Hutchinson, 1961).

Berkeley, Mildred, and C. E. Jenkins, *A Worcestershire Book* (Worcester: Worcestershire Fed. of Women's Institutes, 1932).

Berks. Arch. Soc., *Quarterly Journal of the Berkshire Archaeological and Architectural Society*.

Besterman, Theodore, 'The Folklore of Dowsing', *Folk-Lore* 37 (1926) 113–33.

Betts, P. Y., *People Who Say Goodbye: Memories of Childhood* (London: Souvenir, 1989).

Bigge, John F., 'Local Superstitions at Stamfordham', *Transactions of the Tyneside Naturalists' Field Club* 5 (1860–1862) 88–98.

Billingsley, John, *Stony Gaze: Investigating Celtic and Other Stone Heads* (Chieveley: Capall Bann, 1998).

Billson, C. J., *County Folklore Printed Extracts 3: Leicestershire and Rutland* (London: Folklore Society, 1895; reprint, Llanerch, 1997).

Black, G. F., *County Folklore: Orkney and Shetland Islands* (London: David Nutt, 1903).

Black, William George, *Folk-Medicine: A Chapter in the History of Culture* (London: Folklore Society, 1883).

Blackburn, Elizabeth K., *In and Out the Windows* (Burnley: F. H. Brown, 1978).

Blakeborough, Richard, *Wit, Character, Folklore and Customs of the North Riding of Yorkshire* (London: Frowde, 1898).

Blishen, Edward, *A Cackhanded War* (London: Thames & Hudson, 1972).

Bloom, J. Harvey, *Folk Lore, Old Customs and Superstitions in Shakespeare Land* (London: Mitchell Hughes & Clarke (c.1930).

Bonser, Wilfrid, 'The Dissimilarity of Ancient Irish Magic from that of the Anglo-Saxons', *Folk-Lore* 37 (1926a) 271–88.

——, 'Magical Practices against Elves', *Folk-Lore* 37 (1926b) 350–63.

——, 'Anglo-Saxon Laws and Charms relating to Theft', *Folk-Lore* 57 (1946) 7–11.

——, *The Medical Background of Anglo-Saxon England* (London: Wellcome Historical Medical Library, 1963).

Booth, J. B., *Pink Parade* (London: Thornton Butterworth, 1933).

Bord, Janet, and Colin Bord, *Sacred Waters: Holy Wells and Water Lore in Britain and Ireland* (London, New York: Granada, 1985).

Bosanquet, Rosalie E., *In the Troublesome Times* (Northumberland Press, 1929; reprint, Stocksfield: Spredden Press, 1989).

Borlase, William, *Observations on Antiquities, Historical and Monumental of the County of Cornwall* (Oxford: Jackson, 1754).

Boswell, Annabella, *Annabella Boswell's Journal* (Sydney: Angus & Robertson, 1965).

Boswell, James, *The Life of Samuel Johnson* (1791; London: Robert Riviere, 1906).

Bourne, George, *The Bettesworth Book: Talks with a Surrey Peasant* (London: Duckworth, 1901).

Bourne, Henry, *Antiquitates Vulgares, or the Antiquities of the Common People* (Newcastle: The Author, 1725).

Brand, John, *A New Description of Orkney, Zetland, Pightland-Firth, and Caithness* (Edinburgh: George Mosman, 1703) [selections published in Black (1903)].

——, *Observations on Popular Antiquities* (Newcastle: J. Johnson, 1777).

Brand John, *Observations on Popular Antiquities* (London: Vernor, Bood & Sharpe, 1810).

——, *Observations on Popular Antiquities* (2 vols, London: Rivington, 1813).

——, *Observations on the Popular Antiquities of Great Britain* (new edn, ed. Henry Ellis; 3 vols, London: Bohn, 1849).

Bray, Mrs A. E., *The Borders of the Tamar and the Tavy* (London: Murray, 1836; reissued, 1879).

——, *Traditions, Legends, Superstitions, and Sketches of Devonshire* (London: Murray, 1838).

Bridge, Joseph Cox, *Cheshire Proverbs* (London: Simpkin Marshall, 1917).

Briggs, Katharine, *A Dictionary of British Folk-Tales* (London: Routledge, 1970–1).

——, *The Folklore of the Cotswolds* (London: Batsford, 1974).

——, *Nine Lives: Cats in Folklore* (London: Routledge & Kegan Paul, 1980).

Briscoe, J. Potter, 'Witchcraft in Leicestershire', in Andrews (1892) 126–9.

Brockett, John Trotter, *A Glossary of North Country Words* (Newcastle: Charnley, 1825; 2nd edn, 1829; 3rd edn, Newcastle: Emerson Charnley, 1846).

Brockie, William, *Legends and Superstitions of the County of Durham* (Sunderland, 1886; reprint, Wakefield: EP, 1974).

Brogden, J. Ellett, *Provincial Words and Expressions current in Lincolnshire* (London: Hardwicke, 1866).

Bromehead, C. N., 'Aetites or the Eagle Stone', *Antiquity* 21 (1947) 16–22.

Brown, James Walter, *Round Carlisle Cross: Old Stories Retold* (4th series, Carlisle: Thurnam, 1924).

Brown, Theo, *The Fate of the Dead: Folk Eschatology in the West Country after the Reformation* (Ipswich: D. S. Brewer, 1979).

Browne, Thomas, *The Works of Sir Thomas Browne* (Edinburgh: John Grant, 1927) [includes reprint of 6th edn (1672) of *Pseudodoxia Epidemica*, first published 1646].

Buckley, Anthony D., 'Unofficial Healing in Ulster', *Ulster Folklife* 26 (1980) 15–34.

Buckley, Thomas Edward, and Brown, John Alexander Harvie, *A Vertebrate Fauna of the Orkney Islands* (Edinburgh: David Douglas, 1891).

Bulkeley, H. J., 'Some East Cumberland Superstitions', *Transactions of the Cumberland and Westmorland Antiquarian and Archaeological Society* 8 (1886) 225–32.

Bühler, Curt F., 'Prayers and Charms in Certain Middle English Scrolls', *Speculum* 39 (1964) 270–78.

Bullen, Frank T., 'Sea-Superstitions', *The Spectator* (22 July 1899) 119–20 [also reprinted in Bullen, Frank T., *A Sack of Shakings* (New York: McLure Phillips, 1901)].

Burgess, S. and E. H. Rann, 'Superstitions and Curious Events', in Walters (1897) 112–21.

Burne, Charlotte, *Shropshire Folk-Lore: A Sheaf of Gleanings* (London: Trübner, 1883).

Burnett, John, *Useful Toil: Autobiographies of Working People from the 1820s to the 1920s* (London: Allen Lane, 1975).

———, *Destiny Obscure: Autobiographies of Childhood, Education and Family from the 1820s to the 1920s* (London: Allen Lane, 1982).

Burrell, Philippa, *The Golden Thread* (Hull: University of Hull Press, 1997).

Burstein, Sona Rosa, 'Demonology and Medicine in the Sixteenth and Seventeenth Centuries', *Folk-Lore* 67 (1956) 16–33.

Burt, Edmund, *Letters from a Gentleman in the North of Scotland* (London: S. Birt, 1754).

Butler, G. Slade, 'Appearance of Spirits in Sussex', *Sussex Archaeological Collections* 14 (1862) 25–34.

Calder, James T., *Sketches from John O' Groat's* (Wick: Peter Reid, 1842).

Camp, John, *In Praise of Bells: The Folklore and Traditions of British Bells* (London: Robert Hale, 1988).

Campbell, A. B., *Customs and Traditions of the Royal Navy* (Aldershot: Gale & Polden, 1956).

Campbell, John Gregorson, *Superstitions of the Highlands and Islands of Scotland* (Glasgow: MacLehose, 1900).

———, *Witchcraft and Second Sight in the Highlands and Islands of Scotland* (Glasgow: MacLehose, 1902).

Campbell, J. L., *A Collection of Highland Rites and Customs Copied by Edward Lhuyd from the Manuscript of the Rev. James Kirkwood (1650–1709)* (Woodbridge: Brewer, 1975).

Capp, Bernard, *Astrology and the Popular Press: English Almanacs 1500–1800* (London: Faber, 1979).

Carew, Richard, *The Survey of Cornwall* (1602; reprinted London: Adams & Dart, 1969).

Carey, Edith, *Guernsey Folk Lore* (London: Elliot Stock, 1903) [mostly material from the MacCulloch MS].

Carleton, William, *Traits and Stories of the Irish Peasantry* (Dublin: Wm. Curry, 1844).

Carmichael, Alexander, *Carmina Gadelica* (Edinburgh: Macleod, 1900).

Carr, William, *The Dialect of Craven* (London: Crofts, 1824; 2nd edn, 1828).

Carter, Ian, *Farmlife in Northeast Scotland 1840–1914* (Edinburgh: John Donald, 1979).

Cashen, William, *William Cashen's Manx Folk-Lore* (Douglas: Johnson, 1912).

Cassell's Saturday Journal, 'Queer West-Country

Remedies of To-Day (By a Rural Parson)', *Cassell's Saturday Journal* (17 May 1893).

Chadwick, Owen, *Victorian Miniature* (London: Hodder & Stoughton, 1960).

Chamberlain, Mary, *Old Wives' Tales: Their History, Remedies and Spells* (London: Virago, 1981).

Chambers, Robert, *The Popular Rhymes of Scotland* (Edinburgh: William Hunter, 1826, 1842, 1847).

———, *Popular Rhymes of Scotland* (new edn, London: Chambers, 1870).

———, *The Book of Days: A Miscellany of Popular Antiquities* (2 vols, London: Chambers, 1864/1878).

Chambers, William, *Memoir of Robert Chambers* (Edinburgh: Chambers, 1872).

Chanter, J. R., 'North Devon Customs and Superstitions', *Transactions of the Devonshire Association* 2 (1867–8) 38–42.

Charsley, Simon R., *Wedding Cakes and Cultural History* (London: Routledge, 1992).

Chetwynd-Stapylton, Mark, *Discovering Wayside Graves and Memorial Stones* (Tring: Shire, 1968).

Choice Notes from 'Notes and Queries': Folk-Lore (London: Bell and Daldy, 1859).

Chope, R. Pearse, 'Devonshire Calendar Customs: Part 2, Fixed Festivals', *Transactions of the Devonshire Association* 70 (1938) 341–404.

Clague, John, *Manx Reminiscences* (Castletown: Blackwell, 1911).

Clare, John, *The Midsummer Cushion* (Manchester: Carcanet, 1990).

———, *Cottage Tales* (Manchester: Carcanet, 1993).

Clark, David, *Between Pulpit and Pew: Folk Religion in a North Yorkshire Fishing Village* (Cambridge: Cambridge University Press, 1982).

Claxton, A. O. D., *The Suffolk Dialect of the 20th Century* (Ipswich: Norman Adlard, 1954).

Clegg, *The Diary of James Clegg* (ed. V. S. Doe, Derbyshire Record Society, 1981).

Cobbett, William, *Rural Rides* (London: Wm Cobbett, 1830).

Cockayne, Oswald, *Leechdoms, Wortcunning and Starcraft of Early England* (3 vols, London: Longman Green, 1864–6).

Cohen, Herman, 'Sortes Virgilianae', *Fortnightly Review* (Mar. 1924) 440–52.

Cohn, Shari A., 'A Historical Review of Second Sight: The Collectors, their Accounts and Ideas', *Scottish Studies* 33 (1999) 146–85.

Cole, R. E. G., *A Glossary of Words Used in South-West Lincolnshire* (London: English Dialect Society, 1886).

Cook, Judith, *Dr Simon Forman: A Most Notorious Physician* (London: Chatto & Windus, 2001).

Coppard, George, *With a Machine Gun to Cambrai* (London: HMSO, 1968).

Copper, Bob, *A Song for Every Season: A Hundred Years of a Sussex Farming Family* (London: Heinemann, 1971).

Corbridge, Sylvia Lovat, *It's an Old Lancashire Custom* (2nd edn, Preston: Guardian Press, 1964).

Cornhill Magazine, 'Superstition', *Cornhill Magazine* 5 (1862) 537–49.

Corrie, John, 'Folk-Lore of Glencairn', *Transactions of the Dumfriesshire and Galloway Natural History and Antiquarian Society* (1890/91) 37–45, 75–83.

Couch, Jonathan, *The History of Polperro* (Truro: W. Lake, 1871).

Coulter, John, *Norwood Past* (London: Historical Publications, 1996).

Courtney, M. A., *Cornish Feasts and Folk-Lore* (Penzance: Beare, 1890).

Cowper, H. S., 'Hawkshead Folklore', *Transactions of the Cumberland and Westmorland Antiquarian and Archaeological Society* 14 (1897) 371–89.

Cowper, Henry Swainson, *Hawkshead* (London: Bemrose, 1899).

Cox, J. Charles, *Memorials of Old Derbyshire* (London: Bemrose, 1907).

Crawford, Phyllis, *In England Still* (London: Arrowsmith, 1938).

Crawfurd, Raymond, *The King's Evil* (Oxford: Clarendon Press, 1911).

Cressy, David, *Bonfires and Bells: National Memory and the Protestant Calendar in Elizabethan and Stuart England* (London: Weidenfeld & Nicolson, 1989).

——, 'Purification, Thanksgiving and the Churching of Women in Post-Reformation England', *Past and Present* 141 (1993) 106–46.

Crippen, Thomas George, *Christmas and Christmas Lore* (London: Blackie, 1923).

Crombie, James E., 'First-Footing in Aberdeenshire', *Folk-Lore* 4 (1893) 315–21.

——, 'Shoe-Throwing at Weddings', *Folk-Lore* 6 (1895) 258–81.

Cromek, Robert H., *Remains of Nithsdale and Galloway Song* (London: Cadell & Davies, 1810).

Crossing, William, *Folk Rhymes of Devon* (Exeter: James G. Commin, 1911).

Culloty, A. T., *Drinking from the Well* (Ballydesmond: Desmond, 1993).

Cullum, John, *The History and Antiquities of Hawsted, in the County of Suffolk* (London: J. Nichols, 1984).

Cullwick, Hannah, *The Diaries of Hannah Cullwick, Victorian Maidservant* (ed. Liz Stanley, London: Virago, 1984).

Curry, Patrick, *Prophecy and Power: Astrology in Early Modern England* (Princeton: Princeton University Press, 1989).

——, *A Confusion of Prophets: Victorian and Edwardian Astrology* (London: Collins & Brown, 1992).

Dacombe, Marianne R., *Dorset Up Down and Along* (Dorchester: Dorset Fed. of Women's Institutes, 1935).

Dalyell, John Graham, *The Darker Superstitions of Scotland* (Edinburgh: Waugh & Innes, 1834).

Danaher, Kevin, *The Year in Ireland* (Dublin: Mercier, 1972).

Davey, Frederick Hamilton, *Flora of Cornwall* (Penryn: Chegwidden, 1909).

Davidson, Hilda Ellis (ed.), *The Seer in Celtic and Other Traditions* (Edinburgh: John Donald, 1989).

Davidson, Thomas, 'Animal Charm Cures and Amulets', *The Amateur Historian* 3 (1856–8) 237–48.

Davies, Jennifer, *Saying it with Flowers: The Story of the Flower Shop* (London: Headline, 2000).

Davies, Jonathan Caredig, *Folk-Lore of West and Mid-Wales* (Aberystwyth, 1911; reprint, Felinfach: Llanerch, 1992).

Davies, Owen, 'Healing Charms in Use in England and Wales 1700–1950', *Folklore* 107 (1996), 19–32.

——, 'Hag-Riding in Nineteenth-Century West Country England and Modern Newfoundland', *Folk Life* 35 (1996–7) 36–53.

——, 'Cunning Folk in England and Wales during the Eighteenth and Nineteenth Centuries', *Rural History* 8 (1997), 91–107.

——, 'Charmers and Charming in England and Wales from the Eighteenth to the Twentieth Century', *Folklore* 109 (1998a), 41–52.

——, 'Newspapers and the Popular Belief in Magic in the Modern Period', *Journal of British Studies* 37 (1998b), 139–65.

——, 'Witchcraft: The Spell that Didn't Break', *History Today* (Aug. 1999) 7–13.

——, *A People Bewitched: Witchcraft and Magic in Nineteenth-Century Somerset* (Bruton: The Author, 1999a).

——, *Witchcraft, Magic and Culture 1736–1951* (Manchester: Manchester University Press, 1999b).

Davies, W. L., 'The Conjuror in Montgomeryshire', *Montgomeryshire Collections* 45 (1938) 158–70.

Dawson, W. Harbutt, 'An Old Yorkshire Astrologer and Magician 1694–1760', *The Reliquary* 23 (1882) 197–202.

Dawson, Warren R., 'A Norfolk Vicar's Charm against Ague', *Norfolk Archaeology* 24 (1932) 233–8.

De Garis, Marie, *Folklore of Guernsey* (Guernsey: The Author, 1975).

Deacon, E., 'Some Quaint Customs and Superstitions in North Staffordshire and Elsewhere', *North Staffordshire Field Club Transactions* 64 (1929–30) 18–32.

Deane, Tony, and Tony Shaw, *The Folklore of Cornwall* (London: Batsford, 1975).

Defoe, Daniel, *The History of the Life and Surprising Adventures of Duncan Campbell* (London: Curll, 1720; 3rd edn, 1728).

——, *Secret Memoirs of the Late Mr D. Campbell* (1732).

Denham Tracts: A Collection of Folklore by Michael Aislabie Denham (ed. James Hardy, 2 vols, London: Folklore Society, 1892–5).

Dent, J. G., 'The Witchstone in Ulster and England', *Ulster Folklife* 10 (1964) 46–8.

——, 'The Holed Stone Amulet and its Uses', *Folk Life* 3 (1965) 68–78.

Dew, Walton N., *A Dyshe of Norfolke Dumplings* (London: Jarrold, 1898).

Dickinson, William, *Cumbriana, or Fragments of Cumbrian Life* (London: Whittaker, 1875) esp. 105–23.

——, *A Glossary of Words and Phrases of Cumberland* (London: Bemrose, 1899).

Dilling, Walter J., 'Girdles: Their Origin and Development, Particularly with Regard to their Use as Charms in Medicine, Marriage, and Midwifery', *Caledonian Medical Journal* 9 (1912/14) 337–57.

Ditchfield, P. H., *Old English Customs* (London: Methuen, 1901).

Dives and Pauper (c.1405–1410; London: Early English Text Society, 1976/1980).

Dudeney, Mrs Henry, *A Lewes Diary, 1916–1944* (ed. Diana Crook, Heathfield: Tartus, 1998).

Duncan, Ronald, *Where I Live* (London: Museum Press, 1953).

Duncomb, John, *Words Used in Herefordshire, in* Walter W. Skeat, *Reprinted Glossaries, Series B* (London: English Dialect Society, 1874) [first published in *Collections Towards the History and Antiquities of the County of Hereford* (1804)].

Dundes, Alan, *The Evil Eye: A Casebook* (New York: Garland, 1981).

Durston, Chris, 'Signs and Wonders and the English Civil War', *History Today* 37 (Oct. 1987) 22–8.

Durston, Gregory, *Witchcraft and Witch Trials: A History of English Witchcraft and its Legal Perspectives, 1542 to 1736* (London: Barry Rose, 2000).

Dyer, T. F. Thiselton, *British Popular Customs, Past and Present* (London: George Bell, 1876).

———, *English Folk-Lore* (London: Bogue, 1878; 2nd edn, 1880).

———, *Domestic Folk-Lore* (London: Cassell, 1881).

———, *Folk-Lore of Shakespeare* (London; Griffith & Farran, 1883).

———, *The Folk-Lore of Plants* (London: Chatto & Windus, 1889).

———, *Folk-Lore of Women* (London: Elliot Stock, 1905).

E. P. E., 'Passing Children through a Cleft Ash Tree to Cure Rupture', *Wiltshire Archaeological and Natural History Magazine* 24 (1889) 344–5.

Earwood, Caroline, 'Trees and Folk Medicine', *Folk Life* 38 (1999–2000) 22–31.

Eddrup, Revd Canon, 'Notes on some Wiltshire Superstitions', *Wiltshire Archaeological and Natural History Magazine* 22 (1885) 330–4.

Edmonston, A., *Zetland Islands* (Edinburgh: 1809).

Edmonston, B., and Jessie M. E. Saxby, *The Home of a Naturalist* (London: Nisbet, 1888).

Eggar, J. Alfred, *Remembrances of Life and Customs in Gilbert White's, Cobbett's and Charles Kingsley's Country* (London: Simpkin & Marshall, 1924).

Elder, Eileen, *The Peacock Lincolnshire Word Books 1884–1920* (Scunthorpe: Scunthorpe Museum Society, 1997).

Elworthy, Frederic Thomas, *The West Somerset Word-Book* (London: English Dialect Society, 1886).

———, *The Evil Eye* (1895; reprint, New York: The Julian Press, 1958).

Ettlinger, Ellen, 'British Amulets in London Museums', *Folk-Lore* 50 (1939), 148–75.

Evans, George Ewart, *Ask the Fellows who Cut the Hay* (London: Faber, 1956; 2nd edn, 1965).

———, *The Horse in the Furrow* (London: Faber, 1960).

———, *The Pattern Under the Plough: Aspects of Folk-Life in East Anglia* (London: Faber, 1966).

———, *The Farm and the Village* (London: Faber, 1969).

———, *Where Beards Wag All: The Relevance of the Oral Tradition* (London: Faber, 1970).

———, *Horse Power and Magic* (London: Faber, 1979).

Evans, George Ewart, and David Thomson, *The Leaping Hare* (London: Faber, 1972).

Evans, Joan, *Magical Jewels of the Middle Ages and Renaissance* (Oxford: Clarendon Press, 1922).

Farmer, David, *Oxford Dictionary of Saints* (Oxford: Oxford University Press, 1978).

Ferguson, Robert, *The Dialect of Cumberland* (London: Williams & Norgate, 1873).

Fergusson, R. Menzies, *Rambling Sketches in the Far North* (London: Simpkin Marshall, 1884).

Festing, Sally, *Fishermen: A Community Living from the Sea* (Newton Abbot: David & Charles, 1977).

Finucane, R. C., *Miracles and Pilgrims: Popular Beliefs in Medieval England* (London: Dent, 1977).

———, *Appearances of the Dead: A Cultural History of Ghosts* (London: Junction Books, 1982).

Firth, John, *Reminiscences of an Orkney Parish* (Stromness: Orkney Natural History Society, 1920).

Fitz Stephen, William, *Norman London* (c.1180, New York: Italica, 1990).

Fitzgerald, Edward, *Works* (London: Quaritch, 1887) [Vol.

2 includes 'Sea Words and Phrases Along the Suffolk Coast'].

Fletcher, J. S., *Recollections of a Yorkshire Village* (London: Digby Long, 1910).

Fliess, Robert, 'Knocking on Wood: A Note on the Precedipal Nature of the Magic Effect', *Psychoanalytic Quarterly* 13 (1944) 327–40.

Foli, Prof. P. R. S., *Pearson's Fortune Teller* (London: Pearson, 1902).

Folkard, Richard, *Plant-Lore, Legends and Lyrics* (London: Sampson Low, 1884).

Forbes, Alexander Robert, *Gaelic Names of Beasts* (Edinburgh: Oliver & Boyd, 1905).

Forbes, Thomas R., *The Midwife and the Witch* (New Haven and London: Yale University Press, 1966).

———, 'Verbal Charms in British Folk Medicine', *Proceedings of the American Philological Society* 115:4 (1971), 293–316.

Forby, Robert, *The Vocabulary of East Anglia* (London: Nichols, 1830).

Ford, Joseph, *Some Reminiscences and Folk Lore of Danby Parish and District* (Whitby: Home, 1953).

Fosbroke, Thomas Dudley, *Ariconensia* (Ross: W. Farror, 1821).

Foster, Jeanne Cooper, *Ulster Folklore* (Belfast: H. R. Carter, 1951).

Fowler, M. W. E., 'Yorkshire Folk-Lore', in T. M. Fallow, *Memorials of Old Yorkshire* (London: George Allen, 1909) 286–305.

Friend, Hilderic, *Flowers and Flower Lore* (London: Swan Sonnenschein, 1884).

Fulcher Collection [Norfolk, 1890s] in Folklore Society Archives, London.

Furnivall, Frederick J., *Love-Poems and Humourous* [sic] *Ones* (London: Ballad Society, 1874).

Gales, R. L., *The Vanished Country Folk and other Studies in Arcady* (London: Simpkin Marshall, 1914).

Gamble, Rose, *Chelsea Child* (London: BBC, 1979).

Gaskell, Catherine Milnes, 'Old Wenlock and its Folklore', *The Nineteenth Century* 35 (1894) 259–67.

Gaskill, Malcolm, 'Britain's Last Witch', *History Today* 51:5 (May 2001a) 6–7.

———, *Hellish Nell: Last of Britain's Witches* (London: Fourth Dimension, 2001b).

Gathorne-Hardy, Robert, *The Berkshire Book* (Reading: Berkshire Fed. Of Women's Institutes, 1951) [*Berkshire Book* for first edition].

Gaule, John, *Mag-astro-mances, The* (London: 1652).

Gélis, Jacques, *History of Childbirth* (Oxford: Polity Press, 1991).

Gibson, A. Craig, 'Ancient Customs and Superstitions in Cumberland', *Transactions of the Historical Society of Lancashire and Cheshire* 10 (1858) 96–110.

Gifford, Edward S., *The Evil Eye: Studies in the Folklore of Vision* (New York: London, 1958).

Gill, Alec, *Superstition: Folk Magic in Hull's Fishing Community* (Beverley: Hutton Press, 1993).

Gill, W. Walter, *Manx Dialect: Words and Phrases* (London: Arrowsmith, 1934).

———, *A Third Manx Scrapbook* (London: Arrowsmith, 1963).

Gittings, Clare, *Death, Burial and the Individual in Early Modern England* (London: Croom Helm, 1984).

Glos. N&Q, *Gloucestershire Notes and Queries* (1881–1902).

Glyde, John, *Folklore and Customs of Suffolk* (Wakefield:

EP, 1976) [reprint of part of *The New Suffolk Garland*, 1866].

Goddard, E. H., 'Witchcraft in Wiltshire', *Wiltshire Archaeological and Natural History Magazine* 29 (1896–7) 159–65.

Gomme, G. L. (ed.), *Manners and Customs* (London: Eliot Stock, 1883).

———, *The Gentleman's Magazine Library: Popular Superstitions* (London: Elliot Stock, 1884).

———, *English Traditions and Foreign Customs* (London: Elliot Stock, 1885).

Gomme Collection, Miscellaneous papers of Sir George Laurence Gomme and Lady Alice Gomme: Folklore Society Archives, London.

Good, Jabez, *A Glossary of Words, Phrases, etc. Current in East Lincolnshire* (No publisher, 1900).

Goodland, Norman, *Old Stan's Diary: Autumn and Winter on the Farm* (London: Macdonald, 1963).

Gospelles of Dystaves, English translation of *Les Evangiles des Quenouilles*, composed by Fouquart de Cambrai, Antoine du Val, and Jean d'Arras (c.1507–15, probably in Belgium). Reprinted in Diane Bornstein, *Distaves and Dames: Renaissance Treatises for and about Women* (New York, Scholars' Facsimiles & Reprints, 1978).

Gough, Richard, *The History of Myddle* (1601–1607; Firle: Caliban, 1979).

Gould, George M. and Walter L. Pyle, *Anomalies and Curiosities of Medicine* (London: Saunders, 1900).

Graham, Patrick, *Sketches Descriptive of Picturesque Scenery on the Southern Confines of Perthshire* (Edinburgh: 1806).

Grahame, Kenneth, *The Golden Age* (London: John Lane, 1898).

Grant, Mrs Ann, *Essays on the Superstitions of the Highlanders of Scotland* (London: Longman Hurst, 1811).

Granville, Wilfred, *A Dictionary of Theatrical Terms* (London: André Deutsch, 1952).

Grattan, J. H. G., and C. Singer, *Anglo-Saxon Magic and Medicine* (London: Oxford University Press, 1952).

Greenwood, Harry, *Memories* (Heptonstall: Arvon Press, 1977).

Gregor, Walter, 'The Healing Art in the North of Scotland', *Journal of the Anthropological Institute* 3 (1874) 266–72.

———, *Notes on the Folk-Lore of the North-East of Scotland* (London: Folk-Lore Society, 1881).

Gribben, Arthur, *Holy Wells and Sacred Water Sources in Britain and Ireland: An Annotated Bibliography* (New York: Garland, 1992).

Grinsell, Leslie V., *Folklore of Prehistoric Sites in Britain* (Newton Abbot: David & Charles, 1976).

Groome, Francis Hindes, *In Gipsy Tents* (Edinburgh: Nimmo, 1880).

Grose, Francis, *A Provincial Glossary: With a Collection of Local Proverbs and Popular Superstitions* (London: S. Hooper, 1787; 2nd ed, 1790) [NB: section on superstitions paginated separately from the rest of the book].

Gunn, John, *The Orkney Book* (London: Nelson, 1909).

Gurdon, E. C., *County Folk-Lore of Suffolk* (London: Folklore Society, 1893; reprint Felinfach: Llanerch, 1997).

Guskin, Phyllis J., 'The Context of Witchcraft: the Case of Jane Wenham', *Eighteenth-Century Studies* 15 (1981–2) 48–71.

Gutch, Mrs, *County Folk-Lore: North Riding of Yorkshire and the Ainsty* (London: Nutt, 1901).

Gutch, Mrs and Mabel Peacock, *County Folk-Lore Vol. 5: Lincolnshire* (London: David Nutt, 1908).

Guthrie, E. J., *Old Scottish Customs* (London: Hamilton, Adams, 1885).

Gwyndaf, Robin, 'The Sorrow of All People: Death, Grief and Comfort in a Welsh Rural Community', *Folk Life* 36 (1997–8) 84–105.

Hackwood, Frederick William, *Staffordshire Customs, Superstitions and Folklore* (Lichfield: Mercury Press, 1924).

Haggard, Lilias Rider (ed.), *I Walked by Night* (London: Nicholson & Watson, 1935).

Haining, Peter, *Superstitions* (London: Sidgwick & Jackson, 1979).

Haliburton, Hugh, *Furth in the Field* (London: Fisher Unwin, 1894).

Halliwell, James Orchard, *The Nursery Rhymes of England* (London: Percy Society, 1842; reprint, London: Bodley Head, 1970).

———, *The Popular Rhymes and Nursery Tales of England* (London: 1849; reprint, London: Bodley Head, 1970).

Hamer, Edward, 'Parochial Account of Llandidloes: Ch. 10, Folk-Lore', *Montgomeryshire Collections* 10 (1877) 231–76.

Hammond, Eleanor Prescott, 'The Chance of the Dice', *Englische Studien* 59 (1925) 1–16.

Hampshire Fed. of Women's Institutes, *Hampshire Within Living Memory* (Newbury: Countryside Books, 1994).

Hampson, R. T., *Medii Aevi Kalendarium* (London: Causton, 1841).

Hardwick, Charles, *Traditions, Superstitions and Folk-Lore (Chiefly Lancashire and the North of England)* (London: Simpkin Marshall, 1872; reprint, Didsbury: Morten, 1973).

Hardy, James, 'Popular History of the Cuckoo', *Folk-Lore Record* 2 (1879) 47–91; *see also* Denham Tracts.

Hardy, Thomas, *Moments of Vision and Miscellaneous Voices* (London: Macmillan, 1917).

———, *Human Shows, Far Phantasies, Songs and Trifles* (London: Macmillan, 1925).

———, *Winter Words in Various Moods and Metres* (London: Macmillan, 1928).

Hare, Augustus J. C., *The Years with Mother* (London: Allen & Unwin, 1952).

Harland, John, and Wilkinson, T. T., *Lancashire Legends, Traditions, Pageants and Sports* (London: Routledge, 1873).

———, *Lancashire Folk-Lore* (Manchester: Heywood, 1882).

Harris, Mary Corbett, 'Legends and Folklore of Llan-fachreth Parish', *Journal of the Merioneth Historical and Record Society* 5 (1965–8) 9–20.

Harris, Mollie, *A Kind of Magic: An Oxfordshire Childhood in the 1920s* (London: Chatto & Windus, 1969).

Harrison, William, *The Description of England* (1587; reprint, New York: Dover, 1994).

Harrison, William, *Mona Miscellany* (Douglas: Manx Society Publications, Vol. 16, 1869).

———, *Mona Miscellany* (2nd series) (Douglas: Manx Society Publications, Vol. 21, 1873).

Hart, Kingsley, *The Letters of Dorothy Osborne to Sir William Temple 1652–54* (London: Folio Society, 1968).

Hartland, Edwin Sidney, *County Folklore: Gloucestershire* (London: Folklore Society, 1895; reprint, Felinfach: Llanerch, 1997).

Hastie, G., 'First-Footing in Scotland', *Folk-Lore* 4 (1893) 309–14.

Hatfield, Gabrielle, *Country Remedies* (Woodbridge: Boydell Press, 1994).

———, *Warts: Summary of Wart-Cure Survey for the Folklore Society* (London: Folklore Society, 1998).

Havergal, Francis T., *Herefordshire Words and Phrases* (Walsall: W. Henry Robinson, 1887).

Haworth, D. and W. M. Comber, *Cheshire Village Memories* (Malpas: Cheshire Fed. of Women's Institutes, 1952).

Haymon, Sylvia, *The Quivering Tree: An East Anglian Childhood* (London: Constable, 1990).

Hazlitt, W. C., *A Dictionary of Faiths and Folk-Lore* (London: Reeves & Turner, 1905).

———, *English Proverbs and Proverbial Phrases* (London: Reeves & Turner, 1907).

Heanley, R. M., 'The Vikings: Traces of their Folklore in Marshland', *Viking Club Saga Book* 3:1 (1902).

Henderson, Andrew, *Scottish Proverbs* (Edinburgh: Oliver & Boyd, 1832).

Henderson, George, *The Popular Rhymes, Sayings and Proverbs of the County of Berwick* (Newcastle: Wilson, 1856).

Henderson, William, *Notes on the Folk Lore of the Northern Counties of England and the Border* (London: Longmans Green, 1866; reprint, Wakefield: EP, 1973; 2nd edn, London: Folklore Society, 1879).

Henrey, Mrs Robert, *Bloomsbury Fair* (London: Dent, 1955).

Heslop, Richard Oliver, *Northumberland Words: A Glossary of the Words Used in the County of Northumberland* (London: English Dialect Society, 1892–4).

Hester, Marianne, *Lewd Women and Wicked Witches: A Study of the Dynamics of Male Domination* (London: Routledge, 1992).

Hewett, Sarah, *The Peasant Speech of Devon* (2nd edn, London: Elliot Stock, 1892).

———, *Nummits and Crummits: Devonshire Customs, Characteristics and Folk-Lore* (London: Burleigh, 1900).

Hewins, Angela, *Mary, After the Queen: Memories of a Working Girl* (Oxford: Oxford University Press, 1985).

Hibbert, Samuel, *A Description of the Shetland Islands* (Edinburgh: Constable, 1822; reprint, Lerwick: Manson: 1891).

Hickey, Eileen M., 'Medical Superstitions in Ireland', *Ulster Medical Journal* 7 (1938) 268–70.

Higgins, Robert McR., 'Popular Beliefs about Witches: The Evidence from East London, 1645–1660', *East London Record* 4 (1981) 36–41.

Higgens, T. W. E., 'First Foot in the British Isles', *Folk-Lore* 3 (1892) 253–64.

Hillaby, John, *Journey Through Britain* (London: Paladin, 1970).

Hindley, Charles, *Curiosities of Street Literature* (London: Reeves & Turner, 1871).

History of Mother Bunch of the Weste, The [Chapbook, c.1780]; reprint, ed. George Laurence Gomme (London, Villon Society, 1885) [page numbers refer to 1885 reprint].

Hobsbawm, Eric and Terence Ranger, *The Invention of Tradition* (Cambridge: Cambridge University Press, 1983).

Hodgson, Vere, *Few Eggs and No Oranges* (London: Dobson, 1976).

Hoggart, Richard, *The Uses of Literacy* (London: Chatto & Windus, 1957).

Hole, Christina, *Traditions and Customs of Cheshire* (London: Williams and Norgate, 1937).

———, *English Sports and Pastimes* (London: Batsford, 1949).

———, 'Some Instances of Image-Magic in Great Britain', in *The Witch Figure*, ed. V. Newall (London: Routledge & Kegan Paul, 1973).

———, *English Traditional Customs* (London: Batsford, 1975).

———, *British Folk Customs* (London: Hutchinson, 1976a).

———, *Dictionary of British Folk Customs* (London: Hutchinson, 1976b).

Holman-Hunt, Diana, *My Grandmothers and I* (London: Hamish Hamilton, 1960).

Holt, Alan, *Folklore of Somerset* (Stroud: Alan Sutton, 1992).

Home, Gordon, *The Evolution of an English Town* (London: Dent, 1905) [includes section from an MS compiled by George Calvert, 1823].

Hone, Nathaniel, 'The Hallowing of Cramp Rings', *Month* 79 (1893) 99–103.

Hone, William, *The Every-Day Book* (2 vols, London: Thomas Tegg, 1827).

———, *The Table Book* (London: Thomas Tegg, 1827).

———, *The Year-Book* (London: Thomas Tegg, 1832).

Hope, R. C., *The Legendary Lore of the Holy Wells of England* (London: Elliot Stock, 1893; reprint, Detroit: Singing Tree Press, 1968).

Hope-Nicholson, Jaqueline, *Life Among the Troubridges* [Journals of Laura Troubridge 1873–1884] (London: John Murray, 1966).

Howells, W., *Cambrian Superstitions* (London: Longman, 1831).

Howitt, William, *Rural Life in England* (2 vols, London: Longmans Green, 1838).

Howse, W. H., *Radnorshire* (Hereford: Thurston, 1949).

Hudson, John, *A Surrey Christmas* (Stroud: Sutton, 1996).

Hufford, David J., *The Terror That Comes in the Night: An Experience-Centred Study of Supernatural Assault Traditions* (Philadelphia: University of Pennsylvania Press, 1982).

Huggett, Richard, *The Course of Macbeth and Other Theatrical Superstitions* (London: Picton, 1981).

Hughes, M. V., *A London Child of the Seventies* (Oxford: Oxford University Press, 1934).

Hughes Marian, *No Cake, No Jam* (London: Heinemann, 1994).

Hunt, Robert, *Popular Romances of the West of England* (2nd series; London: Hotten, 1865).

Hunt, Tony, *Popular Medicine in Thirteenth-Century England* (London: Brewer, 1990).

Hunter, Michael, 'The Discovery of Second Sight in Late-17th Century Scotland', *History Today* (June 2001) 48–53.

Hutchinson, William, *A View of Northumberland* (Newcastle: Charnley, 1778).

Hutton, Ronald, *The Pagan Religions of the Ancient British Isles: Their Nature and Legacy* (Oxford: Blackwell, 1991).

———, *Stations of the Sun: A History of the Ritual Year in Britain* (Oxford: Oxford University Press, 1996).

———, *The Triumph of the Moon: A History of Modern Pagan Witchcraft* (Oxford: Oxford University Press, 1999).

Igglesden, Charles, *Those Superstitions* (London: Jarrolds, c.1932).

Illustrated London News, 'Thirteen at Table', *Illustrated London News* (27 Dec. 1851) 779.

Irving, Washington, *The Sketch-Book* (1820; rev. edn, New York: Putnam, 1848).

Isle of Wight Federation of Women's Institutes, *Isle of Wight, Within Living Memory* (Newbury: Countryside Bks., 1994).

James, Louis, *Print and the People 1818–1851* (London: Allen Lane, 1976).

James, Simon, *The Atlantic Celts: Ancient People or Modern Invention* (Madison: University of Wisconsin Press, 1999).

Jamieson, John, *An Etymological Dictionary of the Scottish Language* (2 vols, Edinburgh: 1808; *supplement* (2 vols, 1825).

Jarman, A. O. H. and Eldra Jarman, *The Welsh Gypsies: Children of Abram Wood* (Cardiff: University of Wales Press, 1991).

Jeacock, R., *Plants and Trees in Legend, Fact and Fiction* (Chester: Mothers' Union, 1982).

Jeaffreson, John Cordy, *Brides and Bridals* (London: Hurst & Blackett, 1872).

Jefferies, Richard, *The Gamekeeper at Home* (London: Smith Elder: 1878).

——, *Wild Life in a Southern County* (London: Smith Elder, 1879).

——, *Field and Hedgerow* (London: Longmans Green, 1889).

Jeffrey, Percy Shaw, *Whitby Lore and Legend* (2nd edn, Whitby: Horne, 1923).

Jenkin, A. K. Hamilton, *Cornish Homes and Customs* (London: Dent, 1934).

Jenkins, Richard P., 'Witches and Fairies: Supernatural Aggression and Deviance Among the Irish Peasantry', *Ulster Folklife* 23 (1977) 33–56.

Jennings, Louis John, *Rambles Among the Hills* (London: Murray, 1880).

Jesse, Edward, *Gleanings in Natural History* (2nd series, London: John Murray, 1834).

Jones, T. Gwynn, *Welsh Folklore and Folk-Custom* (London: Methuen, 1930).

Jones, William, *Credulities Past and Present* (London: Chatto & Windus, 1880).

——, *Crowns and Coronations* (London: Chatto & Windus, 1898).

Jones, William Glynne, *Summer Long Ago* (London: Nevill, 1954).

Jones-Baker, Doris, *The Folklore of Hertfordshire* (London: Batsford, 1977).

Josselin, Ralph, *The Diary of Ralph Josselin 1616–1683* (London: Camden Society 3S:15, 1908).

Joyce, Nan, *Traveller* (Dublin: Gill & Macmillan, 1985; reprinted as *My Life on the Road*, Dublin: Farmar, 2000).

Jupp, Peter C., and Clare Gittings, *Death in England: An Illustrated History* (Manchester: Manchester University Press, 1999).

Karkeek, Paul Q., 'A Budget of Witch Stories', *Transactions of the Devonshire Association* 14 (1882) 387–94.

Kearton, Richard, *At Home with Wild Nature* (London: Cassell, 1922).

Keightley, Thomas, *The Fairy Mythology* (London: Bohn, 1850).

Kelly, James, *A Complete Collection of Scottish Proverbs* (London: Innys & Osborn, 1721).

Kelly, Walter, *Curiosities of Indo-European Tradition and Folk-Lore* (London: Chapman & Hall, 1863).

Kemble, John Mitchell, *The Saxons in England* (London: Longman, 1849).

Kendall, Samuel George, *Farming Memoirs of a West Country Yeoman* (London: Faber, 1944).

Kennedy, Patrick, *Banks of the Boro* (London: Simpkin Marshall, 1867).

Kent, Joan, *Binder Twine and Rabbit Stew* (London: Bailey Bros. & Swinfen, 1976).

——, *Wood Smoke and Pigeon Pie* (London: Bailey Bros. & Swinfen, 1977).

Ketteridge, Christopher and Spike Mays, *Five Miles from Bunkum: A Village and its Crafts* (London: Eyre Methuen, 1972).

Kettlewell, F. B., *Trinkum-Trinkums of Fifty Years* (Taunton: Barnicott & Pearce, 1927).

Killip, Margaret, *The Folklore of the Isle of Man* (London: Batsford, 1975).

Kilvert, Francis, *Kilvert's Diary* (ed. William Plomer, London: Jonathan Cape, 1938–9).

Kirk, Robert, *The Secret Common-Wealth* (1691; reprint, Cambridge: Brewer, 1976).

Kirkup, James Falconer, *The Only Child* (London: Collins, 1957).

Kitchen, Fred, *Brother to the Ox: The Autobiography of a Farmer's Boy* (London: Dent, 1940).

Kittredge, George Lyman, *Witchcraft in Old and New England* (Cambridge, Mass.: Harvard University Press, 1929).

Knapp, J. L., *The Journal of a Naturalist* (3rd edn, London: John Murray, 1830).

Knight, Sid, *Cotswold Lad* (London: Phoenix House, 1960).

Knott, Olive, 'Dorset Superstitions', *Dorset Year Book* (1954–5) 175–6.

——, 'Dorset Superstitions', *Dorset Year Book* (1961–2) 73–7.

Knowlson, T. Sharper, *The Origins of Popular Superstitions and Customs* (London: Werner Laurie, 1910).

Kramer, Heinrich, and James Sprenger, *Malleus Maleficarum* (1486; reprint, London: Brachen, 1996, trans. Montague Summers).

Lageniensis [John O'Hanlon], *Irish Folklore* (Dublin: J. Duffy, 1870).

Laing, Jeanie M., *Notes on Superstition and Folk Lore* (Brechin: Brechin Advertiser, 1885).

Lakeham, Joy, *Them Days: From the Memories of Joan Bellan* (Padstow: Tabb House, 1982).

Lambkin, Romie, *My Time in the War: An Irishwoman's Diary* (Dublin: Wolfhound, 1992).

L'Amy, John H., *Jersey Folk Lore* (Jersey: J. T. Bigwood, 1927).

Lancashire Lore (Preston: Lancashire Fed. of Women's Institutes, 1971).

Langford, J. A., 'Warwickshire Folk-Lore and Superstitions', *Transactions of the Birmingham and Midlands Institute* 6 (1875) 9–24.

Latham, Charlotte, 'Some West Sussex Superstitions Lingering in 1868,' *Folk-Lore Record* 1 (1878), 1–67.

Laurenson, Arthur, 'On Certain Beliefs and Phrases of Shetland Fishermen', *Proceedings of the Society of Antiquaries of Scotland* 14 (1879/80) 711–16.

Lea, Hermann, 'Wessex Witches, Witchery, and Witchcraft', *Nineteenth Century* 19/20 (1903) 1010–24.

Lean, Vincent Stuckey, *Lean's Collectanea* (5 vols, Bristol: Arrowsmith, 1902–4).

Leather, Ella Mary, *The Folk-Lore of Herefordshire* (London: Sidgwick & Jackson, 1912).

Leeds Mercury (4 Oct. 1879), 'Notes & Queries No. XL: Yorkshire Folk Lore' [contributed by Samuel Smith].

Lee-Warner, Henry James, 'The Walsingham Wishing Wells', *Norfolk Archaeology* 8 (1879) 51–6.

Lees, Edwin, *Pictures of Nature in the Silurian Region around the Malvern Hills and Vale of Severn* (Malvern, 1856).

Leighton, Henry R., *Memorials of Old Durham* (London: George Allen, 1910).

Leland, Charles G., *The Gypsies* (Boston: Houghton Mifflin, 1882).

Lightfoot, John, *Flora Scotia* (London: B. White, 1777).

Litten, Julian, *The English Way of Death* (London: Robert Hale, 1991).

Liverani, Mary Rose, *The Winter Sparrows: A Glasgow Childhood* (Melbourne: Nelson, 1975).

Lloyd, Virginia, *The Ritual Protection of Post-Medieval Houses in East Anglia* (London: Folklore Society, 1999).

Lockley, R. M., *Pembrokeshire* (London: Hale, 1957).

Logan, Patrick, 'Folk Medicine of the Cavan-Leitrim Area, part 1', *Ulster Folklife* 9 (1963) 89–92.

——, 'Folk Medicine of the Cavan-Leitrim Area, part 2', *Ulster Folklife* 11 (1965) 51–53.

——, *Irish Country Cures* (Belfast: Appletree, 1981) [also published as *Irish Folk Medicine*].

Lovett, Edward, *Magic in Modern London* (Croydon: Croydon Advertiser, 1925).

——, *Folk-Lore and Legend of the Surrey Hills and the Sussex Downs and Forest* (Caterham: The Author, 1928).

Low, George, *A Tour through the Islands of Orkney and Shetland* (1774; Kirkwall: 1879) [selections published in Black (1903)].

Low, George, *Fauna Orcadensis* (Edinburgh: A. Constable, 1813).

Lowsley, Major B, *A Glossary of Berkshire Words and Phrases* (London: Trubner, 1888).

Lucas, E. V., *Highways and Byways in Sussex* (London: Macmillan, 1904).

Lucy, Mary Elizabeth, *Mistress of Charlecote: The Memoirs of Mary Elizabeth Lucy* (London: Gollancz, 1983).

Lupton, Thomas, *A Thousand Notable Things* (1586; enlarged edn, 1660; numerous other editions).

Luxton, Brian C., 'William Jenkin, the Wizard of Cadoxton-juxta-Barry', *Morgannwg* 24 (1980) 31–60.

Lykiardopoulos, Amica, 'The Evil Eye: Towards an Exhaustive Study', *Folklore* 92 (1981) 221–30.

Lynd, Robert, *Solomon in All His Glory* (London: Grant Richards, 1922).

Macbain, Alexander, 'Highland Superstition', *Transactions of the Gaelic Society of Inverness* 14 (1887/88) 232–72.

MacColl, Ewan, and Peggy Seeger, *Till Doomsday in the Afternoon: The Folklore of a Family of Scots Travellers* (Manchester: Manchester University Press, 1986).

MacCulloch MS, Materials gathered on Guernsey Folklore (1864; ed. Edith Carey and published as *Guernsey Folk Lore*, 1903) [NB: the page numbers given in references in this dictionary are to the published Carey edition].

MacDonald, Colin, *Echoes of the Glen* (Edinburgh: Moray Press, 1936).

——, *Highland Journey* (Edinburgh: Moray Press, 1943).

MacDonald, Michael, and Terence R. Murphy, *Sleepless Souls: Suicide in Early Modern England* (Oxford: Oxford University Press, 1990).

McDowell, Florence Mary, *Roses and Rainbows* (Belfast: Blackstaff, 1972).

Macfarlane, Alan, *Witchcraft in Tudor and Stuart England* (London: Routledge & Kegan Paul, 1970; reprint, 1999).

Macgregor, Alexander, *The Prophesies of the Brahan Seer* (Inverness: Mackenzie, 1878).

Mackay, Charles, *Extraordinary Popular Delusions and the Madness of Crowds* (London: Bentley, 1841; 2nd edn, National Illustrated Library, 1852).

Mackenzie, William, *Gaelic Incantations, Charms and Blessings of the Hebrides* (Inverness: Northern Counties Newspaper, 1895).

Maclagan, Robert Craig, *The Games and Diversions of Argyllshire* (London: Nutt, 1901).

Maclean, Calum, 'Traditional Beliefs in Scotland', *Scottish Studies* 3:2 (1959) 189–200.

MacLeay, John, 'Glasgow's Glamourie', *Scots Magazine* 134 (Oct. 1990) 43–51.

McPhee, John, *The Crofter and the Laird* (New York: Farrar, Straus & Giroux, 1970).

MacTaggart, John, *The Scottish Gallovidian Encyclopedia* (London: The Author, 1824).

Maloney, Beatrice, 'Traditional Herbal Cures in County Cavan; part 1', *Ulster Folklife* 18 (1972) 66–79.

Manning, George T., *Rural Rhymes* (London: 1837).

Mansell-Pleydell, J. C., 'On Sorcery and Witchcraft', *Proceedings of the Dorset Natural History and Antiquarian Field Club* 5 (1883) 1–15.

Maple, Eric, 'Cunning Murrell', *Folklore* 71 (1960), 37–43.

——, 'The Witches of Canewdon', *Folklore* 71 (1960), 241–50.

Marples, Morris, *White Horses and Other Hill Figures* (London: Country Life, 1949).

Marryat, Florence, *Life and Letters of Captain Marryat* (London: Bentley, 1872).

Marshall, Sibyl, *Fenland Chronicle* (Cambridge: Cambridge University Press, 1967).

Marsom, F. W., 'County Cures', *Bedfordshire Magazine* 2 (1950) 182–4.

Martin, Angus, *Kintyre Country Life* (Edinburgh: John Donald, 1987).

Martin, Martin, *A Description of the Western Islands of Scotland* (1703; 2nd edn, London: Bell etc., 1716).

Mason, William Shaw, *A Statistical Account or Parochial Survey of Ireland* (Dublin: 1814–19).

Mason, Donald, 'Popular Domestic Medicine in the Highlands Fifty Years Ago', *Transactions of the Gaelic Society of Inverness* 14 (1887/88) 298–313.

Mayes, Nellie, *Nellie Mayes' Nature Notebook* (London: Mirror Books, 1978).

Mays, Spike, *Reuben's Corner* (London: Eyre & Spottiswoode, 1969).

Melton, John, *Astrologaster, or the Figurecaster* (1620; reprint, Los Angeles: Augustin Reprint Society, 1975).

Menefee, Samuel Pyeatt, 'Dead Reckoning the Church Porch Watch in British Society', in Hilda Ellis Davidson, *The Seer in Celtic and Other Traditions* (Edinburgh: John Donald, 1989) 80–99.

Merrifield, Ralph, 'Witch Bottles and Magical Jugs', *Folk-Lore* 66 (1955) 195–207.

————, *The Archaeology of Ritual and Magic* (London: Batsford, 1987).

Miall, Agnes M., *Complete Fortune Telling* (London: Pearson, 1951).

Mitchell, John and Robert J. M. Rickard, *Phenomena: A Book of Wonders* (London: Thames & Hudson, 1977).

————, *Living Wonders: Mysteries and Curiosities of the Animal World* (London: Thames & Hudson, 1982).

Middelboe, Penelope, *Edith Olivier from her Journals 1924–48* (London: Weidenfeld & Nicolson, 1989).

Midland Garner (Banbury: Banbury Guardian, 1884).

Miller, Hugh, *Scenes and Legends of the North of Scotland* (Edinburgh: Black, 1835; reprint, Edinburgh: B&W, 1994).

Milne, John, *Myths and Superstitions of the Buchan District*, ed. Rosalind A. Jack (Maud: R. Jack, 1987) [reprinting articles from 1891 and 1903].

Milton, A. R., 'The Wicked Old Woman', *Sussex County Magazine* 17 (1943) 47–9.

Mirror, The, 'Superstitions, Fables &c. Relative to Animals', *The Mirror* (10 Mar. 1832) 170–1; (17 Mar. 1832) 179–80; (31 Mar. 1832) 211–13.

Mitford, Mary Russell, *Our Village: Sketches of Rural character and Scenery* (5 vols, London: G. B. Whittaker, 1824–32).

Monsarrat, Ann, *And the Bride Wore . . . The Story of the White Wedding* (London: Gentry, 1973).

Monthly Packet, 'West Riding Folk Lore', *Monthly Packet* 25 (1863) 549–51.

Monthly Packet, 'Quaint Customs in Quiet Nooks [South Wales]', *Monthly Packet* 26 (1863) 676–83.

Monthly Packet, 'Devonshire Folk Lore', *Monthly Packet* 28 (1864) 443–7.

Moor, Edward, *Suffolk Words and Phrases* (Woodbridge: Loder, 1823).

Moore, A. W., *The Folk-Lore of the Isle of Man* (London: Nutt, 1891).

More, Hannah, *Tawney Rachel, or The Fortune-Teller* (London: Cheap Repository Tracts, c.1810).

Morgan, Prys, 'A Welsh Snakestone, its Tradition and Folklore', *Folk-Lore* 94 (1983) 184–91.

Morris, Desmond, *Gestures* (London: Cape, 1979).

Morris, M. C. F., *Yorkshire Folk-Talk* (2nd edn, London: A. Brown, 1911).

Morsley, Clifford, *News from the English Countryside 1750–1850* (London: Harrap, 1979).

Morton, H. V., *In Search of Scotland* (London: Methuen, 1929).

Moss, Fletcher, *Folklore: Old Customs and Tales of my Neighbours* (Didsbury: The Author, 1898).

Mother Bunch's Closet Newly Broke Open (chapbook, 1685; reprint, ed. George Laurence Gomme, London: Villon Society, 1885) [page numbers refer to 1885 reprint].

Murphy, Michael J., 'Folktales and Traditions from County Cavan and South Armagh', *Ulster Folklife* 19 (1973) 30–37.

Murray, Walter J. C., *Copsford* (London: Allen & Unwin, 1948).

Naish, Thomas, *The Diary of Thomas Naish*, edited by Doreen Slater (Devizes: Wiltshire Archaeological & Natural History Society, 1965).

Napier, James, 'On Some Popular Superstitions in Partick Forty Years Ago', *Transactions of the Glasgow Archaeological Society* 1 (1859–1882) 391–8 [NB: paper delivered to the Society, 2 May 1864].

————, *Folk Lore in the West of Scotland* (Paisley: Gardner, 1879; reprint, East Ardsley: EP, 1976).

Nares, Robert, *A Glossary, or Collection of Words, Phrases, Names and Allusions to Customs, Proverbs, etc.* (London: Triphook, 1822; new edn ed. James O. Halliwell and Thomas Wright, London: Reeves & Turner, 1888).

Narvaez, Peter (ed.), *The Good People: New Fairylore Essays* (New York; Garland, 1991).

Naughton, Bill, *Saintly Billy: A Catholic Boyhood* (Oxford: Oxford University Press, 1988).

Neasham, George, *North-Country Sketches* (Durham: The Author, 1893).

Neville, Hastings M., *A Corner in the North: Yesterday and Today with Border Folk* (Newcastle: Andrew Reid, 1909).

New Statistical Account of Scotland (Edinburgh: Blackwood, 1845).

Newall, Venetia, *Discovering the Folklore of Birds and Beasts* (Tring: Shire, 1971a).

————, *An Egg at Easter* (London: Routledge & Kegan Paul, 1971b).

Newman, L. F., 'Some Notes on the Nutmeg Graters Used in Folk-Medicine' *Folk-Lore* 54 (1943) 334–7.

Nicholson, John, *Folk Lore of East Yorkshire* (London: Simpkin Marshall, 1890; reprint, Felinfach: Llanerch, 1998).

Nicholson, Phyllis, *Country Bouquet* (London: John Murray, 1947).

Nicol, James, *Poems, Chiefly in the Scottish Dialect* (Edinburgh: 1805).

Noake, J., 'Superstitions of Worcestershire', *Gentleman's Magazine* (1855) 384–6, (1856) 38–40; reprinted in Gomme (1884) 133–9.

Northall, G. F., *English Folk Rhymes* (London: Kegan Paul, 1892).

O'Keeffe, C. M., 'The Formulas of Marcellus', *Ulster Journal of Archaeology* 4 (1856) 261–8.

Old Women's Sayings, broadside ballad [c.1835] printed by Pitts, Catnach, and others; text reprinted in John Ashton, *Modern Street Ballads* (London: Chatto & Windus, 1888).

Oldridge, Darren, *The Devil in Early Modern England* (Stroud: Sutton, 2000).

Oliver, George, 'Popular Superstitions of Lincolnshire', *Gentleman's Magazine* (1833) 590–3; reprinted in Gomme (1884) 116–20.

Oliver, Stephen, *Rambles in Northumberland and on the Scottish Border* (London: Chapman & Hall, 1835).

Ó Muirithe, Diarmaid, and Deirdre Nuttall, *Folklore of County Wexford* (Dublin: Four Courts, 1999).

O'Neill, Gilda, *My East End: Memories of Life in Cockney London* (London: Viking, 1999).

Opie, Iona and Peter, *The Lore and Language of Schoolchildren* (Oxford: Oxford University Press, 1959).

Opie, Iona and Peter, *Oxford Dictionary of Nursery Rhymes* (2nd edn, Oxford: Oxford University Press, 1997).

Opie, Iona, and Moira Tatem, *A Dictionary of Superstitions* (Oxford: Oxford University Press, 1989).

Opie, Peter, 'England the Great Undiscovered', *Folk-Lore* 65 (1954) 149–64.

Opie Collection, Papers of Peter Opie and Iona Opie: Folklore Society Archives, London.

Osborne, Dorothy, *Letters of; see* Hart (1968).

Oxon. Folklore Soc., Oxfordshire and District Folklore Society *Annual Record*.

Owen Elias, 'Folk-Lore, Superstitions, or What-Not, in

Montgomeryshire', *Montgomeryshire Collections* 15 (1882) 121–54; 16 (1883) 131–60; 17 (1884) 165–74; 18 (1885) 135–48.

Owen, Trefor M., *Welsh Folk Customs* (1959; new edn, Dyfed: Gomer, 1987).

Palmer, Kingsley, *Oral Folk-Tales of Wessex* (Newton Abbot: David and Charles, 1973).

———, *The Folklore of Somerset* (London: Batsford, 1976a).

———, *The Folklore of Warwickshire* (London: Batsford, 1976b).

Palmer, Roy, *The Folklore of Leicestershire and Rutland* (Wymondham: Sycamore Press, 1985).

———, *Britain's Living Folklore* (Newton Abbott: David & Charles, 1991).

———, *The Folklore of Gloucestershire* (Tiverton: Westcountry Books, 1994).

Parish, W. D., *A Dictionary of the Sussex Dialect* (Lewes: Farncombe, 1875).

Parsons, Coleman O., *Witchcraft and Demonology in Scott's Fiction* (Edinburgh: Oliver & Boyd, 1964).

Partridge, Eric, *A Dictionary of Slang and Unconventional English* (5th edn, London: Routledge, 1961).

Patterson, Sheila, *Dark Strangers* (London: Tavistock, 1963).

Patterson, William Hugh, *A Glossary of Words in use in the Counties of Antrim and Down* (London: Trubner, 1880).

Paynter, William H., 'Tales of Cornish Witches', *Old Cornwall* 9 (1929) 28–33.

Peacock, Basil, *A Newcastle Boyhood 1898–1914* (Sutton: London Borough of Sutton, 1986).

Peacock, Edward, *A Glossary of Words used in the Wapentakes of Manley and Corringham, Lincolnshire* (London: Trubner, 1877).

Peacock, Edward; *see also* Elder, Eileen.

Pearson, Harry, *North Country Fair* (London: Little Brown, 1966).

Penfold Henry, 'Superstitions Connected with Illness, Burial, and Death in East Cumberland', *Transactions of the Cumberland and Westmorland Antiquarian and Archaeological Society* NS:7 (1907) 54–63.

Pennant, William, *A Tour in Scotland 1769* (Chester: John Monk, 1771; reprint, Edinburgh: Birlinn, 2000) [page numbers refer to reprint edn].

———, *A Tour in Scotland and Voyage to the Hebrides 1772* (Chester: John Monk, 1774–6; reprint, Edinburgh: Birlinn, 1998) [page numbers refer to reprint edn].

Penny, James Alpass, *Folklore Around Horncastle* (Horncastle: Morton, 1915).

Perkins, Maureen, *Visions of the Future: Almanacs, Time, and Cultural Change* (Oxford: Clarendon Press, 1996).

Pettigrew, T. J., 'Observations upon the Extracts from an Ancient English Medical MS in the Royal Library of Stockholm', *Archaeologia* 30 (1844) 419–29.

Phillips, D. Rhys, *The History of the Vale of Neath* (Swansea: The Author, 1925).

Physicians of Myddvai, The (trans. John Pughe: London: Longman, 1861) [NB: the reprint by Llanerch Press, 1993, has title as *The Physicians of Myddfai*].

Picard, Liza, *Restoration London* (London: Weidenfeld & Nicholson, 1997).

Pitcairn, Robert, *Criminal Trials of Scotland* (Edinburgh: Tait, 1833).

Plot, Robert, *The Natural History of Staffordshire* (Oxford: 1686).

Plowman, Thomas F., *Fifty Years of a Showman's Life* (London: John Lane, 1919).

Polson, Alexander, *Our Highland Folklore Heritage* (Dingwall: Geo. Souter, 1926).

———, *Scottish Witchcraft Lore* (Inverness: Alexander, 1932).

Polwhele, R., *Traditions and Recollections; Domestic, Clerical and Literary* (London: John Nichols, 1826).

Poole, Charles Henry, *The Customs, Superstitions and Legends of the County of Stafford* (London: Rowney, 1875).

———, *The Customs. Superstitions, and Legends of the County of Somerset* (London: Sampson Low, 1877).

Porter, Enid, 'Some Folk Beliefs of the Fens', *Folklore* 69 (1958), 112–22.

———, *Cambridgeshire Customs and Folklore* (London: Routledge & Kegan Paul, 1969).

———, *The Folklore of East Anglia* (London: Batsford, 1974).

Potter, Carole, *Touch Wood: An Encyclopaedia of Superstition* (London: O'Mara, 1990).

Potter, Stephen, and Laurens Sargent, *Pedigree* (London: Collins, 1973).

Poulsen, Charles, *Scenes from a Stepney Youth* (London: THAP, 1988).

Power, Patrick C., *The Book of Irish Curses* (Cork: Mercier, 1974).

Pratt, John Burnett, *Buchan* (Aberdeen: Lewis & Smith, 1858).

Price, William Frederick, 'Notes on some of the Places, Traditions, and Folk-Lore of the Douglas Valley', *Transactions of the Historic Society of Lancashire and Cheshire* 51 (1901) 181–220.

Puckle, Bertram, *Funeral Customs: Their Origin and Development* (London: Werner Laurie, 1926).

Puhvel, Martin, 'The Legend of the Devil-Haunted Card Players in Northern Europe', *Folklore* 76 (1965) 33–8.

Radford, E. and M. A., and Christina Hole, *Encyclopedia of Superstitions* (London: Hutchinson, 1971).

Ramsay, Edward Bannerman, *Reminiscences of Scottish Life and Character* (2nd series; Edinburgh: Edmonston & Douglas, 1861).

Randell, Arthur, *Sixty Years a Fenman* (London: Routledge, 1966).

Ransome, Hilda M., *The Sacred Bee* (London: Allen & Unwin, 1937).

Rattue, James, *The Living Stream: Holy Wells In Historical Context* (Woodbridge: Boydell, 1995).

Raverat, Gwen, *Period Piece: A Cambridge Childhood* (London: Faber, 1952).

Raymond, Walter, *English Country Life* (London: Dent, 1934).

Rees, Nigel, *Oops, Pardon Mrs Arden! An Embarrassment of Domestic Catchphrases* (London: Robson, 2001a).

———, *As We Say in Our House: A Book of Family Sayings* (London: Robson, 2001b).

Reid, John T., *Art Rambles in Shetland* (Edinburgh: 1869).

Rhys, John, *Celtic Folklore: Welsh and Manx* (Oxford: Oxford University Press, 1901).

Rinder, Frank, 'Fragments of Caithness Folk-Lore', *Scottish Review* 26 (1895) 49–63.

Robbins, Rossell Hope, *The Encyclopedia of Witchcraft and Demonology* (London: Peter Nevill, 1959).

Roberts, Andy and Clarke, David, 'Heads and Tales: The Screaming Skull Legends of Britain', *Fortean Times* 3 (1996) 126–58.

Roberts, George, *The History and Antiquities of the Borough of Lyme Regis and Charmouth* (London: 1834).

Robinson, C. C., *Dialect of Leeds* (London: J. R. Smith, 1861).

Robinson, Francis Kildale, *Yorkshire Words* (London: Smith, 1855).

——, *A Glossary of Words Used in the Neighbourhood of Whitby* (London: Trubner, 1876).

Rodger, Jean C., *Lang Strang* (Forfar: Forfar Press, 1948).

Rolleston, J. D. 'The Folk-Lore of Venereal Disease', *British Journal of Venereal Diseases* 18 (1942) 1–13.

——, 'Ophthalmic Folk-Lore', *British Journal of Ophthalmology* 26 (1942) 481–96.

——, 'The Folklore of Children's Diseases', *Folk-Lore* 54 (1943) 287–307.

Rolph, C. H., *London Particulars* (Oxford: Oxford University Press, 1980).

Rowling, Marjorie, *The Folklore of the Lake District* (London: Batsford, 1976).

Rowse, A. L., *A Cornish Childhood* (London: Jonathan Cape, 1942).

Rudkin, E. M., *Lincolnshire Folklore* (Gainsborough, 1936; reprint, East Ardsley: EP Publications, 1976).

Ruskin, John, *Praeterita*, Vol. 2 (London: George Allen, 1887).

Russell, Constance, 'Dr. Dee's Cabalistic Bracelet', *The Connoisseur* 69 (1924) 161–3.

Russell, Jeffrey B., *A History of Witchcraft* (London: Thames & Hudson, 1980).

S–llm–n, J–s, 'Superstitions 1831', in William Hone, *The Year Book* (London: Thomas Tegg, 1832) 126–8.

St Clair, Sheila, *Folklore of the Ulster People* (Cork: Mercier, 1971).

Salisbury, Jesse, *A Glossary of Words and Phrases used in S. E. Worcestershire* (London: Salisbury, 1893).

Salmon, L., 'Folklore in the Kennet Valley', *Folk-Lore* 13 (1902) 418–29.

Sargent, Gilbert, *Memories of; see* Arthur (1989).

Saunders, W. H. Bernard, *Legends and Traditions of Huntingdonshire* (London: Simpkin Marshall, 1888).

Saxby, Henry Linkmyer, *The Birds of Shetland* (Edinburgh: Maclachlan & Stewart, 1874).

Saxby, Jessie Margaret Edmonston, *Shetland Traditional Lore* (Edinburgh: Grant & Murray, 1932).

Scot, Reginald, *The Discoverie of Witchcraft* (1584; reprint, New York: Dover, 1972).

Scott, Walter, *Minstrelsy of the Scottish Border* (3 vols., Edinburgh; Ballantyne: 1802).

——, *Letters on Demonology and Witchcraft* (London: Murray, 1830).

Seymour, St John D., *Irish Witchcraft and Demonology* (Dublin: Hodges Figgis, 1913).

Sharpe, James, *Instruments of Darkness: Witchcraft in England 1550–1750* (London: Hamish Hamilton, 1996).

Shaw, James, 'Folk Lore in Tynron', *Transactions of the Dumfriesshire and Galloway Natural History and Antiquarian Society* (1890) 9–13.

——, *A Country Schoolmaster* (Edinburgh: Oliver & Boyd, 1899).

Shaw, Lachlan, *The History of the Province of Moray* (Edinburgh: William Auld, 1775).

Shepard, Odell, *The Lore of the Unicorn* (London: Allen and Unwin, 1930; Random House, 1996).

Sheridan, Dorothy, *Wartime Women: A Mass-Observation Anthology* (London: Heinemann, 1990).

Sheridan, Ronald, and Anne Ross, *Grotesques and Gargoyles: Paganism in the Medieval Church* (Newton Abbot: David & Charles, 1975).

Sieveking, Paul, *Man Bites Man: The Scrapbook of an Edwardian Eccentric, George Ives* (London: Landesman, 1980).

Sikes, Wirt, *British Goblins: Welsh Folklore, Fairy Mythology, Legends and Superstitions* (London: Sampson Low, 1880).

Simpkins, John Ewart, *County Folklore: Fife* (London: Folklore Society, 1912).

Simpson, Jacqueline, *The Folklore of Sussex* (London: Batsford, 1973).

——, *The Folklore of the Welsh Border* (London: Batsford, 1976).

——, 'God's Visible Judgements: The Christian Dimension of Landscape Legends', *Landscape History* 8 (1987), 53–8.

——, and Steve Roud, *A Dictionary of English Folklore* (Oxford: Oxford University Press, 2000).

Sinclair, George, *Satan's Invisible World Discovered* (Edinburgh: William Martin, 1685).

Singer, Charles, 'Early English Magic and Medicine', *Proceedings of the British Academy* 9 (1919–20) 341–74.

Skeat, T. C., 'An Early Mediaeval Book of Fate: The Sortes XII Patriarcharum', *Mediaeval and Renaissance Studies* 3 (1954) 41–54.

Skeat, Walter W., 'Snakestones and Stone Thunderbolts as Subjects for Systematic Investigation', *Folk-Lore* 23 (1912) 45–80.

Skinner, Bob, *Toad in the Hole* (London: Fortean Times, 1985).

Smith, A. C., 'On Certain Wiltshire Traditions, Charms and Superstitions', *Wiltshire Archaeological and Natural History Magazine* 14 (1874) 320–31.

Smith, Alan, *Discovering Folklore in Industry* (Tring: Shire, 1969).

Smith, Mrs Charlotte, *The Natural History of Birds* (London: J. Johnson, 1807).

Smith, Emma (Pseud.), *A Cornish Waif's Story* (London: Odhams, 1954).

Smith, John Thomas, *A Book for a Rainy Day* (London: Bentley, 1861).

Smith, T. C., and J. Shortt, *History of Ribchester* (London: Bemrose, 1890).

Smith, William George and Paul Harvey, *The Oxford Dictionary of Proverbs* (2nd edn, Oxford: Clarendon Press, 1948).

Smollett, Tobias, *The Expedition of Humphry Clinker* (London: Johnston, 1771) [page numbers refer to Penguin edn, 1967].

Smyth, Admiral W. H., *The Sailor's Word-Book* (London: Blackie, 1867).

Snell, F. J., *The Customs of Old England* (London: Methuen, 1911).

Southey, Charles Cuthbert, *The Life and Correspondence of Robert Southey* (6 vols, London: Longman, 1850).

Southey, Robert, *Southey's Common-Place Book* (2nd series, ed. John Wood Warter, London: Longman, 1849).

Spectator, 'Some West of Ireland Superstitions', *The Spectator* (10 Aug. 1907) 190–1.

Spence, John, *Shetland Folk-Lore* (Lerwick: Johnson & Greig, 1899).

Spencer, K. G., 'Wild Birds in Lancashire Folk-Lore', *Journal of the Lancashire Dialect Society* 15 (1966) 2–15.

Statistical Account of Scotland (Edinburgh: Wm. Creech, 1791–99).

Sternberg, Thomas, *The Dialect and Folk-Lore of Northamptonshire* (London: Russell Smith, 1851; reprint, East Ardsley: S. R. Publishers, 1971).

Stewart, Alexander, 'Notice of a Highland Charm-Stone', *Proceedings of the Society of Antiquaries of Scotland* 24 (1890) 157–60.

——, 'Examples of the Survival in Scotland of Superstitions Relating to Fire', *Proceedings of the Society of Antiquaries of Scotland* 24 (1890) 391–5.

Stewart, Sheila, *Country Kate* (Kineton: Roundwood, 1971).

Stewart, W. Grant, *The Popular Superstitions and Festive Amusements of the Highlanders of Scotland* (Edinburgh: 1823).

Storms, G., *Anglo-Saxon Magic* (The Hague: Nijhoff, 1948).

Stow, John, *A Survey of London* (1598; 2nd edn, 1602; reprint, Stroud: Alan Sutton, 1994).

Strickland, Agnes, *Old Friends and New Acquaintances* (2nd series, London: Simpkin Marshall, 1861).

Stroud, Nell, *Josser: Days and Nights in the Circus* (London: Little Brown, 1999).

Strutt, Joseph, *Glig-Gamena Angel-Deod, or The Sports and Pastimes of the People of England* (1801; later edition: as *The Sports and Pastimes of the People of England*, ed. William Hone, London: Chatto & Windus, 1876).

Stubbes, Philip, *Anatomy of Abuses* (1583; reprint, London: New Shakespeare Society, 1877, 1882).

Sturt, George, *A Small Boy in the Sixties* (Cambridge: Cambridge University Press, 1927).

Summers, Gerald, *The Lure of the Falcon* (London: Collins, 1972).

Surman, Phyl, *Pride of the Morning: An Oxford Childhood* (Stroud: Alan Sutton, 1992).

Surrey Fed. of Women's Institutes, *Surrey Within Living Memory* (Newbury: Countryside Books, 1993).

Surtees Society, *Six North Country Diaries* (Durham Publications of the Surtees Society, Vol. 118, 1910).

Sutherland, George, 'Folk-Lore Gleanings and Character Sketches from the Far North' (Wick: *John O'Groat Journal*, 1937).

Sutton, Maureen, *We Didn't Know Aught* (Stamford: Paul Watkins, 1992).

——, *A Lincolnshire Calendar* (Stamford: Paul Watkins, 1997).

Swaby, William Proctor, 'Superstitious Beliefs and Customs of Lincolnshire', in Andrews (1891) 80–95.

Swainson, Revd Charles, *The Folklore and Provincial Names of British Birds* (London: Folklore Society, 1886).

Swift, Jonathan [as 'Simon Wagstaff'], *A Complete Collection of Genteel and Ingenious Conversation* [*Polite Conversation*] (1738).

Tebbutt, C. F., *Huntingdonshire Folklore* (St Neots: Tomson & Lendrum, 1952).

——, *Huntingdonshire Folklore* (St Ives: Friends of Norris Museum, 1984).

Teignmouth, Lord, *Sketches of the Coasts and Islands of Scotland* (London: J. W. Parker, 1836).

Thomas, Dylan, *Portrait of the Artist as a Young Dog* (London: Dent, 1940).

Thomas, Henry, 'Arise Evans, the Welsh Conjuror', *Journal of the Merioneth Historical and Record Society* 3 (1957–60) 280–3.

Thomas, Keith, *Religion and the Decline of Magic* (London: Weidenfeld & Nicolson, 1971).

——, *Man and the Natural World* (London: Allen Lane, 1983).

Thompson, C. J. S., *The Hand of Destiny: Everyday Folklore and Superstitions* (London: Rider, 1932).

Thompson, Flora, *Lark Rise* (Oxford: Oxford University Press, 1939).

——, *Over to Candleford* (Oxford: Oxford University Press, 1941).

——, *Candleford Green* (Oxford: Oxford University Press, 1943).

Thompson, Pishey, *The History and Antiquities of Boston* (Boston: 1856).

Thornton, Alice, *The Autobiography of Mrs. Alice Thornton* (Durham: Publications of the Surtees Society, 1875).

Thrupp, J., 'British Superstitions as to Hares, Geese and Poultry', *Transactions of the Ethnological Society of London* NS: 5 (1867) 162–7.

Timbs, John, *Things Not Generally Known* (London: Kent & Co., 1856; 9th edn, 1860).

——, *Nooks and Corners of English Life* (London: Griffith & Farran, 1867).

——, *Things Not Generally Known* (2nd series, London: Kent & Co., 1859).

Tongue, Ruth L., *Somerset Folklore* (London: Folklore Society, 1965).

Topsell, Edward, *The Historie of Foure-Footed Beastes* (London: Jaggard, 1607).

Toynbee, M. E., 'Charles I and the King's Evil', *Folk-Lore* 61 (1950) 1–14.

Train, J. *Strains of the Mountain Muse* (Edinburgh: Goldie, 1814).

Train, Joseph, *A Historical and Statistical Account of the Isle of Man* (Douglas: Quiggin, 1845).

Trevelyan, Marie, *Folk-Lore and Folk-Stories of Wales* (London: Elliot Stock, 1909).

Tristram, H. B., 'Local Superstitions', *Transactions of the Tyneside Naturalists' Field Club* 5 (1860–62) 98.

Troubridge, Laura; *see* Hope-Nicholson, Jacqueline (1966).

Tudor, John R., *The Orkneys and Shetland: Their Past and Present State* (London: Stanford, 1883).

Tuleja, Tad, 'The Tooth Fairy: Perspectives on Money and Magic', in Narvaez (1991) 406–25.

Tusser, Thomas, *Five Hundred Points of Good Husbandrie* (1557, 1573, 1580; new edn, London: Trubner, 1878).

Tyack, G. S., *Lore and Legend of the English Church* (London: Wm. Andrews, 1899).

Udal, J. S., 'Dorsetshire Folk-Speech and Superstitions Relating to Natural History', *Proceedings of the Dorset Natural History and Antiquarian Field Club* 10 (1889) 19–46.

——, *Dorsetshire Folk-Lore* (Hertford: Stephen Austin & Sons, 1922).

Uttley, Alison, *Country Things* (London: Faber, 1946).

——, *A Year in the Country* (London: Faber, 1957).

Valenze, Deborah M., 'Prophecy and Popular Literature in Eighteenth-Century England', *Journal of Ecclesiastical History* 29:1 (1978) 75–92.

Valiente, Doreen, *An ABC of Witchcraft Past and Present* (London: Robert Hale, 1973).

——, *The Rebirth of Witchcraft* (London: Robert Hale, 1989).

Varden, John T., 'Traditions, Superstitions, and Folklore, Chiefly Relating to the Counties of Norfolk and Suffolk', in *The East Anglian Handbook or*

Agricultural Annual for 1885 (Norwich: Argus Office, 1885) 65–132.

———, 'Traditions, Superstitions, and Folklore', in *The East Anglian Handbook and Agricultural Annual for 1885* (Norwich: Argus Office, 1885).

Vaughan, Mary, 'An Old "Receipt" Book', *Journal of the Merioneth Historical and Record Society* 4 (1961–4) 318–323.

Vaux, J. Edward, *Church Folklore* (London: Griffith Farran, 1894).

Vesey-Fitzgerald, Brian, *Gypsies of Britain* (Newton Abbot: David & Charles, 1973).

Vickery, Roy (ed.), *Plant-Lore Studies* (London: Folklore Society, 1984).

———, *Unlucky Plants* (London: Folklore Society, 1985).

———, *A Dictionary of Plant Lore* (Oxford: Oxford University Press, 1995).

Visser, Margaret, *The Rituals of Dinner* (London: HarperCollins, 1991).

Waldron, George W., *The History and Description of the Isle of Man* (London: W. Bickerton, 1744).

Wales, Tony, *A Sussex Garland* (Newbury: Countryside Books, 1979).

———, *Sussex Customs, Curiosities and Country Lore* (Southampton: Ensign, 1990).

Walsham, Alexandra, 'Sermons in the Sky: Apparitions in Early Modern Europe', *History Today* (Apr. 2001) 57–63.

Walter, Tony, *Funerals and How to Improve Them* (London: Hodder & Stoughton, 1990).

Walters, Cuming, *Bygone Somerset* (London: William Andrews, 1897).

Waring, Philippa, *A Dictionary of Omens and Superstitions* (London: Souvenir, 1978).

Watkins, M. G., 'The Folk-Lore of a North Lincolnshire Village', *Antiquary* 14 (1886) 9–12.

Webster, Mary McCallum, *Flora of Moray, Nairn and East Inverness* (Aberdeen: Aberdeen University Press, 1978).

Weeks, W. Self, 'Witch stones and Charms in Clitheroe and District', *Transactions of the Lancashire and Cheshire Antiquarian Society* 27 (1910) 104–110.

Weightman, Gavin, and Steve Humphries, *Christmas Past* (London: Sidgwick & Jackson, 1987).

Weir, Anthony, and James Jerman, *Images of Lust: Sexual Carvings on Medieval Churches* (London: Batsford, 1986).

Wells, Rosemary, 'The Making of an Icon: The Tooth Fairy in North American Folklore and Popular Culture', in Narvaez (1991) 426–53.

Werenfels, Samuel, *A Dissertation upon Superstition in Natural Things* (London: Robinson, 1748).

Wesley, John, *Primitive Physick, or An Easy and Natural Method of Curing Most Diseases* (1747; 13th edn, Bristol: William Pine, 1768).

West Midlands Fed. of Women's Institutes, *The West Midlands: Within Living Memory* (Newbury: Countryside Books, 1996).

Westwood, Jennifer, *Albion: A Guide to Legendary Britain* (London: Grafton, 1985).

Wheater, William, 'Yorkshire Superstitions', *Old Yorkshire* 4 (1883) 265–71.

Wherry, B. A., 'Wizardry on the Welsh Border', *Folk-Lore* 15 (1904), 75–86.

White, Gilbert, *The Natural History and Antiquities of Selborne* (London: Benjamin White, 1788) [page numbers given are from the Folio Society edition, 1994].

White, Newman Ivey, *North Carolina Folklore 6: Popular Beliefs and Superstitions* (Durham, NC: Duke University Press, 1961).

———, *North Carolina Folklore 7: Popular Beliefs and Superstitions* (Durham, NC: Duke University Press, 1964).

Whitlock, Ralph, *The Folklore of Wiltshire* (London: Batsford, 1976).

———, *The Folklore of Devon* (London: Batsford, 1977).

Wigby, Frederick C., *Just a Country Boy* (Wymondham: George R. Reeve, 1976).

Wilde, Lady 'Speranza', *Ancient Legends, Mystic Charms and Superstitions of Ireland* (London: Ward & Downey, 1888).

Wilkinson, T. T., 'On the Popular Customs and Superstitions of Lancashire', *Transactions of the Historic Society of Lancashire and Cheshire* 11 (1858–9) 155–62; 12 (1860) 85–98; NS:1 (1860–1) 1–16.

Williams, Fionnuala, 'A Fire of Stones Curse', *Folk Life* 35 (1996–7) 63–73.

Williamson, Stanley, *The Third Northcountryman* (Clapham: Dalesman, 1962).

Willmott, Peter, and Michael Young, *Family and Kinship in East London* (London: Routledge, 1957).

Wilson, David, *Anglo-Saxon Paganism* (London: Routledge & Kegan Paul, 1992).

Wilson, Michael, *Performance and Practice: Oral Narrative Traditions Among Teenagers in Britain and Ireland* (Aldershot: Ashgate Publishing, 1997).

Wilson, William, *Folk Lore and Genealogies of Uppermost Nithsdale* (Dumfries: Mann, 1904).

Wilts. N&Q, Wiltshire Notes and Queries (1893–1916).

Wiltshire, Kathleen, *Wiltshire Folklore* (Salisbury: Compton Russell, 1975).

Windele, John, 'Irish Medical Superstitions', *Journal of the Kilkenny and South-East of Ireland Archaeological Society* NS:5 (1864–6) 306–26).

Wise, John R., *The New Forest: Its History and its Scenery* (London: Smith Elder, 1867).

Wood, Mrs Henry, *Johnny Ludlow* (4th series; London: Macmillan, 1899).

Wood, J. Maxwell, *Witchcraft and Superstitious Record in the South-Western District of Scotland* (Dumfries: Maxwell, 1911).

Wood-Martin, W. G., *Traces of the Elder Faiths of Ireland* (London: Longmans Green, 1902).

Woodford, Cecile, *Sussex Ways and Byways* (Willingdon: Crown Books, 1968).

Woodman, Mary, *Wedding Etiquette* (London: Foulsham, 1949).

Woodruff, Maurice, *Woody* (London: Cassell, 1967).

Wootton, Anthony, *Animal Folklore, Myth and Legend* (Poole: Blandford 1986).

Wright, Ann, *The Folk Lore of Holderness* (Beverley: Hedon & District Local History Society, 1978).

Wright, A. R., *English Folklore* (London: Benn, 1928).

———, and T. E. Lones, *British Calendar Customs: England* (3 vols, London: Folklore Society, 1936–40).

Wright, E. M., *Rustic Speech and Folk-Lore* (Oxford: Oxford University Press, 1913).

Yonge, Charlotte M., *An Old Woman's Outlook in a Hampshire Village* (London: Macmillan, 1892).

———, *John Keble's Parishes* (London: Macmillan, 1898).

Young, George, *A History of Whitby and Streoneshalh Abbey* (Whitby: Clark & Medd, 1817).

Zincke, F. Barham, *Some Materials for the History Of Wherstead* (Ipswich: Read & Barrett, 1887).